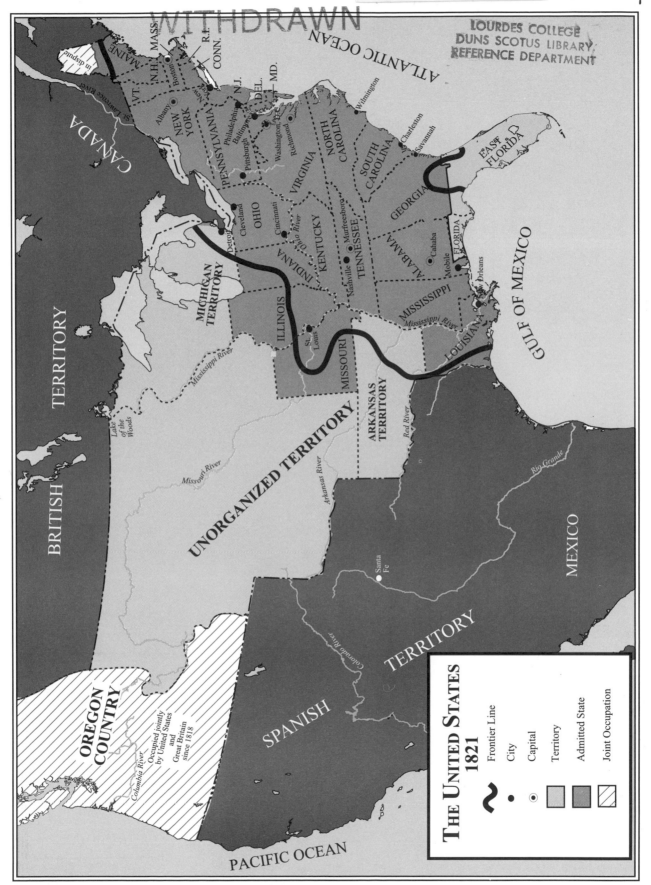

THE UNITED STATES
1821

Frontier Line
City
Capital
Territory
Admitted State
Joint Occupation

ENCYCLOPEDIA
OF THE
UNITED STATES
IN THE
NINETEENTH
CENTURY

ENCYCLOPEDIA
OF THE
UNITED STATES
IN THE
NINETEENTH
CENTURY

Paul Finkelman

Editor in Chief

VOLUME 2

Grand Tour–Presidency

CHARLES SCRIBNER'S SONS

An Imprint of The Gale Group

NEW YORK   DETROIT   SAN FRANCISCO
LONDON   BOSTON   WOODBRIDGE, CT

Charles Scribner's Sons
1633 Broadway
New York, New York 10019

3 5 7 9 11 13 15 17 19   20 18 16 14 12 10 8 6 4 2

PRINTED IN THE UNITED STATES OF AMERICA

Library of Congress Cataloging-in-Publication Data

Encyclopedia of the United States in the nineteenth century / Paul Finkelman, editor in chief.
    p.   cm.
    Includes bibliographical references and index.
    ISBN 0-684-80500-6 (set : hardcover : alk. paper)—ISBN 0-684-80497-2 (vol. 1 :
hardcover : alk. paper)—ISBN 0-684-80498-0 (vol. 2 : hardcover : alk. paper)—ISBN
0-684-80499-9 (vol. 3 : hardcover : alk. paper)
    1. United States—Civilization—19th century—Encyclopedias. I. Finkelman, Paul, 1949–

E169.1 .E626 2001
973.5—dc21   00-045811

Cover image credits *(clockwise, starting from the top left corner):* U.S. Capitol © Corbis; Native American group portrait © Planet Art; Andrew Jackson © Planet Art; Forty-niners © Planet Art; *Whistler's Mother* © EclectiCollections™; Frontier town © Planet Art; Frederick Douglass © Corbis; Drummer boy © Corbis; Abraham Lincoln © Corbis; Train © Planet Art.

The paper used in this publication meets the requirements of ANSI/NISO Z39.48–1992 (Permanence of Paper).

CONTENTS OF OTHER VOLUMES

ENCYCLOPEDIA
OF THE
UNITED STATES
IN THE
NINETEENTH
CENTURY

G

(continued)

GRAND TOUR The grand tour, a phrase borrowed from the British, refers to a practice, widespread among well-to-do Americans in the nineteenth century, of traveling through Europe along routes forged by British nobility during the seventeenth and eighteenth centuries. Beginning in 1818, when the Black Ball Line began transatlantic passenger service between New York and Liverpool, many Americans embarked upon a tour of Europe hoping to absorb the highest elements of European culture and sophistication. While some went with the intention of pursuing artistic or literary aims, others hoped to make or consolidate contacts among the European upper classes. A heightened self-consciousness pervades the written reminiscences of tourists who expected the grand tour to add to their prestige back home.

Americans usually began their tours with a substantial sojourn in Britain before moving on to the Continent. Traveling first by stagecoach and later by railway, most tourists concentrated on sightseeing in France and Italy, often ending their travels with brief excursions through Switzerland, Germany, and the Low Countries (Holland and Belgium). A grand tour typically comprised several months but could stretch to one or more years if it included study at a university or an art apprenticeship. Grand tours inevitably included visits to the European historical monuments and battlegrounds, museums and cathedrals, cafés and spas, about which middle-class Americans would have already read.

New opportunities for leisure and a growing curiosity about Europe, a curiosity more whetted than sated by the profusion of private letters and accounts of grand tours published by Americans, made travel to Europe increasingly accessible and desirable to a large number of middle-class Americans by the century's end. Coinciding with innovations in transportation and communication, the publication of new guidebooks and the extension of Thomas Cook tours helped simplify European travel for the American initiate. Owing to the introduction of faster, larger, and more commodious transatlantic steamers between the 1860s and the 1880s, the annual flow of Americans traveling to Europe, thirty thousand or more in mid-century, trebled by 1900.

Most American writers of the century embarked on grand tours. Their published accounts compare the Old World with the New in ways that speak to the significance of European travel in the construction of American national identities and selfhood in this period. Despite the widespread American middle-class desire to emulate European sophisticates, the nineteenth-century American fascination with European styles and aristocratic grandeur competed with a general scorn for what Americans often viewed as European decadence. Consequently American travel accounts make pointed references to Europe's lack of republican institutions or democratic ideals. For example, one of the most important and widely read texts of the century was *The Innocents Abroad* (1869) by Mark Twain (1835–1910). This book outsold all rival publications on travel in Europe, and its implied critique of the fawning American set alongside a humorous defense of American innocence brought Twain international fame and quickly catapulted him to the position of national spokesperson.

1

Although the grand tour as experienced by Americans in the nineteenth century is most often associated with significant literary production, travel to Europe increasingly played an integral role in the lives of American statesmen and reformers as well. Such causes as antislavery, women's rights, temperance, labor, public education, settlement houses, prison reform, antilynching, and international peace were furthered and sometimes propelled by American reformers on tour who interacted with European dignitaries, officials, like-minded intellectuals, patrons, and activists. Finally, the development of graduate education in the last quarter of the century took American students to European universities, where they earned doctorates.

Although American tourism in Europe did not abate in the twentieth century, the phenomenon of the grand tour is confined most properly to the period between 1818 and 1914. In addition, the need for Americans to appropriate, connect with, or separate from a European cultural heritage diminished, diluting the tour's social significance. Further democratization of travel and tourism in the mid-twentieth century weakened its prestige.

See also **Class, Social; Education,** *subentry on* **Graduate and Professional Education; Gilded Age; Nationalism.**

Bibliography

Dulles, Foster Rhea. *Americans Abroad: Two Centuries of European Travel.* Ann Arbor: University of Michigan Press, 1964.

Earnest, Ernest. *Expatriates and Patriots: American Artists, Scholars, and Writers in Europe.* Durham, N.C.: Duke University Press, 1968.

Metwalli, Ahmed M. "Americans Abroad: The Popular Art of Travel Writing in the Nineteenth Century." In *America: Exploration and Travel.* Edited by Steven E. Kagle. Bowling Green, Ohio: Bowling Green State University Popular Press, 1979.

Stowe, William W. *Going Abroad: European Travel in Nineteenth-Century American Culture.* Princeton, N.J.: Princeton University Press, 1994.

TRACEY JEAN BOISSEAU

GREAT BRITAIN, FOREIGN RELATIONS WITH

Relations with Great Britain dominated the foreign policy of the United States throughout the nineteenth century. The first important issue in these relations involved the rights of neutrals during the Napoleonic Wars (1799–1815).

The Napoleonic Wars

In 1793, when the new French Republic called upon the United States to fulfill the provisions of its treaty of alliance born in the American Revolution, President George Washington issued a Proclamation of Neutrality. That action effectively abrogated the treaty and set the course of American foreign policy for the next century and a half by eschewing "entangling foreign alliances," as Washington phrased it in his Farewell Address. Complicating U.S. neutrality, the new American political parties were divided in their feelings toward the belligerents. The Jeffersonians, or Republicans, had welcomed the French Revolution, continuing in their marked preference for France. The Hamiltonians, or Federalists, detested the French Revolution and had a genuine fondness for Britain.

The most difficult aspect of U.S. neutrality involved freedom of the seas. As the Napoleonic struggle intensified, each side undertook to impede the commerce of the other through a naval blockade. During the administration of President John Adams, French depredations on American maritime commerce led to the creation of a permanent U.S. Navy, overseen by a Department of the Navy, and to an undeclared naval war with France.

With the presidency of Thomas Jefferson, beginning in 1801, American policy took on a more pro-French coloration. But commensurate with American military weakness and with Jefferson's own political philosophy, the administration made extraordinary efforts to preserve the peace with both combatants. U.S. relations with France greatly improved when, after he lost Haiti, Napoleon abandoned his hope for a New World empire and subsequently sold the vast Louisiana Territory to the United States in 1803.

As Britain enforced its Orders in Council and France adopted the Continental System to exclude Britain from European trade, the United States was severely challenged to maintain its neutral rights without resorting to warfare. The British impressment of seamen further troubled Anglo-American relations. In 1807 the British pursuit of deserters from the Royal Navy brought about the *Chesapeake* affair. The HMS *Leopard* fired upon the USS *Chesapeake* within U.S. waters to force the frigate to submit to a search. The Non-Intercourse Act (1806) gave the president the power to stop trade with the belligerents, and an embargo issued by Jefferson in 1807 essentially prohibited U.S. merchant ships from leaving their harbors except to ply the coastal trade. The high cost of the embargo in lost commerce, and its extreme unpopularity, eventually forced the resumption of overseas trade, and pressures for war with Britain increased. The so-called War Hawks were especially eager to use such a war for territorial expansion through the annexation of Canada, and the southern states hoped to gain new slave territories by seizing Florida, and possibly Texas, from Spain.

In terms of American goals, things went wrong from the beginning in the War of 1812. The Spanish Empire, allied with Britain after the 1808 seizure of King Ferdinand VII by Napoleon, declared itself neutral in the Anglo-American struggle, thereby putting Florida outside the U.S. grasp. American armies were driven from Canada, and by 1814 only the diplomatic skills of John Quincy Adams prevented a treaty seriously unfavorable to American interests. In fact, the Treaty of Ghent (1814) resolved none of the difficulties that had beset Anglo-American relations. The most significant U.S. victory in the war, the Battle of New Orleans, was actually fought after the peace treaty was signed in Europe, but before the treaty arrived in the United States.

Border Disputes

Border questions between the United States and Canada, a British colony, were sore points from the time of U.S. independence until 1903. The Treaty of Ghent provided for arbitration of some minor land disputes around the Great Lakes and in the West. In the late 1830s the simmering boundary dispute between the province of New Brunswick and the state of Maine exploded in a round of confrontations involving competing lumbermen. The Maine militia prevented any actual fighting or casualties in the so-called Aroostook War. In 1842 the Webster-Ashburton Treaty avoided a larger war and provided for an equitable distribution of the disputed land.

Another serious border crisis involved the Oregon Territory, which consisted of the present-day states of Oregon and Washington and the province of British Columbia. This northwestern territory had been claimed by Spain, Russia, Britain, and the United States, with the latter two possessing the clearest title. An informal condominium was established in 1818 and was renewed by a convention in 1827. Obviously, however, this situation could not continue indefinitely with an expanding population. James K. Polk's 1844 presidential campaign slogan of "Fifty-four forty or fight!" and pressures in Congress threatened to make the Oregon Territory a cause of war.

Anti-British Satire. Cartoon by Edward Williams Clay depicting John Bull, who represents Britain, as a deal breaker, concerning the fishing rights of Americans in Canadian waters. Lithograph, 1852. LIBRARY OF CONGRESS: PRINTS AND PHOTOGRAPHS DIVISION

After saber rattling on both sides, negotiations in 1846 yielded the Treaty of Washington, establishing the forty-ninth parallel as the boundary.

The final U.S.-Canadian boundary dispute, over the Alaska-Canada border, culminated in arbitration in 1903 during President Theodore Roosevelt's administration. The arbitration found substantially for the U.S. claims.

Canada

Concern with Canada in U.S. foreign policy was not limited to border disputes. For many Americans the Canadian border was an artificial barrier that prevented the natural union of these two English-speaking nations. When discontent and rebellion spread through Canada in 1837–1838, many Americans assumed that it would lead to Canadian independence, followed by Canada's inevitable union with the American Republic. Ultimately, British regulars and Canadian militia put down the armed resistance, but not before Anglo-American relations suffered serious strains. In one of the most stressful incidents, Irish sympathizers set up camps in upstate New York, where they prepared for military operations against Canada. They planned to seize control of a portion of Canada, which they would then trade for the independence of Ireland.

When diplomatic protests produced no satisfaction for London, Canadian militia struck across the border into New York on 29–30 December 1837, burning several camps and setting adrift the brigantine *Caroline*, which the Irish sympathizers intended to use in their invasion. U.S. secretary of state Daniel Webster, well known for his pro-British sympathies, prevented an escalation into war. In his diplomatic note to the British government, Webster succinctly contended that the United States had not violated its neutrality, making the attack an unwarranted intervention. In the aftermath of the *Caroline* affair, Alexander McLeod, the Canadian sheriff who had led the militia assault into New York, was arrested in 1841 and tried for murder in Utica under New York State law (McLeod had come to New York to pick up a prisoner for extradition to Canada). The British government threatened war if New York executed McLeod, but fortunately the jury in Utica acquitted him.

The ultimate outcome of the Canadian rebellion was the creation in British North America in 1867 of a national government with a parliament and a responsible ministry. The separate colonies were transformed into provinces. In the same year, the British North America Act created the Dominion of Canada, and over the succeeding years various North American British colonies were added as provinces or territories. While the uniting of Canada was significant for U.S. foreign policy, the new mode of Canadian government was equally important. As a dominion, Canada had virtually complete authority over its internal affairs, and London controlled only defense and foreign policy.

In 1854 a virtual common market was established between Canada and the United States under the Elgin-Marcy Treaty, but in 1865 the United States repudiated the treaty out of anger over the British pro-Confederacy policies during the Civil War. The protectionist policies of the dominant Republican Party created further opposition to renewing the treaty.

In the period immediately following the U.S. Civil War, Fenian veterans of the Union army created camps on the Canadian border in New York and New England, preparing to invade Canada in pursuit of their scheme to achieve Irish independence. The intervention of U.S. authorities prevented the invasion, but Irish Americans remained the single most persistent complication in Anglo-American relations. Irish hatred of Britain influenced U.S. politics, and politicians of both U.S. parties were said to "twist the lion's tail," meaning they denounced British imperialism in the course of their political campaigns.

Slavery

Slavery produced several contentious quarrels between the United States and Britain throughout the first half of the nineteenth century. Both nations abolished the slave trade in 1807, but Britain used its diplomatic service to press other nations to follow suit and the Royal Navy to suppress the trade. The U.S. Navy lacked the resources to restrain American involvement in the outlawed trade, but concern over past British interference with seaborne commerce militated against a U.S. agreement to allow the Royal Navy to search U.S. vessels. Because the Royal Navy did not have that right of visitation, many slavers flew the U.S. flag to escape British interference. The United States granted the Royal Navy the right of visitation in 1862.

Although the British Empire did not pass an act to abolish slavery until 1833, Upper Canada (now Ontario) adopted a gradual emancipation program in 1793. As a result Canada became a major refuge for escaped American slaves and was the ultimate terminus on the Underground Railroad. The United States bitterly protested the refusal of British officials to surrender fugitive slaves.

The British abolition of slavery caused further problems. American ships bearing slaves from one

U.S. port to another occasionally were driven off course by storms into British territorial waters in Bermuda, the Bahamas, or the British West Indies. The British would free any slaves inadvertently brought into their waters despite U.S. protests. The *Creole* incident was particularly troublesome. In 1841 that American brig was transporting one hundred slaves, who mutinied and forced the ship to the Bahamas. The British authorities freed the slaves, refusing their rendition as slaves or their extradition as criminals. In an exchange of notes at the time of the Webster-Ashburton Treaty, Britain repudiated "officious interference" with U.S. shipping forced into its waters by "violence or accident." Americans often pressured Canada to return fugitive slaves, but with one exception in the 1830s, U.S. attempts accomplished nothing. In 1860 the United States sought formal extradition of John Anderson, a black man who had killed a white person while escaping from slavery in Missouri. Although arrested in Upper Canada, Anderson was never extradited. The case caused diplomatic tension, especially after the Court of Queen's Bench in England issued a writ of habeas corpus directing the sheriff of Toronto to release Anderson. The crisis evaporated when Abraham Lincoln became president.

The Civil War

The U.S. Civil War occasioned a dramatic series of crises in Anglo-American relations. British attitudes toward the Confederacy were divided. Slavery was unpopular in Britain, but the Southern states were major markets for British manufactures and the source of much of the cotton fiber used by British textile mills. In addition, the aristocratic society of the South appealed more to British taste than did the mass democracy of the North. Many British statesmen thought a weakened United States would expedite long-term British interests.

The *Trent* affair and the *Alabama* claims produced the most serious friction. The North's naval blockade of the South was a cause of serious antagonisms with Britain. In November 1861 the USS *San Jacinto* seized the RMS *Trent*, en route from Havana, Cuba, to Saint Thomas, Danish West Indies, and removed James M. Mason and John Slidell, Confederate commissioners to Great Britain and France. Prime Minister John Russell was outraged and demanded the return of the commissioners and a formal apology. Intervention by Albert, the prince consort, softened the communiqué of the British government. The pressures of conducting the war forced Secretary of State William H. Seward to adopt a conciliatory approach, and the seized commissioners were freed.

The conflict arising from alleged British violations of neutrality in the *Alabama* claims was less easily resolved. British shipyards built a number of Confederate warships, including the *Alabama*, the *Shenandoah*, and the *Florida*. Through negligence, the British government allowed these ships to escape to the open sea, where they waged war on Union commerce. After strenuous U.S. diplomatic protests, Britain took possession of some Confederate ships still in English ports.

Upon the conclusion of the war, the United States insisted that British aid and encouragement of the South had prolonged the war significantly and demanded from Britain $2 billion, half of the total cost of the war. If the British did not wish to pay that sum, they could cede their North American possessions to the United States. This issue poisoned Anglo-American relations from the end of the Civil War until 1871, when the Treaty of Washington established procedures for international arbitration of the *Alabama* claims and settled several other issues. Among the side issues were the ownership of the San Juan Islands in the Vancouver Island Channel, which were awarded to the United States; mutual access to fisheries; and mutual navigation rights on the Saint Lawrence River and the Great Lakes. The final disposition of the *Alabama* claims arbitration required Britain to pay compensation for the direct depredations of the Confederate raiders to the amount of $15.5 million but rejected indirect damages.

Canadian and American fishing rights were a perpetual source of difficulties, and the issue came to a head in 1886–1887. Canadian police boats seized American fishing vessels in inland waters, while U.S. Treasury cutters seized Canadian pelagic sealers in international waters in the Bering Sea off the Pribilof Islands. Pelagic sealing threatened devastation of the seal herds, but the U.S. policy of interfering with it in international waters was contrary to international law at the time. The Bayard-Chamberlain Treaty, signed in 1888, ostensibly resolved these issues, but the U.S. Senate refused to ratify it. Britain proffered a modus vivendi at the time of the treaty negotiations, and both governments followed its provisions without any formal ratification of terms.

The Monroe Doctrine

The Monroe Doctrine (1823) began in a convergence of Anglo-American interests. In the early 1820s, most of the Spanish colonies in Latin America rebelled. Triggered by the French usurpation of the Spanish throne during the Napoleonic Wars, the drive for independence was fueled by the Spanish denial of political rights for those born in the colonies and by the severe economic regulations imposed under Spanish theories of mercantilism.

In the aftermath of the Napoleonic Wars, Russia, Prussia, and Austria formed the Holy Alliance to promote the influence of Christian principles in international affairs; in practice, however, it symbolized the repression of democracy, liberalism, nationalism, republicanism, and religious free thinking. Britain joined it in 1815 to form the Quadruple Alliance. Reacting to the South American revolts, the alliance entertained the idea of intervening militarily to restore the colonies to the Spanish throne. The British opposed such a recolonization on strategic grounds. In addition the British had developed an enormous trade with Latin America, and reconquest threatened to extinguish that trade through mercantilist regulation.

In 1823 British foreign secretary George Canning proposed to U.S. secretary of state John Quincy Adams a military-diplomatic alliance to oppose Quadruple Alliance intervention in the New World. Adams recommended to President James Monroe that the United States announce such a policy on its own, not merely "as a cock-boat in the wake of the British man-of-war." In December 1823 the president unilaterally proclaimed the Monroe Doctrine in his annual message to Congress, which sought to exclude European intervention in the Western Hemisphere. On a practical level, however, the U.S. policy required the commitment of British naval power to back the American position. Along with nationalism, the reason the United States excluded Britain from the formal proclamation of the new geopolitical doctrine was because American statesmen were concerned about British intentions regarding Cuba.

In 1842 U.S. secretary of state Webster prevailed upon Great Britain not to validate the protectorate that its diplomatic representative had proclaimed over the Sandwich Islands (Hawaii). Webster simultaneously declared that the United States opposed the colonization of Hawaii by any foreign power.

In Central America, U.S. interest in an interoceanic canal combined with the no-colonization policy of the Monroe Doctrine to create a small crisis in Anglo-American relations. In 1850, prompted by the Clayton-Bulwer Treaty, the British abandoned their territorial claims on the Mosquito Coast, although Britain continued to exert an unofficial protectorate over that region until 1860. In 1895, Royal Marines seized the Nicaraguan town of Corinto in a dispute over Nicaragua's actions in the coastal area. Reacting to the treaty, Britain elevated British Honduras (present-day Belize) to the status of a crown colony.

A key provision of the Clayton-Bulwer Treaty was the mutual commitment by Great Britain and the United States that any interoceanic canal through Central America would be a joint undertaking by the two powers. When President Theodore Roosevelt proposed to construct a U.S. canal through the Isthmus of Panama, he first had to obtain an abrogation of the 1850 treaty through the Hay-Pauncefote Treaty of 1901, which recognized the U.S. right to build and operate such a canal alone, provided that the canal be open to vessels of commerce and war from all nations on terms of entire equality.

The most serious confrontation in Anglo-American relations involving Latin America arose in 1895 over the border between the British Guiana (present-day Guyana) and Venezuela. This border had never been properly delineated by a treaty, and the discovery of gold in the disputed area led to a crisis. The United States pressed the parties to agree to arbitration, but Britain was unwilling to have its ownership of this long-occupied territory judged. President Grover Cleveland, through Secretary of State Richard Olney, issued an ultimatum, and many on both sides of the Atlantic feared war. That outcome was averted, however, when Britain agreed to arbitration in the dispute.

In another incident, Britain and Germany attempted in 1902 to force the Venezuelan dictator Cipriano Castro to honor his nation's debt. British and German naval forces blockaded Venezuela's ports that year. The United States forced Venezuela to repay its legitimate international debts, but President Theodore Roosevelt realized that the Monroe Doctrine posed a dilemma for American foreign policy. Misbehaving American nations could force the United States either to defend them in an unrighteous cause or to allow a violation of the doctrine. The president found his answer to the problem in 1904, when, in response to a similar debt problem in the Dominican Republic, he issued the Roosevelt Corollary. The doctrine asserted that chronic wrongdoing or severe impotence on the part of an American nation would require U.S. enforcement of international legal obligations.

Toward Cooperation

The United States, Great Britain, and Germany were parties in an international rivalry for control of the Samoan Islands in the 1880s. In this instance the bitterest friction was between the United States and Germany. The situation was resolved by the Treaty of Berlin (1889), which created a three-power protectorate that maintained the semblance of Samoan independence.

In 1899 the United States adopted the Open Door policy, which opposed the further territorial partition of China and proposed opening China to the commerce of all nations on an equal footing. In adopting this policy, which had been essentially the British attitude toward China prior to 1899, Washington pursued its own commercial interests in China as a market for U.S. manufactures. Imperial and European demands for British resources were rendering Britain unable to pursue this policy vigorously, thus, for the most part, London welcomed the U.S. initiative.

When the United States and Spain drifted toward war over Cuba in the final years of the nineteenth century, Britain refused to countenance Kaiser Wilhelm II's attempt to put together a European coalition to restrain the United States. Despite the severe storms that sometimes buffeted their relations, by the beginning of the twentieth century the United States and Britain were linked in an informal cooperative alliance prompted by mutual interests and cultural affinities.

See also **Canada; Central America and the Caribbean; Fisheries; Foreign Relations; Maine; Monroe Doctrine; Oregon; War of 1812.**

Bibliography

Campbell, Charles S. *The Transformation of American Foreign Relations, 1865–1900.* New York: Harper and Row, 1976.

Hickey, Donald R. *The War of 1812: A Forgotten Conflict.* Urbana: University of Illinois Press, 1989.

Horsman, Reginald. *The Causes of the War of 1812.* New York: Barnes, 1962.

Pratt, Julius W., Vincent P. De Santis, and Joseph M. Siracusa. *A History of United States Foreign Policy.* 4th ed. Englewood Cliffs, N.J.: Prentice-Hall, 1980.

PATRICK M. O'NEIL

GREAT PLAINS   The Great Plains lie in the heart of North America, stretching twenty-five hundred miles from the Rio Grande in the south to Canada's Parkland Belt in the north.

The Land and Environment

The Rocky Mountains generally mark the Plains' western limits. A lack of a distinct geographic marker in the east, however, makes delineating the boundary there difficult. Scholars have sometimes used the ninety-eighth or hundredth meridian as the eastern edge. A better boundary might be the eastern edge of North and South Dakota, Nebraska, and Kansas— an area linked historically and culturally to the Great Plains rather than the Midwest. The Great Plains includes all or part of ten states: Texas, New Mexico, Oklahoma, Colorado, Kansas, Nebraska, Wyoming, South Dakota, Montana, and North Dakota.

The Great Plains have been called "the great American desert," "the world's breadbasket," "the dust bowl," and "the heartland." Although "Great Plains" has been used to define the region since the seventeenth century, it was Walter Prescott Webb's 1931 book of the same title that popularized it as a regional designation. Webb argued that the Plains' aridity, flat land, and lack of timber forced everyone and everything there to adapt to the harsh conditions. Although scholars have largely discredited Webb's environmental determinism, his concept of the Great Plains as a distinct geographic and cultural region remains vibrant.

The physical environment of the Plains is one of climatic extremes where arctic and tropical weather systems collide, creating violent storms and tornadoes. Temperatures frequently climb to over one hundred degrees Fahrenheit in the summer and plunge to well below zero in the winter. Generally, the region is composed of flat or rolling grasslands that gradually climb from fifteen hundred feet on the eastern edge to seven thousand feet along the foothills of its western boundary. Notable exceptions to the flat terrain are the Black Hills in western South Dakota, the canyonlands of western Texas, Nebraska's Sandhills, and the Flint Hills of Kansas. A lack of sufficient rainfall is probably the most defining characteristic that separates the Great Plains from the Midwest; the Plains' average annual rainfall is between twenty and twenty-five inches. Long periods of drought during the late nineteenth century dramatically affected the Plains' agricultural productivity and the survival of its population. The semiarid climate is made evident by the region's few primary rivers. The upper Missouri, Platte, Republican, Kansas, Arkansas, and Red are shallow and generally slow-moving rivers that meander eastward across the Plains. Only the Rio Grande and its tributaries constitute a major southward-flowing Plains river system.

Plains Peoples

The Great Plains are racially and ethnically diverse. During the first half of the nineteenth century, the peoples living on the Plains included two major groups. The Spanish had first settled in New Mexico and the Rio Grande Valley in the early seventeenth century, and they resided in parts of western Texas, southern Colorado, and New Mexico. On a mission, presidio, and ranching frontier they maintained their presence by suppressing Indian revolts, concluding alliances with Indian nations, and intermarrying with the Indian population.

The rest of the region was the domain of Plains

Indians. By 1800 these Indians generally were either semisedentary agricultural villagers or horse-mounted hunters. Nations such as the Mandans, Pawnees, Wichitas, and Osages lived in semipermanent villages along the river valleys, mostly in the eastern Plains. These tribes cultivated corn, periodically hunted bison, and participated in a complex trade network that brought them into contact with Euro-American traders. Their sedentary world and sustained contact with Euro-Americans exposed them to diseases against which they had no immunities; some, like the Mandans, lost up to 90 percent of their population in the 1830s. Such devastating losses weakened their economic, political, social, and military institutions, making them vulnerable to an expanding American nation and to mounted Indian warriors who frequently raided their villages for horses, food stores, and captives.

On the western Plains a true horse-based life emerged. Tribes such as the Lakotas (the Sioux), Blackfeet, Cheyennes, Comanches, and Kiowas incorporated the horse into their culture and became highly efficient hunters. They followed the massive buffalo herds, which provided food, shelter, and clothing. These mounted Indian nations managed to live in their homelands until the 1850s, when the United States began pushing into the region with force.

In the last half of the nineteenth century, diverse populations flooded onto the Great Plains from the east. Central Plains states such as Nebraska and Kansas attracted immigrants from England, Poland, Ireland, Denmark, Germany, Czechoslovakia, and Russia; sizable numbers of Norwegians and Swedes settled there and in the Dakotas and Montana. Beginning in the 1870s, African Americans moved onto the Plains, founding farming communities and black towns such as Nicodemus, Kansas, and Boley, Oklahoma. At the same time, enterprising individuals drove herds of Texas longhorn cattle to cow towns that sprang up along railroads in Kansas, Nebraska, Colorado, and Wyoming.

Western settlers traditionally have been admired for their independence, individualism, and ingenuity. This image, however, ignores the crucial role played by the U.S. government in the settlement of the Great Plains. Several important pieces of legislation provided for the distribution of the public domain and for the construction of transcontinental railroads. The Homestead Act of 1862 provided 160 acres to those who would take out a claim, live on the land for five years, and improve their farms. Subsequent land laws, such as the Timber Culture Act (1873) and the Desert Land Act (1877), distributed additional federal lands to the public. The Pacific Railroad Act of 1862 gave railroad companies generous loans and granted extensive tracts of land to complete a transcontinental railroad. The Union Pacific Railroad, part of the first transcontinental railroad (completed in 1869), traversed the central Plains. Western railroads caused construction of hundreds of Great Plains towns and villages. Communities such as Cheyenne, Wyoming; Julesburg, Colorado; and North Platte, Nebraska, began as railroad construction camps. Railroads also promoted settlement by establishing immigration societies, providing cheap fares to prospective settlers, and selling them the land granted by the federal government.

A combination of drought, credit problems, plunging land values, and a nationwide depression during the late 1880s turned farmers throughout the nation against corporate America, particularly the railroads. To vent their frustrations, they organized political movements such as the Farmers' Alliance, Greenbackers, Antimonopolists, and the Grangers. These reform groups eventually culminated in the formation of the People's or Populist Party. The Populists outlined their grievances in a manifesto adopted at a national convention in Omaha, Nebraska, in 1892. It called for reforms in national monetary policy, government ownership of the railroads and public utilities, a graduated income tax, the direct election of U.S. senators, and the referendum, recall, and initiative—reforms making lawmakers and officeholders more responsible to the people. Great Plains states enthusiastically supported the party and elected several Populist governors, congressmen, and state legislators. William Jennings Bryan, the Great Plains' most famous nineteenth-century political figure, ran unsuccessfully for president in 1896 on both the Democratic and the Populist tickets. Although the Populists failed to enact a majority of their reforms at the national level, they had some success in the states, particularly South Dakota, Colorado, Oklahoma, Texas, Nebraska, and Kansas.

Despite the varied racial and ethnic backgrounds of Plains peoples, a Great Plains culture emerged during the nineteenth century. An extractive economy based on farming and ranching, a prevalence of small towns over large cities, a shared climate and geography, and a dependence on the U.S. government bonded Plains residents together.

Conquest of the Great Plains

During the nineteenth century the United States acquired most of the Great Plains and subjugated the Indian population. The Great Plains has only once in its history been united under the domination of one people—the Apaches, during the sixteenth century—and by the end of the nineteenth century it was controlled by two nations, Canada and the United States.

In the early 1800s the central and northern Plains were in the process of being consolidated under the control of the Sioux and their Cheyenne and Arapaho allies. The southern Plains were the primary domain of the Comanches and Kiowas. Spain controlled much of New Mexico and parts of Colorado and Texas until the Mexican Revolution of 1821, when Mexico attained its independence. Mexico maintained ownership of the southern Plains from 1821 to 1848.

The United States purchased Louisiana, the western lands that drained into the Mississippi Valley, from France in 1803. This included most of the Plains north of the Red River to what is today the Canada–United States boundary. The northern Plains boundary was solidified by the Oregon Treaty of 1846, between the United States and Britain, at the forty-ninth parallel. Americans largely avoided the region until after the Civil War. Early nineteenth-century explorers such as Meriwether Lewis and William Clark (1803–1806), Zebulon Pike (1806–1807), and Stephen Long (1819–1820) identified the Great Plains as an inhospitable desert that was nonetheless essential for American military security. Nevertheless, between 1840 and 1860, more than 300,000 overland emigrants crossed the Great Plains en route to California, Oregon, and Utah.

Also in the 1840s the United States aggressively pursued a policy to obtain the southern Plains. In 1836 Texans successfully revolted against Mexico and claimed their independence. The Republic of Texas lasted from 1836 to 1845, when it requested and was granted annexation to the United States. The boundary between Texas and Mexico had never been agreed upon, and its resolution provided the backdrop for the Mexican War in 1846. This concluded with an American army in Mexico City and the signing of the Treaty of Guadalupe Hidalgo of 1848, which gave the southern Plains plus the Great Basin and California to the United States. In 1853 the United States acquired its final piece of Great Plains real estate: a sliver of southern New Mexico as a part of the Gadsden Purchase from Mexico.

Plains Wars

The nineteenth century was a time of significant warfare on the Great Plains. Although the Mexican War was fought almost exclusively in Mexico, its ramifications affected the Plains. Of greater importance to Plains residents were the American Civil War and especially the United States–Plains Indian wars.

The Civil War crisis began with confrontations in Kansas over the implementation of the Kansas-Nebraska Act of 1854. Under this compromise legislation the new territories on the Plains could choose whether to allow slavery. This popular sovereignty provoked a movement to Kansas of pro- and anti-slavery forces. One northerner, John Brown, led the killing of several southerners at Pottawatamie Creek in 1856, and "bleeding" Kansas became a prelude to the Civil War (1861–1865). During the Civil War the Battle of Glorieta in New Mexico (1862) established the Union presence and confined the Confederate Army to Texas. The war also split many Indian nations that had been removed to the Indian Territory (later renamed Oklahoma) prior to the Civil War, and they lost extensive landholdings as a result.

In 1864, at Sand Creek in southeastern Colorado, the Colorado militia, led by a Methodist minister, John Chivington, attacked and brutally slaughtered a peaceful village of Cheyennes and Arapahos. The Sand Creek massacre marked the beginning of confrontations between the United States and Plains Indian nations that would not subside until 1890 and the Wounded Knee massacre in South Dakota. The incorporation of the Great Plains into the United States had a profound impact on its indigenous population. The greatest consequence for Plains Indians was the near annihilation of the bison by Euro-American hunters during the 1870s. The Lakotas and Cheyennes on the northern Plains and the Comanches and Kiowas on the southern Plains fought bitterly to maintain control of their native lands and culture. In perhaps the most famous battle between American Indians and the U.S. Army, an alliance of Lakotas, Cheyennes, and Arapahos annihilated George A. Custer's Seventh Cavalry at the Battle of the Little Bighorn in 1876. Armed resistance could do little more than temporarily halt the advancement of Euro-American settlers, however, and by the early 1880s all Plains tribes lived on reservations. Several important Native American leaders emerged out of the Plains wars, such as the Lakota patriots Crazy Horse, Red Cloud, and Sitting Bull.

The federal government devised a strict reservation system on the Plains that prevented travel and forced Indian parents to place their children in boarding schools, drafted legislation to stifle Native American sovereignty, and passed the Dawes Severalty Act to encourage the taking of Indian lands. The Dawes Act remained the cornerstone of U.S. Indian policy from its passage in 1887 until 1934. More land was lost by American Indians under the Dawes Severalty Act than through any war.

By 1900 the Great Plains was incorporated into the United States. Eight states and two territories (New Mexico and Oklahoma) had been carved out of the Plains. The 1900 U.S. census reported more than 5.5 million people residing on the Great Plains, with the largest populations in Kansas and Nebraska. The Plains as it entered the twentieth century was a place of small towns, Spanish-speaking villages, and Indian reservations where farming and ranching were the primary economic activities.

See also **American Indians,** *subentries on* **Wars and Warfare; American Indian Societies,** *subentry on* **The Plains; Kansas-Nebraska Act; Mexican War; Populism.**

Bibliography

Kraenzel, Carl. *The Great Plains in Transition.* Norman: University of Oklahoma Press, 1955.

Lowie, Robert H. *Indians of the Plains.* Lincoln: University of Nebraska Press, 1954.

Luebke, Frederick C., ed. *Ethnicity on the Great Plains.* Lincoln: University of Nebraska Press, 1980.

Ortiz, Roxanne Dunbar. *The Great Sioux Nation: Sitting in Judgement on America.* Berkeley, Calif.: Moon, 1977.

Utley, Robert. *The Last Days of the Sioux Nation.* New Haven, Conn.: Yale University Press, 1963.

Vigil, Ralph H., Frances W. Kaye, and John R. Wunder, eds. *Spain and the Plains: Myths and Reality of Spanish Exploration and Settlement.* Niwot: University Press of Colorado, 1994.

Webb, Walter Prescott. *The Great Plains.* Boston: Ginn, 1931. New York: Grosset and Dunlap, 1957.

Wright, James E., and Sarah Z. Rosenberg, eds. *The Great Plains Experience: Readings in the History of a Region.* Lincoln: University of Mid-America [Nebraska Educational TV], 1978.

Wunder, John R., ed. *Law and the Great Plains: Essays on the Legal History of the Heartland.* Westport, Conn.: Greenwood, 1996.

MARK R. ELLIS
JOHN R. WUNDER

GUNFIGHTERS   The first image of the American West that comes to mind is that of the gunfighter: a tall, lean, leathery-looking man riding his horse across the plains from town to town, ruthlessly using his quick draw to kill anyone standing in his way. This, however, is not a true picture of the American gunfighter. It is a glorified depiction created by books, movies, and other media in the nineteenth and twentieth centuries. Regardless, the American gunfighter endures as an item of fascination worldwide.

Creating a Legend

The myth of the American gunfighter was created in the 1840s in Richard Fox's *Police Gazette.* This weekly periodical had an enormous circulation, and its editors realized there was tremendous profit potential in the drama of the gunfighter. They portrayed the gunfighter as handsome, an experienced horseman, and a skilled marksman. In *Police Gazette* stories, the gunfighter provided the oppressed with life, liberty, and the right to pursue happiness. The make-believe gunfighter usually was motivated by his father's murder by a corrupt lawman or was a Confederate soldier driven to his vocation by ruthless northerners.

Other publications of the mid and late 1800s, such as *Frank Leslie's Weekly* and *Harper's,* saw the potential of gunfighter stories but were more factual than the *Police Gazette.* Such correspondents as Theodore Davis (1840–1894), a renowned Civil War artist, provided stories that ranged from descriptions of cattle rustlers and Indian attacks to interviews (including sketches) with gunfighters. These contemporary portrayals of gunfighters were of great interest to readers in the eastern United States and throughout the world. These accounts helped fuel the egos of the handful of gunfighters who attempted to live up to the legends and also made heroes out of the outlaw gunfighters.

Buffalo Bill Cody brought the image of the gunfighter to life in Buffalo Bill's Wild West Show, which toured the world. In this troupe's performances, actors portrayed gunfighters, outlaws, and thieves. In some cases an actual gunfighter, such as the famous marshal Wild Bill Hickok, appeared in the show.

Another myth created around the gunfighter was the quick draw. Legends described two men on a dusty street; in a blur, they both fire and one falls to the ground. In reality, accuracy was valued over speed, and many gunfighters preferred to use rifles or shotguns in a gunfight.

Profile of a Gunfighter

Outlaws and lawmen were all considered gunfighters. The typical gunfighter was a man who used his gun for a living. He was a law officer, hunter, soldier, thief, cattle rustler, bounty hunter, gambler, or hired killer. He robbed banks, trains, and stagecoaches. He could be Anglo or Hispanic, and it was not uncommon for a gunfighter to be on both sides of the law from one moment to the next. One example was Sam Bass (1851–1878), known as the "good badman" because he gave some of what he stole from the rich to the poor. In 1875 he left the employment of a sheriff in Denton, Texas, and became an outlaw. Bass formed a gang to rob stagecoaches and trains and eventually was shot by Texas Rangers during an attempted bank robbery. Unlike Bass, some men became gunfighters by accident. Ranchers, cowboys, teachers, and prospectors could all find themselves participating in a gunfight.

Even though gunfights and robberies primarily involved men, women also were known to take part. The role of women in the American West differed from that of women in the East. On the frontier, a strong and resourceful woman could forge her way more freely than in any other place. Belle Starr (1848–1889), the "bandit queen," is the best-known female outlaw. Legends say she was wanted dead or alive for robbery, murder, treason, and other acts against the peace and dignity of the United States. Starr probably was a horse thief. She was shot in the back in 1889.

Law and the West

A period of lawlessness spread throughout the American West following the Civil War, and gunfighting flourished in the 1870s and 1880s. This trend was caused by several factors, led by a lack of adequate law enforcement. Policing primarily fell to county sheriffs and constables. Most of these men were stationed in county seats and thus were virtually nonexistent throughout the mountains and plains. Occasionally, soldiers were used to bring outlaws to justice, and the Texas Rangers developed a reputation based on their toughness and ability to capture outlaws either dead or alive. The Texas Rangers occasionally crossed into Mexico while chasing gunfighters and desperadoes, which kept hostilities between Texans and Mexicans high.

Another cause of the spread of lawlessness was the universal acceptance of the "code of the West." This unwritten moral standard was vaguely similar to the dueling code used in the American South before the Civil War. However, many differences existed between the "code duello" of the South and the "code of the West." For example, southerners did not duel outside their social class; in the West, social standing made no difference. In the South, society regulated the code; in the West, each man developed his own version of the code. Courage, pride, and disregard for personal safety were necessary in the West when one was insulted or wronged. These insults, real or imagined, led to many gunfights, which often were cold-blooded killings or ambushes. A wide range of westerners, from drifters to prominent citizens, participated in these events.

Tensions between Hispanics and Anglos also led to violence. Beyond the inevitable cultural clashes, there was contempt between the two groups based on

their history. Anglos tended to distrust the Hispanics, and the feeling was mutual. Texans moving west brought a well-developed sense of superiority to and contempt for the Hispanics. The Texas revolution (1835–1836) and the Mexican War (1846–1848) were not forgotten easily, and the Hispanics and Anglos clashed frequently, leading to gunfights that advanced almost to the point of a racial war in places like Lincoln County, New Mexico.

Famous Gunfighters

Nicknames based on appearance, personality, or occupation often were used by gunfighters. These nicknames were self-chosen, given by gang members or adversaries, or assigned by reporters creating good copy for eastern readers. One of the most famous gunfighters is known by his nickname, "Billy the Kid."

Born in New York City, Billy the Kid (1859–1881) was known by many names, including William H. Bonney, Henry McCarty, and Kid Antrim. In 1873 he moved with his mother and her new husband to Silver City, New Mexico, where he spent much of his youth in saloons. He reportedly killed twenty-one men in his lifetime and committed his first murder at age twelve. He became notorious for robbery and murder and even became involved in the cattle wars in Lincoln County. Sheriff Pat Garrett (1850–1908) captured Billy the Kid in 1880. The outlaw escaped in early 1881, killing two guards. Soon after, Garrett shot and killed Billy the Kid in Fort Sumner, New Mexico.

It was not uncommon for brothers to participate in gunfights together. The most famous gunfighting brothers were Jesse (1847–1882) and Frank (1843–1915) James. At age fifteen Jesse James joined a band of pro-Confederate raiders led by William Clarke Quantrill (1837–1865). Jesse earned a reputation for recklessness and, following the war, formed his own gang, including his brother, Frank, and the Younger brothers (Cole, James, and Robert). In 1876 the gang was involved in a shootout where everyone in the gang was killed except Jesse and Frank James. Jesse was shot by a new member of his own gang seeking reward money in 1882, and shortly thereafter Frank James surrendered. The American public treated Frank James as a hero.

One of the most famous lawmen of the American West was Wyatt Earp (1848–1929). He was born in Illinois and had many occupations. In 1878 he became assistant marshal of Dodge City, Kansas, and later moved to several frontier towns. His reputation as a gunfighter grew as he went to Tombstone, Arizona, and became deputy U.S. marshal for the entire Arizona Territory. Earp, his two brothers, and Doc

Holliday (1852–1887) participated in the famous, but inappropriately named, gunfight at the O.K. Corral in 1881. The gunfight actually took place on another street.

The gunfighters of the American West knew the risks involved with their vocation and understood that at any moment their actions and reactions easily could become violent. The stories of frontier lawlessness in the second half of the nineteenth century are very colorful and often embellished. But the "code of the West" and the gunfighter are historical reminders of the rapid westward growth experienced by the young United States.

See also **Dueling; Interpretations of the Nineteenth Century,** *subentry on* **Popular Interpretations of the Frontier West; Outlaws; West, The.**

Bibliography

Bryan, Howard. *Wildest of the Wild: True Tales of a Frontier Town on the Santa Fe Trail*. Santa Fe, N.Mex.: Clear Light, 1988.

Horan, James D. *The Authentic West*. 3 vols. New York: Crown, 1976–1980.

O'Neal, Bill. *Encyclopedia of Western Gunfighters*. Norman: University of Oklahoma Press, 1979.

Utley, Robert M. *High Noon in Lincoln: Violence on the Western Frontier*. Albuquerque: University of New Mexico Press, 1987.

FRANK T. WHEELER

GUNS   See **Firearms.**

H

HAITI Relations between the United States and Haiti during the nineteenth century revolved around issues of trade, strategic concerns, and, overhanging all affairs, race. The "Negro republic" posed immense problems for U.S. policymakers as they struggled to balance the economic, political, and strategic gains that closer relations with Haiti might bring against their own deeply ingrained racism, which viewed the black nation as a threat to American social sensibilities.

American Ambiguity

By the time Jean-Jacques Dessalines declared Haiti (which until 1844 comprised both present-day Haiti and the Dominican Republic) an independent nation in 1804, the U.S. attitude toward the new republic was clear. Trade was one matter, and it had flourished ever since Haiti was a Spanish colony, and then a French colony known as St. Domingue. Sugar and molasses were Haiti's main exports to the United States; in return Haiti imported lumber and foodstuffs. By 1790 only Great Britain was ahead of Haiti in trade with the United States, and by the early 1800s U.S. trade with Haiti outpaced U.S. trade with all of South America.

Political relations, particularly the establishment of diplomatic recognition of Haiti, was quite another matter. U.S. policy toward the independence movement in Haiti was generally one of aloofness, though the dominant assumption was that America's prosperous trade with the island could best be protected through French control. In 1806, pressured by Na-

poleon, who seemed reluctant to give up the notion that Haiti could somehow be brought again under French control, the United States established a trade embargo against Haiti. The embargo was not intended as a particularly anti-Haiti act. The United States, heavily involved with both France and Spain in issues of territorial expansion and boundaries, simply passed the act to placate French sensibilities.

Beyond issues of trade and security, however, loomed the issue of race. Southern planters and politicians, even the more enlightened ones such as Thomas Jefferson, viewed Haiti through eyes indelibly tinted with their own racism. Initial disdain regarding the idea that the former slaves on the island could possibly engage in self-government turned to horror and revulsion at the slaughter of whites during the insurrection of 1804. Slave owners in the United States, always fearful of rebellion among their own human chattel, were steadfast in their opposition to any formal recognition of the "Negro republic." Such action by the United States might, after all, suggest that slavery was not the natural state for black Africans forcibly brought to the New World. Throughout the pre–Civil War years, therefore, the United States adamantly refused to grant recognition to Haiti. As a result Haiti was precluded from the protection, slight as it may have been, of the Monroe Doctrine, since it was not recognized as a nation that had won and preserved its independence. While other nations, such as Great Britain and Denmark, began to recognize Haiti in the mid-1820s, the United States remained unmoved.

Beyond trade, therefore, the United States and

Haiti had little contact aside from a rather ill-fated attempt to resettle free American blacks in Haiti during the 1820s. Anywhere from eight thousand to thirteen thousand blacks made the journey, but enmity between the newcomers and native Haitians, poor planning, and general dissatisfaction on the part of both the American and the Haitian governments scuttled the venture. A small-scale effort during the Civil War met a similar fate. Petitions from abolitionist groups in the 1830s asking Congress for U.S. recognition of Haiti were similarly unsuccessful.

When the American Civil War began in 1861, Americans expected relations between Haiti and the United States to remain as they had for decades. However, the occupation of Haiti's neighbor, Santo Domingo, by Spanish forces in that year revived the recognition issue. Though President Abraham Lincoln did not want to do anything to offend the slave-owning but still loyal border states, Secretary of State William Seward argued that U.S. recognition of Haiti might serve as a useful counterweight to the Spanish presence. Given the go-ahead by Lincoln, Seward presented the issue to Congress, emphasizing the Spanish threat and the economic factor: both U.S. exports to Haiti and imports from Haiti amounted to more than $2 million. In June 1862 the United States formally extended diplomatic recognition, and Benjamin Whidden became U.S. commissioner and consul general. Following Haitian complaints that this was a rather low-level appointment, the status of the U.S. representative was raised to minister resident in 1866.

Recognition and Trade

Following U.S. recognition of Haiti, the two countries found few sources of friction. Claims against Haiti by U.S. citizens arising from the destruction of years of revolution and war were wrestled with, and U.S. diplomats in Haiti were often pressured and courted by opposing sides during Haiti's various political upheavals of the late nineteenth century. The "Negro republic" also became one of the official "Negro posts" in the U.S. diplomatic service, along with Liberia. Republicans saw the appointment of African Americans to such posts as rewards for black political support. Beginning in 1869 and continuing almost without interruption until the 1910s, African Americans, including Frederick Douglass, held the position of minister resident. In 1897 the minister's position became envoy extraordinary–minister plenipotentiary.

The years after the Civil War were marked by an increase in Haitian-U.S. trade and the development of U.S. strategic interest in Haiti. The growth in trade was but one example of the aggressive commercial expansionism pursued by the United States in the last decades of the nineteenth century. By the 1890s the United States had become Haiti's second most important trading partner, barely behind France. America's strategic interest in Haiti was also related to the overseas commercial surge of the post–Civil War era. The U.S. Navy demanded a coaling station in the Caribbean from which it could protect American shipping and transportation routes across the Central American isthmus; one of its preferred sites was Môle St.-Nicolas in Haiti. American persistence in trying to persuade Haiti to lease the harbor to the United States resulted in some tense diplomatic exchanges during the late 1880s and early 1890s. Eventually the United States, sensing that the Haitians were inflexible on the matter, backed off from its position. However, the same arguments reappeared just prior to the U.S. intervention in Haiti in 1915.

See also **Central America and the Caribbean; Cuba.**

Bibliography
Logan, Rayford. *The Diplomatic Relations of the United States with Haiti, 1776–1891*. Chapel Hill: University of North Carolina Press, 1941.
Montague, Ludwell Lee. *Haiti and the United States, 1714–1938*. Durham, N.C.: Duke University Press, 1940.
Plummer, Brenda Gayle. *Haiti and the United States: The Psychological Moment*. Athens, Ga.: University of Georgia Press, 1992.

MICHAEL L. KRENN

HARPERS FERRY AND JOHN BROWN
Born in Torrington, Connecticut, John Brown (1800–1859) grew up in Hudson, Ohio. After receiving a rudimentary education he attempted but failed at careers as a tanner, wool dealer, and farmer. Strong religious principles moved Brown toward abolitionism. Although not affiliated with any antislavery society, he befriended leading abolitionists Gerrit Smith and Frederick Douglass. Passage of the Fugitive Slave Law of 1850 encouraged Brown to become more militant in his antislavery activities. In Springfield, Massachusetts, he helped blacks form the League of Gileadites, an armed society that resisted efforts to recapture runaway slaves. In 1855 Brown followed five of his sons to Kansas, where he became a minor leader of the armed opposition to that territory's admission as a slave state. He became notorious for his role in the massacre of five proslavery settlers at Pottawatomie Creek in May 1856 in retaliation for attacks on the free-state settlement of Lawrence.

In 1857 Brown secretly began to recruit men and raise funds to establish a base in the southern Appalachian Mountains from which to raid plantations and free slaves. Financing came from a group of white abolitionists, dubbed the "Secret Six," and from Canadian and northern free blacks, including Frederick Douglass. When fear of exposure forced Brown to postpone his southern invasion, his band raided a Missouri plantation and liberated eleven slaves. Brown's plotting culminated in the unsuccessful attack by twenty-one men, including three of his sons and five blacks, on the federal armory at Harpers Ferry, Virginia, on 16 October 1859. Only about twelve slaves were liberated, but a number of white citizens were taken hostage. By the second day of Brown's occupation, the local militia had sealed off his escape route. On 18 October a detachment of U.S. Marines, commanded by Brevet Colonel Robert E. Lee, overran the engine house in which Brown held his captives. In two days of fighting, Brown's insurgents killed six people, including one marine, while losing ten men, among them Brown's sons Oliver and Watson. Five raiders, including Brown's son Owen, evaded capture and with the help of abolitionist sympathizers went into hiding.

Tried for treason under Virginia law, Brown was found guilty and sentenced to be hanged on 2 December 1859. His fortitude while imprisoned, along with propaganda published by his abolitionist allies, helped make Brown a martyr to many northerners. Despite pleas from Brown's friends, Governor Henry Wise allowed the abolitionist to be executed as scheduled. Six other captured raiders were also hanged.

See also **Abolition and Antislavery.**

Bibliography

Boyer, Richard Owen. *The Legend of John Brown: A Biography and a History.* New York: Knopf, 1973.
Finkelman, Paul, ed. *His Soul Goes Marching On: Responses to John Brown and the Harpers Ferry Raid.* Charlottesville: University Press of Virginia, 1993.
Oates, Stephen B. *To Purge This Land with Blood: A Biography of John Brown.* New York: Harper and Row, 1970.

JOHN R. MCKIVIGAN

HAWAII Consisting of eight major islands (Kauai, Niihau, Oahu, Molokai, Maui, Lānai, Kahoolawe, and Hawai'i Island) located 2,400 miles WSW of San Francisco, the Hawaiian Islands lie entirely within the tropics and are of volcanic origin, with the tallest volcanoes rising 13,600 feet above the Pacific Ocean. The Hawaiian archipelago was discovered and populated by Polynesian voyagers around A.D. 300. At the time of Western discovery by the English explorer captain James Cook on 18 January 1778, these islands supported four complex chiefdoms. Cook named the islands after the English earl of Sandwich, and the present collective name, the Hawaiian Islands or simply Hawaii, only became used commonly after 1840. The first American in Hawaii was Cook's corporal of marines, John Ledyard, who, like many of Cook's officers, went on to become a great explorer in his own right.

The Kingdom of Hawaii

Accounts of Cook's last voyage stimulated commerce in the North Pacific. Cook had discovered an abundance of fur-bearing animals in the Pacific Northwest, and his men were impressed at the eagerness for trade of these pelts in Canton, China. This news sparked the Pacific fur trade, in which manufactured trinkets were traded to the Northwest Indians for pelts that were then traded to the Chinese for tea, silks, and porcelains, which fetched a high price in London or Boston. The Hawaiian Islands were conveniently situated to provide food, recreation, and a winter haven for this trade. The political unification of the islands in 1810, under the Hawaiian king Kamehameha the Great provided safety and encouraged commerce. By 1785, Yankee traders were visiting Hawaii, and by 1800 the transpacific fur trade was virtually monopolized by New England traders. Between 1800 and 1830, these traders did a booming business selling Hawaiian sandalwood in China. Yankee traders offered the Hawaiian aristocracy everything from pins to luxury yachts on credit for the aromatic wood, and soon the Hawaiian Kingdom had run up a considerable debt.

Many Hawaiians were recruited as sailors or workers in the Pacific Northwest. One Hawaiian youth, Henry Obookiah (Opukahaia), ended up in New England and became the first Hawaiian convert to Christianity. The publication of his posthumous *Memoirs* in 1818 stimulated the American Board of Commissioners for Foreign Missions (ABCFM) to send Congregational missionaries to Hawaii. Approximately 200 missionaries arrived in Hawaii between 1820 and 1864 and had an impact that is still debated today. The ABCFM missionaries standardized a Hawaiian alphabet and promoted literacy, printing more than a hundred million pages in the Hawaiian language between 1822 and 1842. The missionaries also became increasingly involved in political life as advisers to the aristocracy, and several left the mission to enter government service.

The first written laws of the Kingdom of Hawaii were modeled after the Ten Commandments. The

Liliuokalani

Liliuokalani (1839–1917) was the last reigning monarch of the Kingdom of Hawaii, ruling from 29 January 1891 until she was deposed on 17 January 1893. She was a strong-willed woman who sought to restore the power to the throne she felt that her brother, King David Kalākaua, had lost. The circumstances leading up to the overthrow are still a matter of debate. On 14 January 1893 the Queen prorogued the legislature and attempted to promulgate a new constitution that would have greatly increased the power of the monarchy. A relatively small group of white businessmen declared her in attempted revolution and seized the opportunity to depose the Queen. This was effectively facilitated by the actions of the U.S. minister John L. Stevens and the presence of the Marines of the USS *Boston*. The Queen capitulated, writing:

> I yield to the superior force of the United States of America . . . I do this under protest and impelled by said force yield my authority until such time as the Government of the United States shall upon the facts being presented to it undo the action of its representative and reinstate me in the authority which I claim as Constitutional Sovereign of the Hawaiian Islands.

President Cleveland made an attempt to reinstate Liliuokalani to the throne but was unsuccessful. Liliuokalani was an accomplished composer, particularly known for the song "Aloha `oe" (Farewell to thee). She became much beloved by the Hawaiian people and a potent symbol of Hawaiian aspirations.

DAVID W. SHIDELER

Declaration of Rights of 1839 and the first Constitution of the Kingdom of 1840, though composed by Hawaiians in the Hawaiian language, drew on the American Declaration of Independence and the Bible, illustrating the influence of missionary advisers.

In the same year that the missionaries arrived in Hawaii, so did the whaling industry, which was similarly dominated by New Englanders. These whalers deservedly earned a reputation as brawlers intent on carousing, and they did not appreciate missionary meddling.

Relations with the United States

Foreign businessmen offered the Hawaiian aristocracy luxury goods on credit, which was to be paid in sandalwood. Unfamiliar with credit, the aristocracy acquired mounting debt, resulting in merchants' calling on their governments to aid their cause in gaining payment. This "Sandalwood debt" gave rise to American "gunboat diplomacy" with the arrival of the first American naval vessel, the *Dolphin,* under Captain "Mad Jack" Percival in 1826. Percival managed to get the Hawaiian chiefs to acknowledge a $300,000 debt to American merchants; but he is better known for the riot his men committed, breaking windows and attacking the missionary preacher Hiram Bingham, and for forcing the Hawaiian Kingdom to repeal its anti-prostitution laws.

A number of Americans, including the medical missionary Gerrit P. Judd, the lawyer William Little Lee, and the U.S. commissioner Anthony Ten Eyck were instrumental in land reform (1848–1850). Americans soon dominated ownership of Hawaii's fee-simple lands.

The California gold rush of 1849 and the American Civil War (1861–1865) created a great demand for food stuffs, particularly Hawaiian sugar. While English and German interests were considerable in Hawaiian commercial agriculture, Americans dominated the enterprise from the beginning.

From as early as 1848, the Kingdom of Hawaii had sought a reciprocity agreement with the United States to allow Hawaiian goods (particularly sugar) into America with little or no duty. In 1876 a Reciprocity Treaty with the United States went into effect. Sugar production in Hawaii increased eightfold during the next decade. The McKinley Tariff Act of 1890 wiped out the advantages of the treaty by removing the tariff on raw sugar from foreign countries and granting domestic producers a two-cent-a-pound bounty. This produced a major incentive for members of the foreign business community to seek annexation of Hawaii to the United States.

In 1893 a revolution led by a small group of mostly American businessmen deposed Queen Liliuokalani, the last monarch of the Hawaiian Kingdom. While specifics are still contested, there is general consensus that U.S. minister John L. Stevens and the Marines of the USS *Boston* were instrumental in bringing about the overthrow.

The United States declined to annex Hawaii in 1893 and indeed by the end of the year was attempting to restore Liliuokalani to the throne. President Grover Cleveland denounced the "lawless occupation of Honolulu under false pretexts by the United States forces" (*President's Message Relating to the Hawaiian Islands,* 18 December 1893). Hawaii was finally annexed on 12 August 1898, as a result of its perceived strategic importance in the Spanish-American War. The signing of the Organic Act of 1900 incorporated the Territory of Hawaii, with its population of 154,000, into the United States. Hawaii acquired statehood in 1959. By the end of the twentieth century, many Hawaiians had begun to seek some form of sovereign self-governance and reparations. Public Law 103-150, a joint resolution of the U.S. Congress dated 23 November 1993 and signed by President Bill Clinton one hundred years after the overthrow of Queen Liliuokalani, the Hawaiian monarchy, and the Kingdom of Hawaii on 17 January 1893, expresses "deep regret . . . [for] the suppression of the inherent sovereignty of the Native Hawaiian people."

See also **Exploration and Explorers; Foreign Trade and Tariffs; Missions,** *subentry on* **Foreign Missions; Statehood and Admission.**

Bibliography

Bradley, Harold Whitman. *The American Frontier in Hawaii: The Pioneers, 1789–1843.* Stanford, Calif.: Stanford University Press, 1942.

Daws, Gavan. *Shoal of Time: A History of the Hawaiian Islands.* Honolulu: University of Hawaii Press, 1974.

Kuykendall, Ralph Simpson. *The Hawaiian Kingdom.* 3 vols. Honolulu: University of Hawaii Press, 1938–1965.

Liliuokalani, Queen of Hawaii. *Hawaii's Story by Hawaii's Queen.* Honolulu: Mutual, 1990.

Russ, William. *The Hawaiian Revolution (1893–1894).* Selinsgrove, Pa.: Susquehanna University Press, 1959.

Takaki, Ronald. *Pau Hana: Plantation Life and Labor in Hawaii, 1835–1920.* Honolulu: University of Hawaii Press, 1983.

DAVID W. SHIDELER

HEALTH AND DISEASE Three broad factors shaped Americans' experience of health and disease during the nineteenth century: the kinds of diseases that afflicted large numbers of people; the local, domestic setting for sickness and caregiving; and the growing dominance after 1880 of orthodox medical doctors and the institutions in which they housed their particular style of medicine.

The Threat of Infectious Disease

Overall, infectious diseases borne by air, water, food, and insects were the most widespread threat to Americans' health throughout the nineteenth century. This is not to say that genetic diseases, mental illness, or chronic degenerative diseases, such as cancer, were inconsequential or ignored. Nor did Americans discount the increase in occupational diseases, especially respiratory ailments plaguing coal minors and textile mill workers, which affected increasing numbers of workers after 1870. But no kind of sickness surpassed the power of infectious disease both to inflict acute suffering and to mobilize efforts at relief. These diseases sometimes took epidemic form, such as the

nearly annual surges of yellow fever along the Atlantic seaboard in the early 1800s; the widespread outbreaks of Asiatic cholera in 1832, 1849, and 1868; and the deadly malarial outbreaks in the Mississippi and Ohio River valleys of the late 1870s. At other times, infections were endemic, such as widespread instances of tuberculosis, especially in cities.

Because the microbiological sources of such infections were imperfectly understood until the last two decades of the century, all groups of Americans were to some extent at risk. Such diseases, however, fell with particular force on poorer citizens, who lived in crowded conditions ideal for the spread of infection and whose malnourishment further weakened their resistance. African Americans, especially in the antebellum South, and the increasing number of urban immigrants in the North and Midwest clearly were two such groups at comparatively high risk. Moreover, Native Americans throughout the century were caught up in cycles of first-time exposure to infectious diseases (most dramatically smallpox) carried to them by Anglo settlers, which killed them in large numbers.

The sudden symptomatic onset characteristic of epidemic disease, along with the dread inspired by it, drastically shaped the health experience of large numbers of Americans for most of the century. And yet endemic infectious disease—sickness typically present among a group of people and therefore comparatively familiar—doubtless resulted in more suffering and death in the long run than even the fiercest of epidemics. Poverty, habits of diet, work, and leisure, and differential immunities also shaped the spread of endemic diseases in the population. Many African Americans were comparatively immune to certain strains of malaria because of a genetic trait that caused sickle cell anemia. The poor in warmer climates were susceptible to parasitic diseases or such dietary deficiency ailments as pellagra; Native Americans and Irish immigrants were plagued by alcoholism.

Other demographic characteristics were important as well. The vulnerability of children, for example, to measles, diphtheria, scarlet fever, and other potentially lethal viral and bacterial infections made childhood a time of life as vulnerable to serious disease as extreme old age. Women of childbearing age faced not only the physical stresses of pregnancy and birth but also the severe risk of postpartum infection that made sickness associated with childbirth probably the greatest single threat to the health of most women across class and racial lines. Malarial fevers were endemic to certain portions of the South, and in the colder northern states pneumonia and gastrointestinal infections often proved fatal. Tuberculosis, especially after 1850, was deeply seated in both the North and the South, and through the middle decades of the century it appears that various forms of kidney failure or heart failure (which likely were behind the widespread diagnoses of "dropsy" and "rheumatism") accounted for high levels of morbidity and mortality in all regions.

Diagnostic terms that shift over time pose a problem for knowing what really afflicted sick people. Neither diagnostic procedures nor disease categories were standardized to any reliable degree throughout the century; published case studies, too, are idiosyncratic by modern standards, making retrospective diagnosis highly speculative. Broadly speaking, Americans' life expectancy (at birth) appears to have risen during the century, from perhaps thirty to thirty-five to forty to forty-five years. While still reflecting the toll taken by childhood diseases, the gradual rise suggests that by the end of the century, Americans were somewhat less likely to succumb to the major infections. The extent to which this change occurred, however, was not due to breakthroughs in therapeutic drugs or other interventions used by doctors. The change took place, first, because nutrition improved for most people, conferring added resistance to disease; and, second, because larger numbers of Americans were receptive to the heightened regulation of public health and to new standards of personal cleanliness as a shield against becoming sick.

Family, Community, and the Culture of Health

The way in which Americans cope with sickness and the skills and substances that were brought to the sickbed are crucial to understanding the experience of health and disease. For nearly everyone, regardless of wealth or social background, care for the sick was profoundly local in its resources and was delivered in a domestic setting. Although there were exceptions to this general rule—tubercular patients journeying to restorative places, late-century urban immigrants ending up in warehouse-like hospital wards—for the most part, sick people received care and got better or worse in familiar settings at the hands of people known to them. Moreover, although we now know that nearly all medicines in widespread use were ineffective against the major infectious diseases, Americans were notably partial to taking drugs as a first resort, whether preventive or remedial. Certain therapies in use throughout the century did have beneficial effects confirmed a century later: vaccination against smallpox, quinine as a hedge against malaria, carbolic acid as an antiseptic. In the main, however, Americans used a far greater range of substances that had dramatic effects on physical symptoms, altering

"Sowing for Diphtheria." Diseases such as diphtheria spread quickly in both rural and urban areas where ventilation and sanitation were poor. Wood engraving of a drawing by Gaston Fay. *Harper's Weekly*, 15 January 1881. LIBRARY OF CONGRESS

or masking them, if not the therapeutic power that people imagined. Like drugs, ideas about the origins and nature of disease were drawn from a combination of sources—professional, vernacular, and exotic. Americans were open to overlapping spiritual, moral, and behavioral explanations of why they were sick, and they rarely dismissed any theory that seemed plausible. In sum, they gave and received care in a context that might not lead to cure (and might unwittingly lead to harm) but nevertheless bolstered a sense of the ability to act, choose, and try.

Family was central to this health care context in ways that had important consequences for Americans' experience of health and disease. Birth and death remained domestic events for most people. Women of all classes were the primary birth attendants and caregivers; at death, they prepared the body and oversaw burial and mourning. In most homes, therefore, women were the sources of local knowledge about both sickness and basic therapies. In their diaries and letters, women frequently commented on health and illness—sharing medicinal recipes, critically comparing physicians, and in general organizing the household's watchfulness in the face of disease.

Americans traded views on the relative "healthiness" of their surroundings, making the assessment of climate and hearsay into a touchstone of well-being that extended from the household to the community at large. The relationship of disease to religious faith also was a matter of general popular concern, cutting across social and gender divisions. The will of God or the power of the supernatural was never far from people's sense of the meaning of sickness. Although the most inclusive public expressions of the tie between religious faith and the onset of disease—days of fasting and prayer during epidemics, for example—diminished somewhat during the century, Americans from various backgrounds privately continued to see clear ties between physical symptoms and possible moral or social transgressions. They acted in ways that affirmed an unbreakable link between spiritual and physical well-being, searching for ways to atone, to revitalize faith, or to give testimony to the wisdom of God's trials and the mercy of his acts. Preachers and holy healers, as well as doctors, gathered around the sickbed. The demonstration of religious faith, through prayer or a reliance on a traditional world of spirits or by seeking other portals to the supernatural world, was for many social groups a distinct way to mobilize collective resources of health.

Indeed, there arose in many areas a blended culture of faith healing and mental resistance to disease that in no way denied disease's physical seat in the body. In the decades before 1880, especially, there was surging interest among middle-class Americans in the connections between God's grace and the wonders of the natural world. They took an interest in learning about the natural environment, cultivating physical exercise and physiological information. Americans "botanized," collecting samples of local flora and fauna; they became interested in weather, many keeping meteorological records; and they joined "physiological clubs." Combining such knowledge with prayer or spiritualism, along with drugs, these Americans created a broad context for health and disease that was testimony to health as a spiritual condition as well as a physical one.

These domestic practices took place in a medical marketplace characterized by a vast array of healers who put forward their ideas and substances for popular use. A few cities and other local jurisdictions taxed or otherwise kept tabs on certain healers—midwives, for instance. But regulations were fragmentary or unenforced, and during the greater part of the century, sects of healers flourished or withered in a competition where the byword was "caveat emptor." Powerful drugs were available with no restriction and at comparatively low cost. The domestic context for healing—indeed, for much of basic medical knowledge itself—gave households the ultimate authority to decide which brand of medicine would best serve.

The engine that drove this competitive medical world for all but the last decade of the century depended on several factors. First, no single medical sect was able to demonstrate that it was most effective across the entire range of risks and maladies; thus none could place sufficient pressure on people or lawmaking bodies to give them sole license to heal. Second, the dominant political climate in general, especially during the antebellum years, tended to be one in which professional hegemony over popular choice looked like a bid for monopoly power and was regarded with a powerful skepticism. Finally, medical sects tended to borrow certain therapies and procedures from each other and, in practice if not in theory, acted in ways that blurred lines between them. For example, even though orthodox physicians officially scorned hydrotherapists' enthusiasm for water as a panacea, in practice, after the 1840s many physicians recommended pure drinking water to their patients as a "tonic" and advocated bathing as a disease preventive rather than a risky behavior. To take another example, physicians themselves split into warring factions during the early decades of the century, with a minority of homeopaths (who favored infinitesimal doses of drugs that mimicked disease symptoms, rallying the body's natural healing powers) contesting therapies with allopaths (who prescribed large amounts of harshly acting drugs that reversed symptoms). In actual practice, however, many physicians adopted an eclectic stance, using remedies dictated less by dogma than by their own or their patients' experience. Although it was risky and open to abuse by charlatans, this wide-open medical world also was testimony to the power of popular ideas about health and medicine to dominate decisions about care.

The Significance of Physicians

In the deepest sense, the struggle among sects of healers during the century had a significance that went far beyond the competition for economic rewards. It was a struggle over the definition of medical knowledge itself—how it would be intellectually organized and institutionally structured and how health itself

Vaccination of Infants for Smallpox. Edward Jenner (1749–1823) determined that vaccinating humans with the cowpox virus gave immunity against smallpox. The practice was accepted by physicians by 1797. *The Graphic*, 13 January 1883. LIBRARY OF CONGRESS

was to be defined. The rise of orthodox, mostly allopathic physicians—healers holding medical degrees and claiming descent from such ancient authorities as Galen and Hippocrates—as a result of this debate is a particularly sharp way to focus the key changes in health and disease that, gathering force in the 1840s, became dominant during the last twenty years of the century.

The U.S. Census counted 40,755 people identifying themselves as physicians in 1850, a number that rose to 64,414 in 1870 and to 104,805 twenty years later. These were practitioners who claimed to possess a medical degree or who professed to practice in an orthodox fashion. Physicians were by far the largest group among medical sects, and, with the possible exception of such virulently anti-allopathic healers as Thomsonian botanical doctors, followers of doctor and entrepreneur Samuel Thomson (1769–1843) in the antebellum years, they were the most aggressively organized in their efforts to dominate the medical world. Along with the prestige of their ancient lineage and their dedication to scholarly tradition, physicians were notable as early as the 1820s for the social visibility of their medical societies, journals, and, most important, formal education. Even in the dispersed, domestic-centered world of medical practice, orthodox medical schools grew rapidly during the years after 1820, with the 10 schools in that

year increasing to 44 in 1850 and some 106 by 1890. These schools increasingly focused physicians' claims to superiority, becoming centers for orthodox medicine's search for a more effective medicine, for new standards of professionalism, and thus, especially by the 1880s, for the authority to define broadly what mattered in health care.

A great part of physicians' struggle for hegemony was a struggle over the tenets of orthodoxy itself. A chief marker of orthodoxy before the 1830s was its comparatively heavy reliance on broad (and, with hindsight, strikingly a priori) theoretical constructs of disease and the corresponding principles that explained how a person became vulnerable to it. Exact definition of these principles varied somewhat among physicians, but most held that an individual's health depended on moderation in all things, which would maintain a balance of bodily qualities, variously described as "humors" or as properties of "vitalism," components of healthiness understood as partly organic, partly mental phenomena. Moreover, individuals possessed a basic constitution that was specific to gender, race, and age and largely unalterable, though tempered by a propensity for sickness that consisted of diet, work, prudent (or imprudent) behavior, and the use of medicines. Such abstract principles permitted physicians easily to conflate moral judgments with observations of what was "natural" and led them to think in terms of polarities: dangerous versus healthy behavior, strong as opposed to weak constitutions, and stimulating compared with depleting medicines.

This approach to defining disease and health care began to change by the 1830s, in large part because of the pressure on orthodoxy from alternative forms of medicine that were less harsh and dogmatic. But change also was rooted in increasing numbers of physicians being dissatisfied with the inability of traditional theory to guide actual practice. A new clinical empiricism, with roots not only in the innovative, anatomy-based "Paris school" of French doctors but also in the trials and errors of American physicians who were frustrated with the mismatch between orthodox theory and health care, led numbers of physicians to curb (or at least postpone using) their traditionally aggressive ("heroic") therapies in favor of observing, recording, and thus reevaluating what they saw at the bedside. Following this slow but profound change in practice, rigid theories of medicine based on balancing physical constitutions and the like began to be replaced by a more flexible sense of medicine as rooted in a dynamic of disease and health, pathologic conditions, and physiologic factors—each depending on the other and requiring careful, systematic study and broad, experimental application.

By mid-century, these changes—fitful and often frustrating to doctors and patients alike—were especially visible in three arenas of orthodox health care. It should be noted in passing that the Civil War, occurring in the midst of this change, shaped certain aspects of it. The growth of medical schools in the South, like that of other institutions, was retarded by the war's destruction. The large numbers of white Southern men killed in the war, along with the new population of freed slaves seeking medicine outside the bonds of slavery, changed the gender and racial profile of Southern patients. African American physicians began to appear in larger numbers toward the end of the century, founding their own medical schools when white schools refused black students. Physicians of all descriptions relocated their practices because of the war, and, whether returning to their communities or not, many doctors retained and developed new techniques, particularly with regard to surgery. Except in these broad ways, however, the Civil War neither initiated watershed changes in mainstream health and health care nor diverted them.

The first key change that would dramatically reshape the American medical scene by the 1890s involved the relatively greater prominence of basic science—initially physiology—in orthodox medicine. As physicians became more willing to hold back from immediate bedside intervention and to observe and record their findings, medical educators began arguing for making basic science—expanded by the 1870s to include pathology, pharmacology, and the beginnings of organic chemistry—an essential first step in learning. This movement was reflected in the expansion of medical education from two years to four, with basic sciences taught before clinical or bedside techniques. The rise of bacteriology as a science in the 1880s was a prime example of the effects of this change. As physicians and people in general began to appreciate the role of microorganisms in infectious diseases, it began to make sense to focus on the essential relationship of the well body and the legion of germs. Reformers argued that an effective application of bacteriology to medicine made it imperative to study people in aggregate, collecting data about what was statistically normal to a population, not what was deemed typical or natural to individual patients. Medical careers in basic sciences and in laboratory work thus began to open up by the 1890s.

The clinical promise of basic science and its popular appeal continued to grow, as did a second key change in mainstream health care: the rise of hospitals combining general caregiving with the practical education of physicians. Faculties in larger medical schools had been taking their students on hospital rounds since the mid-1830s, but such experience varied greatly in quality from mentor to mentor, not to mention the fact that hospitals before the 1870s were more custodial than therapeutic institutions. As formal schooling became more complex, however, both students and faculty sought a more regular way to integrate actual patient care into the new configuration of medical learning.

As urban populations of poor grew substantially in the decades following the Civil War, hospitals and medical schools combined their efforts to standardize charity care by giving over the bodies of poor patients to medical study. This, too, had a long tradition, but the difference by 1880 was the number of new general care hospitals that not only attracted funding from benefactors impressed by medical science but also gathered support from urban political leaders eager for institutions that so loudly announced progress. The medical profession, too (though not without resistance from the older generation of doctors), came to embrace an ideal of practice centered not in the patient's home but amid the growing array of complicated instruments (in the new operating room, for example) as well as baseline requirements (antisepsis, professional nurses) that by the 1890s testified to orthodox power. It followed that by the end of the century, increasing numbers of middle-class patients as well as the poor began to receive care in hospitals.

Finally, these transformations in knowledge and institutions, affecting the very definition of health and disease, were joined to a change in orthodox medicine's claim to unique legal privileges. Physicians were able to argue for the first time that the therapeutic promise in orthodox medicine, along with the ability of its institutions to attract well-funded support, made it by far the best repository for the collective interest in good health. Orthodox professional organizations like the American Medical Association grew rapidly in membership and lobbying force. Opponents wary of orthodox monopoly power continued to object to physicians' drive for privilege, but, increasingly, lawmaking bodies were inclined to agree with the physicians, passing licensure laws and other regulations that restricted and marginalized alternative forms of medicine by 1900.

Thus, physicians' rise in status to become a dominant profession with unparalleled authority to practice medicine and define disease was the sharpest single change in the organization of health care during the century. And yet there remained a gap between organization and effective cure. Although after 1880 the new science boosted successful efforts in public health and sanitation, and physicians' institutions and professional power to some extent stabilized a risky commercial world of drugs and healers, these changes did not lead immediately to effective new drugs; specific medicines for most infections still were thirty to fifty years in the future. Indeed, at the end of the century many Americans (including some physicians) worried that despite gains in public health measures, orthodoxy's new emphasis on laboratory findings and the ideal of the doctor-scientist might actually harm patient care. They feared physicians would become more remote from communities, and thus less sensitive to the social roots of caregiving traditionally nourished by bedside relationships based on personal knowledge and trust.

See also **Birth and Childbearing; Contraception and Abortion; Death and Dying; Health Consciousness and Fitness; Hospitals; Medicine; Midwives.**

Bibliography

Leavitt, Judith Walzer. *Brought to Bed: Childbearing in America, 1750 to 1950.* New York: Oxford University Press, 1986.

———. *Typhoid Mary: Captive to the Public's Health.* Boston: Beacon Press, 1996.

Leavitt, Judith Walzer, and Ronald L. Numbers, eds. *Sickness and Health in America: Readings in the History of Medicine and Public Health.* 3d ed. Madison: University of Wisconsin Press, 1997.

Ludmerer, Kenneth M. *Learning to Heal: The Development of American Medical Education.* New York: Basic Books, 1985.

Morantz-Sanchez, Regina Markell. *Sympathy and Science: Women Physicians in American Medicine.* New York: Oxford University Press, 1985.

Pernick, Martin S. *A Calculus of Suffering: Pain, Professionalism, and Anesthesia in 19th Century America.* New York: Columbia University Press, 1985.

Rosenberg, Charles E. *The Care of Strangers: The Rise of America's Hospital System.* New York: Basic Books, 1987.

———. *Explaining Epidemics and Other Studies in the History of Medicine.* Cambridge, U.K.: Cambridge University Press, 1992.

Rothman, Sheila M. *Living in the Shadow of Death: Tuberculosis and the Social Experience of Illness in American History.* New York: Basic Books, 1994.

Savitt, Todd L. *Medicine and Slavery: The Diseases and Health Care of Blacks in Antebellum Virginia.* Urbana: University of Illinois Press, 1978.

Starr, Paul. *The Social Transformation of American Medicine.* New York: Basic Books, 1982.

Tomes, Nancy. *The Gospel of Germs: Men, Women, and the Microbe in American Life, 1870–1930.* Cambridge, Mass.: Harvard University Press, 1998.

Vogel, Virgil. *American Indian Medicine.* Norman: University of Oklahoma Press, 1970.

Warner, John Harley. *Against the Spirit of System: The French Impulse in Nineteenth-Century American Medicine.* Princeton, N. J.: Princeton University Press, 1998.

———. *The Therapeutic Perspective: Medical Practice, Knowledge, and Professional Identity in America, 1820–1885.* Cambridge, Mass.: Harvard University Press, 1986.

STEVEN M. STOWE

HEALTH CONSCIOUSNESS AND FITNESS

The nineteenth century was a time of social reform. Reformers were not only interested in emotional and spiritual well-being but also that of the body, specifically physical health. During the 1800s America's health consciousness reached new heights. Illness, health, and diet were of as much concern as physical attributes and capabilities. Early on Samuel Thomson believed that the best cure was to sweat and purge the body. Instead of bloodletting as used formerly by "heroic" physicians, Thomson advocated exclusive use of liquids procured from "native vegetable flora" (Green, *Fit for America*, p. 6). He and his followers became known as "botanic" physicians who rejected formal medical education. Even though the Thomsonians attended conventions, published newsletters, and established their own schools, they dwindled in numbers, and by mid-century other ideas flourished.

Chief among these new ideas was homeopathic medicine, which also began early in the century. Its main advocates were German immigrants, who insisted on greater personal interaction between doctor and patient and medication in dosages that could be endured. In contrast, the Thomson cure reportedly used enemas laced with cayenne pepper. If purging was the way to fight disease, what was one to do to remain healthy? The more zealous promoted a vegetarian diet, water as a cure-all, breathing fresh air, daily exercise, temperance, and regular portions of bran bread. The main advocate for the bran bread diet was the minister Sylvester Graham, whose name lives on in the graham cracker, although he would not recognize the twentieth-century graham cracker as his invention. Graham taught that it was important to retain the bran in bread because of its nutritional value. Following a two-year ministry for the Presbyterian Church, he came to the fore as a spokesman for the Pennsylvania Temperance Society. Because alcohol was the chief cause of many of life's ills, alcohol had to be quashed. Such were the beginnings of Grahamism, as the health reform movement he founded became known. In building his case for temperance, he argued that true moderation in regard to alcohol consumption meant abstinence.

Russell Trall, a physician who in 1857 published the *New Hydropathic Cook-Book*, was one of the first to subscribe to the water cure as the ultimate in combating disease and maintaining health. Between 1844 and 1854 more than sixty water-cure institutions offered a therapy that consisted of baths and drinking pure water. Trall used his medical knowledge to create a program of hydropathy, gymnastics, diet, sleep, and exercise. Also by 1854 Trall had established his own medical college, the New York Hydropathic and Physiological School, which enrolled students from locations as diverse as Michigan, Louisiana, and Nova Scotia. Almost half of the students were women. More important, he taught moderation in all things, "in passions, exercise, and quantity of food" (Green, p. 64).

In the nineteenth century the dominant belief was that bodily secretions and excretions controlled both health and illness. Therefore, to control illness by promulgating health required knowing what foods to eat and what foods to avoid. A few of the more noteworthy reform movements involved herbs, alcohol, bran, vegetables, water, mineral water, and ultimately certain cereals. Each of the movements had its leaders, followers, and naysayers, and each attracted devoted adherents through the twentieth century. Medicinal herbs remained particularly attractive. Although prohibition of alcohol was short-lived, a number of religious sects continued to ban alcohol and advocated temperance. Graham started the crusade for bran, and nearly one hundred years later scientific data suggested that a shorter mean fecal transit time may reduce the incidence of colon and rectal cancers. Many researchers have studied links between unhealthful lifestyle choices and disease. Graham denounced red meat, fish, beer, wine, liquor, white bread, tobacco, coffee, tea, molasses, sugar, honey, and sedentary living.

Many espoused habits had religious underpinnings. Joseph Smith, the founder of the Church of Jesus Christ of Latter-day Saints, or Mormons (1830); Ellen G. White, the founder of the Seventh-Day Adventists (1860); and Mary Baker Eddy, the founder of Christian Science (1879), each reported visions and prophesies indicating that true believers should abstain from coffee, tea, alcohol, tobacco, and other unwholesome practices. Along with the some-

Turco-Russian Baths, Washington, D.C. The water cure was enjoyed by those who wanted to maintain good health. LIBRARY OF CONGRESS

what extreme habits of eating and purging the body, some reformers advocated a diet composed solely of vegetables. The "Bible" Christians demonstrated to their own satisfaction through careful reading of the Bible that it was God's word that animals should not be slaughtered for meat.

As the century wound down, the cereal wars were just starting between C. W. Post and the Kellogg brothers, John Harvey and Will Keith. The Kelloggs created wheat flakes in 1894, but they raced to develop a method of mass-production before someone else discovered a technique. In 1898 Post introduced his cereal Grape-Nuts, containing neither grapes nor nuts. Post not only determined how to mass-produce his cereals but was also among the first to take advantage of "nationwide mass market advertising" (Armstrong and Armstrong, *The Great American Medicine Show*, p. 111) in direct competition with the Kellogg cereals. In retaliation the Kellogg Company created a presweetened cornflake cereal, which turned the health-food craze upside down. The company marketed cereal for its taste rather than for its medicinal value.

Another prevalent idea was that regular exercise could also be beneficial for maintaining health and thwarting disease. In 1829 Edward Hitchcock wrote in the *Journal of Health*, "There is scarcely any individual among the sedentary and literary, who does not acknowledge, in general terms, the necessity of exercise" (Green, p. 85). Hitchcock devoted his life to exercise and in 1897 his son, Edward, became the first president of the National College Physical Education Association for Men (NCPEAM), the forerunner of the National Association for Physical Education in Higher Education (NAPEHE). The revival of athleticism has been ascribed to Hitchcock and others, notably Dudley Allen Sargent, the third president of NCPEAM, and the movement known as "muscular Christianity," which had its origins in England in the mid–eighteenth century.

Although a number of reforms created commotions in the United States during the nineteenth century, none had a more charismatic leader than Bernarr Macfadden of the physical culture movement. Born in 1868 in Mill Spring, Missouri, Macfadden was known as the "Father of Physical Culture." He advocated much of what Graham and others had promulgated, including proper breathing, vegetables and natural wheat bran foods, and an empirically founded health regimen that shunned doctors, medicine, and hospitals in favor of regular exercise. In 1899 Macfadden began publishing the magazine *Physical Culture* with the motto Weakness Is a Crime; Don't Be a Criminal (Ernst, *Weakness Is a Crime*, p. 21). An international celebrity, he combated what he perceived as the "great curses" of the age: corsets, sexual ignorance, muscular inactivity, overeating, drugs, alcohol, and tobacco. Along with exercise he advocated a significant portion of whole wheat in the diet and occasional fasting. Macfadden supported his claims with anecdotal data collected on himself and his followers without scientific experimentation, which brought him into conflict with trained physicians and the American Medical Association.

Physicians and others challenged many health practices promulgated in the nineteenth century. Nevertheless subsequent research has supported the importance of lifestyle, including a nutritious diet, adequate sleep and rest, and daily exercise, as key to a healthy life.

See also **Food; Health and Disease; Medicine; Patent Medicines; Recreation; Temperance Movement.**

Bibliography

Armstrong, Davis, and Elizabeth Metzger Armstrong. *The Great American Medicine Show: Being an Illustrated History of Hucksters, Healers, Health Evangelists, and Heroes from Plymouth Rock to the Present.* New York: Prentice-Hall, 1991.

Cordain, Loren, Richard Latin, and James Behnke. "The Effects of an Aerobic Running Program on Bowel Transit Time." *Journal of Sports Medicine and Physical Fitness* 26 (1986): 101–104.

Ernst, Robert. *Weakness Is a Crime: The Life of Bernarr Macfadden.* Syracuse, N.Y.: Syracuse University Press, 1991.

Green, Harvey. *Fit for America: Health, Fitness, Sport, and American Society.* New York: Pantheon, 1986.

Park, Roberta J. "Physiologists, Physicians, and Physical Educators: Nineteenth-Century Biology and Exercise, Hygienic and Educative." *Journal of Sport History* 14, no. 1 (spring 1987): 28–60.

Swanson, Richard A., and Betty Spears. *History of Sport and Physical Education in the United States.* Madison, Wis.: Brown and Benchmark, 1995.

Todd, Jan. "Bernarr Macfadden: Reformer of Feminine Form." *Journal of Sport History* 14, no. 1 (spring 1987): 61–75.

Whorton, James C. *Crusaders for Fitness: The History of American Health Reformers.* Princeton, N.J.: Princeton University Press, 1982.

Willett, W. C., et al. "Relation of Meat, Fat, and Fiber Intake to the Risk of Colon Cancer in a Prospective Study among Women." *New England Journal of Medicine* 323 (1990): 1664–1672.

ROBERT O. RUHLING

HISPANICS.   See **Mexican Americans.**

HISTORY   History is shaped by the assumptions of the age in which it is written. At the end of the

George Bancroft (1800–1891). Bancroft, trained at Harvard and Göttingen, wrote the influential *History of the United States,* a ten-volume work. LIBRARY OF CONGRESS

twentieth century, history as a concept was rooted in empirical observation and the recounting of facts. Although nineteenth-century historians examined whatever documentation they could to write the story of the past, they understood history as much more of a literary genre, rather than an objective analysis of historical data. Only at the end of the nineteenth century did the modern scientific approach to history begin to take root, and only then was history established as a distinct discipline in school and college curricula.

For much of the nineteenth century, historical study and writing in the United States were influenced strongly by Americans' sense of their special destiny. At the time of the Revolutionary War, Americans invoked the history of ancient Greece and Rome to explain the meaning of good republican government. In the decline of the Roman Republic and the rise of the Roman Empire, they found lessons on how to govern and to avoid corrupt and venal leaders. *The Federalist* (1788), by James Madison, and other writings about the U.S. Constitution allude constantly to the problems of past republics to make their case.

By the early nineteenth century this classical vision had been tied to a new strain in American thinking—the country's millennial role. A religious and romantic idea of national destiny was replacing the eighteenth-century vision of the past, which focused on human folly. Americans continued to rely on history for political and moral lessons, but increasingly they believed they had been chosen to escape the burdens of other people's histories. The unique economic opportunities and social conditions of the vast West would allow Americans to avoid the class struggles that had blighted European history.

This sense of American destiny actually took the United States outside the processes of history. It provided the constant theme that invested America's history with special meaning. The dominance of Protestant Christianity meant that historians rarely wrote about cause and effect; instead they pictured American history as guided by Providence. George Bancroft's (1800–1891) multivolume *History of the United States* (1834–1874) explained the nation's fate in this way and became a contemporary best-seller. The idea of "progress" dominated Bancroft's description of the unfolding of liberty in American history. Later historians took up similar themes. In a series of works, Francis Parkman (1823–1893) wrote of the epic struggle between Anglo-Protestant liberty and the darker forces of Catholic France, whose defeat seemed preordained. Nineteenth-century U.S. history always remained a question of destiny.

After the Civil War, American historians began explaining how democratic ideals had survived the centuries from pre-Norman, Anglo-Saxon society to find their finest flowering in New England. Henry Adams (1838–1918) taught one variant of this premise at Harvard in the 1870s, and it became the prevailing view of professional historians, such as Herbert Baxter Adams (1850–1901) at Johns Hopkins University's new center for graduate research.

The twentieth-century sense of history as a branch of social science also emerged in the last three decades of the nineteenth century. Among intellectuals, at least, science became the model for knowledge, and so historians in Europe and the United States tried to model their work on natural science. The religious notions that had shaped historical interpretations earlier in the century gradually were displaced by a scientific perspective. Historians after the Civil War modeled American history on the new process of evolutionary change, rather than seeing it as the embodiment of immutable principles. The rapid societal transformations brought about by migration and industrialization at the end of the nineteenth century encouraged historians' new emphasis on change.

After the Civil War, history increasingly was considered a social science instead of a literary form. Historians emphasized the scientific research they were performing by sifting archival documents. They generally understood their work as a contribution to a definitive account of the past. By the end of the century, history was a profession rather than a literary calling. Historians were scholars based in universities and, to ensure that professional standards were maintained, they founded the American Historical Association in 1884.

See also **Manifest Destiny; Progress, Idea of.**

Bibliography

FitzGerald, Frances. *America Revised: History Schoolbooks in the Twentieth Century.* Boston: Little, Brown, 1979.

Higham, John. *History: Professional Scholarship in America.* Baltimore: Johns Hopkins University Press, 1989.

Novick, Peter. *That Noble Dream: "Objectivity Question" and the American Historical Profession.* Cambridge, U.K.: Cambridge University Press, 1988.

Smith, John David. *An Old Creed for the New South: Proslavery Ideology and Historiography, 1865–1918.* Athens: University of Georgia Press, 1991.

IAN MYLCHREEST

HOBOS, TRAMPS, AND THE HOMELESS

American workers in the nineteenth century were undoubtedly the most mobile in the world. Itinerant carpenters and printers had always existed to some degree. Beginning in the 1820s, they were joined by transient laborers building canals and (after 1840) railroads. After the Civil War, seasonal harvesters and lumberjacks became more important, and the number of unemployed men traveling around the country in search of work also increased dramatically. Section workers on railways were usually housed (in boxcars fitted with bunks) and fed by the companies that hired them. Timber cutters and harvesters received temporary housing but were not transported to their jobs. To some extent the lifestyle of migratory workers, known as hobos, and the homeless unemployed overlapped. They shared the informal facilities of hobo "jungles" (makeshift camps near railroad tracks), and both groups usually spent the winter in the emerging skid row areas of cities, working as casual laborers.

Gangs of transient laborers were needed to lay or maintain railroad tracks throughout the country. Prior to the Civil War, most of this work was done by Irish immigrants or, in the South, by slaves. In the postwar decades the Irish were joined by other European immigrants and, in the Far West, by Chinese laborers. The need for this type of labor declined in the 1890s as the national railroad network neared completion, but the use of migratory workers in other areas expanded. As postwar urbanization increased the need for wood and paper, the timber industry sought out new sources of lumber, first in the Upper Midwest and, at the end of the century, in Idaho, Oregon, and Washington State. Beginning in the 1880s the growth of large farms in the Plains states expanded the demand for temporary harvest workers. From the 1880s to about 1920, an estimated 200,000 hobos took part in wheat harvesting each year, traveling to their jobs by boxcar. After 1920, technological innovations in reaping made this type of labor much less necessary.

In the late nineteenth century, migratory workers were joined on the road by a growing number of homeless men (often called tramps or vagabonds) traveling between jobs or, in most cases, seeking work. The homeless unemployed were a relatively minor factor prior to 1815, but their numbers increased significantly during the antebellum period, especially during depressions. At that time, however, the mobility of such individuals was limited to walking along turnpikes; except on the East Coast, most homeless people remained in or near major cities. During the depression from 1873 to 1878, however, the homeless population burgeoned in size and began, for the first time, to use the railroads. Tramps traveled in open boxcars, on the "bumpers" between cars, or sometimes even on top of or underneath cars (a technique called "riding the rods").

Commentators predicted that tramps would disappear with the return of prosperity, but this did not happen. A much-enlarged homeless population became a permanent element of industrializing America in the late nineteenth and early twentieth centuries. The absolute size of the vagabond population is impossible to determine, but comparative data indicate that the homeless were greater during the period from 1865 to 1940 than at any other time in American history. The homeless were also more visible at that time than later. Most citizens regularly encountered beggars, either at their back door or on a city street corner.

Economic depressions were only one cause of homelessness. Even during prosperous times workers might be forced into the vagrant class as a result of seasonal unemployment, automation, or industrial accidents. In addition, many workers voluntarily went on the road, either because they were seeking better jobs in a new locale or because they temporarily decided to opt out of the industrial workforce. Whether forced or voluntary, tramping was a direct product of industrialization. Most tramps had grown up or lived for some time in cities.

Before 1865, women made up a substantial minority of the homeless. After the Civil War, however, young males increasingly predominated, and by 1900 women made up no more than 10 to 15 percent of this group. During the Gilded Age, the rapid growth of charities aiding destitute women retarded the growth of female homelessness. Homeless women were far more likely to remain in the city where they were born, and they rarely traveled on trains. African Americans, in contrast, were well represented among tramps on the road, partly because of their poverty but also because an open boxcar was a convenient way to escape racial oppression in the South. As late as 1870, immigrants (mostly Irish) comprised perhaps two-thirds of the homeless. By the turn of the century, however, native-born whites made up an increasing majority of this group. One possible cause was the smaller size of white Protestant families, which may have made it more difficult for them when breadwinners suffered unemployment or industrial accidents.

Municipal authorities felt little obligation to assist the homeless. The elderly or sick might be placed in almshouses, but the only facilities for the able-bodied were "tramp rooms" in police stations, where the homeless slept on the floor, packed together. People arrested for vagrancy were usually sentenced to three months in a house of correction. In the 1880s and 1890s the Charity Organization Society (COS) attempted to "reform" tramps by building wayfarers' lodges, where homeless men were required to saw a certain amount of wood (a "work test") in return for

a day's food and lodging. Unless they were absolutely destitute, however, most tramps and hobos preferred to stay in private lodging houses in skid row areas, where rented rooms cost from ten to twenty-five cents a night.

The societal response to the homeless varied according to class, ethnicity, and religion. Personal experience with poverty made many workers, immigrants, and blacks sympathetic to the down-and-out, and evangelical groups, such as the Salvation Army, were more responsive to their needs than were mainstream Protestant churches. Anti-begging campaigns by the COS failed to deter the average citizen from giving food or money to beggars. In a society lacking even a rudimentary social safety net, perhaps these mendicants reminded employed people that they, too, given the right combination of unfortunate circumstances, might become homeless.

See also **Panics and Depressions; Poverty.**

Bibliography

Anderson, Nels. *The Hobo: The Sociology of the Homeless Man.* Chicago: University of Chicago Press, 1923.

Holbrook, Stewart. *Holy Old Mackinaw: A Natural History of the American Lumberjack.* New York: Macmillan, 1938.

Kusmer, Kenneth L. *Down and Out, on the Road: The Homeless in American History.* New York: Oxford University Press, 2000.

Schneider, John C. "Homeless Men and Housing Policy in Urban America, 1850–1920." *Urban Studies* 26, no. 1 (February 1989): 90–99.

Solenberger, Alice W. *One Thousand Homeless Men: A Study of Original Records.* New York: Charities Publication Committee, 1911.

Tygiel, Jules. "Tramping Artisans: Carpenters in Industrial America, 1880–90." In *Walking to Work: Tramps in America, 1790–1935.* Edited by Eric Monkkonen. Lincoln: University of Nebraska Press, 1984.

KENNETH L. KUSMER

HOLIDAYS   Originally "holiday" meant a holy day, a day for prayer and religious services. In turn the holy day was part of a longer religious season. Each Protestant denomination had its own, distinctive marking of the calendar. At the beginning of the nineteenth century, Anglicans and Lutherans imbued the Christmas and Easter seasons with special significance, while Congregationalists took little notice of either. Catholics and Jews had their own religious calendars, which included a variety of holy days and seasons. Special holidays were often celebrated on two days, such as the second Christmas or Easter Monday, rather than one. Catholics and Jews also celebrated some special holy days with outdoor

"Grandpa's Visit Christmas Morning." Three generations of a family celebrate Christmas. By the end of the century, Christmas was one of the few legal holidays celebrated on the same date every year. Photograph, Griffith & Griffith, Philadelphia, c. 1897. LIBRARY OF CONGRESS

pranks and merrymaking as a temporary release from the pieties and deference required of observants during the rest of the year. Such days included Shrove Tuesday, or Mardi Gras; Easter Monday; Pinkster, or Pentecost; and Purim.

In comparison with England or the Catholic countries of Europe, the United States had few days off from work. This can be explained by the aversion of a largely Protestant country to the celebration of Catholic festivals and saints' days and by ambitious Americans' often-observed passion for work. Moreover many Americans believed that the weekly Sabbath was a sufficient special day of rest. The few holidays observed in the United States were not celebrated uniformly throughout the nation. Each religion and ethnic group had its own set of special days, and many groups also had their own calendars.

After breaking free from British rule, Americans reserved to the states the power to declare holidays. Thus in 1800 the United States had no national holidays. The Fourth of July was a national day but not a legal holiday in every state. In the early part of the century it was not even an occasion for affirming national unity, since the Republicans and the Federalists held rival celebrations in many cities. While the dates on which to celebrate the Fourth of July and Christmas were clearly established, the date for cel-

ebrating Thanksgiving varied widely. State governors might proclaim a day of Thanksgiving in November or in December.

During the Civil War many women mourners, especially in the South, placed flowers on the graves of their beloved dead, either at home or at the battlefield. The exact origins of an official commemoration day for losses during the war are disputed. It seems likely that a parade of blacks and former abolitionists to the graves of black Union soldiers in Charleston, South Carolina, on 1 May 1865 was the "First Decoration Day." In the white South, by 1866, local memorial associations, usually headed by women, began organizing Confederate Memorial Days to decorate the graves of their dead and espouse their view of the Civil War as a noble but lost cause. By 1868 or 1869 the leaders of veterans' associations in the North countered, calling for a national Decoration Day to commemorate the graves of the Union dead.

By 1900 four holidays were generally observed as legal days off from work on a distinct date: New Year's Day, Independence Day, Thanksgiving, and Christmas. The adoption of these four followed distinct regional patterns. Thanksgiving was originally considered a New England festival. Because the South thought of Thanksgiving as a Yankee holiday, it was slow to catch on there. Similarly Fourth of July celebrations were more common in the North than the South. Charlestonians celebrated their state holiday Palmetto Day (28 June) as often as July Fourth. New Year's Day was recognized everywhere, but the style of celebration varied from shooting off guns in the South to parades and house-to-house visiting in northern cities.

In 1837 Louisiana became the first state to make Christmas a state holiday. Even then Christmas was easily ignored, celebrated merely as a day for hunting and shooting off guns or noted as a day when devout Catholics attended mass. Gaining the attention of the urban middle class, Christmas emerged as a family holiday and a special time for children by the 1830s. Christmas also became a shopping holiday, when the prized gifts were store-bought rather than homemade. Advertisers and merchants encouraged this development. But churches and middle-class families, especially women, regarded Christmas as a way of celebrating the idea of "an affectionate family" and of antebellum Protestant beliefs affirming both religious and family ideals.

See also **Recreation; Religion,** *subentry on* **Religion in Nineteenth-Century America; Social Life.**

Bibliography

Nissenbaum, Stephen. *The Battle for Christmas.* New York: Knopf, 1996.

Commemorating the Nation's Military Dead. Decoration Day was the precursor of Memorial Day. Photograph, 30 May 1899. LIBRARY OF CONGRESS

Pleck, Elizabeth H. *Celebrating the Family: Ethnicity, Consumer Culture, and Family Rituals.* Cambridge, Mass.: Harvard University Press, 2000.

Schmidt, Leigh Eric. *Consumer Rites: The Buying and Selling of American Holidays.* Princeton, N.J.: Princeton University Press, 1995.

Travers, Len. *Celebrating the Fourth: Independence Day and the Rites of Nationalism in the Early Republic.* Amherst: University of Massachusetts Press, 1997.

Waldstreicher, David. *In the Midst of Perpetual Fetes: The Making of American Nationalism, 1776–1820.* Chapel Hill: University of North Carolina Press, 1997.

ELIZABETH PLECK

HOME   By the 1830s, the word "home" had acquired a meaning derived from Victorian values. Previously it had meant an abode where people or animals slept and raised their young. In the early 1800s, as the middle and upper classes increasingly participated in a national economy, "home" came to mean a place from which men went to work and where wives and children resided. Accustomed to universalizing their experience, middle-class Americans had no notion that their definitions were time bound; therefore they thought their ideal home was an oasis of timeless values. Because Victorians attributed certain qualities to men and others to women, women's nurturing qualities supposedly determined the home's meaning. Though anthropomorphizing, Emily Dickinson (1830–1886) expressed the connection:

The smallest housewife in the grass,
Yet take her from the lawn,
And somebody has lost the face
That made existence home!

Historians of the early 1800s, including Richard Bushman, Laurel Ulrich, and Jeanne Boydston, have described the ties between the economy of the home and the market. Bartering, exchange of household manufactures, and the putting out of children and dependents to work connected households in the late 1700s and early 1800s. Further development of the market economy in ensuing decades reduced home manufactures and increased the prevalence of store-bought goods. Concomitantly, city and town centers with sites for exchange, manufacture, and finance became standard urban features. In these years, the concepts of "going to work" for men, and of "staying at home" for women arose along with implications for the proper work for each sex. In 1829, the antislavery paper *Freedom's Journal* argued that the duties of wives included "the absolute necessity of making and keeping that house really a home, which it is a husband's duty to be fond of and constant to." Demanding of the husband only the duty to be devoted, the *Journal* called for a wife to endow her home with "temper, order, and cleanliness."

Accompanying commercial development was change in how people located and constructed their houses. In the eighteenth-century cities, rich and poor had lived in geographical proximity; the rich in grand houses and the poor in far smaller dwellings along the alleyways behind the mansions. Transportation improvements, especially the horse-drawn streetcar in the 1850s, permitted middle-class families to build residences distant from working-class neighborhoods. Their suburbs usually held single-family detached houses distinguished by historically derived architectural styles, whether the Gothic revival in the century's second quarter or the colonial revival in its fourth quarter. Front yards, front porches, and front halls separated residents from street life while house styles evoked associations with grand historical periods. Andrew Jackson Downing, an architect known for domestic housing, extolled the home as a "powerful means of civilization."

As the middle classes withdrew into their own neighborhoods, their members came to view aspects of workingpeople's lives as coarse and vulgar. Their disdain stemmed from the need for those earning less than subsistence wages to have women and children supplement family incomes by working—sometimes for pay and sometimes by scavenging and bartering. In the middle-class world, ladies ideally did not work, for they existed on an elevated plane above manual domestic labor. There they could dedicate their efforts to refined tasks, household management, and child raising. Thus, the fiction predominated that real work belonged to men and occurred at a distance from the home.

All but the least prosperous members of the nineteenth-century middle class hired maids and shed much of the manual labor necessary for the maintenance of homes. As immigration from the countryside and foreign countries filled cities with large pools of unskilled women workers, middle-class women gained the opportunity to promote themselves, at little cost, to nonmanual household positions, much as their husbands had done in the paid work force. As household manuals pointed out, middle-class women were called upon to perform manual labor only when they could not afford to hire servants.

By evoking the idea of the middle-class home as the true home, the rhetoric of genteel literature tended to reserve the term for its own use. Throughout the century, a debate continued about whether the home was defined less by material circumstances and more by the feelings expressed within. According to some, true homes did not depend on material things. In 1851, a poet for an abolitionist paper defended the merit of a slave's home thus:

a low humble cottage,
But still it is home, and I love it full well,
And the little white children that live in the village
Are no more content than black Rose of the dell.

In 1906, a writer for the reformist *Living Age* explained that the slums were "homes to the people who lived in them" and reminded readers that "the relations of husband and wife" lay "at the foundations of home life."

The largely Protestant middle class invoked the name of their God and the concept of divine order that he had created to justify their ideal culture and society. Writing for this audience, Catharine Beecher and her sister Harriet Beecher Stowe explained in *The American Woman's Home* (1869) that God had made the world so that men would do the outdoor work while women "ministered" over home life. Nineteenth-century popular music also extolled the home. John Howard Payne's "Home, Sweet Home" (1823) had the lines

Mid pleasures and palaces, though we may roam,
Be it ever so humble, there's no place like home!

Though the middle classes debated whether the poor might have true homes and whether their true nature was vitiated by women's work outside the home, their members agreed almost unanimously about the sexual arrangements and division of work within proper homes. The experiments of some people with different forms of home life reveal the boundaries of agreement. These experiments existed at the geographic edges of society, in what one historian has called backwoods utopias, where mainstream society could not prohibit their novel living and working arrangements. In Tennessee, Frances Wright's Nashoba community experimented with racial integration in the 1820s. At one extreme, the Shaker communities excluded units of sexual reproduction from their settlements, and at the other extreme, the Mormons permitted families with one husband and several wives. Still other utopias, such as Robert

Dale Owen's New Harmony community in Indiana, transformed work into a communal project, thus departing from the norm of one wage earner per man-woman family unit.

A religious dimension also was crucial to the meaning of home. The word might mean one's home on earth while also implying one's ultimate home in an existence beyond death. Authors, social commentators, ministers, and poets all used "home" to suggest the dual nature of existence. That is, they saw people as having an earthly home now and as having a divine home after death. Or, as Ralph Waldo Emerson wrote, home might be the place where his soul felt as one with the universe:

> Good-bye, proud world! I'm going home;
> Thou art not my friend, and I'm not thine.
> . . .
> Long I've been tossed like the driven foam;
> But now, proud world! I'm going home.

The image of home as a universal center of life provided an instantly familiar image for authors. Much literature took as a dominant theme the growth of a young person. Women authors often commenced novels with the dissolution of the heroine's home. In Susan Bogert Warner's *The Wide, Wide World* (1850) and Augusta Jane Evans's *St. Elmo* (1866), the heroine negotiates a series of learning experiences before finding an eligible mate. The maturation process thus ends with the central character ready to marry. In some books, such as Horatio Alger's *Ragged Dick* series (first volume 1867), this coming-of-age journey supplies the theme. Other authors, such as James Fenimore Cooper, Harriet Beecher Stowe, and William Dean Howells, locate the maturation theme in minor characters while the major characters' adventures reveal significant cultural or national issues, such as the disappearance of the frontier.

As historians have investigated nineteenth-century reform, especially reform led by women, they have discovered the dynamism of the concept "home." Though it contained women's lives within it, it also propelled them into social engagement by providing them with a rationale for social reform. Prospective reformers had only to ask, "If the home is the basis of a moral life and the source of earthly happiness, then shouldn't all people have one?"

Beginning in the 1830s, the most powerful reform movements of the century took hold, and their rhetoric gained force from exhortations to protect homes. Slavery and drink, according to the reformers, corrupted home life. Drinking husbands squandered wages, depriving their families of financial support

and moral guidance. Calling for temperance reform, Amelia Bloomer, known today mostly for innovations in women's clothing, asked New York women in 1852 to petition their legislature and speak out against drink—or as she called it "this monster" threatening to enter "the home circle and drag from thence children of her love, to corrupt and destroy them, body and soul, forever." Thirty years later, Frances Willard, leader of the National Woman's Christian Temperance Union, called her campaign to win temperance legislation "Home Protection."

Perhaps the most influential evocation of the home in the name of reform came from Harriet Beecher Stowe, whose *Uncle Tom's Cabin* (1852) reached a transatlantic audience and was commemorated in innumerable mementos for home decoration. The novel turns on the insidious influence of materialism on human institutions, especially on homes. Wrenched from wife and children, Tom is sold because his owners want to preserve their homestead from creditors. Eventually, a series of sales deposits Tom at a plantation in the deep South. Totally committed to maximizing profits and the materialistic pleasures of drink and sensuality, his new owner, Simon Legree, has no home, no wife, no friends—merely an abode, a concubine, two thug henchmen, and dreaded dreams. The novel shows America as it is with slavery, a land where no home is safe. Its secondary plot, the flight of Eliza and her family from American slavery to Canadian freedom, reveals America as it might be—a country with a home for everyone.

African Americans used the rhetoric of home in their campaign against slavery and racism. They referred to home in folk stories and spirituals to remind themselves of their true home. In the words of a spiritual, when the chariot would "swing low," it would carry them home—either north to freedom or to their ultimate home in heaven. The slave narrative of Harriet Jacobs, *Incidents in the Life of a Slave Girl* (1861), and Harriet Wilson's novel *Our Nig* (1859) share many of the conventions of women's fiction. In predictable beginnings, the heroine's family dissolves. Then the heroine tries to reassemble her family and create a home. However, these African Americans never reach their goal. Racism bars Nig from the gainful employment necessary to support a home, and Jacobs's fear of implementation of the Fugitive Slave law (1850) bars a permanent home.

Documentary photographers including Lewis Hine and Jacob Riis found in the ideal of the home bold contrasts for their images of immigrant life. Riis's photographs in his *How the Other Half Lives* (1890) inspired middle-class viewers to measure the conditions of immigrant neighborhoods against their ideal of home. They saw clutter, dirt, and lack of ventilation in photographs of immigrant mothers and children at work assembling artificial flowers or sewing garments. Consternation followed as they reacted to the homes that immigrants did not have. Thus middle-class ideals helped to motivate support for legislation regulating housing and work conditions. Ironically, immigrants' actual homes were no oases from government intervention on behalf of middle-class ideals of the proper home.

Debate over the home and women's relationship to it became intense when some women assumed public roles as reformers. Opposing women's involvement in temperance and antislavery campaigns, Mrs. A. J. Graves argued in 1841: "Home is her appropriate sphere of action; and . . . whenever she [mingles] in any of the great public movements of the day, she is deserting the station which God and nature have assigned to her." During the 1860s debate over women's potential inclusion in the Fifteenth Amendment, antisuffragists argued that home life was woman's true calling. In the 1890s, as reformers worked for woman suffrage in school board, municipal, and national elections, antisuffragists deployed the rhetoric of the home. First, they described it as fundamental to American democracy. Then they explained that the act of women's voting compromised the home as an oasis. Thus, the home's power would diminish and the foundation of the nation would be destroyed. In opposition, suffragists contended that woman suffrage would extend women's positive influence to urban life. Social reformer Jane Addams pointed out that the functions of municipal government had multiplied. Cities needed women's attention to improve sanitation, children's education, food inspection, and other issues of municipal housekeeping.

Starting in the 1870s, some commentators questioned whether the home promoted personal growth. In *The Adventures of Huckleberry Finn* (1885), Huck flees a conventional middle-class home for adventure on the Mississippi River. After his river adventures, he chooses to "light out for the territories" rather than return home. Women writers also started to deride the bourgeois home. Whereas earlier reformers had argued that it provided for women's happiness and moral development, socialists such as Charlotte Perkins Gilman proposed in *The Home* (1903) that it no longer did. Believing that the home had to evolve with society, Gilman called for its overhaul in order to eliminate "the maintenance of primitive industries in a modern industrial community, and the confinement of women to those industries and their limited area of expression."

Thus, the term "home" helped the nineteenth-century middle class both to affirm its core beliefs and to debate crucial issues. Essentially, the debate centered on the issue of women's inclusion in paid work and civic life, and the terms of inclusion of all races and religions in public life. Politicians, social commentators, and writers engaged their publics by deploying universally meaningful terms while debating their finer meanings. Consensus prevailed on the big issue—that the home should be the foundation of American social life—and contention prevailed on peripheral issues such as inclusion of minorities and women in public and civic life. Middle-class rhetoric to the contrary, the home was never isolated from the central issues of the century.

By 1900, dictionaries had added a meaning to the entry for the word "home." The rise of baseball to national pastime in the post–Civil War years made popular the term "home base." It became a term that people used generally to mean both a point of departure and a final destination. This new meaning speaks to larger changes that separate 1800s discourse from that of the 1900s. For the twentieth-century middle class, the word "home" had lost its divine sanction while gaining new meanings derived from the rise of commercialized leisure.

See also **Architecture,** *subentry on* **Vernacular Architecture; Communitarian Movements and Groups; Domestic Life; Gender,** *subentry on* **Interpretations of Gender; Housing.**

Bibliography

Blumin, Stuart M. *The Emergence of the Middle Class: Social Experience in the American City, 1760–1900.* New York: Cambridge University Press, 1989.

Baym, Nina. *Woman's Fiction: A Guide to Novels by and About Women in America, 1820–1870.* Ithaca, N.Y.: Cornell University Press, 1978.

Boydston, Jeanne. *Home and Work: Housework, Wages, and the Ideology of Labor in the Early Republic.* New York: Oxford University Press, 1990.

Bushman, Richard L. *The Refinement of America: Persons, Houses, Cities.* New York: Knopf, 1992.

Clark, Clifford Edward. *The American Family Home, 1800–1960.* Chapel Hill: University of North Carolina Press, 1986.

Hedrick, Joan D. *Harriet Beecher Stowe: A Life.* New York: Oxford University Press, 1995.

Ryan, Mary P. *Cradle of the Middle Class: The Family in Oneida County, New York, 1790–1865.* New York: Cambridge University Press, 1981.

Sklar, Kathryn Kish. *Catharine Beecher: A Study in American Domesticity.* New York: Norton, 1976.

Stevenson, Louise L. *The Victorian Homefront: American Thought and Culture, 1860–1880.* New York: Twayne, 1991.

LOUISE L. STEVENSON

HOMELESSNESS. See **Hobos, Tramps, and the Homeless.**

HOMESTEADING   George Henry Evans, a labor reformer in the antebellum North, advocated free land as a cure-all for American social problems. Through the National Land Reform Association he and other reformers sought to stop land speculation and to promote small, independent farmers. Horace Greeley, the influential editor of the *New York Tribune,* joined the National Land Reform Association and became its main voice. By the late 1850s the newly formed Republican party had incorporated the "free lands" idea into its platforms.

The departure of the Southern Democrats from Congress in 1861 allowed the Republicans to pass an act in May 1862 that was in keeping with the aspirations of the National Land Reform Association; the law went into effect 1 January 1863. The Homestead Act allowed any "person" who was over the age of twenty-one, or was a head of a family, or was a citizen, to file claim to 160 acres of public land already surveyed. After filing, homesteaders had six months to begin living on their land, and after five years they could gain title to it if they had improved it by building a residence, putting up a fence, or planting crops. Until they possessed title to the land, homesteaders could neither mortgage nor sell it.

While the Homestead Act appears to be a form of congressional generosity, settlers encountered difficulties in "proving up" their claims. For one, the law failed to consider environments where a farmer needed more than 160 acres for economic success. A settler often needed more than $1,000 in capital to fund the improvements on a claim. The preemption laws of 1853, 1854, and 1862 allowed settlers to buy eighty acres of unsurveyed public domain for $100, and required no improvements. The amount of land available for homesteading was somewhat limited, with nearly 84 million acres set aside for homesteading. In comparison, three times that amount went to railroads; 140 million acres were donated to the states; and 175 million acres were in Indian reservations.

Frequently success eluded homesteaders. Many gave up their homesteads long before they made their claim final. In the Dakotas less than half received final title to their land; in Wisconsin about 63 percent gained title; and in Iowa around 60 percent came to own their land. In Kansas 10 percent of the homesteaders decided to buy their claims outright rather than wait five years to gain title; 41 percent stayed on to gain title to the land; and 49 percent relinquished their claims.

The act, by referring to homesteaders as "persons," opened the door for many women to acquire land. Before 1900 in Trego County, Kansas, four women numbered among the thirty-nine homesteaders who acquired title to their land. After 1900 in Logan and Washington Counties in eastern Colorado, women accounted for 18 percent of the claimants, and of these, 55 percent "proved up" their claims. The success rate of women homesteaders compared favorably with that of men.

The Homestead Act never produced the ideal nation envisioned by reformers such as Evans and Greeley. Regardless of the legislation's shortcomings, however, hundreds of thousands of American men and women created new farms through its provisions.

See also **Federal Land Policy.**

Bibliography

Gates, Paul W. *History of Public Land Law Development.* New York: Arno, 1979.

Opie, John. *The Law of the Land: Two Hundred Years of American Farmland Policy.* Lincoln: University of Nebraska Press, 1987.

JAMES E. SHEROW

HOMOSEXUALITY   Intellectual historian Peter Gay has remarked in *The Tender Passion* that nineteenth-century society did not label homosexuality, choosing instead "the spurious safety of ignorance over the risky benefits of knowledge" (Gay, 202). Walt Whitman, the American poet (1819–1892), chose deliberately vague and imprecise terms for homosexuality, "love of comrades" or "adhesiveness." The cataloging of homosexuality was ultimately left to psychiatrists and sexologists who would pronounce homosexuality deviant and perverse. The first reference to and definition of "homosexuality" appeared in Prussia: Dr. Károly Mária Kertbeny, a Hungarian physician, has been associated with coining the term "homosexuality" in 1869. By 1871, a criminal provision banning homosexual acts among males was incorporated in Germany into the Second Reich's penal code. Throughout the nineteenth century, the definition of homosexuality shifted from a criminal act to a diseased condition. In the United States the shift from "namelessness" to identity came largely from individuals who developed a modern sense of "gay" identity by the end of the nineteenth century and beginning of the twentieth century.

Changes throughout the Nineteenth Century

During the nineteenth century, the development in the United States of large urban populations and regions produced greater anonymity, and economic and personal independence. Working-class and farm women were drawn to work outside the home, giving new dimensions to interactions among and between the sexes. Men from diverse educational, racial, and economic backgrounds found their lives intertwined within the crowded and bustling rhythms of city life. Increased social outlets led to new patterns of social and personal life. The restructuring of family and gender relations resulted in a separation of middle-class society into male and female spheres. In the face of such rigid gender prescriptions, homosexual desire became manifested in intense, passionate friendships.

By the end of the century, negative societal attitudes toward homosexuality eclipsed any open tolerance. Homosexuality during this period was viewed with dread. Medical science played an important role in demonizing homosexual desire. The medical profession, both in its scholarship and practice, became fully involved in theorizing and treating homosexuality. Remedies for homosexuality were robustly taken up by medical professionals. Treatments included hysterectomy, lobotomy, electroshock, and aversion therapy. Dr. F. E. Daniel, a physician in Texas in 1893, advocated castration of homosexual males.

During the same period, however, voices sympathetic to homosexuality emerged. Dr. Havelock Ellis, an English sexologist who published highly influential works, including *Studies in the Psychology of Sex* (1897–1910), advocated sexual abstinence for homosexuals who desired a treatment plan yet argued that homosexuals were a natural anomaly. The contributions of homosexuals to the arts and sciences were monumental, according to Ellis. Dr. Richard von Krafft-Ebing, an Austrian psychiatrist and academic who wrote extensively on the subject of homosexuality, urged repeal of the German law that criminalized male homosexuality. Krafft-Ebing argued that homosexuality was a congenital disease.

Difference by Race, Class, Gender, and Region

By the 1890s, homosexuals from all walks of life and social backgrounds began associating and organizing businesses and meeting places. These institutions fostered a sense of identity and cohesion where utter alienation and despair had existed previously. For men, certain parks, streets, and bathhouses became common ground. Red-light districts began to incorporate or house near them bars and clubs where men met other men for sex and social activities. For women, friendship networks emerged. Upper-class women, with inheritances and private wealth, often made use of their country homes for these special friends gatherings.

Race

The U.S. Department of the Interior Census Office of 1880 document "The Prisoners of the United States" lists those jailed for sodomy and buggery as extremely disproportionate to the racial make-up of the population. Of the total of sixty-three prisoners incarcerated for sodomy or buggery, thirty-two are listed as "colored," eleven as "foreign born white," and one as female. By 1890, the Census "Report on Crime, Pauperism, and Benevolence in the United States at the Eleventh Census, 1890," lists 224 crimes against nature or "[a]gainst public morals." Of these, nearly one-third of the perpetrators are listed as "Negroes" and "Chinese"; again, racial make-up is disproportionate to the numbers of each group in the general population.

Documents of the time illuminate the bias and horror of nineteenth-century society toward homosexuality. Historical records depict black male homosexuals in particularly derogatory, prudish, and judgmental tones. In 1893 physician Charles H. Hughes commented on an annual event in which black male transvestites gathered in Washington, D.C., for a "drag dance." According to Hughes, the "Negroes" met to dress and dance in public in frilly women's clothing. Hughes observed that those assembled were workers in the service industry. Hughes further observed that homosexual black and white men often socialized together in private homes. Yet, white men were not arrested for violating laws against public morality as often as black men.

Class

Within large American cities, homosexuals of all classes began to establish a cohesive socio-political identity in the late nineteenth century. For working-class men, such as butlers, cooks, and chauffeurs, resorts consisted of modest houses with apartments appointed for entertaining and meeting. For upper-class men, sexual affairs with other men were deterred by fear of loss of reputation and damage to one's business or profession and personal life. For women, friendship organizations in factories or other female-dominated labor sites or social circles fomented bonds with other women.

Gender

According to historical records of the period, women seldom were arrested or tried for homosexual acts. Before 1920, when Freudian analysis became highly influential, women enjoyed intense emotional bonds without shame and ridicule. These relationships were carried on in the light of public eye by middle-class white women, usually those who were part of a well-educated class. The situation of two women living together in a long-term relationship was popularly dubbed a "Boston marriage."

Several female leaders in nineteenth-century political and intellectual life exchanged letters evidencing powerful love feelings toward each other. The suffrage movement leader Susan B. Anthony, actress and political speaker Anna E. Dickinson, and novelist Willa Cather were all part of a circle of women who loved other women that existed in the 1850 to 1900 period. Of particular significance in this history are the crushes, then referred to as "smashes," that young women developed toward each other at the newly established women's colleges, Mount Holyoke (1837), Vassar (1861), Smith (1871), Wellesley (1875), and Bryn Mawr (1880). Common belief is that these "smashes" were kept platonically affectionate, and did not involve sexual or genital intimacy or gratification. Sexual contact, it is believed, more likely occurred in a female couple where one of the females "passed" as a man.

The incidence of women's attempts to appear to be men dates from as early as the American Revolution, in 1782. At least three documented cases exist of women serving as Civil War soldiers, disguised as men. In peacetime, women passed as men for a variety of reasons, including economic, intellectual, professional, and perhaps sexual opportunities. One particularly daring life was that of "Murray Hall" (1830–1901), a Scottish émigré who lived out her life in New York City. Dressing and presenting herself to the world as a man, she achieved the occupation of politician and enjoyed the admiration of many in the highest political ranks of New York. She was a respected and powerful member of Tammany Hall, the Democratic Party's club. She also married at least one wife during her lifetime.

Region

The available documents suggest that the New England and eastern states were more harsh on homosexuals than the other states. New York and Pennsylvania led the states in number of prisoners jailed in 1880, for "Crime[s] against nature" synonymous with sodomy and buggery. Ironically, these states also developed institutions to cater to homosexual clientele. In New York, author Charles W. Gardener wrote of "the worst vice that N.Y. holds." He recounts his experience of discovering this vice in the "Golden Rule Pleasure Club," a dive located in downtown New York where patrons could meet in small private rooms or share time with a "youth." By 1892, large American cities had developed a homosexual underground culture.

Legislation

During the colonial period, sodomy statutes followed biblical wording, particularly that of Leviticus 20:13.

In Connecticut, for example, the sodomy statute quoted directly from the Bible: "If a man also lie with mankind, as he lieth with a woman, both of them have committed an abomination: they shall surely be put to death; their blood shall be upon them."

After the Revolution, the states reformed their criminal codes in the spirit of Enlightenment philosophy, and sodomy was classified as a "crime against nature," carrying a lesser penalty than capital punishment. In 1810 a Maryland Court incarcerated a man for four months for approaching another man. He was also sentenced to stand in the pillory for one day and pay a fine of $500. North Carolina did not eliminate capital punishment for sodomy until 1869. Thomas Jefferson proposed a lighter and more progressive measure; "sodomitical acts" ought not be capital offenses but merely replaced by castration. Although the ties between church and state were lessened, religion continued to play a role in crimes involving morality. In 1897, for example, an Illinois court described sodomy as a crime "not fit to be named among Christians."

Two-Spirits

In Western culture, homosexuality referred to one's choice of sexual partner; while in many Native American cultures and other non-European cultures, same-sex relationships were merely one possible aspect of an individual's gender expression.

Native American life in the nineteenth-century allowed for social persona which overrode sexual categorization. In Navajo culture, even in the twentieth century, sexual relations were based on one's gender, identified as masculine-man, or feminine-woman, and not based on biological sex, male or female. The notion of "two-spirit" allows for fluid gender expression, where an individual need not engage in activities assigned to any particular biological sex.

While homosexuals were seen as deviant and unnatural in white Western culture, Native Americans often revered transgendered persons. An individual who took on the gender role of the opposite sex in Zuni culture was called a "berdache" or "joya." A berdache man or "not-man" cooked, took care of the young, quilted, did pottery and bead work—all tasks traditionally performed by women—and took a sacred role in tribal rituals. The most famous Zuni berdache was We'Wha (1849–1896), who, known for his pottery and weaving, traveled in 1886 to Washington, D.C., the guest of Matilda Coxe Stevenson, an anthropologist. He reportedly appeared at the National Theatre in an amateur theatrical event, became friends with the Speaker of the House of Representatives and his wife, and presented President

Grover Cleveland a gift of his artwork. It has been noted that 130 different Native American tribes included berdache gender in their culture.

See also **Class, Social; Clubs,** *subentries on* **Fraternal Societies and Clubs, Women's Clubs and Associations; Gender; Race and Racial Thinking; Recreation; Women,** *subentry on* **Women's Rights.**

Bibliography

Barry, Kathleen. *Female Sexual Slavery.* New York: Prentice Hall, 1979.

Boswell, John. *Christianity, Social Tolerance, and Homosexuality.* Chicago: University of Chicago Press, 1980.

———. *Same-Sex Unions in Premodern Europe.* New York: Villiard, 1994.

D'Emilio, John, and Estelle B. Freedman. *Intimate Matters: A History of Sexuality in America.* Chicago: University of Chicago Press, 1997.

Duberman, Martin Bauml, Martha Vicinus, and George Chauncey, Jr., eds. *Hidden From History: Reclaiming the Gay and Lesbian Past.* New York: New American Library, 1989.

Gay, Peter. *The Tender Passion.* Oxford: Oxford University Press, 1986.

Jacobs, Sue-Ellen, Wesley Thomas, and Sabine Lang, eds. *Two-Spirit People: Native American Gender Identity, Sexuality, and Spirituality.* Chicago: University of Illinois Press, 1997.

Katz, Jonathan. *Gay/Lesbian Almanac.* New York: Harper and Row, 1983.

———. *Gay American History.* New York: Crowell, 1976.

Lang, Sabine. *Men as Women, Women as Men: Changing Gender in Native American Cultures.* Austin: University of Texas Press, 1998.

Lauritsen, John, and David Thorstad. *The Early Homosexual Rights Movement, 1864–1935.* New York: Times Change Press, 1974.

MacNamara, Donal E. J., and Edward Sagarin. *Sex, Crime, and the Law.* New York: Free Press, 1977.

Miller, Neil. *Out of the Past: Gay and Lesbian History from 1869 to the Present.* New York: Vintage, 1995.

Mondimore, Francis Mark. *A Natural History of Homosexuality.* Baltimore: Johns Hopkins University Press, 1996.

Quinn, D. Michael. *Same-Sex Dynamics Among Nineteenth-Century Americans: A Mormon Example.* Chicago: University of Illinois Press, 1996.

Roscoe, Will. *Changing Ones: Third and Fourth Genders in Native North America.* New York: St. Martin's, 1998.

MADELINE PLASENCIA

HOSPITALS

HOSPITALS   The nineteenth century was a period of growth and change for American hospitals. Many early hospitals were extensions of public almshouses, and initially hospitalization was the last refuge of a desperate and needy population. In the early part of the century, religious and benevolent groups began to organize hospitals as alternatives to these municipal institutions. Like the almshouse hospitals these were charity institutions but in some cases patients paid something toward the cost of their care. (In *The Care of Strangers,* an analysis of the development of the American hospital, the historian Charles E. Rosenberg suggests that payments may have lessened the stigma attached to hospitalization.) Patients were often referred to as inmates, and hospital treatment assumed a moral as well as a physical recovery. Hospital admission required the permission of administrators or a trustee.

Both Union and Confederate armies organized hospitals on and off the battlefields during the Civil War. With the exception of anesthesia, there was nothing new about the therapeutics of Civil War medical care; the organization and methods that followed new ideas about hospital administration and sanitation along the Nightingale model distinguished them from earlier ones, however, and contributed to relatively low death rates. For many Americans— the soldiers who were patients and the numerous civilian volunteers (nurses and physicians) who staffed military hospitals—this would be their first exposure to hospitals and experience with hospital medical care. Military hospitals were disbanded after the war and federal involvement in medical care continued for only a very limited population: merchant seamen, professional soldiers, and, for a time, former slaves through the Freedmen's Bureau. The United States Soldiers Home was organized to care for disabled veterans.

The number of American hospitals rose dramatically after the Civil War, especially voluntary hospitals, those organized under private auspices. (While privately managed, many of these would receive financial assistance from local governments.) Nevertheless, the majority of Americans continued to receive medical care elsewhere. Patients who could afford private treatment were cared for in their own homes or in a physician's office, and others went to dispensaries, outpatient facilities sometimes affiliated with hospitals, for medical attention.

The term "hospital" referred to a variety of institutions over the course of the century. General hospitals treated a range of illnesses and patients. Others included maternity hospitals, foundling hospitals, and hospitals for the care of the blind, the deaf, crippled children, and the insane. Some hospitals were also called "asylums," emphasizing the institutions' function as refuges.

During the later decades of the century many specialized institutions reorganized as general hospitals. At the same time, general hospitals shifted from chronic care to acute care facilities. This change, a product of industrialization and urbanization, was as much a response to social and economic factors as to medical ones. Americans increasingly were unable to rely on familial support and comfort in times of illness. The introduction of aseptic and antiseptic techniques made surgeries more frequently successful and multiplied the number of surgical patients in the 1890s. The length of hospital stays shortened. Contrary to the conversion to general hospitals, institutions called sanitaria began to specialize in care for the mentally ill or for tubercular patients, previously a large percentage of general hospital patients. The first tuberculosis sanitarium opened in Saranac Lake, New York, in 1884.

The roles and status of caregivers in hospitals changed too. After the Civil War, American women actively sought to reform and professionalize nursing. Nursing education was linked to the development of the general hospital as nursing students became the backbone of the hospital nursing staff. Training schools for hospital nurses began opening in the 1870s. At the same time clinical hospital training became an important component of medical education. Furthermore, in the shift from chronic to acute care in hospitals, physicians assumed more central roles in treatment and decision making in hospitals. The modern hospital, an acute care facility central to the American health care delivery system, was ascending as the nineteenth century ended. Reflecting the enormous upheaval in American society, the hospital was an institution in transition when the twentieth century began.

See also **Asylums; Health and Disease; Medicine; Mental Illness; Midwives.**

Bibliography

Rosenberg, Charles E. *The Care of Strangers*. New York: Basic Books, 1987.
Rosner, David. *A Once Charitable Enterprise*. Cambridge, U.K., and New York: Cambridge University Press, 1982.
Vogel, Morris J. *The Invention of the Modern Hospital: Boston, 1870–1930*. Chicago: University of Chicago Press, 1980.

BERNADETTE MCCAULEY

HOUSING   In the nineteenth century, Americans moved from farms to cities, from cities out to suburbs, and to the West, taking traditional forms of housing with them as well as developing new ones to meet new needs. The row houses of colonial seaboard cities like Philadelphia, Baltimore, and Boston evolved into larger row houses or semidetached houses as housing demands in these cities grew.

Apartment buildings in Boston and New York replaced single-family houses that had been subdivided to accommodate numerous families. Where more land was available, families built spacious suburban homes, following the model of the wealthy who had been able to escape the heat, disease, and congestion of colonial cities. If land was not available for a large lawn, a patch of grass sufficed. Those who settled on the frontier built homes from logs, sod, or any other available materials that would provide temporary shelter until they had the resources to build more permanent homes. Great Plains and southwestern tribes of Native Americans lived in hogans, tepees, pueblos, and other forms of traditional housing until the federal government forced them off their lands and onto reservations and, after the Dawes General Allotment Act of 1887, onto individual allotments. Indeed, the range of housing options expanded dramatically in the nineteenth century, depending on one's location, access to transportation, social and economic status, race, family structure, and the availability of building materials and utilities.

Social and Economic Factors

One of the most obvious factors influencing housing was the social and economic status of the owners. At the beginning of the century, most cities were still walking cities, with the wealthiest residents living in brick row houses in the center of the city, within walking distance of jobs and shops; cities often mandated brick buildings to protect against fire danger. The poorest residents lived on the urban outskirts, farthest from the heart of the city and the jobs and shops. By the end of the century, most cities had reversed this pattern. The wealthy then lived in large, detached suburban houses of wood, brick, or stone, while the poor (often newly arrived immigrants and African Americans) were crowded into center-city dilapidated housing or apartments, such as New York City's infamous dumbbell tenements, so named because the plan resembled the shape of a dumbbell (see sidebar). In between were the middle-class residents who lived in detached, semidetached, or row houses with varying lawn sizes. This transformation took place because the transportation revolution of the nineteenth century made it possible for people to commute to work by horsecar, streetcar, railroad, trolley, incline, or ferry, leaving behind the increasing pollution and congestion of the city center.

Household and family structure also were linked to the evolution of housing throughout the century. In cities, slaves lived in the master's home or in outbuildings on the property. On plantations, slaves often had cabins where they could attempt to maintain

The Tenements of New York

"To-day, what is a tenement? The law defines it as a house 'occupied by three or more families, living independently and doing their cooking on the premises; or by more than two families on a floor, so living and cooking and having a common right in the halls, stairways, yards, etc.' That is the legal meaning, and includes flats and apartment-houses, with which we have nothing to do. In its narrower sense the typical tenement was thus described when last arraigned before the bar of public justice: 'It is generally a brick building from four to six stories high on the street, frequently with a store on the first floor which, when used for the sale of liquor, has a side opening for the benefit of the inmates and to evade the Sunday law; four families occupy each floor, and a set of rooms consists of one or two dark closets, used as bedrooms, with a living room twelve feet by ten. The staircase is too often a dark well in the centre of the house, and no direct through ventilation is possible, each family being separated from the other by partitions. Frequently the rear of the lot is occupied by another building of three stories high with two families on a floor.'" Jacob A. Riis. *How the Other Half Lives.* New York: (Scribners, 1890)

their own family life. Servants, who were often young, single immigrant women, also lived in their employer's home, usually on the top floor in the smallest bedrooms. Large mansions like Biltmore in Asheville, North Carolina, had numerous servants' rooms. The nineteenth century's cult of domesticity emphasized the woman's role in making houses into homes and, for Christians, into centers of religious life for families. Catharine Beecher's (1800–1878) popular *A Treatise on Domestic Economy* (1841) provided homemakers with advice on everything from doing laundry to interior decoration. By the late nineteenth century, husbands and wives often slept in separate bedrooms if the house was big enough to afford this space. Larger houses had ballrooms for entertaining, and the largest had libraries (men's space) and parlors (where women entertained their friends).

Homes also were centers of economic activity. Servants, laundresses, and cooks earned their livings by working in others' houses. Families took in boarders if local housing was scarce, when newcomers to the city did not want to live on their own, or if families needed extra income. Women usually shouldered most of the responsibility for caring for these boarders. Some women and children did piecework at home, making items such as clothing or artificial flowers, so that the mothers could combine work and

child care. Those living on plantations, farms, and ranches, with their barns, smokehouses, corncribs, springhouses, and laundry sheds, provided most of their own food for people and animals, while selling crops or livestock to raise cash.

Certain employers also provided housing as an employee benefit or as a form of social control over workers. George Pullman (1831–1897) built brick houses in his model community of Pullman, just south of Chicago, for the workers who produced his Pullman railroad cars. Coal-company owners in southern West Virginia built small wooden houses for miners because they were importing workers to new communities in sparsely populated areas.

Occasionally, individuals and governments worked to reform poor housing conditions, while tenants took reform into their own hands by rebelling against negligent landlords. There were several tenant strikes in New York State: male renters organized to get the right to vote early in the century (only landowners could vote at that time), and tenants along the Hudson River fought what they called a second American Revolution against landowners in the twenty-year-long Antirent Movement at mid-century. The New York Tenants' League called for rent regulation, protection against eviction, and better-quality, affordable housing. In response, the state passed its first housing codes in 1865. New York City's Act for the Regulation of Tenement and Lodging Houses in the Cities of New York and Brooklyn, passed in 1867, was the first comprehensive housing law in the nation. The law helped to improve the city's squalid housing conditions by requiring, among other things, that bedrooms have at least one window and that there be one privy for every twenty tenants. Housing cooperatives had developed in France as early as 1720, but did not appear in the United States until the 1870s and 1880s as "home clubs" developed in New York City. The more affluent club members owned the property together and could sell their shares in the apartments. Elsewhere, especially in cities like Boston, women experimented with cooking clubs and communal dining rooms so they did not need to have kitchens in their own homes.

There were also many examples of communal housing in the nineteenth century. Utopian communities built houses that served their unique religious purposes. For example, because the Shakers were a celibate community, they divided their large houses at Pleasant Hill in Kentucky into separate quarters for men and women, with separate stairways leading to the common dining rooms and worship areas. Roman Catholics built homes for priests next to churches, as well as monasteries and convents. Religious and philanthropic groups built homes for "aged

Southern Grandeur. Home in the style of the plantation. Natchez, Mississippi. LIBRARY OF CONGRESS

and friendless women" and orphanages. Colleges provided some housing for their students, although students also lived in boardinghouses or fraternity houses. Seminaries, academies, collegiate institutes, and other private or parochial schools often provided housing to students who lived too far away to commute. State and local governments housed the mentally ill in insane asylums and criminals in massive workhouses or prisons.

New Building Techniques and Utilities

Housing options expanded rapidly in the nineteenth century in part due to technological advances in construction. At the beginning of the century, wood-frame houses were built of heavy timbers held in place by pegs. Then, in 1833, the balloon-framing system was invented in Chicago to meet the needs of that rapidly growing city. This system used relatively small studs sawed to standard lengths and typically spaced sixteen inches apart to form a frame for the house. The frame looked so flimsy that it earned the name "balloon frame." By the time of the Civil War, nail makers could make cut-wire nails much more cheaply and faster than blacksmiths could make traditional nails by hand. Soon, there were machines to put the heads on nails, followed by machines that

Cigar-Making in a Tenement. In New York City a common form of housing was the dumbbell tenement, so named for the shape of its floor plan. The home also served as a site of work for the entire family. Photogragh by Jacob A. Riis, 1889. LIBRARY OF CONGRESS

made wire nails even more quickly and cheaply than cut nails. By the 1880s, timber companies were cutting over the virgin forests of Pennsylvania and West Virginia, among other states, using giant band saws to cut the trees into lumber for houses, and shipping the wood across the country for houses held together by wire nails. Owners who wanted their wood-frame house to look more expensive could add a layer of brick veneer to the outside.

As cities became more crowded and land more expensive, contractors and architects needed to find new ways to provide housing. The Chicago fire of 1871 provided the impetus to use steel, a more fireproof material than iron, in high-rise construction for office buildings and apartments. Elisha Otis's (1811–1861) steam elevator, invented in 1853, made it possible to build apartment buildings taller than the five or six stories that people were willing to walk up.

There were other uses for metal products in housing. Beginning in the 1840s, house builders began using corrugated and standing-seam metal roofs, which were lightweight, weatherproof, fireproof, and inexpensive. Companies made pressed metal sheets with elaborate designs that replicated plaster to use as cornices or ceilings. Sheets of metal could be used on the exterior of houses. All of these products were advertised in catalogs that companies mailed across the country, with the products shipped by rail.

The first American use of concrete reinforced with steel in housing was the construction of the Ward House in Westchester County, New York, in the 1870s. Most often, concrete was used for foundations or, if there was no basement, for slabs on grade.

New techniques for making glass also affected housing construction. At the beginning of the century, all glass was hand blown, so each piece of glass (or pane) in a window was small. By mid-century, it was possible to make sheet and plate glass by machine, eliminating the need to make window glass by hand and also allowing the glass industry to meet the increasing demand for window glass. By 1900, windows had large panes, unless they were designed to

Over the course of the century it became easier to light and heat houses and to cook because of the availability of gas and electricity for people who could afford these conveniences. In the 1830s, American homes began to have open gas flames to provide light. Iron stoves for heating and for cooking replaced fireplaces. Central-heating systems used gas or coal to produce hot air or hot water to heat homes by the end of the century. By that time, natural gas was readily available throughout the country at affordable prices. Edison Electric Company built the first electric power plant in New York in 1882, and gradually, Americans in towns and cities began to light their homes with electricity instead of gas.

See also **Architecture; Civil Engineering,** *subentry on* **Building Technology; Home.**

Bibliography

Beecher, Catharine E. *A Treatise on Domestic Economy.* 1841. Reprint, New York: Source Book Press, 1970.

Hayden, Dolores. *The Grand Domestic Revolution: A History of Feminist Designs for American Homes, Neighborhoods, and Cities.* Cambridge, Mass.: MIT Press, 1981.

Howe, Barbara J., et al. *Houses and Homes: Exploring Their History.* Nashville, Tenn.: American Association for State and Local History, 1987.

McDannell, Colleen. *The Christian Home in Victorian America, 1840–1900.* Bloomington: Indiana University Press, 1986.

Smeins, Linda E. *Building an American Identity: Pattern Book Homes and Communities, 1870–1900.* Walnut Creek, Calif.: AltaMira, 1999.

Van Vliet, Willem, ed. *The Encyclopedia of Housing.* Thousand Oaks, Calif.: Sage, 1998.

BARBARA J. HOWE

Farm Home. The bucolic setting belies the less savory aspects of housing: lack of adequate ventilation, light, and heat. LIBRARY OF CONGRESS

replicate earlier architectural styles. These large windows, combined with high ceilings, helped to keep houses cool in the summer.

Some of the most important advances in housing also were significant advances in public health. These included efforts to provide clean water and sewage systems to houses. Many houses in eastern cities such as Boston, New York, Philadelphia, and Richmond had piped water in the first third of the century. By the late nineteenth century, most homes in cities and towns had piped water and even had gas-fired heaters to provide hot water. Bathrooms and kitchens, by 1900, had gleaming tile and metal fixtures that were easy to keep clean and sanitary. Flush toilets replaced outdoor privies. Rural houses still relied on wells, springs, or streams to provide water and on outhouses.

HUMOR   Humor was one of the major ways in which nineteenth-century Americans responded to political developments, the rise of middle-class gentility, and a process of national expansion through the acquisition of new territories and the arrival of large numbers of European immigrants. Humorous expression—in almanacs, newspapers, magazines, political satires, stage productions, and cartoons—helped Americans assimilate the new and unfamiliar, to become acquainted with different regions of the country, and to forge a sense of national identity. Washington Irving, one of the first American authors to attract a European audience, was noted for his satires on New York society and Jeffersonian democracy written in the first decade of the century. Irving later created the characters Rip Van Winkle and Ichabod Crane, both of whom prefer to dream rather than deal with everyday reality. In fact, the scholar Louis

D. Rubin Jr. has identified the conflict between the ideal and the real as a central characteristic of American humor. Rubin suggested that the "great American joke" is the disparity between the lofty promises of American democracy and the mundane realities of inequality, conflict, and injustice. Such disparity was widely apparent in a country in which thousands of immigrants responded to the promise of the "American dream" even as Native Americans were systematically driven from their lands and hundreds of thousands of Africans and their descendants were enslaved.

An American Comic Style

An important part of the development of a distinctly national culture and literature, humor flourished by playing on the peculiar qualities of American geography, speech patterns, and manners. Walter Blair and Hamlin Hill have contended that the "golden age" of American humor began in the 1830s and was characterized by exaggeration, anti-intellectualism, and the use of regional dialects. As the frontier expanded westward and the "common man" was celebrated by Jacksonian democracy, comic characters were frequently rural figures who either used common sense to unmask political hypocrisy and corruption, as did Seba Smith's character Jack Downing in Maine, or, like George Washington Harris's character Sut Lovingood in Tennessee, expressed their individuality by playing practical jokes on those in positions of authority and boasting loudly about their exploits. Boasting and exaggeration joined in one of the indigenous forms of American humor, the tall tale. These stories feature human encounters with larger-than-life elements of the natural world, such as giant bears and alligators, or impossible practical jokes, such as a competitor filling Jim Smiley's prizewinning frog with buckshot, recounted in Mark Twain's "The Celebrated Jumping Frog of Calaveras County" (1865).

The narrative strategy of many tall tales, in which an educated narrator, often from the East, confronts the rustic, dialect-speaking teller of the tale, reflects the tensions between urban and rural, book learning and practical knowledge, genteel manners and backwoods roughness that arose in an increasingly competitive and class-conscious young society. Such tensions plus the all-important conflict between slavery and freedom were captured in the best-known novel of the century, Mark Twain's *The Adventures of Huckleberry Finn*, which was published in Great Britain in 1884 and in the United States in 1885 but is set in the 1840s. As the adolescent Huck travels with the escaped slave Jim down the Mississippi River, Twain (Samuel Clemens) makes pointed fun of pretensions to middle-class gentility, religious hypocrisy, bookish romanticism, and entrepreneurial opportunists, all of which are contrasted to Huck's untutored innocence.

Women writers of humor had a somewhat different slant on issues of gentility and propriety, which were closely tied to their presumed roles as domestic arbiters of manners and morality. Whereas in *Huck Finn* the women, whose task it is to "civilize" unruly boys and men, are portrayed as ineffectual and somewhat ridiculous, writers such as Frances Whitcher in the 1840s implicitly satirized the cultural expectations that pitted women against one another in a competition for marriageable men and, hence, economic security. Fanny Fern (pseudonym of Sara Willis Parton), who in the 1850s was the highest-paid newspaper columnist in the country, used that forum to make fun of women's clothing styles, husbands who were stingy with household money, and even the institution of marriage itself. By the last decades of the century the work of the popular humorist Marietta Holley demonstrated that pressures on women to dress and behave in certain ways remained in force. Those strictures are staunchly opposed by Holley's sturdy, sensible protagonist, Samantha Allen, who argues in her rural New York dialect against foolish sentimentality and in favor of women's right to vote and enjoy other equalities with men.

The Prevalence of Stereotypes

Regional differences and the arrival of immigrants from various parts of the world provided the material for enduring comic stereotypes. The figure of the "Yankee" originated before the Revolutionary War as representative of the colonist, but by the early nineteenth century the Yankee—shrewd, practical, and patriotic—had come to be identified with the North. The southerner, when not a renegade such as Sut Lovingood, was typed as an aristocrat. Humorous stereotypes of members of ethnic groups were more pernicious. The Irish were portrayed as drunk and lazy, Jews as avaricious, and African Americans as either childishly docile or sneaky and dangerous. Such stereotypes were commonplace in jokes, sketches, and theatrical performances. When, for example, Harriet Beecher Stowe's antislavery novel, *Uncle Tom's Cabin* (1852), was adapted for the stage in the decades following the Civil War, Stowe's characters Uncle Tom and Topsy became stereotypical African Americans, singing, dancing, and performing comic routines. Also in the mid–nineteenth century the minstrel show, featuring white actors in black-

Buford's Comic Sheet, c. 1870s. Cartoons poked fun at all stations of life and situations. Unfortunately, the medium employed stereotypes—for example, racial slurs. LIBRARY OF CONGRESS

face, presented blacks as ignorant and slow-witted, speaking in heavy dialects. While sexuality was taboo as a subject for nineteenth-century humor, making fun of the supposed characteristics of groups of people was commonplace, and many Americans became acquainted with the Irish, Dutch, and Native Americans through their stereotyped images on the stage. By the end of the century that stage was likely to present a vaudeville show, a variety show featuring slapstick comedy, jokes, and monologues that often turned upon racial and ethnic "types." By one estimate, two thousand vaudeville theaters were in operation in 1900.

Not all nineteenth-century American humor, of course, played upon sectional and ethnic differences, nor was it intended to appeal to anxieties about these differences. While Mark Twain and Artemus Ward (Charles Farrar Browne) attracted public attention to their folksy, semiliterate creations by going on the lecture circuit, a more urbane and sophisticated humor caught the attention of better-educated Americans. Augustus Baldwin Longstreet's *Georgia Scenes* (1835) makes fun of the pretensions of the socially elite, employing pedantic narrators who themselves become figures of fun. In the 1840s James Russell Lowell, a Harvard-educated New Englander, took on the literary establishment of the time in *A Fable for Critics* (1848), a long poem in heroic couplets that pokes fun at the work and the personal characteristics of such luminaries as Ralph Waldo Emerson, Nathaniel Hawthorne, Henry Wadsworth Longfellow, and Edgar Allan Poe. *Knickerbocker* magazine (1833–1865) continued the tradition of genial humor made popular by Irving, and the *Spirit of the Times* (1831–1861), intended for the "gentleman" reader, published a wide variety of humorous pieces and introduced the southwestern humor of such writers as George Washington Harris, Johnson Jones Hooper, and Thomas Bangs Thorpe to eastern readers. Toward the end of the century several comic periodicals in New York, including *Punch* (1877), *Judge* (1881), and *Life* (1883), specialized in urbane wit. These magazines reflected their urban environment by presenting both the ethnic humor of the streets and sophisticated sketches and verses written by well-educated humorists.

Political Humor

The fact that the New York humor magazines of the nineteenth century published political cartoons and were sometimes quite partisan was nothing new in American humor. Since before the American Revolution humor had been an effective weapon in political controversy, and upon the establishment of na-

tionhood and freedom of speech, citizens mocked and satirized those with whom they disagreed. Lowell published two sets of *The Biglow Papers*, the first (1848) satirizing U.S. imperialism against Mexico and the southern drive to expand slavery and the second (1867) criticizing England's pro-Confederate policies during the Civil War. Joel Chandler Harris, who began writing his Uncle Remus sketches in the 1870s, commented in 1906 that humor was almost as important in American politics as was principle. As Harris's comment suggests, humorists reflected Americans' skepticism about the motives and the methods of politicians, and humorists mocked both their platforms and their rhetoric. Hooper created his comic character Simon Suggs in the form of a campaign biography, that common vehicle of political flattery. Yet politicians also enjoyed humor. Abraham Lincoln was especially noteworthy for his love of jokes, and he was fond of reading aloud bits of frontier humor.

Although scholars often distinguish between "serious" and "humorous" literary works, such a distinction is in fact artificial. Mark Twain was not the only nineteenth-century author who used comic elements to help convey a serious message. Henry David Thoreau's classic *Walden* (1854) contains a great deal of wit and wordplay, as does the poetry of Emily Dickinson. Herman Melville's short story "Bartleby the Scrivener" (1856) includes characters who are essentially caricatures, and Stowe's *Uncle Tom's Cabin* uses comic stereotypes, such as Miss Ophelia, the finicky and efficient New England spinster. As such regional types became popular in local-color fiction in the later decades of the century, authors' interest in preserving distinctive manners, customs, and speech patterns frequently inspired humorous portrayals. New England writers such as Rose Terry Cooke and Mary Wilkins Freeman and southern writers such as Grace King and Kate Chopin, in rendering the dialects and folkways of their respective regions, both enlightened and amused readers in other parts of the country. Despite the fact that novels by nineteenth-century women were for a long time dismissively characterized as sentimental, many of these writers employed clever comic devices. Fanny Fern's novel *Ruth Hall* (1855), for example, sharply satirizes religious hypocrisy, the "science" of phrenology, and people who write fan letters to newspaper columnists. The practice of assigning the comic and the sentimental to the realm of "popular" literature—a realm defined as inferior to "serious" or "elite" literature— was a twentieth-century phenomenon. Nineteenth-century authors felt free to combine different modes in their works.

Cartoons and Comics

Visual humor, almost exclusively in the form of drawings, abounded in nineteenth-century culture. Most published novels and short stories were profusely illustrated, which underscored scenes of slapstick comedy and the outstanding physical and behavioral traits of characters. Political cartoons were pervasive during a century in which the newspaper was the most common form of printed communication. Thomas Nast popularized the political cartoon with his illustrations in *Harper's Weekly* during the Civil War. Following the war, newspapers found that they could attract readers by printing both graphic renderings of newsworthy events and cartoons that made fun of political personalities, policies, and parties. With literacy by no means universal, such visual messages had wide impact. The next step in the development of comic art was the comic strip, which, like the tall tale, originated in the United States. The first true comic strip was developed by Richard F. Outcault, who began in 1894 to illustrate the antics of children on the streets of New York's slums in a series of panels. Originally titled "Hogan's Alley," the strip was renamed "The Yellow Kid" in 1896, when the advent of color printing allowed the depiction of one of the characters in a yellow shirt. Outcault added dialogue in balloons above the characters' heads, launching one of the most ubiquitous forms of American humor.

See also **Book Publishing; Cartoons, Political; Folktales and Tall Tales; Popular Culture, Vaudeville, and Burlesque.**

Bibliography

Blair, Walter, and Hamlin Hill. *America's Humor: From Poor Richard to Doonesbury*. New York: Oxford University Press, 1978.

Blair, Walter, and Raven I. McDavid Jr., eds. *The Mirth of a Nation: America's Great Dialect Humor*. Minneapolis: University of Minnesota Press, 1983.

Brown, Carolyn S. *The Tall Tale in American Folklore and Literature*. Knoxville: University of Tennessee Press, 1987.

Inge, M. Thomas. *Comics as Culture*. Jackson: University Press of Mississippi, 1990.

Rourke, Constance. *American Humor: A Study of the National Character*. Garden City, N.Y.: Doubleday, 1931.

Rubin, Louis D., Jr., ed. *The Comic Imagination in American Literature*. New Brunswick, N.J.: Rutgers University Press, 1973.

Sloane, David E. E., ed. *American Humor Magazines and Comic Periodicals*. Westport, Conn.: Greenwood, 1987.

Walker, Nancy A. *A Very Serious Thing: Women's Humor and American Culture*. Minneapolis: University of Minnesota Press, 1988.

NANCY A. WALKER

HUNTING AND TRAPPING

At the beginning of the nineteenth century most Americans believed that North American wildlife was inexhaustible. Hunting and trapping were considered individual and corporate natural rights protected by the Constitution and sanctioned by state and federal laws and local customs for white Americans. Before they were moved onto reservations, Native Americans considered taking game and trapping furbearers essential for survival. They therefore insisted on provisions in treaties signed with the United States to guarantee traditional hunting, fishing, and gathering rights. Hunting and trapping were also important for blacks, both slave and free, who supplemented their daily fare with products of the hunt and trapline.

Hunting and Trapping throughout the Century

In 1800, as in colonial times, members of the deer (Cervidae) family, which includes moose, elk, and caribou, were the mammals most sought after by individual American Indian and white hunters in North America. In the United States whitetails, or Virginia deer (*Odocoileus virginianus*), were the most widespread species hunted for personal consumptive and utilitarian needs. Many Americans, especially those in the backcountry and on the frontier, wore buckskin and regularly ate venison. The "long hunter" tradition associated with Kentuckians such as Daniel Boone continued to influence costume and culinary preferences as Americans expanded west into woodlands and grasslands, where they took animals individually with single-shot rifles designed for long-distance accuracy. Squirrels, opossums, raccoons, muskrats, and bears were also eaten regularly where available. Trade in deerskins, red deer or elk hides, and bearskins was secondary to the more dominant fur and robe trade that expanded markedly in the United States during the nineteenth century. Skins of smaller game animals, especially raccoons and muskrats, were bartered or sold and became important in regional economies.

Americans expanded westward, filling in landscapes once managed with fire and as open clearings by Native Americans. Game grew scarce anywhere settlements endured and fire was repressed but most rapidly along coastlines and in river valleys. By midcentury the great auk (*Pinguinus impennis*) joined a small but significant list of species no longer sighted in North America. Also on the list were Steller's sea cow (*Hydrodamalis gigas*), extinct by 1768; the eastern bison (*Bison bison pennsylvanicus*), gone by 1832; and the spectacled cormorant (*Phalacrocorax perspicillatus*), a food source of Aleuts and Russian fur traders that was last eaten in 1850. Species that were rarely seen, owing to their easy capture or localized habitat, included the heath hen (*Tympanuchus cupido cupido*), which graced tables throughout the eastern United States during colonial and revolutionary times; the carolina parakeet (*Conuropsis carolinensis*), prized as a cage bird and for its colorful feathers; the labrador duck (*Camptorhynchus labradorius*); and the eastern elk, or wapiti (*Cervus canadensis*), found nowhere east of the Mississippi by the Civil War.

Some species plentiful in 1860 had become threatened or were on the brink of extinction by the end of the nineteenth century. The sea otter (*Enhydra lutris*); the northern elephant seal (*Mirounga angustirostris*); the American bison (*Bison bison*); and three remarkable birds, the trumpeter swan (*Cygnus buccinator*, the world's largest waterfowl), the great egret (*Casmerodius albus*, desired for its plumage), and the passenger pigeon (*Ectopistes migratorius*, which traveled and bred in flocks numbering in the billions) were down to a few hundred by 1900.

Target Species of Fur Companies

Beaver (*Castor canadensis*), more than any other animal, motivated exploration and exploitation of North America from the sixteenth century through the nineteenth century. The beaver population was depleted in Europe, where the military and all classes of civilians valued the nearly waterproof underhair of this animal for felt hats. As many as 250,000 beaver pelts were sent to Europe each year from American and Canadian firms during the eighteenth and nineteenth centuries, and beaver dominated American exports of furs from 1790 into the 1820s. During the decade 1800 to 1810 beaver pelts worth $160,000 were sold to England alone. The War of 1812 virtually halted exports, but after the war high prices kept beaver trappers active through the mid-1830s, especially in the Rocky Mountains. By the 1840s hats made from South American nutria as well as silk and wool had replaced beaver hats in popularity, and the beaver trade collapsed. Pelts that had sold for as much as $6 a pound in the early 1830s were worth only $2.62 per pound in 1843, the lowest price since 1809 and the crisis with England.

By the 1830s raccoons from the Great Lakes region had replaced beaver as the largest export in total volume. In the 1830s England purchased 2.5 million raccoon pelts worth more than $1.4 million to American exporters. Over 13 million coonskins, most destined for Russian and German consumers, reached European markets from 1840 to 1870.

In Missouri River country and on the Great Plains buffalo (*Bison bison*) superseded beaver in importance by the mid-1830s. Most were killed by Native American hunters, whose women scraped and cured the hides for trade to whites in exchange for guns, blankets, and other goods. On average the fur companies in 1835 received $4 per robe or 25 percent profit at market. During the 1840s an average of ninety thousand buffalo robes were sent down the Missouri River to St. Louis each year. This increased to approximately one hundred thousand per year in the period 1850 to 1870. After the Civil War fur companies turned to professional (white) hide hunters, who slaughtered buffalo for industry, which used hides as power belts for water-driven and steam-fired factories; for the military to make into winter coats; and for civilians, who wanted them for area rugs and lap robes. The hunters also took the tongue, considered a delicacy when salted, pickled, or smoked. Between 1872 and 1874 over three million buffalo on the southern plains were killed by hide hunters, who received on average $1 per hide. In the 1870s the Sharps Manufacturing Company introduced the .50-caliber rifle, which gave shooters additional firepower. The southern buffalo herd was literally exterminated by 1878, and attention turned thereafter to the northern herd. From 1878 to 1885 market hunters moved in small squads, leaving only one thousand buffalo alive by the end of the decade.

Sea otters, in great demand in China for high-status clothing, lured ships representing many nationalities into Pacific Coast waters during the eighteenth century and prompted American interest in a lucrative China trade during the first two decades of the nineteenth century. Following the U.S. purchase of Alaska in 1867, fur seals became prime targets. The Alaska Commercial Company alone harvested 1.8 million seals from 1870 to 1890. Individual seal skins sold for as much as $70, adding $40 million to the U.S. economy, but the rookeries were depleted in the process. By 1910 an estimated 133,000 fur seals remained, not enough to sustain the industry.

Changes in Technologies and the Rise of Market Hunters

Snares, deadfall traps, pitfalls, box traps, net traps, and cage traps were all common among early settlers in America. From the sixteenth century on, Europeans had iron traps available, but these were rare in colonial America. In 1820 Samuel Newhouse of Oneida, New York, began manufacturing spring steel foot traps for Iroquois trappers. His various traps for all types of quadrupeds became standard in the antebellum United States, and Oneida became the center of trap manufacturing in the country. In 1867 over a million Newhouse traps in eight sizes were in circulation. Jump and coil-spring, leg-hold traps were also common in the second half of the nineteenth century because they entrapped animals without perfo-

Bear Trappers. Trappers set a trap for bears in Colorado, 1895. Traps were built to restrain the animal without damaging the hide. LIBRARY OF CONGRESS: PRINTS AND PHOTO-GRAPHS DIVISION

rating the hide and prevented "wringing off," or self-amputation, of a foot, a common occurrence with foot traps. Victor brand traps began production in 1886 and quickly became America's most popular trap, lasting well into the twentieth century.

Although guns were used by American hunters in the early part of the nineteenth century, most of the game taken was trapped rather than shot. Muzzle loaders and muskets were awkward, noisy, unreliable, and very slow to reload. Flintlocks were reliable for terrestrial hunts but were unsuitable for wetlands or hunting waterfowl generally. After 1820 percussion caps used as a waterproof firing mechanism gave hunters a new advantage, as did double-barrel shotguns. In addition the punt gun with a bore up to two inches in diameter that spread shot up to eight feet wide and one hundred yards in distance allowed hunters to kill dozens and sometimes hundreds of birds with a single shot. Market hunters used a variety of decoys and heavily baited drop or clap nets, which could take hundreds of birds at a time. In 1878 near Petoskey, Michigan, twenty-five hundred netters surrounded a nesting colony of passenger pigeons and within weeks had marketed more than 1.1 billion birds. Market hunters faced few restrictions prior to

the Lacey Act of 1900, which was designed to stop the interstate transportation of rare-bird plumage. On Chesapeake Bay single "big gunners" with punt guns were known to kill as many as fifteen thousand ducks in one day until they were stopped by legislation in 1918. Similarly, on flyways throughout the country migratory birds were brought down in the thousands by hunters using shotguns. After 1897 hunters had a further advantage with the introduction of the Winchester Model 97 pump gun, which used smokeless powder and paper shells rather than brass shells. New technology also benefited buffalo hunters after 1874. The Sharps .50-caliber, single-shot breech loader, accurate and lethal at several hundred yards, enabled individual hunters to kill up to five thousand animals per season in stands that sometimes left one hundred animals dead in the course of an hour.

Early Conservation Efforts, 1870–1914

By the 1870s it was clear that the nation's supply of wildlife was dwindling. In 1878 both California and New Hampshire established the first state game departments. In 1879 Congress created the Public Lands Commission to codify the federal game protection statutes and make them consistent. The American Ornithological Union was organized in 1883 to determine species distribution and the rate of depletion. In 1885 the Biological Survey of the United States was created within the Department of Agriculture; it was moved in 1930 to the Department of the Interior, and in 1940 it was renamed the U.S. Fish and Wildlife Service. The loss of species was slowed, with additional protection, in national parks (after 1872), forest reserves (after 1891), and wildlife refuges (beginning in 1903). Private organizations, especially the Boone and Crockett Club, founded in 1887, promoted commercial restrictions and hunting seasons to ensure viable populations of animals. Progressive Era legislation, particularly the Lacey Act of 1900, which regulated interstate shipments of game and feathers, and international agreements such as the Fur Seal Treaty of 1911 between the United States, Japan, Great Britain, and Canada slowed down the precipitous decline of some target species, but population restoration was not always successful. The last recorded wild passenger pigeon was shot in 1899, and Martha, the final member of the species, died in the Cincinnati Zoo in 1914.

See also **Conservation; Fur Trade.**

Bibliography

Bateman, James. *Animal Traps and Trapping*. Harrisburg, Pa.: Stackpole, 1971.

———. *Trapping*. Harrisburg, Pa.: Stackpole, 1979.

Clayton, James L. "The Growth and Significance of the American Fur Trade, 1790–1890." In *Aspects of the Fur Trade: Selected Papers of the 1965 North American Fur Trade Conference*. St. Paul: Minnesota Historical Society, 1967.

Dunlap, Thomas R. *Saving America's Wildlife*. Princeton, N.J.: Princeton University Press, 1988.

Kimball, David, and Jim Kimball. *The Market Hunter*. Minneapolis, Minn.: Dillon, 1969.

Matthiessen, Peter. *Wildlife in America*. New York: Viking, 1959.

McClung, Robert M. *Lost Wild America: The Story of Our Extinct and Vanishing Wildlife*. Rev. ed., Hamden, Conn.: Shoe String, 1993.

Ray, Arthur J. "The Fur Trade in North America: An Overview from a Historical Geographical Perspective." In *Wild Furbearer Management and Conservation in North America*. Edited by Milan Novak, et al. Toronto: Ministry of Natural Resources, 1987.

Russell, Carl P. *Firearms, Traps, and Tools of the Mountain Men*. New York: Knopf, 1977.

Trefethen, James B. *An American Crusade for Wildlife*. New York: Winchester, 1975.

WILLIAM R. SWAGERTY

I-J

IDAHO The difficult terrain of the Northwest Territory meant that Idaho was untouched by Europeans until 1805, when Meriwether Lewis (1774–1809) and William Clark (1770–1838) traversed it in their famous expedition. French Canadian Catholics and New England Protestants both tried in the 1830s and 1840s to build missions for converting the Indians, and a Mormon settlement was founded in 1855, but all of these attempts to establish outposts of European civilization had collapsed by 1858.

The lack of any lasting white settlements did not prevent the United States from trying to organize formal sovereignty over the entire region. The area of the future state was secured from the British in 1846, and then was controlled by various combinations of the Oregon and Washington Territories from 1848 to 1863. As in other western states, the first significant non-Indian population arrived with the discovery of valuable metals—in this case gold, in 1860 in northern Idaho. The territorial legislature soon organized four counties. The population grew so rapidly that the new mining regions threatened to become the tail that wagged the territorial dog. The legislative solution, pushed through by politicians in the western part of the territory, created a separate Idaho Territory in 1863.

From the Civil War until 1890, when Idaho became a state, sectional divisions underpinned territorial politics. In 1864 the capital was moved from Lewiston to Boise. This prompted people to divide the state at the Salmon River. Residents of the northern section talked of being annexed to either Washington or Montana, and the southern residents talked of joining the state of Nevada. When these annexation proposals finally emerged from Congress in 1887, President Grover Cleveland (1837–1908) vetoed the bill. Yet that veto marked the first serious attempt to create common interests in the future state. The promise of real self-government and federal financing proved irresistible. In 1889 the University of Idaho was created at Moscow, and the new state soon began building a road linking the northern and southern sections. In the 1890s, Idaho's first decade as a state, its population grew from 88,548 to 161,772.

Into the twentieth century, the building of railroads and the development of irrigated agriculture supplemented Idaho's initial rush to gold mining. Farmers had to irrigate the region's semiarid land, which set up a major source of tension with the mining interests. The state also experienced less stereotypical "frontier" issues in the 1890s. Seven of ten voters supported a prohibition clause in Idaho's constitution, which in effect meant they were endorsing the views of the Women's Christian Temperance Union.

During Idaho's push for statehood, the territory's politics were dominated by Republicans, who firmly believed that organization of the western lands was critical to maintaining the country's democratic characteristics. Most of the state's leaders were experienced westerners, so the spasmodic and often corporate nature of economic development did nothing to shake their faith in the future of the West.

See also **Frontier; Gold Rushes and Silver Strikes; Oregon; Washington State.**

Bibliography

Arrington, Leonard J. *History of Idaho*. 2 vols. Moscow: University of Idaho Press, 1994.

Bentley, E. B., et al. *Snake: The Plain and Its People*. Edited by Todd Shallat. Boise, Idaho: Boise State University, 1994.

Schwantes, Carlos A. *In Mountain Shadows: A History of Idaho*. Lincoln: University of Nebraska Press, 1991.

IAN MYLCHREEST

IDEOLOGY. See **Politics**, subentry on **Political Thought**.

ILLINOIS

Illinois originally comprised prairies, particularly in the central and northern portions of the state, which were later converted to farmland. Southern Illinois has more timber and hills. The land is rich with glacial mineral deposits, and the absence of mountain ranges to the south permits warm air from the Gulf of Mexico to reach the state, giving it mild weather and a five- to seven-month growing season.

Politics and Society in Early Illinois

The land that became the state of Illinois was part of the vast territorial expanse covered by the Northwest Ordinance of 1787, which prohibited slavery. Illinois at the beginning of the nineteenth century was sparsely settled and part of the Indiana Territory. Complaints from residents of the Illinois country that territorial governor William Henry Harrison was too remote and too partial to the concerns of Indiana residents prompted calls for Congress to organize a separate territory for Illinois. This was accomplished in 1809, with Kaskaskia designated as the capital. Ninian Edwards, from Kentucky, was named territorial governor, his origins reflective of the predominantly southern character of the early settlers, often characterized as upland southerners. Their attitudes on slavery generally mirrored those of the South.

Statehood followed in 1818, thanks to the efforts of Daniel Pope Cook (1794–1827), clerk of the Illinois House of Representatives, and a generous reading of the required census. While the Illinois constitution prohibited slavery, the weak clause provided no mechanism for freeing the thousand or so slaves bound by contract in the state. Indeed, people were held in slavery until the state's second constitution was formed in 1847. Under the first constitution, French residents were allowed to retain their slaves, the salt wells at Shawneetown were worked by slaves under contract from border-state owners, and legal loopholes permitted others to keep their slaves as indentured or registered servants. A referendum in 1824 defeated a strong effort to legalize slavery in Illinois, because of the staunch antislavery efforts of Governor Edward Coles, a former Virginian who had urged Thomas Jefferson to back national emancipation. Slavery and race continued to bedevil Illinois, as it did the United States, until its abolition.

Politics in Illinois in the years immediately following statehood was driven by personality, as factions formed under the leadership of such men as Ninian Edwards and Jesse Thomas, both U.S. senators. With the rise of Andrew Jackson, who embodied common man politics, on the national scene, party development began in Illinois and was helped along by a young Vermont-born lawyer, Stephen A. Douglas. The Jacksonian Democrats emerged as the majority party due to their organizational skills and the popularity of their land reform (specifically, lower prices and squatters rights) and Indian removal policies. The Illinois Whig Party formed in 1834 and advocated Senator Henry Clay's American system of tariff, internal improvements, and a national bank. Internal improvements were tremendously popular in developing Illinois, whose citizens were anxious to get their products to market, and both political parties found it expedient to support them. The result was the disastrous state bond issue of 1837—over $10 million for railroad development—that foundered completely when the panic of 1837 struck, leaving the state saddled with debt that took decades to retire.

Migration into Illinois was restricted to the southern portion of the state until it became clear that it was possible to farm the vast prairie of central Illinois. Settlement was spurred by ceding an immense tract in west central Illinois to veterans of the War of 1812, by rivers that provided easy access to virgin lands, by the ease of railroad construction and locomotion on the level prairie, and by the invention of the steel plow and McCormick's reaper. The natives in the region were pushed out; their final stand was the hapless Black Hawk War (1832). In 1833, the Indians were forced to abandon all territorial claims in Illinois.

Settlers poured into Illinois after the Indian exodus, and the state's population began to shift northward. So, too, did the state capital, which was moved from Vandalia to Springfield in 1839 (earlier it had been moved from Kaskaskia to Vandalia). Chicago's location on Lake Michigan made it the terminus of settlers' journeys that began with a trip on the Erie Canal to the Great Lakes. With a population of 4,170

Peru, Illinois. The early stages of commercial development along Water Street. Photograph by D. W. S. Rawson, taken in 1866, published in *The Valley of the Illinois: A Series of Photographic Views of the Illinois River and its Tributaries.* LIBRARY OF CONGRESS

when incorporated in 1837, Chicago became a trading center and a railroad and shipping hub for the livestock and produce of the Midwest, growing tremendously throughout the century to become the nation's second-largest city by 1900.

Slavery in Politics and War

Political consensus was scarce in the decades preceding the Civil War. The rise of the abolition movement and the migration of New Englanders of abolitionist sympathies into the state prompted a sometimes violent anti-abolition reaction. In 1837 the state legislature passed a resolution condemning antislavery agitation and affirming the constitutional right of southern states to own slaves. This act prompted Abraham Lincoln's first public remonstrance against slavery. He was then a young state legislator representing Sangamon County. Yet even Lincoln's counterresolution, which condemned slavery as bad policy, decried abolitionist unrest. That same year, the newspaper editor and abolitionist Elijah Lovejoy was murdered in Alton while defending his fourth printing press from an anti-abolition mob; similar mobs had destroyed the previous three.

Slavery as an issue assumed new urgency in the 1850s when Stephen A. Douglas, Lincoln's great Democratic foe, shepherded a bill through Congress organizing the Kansas and Nebraska territories, at the price of an explicit repeal of the Missouri Compromise's slavery restriction. Called "Little Giant," Douglas dominated Illinois politics and had presidential aspirations, but his ill-judged concession to southern congressmen unleashed a sectional firestorm. Illinois was convulsed too, as political leaders, the press, churches, and social groups weighed in on the question, with those opposed to the Kansas-Nebraska Act far outnumbering those in support. Douglas returned to the state to rally support and was stunned at the negative reaction; he was heckled when he tried to speak on the issue. Illinois politics was changed, with a nascent Republican Party growing out of the ashes of the defunct Whigs, a new coalition whose main unifying force was opposition to the spread of slavery.

The 1858 senate race pitted Lincoln against Douglas in one of the great political contests in American history. Lincoln argued that the founding fathers had explicitly placed slavery on a course of eventual extinction and that slavery's expansion was unthinkable. Douglas contended that it was best to defuse the issue by allowing the people in the territories to decide its fate, a concept called "popular sovereignty." Douglas won the election as the Democrats captured the state legislature, but Lincoln received the national recognition that helped propel him into the presidency.

When the war came, Illinois furnished 259,092 men for the Union cause. Illinoisans participated in some of the bloodiest battles of the war, such as Shiloh and Chickamauga. Illinois regiments formed a critical part of William T. Sherman's army as it marched through Georgia to the sea and crushed the South's will and capacity to fight. Not all Illinoisans supported the war though; many in southern Illinois were of southern heritage and sympathies. Democrats were divided on the war: some supported it, others utterly opposed it, and still others supported the war but condemned the Lincoln administration's conduct of it. A crisis of sorts was reached in 1862, when the paucity of Union victories, perceived violations of civil rights, the preliminary Emancipation Proclamation, and fear of an influx of former slaves weakened the Republican effort in Illinois. Thousands of Republicans and War Democrats (Democrats who supported the Union and the use of military force to reconstitute it) serving in the army were unable to cast a vote. The outcome was a Democratic landslide, as Democrats captured eight of fourteen congressional seats and the state legislature. Even Lincoln's old friend Leonard Swett, who practiced law with Lincoln on the Eighth Judicial Circuit, was defeated for a congressional seat. Soon resolutions were floated in the General Assembly condemning the Emancipation Proclamation and urging a negotiated settlement. On 13 January 1863, the Chicago *Tribune* warned that Illinois is "on the brink of revolution." Subsequent Union victories blunted the peace movement, though strong peace rallies and occasional violence continued into 1864.

Late-Nineteenth-Century Industry

Illinois emerged at war's end saddened at the death of its favorite son, Abraham Lincoln, who was given a martyr's funeral and interred in Oak Ridge cemetery near his beloved Springfield. But there were also grounds for hope. Thousands of miles of railroad track had been laid in the 1850s, leaving the state poised for growth. The population of Illinois roughly doubled, to 4,821,550, in the period between the Civil War's conclusion and the century's end. Most of the growth came in Chicago, which grew from a population of 109,260 in 1860 to its 1900 total of 1,698,575. The Union Stock Yards Company in Chicago was perhaps the busiest in the world, and the great meatpacking magnates Philip D. Armour and Gustavus Swift pioneered the safe transportation of meat from the Chicago stockyards to distant markets. Montgomery Ward and Richard Sears invented mail order houses, and Marshall Field built an unforgettable department store. Illinois became a leading manufacturing state, and coal mining became an important industry as well.

With this growth came labor strife as workers struggled with management for better wages and working conditions. The 1886 Haymarket Riot that left seven policemen dead began as a rally in support of striking McCormick workers. When George Pullman cut his employees' pay in response to the depression of 1893, his workers went on strike, an effort that was foiled by President Grover Cleveland's intervention. The use of black strikebreakers by management in coal mining, meatpacking, and other industries probably fueled racial animosities that ultimately boiled over in race riots early in the twentieth century. Jane Addams, Florence Kelly, and other progressive reformers sought to aid alienated workers and the poor. Illinois had come a long way in a century and had much of which to be proud, but much remained to be done before all its citizens shared a measure of prosperity.

See also **Abolition and Antislavery; Chicago; Indiana; Kansas-Nebraska Act; Meatpacking; Midwest, The; Missouri Compromise; Politics,** *subentry on* **The Second Party System.**

Bibliography

Howard, Robert P. *Illinois: A History of the Prairie State.* Grand Rapids, Mich.: William B. Eerdmans, 1972.

Johannsen, Robert W. *Stephen A. Douglas.* New York: Oxford University Press, 1973.

Keiser, John H. "Black Strikebreakers and Racism in Illinois, 1865–1900." *Journal of the Illinois State Historical Society* 65 (Autumn 1972):313–326.

Leichtle, Kurt E. "The Rise of Jacksonian Politics in Illinois." *Illinois Historical Journal* 82 (Summer 1989):93–107.

Pease, Theodore Calvin. *The Frontier State, 1818–1848.* 1918. Reprint, Urbana: University of Illinois Press, 1987.

DAN MONROE

IMMIGRATION AND IMMIGRANTS

[The entry begins with an overview; continues with three subentries on **The Immigrant Experience, Im-**

migration Policy and Law, and Anti-immigrant Sentiment; and concludes with twelve subentries on immigrants from **Ireland**, **Great Britain**, **France and the Low Countries**, **Germany**, **Central and Eastern Europe**, **Jewish Immigrants**, immigrants from **Scandinavia and Finland**, **Southern Europe**, **The Ottoman Empire and the Middle East**, **Canada**, **Mexico and Latin America**, and **Asia**.]

AN OVERVIEW

According to official statistics, 19,123,606 persons immigrated to the United States during the nineteenth century. The actual number is in fact higher, since no statistics were kept before 1820 and persons immigrating via the unmonitored Canadian and Mexican borders were largely uncounted.

Although no hard data exist for the period before 1820, immigration was relatively light from the mid-1770s through 1819, due largely to the American and French Revolutions and the Napoleonic Wars. The 80,000 to 100,000 American Loyalists or Tories who emigrated, largely to Canada, during and just after the American Revolution plus the several thousand former slaves and free African Americans who left with British troops probably outnumbered the immigrants of the 1775–1820 era. As Table 1 shows, immigration increased in every decade from 1820 to 1900 with two exceptions. Immigration was held down in the 1860s by the Civil War and in the 1890s by the severe depression that plagued most of that decade, even though the total immigration for the 1890s was the second highest of the century. Immigration declined during economic downturns, such as the panic of 1857 and the depression of the mid-1870s, but overall immigration in those decades still exceeded that of the 1840s.

While a glance at Table 1 suggests that immigration was most significant in the latter decades of the century, that is, more persons immigrated to the United States in the three final decades than in all previous history, data showing the percentage of immigrants in the country at any one time portray its constant importance. Tables 2 and 3 provide a more complete picture. Table 2 is a measure of the incidence of arrivals, and Table 3 shows immigrants as a percentage of the total population. The rate of immigration is the calculation of the number of immigrants arriving in a given period as a percentage of the total population at the start of that period. Thus, in 1854 nearly half a million immigrants arrived in the United States, and the total population was just over 25 million. So about 20 immigrants arrived for

Table 1. Immigration to the United States: Fiscal Years 1820–1900*

Years	Number
1820–1830	151,824
1831–1840	599,125
1841–1850	1,713,251
1851–1860	2,598,214
1861–1870	2,314,824
1871–1880	2,812,191
1881–1890	5,246,613
1891–1900	3,687,564
Total	19,123,606

* Fiscal years in the nineteenth century began 1 July; data are for the period 1 July 1819–30 June 1900.

Source: U.S. Department of Justice, Immigration and Naturalization Service. *Statistical Yearbook of the Immigration and Naturalization Service.* Washington, D.C.: Government Printing Office, 1997. Table 1, p. 25.

Table 2. Rate of Immigration per 1,000, 1820–1900

Years	Rate
1821–1830	1.2%
1831–1840	3.9%
1841–1850	8.4%
1851–1860	9.3%
1861–1870	6.4%
1871–1880	6.2%
1881–1890	9.2%
1891–1900	5.3%

Source: Author's calculations from U.S. census data.

Table 3. Foreign-Born as a Percentage of Population, 1850–1920

Year	Percentage
1850	9.7%
1860	13.2%
1870	14.0%
1880	13.3%
1890	14.7%
1900	13.6%
1910	14.7%
1920	13.2%

Source: U.S. census data.

every thousand members of the population, a rate of about 2 percent, which is extremely heavy. In comparison, had 1996 experienced a similar rate, immigrants would have numbered 5.3 million instead of the 915,000 who were recorded. Had the 2 percent rate of 1854 been maintained throughout the 1850s, the decennial figure would be 20 percent. Table 2 shows the rate of immigration per thousand expressed in crude decennial cumulations.

The census data, which give the foreign-born only from the seventh census of 1850, are shown in Table 3. Foreign-born persons were between 13 and 14 percent of the population in every census between 1860 and 1920. (The 1990 figure was 6.2 percent.) In relation to the transformation of the United States in that period from a predominantly rural, agricultural nation to one that was predominantly urban and industrial, this consistency in the size of the foreign-born segment of the population—about one person in seven—is truly remarkable.

Why They Came

The numbers tell us a great deal about the nature of immigration to the United States. Despite much talk, then and now, about America being a refuge for mankind, the overwhelming number of nineteenth-century immigrants came for economic reasons. Large numbers of them came intending to return, as perhaps a third of them did. (The government did not begin keeping records of departing immigrants until 1909.) A definitive study by Harry Jerome, *Migration and Business Cycles* (1926), established that for the nineteenth century and the first decades of the twentieth century the volume of immigration correlated strongly with the major ups and downs of the business cycle.

This is not to say that seeking asylum was an unimportant factor in migration to the United States. Refugees from revolution and persecution, both political and religious, came to the country in large numbers. Political refugees fled from failed revolutions and reform movements, from overthrown monarchies and autocracies, and from a victorious slave rebellion in Haiti. Religious refugees fled from oppressive state churches in places like Sweden, from sectarian persecution in both Catholic and Protestant countries, and from the terror of Eastern European pogroms. Many political refugees planned to return to their native lands when conditions changed, while most religious refugees planned to remain, many of them in backwoods utopias established all over the United States. To be sure, foreign domination of oppressed national groups, the Irish and Poles in particular, heightened what was essentially an economic movement. Most migrants came, as the Poles put it, *za chlebem* (for bread). Similar phrases exist in other languages.

In the first half of the century large numbers of immigrants settled on the land. Although some ag-ricultural settlement continued, immigration was heavily urban in the second half of the century. But from the end of the eighteenth century and the beginning of the nineteenth century, the percentage of immigrants in cities was higher than the percentage of native-born Americans in cities. The switch from agricultural migrants can be seen both within groups and between groups. For example, some of the earliest Polish settlers were agricultural pioneers in Texas, but many more nineteenth-century Polish immigrants earned their bread in the factories of the north central states.

Who They Were

Although nineteenth-century immigrants to the United States came from the four corners of the earth, 17.3 million or 90.4 percent of those enumerated came from Europe. Another 1.1 million came from Canada. All told, 95.9 percent were either Europeans or the descendants of Europeans. Most of the rest, 375,000 immigrants, came from Asia, chiefly China. (Immigration to Hawaii before statehood in 1959 is not generally counted as U.S. immigration.) Mexico, a prime source of twentieth-century immigration, contributed fewer than 30,000 to the mix, while 126,000 came from the Caribbean region.

In the earlier decades of the century immigrants from northwestern Europe, chiefly British, Germans, and Scandinavians, dominated, while in the final decades emigration from eastern and southern Europe grew rapidly. Only in the 1890s, however, did eastern and southern European immigration outnumber that of northwestern Europe. The data for the 1880s show almost 3.6 million from northwestern Europe and just over 900,000 from southern and eastern Europe. Those for the 1890s show immigrants from eastern European sources outnumbering those from western European ones by 1.8 million to 1.5 million. The chief national sources of the southeastern migration were Italy and the Austro-Hungarian and Russian empires. The chief ethnic groups from the two multinational empires were Poles and eastern European Jews.

A variety of reasons explain the expansion of emigration from eastern and southern Europe, but chief among them was the growth and improvement of the transportation networks that brought Europeans to the United States. First, steamships replaced sailing vessels. In 1856 more than 95 percent of European immigrants came to the United States under sail, while in 1873 more than 95 percent came by steam. The extension of increasingly efficient railway networks to all but the most isolated corners of Europe was another obvious change. But entrepreneurial

Main Building, Ellis Island. The Immigrant Station on Ellis Island in New York Harbor first opened its doors in 1892. From that year until 1954, twelve million immigrants were processed here. As a result, over 100 million—more than 40 percent—of Americans living today have an ancestor who passed through Ellis Island. Photograph, 1898. LIBRARY OF CONGRESS

innovation was also important. In the latter part of the century the immigrant trade was dominated by three great European companies: the Liverpool-based Cunard, the Bremen-based North German Lloyd, and the Hamburg-America line. These and other firms developed extensive networks of largely part-time ticket agents in both the United States and Europe. In the United States these agents were usually immigrant entrepreneurs, often saloon keepers and grocers. Thus, a Czech immigrant in Chicago or a Pole in Detroit, without leaving his or her own community or having to use English for a complex transaction, could order and pay for, perhaps on credit, a combination ticket from a Hamburg-America agent that would be delivered to a spouse, a fiancée, a relative, or a friend in Prague or Kraków by a company agent in Europe. That traveler, using one ticket, could go to Hamburg by train, spend waiting time in the line's immigrant depot in Hamburg, cross the ocean, and take a train to the final American destination.

Pioneer immigrants from a family or group were almost invariably male, as were perhaps two of every three nineteenth-century immigrants. Males also predominated, probably even more heavily, among returning immigrants. Regardless of gender, immi-grants were usually young adults, from the late teens into the thirties. The demographic profile varied from group to group and within groups. Among the immigrants who came intending to be farmers there was significantly more family immigration than among those who were headed for industrial pursuits. Among the Irish, for example, male immigration prevailed in the century's early decades and was succeeded by a largely family or survivor immigration in the famine and postfamine migration of the middle decades. That in turn was followed by a distinctly female immigration toward the century's end.

Where They Settled

Settlement patterns were complex and changed as the country grew and economic development proceeded. Two constant generalizations were, first, as noted above, a strong propensity for immigrants to be overrepresented in cities and, second, for them to avoid the South, although Gulf of Mexico ports, particularly New Orleans, Galveston, and Tampa, were popular destinations. Except for the 300,000 Chinese and 30,000 Japanese who generally remained in the Far West, most immigrants settled in the northeast-

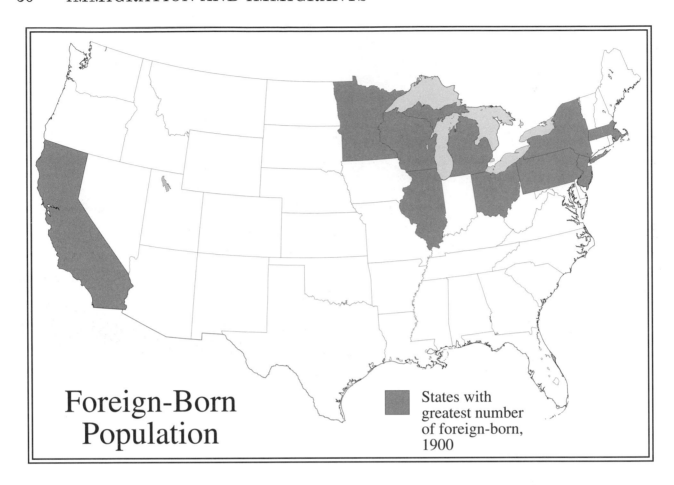

Foreign-Born
Population

States with
greatest number
of foreign-born,
1900

ern United States from the Atlantic seaboard to the Great Plains. All European groups were well represented in New York City. The Irish were the only group heavily concentrated in New England, where they were almost exclusively urban. British immigrants were well distributed, while Germans and Scandinavians were most prominent in the Midwest. British and Germans were both urban and rural, while Scandinavians were chiefly rural. Italians and Jews, both German and eastern European, settled mainly in East Coast cities, although both were well represented in Chicago. Poles and other Slavic groups were concentrated in industrial cities from Buffalo and Pittsburgh to Chicago and Milwaukee.

Whether in towns or in the country, immigrant groups, with one exception, tended to settle initially in ethnic enclaves to be with their own kind whenever it was feasible. The one exception was the English, whom the historian Charlotte Erickson labeled "invisible immigrants." The enclaves were communities where foreign languages, ethnic churches, and immigrant cultures, which became a mix of old and new, created zones of transition. There, for a generation or so, Europeans maintained much of their culture.

Reception in the United States

Although the Constitution does not mention the word "immigrant," the founding fathers mandated a "uniform system of naturalization" and made naturalized citizens eligible for every level of office save president and vice president. From the earliest U.S. history, immigrants have been cabinet officers, Supreme Court justices, senators, representatives, and governors and have held the entire range of lesser offices. Except for the ending of the African slave trade, immigration was generally encouraged. After all, the United States was an empty country to be filled. President John Tyler's message to Congress in June 1841 typified what passed for immigration policy: "We hold out to the people of other countries an invitation to come and settle among us as members of our rapidly growing family" (Richardson, *Compilation of the Messages*, p. 41).

Some elements of the public objected to Catholic immigrants in particular. The Know-Nothing movement tried to curtail both immigration and the rights of immigrant citizens, but it met with only brief, local successes in the 1850s. Masses of immigrant soldiers, many of them in ethnic regiments, proved their patriotism during the Civil War. No significant restrictions on free immigration were enacted until 1882, and that only affected Chinese laborers. Chinese exclusion was the hinge on which immigration policy eventually turned, but that was not clear in the nineteenth century.

Two events late in the century symbolized a growing ambivalence about immigration. On the one hand the government opened the receiving station on Ellis Island in 1892, and on the other anti-immigrant forces began to organize politically. A number of minor restrictive measures were enacted in the 1880s and 1890s, but a literacy test advanced by nativists eventually failed, vetoed by President Grover Cleveland in 1897. Effective general immigration restriction would not occur until the twentieth century.

See also **Chinese Exclusion Act; Cities and Urbanization.**

Bibliography

Daniels, Roger. *Coming to America: A History of Immigration and Ethnicity in American Life.* New York: HarperCollins, 1990. A general history.

Diner, Hasia R. *Erin's Daughters in America: Irish Immigrant Women in the Nineteenth Century.* Baltimore: Johns Hopkins University Press, 1983. A pioneering study of immigrant women.

Jerome, Harry. *Migration and Business Cycles.* New York: National Bureau of Economic Research, 1926. A classic study of economic factors and migration.

Richardson, James D., ed. *A Compilation of the Messages and Papers of the President, 1789–1901.* Vol. 4. New York: Bureau of National Literature and Art, 1905.

Vecoli, Rudolph J., and Suzanne Sinke, eds. *A Century of European Migrations, 1830–1930.* Urbana: University of Illinois Press, 1991. A state-of-the-art survey.

Ward, David. *Cities and Immigrants: A Geography of Change in Nineteenth-Century America.* New York: Oxford University Press, 1971. A careful study of immigrant settlement.

ROGER DANIELS

THE IMMIGRANT EXPERIENCE

Nearly twenty million immigrants came to the United States during the nineteenth century. The official data, which begin in 1820, list 19,123,606 entries. Although the circumstances of both the immigrants and the United States changed drastically during the century, some questions arise about the immigration process regardless of time or place. Where did immigrants come from? Why did they leave their homeland? Why did they come here? How did they get here? Where did they settle? What did they do? How did they live? In what ways did their culture change? How did they interact with their environment?

Throughout the century the vast majority of immigrants were Europeans. Fewer than 750,000 came from Africa and Asia. All but a handful of the perhaps 1.25 million persons who came from Canada were either Europeans—mostly Irish—or French Canadians. Between 1830 and 1870 Germans and Irish accounted for an absolute majority of the immigrants with a peak incidence of more than 70 percent between 1840 and 1860 (see table 1). After that immigration became more diverse.

In the four decades between 1860 and the end of the century, some fourteen million persons immigrated to the United States, considerably more than had come in the seventeenth, eighteenth, and early nineteenth centuries combined. Slightly more came in the first two decades of the twentieth century. Although immigration in the later part of the nineteenth century is often described as dominated by the so-called new immigrants from southern and eastern Europe, western Europeans were in the majority until the 1890s. In fact more Germans immigrated in the 1880s than in any other single decade, although their incidence was not as large as it had been at mid-century. Western European predominance shrank steadily from 84.5 percent in the 1860s to 79.4 percent in the 1880s. Table 2 indicates the number of immigrants who came from the major European immigrant sources. It is important to note that, despite the increase in the volume of immigration, the incidence of foreign-born people in the American population remained remarkably constant during the second half of the century. Every census between 1860 and 1920 reported that about one American in seven was of foreign birth.

One of the great myths of American immigration is that a large percentage of immigrants came because of religious or political persecution. The fact is that the overwhelming majority of immigrants in every century came in hope of bettering their economic statuses. Students of migration have long used a "push-pull" dichotomy to analyze motives for migration. Push is shorthand for factors in the place of origin that make people want to leave, while pull describes those factors that attract the migrant to the new locale. Many, perhaps most, nineteenth-century migrants were both pushed and pulled. Classic examples of predominantly "push" migration include the refugees and their slaves who fled from the Haitian Revolution in the first decade of the century, the Irish in the potato famine years of the late 1840s, and Norwegians leaving a country that simply had no room for them in the middle decades of the century. But most nineteenth-century immigrants, who were not the poorest of the poor in their home countries, came to improve their lots. Many planned to be or became sojourners, immigrants who stayed for a while and then returned home, often with savings to buy land. Perhaps one in every three nineteenth-century immigrants returned, although some of those reemigrated

Most Europeans who migrated in the nineteenth century moved within Europe. Of those who left the Continent, the overwhelming majority came to the United States because economic opportunity seemed greater there. The settler-attracting areas of the British Empire—Canada, Australia, New Zealand, and southern Africa—were the second choice of emigrating Europeans, but even among emigrating Britons the target of choice was the United States. In addition the most populous British colony, Canada, constantly suffered a net drain of persons emigrating or reemigrating across the forty-ninth parallel. Outside of the British Empire the greatest area of attraction for European emigrants was the southern cone of South America—Argentina, Brazil, and Chile.

Large numbers of French Canadians came to the United States by train, and a few Mexicans came on foot. Otherwise nineteenth-century immigrants were ocean-borne, but the nature of their passage changed dramatically about mid-century. As late as the mid-1850s more than 95 percent of European immigrants came to the United States under sail. By the mid-1860s, 75 percent of them came on steam-powered vessels. A passage that had been measured in weeks and months in the early part of the century took only days toward its end. While the conditions on board ship for most immigrant passengers remained miserable, steamships were faster and charged less. Toward the end of the century the North Atlantic immigrant trade was dominated by three firms, the German Hamburg Amerika line, the North German Lloyd line, and the British Cunard line. These firms set up networks of ticket agents in Europe and the United States and rationalized facilities. Early in the century agents offered no schedules and no passenger ships. By the 1890s firms built special ships for the immigrant trade. A person in Poland, for example, could buy one ticket that would cover rail fare to Hamburg, accommodations in the steamship company's barracks, an ocean passage, and a railroad ticket to an American city. As often happened, a recent immigrant in an American city, such as Detroit, could buy a ticket for a family member or friend in a European city, like Kraków, and have it delivered to that person. Conditions for persons emigrating from the Mediterranean were not as well organized. European governments, beginning with the British, and later the American government passed rudimentary

Table 1. Immigration by Nationality, 1820–1900

Immigrants from Ireland

Decade	Number	Percentage of Total Immigration
1820–1830	54,338	35.8
1831–1840	207,381	34.6
1841–1850	780,719	45.6
1851–1860	914,119	35.2
1861–1870	435,778	18.8
1871–1880	436,871	15.5
1881–1890	655,482	12.5
1891–1900	388,416	10.5
Total	3,873,104	20.3

Immigrants from Germany

Decade	Number	Percentage of Total Immigration
1820–1830	7,729	5.1
1831–1840	153,454	25.4
1841–1850	434,626	25.3
1851–1860	951,667	36.6
1861–1870	787,468	34.0
1871–1880	718,182	25.5
1881–1890	1,452,970	27.7
1891–1900	505,152	13.7
Total	5,010,248	26.2

Immigrants from Scandinavia

Decade	Sweden	Norway	Denmark	Scandinavia
1820–1830	94		189	283
1831–1840	1,201		1,063	2,264
1841–1850	13,903		539	14,442
1851–1860	20,931		3,749	24,680
1861–1870	37,667	71,631	17,094	126,392
1871–1880	115,922	95,323	31,771	243,016
1881–1890	391,772	176,586	88,132	656,484
1891–1900	226,266	95,015	50,231	371,512
Total	771,627	438,555	192,769	1,439,073

Swedes and Norwegians were enumerated together before 1861. These immigrants are not included for either country, but they are included in the Scandinavian aggregate, which was 7.5 percent over the century.

The enumerated U.S. immigrants for 1820–1900 total 19,123,606.

protective legislation for immigrant passengers that was not always enforced. In the Pacific a complicated arrangement called the credit ticket system enabled many if not most of the quarter-million Chinese immigrants to travel now, pay later. From Quebec sophisticated arrangements brought families of French

Table 2. Major Sources of European Immigration, 1871–1900

Nation or Region	1870s	1880s	1890s	Total
Germany	718,182	1,452,970	505,152	2,676,304
Ireland	436,871	655,482	388,416	1,480,769
Britain	548,043	807,357	271,538	1,626,938
Scandinavia	243,016	656,494	371,512	1,271,022
Western Europe Total	1,946,112	3,572,303	1,536,618	7,055,033
Austria-Hungary	72,969	353,719	592,707	1,019,395
Italy	55,759	307,309	651,893	1,014,961
Russia	39,284	213,282	505,290	757,856
Poland	12,970	51,806	96,720	161,496
Southeastern Europe Total	180,982	926,116	1,846,610	2,953,708
Western and Southeastern Europe Total				10,008,741
Europe Total				10,562,761

The total number of immigrants to the United States between 1871 and 1900 was 11,746,190.

Canadians to New England mill towns by train. These immigrants often had jobs in the mills and company housing even before they left.

Settlement patterns changed as the nation expanded. Early in the century most immigrants went to rural areas, but those from southern and eastern Europe were likely to reside in cities. The Irish, however, largely settled in cities from early in the century. Their agricultural experience was ill adapted to American conditions, and few had the resources necessary to survive until the first crops came in. Initially, the concentration of Irish immigrants was greatest in New England, but by mid-century most American cities had significant Irish populations. German settlement patterns were more varied. Divided between city and country, Germans gathered in the Middle West, particularly in the so-called German Triangle, whose apexes were the cities of St. Louis, Cincinnati, and Milwaukee, with Chicago inside the triangle. Scholars have estimated that perhaps two-thirds of nineteenth-century German immigrants settled in this area. Scandinavians settled largely in the upper Midwest, from Wisconsin to the Dakotas, and as far south as Nebraska. Toward the end of the century a large secondary migration took immigrants from this area to the Pacific Northwest. French Canadians, as noted above, settled largely in New England mill towns, particularly in Massachusetts and Rhode Island, but some others settled close to the Canadian-American border.

As cheap arable land disappeared, more and more immigrants followed industrial pursuits. The Irish dug canals, built railroads, and pioneered a host of new urban occupations during the middle decades of the century. The Irish American policeman and fireman, more than a stereotype, represented an important segment of the immigrant and ethnic community. The Poles, Italians, eastern European Jews, and Greeks who came late in the century were rarely involved in the expanding American agriculture. Most Italian men worked in construction and other kinds of seasonal outdoor employment. Polish men and other eastern European men worked at the dirtiest jobs in heavy industry and mining. Jewish men and women and Italian women worked in the garment factories that clothed the United States. Like many earlier immigrants, large numbers of late-nineteenth-century immigrants would have preferred to work on their own farms, but the era of free land was long past. Even if free land had been available, few of these immigrants had the capital necessary to get started. The Chinese began working in mining, but later they were instrumental in building the transcontinental railroads and were significant in western agriculture both as laborers and market gardeners. Immigrant women of many ethnicities became domestic servants. For some, particularly unmarried young, rural women, it was training for homemaking, but for many it was a lifelong trade.

A significant minority of most immigrant groups became entrepreneurs. Such persons often began, for example, as labor contractors and boardinghouse keepers and moved up to become proprietors of immigrant businesses, such as grocery stores and saloons. Many such entrepreneurs provided services to fellow immigrants. The ethnic saloon keeper was often employment agent, banker, and travel agent. Some also became the first links between urban immigrant groups and local political machines.

In addition a number of important enterprises were started by immigrants, and some lines may be thought of as ethnic industries. A classic example is the lager beer industry, which involved several cities, German and German American capital, skilled labor,

Entering New York Harbor. Immigrants on the deck of the steamer *Germanic* marvel at the sight of the Statue of Liberty. From *Frank Leslie's Illustrated Newspaper,* 1887. LIBRARY OF CONGRESS: PRINTS AND PHOTOGRAPHS DIVISION

and consumers. It is no accident that each of the corner cities of the German triangle became a center of beer manufacturing. Similarly the California wine industry was largely the product of immigrant entrepreneurs from Italy, Switzerland, and Hungary. Jewish entrepreneurs developed the American garment industry, which was dominated by Jewish workers, male and female. The earliest Chinese entrepreneurs were importers of merchandise both for the ethnic community and for the larger public. Other Chinese carved a place for themselves by creating necessary urban services, particularly hand laundries and restaurants. Many Greeks also became restaurant operators, while a number of Italians became barbers. Nothing better describes the contribution of nineteenth-century immigrant labor than Carl Wittke's titular phrase for his 1939 book, "We Who Built America."

Whether they went to the country or to the cities, immigrants tended to cluster. In nineteenth-century rural America, various areas were heavily German, Swedish, and Norwegian, to name only the three most numerous farming groups. In some districts

there were so many German immigrants that the public schools were conducted in German rather than in English. Ethnic enclaves developed quickly, so that communities of Irish, German, Swedish, Italian, Greek, Polish, eastern European Jewish, and Chinese—to name only the most prominent groups—became a distinct part of American cities. These were usually among the poorest areas, such as *Kleindeutschlands* and Little Italies. A kind of ethnic succession often ensued, as in Chicago, where Swedes were replaced by Italians.

The enclaves were not just residential areas. They included businesses, places of worship, amusements, and civil organizations. A nineteenth-century Swedish American journalist reminisced about Chicago's Swedetown, "Wherever one goes one hears Swedish sounds generally, and if one's thoughts are somewhat occupied, one can believe one has been quickly transported back to Sweden" (Daniels, *Coming to America,* p. 170). The variety of businesses emerge from a San Francisco city directory for 1876, which devoted nine double-columned pages to what it called Chinese business houses. These included an asylum, barbers,

Immigrants in Omaha, Nebraska. While millions of immigrants made large eastern cities their home, many others traveled west after their arrival in their port city. The immigrants depicted here have arrived at the Union Pacific Railroad depot in Omaha, Nebraska. From *Frank Leslie's Illustrated Newspaper*, c. 1877. LIBRARY OF CONGRESS

butchers, bakers, carpenters, carvers and engravers, a cheese manufacturer, clothing manufacturers, drugstores, dry goods stores, employment offices, grocery stores, hotels, interpreters, Japanese and Chinese fancy goods, watchmakers and jewelers, laundries, lodging houses, merchants, a purveyor of opium, a painter, pawnbrokers, a photographer, physicians, restaurants, a shirt manufacturer, shoe manufacturers, a silk factory, slipper manufacturers, tailors, two theaters, tinsmiths, umbrellas and fans, varieties, and wood and lumber. Residential concentration was not determined just by nationality. For example, Rudolph Vecoli's 1963 study of Chicago's Italians showed that one tenement might be dominated by people from Palermo while another might be filled principally with Neapolitans. The historian Charlotte Erickson dubbed Britons the "invisible immigrants" because they did not cluster significantly and blended easily into the general population.

Obviously immigrants brought much of their culture with them. Neither their inherited culture nor the surrounding "American" culture remained the same. While much has been written about Americanizing the immigrant, the immigrants also changed America. Nowhere is this more obvious than on the religious landscape. By the century's end Roman Catholicism was the American religion with the greatest number of adherents. Immigrant churches became what the historian Jay P. Dolan has called "fortresses," in which immigrants not only huddled for protection but also organized attacks against oppressive aspects of American culture. The other lineaments of immigrant culture—language, entertainments, and ethnic folkways—in most circumstances lasted for a generation or so before surrendering to the American environment. But in the process each immigrant culture modified that environment to some degree. Religion alone did endure but was modified by the American experience.

The immigrant experience has always been a bittersweet one. Many immigrants never found what they were seeking in the new land. Almost all were exploited and discriminated against to some degree. Many had no success at all. But millions—no one can say how many—realized at least some of their dreams and found satisfaction, if not in their own lives then in those of their children.

See also Cities and Urbanization; Nationalism; Population; Work.

Bibliography

Conzen, Kathleen Neils. *Immigrant Milwaukee, 1836–1860: Accommodation and Community in a Frontier City*. Cambridge, Mass.: Harvard University Press, 1976.

Daniels, Roger. *Coming to America: A History of Immigration and Ethnicity in American Life*. New York: HarperCollins, 1990.

Gjerde, Jon. *The Minds of the West: Ethnocultural Evolution in the Rural Middle West, 1830–1917*. Chapel Hill: University of North Carolina Press, 1997.

Miller, Kerby A. *Emigrants and Exiles: Ireland and the Irish Exodus to North America*. New York: Oxford University Press, 1985.

Nugent, Walter. *Crossings: The Great Transatlantic Migrations, 1870–1914*. Bloomington: Indiana University Press, 1992.

Rischin, Moses. *The Promised City: New York's Jews, 1870–1914*. Cambridge, Mass.: Harvard University Press, 1977.

Schneider, Dorothee. *Trade Unions and Community: The German Working Class in New York City, 1870–1900*. Urbana: University of Illinois Press, 1994.

Van Vugt, William E. *Britain to America: Mid-Nineteenth-Century Immigrants to the United States*. Urbana: University of Illinois Press. 1999.

ROGER DANIELS

IMMIGRATION POLICY AND LAW

Often described as a nation of immigrants, the United States was transformed by immigration in the nineteenth century from a country small in population and size to a world power dominating the continent from ocean to ocean. As historian Oscar Handlin recounts in *The Uprooted*, "Once I thought to write a history of the immigrants in America. Then I discovered that the immigrants *were* American history."

In 1800, 5,297,000 people lived in the United States; a century later, immigrants and their descendants had helped to increase this number to more than seventy-six million. Five million people immigrated to the United States between 1815 and 1860, mainly from Britain and Ireland. Ten million more arrived between 1860 and 1890, predominantly Germans and Scandinavians as well as other northwestern Europeans. A third wave of immigration began around 1890; before it tapered off at the start of World War I in 1914, about fifteen million came, many from Italy, Austria-Hungary, Russia, and other parts of southern and eastern Europe. Although in smaller numbers, immigrants also came from Asia, Africa, the Americas, and other parts of the world.

As a social force, immigration in the nineteenth century is in large part an inspiring story. Millions came in search of freedom and prosperity, and though not without travail, many of them found it. The legal and political story is less optimistic. As part of a growing country's project of self-definition, the United States regulated which aliens could enter and who among them would be allowed to become citizens. This regulation was often based on racial and religious bigotry.

Citizenship Law

In the nineteenth century, the issue of whether a person was or could become a citizen was consequential; citizens had rights which aliens did not, and aliens were subject to various forms of governmental disadvantage, such as prohibitions on land ownership and the possibility of deportation. In common law, under the principle of *jus soli* (right of the soil), an individual became a citizen by being born in the nation's territory. A person born to parents who were already citizens became a citizen under the principle of *jus sanguinis* (right of blood). Article I of the U.S. Constitution gave Congress the power to grant citizenship through naturalization to those born citizens of other countries. The central legal question faced by nineteenth-century nationality law was whether non-Caucasians were eligible for citizenship by naturalization or birth.

The naturalization law passed by the first Congress in 1790 authorized naturalization only of free whites. From the beginning of the nineteenth century, therefore, immigrants of African or Asian racial ancestry could not naturalize. However, through treaties or statutes, the United States granted citizenship to groups that might not have been eligible for naturalization. Congress frequently offered citizenship to residents of territories acquired from foreign countries; for example, Mexicans in territory ceded to the United States after the Mexican War were made citizens by virtue of the Treaty of Guadalupe Hidalgo (1848). Moreover, some Native Americans were made citizens by treaty or statute.

Court decisions established early in the century that people born in the United States were citizens under the *jus soli* principle. However, the original Constitution did not explicitly define the scope of *jus soli* citizenship. In the case of *Dred Scott v. Sandford* (1857), the Supreme Court decided that African Americans born in the United States were not citizens of the nation, even if they were free and considered citizens of the state in which they lived. In reaching

Immigration Restriction. In this depiction of President Benjamin Harrison's recommendation that immigration be restricted, Uncle Sam draws a line on the ground with his cane, separating himself and Harrison from a crowd of penniless Europeans, including a "played-out German opera singer," a "ruined marquis" seeking an American heiress, and an Italian count. From *Judge*, 1889. LIBRARY OF CONGRESS

this conclusion, Chief Justice Roger B. Taney asserted that at the time of the adoption of the Constitution, blacks had been "regarded as beings of an inferior order, and altogether unfit to associate with the white race, either in social or political relations; and so far inferior, that they had no rights which the white man was bound to respect; and that the negro might justly and lawfully be reduced to slavery for his benefit."

The *Dred Scott* decision held for little more than a decade. During Reconstruction following the Civil War, Congress and the states amended the Constitution to overrule *Dred Scott*. The Thirteenth Amendment (1865) abolished slavery. Section 1 of the Fourteenth Amendment (1868) provided in part that "all persons born or naturalized in the United States, and subject to the jurisdiction thereof, are citizens of the United States and of the State wherein they reside." By ending slavery and making African Americans citizens, the amendments rendered *Dred Scott* ineffective. Congress amended the naturalization statute in 1870 to extend benefits to aliens of

African nativity or descent, as well as the free white persons already eligible.

Although the citizenship clause of the Fourteenth Amendment was broad on its face, it was not clear whether or how far it extended beyond whites and African Americans. In *Elk v. Wilkins* (1884), the Supreme Court held that John Elk, a Native American who had severed his relationship with his tribe, was not a citizen of the United States and therefore not entitled to vote. The court reasoned that tribal governments were "distinct political communities" and members of tribes were not fully "subject to the jurisdiction" of the United States. Accordingly, in the absence of a treaty or statute granting citizenship to a particular tribe, a Native American could become a citizen only through naturalization. The federal government continued to extend citizenship to tribes on a piecemeal basis; finally, in 1924, Congress granted citizenship to all Native Americans who did not already enjoy it.

In *United States v. Wong Kim Ark* (1898), the Supreme Court revisited the issue of whether the Con-

Detained Immigrants on Ellis Island. While many immigrants were quickly processed after arrival on Ellis Island, significant numbers were detained for various reasons, including health and financial problems. Detainees were separated from their families, sometimes for weeks. Drawing by M. Colin, published in *Harper's Weekly*, 1893. LIBRARY OF CONGRESS

stitution's grant of *jus soli* citizenship was limited by race. Specifically, the court had to decide whether children born in the United States to Chinese immigrants were citizens by virtue of the Fourteenth Amendment. Noting that Chinese had been prohibited from naturalizing since 1790 and from immigrating after 1882, the Justice Department insisted that children of Chinese were not citizens and that Chinese were not fully "subject to the jurisdiction" of the United States because Imperial China refused to allow any of its subjects to expatriate. A majority of the Court rejected this argument, concluding that everyone born in the United States was a citizen, with the traditional exceptions of children born to enemy aliens in hostile occupation of the nation, children of foreign ambassadors, and Indians who were members of tribes; the rule "includes the children born within the territory of the United States of all other persons, of whatever race or color, domiciled within the United States."

During the nineteenth century, the United States acquired several overseas territories. The Supreme Court had to decide whether children born in the territories were automatically citizens under the *jus soli* principle. The court found that Alaska, acquired in 1867, and Hawaii, taken in 1898, were "incorporated" into the United States even before they became states. Persons born in the territories after incorporation were *jus soli* citizens; those already resident were given the right to citizenship by treaty or statute.

Other territories were deemed "unincorporated." Unincorporated territories enjoyed second-class status; they were mere possessions that were not part of the United States for constitutional purposes, including *jus soli* citizenship. Unincorporated territories included Puerto Rico, the Philippines, and Guam, acquired from Spain in 1898 following the Spanish-American War, and American Samoa, acquired from Great Britain and Germany in 1899. Residents at the time of acquisition as well as children born there subsequently were noncitizen "nationals" who had limited political rights, unless and until Congress elected to offer them citizenship. The Philippines became independent in 1946, but with respect to Puerto Rico, Guam, and American Samoa, through a series of statutes, Congress granted or offered citizenship to virtually all who were residents at the time of acquisition or were born there subsequently. At the beginning of the twenty-first century, residents of American Samoa remained noncitizen nationals.

Immigration Policy and Politics

Waves of nativism and racism periodically made immigration a national political issue in the nineteenth century. However, the federal government imposed few significant immigration restrictions until 1882, and no numerical restrictions of any kind until the 1920s. One exception was a group of laws called the Alien and Sedition Laws, passed by Congress in 1798. The laws reflected a deep suspicion of aliens; one of the alien acts gave the president the authority to order out of the country "all such aliens as he shall judge dangerous to the peace and safety of the United States."

Another episode of nativism began in the 1830s, in reaction to the increasing Catholic presence in the United States and a growing belief that European immigrants were paupers and criminals—a perennial canard about immigrant groups. By the early 1850s, the anti-Catholic American Party, popularly known as the Know-Nothing Party, was a substantial political force. Its slogan "America for Americans" was reflected in its platform of excluding immigrants from electoral politics by, for example, limiting officeholding to native-born citizens, and requiring twenty-one years' residence prior to naturalization. In 1854 and 1855, the American Party elected seven governors, controlled several state legislatures, and won five Senate and forty-three House seats. The party faded without achieving any of its national policy goals after its candidate, former president Millard Fillmore, ran a distant third in the presidential election of 1856.

While efforts at federal regulation fizzled for most of the nineteenth century, individual states created a substantial system of immigration regulation. Almost every slave state and a few northern states prohibited the entrance of free African Americans. Many states prohibited aliens who were poor and those who had contagious diseases or criminal convictions. In *Chy Lung v. Freeman* (1876) and *Henderson v. Mayor of New York* (1876), the Supreme Court curtailed state authority to regulate aliens, concluding that immigration was commerce, and therefore primarily the domain of the national government.

In 1882, with the passage of the Chinese Exclusion Act, Congress initiated a prohibition of virtually all Chinese immigration, a policy that would continue in various forms until 1965. Responding to political pressure from the West Coast, Congress decreed that the Chinese were an undesirable, unassimilable race. Although the 1882 statute provided only for a ten-year "suspension," it was ultimately made permanent and in the twentieth century extended beyond Chinese to virtually all persons of Asian racial ancestry. The Supreme Court upheld restrictions on Chinese immigrants in a series of cases between 1889 and 1893 that established that Congress has "plenary power" over immigration which is subject to virtually no judicial review. These cases form the basis of modern constitutional immigration law.

Congress also adopted on a national basis some of the regulations of aliens that individual states had imposed earlier in the century. In 1882 Congress provided that a "lunatic, idiot, or any person unable to take care of himself or herself without becoming a public charge . . . shall not be permitted to land," adding these categories to the prostitutes and convicts who had been banned in 1875. Mormon immigration was discouraged by the prohibition on polygamists passed in 1891. Some have observed the irony that Emma Lazarus's famous poem "The New Colossus," beseeching the nations of the world to "give me your tired, your poor, Your huddled masses yearning to breathe free," was a false sentiment by the time it was placed on the Statue of Liberty in 1886.

Even with qualitative limits, some Americans continued to object to the newcomers. Just as it had with the Chinese and other Asians, criticism of Jewish and other southern and eastern European immigrants rested on their supposed racial inferiority. In 1896 Congress voted to impose a literacy requirement on prospective immigrants to stem the flow of "new immigration"; this and subsequent bills were vetoed by a succession of presidents. Nevertheless, anti-immigrant sentiment proved irresistible; the literacy test became law in 1917. A more comprehensive solution was imposed in the 1920s when the national origins quota system allocated most visas to Germany, England, and Ireland, even though the demand in southern and eastern Europe was much higher. This discriminatory law would be in effect, as modified, until 1965, when the race, religion, and color-neutral system of the Immigration and Nationalities Act Amendments was adopted.

See also **Anti-Catholicism; Chinese Exclusion Act; Race and Racial Thinking.**

Bibliography

Bureau of the Census, U.S. Department of Commerce. *Historical Statistics of the United States, Colonial Times to 1970.* Washington, D.C.: U.S. Government Printing Office, 1975. The charts in volume 1, chapter C, compile numerous statistics about the quantity and origin of nineteenth-century immigration.

Chin, Gabriel J. "The Civil Rights Revolution Comes to Immigration Law: A New Look at the Immigration and Nationality Act of 1965." *North Carolina Law Review* 75 (1996): 273–345.

Finkelman, Paul. *Dred Scott v. Sandford: A Brief History with Documents.* Boston: Bedford, 1997.

Gordon, Charles, Stanley Mailman, and Stephen Yale-Loehr. *Immigration Law and Procedure.* New York: Matthew Bender, 1998.

Handlin, Oscar. *Immigration as a Factor in American History.* Englewood Cliffs, N.J.: Prentice Hall, 1959.

———. *The Uprooted: The Epic Story of the Great Migrations*

that Made the American People. Boston: Little, Brown, 1951.

Hutchinson, Edward P. *Legislative History of American Immigration Policy, 1798–1965.* Philadelphia: University of Pennsylvania Press, 1981.

Jones, Maldwyn Allen. *American Immigration.* 2d ed. Chicago: University of Chicago Press, 1992.

Neuman, Gerald. *Strangers to the Constitution: Immigrants, Borders, and Fundamental Law.* Princeton, N.J.: Princeton University Press, 1996.

Schuck, Peter H., and Rogers M. Smith. *Citizenship without Consent: Illegal Aliens in the American Polity.* New Haven, Conn.: Yale University Press, 1985.

GABRIEL J. CHIN

ANTI-IMMIGRANT SENTIMENT

A sweeping tide of immigration across the nineteenth century brought new ethnic and religious diversity to a growing nation. But the newcomers would face intense hostility: antialien movements flourished in the years before the Civil War and in the last two decades of the century.

After relatively modest increases in immigration up to 1827, economic expansion in the United States and worsening conditions in Europe—particularly in Ireland—led to rapid growth in the number of émigrés to the New World. In 1832, 60,000 alien passengers arrived at U.S. ports. In a pattern tied to the economic cycle of boom and bust, the annual influx of foreigners grew slowly, and in 1844 more than 75,000 sought entry to the United States. These numbers soon rose dramatically, however, as a result of potato famines in Ireland and Germany, as well as failed revolutions and political upheaval in Germany and central Europe. In 1847, 234,000 newcomers reached the U.S. ports of entry. By 1851 the number approached 380,000, and immigration continued at this unprecedented rate through 1854. From 1847 to 1854, almost 2.7 million prospective new Americans entered the country.

The majority of these immigrants were Catholic. In 1807 there were 70,000 Roman Catholics in the United States. By 1840 there were 660,000, and that was before the famine, which caused this population to triple. In 1850 there were two million Roman Catholics in the United States, most of them new arrivals in a nation where fear and hatred of Catholicism had been present since colonial times.

Anti-Catholicism had been rampant in England for many years before the first colonists sailed for America. It took root in the threat to English nationalism presented by the rival imperial ambitions of Catholic Spain and France, and was fed by quasi-historical, post-Reformation propaganda. In some of the American colonies, Catholics were denied the franchise; in others, the Mass could not be celebrated publicly and priests were banished on pain of execution. There was bitter opposition to the creation of Catholic churches and schools.

The increasing number of immigrants in the first half of the nineteenth century created new tensions. Catholic immigrants drew public hostility because of their poverty; the diseases they brought with them after the perilous ocean voyage; the slum housing they were forced to live in; and the dramatic rise in crime rates, alcoholism, and the poverty rolls that occurred after their arrival. Many American-born Protestants, equating their English heritage with "true" Americanism, despised the desperately poor Irish and feared the Germans, who spoke a strange new language. The antialiens were nativists, convinced that opposition to the growing minority of Catholic immigrants was necessary to protect their America.

Nativism took many forms in the first half of the century. Catholic convents, churches, and schools were attacked, and dozens of anti-Catholic newspapers found large audiences. Anti-Catholic books were published, warning of Jesuitic conspiracies to undermine America. A new "convent literature" featured best sellers like *The Awful Disclosures of Maria Monk* (1836), which recounted tales of rape and sadism inflicted on innocent girls by evil priests in the inner sanctums of Catholic institutions. There were massive demonstrations by "true" Americans, notably the 4 July 1844 procession in Philadelphia, which led to violent conflict and widespread destruction of Catholic property throughout the city.

The antialiens turned to political activism to arrest immigration and to prevent the establishment of Catholic schools. National anti-Catholic, anti-immigrant political parties emerged, particularly the American Republican Party in the 1840s and the American Party in the next decade. The American Party was created out of one of the proliferating nativist secret societies—the Order of the Star Spangled Banner. Its leaders, fearing that the party could be undermined by an imagined secret cabal of Jesuits, forbade party members to acknowledge they knew anything about any such cabal. Hence the party's more familiar name: the Know-Nothing Party.

With the breakup of the Whig Party, fractured by divisions over slavery, the Know-Nothings became the second most powerful political organization in the nation by 1854, when they elected five senators and forty-three representatives. In the end, this nativist party also could not contain divisive sectional conflicts. The organization splintered in the years before the Civil War and was already in decline by 1856.

"**Where the Blame Lies.**" This 1891 political cartoon by Grant E. Hamilton depicts immigrants as a mass of dirty, animalistic, threatening men. Uncle Sam is urged to blame them for the spread of political evil throughout the nation, indicated in the list at his feet. LIBRARY OF CONGRESS: PRINTS AND PHOTOGRAPHS DIVISION

In that year, former president Millard Fillmore, the Know-Nothing candidate for president, received only 875,000 votes of the more than four million cast. But its brief period of success was an indication of the intensity of antialien feeling.

The Civil War proved a bonding experience for all people supporting the Union, and after the Confederacy's surrender at Appomattox there was a striking decline in nativist activity. Yet as industrial revolution transformed the United States in the postwar years and attracted a vast new influx of immigrants, the antialien animus rose again. In the 1870s more than 2.7 million newcomers arrived at U.S. ports.

For example, more than eighty thousand immigrants from China arrived between 1870 and 1875, brought to America by companies that had contracted to supply cheap labor to mines, railways, and other enterprises needing unskilled labor. With 30 percent of California's workforce unemployed following the panic of 1873, many workers attacked these newcomers as "coolies" willing to work for slave wages. Outbreaks of violence against the Chinese spread through-

out the West, from Los Angeles to Seattle to Denver. In 1882, Congress responded to anti-Asian nativism with the Chinese Exclusion Act, which suspended immigration from China for ten years.

In the 1880s there were 5.2 million more, the greatest number of immigrants in a decade up to that point. Almost 3.7 million more came in the 1890s, despite the economic panic and depression in the United States during those years.

At first, most of the newcomers came from familiar locales, often from cultures the nativists had feared and opposed in the past. More than half of the arrivals through the mid-1880s were from Ireland, Germany, and central Europe. But by the late 1880s, "new immigration" from southern and eastern Europe had begun to change the ethnic landscape of dozens of American cities. Poor Catholic peasant farmers—the *contadini*—from southern Italy, Jews from the "pale of settlement" in the Russian Empire, and Polish and Slavic immigrants arrived in growing numbers. The response was a rebirth of antialien activities.

A striking number of new nativist fraternal groups

were formed, the most important being the American Protective Association (APA). Founded in Iowa in 1887, the APA had attracted a membership of 500,000 by 1895. While its leaders focused on fears of Irish Catholic control of big-city political machines and educational institutions, the organization's members focused on assaulting the "alien" ways of the "new immigrants." They believed these people were the inferior "refuse of Europe" and could never be assimilated into U.S. culture.

By the end of the nineteenth century, the APA had disappeared. Nativist activism did not flourish in the first decades of the twentieth century, the years of the Progressive Era. It rose again in the form of the post–World War I Red Scare in 1919, and in the powerful but short-lived Ku Klux Klan in the 1920s. It was in the nineteenth century that antialien movements had their greatest impact in American history.

See also **Anti-Catholicism; Anti-Semitism; Chinese Exclusion Act; Clubs,** *subentry on* **Fraternal Societies and Clubs; Third Parties.**

Bibliography

Anbinder, Tyler Gregory. *Nativism and Slavery: The Northern Know-Nothings and the Politics of the 1850s.* New York: Oxford University Press, 1992.

Bennett, David H. *The Party of Fear: The American Far Right from Nativism to the Militia Movement.* New York: Vintage, 1995.

Billington, Ray Allen. *The Protestant Crusade, 1800–1860.* 1938. Reprint, Chicago: Quadrangle, 1964.

Higham, John. *Strangers in the Land: Patterns of American Nativism, 1860–1925.* New Brunswick, N.J.: Rutgers University Press, 1955. 2d ed., New York: Atheneum, 1963.

DAVID H. BENNETT

IRELAND

Irish immigration to America changed radically in the nineteenth century, powerfully reshaping the community and culture of Irish Americans. Irish immigration to America had been more or less continuous since the founding of the English colonies on the North American coast, but in the 1830s and 1840s it became a mass movement involving tens of thousands of people each year. Irish immigrants thus were pioneers in what the historian Marcus Lee Hansen called one of the great folk migrations of all time, the mass migration from Europe to the United States of the "long" nineteenth century (from 1800 to 1914).

Yet it was not just the skyrocketing numbers that marked the mid–nineteenth century as such a critical turning point in the history of Irish migration to America. The shifts in the geographic, religious, and to a lesser extent class and origin of the migrants were conspicuous, as were the changes in their destinations and the nature of their social, political, and cultural adjustments in the United States. What had been a migration largely of Protestants from the northern Irish province of Ulster to the middle and southern parts of the United States during the colonial and early national eras became in the nineteenth century a flood of Catholics from southern Ireland that headed to northern cities, such as New York City, Boston, Chicago, and Philadelphia in the East, and San Francisco in the West. The relatively quick assimilation of those earlier Protestant Irish into the rural societies in the Pennsylvania and southern Appalachian backcountry became for the later Irish Catholic immigrants a process of creating a separate Irish American identity focused on Catholicism, Irish nationalism, and the Democratic Party.

Irish Catholic Migration in the Nineteenth Century

Throughout the seventeenth and eighteenth centuries, most immigrants to British North America were Protestant. Even after the new American Republic emerged and guaranteed religious freedom, Catholics were still reluctant to emigrate before the early 1830s. Several trends combined to convince Ireland's Catholics to uproot themselves and brave the North Atlantic for new homes.

One reason was simply that it became easier and cheaper to go. Burgeoning trade between England and North America dramatically increased opportunities for travel and dramatically reduced its cost. Liverpool became the center of a vast trade with North America, and eventually its trade included the immigrant traffic. By the mid–nineteenth century two out of three Irish immigrants to North America shipped out from Liverpool. Initially the trip to Canada was cheaper than the trip to ports in the United States, and thousands of migrants sailed to Canada then made their way south. Yet the ease and price of passage directly to the United States improved substantially. By 1831 travel from Ireland to Canada cost one pound ten shillings, and travel from Liverpool to New York cost only two to three pounds.

Irish Catholics migrated to the United States primarily because changes in Ireland forced them to look abroad. Beginning in the eighteenth century and continuing relentlessly through the nineteenth, transportation improvements drew Ireland tightly into a larger economy centered in England. This had several effects, some of which were cultural. English was the language of the market, and Irish Catholic peasants had to become conversant in that language to survive. As early as 1800 probably half of all Irish spoke English. The chief effects of market integration were, of course, economic. During the Napoleonic Wars in the late eighteenth and early nineteenth centuries, Ireland and the markets both benefited from a rise in the demand for Irish farm products. Grain prices, in particular, increased, encouraging Irish farmers to devote land to tillage rather than to pasture. It was, some have said, a golden age for the Irish economy. Yet this market integration made Irish landlords and thus their peasants more vulnerable to economic fluctuations, and when prices for Irish farm products began to stagger after Waterloo, both landlords and tenants suffered. Many landlords sought to rid their land of small inefficient tenants and introduce new techniques of cultivation or to convert their land from labor-intensive tillage to pasture.

The faltering economy was especially cruel for Irish Catholic peasants because the growing population incited a desperate and vicious competition for land. Between the 1740s and 1845 the population of Ireland rose from a little more than 2 million to more than 8 million. Explanations vary for the cause of this growth. Undoubtedly the newly introduced potato provided cheap, nutritious, and bountiful food for poor farmers. Some historians have suggested that the combination of the potato's abundance and the vibrant grain economy during the Napoleonic Wars may have encouraged the Irish to marry early and have large families. As the economy turned sour after 1815, the pressure on the land grew more intense.

These trends uprooted Catholics in the early nineteenth century and convinced them to make the journey to North America. Market integration in Ireland moved roughly from east to west, and thus Catholic migration began first in the eastern province of Leinster and parts of the southern province of Munster in the 1820s and 1830s. Most of those Catholics were probably English speakers and the younger sons of middling farmers who fled to help themselves or their families as opportunities shriveled in Ireland.

Over the course of the 1830s Catholic migration affected most of Ireland. Between 1838 and 1844, before the famine, an average of 55,000 people from Ireland poured into the United States a year. As the numbers rose the economic status and education of the average migrant probably declined. Mass migration to North America by the Catholic Irish, therefore, began while the potato crop remained bountiful.

Potatoes did not remain bountiful for long, however. In the fall of 1845 a fungus infected potatoes both in the ground and in storage, turning them into a blackened, putrid mass. In 1845 half the potato crop was ruined, and in 1846 it was destroyed entirely. The blight wreaked havoc through the end of the decade, and since the vast majority of the Irish peasantry depended on potatoes for food, its destruction was catastrophic. Perhaps as many as a million

Irish Emigration Office. Irish emigrants pay their passage fees to sail to the United States. From *Frank Leslie's Illustrated Newspaper*, 12 January 1856. LIBRARY OF CONGRESS

people died in the famine, primarily in the poorer and more densely settled west. The famine spurred many to flee to the United States and Canada. Initially the migration came from the midlands and the east, as farmers of some means and their families tried to escape before the disaster engulfed them. Eventually, however, western peasants long rooted in their traditional communal settlements had to leave or risk almost certain death.

The migration that began during the famine continued to the end of the nineteenth century. Irish industry outside of Ulster declined in the nineteenth century, and in the 1870s and 1880s plunging agricultural prices and crop failures sent tens of thousands fleeing once again. However, after 1850 the vast majority left because Ireland did not have enough land to sustain its population. Irish peasants passed on their whole farms to only one son and gave a dowry to only one daughter, forcing the other children to either leave home or remain without hope of marriage or economic autonomy. Between 1856 and 1900 just under 3 million people left Ireland, most for the United States, peaking in 1890. After 1850 the characteristics of Irish immigrants changed. Most were Catholics, but by the 1880s they came primarily from the western province of Connacht. As the century wore on more women immigrated, and they outnumbered men in many years of the 1880s and 1890s. Without chances to marry or find jobs, women had no hope in Ireland.

Forging an Irish Catholic Community and Identity

Irish Catholic immigrants entered a world they were not prepared to master despite their advantages over many other immigrants. By the end of the nineteenth century most Irish immigrants had received a sound elementary education in Ireland because the national schools, introduced in 1831, reduced Irish illiteracy below American proportions. By that time almost all Irish spoke English, and about one-seventh spoke both Irish and English. Such advantages should have translated into economic success, but they did not. Irish men were still peasant farmers or agricultural laborers with nothing to sell but strong backs and arms. Women, too, had little experience beyond their family farms and, perhaps, brief tenures as servants to local gentry. They lacked industrial skills then. In other environments, such as Canada or Australia, where access to land was easy in the early and middle years of the nineteenth century, this lack might not have mattered. In the United States, however, it hindered them and their inability to make much economic headway reinforced the peasant communalism

of the old country. These reinforced traditions of communal reciprocity helped Irish immigrants to survive the sometimes brutal world of urban industrial America, but, in a cruel irony, those traditions may have also limited their ability to move up in it. At the end of the nineteenth century one-quarter of Irish immigrant men were laborers, and more than half of the immigrant women were domestic servants.

Stepping into that new world of America, they not only encountered a new kind of economy, but a new social and cultural world riven with inter-group enmities and conflicts. Some of these were familiar—religious divisions between Protestants and Catholics, for example—but others were new—racial battles between African and Asian Americans on the one hand, and European Americans, on the other.

The enmity between Catholics and Protestants fundamentally divided society and politics in much of America throughout the nineteenth century. It structured political partisanship, nourished economic discrimination and social prejudice, and erupted into full-fledged nativist political movements at mid-century with the Know Nothing and in the late nineteenth century with the American Protective Association. Though Irish Protestants would continue to come to America (if in diminished proportions) through the nineteenth century, the nature of this divide would encourage their quick assimilation into an undifferentiated Protestant mainstream. The same divide would simultaneously starkly separate out and mark their Catholic Irish countrymen as different.

If America's religious division pushed Irish Catholics and Protestants apart, the new nation's racism underlined what both Irish Catholics and Protestants had in common with the European American majority: white skin. Irish relations with nonwhite African and Asian Americans were complex in the nineteenth century. Irish immigrants often lived in the same neighborhoods as African and Asian Americans, in the Lower East Side in New York City, for example, and they probably made up a disproportionate number of the partners in interracial marriages and couples from New York to New Orleans. Irish immigrant soldiers also won acclaim for their exploits in the Civil War, particularly the Irish Brigade's gallant charges at Antietam, Fredericksburg, and Gettysburg. On the other hand, Irish American mobs attacked African Americans in a number of riots throughout the Northeast from the 1820s to the 1860s, culminating in the great Draft Riot in New York (and a smaller one in Boston), just days after the Irish Brigade's heroism at Gettysburg. Led by the Irish immigrant Dennis Kearney, Irish Americans also played a prominent role in the anti-Chinese ag-

Dressing for Saint Patrick's Day. This painting depicts the double-sided patriotism typical of Irish immigrants. The room is decorated with the U.S. flag and the portrait of Ulysses S. Grant—symbols of American pride—as well as a portrait of the pope and a religious statue—symbols that commemorate Irish Catholic beliefs. Painting by John Reid, 1872. LIBRARY OF CONGRESS

itation on the West Coast that led eventually to the exclusion of Chinese immigrants from America.

Irish Catholic immigrants did create stable, thickly networked communities, and they asserted the power of their accumulating numbers. At the center of the new communities and the heart of Irish American identity were the Catholic Church, the Irish nationalist movement, and the Democratic Party.

In the early nineteenth century the Catholic Church in Ireland had few priests or churches and suffered from poor clerical discipline and a laity that was more Catholic in loyalty than in practice. In the early and mid–nineteenth century many Irish Catholic immigrants had little knowledge of their faith or experience in its institutional practice. In the United States in the 1840s mass attendance lagged, as it did in Ireland. Historians estimate that only 40 percent of Irish Catholics attended mass regularly in New York City in the 1860s. Impoverished lay immigrants, inexperienced in institutional Catholicism, bridled at the demands of maintaining expensive parishes and chafed at the impersonal religion they encountered in such parishes as St. James or Immaculate Conception in New York City, where memberships ran to 20,000 or more. In some places the new immigrants rebelled. Irish parishioners in the North

End of Boston hooted their bishop off the altar in 1842, for example, and in nearby Worcester in 1846 famine refugees beat up the local pastor and forced him to flee for his life.

The church, however, ultimately escaped this chaos. In part the confusion and hysteria unleashed by the cataclysm of the famine and the torrent of immigrants subsided as the famine ended and immigration slowed. In addition, the rise of anti-Catholic, anti-Irish nativism in the Know-Nothing Party of the 1850s forced a unified front against the common enemy. The church itself built loyalty and established its authority among the immigrants. Diocesan synods in Boston and New York in 1842 clarified rule and tightened clerical discipline. A "devotional revolution," a Catholic religious revival that swept the European continent, Ireland, and America in the middle and late nineteenth century perhaps had the greatest impact. These revivals were usually clerically inspired and directed, abetted by new technologies in printing and lithography, and embraced by laypeople seeking order and meaning in worlds transformed by economic change. They renewed old Catholic devotions to the Sacred Heart of Jesus, for example, and helped popularize new ones, such as Our Lady of Lourdes. At work on both sides of the Atlantic, the devotional revolution made emigrants leaving Ireland and Catholics of longtime residence in the United States more disciplined and institutionalized. It also produced in Ireland a surplus of priests and nuns for foreign missions, such as the United States, and encouraged a rush of clerical vocations among the children of famine immigrants.

As a result, by the end of the nineteenth century Catholicism was firmly established as the principal pillar of the Irish American community. Although immigrant heads of households advanced little economically over the course of the nineteenth century, their multiple-income families of working sons and daughters made the Irish Catholic community immensely wealthier than it had been at mid-century. Tapping this newly disciplined and richer Irish American laity, clerics built a huge network of parishes, schools, and charitable institutions. Between the middle of the nineteenth century and the beginning of the twentieth, Irish Catholics in Boston built a huge new cathedral, rebuilt most of the churches in the old neighborhoods, such as St. Mary's in the North End or St. James in South Cove, and added three new parishes in the emerging Irish stronghold of South Boston and six new ones in the Irish "second settlement" of Dorchester. Catholicism had become the core of the Irish American community, both the center of its institutional network and the heart of its self-definition.

By the end of the nineteenth century, Catholicism was not only central to the Irish American community, Irish Americans were central to the Catholic church in America. Irish Americans dominated American Catholicism, first overwhelming the few French and English clerics in the early nineteenth century and then fending off the challenges of German, French Canadian, and Polish rivals at the century's end.

The church was not the only glue holding this community together or giving substance to its identity. Nationalism, support for an independent Ireland, was also a critical element in defining the Irish American community, and like Catholicism, it was not a given but emerged over time. Irish immigrants, like immigrants from most countries, identified with their towns or regions as much or more than with a broader nation. Battles among Irishmen from different counties or provinces broke out frequently on canals and railroad construction sites in the 1830s and 1840s. Moreover nationalist movements, like the Repeal Associations or Young Ireland, that might have united Irish immigrants from different regions in the 1830s and 1840s failed to take root either in Ireland or in the United States, and their demise left nationalism without an organizational core. The Fenians, who conspired to overthrow British rule and establish an Irish republic, were founded simultaneously in Ireland and the United States and finally mobilized Irish American nationalism, making it a critical element in the community. Despite the failure of their comic opera attempts to seize Canada in 1866 and 1870, the Fenians were broadly popular in the United States. They established branches or circles across the country, enrolling an estimated 50,000 members. Their relentless agitation and prolific propaganda reached far beyond those numbers and educated and enlisted hundreds of thousands of sympathizers for their brand of republican nationalism. Nationalism ebbed and flowed in Irish American communities throughout the rest of the century, peaking during Ireland's land crisis in the 1880s and falling with the demise of Ireland's Home Rule Party in the 1890s. Not as constant and powerful a presence in Irish American communities as the Catholic Church, it was essential to building community and defining identity.

Whatever symbolic importance nationalism had, Irish Americans had more concrete and political interests closer to home. Irish American Catholics were affiliated with the Democratic Party as far back as Thomas Jefferson's era, and that allegiance continued and deepened in the famine immigrant era of the mid–nineteenth century. At that point Irish Catholic immigrants were largely foot soldiers in the emerging urban political machines of the Democratic Party. In the last two decades of the nineteenth century, however, Irish Catholics broke into the political elite. New York City elected its first Irish American mayor, William R. Grace, in 1880. Boston elected its first Irishman, Hugh O'Brien, in 1884, and Chicago elected John Patrick Hopkins in 1893. Just as important, Irish Americans, mostly American-born, took over city, factional, or critical ward party organizations in New York City, Boston, Chicago, and a host of other cities. Historians have argued over whether or not such political power translated into economic mobility for Irish Catholics. But it certainly cemented Irish allegiances to the Democratic Party, and that loyalty was essential in the trinity of allegiances, the Catholic Church, Irish nationalism, and the Democratic Party, that gave substance to Irish American identity.

The nineteenth century experienced a revolution in what it meant to be Irish in America. As the century began Irish Americans were more Protestant than Catholic, and though most of both denominations were passionate Democrats, many Protestant Irish Americans were indifferent to or skeptical about an independent Ireland. The mass migration of Catholics began just before the famine, became a flood during that catastrophe, and continued in a steady flow after it, changing the nature of the Irish American community and identity.

It was not the last change, however. As the century closed a new generation of Irish, born in the United States, was growing to maturity. Few of these American-born Irish rose "from rags to riches," but most were more successful than their fathers and mothers or even their recently arrived immigrant cousins. Significantly, they cherished their American birthright and eagerly embraced American culture. In the twentieth century they struggled to reconcile their inheritance of Catholicism and nationalism with their American loyalties and eventually defined for themselves what it meant to be Irish in America. Yet their redefined Irish American identity was within the context of the revolution wrought by their Catholic immigrant parents, who had radically changed Irish American identity in the nineteenth century.

See also **Anti-Catholicism; Boston; Catholicism; Chicago; Democratic Party; New York City; Philadelphia; Politics,** *subentry on* **Machines and Bosses; Religion,** *subentry on* **Religion in Nineteenth-Century America; Revivalism.**

Bibliography

Bayor, Ronald H., and Timothy J. Meagher, eds. *The New York Irish*. Baltimore: Johns Hopkins University Press, 1996.

Brown, Thomas N. *Irish-American Nationalism: 1870–1890*. Philadelphia: Lippincott, 1966.

Brundage, David. *The Making of Western Labor Radicalism: Denver's Organized Workers, 1878–1905*. Urbana: University of Illinois Press, 1994.

Clark, Dennis. *The Irish in Philadelphia: Ten Generations of Urban Experience*. Philadelphia: Temple University Press, 1973.

Diner, Hasia R. *Erin's Daughters in America: Irish Immigrant Women in the Nineteenth Century*. Baltimore: Johns Hopkins University Press, 1983.

Dolan Jay P. *Catholic Revivalism: The American Experience, 1830–1900*. Notre Dame, Ind.: University of Notre Dame Press, 1978.

———. *The Immigrant Church: New York's Irish and German Catholics, 1815–1865*. Baltimore: Johns Hopkins University Press, 1975.

Doyle, David Noel. *Ireland, Irishmen, and Revolutionary America, 1760–1820*. Dublin, Ireland: Mercier Press, 1981.

Emmons, David M. *The Butte Irish: Class and Ethnicity in an American Mining Town, 1875–1925*. Urbana: University of Illinois Press, 1989.

Erie, Steven P. *Rainbow's End: Irish-Americans and the Dilemmas of Urban Machine Politics, 1840–1985*. Berkeley: University of California Press, 1988.

Fanning, Charles. *The Irish Voice in America: Irish-American Fiction from the 1760s to the 1980s*. Lexington: University of Kentucky Press, 1990.

Kenny, Kevin. *Making Sense of the Molly Maguires*. New York: Oxford University Press, 1998.

Miller, Kerby A. *Emigrants and Exiles: Ireland and the Irish Exodus to North America*. New York: Oxford University Press, 1985.

Mitchell, Brian C. *The Paddy Camps: The Irish of Lowell, 1821–61*. Urbana: University of Illinois Press, 1988.

Nolan, Janet A. *Ourselves Alone: Women's Emigration from Ireland, 1885–1920*. Lexington: University of Kentucky Press, 1989.

TIMOTHY J. MEAGHER

GREAT BRITAIN

Between 1820 and 1900 approximately 3 million people emigrated from England, Scotland, and Wales to the United States. Figures for the century's first two decades are not available. The total for the rest of the century breaks down as follows: 1,825,000 English; 369,000 Scottish; 42,000 Welsh; and almost 800,000 of unknown origins other than "British." In addition almost 3.9 million people from Ireland came to the United States during the same period. However, probably no more than 200,000 of them were from the six counties of Ulster. The experiences of Irish immigrants differed significantly from those of other British immigrants and thus are addressed in another article.

British immigrants differed in several significant ways from immigrants of other nationalities. Most of them crossed the Atlantic for purely economic reasons, and when the U.S. economy took a downturn, many of them returned to Great Britain. Most British immigrants retained a strong sense of loyalty to the crown long after arriving in the United States. Their exposure to industrialization for a much longer period than peasants from eastern and southern Europe made British immigrants much more useful to factory owners. Almost half of them were skilled laborers, a much higher percentage than for any other national group, therefore they were better able to find and keep good-paying jobs than any other national group. British immigrants looked and thought like American natives, and they could read, speak, and write English. For these reasons British immigrants had little difficulty being accepted as equals into U.S. society.

The English

Unlike immigrants from other nations, Englishmen came to the United States expecting rather than hoping to find the high-paying jobs of their choice. This is because about half of them were skilled workers in industries that were well established in England but still in their infancy in the United States. Skilled English laborers dominated the textile, mining, metalworking, and pottery industries during their formative years in the United States. English workers also played important roles in the development of the glass, paper, boot and shoe, glove, furniture, and printing industries.

When power looms threw many British hand-loom weavers out of work in the 1820s, a number of unemployed weavers in England and Ulster packed their bags and moved to Philadelphia, Pennsylvania, where they helped establish the U.S. fine cotton goods industry. After 1840 experienced English textile workers found plenty of jobs in the mills in New Bedford and Fall River, Massachusetts. Carders, weavers, spinners, dyers, printers, and loom fixers left England because wages were almost twice as high in New England as in Lancashire, the center of the English cotton textile industry, and Yorkshire, the center of the woolen textile industry. After the Cobden Treaty (1860) opened British markets to French silk, practically the entire English silk industry relocated to the United States, centering itself in Paterson, New Jersey. Meanwhile lace workers from Nottingham established the lace industry in Pennsylvania, New York, and Connecticut. After 1870, when American textile mills began to mechanize, their demand for skilled English workers decreased. However, instead of returning to England, many of these workers moved into supervisory positions or, in some cases, became owners of textile mills.

After 1830 the transition in the iron-making industry from wood-burning furnaces to coal-burning furnaces led to an increased demand for English coal miners, particularly in the bituminous fields west of the Allegheny Mountains. After 1850 the demand for skilled laborers to extract copper, iron, lead, silver, and gold from rich American deposits induced a number of copper and tin miners from Cornwall to move to the United States to work in mines in Pennsylvania, Minnesota, and Nevada. As in the textile industry, mechanization after 1870 shifted the demand for labor from skilled to unskilled, so a number of English miners were replaced in the mines by unskilled immigrants from other parts of Europe. However, also as in the textile industry, many English miners became supervisors, foremen, or owners.

During the 1840s potters from Staffordshire played an integral part in starting up the American pottery industry, which centered in East Liverpool, Ohio; Trenton, New Jersey; and Baltimore, Maryland. After 1850 English ironworkers easily found jobs in the expanding U.S. iron industry and played a major role in developing the American iron and steel industry. For example, the boiling method of iron puddling was first practiced in Pittsburgh by the Englishman Edward Nock, and the first American

cold-blast furnace to burn coke was developed by an Englishman, William Firmstone. Cutlers from Sheffield helped to establish the saw-making industry in the United States. The same pattern appeared in pottery and metalworking as in textiles and mining. Once mechanization took command, skilled English labor either returned to England or remained in the United States to hold supervisory positions.

About half of all English immigrants came to the United States to farm. Of these about half went west, while the other half remained east and north of St. Louis, Missouri. Very few settled in the South. Many English farmers settled in Kansas and Minnesota during the railroad boom of the 1870s, but for the most part they did not form ethnic communities as did many other national groups. Instead they blended in with the residents of existing farm communities and became virtually indistinguishable from American natives.

The Scots

Like the English, skilled Scottish workers were in great demand in the United States. Scottish carpet weavers helped establish that industry in Philadelphia prior to 1840, then successfully resisted mechanization until well after 1880. Between 1850 and 1870 Scottish weavers became a prominent part of the workforce in the cotton mills of Holyoke, Massachusetts, and Manchester, New Hampshire. In the 1880s Scottish workers in Fall River, Massachusetts, produced the first high-quality gingham made in the United States. Thread making was dominated by Scots and Ulstermen, who established Paterson, New Jersey, and Fall River as the U.S. centers for that industry. Scottish coal miners were drawn to the soft coal deposits west of the Alleghenies, where they labored alongside English miners. During the 1880s Scottish quarrymen dominated the granite quarries of Vermont, and a large number of Scots worked in the sandstone quarries in northern Ohio.

Like English immigrants who came to the United States to farm, Scottish farmers rarely settled in ethnic communities. However, several such communities are worth noting. In the 1820s Scots settled in western New York in communities such as Caledonia, Le Roy, and Scottsville, and in the 1830s Scots established farming communities at Argyle and Dundee, Illinois. Other Scottish farm communities of note were created near Janesville, Wisconsin, and Sarasota, Florida. In 1871 a group of Scots migrated to western Minnesota, where they raised purebred cattle, and in 1882 northeastern Pennsylvania became home to several groups of Scottish farmers.

The Welsh

Although Welshmen came to the United States in relatively small numbers (by 1870 only eleven thousand had reached America), they played important roles in the development of certain industries. Many experienced Welsh woolen workers settled in western Massachusetts, and by 1870 they had become the dominant nationality in at least one mill town. Welsh miners made a more important contribution to American industry. Having learned to mine anthracite coal in South Wales, Welshmen flocked to the coalfields of Pennsylvania after 1830 and settled in significant numbers in Scranton and Wilkes-Barre. Within a short time they dominated the mining of hard coal in the United States. In the 1830s and 1840s quarrymen from the slate quarries of North Wales began settling in eastern Pennsylvania and western Vermont, and soon took over that industry. After 1850 the rapid growth of the U.S. iron industry created a great demand for Welsh iron puddlers, who soon established a sizable colony in Pittsburgh, Pennsylvania. Among these Welshmen was David Thomas, who set up the first successful hot-blast iron furnace in the United States and helped lead the move away from wood in favor of coal as the fuel of choice in iron foundries. After the McKinley Tariff of 1890 raised the tariffs on tinned sheet iron, most of which was made in Wales, virtually all the Welsh producers of this commodity relocated their operations to the United States, bringing with them scores of skilled Welsh metalworkers.

A number of Welshmen settled in the United States to farm. Perhaps because they spoke their own Celtic language in addition to English, Welshmen tended to congregate in tighter communities than did the English and Scots. Early in the century Welsh farm communities sprang up across Ohio in places such as Gomer, Radnor, and the Welsh Hills of Licking County. Between 1830 and 1850 Welsh farmers settled near Waukesha and La Crosse, Wisconsin; in Blue Earth and Fillmore counties, Minnesota; and in Howard and Iowa counties, Iowa.

Assimilation

For the English, Scots, and Welsh, assimilation into U.S. culture was relatively easy, given their ability to speak English. In addition British immigrants shared several very important cultural traits with American natives, such as similar tastes in food, literature, and music. The vast majority of British immigrants were Protestants, usually either Episcopalian or Presbyterian, which made them much more acceptable to American natives than the hordes of Catholics entering the country from Ireland, Italy, Germany, and Poland. Except for the Welsh, who sometimes insisted on living together in ethnic communities and speaking their own language, most British immigrants were virtually indistinguishable from American natives. Consequently they intermarried with natives to a much higher degree than did any other national group.

Despite their ability to fit in, many British immigrants were unimpressed with American society. Because of the higher wages paid by American mills, Englishmen who had been members of the working class in England rose to the lower middle class in the United States. Although wages were higher in the United States, the workweek was longer. Workers in Great Britain typically worked an average of fifty-five hours per week, whereas the American workweek started at sixty hours and went up from there. This situation distressed a great number of British immigrants, so many stayed only until the U.S. economy took a turn for the worse. Then they returned to Great Britain and resumed working in mills there. In fact, some British textile workers traveled back and forth between Great Britain and the United States on a regular basis, depending on which country offered higher wages for their particular skills.

For the most part British immigrants regarded Americans as uncouth, too egalitarian, and too disrespectful to their "betters," and they thought that American society and culture were poor imitations of British society and culture. Like other national groups British immigrants established their own newspapers, patronized their own clubs and saloons, and continued to play their own sports, especially soccer and rugby. They also observed their own holidays, especially Christmas, which the British celebrated with great enthusiasm, and the feast days of Saint George, Saint Andrew, and Saint David, the patron saints of England, Scotland, and Wales, respectively. Many retained their fondness for home and their allegiance to the crown long after they had settled permanently in the United States. British immigrants were less likely to become U.S. citizens than any other national group. Prior to 1870, when a U.S.–British naturalization treaty outlawed the practice, many British immigrants claimed dual citizenship even after they had become naturalized citizens of the United States.

The job skills and cultural background of British immigrants led American natives to hire them readily and accept them as neighbors, more so than any other national group. Ironically, the availability of good jobs in Great Britain and the immigrants' preference for British culture and society led them to accept life in the United States less readily.

See also **Iron; Mining and Extraction; Textiles.**

Bibliography

Berthoff, Roland. *British Immigrants in Industrial America, 1790–1950.* Cambridge, Mass.: Harvard University Press, 1953.

Erickson, Charlotte. *Invisible Immigrants: The Adaptation of English and Scottish Immigrants in Nineteenth-Century America.* Coral Gables, Fla.: University of Miami Press, 1972.

CHARLES W. CAREY JR.

FRANCE AND THE LOW COUNTRIES

Immigrants from France, Belgium, Luxembourg, and the Netherlands migrated to the United States throughout the nineteenth century, but they represented the smallest group from northwestern Europe. From 1820, when the U.S. Bureau of the Census began recording immigration statistics, to 1900, fewer than 800,000 immigrants arrived from these four nations. They came not as part of a mass exodus but in a flow that increased only slightly during peak waves of migration resulting principally from agricultural crises and industrialization.

They were primarily rural immigrants. Most Belgians, Luxembourgers, and Dutch were peasant farmers before migration. Some Dutch artisans and craftsmen originated from urban areas, but they represented only a small percentage of those migrating to the United States. The French were mostly professionals and merchants who emanated from eastern France and the Paris basin.

Preferring to remain farmers, the Belgians and Luxembourgers tended to settle in New York State and in the Midwest, where they found inexpensive farmland. Belgians migrated to Michigan, Illinois, Wisconsin, and Indiana, especially favoring northern Michigan and Detroit. Luxembourgers moved to the southeastern coast of Lake Erie in New York and to Ohio in the 1830s. From the 1840s forward most chose Illinois and Wisconsin, settling an area that stretched from Chicago and along Lake Michigan to north of Milwaukee, Wisconsin. Other Luxembourgers chose to reside in Iowa, Minnesota, North Dakota, South Dakota, Nebraska, and Kansas.

Although early Dutch immigrants had settled in and around New York City (formerly New Amsterdam), those who arrived in the nineteenth century changed that pattern. In the 1830s Dutch migrants moved to western New York State and Milwaukee. The next decade, a time of increased immigration for the Dutch, saw several groups establish settlements in the rural Midwest, which they found attractive due to favorable reports from a Dutchman who had settled in Indiana. In 1846 the Reverend Albertus Van Raalte (1811–1876) led a group of conservative Calvinists to western Michigan in search of religious freedom; the Reverend Hendrik Scholte (1805–1868) headed a similar party to Iowa the next year. In 1848 Father Theodorus Van den Broek (1783–1851) sponsored a Catholic colony that settled in Little Chute, Wisconsin. Soon after, the Dutch began settling in Chicago, Cleveland, St. Louis, and cities in western Michigan as well. Later, in the 1880s, a few Dutch migrated as far west as California and Oregon.

In contrast to the Belgians, Luxembourgers, and Dutch, who preferred to settle in ethnic communities in the Great Lakes and Midwest regions, the French settled wherever economic opportunity seemed favorable. When the Mississippi River was a prime trade route, the French congregated along it, but as railroads took prominence in the second half of the nineteenth century, they went elsewhere. After the fall of Napoleon I in 1815, former Bonapartists and Republican farmers migrated to rural Pennsylvania, Ohio, Texas, Louisiana, and Alabama. With the 1848 discovery of gold in California, a number of French sought their fortunes there. By the 1850s French proponents of utopian societies had established model communities in Texas and Louisiana, which soon failed.

Immigrants had a variety of motivations for coming to America, which changed with the prevailing conditions in their homelands. Early in the nineteenth century they left Europe for religious and political reasons. French, Belgian, and Dutch Catholic clerics served as missionaries, and Protestants left Belgium after a Catholic state was established in the 1830s. Dutch Jews and Calvinists in the 1840s sought freedom from a state-controlled church as well. Politically motivated French Bonapartists were exiles, expelled by the royalist regime in the second decade of the nineteenth century. For the last sixty years of the century, economic factors played a larger role. Land shortages and other agricultural crises in Belgium, Luxembourg, and the Netherlands in the 1840s, 1870s, and 1880s encouraged farmers to go to America. In the 1870s they took advantage of inexpensive land on the prairies offered by the 1862 Homestead Act. About the same time, craftsmen were being displaced because of industrialization and they came looking for work. These immigrants all arrived in America searching for a better life and often were lured by newspapers, family, and friends who gave encouraging reports.

While some immigrants prospered as they expected, others did not. For Belgian, Dutch, and Luxembourger farmers, success was relative. Europe offered little chance of land ownership, and America held greater promise; farming, however, required hard work and good luck. Dutch urban immigrants also were only moderately successful. The French fared better as many came with professional skills, such as engineering and medicine; some, like the Du Ponts, founders of a chemical company, even became wealthy.

Life in America differed among the ethnic groups. Belgians, Luxembourgers, and especially the Dutch formed communities that allowed them to retain their ethnic identities. In the case of the Dutch, whole communities from the Netherlands resettled together in the United States. The French, on the other hand, preferred to assimilate into the local culture.

Because these immigrants amounted to a relatively small group and they originated from northwestern Europe, they suffered less from American xenophobia than other ethnic groups. The Dutch of western Michigan and Iowa fared especially well because they maintained strong, ethnocentric settlements. This experience, however, was not true for all. In the second quarter of the century a wave of anti-Catholic sentiment swept the nation, and Catholic immigrants faced violence and verbal abuse. For example, a French Ursuline convent was destroyed in Charlestown, Massachusetts, in 1834.

Immigrants from France, Belgium, Luxembourg, and the Netherlands differed from other ethnic migrants in several ways. Unlike the immigrants from south, central, and eastern Europe, they arrived in America throughout the nineteenth century and they came in small numbers. Although they were from northwestern Europe, they did not speak English as did the British and the Irish. In addition, they were not all Protestant as were the Scandinavians, the British, and many Germans. Finally, they tended to settle in rural areas, pursuing farming as opposed to industrial work.

See also **Anti-Catholicism; Homesteading; Midwest, The; New York State; Work,** *subentry on* **Agricultural Labor.**

Bibliography

Blumenthal, Henry. *American and French Culture, 1800–1900: Interchanges in Art, Science, Literature, and Society.* Baton Rouge: Louisiana State University, 1975.

Brinks, Herbert J., ed. *Dutch American Voices: Letters from the United States, 1850–1930.* Ithaca, N.Y.: Cornell University Press, 1995.

Eyck, F. Gunther. *The Benelux Countries: An Historical Survey.* Princeton, N.J.: D. Van Nostrand, 1959.

Lucas, Henry Stephen. *Netherlanders in America: Dutch Immigration to the United States and Canada, 1789–1950.* Ann Arbor: University of Michigan Press, 1955. Reprint, Grand Rapids, Mich.: Eerdman's, 1989.

Sabbe, Philemon D., and Leon Buyse. *Belgians in America.* Tielt, Belgium: Lannoo, 1960.

Swierenga, Robert P., ed. *The Dutch in America: Immigration, Settlement, and Cultural Change.* New Brunswick, N.J.: Rutgers University Press, 1985.

RACHAEL L. DRENOVSKY

GERMANY

German immigration has significantly contributed to the development of the United States. Since colonial times more than seven million Germans have immigrated to America; the majority, about five million, left the Old World in the nineteenth century. In the postcolonial period Germany contributed more immigrants to America than any other country.

Immigrant influx from Germany increased steadily throughout the nineteenth century. During the 1820s, fewer than six thousand Germans came to America. In the 1850s, 950,000 immigrated (peaking at 215,000 in 1854), and by the 1880s, almost a million German immigrants were counted, with more than 250,000 Germans immigrating in 1882 alone. The United States was the preferred destination for almost 90 percent of all registered German immigrants between the 1830s and the turn of the century.

Motivations for Immigration

In nineteenth-century Germany, information about America was readily available from emigration agents and guidebooks, newspapers, and journals specializing in immigration issues. These resources, combined with increasing literacy and discontent with economic, political, and religious conditions, provided motivation for many to leave Germany.

Another important impetus for transatlantic migration was communication by mail, particularly for people who had relatives or friends in the United States. The historian Wolfgang Helbich has estimated that at least 250 million letters were sent to Germany from the United States between 1820 and 1914. Although nine out of ten emigrants from Germany had only rudimentary schooling, as many as 100 million private letters may have been sent during those years. In those letters, family members found words of both encouragement and caution regarding emigration, and a wealth of data about economic and social conditions in the New World. Kathleen Neils Conzen has argued that of all the channels of communication available to potential immigrants, private letters were the most important source of advice and stimulus to emigration.

The majority of the German emigrants came from the lower classes. Small farmers dominated the migration from the southwest, artisans and household manufacturers were prominent among those from the central regions, and day laborers and servants were predominant among emigrants from the northeast.

A small number of the emigrants, less than 1 percent, were paupers and criminals whose trip was financed by their home communities. Between 1845 and 1855, a number of communities in southwestern Germany sponsored such migration to relieve local authorities of the economic burden of providing welfare for an indefinite period of time. This practice was eventually abandoned in the face of American opposition and the concerns of immigrant organizations about its potentially harmful effects on regular immigration.

As a rule, however, in the nineteenth century the very poor did not migrate from Germany to America. During the 1820s, the redemptionist system had disappeared. This system, sometimes called "white slavery," had offered immigrants free passage to America in return for unpaid services to a master for several years. As a proportion of eighteenth-century German immigration to the United States, redemptioners may have accounted for 50 to 60 percent. The end of the indenture system meant that poor people could no longer emigrate to America. Only those who could raise the cost of the passage joined the large migration waves.

Numerous associations existed to provide an organizational basis for group migration. Among the most noted of these organizations were the Giessen Emigration Society and the *Adelsverein*. The Giessen organization was a group of about five hundred young liberals who emigrated after the failed revolution of 1830 to form a model republic in the American West. Their enterprise failed, and the group dispersed into smaller settlements. Other groups from Solingen and Thuringia shared the same fate. The *Adelsverein* (Society of Nobles) promoted the idea of colonizing Texas and transported more than seven thousand immigrants to Texas between 1844 and 1846. Many of the immigrants died on the march from the Texas port of Galveston to the interior, and the association went bankrupt in 1847. After news about this experience reached Germany, potential immigrants became highly skeptical of colonization societies.

Germans emigrated not only for economic and social gain but also for religious reasons. Dissident religious groups wished to escape the pressures of the authorities in Germany. The largest religious migra-

Naturalization Certificate. Certificate of Naturalization for John Menz, a German immigrant born in Prussia; issued in 1859 in Madison County, Illinois. LIBRARY OF CONGRESS

tion was that of the Old Lutherans, to protest Prussia's forced unification of the Lutheran and Reformed churches in 1837. In 1843, the peak year of migration, sixteen hundred Old Lutherans left Germany, and by 1854, five thousand had immigrated to the United States in three main groups. Emigrants from Pomerania and Silesia went to Buffalo and Milwaukee, Bavarian Franconians settled in Michigan, and Saxonians colonized in Missouri.

In addition, a number of Pietists founded communities such as Harmony (1805) and Economy (1825) in Pennsylvania, Zoar (1817) in Ohio, and Amana (1859) in Iowa. In the later decades of the century, this migration was complemented by the exodus of Catholic Germans during the *Kulturkampf* (1871–1887).

Political emigration was relatively rare, although the desire for personal freedom naturally played an important role in individual decisions to migrate. The reactionary and repressive political climate and the repression of German liberalism in the early 1830s motivated some immigration to the United States, as did the abortive revolution of 1848. In addition, some emigrants tried to escape military service, and others left between 1878 and 1890 because of the strict antisocialist law.

Settlement Patterns

In choosing their new homes, German immigrants followed guiding principles that included availability of land, economic opportunity, and climate. Emigration guides promoted certain areas. Some states (for example, Wisconsin in 1852) appointed emigration commissioners to promote their state for settlement. Private businessmen and railroads vigorously promoted land grants. Religion also played a role; some German churches attempted to direct their members to areas where ministers were available.

Up to mid-century, when the railroad connected all main points east of the Mississippi, German immigration followed two routes. Immigrants who arrived in New York or Philadelphia and did not stay in the Middle Atlantic states traveled via the Hudson, the Erie Canal, and the Great Lakes to Illinois, Wisconsin, and Michigan. Those arriving in New Orleans traveled up the Mississippi into the Ohio and Missouri valleys. By the 1860s, both routes connected in the settlement of Minnesota. After the Civil War, agricultural settlers traveled beyond the Mississippi and formed communities in Kansas, Nebraska, and the Dakotas. Only a minority of German immigrants settled directly on the frontier, though a majority of the farmers followed its westward expansion closely.

Throughout the century, New York claimed more German immigrants than any other state. In 1880, 18 percent of German immigrants lived in New York, Illinois counted 12 percent, Ohio 10 percent, Wisconsin 9.5 percent, and Pennsylvania 8.6 percent. States with an above-average German population stretched from Ohio in the east to Nebraska in the west, from Missouri in the south to Wisconsin in the north. Within that region, 39.8 percent lived in the east north-central states, followed by 30 percent in the Middle Atlantic states, and 16.1 percent in the west north-central states.

In general, German immigrants avoided New England and the South. In 1880, only 3.6 percent of the German immigrants lived in the south Atlantic states, 4.9 percent in the rest of the South, and 1.8 percent in New England. Both regions offered little economic opportunity to the newcomers. Harsh climatic conditions in the North and the persistence of slavery in the South proved additional deterrents, despite the massive promotion of immigration to the southern states by local governments after 1865.

It is a persistent myth that most Germans lived in rural areas. German immigrants, most with a small-town background, settled in urban areas to a much greater extent than their relatives in Germany or their American neighbors. In 1850, almost 30 percent of German immigrants, but only 8 percent of the American population, lived in the eight largest cities of the country. In 1890, 69 percent of all immigrants in Milwaukee were German, 60 percent in Louisville, 59 percent in Baltimore, 58 percent in St. Louis, and 55 percent in Indianapolis. By 1900, 49 percent of German immigrants lived in cities with populations of twenty-five thousand or more.

The Evolution of a German American Ethnic Culture

In the era before urban mass transportation, the need to live close to the workplace tended to disperse immigrant populations. However, Germans were more successful in carving out ethnic enclaves than many other nineteenth-century immigrants. Although not all German immigrants lived in quarters called Little Germany, Over the Rhine, Little Saxony, or Nordseite, German neighborhoods were a common feature of the nineteenth century. Particularly in the newer cities of the Midwest, Germans arrived early enough and in sufficient numbers to dominate entire neighborhoods, and their tendency to settle close together encouraged the continuation of familiar lifestyles.

German clubs and associations, many of which were originally formed to serve practical needs, were an important part of community life. The volunteer fire and militia companies combined several goals— protection, demonstration of American patriotism, defense against nativist bullying—with community service. Mutual benefits associations provided insurance against sickness and death. Numerous aid societies assisted newly arrived immigrants. By 1892, the National Federation of Benefit Societies had become the largest secular German organization.

German-speaking lodges were a second focal point of community life. By 1871, over three hundred of the forty-eight hundred Odd Fellows lodges in the United States were German. Germans also created their own lodges, such as the Sons of Hermann, which was founded in 1840.

Along with the fraternal orders, educational, conversational, and debating societies played an important role. They were often linked to political activities and promoted liberal political thought in the 1840s and 1850s. A prominent association, the *Turnerbund*, was formed by the followers of Friedrich Ludwig Jahn (1778–1852), who had stressed a mixture of physical culture and liberal nationalism with his *Turnverein* (gymnastic club) movement. Liberal exiles brought gymnastics to the United States in the 1820s, and after the late 1840s gymnastic associations were formed nationwide. After the distinct contribution of the Turners to Union victory in the Civil

War, the *Turnerbund* served for a while as a national symbol of German American ethnic culture.

Early on, however, German Americans had a reputation for political apathy. They failed to produce officeholders commensurate with their numbers. Carl Schurz (1829–1906), the most prominent exception, served as senator from Missouri and secretary of the Interior under President Rutherford B. Hayes.

Music provided another focal point of German American festive culture and community life. Starting in the 1830s, choirs and singing clubs were formed in many German immigrant communities. The first *Sängerfest* (singing contest) was held in Cincinnati in 1849. Such festivals became massive public events. In 1900 the national competition, held in Brooklyn, brought together six thousand singers from 174 associations.

The ethnic culture of German immigrants was also shaped by churches, schools, and the press. Roughly one-third of German immigrants were Catholic. The rest belonged to the Lutheran, Reformed, and Evangelical churches, and a small number were Methodists, Unitarians, Jews, Baptists, and Pietists. Both Catholics and Lutherans agreed that German should be spoken by German Americans as long as possible. The Protestants wanted to preserve their rich doctrinal and liturgical tradition, and the Catholics feared that if they did not preach in German, parish members might leave for Protestant churches that did.

Hoping to ward off threats to their religion from the English-language schools, churches operated parish schools long before public school systems were mandated by the state legislatures. The available public schools in nineteenth-century America appeared to have an anti-Catholic and Anglo-Protestant bias, and the Old Lutherans in particular rejected their ecumenical tendencies. The largest faction of the Old Lutherans, the Missouri Synod, operated almost 2,100 schools with nearly 100,000 pupils by the end of the century. The 700 German Catholic communities counted more than 130,000 pupils. Although these are impressive numbers, no more than one-third to one-half of all Catholic and Lutheran children attended confessional schools.

From colonial times well into the nineteenth century, all German schools in Pennsylvania, Maryland, Virginia, and the Carolinas were parochial schools. From the 1850s on, there were nonreligious German schools run by freethinkers in Texas and the Midwest. These latter schools incorporated new educational principles that had a lasting effect on the educational system: kindergarten, sports as part of the school program, music, and manual arts.

German-language instruction in public schools became widespread in the last third of the nineteenth century. Beginning with Ohio and Pennsylvania, numerous states permitted, and some—including Ohio, Wisconsin, and Indiana—even mandated German instruction when local demand warranted it. In Chicago and New York, the curriculum was confined to language instruction, but Cleveland, Baltimore, and Cincinnati strove for a truly bilingual instruction system.

The availability of German-language instruction strengthened immigrants' support for the public school system. It is estimated that in 1886, 430,000 pupils nationwide were in German-instruction schools: 38 percent in Catholic schools, 23 percent in Protestant schools, 35 percent in public schools, and 3.7 percent in secular private schools. Toward the end of the century, the public school system became more attractive for German immigrant children. In 1860, four out of five German children in St. Louis attended private (German-language) schools. Twenty years later, the same proportion was enrolled in public bilingual schools.

Like the schools, the German-language press played a central role in creating an ethnic identity for German immigrants. At the same time, it also encouraged assimilation by familiarizing immigrants with American life, habits, and customs. The German press, originating in the eighteenth century, was the largest, best-edited, and most influential foreign-language press in the United States. By the nineteenth century, waves of German immigrants included not only professional journalists but also a new population of interested readers. In 1843, the Cincinnati *Volksblatt*, founded in 1836, was the only German daily in the United States. Seven years later there were twenty daily papers, including four in New York, three in Cincinnati and in Milwaukee, and two in Baltimore, Philadelphia, and Chicago. By 1860, German journals numbered more than 250, and by the 1880s, the German press constituted about 80 percent of the foreign-language press in the United States. The total number of newspapers peaked at eight hundred between 1893 and 1894.

Nativism and Ethnic Politics

In contrast to emigrants from eastern and southern Europe and Asia, newcomers of German origin were extended support and often a sympathetic welcome. Even in the darkest moments of xenophobic nativism, public opinion hardly emphasized differences but stressed perceived similarities in the values and cultural outlooks of Germans and Americans.

Still, non-German residents viewed the development of a German American ethnic culture not only with curiosity and interest, but also with concern. The strong influx of large numbers of Catholic immigrants from Germany and Ireland fostered the fear that the traditional character of Euro-American society—its Anglo-conformity and its Protestantism—would be endangered. In the 1850s, when Germans became the largest group of immigrants, nativism and xenophobia reached a high point.

Although organized nativism had existed since the 1830s, a party of national prominence with a nativist platform did not form until the 1850s. The American Party, also known as the Know-Nothings because of its origins as a secret order, fought to extend the waiting period for naturalization and voting from five to twenty-one years. In addition, the party favored legislation to permanently exclude immigrants from holding public office and to refuse entry to criminals, the poor, and loyal subjects of a "foreign power"—in particular, members of the Roman Catholic Church.

The Know-Nothing movement became popular in the mid-1850s and caused outbreaks of violence in Chicago, St. Louis, Baltimore, and Louisville. After the demise of the party, most of its members joined the Republican Party but did not influence its political course; in fact, the Republican platform of 1860 contained many provisions designed to attract German voters.

Conclusion

German immigration exerted a lasting influence on American architecture, painting, music, festive culture, education, and technological innovation. German ethnic culture was sufficiently broad to encompass the entire spectrum of German migration, transcending regional, professional, political, and religious boundaries. As such it presented and mirrored a microcosm of America's emerging multicultural society in the nineteenth century, with all its limits but also its strengths.

See also **Anti-Catholicism; Catholicism; Clubs,** *subentry* on **Fraternal Societies and Clubs; Protestantism,** *subentry* on **Lutherans; Religion,** *subentry* on **Religion as a Political Issue.**

Bibliography

Adams, Willi Paul. *The German-Americans: An Ethnic Experience.* Translated and adapted by LaVern J. Rippley and Eberhard Reichmann. Indianapolis: Max Kade German American Center, 1993.

Conzen, Kathleen Neils. "Germans." In *Harvard Encyclopedia of American Ethnic Groups.* Edited by Stephan Thernstrom et al. Cambridge, Mass.: Harvard University Press, 1980.

Daniels, Roger. *Coming to America: A History of Immigration and Ethnicity in American Life.* New York: HarperCollins, 1991.

Doerries, Reinhard R. *Iren und Deutsche in der Neuen Welt: Akkulturationsprozesse in der amerikanischen Gesellschaft im späten neunzehnten Jahrhundert.* Stuttgart: F. Steiner, 1986.

Harzig, Christiane. "There Is No 'Kaiser' Here: The United States as a Country of Immigration." In *Fame, Fortune, and Sweet Liberty: The Great European Emigration.* Edited by Dirk Hoerder and Diethelm Knauf. Bremen: Edition Temmen, 1992.

Hoerder, Dirk. "Research on the German Migrations, 1820s to 1930s: A Report on the State of German Scholarship." In *People in Transit: German Migrations in Comparative Perspective, 1820–1930.* Edited by Dirk Hoerder and Jörg Nagler. Cambridge, U.K.: Cambridge University Press, 1995.

Kamphoefner, Walter D. *The Westfalians: From Germany to Missouri.* Princeton, N.J.: Princeton University Press, 1987.

Kamphoefner, Walter D., Wolfgang Helbich, and Ulrike Sommer, eds. *News from the Land of Freedom: German Immigrants Write Home.* Ithaca, N.Y.: Cornell University Press, 1991.

Moltmann, Gunther. "The Pattern of German Immigration to the United States in the Nineteenth Century." In *Americans and the Germans: An Assessment of a Three-Hundred-Year History.* Edited by Frank Trommler and Joseph McVeigh. Volume 1: *Immigration, Language, Ethnicity.* Philadelphia: University of Pennsylvania Press, 1985.

Trommler, Frank, and Joseph McVeigh. *America and the Germans. An Assessment of a Three-Hundred-Year History.* 2 vols. Philadelphia: University of Pennsylvania Press, 1985.

FRANK SCHUMACHER

CENTRAL AND EASTERN EUROPE

They were called "new" immigrants: those who left central and eastern Europe, a region stretching west from the Baltic Sea and German-controlled Poland, east across Russia, and south to the Balkan Peninsula. Between 1820 (when the U.S. Census Bureau began keeping immigration statistics) and 1900, over 6.9 million immigrants came to America from central and eastern Europe, with the bulk arriving from 1880 to the turn of the century.

Home Regions

Most of the "new" immigrants were poor, rural peasants (former serfs). They came from overpopulated areas that could not support their numbers. Industrialization—and its promise of new jobs—was limited in central and eastern Europe. Often, governments restricted the industrialization advancing from the west, as in the Polish region of Galicia and in Slovakia.

The immigrants' home regions were dominated by imperialist nations—Germany, Russia, and Austria-Hungary—that suppressed ethnic and religious minorities. Programs like "Germanization," "Russification," and "Magyarization" all repressed ethnic identity. Jews suffered additional hardships because of their non-Christian beliefs. The Russian government oppressed Jews systematically and late in the century encouraged mob violence against them.

U.S. Settlement Patterns

Although most central and eastern European immigrants came from rural areas, they tended to settle in U.S. cities. Often they established enclaves that attracted more immigrants of the same ethnicity. Relatively few resumed agrarian lives, preferring the higher wages of industrial jobs. In addition, many planned to return home after making enough money and did not want to be tied to a piece of land.

Central and eastern Europeans clustered in the mining and industrial states of the North and Northeast, particularly New York, Pennsylvania, New Jersey, and Massachusetts. In the Midwest, they settled mostly in Illinois, Wisconsin, Ohio, Minnesota, and Michigan. Cities in these states, including New York, Chicago, Cleveland, Detroit, Philadelphia, Boston, and Pittsburgh, became great ethnic centers.

Central and eastern Europeans settled in other places as well. Poles, Czechs, and Hungarians established communities in Texas. In 1854, Father Leopold Moczygemba (1825–1891), a Catholic missionary, convinced a group of poor Poles from Upper Silesia to join him there. Czechs also farmed in Nebraska, Iowa, Kansas, Missouri, and the Dakotas. Farming attracted Ukrainians to Virginia and North Dakota; it also brought Poles, Ukrainians, and Carpatho-Rusyns to Connecticut. Lithuanians went to lumber communities in Maine. Russians, Latvians, and Cossacks also migrated to the West Coast, settling in Oregon and California, as well as Alaska and other areas.

Reasons for Migration

During the first half of the nineteenth century, before the mass migration of the 1890s, a small but visible population of political exiles sought freedom in America. European nationalism reached its height in the 1800s, and some central and eastern Europeans came to the United States as a result of failed revolutionary efforts. In 1834 a party of over two hundred Polish émigrés settled in New York, Boston, Washington, D.C., and Ohio after an uprising against Russia. Polish expatriates also arrived in America following revolutions in 1830 and 1863. The late 1840s saw a small influx of Czech exiles—soldiers, intellectuals, and craftsmen—who came after a failed revolution there. Lajos Kossuth (1802–1894), the leader of Hungarian nationalists, and a few followers visited the United States looking for support in 1851. Some stayed and established settlements in Iowa and Texas.

While some central and eastern European immigrants sought political, religious, and cultural freedom in the United States, most came because of the economic opportunities. At home, they faced agricultural crises, land shortages, and problems from industrialization or lack of it. Most immigrants of the late 1800s wanted to make money in America and then return home to buy land. A number of immigrants went back, but many did not.

Additional factors encouraged migration. Peasants were able to travel after their release from serfdom by the 1860s. The more widespread use of steamships by mid-century meant cheaper and faster transportation to America. Also, family and friends sent positive, though sometimes exaggerated, reports of their success in the United States. Some, like the Latvian Jacob Sieberg (1863–1963), who arrived in Boston in 1888, actively encouraged others to follow.

Occupations

Initially, most central and eastern European immigrants were young males who wanted to improve their families' lives by making quick money in the United States and then returning home. Therefore, they accepted jobs that required hard work and few skills, gravitating toward manufacturing, food processing, mining, and construction. Those who worked in seasonal jobs often arrived in the spring and returned home in the autumn. Working conditions often were unhealthy and unsafe, and numerous laborers were injured or killed. Most did not become wealthy, but many did well enough to forward money home, send for their families, and buy houses. Workers often moved from unskilled to semiskilled labor, and some were able to start their own businesses.

Great numbers of immigrants labored as coal miners in Pennsylvania and other mining states. They worked long hours, and fatalities, injuries, and lung disease were commonplace. Although unions typically did not attract them in the nineteenth century, in 1897 a group of Poles, Slovaks, Lithuanians, and Ukrainians undertook a successful strike against the Lehigh and Wilkes-Barre Company in eastern Pennsylvania. Victory came with a price, however, as nineteen demonstrators were killed by sheriffs prompted into action by fearful native-born citizens.

Other industries attracted central and eastern Europeans. Czechs, Slovaks, and Latvians worked in textile mills in Chicago, in Rochester, New York and in New England. Steel mills and foundries in Pittsburgh, Cleveland, Buffalo, and Chicago employed Poles, Czechs, Hungarians, Latvians, and Carpatho-

Women and Children on Deck. Eastern European families voyage to America aboard the SS *Amsterdam*, 1899. LIBRARY OF CONGRESS: PRINTS AND PHOTOGRAPHS DIVISION

Rusyns. Lithuanians labored in the oil refineries of New York and New Jersey and became lumberjacks in Maine and Michigan. Polish immigrants constructed railroads, streetcar lines, and ships.

Immigrants also provided labor for the food-processing industry. Poles, Czechs, Latvians, and Carpatho-Rusyns worked in meat-packing houses of the Midwest, primarily in Chicago. Canneries employed many Slovaks and Czechs, including women. Carpatho-Rusyns and others worked in sugar refineries in New York, Philadelphia, and Boston.

While most labored in industry, some worked in agriculture. Czechs farmed in the Midwest and the Southwest beginning in the 1860s, attracted by the inexpensive land provided by the Homestead Act. A few Poles owned truck farms in Connecticut, and Ukrainians became farmers in Illinois, Virginia, and North Dakota. Some Russians established utopian farming communities, like New Odessa, Oregon, founded by William Frey (d. 1870).

Most central and eastern European Jews became industrial workers, particularly in the garment industry of the urban East. However, many Jewish immigrants gravitated toward business ownership. In their homelands they had been forced into commerce by laws and attitudes, and they brought their business know-how with them. In America they frequently became peddlers, petty tradesmen, and retail merchants. Densely populated Jewish ghettos in cities offered Jews many opportunities to serve their own people, who—unlike their Christian counterparts—had come to stay.

Immigrant Life

For most immigrants, life in America was very different from life in Europe. Men had left families and wives in their homelands. U.S. cities were not prepared to accommodate large influxes of people, and urban tenement "dumbbell" buildings (nicknamed for their resemblance to the popular weight), constructed in the 1880s, were unsanitary and unsafe. Food was expensive and different from European fare. For the first time, women worked outside the home as domestics and factory workers. Immigrants responded to this new way of life with an emphasis on their ethnicity. Groups clustered, socializing only among themselves and speaking their own language. They established clubs, church congregations, and parochial schools.

Religion was very important to the central and eastern European immigrants, whether they were Catholic, Protestant, Orthodox, or Jewish. Ethnic differences, though, sometimes led to tensions and the establishment of separate congregations. For example, Roman Catholics at first attended predominantly Irish or German parishes, but soon established their own Polish, Czech, Slovak, Lithuanian, and Hungarian congregations. Eastern-rite Ukrainian Catholics had difficulty keeping a separate identity from Latin-rite churches, so many responded by converting to Orthodoxy or Protestantism. The Russian Orthodox church, which established itself in Alaska during the 1840s by sending missionaries there, remained small in the rest of the United States, with churches in San Francisco, New Orleans, and New York. Like the Catholics and Orthodox, Protestants, including Slovaks, Hungarians, Latvians, and Estonians, formed ethnically based congregations. The Reverend Hans Rebane (1863–1911) helped many Estonians and Latvians to establish Lutheran churches in the nineteenth century. Jews also built congregations that were based upon their European regional origins.

Foreign-language newspapers proliferated during the late 1800s, keeping immigrants in touch with their homelands and easing the transition to American life. Two popular Polish papers were Chicago's *Gazeta Polski*, headed by Wladyslaw Dyniewicz (1843–1928), and Toledo's *Ameryka-Echo*, published by Antoni Paryski (1865–1935). A Ukrainian priest, Agapius Honcharenko (1832–1916), established the first Russian-language newspaper, *Svoboda/ The Alaska Herald*, in 1868. The Lithuanians Jonas Šliūpas (1861–1944) and Aleksandras Burba (1854–1898) also began foreign-language newspapers. A number of Yiddish papers started at this time, including the well-known *Jewish Daily Forward* (1897).

Ethnic groups also established mutual-benefit societies that reimbursed beneficiaries for injuries or fatalities. For example, Slovaks belonged to the National Slovak Society and the First Catholic Slovak Union, founded by Peter Rovnianek (1867–1933) and Stefan Furdek (1855–1915) in 1890.

To assimilate, immigrants dressed in American clothing, attended classes to learn English, and Americanized their courtship practices. Often, the question of remaining ethnic or becoming American created tension between parents and children.

U.S. Acceptance of Immigrants

Typically, native-born Americans did not welcome the central and eastern Europeans; many Americans were frightened by the sizable numbers of "new" immigrants arriving at the end of the century. These immigrants were classified as "new" for several reasons. Unlike the British and Irish, they did not speak English. Also, they were mostly Catholic or Orthodox or Jewish, in contrast with the Protestant Germans, Scandinavians, and British. They had different clothing, tended to settle in urban areas, and usually pursued industrial work instead of farming or business ownership. Nativists equated the "new" immigrants with radicalism and lawlessness. "Old" immigrants, like the Irish, did not accept them either.

Americans took various measures to reduce the impact of foreigners. Protestants attempted to convert Catholics. Reformers built settlement houses to assist immigrants and ran schools to help migrants assimilate. In 1885 the federal government began restricting immigration. By the end of the century, criminals, lunatics, polygamists, and those under labor contracts or with certain diseases could not enter the United States.

Implementing these restrictions was possible, in part, because of central and eastern European immigrants' attitudes toward politics. With little democratic experience and a language barrier, these migrants tended to remain apathetic. Furthermore, most saw themselves as temporary residents, so they did not seek naturalization or involve themselves in American issues. Those who did vote often stuck to local matters and voted as a bloc, which dispersed their power at the state and national levels. Generally, these immigrants leaned toward the Democratic Party. Some Russian Jews, who happened to be socialist thinkers, were the exception. They founded the Russian Social-Democratic Society in 1891, out of which came the Russian sections of the American Socialist Party.

Despite anti-immigrant sentiment, the wave of central and eastern European immigration to the United States did not end with the turn of the twentieth century. It continued to increase until World War I began in 1914 and remained steady after the 1918 armistice, until quotas were instituted by the immigration acts of the early 1920s.

See also **Immigrants,** *subentry on* **Jewish Immigrants; Labor Force; Mining and Extraction; Religion,** *subentry on* **Religion in Nineteenth-Century America; Work.**

Bibliography

Balch, Emily Greene. *Our Slavic Fellow Citizens*. New York: Charities Publication Committee, 1910. Reprint, New York: Arno, 1969.

Capek, Thomas. *The Cechs (Bohemians) in America: A Study of Their National, Cultural, Political, Social, Economic, and Religious Life*. Boston and New York: Houghton Mifflin, 1920. Reprint, Westport, Conn.: Greenwood, 1970.

Kuropas, Myron B. *The Ukrainian Americans: Roots and As-pirations, 1884–1954.* Toronto: University of Toronto Press, 1991.

Pula, James S. *Polish Americans: An Ethnic Community.* New York: Twayne, 1995.

Thernstrom, Stephan, ed. *Harvard Encyclopedia of American Ethnic Groups.* Cambridge, Mass.: Belknap Press of Harvard University Press, 1980.

Várdy, Steven Béla. *The Hungarian-Americans.* Boston: Twayne, 1985.

Wytrwal, Joseph A. *America's Polish Heritage: A Social History of the Poles in America.* Detroit: Endurance, 1961.

RACHAEL L. DRENOVSKY

JEWISH IMMIGRANTS

Jewish immigration to the United States generally followed European patterns of immigration during the nineteenth century. Before 1830 there were perhaps six thousand Jews in the United States. (Statistics for Jewish immigrants are notoriously inexact because people were counted by country of origin, not by religious preference.)

Jewish Market, New York City. During the middle of the nineteenth century, the Lower East Side of New York became an energetic commercial center for Jewish immigrants and their retail businesses. LIBRARY OF CONGRESS

Immigration and Settlement

The first major wave of European immigration to the United States began in the late 1830s, reached a crescendo in 1854, and then began to decline. Most of the people in this wave came from either Ireland or the German states in Europe. By the time the Civil War began in 1861, the nation had received more than four million immigrants in a twenty-five-year period. Of that number, approximately 250,000 Jews came from the central states of Europe (they are often referred to as German Jews even though only about half actually came from German-speaking areas). Beginning in the early 1880s another major wave started, and that wave reached its peak in 1914, just before the outbreak of World War I. During the last two decades of the nineteenth century, there were more than eight million immigrants to the United States. That number included slightly more than half a million Jews, most of whom came from eastern Europe.

All nineteenth-century immigrants, including Jews, tended to come to the United States during the period in which the industrial revolution was creating turmoil and upheaval in their countries of origin. Since industrialization began in northern and western Europe and then moved west and south, it can be assumed that whenever a large stream of people left a country, the industrial revolution had begun to impact that area.

Most Jews coming to America settled initially in and around the New York City area. During the mid-nineteenth century, however, Philadelphia, Cincinnati, and Baltimore attracted sizable numbers of Jews, while in the 1880s and 1890s Jewish immigrants also went to cities like Boston, Pittsburgh, Cleveland, Detroit, and Chicago. Also in the middle of the nineteenth century, hundreds if not thousands of Jewish newcomers put packs on their backs and peddled in the backcountry, settling down when they had made enough money to open a store. Many of these establishments later became major department stores in cities like Dallas, Texas; Atlanta, Georgia; and Omaha, Nebraska. Likewise, stores in Arizona, New Mexico, Colorado, Oklahoma, or Arkansas often had their origins in small businesses opened by Jewish immigrants.

Occupations and Social Status

Most Jews engaged in retail businesses because they found it difficult to get hired in other industries by non-Jews. On the other hand, many Jews throughout the country were able to start and build their firms with credit provided by fellow Jews in the United States. A small number of Jews engaged in banking, and some of them, including the Seligman brothers, Solomon Loeb, and the Lehman brothers, eventually opened major banking houses. New York City, where most of the Jews in the United States lived, provided myriad opportunities for both the self-employed and menial laborers, many of whom found employment in the garment industry, as well as in printing, painting, and other blue-collar occupations. A much smaller percentage of Jewish women worked outside of the home compared with the number of other European women. Unmarried Jewish women often found jobs sewing, while both daughters and wives worked in family businesses with their parents and husbands. Some women assumed the reigns of leadership upon the death of their spouse. Throughout the country one also found Jewish widows running boardinghouses.

Economically, the Jews who arrived in the middle of the nineteenth century moved up the ladder of success more quickly than the east Europeans who came at the end of the century. In 1894, for example, it was estimated that two-thirds of all the Jewish families in the United States had servants. Most of the east Europeans, however, who started coming en masse at the end of the century, barely lived above what we now regard as the poverty line.

The earlier Jewish arrivals, who had moved up the socioeconomic ladder, often resented those who came later. The earlier immigrants had already acculturated, often lived in substantial homes, interacted with non-Jews in business and politics, and, to all outward appearances, looked like other Americans. The newcomers, on the other hand, were perceived as poor, more devoutly orthodox in their religious practices, European in their dress and mannerisms, and dependent on Yiddish as their language of communication. All of these characteristics embarrassed and alarmed established American Jews, who feared that the newcomers might engender or lead to the intensification of anti-Semitism among Christian Americans. On the other hand, acculturated Jews also felt responsible for their coreligionists and sought to establish orphanages, hospitals, recreational centers, educational facilities, and newspapers to help their brethren adjust to life in the United States. They felt the need not only to assist their Jewish "cousins," but also to help acculturate them as quickly as possible.

The half-million east European Jews who arrived in the last two decades of the nineteenth century were the forerunners of more than a million others, and they eventually outnumbered the Germans Jews who had come before them. They too established their own institutions and communal organizations, and during the first half of the twentieth century the two groups lived uneasily with one another.

One major area of difference between the more established Jews whose ancestors had come in the middle of the nineteenth century and the east Europeans who came later revolved around Jewish religious practices. The newcomers adhered to a much more rigid orthodox code of worship; those who had come earlier in the century were more likely to have embraced Reform Judaism, which reflected the need of some Jews to adapt the practices of their faith to the modern world. Reform Judaism had its origins in central Europe and in South Carolina, as well, and during the 1840s became a factor in American Jewish life.

When looking back at nineteenth-century Jewish immigrants one can easily say that practically all came for similar economic opportunities but that conditions in the United States differed at their respective times of arrival. Whereas the mid-nineteenth-century wave of newcomers immigrated to both urban and rural areas, at the end of the century, Jewish immigrants settled for the most part in urban areas where they could find hundreds of thousands of others who shared their culture; this tendency delayed acculturation to a greater extent than it had for their forerunners, who had had a greater need to adapt quickly to a predominantly Christian world.

See also **Anti-Semitism; Immigration and Immigrants,** *subentries on* **Anti-immigrant Sentiment, Central and Eastern Europe, The Immigrant Experience; Judaism.**

Bibliography

Diner, Hasia R. *A Time for Gathering: The Second Migration, 1820–1880* Baltimore: Johns Hopkins University Press, 1992.

Cohen, Naomi W. *Encounter with Emancipation: The German Jews in the United States, 1830–1914.* Philadelphia: Jewish Publication Society, 1984.

Korn, Bertram Wallace. *Eventful Years and Experiences: Studies in Nineteenth Century American Jewish History.* Cincinnati: American Jewish Archives, 1954.

LEONARD DINNERSTEIN

SCANDINAVIA AND FINLAND

Although extending well into the twentieth century, the transatlantic migration from the five Nordic countries of Norway, Sweden, Denmark, Iceland, and Finland was to a great extent a nineteenth-century phenomenon. In 1800, as the new century dawned, these nations existed politically within the realms of two kingdoms, Denmark-Norway and Sweden. Finland, until 1809 an integral part of Sweden, was thereafter a grand duchy under the Russian tsar until its independence as a republic in 1917; in 1814 Denmark lost Norway, which as an independent kingdom entered into a union with Sweden under a common king until 1905, when the union was dissolved. Iceland declared its independence from Denmark as a republic in 1944. Because a striving for political unity of the entire region—based on ethnic, linguistic, and historical commonalities—has characterized the history of the North back to the age of the Vikings, migrations old and new should be viewed within a common Nordic geographic and cultural framework.

Emigration from the North to the United States started dramatically—and in a Nordic context early—on 4 July 1825, with the sailing of the tiny sloop *Restauration* from Stavanger on the southwestern coast of Norway. The pathfinders of Norwegian emigration numbered fifty-three crew and passengers, including a baby girl born during the fourteen-week voyage. They landed in the port of New York on 9 October 1825 and became known as the "Sloopers" because of the type of ship on which they crossed the Atlantic. Their agent, Cleng Peerson, sometimes referred to as "the father of Norwegian immigration," had investigated and reported back on opportunities in the New World, and he met them as they debarked. These Norwegian immigrants were Quakers, Quaker sympathizers, and Haugeans—pietistic followers of the lay preacher Hans Nielsen Hauge—who left the homeland because of persecution by the religiously monopolistic Norwegian Lutheran state church. In addition to America's promise of economic betterment, they were attracted by its religious liberties, communicated to them by English Quakers with whom they had contact.

Religion did not remain a major force in Nordic emigration, although the Swedish farmer-preacher Erik Jansson in the mid-1840s led members of his sect to Bishop Hill, Illinois, where they established a colony. An earlier group of Swedes with Gustaf Unonius as leader had left in 1841. The early Norwegian and Swedish colonies established bridgeheads in America and gave information and encouragement for later emigration. From 1836, emigration from Norway became a yearly phenomenon; it had its rise in the 1840s as the Swedish movement was getting under way. These Norwegian and Swedish pioneers left to obtain land, which for several decades attracted footloose peasants to America from the North. Danish group emigration began in the 1850s, though some Danes had left earlier; Danish emigration was, however, not nearly as extensive as that from Norway and Sweden. Icelanders did not follow the examples of other Scandinavians; only from the 1870s did Iceland experience a brief but intense departure of its citizens. The most popular Icelandic destination was not the United States, but Canada. The Finnish overseas migration commenced in the late 1860s; many Finnish emigrants found work in the mines in northern Michigan.

Mass emigration occurred in the post–Civil War decades. Heroic ethnic figures such as the Norwegian colonel Hans Christian Heg of Civil War fame and the Swedish naval engineer John Ericsson, who built the Union's first ironclad, the USS *Monitor,* helped to create a new patriotism among the immigrants and a sense of having earned a legitimate place in America. Later immigrants admired prominent politicians like Knute Nelson, who as United States senator from Minnesota from 1895 to 1923 was the first midwestern Scandinavian to attain political prominence at the national level.

In numbers, occupants of the Nordic countryside dominated the mass overseas movement. With the exception of Sweden, however, proportionately more people left an urban area than left a rural environment. The ebb and flow of the movement was largely dictated by the needs of the American marketplace, which, as the migration from the 1870s onward increasingly responded to the American urban economy and industrial growth, changed the character of the exodus from a family movement in the early period to an individual youth migration that was predominantly male toward the end of the nineteenth century. The immigrants were mainly ordinary workers, but as the homelands modernized, engineers, artists, and professionally trained people responded to the lure of America. Improved transatlantic communication created an international labor market and a greater exchange of ideas and people across the Atlantic.

In its basic contours the Nordic exodus did not differ substantially from the general contemporaneous European overseas movement. Mass emigration throughout Europe followed an unparalleled growth in population and occurred during a time of fundamental demographic and social change. The Nordic countries grew from 5.2 million people in 1800 to 7.9 million in 1850, and, despite a massive departure of citizens, by 1900 the population had increased to 12.5 million. It has been claimed that industrialization and emigration saved the Nordic countries as surplus populations were siphoned off through transoceanic migration. Nearly 2.5 million people left the sparsely populated Nordic countries before World War I; Norway accounted for 30 percent and had the highest proportionate rate throughout the era of mass migration; Sweden contributed 44 percent, Denmark and Finland each approximately 12 percent, and Iceland less than 1 percent.

Historians have found a correlation between the

latitude of the emigrants' location in the homeland and the latitude of settlement in North America. It is a circumstance that can be explained in part by the timing of emigration as it related to the westward movement of the American frontier. The Icelanders went to Manitoba and Saskatchewan; the Finns to northern Michigan and northern Minnesota; the Norwegians to the upper Middle West; the Swedes to the Middle West; and the Danes to Wisconsin, Iowa, Nebraska, and California. The Middle West and Great Plains were clearly the most important destinations for nineteenth-century Nordics, but they also settled in substantial numbers on both coasts.

Nordic harmony in America suffered defeat on many occasions. It was obvious that nationalistic feelings could not entirely surrender to a common Scandinavian or Nordic identity. Nordic immigrants were fragmented along national lines, and deep divisions existed within each nationality. Finnish political radicalism in a segment of that population created both extreme tensions within the Finnish American community and strong prejudice against it.

But, when the variables relating to time of emigration and place of settlement are taken into account, the experiences of Nordic immigrants in America exhibit remarkable similarities. Rural areas, for instance, exerted a powerful attraction on all Nordic nationalities. They became dedicated to the family farm as a way of life and exalted traditional rural values. Unique to the Finns was a movement from their initial employment in mining and industry to subsistence farming. The Lutheran Church was influential in the rural settlements and represented the most visible link among the Nordic immigrants themselves and of this population to the homelands. Scandinavian cooperation manifested itself most clearly in large multiethnic centers; complex ethnic communities were constructed to serve the needs of the immigrants. Nordic accord was evidenced in residential and occupational patterns in the building trades—which became a special economic niche for Nordic men—and in the maritime activities of fishing and shipping, in political mobilization with a strong loyalty to the Republican party, in public commemorations, and in intermarriage, which promoted interethnic assimilation. A Nordic melting pot existed in the Scandinavian urban social world. In general the American environment encouraged the immigrants to find a common Scandinavian ground. Nevertheless, individual national identities were not lost in America, in urban or rural surroundings; rather they were celebrated as the immigrants and their children adjusted to a multicultural American environment and the demands of American society.

Bibliography

Hvidt, Kristian. *Flight to America: The Social Background of 300,000 Danish Emigrants.* New York: Academic, 1975.

Hvidt, Kristian, ed. *Emigration fra Norden indtil 1. Verdenskrig: Rapporter til Det Nordiske Historikermøde i København 1871, 9–12 August.* Copenhagen: Fr. Bagges Kgl. Hofbogtrykkeri, 1971.

Kastrup, Allan. *The Swedish Heritage in America.* St. Paul, Minn.: Swedish Council of America, 1975.

Lovoll, Odd S. *The Promise of America: A History of the Norwegian-American People.* Rev. ed. Minneapolis: University of Minnesota Press, 1999.

Lovoll, Odd S., ed. *Nordics in America: The Future of Their Past.* Northfield, Minn.: Norwegian-American Historical Association, 1993.

———, ed. *Scandinavians and Other Immigrants in Urban America.* Northfield, Minn.: St. Olaf College Press, 1985.

Nielsen, George R. *The Danish Americans.* Boston: Twayne, 1981.

Norman, Hans, and Harald Runblom. *Transatlantic Connections: Nordic Migration to the New World after 1800.* Oslo: Norwegian University Press, 1987.

Ross, Carl. *The Finn Factor in American Labor, Culture, and Society.* New York Mills, Minn.: Parta, 1977.

Semmingsen, Ingrid. *Norway to America: A History of the Migration.* Minneapolis: University of Minnesota Press, 1978.

ODD S. LOVOLL

SOUTHERN EUROPE

The majority of immigrants to the United States from southern Europe—Italy, Greece, and the Balkan Peninsula—were part of the immigration wave during the nineteenth century's last two decades. Primarily poor, male peasants, they came to make their fortunes, supplying a large, transitory unskilled labor force. Between 1820, when the U.S. Census Bureau began keeping immigration statistics, and 1900 more than 1.1 million immigrants arrived in the United States from southern Europe. These statistics do not, however, reveal the repatriation rate. Scholars estimate that about half of the southern Europeans who came eventually returned home.

Italians were the predominant southern European group, amounting to more than a million in the census count. Prior to the 1880s most were merchants and artisans from northern Italy. Some, like Giuseppe Garibaldi, were nationalist exiles who had fought to unite Italy. After Italian unification in 1870, poor, rural peasants from southern Italy became the dominant immigrant group.

Greece contributed a smaller number of immigrants. In the 1820s American supporters of Greek independence sponsored the migration of forty orphans, and at mid-century a small number of Greek fishermen and businesspeople arrived. The new immigration in the 1870s began with males from Sparta, and within a decade peasants from the entire rural population followed.

Balkan immigrants, primarily Croatians, Serbs, and Slovenes, also came in small numbers, especially at the beginning of the century. Serbian and Croatian sailors and fishermen settled on the Gulf Coast in the 1830s. About the same time Catholic missionaries, such as the Reverend Frederic Baraga and other Slovenes, settled in Michigan, Minnesota, and the Dakotas. Like other new immigrants, Balkans flowed into the country in larger numbers late in the century.

Most southern Europeans, who had lived in rural areas in their homelands, amassed in cities in the United States because they equated agricultural work with hardship. They planned to return home once they made enough money, so they also sought the higher wages that urban, industrial jobs offered. Owning land would tie them to America more than they wished. Once established, the urban enclaves attracted more immigrants of the same ethnicity.

Throughout the century Italians preferred urban settlements. Even before the Civil War, Italian districts existed in Boston, New York, San Francisco, and New Orleans. When mass migration began in the 1880s, the majority located in such large cities as New York, Chicago, and Philadelphia. Some established agricultural communities in Texas, New Jersey, Wisconsin, and California. A few Italians lived in the mining regions of Pennsylvania and Michigan's Upper Peninsula. Greeks also centered in urban areas, particularly New York, Chicago, and the mill towns of New England. California attracted Greeks, who established a significant community in San Francisco.

Balkan immigrants went to the Midwest, the West, and the Gulf Coast. In the 1830s Croat sailors settled in New Orleans; Biloxi, Mississippi; and Mobile, Alabama. During the gold and silver rushes of the 1840s and 1850s, Croats also went to California, Nevada, and Arizona. Later they preferred industrial Chicago. Slovenes congregated in the mining towns of Michigan, Minnesota, and Montana, and Chicago and Cleveland became important urban centers for them in the 1880s and 1890s. Serbs settled in north-

Italian Quarter, New York City. Italian men return to Mulberry Street, in the heart of the city's Italian enclave, after a day's work. Many Italian men in urban areas found jobs in construction. From *Harper's Weekly*, 1890. LIBRARY OF CONGRESS

ern industrial cities, mining areas of Ohio and Pennsylvania, lumbering regions in the North and West, and port cities on the Gulf of Mexico.

Many factors convinced southern European immigrants to leave their homes. The commercialization and inefficiency of agriculture, industrialization, and land shortages were the most prominent. Southern Europeans saw opportunities to make money in the United States and responded to positive reports from family members and friends who had immigrated, enticements of labor recruiters, and advertisements by shipping companies.

Italian conditions were typical. Poor northern Italians began their exodus as early as the 1840s. Southern Italians left in droves starting in 1880, and sometimes entire villages went to the United States. Greeks began seeking prosperity in America around the middle of the century, when a small number of fishermen found work on the Great Lakes, the Mississippi River, and the Gulf of Mexico. By the 1870s Greeks left Sparta, and in the 1890s emigration escalated in response to crop failures, an indifferent government, and a poor economy. Rural peasants from the Balkans also migrated for economic reasons. Slovenes began arriving in the 1850s because their farms could not sustain the population. The wave of Balkan immigration started in the 1880s.

Southern Europeans, overwhelmingly young males, immigrated hoping to better their families' lives. They wished to make quick money in the United States, then return home. Therefore, they accepted jobs that required hard labor but few skills, gravitating toward manufacturing, food processing, mining, and construction. Many worked in seasonal jobs, arriving in spring when work began and returning home after it ended. Most did not become wealthy but did well enough to forward money to Europe or send for their families.

Typically Italians were unskilled laborers, but they held other jobs as well. A large number worked in the construction industry, building railroads, subways, roads, and bridges. Some, especially women, worked in textile mills and the garment industry. Mining rarely attracted Italians, but a few followed that line. Italians fished off San Francisco, and they were employed as fishermen, stevedores, and longshoremen in New Orleans. Others owned businesses, selling fruits, vegetables, pasta, and candy; and some, including children, peddled wares. A small number of Italians were restaurateurs, bankers, and civil servants.

The padrone, or agent, was a central figure in Italian labor. Prior to 1885 agents recruited laborers in Italy, but after the practice was outlawed there they shifted their efforts to the United States. Padrones, who understood the immigrants' language and culture, acted as intermediaries between newcomers and business owners. Each worker paid the padrone a commission in exchange for a job. Often agents hired laborers in New York or Chicago and shipped them to job sites. Padrones paid wages, wrote letters, acted as bankers, and supplied room and board. Not all agents exploited immigrants, but those who did tarnished the reputation of all. The Italian padrone system flourished from 1880 to 1900. Similar systems were common for most non-English-speaking immigrant groups. Although the padrone system has superficial similarities to the activities of the mafia in the twentieth century, Italian crime bosses did not establish themselves in the United States until the 1920s.

Greeks held similar jobs. Late in the century Greeks constructed railroads, sold fruits and vegetables, and shined shoes; and they were restaurateurs, confectioners, and peddlers. Beginning in the 1850s many ran import-export firms out of New York, New Orleans, and Savannah. Like the Italians, some Greeks recruited workers under a padrone system.

Balkan immigrants tended toward manufacturing, lumbering, and mining gold, silver, copper, iron, and coal. In the 1880s they began moving to cities like Cleveland and Chicago to work in factories. Many cut timber in West Virginia and in the West, while still others became busboys, dishwashers, or peddlers.

Life in the United States contrasted sharply with life in Europe. Most men left families and wives at home, and women who did immigrate worked outside the home for the first time. American cities were not prepared to accommodate large influxes of people, and the tenements constructed in the 1880s were unsanitary and unsafe. Those on work gangs lived in boxcars or shanties. American food, which took a good portion of immigrants' pay, seemed strange to those used to a Mediterranean diet.

Immigrants preserved their ethnicity, clustering and socializing only with others of their ethnic groups. They established their own clubs, church congregations, and parochial schools. Foreign-language newspapers proliferated, keeping immigrants in touch with their homelands and translating American ways, and publishers became ethnic leaders. Giovanni Francesco Secchi de Casali and Charles Barsotti published two Italian newspapers, and the Reverend Joseph Buh established a Slovene newspaper. Work-related injuries or fatalities were common, so ethnic groups established mutual benefit societies that reimbursed families for lost pay.

Responding to the pressures of life in the United States, immigrants also assimilated. They learned English at immigrant schools, dressed like other

Italian Railroad Workers. Italian workmen lay the street railroad line at Union Square, New York City. From *Harper's Weekly*, 26 September 1891. LIBRARY OF CONGRESS

Americans, and Americanized their courtship practices. Often the second and third generations expressed a wish to become more American than their parents, creating family tensions.

Typically southern Europeans received a cold welcome from native-born Americans. Numerous Americans were frightened by the large numbers of immigrants, who did not speak English, wore peasant clothing, and were mostly Catholic or Orthodox. Nativists worried that immigration brought radicalism and lawlessness. Older immigrant groups, like the Irish, did not accept newcomers any more readily.

Americans attempted to reduce the impact of foreigners in several ways. Reformers established schools to aid in assimilation and campaigned for child labor laws to encourage immigrant children toward an education instead of work. Prior to the 1920s only a small percentage of southern Europeans attended school past sixth grade. Further, Protestants tried unsuccessfully to convert Catholic populations. During the last quarter of the century the federal government tightened restrictions on aliens. By 1900 criminals, prostitutes, lunatics, polygamists, those under labor contracts, or people with diseases could not enter the United States. Congress added more limitations in the twentieth century.

In part southern European immigrants' attitudes toward politics prompted restrictions. Because most were transient, they did not learn English, become citizens, or take an interest in American elections. Consequently they lacked political power, especially at the state and national levels. Those who did vote generally followed the suggestions of community leaders and ethnic newspapers, which revolved around U.S. relations with their homelands or rewards city ward bosses offered them.

Southern European immigrants were considered new immigrants because they came in significant numbers only at the end of the century; they did not speak English; the majority were not Protestant like most Germans, Scandinavians, and British; and they settled in urban areas to pursue industrial work as opposed to farming. The wave of southern European immigration continued into the twentieth century. The tide rose until the onset of World War I in 1914 and resumed after the armistice in 1919. Only quota laws in the 1920s slowed their numbers.

See also **Anti-Catholicism; Catholicism; Labor Force; Language; Lumber and Timber Industry; Mining and Extraction; Politics,** *subentry on* **Machines and Bosses; Railroad Industry, The; Work.**

Bibliography

Govorchin, Gerald Gilbert. *Americans from Yugoslavia.* Gainesville: University of Florida Press, 1961.

Iorizzo, Luciano J., and Salvatore Mondello. *The Italian Americans.* Rev. ed. Boston: G. K. Hall, 1980.

La Sorte, Michael. *La Merica: Images of Italian Greenhorn Experience.* Philadelphia: Temple University Press, 1985.

Moskos, Charles C. *Greek Americans: Struggle and Success.* 2d ed. New Brunswick, N.J.: Transaction, 1989.

Saloutos, Theodore. *The Greeks in the United States.* Cambridge, Mass.: Harvard University Press, 1964.

Scourby, Alice. *The Greek Americans.* Boston: Twayne, 1984.

Thernstrom, Stephan, ed. *Harvard Encyclopedia of American Ethnic Groups.* Cambridge, Mass.: Belknap Press of Harvard University Press, 1980.

RACHAEL L. DRENOVSKY

THE OTTOMAN EMPIRE AND THE MIDDLE EAST

Although Christopher Columbus chose a Spanish Arab, a Moor, as his primary translator for his trip to India in 1492, the Arabs were latecomers to the United States. Full-scale Arab immigration did not begin until the late nineteenth century, reaching its peak at the onset of World War I. Small numbers of Turks, Persians, Egyptians, Omanis, and others came with a larger group of Armenians. However, the sizable majority of nineteenth-century immigrants from the Middle East were Arabs from the Levant, that is, the littoral bordering the eastern Mediterranean, known then as the Ottoman *vilayet* of Syria, encompassing Syria, Lebanon, and Palestine. Indeed, Lebanese and Palestinians were referred to and referred to themselves as Syrians.

Syrians

Incomplete U.S. immigration records up to 1898 listed Syrians under the unnerving label "Turkey in Asia." Official sources recorded that 24,398 Syrians arrived in the United States by 1900, though actual numbers were probably closer to 30,000. By the turn of the century the number of Armenian immigrants was about half that, 14,000.

The first Arab adventurers to the New World embodied the intrepidness, daring, and entrepreneurialism of their later Syrian brethren. Syrians established their first colony on the Lower West Side of Manhattan, directly across the island from their Semitic cousins, the Jews, on the Lower East Side. It seemed the Syrians did not want to be too far from Old World relationships or for that matter from the point of debarkation, Ellis Island, which is visible from the Lower West Side shoreline.

In addition to Louis de Torre, Columbus's Moor-ish translator, other early wayfarers to America were from North Africa. One North Carolina family, the Wahabs, claim to trace their ancestry back to an Algerian shipwreck in 1779. Algeria then was stocking George Washington's depleted cavalry with horses. In 1790 South Carolina made a distinction in its code of laws between "sundry Moors, Subjects of the Emperor of Morocco" and blacks, giving the former the voting rights denied the latter. Strangely enough, a century later Syrians were declared a "yellow race" and were denied the right to vote on that basis. The chronic question of what color hole to fit the Arabs in compounded the identity crisis of a people who had been dominated by the Ottoman Turks for five hundred years and who had difficulty showing fealty outside their own villages.

The following three pre–Civil War immigrants from the Arab world established roots in the United States. Jeremiah Mahomet raised horses and worked in real estate in Frederick, Maryland, in the early 1800s. In 1854 Antonios Bishallany followed a New York businessman, for whom he had been a dragoman, or interpreter, from the Holy Land to New York City to become the man's butler. Hadji Ali, also known as "Hi Jolly," imported thirty-two camels to the United States from Cairo in 1856 for Secretary of War Jefferson Davis's fruitless attempt to carve a "camel highway" to the American Southwest from Texas.

The first wave of Syrian immigration to the United States from the Ottoman Empire, hundreds by 1887 and thousands by 1891, peaked at 9,210 in 1913. They came for many reasons, some push factors and some pull factors. The events that pushed the Syrians away from their land included a shattering of the religious mosaic that broke into full-scale civil war between Maronite Catholics and Druze in 1860; economic gyrations, including a horrific silkworm blight caused by locusts from 1865 to 1871 that virtually destroyed Lebanon's prosperous silk trade; a land squeeze and overpopulation, especially in the Lebanon mountains; and the hard hand of the Turkish sultan, who threw Arabs into the front lines of battle during World War I, a fight in which the Arabs had no interest or stake. The Arab mortality rate was high, 17 percent. This all culminated in the most traumatic event in the early Syrians' lives, mass starvation in the Levant during World War I that killed 100,000 people, one-quarter of Lebanon's population alone.

As for pull factors, Christian missionaries from New England went to Syria early in the nineteenth century and stimulated the growth of Arabic printing presses; established schools, such as the Syrian Protestant College, which became the American University of Beirut; and introduced medical assistance into

Turkish Immigrant, New York City. A Turkish immigrant and his wagon on the streets of New York, 1898. LIBRARY OF CONGRESS

this province of the Ottoman Empire that lacked social services. The French and British took sides with the Maronites and Druze, respectively, in the Lebanese civil war of 1860. But the Americans were unbiased, and the populace respected them for that stand. A Druze businessman in New York called the Americans "angels in our land" (Orfalea, *Before the Flames,* p. 56). Not surprisingly, when the situation in Syria and Lebanon darkened toward the century's end and during World War I, the United States became the land of first choice as a safe haven. Ellis Island was known as *bayt al-hurriyah* (the house of freedom). One pregnant Syrian woman, who was detained on Ellis Island with trachoma, gave birth to a girl there. When the woman and her baby finally proceeded to New York City, the family proudly named the infant "Elsie" in honor of the island of first berth.

Armenians

A somewhat similar set of push and pull factors led Armenians to the United States. Before 1890 grind-

ing poverty and taxes under the Ottomans lured this group of tough-minded, independent-thinking mountain people to emigrate. A few Armenians entered the United States as early as 1834. Indeed, thirty Armenians fought for the Union during the American Civil War, and three Armenian doctors nursed the wounded in a Philadelphia hospital.

Unlike the Syrian situation, however, a series of vicious pogroms toward the end of the nineteenth century propelled Armenians out of their native land. In 1876 loyalists of the repressive sultan Abdülhamid II burned the Armenian headquarters in Istanbul, forcing many democratic-minded students to emigrate and pursue studies at Princeton, Yale, Amherst, and other American universities. The big blow came in the period 1894–1896, when at least 100,000 Armenians were massacred throughout Ottoman Turkey. The out-migration swelled, and new Armenian immigrant communities formed in Massachusetts, New York, Rhode Island, and especially California, where in 1908 the Armenian writer William Saroyan was born in Fresno. The pogroms culminated in what some have termed the first genocide of the twentieth century, the killing of at least one million Armenians by the Turks in World War I.

Destinations and Occupations

By 1900 more than half of the Syrian immigrants lived in New York City, most of them crowded in with the "shanty" Irish, with whom they often squabbled, on Washington Street in the Lower West Side. It was the closest area the early Syrians had to a "little Italy." Washington Street institutions, such as the Shiek restaurant, over time moved to Atlantic Avenue in Brooklyn. The Syrians resurrected their silk industry in Manhattan and New Jersey. By 1924 twenty-five Syrian silk factories operated in Paterson and West Hoboken. On Washington Street thirty-five establishments, almost all Syrian, manufactured kimonos. Syrians ran most of the Madeira lace outlets, and half the sweaters produced in New York were made by the early Syrians. The N. P. and J. Trabulsi Company was called the king of the woolen knits. F. A. Kalil on Broadway won a national competition for the right to use "Red Grange" on a sweater. Armenians often lived in Syrian neighborhoods and intermarried with Syrians. Some Armenians took up various garment trades as well, while others imported rugs from the native land.

Life in a sweatshop was a hard one. Pay was poor, $10 a week for men and half that for women, and conditions were miserable, sweltering in the summer and freezing in the winter. Because a peddler could earn between $200 and $1,500 a year, many Syrians took to the road. Soon the olive-skinned Syrian peddler carrying his *qashshah* case of laces, needles, threads, and notions of all kinds was a staple of the American landscape, even in the farthest reaches of the country. By 1910 it was a $60 million business. Years after the peddler boom, the peddler in Richard Rodgers and Oscar Hammerstein's 1943 Broadway musical *Oklahoma!* was a Syrian named Ali Hakim.

Syrian peddlers went everywhere. From Washington Street in New York City they fanned toward Utica and Buffalo. From New Orleans they peddled up the Mississippi River and established a major colony in Vicksburg, Mississippi, because its promontory along the water reminded them of Lebanon along the sea. They peddled in border towns along the Rio Grande and into Texas. The founders of both Haggar Slacks in Dallas and Farah Slacks in El Paso were originally peddlers. Soon Syrian settlements grew up in South Dakota, Iowa, Oklahoma, Arizona, Washington State, and California. The father of Casey Kasem, a popular twentieth-century American disc jockey, was a Druze peddler who arrived from Lebanon in 1895 by fording the Rio Grande.

Some early Syrians worked in factories. Detroit, destined to have the largest twentieth-century Arab American population, had fifty Lebanese Christians in town in 1900. Sixteen years later 555 Syrian men worked at the Ford car plants. Syrians were numerous in the woolen and cotton textile mills of Lawrence and Fall River, Massachusetts.

Muslim communities sprang up in places like Toledo, Ohio, where Arabs worked in the box factories or Willis Auto, and Michigan City, Indiana, where Muslim Syrians fabricated Pullman train cars. One man who arrived in Newark, New Jersey, at the end of the nineteenth century found employment in a machine shop for one year, then quit, saying, "I see how factories work" (Orfalea, p. 84). This man was Nathra Nader, father of the consumer advocate Ralph Nader.

A few Arabs tried farming. Ross, North Dakota, was founded in 1900 by Syrians, who later built the first mosque in the United States. The California Armenians developed prodigious farms in the San Joaquin Valley, celebrated by Saroyan in *My Name Is Aram* (1940).

A few Syrians were Jews, but most of the early Syrians and all the Armenians were Christians. By 1890 the Melkite, Maronite, and Syrian Orthodox communities each had established one church in Manhattan, and Armenian Catholics had built their first church in Jersey City, New Jersey.

Though the arts were not pushed by Syrian immigrants struggling to make a living in the New World, the native Arab love of poetry transplanted itself with startling results. In 1895 two young men who were destined to launch a revolution in Arab letters emigrated with their families from Lebanon. Amin Rihani immigrated with his silk-making family to Manhattan, and Kahlil Gibran, author of *The Prophet* (1923), immigrated with his impoverished mother to Boston.

Syrians were acclaimed as hardy and venturesome. Nevertheless, in 1899 the Associated Charities of Boston reported its opinion that "next to the Chinese, who can never in any real sense be American, [the Syrians] are the most foreign of all foreigners" (Orfalea, p. 78). On 24 October 1905 a murder on Washington Street made the front page of the *New York Times*, speaking of "wild-eyed Syrians [showing] the glint of steel in two hundred swarthy hands." In contrast, in 1904 Lucius Miller wrote: "In his love of law and order the Syrian cannot be excelled. . . . The universal testimony of the police authorities is that there is no more peaceful and law-abiding race in New York City" (p. 51).

By the end of the nineteenth century many Syrians had turned their entrepreneurial instincts away from peddling to settle into communities, where they set up general stores, auto repair shops, restaurants, and garment and furniture manufacturing plants. When immigration slowed in 1924, 150,000 Syrians lived in the United States. During the twentieth century the Arab American community grew to two million. Involved in almost every area of American commercial life, Arab Americans had the second-largest rate of business ownership of any U.S. ethnic group. Among those businesses was the Kinko's photocopy chain, one thousand stores at the end of the twentieth century, founded by a man whose Syrian grandfather was a garment maker who started as a peddler.

See also **Entrepreneurs; Literature,** *subentries on* **Poetry, The Influence of Foreign Literature; Non-Western Religions; Work.**

Bibliography

Hitti, Philip K. *The Syrians in America.* New York: George H. Doran, 1924.

Hooglund, Eric J., ed. *Crossing the Waters: Arabic-Speaking Immigrants to the United States before 1940.* Washington, D.C.: Smithsonian Institution Press, 1987.

Houghton, Louis Seymour. "The Syrians in the United States." *Survey* 26, nos. 1–4 (1911): 480–495, 647–665, 786–802, 957–968.

Kayal, Philip M., and Joseph M. Kayal. *The Syrian-Lebanese in America: A Study in Religion and Assimilation.* New York: Twayne, 1975.

Miller, Lucius Hopkins. *Our Syrian Population: A Study of the Syrian Communities of Greater New York.* 1904. Reprint, San Francisco: Reed, 1969.

Mirak, Robert. *Torn between Two Lands: Armenians in America, 1890 to World War I.* Cambridge, Mass.: Harvard University Press, 1983.

Naff, Alixa. *Becoming American: The Early Arab Immigrant Experience.* Carbondale: Southern Illinois University Press, 1985.

Orfalea, Gregory. *Before the Flames: A Quest for the History of Arab Americans.* Austin: University of Texas Press, 1988.

Orfalea, Gregory, and Sharif Elmusa, eds. *Grape Leaves: A Century of Arab American Poetry.* Northampton, Mass.: Interlink, 2000.

Rihbany, Abraham Mitrie. *A Far Journey.* Boston: Houghton Mifflin, 1914.

Wertsman, Vladimir. *The Americans in America, 1618–1976.* Dobbs Ferry, N.Y.: Oceana, 1978.

Younis, Adele L. *The Coming of the Arabic-Speaking People to the United States.* Staten Island, N.Y.: Center for Migration Studies, 1995.

GREGORY ORFALEA

CANADA

Economic circumstance or opportunity generally framed the nineteenth-century migration of British North Americans to the United States. On the eastern seaboard rising U.S. tariffs rendered Canadian fisheries and forestry uncompetitive, and after the 1830s approximately 427,000 residents of New Brunswick and Nova Scotia pulled up stakes and moved to New England. Elsewhere, once the arable land south of the Canadian Shield was filled, aggressive land and transportation companies ferried aspiring farm families to the U.S. Northeast and Midwest. In response to these and other inducements, 521,000 Ontarians immigrated to New York, Michigan, Wisconsin, and Minnesota in the sixty years after 1840. The greatest migration south was that of French Canadians fleeing Quebec's overworked countryside and failing timber industry. Between 1840 and 1900, 582,000 French Canadians migrated to Massachusetts, New York, and Michigan to work in factories and the forests. In the 1850s alone an estimated 30,000 French Canadians left for the United States. Not always welcome because of their resistance to assimilation, these Francophone newcomers were soon labeled the Chinese of New England.

Although not all immigrants settled down, the majority did. The 1900 U.S. census recorded 1,179,461 Canadian-born residents: 785,461 English-speaking and 394,461 French-speaking. These figures represented almost one-quarter of the Canadian population recorded in 1901.

Uncounted in these statistics were the aboriginal peoples and métis, who had little reason to heed the boundary separating British North America and the United States. Untold thousands regularly crossed and recrossed the border in pursuit of game, especially the dwindling bison herds. Also unrecorded were fur company employees, whose activities acknowledged few borders even after the Oregon Territory settlement of June 1846 extended the forty-ninth parallel to the Pacific Coast as the boundary between British and American territory in the Far West.

Those who migrated south included a wide variety of individuals. The leaders of the failed revolt of 1836–1837, Louis-Joseph Papineau and William Lyon Mackenzie, sought refuge in the United States. During the Civil War it was estimated that more than fifty-three thousand Union soldiers were born in British North America, among them Fred Howe of the Twenty-third Ohio Regiment, who was the son of the Nova Scotian premier Joseph Howe. Others, such Edward Cunard Jr., son of the shipping magnate Sir Samuel Cunard, relocated to New York for business reasons, and the railway entrepreneur James J. Hill launched his railway empire in Canada before expanding into the U.S. market. After moving to Springfield, Massachusetts, James Naismith, improvising an indoor sport to fill the season between football and baseball, nailed a peach basket to the YMCA gymnasium wall in 1891, and basketball was born.

Many Canadian immigrants left a mark on U.S. society without completely abandoning their birthplace. British North Americans shared an economic motivation for relocating to the United States, and nineteenth-century French and English Canadians were, despite their migration, disproportionately uninterested in becoming naturalized American citizens.

See also **Canada.**

Bibliography

Brebner, John Bartlet. *North Atlantic Triangle.* Toronto: McClelland and Stewart, 1966.

Thompson, John Herd, and Stephen J. Randall. *Canada and the United States: Ambivalent Allies.* Montreal and Kingston, Ontario: McGill Queen's University Press, 1994.

JONATHAN SWAINGER

MEXICO AND LATIN AMERICA

Europeans dominated immigration to the United States during the 1800s, but Mexicans dominated Latin American immigration. Approximately one hundred thousand people of Mexican descent suddenly became residents of a foreign country when the United States acquired a vast territory after winning the Mexican War of 1846–1848. The Mexicans in the territories that became the states of California, Texas, New Mexico, and Arizona lived uneasily with whites after the Treaty of Guadalupe Hidalgo ended the war, and segregation was common. But the United States took no actions to impede Mexican immigration, and people from both sides moved freely across the border. The most significant reason Latin Americans, particularly Mexicans, immigrated was economics. They wanted greater socioeconomic mobility, and the United States needed labor. Much of their collective experience, however, was negative, owing to the social contexts they entered. Mexicans faced language barriers, and whites saw them as unequal.

Mexico's population steadfastly increased, especially during the second half of the nineteenth century. However, available land declined, and the rural regions offered less farmland. As a result, Mexicans anticipated more opportunities in the United States. Immigrants came mainly from rural backgrounds, and immigration increasingly became a family endeavor. Mexicans labored in family units as well as individually. They were more mobile than other Latin American immigrants. Mexicans immigrated particularly to California after the discovery of gold there in 1848. Immigrants also came from Chile, Argentina, and other South American nations in search of gold in California. Chileans responded fervently to the frantic search for gold. Chilean miners worked very hard alongside Mexicans, Frenchmen, Englishmen, and other Europeans in the streams and mountainsides in Northern California. Few people, however, got rich from the California gold rush. South Americans did not come into the United States in large numbers compared to other groups like the Europeans and Chinese. But when they did come to places like the West they were in search of new economic opportunities and the chance to better their social and financial lot as opposed to anything else.

By the 1880s the U.S. agricultural industry sought Mexican immigrant labor. Mexicans worked in the California sugar beet industry and in the cotton-growing regions of Texas. Mexican immigrants also toiled in the emerging railroad industry of the Southwest and in mining. U.S. labor organizations considered Mexicans a threat to domestic white labor, as the typical Latin American workers were young, uneducated, and willing to work for little pay in low-skill jobs.

The agriculture, railroad, and mining industries were nonurban industries and, unlike other Latin Americans who came to the United States, Mexican immigrants were a rural population. This set Mexicans' experience apart from that of other Latin Americans like Cubans, who immigrated to the United States in large numbers during the war for Cuban independence in the late 1860s. Cuban workers, professionals, and business leaders went to New York, Philadelphia, Boston, and the southeastern United States.

The Cuban cigar industry flourished in Key West, Florida, in the 1800s. The first cigar factory in that city began operating in 1831, and by the mid-1800s Key West had assumed the title as the cigar manufacturing capital of the world. During the Cuban Revolution in 1868, additional Cubans migrated to Key West so that by the end of the century there were more than one hundred cigar factories in Key West alone. The cigar industry was an invaluable connection between Key West and Cuba, and the Cuban culture thrived in southern Florida. Many of the Cubans who lived in Key West and worked in the cigar industry supported Cuba's struggle for independence from Spain. Some Cuban immigrants returned home after their country won independence in 1898.

Mexican and Latin American immigration to the United States in the nineteenth century was tied to the rise of the U.S. agricultural, railroad, and mining industries and to the socioeconomic conditions in the home countries. Compared with other groups, Latin Americans did not come into the United States in massive numbers in the 1800s. As the century progressed they overcame adversities and contributed to the unique, growing cultures of the United States.

See also **Agriculture; Barrios; California; Cuba; Labor Force; Language; Mexican Americans; Mexican War; Mexico; Mining and Extraction; Nationalism; Railroad Industry, The; Texas**

Bibliography

Briggs, Vernon M., Jr. *Immigration Policy and the American Labor Force.* Baltimore: Johns Hopkins University Press, 1984.

Glazer, Nathan, ed. *Clamor at the Gates: The New American Immigration.* San Francisco: Institute for Contemporary Studies, 1985.

Miller, E. Willard, and Ruby M. Miller. *United States Immigration: A Reference Handbook.* Santa Barbara, Calif.: ABC-CLIO, 1996.

Samora, Julian. *Los Mojados: The Wetback Story.* Notre Dame, Ind.: University of Notre Dame Press, 1971.

Santibáñez, Enrique. *Ensayo acerca de la inmigración Mexicana en los Estados Unidos* (Essay concerning Mexican immigration to the United States). San Antonio, Tex.: Clegg, 1930.

DAVID TREVIÑO

ASIA

Although few Chinese and even fewer Japanese came to the United States in the closing decades of the eighteenth century and the first four decades of the nineteenth, numerically significant immigration began at the time of the California gold rush of 1849. No other Asian groups came in significant numbers in the nineteenth century. Asian Indian, Filipino, and Korean immigration did not begin until the first decade of the twentieth century. The Immigration and Naturalization Service lists almost forty thousand immigrants from Turkey in the nineteenth century, two-thirds of whom were Greek, and about six thousand other immigrants originating in Asia. The latter were largely Middle Easterners who did not suffer the legal discriminations that were raised against first East Asians and then South Asians.

Chinese

Most of the roughly forty thousand Chinese who came to antebellum California were part of the migration of hundreds of thousands of gold seekers who flocked there from the rest of the United States; Latin America, largely Mexico and Chile; Europe, chiefly the British Isles and France; and Australia. The Chinese characters for the word "California" can be read as "gold mountain." Chinese, some of them from California, also participated in the Australian gold rush of 1854, and the Chinese characters for "Australia" can be read as "new gold mountain."

Chinese immigrants were predominantly male. Gender ratios were 18 to 1 or larger in every late-nineteenth-century census save that of 1870, which was defective. Most immigrants came from south Chinese counties, where many had families. Often denounced as coolies, that is, indentured laborers, they were in fact free people. Some historians have written that the Chinese were not really immigrants because most were sojourners or, as they called themselves, *gamsaanhack* (gold mountain guests). But members of many other immigrant groups were also involved in temporary, sometimes circular or back and forth migration. Many members of all immigrant groups who came intending to sojourn actually stayed, and some who planned to stay returned home. What set the Chinese and later the Japanese apart from members of other nineteenth-century immigrant groups was race.

The Chinese quickly became targets of discrimination in California and the rest of the West. A special foreign miners' tax was collected from them but not generally from other foreigners. Until 1870 Chinese could not testify in court against whites, and since federal law denied them the right to become naturalized, they were perpetual aliens. The original naturalization statute (1790) restricted that process to "free white persons." The statute was amended in 1870 to extend naturalization to "aliens of African nativity and to persons of African descent." Chinese and other East Asians and South Asians were not granted naturalization rights until a series of statutes between 1943 and 1952 eventually made naturalization color-blind.

Nineteenth-century entrepreneurs soon discovered that Chinese labor was vital to the development of the American West. The most prodigious feat of the Chinese workers was building the western leg of the first transcontinental railroad, and they were a major factor in railroad construction in both the western United States and Canada. They also were important in the development of hydraulic mining, agriculture, and light manufacturing, particularly shoes, clothing, and cigars. Charles Crocker, a principal of the Central Pacific Railroad, testified before a congressional committee in 1876, "If I had a big job of work to do . . . I should take Chinese labor . . . because of its greater reliability and steadiness, and their aptitude and capacity for hard work" (U.S. Senate, 44th Cong., 2d sess., 1877, S. Rept. 689, pp. 666–688).

Workingmen and their organizations felt otherwise. Their view was that the Chinese "worked cheap and smelled bad." At the end of the 1860s almost all supported the anti-Chinese campaign led by the Irish immigrant Denis Kearney, whose slogan was "the Chinese must go!" This agitation was eventually supported by almost every western politician. Most believed or claimed to believe that the Chinese were a threat both to American living standards and to American culture. The legislative result was the Chinese Exclusion Act of 1882, which did allow some Chinese immigration, as Table 1 indicates.

The anti-Chinese movement was accompanied by a high degree of mob violence, which was almost never punished by local authorities. From the 1860s through the 1880s assaults in both town and country killed dozens of unarmed Chinese. On the Pacific Coast anti-Chinese riots occurred from Los Angeles to Seattle and stretched as far east as Rock Springs, Wyoming, and Denver, Colorado. The most destructive urban violence of the century, the New York City draft riots of 1863, claimed Chinese victims, although it was alleged that Asians were incidental targets of opportunity to the rioters.

After the passage of the 1882 act, the Chinese American population declined steadily until 1930, as shown in Table 2. (Hawaii's population is not usually included in U.S. population figures until statehood in 1959.) Chinese immigrants, often described as largely impervious to American influences, quickly learned to use U.S. courts in sometimes successful attempts to protect their rights. Not surprisingly they were more successful in defending their property and less so in defending themselves against immigration statutes that they regarded as "laws harsh as tigers." Chinese cases, as the legal historians Charles McClain and Lucy Salyer have demonstrated, had a ma-

jor effect on two separate aspects of American law. They helped strengthen due process and equal protection jurisprudence under the Fourteenth Amendment and shaped newly developing U.S. immigration law, of which the Chinese were the major target for decades.

Most nineteenth-century Chinese Americans were laborers or all-but-anonymous merchants. But 120 Chinese youths were sent to Connecticut in the Chinese Educational Mission of 1872–1881, the first group of foreign students ever sent to learn American ways. Their forerunner was Yung Wing (1828–1912), the South China–born protégé of Christian missionaries who in 1854 became the first Asian to graduate from an American college, Yale. Yung married a Caucasian woman, had sons who were U.S. citizens, and wrote the first Chinese American autobiography, *My Life in China and America* (1909).

Japanese

Unlike the Chinese, who were part of a large and far-flung diaspora of laborers and merchants, the Japanese had no immigrant tradition. The first Japanese to reach the United States were accidental immigrants, castaways whom the Japanese current brought into the American orbit. One of them, who took the Americanized name Joseph Heco, served the United States as an interpreter and intermediary during Commodore Matthew C. Perry's missions to Japan in the 1850s. The first Japanese who can be called settlers, two small groups of refugees from the Meiji Revolution, founded short-lived colonies near San Francisco and Sacramento in California in 1868 and 1869. As late as 1890 not more than three thousand Japanese had come to the United States, and a third of those had already left.

Before a sizable number of Japanese had come to the United States, some thirty thousand Japanese contract laborers were recruited by the Hawaiian Sugar Planter's Association (HSPA) to work on Hawaii's plantations. Many of them subsequently moved on to the U.S. mainland before and after the United States annexed Hawaii in 1898. The migration both to Hawaii and to the United States was heavily male before 1908 but not so heavily male as Chinese immigration had been. The precise records of the HSPA show that during the nine-year period ending in 1894, 23,204 men and 5,487 women entered Hawaii under contract, a ratio of about 4.5 to 1. On the mainland, gender ratios resembled those of the Chinese in earlier decades. In 1900 California had just over ten thousand Japanese, of whom fewer than six hundred were women. But whereas Chinese immigrants were fleeing from an impoverished economy,

Table 1. Asian Immigration to the United States, 1850–1910

Years	Chinese	Japanese
1851–1860	41,397	—
1861–1870	64,301	186
1871–1880	123,201	149
1881–1890	61,711	2,270
1891–1900	14,799	25,942
1901–1910	20,605	129,797

Source: U.S. Department of Justice, Immigration and Naturalization Service. *Statistical Yearbook of the Immigration and Naturalization Service.* Washington, D.C.: Government Printing Office, 1997. Table 2, pp. 26–27.

Table 2. Chinese and Japanese Population, United States and California, 1860–1910

CHINESE

Year	United States	California	California as Percentage of United States
1860	—	34,933	—
1870	63,199	42,277	66.9
1880	105,465	75,132	71.3
1890	107,488	72,472	67.7
1900	89,863	45,753	50.9
1910	71,531	36,248	50.7

JAPANESE

Year	United States	California	California as Percentage of United States
1860	—	—	—
1870	—	—	—
1880	148	86	58.1
1890	2,039	1,147	56.3
1900	24,326	10,151	41.7
1910	72,154	41,356	57.3

Source: U.S. census data.

Japanese immigrants were fleeing from a thriving one. The economic growth that transformed Meiji Japan (1868–1912) was devastating for many small-scale agriculturalists, and it was from this group that most early Japanese immigrants came. In addition a number of upwardly mobile young Japanese men sought a Western education, but they had to work, often at menial jobs, to be able to go to school.

Most white Californians regarded the growing number of Japanese laborers as successors to the excluded Chinese and as representing precisely the same kind of threat. As early as 1892, when fewer than five thousand Japanese lived in the United States, a few West Coast zealots tried to raise an anti-Japanese hue and cry but without success. Around the turn of the century, as the Japanese immigrant population grew, a real anti-Japanese movement developed. This was something the government in Tokyo had long feared, convinced that discrimination against Japanese immigrants would be prejudicial to Japan's aspirations to great-power status. Thus Japan as early as the 1890s sought to police the behavior of its immigrants in the United States and proved amenable to negotiated settlements of disputes over immigration.

After Japan's stunning victory over the forces of the tsar in the Russo-Japanese War of 1904–1905, the U.S. government was ready to exercise its influence to moderate anti-Japanese behavior. There can be no serious doubt that, had Japan been a weak power, as China was, pressure from the Far West would have pushed a Japanese exclusion act through Congress sometime in the first decade of the twentieth century. Three successive administrations—those of Theodore Roosevelt, William Howard Taft, and Woodrow Wilson—tried to moderate discriminatory anti-Japanese legislation and actions by Californians. Only Roosevelt's will be discussed here.

In a time of turmoil in San Francisco politics and following the devastating earthquake and fire of April 1906, the San Francisco School Board ordered that all Japanese pupils in the city attend the long-established school for Chinese located in Chinatown. Although segregation of Chinese had never been a diplomatic problem, Tokyo saw segregation as an affront and eventually provoked the intervention of Theodore Roosevelt. He summoned the school board to the White House and, by a combination of cajolery, threats, and promises, got it to rescind its order. The chief threat was a suit, actually filed by Secretary of State Elihu Root, seeking to enjoin the school board from segregating pupils who were Japanese nationals. Their rights, it was argued, were protected by an existing commercial treaty with Japan. In the light of

Chinese Arrive at San Francisco. The inspection of Chinese immigrants by customs officers, 1877. Hostility to Chinese immigration led to the nation's first immigration restrictions in the Chinese Exclusion Act of 1882. © BETTMANN/CORBIS

the Supreme Court's recent sanctioning of the "separate but equal" doctrine in *Plessy v. Ferguson* (1896), the government could do nothing for American-born Japanese children. The school board's retreat made the suit moot, and subsequent segregation by rural school boards in the strawberry country around Sacramento was ignored by both governments.

Roosevelt fulfilled his promise to do something about Japanese immigration by supervising the complicated negotiations that produced the Gentlemen's Agreement of 1907–1908. Tokyo promised to stop issuing to male laborers passports good for travel to the United States, and Washington promised not to pass anti-Japanese legislation. In a provision whose effects neither side anticipated, family reunification for laborers already present in the United States was permitted, which initiated a period of female immigration from Japan. During the fifteen years the Gentlemen's Agreement was in effect, from 1909 to 1924, some 118,000 Japanese, nearly 8,000 a year, came to the United States. Most of them were women. Some had married before their husbands emigrated, but most were postemigration brides. Some Japanese men returned to Japan to get married, but many others entered into arranged marriages with women they had never seen, known as "picture brides." Californians came to feel betrayed. They had been promised "exclusion," but they got women who had babies who were U.S. citizens.

Unintended Consequences

The actions of the federal government in regard to the two Asian immigrant groups, although inspired by a common racism, had diametrically opposed effects. The Chinese were largely prevented from having families, while the Japanese were encouraged to have families more quickly than they would have otherwise. The Chinese existed for decades as a largely bachelor society, while the Japanese developed a familial society much quicker than most other immigrant groups. The latter development, of course, was not planned or foreseen. It would not be the last time that unintended consequences would stem from ill-considered immigration laws and regulations.

See also **Asia, Foreign Relations with; Chinatowns; Chinese Exclusion Act.**

Bibliography

Chan, Sucheng. *Asian Americans: An Interpretive History.* Boston: Twayne, 1991. A good brief account.

———. *This Bittersweet Soil: The Chinese in California Agriculture, 1860–1910.* Berkeley: University of California Press, 1986. Best work on nineteenth-century Chinese.

Daniels, Roger. *Asian America: Chinese and Japanese in the United States since 1850.* Seattle: University of Washington Press, 1988. The best comparative account.

———. *The Politics of Prejudice: The Anti-Japanese Movement in California and the Struggle for Japanese Exclusion.* Berkeley: University of California Press, 1962. The standard work.

Kitano, Harry H. L., and Roger Daniels. *Asian Americans: Emerging Minorities.* 2d ed. Englewood Cliffs, N.J.: Prentice Hall, 1995. A good brief account.

McClain, Charles J. *In Search of Equality: The Chinese Struggle against Discrimination in Nineteenth-Century America.* Berkeley: University of California Press, 1994. Analyzes how federal courts limited state and local discrimination.

Miller, Stuart Creighton. *The Unwelcome Immigrant: The American Image of the Chinese, 1785–1882.* Berkeley: University of California Press, 1969. An intellectual history.

Peffer, George Anthony. *If They Don't Bring Women Here: Chinese Female Immigration before Exclusion.* Urbana: University of Illinois Press, 1999. Emphasizes legal issues.

Salyer, Lucy E. *Laws Harsh as Tigers: Chinese Immigrants and the Shaping of Modern Immigration Law.* Chapel Hill: University of North Carolina Press, 1995. Shows how the Chinese experience shaped immigration law.

Sandmeyer, Elmer C. *The Anti-Chinese Movement in California.* Rev. ed. Urbana: University of Illinois Press, 1991. The original edition of this classic account was published in 1939.

Saxton, Alexander. *The Indispensable Enemy: Labor and the Anti-Chinese Movement in California*. Berkeley: University of California Press, 1971. An analysis of racist thought and action in the labor movement.

ROGER DANIELS

INCOME TAX.   See **Taxation and Public Finance.**

INDIANA   The nineteenth state, Indiana was admitted to the Union on 11 December 1816, the second state created from the Northwest Territory. Its population was officially estimated at 63,897, which was above the 60,000 required for statehood.

Early Indiana

The Indiana Territory, established on 7 May 1800, originally included Michigan, Illinois, Wisconsin, and eastern Minnesota as well as Indiana. Its boundaries were reduced to the state's present limits by 1809. Most of the state was heavily forested, with prairie openings and extensive marshland toward the northwest. Indiana was settled chiefly by an English and Scots-Irish population that came down the Ohio River from Pennsylvania or across the river from Kentucky. Only the northern counties were settled by families moving directly westward through Ohio. The two streams of settlement produced lasting differences in speech patterns, folkways, farming techniques, and religion.

Indiana was much like the other states of the Old Northwest. Democratic in its ideals, hostile to slavery, it nonetheless excluded African American men from voting and militia service. The state constitution of 1816 strictly prohibited slavery, but only in the 1820s did the courts eliminate the last legal vestiges of slavery. Abolitionists were few in Indiana, but there was widespread opposition to the return of fugitive slaves. In 1851 white male voters overwhelmingly approved Article XIII of the new constitution, prohibiting African Americans from settling within Indiana. American Indian resistance was broken by Governor William Henry Harrison at the Battle of Tippecanoe in 1811 and ended with the defeat of Tecumseh in 1813. Indian removal was gradual, and many of the Miamis remained until the mid-1840s. Most white residents made a living on family farms, raising corn, wheat, cattle, and hogs.

The most exceptional town of frontier Indiana was Harmonie near the lower Wabash, where a community of German Pietists settled in 1815. They prospered economically but left for religious reasons, selling their entire town in 1825 to Robert Owen, a British industrialist who envisioned a secular and scientific utopia that he named New Harmony. Owen's dream failed within two years, but he left a marvelous scientific and educational tradition along with several members of his remarkable family.

Indiana struggled for many years with transportation problems founded on poor roads and streams that were navigable only during springtime. Seeking to overcome these deficiencies, Governor Noah Noble implemented a mammoth improvements plan in 1836. However, his overambitious canal and railroad projects virtually bankrupted the state.

Except for wetlands along the Kankakee River, most of the public land in Indiana was sold at the federal land offices by 1837, although another two generations worked to clear the timber for cropland and pasture. The territorial capital was originally in Vincennes on the Wabash River but was moved to Corydon in 1813. The permanent capital, Indianapolis, was established in the center of the state in 1825. Indianapolis grew from wilderness to the state's largest city by the mid-1850s as the expanding railroads shifted trade and population from the Ohio River towns of Madison and New Albany. By 1860 Indiana's population had reached 1,350,428, but only 18,611 people lived in Indianapolis.

Indiana was closely contested by the Democratic and Whig Parties from the early 1830s until the early 1850s and thereafter by the Democrats and the Republicans. Reported voter turnout sometimes reached 90 percent of the adult male population, and politics attracted enormous attention. The Republicans won control of the state in 1860 and generally prevailed for the rest of the century, although the Democrats were occasionally victorious.

The Civil War

During the Civil War, Governor Oliver P. Morton was an effective champion of the Union war effort. Most Indiana troops fought in the western campaigns, but the Nineteenth Indiana Infantry won fame as part of the Iron Brigade with the Army of the Potomac. Altogether 196,363 Hoosiers served in the armed forces during the Civil War, and more than 25,000 of them died for the Union cause. For the remainder of the century the Grand Army of the Republic, the organization of Union veterans, played a major role in Indiana politics and social life. Fighting was a duty for men, but women had to manage the farms and shops the soldiers left behind. A few Indiana women, most notably the Sisters of the Holy Cross from Saint Mary's Academy at Notre Dame, nursed the wounded. Mother Angela Gillespie overcame the objections of army surgeons by appealing to an old family friend, General William T. Sherman. The Civil War meant the effective end of African American exclusion under Indiana's 1851 constitution, but the exclusion article was not formally repealed until 1881. Evansville and Indianapolis soon had significant African American populations.

Late Nineteenth Century

Because Indiana was a swing state that either party might carry, it often provided national candidates. Schuyler Colfax, a Republican, won election as U.S. vice president in 1868, and Thomas A. Hendricks, a Democrat, was defeated for vice president in 1876 before his successful second attempt in 1884. William H. English, a Democrat, was more banker than politician, but he was nominated for vice president in 1880. Benjamin Harrison, a Republican and a grandson of the first territorial governor, was a lawyer and politician. After advancing to the rank of brigadier general during the Civil War, Harrison lost his race for governor in 1876 but won election to the Senate four years later. In 1888 he won the presidency, but he was defeated for reelection in 1892.

Although most Hoosiers made their livings as farmers throughout the century, the state enjoyed extensive development after the Civil War in industries based on agriculture. Indianapolis and Hammond became major meatpacking centers, while Studebaker wagons and Oliver plows from South Bend found nationwide markets. Evansville, Fort Wayne, and Terre Haute were important railroad and manufacturing cities, while coal mining became a major business in southwestern Indiana after 1880. East Central Indiana experienced a major gas boom in 1888 followed by a minor oil boom five years later. The abundance of cheap gas encouraged the establishment of extensive glass-making enterprises, notably the Ball Brothers (1886) of Muncie, which became the nation's leading manufacturer of glass jars. Eli Lilly and Company began manufacturing pharmaceutical products in Indianapolis in 1876.

Beginning in the late 1840s Indiana attracted significant numbers of Irish and German immigrants, particularly in Evansville, Indianapolis, Hammond, and Fort Wayne, and in the 1870s South Bend drew large numbers of Polish and Hungarian immigrants to its booming factories. Nevertheless, Indiana had a lower proportion of immigrants than most northern states, and only the Germans had a significant cultural influence.

Indiana did not begin to build a properly financed public school system until the 1850s, and its educational levels were the lowest in the Midwest through the rest of the century. Purdue University, the state's land-grant college, and Indiana University were relatively small and weak until the 1890s, but a number of denominational colleges flourished, particularly DePauw University (Methodist) and Wabash College (Presbyterian).

Often writing of local scenes, Hoosier authors enjoyed widespread national attention during the last quarter of the nineteenth century. The period from 1871 until the early 1920s became known as the golden age of Indiana literature. The first best-seller was Edward Eggleston's *The Hoosier Schoolmaster* (1871), a tale of frontier life, followed by Maurice Thompson's *Hoosier Mosaics* (1875), a collection of short stories about rural Indiana. Lew Wallace's *Ben-Hur* (1880) had nothing to do with Indiana, but all of James Whitcomb Riley's poetry celebrated Hoosier themes. Indiana's reputation as the "American heartland" was marked at the turn of the century by three bestsellers, *The Gentleman from Indiana* (1899), the first novel by the young Booth Tarkington; Meredith Nicholson's *The Hoosiers* (1900), a historical study; and Thompson's *Alice of Old Vincennes* (1900), a romance of the Revolutionary War. By this time a well-known "Hoosier School" of landscape painters, including T. C. Steele, worked in the colorful hills of southern Indiana.

By 1900 Indiana was a mature state with a population of 2,516,462 that still lived mostly on farms and in small towns. However, industrial cities of modest size were attracting residents. Indianapolis, with 169,164 residents, was the only large city. Only 5.6 percent of the state's population was foreign-born, and less than 2.3 percent was African American. Hoosiers were proud, prosperous, and self-confident as they entered the twentieth century. Those with a bleaker view of life, like the novelist Theodore Dreiser, were not regarded as true Hoosiers.

See also **American Indian Societies,** *subentry on* **The Great Lakes; Glass; Immigration and Immigrants; Indian Territory; Meatpacking; Midwest, The; Northwest Territory.**

Bibliography

Barnhart, John D., and Dorothy L. Riker. *Indiana to 1816: The Colonial Period.* Volume 1 of History of Indiana. Indianapolis: Indiana Historical Bureau, 1971. The comprehensive History of Indiana series is the fundamental source for any serious study of the state's history, and all volumes include extensive bibliographies.

Carmony, Donald F. *Indiana, 1816–1850: The Pioneer Era.* Volume 2 of History of Indiana. Indianapolis: Indiana Historical Bureau and Indiana Historical Society, 1998.

Furlong, Patrick J. *Indiana: An Illustrated History.* Northridge, Calif.: Windsor Publications, 1985. A readable single-volume survey.

Gray, Ralph D., ed. *Indiana History: A Book of Readings.* Bloomington: Indiana University Press, 1994. A rich selection on a variety of Hoosier topics.

Madison, James H. *The Indiana Way: A State History.* Bloomington: Indiana University Press, 1986. A fine interpretative study.

Phillips, Clifton J. *Indiana in Transition: The Emergence of an Industrial Commonwealth, 1880–1920.* Volume 4 of History of Indiana. Indianapolis: Indiana Historical Bureau, 1968.

Thornbrough, Emma Lou. *Indiana in the Civil War Era, 1850–1880.* Volume 3 of History of Indiana. Indianapolis: Indiana Historical Bureau, 1965.

PATRICK J. FURLONG

INDIANS.   See **American Indians.**

INDIAN TERRITORY   Created for resettlement of Indian peoples removed from the East, Indian Territory eventually was home to members of fifty tribes. Its history, which ended with the creation of the present state of Oklahoma in 1907, was one of both bitter conflict and remarkable persistence among the Native Americans whose descendants live there today.

In 1825 Congress set aside for Indian colonization the country west of Missouri and Arkansas, south of the Platte River, north of the Red River, and westward to the hundredth meridian and the Rocky Mountains. Closed to white settlement, it was first called Indian Country and then, by 1830, Indian Territory.

It had three purposes, all arising from the westward expansion of white society and the resulting tensions with native peoples. Eastern land would be opened to white settlement by the removal of Indians to the Territory. Relocated Indians would be protected from land-hungry whites. Isolating Indians from outside pressures would buy the time needed to assimilate them gradually into the dominant white culture with the help of missionaries and government programs.

These strategies assumed that Indian Territory would be the far western edge of the United States. The Louisiana Purchase (1803) had set the nation's western boundary at the crest of the Rocky Mountains, and the Adams-Onís Treaty (1819) established the Red River as the Purchase's southern border. Indian Territory was thought to be far enough beyond white settlements to escape their worst influences, yet much of it was still part of the humid, well-timbered terrain more familiar to the removed eastern tribes than the semiarid plains farther to the west.

Some Indian peoples already had emigrated from the east, and others soon followed. Cherokees known as the Old Settlers moved in 1828 onto land immediately west of the Arkansas line and north of the Arkansas River. The government also granted them a large rectangle of land to the west, the Cherokee Outlet. Before 1830 some Choctaws had settled south of the Arkansas River.

The great migration, however, came during the presidential administrations of Andrew Jackson and Martin Van Buren. Under Jackson, long an advocate of the removal of eastern tribes, Congress passed the Indian Removal Act (1830), which authorized negotiations and funds to extinguish tribal holdings in exchange for lands in the West and to organize emigration to Indian Territory. During the next decade most Choctaws, Chickasaws, Cherokees, Creeks, and Seminoles were removed from their homelands in Mississippi, Alabama, Tennessee, and Georgia.

These groups, often called the Five Civilized Tribes, emigrated under pressure from the white frontier and from state and federal governments, although some among them chose to cooperate or resist more than others. Whatever the circumstances, their uprooting took a terrible toll in lives, tribal disharmony, and cultural trauma. Their removal to Indian Territory is known collectively as the Trail of Tears, a phrase describing both the process of uprooting and the various routes taken.

Choctaws came first, signing a removal treaty in 1830 and settling with those already living south of the Arkansas River. Their relatives the Chickasaws soon followed and took up a purchased western portion of the Choctaw lands. Following the "Creek War" of 1836, actually a brief clash involving a tiny minority of that group, federal troops forced virtually all Creeks to emigrate, some under armed guard. They were assigned lands between the Cherokees and the Choctaws along the Arkansas and Canadian rivers.

The Cherokees, the largest of these groups, were divided between a minority advocating removal, led by members of the Ridge family, and the majority, led by John Ross, who resisted. After the first group signed a treaty and emigrated in 1835, the second fought their case in the courts. Despite a favorable opinion by the U.S. Supreme Court (*Cherokee Nation v. Georgia*, 1831), all but a small portion were rounded by federal troops and militia in 1838 and confined to holding camps. Ross then agreed to oversee the journey of his followers to join those already settled in the northeastern part of Indian Territory.

Fiercest resistance came from the Seminoles. After a protracted war in the swamps of Florida, all but a fragment had been forced westward by 1842. They were placed first among the Creeks, their nearest relatives among the tribes, and later given land immediately to the west.

Tribal governments were reestablished, fields were planted, and schools were founded. Customs of daily life, religions, and cultural traditions were transplanted and adapted to the new setting. Several missionaries made the move with the tribes and continued their work in the Territory.

Meanwhile, many other less numerous eastern tribes were being pressed to emigrate. From New York came Senecas and others from the Iroquois Confederation. Out of the Great Lakes region and Ohio valley came Potawatomis, Shawnees, Delawares, Wyandots, Kickapoos, Miamis, and others. Quapaws were displaced from Arkansas. All these were assigned lands immediately west of the Missouri border. With one exception these emigrations were mostly peaceful. Part of the Sac and Fox people, led by Black Hawk, resisted removal from Illinois, and after several bloody encounters with state militiamen, they were forced to resettle in Iowa, then part of Indian Territory.

Conflict and suffering by no means ended with removal. Eastern tribes were set on lands long occupied or used by others as hunting grounds. The militarily formidable Osages, Kiowas, and Comanches were especially vigorous in attacking the newcomers. By 1840 government negotiations and a growing military presence had dampened this conflict, although tensions remained. Conflict also flared among and within the newly arrived groups. Creek and Seminoles disagreed on treatment of African American slaves brought with them, and old antagonisms were rekindled between Choctaws and Chickasaws. Boundary disputes arose between the Creek and Cherokees. Previous intratribal hostilities also arrived with the emigrants. The Upper and Lower Creeks drew apart, the former settling along the Canadian River and the latter along the Arkansas.

Divisions among the Cherokees were especially bitter. The Old Settlers resented the more numerous newcomers. Relations between the followers of John Ross and the minority who had supported the removal treaty flashed into violence, as when leaders of the treaty faction were killed shortly after the last of the Ross party finished their trek along the Trail of Tears. Strife abated after 1846 but resurfaced later.

The government meanwhile established military posts: Fort Smith, on the Arkansas River at the Territory's eastern edge: Fort Gibson, upriver between the Cherokees and Creeks; Fort Scott, on the line between the Territory and southern Missouri; and Fort Leavenworth, farther north on that boundary, on the Missouri River. Their twofold purpose was to maintain peace among and within the tribes and to form a "permanent Indian frontier," keeping whites and Indians apart and allowing the gradual assimilation of native peoples now on the far western fringe of the nation.

Events of the mid-1840s, however, undercut the original assumptions behind Indian Territory. First Texas was annexed (1845), then the Oregon country was acquired from Great Britain (1846), and finally the vast Mexican Cession was acquired in 1848, following the Mexican War. With the United States now stretching to the Pacific Ocean, Indian Territory suddenly was in the middle of the nation, not on its far edge, and as white settlers pressed westward, around and through the Territory, the tribes there soon faced a new set of demands.

During the 1850s Indian holdings in the Territory were reduced dramatically. The organization of the Kansas and Nebraska territories in 1854 established the thirty-seventh parallel as the Indian Territory's northern boundary, removing more than half of its former area. Tribes in Kansas and Nebraska were urged to surrender land to white settlers now swarming across the Missouri River. Within a year, nine tribes agreed to withdraw to a small portion of their holdings and to sell the rest. Buffeted by the violent free soil conflict and beset by land-hungry white farmers, these groups soon faced pressures as powerful as those on the eastern frontier a generation earlier.

This turbulence increased immeasurably with the Civil War. Older political divisions reopened with a new ferocity. Many among the Five Tribes, frustrated by Washington's lack of support and wooed by the charismatic Arkansan Albert Pike, allied with the Confederacy. A large minority of Creeks and Cherokees, however, supported the Union. They were driven into southern Kansas, where they suffered horribly from exposure and starvation while Confederate supporters fought in Missouri and Arkansas in 1861 and 1862. By 1863 the Union was in formal control of that region, but bitter warfare continued, some of the bloodiest in Indian Territory.

Despite the support and sacrifice of pro-Union factions, the victorious federal government forced a new series of land cessions. In what has been called the "Second Trail of Tears," many smaller tribes were removed from what had been the Territory's northern portion. The Osages, Kaws, Poncas, Otoes, and Missouris were resettled on land surrendered by Cherokees. Iowas, Sac and Fox, Kickapoos, and Potawatomies were removed to land taken from Creeks and Seminoles.

Following massacres and military defeats, the nomadic tribes of the central and southern plains were sent into the increasingly crowded Territory—Cheyennes and Arapahoes in the west-central portion, and south of them the Comanches, Kiowas, and Eastern Apaches. Military posts were established in the West—Fort Supply in the Cherokee Outlet, Fort Reno among the Cheyennes, and Fort Sill among the Comanches and Apaches. Several million acres near the center of the Territory, the Unassigned Lands, remained uncommitted to any tribes.

These years were among the bleakest of the Territory's generally troubled history. Western tribes struggled with the hopeless demand that they take up farming on the semiarid high plains. Angry rivalries and bitter memories continued to foul relations among the Five Tribes, and as another penalty for their support of the Confederacy, these tribes were denied effective self-government. The war's violent legacy as well as the lack of effective authority, made eastern Indian Territory a haven for outlaws. Deputies from the federal court in Fort Smith, just over the Arkansas line, prowled the region in an abortive effort to maintain some order.

Outside economic interests also were closing in on what had been conceived as a place of isolation from frontier pressures. After the Civil War, Texas cattlemen began driving herds across Indian Territory to Kansas railheads, and by the 1870s ranchers were pasturing their animals on Indian lands. The Missouri, Kansas, and Texas Railroad was built southward across the Territory by 1872, followed by the Atlantic and Pacific and a branch of the Atchison, Topeka, and Santa Fe. As these developments introduced thousands of whites to the area, pressure grew to open Indian lands to outside settlement. By 1894 an estimated 250,000 whites lived in the Territory.

The Dawes Severalty (or General Allotment) Act (1887), which provided for breaking up land collectively held by Indian tribes into individual holdings, or allotments, with the remainder opened to white settlement, did not extend to the Five Civilized Tribes. When special commissioners tried to set this process in motion, they were vigorously opposed by native leaders. Congress finally compelled the Five Tribes to comply, and their lands were distributed among those on the tribal rolls or set aside for town sites and schools. Meanwhile, federal courts had taken full jurisdiction in the Territory, effectively ending tribal governments.

In the western portion of Indian Territory, much of the land was distributed through a series of dramatic "land rushes" or "runs." On 22 April 1889, at least fifty thousand persons dashed into the Unassigned Lands to take up claims and to organize Oklahoma City, Guthrie, and other towns. The largest of these rushes came on 13 September 1893, when the

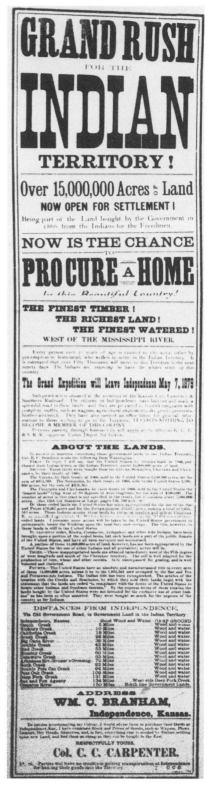

Indian Territory Land Rush. Declaring a "grand rush for the Indian Territory," this poster advertises over 15 million acres of land available for settlement, which was purchased by the government from the Indians in 1866 and given to former slaves. The land was opened to whites in 1879 as advertised here. LIBRARY OF CONGRESS

Cherokee Outlet, sold in 1890, was overrun by more than a hundred thousand "boomers."

As other former Indian lands were disposed of in rushes and auctions, roughly the western half of the Territory, plus the "No Man's Land," a strip immediately north of the Texas panhandle, was organized into Oklahoma Territory. Sentiment was strong in what remained of Indian Territory to form a separate state, and a referendum in 1905 asked Congress to create the state of Sequoyah. This was refused, however. In 1907, with all tribal lands distributed, Indian Territory formally disappeared when Congress merged it with Oklahoma Territory to create the state of Oklahoma.

See also **American Indians,** *subentry on* **Indian Removal.**

Bibliography

Burton, Jeffrey, *Indian Territory and the United States, 1866–1906: Courts, Government, and the Movement for Oklahoma Statehood.* Norman: University of Oklahoma Press, 1995.

Debo, Angie. *And Still the Waters Run: The Betrayal of the Five Civilized Tribes.* Princeton, N.J.: Princeton University Press, 1940. Reprint, Norman: University of Oklahoma, 1984.

Gibson, Arrell Morgan. *Oklahoma: A History of Five Centuries.* Norman: University of Oklahoma Press, 1981.

La Vere, David. *Contrary Neighbors: Southern Plains and Removed Indians in Indian Territory.* Norman: University of Oklahoma Press, 2000.

Miner, H. Craig. *The Corporation and the Indian: Tribal Sovereignty and Industrial Civilization in Indian Territory, 1865–1907.* Norman: University of Oklahoma Press, 1989.

ELLIOT WEST

INDUSTRIALIZATION AND THE MARKET

Industrialization transformed the economy of the United States during the nineteenth century. The expansion of the industrial sector accelerated the rate of economic development and growth and caused a steady increase in the gross national product and the per capita income of a majority of Americans by the end of the century. Industrialization could advance only if manufacturers could expand the market for their goods while continuing to increase production. Industrialization, therefore, drove and was driven by the expansion of local and regional markets into national and international ones, and the creation of a market-oriented culture. Industrialization and the "market revolution" were symbiotically locked in a cause-and-effect interaction as together they transformed American life.

Industrialization was not, however, a monolithic process that spread its benefits to all Americans equally over time or to every community, state, or region simultaneously or equitably during the nineteenth century. The different adaptability of different products to industrial processes; the variable access of producers in different lines of production to power, capital, knowledge, skilled labor, and raw materials; the diversity of the scale, structure, and dynamics of local, regional, and national markets for different goods; and the varying degree to which new transportation, communication, financial, institutional, and legal frameworks converged to trigger the emergence of a dynamic national economy discursively and unevenly filtered the effects of industrialization across the economy. Nevertheless, in industrialization's seemingly contradictory power to centralize, integrate, and homogenize while differentiating, segmenting, and separating various aspects of the American economy, it became the engine of change that structured and drove the complex economic, social, political, and cultural transformation of the United States in the nineteenth century.

Industrialization began with the transformation of the craft shop, through the division of labor, into a new "manufactory" production system before 1820. By the 1840s industrialists sought to improve their market position by taking advantage of the external economies—raw materials, transport, labor, capital, know-how—that cities provided, which would enable them to diversify and expand within a growing cluster of related industries. After the Civil War, pressure to maintain market shares encouraged some producers to establish industrial corporations in which a growing cadre of managers, forming the bureaucracy of new industrial enterprises, situated their main production plants at the centers of vast vertically integrated systems of raw material acquisition, production, and marketing. Greater competition compelled some firms to diversify and enlarge the scope of production or to establish branch plants at various places across the country. Others pursued control over the competition by means of horizontal integration. Either way, as struggles for market shares intensified, efforts to reduce competition led in the 1890s to a wave of mergers, setting the stage for the creation of the modern industrial economy of the twentieth century.

Technological innovation and increased production occurred in direct response to the need to generate more sales. Soon after 1800, when initial changes in the division of labor in the craft shop replaced production of "bespoken goods" with the production of goods to be sold in the market, a manufacturer, by necessity, entered into the market to sell his goods. In time, as markets expanded in tandem with production, large-scale industrial production outstripped the market capacity for industrial goods, causing, at increasingly regular intervals, retrenchments and declines in investment and production that triggered panics or crashes in 1819, 1837, 1857, 1873, and 1893. Industrial activity responded to growing market activity in local, regional, and international markets that were in place by the end of the eighteenth century. As industrialization developed, its impact advanced unevenly across the variegated market terrain, transforming the size and dynamics of the "market" in a gradual and haphazard fashion. The impact of the "market revolution" also was uneven across space and time. Thus, the transition from economic activity in local, regional, and international markets to an increasingly integrated national market economy in which most people acted within the same context and rules was equally uneven.

Industrialization developed as a response to changes in the scale and dynamics of some of the many local and regional marketplaces that made up the broader American market. Most American farmers, craftsmen, and merchants in the eighteenth century produced, made, and traded goods and services locally, if they traded them at all. Those who produced a small surplus for market found roads lacking, markets unpredictable, currency scarce, and information faulty and experienced uneven success. Market farming was not a priority, nor, as a result of limited demand, was any kind of specialized production of goods. Unspecialized local craftsmen produced furniture, clothes, candles, or ironware and provided blacksmith, tanning, and livery services for a limited market in which bartering of specific goods and services prevailed over monetary exchange at a merchant's shop. More specialized town merchants produced better-quality furniture, utensils, cutlery, dinnerware, clothes, shoes, books, and other luxury items primarily for cash from the wealthiest farmers in the nearby hinterland and members of the elite urban merchant class.

As prices for grain increased and roads were "improved," competition among farmers intensified. Many farmers tried to implement new scientific farming techniques to boost yields as a way to maintain self-sufficiency. In so doing, they triggered the agrarian revolution. Those smaller farmers unable to get more production from their lands eventually sold out to larger farmers and went either west or into the city. And larger farmers, employing more efficient techniques and achieving some level of economies of scale, began producing more for the market. By about 1800, more incentive to specialize and higher incomes accelerated the demand by farmers for a broader range of manufactured goods. In response, craftsmen in small villages and towns across the northern states sought to increase the scale and efficiency of their production. They did so in a world in which most markets were local, only loosely and occasionally connected to the more specialized regional and international markets in which farmers producing surpluses and city merchants acted. These diverse responses initiated the industrial revolution in America around 1800.

Industrialization emerged from the response of local entrepreneurs and producers to the rising demand for goods. Entrepreneurs responded early in the century by employing new organizational techniques in management, labor, and technology to improve productivity, limit production costs, and raise profits. Walter Licht has suggested that among the wide variety of ways industrialization developed, most responses occurred along one of four distinctive paths. Perhaps the most universal path, though least associated with the industrial revolution, was the rearrangement and expansion of the craft shop in the town or city through division of labor. As cities grew after 1800, demand for goods rose. More and more master craftsmen found that to meet that demand, and avoid its being satisfied entirely by imported British goods, they had to step up production while lowering costs. Masters divided their labor, increased the number of workers to ten to twenty individuals, and specialized their production. These modest "manufactories"—most of which did not extensively employ machines before the Civil War—lowered costs while significantly enlarging the scale and diversity of most lines of production.

By the 1820s the rapid growth of cities concentrated this small-scale industrialization in the metropolis, where external economies, specialization, and diversity, far more than scale economies, triggered a rapid increase in the production and sales of machines, tools, hardware, bricks and tiles, drugs and chemicals, books, and a vast array of household items demanded by the burgeoning middle class. By the 1840s, advances in house-building technology, involving the balloon frame wooden house or the taller brick row building, and road, sewer, and water system technology made city construction an integral part of market expansion, further feeding and stimulating the drive for metropolitan industrialization.

Those producers who expanded production to a larger scale did so, at first, in smaller cities located near fast-flowing water, the source of power necessary to run larger factories. Some producers established an outwork system of production, whereas others centralized production under one roof; but it was only with the development of steam engines that manu-

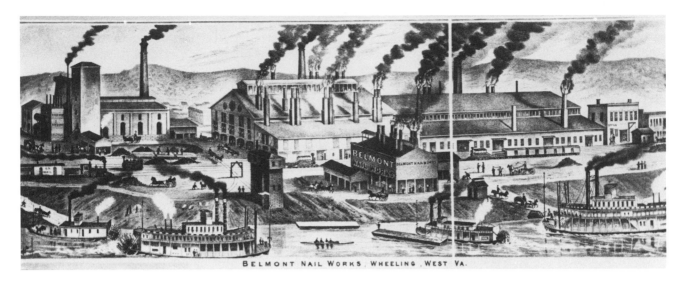

BELMONT NAIL WORKS, WHEELING, WEST VA.

Industrialization in Wheeling, West Virginia. Wheeling was one of many cities that became an industrial center, due in part to its advantageous position on the banks of a major river, the Ohio. The Ohio's busy river traffic is shown in the foreground of this lithograph, printed in 1877. LIBRARY OF CONGRESS

factories could become factories and the towns could develop into industrial towns or cities. Such was the case in the shoe industry, centered, since colonial times, at Lynn, Massachusetts. Elsewhere, industrialists established large factories in small towns at the fall line along the hills and low mountains away from the Atlantic coast. Chester Creek to the south and the Delaware and Lehigh Rivers to the north of Philadelphia, the rivers above Baltimore, and the towns along the rivers in interior New England were early locales where industrialists established textile, iron, lumber, and flour mills. These mill towns, which often became company towns, usually had two or three different medium-sized mills, developed by local entrepreneurs who owned the firm employing members of families who lived in town or in the nearby hinterland. This kind of early industrialization had, therefore, a strong rural or communal element. A significant variant occurred in the urban South. Using both slave and free labor, southern industrialists achieved more than is usually recognized, producing about 10 percent of the nation's industrial output by 1860, mostly in textiles, iron, and small machinery, especially cotton gins.

The most dramatic form of industrialization was the creation of the one-industry city, such as Lowell or Waltham, Massachusetts, established as larger-scale textile industrial centers by entrepreneurs in nearby Boston. Organized as a corporation in 1813, the Boston Manufacturing Company employed large amounts of capital to consolidate production in fully mechanized factories at Waltham and later at nearby Lowell. By the 1830s scores of mills employed thousands of workers—through 1850, mostly farm

women and, after that, Irish immigrants—to achieve massive economies of scale and scope that allowed the respective companies to control the American market. Once these companies achieved market dominance through scale and scope economies, others sought to compete through specialization and diversity and located mills and factories in towns and cities throughout New England. By the 1850s, the manufacturing sector became the predominant driving force of the regional economy, making the northeastern United States the manufacturing center of the national economy.

As industry evolved along these four paths between the 1800s and the 1840s, the boundaries of local and regional markets were stretched. Meanwhile, as farmers sought new lands, the national market continued to expand and grow. With production in some lines now exceeding local demand, industrialization began to drive the transformation of the market by pushing for more transportation innovation. Large programs were launched to improve the means of transportation. Market demand and industrial production began to move in tandem, opening up larger regional markets and encouraging industrial firms to produce more for those markets.

This process moved outward from a developing group of industrial centers along the northeastern coastal region. Within that core, at first state governments and then the federal government supported innovations in transportation technology, mail service, and communications as well as canal construction and road and turnpike improvement before 1830 and railroad development thereafter.

Rapid urban development in the core region made

it the strongest market for its own goods. But western migration and the development of specialized agricultural regions in the West and South increased demand for manufactured goods. Again the federal and state governments supported massive canal construction, followed by the development of a railroad network that connected the East to Buffalo, Cleveland, and Chicago by water in 1825 and by railroad in the 1840s. The National Road was proposed in 1802 to connect Pittsburgh with St. Louis, but it was extended across Illinois to St. Louis only in the 1840s. The Baltimore and Ohio Railroad began its trek west over the Appalachians in 1828, reaching Harpers Ferry, (West) Virginia, by 1834; it reached Wheeling, (West) Virginia, in 1852, and arrived in St. Louis in 1857. The New York Central arrived in Chicago by 1848, and from there, the Chicago, Burlington, and Quincy Railroad and the Illinois Central drove south and west, crossing the Mississippi to towns in Iowa in 1856 (Davenport), 1865 (Clinton), and 1868 (Dubuque and Burlington) and reaching St. Louis in 1874. Meanwhile, the Pacific Railroad Acts of 1862 and 1864 finalized plans for four transcontinental railroads to connect California to the burgeoning national market, a long-held dream that became reality in the 1870s and especially in the 1880s, when improvements in management enhanced the efficiency and capacity of railroad service. By the 1890s, nearly a quarter of a million miles of track stretched from coast to coast.

Whereas technology, innovation, and capital fueled the industrial revolution after 1850, the city—more particularly the industrial metropolis—became the central engine that enabled the impact of that revolution to penetrate the farthest reaches of the national economy and beyond. As early as the 1830s, cities were able to generate significant external economies that enhanced the scale-economy advantages of larger firms and allowed them to maintain or achieve a greater share of the market. Cities became the nexus between industrialization and the market, and as urbanization accelerated and Americans began moving to cities in ever greater numbers, cities became the focal points of national market as well.

The construction of the railroads not only expanded the market in which industrial production occurred but also was an agent of industrialization itself. The construction of the railroad system demanded technological innovation and improvements in communications and management as well as massive amounts of wood, coal, iron, and, by the late 1870s, steel. Rising demand stimulated innovation and then rapid centralization in the metal industries, especially steel, silver, gold, and copper. The steel industry tapped the Appalachians and Midwest for coal—which was also in great demand by all industries, causing mining towns to develop across the Appalachians and lower Midwest—and the Mesabi Range of Minnesota for iron ore. The rising industrial demand for other minerals touched off massive efforts to tap the mineral wealth of the Rockies, causing industrial towns to spring up, such as Bisbee, Arizona, near the Mexican border; Leadville and Denver, Colorado; and Butte and Billings, Montana. In the Sierras industrialized mining quickly replaced the placer mining of the earlier era that began with the California gold rush and the Nevada silver rush at Virginia City and Carson City in the 1850s through the 1880s.

As the steel industry drew the industrial core west, between Pittsburgh and Chicago, specialized industries established themselves. The large cities of the West—Buffalo, Cincinnati, St. Louis, Milwaukee, and especially Chicago—developed vibrant industrial sectors by the 1850s and 1860s. Each mixed a distinctive combination of core industries, which took advantage of their location to process the hinterland's abundance—grain, coal, oil, livestock, wood, and iron and steel—and their derivatives— flour, cornstarch, liquor, beer, coke, glass, processed meat, lumber, furniture, agricultural implements, hardware, machinery, carriages and wagons, tanning, soap, petroleum—with a wide range of smaller industries related to urban development and consumption. Within or near these cities, some of the largest manufacturers invented a new institutional form: the managerial industrial enterprise. They did this by first investing in production facilities large enough to tap a technology's economies of scale. More important, they then invested in a national and international purchasing, marketing, and distribution network that maintained levels of production and enabled sales to keep up with those levels. To carry out such vertical integration, managers trained large cadres of middle-level managers who, though having no stake in it, ran the firm and maintained its market position through what Alfred Chandler calls functional management (improving some aspect of the purchasing, production, and distribution system) or strategic management (developing more products and moving in and out of markets efficiently and quickly).

By the 1890s, the Carnegie Steel plant in Homestead, outside Pittsburgh; the Standard Oil refinery in Cleveland; the McCormick Reaper works, the Pullman Company plant, and the Armour Meat Packing Company facility in Chicago; the Procter and Gamble plant in Cincinnati; and the Crosby-Washburn Mills (precursor of General Mills) plant in St. Paul employed thousands of workers in mass-production systems that were the linchpins of vertically integrated purchasing and marketing and distribution systems stretching across the nation. Having so few competitors, some of these firms were able to form massive conglomerates from scores of companies in the great merger movement of the late 1890s. As national conglomerates these firms responded to the broadening national market by establishing branch plants in the West, thus pointing the way to an increase in manufacturing activity outside the industrial core in the urban West in the twentieth century.

By the end of the nineteenth century, the industrial sector serving a national marketplace dominated the American economy. Improvements in railroad service and the development of mail order catalogs and rural free delivery allowed the market for manufactured goods to penetrate nearly every corner of the nation. While large-scale industrialization continued to navigate the creation of a mass national market at the turn of the twentieth century, metropolitan industrialization involving countless smaller-scale factories producing machines and tools, hardware, housing and building materials, household goods, clothing, and food products continued to develop and intensify. Thus, within the framework of the "national market," many pockets of local and regional markets, and blockages and inefficiencies, that seem primitive from today's perspective remained.

See also **Consumerism and Consumption; Corporations and Big Business; Electricity; Entrepreneurs; Interstate Commerce; Investment and Capital Formation; Labor Movement,** *subentry on* **Unions and Strikes; Market Revolution; Steel and the Steel Industry; Stock Markets; Trusts; Waterpower; Work,** *subentry on* **Factory Labor.**

Bibliography

Chandler, Alfred D. *The Visible Hand: The Managerial Revolution in American Business.* Cambridge, Mass.: The Belknap Press of Harvard University Press, 1977.

Chandler, Alfred D., with Takashi Hikino. *Scale and Scope: The Dynamics of Industrial Capitalism.* Cambridge, Mass.: The Belknap Press of Harvard University Press, 1990.

Clark, Christopher. "The Consequence of the Market Revolution in the Antebellum North." In *The Market Revolution in America: Social, Political, and Religious Expressions, 1800–1880.* Edited by Melvyn Stokes and Stephen Conway. Charlottesville: University Press of Virginia, 1996.

Cochran, Thomas C. *Frontiers of Change: Early Industrialism in America.* New York: Oxford University Press, 1981.

Hindle, Brooke, and Stephen Lubar. *Engines of Change: The American Industrial Revolution, 1790–1860.* Washington, D.C.: Smithsonian Institution Press, 1986.

Kirkland, Edward C. *Industry Comes of Age: Business, Labor and Public Policy, 1860–1897.* Volume 6. New York: Holt, Rinehart, and Winston, 1961.

Licht, Walter. *Industrializing America: The Nineteenth Century.* Baltimore: Johns Hopkins University Press, 1995.

Ratner, Sidney, James H. Soltow, and Richard Sylla. *The Evolution of the American Economy: Growth, Welfare, and Decision Making.* New York: Basic Books, 1979.

Stokes, Melvyn, and Stephen Conway, eds. *The Market Revolution in America: Social, Political, and Religious Expressions, 1800–1880.* Charlottesville: University Press of Virginia, 1996.

TIMOTHY R. MAHONEY

INDUSTRY (THE WORK ETHIC)   Often called "the work ethic," the personal characteristic of "industry" was understood as one's capacity to harness resources industriously and to provide a living through work for oneself and one's family. The German sociologist Max Weber wrote in *The Protestant Ethic and Spirit of Capitalism* (in German, 1904–1905) that America's expansive industrial and commercial sectors owed their vivacity to an ethic of work peculiar to Protestant ideology. Protestants, according to Weber, worked diligently in order to demonstrate either that they were among the saved or were worthy of salvation. They then invested the money their work produced back into the community. Weber considered America to be the prime example of how the Protestant ethic created a powerful work ethic. A secular influence that also promoted "industry" was the promise and abundance of the American landscape.

Origins of the Concept

The foremost expositor and promoter of the work ethic in early America was Benjamin Franklin. His *Poor Richard's Almanack* (1732–1757), particularly his almanac essay "The Way to Wealth" (1758); his continuously popular *Autobiography* (1793); and his essay "Information to Those Who Would Remove to America" (1784), all encouraged industry, hard work, and moderation for anyone seeking success in America.

"The Way to Wealth"

"In short, the way to wealth, if you desire it, is as plain as the way to market. It depends chiefly on two words, INDUSTRY and FRUGALITY: i.e. waste neither time nor money, but make the best use of both. He that gets all he can honestly, and saves all he gets (necessary expenses excepted) will certainly become RICH."

BENJAMIN FRANKLIN

Autobiography and Other Writings. Edited by L. Jesse Lemisch. New York: Signet, 1961, p. 187.

By the nineteenth century, the work ethic became the dominant theme of rhetoric about work and economy in America. The French statesman Alexis de Tocqueville wrote in *Democracy in America* (1835) that American dedication to "industry" spurred powerfully the growth of the American economy, particularly its manufacturing centers. The American Industrial Revolution was complemented and in many ways supported by the work ethic. In America, Tocqueville argued, work was not seen as a dishonorable obligation as it often was in aristocratic Europe, but he also warned that as the industrial sector grew, it threatened to place workers and owners in adversarial class positions.

As industrialization did indeed widen class division, the work ethic began to be deployed against the interests of the growing working class. Under the ethos of the work ethic, a person's economic fate was determined by how effectively he or she worked. When tied to a rags-to-riches ideology that was popular in middle-to-late nineteenth-century America, the work ethic helped the middle class to justify laissez-faire policies toward the urban and rural poor. Popular literature, such as Horatio Algers's novel *Ragged Dick* (1868), encouraged this ideology. Charles Darwin's *On the Origin of Species* (1859) added a purported scientific basis to the practice of blaming the poor for a lack of industry.

In many ways, though, Northern workers appropriated the rhetoric of industry for their own purposes. As the artisanal shop gave way to the factory system, workers, who felt they were losing important rights, banded together under the ideals of the work ethic. Workers used the positive connotation of the work ethic in order to demand more from factory owners. They called themselves "mechanics" and "producers," as opposed to "hands." They accused owners of being nonworking "parasites" who preyed upon their employees. Although the work ethic was connected to an ideal of bread-winning masculinity, women workers also used its rhetoric. In the Lowell Mills' protests in Massachusetts, women workers exhorted that they were "daughters of freemen" and not slaves. In the culture of workers, liberty grew to be associated with fairly compensated work, just as it was connected to individual achievement in the minds of employers and capitalists. This connection between liberty and fair pay solidified the work ethic's relationship to Northern capitalism for both workers and owners.

The Work Ethic and Slavery

As the work ethic was increasingly linked to a capitalist ethic of fairly paid work, it threw into high relief the differentness of slavery, a labor system that challenged all of the premises of free labor. A permanent class of noncitizens who performed unpaid labor contradicted the idea that if one works hard enough in the United States one can become rich. Yet as much as slavery seemed to contradict the work ethic, it was ironically often defended under the

"Strive to Excel." The motto served as a constant reminder of the proper work ethic to the women sewing skirts at the W. S. and C. H. Thomson factory. From *Harper's Weekly*, 19 February 1859. LIBRARY OF CONGRESS

terms of the work ethic. Proslavery advocates claimed that slaves deserved enslavement because they did not possess the characteristic of "industry." The stereotype of the "sambo" perpetuated the myth of the "lazy slave" who needed to be kept busy forcibly or would never be industrious, furthering justifications for slavery.

Although the most visibly exploited group, slaves were not the only population derided for their inability to be industrious workers. Laziness became a standard slur against the Catholic Irish and Italians in New York, the Mexicans in the Southwest, the Chinese in the West, and, after the Civil War, the African American sharecroppers and domestic servants of the South. These groups often were concentrated together in the lowest and most dangerous jobs, and their "failure" to move up was often attributed to a lack of desire to better themselves, or, similarly, a "failure" to assimilate. One of the aims of late-nineteenth-century and early-twentieth-century "Americanization" programs for immigrants, which grew in response to the fears engendered by rising immigration, was to instill the Protestant work ethic in the populations of alleged idlers.

By late in the nineteenth century, unions had abandoned their producer rhetoric, and instead began to fight more aggressively the abuses of the factory system and the employers' rationalization of it through the work ethic. The labor movement took on issues and planned actions that appeared to contradict the ideals of the work ethic, such as fighting for the eight-hour day and mounting strikes, such as the Homestead strike of 1892 and the Pullman strike of 1894. Owners continued to use the work ethic, with its connections to liberty and prosperity, as a way to delegitimize unionization. The steel baron Andrew Carnegie became the great exemplar and prophet of the rags-to-riches myth that turned the work ethic to the purposes of class propaganda, justifying the wealth of affluent individuals and discrediting the claims of the working poor.

The ideology of the work ethic was also applied outside of discourse about work and labor. By the middle of the nineteenth century, its rhetoric was being used to defend Manifest Destiny; and by the end of the century, the combination of manifest destiny and the work ethic pervaded popular conceptions of American history. In his address "The Significance of the Frontier in American History" in 1893, Frederick Jackson Turner argued that American history was one of triumph and progress across the continent through the hard work of its citizens. As the century turned, Theodore Roosevelt would encourage Americans to keep living the "Strenuous Life" (1902), a vision that would stretch both the American work ethic and the aspirations of American nationalism beyond the continent.

See also **Entrepreneurs; Foreign Observers; Industrialization and the Market; Labor Movement,** *subentry on* **Unions and Strikes; Offices and Office Work; Work.**

Bibliography

Dublin, Thomas. *Women at Work.* New York: Columbia University Press, 1979.

Gilje, Paul A., and Howard B. Rock, eds. *Keepers of the Revolution: New Yorkers at Work in the Early Republic.* Ithaca, N.Y.: Cornell University Press, 1992.

Glickstein, Jonathan. *Concepts of Free Labor in Antebellum America.* New Haven, Conn.: Yale University Press, 1991.

Johnson, Paul E. *A Shopkeeper's Millennium.* New York: Hill and Wang, 1978.

Morgan, Edmund S. *American Slavery, American Freedom.* New York: Norton, 1975.

Rodgers, Daniel T. *The Work Ethic in Industrial America, 1850–1920.* Chicago: University of Chicago Press, 1978.

Roediger, David R. *The Wages of Whiteness.* London: Verso Press, 1991.

Schultz, Ronald. *The Republic of Labor.* New York: Oxford University Press, 1993.

Tocqueville, Alexis de. *Democracy in America.* Edited by J. P. Mayer and Max Lerner. Translated by George Lawrence. New York: Harper and Row, 1966.

White, Deborah Gray. *Ar'n't I a Woman? Female Slaves in the Plantation South.* New York: Norton, 1985.

Wilentz, Sean. *Chants Democratic: New York City and the Rise of the American Working Class, 1788–1850.* New York: Oxford University Press, 1984.

JUSTINE S. MURISON

INSURANCE   As a vehicle for managing risk and accumulating resources, insurance profoundly shaped the development of the economy, urbanization, and the evolution of regulation in the United States during the nineteenth century. Insurance is a system by which groups of individuals spread the burdens of loss by using the contributions of the many to bear the losses of the few. Insurance per se does not eliminate risk or loss. Rather, it eliminates uncertainty about loss and transfers risk from the individual to the group by combining risks, by using the "laws of large numbers" to predict the chances of loss, and by accumulating premiums from group members to cover current or future losses.

With very few exceptions insurance in the United States during the nineteenth century was provided privately by for-profit stock companies, mutual insurers, the English underwriters Lloyd's of London, reciprocal exchanges, and fraternal societies. The insurance business was regulated by the states, which drew a sharp line between life insurance and property insurance and required providers to specialize in a single form of coverage. This system led to distinctive developments in life and fire insurance, the century's preeminent property-casualty line, and in the marine and workers' compensation branches of the insurance business.

The early development of life insurance was retarded by moral objections to placing a monetary value on life. But economic growth, the invention of the agency system, and entrepreneurs' success in reframing life insurance as the mark of a prudent householder set the stage in the 1840s for rapid expansion. Life insurers' first markets were the urban middle classes, who enthusiastically consumed whole-life products, including deferred dividend policies, in which each policyholder gambled on outliving his or her peers. Industry expansion continued in the 1860s and 1870s with the adoption of the "American Experience Table of Mortality" and the introduction of industrial life or small, weekly payment policies sold to the working classes.

Growth coincided with concentration of population. Fraternal societies issued a substantial fraction of life insurance up to the 1890s, but by 1900 the industry was dominated by five giant, northeastern companies, Mutual Life, Equitable, New York Life, Prudential, and Metropolitan Life, and six regional powerhouses (John Hancock, Aetna, Connecticut Mutual, Pennsylvania Mutual, Mutual Benefit of Newark, and Northeastern Mutual of Milwaukee) who, with one exception, were also based in the Northeast.

Industry development posed two regulatory problems. First, life insurance entailed long-term contracts that entrusted accumulated premiums to the companies for upwards of twenty years. Companies were supposed to build reserves, invest reserves prudently, and pay dividends and benefits on time. However, company officials canceled policies when insured policyholders missed payments, used premiums to finance personal undertakings, and otherwise appropriated policyholder contributions. In response state governments intervened to require reserves, ban certain policies, and otherwise safeguard consumers. Second, growth and centralization made life insurance an important source of capital while concentrating funds in a few large firms and channeling investment capital into New York financial markets. These trends sparked efforts to control industry resources that ranged from taxes and discriminatory measures against companies from other states to attempts by Texas and Kansas populists to require insurers to invest in their state economies.

Fire insurance was also decisive in the United States for economic development, urbanization, and the general welfare. This industry was the nation's primary mechanism for mobilizing resources in the aftermath of fires. American cities and towns burned with distressing frequency during the nineteenth century. More than thirty major conflagrations created huge demands for funds to rebuild devastated areas. Banks and other lenders universally required fire insurance on collateral for mortgages and credit, making insurance purchases mandatory for property owners and businesses throughout the United States. Indeed, in a credit-dependent economy these requirements made steady supplies of fire insurance necessary for the expansion of trade and commerce and established fire insurance as a critical infrastructure industry.

Fire insurance emerged during the 1810s and 1820s as local businesses in urban centers and evolved into a national industry during the 1850s. Companies grew by selling coverage against property loss from fire, hail, or windstorms to owners of small "preferred risks" like single-family dwellings, barns, and schoolhouses and to owners of large "special hazards" like grain elevators, stockyards, and multiplant factories. Here, too, growth fostered large corporations, yet the industry remained relatively fragmented. Mutual, state, and local insurers competed effectively with nationally operating stock companies and captured significant market shares in many midwestern states.

Fragmentation and price warfare prevented fire insurers from pooling loss data and placing rates on a rational basis. Those problems also left the industry vulnerable to widespread insolvency when conflagrations occurred. Insurers worked to control competition through price-fixing associations and various collaborative schemes, thereby provoking rate protests, antitrust laws, and other hostile legislation during the 1880s and 1890s. However, political struggles yielded compromises that endorsed, regulated, and rationalized cooperative rates. The resulting system of associates and rate regulation encompassed collective bargaining, actuarial boards, prevention organizations, and collaborative rate making. In fact this system supported a nationwide movement to reduce fire losses and qualified fire insurance as a regionally decentralized, cooperatively organized alternative to large-firm models of industrial order.

Marine insurance and workers' compensation, although important providers of insurance, played a relatively small role in domestic politics and economic development in the nineteenth century. Marine insurance, which covered property in transit, was a leading line at the beginning of the century but was mainly associated with shipping interests and international trade. In contrast, workers' compensation for work-related injuries was central to domestic industrial development and stability and entailed extensive state intervention, including intervention in cases involving rate regulation, mandated coverage, and even monopoly public insurance in some states. This insurance line, however, did not emerge until the first two decades of the twentieth century.

See also **Death and Dying; Disasters; Fires and Firefighting; Investment and Capital Formation; Regulation of Business.**

Bibliography

Grant, H. Roger. *Insurance Reform: Consumer Action in the Progressive Era.* Ames: Iowa State University Press, 1979.

Keller, Morton. *The Life Insurance Enterprise, 1885–1910.* Cambridge, Mass.: Belknap Press of Harvard University Press, 1963.

Meier, Kenneth J. *The Political Economy of Regulation: The Case of Insurance.* Albany: State University of New York Press, 1988.

Schneiberg, Marc. "Political and Institutional Conditions for Governance by Association: Private Order and Price Controls in American Fire Insurance." *Politics and Society* 27, no. 1 (March 1999): 66–102.

Zelizer, Viviana A. Rotman. *Morals and Markets: The Development of Life Insurance in the United States.* New Brunswick, N.J.: Transaction, 1983.

MARC SCHNEIBERG

INTELLECTUAL AND CULTURAL MOVEMENTS. See Lyceums.

INTERNAL IMPROVEMENTS

During the first half of the nineteenth century numerous American groups sought to improve transportation within the United States. Because the construction of roads, canals, and railroads involved a tremendous amount of capital, these groups tried to involve government in their projects. Although the federal government ultimately played a secondary role in the funding of internal improvements prior to the Civil War, state governments played a major role in the construction of antebellum transportation projects. Between 1817 and 1860 thousands of miles of roads, canals, and railroads were constructed east of the Mississippi River. After the Civil War the federal government replaced state governments as the primary sponsor of transportation projects. Between 1865 and 1900 the vast tracts of the Far West were crisscrossed by thousands of miles of federally subsidized railroads. Throughout the century private investors supplemented government funding by contributing huge amounts of capital to the construction of long-distance transportation projects. Consequently the development of internal improvements in the United States can best be seen as a mixed enterprise involving both public and private sources of capital.

Early Plans

In the early 1800s three groups in particular were interested in developing the nation's internal transportation and communication facilities. American nationalists wanted to create a countrywide transportation network to improve communications and thereby cement relationships among the country's different regions and also enable troops to respond speedily to foreign invasion. Civic boosters, land speculators, and western farmers wanted access to eastern markets, and millers in places like Rochester, New York, hoped to have wheat shipped to them. Merchant capitalists, who began to experience increased competition in the foreign market from European traders immediately after the end of the Napoleonic Wars, wanted to improve transportation between the major commercial cities of the eastern seaboard and the rural portions of their states so as to create a larger domestic market for their goods.

Although earlier attempts at constructing colonial turnpikes were financed in part by government money, most of the nation's earliest transportation projects were funded primarily by private capital. The century's first canals, the Santee and Cooper in South Carolina and the Middlesex in Massachusetts, were paid for by private investors exclusively. As the distances increased between the points that transportation projects attempted to connect, so too did the amount of capital required to complete them. Because private groups could not hope to raise enough money to fund a major road or canal, backers of such projects initially turned to the federal government for financial assistance.

The first internal improvements proposal presented to the federal government was the Gallatin Plan, advanced in 1808 by Albert Gallatin, secretary of the Treasury under President Thomas Jefferson. The plan called for federal financing and supervision of the construction of a turnpike from present-day Maine to Georgia, an intracoastal waterway running roughly parallel to this turnpike, a system of roads crossing the Appalachian Mountains at several key places, major improvements to the navigability of the major east-west river systems east of the Appalachians, and a system of canals linking these rivers to the Great Lakes. The plan carried with it a proposed budget of $30 million, a sum equal to three times the federal government's annual outlay at that time.

Although nearly all agreed that such a system of roads and canals would provide great economic benefits, few agreed on who would reap those benefits. Because a national market did not yet exist, largely owing to the deficiencies of land and water transportation, most people thought only in terms of their local or state economies. For this reason many believed such a network would benefit only those communities through which it passed. Members of Congress from districts not adjacent to the proposed routes were loathe to vote in favor of the plan, particularly given its immense price tag. Although Congress did appropriate enough money in 1811 to construct the National, or Cumberland, Road, a toll-free pike running from Cumberland, Maryland, to Wheeling, Virginia, the rest of the Gallatin Plan was tabled.

Undeterred by the Gallatin Plan's failure in Congress, nationalists, led by Senators Henry Clay of Kentucky and John C. Calhoun of South Carolina, tried a second time to obtain federal money for internal improvements. Encouraged by President James Madison's annual message to Congress in 1815, in which he declared that internal improvements were an excellent idea and that the federal government was in a much better position to create a national transportation network than were the individual states, they began touting the benefits of a nationwide transportation network. They designed the American System, which proposed in part to stimulate the development of a national market by linking the nation's three regions via roads and canals in much the same way that Gallatin had advocated. In 1817 Clay and Calhoun succeeded in gaining passage of the Bonus Bill, which allocated monies acquired from chartering the second Bank of the United States to transportation projects. Although Madison supported such projects, he doubted the bill's constitutionality because it used public money to promote private gain, so he vetoed it. In 1819 Calhoun developed an elaborate plan to secure federal funding for internal improvements, then he spent the next three years securing sufficient congressional support for passage. However, his bill was also vetoed, this time by President James Monroe, for the same reason. Monroe suggested that the obstacle should be removed by amending the Constitution. Proponents of a federally sponsored nationwide transportation network finally gave up the struggle in 1830, when President Andrew Jackson, demonstrating that he, too, believed that such expenditures were unconstitutional, vetoed federal support for the Maysville Road in Kentucky.

Despite presidential reluctance to provide funds for internal improvements, the federal government did participate to a limited degree in the construction of antebellum transportation projects. It eventually donated several million acres to canal construction in Ohio, Michigan, Indiana, Illinois, and Wisconsin and bought about $3 million in stock in various canal companies, primarily the Chesapeake and Ohio. Between 1830 and 1849 the federal government also donated approximately twenty-two million acres of public land to help finance various railroad projects, and in 1854 the government paid $10 million for the Gadsden Purchase, three thousand miles of land in present-day Arizona and New Mexico, so that a transcontinental railroad might be built along the most practical route. However, as a percentage of total capital contributed to transportation projects, the federal government's involvement in funding internal improvements prior to the Civil War was of secondary importance.

Canals

While nationalists lobbied the federal government for funding, local entrepreneurs sought public money from state governments, which proved to be much more amenable to funding internal improvements. Congressmen looked with suspicion on long-distance transportation projects because the economic advantage might fall to someone in another district, but state legislators had no such difficulty. Politicians in New York, Pennsylvania, Maryland, and Virginia, many of whom came from mercantile families, clearly understood that improving transportation between New York City, Philadelphia, Baltimore, or Richmond and their state's western regions would increase business activity and benefit the state's residents. Consequently these states appropriated significant amounts of money to build canals.

Between 1817 and 1837 New York built the Erie Canal from New York City to Buffalo, Pennsylvania completed the Main Line Canal from Philadelphia to Pittsburgh, Maryland and Virginia struggled to construct the Chesapeake and Ohio Canal along the upper reaches of the Potomac River, and Virginia provided capital to finish the James River and Kanawha Canal from Richmond into its western highlands. Inspired by the success of the Erie Canal, between 1830 and 1860 Ohio and Indiana provided enough capital to build the Ohio and Erie, the Miami and Erie, and the Wabash and Erie Canals. During this period New Jersey funded the Delaware and Raritan Canal, one of the intracoastal waterway links proposed in the

Gallatin Plan, and New York completed a system of five feeder canals linking upstate and western New York to New York City via the Erie. In 1850 the federal government concluded the Clayton-Bulwer Treaty with Great Britain as a step toward constructing a canal across the Isthmus of Panama, thereby providing a sea link between the eastern seaboard and the West Coast. Altogether approximately four thousand miles of canals were constructed between 1817 and 1860. Although municipal and private sources also played a role in financing their construction, state funds accounted for approximately two-thirds of the necessary capital. Most of this money was provided via state purchase of canal company stock, the funds for which were raised by the sale of state land, special bond issues, and canal taxes and tolls.

Railroads

After 1840 the passion to build canals began to decline as railroads became increasingly popular. Railroads appealed particularly to commercial interests in states where extensive water routes did not exist or where mountains presented a daunting engineering challenge, but their construction costs were considerably higher than canals. Because railroads came into existence after the U.S. domestic market had taken off, railroad builders had better access to domestic private capital, which was generated in far greater amounts than it had been during the canal age. The development of stock exchanges in New York City also made it easier for private investors to buy and sell shares in railroad corporations than it had been to invest in canal companies. For these reasons state government support of railroad construction was not as extensive as it had been for canal building. Although state governments provided much capital for railroad construction, their contributions amounted to about 25 percent of the capital invested in railroad construction during the antebellum period. Most of the remaining 75 percent was provided by private investors.

Unfortunately for the states, railroads provided ruinous competition for canals, many of which went bankrupt. In addition many of the state-supported railroads overextended themselves financially, and their failures often forced a state to default on the bond issue that had funded the project. These defaults had near-disastrous effects on state credit, in large part because many of the bonds involved were held by English investors who subscribed freely to new securities; those who lost money on a state issue were reluctant to take a second chance. Consequently, several states passed bills or amended their constitutions to prohibit their states from underwriting such projects. By 1850 state governments had lost most of their enthusiasm for large-scale transportation projects. Nevertheless between 1861 and 1890 various states, particularly those in the South, contributed a total of $350 million for the construction of railroads within their borders.

As the states got out of the transportation business, the federal government assumed a larger profile in the development of a national transportation system. Although federal funding did not become widespread until after the Civil War, federal land grants were an important source of capital for internal improvement projects. The Illinois Central Act of 1850, which contributed approximately four million acres to the construction of the Illinois Central Railroad, opened the door to even larger federal land grants later in the century. Altogether the Union Pacific, Northern Pacific, and Atlantic and Pacific Railroads received approximately ninety million acres during the remainder of the century. Nevertheless, federal funding still did not serve as the primary source of capital for railroad construction. Despite their propensity to overextend themselves and go bankrupt, railroads remained attractive to private investors, particularly those with considerable sums of money to invest.

The development of a national transportation network in the United States during the nineteenth century was accomplished through cooperation between the public and private sectors. On the one hand, private entrepreneurs sought to protect themselves from financial ruin by availing themselves of the superior financial strength of state and federal governments. On the other hand, legislators seeking to expand the economic prospects of their polity attracted private money to the construction of transportation projects by offering to assume some but not all of the financial risks involved. The canals and railroads that were built led in turn to the creation of a national market.

See also **Market Revolution; Transportation; Travel, Technology of.**

Bibliography

Gordon, Sarah H. *Passage to Union: How the Railroads Transformed American Life, 1829–1929.* Chicago: Ivan R. Dee, 1996.

Hughes, Jonathan R. T. *The Governmental Habit Redux: Economic Controls from Colonial Times to the Present.* Princeton, N.J.: Princeton University Press, 1991.

Parkman, Aubrey. *History of the Waterways of the Atlantic Coast of the United States.* Washington, D.C.: Government Printing Office, 1983.

Taylor, George Rogers. *The Transportation Revolution, 1815–1860.* New York: Rinehart, 1951.

CHARLES W. CAREY JR.

INTERPRETATIONS OF THE NINETEENTH CENTURY

[This entry includes subentries on **Popular Interpretation of the Frontier West** and **Twentieth-Century Film and Media**.]

POPULAR INTERPRETATIONS OF THE FRONTIER WEST

While popular interpretations and misinterpretations of nineteenth-century events are part of American culture, many Americans have little sense of the nineteenth century as a whole. Few if any nineteenth-century decades resonate in the public mind, even in broad stereotypes. Until the early or mid–twentieth century the public was conscious of the 1890s as a decade marked by industrial conflict, agrarian unrest, economic depression, and a war with Spain, but that sense did not exist by the century's end. The two nineteenth-century events that have had an enduring effect on the public imagination are the Civil War and the "winning" of the West.

Western Literature

The march of white American civilization westward, the story of the frontier, had become the subject of popular interpretations long before the twentieth century. The conquest and settlement of the West became the nation's creation myth. Colorful renditions of frontiersmen, cowboys, American Indians, wagon trains, and rugged yet romantic landscapes together constituted an established genre of Western art by the end of the nineteenth century. From the 1860s into the next century, dime novels shaped legends of real Western figures, including Billy the Kid, Kit Carson, Wild Bill Hickok, Calamity Jane, and Annie Oakley, and fictional ones, such as Deadwood Dick.

By the early twentieth century the popular human centerpiece of the Wild West, the cowboy, had become the subject of an immensely popular novel by Owen Wister, *The Virginian* (1902), and a series of huge sellers by Zane Grey, most notably *Riders of the Purple Sage* (1912). Andy Adams, a bona fide cowboy, wrote unromantically of the realities and hardships of the trail drive in *The Log of a Cowboy* (1903). But it was the mythic heroes of Wister and Grey who captured the public imagination, not Adams's plainer, truer portrayal. For example, more than 1.5 million copies of *The Virginian* had been sold by 1938, and around 6 million copies of *Riders of the Purple Sage* have been purchased. Clearly, for the reading public the mythology of cowboy life—characterized by freedom, independence, peace of mind, and stunning vistas of the West—was far more palatable than the grim realities of what was essentially low-paid wage labor marked by long hours, dangerous conditions, and the absence of family life. More than a century after the great cattle drives of the late nineteenth century, the romantic cowboy image still abounds in film, television, and advertising.

Early Western Films

The Western movie industry, building on a wealth of literary and artistic precedent, helped create the popular image of western settlement as a noble, heroic effort by well-intentioned white settlers who faced the dangers of a savage wilderness and even more savage Indians. It is a simple story of struggle against and triumph over adversity with little attention paid to what Native Americans suffered as a consequence of the white advance. One of the most enduring images of the Western film genre features a wagon train being attacked by Indians, effectively turning the mainstream majority into an innocent minority victimized by savages. The scene was played out in countless Westerns, most famously in producer John Ford's classic *Stagecoach* (1939), which drew heavily on Frederic Remington's vivid, action-packed painting *Downing the Nigh Leader* (1907). In much the same way that Puritan captivity narratives suggested that whites were constantly being abducted by Indians, Western movies usually perpetuated the misperception that peaceful white settlers and soldiers were constantly under attack by Indians. Such misperceptions perhaps served to ease the conscience of a nation whose real past was characterized far more by the subjugation of native peoples than by victimization by them.

Another staple of the Western movie industry was the direct juxtaposition of good and evil with few discernible shades of gray in human nature. Celluloid legends such as John Wayne had to use force and take lives to ensure the triumph of good over evil; they were forced, by the magnitude of the evils they faced, to resort to violence. Not surprisingly, this genre reached its heyday in the late 1940s and the 1950s, when the cold war between the United States and the Soviet Union was at its most intense. As Dwight Eisenhower's secretary of state, John Foster Dulles, and other cold warriors painted the ideological conflict between the two superpowers in stark, absolutist terms—a struggle between the forces of light and those of darkness—Western movies did essentially the same thing.

Westerns were a thoroughly male genre and an almost exclusively white one. African Americans, a significant presence in the nineteenth-century West, were conspicuously absent from the West of the silver screen. With only occasional Chinese laundrymen, Indian sidekicks such as Tonto for the Lone Ranger, and Mexican villains and senoritas, Hollywood portrayed a decidedly Anglo West that mainstream America could relate to. In the first half of the twentieth century, the Hollywood West was filled with prideful reminders of a noble heritage for European Americans.

Revisionist Westerns

By the mid-1960s, however, Westerns were no longer as unabashedly nationalistic and simplistic as they had been. A classic example of the shift is the 1970 movie version of Thomas Berger's novel *Little Big Man* (1964), starring Dustin Hoffman as Jack Crabb, who recounts his life among Indians and whites on the late-nineteenth-century Plains frontier. The movie poked fun at hallowed Western icons, such as the snake-eyed gunfighter, and graphically depicted the U.S. Cavalry, under an egomaniacal General George Armstrong Custer, slaughtering Indian women and children. The movie's mix of tragedy, irony, and black humor is a significant departure from the classic Western format.

In the 1990s two Oscar-winning movies demonstrated the enduring appeal of the movie Western and a growing appreciation for the complexity of the western past. Kevin Costner's *Dances with Wolves* (1990), while in the last analysis a romantic movie about a white hero and heroine in an Indian setting, nonetheless exhibits an environmental consciousness and an emphasis on the consequences of the white advance onto the Plains. Clint Eastwood's *Unforgiven* (1992) paints a grim picture of an aging gunfighter trying to escape his past and live a decent life, but even the fond memory of his "dear departed wife" cannot prevent Will Monnie from succumbing to the lure of easy money. The money is put up as a bounty by a group of prostitutes seeking revenge for the brutal slashing of one of their coworkers. The young prostitute was attacked by her customer because she giggled at his lack of endowment. *Unforgiven* also chronicles the process by which Western myths were spun by dime novelists and by ordinary people embellishing a story with every retelling. Eastwood's movie also features a black sidekick with an Indian wife and a young, would-be gunfighter and killer who is sickened by his first and only violent act—the murder of a man sitting on a toilet.

Dances with Wolves, Unforgiven, and the 1989 television miniseries adaptation of Larry McMurtry's novel *Lonesome Dove* (1985) give a more complex picture of the "winning" of the West that shows consequences, avoids moral absolutes, and eschews romance in favor of gritty realism.

Reinterpretations in Art and History

These revisionist Westerns have their parallel in recent appraisals of Western art. A controversial exhibit, *The West as America*, at the Smithsonian Institution in 1991 reevaluated the heroic, romantic images of westward expansion as justifications for Euro-American imperialism and conquest and as fundamentally racist and materialist images. The more than seven hundred written reactions to the exhibit in the comment books provided evidence of the enduring legacy of the West and its centrality to American culture. Some visitors praised the exhibit for trying to present a more honest, less romantic western past. Others viewed it as "a mean spirited and cynical attack on western art and artists."

The efforts of some moviemakers and art critics to reinterpret the nation's western legacy have been mirrored in and inspired by the writings of a new generation of historians who since the mid-1980s have worked to demythologize the West for an audience outside of academia. The most influential of these self-labeled new western historians, Patricia Nelson Limerick, wrote the book *The Legacy of Conquest: The Unbroken Past of the American West* (1987), which plays down the triumphal, romantic story of frontier advance and emphasizes the conquest, subjugation, and resistance of women, Native Americans, and other peoples of color in the West; the despoliation of the fragile environment; and the less-than-romantic motivations that brought European Americans to the West. Limerick and a host of other revisionists to some degree have put the story of a less mythic, more complex and morally ambiguous western heritage before the public.

Advertising Images

The task of the new western historians is daunting. They contend less with other historians who wish to sustain the mythic West within the walls of academia and more with advertising agencies that understand the awesome power of traditional western images to sell everything from cars and trucks to clothing, cosmetics, colognes, alcohol, cigarettes, and real estate. Their interpretations of the West have reached a broad audience that is bombarded daily with images that play up the classic western frontier themes of freedom, independence, self-reliance, and ruggedness against a background of stunning scenery.

The sports utility vehicle (SUV) craze of the 1990s offers a good example of the power of western themes

Indians Trading at a Frontier Town. Note the use of popular images of the western frontier: American Indians, traders, coonskin caps and furs hanging from the door frame. From *Harper's Weekly*, 3 July and 31 November 1875. LIBRARY OF CONGRESS

in advertising. For men and women wishing to reassert their independence and regain control of their lives, the Ford Motor Company has offered the Explorer and the Expedition, Mazda has offered the Navaho, Jeep has offered the Cherokee and the Grand Cherokee, and Nissan has offered the Pathfinder. Cars with names evocative of cowboys or horses, such as the Mustang, Bronco, Dakota, and Wrangler, provide further evidence of the utilization of frontier themes by automobile manufacturers. Typically, newspaper and television ads for these vehicles are set against a rugged western landscape and promise a touch of the nineteenth-century West at the dawning of the new millennium. Advertisements that draw on the Old West as an escape from the present keep alive, in a strange sense, the nineteenth-century notion of the frontier as a safety valve—a new beginning for overworked, underpaid eastern industrial laborers. Of course, the vast majority of nineteenth-century eastern laborers did not head for the frontier to stake out homesteads, and the vast majority of SUV owners do not actually take their four-wheel-drive vehicles off-road and explore the wilderness.

Drawing on the public's familiarity with Western themes, advertisers strike a familiar set of chords: western backdrops emphasize the toughness and the ruggedness of vehicles, the comfort and durability of clothing, and so on. Such ads appeal to the public's yearning for the simplicity and purity of the past. These ads do not sell the Old West, something very few contemporary Americans would wish to buy in unmythologized form; instead they depict a faint semblance of it, a taste of the frontier, echoes of freedom, ruggedness, and self-reliance.

Walt Disney began offering a semblance of the Old West to the American public in 1955 through Frontierland and Main Street U.S.A., an idealized rendering of a typical late-nineteenth-century small town's main thoroughfare, at Disneyland in Anaheim, California. The creatively constructed landscape of Frontierland works in a way similar to Western advertisements. A trip to Frontierland provides the visitor with a mélange of Old West images—cowboys, Indians, stockaded forts, the *Mark Twain* steamboat—that together offer a chance to wander into the past and imagine oneself as a fearless, self-reliant pioneer. The images are drawn from the whole of the nineteenth century and from the early trans-Appalachian frontier to the dramatic scenery of the Far West, particularly the southwestern desert. The images resonate individually and collectively by evoking a romantic, adventurous frontier setting and by placing the visitor in its midst as a participant.

The lack of exact chronology in Frontierland may actually help to explain the place's popularity a hundred years after the nineteenth century came to a close. In the popular imagination the frontier is a mood, a spirit, a metaphor for promise, freedom, and opportunity. On a largely subconscious level it is an antidote of sorts to the technological excesses of a society that has urbanized, suburbanized, industrialized, and modernized at a rapid pace for well over a century. Popular interpretations of the nineteenth century as a whole are formed from agrarian simplicity and purity, simple small-town living, wholesome values, and skilled artisanship as opposed to mass production, all of which are captured in Main Street U.S.A. In addition, the supposed frontier qualities of independence, freedom, self-reliance, ruggedness, and ingenuity evoke a world where the challenges were greater than the modern ones of fighting traffic and completing one's Christmas shopping. To experience that spiritual and psychological rejuvenation, Billy Crystal and his urban sidekicks head to the West in the movie *City Slickers* (1991), and after successfully facing the challenges of the frontier on a cattle drive, they return to their wives and girlfriends with enough frontier spirit to sustain them until the sequel, *City Slickers II: The Legend of Curly's Gold* (1994).

The historian Frederick Jackson Turner proclaimed in his essay *The Significance of the Frontier in American History* (1893) that the frontier was closed, and a host of other writers began to lament the passing of a wild, untamed West. Nevertheless, that mythic concept and place continue to provide fertile ground for popular interpretations and reinterpretations. The mythology of the nineteenth-century frontier West is an integral component of the national heritage and culture, and it is likely to endure well into the twenty-first century and beyond.

See also **American Indians,** *subentry on* **The Image of the Indian; Cowboys and Cowgirls; Frontier; West, The.**

Bibliography

Butler, Anne M. "Selling the Popular Myth." In *The Oxford History of the American West.* Edited by Clyde A. Milner II, Carol A. O'Connor, and Martha A. Sandweiss. New York: Oxford University Press, 1994.

Etulain, Richard. *Re-Imagining the Modern American West: A Century of Fiction, History, and Art.* Tucson: University of Arizona Press, 1996.

Grossman, James R., ed. *The Frontier in American Culture: Essays by Richard White and Patricia Nelson Limerick.* Berkeley: University of California Press, 1994.

Kammen, Michael. *Mystic Chords of Memory: The Transformation of Tradition in American Culture.* New York: Vintage, 1993.

Nash, Gerald D. "Historical Commentary: The West as Utopia and Myth." *Montana: The Magazine of Western History* 41 (winter 1991): 69–75.

Slotkin, Richard. *Gunfighter Nation: The Myth of the West in Twentieth-Century America.* New York: Harper Perennial, 1992.

Steiner, Michael. "Frontierland as Tomorrowland: Walt Disney and the Architectural Packaging of the Mythic West." *Montana: The Magazine of Western History* 48 (spring 1998): 2–17.

Truettner, William H., ed. *The West as America: Reinterpreting Images of the Frontier, 1820–1920.* Washington, D.C.: Smithsonian, 1991.

West, Elliott, "Selling the Myth: Western Images in Advertising." *Montana: The Magazine of Western History* 46 (summer 1996): 36–49.

DAVID M. WROBEL

TWENTIETH-CENTURY FILM AND MEDIA

America's nineteenth century has been represented in film and television chiefly as the celebratory epic of the Civil War and the western frontier and somewhat as the melodrama of increasingly urbanized, industrialized life. Most films about nineteenth-century history have focused on events of the period extending from the Civil War to the end of the century. The first half of the century, the War of 1812, the slave rebellion led by Nat Turner, and the Mexican War, have gone virtually without recognition in significant films. A strong cinematic record, however, portrays Civil War battles, frontier adventures, and wry social dramas about class and politics.

The general question of how to represent American history accurately on film has been much debated. Some scholars have taken filmmakers to task for working freely with factual details, as in films that change a life story to offer a happy ending or that play loosely with the period. In *Santa Fe Trail* (1940), for example, John Brown, brilliantly played by Raymond Massey, is captured by an army with cannon and cavalry although neither was present at Harpers Ferry. A Civil War battle may be retold to highlight the untrue but dramatic contribution of a particular soldier, the troops may be dressed in an incorrect costume, or soldiers may fire the wrong weapons for the period. Some films indulge in deliberate anachronism for comic effect, as in the Marx brothers' film *Go West* (1940). During a crisis, when Groucho Marx is asked to telephone for the sheriff, he shouts: "Telephone? This is 1879! The telephone hasn't been invented yet!"

Others have defended the privilege of filmmakers to depict historical events just as they wish in the interest not of history but of a story. Even if events are retold with imperfect accuracy, they reason, a skillful historical drama at least exposes viewers to information about their own pasts and perhaps motivates them to learn more. Thus Ken Burns, the creator of the acclaimed eleven-hour television documentary *The Civil War* (1990), asserted that his obligations to history are not as important as "the demands of the ultimate master, which is narrative" ("In Search of the Painful, Essential Images of War").

Early Themes: The Civil War and the Wild West

It is no accident that the first American feature film was a Western, *The Great Train Robbery* (1903), or that the first blockbuster film was about the Civil War and Reconstruction, *The Birth of a Nation* (1915). Both films were made during the Progressive Era. The racial and ethnic composition of the American population had diversified enormously in this period owing to increases in immigration from Europe. Many scholars have examined early films as guides to American life, meant for immigrants and natives alike, to explain and justify the dominance of Anglo-Saxons. Both films indulge white paranoia by telling the story of threats by nonwhites to imagined racial purity.

In *The Great Train Robbery,* Edwin S. Porter established a number of the standard visual practices of the Western, including thrilling stunts, such as jumping off a moving train on to a galloping horse, and a variety of wide shots and close-ups. The adaptation of cinematic technology to a popular set of stories about the recent past was, in many ways, the obvious course for American films to take. Westerns were already the best-selling genre of the "dime novels," popular stories about adventure and romance in frontier towns, with stock characters such as white-hatted heroes and black-hatted villains. Westerns were an instant hit. They were also the immediate subject of disputes about how to represent Native Americans. Frequently played by white actors in dark makeup, American Indians were inevitably the losers in battles with whites, and they displayed the imagined Indian traits of verbal terseness, vague spirituality, savagery, and bloodthirstiness.

The Birth of a Nation is significant in film history because of the technical genius of D. W. Griffith and his determination to make an American epic. After decades of debate, it was acknowledged as "a flawed masterpiece." The film is a simpleminded morality tale about white supremacy based on Thomas Dixon's racist novel *The Clansman* (1905), which glorified the exploits of the Ku Klux Klan (KKK) in terrorizing newly freed blacks in the Reconstruction South. *The Birth of a Nation* represents southern blacks as clownish, imbecilic, and savage. The "birth" in the title refers to the rise of the KKK, white men outraged by what the film depicts as the brutish behavior of the blacks who had recently acquired control of the South. This brutishness climaxes with the attempted rape of one white woman and the attempted forced marriage of another. The Klan sweeps in and eliminates the menace. The "nation" is therefore actually reborn for whites, who rescue white womanhood from bestial blacks and in general reestablish the social arrangement of plantation slavery.

Used as a recruiting tool by the revived Ku Klux Klan in 1915, *The Birth of a Nation* had an enormous negative effect on white Americans' understanding of black culture and on whites' willingness to extend blacks full citizenship. Many northerners found in the film a justification for southern racism toward black people and largely accepted the reborn KKK as a reasonable social movement. Later films about the nineteenth century routinely purveyed demeaning images of blacks, notably as grinning plantation inferiors in the hugely popular *Gone with the Wind* (1939). Strong protests against *The Birth of a Nation* organized by the young National Association for the Advancement of Colored People (NAACP) failed to stop distribution of the film but at least raised public questions about the unjust portrayal of blacks in films.

These formative films gave rise to two principal types of American cinematic epic. The Western became the most successful Hollywood genre, and it changed as filmmakers' views of the past changed. The so-called horse opera found an early master in the director John Ford, whose *Stagecoach* (1939) is probably his finest film. The tale of a perilous journey by a group of passengers, *Stagecoach* offers many classic ingredients of the romantic Western, including a mix of classes and races, gorgeous wide shots of natural scenery, and a redemptive, happy ending marked by the cathartic violence of the hero. John Wayne played Ringo, a Civil War veteran traveling west to settle an old score. He is accompanied by a variety of character types: a gambler, a pregnant genteel lady, a traveling salesman, a drunkard, and a prostitute named Stella, with the proverbial heart of gold. The stagecoach passengers endure the rigors of an Indian attack, childbirth in a wayside inn, bitter fights over propriety and social customs, and the tempestuous courtship of Stella by Ringo.

Ford's West is, for whites, a democratic zone,

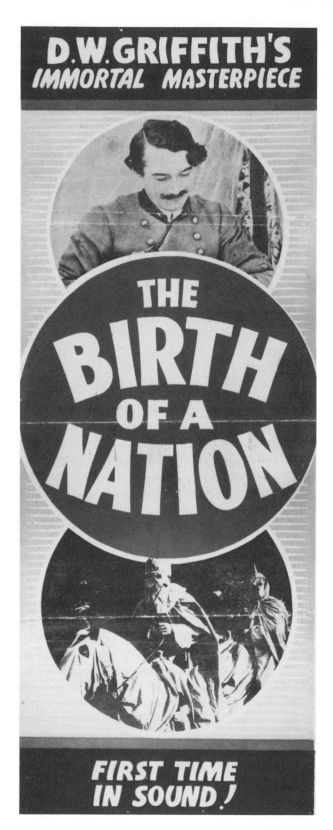

The Birth of a Nation. This 1936 movie poster announced the first use of sound in D. W. Griffith's 1915 cinematic triumph, a film that celebrated white supremacy and the Ku Klux Klan. LIBRARY OF CONGRESS: PRINTS AND PHOTOGRAPHS DIVISION.

where social differences tend to matter less then innate goodness. Ford, from the vantage of the 1930s, viewed the 1870s and 1880s as lawless but admirably rugged and open to individuals' efforts to improve their lots. His later films, such as *The Searchers* (1956) and *The Man Who Shot Liberty Valance* (1962), are more elegiac, depicting in the West the lost innocence of the American nation. His legendary photography of desert landscapes, especially of Arizona's Monument Valley, are symbolic representations of the West's idealized freedoms and have been widely imitated.

While Ford created his fictional West, other directors explored variations on the Ford pastoral. Fred Zinneman created the somber Western *High Noon* (1952), an exploration of conformity and terror in a town afraid to help the marshal, played splendidly by Gary Cooper, in his fight against evil. The film is frequently read as a comment on the fearful 1950s of Senator Joseph McCarthy. Likewise, George Stevens's *Shane* (1953) presents a lone gunfighter, played by Alan Ladd, whose knightly qualities duly involve him in a classic morality tale of good small farmers against evil big farmers. John Sturges's *Gunfight at the OK Corral* (1957), the story of Wyatt Earp and Doc Holliday, also represents the American West as a testing ground of individual character.

By the late 1960s directors of Westerns found less to celebrate in the genre. The Vietnam War and the general climate of protest and unrest in the United States inspired Westerns that inverted the conventions of the genre, depicting the senselessness of gunfights that were formerly seen as heroic and liberating. Sam Peckinpah's *The Wild Bunch* (1969) is the best-known example of this revisionist kind of Western. Its opening scene, in which the participants in a temperance parade in a western town are massacred by a posse of criminals, is a tour de force of brutality and lawlessness. Sergio Leone's "Spaghetti Westerns," so called because they were made in Italy, continued this trend of picaresque violence with *A Fistful of Dollars* (1964), *For a Few Dollars More* (1965), and *The Good, the Bad, and the Ugly* (1966), all starring Clint Eastwood. After the 1980s the Western enjoyed a revival with eclectic and brilliant works describing the forgotten constituencies of the nineteenth-century West, including antiheroic men, as in *Unforgiven* (1992); black cowboys, as in *Posse* (1993); and Native Americans, as in *Thunderheart* (1992) and *Dances with Wolves* (1990).

Television was a blander and more conservative medium in the United States, producing relatively tame additions to the narrative interest in the frontier, such as *Bonanza* (1959–1973), *The Wild Wild West* (1965–1968), *Gunsmoke* (1955–1975), *Bat Mas-*

terson (1958–1960), *Have Gun Will Travel* (1957–1962), *The Adventures of Rin Tin Tin* (1954–1956), and *Little House on the Prairie* (1974–1982). The last, adapted from Laura Ingalls Wilder's charming books, follows the Ingalls family in their struggle to homestead on the frontier. Both *Little House* and *Bonanza* were praised for their wholesome depictions of family frontier life, but most of the gunfighter television series presented formulaic action sequences, melodramatic plots, and witless dialogue.

The Public Broadcasting Service (PBS) became the main source of high-quality examinations of western life and history. Its 1990s series *The American Experience* is comprised of dozens of short documentaries, including five on the nineteenth-century West: *The Donner Party* on the cannibalism of a party of stranded pioneers; *Gold Fever* on the Alaskan gold rush; *The Iron Road* on the race to complete transcontinental rail lines; *Lost in the Grand Canyon* on John Wesley Powell's romantic exploration of the Colorado River; and *The Orphan Trains* on a philanthropic society that in the 1850s shipped homeless children from East Coast urban poverty to "wholesome" lives out West. PBS produced other fine work, such as the Ken Burns series *The West*, *In Search of the Oregon Trail*, and documentaries on the Mexican-American and Spanish-American Wars. The History Channel, produced by A&E, began to offer history documentaries twenty-four hours a day on cable television in the late twentieth century, again representing the American nineteenth century in frontier stories and the drama of the Civil War.

The other great subject of cinematic interest in nineteenth-century America, the Civil War, generated fewer films, but those we have are important in Hollywood history. Among them, *Gone with the Wind* has been called by some historians the most popular historical film ever made. Produced by David O. Selznick and based on the best-selling 1936 novel by Margaret Mitchell, *Gone with the Wind* is both a fantasy about the Civil War and a depiction, in some respects fairly accurate, of white southern plantation life. Through the character of Scarlett O'Hara the film describes the work and social power of plantation mistresses in the Old South. Scarlett's mother is in full command of domestic life at "Tara," the O'Hara plantation, and her tasks range from tending the sick to keeping the account books. Scarlett, in her mercenary drive during Reconstruction to survive financial ruin, suggests the situation of many Civil War widows, who had to defy gender conventions and run businesses.

The distortions of history in *Gone with the Wind* lie chiefly in its demeaning portrayals of blacks. The stereotypes of mincing domestics and loyal "darkies" in the film were scarcely more dignified than the more sinister images of blacks that Griffith created in 1915, and they reportedly made Malcolm X cringe when he first saw the film (Clinton, "Gone with the Wind," p. 134). The director Victor Fleming offered audiences a diaphanous fiction of "the land of Cavaliers and Cotton Fields called the Old South. . . . Look for it only in books, for it is no more than a dream remembered, a Civilization gone with the wind."

A significant corrective to this set of clichés about southern blacks during the Civil War, *Glory* (1989) is also an extraordinarily gripping film. *Glory* was the first film that told the story of the Fifty-fourth Massachusetts Volunteer Infantry, a regiment of black soldiers led by a white officer, Colonel Robert Gould Shaw. Frederick Douglass's two sons served among its ranks. This unit made an unsuccessful but heroic assault on South Carolina's Fort Wagner. The skeptical *New York Tribune* in 1863 asked, "Will the Negro fight?" The doubts of whites were dispelled by the exemplary bravery of the Fifty-fourth, one among many regiments formed by the 178,000 black soldiers who were finally allowed to join the Union army following the Emancipation Proclamation (1863). *Glory* contributes to historical films about the Civil War with complex, humane portraits of the black soldiers, who face not only battle terrors (just as do white soldiers) but also the contempt of whites who think them unfit for combat. They achieve glory in their victory over both obstacles.

Another noteworthy exploration of the war that moves beyond romantic myth is Ken Burns's television documentary *The Civil War*. Narrated by over twenty historians and praised for its use of archival materials and previously unknown letters and photographs, the series has been hailed as the American *Iliad*, Homer's epic about the Trojan War. But even this extensively researched film has been criticized for its excessive attention to military affairs, its neglect of war motives and black voices, and other points of interpretation. Less satisfying was Burns's later documentary *Lewis and Clark* (1997), which depicted the opening of the West in the terms of a recognizable national myth. Exploring expeditions are pleasing reenactments of American Manifest Destiny.

Of course the mythical side of the Civil War and the issue of slavery continued to inspire feature films, though none memorably. Richard Fleischer's *Mandingo* (1975) rehearses the most threadbare of racial stereotypes in its depiction of interracial sex on an antebellum Louisiana plantation. Stephen Spielberg's sentimental *Amistad* (1997) transforms an 1839 slave revolt into a reprise of his successful film *E.T.* (1982), only this time the aliens are West Africans. Even Shirley Temple contributed to the maudlin portrayal of the Old South in the 1935 film *The Littlest Rebel,* in which she charms Abraham Lincoln into sparing her Confederate father's life.

Heroic Biography and Urban Life

Another type of film about the nineteenth century is the heroic biography. Andrew Jackson inspired three "bio-pics," as they are called: *The Gorgeous Hussy* (1936) starring Joan Crawford, who after her wild days as an innkeeper's daughter reforms to marry the president; and two versions of *The Buccaneer,* one by Cecil B. DeMille in 1938 and another by Anthony Quinn in 1958. Lincoln inspired two well-known film biographies. Henry Fonda played the title role in John Ford's *Young Mr. Lincoln* in 1939, and Raymond Massey is the star of John Cromwell's *Abe Lincoln in Illinois* in 1940. All of these films offer sentimental stories of rising to the White House from rustic log cabins. None deals profoundly with political issues, settling instead for harmless pieties about the virtues of hard work. PBS produced creditable biographical documentaries of both the woman suffrage movement in *Not for Ourselves Alone: The Story of Elizabeth Cady Stanton and Susan B. Anthony* (1999) and of Alexander Hamilton and Aaron Burr in *The Duel* (2000).

Many historical films have attempted to resist the temptations and the sweep of national epic. Their topics are generally domestic melodrama. Three film versions of Louisa May Alcott's semiautobiographical novel *Little Women* (1868), for example, relate the tribulations of the four March sisters in Concord, Massachusetts, in the mid–nineteenth century. Unburdened by the rustling silks and stiff corsets of conventional "costume drama," in which ladies and gentlemen speak to each other as if through Victorian gauze, *Little Women* has consistently appealed to audiences who cherish the personal miseries and triumphs of the four female protagonists. Alcott's roots in the idealistic New England philosophical movement known as transcendentalism are emphasized in the 1994 version, which also delves into the details of social movements in the 1850s and 1860s, including diet and dress reform for women, abolitionism, and education reform.

Joan Micklin Silver's excellent *Hester Street* (1974), about Jewish immigrant life on New York's Lower East Side, depicts with thoughtfulness the difficulties of the immigrant experience. A woman, Gitl, recently arrived in New York from Poland to join her husband Jake, is shocked that he has shaved off his beard "Yankee style." Jake is ashamed that Gitl still wears the Old World, orthodox *sheitl* or wig to cover her hair according to Jewish marital custom. The two

eventually divorce and find more suitable partners, but not before Gitl acquires from Jake his American girlfriend's fortune. Another little-known film, *The Molly Maguires* (1970), about the early movement to unionize miners in Pennsylvania, features actors Richard Harris and Sean Connery. The protagonists' conflict on opposing sides of a unionization battle illustrates two kinds of immigrant adaptation to the United States. One character is irrationally loyal to his origins, and the other turns cruelly away from his roots. The film maintains an impressive ambiguity about which kind is better off. Immigration and the labor movement, despite their importance in American life after the Civil War, have been overlooked by major films.

Perhaps the best of all the costume dramas that have been made about the intrigues and intricacies of upper-class society in the nineteenth century, Martin Scorsese's *The Age of Innocence* (1993), is adapted from Edith Wharton's 1920 novel about New York society in the 1870s. Wharton carefully anatomized the materials of upper-class life, from its china patterns to its opera boxes to its flower arrangements, as the background for a story of unconsummated passion between Newland Archer and Ellen Olenska. Scorsese's adaptation brilliantly conveys the textures and opulence of this life. The 1870s were known for their decorative luxury, and Scorsese's research team accordingly investigated the precise cuts of dress for married versus unmarried ladies, the paintings hung in fashionable drawing rooms, the style of carriages kept by "old" New York families and those vaunted by the nouveaux riches, the number of courses served at a going-away dinner in winter, and the European literature a bookish young man might import from a London bookseller. The film offers perhaps as clear a picture of a single social stratum of nineteenth-century America as is possible.

Conclusion

Filmmakers turned to historians for guidance in their work only in the late twentieth century. The collaboration can result in exceptional richness and accuracy of detail, as in *The Age of Innocence.* But in general the question of faithfulness to historical facts has not troubled most filmmakers, who try for an emotional and impressionistic understanding of a historical period and would rather tell a good story than accurately present the historical record. Given the capacity of film to dazzle and mesmerize viewers, it is fortunate that, amid a profusion of melodrama and sentiment, a number of incisive and balanced films look at nineteenth-century American history.

See also **American Indians,** *subentry on* **The Image of** the Indian; Civil War, *subentry on* Remembering the Civil War; History; Ku Klux Klan; Movies; Race and Racial Thinking; West, The.

Bibliography

Burns, Ken. "In Search of the Painful, Essential Images of War." *New York Times*, 27 January 1991.

Clinton, Catherine. "Gone with the Wind." In *Past Imperfect: History According to the Movies*. Edited by Mark C. Carnes. New York: Holt, 1995.

KRIS FRESONKE

INTERSTATE COMMERCE   In September 1786, commissioners from five states met at a special commercial convention in Annapolis, Maryland, to discuss tariff and taxation issues that were creating increased economic tensions within and among the states of the new Republic. They, like other nationalists, feared that a diversity of state tariffs, duties, monopolies, and regulations would restrict interstate commerce and thwart the development of a national free trade economy. Though the convention had no formal standing, the delegates present proposed a meeting in 1787 to amend the Articles of Confederation. Congress passed a resolution that made the call of the Annapolis convention legal.

When members of the Constitutional Convention met eight months later, they brought with them a deep concern that national political unity could be undermined by economic civil war, or as James Madison described it in Federalist No. 42, "unceasing animosities" among the states. Determined that the national government should promote economic harmony among the states, the framers of the Constitution formulated the so-called commerce clause (Article I, Section 8, Clause 3), which gave Congress the power to "regulate Commerce with foreign Nations, and among the several States, and with the Indian Tribes."

Antebellum Interpretations of the Commerce Clause

In the nineteenth century, the commerce clause became one of the focal points of ongoing constitutional debates over the scope of federal power and its relation to that of the states. As the territory of the United States expanded, the economy shifted from international trade to the production and exchange of goods and services for domestic consumption. In response, politicians who supported national development called for the federal government to promote a national economy. One aspect of this developmental program—which included a national bank, federal

funding for internal improvements, and high tariffs to foster and protect American manufacturing—was the use of federal power to promote interstate trade and the creation of a national free market. Though the commerce clause gave Congress the power to regulate interstate commerce, how Congress would assert that power and what its interaction with the states would be remained unclear.

Initially, the power of the federal government was defined through the efforts of entrepreneurs, capitalists, and merchants who used the courts to challenge state efforts to interfere with interstate trade or rights over personal property carried across state lines. In *Gibbons v. Ogden* (1824), Aaron Ogden sued Thomas Gibbons, a rival operator of a steamboat ferry between New Jersey and New York City, for infringing on his monopoly rights to navigate in New York waters that he had purchased in 1815 from Robert R. Livingston and Robert Fulton, who had received a monopoly to operate steamboats from the state of New York as early as 1803. Though the right of New York to grant a monopoly was upheld in the lower courts as within the concurrent rights of states to regulate commerce within their territory, an appeal brought the case before the Supreme Court.

In his opinion, Chief Justice John Marshall reaffirmed the principles of federal supremacy and static, traditional property rights that he had previously articulated by prohibiting states from interfering with federal activity within their borders (*McCulloch v. Maryland*, 1819) or abridging contracts in any way (*Fletcher v. Peck*, 1810, and *Dartmouth College v. Woodward*, 1819). Marshall argued that transportation was indeed "commerce" and that a state monopoly that limited interstate commerce abridged the power of the federal government. He affirmed that the power to regulate commerce was exclusively held by the federal government and also, by overruling the state's effort to limit and control commerce into or across its territory, implied that the federal government had the power to limit the regulatory power of the states. Within weeks of the opinion, unrestricted interstate shipping entered New York Harbor, ending interstate rivalries and opening the way for the creation of a national free trade economy.

Though it has been argued that most subsequent cases on interstate trade were "merely commentary on *Gibbons*" (Hall, Wiecek, and Finkelman, p. 125), the Supreme Court gradually established a more nuanced interpretation of the respective rights of the federal government and the states to regulate commerce in the antebellum period. In *Brown v. Maryland* (1827) Marshall struck down the validity of state license taxes on wholesalers as a violation of Article I, Section 10 of the Constitution, which prohibits states from imposing any duties or tariffs. In *City of New York v. Miln* (1837), however, Justice Philip P. Barbour held that a law requiring ships to report data on immigrants was a legitimate use of the state's police power. In *License Cases* (1847), Chief Justice Roger B. Taney further confused the issue by contending that in the absence of federal power, a state still had a concurrent power to regulate commerce, which he defined as "the power to govern men and things within the limits of its dominion." In *Cooley v. The Board of Wardens of the Port of Philadelphia* (1852), the court refined the meaning of this power by noting that some commerce was national in character and thus demanded uniform regulation, while other commerce was local and demanded a diversity of regulation. In the "local" realm, the states had the power to regulate commerce or subjects that the federal government had not yet regulated. In shifting its focus to the subjects of regulation, the court opened up a broad area of commerce in which states had "concurrent" regulatory power, but it also reserved for itself and the federal government the centralized power to regulate and control interstate commerce in ways that helped create a unified national economy.

Federal Regulatory Power in the Free Market Economy

In a series of rulings after the Civil War, the Supreme Court examined the exclusive regulatory power of the federal government. The court reinforced the view that states maintained concurrent powers or police power over trade originating or carried out within their borders, or trade matters of a "local" nature, or even over "instruments of trade" (for example, dams, bridges, ferries, or turnpikes) within a state (*Hall v. DeCuir*, 1878). But even as the courts conceded certain regulatory powers to the states, they expanded the power of the commerce clause to prohibit state regulations that directly discriminated against or exerted a "direct burden" on interstate trade. This two-tiered or "dual approach" interpretation of the commerce clause resulted in an increasingly complex understanding of the interaction between federal and state powers to regulate trade in the twentieth century.

Meanwhile, the federal government moved only reluctantly toward developing a federal police presence by the end of the nineteenth century. The rapid growth of the free market economy after the Civil War, assisted by the construction of a national railroad network, accelerated the concentration of economic power and the growth of ever larger corporations. These firms initially achieved and maintained their share of highly competitive markets through economies of scale and vertical integration.

By the 1870s, reduced revenues caused by economic recession compelled many firms to limit competition in the marketplace by colluding with other firms to set prices and rates and discriminate against customers. In response, the Populists rose to power in several midwestern states and enacted a flurry of hastily drafted laws that regulated railroad rates, prohibited the free pass system, and established state commissions to control the railroads. Though the Supreme Court regularly overturned state legislation on the grounds that state laws impeded the free flow of interstate commerce (the Wabash Case, 1886), it was increasingly compelled to distinguish between the rights of private property and the power of the state to regulate business.

In the Slaughterhouse Cases (1873), and the Granger Cases, including *Munn v. Illinois* (1877), the Supreme Court concluded that businesses "affected with the public interest" could indeed be regulated by the government, though it continued to support the rights of companies involved in "ordinary trade" to operate free from government regulation. Railroad corporations, as owners and operators of what the federal government considered the public conduits of national economy, clearly came within the newly defined scope of federal regulatory powers. In response to the efforts of a number of states to regulate railroads, the Supreme Court, in the Railroad Cases (1886), clearly limited those powers to regulation that did not abridge the right of private companies to due process.

With the support of the railroads, which desired an end to ruinous rate competition, Congress established the Interstate Commerce Commission in 1887. The narrow manner in which the commission's power was initially defined, the influence of the railroads over board members, and the board's case-by-case approach to regulation precluded the development of a comprehensive regulatory policy and limited the commission's effectiveness in controlling interstate commerce. Many of the commission's decisions either went in favor of the railroads (for example, see *The Lincoln Board of Trade v. The Burlington and Missouri River Railroad Company and the Chicago, Burlington, and Quincy Railroad Company*, 1888, in which the commission rejected the arguments of the city board of trade that the Burlington's railroad rates were unjustly discriminatory to Lincoln) or were overturned by the Supreme Court. Undaunted, Congress sought to further broaden its regulatory power by passing the Sherman Antitrust Act in 1890, which asserted the illegality of unfair restraints of economic activity. Though the Supreme Court initially sought to limit the impact of the Sherman Act power by making separate distinctions between its power to suppress monopolies, control commerce, or regulate manufacturing (*United States v. E. C. Knight*, 1895), the Department of Justice launched several efforts to limit business combinations in the 1890s.

The federal government did not assume its role as a regulatory force having police power over interstate commerce until the twentieth century. Spurred on by the rising tide of Progressive reform, the Justice Department continued to prosecute business monopolies and Congress broadened the ICC's regulatory powers over the railroads in the Hepburn Act of 1906. It also began to pass legislation on matters involving public health and safety such as the Pure Food and Drug Act (which formed the Food and Drug Administration), and the Meat Inspection Act (which empowered the Department of Agriculture to establish a meat inspection system). These opened the door to more aggressive government regulation of commerce, industry, and transportation.

See also **Economic Regulation; Federal-State Relations; Industrialization and the Market; Market Revolution; Railroad Industry, The; Regulation of Business; States' Rights; Supreme Court,** *subentry on* **The Economy.**

Bibliography

Bassinger, Kenneth D. "Dormant Clause Limits on the State Regulation of the Internet: The Transportation Analogy." *Georgia Law Review* 32 (1998): 895–898.

Benson, Paul R. *The Supreme Court and the Commerce Clause, 1937–1970.* New York: Dunellen, 1970.

Hall, Kermit, William M. Wiecek, and Paul Finkelman, eds. *American Legal History: Cases and Materials.* New York: Oxford University Press, 1991.

Palmore, Joseph R. "The Not So Strange Career of Interstate Jim Crow: Race, Transportation, and the Dormant Commerce Clause." *Virginia Law Review* 83 (1997): 1773–1782.

Sellers, Charles Grier. *The Market Revolution: Jacksonian America, 1815–1846.* New York: Oxford University Press, 1991.

Stone, Richard D. *The Interstate Commerce Commission and the Railroad Industry: A History of Regulatory Policy.* New York: Praeger, 1991.

TIMOTHY R. MAHONEY

INVENTORS AND INVENTIONS The United States led all other nations in the development and application of new technologies in the 1800s. By the end of the century, Americans' facility and fascination with machines had helped to change the United States from an overwhelmingly agrarian nation to an industrial power firmly positioned on the cutting edge of technological advancement.

In 1789 Thomas Paine (1737–1809) remarked, "Great scenes inspire great ideas. The nature of America expands the mind, and it partakes of the greatness it contemplates" (Hawke, *Nuts and Bolts of the Past,* p. 24). It seems the very essence of the American experience engendered an atmosphere for innovation. Early settlers brought with them the desire to re-create what had been left behind in the Old World. Separated from familiar ways of life by a vast ocean, these unskilled immigrants were forced to learn the tasks formerly performed by blacksmiths, coopers, and other artisans. Frequently, as the immigrants taught themselves traditional trades, they developed novel ways to reach a desired end. Of necessity the new settlers lived by the maxim, "If at first you don't succeed, try, try again."

At the beginning of the nineteenth century, many young farmers were lured to towns and cities by an industrial revolution that was unfolding in a uniquely American way. By virtue of their rural backgrounds, these unschooled tradesmen were generalists: they could switch between varying tasks and often understood the job at hand intuitively. They conceived of and carried with them new ideas as they roamed from workplace to workplace. In sharing innovative concepts, they often achieved a cross-fertilization of techniques that resulted in improved ways of doing things.

Eli Whitney (1765–1825), best known for inventing the cotton gin in 1792, helped to lay the foundation for America's industrial transformation by proposing in 1801 to manufacture muskets made of interchangeable parts. Whitney was aware that identical, interchangeable parts were the key to mass production.

The steam engine proved to be essential to the nation's industrial development. John Fitch (1743–1798) successfully operated a steam-powered craft on the Delaware River in 1787. Then in the early 1800s, John Stevens (1749–1838) and Oliver Evans (1755–1819) built upon Fitch's work and constructed several steam-powered vessels. Evans went so far as to build an amphibious "steam carriage," the *Orukter Amphibolos,* which was powered by steam on both land and water. Robert Fulton (1765–1815) debuted his steamboat, the *Clermont,* in 1807. While Fulton is commonly remembered as the first American to build a successful steamboat, he openly acknowledged his debt to Fitch, Stevens, and Evans.

The 1830s saw the opportune birth of new farming technology in America, with both the Maine-born Obed Hussey (1792–1860) and the Virginian Cyrus McCormick (1809–1884) building reaping machines.

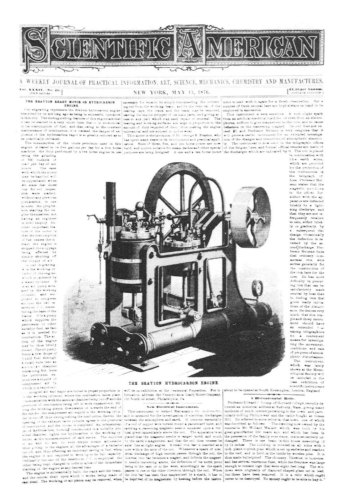

THE BRAYTON HYDROCARBON ENGINE.

Front Page of *Scientific American*. The magazine was devoted to the unprecedented technological progress and innovation of the era; this 13 May 1876 issue featured the Brayton Hydrocarbon Engine. LIBRARY OF CONGRESS

Hussey's reaper was patented several months before McCormick's, and initially was a more effective machine. But McCormick's subsequent improvements and aggressive marketing made his device preeminent. The development of the steel plow in 1838 by John Deere (1804–1886) also was crucial to improving agricultural productivity.

Samuel Morse's (1791–1872) introduction of the electromagnetic telegraph in 1837 helped to make America a more closely knit society. Morse's invention was an outgrowth of Joseph Henry's (1797–1878) work with electromagnets. (Henry later was appointed head of the new Smithsonian Institution in Washington, D.C., an organization devoted to the promotion of science and technology.) Along with the railroad, the telegraph made it possible for companies selling Deere's and McCormick's inventions to grow into national corporations that used mechanized techniques of mass production and distribution.

During the same time period, Charles Goodyear (1800–1860) was single-mindedly pursuing the commercial improvement of rubber, a fickle substance that is vulnerable to temperature and humidity changes. Goodyear's discovery of the vulcanizing process in 1839 made it possible to use rubber products in virtually all spheres of life. Unfortunately, he did not profit personally from the invention, and he died in poverty.

Technological breakthroughs also affected the domestic sphere. Elias Howe (1819–1867) patented his sewing machine in 1846, but it was poorly received. By 1850 Isaac Singer (1811–1875) had redesigned Howe's machine by adding a metal "foot" that held the cloth in place and a continuous feed mechanism that moved the fabric along as each stitch was placed. These innovations made the device a success. After prolonged legal battles, both Howe and Singer were able to enjoy the financial rewards of their work.

The 1850s brought a variety of new ideas. George Corliss (1817–1888) refined the design of his valve gear mechanism, which dramatically increased the efficiency of steam engines. Elevators became safe for passengers with the addition of Elisha Otis's (1811–1861) automatic braking device. Gail Borden (1801–1874) patented a commercial process for producing condensed milk, which became widely used in the next decade.

The Civil War engendered many inventions, although often of a deadly sort. Richard Gatling (1818–1903) designed a hand-cranked, rapid-fire machine gun. (More than twenty years earlier, Gatling had invented a screw propeller for steamboats.) John Ericsson (1803–1889), the personification of American mechanical genius, incorporated several new technological ideas in the Union's *Monitor,* an iron-clad warship. Samuel Colt (1814–1862), known for inventing a revolving pistol, manufactured tens of thousands of weapons during the war at his state-of-the-art arms factory in Hartford, Connecticut. Colt's factory became a hotbed of innovation in the machine-tool trade.

With peace came a tidal wave of U.S. technological developments. In 1868 George Westinghouse (1846–1914) patented an air brake system that markedly improved railroad safety. That same year, Christopher Latham Sholes (1819–1890) introduced the first practical typewriter and later created its familiar keyboard layout. Alexander Graham Bell's invention of the telephone in 1876 and Thomas Edison's rapid succession of inventions in the 1870s and 1880s—among them the phonograph, a practical electric light, and the Kinetoscope—ushered in a new era. George Eastman (1854–1932) revolutionized the art of photography with his inventions of film rolls, the Kodak camera, and flexible, transparent film in the 1880s.

The development of the alternating-current power system by Nikola Tesla (1856–1943) transformed American industry. Tesla's system and its marketing by George Westinghouse were fiercely opposed by Edison and his backers, who supported the direct-current system. But by the mid-1890s, alternating current had been recognized as the most efficient system for generating and distributing electric power. The new abundance of inexpensive electricity made it viable to produce aluminum using Charles Martin Hall's (1863–1914) electrolytic method and to manufacture Carborundum (silicon carbide), the artificial abrasive discovered by Edward G. Acheson (1856–1931).

The first successful U.S. automobile was produced by Charles Duryea (1861–1938) and J. Frank Duryea (1869–1967) in 1893, three years before Henry Ford built his first vehicle. Little did these inventors know how the automobile would come to dominate the twentieth century. In 1884 Herman Hollerith (1860–1929) patented his electromechanical system of encoding data on cards with punched holes. Little, too, did he realize how his invention would become crucial to the development of the digital computer, which would, in its turn, lead the way into the twenty-first century.

See also **Agricultural Technology; Electricity; Military Technology; Steam Power; Travel, Technology of.**

Bibliography

Gies, Joseph, and Frances Gies. *The Ingenious Yankees.* New York: Crowell, 1976.

Hawke, David Freeman. *Nuts and Bolts of the Past: A History of American Technology, 1776–1860.* New York: Harper and Row, 1988.

Hindle, Brooke, and Steven Lubar. *Engines of Change: The American Industrial Revolution, 1790–1860.* Washington, D.C.: Smithsonian Institution Press, 1986.

Hughes, Thomas Parke. *American Genesis: A Century of Invention and Technological Enthusiasm, 1870–1970.* New York: Viking, 1989.

DANIEL MARTIN DUMYCH

INVESTMENT AND CAPITAL FORMATION

High and rising levels of investment and capital formation throughout the nineteenth century propelled the United States to world economic leadership. When the century began, the new nation was a small, predominantly agricultural economy on the periphery of a Europe-centered world system. But its tiny modernizing sectors—commerce, manufacturing, and transportation—were already expanding rapidly. It was the continued growth of these sectors at high rates, compared with those elsewhere, that by mid-century made the country a major world economy. By the end of the century, the United States, vastly larger than European countries in territory and population, was by far the world's largest national economy. Capital formation, the end result of investment in productive assets, was crucial to what some have called this "grand traverse."

Growth of the Capital Stock

A nation's capital stock is the value of the durable goods that it credits and uses to produce other goods and services. It is made up of items such as factories, machinery, and transportation and communications networks. Economic historians have provided us with estimates of the U.S. capital stock at benchmark dates for the entire nineteenth century. Because estimates of aggregate economic income and product flows are available only since the 1840s, the capital stock estimates furnish the best record available of the U.S. economy's early growth.

Benchmark index numbers of the real capital stock ("real" here meaning adjusted for changes in the price level) and the real capital stock per capita are given in the accompanying table. They indicate that

Index Numbers of U.S. Real Capital Stock, Total and Per Capita, 1799–1900

Year	Total Capital Stock	Per Capita Capital Stock
1799	100	100
1805	153	125
1815	200	123
1840	562	168
1850	1,017	225
1860	1,965	320
1870	2,036	263
1880	3,556	363
1890	6,983	569
1900	10,056	679

Source: Adapted from Robert E. Gallman, "American Economic Growth before the Civil War," Table 2.4, p. 89, and Table 2.6, p. 92.

Note: For both series Gallman's capital stock deflated by the Consumer Price Index was used to derive the real capital stock in 1860 prices, and his "conventional concept" of the capital stock. His series were converted to a base of 1799 = 100 from his base of 1774 = 100 to better show the relative movements of the two series over the nineteenth century.

the U.S. economy in 1900 possessed one hundred times the capital it had in 1799. This implies that the capital stock grew at a rate of 4.6 percent per year over the century.

The country's population also expanded at a high rate, growing from 5.3 million in 1800 to 76 million in 1900. But the capital stock grew even faster. Consequently, as the table indicates, capital per person increased nearly sevenfold over the course of the century, growing at an average annual rate of 1.9 percent. This large increase over time in capital per person, in facilities and equipment per worker, helped raise U.S. labor productivity to high levels, thereby increasing American living standards.

The rate of growth of the capital stock, and the rates of investment and savings that contributed to it, exhibited a tendency to increase over time. Total capital grew marginally faster (4.6 percent per year) between 1850 and 1900 than it did between 1799 and 1850 (4.5 percent). Because population growth slowed after 1850, the difference between the two eras is more pronounced in the per capita capital stock estimates, which grew 2.2 percent per year in the latter half of the century, compared with 1.6 percent during the first half.

Net investment and savings rates, the proportions of net national income and net national product devoted to capital formation, exhibit a similar pattern. They are estimated at 6–7 percent early in the century, with a rise to a range of 10–12 percent before the Civil War and a further rise to 18–20 percent by the end of the century.

Overall economic growth, in keeping with the investment pattern, also probably accelerated in the early decades of the century. This appears to have been the result of an initially small but rapidly growing nonagricultural sector steadily accounting for an ever-larger share of aggregate economic activity. It does not seem to have been a consequence of some dramatic breakthrough in manufacturing or transportation technologies concentrated in any one or two early decades.

Some comparisons with the experience of Great Britain, another of the great economic success stories of the nineteenth century, lend perspective to U.S. achievements in capital formation. The British capital stock expanded at a rate of 1.7 percent per year from 1800 to 1860, far lower than the U.S. growth rate of 4.9 percent in the same decades. Britain, of course, did not have the territorial expansion of the United States in these years, and its population grew more slowly. But that made little difference. In these six decades Britain's capital stock per capita grew at a rate of 0.4 percent per year, far below the 1.9 percent per year in the United States.

Sources of Investment and Capital Stock Growth

Why did nineteenth-century Americans invest so much and form so much more capital than people in other countries? One answer is that other countries helped by investing in the emerging U.S. market. As early as the 1790s foreign investors, attracted by high returns and stable U.S. political institutions, bought large quantities of U.S. government bonds and bank stocks, thereby transferring capital to the United States. Immigrants brought capital with them as well; all but the very poorest came with some money. This was the beginning of a great long-term flow of capital, mostly from Europe, cresting in the railroad age and lasting throughout the nineteenth century. Great as it was, however, the inflow of foreign capital was a marginal addition to what Americans themselves formed. Net foreign investment in the United States rose from $80 million in 1800 to $380 million in 1860 to $2.5 billion in 1900. It accounted in 1900 for about 3 percent of the U.S. capital stock in that year.

The same economic and institutional factors that attracted foreign investment encouraged Americans to save and invest. High returns to capital led individuals and businesses, agricultural and nonagricultural, to plow back portions of their earnings into further investment.

The corporate form of business organization, in which the United States was a pioneer, facilitated the pooling of small sums of capital to form large enterprises. In the early years it spread from banks and other financial institutions to railroads and eventually to manufacturing firms. Numerous banking and insurance corporations were chartered by states to attract and consolidate the funds of savers and make them available to finance rising levels of investment in productive facilities.

Governments were frugal. Debts incurred by the federal government, mostly in wartime, were repaid, returning financial capital to productive uses. State and local governmental debts were incurred for capital purposes—roads, canals, railroads, and urban infrastructure—that increased productive potential.

Businesses, corporate and noncorporate, and governments provided individual savers and investors with a large array of financial and real assets in which to invest and markets in which to trade them. Compared with other countries, the United States from its first years was blessed with a stable government, secure property rights, and an innovative financial system featuring banks and securities markets second to none. These initial advantages fostered the high rates of investment and capital formation that made the United States an economic giant among nations.

See also **Government; Industrialization and the Market; Stock Markets.**

Bibliography

Davis, Lance E., and Robert E. Gallman. "Capital Formation in the United States during the Nineteenth Century." In *The Cambridge Economic History of Europe.* Edited by Peter Mathias and M. M. Postan. Volume 7, part 2. Cambridge, U.K.: Cambridge University Press, 1978.

Gallman, Robert E. "American Economic Growth before the Civil War: The Testimony of the Capital Stock Estimates." In *American Economic Growth and Standards of Living before the Civil War.* Edited by Robert E. Gallman and John Joseph Wallis. Chicago: University of Chicago Press, 1992.

Sylla, Richard. "U.S. Securities Markets and the Banking System, 1790–1840." In *Federal Reserve Bank of St. Louis Review* 80, no. 3 (May-June 1998): 83–98.

Wilkins, Mira. *The History of Foreign Investment in the United States to 1914.* Cambridge, Mass.: Harvard University Press, 1989.

RICHARD SYLLA

IOWA   Located in the center of the Midwest, Iowa, with its fertile soil, adequate rainfall, and gentle, undulating topography, soon became known for its agricultural bounty. Iowa's most distinctive physical characteristic in the nineteenth century was the prairie, which covered about four-fifths of the state; the remaining area was covered with hardwood trees. Given its central location in the nation and its centrist position in political and social issues, Iowa has come to epitomize the middle West.

Early explorers like Frenchmen Jacques Marquette and Louis Joliet and later the Americans Meriwether Lewis and William Clark described numerous Native American tribes that resided in Iowa from 1600 to 1851. Numbering at least seventeen and including the Sauks, Meskwakis, Ioways, Santee Sioux, and Potawatomis, these tribes were part of the prairie-plains Indian culture, whose members relied on hunting and agriculture for sustenance. Through a series of treaties between the federal government and tribal leaders, most Native Americans were removed to reservations outside the state by 1851. The Meskwakis proved an exception as some members refused to leave Iowa and others returned; the Meskwakis later purchased about three thousand acres in Tama County, and their home became known as the Tama Reservation.

Permanent white settlement began in Iowa in 1833 along the Mississippi River. Political organization quickly followed as Iowa became a territory in 1838 and a state in 1846. The 1850 census counted 191,881 whites and 333 black residents, all free. By the early 1870s the frontier period had ended, and farms and small towns dotted the entire state. In general, settlement moved from southeast to northwest Iowa. Railroad building greatly sped up the final decades of settlement. Construction started in Iowa in 1853, and the first railroad, the Chicago and North Western, reached Council Bluffs in 1867. By 1870 three more railroads had reached Iowa's western border. In the eastern half of the state railroads connected existing towns. In the western half, where railroad building preceded settlement, the railroads created towns along the right of way.

Like other northern states, Iowans made major contributions to the Civil War. More than 70,000 Iowans served in the war: 3,540 men were either killed in battle or mortally wounded; another 8,498 died of disease. Many Iowans served with distinction: Major General Grenville Dodge was noted for rebuilding railroads throughout the South; Annie Wittenmyer served as the state's agent for the U.S. Sanitary Commission and is credited with starting diet kitchens in Union military hospitals. At war's end, Iowa had entered a new phase. Settlement was nearing completion, and, as a result of earlier agricultural expansion and diversification, Iowans would enjoy stability and considerable, although periodic, prosperity between 1870 and 1900.

Both before and after the Civil War, Iowa attracted a continual stream of immigrants. The four largest immigrant groups, in numerical order, were Germans, Irish, Norwegians, and English. The 1890 census recorded the largest number of foreign-born residents, 324,069 (19 percent). Foreign populations assimilated gradually into Iowa society with few difficulties. German Americans imported their version of the Continental Sunday, which included such leisure activities as skeet shooting, polka dancing, and beer drinking. These activities clashed with the custom of the Puritan Sunday, the dominant tradition of native-born residents, who believed Sunday to be a day for churchgoing and abstention from secular interests.

The major social issues confronting Iowans in the nineteenth century were prohibition and woman suffrage. Iowa's legislature passed numerous prohibition acts between 1855 and 1900, ranging from prohibiting all manufacturing and consumption of alcoholic beverages to the infamous Mulct Law of 1894, which allowed saloon keepers to pay a fine of six hundred dollars for the privilege of ignoring the state's prohibition law and remaining open. By 1900 the liquor issue remained unresolved, even though Iowa's Protestant majority strongly supported prohibition.

Iowans also demonstrated ambivalence toward woman suffrage. Iowa would be one of the first states to consider woman suffrage, but in the nineteenth century the proposed state amendment never reached the electorate because it failed to be approved by appropriate legislative action. Women did gain a small concession in 1894 when they won the right to vote in certain school and municipal elections.

Throughout the nineteenth century Iowa remained an agricultural state. By 1870 Iowa farmers were diversifying their operations, raising not only corn but oats, hay, hogs, and other livestock. From the 1870s through the end of the century Iowa ranked either first or second nationally in the production of corn and hogs.

Industries developed in Iowa but all remained small. Davenport early became a flour milling center, while Clinton became a major lumber production center. Many Mississippi River communities had breweries and meatpacking plants. Cedar Rapids, along the Cedar River, became home to an oats-processing plant in the 1870s, later to be named Quaker Oats. Smaller towns also developed industries, including Newton, where Frederick Maytag originally produced band-cutter attachments for threshing machines; Maytag would later produce washing machines. By 1900 Iowa's industries, although small, served both regional and national markets.

In the 1840s Iowans voted for Democratic candidates, but by the mid-1850s they had switched allegiance to the new Republican Party. The Republican principles of free soil, free labor, and free men appealed to Iowa's pioneering generation. James Grimes, who served two terms as governor, first as a Whig and then as a Republican, played a prominent part in the transition. After the Civil War, Democrats controlled the governorship for only four years when Horace Boies was elected governor in 1889 and again in 1891.

In the postwar years, Iowans listened to the rhetoric of radical agrarian reformers but generally remained loyal to the Republican Party. Few Iowa farmers joined the Populist Party or the People's Party in the 1890s. One Iowan, James B. Weaver, had the distinction of serving twice as a presidential candidate, first for the Greenback Party in 1880 and then for the People's Party in 1892.

At the end of the nineteenth century Iowa remained predominantly rural, with a national reputation for its agricultural production. Manufacturing and industry were evident both in large and small communities, but these operations clearly ranked second in importance to agriculture. With a population of 2,231,853 in 1900, Iowa also remained a state dominated by political and social moderates.

See also **Agriculture; Midwest, The; Transportation,** *subentry on* **Railroads.**

Bibliography

Bogue, Allan G. *From Prairie to Corn Belt: Farming on the Illinois and Iowa Prairies in the Nineteenth Century.* Chicago: University of Chicago Press, 1963.

Riley, Glenda. *Frontierswomen: The Iowa Experience.* Ames: Iowa State University Press, 1981.

Sage, Leland. *A History of Iowa.* Ames: Iowa State University Press, 1974.

Schwieder, Dorothy. *Iowa: The Middle Land.* Ames: Iowa State University Press, 1996.

Wall, Joseph F. *Iowa: A Bicentennial History.* New York: Norton, 1978.

DOROTHY A. SCHWIEDER

IRON   The growth of the iron and steel industry was a driving force in the dynamic industrial economy of nineteenth-century America. During the antebellum era American iron evolved from a small-scale trade dominated by individual furnaces into an industry capable of rapid technological change and increased productivity. Following the Civil War the emergence of the American steel industry triggered a number of innovations in the industrial economy. Along with the attendant benefits of stronger and more durable materials for constructing buildings, bridges, and railroads, developments in the making of iron and steel helped revolutionize U.S. industry from the boardroom to the shop floor. Iron and steel served as essential building blocks of nineteenth-century economic growth in the United States.

American Iron in the Antebellum Years

American ironmaking at the beginning of the nineteenth century was a small and decentralized trade. Most iron furnaces operated as "iron plantations," requiring close proximity to essential resources such as waterpower, iron ore, and wood for charcoal fuel. A small workforce consisting of an ironmaster, skilled employees, and manual laborers gathered fuel, fired the furnace, and smelted the raw ore into pig iron (as the most basic form of iron is commonly called) in remote locations across the Atlantic seaboard states of New York, New Jersey, Pennsylvania, Maryland, and Virginia. Production was sporadic. At peak performance a good furnace could produce twenty-five to thirty tons of pig iron a week. When nearby fuel reserves became depleted, many proprietors simply abandoned their iron plantations and rebuilt in another location. Specialized facilities, such as rolling mills, nailworks, and wireworks that produced more refined types of iron products, were independent firms, usually under the supervision of a single entrepreneur and located close to urban centers. The limited production of early iron furnaces, along with the lack of concentrated production centers, placed severe constraints on the early iron trade in the United States. But two important developments triggered massive changes in the shape and scope of the antebellum iron industry and paved the way for American iron and steel to dominate global markets by the close of the nineteenth century.

First, a series of technological innovations centered in Pennsylvania allowed mineral coal to be substituted for charcoal as a fuel, which in turn freed iron furnaces from their dependence on nearby resources and dramatically reduced the cost of making pig iron. In British and U.S. iron furnaces of the early nineteenth century the high heat needed to smelt iron ore required a blast of excess air to aid the combustion of the fuel, which was usually charcoal. During the 1820s British ironmakers using mineral fuel attempted to increase the efficiency of the process by injecting superheated air into the furnace, known commonly as the "hot blast." American ironmakers still used a "cold blast" to stoke their furnaces, which limited them to charcoal fuel. At about the same time discoveries of large deposits of anthracite coal in Pennsylvania suggested that an adaptation to the hot blast could facilitate the use of mineral fuel in American iron, thus reducing the dependence of iron furnaces on charcoal. A number of institutions promoted this innovation. Philadelphia's Franklin Institute offered awards for the first practical anthracite furnace, and in 1836 the Pennsylvania legislature passed an act offering corporate charters to firms that used coal as fuel. In 1840 David Thomas brought Welsh hot-blast technology to the Lehigh Crane Iron Company, a firm near Allentown chartered by the Pennsylvania incorporation act. Iron produced with a hot blast fired by anthracite coal became a reality, and by 1841 eleven anthracite iron furnaces were in operation in Pennsylvania alone.

As a result of technological innovation, entrepreneurial effort, and state promotion, anthracite coal eventually became an essential fuel for U.S. iron production. In 1854 anthracite was responsible for more than 46 percent of all U.S. pig iron production; by 1860 its share was more than 56 percent. The fuel revolution in iron was by no means limited to the anthracite region. In western Pennsylvania iron furnaces burning bituminous coal as fuel accounted for about 10 percent of American pig iron on the eve of the Civil War. As ironmakers there continued to develop methods of burning coke, a refined form of bituminous coal with the impurities removed, coal's share of pig iron production accelerated. Although charcoal accounted for about a third of pig iron production in 1860, its use declined steadily, and it was rarely used by the end of the century. The substitution of coal for charcoal halved the fuel cost of making a ton of pig iron and eliminated the dependence of iron furnaces on nearby stocks of wood, thus allowing them to be nearer to urban centers.

The second major development to spur the growth of the antebellum U.S. iron industry was the increased demand for iron rails by the nation's growing railroad network. From 1830 to 1860 the railroad network of the United States grew tenfold, creating an unprecedented market for such iron products as rails, cars, and other railroad components. American firms scrambled to satisfy the ravenous appetite of railroads for iron, but at first lost ground to cheaper British imports, especially in the critical iron rail market. In 1850, for example, U.S. roll mills produced 39,000 gross tons of iron rails, while 142,000 gross tons of rails made by British firms were imported.

During the antebellum era the fortunes of America's early iron trade in the rails market was linked to tariff policy and protection, which spurred iron producers to organize into trade associations. Throughout the antebellum era, specific rates on rails and other iron products rose and fell in accordance with the volatility of national politics. In response, iron producers formed such organizations as the Home League to combat these measures, and they won an increase in tariff levels in 1842. However, the Walker Tariff of 1846 reduced rates again until the advent of the Civil War. In 1855 iron interests formed the American Iron Association to collect statistics and advocate the return of a protective tariff, but rates would not rise significantly until the passage of the Morrill Tariff in 1861. Supporters of a protective tariff found little to cheer about in the antebellum years, but the response of iron producers to federal tariff policy resulted in trade organizations that would later aid in disseminating technological knowledge, promoting the use of iron, and pushing for higher tariffs to protect U.S. industry.

British imports actually supplied about three-fourths of the rails used to build American railroads in the 1850s. But the competition to fulfill the demands of railroad construction helped the U.S. iron trade in a number of ways. First, the competition in rails during the 1840s created incentives for American ironmakers to build integrated rail mills. These new facilities contained coal-burning smelting furnaces and utilized steam power to roll the rails. This process required a great deal of coordination to operate smoothly. In place of individual proprietors,

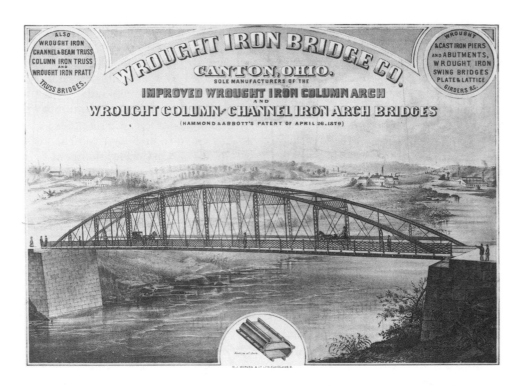

Wrought Iron Bridge Company. The company, based in Canton, Ohio, produced trusses, arches, girders, and other bridge parts; it advertised its capability with an illustration of the Fox River bridge in Ottawa, Illinois. LIBRARY OF CONGRESS: PRINTS AND PHOTOGRAPHS DIVISION

many of these new rail mills utilized a corporate form of organization to raise the capital required for the construction and operation of their facilities. Since many of the stockholders in these corporations came from outside the iron business, firms often hired superintendents to run the mills, separating ownership from management. Technological innovation also played a role in this market, and American rails were given a vital boost by the successful operation of the three-high rail mill by John Fritz of the Cambria Iron Works in Johnstown, Pennsylvania, in 1857. The three-high mill process reduced the cost of making iron rails by 80 percent and allowed U.S. rolling mills to cut into British imports even further. In 1860 American rail mills produced 175,000 tons of iron rails and recaptured this vital market from British imports. More important, the competition for rails helped transform the structure of many ironmaking firms. It is nevertheless important to remember that variety rather than uniformity characterized the overall iron trade at this time and that innovation among rail mills did not instantaneously persuade all ironmakers to abandon traditional techniques. For example, although the four largest ironworks in the United States in 1860 were integrated rail mills, small independent furnaces still smelted more than 75 percent of America's pig iron.

The organization of labor in the antebellum iron industry was as varied as the organization of capital. In northern states the high level of skill demanded of iron workers meant that employees exerted a great deal of control over the pace of work, and they commanded relatively high wages. In Maryland and Virginia, however, ironmasters often used slave labor in their furnaces, with varying degrees of success. Iron making required a variety of skilled workers. For example, the puddling method of refining involved melting pig iron using the heat of a coal fire reflected off the ceiling of a furnace while an experienced "puddler" stirred the molten iron, thus burning off impurities. The purer iron formed a pool, or "puddled," in the furnace. Working pig iron into rails, wrought iron, or nails also required a great deal of skilled labor. Despite the rise of the integrated rail mills that combined a number of functions at one location, the rhythm and organization of ironmaking at mid-century was very much controlled by the workers on the shop floor.

The Rise of American Steel

Because steel is more flexible and stronger than cast or wrought iron, it is in many ways a preferable metal for rails and building materials. During most of the antebellum period, the bulk of American steel was made as "blister steel," an expensive process that required the repeated application of powdered carbon to superheated wrought iron. In 1856, however, Henry Bessemer obtained a patent for a revolutionary process of converting iron into steel, using the injection of a cold blast of air through molten iron in an egg-shaped furnace. Alexander Holley successfully operated the first Bessemer plant in the United States at Troy, New York, in 1865. The Bessemer process reduced the time required for steelmaking to a matter of minutes and provided enormous savings on fuel costs. Steel rails became an affordable, high-quality alternative to iron rails by the 1870s. Such innovative firms as the Cambria Iron Works and the Bethlehem Iron Company quickly adapted Bessemer furnaces in their plants, and by 1877 American steelmakers surpassed ironmakers in the rail market by producing 432,169 tons of steel rails. In the same year 332,540 tons of iron rails were produced.

The budding American steel industry benefited from a postwar tariff regime geared largely toward protectionism, thanks in no small part to the American Iron and Steel Association (reorganized from the American Iron Association in 1864) and the efforts of active protectionists in the U.S. Congress, including the Pennsylvania representative William "Pig Iron" Kelley. Their efforts ensured that despite fluctuations in the years prior to 1900, tariff levels remained firmly protectionist. Operating with strong tariff protection and utilizing new technologies such as the Bessemer process, the U.S. iron and steel industry blossomed in the postwar years. Railroad construction showed no signs of dropping off, which meant that iron and steel rails still commanded a large share of domestic consumption, and the application of steel beams to the construction of buildings and bridges dramatically increased the demand for steel.

Firms responded to the growing demand for iron and steel by repeating the expansionist strategy pioneered by the rolling mills in the 1840s. The Cleveland Rolling Mill Company, for example, expanded in the 1860s and 1870s by adding four Bessemer converters, an iron rod mill, and a wire mill to their already profitable iron rail business. The growth of the iron and steel industry in the nineteenth century was thus linked to an increase in operations under the control of a single firm rather than an increase in the number of individual furnaces, steelworks, or rolling mills. The size of firms continued to rise throughout the nineteenth century, culminating in the appearance of massive firms by the turn of the century. One such firm, Federal Steel, was capitalized at $200 million with manufacturing plants in three cities. An-

drew Carnegie's steel and coke empire was valued at more than $300 million in 1900.

Carnegie, although unusual in his adherence to limited partnerships instead of corporate organization, is perhaps the exemplar of the American steel manufacturer's relentless drive to increase production efficiency while eliminating competition. Carnegie's first major ironworks, the Lucy Furnace, set pig iron production records in the 1870s by utilizing the concept of "hard driving," in which workers maximized output without concern for wear and tear on the furnace. Carnegie made hard driving pay off in his steelmaking operations as well, mostly through his relentless adherence to reducing costs. Simply put, he calculated that it was cheaper for him to completely replace worn-out facilities than to cut back production. By 1892 Carnegie Steel dominated the American steel market by consistently beating competitors on price. Carnegie demonstrated flexibility as well. After the rise of open-hearth steel conversion, a process pioneered in the United States by the Trenton Iron Company of New Jersey in 1868, Carnegie hired chemists to help refine the method and then converted his steelworks to make open-hearth steel. He also arranged a partnership with Henry Clay Frick, the leading producer of mineral coke, and secured ore mining privileges in the rich ore fields of northern Michigan and Minnesota, thus ensuring a supply of raw materials. In 1901 J. P. Morgan acquired Carnegie Steel for $480 million and formed United States Steel, a corporation capitalized at the unprecedented amount of $1.4 billion.

Carnegie's shadow is cast prominently upon the history of American steel, but his operations represented an extreme of the iron and steel trade that was by no means typical in the later half of the nineteenth century. While smaller firms struggled to beat Carnegie Steel's prices among large industrial consumers, they successfully filled niche markets, such as structural steel, wire, wire nails, rods, and hardware. These smaller firms ranged from the individually owned operations so common in the antebellum period to mid-size corporations that specialized in certain areas. In the late 1870s, for example, the Phoenix Iron Company, a family-owned firm for most of the nineteenth century, specialized in steel bridge components and provided forty thousand tons of structural iron to build New York City's elevated railroads. As America's industrial economy created more and more uses for iron and steel, small firms capitalized on their comparative advantage in these niche markets to survive the ruthless price competition that had developed in bulk markets such as steel rails. But even in these niche markets, firms increased in size due to merger and acquisition. Whether in bulk or specialty markets, the late-nineteenth-century iron and steel industry became inundated with larger and larger firms.

As the managers of iron and steel furnaces attempted to overhaul the process of making iron and steel, their employees responded in kind. At no time in the nineteenth century did more than one-fourth of U.S. ironworkers and steelworkers claim membership in a trade union. But labor organizations nonetheless played a large role in the battle for control of the shop floor. For example, in 1865 the Sons of Vulcan, an organization of iron puddlers, secured a sliding scale rate of pay for their members in which wage rates were tied to the price of iron. However, as new techniques eroded the traditional power and prestige of puddlers and other skilled ironworkers, many employees sought to organize themselves into unions. In 1876 in Pittsburgh the Sons of Vulcan combined with a number of other trade unions to form the Amalgamated Association of Iron and Steel Workers. By 1891 the Amalgamated reached its peak membership of more than twenty-four thousand workers organized into 290 locals. The following year the battle over union organization in the steel industry came to a symbolic apex during a strike at Carnegie's Homestead facility outside of Pittsburgh. Carnegie and his ruthless business partner, Frick, broke the strike. By 1894 the Amalgamated dropped to fewer than ten thousand members and claimed only 125 active locals. Organized labor would not make significant inroads in the steel industry again until the 1930s.

From its humble beginnings among the iron plantations of the century's early decades through the operation of the massive steelworks at Homestead, the iron and steel trade's development facilitated the rapid expansion of American manufacturing in the nineteenth century. Cheap and durable iron and steel, for example, helped build the nation's extensive railroad network and enabled skyscrapers to reshape American cities. Managers and workers in the iron and steel industry also provided innovations in technology, business organization, and labor relations that were repeated throughout the U.S. economy. In many ways iron and steel served as the foundation of American industrialization.

See also **Coal; Foreign Trade and Tariffs; Labor Movement,** *subentry on* **Unions and Strikes; Mining and Extraction; Natural Resources; Pennsylvania; Railroad Industry, The; Steel and the Steel Industry.**

Bibliography

Brody, David. *Steelworkers in America: The Nonunion Era.* Cambridge, Mass.: Harvard University Press, 1960.

Dew, Charles B. *Bond of Iron: Master and Slave at Buffalo Forge.* New York: Norton, 1994.

Hogan, William Thomas. *Economic History of the Iron and Steel Industry in the United States.* Volume 1. Lexington, Mass.: D.C. Heath, 1971.

Ingham, John N. *Making Iron and Steel: Independent Mills in Pittsburgh, 1820–1920.* Columbus: Ohio State University Press, 1991.

Krause, Paul. *The Battle for Homestead, 1880–1892: Politics, Culture, and Steel.* Pittsburgh, Pa.: University of Pittsburgh Press, 1992.

Lewis, Ronald L. *Coal, Iron, and Slaves: Industrial Slavery in Maryland and Virginia, 1715–1865.* Westport, Conn.: Greenwood, 1979.

Livesay, Harold. *Andrew Carnegie and the Rise of Big Business.* Boston: Little, Brown, 1975.

Misa, Thomas J. *A Nation of Steel: The Making of Modern America, 1865–1925.* Baltimore: Johns Hopkins University Press, 1995.

Paskoff, Paul F. *Industrial Evolution: Organization, Structure, and Growth of the Pennsylvania Iron Industry, 1750–1860.* Baltimore: Johns Hopkins University Press, 1983.

Temin, Peter. *Iron and Steel in Nineteenth-Century America: An Economic Inquiry.* Cambridge, Mass.: MIT Press, 1964.

SEAN PATRICK ADAMS

JACKSONIAN ERA

The Jacksonian era refers to a period in the second quarter of the nineteenth century dominated by the personality and policies of Andrew Jackson, the seventh president of the United States. While many historians once limited the term to the years of Jackson's presidency (1829–1837), most came to see it as encompassing the period from Jackson's first election through the subsequent administration of his fellow Tennessean and Democrat James K. Polk (1845–1849). While Jackson has always been a controversial figure and the nature of his influence on his age has been much debated, the affixing of Jackson's name to this era was considered useful by historians for nearly the whole of the twentieth century. However, with the waning of interest in political history and the dissatisfaction with writing history from the vantage point of elites, the term gradually has begun to fall out of favor. Increasingly historians characterize the era by references to broader social and economic developments that seem to transcend the influence of any particular politician and even of politics in general.

Central Themes

The most important theme of the era was a market revolution, in which a large part of the population moved from agrarian self-sufficiency into market agriculture. This process was stimulated by swift developments in transportation that involved the improvement of the nation's road system, the building of canals and railroads, and the proliferation of steamboats on America's waterways. The network of cheap, reliable transportation encouraged farmers to abandon the diverse activities of self-sufficiency and to specialize in staples for distant markets. Greater efficiency in agriculture in turn stimulated urban crafts and manufacturing, giving rise to urbanization and a working class. The frequent use of money in transactions increased people's reliance on banks and strengthened the influence of banks. The scope and significance of these changes well justified the use of the term "revolution." Not only was the economy transformed in this process, but politics, the law, society, and values were deeply influenced by the changes this market revolution produced.

Probably the second most important theme of the era was the development of a more democratic political system and the birth of great national political parties. (Some argue that it was a rebirth, that the earlier Federalists and Democratic-Republicans created a true party system.) The era saw a significant widening of suffrage to include almost all adult, white males as religious and property qualifications were eliminated. At the same time more offices became elective, giving the people's vote greater power. This trend included the increased power of the people in electing the president as states allowed voters rather than state legislatures to select presidential electors. Perhaps most important was the emergence, for the first time in American history, of a fully national, competitive, two-party system of Democrats and Whigs whose loyalties reached deeply into the American electorate. This party system resulted in the first modern presidential election in 1840, in which nearly 80 percent of the electorate went to the polls to elect the Whig William Henry Harrison.

At this time the United States saw the full emergence of what has been called the American national character with the public acceptance of the country's democratic, egalitarian, and individualistic tendencies. The term "self-made man" was born, and economic opportunity took center stage. A corresponding literary and artistic flowering took place. A national literature emerged, dominated by such writers as Washington Irving, James Fenimore Cooper, Ralph Waldo Emerson, Henry David Thoreau, Henry Wadsworth Longfellow, Nathaniel Hawthorne, Edgar Allan Poe, and Herman Melville. America's cultural independence from Europe was also signaled by the emergence of the Hudson River School of painters, the country's first indigenous artistic achievement of major significance. At the same time such genre painters as William Sidney Mount and George Caleb Bingham produced a new, democratic art that was both of and for the people.

With regard to women, the era had two tendencies.

The first and most widespread, at least among the middle class, was the marking off of a separate domestic sphere as the woman's proper domain. Within this sphere she reigned supreme, creating a haven for the family away from the emerging world of capitalist striving and competitive politics while she shaped the broader culture through the inculcation of values in the young. In a lesser but in the long run more significant movement, some women strove to break out of the restricted sphere and to open the public arenas of politics and work to women. These reformers demanded equal rights with men and published a manifesto to that effect at a woman's rights convention in Seneca Falls, New York, in 1848.

Women from both camps were important in the many religious and humanitarian reform efforts that swept the era. Stimulated by Enlightenment optimism, economic prosperity, and perhaps most important the wave of religious revivals known as the Second Great Awakening, men and women reformers sought to eradicate both sin and suffering from the American scene in the Jacksonian era. They used primarily propaganda and persuasion but also institutional reforms and governmental coercion to attack slavery; intemperance; war; poverty; cruelty toward the blind, the insane, and the criminal; and a host of other social and moral ills. Voluntary associations to accomplish these ends were created all over the country, though they were perhaps strongest in New England and its cultural provinces to the west.

The rapid settlement and expansion of the national domain was another theme of the era. The American population poured over the Appalachians to settle the area of the Old Northwest Territory and the rich lands of the Old Southwest. The annexation of Texas (1845), the settlement of the Oregon Country boundary dispute with Britain (1846), and most of all the war with Mexico (1846–1848) added vast lands in the West to the national domain. The Oregon, California, and Santa Fe Trails carried large numbers of settlers into these new territories. The discovery of gold in California (1848) ensured the continued rapid pace of this westering.

The more sinister side of all these developments can be seen in the rapid expansion of slavery into new realms and the dispossession of American Indians from their lands east of the Mississippi. The slave population grew by natural increase and by migration, spreading throughout the Old Southwest largely as a consequence of the prosperity wrought by cotton culture. By the end of the era the institution was strongly entrenched from the Tidewater states of the East Coast to the frontiers of Texas. Searching for new cotton lands to develop, Americans mounted a concerted effort to dispossess Indians of their lands

BORN TO COMMAND.

OF VETO MEMORY.

HAD I BEEN CONSULTED.

KING ANDREW THE FIRST.

Andrew Jackson as Monarch. A political cartoon satirizes Jackson's attempt to remove funds from the Bank of the United States in 1833. LIBRARY OF CONGRESS: PRINTS AND PHOTOGRAPHS DIVISION

in the East and remove them to less valuable areas west of the Mississippi. Official government policy in the 1830s forced southern tribes to march along the so-called Trail of Tears to Oklahoma.

Jackson and His Era

Historians originally attached Jackson's name to the era because he dramatically shaped or at least symbolized the striking changes in politics, society, and the economy in the early Republic. Because he was a westerner, a man of humble beginnings, and a popular "man of the people," his rise to the presidency appeared to symbolize the democratic tendencies of the era. Wider suffrage, more elective offices, greater electoral turnouts, and the emergence of the first mass party system in American history either paved the way for his election or were the consequence of his actions in office.

It can also be argued that Jackson was central to

the formation of the entire second party system. The new Democratic Party certainly coalesced around his popularity and readily adopted his stances on public issues during his administration. The Whig Party emerged in 1834 largely in opposition to Jackson and his vetoes. They adopted their name because they rallied, like the Whigs of the Revolutionary Era, in opposition to what they saw as the executive usurpation of "King Andrew I." The Whigs particularly advocated Henry Clay's American System, including government support for a national bank, a protective tariff, and internal improvements, policies that seemed endangered by Jackson's presidency.

Jackson's relationship to the market revolution was more ambiguous. His vetoes of the Maysville Road Bill (1830) and the Bill to Recharter the Bank of the United States (1832) during his first administration arose from objections to the federal government's involvement in the transportation revolution and the banking system, both important engines of the economic development that characterized the market revolution. While some historians have seen Jackson's actions as stemming merely from a desire to reform and democratize economic development, others have argued that Jackson and his party were uncomfortable with development itself and were attempting to stop it or at least slow its pace.

Jackson and his party may have been intent on economic reform, but they were much less interested in social and benevolent reforms than their Whig opponents. Whigs were far more likely to support such reforms, which Jacksonians tended to characterize as busybody meddling or even social control. When reforms required governmental support, such as those related to education, the poor, criminals, and the insane, Jacksonians were likely to vote to withhold support, while Whig legislators voted in favor of funding them. Jacksonians were notably less active in women's concerns as well, whether bent on the promotion of women's "separate sphere" or the campaign for equal rights.

Jackson and his party were, however, in the forefront of the drive for the expansion of the national domain. A Jacksonian Democrat, John L. O'Sullivan, coined the term "manifest destiny." The party advocated low public land prices to open up the West to settlers as rapidly as possible, and Jackson pushed for the annexation of Texas. His protégé Polk settled the Oregon boundary dispute and wrested the Southwest from Mexico at the end of an expansionist war that many Whigs opposed.

Unfortunately its position on expansion also allied the party with some of the darker aspects of the age. The Democratic Party was particularly strong in the South, thus it became associated with the spread of slavery into new territories and a staunch defense of the institution where it already existed. With the spread of plantation agriculture in mind, Democrats were the chief advocates of dispossessing the Indians of their lands east of the Mississippi and pushing them into the West. Jackson, who had made his early reputation in the military in wars with southern tribes, was instrumental in inaugurating the Trail of Tears during his first administration.

When the expansion issue reached its peak at the end of the Mexican War, however, Jackson was already dead (1845), and the second party system was beginning to wane. Sectional differences over slavery caused divisions within the parties, while the economic issues that had provided the basis of their national unity and that had distinguished them from one another lost their significance. Except for abolition, the religious and humanitarian reform impulses of the past two decades were largely spent. In the next decade Americans continued to cope with the market revolution, but their political responses were complicated by the sectional controversy and the issues raised by the heavy Irish and German immigration that began in 1846.

The Jacksonian era was a seminal period in American history. The United States became a continental Republic during these years, and American values and institutions became recognizably modern. Many of the issues that we still struggle with were placed on the national agenda at this time. In the 1830s and 1840s the United States declared its cultural independence from Europe and saw the first flowering of American art and literature. While Andrew Jackson was hardly responsible for all of these developments, his personality towered over the age. By whatever name it is known, this era will never lose its significance, and historians will recognize Jackson's powerful influence in shaping it.

See also **American Indians,** subentry on **Indian Removal; Banking and Finance,** subentry on **The Politics of Banking; Democratic Party; Elections,** subentry on **Presidential Elections; Expansion; Federal Land Policy; Gender,** subentry on **Interpretations of Gender; Internal Improvements; Manifest Destiny; Market Revolution; Nationalism,** subentry on **1800–1865; Politics,** subentry on **The Second Party System; Slavery,** subentries on **Domestic Slave Trade and Migration, Defense of Slavery; Transportation,** subentry on **Railroads; Voters and Voting,** subentry on **White Male Franchise; Whig Party; Woman's Rights.**

Bibliography

Feller, Daniel. *The Jacksonian Promise: America, 1815–1840.* Baltimore: Johns Hopkins University Press, 1995.

———. "Politics and Society: Toward a Jacksonian Synthesis." *Journal of the Early Republic* 10 (1990): 135–161.

Kohl, Lawrence Frederick. *The Politics of Individualism: Parties and the American Character in the Jacksonian Era.* New York: Oxford University Press, 1989.

Pessen, Edward. *Jacksonian America: Society, Personality, and Politics.* Rev. ed. Homewood, Ill.: Dorsey, 1978.

Schlesinger, Arthur M., Jr. *The Age of Jackson.* Boston: Little, Brown, 1945.

Sellers, Charles Grier, Jr. "Andrew Jackson versus the Historians." *Mississippi Valley Historical Review* 44 (1958): 615–634.

———. *The Market Revolution: Jacksonian America, 1815–1846.* New York: Oxford University Press, 1991.

Thornton, J. Mills, III. *Politics and Power in a Slave Society: Alabama, 1800–1860.* Baton Rouge: Louisiana State University Press, 1978.

Van Deusen, Glyndon G. *The Jacksonian Era, 1828–1848.* New York: Harper, 1959.

Walters, Ronald G. *American Reformers, 1815–1860.* Rev. ed. New York: Hill and Wang, 1997.

Watson, Harry L. *Liberty and Power: The Politics of Jacksonian America.* New York: Hill and Wang, 1990.

LAWRENCE FREDERICK KOHL

JEFFERSONIAN ERA

Thomas Jefferson tells Americans something fundamental about themselves. What Jefferson seems to signify, however, has varied enormously. He has been the father of democracy, the champion of liberty, an irreligious infidel, and the embodiment of racist hypocrisy. His presidency (1801–1809) and those of his fellow Virginians James Madison (1809–1817) and James Monroe (1817–1825) form the Jeffersonian era in American political life. Jefferson himself, however, did not list the presidency among the achievements to be recorded on his tomb.

Two Elections

The presidential elections of 1800 and 1824 mark that era's beginning and its end, each revealing a flaw in the procedures for choosing a president. Under the original electoral rules each presidential elector would vote for two candidates, with the expectation of no previous consultation. This process either would find the two men most qualified, who would become president and vice president, respectively, or send the election to the House of Representatives, where each state would cast one vote.

When the election of 1796 led to John Adams as president and Jefferson as vice president, there was no question of both being highly qualified. But they were political opponents, each seeking the highest office, and the voting that chose them was organized. In 1800 they faced each other again, and Jefferson's people organized too well, leading to an equal number of electoral votes for Jefferson and for his expected vice president Aaron Burr. The election did go to the House, and a constitutional crisis resulted when the representatives deadlocked. The Twelfth Amendment to the Constitution, ratified in 1804, which separates electoral college voting for the two offices, was the result.

If the election of 1800 deadlocked because of too much organization, that of 1824 deadlocked because parties were in disarray. Only four years earlier James Monroe's second term had begun with just one dissenting electoral college vote, because the old Federalist party had virtually disappeared. One sign of its demise was Monroe's choice for secretary of state, John Quincy Adams, the son of Jefferson's onetime revolutionary comrade turned political rival. Now the two old men were friends again and the younger Adams was a Jeffersonian, whatever that had come to mean. By then the secretary of state was the presumptive next president, and Secretary Adams did seek the highest office in 1824. His chief rival was Andrew Jackson, but with parties in disarray, two other candidates won electoral votes, leaving none of the four with an electoral college majority. Once more the election went to the House; once more the House deadlocked. Adams won, but the real result was the modern Democratic Party, which won the White House for Jackson in 1828.

Aristocratic Populism

The three presidencies that lay between the crisis elections of 1800 and 1824 were marked by continuity in several dimensions. First, Jefferson, Madison, and Monroe were all Virginia gentlemen. That Jefferson chose to begin his presidency without the quasi-regal pomp of George Washington's first inauguration in 1789 and of John Adams's in 1797 was more than a matter of aesthetics. Jefferson's mansion, Monticello, was the house of a man who lived apart from the common lot, but his mature political style was as a man of the people. In this sense he set a pattern of aristocratic populism that has persisted through such disparate figures as presidents Theodore Roosevelt, Franklin D. Roosevelt, John F. Kennedy, and George Bush. By comparison with Jefferson, Madison was socially awkward and Monroe was bland, but both carried forward the aristocratic populist tradition.

A Strengthened Presidency

The Jeffersonian era presidencies were marked by another contradiction as well. None believed in an activist state. Jefferson set the pattern during his debate in 1791 with Alexander Hamilton about the constitutionality of a Bank of the United States,

while both were in Washington's cabinet. He, Madison, and Monroe all were hostile to federally sponsored "internal improvements," as Madison showed when he vetoed a renewal of that bank's charter in 1811 and an act to build a canal across New York State in 1817, one of his last actions in office. New York built the Erie Canal (completed in 1825) itself, and under Monroe the United States did virtually nothing in the economic realm.

Yet all three strengthened the presidency, particularly in regard to foreign affairs. Jefferson did it by his purchase in 1803 of the whole territory of Louisiana from France, despite doubting his own constitutional right as president to do so. The later stages of his foreign policy, when he used an embargo on exports to convince warring France and Britain to respect American neutrality, proved disastrous. Still, the policy had been Jefferson's own. The War of 1812, into which Madison blundered, resulted in a stalemate after Washington, D.C., was captured and sacked while the government fled. But it had been "Mr. Madison's War."

The End of a Generation

During the Jeffersonian era the American Republic started to become an empire. The purchases of Louisiana from France and of Florida from Spain (1819) added vast territories to the legally recognized American domain. The purchases also added to the American population significant numbers of non-British Europeans, largely Africans and Native Americans, without their consent. The Republic's ambitions reached further, demonstrated by the Lewis and Clark expedition that Jefferson sent to the Pacific Northwest in 1804 and the 1819 acquisition of Spain's legal claim to the Oregon Country (modern Oregon, Washington, and British Columbia). The Monroe Doctrine of 1820 illustrated the Republic's hostility to further European colonization in the Americas, but it also declared the Republic's primacy over the other postcolonial states that were emerging. Politicians considered acquiring Canada and individual "filibusters" raided across the Canadian border. The effort by Moses Austin (1761–1821) and his son Stephen (1793–1836) to colonize Spanish-Mexican Texas with "Anglo" settlers was a private venture, but it harmonized with official policy.

The Jeffersonian era was dominated by aging figures from the Revolution, but it marked a shift from revolutionary concerns. Despite the foreign policy triumphs of Jefferson and Monroe, the dominant American question shifted from the political problem of founding a republic to the economic problem of how that republic might prosper. The Erie Canal is the era's greatest domestic monument. It was a public venture, because no private enterprise could fund it. It was of benefit to the whole American economy. But it was the work of just one state, not of the American people. Jefferson himself had regarded the project as madness.

The era saw the emergence of the next political generation, such men as Martin Van Buren, De Witt Clinton, John C. Calhoun, Henry Clay, and Daniel Webster. It also saw the beginnings of the issue of slavery and freedom with the Missouri Compromise of 1820, which a frightened Jefferson called a "fire bell in the night." The coincidence that Thomas Jefferson and John Adams both died on 4 July 1826 struck almost every contemporary who heard of it as a divine intervention. It did indeed mark the passing of a generation and the end of an era.

See also **Democratic Party; Expansion; Federalist Party; Monroe Doctrine; Nationalism,** *subentry on* **1800–1865; Republicanism.**

Bibliography

Ellis, Joseph. *American Sphinx: The Character of Thomas Jefferson.* New York: Knopf, 1997.

Onuf, Peter, ed. *Jeffersonian Legacies.* Charlottesville: University Press of Virginia, 1993.

Stagg, J. C. A. *Mr. Madison's War: Politics, Diplomacy, and Warfare in the Early American Republic, 1783–1830.* Princeton, N.J.: Princeton University Press, 1983.

Waldstreicher, David. *In the Midst of Perpetual Fetes: The Making of American Nationalism, 1776–1820.* Chapel Hill: University of North Carolina Press, 1997.

EDWARD COUNTRYMAN

JEWS.   See **Anti-Semitism; Immigration and Immigrants,** subentry on **Jewish Immigrants; Judaism.**

JOURNALISM.   See **Newspapers and the Press.**

JUDAISM   Although relatively few Jews lived in the United States during the nineteenth century, steady progress was made toward the creation of major centers of Jewish cultural and religious life in New York City and other large cities by 1900. Already during the colonial period, the five embryonic Jewish communities on the eastern seaboard found ways to transplant Jewish religious life to the New World and adapt to the American environment. While generally ritually lax, colonial Jews did organize kehillot, or synagogue-communities, in Newport, Rhode Island, New York City, Philadelphia, Charleston, South Carolina, and Savannah, Georgia, which followed the sephardic (Iberian) mode of Jewish worship. The kehillot were governed by "juntas" dominated by the socio-economic elite of the community.

Schisms and Adaptations

At the end of the eighteenth century, when the deferential colonial social system was rapidly being undermined by emerging traditions of American republicanism, the Philadelphia Kehillah split in 1798 along Sephardic-Ashkenazic lines. The German (Ashkenazic) Jews of the city organized a separate kehillah called Rodef Shalom, or "Pursuer of Peace," an ironic name for a schismatic group. In 1824 both the New York and Charleston Kehillot also divided, the former for ethnic reasons, the latter because of the emergence of a Reform ideology in the community. Thus, by the middle of the third decade of the nineteenth century, the old, all-inclusive synagogue-community of the colonial era had been replaced by an amorphous community of synagogues and independent Jewish organizations.

A number of other factors defined the religious character of the pre–Civil War American Jewish community. German Jewish immigration swelled the tiny Jewish community from just a few thousand people before the War of 1812 to a substantial community of 150,000 in 1860. In the following quarter century, the Jewish population grew by another 100,000 individuals. The majority settled in the United States' emerging urban centers, particularly in New York City, but also in the Midwest, South, and Far West. The urban character of the Jewish community included the development of Jewish organizations outside of the synagogue, including both male and female benevolent societies and fraternal orders.

The growing number of Jewish communities and organizations did not change the essentially lax nature of American Judaism, however, in spite of the efforts of a number of individuals and groups to invigorate American Jewish religious life in the antebellum period. In particular, the work of Rebecca Gratz, Isaac Harby, and Isaac Leeser propelled a Second Great Awakening in Judaism in the United States in the first half of the nineteenth century. In radically different ways, each leader sought to adapt American Judaism to models provided by the Protestant majority while at the same time devising strategies to resist Christian missionary activity and the secularization inherent in the modernizing of the American Jew.

The general trend toward a feminization of religion in nineteenth-century America has its fullest reflection in the Jewish community in the communal and religious work of Rebecca Gratz (1781–1869). A member of one of Philadelphia's leading Sephardic families, Gratz organized the first Jewish women's organization in the United States, the Female Hebrew Benevolent Society, in 1819. Less than twenty years later, she founded the first Hebrew Sunday School in the United States (1838) and operated it as a women's organization outside of the auspices of the male-dominated synagogues of the period. For the first time in Jewish history, women, not men, became the primary teachers of Judaism for the young. In 1855 Gratz also helped found the first American Jewish foster home.

Early in the 1830s, Gratz, and other women at her home synagogue, Mickveh Israel in Philadelphia, also prevailed on the congregation's hazzan (cantor), to give regular vernacular (English-language) sermons, another important adaptation of America's

Confirmation Certificate. A Jewish confirmation certificate used by Reformed synagogues, c. 1872. LIBRARY OF CONGRESS: BROADSIDE COLLECTION

Protestant religious culture. The hazzan, Isaac Leeser (1806–1868), who had emigrated from Germany in 1824 and made no pretension to having an advanced Jewish education, had accepted Mickveh Israel's invitation to serve the congregation in 1830. He quickly emerged as the leading Jewish religious leader of the period despite his unhappy twenty-year relationship with his congregation. Orthodox in theology, Leeser advocated greater decorum in the synagogue, single-handedly translated the Hebrew bible into English, and published beginning in 1843 the first successful Jewish newspaper in the United States, *The Occident and American Jewish Advocate,* which he used to disseminate his vision of a Protestantized Sephardic orthodoxy and combat the embryonic Reform movement in American Judaism. The Reform movement sought to modernize Judaism's theology and liberalize its ritual practice. The first properly ordained Orthodox rabbi to settle in the United States (1840), Abraham Rice (1802–1862), generally supported Leeser but met with little success of his own in Baltimore's emerging Jewish community.

In 1824, the same year Leeser arrived in the States, Isaac Harby (1788–1828), a young Sephradic Jew in Charleston, South Carolina, influenced by newspaper reports provided by a local Unitarian minister of developments in Germany, launched the Reformed Society of Israelites. A deistic liturgy was quickly developed and even attracted original contributions from a local Jewish woman, Penina Moise (1797–1880). However, the Reformed Society encountered stiff resistance from Charleston's presiding junta. In general, Reform Judaism was slow to develop in the United States in the decades prior to the Civil War. By 1860, only a handful of the nation's two hundred synagogues were fully "reform."

The fortunes of the Reform movement in American Judaism began to change with the arrival in 1846 of Isaac Mayer Wise (1819–1900), a Jewish religious instructor from Bohemia, although he did not meet with success at the national level until the 1870s. Wise's reformist tendencies split his first congregation in Albany, New York, in 1851. Supported by the schismatics, he started his own synagogue in New York's capital and for practical purposes introduced the radical innovation of "mixed seating." In 1854 Wise moved to Cincinnati, Ohio, to serve Congregation Bene Jeshurun. Soon after his arrival in the Midwest, he began publishing two newspapers, *The Israelite* and a German language parallel, *Die Deborah,* to advance his views. A moderate reformer, Wise promoted the idea of a single "American Judaism." In 1855 he convened a "unity" conference in Cleveland, which ultimately failed to gain the support of the traditionalists led by Leeser and was openly attacked by David Einhorn (1809–1879), a recently arrived "Doctor-Rabbi," who immediately emerged as the champion of radical German Reform Judaism in America. Einhorn was a radical reformer, quicker to discard ritual, was highly ideological, and preferred German to English.

Judaism and the Civil War

The Civil War proved deeply traumatic for American Jewry. Rabbis were generally slow to debate the question of slavery in public. Einhorn openly preached for the abolition of the "peculiar institution." On the other hand, Wise emphasized "union" and Leeser, who harbored southern sympathies, largely remained silent on the eve of the Civil War. A few rabbis, including Morris Raphall of New York, argued that slavery was biblically sanctioned. Once the war started, regionalism generally prevailed, with Jewish chaplains and civilian women from both sides ministering to the needs of the wounded and dying. As word spread of Lee's surrender on the first night of Passover in 1865, oscillating waves of grief and relief were felt throughout the American Jewish community as families gathered to celebrate the traditional Seder meal.

Despite the deep divisions in American Judaism at the beginning of Reconstruction, the closing decades of the nineteenth century witnessed an American Jewish Awakening, which ultimately proved responsible for creating the three principal denominational tracks of American Judaism in the twentieth century: Reform, Conservative, and Orthodox. In 1873 followers of Isaac Mayer Wise founded the Union of American Hebrew Congregations (UAHC) in Cincinnati. Originally intended to serve as an umbrella organization for all American synagogues, it mostly attracted moderate Reform congregations. The principal purpose of the UAHC was to serve as the patron of Wise's Hebrew Union College (HUC), which he founded in Cincinnati in 1875. Following HUC's first ordination ceremony in 1883, a scandal erupted when the guests were served shellfish at the so-called "Trefa Banquet." Eastern traditionalists were galvanized by the event, which also resulted in a coalition between moderate and radical reformers. Two years later, Kaufman Kohler (1843–1926) convened a group of radical reform rabbis to articulate a set of religious principles, the first Pittsburgh Platform, which attempted to locate Reform Judaism between the traditionalist camp and the philosophy of Felix Adler's "Ethical Culture" movement.

In the wake of the Pittsburgh Platform, an alliance of German and Sephardic traditionalists led by Sabato Morais (1823–1897), Leeser's successor at Mickveh Israel, and others quickly led to the establishment of the Jewish Theological Seminary of America (JTS) in New York City in 1887. However, the original JTS did not flourish, as the anti-Reform camp grew increasingly complex both in its sub-ethnic and religious composition. East European Jews, who had already organized a synagogue in New York as early as 1852, were quickly becoming a statistical majority in the American Jewish community. In 1887 East European traditionalists established the Etz Chaim Talmudical Academy, which, in turn, was followed by the opening of the Rabbi Isaac Elchanan Theological Seminary in 1896. The two later merged in 1915 to form the basis of the present-day Yeshiva University. Meanwhile, the original JTS was reorganized by Cyrus Adler (1863–1940), a protégé of the "Leeser School" in 1902. Adler aligned the seminary with the positive-historical philosophy of Germany's Jewish Theological Seminary and brought Solomon Schechter (1897–1915), a distinguished Romanian scholar, from England to head the school and the nascent "conservative" movement. Schechter and his uptown German Jewish supporters quickly and successfully sought to attract Americanizing East European Jews to the newly forged middle track in American Judaism. Thus, by World War I, the three tracks of twentieth-century American Judaism were clearly established, and American Jews embarked on a course of massive institution-building unparalleled in the history of American Judaism.

The institutional strength of American Judaism at the end of the nineteenth century was not only found in the world of seminaries and synagogues, but in Jewish women's organizations as well. By the 1890s, women, the principal teachers in Jewish Sunday Schools, were also actively forging other significant gender-based alliances. In 1893 Hannah G. Solomon (1858–1942), after years of activity as a clubwoman, organized the National Council of Jewish Women. Two years later Rosa F. Sonneschein (1847–1932), a Zionist and a feminist, launched the *American Jewess*, the first Jewish newspaper by and for Jewish women in the United States. Short-lived, it achieved a circulation of 29,000 subscribers. But perhaps it was the young, tragic Zionist poet Emma Lazarus (1849–1887) who most fully represented the American Jewish Awakening of the late nineteenth century and whose 1883 sonnet, "The New Colossus," is inscribed on the base of the Statue of Liberty. As the twentieth century dawned, the majority of Jews in the United States, and still millions more in Europe, believed that the Jewish people and the ancient religious heritage of Israel had found a home in America.

See also **Anti-Semitism; Immigration and Immigrants,**
subentry on **Jewish Immigrants; Religion,** *subentry on*
Religion in Nineteenth-Century America.

Bibliography

Ashton, Dianne. *Rebecca Gratz: Women and Judaism in Antebellum America.* Detroit, Mich.: Wayne State University Press, 1997.

Jick, Leon A. *The Americanization of the Synagogue, 1820–1870.* Hanover, N.H.: University Press of New England, 1976.

Sarna, Jonathan D. *Jacksonian Jew: The Two Worlds of Mordecai Manuel Noah.* New York: Holmes and Meier, 1981.

Sussman, Lance J. *Isaac Leeser and the Making of American Judaism.* Detroit, Mich.: Wayne State University Press, 1995.

Wertheimer, Jack, ed. *The American Synagogue: A Sanctuary Transformed.* Cambridge, U.K.: Cambridge University Press, 1987.

LANCE J. SUSSMAN

JUDICIAL REVIEW   Judicial review is the
power of courts to evaluate the acts of the other
branches of government to determine their constitutionality. When legislative acts are found unconstitutional, the courts decline to enforce them. Constitutionally inappropriate decisions of lower courts
are reversed, and unconstitutional actions by executive authorities are enjoined.

The model of judicial review was in Chief Justice
John Marshall's decision in *Marbury v. Madison*
(1803), but some scholars have claimed a long tradition of judicial review. Under the British system,
any law passed by Parliament and given the royal
assent is automatically constitutional. No court can
overturn a parliamentary statute on any grounds
whatsoever. In *Dr. Bonham's Case* (1610) Lord Coke
attempted to establish a kind of judicial review, but
the case produced no judicial progeny and was later
cited in Coke's removal from the bench.

The Judicial Committee of Privy Council repeatedly invalidated colonial legislation held antithetical
to the laws of England, invasive of the royal prerog-
ative, or contrary to natural justice. Some of these
decisions were judicial, primarily appeals from cases
heard in colonial courts, although the bulk appear
political in nature. Various colonial court cases, such
as *Giddings v. Brown* (Massachusetts, 1657), *Frost v.
Leighton* (Massachusetts, 1739), and *Robbin v. Har-
daway* (Virginia, 1772), may be precedents for judicial review, but none could be called an unquestion-
able instance of it. During the period of the Articles
of Confederation, a number of decisions by state
courts tended toward judicial review, including the
Case of Josiah Philips (Virginia, 1778), *Holmes v.*

Walton (New Jersey, 1780), *Commonwealth v. Caton*
(Virginia, 1782), *Rutgers v. Waddington* (New Jersey,
1784), *Trevett v. Weeden* (Rhode Island, 1786), *Syms-
bury Case* (Connecticut, 1785), and *Bayard v. Single-
ton* (North Carolina, 1787).

In a real sense the first U.S. Supreme Court case
involving judicial review was *Hylton v. United States*
(1796), which clarified the taxing power of Congress.
That suit claimed that a sixteen-dollar tax on carriages enacted by Congress should have been appor-
tioned among the states by population as a direct tax.
Although seldom cited as an instance of judicial review because it upheld the congressional act, the case
was heard on the basis of a claim of the unconstitutionality of the tax code.

In *Marbury v. Madison* the Supreme Court took
up William Marbury's claim that Secretary of State
James Madison had improperly withheld the certificate of his appointment as a justice of the peace in
the District of Columbia. The case was fraught with
serious implications for an independent judiciary.
The Jeffersonians contemplated impeachment of
Federalist judges, so a ruling for Marbury would
have been dangerous. A simple decision against him,
however, might have damaged the Court's prestige.
Chief Justice Marshall brilliantly avoided this dilemma by dismissing the case for lack of jurisdiction,
accomplished by invalidating a section of the Judiciary Act of 1789 that expanded the original jurisdiction of the Supreme Court.

In *Fletcher v. Peck* (1810) the Supreme Court held
a Georgia law revoking the corrupt Yazoo land grant
of a previous legislature a nullity because it violated
the obligation of contract clause of the U.S. Constitution. The vast bulk of laws struck down by the federal courts were state enactments, as in *Dartmouth
College v. Woodward* (1819) and *Gibbons v. Ogden*
(1824). The only other federal enactment struck
down before the Civil War was part of the Compromise of 1820 and by implication the Compromise of
1850, invalidated by the decision in *Dred Scott v.
Sandford* (1857) on the grounds that Congress lacked
authority to outlaw slavery in the territories.

The tendency of the federal courts to invalidate
state enactments but to uphold congressional statutes has been attributed by some scholars to the facts
that Congress has considerable power over the federal courts and state legislatures have little recourse.
State courts in the early nineteenth century practiced
judicial review, striking down state laws and local ordinances as contrary to the U.S. Constitution, federal
statutory law, or the appropriate state constitution.

From 1897 until the mid-1930s the doctrine of substantive due process was the primary cause for judicial review of state laws by the federal courts. Aban-

doning the restrictive reading of the privileges and immunities clause of the Fourteenth Amendment adopted in the *Slaughterhouse Cases* (1873), the U.S. Supreme Court in *Munn v. Illinois* (1877) and the associated Granger cases seemed to admit several of the principles of substantive due process while ultimately upholding state regulation of grain elevator rates.

Allgeyer v. Louisiana (1897) applied the principles of substantive due process recognized in the dicta of earlier cases. The Supreme Court invalidated a Louisiana law barring corporations not licensed by the state from insuring property within the state. In the early twentieth century substantive due process provided the main rationale for overturning state legislation under judicial review. After 1937 the incorporation doctrine, which held that the Fourteenth Amendment had applied parts of the Bill of Rights to the states, became the main source of issues for judicial review. As central as judicial review became to the role of the courts, judges occasionally avoided undertaking such a review by holding that particular issues lacked justiciability (that is, the courts lacked a means of granting relief) or by holding that the issue involved constituted a political question beyond the competence of the courts to decide.

From the beginning judicial review was controversial. The Constitution is silent on the issue, and allegedly tension exists between the power of an unelected judiciary that enjoys life tenure and the democratic self-government that forms the cornerstone of republican government.

See also **Constitutional Amendments,** *subentry on* **Thirteenth, Fourteenth, and Fifteenth Amendments; Constitutional Law; Courts, State and Federal; Law; Supreme Court.**

Bibliography

Bickel, Alexander M. *The Least Dangerous Branch: The Supreme Court at the Bar of Politics.* Indianapolis; Ind.: Bobbs-Merrill, 1962.

Bozell, L. Brent. *The Warren Revolution: Reflections on the Concensus Society.* New Rochelle, N.Y.: Arlington House, 1966.

Gunther, Gerald. "Judicial Review." In *Encyclopedia of the American Constitution.* Edited by Leonard W. Levy, Kenneth L. Karst, and Dennis J. Mahoney. 4 vols. New York: Macmillan, 1986.

Hall, Kermit L., ed. *The Oxford Companion to the Supreme Court of the United States.* New York: Oxford University Press, 1992.

McDonald, Forrest. *A Constitutional History of the United States.* Malabar, Fla.: Krieger, 1986.

Russell, Elmer Beecher. *The Review of American Colonial Legislation by the King in Council.* New York: Octagon Books, 1976.

Swindler, William F. *The Constitution and Chief Justice Marshall.* New York: Dodd, Mead, 1978.

PATRICK M. O'NEIL

JUDICIARY AND THE COURTS. See **Courts, State and Federal.**

K

KANSAS Kansas in the nineteenth century was both a bellwether and a laughingstock, a beacon and a whipping boy for the nation. It was a place of extremes in climate and politics, and also the heartland in whose struggles Americans recognized their hopes and frustrations. In Kansas, it was said, idealistic people tried to accomplish what others only talked about—consequently they were wound to a certain tightness. A local editor said that Kansans were subject to "fits." These were "bred in the bone and carried like cottonwood seed in the wind. The ozone of Kansas is congested with hysteria all the time and the public mind is as easily touched off as a natural gas well."

The early history of the region was as full of incongruities, even contradictions, as its landscape. For Native Americans the territory was a bison range that was maintained, with fire, as prairie. The Spanish explorer Coronado did not see in that pasture what he was looking for, and he had the guide who brought him there strangled. To the Santa Fe traders the area was, as it is to some modern-day travelers on I-70, a dull but profitable crossing on the way to someplace else. To those behind the Indian removal policy, it was a protected border utopia for eastern tribes. For the railroad promoter it was the temperate pivot in binding the nation together with steel. To settlers it was a paradise of nearly free land amenable to modern machines and crops. It was a place to make money; it was a place to live well; it was a country of opportunity for the immigrant and the racial minority; it was a locus to create a new and better society where things were, as the *Wichita Eagle*

put it in 1875, "plastic yet and warm." Yet the visions often clashed. And not being capable of being all things to all people, Kansas risked having no distinct identity beyond bad news coming from there of droughts, tornadoes, chaos, and violence.

The region did "bleed" in one way or another throughout the century. John Brown, sinner or saint that he was, became a Kansas icon for his violent protests against slavery in the 1850s, as did James H. Lane, a leader in the Free-State movement and the most meteoric and unstable personality one could imagine in a U.S. senator, which he became following Kansas statehood in 1861. The Kansas cow towns of the 1870s were mythologized before they had passed into myth. Prohibition, which became part of the state constitution in 1880, was aptly called "the Kansas idea." Middle-class Kansas women voted in municipal elections, sang hymns in saloons as "home defenders," and followed Carry Nation on her "raids" of saloons, ready for nonviolent resistance in matters that affected the quality of family life. Populism originated in Kansas in a wave of bitterness on the dusty side of a boom. Congressman Jeremiah "Sockless Jerry" Simpson and Mary E. Lease, who fought for farmers, capped a tradition that put "the Kansas man on the defensive" (the phrase used by William Allen White in the *Emporia Gazette* in 1896), at the same time making a strong case for a better balance between the materials of the economy and the timber of humanity. Maybe the tramp was the offscouring of society as defined by social Darwinism, or maybe he was your neighbor, marginalized by the system and then persecuted for vagabondage. In end-of-the-century Kansas, where tumbleweeds blew through the empty streets of towns that once aspired to county-seat status and where once-prosperous farmers gave up their acreages to banks, the latter picture seemed plausible. People in the state had seen both sides of American opportunity—sometimes more than once. In 1877 an eastern journalist wrote in the *Philadelphia Record* of Kansas, "Its best people are Puritanic and the rest Satanic—the one class being as disagreeable as the other is dangerous."

By 1900, the population of Kansas reached 1,470,495, up from 107,204 in 1860. Below and behind the seemingly mad politics of experiment, there was a rich region with strong people, tempered by difficulties, who were finding their special voice and way. In the nineteenth century Kansas became the wheat state; it discovered oil and gas; it developed institutions; it created cities; and it built more rail miles per capita than any other state in the Union. It was rough around the edges for a time, but vital and energetic. By 1910 Kansas seemed mature enough for Theodore Roosevelt to give his Osawatomie address there. He said little about John Brown, to whom the day was dedicated, but much about his ideas for advancing Progressive reform in the bosom of the state, which could well be seen as the movement's cradle.

See also **Bleeding Kansas; Populism; Progressivism; Temperance Movement.**

Bibliography

Clanton, O. Gene. *Kansas Populism: Ideas and Men.* Lawrence: University Press of Kansas, 1969.

Dykstra, Robert R. *The Cattle Towns.* New York: Knopf, 1968.

Gates, Paul W. *Fifty Million Acres: Conflicts over Kansas Land Policy, 1854–1890.* Ithaca, N.Y.: Cornell University Press, 1954.

Malin, James C. *John Brown and the Legend of Fifty-six.* Philadelphia: American Philosophical Society, 1942.

Miner, Craig. *West of Wichita: Settling the High Plains of Kansas, 1865–1890.* Lawrence: University Press of Kansas, 1986.

CRAIG MINER

KANSAS CITY   Kansas City was founded in 1838 by a syndicate of merchants financed by a St. Louis, Missouri, trading firm, Sublette and Campbell. The settlement, originally called the Town of Kansas, was located on the south bank of the Missouri River, just below the great bend where the river changes course from southeast to east and at the junction where the Kansas River flows into it. The site provided superb transportation advantages, es-

pecially toward the south and west. At first, Kansas City was a backcountry outpost providing a staging area for settlers crossing the plains. The U.S. victory in the Mexican War of 1846–1848 stimulated its development by increasing the westward movement of people and goods. By 1860, six years after the Kansas-Nebraska Act had been passed to organize these western territories, Kansas City had a population of 4,418 and had become a minor transportation, banking, and real estate center. Although its leaders were city boosters who eagerly sought government aid and railroad construction, Kansas City was smaller and less well established than such competing Missouri River towns as Leavenworth and St. Joseph.

The event that let Kansas City overtake its rivals occurred in 1867, when the Hannibal and St. Joseph Railroad decided to build its Missouri River bridge there. Kansas City won the urban competition for this bridge partly because of its accessibility to the burgeoning Southwest and partly because its unified and politically astute business elite mounted an effective campaign. The Hannibal Bridge opened in 1869 as the first rail span across the Missouri River, establishing Kansas City as a rail hub that became a transshipment point for western grain and livestock and a meat-packing center. The city handled nearly one million cattle, sheep, and hogs in 1880. By 1900 Kansas City had a population of 163,752. It was the regional metropolis for the southwestern United States, a position it retained until Houston, Texas, displaced it several decades later.

The city was highly stratified. A white Protestant upper class resided on Quality Hill overlooking the Missouri River, while below the bluffs stood the city's poorest neighborhood, the West Bottoms, inhabited by a polyglot mixture of blacks, immigrants, and native-born whites. These residents performed unskilled labor in the rail yards, stockyards, and packing plants. The proportion of blacks in the total population was higher than in northern industrial cities, while the proportion of immigrants was smaller. The largest ethnic groups were the Irish, Germans, and Italians. In 1892 James F. Prendergast, an Irish American saloonkeeper from the West Bottoms, was elected alderman, laying the groundwork for the political machine later controlled by his brother, Thomas J. Prendergast.

A city beautification movement began in the 1890s that aimed at refining Kansas City's dismal physical appearance and its reputation as a cowtown. In 1914 Kansas City unveiled a new railroad station and neared completion of a system of parks and boulevards that would become a national model for city planning. These projects benefited downtown business interests and affluent residents but did not improve the living conditions of the poor.

See also **Cities and Urbanization; City and Regional Planning; Missouri.**

Bibliography

Brown, A. Theodore, and Lyle W. Dorset, *K.C.: A History of Kansas City, Missouri.* Boulder, Colo.: Pruett, 1978.

Glaab, Charles N. *Kansas City and the Railroads: Community Policy in the Growth of a Regional Metropolis.* Madison: State Historical Commission of Wisconsin, 1962.

CLIFTON HOOD

KANSAS-NEBRASKA ACT   In 1820 the Missouri Compromise prohibited slavery in the federal territories north and west of the state of Missouri. The compromise more or less ended debate over the status of slavery in the federal territories for the next quarter-century. The Mexican War (1846–1848) led to the acquisition of vast new lands, including all or part of the eventual states of California, New Mexico, Arizona, Nevada, Utah, and Colorado. With this new land came new debates over the status of slavery in the territories. Southerners wanted access to the new territories and, equally important, wanted to undo the Missouri Compromise.

The Compromise of 1850 allowed slavery in most of the newly acquired territories, which whetted the appetites of southern expansionists. Northerners remained divided on the issue. Most, for a variety of reasons, wanted to keep slavery out of the territories. Northern opponents of slavery wanted to stop its spread as a first step toward destroying the institution altogether. Other northerners wanted the territories to be free of slavery because they felt that free labor and free farmers could never compete against slave labor and the economic power of slave owners. Some white northerners also wanted the West to be free of slavery for racist reasons: they wanted to keep all blacks out of the West.

Had the issue of slavery in the territories followed a strict sectional vote, the North would have successfully kept human bondage out of the region. But by 1854 the Democratic Party controlled all three branches of the national government, and southerners controlled the party. Thus northern Democrats with political ambitions, such as Senator Stephen A. Douglas of Illinois, tried to avoid any conflict over slavery and, when pushed, often sided with the South. In 1854 Douglas's main interest was neither slavery nor the settlement of the territory west of Missouri known as Nebraska, which encompassed the state of that name as well as Kansas and the Da-

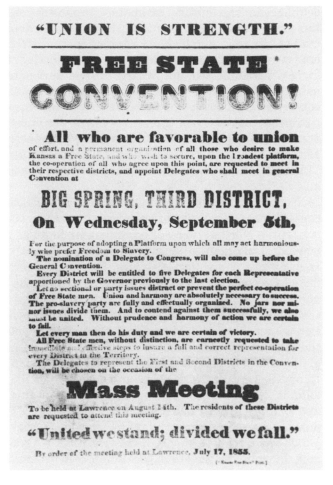

Poster for the Free State Convention, Kansas, 1855. Following the passage of the Kansas-Nebraska Act in 1854, opponents of slavery in Kansas held a "free state convention" and set up their own constitution and government that denounced slavery. The vicious fighting that ensued between opponents and proponents of slavery became known as "Bleeding Kansas" and accelerated the coming of the Civil War. LIBRARY OF CONGRESS

kotas. Douglas wanted to secure federal support for a transcontinental railroad that would begin in his hometown of Chicago and end in San Francisco.

To get congressional support for his Chicago route, Douglas in January 1854 proposed organizing the Nebraska Territory for settlement and letting the people living there at the time of statehood determine the status of slavery. He quickly amended his proposal to say that before statehood the first territorial government would have power to allow slavery in the territory. Through partial repeal of the Missouri Compromise, Douglas hoped to get southern support for his bill. The South, however, wanted a full repeal of the Missouri Compromise in the new territories. Without this repeal the bill would be lost, so Douglas acquiesced. The bill he ultimately proposed contained two territories: Kansas, which was the area west of Missouri, and Nebraska, which contained the land west of Minnesota and Iowa. Two months of fierce debate followed, but in early March the Senate passed the bill 37 to 14. Debate in the House was equally intense. President Franklin Pierce combined patronage, flattery, and threats to line up the votes. Southern Whigs and Democrats joined northern Democrats, and on 22 May the bill passed the House 113 to 100. On 30 May, President Pierce signed it into law.

The Kansas-Nebraska Act had two immediate consequences. First, the unprecedented hostile reaction in the North soon resulted in the formation of a new political organization, the Republican Party. In creating this party, former Whigs, Free-Soilers, and "free" Democrats buried their differences over banking policy, tariffs, internal improvements, and western expansion. They coalesced around their opposition to repeal of the Missouri Compromise, which they saw as virtually a sacred document. The leaders of this party included former Whigs, like William Henry Seward of New York, and Democrats, like Salmon P. Chase of Ohio, Hannibal Hamlin of Maine, and Charles Sumner of Massachusetts. In Douglas's home state the most articulate member of the new party was a relatively obscure lawyer named Abraham Lincoln. In the state, local, and congressional elections of 1854 and 1855 the new party swept Democrats out of office throughout the North. In 1854 the Democrats had won ninety-one northern congressional seats, but after the 1856 election they still held only twenty-five of them.

The second result was a rush of armed settlers from the North and the South into Kansas. The act essentially left the issue of slavery up to the settlers in what was called popular sovereignty. By 1855 Kansas was edging toward civil war as southerners and northerners competed for land and resources. In late 1855 a southern settler killed a northerner in a land dispute. Instead of arresting the killer, the local sheriff, who had proslavery sympathies, went after northerners who threatened to retaliate for the killing. This was only one of many fatal incidents involving northern and southern settlers. In 1856 violence erupted in response to massive vote fraud by southerners entering the territory to vote for a proslavery government. In May 1856 proslavery ruffians attacked the Free-Soil town of Lawrence, Kansas, destroying much of it. In retaliation, men under the command of John Brown, an Ohio abolitionist, killed a group of proslavery settlers at Pottawatomie. By the summer of 1856 the territory was caught in a small civil war.

A new territorial governor, John W. Geary, restored order in late 1856, but the territory remained a tinderbox until the Civil War began. In 1858 President James Buchanan tried to bring Kansas into the Union as a slave state under a constitution that had been approved by a fraudulent referendum. The attempt failed, in part because Douglas would not go along with this misuse of his notion of popular sovereignty. In January 1861, on the eve of the Civil War, Kansas entered the Union as a free state.

Paradoxically, the Kansas-Nebraska Act failed to accomplish the goals of its author and its supporters. Douglas hoped it would lead to a transcontinental railroad, but that had to wait until after the Civil War. Southerners hoped it would produce a slave state in Kansas, but that also did not happen. Instead, the act prompted massive violence and substantial bloodshed in the territory and helped create a new political party wholly dedicated to preventing slavery from spreading to the new territories. With hindsight, clearly the act helped push the nation closer to civil war than it was before the act was passed.

See also **Bleeding Kansas; Civil War,** *subentry on* **Causes of the Civil War; Compromise of 1850; Harpers Ferry and John Brown; Kansas; Missouri Compromise; Nebraska; Republican Party; Slavery,** *subentry on* **Law of Slavery.**

Bibliography

Morrison, Michael A. *Slavery and the American West.* Chapel Hill: University of North Carolina Press, 1997.

Potter, David M. *The Impending Crisis, 1848–1861.* New York: Harper and Row, 1976.

SenGupta, Gunja. *For God and Mammon.* Athens, Ga.: University of Georgia Press, 1996.

PAUL FINKELMAN

KENTUCKY The fifteenth state, having acquired statehood on 1 June 1792, Kentucky entered the nineteenth century in a position of great strength and ended the century declining in almost every category. Nascent Kentucky had modeled its institutions after Virginia, even adopting the designation "Commonwealth." Many of the first settlers from Virginia and North Carolina brought their slaves, so that by 1860 nearly one quarter of Kentucky white families owned slaves. The state's population rose from 179,873 in 1800 to 1,155,684 (20 percent slave) in 1860 to 2,147,174 in 1900.

Because of the state's temperate climate and varied topography, agriculture flourished there from the beginning. The vaunted Bluegrass region of central

Kentucky became famous for its fine cattle and thoroughbred horses. ("Bluegrass" refers to the dominant grass of central Kentucky, which has a bluish tint when it blooms.) Kentucky hemp, corn, tobacco, wheat, pork, whiskey, and other goods were shipped down the Ohio and Mississippi Rivers to New Orleans, Louisiana. Industrial development was limited to small-scale iron, salt making, textiles, and other locally produced products.

The Kentucky, Barren, Green, Licking, and other rivers provided early outlets to the Ohio and the world beyond. Steamboats revolutionized transportation on the western rivers. Owing to a lack of entrepreneurship, Kentucky never developed an internal canal system. Moreover, railroads caught on slowly, with only the Louisville and Nashville Railroad crossing the state before the Civil War. In 1872 the Cincinnati Southern Railway won the right to build southward after a hard-fought battle in the Kentucky General Assembly.

As a leading western state in the early part of the century, Kentucky paid a bitter price in the War of 1812. Nearly two-thirds of the men killed during that war were Kentuckians; many died at the Raisin River in Michigan. Richard M. Johnson, credited for killing Tecumseh at the Battle of the Thames, used his fame to propel himself into the vice presidency in 1836.

In the 1820s an economic and political struggle rocked the state. When debtors could not get cheap credit and relief, they formed their own political party. They took over the governorship and state legislature, creating new banks, known to their enemies as "the forty thieves," and passing a replevin, or debt-relief law. The antirelief forces included Whiggish businessmen who controlled the state's credit. While the reliefers briefly took control of the court system, they eventually had to relinquish power to a resurgent conservatism.

The national development of a second party system coincided with the relief-antirelief struggle in Kentucky. Many of the reliefers joined the party of Andrew Jackson, and many of the antireliefers became adherents of Kentuckian Henry Clay and the new Whig Party.

In the presidential election of 1824, Clay and Jackson clashed for the first time. With no candidate having a majority in the electoral college, Clay encouraged the Kentucky delegation in the U.S. House of Representatives to vote for Adams instead of Jackson, and in so doing elicited the unproven charge of striking a "corrupt bargain," for which Jacksonians condemned him. Although Clay remained Kentucky's favorite son for many years, a surprising number of Kentuckians swore by "Old Hickory."

Jackson later took delight in thwarting Clay's "American System" by vetoing the Maysville Bill, which proposed federal support for the construction of a highway from Maysville to Lexington.

Kentucky's Cassius Marcellus Clay, President Abraham Lincoln's ambassador to Russia, and John G. Fee, an educator, voiced disapproval of slavery, but the majority of Kentuckians went along with Kentucky's southern political attachment in the 1840s and 1850s as abolitionism increasingly fell on deaf ears.

Yet the state did not secede and join the Confederacy. The Civil War was truly a brother's war (dividing families: father against son; brother against brother) for many Kentucky families. Kentucky's participants in the civil war numbered between 25,000 and 40,000 for the Confederacy and between 90,000 and 100,000 for the Union. Moreover, Kentucky contributed presidents to both sides: Abraham Lincoln for the United States and Jefferson Davis for the Confederacy. In the first months of war, Kentucky's leaders, particularly Governor Beriah Magoffin, hoped for neutrality. However, both sides realized Kentucky's strategic position on the Ohio River would prove to be crucial in any battle plans. Numerous skirmishes and small battles took place in Kentucky. The Battle of Perryville in early October 1862, sealed the fate for Confederate hopes in Kentucky. While Confederate raider John Hunt Morgan and guerrillas, such as Sue Mundy and William Clarke Quantrill, continued to stir up trouble in the remaining years of the war, Union forces kept control of most of the state.

Though not one of the eleven Confederate states, Kentucky suffered through many of the pains of Reconstruction. Freedmen fared only slightly better than in the Deep South, as Kentucky's racial mores remained conservative. Close affiliation with the South, racially, politically, and morally, stunted the state's postwar economic development.

By the century's end, Republicans had produced some political competition for conservative Democrats, with a hotly contested gubernatorial race in 1899 between Democrat William Goebel and Republican William S. Taylor. Not long after Goebel's election, on 30 January 1900, a gunman ambushed him just outside the statehouse, leaving Kentucky with the notoriety of being the only state to have had an assassinated governor. This outrage, coupled with the well-publicized Hatfield-McCoy feud, branded an association of Kentucky with violence into the national consciousness.

See also **Appalachia; Civil War,** *subentries on* **Battles and Combatants, The Home Front in the South; Re-**

construction, *subentry on* **The South**; **South**, *subentry on* **The New South after Reconstruction.**

Bibliography

Channing, Steven A. *Kentucky: A Bicentennial History.* New York: W. W. Norton, 1977.

Clark, Thomas D. *A History of Kentucky.* Lexington, Ky.: The John Bradford Press, 1960.

Harrison, Lowell H., and James C. Klotter. *A New History of Kentucky.* Lexington: The University Press of Kentucky, 1997.

Waller, Altina L. *Feud: Hatfields, McCoys, and Social Change in Appalachia, 1860–1900.* Chapel Hill: University of North Carolina Press, 1988.

WILLIAM E. ELLIS

KU KLUX KLAN   The Reconstruction-era Ku Klux Klan was a white-supremacist, paramilitary terrorist organization committed to the preservation of traditional white southern values. Most white southerners considered African Americans inferior, thus they could not accept the former slaves as equal participants in state and national politics. They worried, moreover, that equality under the law would inevitably bring social equality, a possibility even more abhorrent to white southerners. The Klan was born of southern recalcitrance toward Republican Reconstruction policy that attempted to elevate the former slaves. The more aggressively the United States pushed black equality, the more violently white southerners resisted. As Klan violence escalated beyond the ability of the weak southern state governments to control it, the Republican national government moved inexorably toward the federal judicial intervention that ended the reign of terror by 1873.

Origins and Spread of the Klan

The Klan began in early 1866 as a harmless organization of young, former Confederate soldiers looking for a good time in Pulaski, Tennessee. The Klan adopted disguises, secret signs, and rituals similar to other fraternal organizations. Within months, however, the Klan acquired a sinister propensity for frightening emancipated slaves for sport. By mid-1867, the Tennessee Klan's nocturnal rides closely resembled the antebellum slave patrols that had authority to "try" and punish blacks who were found away from home. Like the slave patrols, the Klan supplied an unofficial justice system to keep blacks under control.

The Klan quickly spread across the former Con-federacy, attracting men of every class. Nathan Bedford Forrest, a former Confederate general and war hero who embodied the ideals of white southern manhood, was the Grand Wizard, or supreme commander, of the "Invisible Empire." Klan leaders—many of them former Confederate officers—came from the educated, propertied classes, but poorer whites were often expected to implement Klan atrocities. In such areas as the South Carolina upcountry, where the Klan was particularly strong, whites who preferred to remain aloof were forced into the Klan to maintain white solidarity. But the Klan had few enemies among white southerners, who generally regarded their Republican state governments as unconstitutional usurpations of their own authority and consequently tolerated the Klan as a necessary evil. Southern tradition was a stronger force than the new order the Republican national government sought to impose under the authority of the Thirteenth, Fourteenth, and Fifteenth Amendments.

Influence in Southern Society, Economy, and Politics

The Klan's hatred was directed toward anyone—white or black—who attempted to elevate African Americans. Unlike the twentieth-century Klan, the Reconstruction-era Klan did not burn crosses on the lawns of its victims; its methods were more direct. Attacking under cover of night, the nineteenth-century Klan whipped, robbed, murdered, and raped their victims. Recognizing that education was the key to the blacks' advancement, the Klan whipped and threatened schoolteachers, burned black schools, and destroyed the property of whites bold enough to teach blacks. Whites who sold land to blacks, hired them away from plantations, or paid them decent wages also felt the Klan's wrath. The detested "scalawags"—native white Republicans—suffered enormously for failing to support the Democratic Party. But African Americans suffered even more. On the typical Klan visit, disguised terrorists broke into the home of a black Republican, stole his gun, then applied the lash. If the mangled victim renounced his Republican Party affiliation, he might be spared any future indignities, but hundreds of African Americans were brutally murdered by the Klan. The night-riders especially targeted courageous black political officials, militia leaders, teachers, and ministers whose lives and work encouraged other African Americans to consider themselves worthy of all the attributes of American citizenship. Klan brutality did not even spare the women and children; Klansmen often punished the wives when they could not

Ku Klux Klan Members in Disguise. Like other male societies, disguises, secret signs, and rituals were essential to identify members of the Ku Klux Klan. These accoutrements became symbolic of the organization's murderous activities against blacks. From *Harper's Weekly,* n.d. LIBRARY OF CONGRESS

find their husbands at home. Economic reprisal was as important as physical punishment in the Klan's agenda; Klansmen routinely refused employment to politically active black Republicans. Black landowners were beaten, robbed, and run off their property.

Klan violence peaked around the election of 1870, when the Klan terrorized black Republicans to keep them from the polls, and continued for several months after the election to punish those who had voted. Fearing for their lives, blacks slept in the woods and swamps; in some neighborhoods, a large portion of the agricultural workers fled to nearby towns or to the protection of federal army camps, causing a severe labor shortage. Southern state governments were too weak to stop the violence even after President Ulysses S. Grant sent additional troops into the South. In York County, South Caro-

lina, for example, the grand jury evaded the evidence against the Klan that a federal army officer had painstakingly accumulated over several months. Although justice would require federal intervention and prosecution, burglary, assault, and murder were not federal crimes.

Federal Efforts to Suppress the Klan

To meet the emergency, Congress passed extraordinary new laws extending federal authority to protect the civil and political rights of citizens under the Fourteenth and Fifteenth Amendments. Targeting the Klan, the First Enforcement Act (May 1870) made it a federal crime to conspire or ride the public highways to deprive any citizen of his civil rights. To facilitate making large numbers of arrests quickly, the Ku Klux Act (1871) was passed, empowering the president to suspend habeas corpus in areas where the Klan was out of control. Democrats in the North and South considered the laws an unconstitutional power grab on the part of the Republican national government.

The Enforcement Acts enabled the U.S. government to bring numerous Klansmen to justice. South Carolina was the only state in which President Grant suspended habeas corpus; in North Carolina and Mississippi numerous federal Klan trials proceeded without such extraordinary measures. In Columbia, South Carolina, the federal Klan trials in November and December 1871 took on a deeper constitutional meaning than the guilt or innocence of the defendants, as federal prosecutors attempted to establish a broad nationalization of federal authority under the Fourteenth Amendment, demonstrating that the Second and Fourth Amendments were now federally enforceable rights. These constitutional goals failed, but the government attorneys successfully prosecuted numerous Klansmen in 1871 and 1872, gaining five convictions and forty-nine guilty pleas in the November 1871 court session. The Klan's reign of terror was over. But the traditional southern values had not changed; white supremacists simply turned to other methods of restoring the state governments to their "rightful owners," the white southern Democrats. These methods included fraudulent elections, grandfather clauses, poll taxes, literary tests, and economic coercion. The nineteenth-century Klan was dead, but its memory lingered and took on heroic proportions in D. W. Griffith's *Birth of a Nation,* the 1915 film that helped to inspire the twentieth-century Ku Klux Klan.

See also **African Americans; Race and Racial Thinking; Reconstruction; Vigilantes; Violence.**

Bibliography

Trelease, Allen W. *White Terror: The Ku Klux Klan Conspiracy and Southern Reconstruction*. New York: Harper and Row, 1971.

U.S. Congress. *Report of the Joint Select Committee to Inquire into the Condition of Affairs in the Late Insurrectionary States*. 13 vols. Washington, D.C.: U.S. Government Printing Office, 1872. Volumes for every southern state contain testimony from Klan members and victims, as well as numerous primary source materials pertinent to the Klan.

Wade, Wyn Craig. *The Fiery Cross: The Ku Klux Klan in America*. New York: Simon and Schuster, 1987.

Williams, Lou Falkner. *The Great South Carolina Ku Klux Klan Trials: 1871–1872*. Athens, Ga.: University of Georgia Press, 1996.

LOU FALKNER WILLIAMS

L

LABOR FORCE Economic growth occurs whenever the stock of productive inputs—that is, labor, capital, or natural resources—expands or when more output can be produced with a given amount of inputs, for example, because of technical progress. Compared with the twentieth century, economic growth in nineteenth-century America was relatively more dependent on expansion of the stock of productive inputs than on technical progress. The labor force in the nineteenth century was by far the most important of the three basic productive inputs when measured in terms of its share of national income.

For the census years 1870 to 1900, economic historians consider individuals to have been in the labor force if they reported a "gainful occupation" to census enumerators. Before 1870 it is not possible to apply the "gainful worker" definition to census data consistently for all census years. Various procedures have been developed to estimate labor force participation rates—the ratio of persons in the labor force to population—for specific groups before 1870. Estimates of the national labor force are then built up piece by piece, by applying the group-specific participation rates to population figures.

Table 1 *(overleaf)* gives the best estimates of the labor force and the national labor force participation rate (as of the late 1990s) for the census years 1800 to 1900. At the turn of the nineteenth century, about 1.7 million persons were in the labor force. By 1900 the labor force had increased to 29.1 million persons. Labor force growth was quicker before the Civil War (on average, 3.1 percent per year, from 1800 to 1860) than after the Civil War (2.4 percent per year, from 1860 to 1900), and also varied across decades.

Over the entire course of the nineteenth century, the national labor force participation rate increased from 32 percent (in 1800) to 38 percent (in 1900). The antebellum increase was concentrated in the 1840s, and most of the postbellum increase occurred after 1880.

Who Participated in the Labor Force?

For free males ages fifteen and over, the labor force participation rate before the Civil War was extremely high, near 90 percent. For free females ages sixteen and over, the best current estimate suggests a participation rate of about 8 percent in 1800. By mid-century the female participation rate had risen to about 11 percent, reflecting economic developments that created new employment opportunities in the market economy for young, single women. Chief among these was the emergence of manufacturing, primarily in factories. Young, single women also found work as domestic servants or teachers. North-South differences were pronounced—few young women in the South worked in factories, and proportionately fewer women than in the North were teachers, as men were more likely to be teachers in the South. Participation rates for married women were extremely low throughout the first half of the nineteenth century (5 percent or less), although recent research suggests rates may have been somewhat higher in the late 1700s.

For slaves over age ten, the labor force participation rate was around 90 percent. Age and gender mattered far less in determining a slave's labor force participation than they did among the free population.

Table 1.   Labor Force in the United States, 1800–1900

	Labor Force (thousands)	Labor Force Participation Rate (percent)
1800	1,712	32.3
1810	2,337	32.3
1820	3,150	33.7
1830	4,272	33.2
1840	5,778	33.9
1850	8,192	35.3
1860	11,290	35.9
1870	12,809	33.2
1880	17,392	34.7
1890	23,547	37.4
1900	29,073	38.3

Source: Labor force from unpublished estimates of Thomas Weiss. Population figures are from U.S. Department of Commerce, *Historical Statistics of the United States* (Washington, D.C.: Bureau of the Census, 1975), series A-1, p. 8.

Consequently, the overall participation rate of slave labor considerably exceeded that of free labor. Postbellum census data indicate lower rates of labor force participation among emancipated African Americans in the South, suggesting that once they were free to do so, former slaves worked less than when they were in bondage. Per capita income declined in the South between 1860 and 1880, and some economic historians have pointed to the reduction in labor force participation among former slaves as one of several factors responsible for the decline in income. This also explains part of the decline in the rate of labor force growth after 1860.

Data from the manuscripts of the 1880 census permit a detailed look at labor force participation at about the midpoint of the second half of the nineteenth century. Table 2 shows participation rates for various population groups. Labor force participation among adult men (ages twenty and over) remained very high, declining only after age sixty-five. However, by comparison with late-twentieth-century standards, older males were far more likely to be working than today—"retirement," in other words, was uncommon in the late nineteenth century. Labor force participation by adult women was a more varied function of age, race, marital status, and urban-rural residence than it was for adult men. African American women were more likely to participate in the labor force than were white women. This difference has been attributed to a greater need for African American women to work, owing to the lower average economic status of adult African American men (compared with white men) and to the legacy of slav-

Table 2.   Labor Force Participation Rates in 1880 (percent)

Adults		
Age	Male	Female
20–24	90.5	24.0
25–34	96.3	14.5
35–44	96.8	11.2
45–54	96.6	11.6
55–59	95.6	11.1
60–64	90.3	8.7
65–74	82.6	5.5
>75	58.2	4.6
White	93.2	10.5
Black	96.1	37.8
Native-born	93.5	14.2
Foreign-born	93.9	14.0
Unmarried	88.6	31.2
Married	96.2	5.5
Rural	93.7	10.9
Urban	93.3	20.7
Total	93.6	14.1

Children and Young Adults		
Age	Male	Female
10	14.5	7.2
11	20.0	5.7
12	30.2	9.6
13	33.6	10.3
14	43.4	14.3
15–19	68.7	26.6
White	43.1	13.1
Black	65.5	43.7
Native-born	45.9	16.7
Foreign-born	53.6	32.7
Rural	48.5	15.4
Urban	39.9	23.5
Total	46.4	17.7

Source: Robert A. Margo, "The Labor Force in the Nineteenth Century," Appendix Table 1.

ery. Compared with single women, relatively few married women held gainful occupations. Women in urban areas were much more likely to report a gainful occupation than were women in rural areas.

Among children and young adults (ages ten to nineteen) labor force participation varied by age, gender, race, and ethnicity. Males typically entered the labor force by age fifteen, and were more than twice as likely as females under age twenty to participate in the labor force. African American children had higher participation rates than white children, as did the foreign born compared with the native born.

Young urban males had lower participation rates than rural males, but as was true among adults, the opposite was true among females.

Thus, labor force participation in the nineteenth century was sharply delineated along age, ethnic, racial, and gender lines. Differences in participation rates among population groups suggest three factors behind the long-term upward trend in national participation rates. First, because fertility fell throughout the nineteenth century, the composition of the population shifted toward adults of working age. Second, immigration raised the national participation rate in two ways: foreign-born children had higher participation rates than native-born children, and the foreign-born were more likely to be adults. Third, urbanization boosted the national participation rate by increasing the fraction of women who held gainful occupations.

Structure of the Labor Force

"Structure" is the distribution of workers across industries or occupations. The most important change in the structure of the labor force in the nineteenth century was the shift of labor away from agriculture. In 1800 approximately 75 percent of the labor force was engaged in agriculture. Agriculture's share of the labor force fell by fourteen percentage points between 1800 and 1850. By 1900 approximately 36 percent of the workforce was employed in farming. The shift of labor away from agriculture began earliest in New England; by 1860 less than 40 percent of the region's workers were engaged in farming. The South was the only region to have a majority of workers in farming at the end of the nineteenth century.

Economic historians explain the long-run shift of labor away from agriculture by appealing to technological change and the nature of the demand for agricultural goods. The demand for agricultural goods was relatively insensitive with respect to price, compared with the demand for nonagricultural goods. Improvements in agricultural technology increased the supply of agricultural goods relative to nonagricultural goods. However, because demand for agricultural goods was inelastic, their relative price declined, reducing the value of labor in agriculture compared with the nonfarm sector. In this scenario labor is said to have been pushed out of agriculture. Conversely, improvements in nonfarm technology tended to raise the relative demand for labor in the nonfarm sector, pulling labor from the farm.

Manufacturing was by far the most important sector receiving the growth of nonfarm employment. Virtually nonexistent before 1820, manufacturing employed slightly less than a third of all nonfarm workers by 1840. The proportion in manufacturing reached 37 percent in 1860, and it remained at that figure for the rest of the century. Employment in mining, wholesale and retail trade, and construction also grew over the course of the century. Between 1840 and 1900 employment in mining increased at an average annual rate of 5 percent. Employment growth in wholesale and retail trade and in construction over the same period was a bit slower but still brisk (4.0 and 2.9 percent per year, respectively). By 1900 trade and transportation claimed the most workers, about 32 percent, after manufacturing. Services, including government, employed another 20 percent, followed by mining and construction (12 percent).

The distribution of employment by occupation indicates how the skills embodied in the labor force and the demand for skills change over time. Although some information on occupations was collected in the 1820 and 1840 censuses, the data were very crude and not readily comparable with those of later census years. Evidence on occupations at mid-century can be gleaned from figures published in the 1850 census. The data pertain to free males, ages fifteen and over; unfortunately, similar data for females cannot be extracted from the census volumes.

In 1850 approximately half of the census respondents declared themselves to be farmers. Laborers were the next most numerous, making up nearly 17 percent of all occupations reported. Skilled artisans—in particular, blacksmiths, carpenters, masons, and plasterers—made up another 7 percent of free male workers. Clerks and merchants, the biggest white-collar occupations, made up about 4 percent. The remaining workers were scattered among the several hundred additional occupations listed in the 1850 census.

How did the occupational distribution change over time? By 1900 approximately 40 percent of males were in agriculture. Among the 60 percent of males in nonfarm occupations in 1900, fully 39 percent were in the skilled crafts or closely related semiskilled occupations, and another 30 percent held white-collar occupations, primarily as managers or proprietors. Unskilled labor and various low-skilled service occupations employed another 30 percent of men in nonfarm occupations. Compared with men, women reporting an occupation in 1900 were much less likely to work in agriculture (19 percent) and also were less likely to hold a white-collar or skilled blue-collar job than were men. Approximately two-thirds of female workers were employed as semiskilled operatives in manufacturing, as unskilled laborers, or in the service sector, primarily in domestic service.

Race and ethnicity significantly influenced the occupational structure in 1900. African Americans were far more likely than whites to work in unskilled occupations. The foreign-born were less likely than native-born whites to be white-collar workers or farm operators, but they were more successful than African Americans at obtaining semiskilled and skilled blue-collar jobs. Various studies by economic historians suggest that language skills, work experience, and time in the United States were important factors explaining ethnic differences in occupations. African Americans suffered severely from discriminatory practices that excluded them from the higher-paying occupations.

See also **Labor Movement,** *subentries on* **Women, People of Color; Work,** *subentries on* **Agricultural Labor, Domestic Labor, Artisans and Craftsworkers, Factory Labor, Child Labor, Middle-Class Occupations.**

Bibliography

Fogel, Robert William. *Without Consent or Contract: The Rise and Fall of American Slavery.* New York: W. W. Norton, 1989.

Goldin, Claudia. *Understanding the Gender Gap: An Economic History of American Women.* New York: Oxford University Press, 1990.

Lebergott, Stanley. *Manpower in Economic Growth: The American Record since 1800.* New York: McGraw-Hill, 1964.

Margo, Robert A. "The Labor Force in the Nineteenth Century." In *The Cambridge Economic History of the United States.* Edited by Stanley L. Engerman and Robert E. Gallman. Volume 2. Cambridge, U.K., and New York: Cambridge University Press, 1996–.

Moen, Jon. "From Gainful Employment to Labor Force: Definitions and a New Estimate of Work Rates of American Males, 1860–1980." *Historical Methods* 21 (fall 1988).

Ransom, Roger, and Richard Sutch. *One Kind of Freedom: The Economic Consequences of Emancipation.* New York: Cambridge University Press, 1977.

Weiss, Thomas. "U.S. Labor Force Estimates and Economic Growth, 1800 to 1860." In *American Economic Growth and Standards of Living before the Civil War.* Edited by Robert E. Gallman and John Joseph Wallis. Chicago: University of Chicago Press, 1992.

ROBERT A. MARGO

LABOR MOVEMENT

[This entry includes three subentries: **Unions and Strikes, Women,** and **People of Color.**]

UNIONS AND STRIKES

During the nineteenth century the American labor movement assumed the characteristics that influenced its subsequent development and distinguished it from the labor movements of other nations. Unions arose with the industrial order that transformed the United States from an agrarian, slaveholding republic in 1800 to an industrial giant that boasted the world's most fluid and diverse labor market a century later. That transformation brought to workers uncertainty and disruption, as well as opportunity and improved living conditions. As they struggled with the hardships of industrialism, laborers learned to act collectively in unions. As they built durable organizations, they learned to rely heavily on their most effective economic weapon, the strike.

Emergence of Trade Unions and Strikes

The interplay between trade unions and strikes was evident from the beginning. The last decades of the eighteenth century saw the first true workers' organizations, journeymen's societies, undertake the first true strikes. In New York tailors struck in 1768 and shoemakers in 1785, and in Philadelphia printers struck in 1786 and carpenters in 1791. Each group sought higher wages from its masters.

The Federal Society of Journeymen Cordwainers, established by Philadelphia shoemakers in 1794, was among the most successful of the early journeymen's societies that undertook strikes, or "turnouts" as they were first called, in pursuit of its goals. But it was scarcely the only such organization. Printers, building tradesmen, tailors, coopers, weavers, stonecutters, and millwrights were among the other artisans who formed journeymen's societies by the early nineteenth century. Journeymen's societies struggled to protect their crafts from "bastardized work," opposing the introduction of boys, poorly trained workers, and occasionally women into the trade. As early as 1799, when Philadelphia cordwainers delegated a committee to meet with masters in their trade, organized journeymen also fought for collective bargaining, and in time they struggled to implement the "closed shop," the right to limit work in the trade to union members.

A combination of factors constrained these early unions. Recurrent depressions undermined efforts to elevate wages, the courts frequently declared collective actions illegal, and factory production gradually undermined the craft basis upon which journeymen organized.

For most of the nineteenth century the law proved a great impediment to unionism. In a series of disputes early in the century, employers successfully contended in the courts that journeymen's organizations amounted to monopolistic criminal conspiracies. This argument was first sustained in 1806, when Philadelphia's master shoemakers won a decision against their journeymen. In 1810 New York's journeymen shoemakers suffered a similar legal defeat. In 1815 Pittsburgh cordwainers were convicted of criminal conspiracy, as were New York tailors in 1836. In 1842 Chief Justice Lemuel Shaw of the Massachusetts Supreme Judicial Court drafted a significant decision acknowledging the legality of unions. Yet the courts continued to raise obstacles to successful strikes in the following decades. In the late nineteenth century employers regularly secured judicial injunctions against strikes, a tactic made all the more effective when the courts subjected interstate strikes to regulation under the Sherman Antitrust Act of 1890.

Like skilled journeymen, unskilled workers also waged strikes in the early nineteenth century, though their actions were usually spontaneous and resulted in no durable union organizations. The women textile-mill operatives of Lowell, Massachusetts, "turned out" against wage cuts in 1834 and 1836. New York stevedores struck in 1828 against wage cuts, while many of that city's coal heavers walked out in 1834, demanding a shorter workday. Discontented canal diggers staged fourteen strikes and twenty-five riots across the country in the 1830s, provoking military intervention on a dozen occasions.

During the economic boom of 1824 through 1837 unionism finally began to take deep root in American cities. This period saw the consolidation of the first city central labor federation, the Mechanics' Union of Trade Associations, founded in Philadelphia in 1827 during agitation for the ten-hour workday. Informed by a producerist ethic often called "artisan republicanism" by historians, the Mechanics' Union called for a social order in which wealth would go to those who produced it with their own hands. This model inspired workers elsewhere. By 1836 thirteen city centrals had been founded around the nation. The largest, the General Trades' Union of New York, included fifty-two trade societies.

Surging organization was accompanied by a flourishing labor press, including some sixty-eight labor newspapers by the early 1830s, and the birth of workingmen's parties in at least a dozen states. The first Workingmen's Party, launched in New York City in 1829, attracted prominent leaders, such as the self-educated reformer Thomas Skidmore, the labor editor George Henry Evans, and the radicals Robert Dale Owen and Fanny Wright. Factionalism soon undermined the organization, but not before it encouraged similar efforts in Troy, Albany, Rochester, and other New York cities as well as in cities in eleven other states. Although such initiatives were easily absorbed by mainstream parties willing to take up their

issues, they signaled a period of intense working-class organization.

In the union upsurge of the 1830s, more than 44,000 workers organized by mid-decade. Most organized workers plied artisanal trades, but factory operatives also founded such organizations as the Factory Girls' Association of Massachusetts (1834).

Spreading organization also sparked a strike wave in the 1830s. Local newspapers recorded nearly 170 strikes between 1833 and 1837. Many of these strikes were prompted by workers' efforts to reduce the workday to ten hours. Strikers stressed the need for more leisure time to pursue self-education, considered essential if newly enfranchised workers were to intelligently exercise the ballot. The itinerant New England agitator Seth Luther carried this message effectively. In several cities efforts to secure the ten-hour day erupted into concerted strikes, including a failed strike by seventeen trades in Baltimore in 1833 and a successful effort by Philadelphians in 1835. Such organizing successes gave birth in 1834 to the short-lived National Trades' Union, a federation presided over by the eloquent journeyman printer Ely Moore.

The panic and subsequent depression of 1837 combined with employers' antiunion associations devastated the labor unions of the 1830s. The National Trades' Union collapsed, strikes diminished, and ten-hour agitation dried up by 1840.

In the 1840s workers were attracted to various forms of utopian socialism, to producers' and consumers' cooperatives, and to agrarianism, the notion that the people as a whole had the right to homestead public lands. Ten-hour agitation was again taken up, this time by the National Reform Association, established in 1845, and by "industrial congresses" convened in several states during the decade. Most of these efforts, however, were co-opted by major party politicians or resulted in the passage of ineffectual ten-hour laws in several states.

Revival of Unionism

In the late 1850s labor unions revived and built the first effective national trade organizations. The National Typographical Union and the National Union of Iron Molders were among the first to create structures that transcended state lines. Railroad workers, shoemakers, stonecutters, plumbers, and machinists also formed national unions. These organizations collected dues, established strike funds, and created benefit features. They also waged strikes that were generally less spontaneous and more effective than those in the past.

The first strike coordinated across state lines by one of these early unions erupted in February 1860 over wages in the shoe factories of Lynn, Massachusetts. The "turnout" eventually spread to twenty thousand workers in New England. Although the strike proved too much for the embryonic shoemakers' union to sustain, it did result in significant wage gains for workers.

The coming of the Civil War in 1861 was a boon for unions in the North. With labor scarce and war orders piling up, workers proved willing to strike in coal fields, arms factories, and other workplaces. By the war's end some 270 unions had blossomed into a combined membership of 200,000. Trades assemblies again formed in numerous cities, beginning in Rochester, New York, and by 1872 thirty national trade unions functioned. Organization also broadened during the years after the war. The first coal miners' national union, the Workingmen's Benevolent Association (WBA), was founded in 1868. Collar laundresses in Troy, New York, formed an effective organization after the war. Some freedmen, including the black dockworkers in Pensacola, Florida; Charleston, South Carolina; and New Orleans, Louisiana, and the black sawmill workers in Jacksonville, Florida, experienced organizing successes.

The unionism of this period gave birth to the National Labor Union (NLU) in 1866. The NLU worked in the political field for immigration restriction, especially toward blocking the entry of Chinese workers into the United States; the creation of cooperatives; and the eventual replacement of waged labor with a cooperative commonwealth. Yet nothing animated the postwar labor movement as much as the struggle for the eight-hour workday, inspired in part by the writings of Ira Steward, a Boston machinist and founder of the Grand Eight Hour League of Massachusetts. Steward argued that shortening the workday would stimulate consumer demand, raise wages, and create jobs. His arguments helped secure a federal law limiting the workday of government employees to eight hours, but legislative efforts to implement the eight-hour day more broadly came to naught.

William Sylvis, the dedicated leader of the Iron Molders' International Union, took the helm of the NLU in 1868 and moved it in the direction of a third party. But Sylvis's death in 1869, the NLU's abortive effort to field a presidential candidate in 1872, and the panic of 1873 killed the organization. Working-class political agitation did not cease with the collapse of the NLU. The Greenback Party (1876), which advocated currency reform, and the Socialist Labor Party (1877), a Marxian party, both drew working-class support.

Trade unionism itself, however, fell on hard times during the depression of 1873–1878. The WBA, the coal miners' union, was undermined by a bitter lockout in 1873–1874 and by subsequent accusations that it harbored a terrorist sect known as the Molly Maguires. Indeed most national unions, like the Cigar Makers International Union (CMIU), which saw its membership dwindle from six thousand down to one thousand during this period, suffered significant losses. The great railroad strike of 1877, the most notable labor event of the decade, expressed nothing so much as workers' desperation in the face of mass deprivation. That strike erupted on 16 July 1877, when employees of the B&O Railroad in Martinsburg, West Virginia, walked out to protest a 10 percent wage cut. The strike soon spread throughout much of the Midwest and led to mob actions in the streets of Chicago and Pittsburgh. By the time federal troops put it down, the uprising had demonstrated workers' frustrations and the new capability for mass solidarity generated in densely packed urban, working-class enclaves.

As the economy recovered during the 1880s, so did unionism. From that decade's turbulent social milieu, which nurtured a range of organizations from the anarchists' International Working People's Association to conservative national unions, two great organizational efforts emerged. The Noble and Holy Order of the Knights of Labor experienced a meteoric rise and decline, but the American Federation of Labor (AFL) survived to shape American unionism in the next century.

The Knights of Labor

The Knights of Labor was a secret society formed by skilled Philadelphia garment workers in 1869. Led by Uriah S. Stephens, a one-time student of the Baptist ministry, the order intended to recruit workers of all trades, skilled and unskilled, men and women, black and white, although Asian or "coolie" labor was not welcome. Its secrecy protected the order from employers' efforts to root it out and enhanced the feelings of solidarity that bound the Knights together. The Knights resurrected elements of the earlier artisan republican tradition, preaching the need to establish a cooperative commonwealth through agitation and education and opening the order's doors to all "producers."

Stressing the essential unity of capital and labor, the Knights officially opposed strikes, though in practice the organization was often forced to wage them. The humane vision of the order won it nearly ten thousand members across six states by 1878. These members were organized in regional district assemblies or in national trades assemblies depending upon their crafts or skill levels.

Protest March, New York City. Champions of the eight-hour day stage a strike in the Bowery, 10 June 1872. Drawing by Matt Morgan in *Frank Leslie's Illustrated Newspaper*, 29 June 1872. LIBRARY OF CONGRESS

In 1879 a Pennsylvania machinist named Terence V. Powderly succeeded Stephens as the Knights' leader, and the order entered a phase of rapid growth. Powderly scrapped the organization's secret ritual, which had repelled Roman Catholic workers, and many Catholics subsequently joined the group. Under Powderly the Knights continued to stress cooperative efforts, opening some 135 cooperatives by the mid-1880s. Yet the order's growth was fueled by its successful conduct of several highly publicized strikes. The Knights waged a round of successful walkouts against wage cuts in New York, Pennsylvania, and Massachusetts in 1883 and 1884 and against the railroads of financier Jay Gould in 1884 and 1885. The Knights' victory in a strike against Gould's Wabash Railroad in 1885 sparked an explosion in the order's membership rolls. Between mid-1885 and mid-1886 the number of local assemblies of the Knights of Labor ballooned from 1,610 to 5,892, and membership rose from roughly 100,000 to as many as 700,000.

However, the order grew too quickly to consolidate its gains, and it suffered a profound reversal in the following few years. When the Knights led another strike against the Southwest System in 1886, Gould was prepared, and the walkout collapsed. Meanwhile the paranoia ignited by the Haymarket riot of May 1886 created conditions unfavorable for labor organization. A controversy over the Knights' efforts among black workers erupted at the order's 1886 national convention in Richmond, Virginia, badly dividing the membership.

The American Federation of Labor

Ultimately, though, the Knights collapsed under the challenge of a formidable rival. The American Federation of Labor held its first convention at Columbus, Ohio, in December 1886, bringing together delegates representing twenty-five national trade unions with a combined membership of some 150,000. The Railway Brotherhoods, which represented the operating crafts on the nation's rail lines, were among the few national trade unions that remained aloof from the AFL. Many of the AFL's founding unions had recently won local victories in a nationwide wave of strikes for the eight-hour day, unleashed by the skilled trades in May 1886.

The AFL boasted talented leaders, such as Adolph Strasser of the CMIU and Peter J. McGuire of the United Brotherhood of Carpenters and Joiners. But from the beginning the organization was dominated by Samuel Gompers, a tough-minded immigrant cigar maker of Dutch Jewish extraction. Gompers served as president of the AFL for all but one year between its founding and his death in 1924.

The AFL survived the depression of 1893–1897, the worst economic decline of the century, in part because of its able leadership and in part due to its limited scope and objectives. Its most successful affiliates organized skilled workers into strong national unions that sought to control the labor market in their trades. These unions retained great autonomy and were granted exclusive jurisdictions by the AFL. Such unions generally required hefty initiation fees and high monthly dues. In return they offered sickness and death benefits and fought for higher wages, shorter hours, and increasing control over the terms of work. As they focused on such concrete matters, AFL unions officially steered away from partisan politics, judging past working-class political parties as wasted efforts. AFL leaders distrusted politics and feared that increasing state involvement in labor relations would come at the expense of workers' interests. Thus they advocated voluntarism, the belief that improvements in workers' lives would come not through reform legislation but rather through the organization of unions powerful enough to force employers to bargain collectively with workers free from government interference. The ultimate weapon that the AFL drew upon in its efforts to win collective bargaining was the strike, and AFL unions showed none of the Knights' ambivalence toward the use of this weapon.

Though generally pragmatic in approach, many AFL unions were initially committed to the eventual replacement of capitalism with some form of socialism, and the AFL officially opposed the exclusion of blacks from affiliated unions. Over time, however, the federation's conservative and exclusive tendencies came to the fore. By the end of the 1890s the federation had turned a blind eye to racial discrimination among its affiliates, many of which used their initiation rituals to bar blacks from their ranks. Likewise the federation did not expend much energy organizing among women workers. The AFL's vigorous championship of immigration restriction, as well as its tendency to organize the skilled "aristocrats of labor," meant that it grew increasingly out of touch with the masses of eastern and southern European workers who streamed into American factories in the years after 1886.

Although it survived the 1890s, the AFL's exclusivist tendencies hampered its efforts to confront industrialism, as the disastrous Homestead strike of 1892 illustrated. During that conflict the Amalgamated Iron and Steel Workers, a prominent AFL affiliate that organized skilled workers, suffered a crushing defeat when it took on Andrew Carnegie's steel corporation in Homestead, Pennsylvania. Carnegie locked out the union, ran his mill with semiskilled replacements, and relied on Pennsylvania state militia to smash the union's resistance.

Alternatives to the AFL arose in the 1890s, a decade that saw numerous violent labor conflicts and frequent government repression of strikes. One of the most ambitious rivals was the American Railway Union (ARU). The ARU, led by the future socialist Eugene V. Debs, rejected the craft unionism of the AFL and the Railway Brotherhoods and attempted to organize all railroad workers into one industrial union. The ARU was crushed by federal intervention in 1894, however, when its members attempted a nationwide boycott to aid the striking workers of the Pullman Palace Car Company. The Western Labor Union, a rival federation founded by disaffected hard-rock miners in 1898, provided an equally short-lived challenge to the AFL. It dissolved after the turn of the century.

With the recovery of the economy after 1897, the AFL grew quickly, firmly establishing itself at the center of the American union movement. As its members used sympathy strikes, boycotts, and other effective militant tactics to advance their interests, the AFL grew to 868,500 members by 1900 and to more than two million four years later. Employers again mounted strong resistance to the AFL after 1900, and judicial rulings and the frequent use of injunctions continued to hamper unions and strikes. The combined effects of industrialization, mechanization, and immigration in time revealed the shortcomings of the AFL's narrow craft-organizing strategy. Yet by 1900 the AFL had weathered its infancy and was poised to exert the generally conservative influence that would distinguish American unions for much of the twentieth century.

See also **Industrialization and the Market; Interstate Commerce; Labor Force; Panics and Depressions; Trusts; Work.**

Bibliography

Dawley, Alan. *Class and Community: The Industrial Revolution in Lynn.* Cambridge, Mass.: Harvard University Press, 1976.

Dublin, Thomas. *Women at Work: The Transformation of Work and Community in Lowell, Massachusetts, 1826–1860.* New York: Columbia University Press, 1979.

Dubofsky, Melvyn. *Industrialism and the American Worker, 1865–1920*. Wheeling, Ill.: H. Davidson, 1996.

Fink, Leon. *Workingmen's Democracy: The Knights of Labor and American Politics*. Urbana: University of Illinois Press, 1983.

Foner, Philip S. *Organized Labor and the Black Worker, 1619– 1973*. New York: Praeger, 1974.

Krause, Paul. *The Battle for Homestead, 1880–1892: Politics, Class, and Steel*. Pittsburgh, Pa.: University of Pittsburgh Press, 1992.

Laurie, Bruce. *Artisans into Workers: Labor in Nineteenth-Century America*. New York: Hill and Wang, 1989.

Montgomery, David. *Workers' Control in America: Studies in the History of Work, Technology, and Labor Struggles*. New York: Cambridge University Press, 1979.

Palladino, Grace. *Another Civil War: Labor, Capital, and the State in the Anthracite Regions of Pennsylvania, 1840–68*. Urbana: University of Illinois Press, 1990.

Rock, Howard B., Paul A. Gilje, and Robert Asher, eds. *American Artisans: Crafting Social Identity, 1750–1850*. Baltimore: Johns Hopkins University Press, 1995.

Schneirov, Richard. *Labor and Urban Politics: Class Conflict and the Origins of Modern Liberalism in Chicago, 1864–97*. Urbana: University of Illinois Press, 1998.

Tomlins, Christopher L. *Law, Labor, and Ideology in the Early American Republic*. New York: Cambridge University Press, 1993.

Way, Peter. *Common Labor: Workers and the Digging of North American Canals, 1780–1860*. New York: Cambridge University Press, 1993.

Wilentz, Sean. *Chants Democratic: New York City and the Rise of the American Working Class, 1788–1850*. New York: Oxford University Press, 1984.

JOSEPH A. MCCARTIN

WOMEN

As some of the first wage and factory workers in the United States, women followed their traditional domestic responsibilities for the production of textiles and garments into a variety of industrial settings in the early nineteenth century. They also were recruited for such other industries as the making of paper, iron, and shoes, and were assigned to gender-specific tasks such as rag sorting and sewing uppers. Whatever women did, their jobs invariably brought lower pay and had less status than men's work. Dependent on investment capital and large amounts of freshwater for power and processing, the early factory system was concentrated in New England, drawing women from the surrounding countryside to idyllic new villages and paying wages considerably higher than the domestic work or farmwork available to them at home.

Women garment workers, by contrast, worked in small sweatshops or their own homes in port cities along the Atlantic seaboard, particularly New York and Philadelphia. Seamstresses, among the poorest women in the nation, were often recent immigrants or single heads of households supporting small children, forced to work long hours for a pittance. The sewing machine, introduced in the 1850s, did not so much alleviate the conditions of sewing and stitching as change their character; employers quickly learned they could increase production and lower wages with women poised over foot-pedaled machines, working at a feverish pace.

The character of the shoe, cigar, and garment industries was mixed, with some women employed in factories and others working in small shops managed by their husbands or fathers. These differing modes of production undermined women's ability to organize on common ground with one another and with men. Unburdened with children and earning their own wages in factories, young, single women were the most militant workers. But male workers often discredited the demands of "factory girls" and discouraged their organizing, arguing that male breadwinners with families to support should be the focus of labor organizing. Led by Clara Brown, young women shoe workers in Lynn, Massachusetts, went on strike in 1860 but failed to gain the support of women homeworkers and of men. The shoeworkers' Daughters of Saint Crispin, the first national labor organization for women, was formed in 1868.

Women in large textile mills were in the best position to organize collectively and to make forceful demands. The first known textile mill strike occurred in Pawtucket, Rhode Island, in 1824, when women weavers shut down their looms and took to the streets to protest low wages. The pace of turnouts increased in the 1830s and 1840s as cloth prices plummeted due to overproduction and nationwide depression. Employers turned to the speedup (increasing the pace of machinery), the stretch-out (assigning more machines to each worker), and longer hours to cut costs; they also reduced wages and increased boardinghouse rates. In a series of protests, only a few of which were successful, mill women in Lowell, Massachusetts, used the rhetoric of the American Revolution and of the antislavery movement to justify their militancy. These "daughters of free men" saw themselves as exploited "wage slaves" and demanded better treatment on the premise that their ancestors had fought for, and won, liberty and independence for all citizens. They formed the Lowell Female Reform Association in 1844 and made Sarah Bagley, a mill employee from New Hampshire, its first president. Despite their inability to vote or hold public office, association members petitioned the Massachusetts state legislature for an investigation of working conditions and for a ten-hour-day law. Spurred by male unions of all kinds, women workers continued to agitate for a ten-hour day throughout the century, although little progress was made in passing, let alone enforcing, maximum-hour laws in the states until after 1900.

After the Civil War the ability of all American workers to organize was steadily undermined by immigration, deskilling (reducing the level of skill needed), and the political power of employers. Male workers viewed women as competitors for their jobs. In fact they were, for employers took advantage of women's low wage rates to hire them for new routinized jobs, replacing male artisanal work. Excluded from heavier industry and the skilled trades, women poured into already crowded occupations in light factory work, domestic service, and teaching and were virtually powerless to prevent their own exploitation. A strike of five hundred women textile workers in Lawrence in 1882, for example, drew national attention to their misery, but it also resulted in firings, blacklistings, and city reprisals against self-supporting women. Often characterized as "radicals of the worst sort," female strikers raised the double specter of women escaping the patriarchal tutelage of fathers and husbands and of a threat from below to a civic order based on the holding of property.

Toward the end of the century, textile companies began moving factories to impoverished areas of the South, where energy costs were low, land was cheap, and the racial animosity of whites toward blacks could be used by employers to undermine labor unions. Whether in Lawrence, Massachusetts, or Atlanta, Georgia, whole families of recent immigrants and poor whites were forced to work for the most meager of livings. Since they were excluded from textile mills, industrial employment among African American women was largely limited to stripping tobacco and commercial laundering. In a remarkable strike in Atlanta in 1881, three thousand African American washerwomen and domestic servants protested the city's new vagrancy ordinance designed to prevent them from quitting their jobs and demanded higher wages.

New possibilities for the organization of women in the labor force arose in the 1880s when the Knights of Labor opened its doors to all workers (except the Chinese). By 1886 women constituted 10 percent of the Knights' membership. Leonora Barry, an Irish hosiery worker, was appointed the first director of the Women's Work department. Over the next decade, the demise of the Knights and the ascendency of the more conservative American Federation of Labor exacerbated competition between the genders and focused labor's attention on the skilled trades that excluded women. But the modes of protest used by women workers before 1900—spontaneous walkouts, agitation for maximum-hour and minimum-wage laws, and the creation of separate women's labor organizations—would prove to be more successful and to lead to real gains in women's labor organizing in the next century.

See also **Labor Force; Women,** *subentry on* **Women's Labor; Work,** *subentries on* **The Workshop, Factory Labor.**

Bibliography

Cameron, Ardis. *Radicals of the Worst Sort: Laboring Women in Lawrence, Massachusetts, 1860–1912.* Urbana: University of Illinois Press, 1993.

Dublin, Thomas. *Women at Work: The Transformation of Work and Community in Lowell, Massachusetts, 1826–1860.* New York: Columbia University Press, 1979.

Hunter, Tera W. *To 'Joy My Freedom: Southern Black Women's Lives and Labors after the Civil War.* Cambridge, Mass.: Harvard University Press, 1997.

Kessler-Harris, Alice. *Out to Work: A History of Wage-Earning Women in the United States.* New York: Oxford University Press, 1982.

Murphy, Teresa. *Ten Hours Labor: Religion, Reform, and Gender in Early New England.* Ithaca, N.Y.: Cornell University Press, 1992.

Stansell, Christine. *City of Women: Sex and Class in New York, 1789–1860.* Urbana: University of Illinois Press, 1983.

SHARON HARTMAN STROM

PEOPLE OF COLOR

As the nineteenth century dawned most blacks in the United States were slaves, but about sixty thousand were free. Most black workers were unskilled, but some had metalworking and woodworking skills. Free skilled blacks could earn a living and even dominated certain trades, partly because immigration declined between 1776 and 1815. Women usually worked as seamstresses or servants. The first unions of skilled workers emerged in the 1790s. Throughout the nineteenth century white labor unions excluded blacks, though some attempts at interracial unity were successful.

After the Napoleonic Wars ended in 1815, immigration to the United States increased. Europeans joined the Americans moving into industrial centers and pushed blacks out of the skilled labor force. In the 1840s and 1850s whites, especially the Irish fleeing the 1846 famine, also moved into the unskilled jobs previously held by blacks in northern cities. Job competition was complicated when companies hired blacks to replace strikers, and whites often physically attacked black strikebreakers.

By 1860 nearly 500,000 free blacks lived in the United States, primarily in the Upper South, where

The Caulkers of Baltimore

In Baltimore's shipbuilding industry one of the few occupations dominated by blacks during the nineteenth century was that of caulker, a low-prestige but essential job. When German and Irish immigrants began flocking to Baltimore, an important commercial center, blacks formed the Association of Colored Caulkers in 1858 and for a time defended their jobs. In October 1865, however, whites went on strike, successfully demanding the firing of blacks. In response Isaac Myers, the first important black labor leader in the United States, formed the Colored Caulkers' Trade Union Society of Baltimore, which sponsored a cooperative company to buy a shipyard and railway. The caulkers issued stock and raised ten thousand dollars from blacks in Baltimore and other cities. Frederick Douglass was one of the first investors. The company was in operation by February 1866, and within six months it employed three hundred black workers. Winning government contracts, the company paid off its debt within five years. Subsequently the two Baltimore caulkers' unions, one black and one white, cooperated with each other.

they found work more easily than in the North. Pre–Civil War black organizations, like the New York African Society for Mutual Relief founded in 1808, provided protection, aid, and training for their members.

After Abraham Lincoln issued the Emancipation Proclamation in January 1863, whites who feared competition and increased use of black strikebreakers and who opposed conscription into the army rioted, leaving four hundred people dead. In a wave of unionization between 1863 and 1865, the number of locals rose to three hundred, and workers formed twenty-one national trade unions. The country faced widespread unemployment, renewed immigration, and depression between 1865 and 1867. In 1866 reformers organized the National Labor Union (NLU), a confederation of local and state unions. The NLU ignored blacks, and, in response, black workers began to organize and strike. In December 1869 the black labor leader Isaac Myers and others founded the Colored National Labor Union (CNLU). Conceived as a confederation, the CNLU sought the right to work, apprenticeships, education, and fair pay for workers. Welcoming all races and both sexes, it was the only organization that accepted Chinese workers into its membership.

At the 1870 NLU congress whites insisted that blacks join them in a Labor Reform Party. Blacks, however, were loyal to the Republican Party as the party of emancipation, wanted to participate in the marketplace more than to change it, and were unwilling to join an organization formed by labor unions that excluded them. Following that conflict, the NLU, seen as a political rather than a labor association, declined. The CNLU met for the last time in 1871, the victim of overwhelming difficulties in organizing black workers.

A new organization emerged at that time, however. The Knights of Labor welcomed all male workers regardless of race, politics, or religion. Its active enlistment of unskilled labor and its emphasis on labor solidarity, unity, land reform, education, and workers' cooperatives appealed strongly to blacks. Women were admitted after 1881. At its peak in 1886, the Knights of Labor had at least sixty thousand black members of a total membership of between 700,000 and one million. In 1886 employers launched a counteroffensive. Activists in the movement for an eight-hour workday were convicted on charges of exploding a bomb in Chicago's Haymarket Square, and management used lockouts, blacklists, and further arrests against unions. The Knights of Labor declined rapidly, and after 1895 it was no longer a viable organization.

Workers in a handful of crafts unions founded the American Federation of Labor (AFL) in the early 1880s. Samuel Gompers, the AFL's first leader, was an immigrant cigar maker who advocated improved wages, hours, and conditions through peaceful collective bargaining. During the 1880s and early 1890s, Gompers emphasized that the AFL must organize blacks at all costs. In extreme cases, he said, blacks should be organized temporarily into separate locals with the same rights and privileges. By the end of the century the AFL had almost 600,000 members.

In 1892 twenty-five thousand black and white workers shut down New Orleans. Achieving a ten-hour workday, the New Orleans general strike proved that labor unity could work. But a financial panic in 1893 followed by a depression that lasted until 1898 brought reverses. Most AFL unions continued to refuse to integrate blacks and tried to drive them off jobs. Officially the AFL still advocated organizing all workers, but a new qualification requiring a skill excluded most blacks. Unions refusing blacks were no longer denied membership in the national organization. By the end of the century blacks participated in the AFL almost exclusively in segregated locals

Isaac Myers

Isaac Myers was born free to poor parents in Baltimore in 1835. Although Maryland, a slave state, offered black children no public education, Myers received a private education and was apprenticed to a black caulker at age sixteen. By age twenty-five he was a skilled caulker and supervisor. When whites succeeded in driving many black caulkers from their jobs in 1865, he suggested that the black caulkers of Baltimore form a cooperative company. The venture was a success, and Myers became president of the Colored Caulkers' Trade Union Society of Baltimore. Continuing his labor reform work, Myers founded a statewide black labor organization in Maryland that became the center of a national black labor organization. He attended National Labor Union congresses as a black delegate and became the first president of the Colored National Labor Union in 1869.

organizations provided immigrants with a continuing network of support and mutual aid. Second, the Chinese were met with great hostility. Much of the labor movement, including Samuel Gompers himself, was strongly anti-Chinese and sought to bar them from many occupational branches. Anti-Chinese agitation grew during the mid-1870s, when the Chinese were driven out of many smaller towns, and culminated in the Chinese Exclusion Act of 1882.

See also **African Americans,** *subentry on* **Free Blacks before the Civil War; Emancipation; Labor Force; Work.**

Bibliography

Foner, Philip S. *Organized Labor and the Black Worker, 1619–1973.* New York: Praeger, 1974.
Cahn, William. *A Pictorial History of American Labor.* New York: Crown Publishers, 1972.

SUSAN M. STEINER

LAND POLICY.   See Federal Land Policy.

that were not permitted to send delegates to AFL central labor bodies.

Hispanic peoples in the U.S. during the nineteenth century were usually ranchers or farmers. One instance of union activity can be found, however. A Spanish cigarmaker, Vincente Martinez Ybor, from Havana, Cuba, opened a branch factory on Key West, Florida, in order to evade import duties. Other Cuban cigar producers followed his lead and Cuban settlement spread from Key West north to Tampa. The Cuban workers were better educated and more self-confident than other Hispanics in the United States at the time. They immediately formed Los Caballeros del Trabajo, a branch of the Knights of Labor. A new group formed in 1886 took a more militant name: La Resistencia. By 1900, the Cuban unions felt strong enough to initiate their first strike. It failed due to the overwhelming power of the owners.

Chinese immigration to the United States began slowly around 1820 and increased sharply after the discovery of gold in the late 1840s. Chinese men mined for gold and other minerals throughout the West, worked as fishermen, cooks, and servants, and opened restaurants and laundries. About fifteen thousand Chinese also built part of the first railroad track to cross the country.

Generally, Chinese workers were not organized in unions for two reasons. First, early Chinese immigrants had replicated the system of district and clan associations and tongs they knew from home. These

LANGUAGE   Language was at the center of much discussion and dissent in nineteenth-century America. Arguments about usage reflected deeper conflicts about what it meant to be a citizen of a republic and how democracy related to traditional ideas of gentility. The newly evolving democracy affected the number and types of voices that contributed to public life. For example, for the first time, women spoke in public. Popular participation in politics affected political rhetoric, making it less refined and more raucous. Politicians like Andrew Jackson, who come from the frontier, brought tall-tale language and an anti-English sentiment with them, transforming American political language.

While some scholars contend that dialects of American English can be traced regionally to dialects of British immigrants, other scholars claim that dialects were tied more to economic activity. In any case, the American language, in much the same way the country was establishing itself as a separate entity, was moving away from the British roots that had held so firmly in the eighteenth century. Reports of English visitors to the United States characterized American English words as "barbarisms" and "vulgar." The evolution of a distinct national identity for Americans and the movement westward played strong roles in widening the gap between British and American English. According to writer H. L. Mencken in *The American Language* (1919), the late-eighteenth-century speech of a Philadelphian or Bostonian would have been easily understood by an Englishman, but by the early nineteenth century, speakers from Ohio or points west would not have been understood. At a practical level, the Americans had to find words for the new natural phenomena they were experiencing in America.

According to historian Richard Bailey, linguistic intolerance characterized those who considered themselves arbiters of American linguistic practices (Bailey, p. 82). It was not until the latter half of the century that American English dialects began to be accepted. Following the first edition of John Russell Bartlett's *A Glossary of Words and Phrases Usually Regarded as Peculiar to the United States* (1848) to its fourth edition in 1877, we see this change in attitude exemplified. From the disparagement of Americanisms as vulgar in the first edition, to the inclusion and praise of slang in the fourth edition, Bartlett's text reflected the changing attitude of lexicographers of the nineteenth century toward the developing language.

Noah Webster, prolific writer of, and nationalistic defender of, the American language produced the first dictionary of American English, the *American Dictionary of the English Language,* in 1828. This work was not only well regarded in the United States but was considered the best dictionary of English at the time. In it, Webster defended the language of the common people and criticized eighteenth-century grammarians for trying to force the rules of Latin on an English whose Saxon purity was best exhibited in the speech of Shakespeare and Queen Elizabeth I. Much of the English that was spoken in the United States was believed to have come from the south of England and survived less changed in the United States than in England at the time.

While Webster and like-minded authorities expressed confidence in the language of the Americans, others, such as John Pickering, were more interested in policing American English. His *Vocabulary or Collection of Words and Phrases Which Have Been Supposed to be Peculiar to the United States of America* (1816) presented words cited in critical English reviews of American books as a way of warning against their use and supporting the English reviewers' criticism of Americanisms. This conservative attitude had its proponents through the end of the century.

The nineteenth century heralded a time of unprecedented literacy due in part to innovations in education, business, industry, and technology. As nineteenth-century citizens consumed more and more commercial products, merchants learned to value advertising as a means of increasing trade (Bailey, p. 26). More efficient technology allowed for mass production of books and newspapers that made the written word more accessible to the common people. While there were concerns on the part of the educated and powerful that popular literacy could prove both expensive and dangerous, the new principles of democracy demanded a literate public. Common schooling resulted, and with it the need for textbooks of English. The increase in economic activity also produced an increase in the vocabulary of the people of the United States.

Westward movement had a significant impact on American English. While the New England dialect was confined to regions east of the Hudson River, people moving west from all areas of the eastern United States blended several dialects into what became a homogeneous frontier speech, affected most extensively by the Scots-Irish. Further movement west, linked to such events as the gold rush and the building of the railway system, continued to infuse the language with new vocabulary.

Other languages contributed to the change and development of American English. European languages that enriched American English included French, Spanish, Dutch, and German. French influenced the northern Great Lakes region down the Mississippi River and into Louisiana, where a Creole dialect had developed from the French influence on the area that became the Louisiana Purchase. Spanish influenced the language of the Southwest and the consequent cattle-ranching culture based there. While the United States experienced immigration from all parts of the world during the nineteenth century, the Irish and the Germans dominated. Although Germans had lived in the East since colonization, their influence on English was minimal until millions of Germans, many well educated, began arriving in America at mid-century, making German words second only to Spanish in number in the American language. The century also saw linguistic adaptions from existing Native American languages, the development of Black English, and contributions from Chinese through the medium of Pidgin English.

Separation from British English, widespread education and literacy, the influence of native and immigrant languages, and the leveling of the language, all grounded in the profound social, political, cultural, and technological changes of the time, had by 1900 firmly established American English as an autonomous language.

See also **Book Publishing: Dime Novels and Story Papers; Immigration and Immigrants; Libraries; Literacy and Reading Habits; Magazines; Newspapers and the Press.**

Bibliography

Bailey, Richard W. *Nineteenth-Century English*. Ann Arbor: The University of Michigan Press, 1996.

Cmiel, Kenneth. *Democratic Eloquence: The Fight over Popular Speech in Nineteenth-Century America*. Berkeley: University of California Press, 1990.

Dillard, J. L. *Black English*. New York: Random House, 1972.

———. *A History of American English*. London and New York: Longman, 1992.

Laird, Charlton. *Language in America*. New York and Cleveland, Ohio: World Publishing Company, 1970.

Mencken, H. L. *The American Language*. New York: Knopf, 1936.

Simpson, David. *The Politics of American English, 1776–1850*. New York and Oxford: Oxford University Press, 1986.

Wolfram, Walt. *Dialects and American English*. Englewood Cliffs, N.J.: Prentice Hall, 1991.

REBECCA L. DAMRON

LATTER-DAY SAINTS.　See Mormonism.

LAW

[This entry includes an overview and four subentries on **Federal Law**, **State Law**, **Common Law**, and **Women and the Law**.]

OVERVIEW

Law played a significant role in the development of the American economy and society in the nineteenth century. At the same time, vast social and economic changes led to fundamental changes in the character of the legal process. And legal ways of thinking became a significant factor in the development of American ideology and the sense Americans had of themselves.

Many of the founding fathers, including John Adams, Thomas Jefferson, Alexander Hamilton, and John Jay, were attorneys. James Madison was trained in the law but never practiced. These men brought a strong sense that law was a tool for social change as well as for the preservation of liberty and property. Jefferson's first act as president, in March 1801, was to pardon those convicted under the Sedition Act of 1798, a signal that law was a force of politics and had to be treated as such.

Early in the century Americans sought to create their own legal regime. In 1803 St. George Tucker, a Virginia judge and law professor, published an American edition of *Blackstone's Commentaries*, which was designed to reconceptualize English law for a democratic republic. Part of this process was a modified rejection of common law. In *United States v. Hudson and Goodwin* (1812), the U.S. Supreme Court held that there was no federal common law of crimes, and that any prosecutions by the national government had to be based on statutes. Other treatise writers and law reformers, especially James Kent, Joseph Story, Joseph Angell, and Thomas R. R. Cobb in the first part of the century, and David Dudley Field and Thomas M. Cooley later, helped to shape how lawyers and judges thought about the law while defining what American law was. Indicative of the hope that law held for some was the first treatise on civil rights, *Justice and Jurisprudence* (1889), published by the Brotherhood of Liberty. Sadly, this treatise failed to affect the pervasive racism of the time and the general trend toward segregation at the end of the century.

Law played a vital role in the emerging economy of antebellum America. In *Fletcher v. Peck* (1810) and *Trustees of Dartmouth College v. Woodward* (1819), the U.S. Supreme Court insisted that the states uphold their contractual obligations. Certainty in business transactions became the hallmark of American law. At the same time, as the legal historian J. Willard Hurst has noted, law allowed for the "release of creative energies" by providing mechanisms for development and change. In the West, water and property law evolved to allow for development where water was scarce and landownership was uncertain. In New England and the Middle Atlantic states, innovations in business law allowed for the development of factories and railroads that set the stage for a vast economic revolution in the nation. Innovations in tort law, including the law of industrial accidents, worked to the benefit of emerging industries and the detriment of injured workers and bystanders. The fellow servant rule, first developed in England but borrowed and forcefully articulated in the United States by Chief Justice Lemuel Shaw of the Massachusetts Supreme Judicial Court in *Farwell v. Boston & Worcester Railroad* (1842), altered the common law to place the burden of industrial accidents on the workers, rather than on the owners of the new and more dangerous industries. In the South, innovations in slave law promoted the property interests of the masters both in industrial settings and when slaves were harmed by third parties. Thus, the South applied the fellow servant rule to injured free workers, but most southern states rejected it for slaves because that would have placed the cost of accidents on slave owners.

Whereas some scholars argue that the courts generally favored industries and capitalism, others have noted the tendency of judges to try to bring a measure of humanity to the law, and of the courts to use the law to protect the public interest at the expense of both individuals and corporate players in the economy.

Some antebellum lawyers were trained in proprietary law schools, like Litchfield in Connecticut and the Lumpkin Law School in Georgia, and some studied at the few collegiate law schools, like Harvard. But most lawyers read the law with a member of the bar. In this way the law provided professional opportunities for many young Americans of limited financial means. Abraham Lincoln, the nation's greatest nineteenth-century leader, used the law as a stepping-stone from near poverty to comfortable middle-class status and then enormous political success. Before the Civil War, men who had once practiced law, and often continued to do so, dominated politics. Among them were Henry Clay, John C. Calhoun, Daniel Webster, Stephen A. Douglas, William H. Seward, and Salmon P. Chase, and Presidents Jefferson, Monroe, John Quincy Adams, Andrew Jackson, Martin Van Buren, John Tyler, James Polk, Millard Fillmore, Franklin Pierce, James Buchanan, and Abraham Lincoln. After 1865 fewer lawyers reached the White House, and significant political leaders came increasingly from other fields.

Access to the law also changed. More often the most successful lawyers were college- and law school–trained, a change instituted late in the century by the American Bar Association and local bars to raise barriers that would prevent the poor and new immigrants from entering practice.

Large enterprises in post–Civil War America used law and lawyers to secure markets and to protect their economic interests from state regulation. By the end of the nineteenth century the Supreme Court had become the apparent ally of big business, striking down regulatory schemes proposed by the states and Congress, as well as the income tax, which would have placed the cost of government more fairly on the emerging millionaire class.

Before the Civil War, opponents of slavery tried to use the legal system to dismantle the institution in the North and to attack it in the South. Abolitionists used cases like *United States v. The Amistad* (1839) to rally northern support for their cause. Attorneys such as Salmon P. Chase and William H. Seward combined successful political and legal careers with legal assaults on slavery. In the 1840s and 1850s law became a central aspect of the sectional conflict, and northerners and southerners squared off over the Fugitive Slave Law, the necessity of a slave code in the territories, and the Supreme Court's proslavery jurisprudence in *Prigg v. Pennsylvania* (1842), *Dred Scott v. Sandford* (1857), and *Ableman v. Booth* (1859).

Legal and constitutional developments during and after the Civil War ended slavery, and brought the promise of racial equality with the Fourteenth and Fifteenth Amendments and the Civil Rights Acts of 1866 and 1875. But an increasingly conservative Supreme Court undermined these developments. By the end of the century, the Court held that law could not counter social prejudice; instead, it should in effect condone it. The Court upheld segregation in *Plessy v. Ferguson* (1896) and black disfranchisement in *Williams v. Mississippi* (1898). Nor did the postwar federal courts find a place for women at the bar (*Bradwell v. Illinois,* 1873) or in the voting booth. Law was increasingly the tool of the white, the wealthy, and the empowered, rather than a tool for reform. Although "equal justice under law" remained a goal, reformers could expect little help or sympathy from the federal courts or most state courts. The bar itself was increasingly closed to those who might be most inclined to seek social change.

See also **Constitutional Amendments,** *subentry on* **Thirteenth, Fourteenth, and Fifteenth Amendments; Constitutional Law; Federal-State Relations; Fugitive Slave Laws; Gender,** *subentry on* **Gender and the Law; Immigration and Immigrants,** *subentry on* **Immigration Policy and Law; Slavery,** *subentry on* **Law of Slavery.**

Bibliography

Horwitz, Morton J. *The Transformation of American Law, 1780–1860.* Cambridge, Mass.: Harvard University Press, 1977.

Hurst, J. Willard. *Law and the Conditions of Freedom in the Nineteenth-Century United States.* Madison: University of Wisconsin Press, 1956.

Karsten, Peter. *Heart versus Hand: Judge-Made Law in the Nineteenth Century.* Chapel Hill: University of North Carolina Press, 1997.

Novak, William J. *The People's Welfare: Law and Regulation in Nineteenth-Century America.* Chapel Hill: University of North Carolina Press, 1996.

Urofsky, Melvin I., and Paul Finkelman. *A March of Liberty: A Constitutional History of the United States.* 2d ed. New York: Oxford University Press, 2001.

PAUL FINKELMAN

FEDERAL LAW

Federal law in the nineteenth century was the product of acts of Congress, decisions of the federal courts, rulings of federal administrative agencies, and treaty practices with American Indian tribes. The jurisdiction of the federal courts extended to all federal questions and to disputes between citizens of different states and between states. During the Civil War and Reconstruction, Congress expanded the jurisdiction of the federal courts in a series of twelve removal statutes, starting with the Habeas Corpus Act of 1863 and culminating in the Jurisdiction and Removal Act of 1875. Under these statutes, cases involving federal officials could be removed from state courts and heard in federal courts. The U.S. Constitution and the political process limited the reach of congressional legislation. The future of slavery and the South's political control of the Senate were at stake in land law, the admissions of states, and tax law. Throughout the century, the reach of Congress was limited by the slavery controversy, concepts of federalism and comity, and a political philosophy of limited federal intervention in American life.

The Antebellum Period

The primary business for the Congress in the antebellum period was the disposal of the public domain and providing needful revenues for the federal government. In 1800 Congress altered the provisions of the Land Ordinance of 1785 to lower the minimum purchase from 640 to 320 acres and provide for credit sales to reduce speculator influence in western lands. As the western lands filled with settlers, Congress created territorial governments by statute and authorized constitutional conventions through enabling acts, which would move territories to statehood. Land distribution policy and statehood had important political ramifications due to the South's interest in maintaining a veto in the Senate over any antislavery legislation passed by the House. Political fights over these issues flared in 1820 and continued until the Civil War, when the Republican Party controlled Congress. The Republicans produced the Homestead Act of 1862 to create a free land frontier in the West; expanded the reach of the federal tax system; and passed the Thirteenth, Fourteenth, and Fifteenth amendments, as well as the Civil Rights acts of 1866 and 1875, to lift the vestiges of slavery. However, the Supreme Court effectively nullified these amendments and laws in a series of decisions between 1873 and 1898. The Republican Congresses also created a social welfare and disability system for Civil War veterans and their dependents.

Congress maintained a policy of distributing or selling public land to promote the release of energy inherent in the uses of private property and using tariff legislation to fund federal spending and to protect favored industries. Congress used land to promote its policies in the nineteenth century simply because federal revenues were minimal. Tariff dollars financed government until the Civil War. Protectionism in the 1820s and early 1830s gave way to lower tariffs in 1833, and low custom duties in the Walker Tariff of 1846 were enough to cover 60 percent of the cost of the Mexican War. The Civil War necessitated the federal taxation of virtually anything of value. Congress created the Office of the Commissioner of Internal Revenue, the first income tax, and a welfare state that gobbled up about 45 percent of all federal receipts by the late 1890s. The Republican welfare state forced Congress to search for more money, which led to a progressive income tax the Wilson-Gorman Tariff Act, in 1894. In 1895 the U.S. Supreme Court declared the tax unconstitutional in *Pollock v. Farmers' Loan and Trust Co.*

The Supreme Court frequently faced issues of taxation and liberty during the century. The preference for the dynamic use of property was clearly part of Court doctrine, whether in protecting contracts or in finding public policy reasons for voiding contracts that inhibited creative destruction of property to further the capitalistic economy. The release of energy inherent in private property use was a favored constitutional position. When faced with the regulatory state after the Civil War, the Court found some regulation permissible under the police power, such as the regulation of businesses in which the public has an interest. The Court protected the marketplace by limiting state and municipal regulatory and tax schemes that negatively impacted interstate commerce. One favorite target of states and Jacksonian politicians was the federal banking system, which did not become a permanent part of our national economy until the Civil War. By the end of the century, the Court had rediscovered substantive due process of law and liberty of contract doctrines that enabled justices to strike down legislation that they personally disliked. Pollock, struck down by Justice Stephen J. Field, was one such case.

Despite the public outcry against the decision, the Court was safe in its favored position of judicial supremacy hard won in the early nineteenth century. Between 1801 and 1835 Chief Justice John Marshall had forged this position from assertions of jurisdiction and federal supremacy based on constitutional interpretation that galled politicians yet went institutionally unchallenged. The most divisive issue, slavery in the antebellum period, weakened America as a union because the constitutional questions of federalism and comity were at stake. Ultimately, the Court would decide *Dred Scott v. Sandford* (1857), upholding the slave states' position and bringing a firestorm of criticism down on a divided Court. Yet with the Union's victory in the Civil War, the Court survived with the decision reviled and the judicial supremacy of the Court intact. Even more certainly, Congress gave more authority to the federal courts with the Habeas Corpus Act of 1863, allowing removal from state courts to the federal courts of civil and criminal cases involving the acts of federal officials. The Civil Rights Act of 1866, the Internal Revenue Act of 1866, and the Voting Rights Enforcement Act of 1871 further put such cases in the federal courts. The Jurisdiction and Removal Act of 1875 gave sweeping removal options to litigants and resulted in the wholesale removal of business cases from the state to the federal courts. The creation of a federal commercial law under *Swift v. Tyson* (1842), coupled with removal, made the federal courts increasingly the arbiters of a national marketplace and its needful rules.

Post–Civil War Concerns

Congress had the power to regulate interstate commerce but seldom did so until it passed the Interstate Commerce Act of 1887 to regulate railroads. The states had led in the field of regulation, but the Supreme Court in *Wabash, St. Louis and Pacific Railway Co. v. Illinois* (1886) by concluding that only Congress could regulate interstate transportation charges forced Congress's hand. Subsequently, the Court limited the reach of the administrative agency. Congress also acted to limit the reach of monopoly capitalism in the Sherman Antitrust Act of 1890. Here Congress reacted to public perceptions of increased predatory business practices, vast consolidations, and cartelization. Congress also wanted to promote economic efficiency just as the rise of administrative regulatory agencies sought certainty in the marketplace amid destructive monopoly practices that diminished rational market and profit expectations.

While the Congress and the Court were setting policy for the national marketplace and the federal treasury, federal officials were negotiating treaties with American Indian tribes. The treaty practice lasted until 3 March 1871 and created a body of federal law flowing from a political anomaly. The tribes were sovereign, but only to an extent. The American Indian treaties were not like treaties with England or France. Federal law and policy worked to dispossess Indians from their ancestral lands, remove them to reservations, make them into agricultural entrepreneurs, redistribute their lands, and marginalize them in American society. The Congress created a scheme for the filing of Indian depredation claims processed by the U.S. Court of Claims after its creation in 1855. The depredation claims system lasted until 1890. As the century ended, the sovereignty of the tribes was in retreat, the Ghost Dance (a religious outburst of visionary experience recalling Indian holy men that liberated Indians from misery, death, and disease) seemed the only salvation, and federal policy favored

cultural extinction. Among African Americans, who were now citizens of the United States, males could vote, although by the 1890s Congress and the courts no longer evidenced any desire to protect that right, nor any other civil or political rights of blacks in the face of increasing southern white determination to marginalize and segregate blacks. American Indians were wards of the government under *United States v. Kagama* (1886) and could not vote because the Court had declared them not to be citizens. Neither Congress nor the Court favored Indians' claims to sovereignty.

See also **American Indians,** *subentry on* **U.S. Government Policies; Civil Rights; Congress; Courts, State and Federal; Federal-State Relations; Interstate Commerce.**

Bibliography

Brownlee, W. Elliott. *Federal Taxation in America*. New York: Cambridge University Press, 1996.

Finkelman, Paul. *An Imperfect Union: Slavery, Federalism, and Comity*. Chapel Hill: University of North Carolina Press, 1981.

Hurst, James Willard. *Law and the Conditions of Freedom in the Nineteenth-Century United States*. Madison: University of Wisconsin Press, 1956.

Prucha, Francis Paul. *American Indian Treaties: A History of a Political Anomaly*. Berkeley: University of California Press, 1994.

Purcell, Edward A., Jr. *Litigation and Inequality: Federal Diversity Jurisdiction in Industrial America, 1870–1958*. New York: Oxford University Press, 1992.

GORDON MORRIS BAKKEN

STATE LAW

State legislatures and appellate courts played a leading role in formulating public policy during the nineteenth century. During the antebellum period the emergence of a market economy that valued competition, entrepreneurial risk taking, and the constructive use of property rather than its mere possession challenged traditional legal values, which had favored landholding, social stability, and the encouragement of moral behavior. State legislatures responded by passing laws that encouraged capital investment. For example, business incorporation laws facilitated large-scale enterprises by allowing investors to pool their resources and by limiting their financial liability should the venture fail.

At the same time judges modified common law rules to facilitate market behavior. This utilitarian approach to judging, dubbed "instrumentalism" by historians, promoted commercial relations by encouraging individuals to enter into profitable business arrangements unfettered by governmental supervision. The abandonment of the "sound price" doctrine, which had allowed courts to adjust the terms of a contract if it was deemed unfair, and the imposition of caveat emptor ("let the buyer beware") in the law of sales allowed parties to strike economically advantageous bargains without worrying that a court would negate them.

Although courts and legislatures facilitated the privatization of the marketplace, they did not endorse laissez-faire economic theory. Through the exercise of their "police powers" to protect the health, safety, morals, and general welfare of their citizens, states enacted regulations on everything from banking practices to the packaging of goods. More important, however, they invoked their police powers to favor private enterprises that were deemed to serve a valuable public purpose. Through the exercise of eminent domain, for instance, states transferred land to corporations that promised to build needed improvements, such as railroads and turnpikes. Judges modified common law rules regarding water rights to allow textile mill owners to divert water from preexisting users. These actions constituted a virtual subsidy to entrepreneurs who engaged in activity that benefited the public.

Perhaps the most striking example of the use of legal instrumentalism to provide indirect subsidies involved the law of torts (personal injuries). The technological innovations that accompanied economic development, such as steam boilers, could be quite dangerous, and if entrepreneurs had been required to compensate victims for their injuries they might have been deterred from investing in useful technologies. Judges responded by replacing absolute liability for injuries with a fault standard that held liable only businesses that acted negligently. Additional doctrines—contributory negligence, the fellow-servant rule, and assumption of risk—immunized employers from liability for injuries suffered by their workers. These innovations were especially helpful to the burgeoning railroad industry, which faced financial weakness if it had to compensate for the numerous injuries suffered by its employees.

After the Civil War courts and legislatures began to diverge in their positions regarding law and the economy. Responding to constituents' concerns about the deleterious effects of industrialization, legislators shifted from promotion to regulation of business, passing laws designed to protect workers and consumers. Appellate judges, on the other hand, were more ambivalent about business regulation and were not shy about subjecting legislation to vigorous judicial review. Most regulations passed muster, as long as they were reasonably related to the state's police powers. If the purpose of the legislation appeared to be redistributive—that is, if it attempted to reallocate the costs of industrialization or to aid one group at the expense of another—courts would not hesitate to strike it down. These rulings were justified by such doctrines as "substantive due process" and "liberty of contract" that typically operated in favor of corporate interests. But courts hostile to redistributive legislation also struck down subsidies to private businesses and sales regulations that inflated prices for consumers.

Although economic development dominated lawmakers' attentions, other bodies of substantive law reflected the societal changes wrought by market capitalism. Criminal law, for instance, became less concerned with policing morality and more devoted to protecting property. Prosecutions for blasphemy and fornication gave way to actions against embezzlement and forgery. Family law flourished as the new economy, which separated the workplace from the home and subjected families to the vagaries of the market, altered the roles of husbands, wives, and children. As courts and legislatures increasingly protected children from abuse and neglect and granted married women rights to separate property and access to divorce, the conduct of the household, like the economy, became subject to governmental supervision.

Because legal historians have focused their attention heavily on the northeastern states, the question of whether or not their findings can be generalized to other regions of the United States has been an important one. Twentieth-century scholarship suggested that, while significant variations existed, the main trends of judicial instrumentalism and governmental supervision of economic and social institutions transcended sectional boundaries. Because legislatures were directly influenced by local politics, statutory law exhibited more variation than judge-made law. Judges, after all, read the same case reports and treatises and shared a common understanding about their importance to the formulation of public policy, fostering a national professional consciousness.

The glaring exception to this national coherence involved the body of law governing slavery in the South. Because slavery functioned as a system of labor and social control and because it was premised on both white domination and paternalism, southern states created complex rules that resembled nothing seen in other parts of the nation. Legislatures passed slave codes that asserted the absolute authority of masters over slaves and prescribed harsh penalties for slaves who rebelled or committed crimes. Judges grappled with the inherent contradictions of property in humans. On the one hand, their belief in white supremacy left victimized slaves without any formal protection. On the other hand, their paternalistic impulses led them to extend due process guarantees to slaves accused of crimes. In addition the central role of slavery in the southern economy spawned a commercial law of slavery, governing such issues as warranties for slave sales and liability for accidents caused by slaves.

The Reconstruction amendments to the U.S. Constitution abolished slavery and granted African Americans civil and political rights, but in reality southern law perpetuated racial subordination. After 1876 southern states mandated racial segregation in all public places and passed miscegenation laws to discourage interactions in private. Some northern states followed suit as calls for economic reform crowded pleas for racial justice from legislative agendas, and new "scientific" theories positing the natural superiority of whites convinced many white Americans of the futility of pursuing racial equality. Other northern states, especially in New England and the Mid-Atlantic region, passed civil rights laws that banned most private discrimination. Nevertheless, by the end of the century the laws governing race relations, like those involving business, crime, and families, exhibited more similarities than differences among the states.

See also **Civil Rights; Civil War,** *subentry on* **Consequences of the Civil War; Constitutional Amendments,** *subentry on* **Thirteenth, Fourteenth, and Fifteenth Amendments; Courts, State and Federal; Divorce and Desertion; Economic Regulation; Judicial Review; Miscegenation; Race Laws; Regulation of Business; Slavery,** *subentry on* **Law of Slavery.**

Bibliography

Hall, Kermit L. *The Magic Mirror: Law in American History.* New York: Oxford University Press, 1989.
Horwitz, Morton J. *The Transformation of American Law, 1780–1860.* Cambridge, Mass.: Harvard University Press, 1977.
Huebner, Timothy S. *The Southern Judicial Tradition: State Judges and Sectional Distinctiveness, 1790–1890.* Athens, Ga.: University of Georgia Press, 1999.
Karsten, Peter. *Heart versus Head: Judge-made Law in Nineteenth-Century America.* Chapel Hill: University of North Carolina Press, 1997.

ERIC W. RISE

COMMON LAW

Common, or judge-made, law is the set of rules, principles, and procedures in U.S. courts that are descended from those created over the centuries by the English appellate courts of Common Pleas, King's Bench, and Exchequer. It should not be confused with the laws created by legislatures (which are often designed to alter one or more common-law rules), nor with interpretations of constitutions by state and federal courts.

During the American Revolution the colonial legislatures declared themselves free of the English crown and Parliament but simultaneously adopted most English statutes in existence at the time of settlement, thus formalizing their reception of the English common law. Over the next century state courts, with varying degrees of frequency, referred to both pre- and postreception reports of English decisions, citing them either as binding precedent or as guidance for their principled reasoning and great authority.

But while many English doctrines and rules persisted throughout the nineteenth century, U.S. courts rejected others, or replaced them with rules and doctrines of American origin. Historians differ as to which rules were changed and why. Some, especially Lawrence Friedman and Morton Horwitz, argue that the changes were essentially ones that were of advantage to businesses and entrepreneurs. Others, especially Peter Karsten, argue that there were far fewer changes of this sort than has been claimed and that most of the innovations served the interests of plaintiffs suing corporations.

Property Law

Most of the changes in the common law of property in nineteenth-century America were imposed by legislatures, not courts. These include the granting of eminent domain powers to quasi-public corporations to take (but compensate for) the property of others in order to construct roads, canals, or railways; the requirement that all transfers of or liens against real estate be recorded in a public repository; the abolition of slavery; the abolition of primogeniture—the rule passing all real estate to the eldest son in the event that the father died without a will; and the abolition of entail—the rule permitting a testator to tie up a family's property for more than one generation by naming those to receive the "entailed" estates in each generation. (Throughout most of the century in most states, wives possessed only limited powers with regard to the disposing of property by will.)

When courts interpreted these statutory changes, they tended to read them quite strictly. For example, they rejected arguments advanced by railroad company attorneys that compensation paid to plaintiff property owners in takings cases be offset by the remaining property's increase in value as a consequence of the arrival of the railroad.

Some changes in the common law of property, however, were judge-made. Courts abolished the English ancient lights doctrine, which held that if a property owner had enjoyed the light coming over a neighbor's property through his windows for a certain number of decades, the neighbor was precluded from building anything on his property that blocked that light. Some state courts in the northeastern and north-central regions adopted a prudent investor rule, permitting trustees to invest in private corporations rather than to limit their investments to land and government securities.

Some state courts balanced the equities of plaintiff and defendant in cases alleging that the smoke, smell, or noise from the defendant's business operations had resulted in damage to the plaintiff's property. This was not the case in English common law. But even where this balancing of the relative values of the polluter and the plaintiff property owner was sanctioned, different courts loaded the equation to favor either the property owners (in New York and New Jersey, for example) or polluters (in Pennsylvania).

Most of the law of slavery was created by colonial and state legislatures, but for many years a number of issues, unaddressed by statutes, had to be determined by the rules of the common law and equity, sometimes borrowing a principle or two from European civil law. When slaves were sold, for example, a number of courts posited that a "sound price" paid warranted the "soundness" of the slave. Virtually all southern courts declined to apply the fellow-servant rule to the case of a hired slave injured or killed by a "fellow" worker, on the grounds that the slave lacked the kind of free will presumed by the rule (that would lead to the reporting and firing of careless workers). Slaves placed on trial for their lives were afforded most of the same procedural rights as whites enjoyed, and third-party whites who assaulted a slave without provocation could find themselves charged with a common-law crime, but southern courts held that the killing of an escaping or resistant slave by the master was not a common-law crime. Where sanctioned by statute, courts sanctioned the act of manumission (the freeing of a slave in one's last will and testament). But jurists were unwilling to utilize the equitable *cy pres* doctrine (to enable a testator's intentions to be carried out "as nearly as possible"). Beginning in 1836 northern courts followed the English precedent (Somerset's Case, 1772) to hold that slaves willfully brought into a free state by their owners might sue successfully for their freedom. Some northern courts offered no support to those seeking fugitive slaves, sometimes applying the terms of a personal liberty statute, sometimes a legal fiction, sometimes a higher law. Southern courts responded in kind to these measures, refusing to observe comity with regard to the laws of those northern states.

Criminal Law

Most alterations in the law of crime in nineteenth-century America were made by state legislatures, not courts. For example, in 1820 Indiana's criminal law consisted of thirty-four named felonies and twenty-five named misdemeanors; by 1860 the legislature had raised these to forty felonies and eighty misdemeanors. But a handful of interesting rules were added by the courts. In *Commonwealth v. Selfridge* (1806), the Massachusetts court held that in the event one was confronted with a life-threatening assault, one had "no duty to retreat" from one's attacker, as in England, but could employ deadly force in self-defense. This rule, which courts in Tennessee and Texas later expanded, served in time to justify deaths ensuing from the wearing of side arms. A second innovation consisted of the right of the accused to testify on his or her own behalf. A third went beyond the English rule regarding a defense based on insanity (that the accused must have known the difference between right and wrong). Some state courts followed the "wild beast" test offered by Iowa's Chief Justice John Forrest Dillon in *State v. Felter* (1868), that the accused should not be regarded as criminally responsible if the act was driven by an "irresistible impulse, arising . . . from an insane condition of the mind." Finally, the practice of plea bargaining between the prosecutor and the accused appears to have increased in frequency in the mid–nineteenth century and thereafter.

Contract Law

Few significant changes were made in the common law of contracts throughout the nineteenth century: no replacement of a fairness doctrine or inadequacy of consideration defense with a will of the parties or caveat emptor rule. Similarly, there were no notable changes with regard to conditional sales, chattel mortgages, expectation damages in futures contracts, and the standing in courts of third-party beneficiaries to contracts. Two innovations that might be noted, however, were the sanctioning of contingency fee contracts between attorneys and clients, enabling poor suitors to "have their day in court," and (at least in half of the states) the sanctioning of employer compensation to workers who quit entire contracts (those entered into for a specified sum and period of time).

Inasmuch as marriage was a contract, one should note here another two innovations. First, courts (as well as legislatures) slowly added mental cruelty to physical cruelty as one of the grounds for divorce. Second, courts (as well as legislatures) applied a best interests of the child doctrine to determine custody decisions.

Torts

One historical school has it that the common law in cases of accidental injury or death changed in the nineteenth century from a regimen of strict liability, holding defendants liable if it could simply be established that they or their agents had caused the accident, to one requiring proof that they had also been negligent. But analyses by Robert Kaczorowski and Peter Karsten appear to have demonstrated that there had been a clear negligence standard in English common law for centuries.

Moreover, a case has been made that the changes in the common law of torts introduced by American jurists in the nineteenth century favored plaintiffs suing businesses, not the other way around. Thus passengers injured in derailments and collisions were treated as having made a prima facie case of the railway's negligence simply by establishing that the accident occurred; the companies had an increasingly difficult time of evading liability for equipment that they had purchased (or manufactured themselves), maintained, and retained in service. Similarly, courts held that a passerby injured by the careless act of an unknown party on a construction site had a prima facie case, reasoning that "the thing speaks for itself" (res ipsa loquitur). By mid-century courts and legislatures in most states had abrogated the doctrine of sovereign immunity for persons injured on defective roads or bridges. Children injured on dangerous objects ("attractive nuisances") left unattended and unlocked (such as railroad turntables) were by the 1870s and 1880s being treated by courts not as trespassers, to whom property owners owed few duties, but as "invitees," to whom considerable care was owed. And courts similarly ceased to tolerate the English rule imputing parental contributory negligence to children injured in the streets by careless drivers. The "sins of the fathers," jurists wrote, quoting from the Bible, were "not to be visited upon the child."

Employees injured on the job encountered considerably less friendly rules in court; they had assumed the risks of injury under the terms of their labor contracts, it was said. And if they were injured through the carelessness of a fellow employee, the early decisions held that their only recourse was to sue that employee, not their employer. Many state courts softened these harsh rules with exceptions throughout the second half of the nineteenth century: employers were liable if safe tools, a safe workplace, or competent fellow workers had not been provided. They were liable if the risks demanded of the employee had been extraordinary, or if the fellow employee responsible for the accident had in fact been so senior in rank to the injured worker as to constitute an agent for the company, or if that employee had belonged to a department in the company quite different from that of the injured worker (thus giving him no opportunity to learn of the "fellow-servant's" careless habits).

The law of on-the-job accidents was finally addressed by legislatures, under pressure from labor unions, in the late nineteenth and early twentieth centuries, culminating in virtually no-fault workmen's compensation schemes.

See also **Courts, State and Federal; Market Revolution.**

Bibliography

Bakken, Gordon M. *The Development of Law on the Rocky Mountain Frontier: Civil Law and Society, 1850–1912.* Westport, Conn.: Greenwood, 1983.

Brown, Richard Maxwell. *No Duty to Retreat: Violence and Values in American History and Society.* New York: Oxford University Press, 1991.

Finkelman, Paul. *An Imperfect Union: Slavery, Federalism, and Comity.* Chapel Hill: University of North Carolina Press, 1981.

Friedman, Lawrence M. *A History of American Law.* 2d ed. New York: Simon and Schuster, 1985.

Grossberg, Michael. *Governing the Hearth: Law and the Family in Nineteenth-Century America.* Chapel Hill: University of North Carolina Press, 1985.

Horwitz, Morton J. *The Transformation of American Law, 1780–1860.* Cambridge, Mass.: Harvard University Press, 1977.

Kaczorowski, Robert. "The Common Law Background of Nineteenth Century Tort Law." *Ohio State Law Journal* 51 (1990): 1127–1199.

Karsten, Peter. *Heart Versus Head: Judge-Made Law in Nineteenth Century America.* Chapel Hill: University of North Carolina Press, 1997.

Morris, Thomas D. *Southern Slavery and the Law, 1619–1860.* Chapel Hill: University of North Carolina Press, 1996.

Rosen, Christine. "Differing Perceptions of the Value of Pollution Abatement across Time and Place: Balancing Doctrine in Pollution Nuisance Law, 1840–1906." *Law and History* 11 (1993): 303–381.

Teeven, Kevin M. *A History of the Anglo-American Common Law of Contract.* Westport, Conn.: Greenwood, 1990.

PETER KARSTEN

WOMEN AND THE LAW

While women achieved legal advances throughout the course of the nineteenth century with regard to property rights, divorce, child custody, suffrage, and admission into professions, women's legal progress was hampered by entrenched social and cultural values. Social order was dictated by the middle-class "separate spheres" construct, which proscribed different spheres of action and influence for white men and women. Any societal change that threatened to deteriorate the rigid boundary between women and men, and elevate women above a subordinate role, was resisted by those in power. Actions hinting of legal equality between the sexes posed a tremendous risk to the status quo. Thus, in spite of women's legal gains, the symbiotic relationship between law and culture prevented women's true emancipation. Laws changed, but in many ways women's position remained the same.

Origins in Common Law

The basis of the U.S. legal system, English common-law principles, reflected longstanding customs and cultural patterns that were subject to judicial interpretation. The law was in written form in statutes, the decisions of judges, and legal treatises. They were not interpreted until English jurist William Blackstone attempted a discussion of common law in 1765 in his *Commentaries*. This text served as the main guide to women's legal status throughout the nineteenth century. Single women lived under an oppressively sexist legal system that affirmed their inferiority, as well as denied them the right to vote and serve on juries, but they were able to own property and make contracts. Upon marriage, women's legal identity was subsumed by their husbands, and they lost the few privileges they possessed while single. According to Blackstone, marriage resulted in women's "civil death." "Coverture," or the legal subjugation of married women to their spouses, was partly based in the biblical assertion that husband and wife were united by flesh.

Building on the coverture tradition, the development in the nineteenth century of separate spheres promoted the notion that women were gentle, nurturing, delicate creatures requiring protection from the harsh outside society. Husbands provided this "protection" by assuming their wives' legal responsibilities and privileges, along with their property and wages. Coverture confirmed male dominance by relegating women to a subordinate status. Throughout the nineteenth century, even as legal adjustments began to project women as individuals with interests apart from men's, judicial interpretation of the laws was inextricably bound to the separate spheres ideology; judges were acutely aware of the law's role in social control.

Property Rights

For the first third of the nineteenth century, married women had no right to hold, acquire, or control property, retain their own wages, make contracts, and to sue or be sued in their own names. Married women's only protection was in the form of a "dower right." This gave wives access to one-third of the husband's real property for their own sustenance during widowhood. While it provided some income, they could not dispose of the property. Their lack of control placed them in the positions of tenants rather than owners.

Married women's legal disadvantages were addressed in 1839 when the first Married Women's Property Act was passed in Mississippi. By 1860, seventeen states had some form of legislation on their books that redressed women's legal disabilities. After the Civil War, black women were also protected by Married Women's Property Acts. Within thirty years, twenty-nine states could claim such laws, and by the turn of the century, 75 percent of the states provided legal protection to married women. The laws varied from state to state but generally provided that married women could initiate legal action, own and control property, and retain their wages. The Earnings Acts of 1860 and 1868 further reflected this legal trend by altering husbands' common-law rights to their wives' earnings.

The piecemeal legislation resulted in the expansion of women's self-protection and certainly represented progress. However, judicial construction of the statutes was narrow and inextricably bound to cultural assumptions about male dominance and women's circumscribed role. Thus, Married Women's Property Acts did not change women's condition significantly. For example, in *Switzer v. Valentine* (1854), the New York Superior Court rejected a woman's ability to make a valid contract. Caroline Switzer took out a loan to expand her business, but was unable to pay her debt. The court ruled her contract was not valid because she did not possess a separate estate. This decision made it more difficult for women to acquire credit in their own names. In addition, women who earned wages outside of the home remained shackled by entrenched ideas about the nature of marriage and male control. In *Brooks v. Schwerin* (1873), the New York Court of Appeals decided that if a wife was injured and lost wages, it was actually the husband who suffered the loss, and thus his place to sue for restitution.

Established beliefs about women's subordinate status were not easily dislodged by legislative adjustments. The Property Acts did not interfere with husbands' authority to manage or deplete their wives' assets, and some states did not allow women full control over their property or wages, or permit them to sue without their husbands' consent. This intransigence signaled judicial resistance to legislative attacks on common law.

Family Roles

Laws governing domestic life affected women in their primary roles of wife and mother. When, for example, smaller families became desirable in the industrial era because having too many children had become an economic liability, laws were created to address the increase in the incidence of abortion. Legislative policy cracked down on abortion, making it unconditionally illegal. Previously, pregnancy termination had been permissible in the gestational cycle that preceded "quickening," the mother's awareness of fetal movement. *Commonwealth v. Bangs* (Mass., 1812) demonstrated the trend toward illegalizing all abortion. After the Civil War, the attack on abortion expanded to an assault on all forms of birth control; under the Comstock Act (1873), any discussion of family planning was illegal under the definition of obscenity. The criminalization of birth control was partly a response to fears that the native American population was being squeezed out by immigrants. Thus it was intended to increase the birth rate among native white American women, as seen in *Mills v. Commonwealth* (Pa., 1850). This fear profoundly affected women's reproductive freedom, and is an example of how social concerns are reflected in laws.

The liberalization of divorce statutes, which occurred in several states starting in the antebellum period, benefited women, whose inability to divorce an abusive or irresponsible husband had reinforced their inferior status. Some states expanded the grounds for absolute divorce. Liberalized divorce laws, however, were also taken advantage of by men who could attain divorce on the grounds their wives were "idle," "neglectful," or did not respect husbands' authority. In an effort to encourage family stability and growth, some courts began granting divorce, rather than permanent separation, so that women could remarry. Also, alimony guidelines changed. Before *Prince v. Prince* (1845) alimony came exclusively out of husbands' property, but in that case the South Carolina Court of Equity allowed it to be taken out of a husband's income as well. Changes in alimony helped women materially, but reinforced the idea of husband as wife's protector. Finally, divorce was accessible only to those who could pay legal fees, which presented another obstacle to women.

Where child custody was at issue, common law automatically gave fathers custody in the case of separation and divorce. With the formulation of separate spheres, however, women's natural superiority at child rearing and nurturance was emphasized, and custody decisions began to favor mothers in the event of the dissolution of a marriage. The Rhode Island case *McKim v. McKim* (1879) illustrates the concept that the best interest of the child should prevail in custody issues. This, however, was first and foremost a strong cultural belief rather than a legal right. Men frequently invoked their common-law right to custody in order to force their wives to return to them. Some decisions reflected judicial belief that it was not in the best interest of the child to be reared in an environment where the mother was forced to return to the father. Thus, legal changes with regard to women's roles as wives and mothers represented both advances and setbacks.

Suffrage

As many white males feared, the Married Women's Property Acts reflected a disturbing trend among female activists; in 1848 women's rights advocates, including reformer and suffragist Elizabeth Cady Stanton, convened at Seneca Falls, New York, and drafted the Declaration of Sentiments, formally calling for suffrage. Many of the activists involved had gained experience in the abolitionist movement, equipping them to stage a political movement on their own behalf. Women's desire for an unmediated relationship with the state was a direct attack on the separate spheres ideology and was consequently met with tremendous resistance.

Among women as well as men, women's suffrage was a controversial issue. There were many women, for example, who supported legal rights for women but did not believe women should vote. Even among those who backed suffrage, the movement splintered in 1869 when the issue of black male suffrage surfaced, forcing a chasm between the activists who believed women should gracefully concede their demands for the vote and allow the Fifteenth Amendment to pass, and those who spoke out against the amendment because it gave black men the vote while passing over white women.

The latter group, including Stanton and her partner Susan B. Anthony, embarked on a plan of encouraging women to register to vote on the grounds that they already possessed the right under the Fourteenth Amendment's Privileges and Immunities Clause. This was followed by a series of arrests and criminal trials of women who attempted to register, bringing public attention to the cause. Anthony was arrested for this crime, and in *United States v. Susan B. Anthony* (1873), she was not permitted to testify on her own behalf, and the federal district judge instructed the jurors to return a guilty verdict. Two years later the issue was raised in the Supreme Court in *Minor v. Happersett* (1875). The court's narrow construction threw the issue back into the legislative arena, and the Supreme Court absolved itself of responsibility. While women gained the right to vote in some states, starting with Wyoming in 1869, they did not possess the legal right to vote nationally until the passage of the Nineteenth Amendment in 1920.

Access to Occupations

The momentum created by women's acquisition of property rights and the suffrage movement contributed to their professional advancement. Legal change and suffrage activity resulted in enhancing the perception of women as autonomous individuals, thus positioning them for entrance into professions historically denied them. For example, women first tried to gain admission to the legal profession in 1869. Arabella Babb Mansfield, an extremely qualified candidate, gained entrance to the Iowa bar that year. This was followed by other women seeking admission to the bar, and litigation that responded to those requests. Myra Colby Bradwell, equally as qualified as Mansfield, was denied admission to the Illinois bar. Her case went to the Supreme Court, where reliance on common law principles led to the decision that women had no constitutionally protected right to practice law. Thus, women had to apply for entrance state by state. Their cases were not judged on individual merit, but instead on the larger implications of women practicing law. Female attorneys usually suffered from professional isolation and were not admitted to the American Bar Association until 1918. For most men, the social consequences of allowing women into the legal profession were undeniable; it would enable them to navigate their way to suffrage, endangering the concept of separate spheres and ultimately threatening the male dominance that was the cultural foundation of American life.

Women's legal advances were only as meaningful as judicial interpretation allowed them to be. Fears of women's equality and autonomy and the social disorder that would ensue played vividly in the minds of judges as they assessed the validity of women's legal claims. During the nineteenth century statutory gains were gradual but consistent, yet women's roles continued to be defined by traditional gender assumptions.

See also **Constitutional Amendments,** *subentry on* **Thirteenth, Fourteenth, and Fifteenth Amendments; Contraception and Abortion; Divorce and Desertion; Domestic Life; Gender,** *subentry on* **Gender and the Law;** **Labor Movement,** *subentry on* **Women; Law,** *subentry on* **Common Law; Voters and Voting,** *subentry on* **The Women's Vote; Women,** *subentry on* **Women's Rights.**

Bibliography

Basch, Norma. *In the Eyes of the Law: Women, Marriage, and Property in Nineteenth-Century New York.* Ithaca, N.Y.: Cornell University Press, 1982.

DuBois, Ellen Carol. *Feminism and Suffrage: The Emergence of an Independent Women's Movement in America, 1848–1869.* Ithaca, N.Y.: Cornell University Press, 1978.

Hoff, Joan. *Law, Gender, and Injustice: A Legal History of U.S. Women.* New York: New York University Press, 1991.

Kanowitz, Leo. *Women and the Law: The Unfinished Revolution.* Albuquerque: University of New Mexico Press, 1969.

Lazarou, Kathleen Elizabeth. *Concealed Under Petticoats: Married Women's Property and the Law of Texas, 1840–1913.* New York: Garland, 1986.

Wortman, Marlene Stein, ed. *Women in American Law.* Vol. 1, *From Colonial Times to the New Deal.* New York: Holmes and Meier, 1985.

LIANN E. TSOUKAS

LAW BOOKS American law books and legal publishing changed significantly and in certain respects fundamentally during the nineteenth century. In 1800 American law books were essentially either reprints of English legal treatises, legal self-help manuals, or statute books. By 1900 definitive American legal materials written by American legal scholars, including court reports, legal treatises, and legal encyclopedias, were plentiful.

The most dramatic change occurred in the reporting of court decisions. In 1800 reporting had just begun. Even the obligation of courts to render written opinions explaining their decisions was new, often compelled by recent state statutes. The transition from the occasional and serendipitous printing of a single court decision in a particular case to the systematic publishing of all the decisions of all courts was just underway.

In 1800 court reports were mainly private enterprises undertaken by individual reporters. These earliest reports were referred to by the reporter's name. Thus, the first U.S. Supreme Court reports by Alexander J. Dallas are "Dallas's Reports." Soon after 1800 officially appointed reporters began to replace "entrepreneur" reporters. But the custom of referring to reports by the reporter's name remained for much of the century.

By 1900 a national reporter system had been established, principally through West Publishing Company. West began its series of regional reports, providing the opinions of state supreme courts, in 1877. Its *Federal Reporter,* recording the decisions of the

U.S. courts other than the Supreme Court, started in 1880. At the same time other publishers began offering reports on various subjects, such as cases involving railroads or corporations or selected cases from certain state courts. By 1900 these efforts in their totality had resulted in the comprehensive reporting of American court decisions.

Dramatic change also occurred in the publishing of legal treatises. In 1800 almost all American legal treatises were either self-help works, such as justice of the peace and probate manuals, or reprints of English treatises, such as William Blackstone's *Commentaries on the Laws of England* (1765–1769). Two changes that had just begun accelerated quickly. First, English law books edited by American legal scholars who added significant American content appeared. Good examples are St. George Tucker's edition of *Blackstone's Commentaries* (1803) and the future Supreme Court justice Joseph Story's edition of *A Treatise of the Law Relative to Merchant Ships and Seamen* (1810), originally by Charles Abbott.

Second, works on American law written by American scholars appeared. James Kent's *Commentaries on American Law* was published in four volumes between 1826 and 1830. During the 1830s and 1840s Justice Story produced nine *Commentaries*, all on American law, including his *Commentaries on the Constitution of the United States* (1833). In the 1840s Story's colleague at Harvard, Simon Greenleaf, published the first two volumes of his *Treatise on the Law of Evidence* (1842–1853). These and other treatises, often in many editions, were published throughout the century, on occasion by editors who were themselves noteworthy. The future Supreme Court justice Oliver Wendell Holmes undertook the twelfth edition of Kent's *Commentaries* (1873), and John H. Wigmore prepared the first volume of the sixteenth edition of Greenleaf's *A Treatise on the Law of Evidence* (1899).

Two other types of legal publications complemented the treatises. Law reviews, rich in academic content, appeared at major law schools, the first at Harvard in 1887. Casebooks, the fruits of the revolution in teaching of law introduced by C. C. Langdell at Harvard, entered publication in the early 1870s. By 1900 a legal treatise, a law review article, or a casebook had been written on virtually every legal subject, however obscure.

The paucity of legal materials in 1800 had thus turned to plenty by 1900. This phenomenon led to legal encyclopedias, designed to help the beleaguered lawyer cope. The father of the American legal encyclopedia, James Cockcroft, saw his *American and English Encyclopedia of Law* appear in twenty-nine volumes between 1887 and 1896.

In 1800 American legal publishing was concentrated principally in the East in Boston, New York, Philadelphia, and perhaps surprisingly Albany, New York. Little, Brown and Company, which published the works of Justices Story and Holmes, originated in 1784. The nation's expansion significantly shifted the location of legal publishers. The most influential legal publisher of the twentieth century, West Publishing Company, was founded in 1872 in St. Paul, Minnesota, as a secondhand law bookstore. Even earlier, in 1856, the predecessor of Bancroft-Whitney Company was established in San Francisco.

By 1900 American legal publishing had assumed a form easily recognizable to a mid–twentieth century practitioner. Late in the twentieth century microform and electronic publishing created changes as revolutionary as those effected between 1800 and 1900.

See also **Book Publishing; Courts, State and Federal; Law,** *subentry on* **An Overview; Legal Profession; Printing Technology.**

Bibliography

Cohen, Morris L. *Bibliography of American Law*. Buffalo, N.Y.: William S. Hein, 1998.

Hall, Kermit L. *A Comprehensive Bibliography of American Constitutional and Legal History, 1896–1979*. Millwood, N.Y.: Kraus International Publications, 1984.

Surrency, Erwin C. *A History of American Law Publishing*. New York: Oceana Publications, 1990.

JORDAN D. LUTTRELL

LEGAL PROFESSION

The legal profession during the nineteenth century grew greatly in size, diversity, and efficiency. At the same time it remained highly powerful, stratified, fragmented, and unpopular.

Democratization of the Profession

During the early part of the century the bar tended to be highly elite. Although the incomes of attorneys varied widely and many had difficulty earning a living, they tended to have solid liberal educations and to come from the propertied classes, whose members they usually served in their work. With the rise of Jacksonian democracy and the westward expansion of the frontier during the middle third of the century, the legal profession began to attract more self-made men, many of whom had little formal education of any kind. Western attorneys also represented a more diverse clientele than did their eastern counterparts.

The democratization of the bar stymied efforts by state and county bar associations to tighten regulation and raise professional standards. Requirements for admission became more lax during the mid–nineteenth century then rose somewhat later in the century. The number of lawyers grew from a few thousand to more than one hundred thousand, although the proportion of lawyers to the general population expanded much less markedly.

Despite this democratization, women were completely excluded from the legal profession until a few states admitted women to the bar during the 1870s. In decisions in 1873 and 1894 the U.S. Supreme Court upheld the constitutionality of state legislation that prohibited women from practicing law. Beginning with the University of Michigan in 1870, some law schools accepted women, although barriers to formal legal education remained the norm throughout the century. At the end of the century women attorneys numbered only a few hundred. African American attorneys faced similar obstacles. Only a handful practiced before the Civil War, and they, too, numbered no more than a few hundred by the end of the century.

Throughout the century most attorneys were entrepreneurs who practiced alone or with a single partner. They usually handled a broad range of matters, from criminal defenses to land litigations. The rise of large corporations after the Civil War led to the creation of the first modern law firms that specialized in counseling business clients and avoided courtroom work.

Growth of Legal Literature

Because of the dearth of formal legal education and the lack of reported judicial decisions and uniform rules of law, attorneys during the early part of the century relied heavily upon common sense, logic, emotional appeals to juries, standard legal treatises, and their personal reputations among judges and jurors. The practice of law became more standardized and efficient late in the century as state legislatures codified laws, particularly procedural, commercial, and criminal laws. In addition the number of published volumes of reported case law expanded from eighteen in 1810 to eight thousand by 1910. Beginning in 1879 the West Publishing Company indexed and published judicial decisions to supplement the more disorganized and less comprehensive state systems of publication.

Law practice benefited from a burgeoning literature on law. At the start of the century the only secondary sources available to lawyers were William Blackstone's *Commentaries on the Laws of England* (1765–1769) and a handful of other often outdated, abstruse, and impractical treatises. In 1803 St. George Tucker, a professor at the College of William

Joseph Story (1779–1845). Story, a Republican congressman from Massachusetts from 1808 to 1809, had a long legal career. He was an Associate Justice of the U.S. Supreme Court and a Professor of Law at Harvard University. Daguerreotype, Matthew Brady, c. 1844–1845. LIBRARY OF CONGRESS

and Mary in Virginia, published the first American adaptation of Blackstone, entitled *Blackstone's Commentaries* and known as "Tucker's Blackstone." Several new American law books followed, among them James Kent's *Commentaries on American Law* (1826–1830). Justice Joseph Story of the U.S. Supreme Court published nearly a dozen treatises, including his famous *Commentaries on the Constitution of the United States* (1833). Other scholars produced scores of specialized volumes, such as Joseph Angell's treatises on corporation law and water law, John Bouvier's *Law Dictionary* (1830), and Thomas R. R. Cobb's *An Inquiry into the Law of Negro Slavery* (1858). By the end of the century lawyers could draw from highly practical and up-to-date treatises on a wide range of general subjects, such as evidence and contracts, and a broad array of specializations, such as railroad law and labor law. Several law schools published student-edited law reviews, which provided scholarly and practical articles. A number of nationally circulated legal periodicals, notably the *American Law Review,* the *Central Law Journal,* and the *Green Bag,* offered news and commentary that promoted cohesion in the profession.

The Bar

The organization of the bar was haphazard throughout the century. State, county, and city bar associations, which provided only limited control over professional standards and discipline, waned at midcentury but enjoyed greater prominence near the century's end. With the exception of a short-lived group started in 1849, no national bar organization formed before the American Bar Association (ABA) started with one hundred members in 1878. With a membership of less than two thousand at the end of the century, the ABA consisted of elite attorneys who elevated standards of professionalism and modernized judicial administration, civil procedure, and commercial law.

Although the profession was generally unpopular throughout the century because of its identification with propertied interests and its association with the unpleasantness of litigation and strife, lawyers occupied a disproportionately prominent position in American society, and politicians and businessmen regarded the bar as an ideal avenue for advancement. The unsettled character of the nation bred legal disputes, and the law provided cohesion in a society that lacked established classes and institutions. According to Alexis de Tocqueville and other observers, the legal profession filled the void in the United States created by the absence of an aristocracy. Lawyers were social and political leaders at both the local and the national levels despite widespread carping about the profession among laypersons.

Legal Education

Early in the century legal education was a highly informal apprentice system, under which a student read law and performed clerical tasks in the office of an attorney until he was ready to apply for a license. A few freestanding law schools, particularly Tapping Reeve's Litchfield Law School (1784–1833) in Connecticut, flourished. Some colleges, including William and Mary, had a professor of law but no systematic program. Harvard in 1817 established a law chair, and subsequently other universities offered legal education.

By 1900 the United States had approximately one hundred law schools that enrolled about eight thousand students. Admission and graduation standards were generally lax, however. Few schools required a college degree for entrance, and most granted a law

degree in two years. At the end of the century most practicing lawyers still lacked a degree from a law school. To improve the standards of legal education, in 1900 the Association of American Law Schools (AALS) was formed to accredit schools, beginning with its thirty-two charter members. The AALS also lobbied state legislatures to raise bar admission standards.

For most of the century legal education emphasized rote learning of rules and development of practical skills. The principal modes of instruction were lecture, recitation, and moot court exercises. In 1870 Harvard introduced the case method of instruction, in which students analyzed the decisions of appellate courts and engaged in Socratic dialogue with faculty in class. The developers of the case method intended to make the study of law more "scientific" and less vocational by developing analytical skills based on broad principles. Although the elite schools adopted the case method by 1900, the old emphasis on vocational training prevailed at most schools until well into the twentieth century.

See also **Education,** *subentry on* **Graduate and Professional Education; Law Books; Professions; Women,** *subentry on* **Women in the Professions.**

Bibliography
Bloomfield, Maxwell. *American Lawyers in a Changing Society, 1776–1876.* Cambridge, Mass.: Harvard University Press, 1976.

Chroust, Anton-Hermann. *The Rise of the Legal Profession in America.* Volume 2. *The Revolution and the Post-Revolutionary Era.* Norman: University of Oklahoma Press, 1965.

Finkleman, Paul. "Not Only the Judges' Robes Were Black: African-American Lawyers as Social Engineers." *Stanford Law Review* 47 (November 1994): 161–209.

Friedman, Lawrence M. *A History of American Law.* New York: Simon and Schuster, 1973.

Johnson, William R. *Schooled Lawyers: A Study in the Clash of Professional Cultures.* New York: New York University Press, 1978.

WILLIAM G. ROSS

LEWIS AND CLARK EXPEDITION The famous expedition led by Meriwether Lewis and William Clark was the first of several sent to explore the trans-Mississippi West and to engage its native population in diplomatic and commercial relations with the United States. Traveling by foot, by boat, and on horseback, the expedition began in 1804 and lasted over two years.

President Thomas Jefferson learned in 1802 that Alexander Mackenzie, a member of the North West Company trading for furs in Canada, had traveled

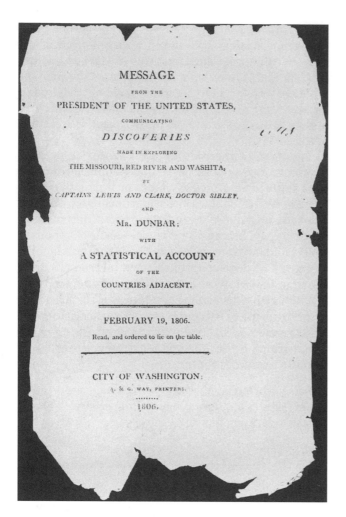

MESSAGE

FROM THE

PRESIDENT OF THE UNITED STATES,

COMMUNICATING

DISCOVERIES

MADE IN EXPLORING

THE MISSOURI, RED RIVER AND WASHITA,

BY

CAPTAINS LEWIS AND CLARK, DOCTOR SIBLEY,

AND

MR. DUNBAR;

WITH

A STATISTICAL ACCOUNT

OF THE

COUNTRIES ADJACENT.

FEBRUARY 19, 1806.

Read, and ordered to lie on the table.

CITY OF WASHINGTON:

A. & G. WAY, PRINTERS.

....

1806.

Wilderness Discovered. Official report from President Jefferson announcing the discoveries made by Lewis and Clark on their expedition of the Missouri, Red, and Washita Rivers, 19 February 1806. LIBRARY OF CONGRESS: PRINTS AND PHOTOGRAPHS DIVISION

overland from central Canada to the Pacific Coast and back in 1792–1793. Jefferson had long been interested in Spanish lands west of the Mississippi River and worried that Mackenzie's feat might open the region to British control. To counter this threat, in January 1803 the president asked Congress to fund a small military party that would enter Spanish territory, search for a practical route between the Missouri and Columbia Rivers, and establish relations with the American Indians living along the rivers. He hoped to give the United States an advantage over Britain in the region and make it possible for Americans to trade more easily with Asian markets.

The president had already chosen his private secretary, Meriwether Lewis, to command the expedition. Lewis had been an army officer in the Ohio Valley for several years during the 1790s, and Jefferson thought him perfectly suited to this new task. Lewis asked William Clark, a comrade from his army days and the younger brother of the Revolutionary War hero George Rogers Clark, to join him as co-commander. Together they picked the rest of their men from among soldiers posted along the Ohio River and French Canadian boatmen living in St. Louis.

The expedition left St. Louis on 14 May 1804. By this time the United States had acquired vast western territory from France through the Louisiana Purchase. For six months the group slowly ascended the Missouri River while the commanders tried to negotiate with Indian tribes in the region, most notably with the Teton Sioux. The explorers spent the winter of 1804–1805 among Mandan Indians in North Dakota. Indians and whites hunted, traded, and socialized together, and the Mandan provided important information about the land and peoples ahead. The expedition also gained a valuable team of interpreters and cultural brokers that winter, when it hired Toussaint Charbonneau, a French Canadian trader, and thus obtained the services of his Shoshone wife, Sacagawea.

Lewis and Clark resumed their journey in April 1805. By August they had reached the upper Missouri Valley and in September, with help and horses provided by the Shoshone Indians, crossed the Rocky Mountains. Descending the Columbia River, they reached the Pacific in mid-November and spent the winter of 1805–1806 at a fort on the Oregon side of the river, where they had relatively little contact with Indians. Lewis and Clark disliked the local Clatsop Indians, and the latter, who were used to trading with visiting ships, had little interest in the Americans' limited supply of goods.

In March 1806 Lewis and Clark set out for home. After recrossing the Rockies in June, the expedition split up in order to explore more territory. Clark went south to the Yellowstone River, while Lewis followed the Marias River nearly to Canada and fought a brief skirmish with Piegan Blackfeet, the only violent episode of the journey. The two commanders met again just below the junction of the Yellowstone and Missouri Rivers and continued to St. Louis, arriving there on 23 September 1806.

Lewis and Clark did not find a practical route between the Missouri and Columbia Rivers and had little success negotiating peace or trade agreements with the Indians. Nevertheless, the geographic information they brought back was a major factor in opening the West to American trappers, traders, and settlers during the next fifty years.

See also **Expansion; Exploration and Explorers.**

Bibliography

Moulton, Gary E., ed. *The Journals of the Lewis & Clark Expedition.* Lincoln: University of Nebraska Press, 1983–1997.

Ronda, James P. *Lewis and Clark among the Indians.* Lincoln: University of Nebraska Press, 1984.

Thorp, Daniel B. *Lewis and Clark: An American Journey.* New York: Friedman/Fairfax, 1998.

DANIEL B. THORP

LIBERALISM   "In the beginning all the world was America," wrote John Locke in *Two Treatises on Government* (1690). In Locke's America people remained close to the state of nature, their liberties not yet eclipsed by the hand of government. A century before the Revolution, America already occupied a privileged place in the imagination of Englishmen who were developing the ideas that later acquired the name "liberalism." Elaborated by David Hume, Adam Smith, Thomas Jefferson, James and John Stuart Mill, and Jeremy Bentham, liberalism became in the nineteenth century the leading school of political and economic thought in the English-speaking world.

At the foundation of liberalism was the proposition that humans are by nature interdependent creatures. From humans' weakness as individuals arises the necessity to cooperate and trade and thus to create markets. From an inborn moral sense and the disposition of the mind to see oneself as others see one arise conscience and sociability. It follows, contended liberal thinkers, that by doing what comes naturally, people develop spontaneously the web of self-adjusting exchange relationships that is called society. Government, in contrast, is an artificial construction, instituted for its usefulness in protecting the "life, liberty, and property" of good people against the predations of bad ones. But take away government, liberals believed, and society—the underlying social order created by markets and mutual sympathy—will endure. Thomas Paine forcefully summarized this core doctrine of liberalism in the great revolutionary pamphlet *Common Sense* (1776): "Society is produced by our wants and government by our wickedness; the former promotes our happiness positively by uniting our affections, the latter negatively by restraining our vices. . . . Society in every state is a blessing, but government, even in its best state, is but a necessary evil."

This was radical thinking, for instead of attributing order to coercive acts of government—as virtually every political thinker since antiquity had done—liberals linked order to the free state of nature. No longer charged with keeping order, government's purpose was reduced to safeguarding men's rights and especially their property. Adam Smith further eroded the rationale for government by severing its associations with material welfare. Left free to pursue their private economic interests in unregulated markets, Smith contended, men would spontaneously coordinate their wants and needs as if guided by a beneficent "invisible hand," and the result would be a level of prosperity far superior to what the clumsy hand of government could produce.

If the foundation of liberalism was the distinction between natural society and unnatural government, on that foundation stood the value of liberty. Liberals believed that human beings do best when they are free to serve their own interests as they define them. Attached to this core belief were several others: humans are naturally rational and moral beings; individuals, though social, possess interests that are distinguishable from those of their fellows; liberty is the key to both intellectual and material progress.

Origins

Although liberals described their ideas as universal and timeless truths, liberalism had its origins in the particular circumstances of early modern Europe. It was a way of thinking born of the tumultuous forces that brought about the Renaissance, the Reformation, the English Revolution, exploration and colonization of the New World, and the rise of commercial capitalism. All of these developments had the effect of releasing people from tradition and opening up new latitudes of social possibility. In its emphasis on freeing the individual, liberalism spoke to the dilemmas of men experiencing the breakup of the corporate, hierarchical, feudal order of the Middle Ages. In its secularism and faith in material progress, liberalism reflected the erosion of medieval otherworldliness and piety. And in Locke's and Smith's emphasis on freeing economic behavior, dismantling state regulation of markets (mercantilism), and protecting the rights of property, early liberalism proclaimed its kinship with capitalism and the entrepreneurial ethos.

This last point merits emphasis, because liberalism originated as the creed of the bourgeoisie—the dynamic mercantile and manufacturing class—that was destined to remake first the Anglo-American and then the whole North Atlantic world in the eighteenth and nineteenth centuries. Historians disagree on the essential spirit of liberalism: some consider it optimistic and progressive, bent on clearing away barriers to human creativity; others portray it as anxious and defensive, a shield for protecting economic gains already made. But virtually all agree that liberalism presumed a connection between liberty and property. The fullest liberties were rightfully enjoyed and properly employed only by persons who either possessed substantial property or who aspired to obtain it.

If liberalism grew out of struggles to free people from constraints sunk deep in European history, would it not flourish in America, where those constraints had shallow roots—where, as Paine grandly said, "We have it in our power to begin the world over again"? Here historical conditions seemed actually to breed liberal ideas; here the abundance of the continent and its distance from imperial centers invited men to acquire property and live as they pleased, while disabling the hand of government. "The great advantage of the Americans," wrote Alexis de Tocqueville, is that, unlike any other people, "they are born equal, instead of becoming so."

The Hartz Thesis

This insight became the seed of a popular interpretation of American political experience put forward by Louis Hartz in *The Liberal Tradition in America* in 1955. Hartz contended that in America the liberal tradition was dominant because monarchy, inherited privilege, and feudal land tenure had never been planted on American soil. Americans believed they lived closer to the state of nature than any other civilized people. They saw in Locke's writings not just a theory but a description of their actual experience. "The revolutionaries of 1776," wrote Hartz, "had inherited the freest society in the world" (p. 47). The liberalism that was a class ideology in Europe became a virtually universal ideology in nineteenth-century America, where a majority of the population either owned productive property or aspired to proprietorship.

In reply to the "Hartz thesis" it could be objected that nineteenth-century Americans seemed oblivious to liberalism, just as they were wary of all ideologies. Even among the intelligentsia, few read the writings of contemporary liberal thinkers like Bentham, Mill, or Tocqueville, and fewer still publicly adopted liberal principles. In Britain a Liberal Party led by one of the great statesmen of the era, William Gladstone, came to power soon after it was formed in 1870. In the United States the only political group to claim the name "liberal" consisted of gentlemen reformers who bolted from the Republican Party to form a short-lived Liberal Republican Party in 1872. To this objection Hartz had a ready reply: nineteenth-century Americans did not talk about liberalism because they assumed it. The premises of liberalism suffused the cultural air they breathed, and like air it was invisible.

Another defense of the Hartz thesis hinges on the understanding that there were many layers of liberal thought in nineteenth-century America. The political philosophy expounded by John Locke and John Stuart Mill may have been known to very few, but related to this philosophy were the liberal economic doctrines, developed originally by Adam Smith, that were widely taught in the nation's colleges. Many Americans who never set foot in a college nonetheless subscribed to the root propositions of this "classical economics." Finally, there was a loose creedal liberalism that was probably embraced—indeed, taken for granted—by a majority of citizens who gave any thought to politics or economics. American liberalism became, as Joyce Appleby has observed, "a description of a modern utopia which could garner the loyalties of a broad range of Americans" (*Liberalism and Republicanism in the Historical Imagination*, p. 187).

Liberalism as a Constellation of Ideals

If, then, liberalism is not a formal system of ideas but rather a loose constellation of ideals, or a language for articulating a visionary faith in liberty, it is difficult to doubt its significance in nineteenth-century America. For liberty was the magnetic pole at the center of the nation's self-conception, tirelessly invoked in all its civic ceremonies. Thomas Jefferson, the greatest champion of liberal principles in early America, inscribed them in the nation's foundations when he listed among men's "inalienable Rights . . . life, liberty, and the pursuit of happiness" and asserted that governments derive "their just powers from the consent of the governed." Almost a half-century later Jefferson held fast to the principles of the Declaration of Independence when he told a correspondent in 1823: "We believed . . . that man was a rational animal, endowed by nature with rights, and with an innate sense of justice; and that he could be restrained from wrong and protected in right, by moderate powers, confided to persons of his own choice, and held to their duties by dependence on his own will" (Arieli, *Individualism and Nationalism in American Ideology*, p. 90). These ideas resonated throughout American society. In 1798 a Massachusetts farmer named William Manning wrote an essay titled "The Key of Libberty" [sic] which, though he never managed to publish it, expressed the core of liberal belief as tidily as anything written by the sage of Monticello: "For the prinsapel hapiness of a Man in this world is to eat & drink and injoy the good of his Labour, & to feal that his Life Libberty & property is secure" (Tomlins, *Law, Labor, and Ideology in the Early American Republic*, p. 4).

Nor was the liberty constantly invoked in nineteenth-century America wispy rhetoric or empty formula. The white males who monopolized citizenship congratulated themselves on being the most lightly governed of civilized people anywhere in the world, and so they probably were. They regarded themselves, and were regarded by friends abroad, as exemplars of liberty. Moreover, those millions of Americans who did not share in the liberties enjoyed by white males made it their highest aspiration to obtain them. Although slavery mocked white Americans' commitment to liberty, emancipation would have been unthinkable without it. And while the continuing subordination of blacks and women called into doubt the sincerity of male citizens' devotion to liberty, African Americans' and women's devotion to liberty lay at the heart of their quest for equal rights.

However difficult it may be to generalize about nineteenth-century liberalism, it seems irrefutable that America's "special conditions" favored the flourishing of liberal principles. The phrase comes from Karl Marx's collaborator Friedrich Engels, but the insight was shared alike by Tocqueville, the historian Frederick Jackson Turner, Hartz, and countless others who read nineteenth-century America as an *experimental* society. The opening of the continent called forth a creed of optimistic striving; the natural wealth and spaciousness of the continent presented a vast market of opportunities to the entrepreneur. Turner's "frontier thesis" (1893) encapsulated a century of thinking about the effects of abundant land on the development of American civilization. With its emphasis on private initiative and its faith in freedom, liberalism seemed a creed made to order for a dynamic and often turbulent young society, wherein it was beguiling to suppose that the spontaneous workings of the market would magically yield "ordered liberty." Moreover, in nineteenth-century America liberalism converged with the promptings of evangelical religion and popular myth. Market hero, converted Christian, self-made man—all seemed variants of the same ideal: the individual who was free to perfect himself, with his economic destiny dictated by his moral character.

The result was an American liberalism that thrived in popular imagination and public policy long after constricting socioeconomic conditions had compelled European liberals to reformulate their beliefs. While the English economist Thomas Malthus was brooding on the exhaustibility of nature and amending the teachings of Adam Smith to acknowledge limits to social progress, his contemporary James Madison was arguing that the plenitude of American land would prove a blessing to the new federal government. With Malthus in mind, Jefferson happily contrasted "the man of the old world . . . crowded within limits either small or overcharged, and steeped in the vices which that situation generates" to the man of the New World, blessed with geographic expanses that insulated his liberties (Wolin, *Politics and Vision*, footnote no. 323, p. 487). Visiting the United States in 1831–1832, Tocqueville famously fretted about pressures for conformity that might eventually distort American democracy, but the most immediate threats, in his view, were excesses of American individualism—not freedom denied, as in the Old World, but freedom abused. For Americans, laissez-faire liberalism remained gospel, with Herbert Spencer and E. L. Godkin its high priests, at a time when English liberals were fast discovering uses for an activist state. And throughout the century, government at all levels in America did, in fact, remain reticent and feeble.

The Narrowing of Late Nineteenth-Century Liberalism

When America's special conditions eroded, when industrialization, concentrations of corporate power, and rising population densities brought with them the compressions and confinements familiar to Jefferson's "man of the old world," American liberalism inevitably changed. Always tethered to the interests of the bourgeoisie, liberalism became increasingly class-bound after the Civil War, as the propertied middle class felt itself besieged by venal politicians, radical ideologues, angry farmers, and alien workers. Liberals lost faith in the vision of order emerging spontaneously from freedom. And losing its universalism, American liberalism lost much of its optimistic, utopian spirit. The balance of emphases within liberal thinking shifted, from an accent on opportunity to an accent on security, from the interests of aspiring entrepreneurs to the interests of established wealth.

At the founding of the Liberal Republican Party in 1872, the Missouri senator Carl Schurz protested "the hand of power" that thrust "through the vast machinery of the public service into local and private affairs" (Goldman, *Rendezvous with Destiny*, p. 22). At the root of liberal republicanism, wrote author William Dean Howells, was the principle that in "the most perfect state . . . moral self-control is substituted for the sanctions of government" (Montgomery, *Beyond Equality*, p. 379). But if these Gilded Age liberals remained faithful to the core doctrine of limited government, they did so less because they had faith in a self-regulating society than because they feared government would be captured by their class enemies. The Liberal Republicans sought "the largest liberty consistent with public order" on behalf of white males only, leaving radicals to champion the rights of emancipated blacks, immigrant workers, and women. In practical politics, to be a liberal after the Civil War meant to advocate free trade, honesty and economy in government, and sound monetary policies. The narrow, nay-saying liberal orthodoxy of judges and politicians who rallied to the defense of corporations in the late nineteenth century expressed a mentality very different from that of Adam Smith and Thomas Jefferson.

Finally, reforming intellectuals like the economist Richard Ely, along with reforming politicians like Robert La Follette and Theodore Roosevelt, began to recast liberalism. Anticipating the Progressive movement of the early twentieth century, these revisionists argued that a political economy transformed by industrialization, prosperity, order, and the preservation of freedom required judicious regulation by the state. In effect, this way of thinking proposed new means for achieving the old liberal goals of maximizing freedom and safeguarding private property. In preindustrial America, liberals had viewed the state as a corrupter of markets serving small producers; in industrialized America, new-model liberals came to view the state as an instrument for policing markets that would otherwise be corrupted by huge business corporations. Moreover, like the antistatist liberalism of Spencer and Godkin, the activist liberalism of Ely and La Follette—destined to become the New Deal liberalism of Franklin Delano Roosevelt—offered itself as a superior alternative to the socialist doctrines that were then making rapid gains. First and last, American liberalism in the nineteenth century remained linked to the health of markets, the fortunes of capitalism, and the interests of property.

See also **Economic Theory; Entrepreneurs; Liberty; Market Revolution; Progressivism; Radicalism.**

Bibliography

Appleby, Joyce. *Capitalism and a New Social Order: The Republican Vision of the 1790s.* New York: New York University Press, 1984.

———. *Liberalism and Republicanism in the Historical Imagination.* Cambridge, Mass.: Harvard University Press, 1992.

Arieli, Yehoshua. *Individualism and Nationalism in American Ideology.* Cambridge, Mass.: Harvard University Press, 1964.

Fine, Sidney. *Laissez Faire and the General-Welfare State: A Study of Conflict in American Thought, 1865–1901.* Ann Arbor: University of Michigan Press, 1956.

Goldman, Eric F. *Rendezvous with Destiny: A History of Modern American Reform.* New York: Vintage, 1956.

Hartz, Louis. *The Liberal Tradition in America: An Interpretation of American Political Thought since the Revolution.* New York: Harcourt, Brace, and World, 1955.

Kammen, Michael G. *Spheres of Liberty: Changing Perceptions of Liberty in American Culture.* Madison: University of Wisconsin Press, 1986.

Laski, Harold J. *The Rise of Liberalism: The Philosophy of a Business Civilization.* New York: Harper and Brothers, 1936.

Montgomery, David. *Beyond Equality: Labor and the Radical Republicans, 1862–1872.* New York: Knopf, 1967.

Ross, Dorothy. "Liberalism." In *Encyclopedia of American Political History.* Vol. 2. Edited by Jack P. Greene. New York: Scribners, 1984.

Sproat, John G. *The Best Men: Liberal Reformers in the Gilded Age.* New York: Oxford University Press, 1968.

Tomlins, Christopher L. *Law, Labor, and Ideology in the Early American Republic.* New York: Cambridge University Press, 1993.

Wolin, Sheldon. *Politics and Vision: Continuity and Innovation in Western Political Thought.* Boston: Little, Brown, 1960.

Wood, Gordon S. *The Radicalism of the American Revolution.* New York: Knopf, 1992.

EUGENE E. LEACH

LIBERIA   After its initial settlement in the 1820s, Liberia remained for most Americans the best-known territory in sub-Saharan Africa. The inspiration for Liberia came from a number of prominent white Americans who viewed emigration or repatriation of freed black Americans as a solution for both the controversial presence of "free persons of color" and the question of what to do with Africans taken from slaving vessels, especially after 1819, when the United States agreed to help suppress the slave trade on the high seas. The American Colonization Society, with some subsidies from the administration of President James Monroe and from Congress, sponsored the first settlements. Liberia declared its independence in 1847, making it Africa's oldest modern state.

From the start African American attitudes toward Liberian colonization experiments were mixed. Some opposed it as the brainchild of slaveholding interests, while others saw it as a positive alternative to integration in American society. For many, however, Liberia came to represent a promised land and a symbol of black independence. Americans in Liberia created their own distinctive settler society with a rich mixture of both African American and African characteristics.

The United States retained a reluctant informal protectorate over Liberia, though the United States did not extend formal recognition until 1862, when opposition from the southern states was no longer a factor. In 1875 and 1879 the United States sent warships to help the Americo-Liberian government contain rebellions by indigenous Africans. In the last two decades of the century the United States brought pressure on the British and French to prevent Liberia from being incorporated into the full-scale European partition of the African continent.

See also **Colonization, African American.**

Bibliography

Cassell, C. Abayomi. *Liberia: History of the First African Republic.* New York: Fountainhead, 1970.

Liebenow, J. Gus. *Liberia: The Quest for Democracy.* Bloomington: Indiana University Press, 1987.

Shick, Tom W. *Behold the Promised Land: A History of Afro-American Settler Society in Nineteenth-Century Liberia.* Baltimore: Johns Hopkins University Press, 1980.

THOMAS C. HOWARD

LIBERTY   "Conceived in liberty, and dedicated to the proposition that all men are created equal," Abraham Lincoln said of the United States at Gettysburg in November 1863. Earlier that year the Emancipation Proclamation had done much to put truth into those words. Lincoln's countrymen boasted of being the freest people in history by virtue of God's grace (the gift of the continent) and human will (the Revolution and the Constitution). But for the majority of Americans, including the newly emancipated, liberty was a project, not a possession. The central drama of American freedom in the nineteenth century lay in struggles to create a universal citizenship guaranteeing "liberty and justice for all."

To understand how the meaning of freedom evolved, it is essential to grasp how differently and narrowly freedom was previously defined. Until the modern period virtually all complex societies organized themselves as hierarchies, in which each individual was bound by law or custom to those above and below him or her. In such societies only those at the top enjoyed a measure of political or economic freedom. All others accepted dependency and subservience as the price of security in a hard world.

Great Britain began to break out of this pattern in the seventeenth and eighteenth centuries, when its thriving commerce and agriculture generated new wealth. Having freed themselves from scarcity, Britons questioned the constraints on liberty that scarcity had traditionally justified. John Locke theorized that, in their presocial state, people enjoyed a natural liberty, which they surrendered only in exchange for the security of living under law. The "end of Law," wrote Locke, "is not to abolish or restrain, but to preserve and enlarge Freedom" (Reid, *The Concept of Liberty in the Age of the American Revolution,* p. 64).

Liberty Awaits Her Final Destination. In France, the head of the Statue of Liberty awaits shipment to America. LIBRARY OF CONGRESS

No freemen enjoyed a greater share of "British liberty" than the white colonists of North America. In prosperous America many men owned property, and monarchical and aristocratic institutions were weak. Nonetheless, only a minority of adults enjoyed full legal freedom. Gordon Wood estimates that as many as half the adult males in colonial America were slaves, indentured servants, or apprentices (*The Radicalism of the American Revolution,* pp. 50–55). Free women, bound to and dependent on their fathers or husbands, had far less liberty than their brothers, fathers, or sons.

Even among freemen in early America "liberty" had meanings different from those the word bore in the twentieth century. Most freemen at the time of the Revolution thought of liberty as a civic privilege that was vital to good government. This view was embedded in a political philosophy inspired by ancient Greece and Rome that historians have labeled "republicanism." As republicans, the patriots fought in 1776 for the right to participate in the state, not the right to do as one pleased. Republicans regarded liberty and law as inseparable. United they protected men against the menace of arbitrary power. Not all men qualified for republican liberty. Since liberty's essence was virtuous citizenship, it could be entrusted only to men of sufficient property and education to think for themselves. Similarly, for Puritans and many other Christians, "true liberty" meant, in the words of the English minister Jonathan Boucher, "a liberty to do everything that is right, and being restrained from doing any thing that is wrong" (Foner, *The Story of American Freedom*, p. 5).

The patriots supported the Revolution to secure this duty-bound species of liberty, but the liberty won in the Revolution rapidly changed. Alongside republican freedom, the natural-rights conception of liberty, elaborated first by English jurists and Locke, evolved into the political philosophy known as liberalism. If republicans thought first of men's public obligations, liberals thought first of individuals' private right to be free of restraint. Following Locke, the Massachusetts House of Representatives declared in 1762, "Freedom of Men under Government, is to have standing fundamental Rules to live by . . . ; a Liberty to follow my own will in all things where that Rules [*sic*] prescribes not, and not to be subject to the inconstant, uncertain, unknown arbitrary will of another Man" (Reid, *The Concept of Liberty*, p. 66). This expansive notion of liberty could serve the economic interests of market operators, the cultural interests of dissenters, and the political interests of citizens. Liberals moved away from the republican and Christian emphasis on freedom balanced by law and duty. Theirs was the liberty of laissez-faire and minimal government, of immunity from interference with private choice, and of the Bill of Rights.

Historians differ on the relative strengths of republican and liberal values following the Revolution. Some contend that the republican ideal of freedom was in retreat by the 1790s. Others insist that it remained robust well into the nineteenth century. But almost all agree that, before the Civil War, the liberal, legal-rights version of liberty had gained ascendancy in the thinking of most white men. Meanwhile freedom was catching; the people of the young Republic carried its spirit to all corners of the national culture. In a country whose founding document declared "all men are created equal," democratic aspirations led to the universal enfranchisement of white men. In a country swept by waves of Protestant perfectionism, reformers sought to liberate their fellow citizens from every kind of sin and error. In a country where fertile land beckoned settlers and opportunity beckoned entrepreneurs as in few other places on earth, men gravitated toward values that favored capitalist enterprise, including hostility to special privilege, suspicion of government, and free markets. In a country where establishments and traditions were weak and ambition and faith were strong, people developed habits of self-reliance that Alexis de Tocqueville, observing the Americans, called "individualism." Liberty as liberals conceived it, the right to go one's way without arbitrary interference, was the pivot and emblem of all these developments. "Liberty is the lesson," said the orator Edward Everett, "which we are appointed to teach" the world (Foner, *The Story of American Freedom*, p. 48).

It was a lesson that nineteenth-century Americans still needed to teach themselves. The mass enslavement of blacks decades after other nations had abolished slavery and the curtailment of free blacks' rights grotesquely contradicted the nation's professed principles. All women were excluded from politics and public affairs and were denied many legal rights. Middle-class women were confined by custom to a domestic "women's sphere." Native Americans, regarded by most whites as unassimilable savages, were hunted down and assigned to reservations. Catholics and Jews suffered under religious disabilities. Mormons were chased from their homeland and faced persecution when Manifest Destiny brought them once again under the Stars and Stripes. Class barriers, too, limited access to freedom by artisans and poor farmers, who were hurt by technological and economic change.

Hypocrisy, bigotry, and the love of power all went into the pattern of white Protestant men reserving liberty for themselves alone, but a double standard may have been another ingredient. Even as white men were shifting their allegiance to liberal principles, they continued to apply the standards of republicanism to women, men of color, and men who worked for wages. The argument was that these groups were ineligible for the freedom enjoyed by propertied white men because they lacked the economic independence, the education, the sound judgment, and thus the civic virtue required for disinterested citizenship.

For their part the unfree in nineteenth-century America demanded freedom as liberals defined it, but they also strove to demonstrate their civic virtue in the older republican style. An example is the abolitionist Frederick Douglass, whose 1845 autobiography emphasized his desire to assume the obligations as well as the rights of a freeman. No sooner had he escaped from slavery in Maryland, Douglass related, than he married, found useful employment, and joined antislavery societies. For him as for most black Americans, the path of freedom pointed not away from society and government but toward them.

Other groups, too, combined the languages of republicanism and liberalism in their quests for freedom. Thus feminist militants like Elizabeth Cady Stanton and Susan B. Anthony demanded the emancipation of women on terms of absolute equality with men, while feminist moderates justified women's freedom on grounds of their womanly aptitude for serving their families, their communities, and the state. At the fringes of feminism a handful of women and men decried the inequities of conventional marriage and called for "free love." Artisans and laborers protested exploitation by employers, which they called "wage slavery," on the strength of their virtuous lives and contributions to the commonwealth. The presence of real slavery in the United States sharpened the edge of white workers' campaigns to win protection for "free labor." For immigrant Catholics and Jews the meaning of American freedom centered on freedom of worship, which they sought to achieve by demonstrating their American patriotism.

Soldiers on both sides of the Civil War saw themselves as crusaders for liberty. In 1864 an English-born corporal from Ohio told his wife that he risked his life "not only for my Country and my Children but for Liberty all over the World . . . , for if Liberty should be crushed here, what hope would there be for the cause of Human Progress anywhere else?" (McPherson, *For Cause and Comrades*, p. 113). Union victory brought emancipation of the slaves and the establishment of equality before the law as indispensable to the freedom of all men. The Thirteenth, Fourteenth, and Fifteenth Amendments, the Civil Rights Acts of 1866 and 1875, and Reconstruction efforts to safeguard the citizenship of southern blacks represented the high-water mark of American commitment to the expansion of freedom in the nineteenth century.

The cause of universal freedom ebbed through the last third of the century, however, as reaction set in and prejudices reasserted themselves. By the 1880s blacks in the South were deprived of much that emancipation had promised them, including the right to vote, access to public accommodations, and prospects to acquire property. It was a measure of blacks' vulnerability that in the 1890s their foremost leader, the educator Booker T. Washington, counseled them to concentrate on the economic freedom they still had rather than fight for social and political rights they were losing. Women's drive for the vote achieved victories in a few western states but stalled in the rest of the country. Accelerating immigration provoked new waves of nativist, anti-Catholic, and anti-Semitic hostility among native-born Americans. Less tangibly, middle-class Americans felt their personal freedom shrinking as the country grew crowded, organized, and urbanized. A more settled America was losing the spirit of boundless possibilities that had fed experiments in reform and religion before the Civil War.

The most dramatic changes in attitudes about American freedom reflected intensifying class conflict in an economy that was creating huge inequities of wealth and power. On one hand, native-born men of property shrank their conception of liberty to the bedrock principles of freedom of contract, sound money, minimal government, and the right to vote. On the other hand, workers, farmers, and reformers enlarged their definition of liberty to include economic rights that only government could guarantee. Men of wealth and conservative principles won most of the battles before 1900. But struggles to expand liberty in the late nineteenth century laid the groundwork for victories—especially for women and workers but not yet for blacks—during the first decades of the next century.

See also **Abolition and Antislavery; Bill of Rights; Civil Rights; Constitutional Amendments; Emancipation; Liberalism; Republicanism; Women,** *subentry on* **Women's Rights.**

Bibliography

Appleby, Joyce. *Capitalism and a New Social Order: The Republican Vision of the 1790s.* New York: New York University Press, 1984.

Foner, Eric. *The Story of American Freedom.* New York: Norton, 1998.

Kammen, Michael. *Spheres of Liberty: Changing Perceptions of Liberty in American Culture.* Ithaca, N.Y.: Cornell University Press, 1989.

Konig, David Thomas, ed. *Devising Liberty: Preserving and Creating Freedom in the New American Republic.* Stanford, Calif.: Stanford University Press, 1995.

McPherson, James M. *For Cause and Comrades: Why Men Fought in the Civil War.* New York: Oxford University Press, 1997.

Reid, John Phillip. *The Concept of Liberty in the Age of the American Revolution.* Chicago: University of Chicago Press, 1988.

Watts, Stephen. *The Republic Reborn: War and the Making of Liberal America, 1790–1820.* Baltimore: Johns Hopkins University Press, 1987.

Wood, Gordon S. *The Radicalism of the American Revolution.* New York: Vintage, 1993.

EUGENE E. LEACH

LIBRARIES   The development of American libraries in the nineteenth century variously reflected the relative prosperity of an industrializing economy, westward migration and settlement, immigration, racial segregation in the South, and urbanization. By the end of the century American library services outside the South had developed a democratic model that few other countries could duplicate. In the late 1990s the U.S. library system achieved its high purpose of providing reference, research, entertainment, literary, and all types of educational materials to millions of readers on a generally equitable basis.

Private Libraries

Private libraries, often owned by members of the clergy or political elite, served for many years as the prime source of reading material in the thirteen colonies and early Republic. A number of these private collections eventually became the core of university or urban public libraries. As the economy expanded and towns grew in the first half of the nineteenth century, many colleges were founded. Few had large book collections or special library buildings. This led many students to form college society libraries, which usually contained collections of books, magazines, and newspapers and often were open longer hours than the university libraries.

Social libraries—essentially groups of people with a shared interest—flourished in the first half of the nineteenth century. Members joined for a fee and contributed money each year in order to purchase new materials. Some social libraries were established by sororal, fraternal, or vocational groups, such as sewing circles, lodges, and fire companies. By 1850 there were more than one thousand social libraries in New England alone. Although closed to the public, many social libraries held general collections, including romantic or popular fiction.

The circulating library was another type of reading group that grew rapidly during this period of increased immigration, urban growth, and lower book prices. These commercial libraries provided reading for a fee. In many ways more democratic than the subscription social libraries, the circulating libraries often allowed women to have books, featured reading rooms with long hours, and provided access to a variety of reading matter, including newspapers, popular pamphlets, and novels. To retain membership these libraries found it necessary to buy the materials their clients wanted. Commercial libraries grew rapidly due to increased literacy, the movement of people to the West, and the expanding U.S. economy.

Mercantile libraries were especially important, with the first established in New York City in 1820. They served the needs of the many young men moving into the cities, providing mechanics, clerks, and general readers with an opportunity to educate themselves in economic and other bodies of knowledge needed for their work. Mechanics' libraries often were paid for by wealthy philanthropists who sought to uplift and instruct the working-class poor, many of whom were recent immigrants. The hope of the

The Astor Library, New York City. The Astor Library was founded in 1861 by John Jacob Astor. The Astor Library, the Lenox Library, and the Tilden Trust combined in 1895 to form the New York Public Library. LIBRARY OF CONGRESS

economic elite and the emerging middle class was that supplying proper reading materials would encourage virtuous habits and improve technical work skills among the poor. Mercantile and Sunday School libraries in the early 1800s also concentrated on serving children and young people, no doubt increasing the national taste for reading as their young patrons grew to adulthood. Other private groups, such as the Women's Christian Temperance Union and the Young Men's Christian Association, provided library services to thousands later in the century.

Another kind of private library was the athenaeum; one in Boston began circulating books in 1826. Athenaeums used membership fees to buy books, pay lecturers, and maintain reading rooms. Although they essentially functioned as social libraries, athenaeums attracted many patrons interested in liberal learning and general culture and expanded the concept of libraries serving whole communities.

Public Libraries

The Peterborough, New Hampshire, library established in 1833 is considered the first modern, tax-supported public library in the United States. Along with the Boston Public Library, opened in 1854, Peterborough qualified as a genuine public institution: it had a collection funded by taxes or by personal gifts, was open to all citizens, and was managed as a public trust. In the last quarter of the nineteenth century, when municipal self-rule enabled cities to form public libraries without state legislation, the number of public libraries quickly grew. The western states greatly increased library services in this period. Women's clubs in many western communities collected books, provided librarians, and campaigned for library funding. More than 257 American public libraries had been formed by 1875. So rapid was their growth that by 1925 almost six thousand public libraries directly served 57 percent of the U.S. population.

The growth of the public library movement in the late nineteenth century was aided by the philanthropy of wealthy men who made their fortunes in the early industrial era. In New York City, John Jacob Astor's will provided for the establishment of the Astor Library in 1861, and James Lenox established the Lenox Library in 1870. Both institutions forbade public circulation of materials, and hours were short and access difficult. A third large bequest for a public library in New York City came from the Samuel J. Tilden Trust. In 1895 the Astor Library and the Lenox Library were merged with the Tilden Trust to create the New York Public Library. Under the direction of Josh Shaw Billings (1896–1913) the New York Public Library sought to serve public needs as well as research functions. In both areas it soon became a model for the world in its effort to provide free public access to reading materials of all kinds. The Newberry Library was founded as a privately endowed independent research library in 1887 in Chicago, supported by a bequest from Walter Loomis Newberry, an early Chicago businessman. The Newberry trustees created a reference and research library, rather than a circulating library, because the Chicago Public Library was already operational. William Frederick Poole, a highly respected senior librarian of the period, assumed direction of the collection until his death in 1894. His goal from the start was to build a collection for scholars. The Newberry first concentrated its major attention on the social sciences and the humanities, as well as on rare books and musical materials.

Much of the creation of public libraries in the last two decades of the nineteenth century was due to the contributions of Andrew Carnegie. Beginning in 1881 the steel magnate made the first of his many gifts linked to library service; he eventually donated more than $60 million to the cause. Typically the construction of a local public library building was funded by the Carnegie Foundation, but only after the local government approved funds to buy books, pay a library staff, and maintain the building and operations. Eventually 1,679 public libraries in 1,412 communities were built in the United States with Carnegie funds.

Once formed, U.S. public libraries also pioneered the formation of branch libraries. Following Boston's example, many large cities established branch libraries in the last two decades of the nineteenth century. These were created to allow people in areas outside the city center to have easier access to library materials. Often, popular reading materials were placed in branch libraries, with the more serious or technical resources remaining in the central building. The need for branch libraries was fed by spreading urbanization and by the tendency of American cities to develop areas separated and defined along economic and ethnic lines. Branch libraries often were shaped to appeal to the reading preferences of the emerging middle class, especially women's interests in romantic fiction and domestic topics. Also, branch collections often were built to provide literature that the middle class felt would best improve the education of new immigrants and properly shape their thinking, as well as influence urban children of all classes.

In 1890 Massachusetts passed the first major library extension act, which led to the establishment of the first state library agency. Many other states followed suit, providing extension services to adults and rural citizens, often in traveling libraries or book-wagons that also were designed to serve the special needs of the blind, young children, or disabled and aged citizens. Melvil Dewey, one of the leading American librarians and creator of the decimal system to catalog and classify reading materials, worked hard to popularize extension services for readers who could not travel easily to library buildings. Dewey often spoke of the need for public library services to function as a true "people's university."

In the nineteenth century the development of new universal classification systems greatly facilitated knowledge retrieval in the library. William Frederick Poole, a leading pioneer librarian, prepared the first general index to periodicals, published in 1848. The bibliographical form he created came to be a foundation of library service throughout the world. The Dewey Decimal Classification, published in 1876, was based on decimal notations that divided subjects from main classes to specific topics. The Library of Congress Classification, devised in 1898, replaced the decimal notation with a combined letter and number form, and left blank spaces for new subjects to develop. Both the Dewey Decimal and the Library of Congress classification systems enormously increased access to learning for millions of people.

The growing number of public libraries created a growing demand for trained librarians and the provision of formal library education. Dewey opened the first librarian's training program at Columbia College in New York City in 1887, with seventeen female and three male students. While most early librarians were male, the library profession quickly became feminized in the last decades of the nineteenth century, although men continued to head most of the major library collections. In 1888 Columbia protested against the predominance of female students in Dewey's school, prompting him to move it to the New York State Library in Albany. Many of Dewey's students went on to head the new library schools opening at the Pratt Institute, Drexel University, and the University of Illinois.

The last decades of the nineteenth century were marked by professionalization in many fields, including the feminized areas of social work and librarianship. The American Library Association was formed in 1876 and the *American Library Journal*, renamed the *Library Journal* in 1877, began publication in the same year. Professionalization of public librarians concentrated on standardizing cataloging and classification; on the role played by the librarian in establishing and maintaining elite and middle-class standards of good reading, especially in fiction; on the provision of library services to children; and on the Americanization of the large numbers of recent immigrants.

Whatever the goals articulated in professional rhetoric, however, in most cases and in most areas nineteenth-century public librarians provided the popular reading materials their public enjoyed most, and they served their clients very well. Even while encouraging the reading of the "best" material their public would accept, librarians understood the need to serve popular tastes and thus to justify continued tax support.

Library of Congress

In 1800 President John Adams approved a new law that appropriated $5,000 to purchase books to be used by Congress. Two years later, President Thomas Jefferson oversaw the implementation of legislation establishing the Library of Congress. The 1802 law made the appointment of the librarian of Congress a presidential responsibility and gave Congress the right to establish the new institution's rules.

President Jefferson, the principal founder of the Library of Congress, greatly influenced its structure and function. Jefferson believed a national library should do more than provide reference and research aid to Congress. He felt that to serve the people well a democratic legislature required information on all subjects. This rationale shaped the comprehensive collection policy of the library. Jefferson also held that the national legislative library should serve the information needs of all U.S. citizens. From the beginning the Library of Congress was open to the general public as well as to legislators and other government officials.

During the War of 1812 British troops invaded Washington in 1814 and burned the materials held in the new Library of Congress. Jefferson offered to sell his personal library of more than six thousand volumes to Congress to replenish the national library. His collection, perhaps the best private library in the nation, was purchased in 1815 after a close vote for about $24,000. The library reflected Jefferson's diverse interests in such subjects as science, literature, and geography and also included volumes in several languages. In 1851 another fire consumed two-thirds of the Library of Congress's collection, burning thirty-five thousand volumes in all.

Ainsworth Rand Spofford, appointed by President Abraham Lincoln, served as the librarian of Congress from 1864 to 1897. He is recognized as the individual who transformed the Library of Congress into an institution of genuine national and even international significance. Like Jefferson, Spofford strongly believed that the library should serve both the legislature and the general public. For him, the general welfare of a democracy required that information on all subjects be provided to all citizens. For more than

..

thirty years, Spofford worked to strengthen the legislative and educational functions of a great national library.

Spofford's enrichment of the Library of Congress's services included the acquisition of the Smithsonian Institution's entire library in 1866. The next year Congress purchased Peter Force's private library for $100,000. In 1870 copyright laws were revised to require deposit in the library of two copies of every work copyrighted in the United States, which greatly increased the number of holdings. A legislative appropriations act of 1897, supported by Spofford and the American Library Association, gave Congress responsibility for determining the regulations governing the Library of Congress and stipulated that the presidential appointment of the librarian of Congress be approved by the Senate. The library's expanding size and services required a larger physical space. After a twenty-six-year struggle to finance the construction of a larger building, Spofford presided over the 1897 opening of a new Library of Congress building on Capitol Hill. At the time, it was the largest library building in the world.

Spofford was succeeded as librarian by John Russell Young, a former journalist and diplomat. Young fully shared the Jeffersonian view of the proper role and operation of the nation's library. Young died after only eighteen months in office. During his short tenure, however, he faithfully followed the example set by Spofford, concentrating his best efforts on the acquisition of research materials from and about many other countries.

The first experienced librarian to be appointed librarian of Congress was Herbert Putnam, formerly the director of the Boston Public Library, in 1899. Under Putnam's direction the Library of Congress increased services to other libraries and to scholarly researchers. The development of sophisticated classification and cataloging systems served to systematize librarianship and knowledge collection and distribution. Putnam also encouraged the inauguration of interlibrary loans and the expansion of the library's foreign-language and research holdings. By the end of its first century the Library of Congress had established the major patterns of professional service that would mark this great national library through the century to come.

See also Cities and Urbanization; Clubs; Jeffersonian Era; Literacy and Reading Habits; Philanthropy.

Bibliography

Carpenter, Kenneth E. *Readers and Libraries: Toward a History of Libraries and Culture in America*. Center for the Book, no. 31. Washington, D.C.: Library of Congress, 1996.

Cole, John Y. *For Congress and the Nation: A Chronological History of the Library of Congress [through 1975]*. Washington, D.C.: Library of Congress, 1979.

Garrison, Dee. *Apostles of Culture: The Public Librarian and American Society, 1876–1920*. New York: Free Press, 1979.

Van Slyck, Abigail A. *Free to All: Carnegie Libraries and American Culture, 1890–1920*. Chicago: University of Chicago Press, 1995.

Wiegand, Wayne A. *The Politics of an Emerging Profession: The American Library Association*, 1876–1917. Westport, Conn.: Greenwood, 1986.

DEE GARRISON

LIFE CYCLE

[This entry includes three subentries: **Childhood and Adolescence**, **Adulthood**, and **Old Age**.]

CHILDHOOD AND ADOLESCENCE

Often labeled the "century of the child," the nineteenth century saw dramatic changes in America's definitions of childhood and adolescence. By the turn of the twentieth century, "modern" children bore little resemblance to their colonial predecessors. Both childhood and adolescence had become recognizable life stages that attracted considerable concern and attention. As revealed through demographic patterns, philosophical descriptions, and institutional and material realities, children and adolescents of the 1800s came to occupy a unique place in their families and in society.

The demographic transformation of the American family was central to the changes that occurred in nineteenth-century childhood and adolescence. At the start of the century, the average fertility rate for white women was 7.04; by 1850 it had fallen to 5.42, and by the end of the century it was 3.56. With the decline in fertility, the median age of Americans rose from 16.7 in 1820 to 22.9 in 1900. America's smaller families and declining proportion of children were, at first, the result of a decreasing amount of arable land; later, they reflected the changing realities of an increasingly industrial and urban world. By the end of the nineteenth century, therefore, children were surrounded by far fewer siblings. Furthermore, parents had begun to perceive their offspring as individuals who merited substantial commitments of adult time and resources.

This parental investment did not, however, bring about a decline in infant mortality. In the mid–nineteenth century, infant mortality remained relatively stable. (Not until 1920 was there a marked decline in childhood deaths.) In the early 1800s, children's deaths were seen as part of God's will. But as the century progressed, the liberalized Protestant belief system of the Second Great Awakening began to define such deaths as human faults to be overcome through progress and reform.

These demographic changes, along with new religious beliefs, contributed to a revolutionary transformation in the way children were perceived and treated. In contrast to the stern doctrines of the Puritans, adults no longer viewed children as sinful and evil, or as small adults who required harsh punishment and a "breaking of the will." Rather, romantic philosophies stressed the innocence of childhood and children's close relationship with God. In turn, adolescence was defined as a time of considerable peril as innocent children evolved into their adult selves. An adolescent's character, sexuality, and morals all needed to be strictly guarded and molded to assure he or she would not be corrupted by the wicked world.

By the mid–nineteenth century, scores of child-rearing books outlined the treacherous course awaiting children as they traveled from innocence to maturity. Advocates agreed that children and youth had special qualities that needed to be separated sharply from the adult world. Where once children were commended for acting like adults, and mixed readily at work and school with older individuals, by the end of the century, age mixing was far less acceptable. The young increasingly occupied a distinct world set off by their age and assumed capabilities.

The work experiences of the nineteenth-century child, therefore, differed considerably from colonial patterns. Children of the eighteenth century contributed to the family economy at an early age, and generally began to learn a trade or skill through apprenticeships at age twelve or thirteen. But the labor of children a century later was an issue of great debate. Although farm children might work alongside their parents by age seven or eight, children generally remained at home until age fifteen or sixteen. With the changing nature of the economy, the expectation no longer existed that they would simply follow the work of their parents; training came through a variety of new institutions. And, although children made up a considerable proportion of the labor force at many of the new nineteenth-century factories, their labor was often a cause for concern. Both in terms of depressing the wages of adults and in destroying their own youthfulness, their employment no longer seemed in keeping with their life stage. By the early twentieth century, child labor laws limited the acceptable age for labor and the hours children could work.

Educational ideals and realities also differed significantly from those in earlier centuries. A school's purpose was not only to teach, but to protect and socialize; ultimately teachers were responsible for molding their students' character and behavior. In the 1830s, school reformers such as Henry Barnard (1811–1900) began to argue that public education was important for all children. By the end of the nineteenth century, compulsory education for individuals age six to sixteen had been instituted, along with a graded curriculum based on chronological age. Reformers argued that children and adolescents could best be served in distinctive grades based on age and surrounded by their peers. The success of these changes was evident: while only 35 percent of all white American children age five to nineteen went to school in 1830, by 1870 the number had risen to over 60 percent.

By the second half of the nineteenth century, the notion that childhood was a unique and separate life stage with its own values and ideals was reflected in a number of innovations. Magazines, such as *Youth's Companion* and *Frank Leslie's Boy's and Girl's Weekly*, were written particularly for children or young adults; clubs, such as the YMCA, limited membership by chronological age. Toys, once shared by adults and children, now mirrored the belief that children required distinct, age-appropriate playthings. Juvenile courts, first established in 1899 in Illinois, separated young offenders from adult criminals. Moreover, the creation of pediatrics as a separate medical discipline in 1888 and the publication of *Adolescence* (1904) by G. Stanley Hall (1844–1924) provided medical and psychological evidence to support the notion that children and adolescents needed to be understood and treated by their own standards. By the beginning of the twentieth century, there seemed little doubt that children and adolescents were to occupy their own place in the world, based on an assessment of their own needs and characteristics.

While reformers stressed that childhood and adolescence was a unique phase in the life cycle, the realities of growing up in the nineteenth century differed considerably by race, gender, class, and region. Calls for mandatory schooling or removal from the labor market were clearly urban, middle-class ideals. For those in the rural West, childhood was markedly shorter than it was for their urban counterparts. Often taught in one-room schoolhouses, children generally attended classes (which were rarely separated by grade or learning ability) for only three months a year. In an agricultural society, their work remained essential to the support and productivity of the family. Similarly, immigrant children often left school at early ages to enter the labor market. Far more likely to be employed in their teens than native-born children, they remained a vital part of the family economy.

Race also affected the character of childhood. During the first half of the century the majority of African American children were slaves. The institution of slavery shaped the parameters of their existence. Masters—not parents—dictated the discipline of slave children, which included the very real threat that they would be permanently separated from their families. After slavery, some African American children were able to obtain formal education at Freedman's Bureau schools, or later at segregated institutions. The demands of sharecropping and tenant farming, however, dictated their continued labor. Even the nation's declining fertility rate was a statistical reality only for white women; although the numbers are unclear for African Americans, they appear to have experienced less of a decline in fertility. Like African Americans, Native American children were strongly affected by race and poverty. The rites of passage that traditionally marked white middle-class youths' entry into adulthood were copied by boarding schools for Native American children that attempted to divest them of their culture and acclimate them to an industrial world.

Nineteenth-century childhood was also influenced by gender. While boys were expected and trained to take part in the new industrial world, it was assumed that girls would become responsible for the home. As a result, children's education, toys, books, clubs, and training all reflected society's sharply segregated world.

Even accounting for these great variations, by the early twentieth century, American children were viewed, and behaved, far differently than their eighteenth-century predecessors. The dramatic transformation in the American economy and the resulting changes in the family established new patterns of behavior and expectations that transformed the colonial boy and girl into the modern child and adolescent.

See also **Education; Population; Republican Motherhood; Work,** *subentry on* **Child Labor.**

Bibliography

Bremner, Robert H., ed. *Children and Youth in America: A Documentary History*. Cambridge, Mass.: Harvard University Press, 1970–1974.

Chudacoff, Howard P. *How Old Are You?: Age Consciousness in American Culture*. Princeton, N.J.: Princeton University Press, 1989.

Clement, Priscilla Ferguson. *Growing Pains: Children in the Industrial Age, 1850–1890*. New York: Twayne, 1997.

Katz, Michael B. *The Irony of Early School Reform: Educational Innovation in Mid-Nineteenth-Century Massachusetts*. Cambridge, Mass.: Harvard University Press, 1968.

Kett, Joseph. "Adolescence and Youth in Nineteenth-Century America." In *The Family in History: Interdisciplinary Essays*. Edited by Theodore K. Rabb and Robert I. Rotberg. New York: Harper and Row, 1973.

Platt, Anthony M. *The Child Savers: The Invention of Delinquency*. 1969. 2d, enl. ed., Chicago: University of Chicago Press, 1977.

Wishy, Bernard. *The Child and the Republic: The Dawn of Modern American Child Nurture*. Philadelphia: University of Pennsylvania Press, 1968.

CAROLE HABER

ADULTHOOD

What did it mean to be an adult in the nineteenth century? Unlike other stages of life, adulthood, as a life stage, was rarely discussed in great detail; neither did distinctive age boundaries set off the middle years. While children and adolescents became the subject of much study, and the elderly were assumed to have become a problem requiring the attention of experts, few authorities specifically discussed what it meant to be an adult, even though both the demographic and ideological markers of adulthood underwent significant transformation. Affected by changing mortality rates, economic patterns, family structure, and cultural beliefs, the lives of nineteenth-century adults and the expectations for the life stage often differed significantly from those of their colonial predecessors.

Throughout the nineteenth century, an increasing proportion of individuals survived to the beginning of old age. Although the greatest changes in mortality rates affected those between birth and age five, throughout the century adults also experienced a significant decline in mortality. From 1840 to 1900, the percentage of the population surviving from age twenty to sixty rose from 59.6 to 73.7 percent. Even including children in the mortality figures, by 1900 a majority of the American population (56.5 percent) lived to age sixty. Moreover, with a significant decline in the number of children in the family—decreasing precipitously from an average of 7.04 in 1800 to 3.56 in 1900—the median age of the population rose throughout the century from 16.6 to 23.3.

Establishing Life Stages

It would be a mistake, however, to set these demographic markers as clearly denoting the beginning or the end of adulthood. In the first half of the century, chronological age itself did not play the important role it was to later attain, nor did numerous institu-

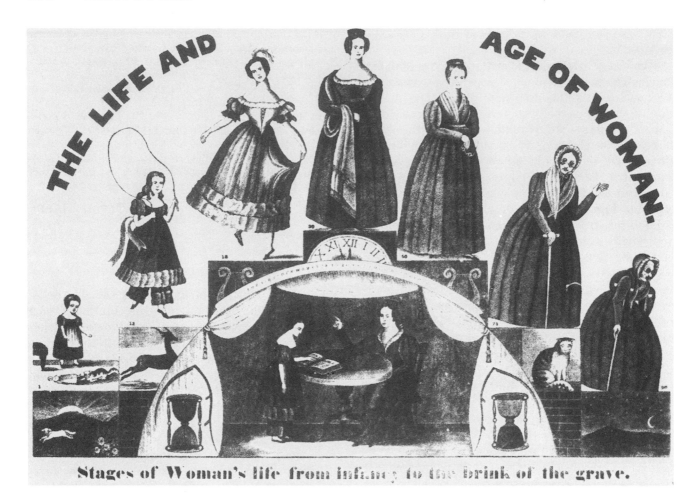

A Woman's Life Cycle. The idealized drawing denies the reality of many women's lives in the nineteenth century, for example, grueling work, sickness, and death from childbirth. LIBRARY OF CONGRESS

tional boundaries sharply define when one stage ended and the next began. In contrast to the established patterns of the twentieth century, the transitions to adulthood, marked by important role exits, such as ending school, leaving home, entering the labor force, marriage, and establishing a household, were often spread across a wide number of years and reflected a broad latitude of patterns. Depending on class, region, gender, and, most importantly, family conditions, the young entered adulthood with irregular patterns and at a variety of ages.

The transitions to adulthood—and their lack of clarity—were clearly affected by changes in the economy. In the first half of the nineteenth century, the decrease in arable land had a significant effect on the start of adulthood. Without access to valuable resources, children began to marry later and delayed establishing their own homes. In the second half of the nineteenth century, urban and industrial growth had a similar impact on adulthood. Required to make contributions to the family, or in need of a residence, aging children often lived for many years in a state of semi-dependence. In Philadelphia in 1880, for example, on average young men and women continued to reside at home for seven years after they entered the labor market. Despite the fact that they had left school, they did not establish their own homes or marry; they played a key role in the family economy.

Throughout much of the nineteenth century, the entry point to old age was also indistinct. The first pension plans were not established until the very end of the century; most workers in the labor force were not subject to a strict retirement requirement. The overwhelming majority of men remained heads of their households and in the labor market well into their sixties. Similarly, until the last decades of the nineteenth century, the empty-nest syndrome was a rare occurrence. Most families had children in their homes. For women, only widowhood clearly marked their status as an elderly individual.

Gender Roles Redefined

Yet while the economy often tended to blur the divisions between stages, it did serve to define the characteristics and behavior of adults. With industrialization, changes in work and family among whites divided age groups and produced distinctive qualities in men and women, as well as in their relationship to each other. With the separation of work and home, and the rise of the factory economy, adult middle- and upper-class men and women came to occupy "separate spheres," in which their dress, activities, and ideal adult qualities were clearly linked to their gender. For men, the notion of adulthood was based on the concept of work and wages. Taking men out of the home, the industrial revolution challenged the ties between fathers and their children. Sons no longer automatically followed their fathers' career nor did they regularly assume their names. Discarding the wigs and stockings of the eighteenth century, adult men acquired gender-specific attire that emphasized their distinctive roles as "breadwinners." Protectors of the home, they were to be noble, virile, just, and brave. Their central role was to acquire the economic resources necessary to provide for their families.

Similarly, in the nineteenth century, adult women were assumed to have social and biological qualities that allowed them to fulfill their "separate sphere." As concepts of marriage were transformed to emphasize the affection between two independent individuals, rather than an economic merger of households, the qualities a woman brought to the family became central to her nature. Characterized as pious, pure, domestic, and submissive, she became the keeper of the hearth, responsible for the care and upbringing of children.

These adult characteristics, however, were the ideal, rather than the reality, and depended strongly on class, race, and region. During slavery, African Americans had little of the autonomy that supposedly characterized adulthood. They generally had limited control over their marriage, children, or labor. In the plantation records and at sales, their adult status was simply linked to their ability to work as "full hands," while the young and old earned the status of "half" or "quarter" hands. Even after emancipation, the frequent references to adult men as "boys" underscored the racism that challenged their adult autonomy. Similarly, the adult life cycle of immigrants often differed from that of their native-born counterparts. Generally delaying the creation of the independent household, recent immigrants often lived in families in which one child gave up marriage entirely to support the aging parents. Nor were the ideal adult roles based on "separate spheres" always the reality. In the West, gender roles that supposedly divided adult men and women were often eclipsed as husband and wife worked together to survive.

By the beginning of the twentieth century, however, the lines separating adulthood from other life stages became far clearer. Chronological age assumed increasing importance. Schools, medical specialties, and industry all began to establish boundaries that separated the child from the adult, and the adult from the aged individual. With increasing regularity, individuals moved consciously from one stage to the next. In the century to come, the notion of adulthood as a unique stage defined by institutional and chronological limits would gain general acceptance.

See also **Class, Social; Domestic Life; Gender,** *subentry on* **Interpretations of Gender; Health Consciousness and Fitness; Industrialization and the Market; Race and Racial Thinking; Work,** *subentry on* **Middle-Class Occupations.**

Bibliography

Chudacoff, Howard P. "Newlyweds and Family Extension: The First Stage of the Family Cycle in Providence, Rhode Island." In Tamara Hareven and Maris A. Vinovskis, *Family and Population in Nineteenth-Century America.* Princeton, N.J.: Princeton University Press, 1978.

Degler, Carl N. *At Odds: Women and the Family in America from the Revolution to the Present.* New York: Oxford University Press, 1980.

Fischer, David Hackett. *Growing Old in America.* New York: Oxford University Press, 1977.

Haber, Carole, and Brian Gratton. *Old Age and the Search for Security.* Bloomington: Indiana University Press, 1994.

Hareven, Tamara, ed. *Transitions: The Family and the Life Course in Historical Perspective.* New York: Academic Press, 1978.

Modell, John, Frank Furstenberg Jr., and Theodore Hershberg. "Social Change and Transitions to Adulthood in Historical Perspective." In *The American Family in Social-Historical Perspective.* 2d ed. Edited by Michael Gordon. New York: St. Martin's Press, 1978.

Stearns, Peter N. *Be a Man! Males in Modern Society.* New York: Holmes and Meier, 1990.

Welter, Barbara. "The Cult of True Womanhood." In *The American Family in Social-Historical Perspective.* 2d ed. Edited by Michael Gordon. New York: St. Martin's Press, 1978.

CAROLE HABER

OLD AGE

Turning points in the history of old age do not neatly coincide with the beginning or the end of the nineteenth century. Ancient and postmodern humans would recognize many of the late-life experiences of older people in the 1800s. These continuities in the meanings and realities of old age are worth emphasizing. That said, it must quickly be added that several aspects of growing older associated with the late twentieth century began to take shape during the nineteenth century.

At least three universal concepts of aging merit consideration. First, throughout recorded history, humans have considered old age the last stage of the normal life course. Although there have been tremendous gains in life expectancy at birth, notably in the twentieth century, nineteenth-century Americans (like their forebears and their descendants) would have assumed that age sixty-five marked the onset of old age, give or take fifteen years. Hence, some would have stated that old age began at fifty, while others would have claimed it could be deferred until the ninth decade. Still others would have picked some benchmark between fifty and eighty. A few would have declared that no single age indicated the beginning of the end.

This thirty-year boundary defining old age is unique among life's stages, and it explains a second universal concept of aging: older people constitute a more diverse group than any other definable age group in the population. Childhood and adolescence, after all, are far briefer in duration. In the nineteenth century physicians attested to the elderly's heterogeneity in terms of their health status and mental capacities. Census takers reported a wide range of household relationships. There was a greater incidence of home ownership among senior citizens than among the middle-aged or youth. Native-born elders tended to be better off financially than those who migrated to the United States in middle age. Older men generally had more assets than older women. Some of the aged lived independently, while others experienced illnesses or reversals of fortune that forced them to rely on family members or neighbors for assistance. Many older people died as paupers (or at least intestate); others left fortunes at their death.

Old age's fuzzy boundaries not only explain the elderly's diverse socioeconomic circumstances; they also have given credence to a wide range of popular and scientific attitudes about old age. In the nineteenth century, everybody knew a few lucky souls like Daniel Boone (c. 1734–1820) who seemed blessed from childhood through ripe old age. By the same token, most families contained a disabled uncle or maiden aunt who had weathered crises at every life stage, surviving past the biblical three-score-and-ten only to endure the vicissitudes of old age (death of a spouse, chronic or acute ailments). Death attacked some elders gradually and stung others viciously. These varying experiences affected popular images of old age, as did people's associations (for good and ill) with their parents and other authority figures. The third universal concept of aging may be simply put: old age was perceived as a mixed bag.

In counterbalance to these three continuities, at least three changes in the meaning and experiences of old age occurred in the nineteenth century. First, although historians disagree as to when and how dramatically images of old age changed, Americans increasingly challenged every favorable notion about the elderly's worth that had been prevalent before the Revolutionary War. Doctors rejected Benjamin Rush's (1745–1813) notion that old age was caused by "natural decay." U.S. scientists embracing the latest theories and technologies from Europe offered proof that senility was pathological, perhaps even a disease that could not be cured. Furthermore, evidence that senectitude impaired mental faculties—the term "geezer" entered the American lexicon after the Civil War—undermined paeans to the wisdom and sagacity of late life. Finally, new industrial priorities devalued veterans' skills.

New conditions made the elderly vulnerable. As the agricultural sector of the economy shrank from 72 percent in 1820 to 42 percent by 1890, employment opportunities for those over age sixty-five diminished, although farming remained the primary occupation for nearly half of all older men. African Americans rarely reaped much from their labors, since they were reduced to sharecropping after being freed from slavery. Less than 10 percent of all elderly women in 1890 were gainfully employed; most of those earning incomes were in domestic or personal service. The growth in the percentage of older almshouse inmates (including those who went in later years as well as those who aged in place) and the increasing number of private old-age homes built by religious bodies and fraternal associations attest to the existence of old-age poverty. Most nineteenth-century reformers discounted the extent of the problem, however.

In one sphere older people mobilized their resources in order to demand recognition and assistance. The federal government grudgingly gave pensions and land to veterans of the Revolutionary War, the War of 1812, and the Mexican War. They waited as long as possible in order to reduce the numbers of survivors who might collect. Civil War veterans learned their lesson: they formed the Grand Army of the Republic to secure benefits that would ease concerns as they grew older. The federal government built national homes for disabled Union soldiers. In 1900 several thousand aging men were housed in the Dayton, Ohio, facility. (Many southern states fell deeper into debt, because the losers had to take care of their own widows and aging veterans.)

Significantly, the U.S. Congress did not grant Civil War pensions on account of age (setting sixty-two as the criterion) until 1907. Proof of advanced age sufficed; veterans did not have to demonstrate that they were disabled in order to qualify. Veterans' pensions were a gratuity given to a select subset of the population, not a right of age. Widows of soldiers and sailors often qualified, in due course, for pensions on the basis of their marital status. Yet the federal government refused to consider similar pensions for industry's superannuated workers or the elderly population as a whole. Germany, New Zealand, and Denmark may have developed assistance measures, and Great Britain enacted a pension plan in 1908. But developing old-age welfare measures was a matter for the states and the U.S. Congress to take up in the twentieth century.

See also **Death and Dying; Health and Disease; Veterans Organizations; Welfare and Charity.**

Bibliography

Achenbaum, W. Andrew. *Old Age in the New Land: The American Experience since 1790.* Baltimore: Johns Hopkins University Press, 1978.

Chudacoff, Howard P. *How Old Are You? Age Consciousness in American Culture.* Princeton, N.J.: Princeton University Press, 1989.

Cole, Thomas R. *The Journey of Life: A Cultural History of Aging in America.* New York: Cambridge University Press, 1992.

Haber, Carole. *Beyond Sixty-five: The Dilemma of Old Age in America's Past.* New York: Cambridge University Press, 1983.

Skocpol, Theda. *Protecting Soldiers and Mothers: The Political Origins of Social Policy in the United States.* Cambridge, Mass.: Belknap Press of Harvard University, 1992.

W. ANDREW ACHENBAUM

LINCOLN-DOUGLAS DEBATES On 16 June 1858 Illinois Republicans took the unusual step of declaring that, should their party secure control of the state house as a result of the fall elections, they would unite in selecting Abraham Lincoln as their choice to succeed the Democrat Stephen A. Douglas in the U.S. Senate. In following this procedure, Lincoln's supporters hoped to head off any efforts to derail Lincoln's political ambitions, which had been frustrated in 1855, when defections had cost him a Senate seat. They also aimed to discourage efforts by some eastern Republicans, led by the newspaper editor Horace Greeley, to unite behind Douglas as a way to worsen current divisions in the Democratic Party. The following month Douglas and Lincoln addressed crowds in Chicago on successive nights. Lincoln decided to follow Douglas wherever he went, rising at the conclusion of the senator's remarks to inform those assembled that he would offer a reply that evening or the next day. This tactic produced mixed results and drew criticism from Democratic newspapers, whereupon Lincoln decided to challenge

Douglas to a series of debates. The senator agreed to a series of seven joint appearances, each to take place in a congressional district where the two men had not already appeared, thus excluding Chicago and Springfield.

In a span of two months the two men engaged each other at Ottawa (21 August), Freeport (27 August), Jonesboro (15 September), Charleston (18 September), Galesburg (7 October), Quincy (13 October), and Alton (15 October). These widely reported encounters proved the highlight of the political contest, although both candidates crisscrossed the state in an effort to win votes. At each stop Douglas accused Lincoln of favoring racial equality and asserted that the Republican opposition to slavery would disrupt the Union. After a dismal performance at Ottawa, Lincoln looked to turn the tide at Freeport, where he asked a series of questions designed to demonstrate that, in light of the Supreme Court's ruling in *Dred Scott v. Sandford* (1857), Douglas could offer no program to stop slavery's expansion. In response Douglas recited what he had long before stated, that the people of a territory could render slavery's expansion unlikely by failing to pass legislation to enforce it. He thereby alerted southern Democrats to the notion that perhaps he was not safe on the issue of slavery. Because the Republican candidate was laboring to prove that Douglas was part of a larger conspiracy to provide for slavery's expansion, it was risky for him to highlight this divergence. In response to Douglas's charges that he favored racial equality, Lincoln drew distinctions between biological, political, social, and legal equality. At the same time he asserted his beliefs in the fundamental humanity and thus equality of blacks and the immorality of slavery, although some of these statements have been used to illustrate his racial attitudes.

In time people referred to these exchanges as political debate of the highest order, but in fact both men resorted to dubious tactics, negative campaigning, and shaky defenses of their own positions. On 2 November, Illinois voters chose a state legislature in which Douglas prevailed when it selected a senator the following January. However, the Republicans claimed a slim plurality of the statewide vote. Even in defeat, however, Lincoln built his political reputation with an eye toward future races. Douglas's answers at Freeport rendered him suspect in the eyes of southern Democrats, damaging his chances to capture a united Democratic Party's nomination for president in 1860.

See also **Democratic Party; Elections; Orators and Oratory; Republican Party; Slavery,** *subentry on* **Defense of Slavery.**

Bibliography

Jaffa, Harry V. *Crisis of the House Divided: An Interpretation of the Issues in the Lincoln-Douglas Debates.* Chicago: University of Chicago Press, 1982.

Johannsen, Robert W., ed. *The Lincoln-Douglas Debates of 1858.* New York: Oxford University Press, 1965.

Zarefsky, David. *Lincoln, Douglas, and Slavery: In the Crucible of Public Debate.* Chicago: University of Chicago Press, 1990.

BROOKS D. SIMPSON

LITERACY AND READING HABITS

Literacy can be defined as the ability to decode and understand written language at a rudimentary level. Literacy rates for the nineteenth-century United States are challenging to assess, but it is generally agreed that the ability to sign a document—such as a will—was roughly correlated with reading ability during these years. Will-signing and other indicators suggest that access to literacy after the American Revolution expanded rapidly but unevenly. Other evidence shows that reading materials and reading habits were segmented and commercialized over the course of the nineteenth century. Taken together, these patterns indicate that expanded literacy in nineteenth-century America can be viewed as a liberating force, a constraining force, or a combination of the two.

Literacy and Social Groups

The principal organs of teaching and learning literacy in the nineteenth century were family, church, and school. Access to literacy was dictated by social class, gender, ethnicity, race, and geographic location. Schools overtook the family and the church as the primary source for literacy instruction during the second half of the century.

Just after the Revolution, 90 percent of white males were able to sign their own names to documents, due in large measure to the Protestant doctrine that individuals should be able to read scripture in order to seek salvation. The gap in literacy rates between white men and women started to close as women began to be seen as the primary instructors of their children. Women would have to be able to read and understand the Bible themselves in order to effectively teach others. By 1850 the literacy rates of white men and women, as reported to the U.S. Census, were almost equal.

The largest gaps in literacy rates in the nineteenth century were between whites, foreign-born whites, and nonwhites; there were regional, income, and urban-rural differences as well. Over the course of the cen-

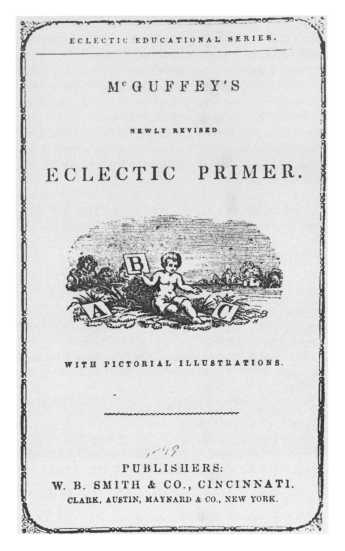

Learning the ABC's. Cover, *McGuffey's Newly Revised Eclectic Primer with Pictorial Illustrations,* 1849. At the time of this printing, men and women had attained almost equal literacy. LIBRARY OF CONGRESS

tury, white illiteracy declined from 10.7 percent in 1850 to 6.2 percent in 1900. Only 4.6 percent of native-born whites admitted illiteracy in 1900, while 12.9 percent of foreign-born whites did. The reported illiteracy rate among nonwhites in 1900 was 44.5 percent.

Literacy was generally withheld from slaves, and most slave states prohibited anyone, including owners, from teaching slaves to read or write. Most masters believed that keeping slaves ignorant was vital to keeping them dependent and tractable. Nevertheless, in spite of legal prohibitions and general fears about slave literacy, some masters taught a few prized slaves basic skills. Moreover, a few slaves learned to read on their own or were taught by other slaves. Literacy was particularly dangerous to the slave system because literate slaves could write out passes and forge other documents that they might use to gain freedom. Thus, white southerners prevented enslaved African Americans from learning to read and write at the same time that literacy for the white masses was being promoted in other parts of the United States as a necessary and positive development. When Lincoln proclaimed the emancipation of the slaves, roughly 10 percent of them were already literate, however, and schools for freed men, women, and children proliferated during Reconstruction.

Immigrant illiteracy rates in their native languages were much higher at the end of the nineteenth century than they would be later, chiefly because so many immigrants came from countries where educational standards were low. Literacy in English was generally not withheld from immigrants willfully, as it was in the case of slaves, but it was sometimes not readily available. Learning to read was often a key to assimilation for immigrants, and by the turn of the century assistance efforts had taken the form primarily of common schooling and instruction in settlement houses. Literacy instruction was the site for the often emotional tug-of-war between various subcultures and the mainstream culture in the increasingly pluralistic United States. No confrontation was more embattled than the one between the U.S. government and a number of Native American tribes, since the government sought to "civilize" Native American children and adults by forcing them to read and write in English.

Reading Matter

By the mid–nineteenth century there was a significant explosion in the availability of print matter, sparked by changing papermaking and printing technology and fueled by rapidly growing increases in literacy rates. A class-segmented reading populace made for differentiated reading habits, and the second half of the nineteenth century saw the publication of many more books, magazines, and newspapers expressly targeted for particular groups of readers. Women of the upper class, for example, were believed to prefer sentimental novels, and records from reading groups and libraries support this assumption. What women took from this reading is less clear. Often sentimental novels reinforced conventional norms about gender, class, and other topics, but sometimes they conveyed subversive messages that contradicted those promoted in school and church texts. Magazine publishers joined book producers in targeting lowbrow as well as highbrow tastes during these years, publishing *Argosy* magazine and dime novels for lowbrow readers, in addition to *Century*

magazine and elegant books of poetry for highbrow readers.

Nineteenth-century producers of books, magazines, and newspapers therefore wielded significant power by controlling available reading materials and commercializing the content of magazines and newspapers. But readers and groups of readers had the power to choose or reject print matter and to judge and interpret its content. Their tastes helped to shape print culture, and they created their own meaning through what they read and wrote.

Conclusion

The extent to which English-language literacy is a liberating or constraining force is an open question that depends on time, place, and the readers and writers involved. For African Americans, literacy seemed to be largely a liberating tool in the nineteenth century, enabling them to dismantle some of the constructs of slavery. For Native Americans, literacy in English was primarily a tool of coercive assimilation by whites, used to strip them of their culture and to substitute another. On the other hand, the creation of an alphabet for the Cherokee and native Hawaiian languages allowed for the preservation of those cultures and for books, papers, and legal documents written in these languages. For many immigrants the experience was mixed: literacy was the route to advancement in their new country, but adopting the English language often forced them to leave behind key features of their cultural heritage. The ability to read and write was an insufficient but necessary condition for maintaining and improving upon one's status. Despite the barriers to education encountered by many in America, access to literacy was fundamental to growing, furthering, and sustaining democracy in the nineteenth-century United States.

See also **Book Publishing; Education,** *subentries on* **Elementary and Secondary Schools, Education of Girls and Women, Education of African Americans, Indian Schools; Language; Literature,** *subentry on* **Women's Literature.**

Bibliography

Cornelius, Janet Duitsman. *"When I Can Read My Title Clear": Literacy, Slavery, and Religion in the Antebellum South.* Charleston: University of South Carolina Press, 1991.

Davidson, Cathy N., ed. *Reading in America: Literature and Social History.* Baltimore: Johns Hopkins University Press, 1989.

Kaestle, Carl F., et al. *Literacy in the United States: Readers and Reading since 1880.* New Haven, Conn.: Yale University Press, 1991.

Radway, Janice A. *Reading the Romance: Women, Patriarchy, and Popular Literature*. Chapel Hill: University of North Carolina Press, 1984.

HELEN DAMON-MOORE

LITERATURE

[This entry includes seven subentries:
Fiction
The Essay
Poetry
Children's Literature
Women's Literature
African American Literature
The Influence of Foreign Literature.]

FICTION

In 1790 the U.S. Congress passed the Federal Copyright Act, granting copyright protection for a period of fourteen years to American authors or their publishers. This act was an explicit effort to establish a national literature. Congress, however, did not anticipate the rise of the American novel. Indeed, at the start of the nineteenth century, fiction was held in contempt by the country's cultural and political elite. Nevertheless, between 1789 and 1820, ninety works of fiction by American authors were issued by U.S. publishers. In most cases, the authors had sold the rights to their works to printers who not only manufactured the books, but also performed the tasks of publishers and marketers.

Creating a National Literature

Prior to 1820, the American fiction industry was intensely localized and small-scale. Northeastern printer-publishers from the revolutionary period typically printed five hundred to fifteen hundred copies of a novel; few publishers risked producing more than one work of fiction in their entire career. Inadequacies in the transportation system and the availability of cheaper British publications limited sales of American fiction. But while the hundreds of British fiction titles outsold American works, they also helped to foster an American market for fiction. In 1891, Congress passed an International Copyright Act that protected American authors abroad and stopped the flood of cheap English reprints onto the U.S. market.

Charles Brockden Brown (1771–1810) was one of the first American novelists to try to make a profession out of writing, although he was ready to give up the effort by 1800. His major works of fiction, including *Wieland; or, The Transformation* (1798) and *Edgar Huntly; or, Memoirs of a Sleep-Walker* (1799), sold only a few hundred copies, and Brown wrote despairingly of the poverty that accompanied fiction writing. Taken in isolation, Brown's experiences suggest there was no place for fiction in the early Republic. But the success of *Charlotte Temple* (1791) by Susanna Rowson (1762–1824) tells a different story. The first American "best-seller," Rowson's novel (originally published as *Charlotte, a Tale of Truth*) describes the seduction and tragic betrayal of a young woman by an eloquent soldier. By 1810 nearly forty thousand copies of *Charlotte Temple* had been sold, and subsequent editions continued to sell well throughout the century. Rowson's novel exemplifies the most popular fictional genre in the early Republic: the "sentimental" novel, or novel of seduction.

Because it was the first work of fiction to be written by an American, published by an American, and set in the postrevolutionary United States, *The Power of Sympathy* (1789) by William Hill Brown (1765–1793) is regarded as the first American novel. Like *The Coquette* (1797) by Hannah Webster Foster (1759–1840), *The Power of Sympathy* owes a great deal to the epistolary novels *Pamela* (1740) and *Clarissa* (1747–1748) by the English author Samuel Richardson (1689–1761). Recently, scholars have drawn attention to the metaphorical correspondences between these seduction novels and the revolutionary discourse of the late eighteenth century: radical political ideas were said to seduce naive Americans, Britain was depicted as a cruel parent, and the youth of independent America were warned against the fanciful attractions of European luxury.

America's early sentimental novels inaugurated a rich tradition of fiction written by and for women. In the postrevolutionary United States, women with more and more time and money to spend on commodities became the target of book and magazine publishers. Fiction written for women far outsold any other kind of fiction in the United States until at least 1870. Some of these popular works and authors include *Hope Leslie* (1827) by Catharine Maria Sedgwick (1789–1867); *Ruth Hall* (1855) by Fanny Fern, the pen name of Sara Payson Willis (1811–1872); *The Lamplighter* (1854) by Maria Cummins (1827–1866); *The Wide, Wide World* (1850) by Susan B. Warner (1819–1885); *Uncle Tom's Cabin* (1852) by Harriet Beecher Stowe (1811–1896); and *Little Women* (1868) by Louisa May Alcott (1832–1888). Warner's tale of the trials and triumphs of an orphan girl brought tears to the eyes of thousands of readers and outsold any previous work of fiction by an American author. Ultimately, more than 500,000 copies of *The Wide, Wide World* were sold in the United States. *Uncle*

Tom's Cabin was one of the most popular books in English in the nineteenth century: over 500,000 copies had been sold by 1857, and the book continued to sell at the rate of 1,000 copies per week six years after its initial publication in Washington's *National Era* magazine.

Irving, Cooper, and Hawthorne

The first American fiction writer to earn critical acclaim internationally was Washington Irving (1783–1859), whose *The Sketch Book* (1819–1820) became an instant transatlantic sensation. For the first time, an American writer could begin to think about living off the proceeds from works of fiction. At the same time, the enormous success of *Waverley* (1814) by Sir Walter Scott (1771–1832) had made reading fiction more respectable in both England and the United States. In 1821 James Fenimore Cooper (1789–1851) met the popular demand for an "American Scott"

The Deerslayer. James Fenimore Cooper wrote *The Deerslayer* (1841) as well as *The Last of the Mohicans* and *The Prairie,* among many other works. LIBRARY OF CONGRESS

when he published *The Spy,* a novel set in New York during the Revolutionary War. Cooper was not only an energetic novelist, he also was unabashedly patriotic. While his first novel, *Precaution* (1820), consciously mimicked the works of Jane Austen (1775–1817), Cooper's subsequent books stressed uniquely American and masculine themes. He implicitly condemned Irving's fawningly nostalgic sketches of English life and stylistic indebtedness to English standards. In his Leatherstocking Tales, including *The Pioneers* (1823) and *The Last of the Mohicans* (1826), Cooper told the story of Natty Bumppo, a white American raised by Indians who is only at home on the edges of the young nation. While Irving's short stories and sketches were admired at home and abroad, Cooper's works earned popular acclaim by combining the stock ingredients of sensational fiction (Indians, war, romance, the wilderness, treachery, and heroic sacrifice) with geographical and historical settings that contributed to the patriotic mythologization of the United States. On the day *The Pioneers* was published, thirty-five hundred copies were sold in New York by noon. Throughout the 1820s Cooper earned an average of $6,500 a year for his writing—a princely sum at the time.

One result of Cooper's success was the expansion of a market for historical romances about America. This demand was met by, among others, Lydia Maria Child (1802–1880), whose works included *Hobomok* (1824) and *The Rebels; or, Boston before the Revolution* (1825); Catharine Maria Sedgwick, whose *Hope Leslie* (1827) was ranked with Cooper's novels by contemporary commentators; and, in the 1830s William Gilmore Simms (1806–1870), the author of *Guy Rivers* (1834) and *The Yemassee* (1835). In the aftermath of Cooper's and Sedgwick's successes, in the 1830s Nathaniel Hawthorne (1804–1864) began mining historical records in New England for material for the fiction he would publish over the next three decades. The fiction of the 1820s and 1830s demonstrates the extent to which comfortably independent Americans felt the need to scrutinize their unique past.

From 1820 through the economic crash of 1837, the amount of American fiction published increased every year. The development of stereotyping (a printing process that allows multiple copies to be printed at once) and improvements in papermaking and bookbinding helped to lower production costs. Also, the completion of the Erie Canal in 1825 helped to extend the market westward for all kinds of publications. An expanding U.S. postal system and cheap "newspaper" rates helped fuel the continual rise in the popularity of magazines. For many Americans, periodicals were their primary source of American fiction. The historian Frank Luther Mott (1886–1964)

Washington Irving (1783–1859). Irving, a chronicler of New York in his humorous *Knickerbocker's History of New York*, is best known for *The Sketch Book* and *Bracebridge Hall*. Photograph by Matthew Brady, c. 1861. LIBRARY OF CONGRESS

claims that while five magazines were published in the United States in 1794, the number had jumped to one hundred in 1825 and to almost six hundred in 1850. *Godey's Lady's Book,* one of many periodicals aimed directly at women, reached a circulation of 50,000 by 1850. By 1860 the *New York Ledger* was the most popular literary weekly in America, with a subscription list of 400,000. The *Ledger's* success owed much to its serialized, popular fiction written by extraordinarily prolific, and usually anonymous, men and women.

In the early 1830s, Hawthorne published his first works of fiction in magazines like the Salem *Gazette* and the Boston *Token* (an annual collection of tales, verse, and illustrations aimed at women readers and sometimes referred to as a "giftbook" or "keepsake"). By 1837, Hawthorne had published nearly fifty items in various periodicals, but had not found a publisher for the books he believed would secure him lasting fame. Financial help from a friend finally allowed Hawthorne to publish nineteen of his stories in book form. *Twice-Told Tales* (1837) did not sell particularly well, but it introduced his name to a growing circle of influential American literary reviewers and publishers. Men like Henry Wadsworth Longfellow (1807–1882) and the brothers Evert Duyckinck (1816–1878) and George Duyckinck (1823–1863) were beginning to establish critical authority in the United States. With their support, it became possible for someone like Hawthorne to move from the role of an underpaid writer of anonymous short pieces to the culturally, if not financially, superior position of a literary man. George Duyckinck, one of the strongest advocates for a unique and powerful American literature, was the general editor of the Library of American Books series published by Wiley and Putnam. This series included *Tales of the Grotesque and Arabesque* (1840) and *The Raven and Other Poems* (1845) by Edgar Allan Poe (1809–1849), *Typee* (1846) by Herman Melville (1819–1891), and *Mosses from an Old Manse* (1846) by Hawthorne. Under Duyckinck's guidance, the series established a bold, new American literature free of the dominating influences of Irving, Cooper, and their British contemporaries. Hawthorne did not achieve popular acclaim, however, until the publication of *The Scarlet Letter* (1850). He tried to capitalize on the book's success by reprinting his earlier collections of tales and by quickly completing two more novels: *The House of the Seven Gables* (1851) and *The Blithedale Romance* (1852). In the meantime, however, Hawthorne watched in dismay as a host of other books met with comparatively vast popular success. (Hawthorne's total lifetime earnings from *The Scarlet Letter* were $1,500; Susan Warner's *The Wide, Wide World* earned royalties of $4,500 in 1853 alone.)

The Dime Novel and Magazine Fiction

One of the most phenomenal publishing successes of the 1840s was *Quaker City* (1844) by George Lippard (1822–1854), which originally was published as a series of pamphlets entitled *The Monks of Monk Hall* (1844). This novel about crime and deprivation in Philadelphia sold 48,000 copies in three months and by 1850 Lippard had issued twenty-seven editions, running from 1,000 to 4,000 copies each. Other examples of sensational, urban pamphlet fiction include *City Crimes; or, Life in New York and Boston* (1849) by George Thompson and the temperance story *Ten Nights in a Barroom and What I Saw There* (1854) by Timothy Shay Arthur (1809–1885). The audience created by such fiction paved the way for the success of the dime novel. From 1860 to the end of the century, the dime novel remained the most popular form of fiction among American readers. The preeminent publishing house in this market was that of Erastus Beadle (1821–1894) and Irwin Beadle of New York. In their first four years of publication, Beadle's Dime Novels sold more than five million copies. These "dollar books for a dime" were published every fortnight and were written by anonymous or pseudonymous professionals who churned out formulaic tales of suspense, crime, and adventure that sported dramatic cover illustrations. Although the first recognized dime novel, *Malaeska: The Indian Wife of the White Hunter* (1860), was written by a woman, Ann S. Stephens (1813–1886), dime novels established a markedly masculine profile in their standard subject matter. Advertisements appealed to "travellers, soldiers, sailors, brakemen on the railroads and hunters in camp."

The major nineteenth-century figure most associated with magazine fiction is Edgar Allan Poe. Financial necessity, as well as a predilection for popular subject matter, led Poe into the world of periodical publication in the early 1830s. Poe published stories in *Burton's Gentleman's Magazine,* the *Broadway Journal,* and *Godey's Lady's Book;* held editing positions at the *Southern Literary Messenger* in Richmond, Virginia, and *Graham's Magazine* in Philadelphia; and dreamed of founding his own American literary journal. Poe grew up in Richmond, and, like his southern contemporaries John Pendleton Kennedy (1795–1870) of Maryland and William Gilmore Simms of South Carolina, he was forced into cultivating a northern audience even as he maintained a tense relationship with the North's literary establishment. The South did not have the commercial infrastructure to support a specifically southern literary economy.

Despite his remarkable sense of aesthetic value, Poe continued to write for a popular audience, although he did not always succeed in capturing their attention. His one attempt at a longer piece of fiction, *The Narrative of Arthur Gordon Pym, of Nantucket* (1838), failed to bring sufficient financial rewards to support him as a full-time novelist. Between 1838 and 1846, Poe published some of the most consistently read pieces of short fiction in the American canon: "The Fall of the House of Usher" (1839), "William Wilson" (1839), "The Black Cat" (1843), "The Tell-Tale Heart" (1843), "The Pit and the Pendulum" (1843), "The Purloined Letter" (1845), and "The Cask of Amontillado" (1846).

Herman Melville

The most aesthetically and philosophically challenging American fiction of the nineteenth century was written by Herman Melville. His first book, *Typee*

(1846), was ostensibly nonfiction, presented as the account of "Four Months' Residence among the Natives of a Valley of the Marquesas Islands" by a "simple seaman." It was clear to Washington Irving and others that *Typee* was the work of a powerful writer, and thus the narrative was republished in the Library of American Books series. The sequel, entitled *Omoo* (1847) for a Polynesian word for "wanderer," was sufficiently well received to enable Melville to move to Manhattan and pursue a career as a professional author. *Mardi* (1849) took more philosophical detours and was less successful, but Melville followed up with two popular books written in one five-month period: *Redburn: His First Voyage* (1849) and *White-Jacket; or, The World in a Man-of-War* (1850). In a letter to his father-in-law, Melville dismissed these novels as "*jobs,* which I have done for money—being forced to it, as other men are to sawing wood." In early 1850 he began work on *Moby-Dick* (1851), a book that he said would tell both the "truth" and the "poetry" of the whaling industry. The novel was a popular failure (many reviewers found it puzzling and readers were disappointed by the digressions), but it later was hailed as one of America's great literary masterpieces. Between 1853 and 1856, Melville supported his family by publishing fourteen tales and sketches in magazines like *Putnam's* and *Harper's,* including "Bartleby, the Scrivener" (1856), "Benito Cereno" (1856), and the serialized novel *Israel Potter* (1855).

African American Literature

In 1845 the American Anti-Slavery Society of Boston published the *Narrative of the Life of Frederick Douglass, an American Slave, Written by Himself.* Although Douglass (1817–1895) wrote his autobiography primarily for abolitionist purposes, he adopted literary modes that became increasingly characteristic of American fiction in the second half of the nineteenth century. In the interests of authenticity, Douglass's story cultivates a simple—though never naive—narrative voice. It recounts a slave boy's struggles for education and freedom, and along the way provides portraits of American types from various backgrounds. Douglass's slave narrative thus incorporates some basic ingredients of the most celebrated novel of the second half of the nineteenth century: *Adventures of Huckleberry Finn* (1884) by Mark Twain (1835–1910). The small quantity of fiction by African Americans in the nineteenth century includes *Clotel; or, The President's Daughter: A Narrative of Slave Life in the United States* (1853) by William Wells Brown (1814–1884); *Our Nig* (1859) by Harriet E. Wilson (c. 1827–?); and *Iola Leroy* (1892) by Frances Ellen Watkins Harper (1825–1911). All of these books draw on the experiences of slavery and the quest for freedom for their literary force.

Realism and Naturalism after the Civil War

In his 1879 study of Nathaniel Hawthorne, Henry James (1843–1916) argued that Americans had been changed radically by the experience of the Civil War. "It introduced into the national consciousness," he wrote, "a certain sense of proportion and relation, of the world being a more complicated place than it had hitherto seemed, the future more treacherous, success more difficult." The war certainly had profound effects on the nation's infrastructure. The completion of the Union Pacific and other railroads radically expanded the market for fiction and allowed other areas of the country to enter the publishing circuit. The war stimulated investment in manufacturing, and steelmaking became a dominant industry. As the size of corporations grew, so did the number of factory hands working for low wages in large manufacturing centers. Technical improvements in printing, the lower cost of paper, and the rise in the number of large national corporations looking for advertising outlets fueled the growth of the periodical industry from seven hundred to more than six thousand titles between 1865 and 1905. Meanwhile, the doubling of the U.S. population between 1860 and 1890, with especially rapid urban growth, resulted in a substantially bigger reading market.

These transformations affected the kinds of fiction being written in the post–Civil War period. The growing discontent among the country's industrial labor force found expression in realist fiction, the genre that dominated literary experimentation in the second half of the nineteenth century. "Life in the Iron Mills" (1861) by Rebecca Harding Davis (1831–1910) is an early example of this work; it examines what some were calling wage slavery, in this case among iron workers in Wheeling, Virginia. One of the distinctive features of Davis's narrative is its summons to educated readers to observe, in an almost scientific fashion, the contours and consequences of a particular social structure. In this respect, Davis's story anticipates the significant influence of the social sciences on the evolution of American fiction (the American Social Science Association was founded in 1865).

A more explicitly reformist perspective informs *Looking Backward: 2000–1887* (1888) by Edward Bellamy (1850–1898), which attacks industrial capitalism's dark consequences while imagining a utopian society at the end of the twentieth century. Stephen Crane (1871–1900) made the city and its squalor the subject of some of his most powerful works of fiction, including *An Experiment in Misery* (1893) and *Maggie: A Girl of the Streets* (1893). *The Octopus* (1901) by Frank Norris (1870–1902) dramatizes the conflict between California wheat farmers and the railroad. The stories in *Main-Travelled Roads* (1891) by Hamlin Garland (1860–1940) tell of the harsh life of midwestern farmers in the latter part of the nineteenth century. Crane and Norris often are referred to as practitioners of naturalism—an intensified realism that unsentimentally portrays the Darwinian struggle to survive in the technological and economic dystopia of late-nineteenth-century America. This fiction shows the influence of the French novelist Émile Zola (1840–1902), and culminated in *Sister Carrie* (1900) by Theodore Dreiser (1871–1945). Dreiser's novel disturbed contemporary readers with its determination to present modern urban crimes and transgressions under a harsh but insistently amoral light. The experiences of some of the ten million immigrants who came to the United States between 1880 and 1900 were recorded in *Yekl: A Tale of the New York Ghetto* (1896), Abraham Cahan's (1860–1951) stories of Jewish immigrant life in New York City.

As part of the expansion of the social sciences in the 1880s, the American Folklore Society, a white liberal movement, started gathering examples of black oral culture from the South. This material constituted a previously unrecognized tradition of American fiction, a tradition that was first explored by the African American writer Charles Chesnutt (1858–1932). Chesnutt's "The Goophered Grapevine" first appeared in the *Atlantic Monthly* in 1887, and became the first story in the collection *The Conjure Woman* (1899). Chesnutt deployed a structural device made popular by Joel Chandler Harris (1848–1908) in his "Uncle Remus" stories of the 1880s, which have an older African American relating plantation stories to a younger white audience. One of the first attempts to collect and translate another American tradition of fiction, the vast body of Native American oral mythology, was *Old Indian Legends* (1901) by Gertrude Bonnin, also known as Zitkala-Ša (1876–1938).

Howells, Twain, and Regional Fiction

The realist imperative at work in much of American fiction from 1861 on found its most influential champion in William Dean Howells (1837–1920). Born in Ohio, Howells eventually moved to Boston where, as editor, he turned the *Atlantic Monthly* into the most important literary magazine of its day. Howells promoted the European realist fiction of George Eliot (1819–1880), Leo Tolstoy (1828–1910), and Ivan Turgenev (1818–1883), and demonstrated his own realist principles in a series of novels; *The Rise of Silas Lapham* (1885), *Annie Kilburn* (1889), and *A Hazard of New Fortunes* (1890) all deal with the moral strug-

Samuel Clemens (1835–1910). Clemens's novels, written under the name Mark Twain, capture nineteenth-century life, manners, and customs. LIBRARY OF CONGRESS

gles of America's rising middle classes. Howells's midwestern origins indicate another aspect of transformation in this period: the development of national transportation and communications networks helped to undermine the Northeast's control over the American literary voice, even as it became more feasible for the major publishing companies to consolidate in New York (as did, for example, Leypoldt and Holt in 1866, Macmillan Company in 1870, and Doubleday in 1900). Regional writers increasingly introduced new accents and dialogues into American fiction as stories of "local color" appeared from every corner of the country. Samuel Langhorne Clemens (Mark Twain) was born in Florida, Missouri, in 1835 and developed his literary voice while exploring the frontiers of the West and Old Southwest. One of Twain's earliest successes was his retelling of a California folktale, "The Celebrated Jumping Frog of Calaveras County" (1865). His masterpiece, *Adventures of Huckleberry Finn* (1884), turns a regionally specific voice into a lasting literary character and finds its inspiration in the slave narrative, the picaresque story, and the folktale, rather than in the tradition of the novel of manners.

This period produced many popular authors of regional fiction. Bret Harte (1836–1902) founded and edited one of California's first literary magazines, *Overland Monthly,* in 1868. Harte's tales of California can be found in *The Luck of Roaring Camp and Other Sketches* (1870). Ambrose Bierce (1842–1914?), the author of *Tales of Soldiers and Civilians* (1891), was born in Ohio but moved to San Francisco after the Civil War and helped to establish that city as a literary center. George Washington Cable (1844–1925) wrote about New Orleans's Creole community in *Old Creole Days* (1879) and *The Grandissimes* (1880). Sarah Orne Jewett (1849–1909) described life in Maine seaport settlements in *The Country of the Pointed Firs* (1896). Kate Chopin (1851–1904), the author of *The Awakening* (1899), was born in St. Louis but moved to and wrote about New Orleans.

Henry James

The author Henry James transformed the observational empiricism of realist writing into a highly wrought narrative style, and in the process produced the most critically acclaimed American fiction of the nineteenth century. Where Hawthorne cultivated a studied attention to historical detail and a penchant for neo-Puritan allegorization, James—who thought of himself as Hawthorne's successor in the tradition of American fiction—tended to write the history of the present, substituting psychological complexity for allegorical weight. *The Portrait of a Lady* (1881) illustrates some of James's most consistent concerns as it follows a young American through Europe, charting the dynamic relationship between her notions of American independence and the opportunities for love and financial stability offered to her by various European suitors. If Davis (and later Crane, Norris, and Dreiser) observed the entrapments of lower-class life in the newly industrialized and urbanized America, James explored the eclipse of individual aspirations at more rarefied social and intellectual levels. Isabel Archer, the heroine of *The Portrait of a Lady*, "had taken all the first steps in the purest confidence," but her eventual marriage transforms the "infinite vista of a multiplied life" into "a dark, narrow alley with a dead wall at the end." James's characters, for all their individual realization, allowed him to articulate a more general American experience at the end of the nineteenth century. James wrote of Isabel Archer's marriage as he might have written of America's great industrial expansion:

> Instead of leading to the high places of happiness from which the world would seem to lie below one, so that one could look down with a sense of exaltation and advantage, and judge and choose and pity, it led rather downward and earthward, into realms of restriction and depression where the sound of other lives, easier and freer, was heard as from above, and where it served to deepen the feeling of failure (New York: Oxford University Press, 1981, p. 461).

If English critics in the early decades of the nineteenth century could declare (with some glee) that no one in the world read American literature, James's works demonstrate the extent to which the American novel evolved over the course of the century. After 1881 no serious student of the novel in English could afford to ignore American fiction.

See also **Dime Novels and Story Papers; Folktales and Tall Tales; Magazines; Magazines, Women's; Realism and Naturalism.**

Bibliography

Bell, Michael Davitt. *The Development of American Romance: The Sacrifice of Relation.* Chicago: University of Chicago Press, 1980.

Bercovitch, Sacvan, gen. ed., and Cyrus R. K. Patell, assoc. ed. *The Cambridge History of American Literature.* Vol. 2. *1820–1865.* Cambridge, U.K., and New York: Cambridge University Press, 1994–.

Bercovitch, Sacvan, and Myra Jehlen, eds. *Ideology and Classic American Literature.* Cambridge, U.K., and New York: Cambridge University Press, 1986.

Charvat, William. *Literary Publishing in America, 1790–1850.* Philadelphia: University of Pennsylvania Press, 1959.

Davidson, Cathy N. *Revolution and the Word: The Rise of the Novel in America.* New York: Oxford University Press, 1986.

Elliott, Emory, gen. ed., and Cathy N. Davidson, et al., assoc. eds. *The Columbia History of the American Novel.* New York: Columbia University Press, 1991.

Fiedler, Leslie A. *Love and Death in the American Novel.* Normal, Ill.: Dalkey Archive Press, 1997.

Fisher, Dexter, and Robert B. Stepto, eds. *Afro-American Literature: The Reconstruction of Instruction.* New York: Modern Language Association of America, 1979.

Hubbell, Jay B. *The South in American Literature, 1607–1900.* Durham, N.C.: Duke University Press, 1954.

Lehmann-Haupt, Hellmut, with Ruth Shepard Granniss and Lawrence C. Wroth. *The Book in America: A History of the Making, the Selling, and the Collecting of Books in the United States.* 1939. 2d ed., rev. and enl., New York: Bowker, 1951.

Marx, Leo. *The Machine in the Garden: Technology and the Pastoral Ideal in America.* New York: Oxford University Press, 1964.

Matthiessen, F. O. *American Renaissance: Art and Expression in the Age of Emerson and Whitman.* London and New York: Oxford University Press, 1941.

McDowell, Deborah E., and Arnold Rampersad, eds. *Slavery and the Literary Imagination.* Baltimore: Johns Hopkins University Press, 1989.

Michaels, Walter Benn. *The Gold Standard and the Logic of Naturalism: American Literature at the Turn of the Century.* Berkeley: University of California Press, 1987.

Michaels, Walter Benn, and Donald E. Pease, eds. *The American Renaissance Reconsidered.* Baltimore: Johns Hopkins University Press, 1985.

Mott, Frank Luther. *A History of American Magazines, 1741–1850.* New York and London: D. Appleton, 1930. Republished as volume 1 of *A History of American Magazines.* 5 vols. Cambridge, Mass.: Harvard University Press, 1938–1968.

Pearson, Edmund. *Dime Novels; or, Following an Old Trail in Popular Literature.* Boston: Little, Brown, 1929.

Slotkin, Richard. *Regeneration through Violence: The Mythology of the American Frontier, 1600–1860.* New York: Harper-Perennial, 1996.

Sundquist, Eric J. *To Wake the Nations: Race in the Making of American Literature.* Cambridge, Mass.: Harvard University Press, Belknap Press of Harvard University Press, 1993.

Ziff, Larzer. *Literary Democracy: The Declaration of Cultural Independence in America.* New York: Viking, 1981.

PAUL DOWNES

THE ESSAY

From intellectual discussions to newspaper editorials to political statements, the essay was the literary genre of choice for public discourse in nineteenth-century America. Traditionally the genre of intellectuals, the essay gained wider popularity in the nineteenth century because of the development of periodic journals, magazines, and newspapers through which editors, writers, and readers could communicate. The development of the American essay paralleled the development of other literary forms, but the essay was unique as it is changed from being the property of the intellectual to becoming an organ of popular expression.

Nationalism

At the dawn of the nineteenth century, there was a desire among the people of the young United States to foster an identifiable American culture. With the defeat of the British monarchy, the ideas of democracy and individual rights were installed at the center of what it meant to be American, at least for white males, and the essay served as a key instrument for expounding these ideas. Following on the heels of political essay writers like Benjamin Franklin, Ralph Waldo Emerson transformed the genre into a form for cultural expression and instruction. In seminal works like "Nature" (1836) and "The American Scholar" (1837), Emerson expounded his ideas about reconciling nature, man, and God in this new country. Emerson sought for the people of the United States to cast off the old European ways and to create their own traditions, values, and purposes.

Another of Emerson's themes was the divinity of the individual person. In "Self-Reliance" (1841), he urged the radical idea that a man should trust his own instincts and act accordingly, writing "Nothing is at last sacred but the integrity of your own mind." Trained as a Unitarian minister, Emerson was also a poet and a popular lecturer, and he drew upon the art of the sermon and the vibrant oral culture of nineteenth-century America to craft the essay into a supple medium for reflection, exhortation, and instruction.

Abolition

Like many intellectuals of the day, Emerson was an abolitionist. The essay became an important means of spreading the call for abolition throughout the states in daily newspapers and magazines like the *Atlantic Monthly*. The rising middle class formed a reading public that eagerly consumed lessons in ethics, aesthetics, and other "higher" realms of thought that the essay seemed well designed to convey. William Lloyd Garrison founded the abolitionist newspaper *The Liberator* in January 1831 and ran it until December 1865, publishing essays and editorials that helped further the cause. Frederick Douglass, a former slave, founded several abolitionist newspapers and published his lectures as essays. He contin-

---

Henry David Thoreau and "Civil Disobedience"

A friend of Emerson and a fellow transcendentalist, Henry David Thoreau took the idea of personal freedom to heart. As a protest against the government's use of tax dollars to support the war in Mexico, the resettlement of Native Americans, the Fugitive Slave Law, and other moral injustices, he refused to pay his poll tax. Thoreau used a nonviolent approach to make a private protest and then wound up in jail for refusing to pay. The essay he later wrote, "Civil Disobedience" (originally titled "Resistance to Civil Government"), has had an important influence on protestors of injustice since its publication in 1849.

---

ued to publish such essays after slavery ended in an effort to forestall any efforts to reinstate it.

Sarah and Angelina Grimké, sisters from Charleston, South Carolina, became the first women from a slaveholding family to speak out against slavery, and they also used lectures and essays to express their views. Sarah Grimké's first essay, "An Epistle to the Clergy of the Southern States," published in 1836, sought to raise the sympathy of southern clergy by appealing to them as Christians. In her "Appeal to the Christian Women of the South" (1836), Angelina Grimké used numerous biblical references to argue forcefully that slavery was not part of God's plan. Lydia Maria Child was another powerful voice for the cause of abolition and other social reforms. Her 1833 essay, "An Appeal in Favor of that Class of Americans Called Africans," incited the public to brand her a radical, although many intellectuals were persuaded by the arguments. Her other essays included "Appeal for the Indians," published in 1868.

Women's Rights

Essayists like Emerson, the Grimkés, and Child were also active in the fight for women's suffrage. For women who fought for abolition, the cause of women's rights was a natural next step, for they were, in a sense, defending their own right to speak out. Sarah Grimké followed her essay on abolition with "Letters on the Equality of the Sexes" (1838). In 1845 the editor of the transcendentalist journal *The Dial*, Margaret Fuller, published "Woman in the Nineteenth Century," an essay that confronted society's treatment of women. Fuller's argument was that if it is wrong to enslave a person because they have the right to be free, then men do not have the right to place restrictions on women.

Literary Criticism

By the 1870s the essay had shifted from being a means of political and social discourse into a literary art form. Writers such as William Dean Howells and Henry James used the essay form for literary discourse, establishing a tradition of American literary criticism. Their efforts were also helped by the tremendous growth of popular journals and magazines. Periodicals such as the *New Yorker* and *Scribner's* became important vehicles for the literary essay. Howells had an especially profound effect on the shaping of American cultural and critical thinking. As the editor of the *Atlantic Monthly* from 1871 to 1881, and through his work at other magazines, he was able to bring many writers to the attention of the public. He helped forward the careers of Mark Twain, Henry James, Stephen Crane, and many others.

As a genre, the essay was an important means of shaping American thought during the nineteenth century, and it played a role in the development of popular and literary periodicals. These were very democratic developments, providing a means of expression for public discussion through essays, while also trying to forge the path of American morals and culture.

See also **Abolition and Antislavery; Literary and Reading Habits; Lyceums; Magazines, Women,** *subentry on* **Women's Rights.**

Bibliography

Cain, William E., ed. *William Lloyd Garrison and the Fight Against Slavery: Selections from the Liberator.* Boston: Bedford, 1995.

Emerson, Ralph Waldo. *Selected Writings.* Edited by Brooks Atkinson. New York: Modern Library, 1950.

Lauter, Paul, ed. *The Hath Anthology of American Literature,* 3d ed., Volume 1. Boston: Houghton-Mifflin, 1998.

MARCY L. TANTER

POETRY

Conceptions of nineteenth-century American poetry have changed dramatically over the last two hundred years. As the readers of poetry shift, so too does its definition. Consequently, there are three canons of nineteenth-century American poetry: the one recognized by nineteenth-century readers, the one created at the beginning of the twentieth century by modernist poets and New Critics, and the one emerging at the end of the twentieth century from the work of historical revisionists.

The Nineteenth-Century's Nineteenth Century

The poetic nineteenth century began with the publication of William Wordsworth's (1770–1850) *Lyrical Ballads* in 1798. Unlike their poetic forefathers, the English romantics located the provenance of a poem in the individual poet rather than in the outside world; they also introduced first-person poetry. The American poetic ego took on many different personae, depending on who said "I."

In response to swift economic, social, and political changes, the American "fireside poets" of the mid-nineteenth century wrote to solace men and women alienated by modernity. William Cullen Bryant (1794–1878), Henry Wadsworth Longfellow (1807–1882), John Greenleaf Whittier (1807–1892), Oliver Wendell Holmes (1809–1894), and James Russell Lowell (1819–1891) wrote verse that affirmed patriotism, familial solidarity, and individual liberty. Stripped of personal idiosyncrasies, the speaking "I" in these poems confronted the trials of modern life and demonstrated the stoic endurance needed to persevere. To reassure, rather than further disturb, their audience, these poets shunned originality in favor of conventional styles and forms, the regularity of which facilitated memorization and the inculcation of moral and social lessons. These methods succeeded hugely: the genteel, middle-class audience eagerly consumed verses both long and short in collections, anthologies, and periodicals. The enormous success of Whittier's *Snow-Bound* (1866), which ensured his financial security for the last twenty-six years of his life, is a testament to the widespread popularity of poetry as a genre. The poetry of the fireside poets was often read aloud among family and friends in the privacy of the reader's home.

Although often considered as a schoolroom poet, Ralph Waldo Emerson (1803–1882) regarded poetry as a means of apprehending transcendent truths, rather than as a way of communicating known truths. He and the transcendentalist poets translated the individual self into the universal self by employing an "I" that was grammatically singular but effectively plural. Equating transcendent truth with harmony, however, Emerson still valued formal regularity and stylistic clarity, which he thought of as ends to be achieved through struggle, rather than as a place to begin.

Having abandoned any idea of transcendent truth, Edgar Allan Poe (1809–1849) embraced harmonious verse as pure artifice. His intensified versification took the jingling rhymes and rhythms of the fireside poets to a mind-numbing extreme and called attention to his poems' hyperbolic musicality, a quality that would resonate later in the poems of fellow

James Russell Lowell (1819–1891). In addition to writing essays and works of poetry such as *Fireside Travels,* Lowell was a diplomat who served as the U.S. minister to Spain (1877–1880) and to Great Britain (1880–1885). LIBRARY OF CONGRESS

southerner Sidney Lanier (1842–1881). Both a poet and musician by profession, Lanier wrote extensively about the intersections of music and verse.

Toward the end of the century, the poetry of the African American poets Paul Laurence Dunbar (1872–1906) and Frances Ellen Watkins Harper (1825–1911) was extremely popular. Working within the conventional, Anglo-American verse forms, Dunbar poeticized African American dialect as well as standard English, depicting the South as idyllic and pastoral. Harper, on the other hand, used her verse for progressive purposes. A recognized abolitionist and suffragette, Harper relied heavily on familiar sentimental and stereotypical images to evoke feelings of sympathy and outrage and to incite political change. Her speeches were often accompanied by her poems. Harper also represented the rising category of the "American poetess." She and her fellow poetesses Lydia Sigourney (1791–1865), Frances Osgood (1811–1850), Alice (1820–1871) and Phoebe Cary (1824–1871), and Sarah Piatt (1836–1919) filled periodicals with their verse and peppered bookshelves with their collections. Women's magazines, which contained both literature and articles on homemaking and child rearing, proliferated in the first half of the nineteenth century and provided consistent publication opportunities that had not existed previ-

ously. Much of women's poetry of the period centered around the domestic sphere and was written within conventional verse forms in a self-consciously poetic language.

The Modernist Nineteenth Century

At the beginning of the twentieth century, poetry began its migration from the hearth to the classroom and became the domain of the academic elite. The poet-critics of the modernist movement—John Crowe Ransom (1888–1974), Allen Tate (1899–1979), and Yvor Winters (1900–1968)—forged a movement that came to be called "New Criticism" and that redefined the standards of poetry: they lauded the recondite, objective, and elusive, and despised the mawkish, mellifluous, and sentimental. The critical focus shifted primarily to poets who had been considered "minor" or "nonpoets" in their own time—Walt Whitman (1819–1892), Emily Dickinson (1830–1886), and Herman Melville (1819–1891)—but came to be seen as protomodernists.

Whitman's free verse did not look or sound like anything his contemporaries in the 1850s called poetry. His overflowing lines defied metric regularity, confused the boundaries between poetry and prose, piled one image on the other, and created a speaking "I" who was at once absolutely individualistic and universally representative. Modernists were drawn to the intense self-absorption of Whitman's poetry and his abandonment of conventional verse forms. Rather than feed his audience's complacency or assuage their fears, Whitman's "barbaric yawp" ("Song of Myself" in *Leaves of Grass*, 1855) cataloged the modern world from which they sought escape. He believed that political conflicts and social unrest could be reconciled by the voice of the poet, a voice he imagined himself assuming. Although Whitman's *Leaves of Grass* was received coolly at first and later banned because of its sexual passages, he continued to rework this single text until his death. What began as a collection of twelve untitled poems grew through eight subsequent editions into the ultimate "deathbed" edition (1891–1892), which contained 293 poems (including *Drum-Taps*, 1865, the verse inspired by his volunteer work in the Civil War) and two annexes.

Unlike the verbose, prophetic Whitman, Emily Dickinson compacted verse into enigmatic metaphors and entered into an intensely private conversation with herself. She revitalized the common topics of poetry—God, love, death, consciousness—in

Walt Whitman (1819–1892). The foremost poet of his era, Whitman wrote *Leaves of Grass* as well as diaries of his impressions during the Civil War. Photograph by Frank Pearsall, c. 1870. FEINBERG-WHITMAN COLLECTION, LIBRARY OF CONGRESS

her heavily imagistic, relentlessly original language. Like Whitman, Dickinson abandoned the prescribed verse of her peers, trading in public expectation for personal experience and exchanging rhetoric for imagery, moves that drew modernists to her work. Once the center and focus of poetry, the audience found themselves spoken in front of rather than spoken to. Whereas her contemporaries provided the audience with a scripted response, Dickinson provided only a fragmented script that required the audience's active involvement in deciphering the poetry. The economy of her language requires that not a character go unread: sporadic capitalization, interruptive dashes, and irregular syntax distinguish her poetry from any that preceded or followed it. The few poems published during her lifetime were done so against her will. Mabel Loomis Todd (1856–1932) and Thomas Wentworth Higginson (1823–1911) compiled the first collection of Dickinson's poems in the 1890s but edited them almost beyond recognition, "correcting" the punctuation and adjusting the language when it was deemed inaccessible. The first edition of her work that resembled what Dickinson had composed was published by Thomas H. Johnson in 1955.

To an extent, Herman Melville's status as a nineteenth-century poet is still uncertain. His unconventional use of conventional verse forms, erudite references, and impervious metaphors have provided excuses to ignore his poetry as the enigmatic jetsam of the author of *Moby-Dick* (1851). Yet Melville was a prolific writer of poetry who published four volumes of poems, including the 18,000-line *Clarel* (1876). In his first published collection, *Battle-Pieces and Aspects of the War* (1866), Melville used the Civil War as a vehicle to consider fundamental dualities—poverty and privilege, experience and innocence. Historic places and events were ancillary to his private meditations. In the mid–twentieth century, Melville came to be, for Robert Penn Warren (1905–1989) and Randall Jarrell (1914–1965), one of the three best American poets of his day, valued for his acceptance of ambiguity as an unavoidable condition and for his "escape from personality" (Eliot, "Tradition and the Individual Talent") through impersonation. As with the modernists to follow, the self of the poet is absent from Melville's poems.

The New Critics also recognized Frederick Goddard Tuckerman (1821–1873) and the early Edwin Arlington Robinson (1869–1935). A lawyer by avocation and tutored by the transcendentalist poet Jones Very (1813–1880) while at Harvard, Tuckerman refracted grief through nature and nature through poetry. But his attempts to achieve consolation through the exploration of grief proved unsuccessful and suspended his poetry in a state of incurable loss; his metaphoric expression of this loss recommended him to the modernists. Robinson, on the other hand, was recognized for his short poems that dramatized the lives and psyches of people in a small New England town. His bleakly terse, ironic portraits of wayward, stunted, and fruitless lives and his refusal to moralize attracted the modernists to his work, though his prosodic style, colloquial language, and concentration on daily life anticipated the poetry of Robert Frost (1874–1963), one of the unmodernist moderns.

The Revisionist Nineteenth Century

In the 1970s, New Criticism gave way to new historicism, and the interest in nineteenth-century poets shifted yet again. Rather than viewing the protomodernist poets as the only poetic voices of the nineteenth century, critics began to contextualize these bards within their own century. Challenging the canon, redefining the genre of poetry, and exhuming texts previously silenced by exclusion uncovered a wealth of poetry that reshaped the conception of American literature in the nineteenth century.

Native American poetry brought to the fore issues of genre, medium, and authorship: issues of primary concern to the historicist movement. There are no original versions of this poetry, only the printed texts of an oral tradition filtered through the language of Puritan missionaries. Issues of translation from one language to another, from one culture to another, and from one medium to another complicate the reading of this work and enrich the analysis done on it. Whereas New Critics did not even call this type of verse "poetry," recent critics have used the missionary transcriptions to investigate nineteenth-century ideology and to query the politics of aesthetics.

The tandem consideration of ideology and aesthetics carries over into late-twentieth-century analysis of nineteenth-century women's verse. Scholars have explored issues of sentimentalism and the reductive, unsophisticated assumptions made about the American poetesses. Nineteenth-century women poets wrote rich, diverse poetry that both represented their own time and foreshadowed the work of poets to come. They helped their readers come to terms with the contradictions of war, threats to stability (both domestic and national), and the impact of modernization. Through multiple lenses—domestic, maternal, political—the poetesses used poetry to articulate their world and the world of their children. Rather than isolate Dickinson from her female contemporaries at the latters' expense, historicist scholars read Dickinson alongside her peers.

Dunbar and Harper have also been recontex-tualized by the poetry of other nineteenth-century African Americans—George Moses Horton (c. 1797–c. 1883), James Edwin Campbell (1867–1895), Charlotte Forten Grimké (1837–1914), and Mary Eliza Tucker Lambert (1838–?). As viewed by scholars of the late twentieth century, the metamorphosis that African-American poetry underwent in the nineteenth century reflects the changing economic, social, and political situations of the time. From poetry opposing slavery to poetry creating a racial identity, from bitter satires of white hypocrisy to nostalgic eulogies of the Old South, this heterogeneous body of work invited discussion of dominant and subordinate languages and poetic forms, the complexities of multiracial ancestors, and the changing representations of the United States before and after the Civil War. Scholars have also investigated the multiple roles of African American dialect verse and uncovered a number of different motivations for writing in this subgenre—to educate black and white Americans, redefine language, appeal to a wider audience, and mock racial stereotypes.

New historicists have also begun to consider the poetry that came out of the Civil War. In addition to Whitman's *Drum-Taps* and Melville's *Battle-Pieces*, critics have considered the poems penned by America's popular poets in honor of their dying countrymen, in horror at the atrocities of war, in moral outrage at both the institution of slavery and the aggression of the North. In keeping with the doctrines of sentimentality, many poets, who were often doctors, teachers, and housewives, avoided the brutal realism of the battlefield in favor of poetically inflected and colorful language that martyred and demonized either side. Julia Ward Howe's (1819–1910) "Battle Hymn of the Republic" (1862) and Longfellow's "Killed at the Ford" (1868) were two of the most popular pieces to come out of the Civil War.

The moral outrage that surrounded the issue of slavery also found its way into verse on both sides of the Mason-Dixon line. Like Harper, African American poets Sarah Louisa Forten ("Ada") (1814–1883) and James M. Whitfield (1822–1871) championed the northern abolitionist movement, along with the fireside poet Whittier, the most esteemed antislavery poet of his time. Whittier's "The Furnace Blast" (1869) exemplified the militant abolitionist verse that saw slavery as the vice that would destroy the country; Harper's "Bible Defense of Slavery" (1854) employed sentimental images to incite emotional responses from her audience. The title of Harper's work is most likely in direct response to the use of a literal reading of the Bible in southern verse to defend the institution of slavery, an example of which can be found in Mary Sophie Shaw Homes's (b. 1830?)

("Millie Mayfield") *Progression; or, the South Defended* (1860). Other defensive tactics deployed by proslavery verse were to paint an idyllic picture of the South in which the slaves lived happily on the plantation, as in Charles T. Daniel's *William and Annie: or, A tale of Love and War and Other Poems* (1864), and to contrast the life of the slave in the South with that of the industrial worker in the North, as in William Grayson's *The Hireling and the Slave* (1856).

Other canonical poets have also been reexamined in light of various branches of cultural criticism. In the same way that feminists have reread Dickinson and African Americanists have reread Dunbar, gay and lesbian studies scholars have reread Whitman through the lens of sexuality.

The extensive scholarly recovery work of the 1980s and 1990s has rescued these poets from oblivion. New historicism has provided scholars with the tools to reevaluate what constitutes literature and how a canon is formed. As the verses of these newly recovered poets are circulated in print, the idea of nineteenth-century American poetry may metamorphose yet again. Shifts in poetic taste will keep its definition in flux and likely will complicate any attempt at permanent canonization.

See also **Magazines, Women's; Romanticism; Transcendentalism.**

Bibliography

Baym, Nina, et al., eds. *The Norton Anthology of American Literature.* 5th ed. New York: Norton, 1998.

Bennett, Paula Bernat, ed. *Nineteenth-Century American Women Poets: An Anthology.* Malden, Mass.: Blackwell, 1998.

Blasing, Mutlu Konuk. *American Poetry: The Rhetoric of Its Forms.* New Haven, Conn.: Yale University Press, 1987.

Duffey, Bernard. *Poetry in America: Expression and Its Values in the Times of Bryant, Whitman, and Pound.* Durham, N.C.: Duke University Press, 1978.

Eliot, T. S. "Tradition and the Individual Talent." In *Selected Prose of T. S. Eliot.* Edited by Frank Kermode. London: Faber, 1975.

Hollander, John, ed. *American Poetry: The Nineteenth Century.* 2 vols. The Library of America Series. New York: Penguin, 1993.

Lee, A. Robert, ed. *Nineteenth-Century American Poetry.* London: Vision, 1985.

Marius, Richard, and Keith Frome, eds. *The Columbia Book of Civil War Poetry.* New York: Columbia University Press, 1994.

Momaday, N. Scott, ed. *Complete Poems,* by Frederick Goddard Tuckerman. New York: Oxford University Press, 1965.

Parini, Jay, ed. *The Columbia History of American Poetry.* New York: Columbia University Press, 1993.

Pearce, Roy Harvey. *The Continuity of American Poetry.* Princeton, N.J.: Princeton University Press, 1961.

Sherman, Joan R., ed. *African American Poetry of the Nineteenth Century: An Anthology.* Urbana: University of Illinois Press, 1992.

Spengemann, William C., with Jessica F. Roberts, eds. *Nineteenth-Century American Poetry.* New York: Penguin, 1996.

Steinmetz, Lee, ed. *The Poetry of the American Civil War.* East Lansing: Michigan State University Press, 1960.

JESSICA FORBES ROBERTS

CHILDREN'S LITERATURE

American literature for children at the beginning of the nineteenth century remained heavily Puritan, dominated by the 1690 *New England Primer,* which asserts, "In Adam's fall/We sinned all," and other books of moral and religious instruction. From a secular perspective, most nineteenth-century children's literature reflects an unquestioning Protestant morality in which the individual's relationship with God and the development of character are inextricably tied to obedience to parents, social responsibility, and citizenship. Not until the end of the century did light-hearted fantasy and pure entertainment become acceptable in such works as Frank Stockton's fanciful *Ting-a-ling* (1870), Palmer Cox's *The Brownies: Their Book* (1887), and L. Frank Baum's *Wonderful Wizard of Oz* (1900).

Although nursery rhymes and fairy tales were available early in the century, usually in inexpensive chapbooks, they were often heavily criticized as unsuitable for children and charged with encouraging "lying, deception and murder," as Samuel Griswold Goodrich (1793–1860) wrote in 1857 in his *Recollections of a Lifetime* (p. 166). The noted printer Isaiah Thomas in about 1785 and others after him reprinted and adapted such books as John Newbery's *Mother Goose's Melody* (c. 1760) and versions of *Cinderella, Little Red Riding Hood,* and *Jack the Giant Killer* for American children. Later in the nineteenth century, translations of the fairy tales of Jacob Grimm and Wilhelm Grimm and the literary tales of Hans Christian Andersen were also popular. Washington Irving's "Rip Van Winkle" (1819) recast a traditional German tale in an American setting. One of the best-loved and best-known works of pure imagination from the early nineteenth century is Clement Clarke Moore's "A Visit from St. Nicholas," first published anonymously in the *Troy* (New York) *Sentinel* in 1823. Nathaniel Hawthorne's *A Wonder-Book for Girls and Boys* (1851) provided romantic and freely rendered retellings of Greek myths within an American framework.

After the War of 1812, reliance on English books lessened, as writers for children, like writers for adults, attempted to create a truly American literature. Biographies of American heroes were popular, the best-known being Mason Locke Weems's *The Life of Washington the Great,* which contains in its 1806 version the apocryphal story of Washington cutting down the cherry tree and declaring, "I can't tell a lie, Pa, you know I can't tell a lie, I did cut it with my hatchet." (The origin of the more familiar quote, "Father, I cannot tell a lie," is not well documented.)

Periodicals, Sunday school literature, and *McGuffey's Readers* also became important forms of literature for children. The longest-lived children's magazine was the *Youth's Companion,* published weekly in Boston from 1827 until 1927. Religious organizations, such as the American Tract Society and the American Sunday School Union, were responsible for publishing and stocking their own libraries with millions of copies of books and periodicals, adding greatly to the volume of religious literature encountered by children. The *McGuffey Eclectic Readers,* first published in 1836, were the most widely read American schoolbooks for at least seventy-five years. Their changing selections of poetry and prose, many by famous writers, influenced several generations of children.

Writings for children contained only a few portrayals of Native American and African American characters, and most of those were condescending. Even ardent abolitionists often portrayed blacks as inferior, and American Indians were usually depicted as savages, noble or otherwise. In the later part of the century, the sensational dime novels often featured conflicts with American Indians on the frontier.

In the years following the War of 1812, Goodrich started his famous Peter Parley series, beginning with *The Tales of Peter Parley about America* (1827). The books combined tales of travel with cultural, historical, and geographical information, some outrageously biased and misinformed by later standards. Ironically, Goodrich is most often remembered for his nursery rhyme "Higgledy, Piggledy Pop," written to satirize the form. Jacob Abbott, also a prolific author, earned praise for the Rollo books that charmingly portray the education and travels of a young boy. Lydia Maria Child, author of several notable books, outspoken opponent of slavery, and defender of Native Americans, founded and edited the periodical *Juvenile Miscellany.*

Important writers after 1850 include Susan Warner, whose lengthy novel *The Wide, Wide World* (1850) became a best-seller on both sides of the Atlantic; Harriet Beecher Stowe, whose influential *Uncle Tom's Cabin* (1851–1852) was eventually issued in several children's editions; Mary Mapes Dodge, editor of the renowned *St. Nicholas* magazine and author of *Hans Brinker; or, The Silver Skates* (1865); Martha

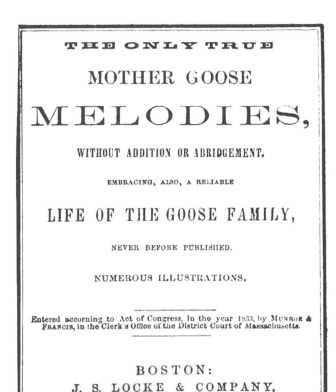

THE ONLY TRUE

MOTHER GOOSE

MELODIES,

WITHOUT ADDITION OR ABRIDGEMENT.

EMBRACING, ALSO, A RELIABLE

LIFE OF THE GOOSE FAMILY,

NEVER BEFORE PUBLISHED.

NUMEROUS ILLUSTRATIONS.

Entered according to Act of Congress, in the year 1833, by MUNROE & FRANCIS, in the Clerk's Office of the District Court of Massachusetts.

BOSTON:
J. S. LOCKE & COMPANY,

Mother Goose Melodies. Familiar children's stories such as *Little Red Riding Hood* were published in America as early as the eighteenth century. Published by Munroe and Francis, Massachusetts, 1833. LIBRARY OF CONGRESS: PRINTS AND PHOTOGRAPHS DIVISION

Finley, author of the sentimental *Elsie Dinsmore* (1867); Louisa May Alcott, whose seminal *Little Women* (1868) became one of the most-loved books of all time; and Susan Coolidge, author of the popular *What Katy Did* (1872).

Popular stories for boys included Oliver Optic's *The Boat Club* (1854); Horatio Alger's *Ragged Dick* (1867); Thomas Bailey Aldrich's *The Story of a Bad Boy* (1870); Mark Twain's *The Adventures of Tom Sawyer* (1876) and *Adventures of Huckleberry Finn* (1884); George Wilbur Peck's *Peck's Bad Boy and His Pa* (1883); and Howard Pyle's exquisitely illustrated *The Merry Adventures of Robin Hood* (1883). Joel Chandler Harris published the first of the Uncle Remus stories in 1880, and that year Lucretia Hale released her humorous book *The Peterkin Papers.* Frances Hodgson Burnett published *Little Lord Fauntleroy* in 1886 and *Sara Crewe* in 1888.

The years 1865 to 1914, between the end of the Civil War and the beginning of World War I, are sometimes considered the golden age of American children's literature. Advances in technology, transportation, printing, and paper manufacturing; rising levels of education; and a general concern for the welfare of children all contributed to the blossoming of children's literature. The separation between literature for children and for adults was less pronounced than it would later become. The tight religious control exerted on publishing for children at the beginning of the century had gradually been replaced by concern on the part of genteel editors with enculturating children with the values necessary to preserve order in a turbulent, rapidly changing age. Although many of those values crumbled in the succeeding century, a significant number of nineteenth-century children's books were read and loved a century and more after they were written.

See also **Education,** *subentry on* **Elementary and Secondary Schools; Life Cycle,** *subentry on* **Childhood and Adolescence; Literature,** *subentry on* **Fiction.**

Bibliography

Avery, Gillian. *Behold the Child: American Children and Their Books, 1621–1922.* Baltimore: Johns Hopkins University Press, 1994.

Estes, Glenn E., ed. *American Writers for Children before 1900.* Volume 42 of *Dictionary of Literary Biography.* Detroit: Gale, 1985.

Kelly, R. Gordon. *Mother Was a Lady: Self and Society in Selected American Children's Periodicals, 1865–1890.* Westport, Conn.: Greenwood, 1974.

MacLeod, Anne Scott. "Children's Literature in America: From Puritan Beginnings to 1870." In *Children's Literature: An Illustrated History,* edited by Peter Hunt. Oxford and New York: Oxford University Press, 1995.

LINNEA HENDRICKSON

WOMEN'S LITERATURE

As a result of the twin efforts of feminist literary scholarship and historians of the printed word, the novelist Nathaniel Hawthorne's expression of exasperation with those "damned scribbling women," his contemporary female writers, can be interpreted as the cry of an angry competitor rather than as a judgment of their literary merit. Throughout the nineteenth century American women writers not only crowded the marketplace with their work, they, as recent scholarly work shows, came to define it. Their engagement with abolition, women's rights, and the cult of true womanhood among other then-current issues coincided with the rise of authorship as a profession, placing the work of women writers at the center of the burgeoning nineteenth-century literary marketplace. Major figures of the century, such as Louisa May Alcott, Lydia Maria Child, Sarah Josepha Hale, Frances Ellen Watkins Harper, Pauline

Elizabeth Hopkins, Catharine Maria Sedgwick, E.D.E.N. Southworth, Harriet Beecher Stowe, Susan Bogart Warner, and Sara Payson Willis Parton (a.k.a. "Fanny Fern") all made their living—unlike many of their male counterparts—by the pen. And perhaps what is most striking about their success as a group is the degree to which, because of their popularity, they had an impact on the development of literary culture.

Literature and literary business played an important role in the plots featured in many of the works by these writers. In *Ruth Hall* (1855), Fanny Fern's runaway bestseller, for instance, the novel's main character is a writer of serial fiction. As the novel's heroine pursues her professional goals, it is copyright law that becomes the de facto hero of the novel, not some gallant suitor proposing marriage. In Louisa May Alcott's seminal work, *Little Women* (1868), writing also figures as a central plot device. Alcott made her most dynamic "little woman"—"Jo"—a writer who finds success as a hack writer producing sensational fiction. Over the course of the novel we come to understand that Jo has learned to aim higher, and we enjoy the results: the novel's fictional conceit is that it is a direct result of that lesson, produced by Jo's pen.

Public Response

Achievement brought limitation. Alcott's post–*Little Women* career, for instance, signals both success and confinement for women writers and women's literature generally. As Alcott enjoyed the financial relief that the popularity of *Little Women* afforded her, we also know, thanks to the literary detective work of Madeline Stern, that she was hemmed into producing children's literature while her interests lay in exploring more adult subjects. Novels such as *Work* (1873) and *Moods* (1864) sought a mature audience but did not pay; after the success of *Little Women,* the market demanded more of the same. Thus, Alcott turned to gothic expressions in stories she published pseudonymously so that she could still have the pleasure of (and the payment for) boiling the pot with literary thrillers, such as *Behind a Mask* (1866).

Role of Domesticity and the Domestic Novel

Women succeeded in the literary marketplace more than many of their male counterparts, in part because they made domestic life a focus for their fictions. Susan Bogart Warner's *Wide, Wide World* (1852) was one of the first (and most popular) to cater to women's interests in home and marriage. But plots from the "domestic" novels often used "home" and its economy as a springboard for larger issues.

AL. W. MARTIN'S MAMMOTH PRODUCTION
"UNCLE TOM'S CABIN"

A SNAP SHOT OF OUR REGAL
TRAIN OF PALACE COACHES AND
PRINCIPAL FEATURES OF OUR
SUMPTUOUS DAILY STREET PARADE.

The Novel That Sparked a War. A poster advertising a theater group performing *Uncle Tom's Cabin* written by Harriet Beecher Stowe. The 1898 date of this poster attests to the longevity of the novel after its publication. LIBRARY OF CONGRESS: PRINTS AND PHOTOGRAPHS DIVISION

Lydia Maria Child's popular novel *Hobomok* (1824) used a domestic setting to develop issues regarding race relations. This historical novel boldly represented miscegenation between a Puritan woman and a Native American man as its central romance. (Catherine Maria Sedgewick's *Hope Leslie* [1827] picks up on this theme.) These popular novels exhibited a reformist tendency with a radical edge that earlier critics—Hawthorne among them—failed to appreciate in women writers.

Themes

Reform as a major impulse powers Harriet Beecher Stowe's *Uncle Tom's Cabin* (1852). Stowe began this work as a piece for serial publication in response to the Fugitive Slave Act of 1850. She projected that the piece would run "three or four numbers"; the completed novel sprawled across forty issues. By the time she brought it out in book form, keeping the public in copies meant keeping the presses running literally all night to satisfy demand. Based on a vi-

sion she had of an old black man being beaten to death, along with several well-known slave narratives, she galvanized reader sentiment into a desire for reform. The significance of *Uncle Tom's Cabin* both in the literary marketplace and the wider world is summed up by President Abraham Lincoln, who on meeting Stowe, asked if she was "the little lady that started this big war."

Another writer that should be recognized as a contributor to the reform movement is Sojourner Truth, whose *Narrative*, written with Olive Gilbert in 1850, went through numerous editions and helped to support her throughout her lifetime. Through that work she adds her voice to a tradition largely defined by the experiences of Southern black males, such as Frederick Douglass and Josiah Henson, who had escaped from slavery.

Truth's work made way for that of Harriet Jacobs—the writer who famously told Harriet Beecher Stowe that her *Incidents in the Life of a Slave Girl* (1861) "needed no romance" to succeed as a literary work. Jacobs used a pseudonym for her autobiographical account and thus began a trend toward blurred boundaries between fact and fiction that has allowed African American writers to expand and innovate genres significantly.

In the first novel written by an African American woman in the United States, *Our Nig* (1859), Harriet Wilson fused the domestic framework popularized by white women writers with the literary genre of slave narrative. Her novel inaugurated important stylistic advances while also uncovering systemic racism in the "slave-free" North. Frances Ellen Watkins Harper's *Iola Leroy, or Shadows Uplifted* (1892)—a novel that develops links between race and gender through what would otherwise be a conventional marriage plot—extended this tradition into the twentieth century.

Development over the Century

Up until the 1870s, New England writers and themes dominated literature. In part, no doubt, because the most powerful publishing houses were located first in Philadelphia and later in Boston, writers who developed subjects drawn from Yankee culture by far outnumber those who set their work in other regions. Even writers who took exception to the "Yankee" patriotism were rewarded with publication and prominence. One such writer, Rose Terry Cooke, contributed to the development of the literary style called "local color" through her critiques of New England customs and the culture's tendency toward self-aggrandizement. One of Cooke's most influential works was *Somebody's Neighbors* (1881). A widely popular writer (to the extent that there are several known cases of people posing as Cooke), Cooke influenced others closely associated with local color writing, such as Sarah Orne Jewett and Mary E. Wilkins Freeman.

Differences by region, class, race, and genre

The local color movement—characterized by an interest in local culture and customs—opened the door for a more diverse group of writers than those who had populated the profession prior to the Civil War. Writers from regions, races, and ethnicities outside of the dominant culture of New England that took advantage of the new interest in belles lettres included Celia Thaxter, Mary Noialles Murfree, Grace Elizabeth King, Kate Chopin, Rebecca Harding Davis, Alice Dunbar-Nelson, Sui Sin Far, Zitkala-Sa, and Mary Austin. Each introduced aspects of her experience to a readership eager for a glimpse into worlds and cultures that remained obscure or outlandish. Their stories are usually told by an outsider who gains access to the community through a particular figure whose perspective strongly influences the narrator's (and hence the reader's) experience. Sarah Orne Jewett, whose, *The Country of the Pointed Firs* (1896) perfects the form, takes the relationship between the narrator and her informant through a series of events. Using the duration of time in much the same way that serial novelists had in an earlier era, Jewett grows and deepens the relationship between the narrator and her informant significantly beyond the "cultural tourism" that dominates this literary form.

Restricting herself to poetry alone, Emily Dickinson, who spent her life in the small New England town of Amherst, Massachusetts, revolutionized the form through her idiosyncratic use of verse and syntax. Although her rejection of publication meant her poetry was not read widely by her contemporaries, her work, now world renowned, offers a subtle commentary on such issues as the Civil War, the artistic process, and spirituality. Her pared-down style invokes a degree of transcendence beyond the specific focus of any single event. The image of an insect at work in a garden, for instance, can yield stunning insight into mortality itself.

Turn-of-the-century writers

Several important figures—Ida B. Wells-Barnett, Pauline Hopkins, and Edith Wharton among them—began their careers in the nineteenth century and continued to work well into the twentieth, leaving their stamp on both eras. Wells-Barnett, an important African American journalist, editor, and activist, wrote extensively on issues affecting the race. Her *Southern Horrors: Lynch Law in All Its Phases* (1892) was the first to attribute violent racism to a form of class anxiety. There and elsewhere, she maintained that lynching was a means for keeping blacks down economically by eliminating those who prospered. Later, in autobiographical works she wrote during her lifetime, she contributed to a growing understanding of the obstacles a black woman must face and overcome in a white world. Her writings continue the tradition of resistance that earlier African American writers had forged through their lives and literary production. Similarly, the works of Pauline Elizabeth Hopkins, a prominent journalist and editor, mark an important step in the development of the African American tradition of resistance. In her serial works, such as *Hagar's Daughter* (1901), *Winona* (1902), and *Of One Blood* (1902), Hopkins reclaims the serial novel form and fits it to the development of a philosophy of race that remains radical even to this day.

Edith Wharton's career, on the other hand, is closer to the commercial roots of women's writing. She published more than thirty-five book-length projects; her works span the genres and include poetry, travel writing, interior design, short stories, and novels. Despite her financial success, she did not need to make her living by her pen. But her success allowed her to define her career as a literary artist through her commitment to her craft in a way that would resonate with many twentieth-century women writers. By 1921, her identity as a writer had been recognized by the culture at large with a Pulitzer Prize for her novel *The Age of Innocence* (1920).

Home: Both Boundary and Point of Departure

While most women writers addressed contemporary morality, considering for instance, the limits of marriage and the treatment of women within the body of their works, a debate continues on how "limiting" and "limited" a focus on the domestic was for women who undertook writing as a profession in the nineteenth century. Certainly many of their works use the home as a setting—and some plots remain exclusively focused on the hearth—but just as many venture beyond the household or deeper into it as a means of exploring race, gender, class, and nationhood in new and exciting ways. Considered as a group, in fact, the diversity reflected in their themes and views is so intense that little unites them aside from the degree of popularity they enjoyed and their collective identification as women.

See also **Book Publishing; Domestic Life; Gender,** subentry on **Interpretations of Gender; Home; Magazines, Women's; Sexual Morality; Women:** *subentry on* **Women in the Professions.**

Bibliography
Ammons, Elizabeth. *Conflicting Stories: American Women Writers at the Turn of the Twentieth Century.* New York: Oxford University Press, 1991.

Baym, Nina. *American Women Writers and the Work of History. 1790–1860.* New Brunswick, N.J.: Rutgers University Press, 1995.

———. *Women's Fiction.* 2d ed. New Brunswick, N.J.: Rutgers University Press, 1993.

Carby, Hazel V. *Reconstructing Womanhood: The Emergence of the Afro-American Woman Novelist.* New York: Oxford University Press, 1987.

Coultrap-McQuin, Susan. *Doing Literary Business: American Women Writers in the Nineteenth Century.* Chapel Hill: University of North Carolina Press, 1990.

DuCille, Ann. *The Coupling Convention: Sex, Text and Tradition in Black Women's Fiction.* New York: Oxford University Press, 1993.

Foster, Frances Smith. *Written by Herself: Literary Production by African American Women, 1746–1892.* Bloomington: University of Indiana Press, 1993.

Pryse, Marjorie, and Hortense, J. Spillers, eds. *Conjuring: Black Women, Fiction, and Tradition.* Bloomington: University of Indiana Press, 1985.

Stern, Madeline. *Louisa May Alcott: A Biography.* Boston: Northeastern University Press, 1996.

Zagarell, Sandra. "Crosscurrents: Registers of Nordicism, Community, and Culture in Jewett's *Country of Pointed Furs.*" *Yale Journal of Criticism* 10, no. 2 (1997): 355–370.

Augusta Rohrbach

AFRICAN AMERICAN LITERATURE

The nineteenth century was the formative period for African American literature, building on the foundations laid by such pioneers as Phillis Wheatley and anticipating twentieth-century literary developments, such as the Harlem Renaissance. Nineteenth-century African American writers struggled to define and give voice to the black experience at a time when slavery, abolition, civil war, emancipation, subjugation, and efforts for equality dominated black consciousness. Against this background black authors sought answers to two questions. Were African American writers simply darker skinned versions of American writers? Was African American literature a distinctive literature based on African and African American themes and folk traditions?

The most significant writer in the early nineteenth century was George Moses Horton, a slave in North Carolina whose first book of poetry, **The Hope of Liberty,** appeared in 1829. Like Wheatley he modeled his poetry on traditional English forms, and also like her he used his poetry to subtly expose the injustices of slavery. Horton's patrons were white northerners and southerners, and his audience largely consisted of the readers of the antislavery journals that published most of his poems.

African American Literature in the Antislavery Era

Slavery was the overriding reality that African Americans confronted during the first two-thirds of the nineteenth century, and African American literature reflected their preoccupation with the fact that the great majority of black Americans lived in bondage. The dominant literary form of this period was the slave narrative, of which the two most widely read were *The Narrative of the Life of Frederick Douglass, an American Slave, Written by Himself* (1845) by Frederick Douglass, and *Narrative of William W. Brown, a Fugitive Slave* (1847) by William Wells Brown. Both Douglass and Brown achieved international fame, and their autobiographical accounts of slavery were popular among readers in both England and the United States. Other examples of this literary genre include Harriet A. Jacobs, *Incidents in the Life of a Slave Girl* (1861), and *The Confessions of*

Nat Turner (1831), based on statements allegedly made by Turner before he was executed for leading a slave rebellion in Virginia in 1831. In total some two dozen slave narratives were published during the two decades preceding the Civil War. The narratives provided literary material for the emerging African American religious and antislavery publications and for white-owned abolitionist journals, and they found audiences among both whites and free blacks.

In the 1850s the turmoil surrounding the antislavery movement as well as the popularity of works about the black experience, such as Harriet Beecher Stowe's *Uncle Tom's Cabin* (1852), stimulated African American literature. In 1853 William Wells Brown became the first black novelist when he published *Clotel; or, The President's Daughter,* which examines the life of a fictional mixed-race daughter of Thomas Jefferson. While this story is an early example of the theme of the tragic mulatto, the character Clotel emerges as a true heroine as she struggles to free her daughter from slavery. Also in 1853 the abolitionist Douglass published *The Heroic Slave,* a novella based on an 1841 slave mutiny. The third African American novel of this decade, Martin R. Delany's *Blake; or, The Huts of America* (1859), also centers on efforts to organize a slave revolt in the South. In 1858 Brown wrote *The Escape; or, A Leap for Freedom,* a play dramatizing the flights from slavery recounted in many slave narratives. During the decade two works of fiction by African American women were published. "The Two Offers" (1859) is a short story by the poet Frances Ellen Watkins Harper, and Harriet E. Wilson's *Our Nig; or, Sketches from the Life of a Free Black* (1859) was the first novel written by an African American woman.

African American Literature after Emancipation

Following emancipation African American literature shifted focus significantly. Memoirs of slave life were popular for a while, but instead of concentrating on the horrors of slavery, they took on a Horatio Alger flavor, emphasizing individualism, self-reliance, and personal achievement. Booker T. Washington's *Up from Slavery* (1901) is the best-known example of this genre. African American literature also responded to changing social and political conditions. The decline of the abolitionist movement and the hardening of racial lines following Reconstruction reduced interest among whites and white publications in African American literature. Instead the education of blacks, the proliferation of black periodicals, and the emergence of small, usually church-affiliated black publishing operations created a new but smaller outlet for black writing within the black community.

As the optimism of emancipation faded before the growing realities of lynching, racial intimidation, and economic oppression, black writers turned to a literature that drew upon African American folk culture and history. Much of the work of uncovering the rich African American folk tradition was done in the black community. The Jubilee Singers of Fisk University, organized in 1871, popularized the spirituals as an art form, while at Hampton Institute writers for the *Southern Workman* collected and published African American folk materials. In the 1880s the Uncle Remus stories of Joel Chandler Harris, a white author, popularized traditional black trickster tales, while black writer-performers like Bob Cole and Rosamond Johnson used spirituals and traditional black musical forms to lay the foundations for black musical theater.

In spite of these developments, black literature was limited by the difficulty blacks faced in getting their works published and distributed. The black press lacked the resources to produce and market on a mass scale, especially works that challenged popular stereotypes of blacks. In the last years of the nineteenth century only two black writers managed to attain anything approaching a national reputation. Discovered and promoted by the prominent novelist, editor, and critic William Dean Howells, the poet Paul Laurence Dunbar and the novelist Charles Waddell Chesnutt were published by commercial presses and marketed nationally. They achieved their greatest popularity when they embraced black folk tradition and white stereotypes of black literature. They were much less successful when they deviated from these forms. After Dunbar privately printed his first book of poetry, *Oak and Ivy* (1893), Dodd and Mead published his next two volumes, *Majors and Minors* (1895) and *Lyrics of Lowly Life* (1896). Dunbar's most famous and most popular verse was dialect poetry that seemed nostalgic for the carefree antebellum plantation life. While Dunbar's dialect poetry can give that impression, the more powerful pieces, such as "When Malindy Sings" (1895), also project a strong sense of African American humanity and dignity. Dunbar was more effective though far less popular when he moved away from dialect poetry and celebrated black history in "The Colored Soldiers" (1895) or addressed the psychological costs of racism in "We Wear the Mask" (1895).

Chesnutt faced many of the same frustrations as Dunbar. His first successful writing utilized dialect and the character of an elderly black man, Uncle Julius, who recited folktales about slavery in Uncle Remus fashion. In spite of surface similarities, Uncle Julius was no Uncle Remus, and the plantation Chesnutt portrayed was a dark, violent, and thoroughly deromanticized setting. With the help of Howells, Chesnutt found a commercial press for his first volume of Uncle Julius stories, *The Conjure Woman* (1899). That same year Chesnutt published a second volume of short stories, *The Wife of His Youth and Other Stories of the Color Line,* which dropped dialect and focused on race relations and the African American urban elite. These stories and the three novels that followed did not achieve the success of his dialect stories.

The nineteenth century left a rich tradition in African American literature. Early in the twentieth century Chesnutt and Dunbar were joined by a host of other black poets and writers, including James Weldon Johnson and W. E. B. Du Bois, who continued to pursue the themes laid out by their predecessors as they searched for meaning in the African American experience and lay the foundations upon which African American literature flourished during the Harlem Renaissance.

See also **Abolition and Antislavery; African Americans; Emancipation; Folktales and Tall Tales; Newspapers, African American; Race and Racial Thinking; Segregation,** *article on* **Segregation and Civil Rights; Slavery.**

Bibliography

Andrews, William L., Frances Smith Foster, and Trudier Harris, eds. *The Oxford Companion to African American Literature.* New York: Oxford University Press, 1997.

Bruce, Dickson D., Jr. *Black American Writing from the Nadir: The Evolution of a Literary Tradition, 1877–1915.* Baton Rouge: Louisiana State University Press, 1989.

Foster, Frances Smith. *Written by Herself: Literary Production by African American Women, 1746–1892.* Bloomington: Indiana University Press, 1993.

Gates, Henry Louis, Jr., and Nellie Y. McKay, eds. *The Norton Anthology of African American Literature.* New York: Norton, 1997.

Jackson, Blyden. *The History of Afro-American Literature.* Volume 1: *The Long Beginning, 1746–1895.* Baton Rouge: Louisiana State University Press, 1989.

Sherman, Joan R. *Invisible Poets: Afro-Americans of the Nineteenth Century.* 2d ed. Urbana: University of Illinois Press, 1989.

Wintz, Cary D. *Black Culture and the Harlem Renaissance.* College Station: Texas A&M University Press, 1997.

CARY DECORDOVA WINTZ

THE INFLUENCE OF FOREIGN LITERATURE

In the nineteenth century American writers were urged to establish their independence from European (especially British) literary imperialism and to develop a literature reflecting American democracy, ideals, manners, culture, forms, and language. But they found it difficult to create a new literature on demand. American writers continued to read European literature, resulting in the continuation of a strong European influence on all literary forms.

The Allure of Scott

The American essayist Washington Irving (1783–1859) relied on satiric models in the English neoclassical tradition in his early works on American subjects, such as his essays in *Salmagundi* (1807–1808) and his burlesque *History of New York* (1809). But during a seventeen-year sojourn in Europe, Irving turned to European subjects, producing *The Sketch Book* (1819–1820), which lauded European culture and was dedicated to the Scottish novelist Sir Walter Scott (1771–1832). *Bracebridge Hall* (1822), set in England, was followed by *The Alhambra* (1832), set in Spain. All of these works reveal the influence of the European romantic movement. In Irving's best-known works, "Rip Van Winkle" and "The Legend of Sleepy Hollow" (from *The Sketch Book*), he grafted the homegrown American characters of Rip and Ichabod Crane onto stories steeped in the European Gothic tradition and based on German folktales.

In 1820 the American novelist James Fenimore Cooper (1789–1851) published *Precaution,* a study of English rural manners modeled after *Persuasion* (1817), by the English novelist Jane Austen (1775–1817). The following year, despite having criticized Irving for falling under the spell of Scott, Cooper himself turned to Scott for inspiration in *The Spy* (1821) and modeled *The Pilot* (1823) after Scott's *The Pirate* (1821), while including a preface criticizing Scott. As with Irving, Cooper's ability to hybridize European models and American subjects established his reputation. In *The Pioneers* (1823), *The Last of the Mohicans* (1826), *The Prairie* (1827), *The Pathfinder* (1840), and *The Deerslayer* (1841), Cooper borrowed from several of Scott's novels. He transferred the British versus Scottish Highlanders story of Scott's *Rob Roy* (1817) to the American wilderness, where he changed it into a struggle between whites and American Indians. Ironically, the Leather-Stocking series gained Cooper the title "the American Scott."

Other Americanized Scott novels include *Swallow Barn* (1832) by John Pendleton Kennedy (1795–1870) and *Guy Rivers* (1834) and *The Yemassee* (1835) by William Gilmore Simms (1806–1870). Scott's popularity also inspired the playwright James Nelson Barker's (1784–1858) dramatization of *Marmion* (1812), the first of many such stage adaptations of Scott's novels.

Although many nineteenth-century American

playwrights wrote about American subjects, they also used the melodramatic form developed in France by Guilbert de Pixérécourt (1773–1844) and in Germany by August Friedrich Ferdinand von Kotzebue (1761–1819). *She Would Be a Soldier* (1819), by Mordecai Manuel Noah (1785–1851), takes place during the War of 1812. It features a noble American Indian, Yankee humor, and patriotic speeches, but its plot utilizes the stock characters and sensational plot devices typical of melodrama. The virtuous heroine, disguised as a soldier, is arrested, condemned to death for treason, and saved by the noble hero; virtue and nobility are rewarded. Once the American public developed a taste for melodrama, dramatists were unable to escape this pervasive but popular European influence. Even George L. Aiken's (1830–1876) adaptation of *Uncle Tom's Cabin* (1852), in which he strove to be true to the American novelist Harriet Beecher Stowe's (1811–1896) semirealistic portrayal of slavery, could not escape the sentimentality and exaggeration of virtue and villainy that are characteristics of the melodramatic form. Another treatment of the slavery issue, *The Octoroon* (1859), by the Irish-born American playwright Dion Boucicault (1820–1890), contains every nuance of melodrama ever invented. The form retained its popularity throughout the century.

Romanticism and the American Renaissance

Early in his career, the poet and short-story writer Edgar Allan Poe (1809–1849) imitated Lord Byron's (1788–1824) romantic poetry, as well as his black clothing and melancholy air. But as a reviewer of European literature, Poe became exposed to other influences, most importantly the English and German Gothic. In his *Anglo-American Encounters* (1981), the American critic Benjamin Lease cites the German romantic E. T. A. Hoffmann's (1776–1822) "The Devil's Elixir" (translated 1824) as a major source for Poe's "William Wilson" (1839). Both stories have a hero who must deal with his double. Lease also notes that in reviewing the English novelist Charles Dickens's (1812–1870) *Pickwick Papers* (1836–1837), Poe admired the *Pickwick* tale "A Madman's Manuscript," which bears similarities to Poe's own "Ligeia" (1838). Both plots deal with a man's desire to murder his wife. A source for Poe's "The Tell-Tale Heart" (1843) is Dickens's short tale "Confession Found in a Prison in the Time of Charles the Second," from *Master Humphrey's Clock* (1840–1841), praised by Poe in his review of *The Old Curiosity Shop* (1840–1841). In both stories, a murderer is haunted by the accusing eye of his victim. In addition, Poe was influenced by the English poet Samuel Taylor Coleridge (1772–1834). Narrative echoes of Coleridge's "Rime of the Ancient Mariner" (1798) appear in Poe's "MS. Found in a Bottle" (1833).

The primary European influence on the American poet William Cullen Bryant (1794–1878) was the English poet William Wordsworth (1770–1850). Adopting ideas from Wordsworth's preface to *Lyrical Ballads* (1798, 1800, 1802, 1805), Bryant asserts, in his essay "Poets and Poetry of the English Language" (1876), that poetry should deal with everyday life and one's communion with nature. Bryant's extensive use of Wordsworthian models can be seen in "Thanatopsis" (1817), "After a Tempest" (1824), "Lines on Revisiting the Country" (1825), and "A Summer Ramble" (1826), among others.

Coleridge, Wordsworth, and the Scottish historian Thomas Carlyle (1795–1881) all influenced the American poet and essayist Ralph Waldo Emerson (1803–1882). In his essay "The Poet" (1844), based on Wordsworth's *Lyrical Ballads*, Emerson extolled Wordsworth's idea that poets possess the ability to explore the relationship not just between humans and nature, but also between humans and the universe. In "Self-Reliance" (1841) and "Nature" (1844), Emerson echoed Wordsworth's belief in the cleansing power of nature. Coleridge's interpretation of the difference between fancy and the imagination in *Biographia Literaria* (1817) inspired Emerson's 1836 lecture "Modern Aspects of Letters." Emerson utilized Coleridge's theory that the imagination sees unity in all things in developing his own theory of the "oversoul." He also agreed with Coleridge that a poem's content, not its traditional meter and rhythm, should mold its organic form. Carlyle's *On Heroes, Hero-Worship, and the Heroic in History* (1841) gave Emerson the inspiration and structure for *Representative Men* (1850). Like Carlyle, he became interested in chants as a basis for new poetic forms and adopted Carlyle's idea of the poet as prophet.

Emerson passed on many of his adopted European ideas to other American writers. In his celebration of nature in *A Week on the Concord and Merrimack Rivers* (1849) and *Walden, or Life in the Woods* (1854), the American essayist Henry David Thoreau (1817–1862) expressed European romantic ideas voiced by Emerson. The American poet Walt Whitman (1819–1892), like Emerson, was inspired by Carlyle's idea of the poet as prophet. In eschewing meter and rhythm, Whitman adopted Emerson's ideas, based on Coleridge's, which helped in his own development of free verse.

Like Cooper, the American novelist Nathaniel Hawthorne (1804–1864) was influenced by Scott. The plot of Hawthorne's *The Scarlet Letter* (1850) is similar to that of Scott's *The Heart of Midlothian*

(1818). Both books deal with a community's punishment of a sinful woman who has given birth to a child but refuses to identify the father. The problem of the individual versus society is explored both in Hawthorne's *The House of the Seven Gables* (1851) and in Scott's *Guy Mannering* (1815). Hawthorne's *House* also shares with Scott's *The Bride of Lammermoor* (1819) a hint of the supernatural: both stories involve a family curse.

The American novelist Herman Melville's (1819–1891) European models included François Rabelais (1483–1553), John Milton (1608–1674), and Coleridge, but Carlyle, William Shakespeare (1564–1616), and the Bible most influenced his fiction. In Melville's *Moby-Dick* (1851), Ahab's name and his desire for eye-for-an-eye vengeance follow Old Testament models. Ahab's language contains nautical terms and colloquial Americanisms, but its style and tone are Shakespearean. In *British Influence on the Birth of American Literature* (1982), Linden Peach traces Melville's use of the analogy between clothes and house from Carlyle's *Sartor Resartus* (1833–1834), his use of the sphinx image from Carlyle's *Past and Present* (1843), and echoes of Carlyle's defense of paganism from *On Heroes, Hero-Worship, and the Heroic in History* in Melville's positive treatment of Queequeg's character.

Realism and Naturalism

Like Emerson before him, the American novelist and essayist William Dean Howells (1837–1920) was an influential advocate and transmitter of European literary trends. The successful author of *A Modern Instance* (1882) and *The Rise of Silas Lapham* (1885), Howells became dissatisfied with American and English literature, considering both too narrow. He pointed to the years 1887–1888 as a turning point in his thinking and writing because he became interested in the doctrines of European socialism and fell under the influence of the Russian novelist Leo Tolstoy (1828–1910), whose ethical ideas affected Howells profoundly. In turn, Howells affected other American writers by writing essays such as "Tolstoy's Creed" (July 1887) and "Breadth in Literature" (September 1887) for *Harper's*. Between 1886 and 1892 Howells's monthly column in *Harper's* denounced romanticism, promoted realism, and praised European continental writers such as Russia's Tolstoy and Ivan Turgenev (1818–1883), the French novelist Émile Zola (1840–1902), and the Norwegian playwright Henrik Ibsen (1828–1906) for their development of realism and their sense of universal brotherhood. In such novels as *Annie Kilburn* (1888) and *A Hazard of New Fortunes* (1890), Howells prac-

ticed what he preached. Like Tolstoy, he championed commonplace characters and commented on problems caused by governmental abuses, social prejudices, and economic inequality.

Some of Howells's fellow American writers listened to him but went beyond his brand of realism, adopting the French naturalism of Zola. This is apparent in Hamlin Garland's (1860–1940) *Main-Travelled Roads* (1891) and Theodore Dreiser's (1871–1945) *Sister Carrie* (1900), which depict the sordid details of their characters' lives and make didactic pronouncements about fixing society's ills.

The expatriate American novelist Henry James (1843–1916), an admirer of Howells, used realistic techniques. But in works like *The Portrait of a Lady* (1881), *What Maisie Knew* (1897), *The Wings of the Dove* (1902), and *The Ambassadors* (1903), James demonstrated a psychological insight into character and a concern for moral choices more reminiscent of Ibsen than of Howells. Ibsen's plays, such as *A Doll's House* (1879) and *Hedda Gabler* (1890), focus on the social, psychological, and philosophical problems of modern times. Both James's and Ibsen's works pointed forward to the twentieth century.

See also **Folktales and Tall Tales; Literature,** *subentries on* **Fiction, Poetry; Realism and Naturalism; Romanticism.**

Bibliography

Lease, Benjamin. *Anglo-American Encounters: England and the Rise of American Literature.* Cambridge and New York: Cambridge University Press, 1981.

Matthiessen, Francis O. *American Renaissance: Art and Expression in the Age of Emerson and Whitman.* London and New York: Oxford University Press, 1968.

Peach, Linden. *British Influence on the Birth of American Literature.* London: Macmillan, 1982.

Ringe, Donald A. *American Gothic: Imagination and Reason in Nineteenth-Century Fiction.* Lexington: University Press of Kentucky, 1982.

Spencer, Benjamin T. *The Quest for Nationality: An American Literary Campaign.* Syracuse, N.Y.: Syracuse University Press, 1957.

Weisbuch, Robert. *Atlantic Double-Cross: American Literature and British Influence in the Age of Emerson.* Chicago: University of Chicago Press, 1986.

Wilson, Garff B. *Three Hundred Years of American Drama and Theatre: From Ye Bare and Ye Cubb to Chorus Line.* Englewood Cliffs, N.J.: Prentice-Hall, 1982.

PEGGY ANNE RUSSO

LITHOGRAPHY AND PRINTS Until the final years of the eighteenth century, printed images were made from incised planks of wood or metal plates. These traditional techniques had been in use in Europe since late medieval times. In the United States, woodcuts and wood engravings were generally used as illustrations in books or on broadsides and ephemera. Engravings from copperplates were made for books and ephemera, but were also made to be sold as larger format, separately published prints.

European Roots

Many engravers came to Philadelphia and New York from Great Britain at the end of the eighteenth century, bringing with them technical skills and a desire to succeed in an emerging commercial market. They produced portrait prints, town and city views, and political and social satires. Patriotic sentiments during and just after the War of 1812 increased the popularity of prints of military and naval battles and political caricatures. British-born engravers William J. Bennett, William Charles, David Edwin, John Hill, William S. Leney, and William Rollinson joined native-born engravers Amos Doolittle, Francis Kearney, James B. Longacre, Abner Reed, and Joseph Yaeger, among others, to produce a body of separately published engravings, often sold by subscription. These engravings, however, appealed only to a small segment of the American public because they were expensive. Each image was tedious to produce and preparing the copperplate for printing was a slow process. Coloring was applied by hand. Framing and glazing were added expenses.

By 1800, artists in Europe had begun to experiment with a new printmaking medium—lithography—which, by mid-century, would transform the market for prints in the United States, expanding it beyond the province of the elite. To make lithographs, draftsmen drew directly on carefully prepared limestone, and the design was affixed chemically. Lithographic inking and printing reduced the amount of labor required to produce impressions. The price of prints dropped to pennies per image, making them available to all but the poorest consumers. As the market for lithographs expanded, so did their subject matter. Portraits of actors, views of disasters, and sentimental scenes proliferated. As the century progressed, steam presses replaced hand printing. By 1850 several firms produced lithographs printed in color; within two decades chromolithographs were published in editions of thousands of impressions. Printed on paper embossed to imitate fabric, varnished, and sold framed, they resembled oil paintings.

American Innovations

The earliest significant American experiments in lithography occurred between 1810 and 1820 in Philadelphia (Bass Otis and Alexandre Lesueur) and in

---

Nathaniel Currier (1813–1888)

Currier moved to New York City in 1834, after leaving the Pendleton printmaking firm in Boston in 1833 and working briefly in Philadelphia. Although there were other competing firms in New York, Currier, who was joined by his brother-in-law James Merritt Ives in 1857, dominated the trade throughout the nineteenth century. Employing such artists as Louis Maurer, Fanny Palmer, Charles Parsons, Arthur Fitzwilliam Tait, and Thomas Worth, the firm produced over 7,500 prints in addition to book illustrations, advertising cards, and other job printing. Their prints appealed to a wide array of tastes and budgets. For recent European immigrants and Spanish missions in the American Southwest, prints of Catholic saints and other religious images poured forth, alongside illustrations of biblical stories that appealed to Protestant taste. Handsome large folio prints, reproducing the New England winter landscapes of George Henry Durrie, competed with more sentimental farmyard scenes and pictures of domestic animals. The firm served maritime tastes by publishing appealing prints of steamships and sailing vessels. The sports-minded were well served by humorous hunting scenes by Thomas Worth and stunning portraits of trotters and race horses. Currier and Ives's prints were distributed widely by mail order throughout the country.

GEORGIA BRADY BARNHILL

New York (Arthur J. Stansbury). The first commercially successful publisher of lithographs was the Boston firm organized in 1825 by John B. Pendleton and his brother William S. Pendleton. Among their apprentices were John H. Bufford, Nathaniel Currier, and Moses Swett, each of whom established their own firms.

William Pendleton continued the firm until 1836, when he sold it to Thomas Moore, a former employee. In 1840 Moore sold the firm to John H. Bufford. These publishers attracted important artists who drew portraits, landscape views, depictions of buildings and cities, and genre prints to be sold in stores and by salesmen. Among the artists who produced these prints were Joseph E. Baker, Robert Cooke, Leopold Grozelier, Winslow Homer, David Claypoole Johnston, Fitz Hugh Lane, John Perry Newell, Rembrandt Peale, and Benjamin F. Nutting.

Other popular print publishers thrived in other cities. In Hartford, Connecticut, for example, the firm established by Daniel W. Kellogg and his various partners published prints similar in subject matter to those of Nathaniel Currier, but of lesser quality. Many of their prints were copied from those of Currier.

William B. Lucas issued the first commercially published lithograph in Philadelphia in 1827. A year later he formed a partnership with David Kennedy, and they published several prints of churches in the city. The engraver Francis Kearney turned to lithography at the end of his career, forming a brief partnership with John B. Pendleton and Cephas G. Childs in 1829. Childs then published lithographs with the artist Henry Inman from 1831 to 1834. This well-connected partnership attracted such artists as Thomas Doughty, George Lehman, and Albert Newsam to draw portraits and views on stone. Sometimes firms, such as Childs and Inman, published prints for themselves, sometimes for dealers in dry goods and household furnishings, importers of prints, and picture framers. As national political life evolved, a few publishers, such as Henry R. Robinson in New York City, focused their efforts on political prints.

The firms of Nathaniel Currier and later Currier & Ives also published political prints. Nathaniel Currier often used the pseudonym Peter Smith for these topical, sometimes controversial, prints. During the Civil War, Currier & Ives published a substantial number of political prints supporting the Union cause. By the time these prints were published, the artists used photographs as sources for the portraits in the caricatures.

In the second half of the century, political unrest in Europe, particularly in Germany, resulted in the emigration of several experienced lithographic pressmen and the introduction of chromolithography to many cities. Louis Prang in Boston specialized in the production of chromolithographs, colored prints made from multiple stones, one for each color. The finest of the prints were made from up to forty-five stones in a complex process. Prang chose his subjects carefully, concentrating his efforts on reproductions of American paintings by such artists as Alfred T. Bricher, Eastman Johnson, and Arthur Fitzwilliam Tait. He also issued small album cards of flowers, birds, and scenery.

Lithographs, whether black and white or colored, did not completely supplant the production of engravings. Throughout the century, publishers produced black-and-white prints for an elite audience.

"American Scenery: The Inn on the Roadside." Representative of many nineteeth-century American lithographs, this scene is a complex depiction of diverse activities. Color lithograph printed by E. Sachse & Company, Baltimore, 1872. LIBRARY OF CONGRESS

Summer Reading. Lithograph by Louis John Rhead for *Century Magazine*, 1894, Midsummer Holiday Number. LIBRARY OF CONGRESS

John Sartain arrived from England in 1830 and settled in Philadelphia, where he produced skillful mezzotint engravings, reproducing portrait paintings, historical subjects, and genre scenes. His sons Samuel and William followed in his tradition. In New York City and elsewhere, art unions flourished. The American Art Union published reproductive engravings after works by George Caleb Bingham, Thomas Cole, John Frederick Kensett, and others in editions of up to ten thousand impressions. The French art dealer Goupil, Vibert and Company had an office in New York, from which they published engravings taken from American works and sold European engravings. Many reproductive engravings, including bird's-eye views of cities, portrait prints, and genre prints were published by subscription.

During the second half of the century, American painters began to experiment with etching, following the lead of European artists. George Loring Brown, Edwin Forbes, Robert Swain Gifford, Otto Bacher, Mary Nimmo Moran, Thomas Moran, Stephen Par-

rish, and J. Alden Weir are among those who produced etchings in limited numbers for a market restricted to collectors of fine art. The so-called etching revival lasted through the 1890s.

Large format photographs emerged in the later decades of the century to compete with separately published prints. Purchasers often framed them for viewing in offices and parlors. Some city views, for example, were published commercially as photographs rather than as lithographs. Toward the end of the century, photographic technology was used by publishers to transfer images to printing plates.

Print publishers served a valuable function during the nineteenth century. Reproductive prints made American painters well known and enhanced the market for their paintings. Print images of political and military leaders educated generations of Americans. Separately published political prints enlivened the discourse surrounding elections and other political activities. Civic pride was expressed in the many prints made of churches, public buildings, and cities.

Today these prints give a valuable visual dimension to historians' understanding of American culture in the nineteenth century.

See also **Cartoons, Political; Printing Technology.**

Bibliography

Bruhn, Thomas. *The American Print: Originality and Experimentation 1790–1890.* Storrs: University of Connecticut, 1993.

Currier & Ives. A Catalogue Raisonne. Detroit, Mich.: Gale, 1984.

Ebert, John, and Katherine Ebert. *Old American Prints for Collectors.* New York: Scribners, 1974.

Marzio, Peter. *The Democratic Art; Chromolithography, 1840–1900: Pictures for a Nineteenth-Century America.* Boston: Godine, 1979.

Pierce, Sally, and Catharina Slautterback. *Boston Lithography, 1825–1880.* Boston: Boston Athenaeum, 1991.

Wainwright, Nicholas. *Philadelphia in the Romantic Age of Lithography.* Philadelphia: Historical Society of Pennsylvania, 1958.

GEORGIA BRADY BARNHILL

LOCAL GOVERNMENT

LOCAL GOVERNMENT   During the first half of the nineteenth century, democratic institutions were not fully developed at the local level. In 1800, major urban areas such as Cincinnati, Brooklyn, Buffalo, and St. Louis did not have city charters. The governor of the Orleans Territory controlled New Orleans before Louisiana became a state, while the U.S. president controlled Washington, D.C. Even when cities or settlements were chartered, it was accepted that local governments were subordinate to their state's government. State constitutions usually ignored the issue of local governance. In the few cases where it was mentioned, the state asserted itself as the governing authority for cities, towns, and villages. For example, in 1821 the Massachusetts Constitution gave its legislature full and final authority to erect and constitute local and municipal governments. State supreme courts upheld the states' authority over local governments. In *Berlin v. Gorham* (1856), the New Hampshire Supreme Court concluded, "the legislature has entire control over municipal corporations, to create, change, or destroy them at pleasure, and they are absolutely created by the act of incorporation (with or) without the acceptance of the people."

Rise of Local Government

John Forrest Dillon (1831–1914), chief justice of the Iowa Supreme Court, established a constitutional basis for state authority over towns and cities. In *City of Clinton v. Cedar Rapids and Missouri River Railroad* (1868), he argued there was no constitutionally guaranteed right of local self-government, calling municipal corporations "mere administrative conveniences of the state." This concept, known as Dillon's Rule, reinforced the right of state governments to intervene in local government affairs.

Despite strong state authority, local governments began to evolve into more independent governing bodies toward the end of the nineteenth century. Growing cities needed political and administrative authority to tax and manage budgets, enforce local regulations, and invest in public works projects. Though these needs were contested at the state level, a legal foundation for local government gradually took shape. Thomas Cooley (1824–1898), chief justice of the Michigan Supreme Court, argued in *People ex rel LeRoy v. Hurblut* (1871) that local government was a right, not a privilege. He contended that although the state constitution did not directly support a system of local government, a right of local governance existed because of its historical and political primacy as a means of securing popular liberty.

Cities also began to solidify their local governing authority by pursuing home rule, a legal concept that limits state intervention in local politics and guarantees some degree of autonomy for municipalities. Adopting home rule gave local governments jurisdiction over their own affairs, and prevented state legislatures from passing laws that applied only to specific localities, instead of to the entire state. In the 1870s Missouri and California became the first states to adopt home rule constitutions, which included the provision that cities "shall have all powers which the state assembly has the authority to confer on the city." The home rule movement, coupled with the sheer complexity of providing services to a rapidly growing population, fostered greater local autonomy. By the end of the nineteenth century, local governments had the right to collect taxes, build public works projects, and pass ordinances that concerned citizens' health, safety, and public welfare.

Formation of Local Government

Local jurisdictions are administered on various geographic levels, including counties, townships, and municipalities. During the nineteenth century, as settlers moved farther and farther west, county governments were formed to administer local services in geographically large, mostly rural areas. Counties, or shires, originally were created in England as political and administrative subdivisions of the regional or central government, and the system was transposed to the British colonies. After the United States became a nation, county administrations served as the local governments in sparsely populated areas. County borders were drawn in accordance with the idea that a farmer from anywhere in the county had to be able to travel by horse and wagon to the county seat, conduct business there, and return home the same day, between his morning and evening chore hours. County governments performed a variety of functions, such as recording deeds and providing law enforcement, judicial review, social welfare assistance, and road construction and maintenance.

As county populations grew throughout the nineteenth century, smaller administrative jurisdictions became necessary. Counties often were subdivided into civil townships. (These differ from survey townships: six-mile-square units of land, which frequently were used in New England counties.) U.S. civil townships were common in the 1800s, especially in the Northeast and Midwest. While the main purpose of townships was to bring local government closer to rural residents, their actual services were very similar to those provided in nondivided counties. Sometimes the township lines doubled as the school district boundaries. After the nineteenth century, townships stopped functioning as a local government unit. By the mid–twentieth century, many townships had been eliminated and had their government functions transferred back to the county.

Unlike counties and townships, municipalities are characterized geographically as single settlements consisting primarily of built structures arranged in a contiguous pattern. They may take the form of towns, villages, or cities. There is no true standard for distinguishing among the various types of municipalities. However, in general villages have fewer residents while towns and cities have more.

Municipalities are chartered or incorporated by states for the purpose of governance at the local level. They are empowered to create local regulations, called ordinances, as long as the ordinances are within the bounds of federal laws and state statutes. The government structure in individual municipalities varied widely during the nineteenth century, particularly with regard to citizen representation, public administration, and political organization.

New England towns, as well as early-nineteenth-century Boston and Providence, maintained a unique form of local government: the town hall. All eligible voters exercised their governing functions directly at scheduled town meetings, without using a mayor or elected council members. As town populations increased, governing using the town hall system became more complicated. Adjustments were made, such as creating "selectmen" who were appointed by the town hall to manage specific civil services. These services covered a broad range of functions, including fire protection, public education, sealing of weights and measures, road surveying, and cording of wood. Some cities made further adjustments to accommodate governing their rapidly growing populations. For example, Boston developed written ballots for its wards, where residents voted. Then, in 1813, the city created a town finance committee for selecting tax collectors and the town treasurer. The committee consisted of board of health members, selectmen, and overseers of the poor. Gradually, Boston's town hall form of government evolved into a system of governance by professional civil servants. In 1822 the city adopted a new charter and elected its first mayor, John Phillips (1770–1823).

Charleston, South Carolina, gave voters the greatest choice in selecting governing officials. The city's system of government, which began in 1783, gave voters the power to elect one warden in each of Charleston's thirteen wards to perform legislative functions. A citywide election decided which warden would serve as the intendant—the official responsible for guiding legislative procedures. A single council, which consisted of the intendant and a single warden chosen by voters, performed executive duties.

New Orleans was chartered as a city in 1805, and was primarily controlled by the governor. For legislative purposes, the city was divided into seven wards. Residents elected two aldermen from each ward. The fourteen aldermen along with the city recorder, who was selected by the governor, created municipal ordinances. The governor had veto power over the city's government.

As the century progressed, local political power gradually moved from neighborhood representatives such as wardens and aldermen to the mayor's office and special commissions. This was most apparent in New York City, which, in the early 1800s, was controlled by a council of neighborhood-elected aldermen. By the middle of the century, authority over services related to health, fire, and police had been given to state-appointed commissions. Further, funding and appropriations were slowly taken away from city councilmen and put in the hands of William M. "Boss" Tweed (1823–1878). In 1870 he revised the city charter to create a board of audit for administering outstanding debts. In 1871 Tweed created the board of apportionment to administer current finances. Finally, in 1873 a further revision created the board of estimate and apportionment. This board had the additional responsibility of drafting the city budget and creating the city tax rate. The new board's officers consisted of the mayor, the comptroller, and the president of the department of taxes and assessments; they were responsible for drafting the budget and adjusting the city tax rate.

Toward the end of the nineteenth century, mayors played an increasingly influential role in governing U.S. cities. Their influence was wielded through the power of the veto. Some cities enacted the line-item veto, which allowed the mayor to reject certain items in an ordinance while still signing the remainder into law. Typically a council would need a two-thirds majority vote to override a veto; this was not accomplished easily. In Chicago only 9 out of 60 vetoes were overridden between the years 1882 and 1889. In Baltimore only 8 out of 118 vetoes were overridden during the same period. Veto power made the mayor the most influential player in local government.

Providing Services and Infrastructure

During the nineteenth century, providing services such as education, fire protection, police, and infrastructure maintenance became major functions of local governments. Education administration was taken out of the hands of counties and municipalities and became the duty of local school districts. Having an autonomous school district ensured that the education system's curriculum and administration would not be burdened by partisan politics. The school districts were run by elected school-board members. Thus, citizens were motivated to vote for candidates based on their expertise or policy goals and not their political party affiliation.

The administration and operation of local fire protection also changed during the nineteenth century. Fire companies evolved from loosely controlled and independently managed volunteer groups into a highly organized and effective local government service. Early-nineteenth-century volunteer firefighting companies were not effective; the unpaid volunteers often lacked ambition, professional competence, and firefighting expertise. Firefighters also were known to be highly politicized and in many cases violent. From the 1850s through the 1870s, cities dismissed volunteer firefighters and replaced them with full-time salaried employees, thus ensuring a stronger degree of expertise and professionalism. In addition, civil-service laws in major cities such as Chicago and New York protected firefighters from dismissal based on political motives.

Police departments also went through a tremendous change in the 1800s. At the beginning of the century, law enforcement was conducted by privately paid constables and volunteer night watchmen. This system was fraught with inefficiency: poor people could not afford the constable's services and the night watchmen frequently were incompetent. In the mid–nineteenth century, organized uniformed police departments officially replaced the constables and night watchmen. The new policemen often were hired and fired at the will of local politicians. Their allegiance was to the aldermen and not necessarily to the public. Thus, police forces frequently were corrupt and racked with incompetence. Toward the end of the century, in order to combat this corruption and favoritism, cities organized separate bipartisan commissions to run their police forces.

Growing cities also needed public works departments to build and maintain their infrastructure. Providing water lines, sewers, electric lines, streets, and bridges required a substantial monetary investment as well as professional engineering. Toward the end of the nineteenth century, local governments began creating special commissions and departments to oversee their infrastructure. These departments usually were headed by professionals such as civil engineers, who were responsible for managing new projects, maintaining existing systems, and reporting to the local government's legislative and executive branches.

See also **City and Regional Planning; Fires and Firefighting; Government; Police; Politics,** *subentry on* **Machines and Bosses; State Government; Territorial Government.**

Bibliography

American Public Works Association. *History of Public Works in the United States, 1776–1976.* Edited by Ellis L. Armstrong. Chicago: American Public Works Association, 1976.

Beard, Charles A. *American City Government: A Survey of Newer Tendencies.* New York: Century, 1912.

Curry, Leonard P. *The Corporate City: The American City as a Political Entity, 1800–1850.* Westport, Conn.: Greenwood, 1997.

McKelvey, Blake. *The City in American History.* London: Allen and Unwin, 1969.

Teaford, Jon C. *The Unheralded Triumph: City Government in America, 1870–1900.* Baltimore: Johns Hopkins University Press, 1984.

BARRY BAIN

LOS ANGELES   Settled in 1781 as part of Spain's efforts to secure a northern frontier, El Pueblo de la Reina de Los Angeles developed from a colonial outpost to a burgeoning international city during the nineteenth century. From its beginning Los Angeles was racially and ethnically mixed, including Native Americans, Africans, Spanish, mestizos, and after the 1840s Europeans and Asians. An ebb and flow of conflict and accommodation among these residents defined the city's nineteenth-century economy, politics, geography, and cultural terrain.

The local economy was initially centered around agricultural production and stock raising on large ranchos surrounding an urban villa. During the nineteenth century the city became a trading center for beef, tallow, and hides. Following the U.S. conquest and acquisition of the area from Mexico in 1848, Californio elites lost most of their land to Euramerican speculators. Subsequent Euramerican investment in large-scale commercial agriculture and stock raising, real estate development, and light manufacturing transformed the local economy.

The population grew from only 11,183 in 1880 to 50,395 in 1890 and 102,479 in 1900. The city divided and segmented along ethnic and class lines, and the Mexican pueblo became a Mexican American barrio in the city's central business district. For many this change symbolized the decreasing political and economic power of the city's Spanish-speaking residents. But the plaza communities were social space for families, political clubs, religious organizations, and a Spanish-language press.

See also **Barrios; California; Immigration and Immigrants**, *subentries on* **Mexico and Latin America, Asia; Mexican Americans; Mexican War.**

Bibliography

Fogelson, Robert M. *The Fragmented Metropolis: Los Angeles, 1850–1930*. Berkeley: University of California Press, 1993. The original edition was published in 1967.

Griswold del Castillo, Richard. *The Los Angeles Barrio, 1850–1890: A Social History*. Berkeley: University of California Press, 1979.

Ríos-Bustamante, Antonio, and Pedro Castillo. *An Illustrated History of Mexican Los Angeles, 1781–1985*. Los Angeles: University of California, Chicano Studies Research Center Publications, 1986.

DAVID A. REICHARD

LOUISIANA   The history of nineteenth-century Louisiana is one of men and their struggle for power. Louisiana began the nineteenth century as a Spanish colony but was retroceded to France in October 1800. Napoleon Bonaparte (1769–1821) wanted to revive France's empire, but his dream went unrealized. On 30 April 1803, he sold his newest prize to the United States for $15 million. Before 1800 Louisiana was underdeveloped and underpopulated; after 1800 its economy prospered as planters in southern Louisiana found a way to granulate sugar and planters in the northern parishes of the state began to profit from ginned cotton. As the region fell under American rule and its planters began to experience prosperity, U.S. settlers began to pour into the sparsely populated territory.

The first years of American rule were difficult for Louisianians of all colors, social classes, and origins. Native Creoles, the white descendants of the region's early European settlers, spoke French. Newcomers, including Governor W. C. C. Claiborne (1775–1817), spoke English. There were French and English courts, French and English police forces, and interpreters for everything else. But the interpreters could not solve all the problems. English-speaking immigrants suffered culture shock as they tried to settle into the rhythms of the budding territory. Americans believed the French-speaking Creoles to be uneducated and provincial, while the Creoles considered the English-speaking Americans to be culturally backward. Even though diversity segregated Creoles from Americans, culturally the groups increasingly were knit together in their attitudes about slavery and the potential for plantation agriculture. White planters, yeoman farmers, merchants, and their poor neighbors—no matter their language—were united in their attitudes about the productivity of plantation slavery.

The growth of Louisiana's economic and population sectors mirrored the growth of its port city. Between 1810 and 1860, New Orleans became the largest city west of the Appalachian Mountains. In 1846 the editor J. D. B. De Bow (1820–1867) predicted that New Orleans would be to the "Father of Waters" (the Mississippi River) as was "London to the Thames and Paris to the Seine." Long before New Orleans took its primacy as an international port, Louisiana was admitted to the Union (1812) as the eighteenth state. Louisianians united in order soundly to defeat the British at the Battle of New Orleans in 1815. English-speaking Americans and French-speaking Creoles, black freed people, and slaves joined together in an attempt to free, once and for all, the United States from domination by Great Britain.

Between 1830 and 1850, as the state's planter elite sought to reinforce the profitability of plantation slavery, new groups of Irish and Germans poured into the state, creating an even more diverse population, especially in the cities. That population grew from approximately 80,000 in 1812 to 708,002 in 1860. The economy grew along with the population. In 1830, $22 million of produce passed through the port of New Orleans. In 1860, the value had increased to $185 million.

Although few Louisianians profited directly from the institution of slavery, the overwhelming number of free residents accepted the notion that white people could own people of African descent and that they could and should earn profits from slave labor. With that mentality, few objected to Louisiana's secession from the Union after Abraham Lincoln's (1809–1865) election to the presidency. By early 1861, Louisiana had joined the other Deep South states at Montgomery, Alabama, to form the Confederate States of America. In July of the same year, Louisianians were fighting at Manassas; they contributed to the ranks of the Confederate Army throughout the war. Between 1861 and 1865, at least fifty thousand Louisianians joined the fighting. A description of the men who joined the Confederate war effort is complex. Most were white, though a significant number were free Creoles of color. These men were later opposed in the fighting by freed slaves, many of whom shared a common heritage, who fought on the side of the Union Army. By the end of the war the state lay in ruins. Some historians place the financial loss suffered by Louisiana at more than $3 billion. By war's end, the state's agriculture was devastated: its slaves had been emancipated and, even though they were still able to produce, the capital they represented had collapsed. Plantations and farms, fields, and fences lay in ruins. Livestock had been eaten or stolen. Roads were rutted, and levees had ruptured, due to the lack of maintenance.

When the war ended white southerners had one agenda: to force newly freed African Americans back into positions of subordination. As African Americans struggled to assert their rights, the legislature passed black codes designed to restrict the freed slaves' movements, require them to work under labor contracts, and punish any "insubordinate" behavior. The legislature also set up the convict-lease system, which leased a prisoner's services, usually to a planter, for a year. By 1866 newly freed slaves, freedpeople of color, and a few northerners had organized the Republican Party in the state and begun to seek to secure the franchise. By 1868 Louisiana's Reconstruction government served as a symbol of black civil and political rights. Although violence aimed at blacks was not rooted out, African Americans in Louisiana made significant political, economic, and social strides during Reconstruction and even after federal troops were withdrawn from the state in 1877.

The Civil War left wrenching poverty in Louisiana. The postwar agricultural systems of tenancy and sharecropping institutionalized that poverty. The war and Reconstruction intensified the harsh racism present in Louisiana and poisoned the state's social relations for the next century.

See also **Civil War; Convict Leasing; Creoles; New Orleans; Reconstruction,** subentry on **The South.**

Bibliography

Cummins, Light Townsend, et al. Louisiana: A History. 3d ed. Edited by Bennett H. Wall. Wheeling, Ill.: Harlan Davidson, 1997.

Malone, Ann Patton. Sweet Chariot: Slave Family and Household Structure in Nineteenth-Century Louisiana. Chapel Hill: University of North Carolina Press, 1992.

Shugg, Roger W. Origins of Class Struggle in Louisiana: A Social History of White Farmers and Laborers During Slavery and After, 1840–1875. 1939. Reprint, Baton Rouge: Louisiana State University Press, 1968.

Taylor, Joe Gray. Louisiana Reconstructed, 1863–1877. Baton Rouge: Louisiana State University Press, 1974.

VIRGINIA MEACHAM GOULD

LOUISIANA PURCHASE   In 1803 the United States obtained a vast territory between the Mississippi River and the Rocky Mountains. President Thomas Jefferson had initially sought France's guarantee that Americans could use the port at New Orleans. He wanted assurance that farmers in the Tennessee River and Ohio River valleys could ship goods down the Mississippi and on to Atlantic basin markets. Instead, Napoleon Bonaparte offered the United States all of France's North American holdings, the western half of the Mississippi Valley. Napoleon concluded that, in view of France's waning fortunes in a war to suppress a slave uprising in Saint Domingue, he no longer needed Louisiana as a military post or breadbasket and that, in view of an imminent return to war with England, it was better to convert the territory to cash.

If Jefferson accepted the offer, the United States would double in territory, and both banks of the Mississippi River would be under American control. As he pondered a constitutional amendment to authorize the purchase, he gave as a major justification the prospect of clearing American Indians from land east of the Mississippi by offering them lands in the West. Given the dim prospects of timely ratification and the unlikelihood that Napoleon's offer would wait, Jefferson decided to go ahead with the deal without express constitutional authority. The river and the territory became America's, though the trade advantages were briefly jeopardized during the War of 1812 when English forces attacked New Orleans. The removal of Indians into present-day Oklahoma, which was part of the new territory, was largely accomplished by 1840 and facilitated the Cotton Kingdom's expansion through Alabama and Mississippi. Trans-Mississippi lands acquired in the purchase permitted slavery's extension through Louisiana and Arkansas.

In 1819, sixteen years after the purchase, political conflict emerged because of the Louisiana Territory.

A New York congressman, James Tallmadge, proposed that Missouri be granted statehood only on the condition that it consent to a gradual end to slavery. Like a "fire bell in the night," Jefferson wrote (Fehrenbacher, *The Dred Scott Case*, p. 111), the news alarmed him. Might the Union break up over the question of slavery in those western lands? Jefferson's stunning diplomatic success in 1803, threatening now to undo a lifetime of work, jeopardized his political legacy, which harkened all the way back to the Declaration of Independence.

Indeed, in the 1850s the Kansas-Nebraska Act, designed to revisit the question of slavery in the areas of the purchase that were not yet organized into states, led to the rise of the Republican Party, which insisted on the exclusion of slavery from all western territories. Just west of Missouri, warfare broke out in Kansas Territory over the extension of slavery, presaging the Civil War.

The territory that Jefferson acquired from France made possible the land-grant college system established under the Morrill Act of 1862. By the late nineteenth century, moreover, the region became one of the world's great producers of grain and meat. Farmers in Iowa produced corn and hogs, while those in the Dakotas raised cattle and wheat. Oklahoma became an important source of crude oil. The Louisiana Purchase, envisioned to secure the political unity of the new nation, endangered it as well. In the longer run it helped the United States become an agricultural and industrial superpower.

See also **American Indians,** *subentry on* **Indian Removal; Expansion; Foreign Relations,** *subentry on* **1789–1860; Kansas-Nebraska Act; Missouri Compromise; Sectionalism; War of 1812.**

Bibliography

DeConde, Alexander. *This Affair of Louisiana.* New York: Scribners, 1976.

Fehrenbacher, Don E. *The Dred Scott Case: Its Significance in American Law and Politics.* New York: Oxford University Press, 1978.

Peterson, Merrill D. *Thomas Jefferson and the New Nation: A Biography.* New York: Oxford University Press, 1970.

PETER WALLENSTEIN

LUMBER AND TIMBER INDUSTRY

The lumbering profession dates back nearly as far as the origins of white European settlement in North America. Beginning along the coast and nearby rivers and streams, lumbering had spread by the early nineteenth century into the interior. Although there were full-time lumbering operations manned by people who depended entirely on the lumber trade for their livelihoods, much of the production of lumber was in the hands of farmers who cut and processed timber for their own use as well as for their neighbors or local marketers.

While early census reports and other sources yield some information about lumbering, constructing the history of the trade is difficult. Many of those who were engaged in logging and lumbering during the early days were illiterate and did not leave correspondence or other written evidence of their activities. Even as small companies emerged, record keeping was sporadic, and boiler explosions and fires in sawmills often destroyed what records existed. Travelers' accounts, newspapers, and other sources were not likely to mention such mundane activities, unless there was an accident or some spectacular reason to notice what was considered a rather humdrum business. Nevertheless, it is evident that cutting timber and processing lumber was pervasive in the forested areas of early nineteenth-century America.

The forests of the northeastern seaboard differed from those to the north and south, but in most areas, inland as well as coastal, there were varieties of pines and hardwoods. The early American landscape was a mosaic of dense, open, pine, and mixed forests, savannas, and grasslands, shaped over the eons by geological change and by the activities of prehistoric societies, Native Americans, and colonial farmers and lumbermen who burned, cut, girdled, and used the forests in various ways. If a "virgin" forest is one not altered by man, much of the early American forest would not have fit that definition.

Many American forests were cleared for agriculture, and much of the wood was destroyed or used for domestic purposes. Timber and lumber were used for buildings, fences, and home-crafted primitive furniture, as well as boats, vehicles, tools, and other manufactured items. Even during the colonial period, colonists had utilized the forests commercially, developing shipbuilding and naval stores industries. In the southeast and on the Gulf Coast, the Spanish and French developed lumbering and naval stores industries. In the interior along the Mississippi River, French colonists built mills powered by runoff waters from flooded areas and horse-powered portable sawmills. The British engaged in similar activities, as well as producing timbers for shipbuilding on the Gulf Coast.

Cypress swamps along the Mississippi River provided raw material for commercial logging and lumbering, but the industry did not become important until the introduction of steam engines and the growth of markets. The first steam sawmill appeared in New Orleans in the early nineteenth century; its success inspired others to apply steam power to the manufacture of lumber. The desirability of longleaf and slash pine and of cypress for various uses was known in England and other areas of Europe, such as France, where the government purchased pine for spars and square timbers for their navy. Markets also developed in Cuba, Mexico, and Texas. New Orleans remained the major market for interior lumber producers; both logs and lumber were rafted down the Mississippi River to be marketed in the Crescent City.

There was significant commercial lumbering during the first half of the nineteenth century in northern New England and the coastal states of the South, as well as the interior. American lumber was sold in domestic markets, Europe, Latin America, and the Caribbean. Even in the early period it was evident that lumbering was a migratory industry, moving from area to area as forests were cut and as markets changed. Lumbermen harvested timber, then moved on to new stands, practices aided by the advent of railroad logging and the use of steam skidders later in the century. Knowledge of the regenerative properties of trees was limited, and little or no thought was given to reforestation.

The growth of domestic lumber markets mirrored the expansion of the American economy. Wood was used for various purposes that would eventually be met by iron, stone, and other materials. There were wooden roads, bridges, nails, hinges, locks, gears, and machinery. Wood was employed for all sorts of mundane uses. Packing containers constituted a major market. Sugar and tobacco were shipped in large-bellied hogsheads and triggered a business in gathering and riving staves. Flour, cornmeal, whiskey, lard, lard oil, pork, pickled beef, tar, and pitch were transported in barrels, feeding a thriving business in common and pipe staves and wine pipes. In 1839 an estimated 84 percent of houses were constructed of wood. Most residences until the late nineteenth century were also heated by wood. Roughly half the trees that were cut for purposes other than land clearing were utilized for heating fuel. As late as 1850, wood supplied approximately 90 percent of the country's fuel.

The first half of the nineteenth century was a period of technological innovation and demographic change. People were fanning out across the eastern half of the continent, and many were moving from farms to cities. From 1810 to 1860 the U.S. population grew from 7.2 to 31 million, creating an enormous increase in the domestic market. Lumbering evolved from an industry characterized by relatively small proprietorships and partnerships into one increasingly dominated by large corporations. By mid-century the railroad had freed lumbering's woods and mill operations from a need for immediate access to water, enabling the industry to operate over a much larger area. Finally, technological change transformed work in both the woods and the mills.

The steam engine, in wide use by the 1840s, was a potent symbol of the American economy in the nineteenth century, associated in the public mind with the advent of an age of coal and iron. But, above all wood had fueled these developments. Railroads were major consumers of wood, for ties, car construction, and fuel. Wood was cheaper and more convenient for railroad use, and by 1860 there were some 4,000 locomotives, of which all but about 350 to 400 were fired with wood. By that time there were thirty thousand miles of track in the United States, and railroads in some parts of the country converted to coal as their wood supplies were depleted. However, in the South, where trains were light and pine abundant, they continued to burn wood into at least the 1880s. Steamboats on the interior waterways became heavy utilizers of wood fuel, mostly supplied by "woodhawks" who cut and sold their products in areas along the rivers. By 1870, approximately ten million cords of wood were consumed for motive power annually, although household wood consumption continued to dominate the market.

National lumber production grew from less than half a million board feet in 1801 to 1.6 million in 1839, and 8 billion board feet by 1859, with an even faster increase after that time. The national center of production shifted from the Northeast to the Great Lakes states. In 1839, New York, Pennsylvania, New Jersey, and the New England states provided about two-thirds of the national lumber total. By mid-century the Northeast was the source of only about one-third of production as the Great Lakes states of Wisconsin, Michigan, and Minnesota became the most important production centers. When improved transportation and marketing networks linked the producing areas to markets across the nation and new technology made work in the woods and the mills more efficient and productive, the stage was set for a massive assault on the forests of the Great Lakes states during the latter half of the century.

Technological change in the forests and mills was rapid. At the beginning of the century woods workers cut trees as their forebears had done for centuries, with axes (although in the eighteenth century American craftsmen made major design improvements over European felling axes). They then used wedges to split the trees into planks. After about mid-century axes gave way to crosscut saws, which two-man teams used to fell trees. Boards were produced

Lumber District, Chicago. View from the westside waterworks of Chicago. The region of the Great Lakes was a primary lumber district by the middle of the nineteenth century. *Harper's Weekly*, 1883. LIBRARY OF CONGRESS: PRINTS AND PHOTOGRAPHS DIVISION

by pitsawing (in which a pit was dug into the ground) or whipsawing (in which a platform was built) so that one worker could stand above the log and another below it, operating a saw that they pulled back and forth to produce at best only a few boards per day. Placing a wooden frame around saws prevented them from warping, and attaching the frame or sash to a waterwheel made the saws vastly more productive. By 1840 there were more than thirty-one thousand waterpowered sawmills in the United States. Sawmills, found in many early settlements, produced the lumber with which the nation's increasingly common frame buildings were constructed. By mid-century, frame houses in the state of New York outnumbered log cabins eight to one.

The next technological step was to mount several parallel saws in a frame, creating "gang saws" that could turn out a significantly greater volume. Sash saws were soon replaced by "muley" saws, in which the sash and frame were lightened and the stroke of the saw speeded up. The sash and muley saws were

driven by animal, water, or eventually steam power. By the early nineteenth century there were circular saws in America, but they warped, bowed, and wobbled as a result of the friction and heat generated by cutting. Thickening them for durability and stability meant a wider saw cut (kerf) and more waste (nearly one-third of the log). Nevertheless, the circular saws were faster and more productive than their predecessors, and they dominated lumber manufacturing until the 1870s, when band saws became important. The band saw, an endless ribbon of tempered steel, was usually twelve to fifteen inches wide and thirty to fifty feet long and revolved around two huge wheels located above and below the cutting area. Band saws were faster and cut a much narrower kerf than the circulars. Finally, steam machinery was developed to move the logs into the mills, set them in place for cutting, and move the lumber on for further processing or sorting.

The conversion from waterpower to steam occurred fairly slowly. In the late 1830s only about two hundred steam engines were used in lumber mills, with some sixty-five employed in wood planing, turning, or lathe making. As late as 1870 there were more than sixteen thousand waterpowered lumber mills, compared with just over eleven thousand steam-powered operations. Eventually, steam engines became more powerful and safer, and because they allowed the mill owner to locate his manufacturing facilities almost anywhere (closer to his timber or to the lumber markets), large steam-powered operations dominated the lumber industry by the turn of the century.

During most of the nineteenth century, logs moved from the woods to the mill by water or animal power. In the Northeast and later in the Great Lakes states, logging was done in winter. The workers prepared paths over which logs were pulled by horses or oxen to streamside landings, where they were held until the spring thaw. They were then rolled into the water and driven downstream to the mills. In the lakes states loggers developed greased skids and "big wheels" to get the logs to the mills year round. The latter were a pair of wheels as much as ten feet in diameter from which logs were suspended and pulled by horses or oxen. Lacking snow and ice, southern loggers transported logs to the mills on carts, wagons, or big wheels, and if streams were available, they constructed log rafts, which were pulled or propelled downstream with poles or paddles. The rafts could be enormous, sometimes covering several acres.

The log-runs downstream from the woods to the mills in the northeastern and Great Lakes states were perhaps the most colorful facet of the nineteenth-century logging and lumbering business. The logs were stored on the banks or in frozen lakes during the winter, sometimes restrained by "booms," or groups of logs chained together. With the thaw the logs tumbled from the lakes and tributary streams into the main waterways. The lumbermen sometimes rode the logs, but usually maneuvered them through the dangers of the downstream trip from flat-bottomed boats. Eventually in some areas steamboats helped to tow the groups or "rafts" of logs downstream. Since the logs came from many producers, they were "branded" with marks chopped or stamped into their surfaces. The greatest danger for the drivers was when the logs "jammed." Some jams covered forty to fifty acres, with the logs stacked from two to ten feet deep. The jams were pried, chopped, or blasted with gunpowder to break them loose.

From the mills the lumber moved to regional wholesaling and marketing centers whose importance rose and fell with the depletion of nearby timber and the migration of the industry. Bangor, Maine; Burlington, Vermont; Albany and Buffalo, New York;

Williamsport, Philadelphia, and Pittsburgh, Pennsylvania; Chicago; Minneapolis; St. Louis and Kansas City, Missouri; Savannah, Georgia; Charleston, South Carolina; Pensacola, Florida; Mobile, Alabama; and New Orleans, Louisiana, each had their time as premier marketing, shipping, or manufacturing centers. But by the late nineteenth century the depletion of timber supplies in the Great Lakes states and new technology were pushing the lumber industry toward the vast forests of the West and the inland South. By that time railroads connected the nation and reached remote interior areas in the South and West, thus freeing loggers and lumbermen from their dependence on water to get the logs to the mill and lumber from mill to market. Chicago and other cities that were remote from the woods and many of the markets nevertheless retained their role as major marketing and wholesale centers because their locations astride major railroads gave them relatively speedy and cheap access to large areas of the nation.

Steam power also transformed work in the woods. Railroad logging became the order of the day as tramways were extended into the forests to supply the mills. Over these lines traveled enormous steam-powered skidders and loaders. Operating from the tracks, cable lines attached to large rotating drums on the skidders were pulled out and fastened to felled logs, which were then pulled or "skidded" back to trackside. There they were picked up by lines from giant steam-powered loaders that placed them on railroad cars for transport to the mill. The system was both faster and more destructive of the woods than earlier logging methods, but few seemed to care. The days of "scientific forestry," "selective cutting," and "sustained yield" operations were in the future. By the end of the nineteenth century, the technology, organizational systems, and national markets were all in place that would enable lumbermen rapidly to level vast forested areas of the West and South during the early years of the twentieth century.

See also **Geography and Ecology; Steam Power; Waterpower.**

Bibliography

Cox, Thomas R. *Mills and Markets: A History of the Pacific Coast Lumber Industry to 1900.* Seattle and London: University of Washington Press, 1974.

Cox, Thomas R., Robert S. Maxwell, Phillip Drennon Thomas, and Joseph J. Malone. *This Well-Wooded Land: Americans and Their Forests from Colonial Times to the Present.* Lincoln and London: University of Nebraska Press, 1985.

Drobney, Jeffrey A. *Lumbermen and Log Sawyers: Life, Labor and Culture in the North Florida Timber Industry, 1830–1930.* Macon, Ga.: Mercer University Press, 1997.

Fickle, James E. *Mississippi Forests and Forestry*. Forthcoming from The University Press of Mississippi.

———. *The New South and the "New Competition": Trade Association Development in the Southern Pine Industry*. Urbana and London: University of Illinois Press, 1980.

Fries, Robert F. *Empire in Pine: The Story of Lumbering in Wisconsin, 1830–1900*. Madison: State Historical Society of Wisconsin, 1951.

Hidy, Ralph W., Frank Ernest Hill, and Allan Nevins. *Timber and Men: The Weyerhaeuser Story*. New York: Macmillan, 1963.

Williams, Michael. *Americans and Their Forests: A Historical Geography*. Cambridge: Cambridge University Press, 1989.

JAMES E. FICKLE

LYCEUMS

Lyceums Before the Civil War: 1826 to 1861

Some of the earliest efforts to promote and provide structure for American adult education were made through the community-based lecture series called lyceums. Borrowing the name "lyceum" from the ancient Greek school established in a garden sacred to Apollo Lyceius, Josiah Holbrook (1788–1854) sponsored the first American lyceum course in 1826 for textile workers in Millbury, Massachusetts. Initially, lyceums mostly provided instruction on vocational topics pertaining to textile work.

The opening of the Erie Canal in 1825 spurred the evolution of the lyceum movement into a cultural and popular educational enterprise. As the canal became a major commercial artery for textile goods, villages and trading posts along the waterway grew into towns and, in some instances, powerful economic centers. The increase in population along the Erie Canal, coupled with an active economy, created towns sufficiently prosperous to pay professionals to conduct lyceum courses. By 1840 there were more than one thousand active lyceum groups operating in New England.

Lyceum lecturers often were noted authors, biographers, explorers, or religious philosophers from New York City or Boston. The literary, philosophical, and cultural subjects broached by these professionals attracted diverse audiences, including women, to lyceum programs. Vocational instruction in textile work, largely dominated by men, became secondary to the new offerings sponsored through local lyceums.

As the lyceum movement developed along the eastern seaboard, it also moved westward. A series of public land disposal acts passed by the U.S. Congress in the 1830s and 1840s, coupled with railroad expansion into the Ohio River Valley throughout the 1840s,

opened up vast areas for settlement to the west. As settlers pushed westward they attempted to preserve what they could of the "civilized" world left behind, which included the lyceum. Lyceum programs made adult education accessible in the isolated areas of the frontier.

Despite the expansion and popularity of lyceums prior to the Civil War, the movement lacked any sort of centralized commercial structure. All attempts to centralize lyceum programming during the 1840s and 1850s failed. The common obstacle to these efforts was communities' refusal to relinquish control of their lyceums to an outside authority. The growth of the lyceum movement was interrupted by the economic depression of 1857. By the time prospects for lyceums again appeared good, the Civil War had begun.

Lyceums After the Civil War

When the lyceum movement reappeared after the Civil War, it was dominated by commercial booking agencies. Commercialization of the lyceums was, in part, initiated by what remained of the pre-war community lyceum organizations. Approximately one hundred of these surviving associations, located primarily in the Midwest, banded together in 1865 to create the Associated Western Literary Society. Through this alliance, members cooperatively booked speakers for their respective lyceum programs and, by coordinating travel schedules, were able to negotiate favorable fees. In the spring of 1868, the Associated Western Literary Society merged with the American Literary Bureau of New York to create the first national commercial lyceum booking agency.

But the most prominent and commercially successful lyceum agency was the Boston Lyceum Bureau, later known as the Redpath Lyceum Bureau. James Redpath (1833–1891) founded the organization in Boston in 1868. There was so much demand in the Midwest for lyceums that by 1871, Redpath had established a regional office in Chicago. Two other notable lyceum bureaus soon started operation: the Williams Lecture and Musical Bureau and the Midland Lyceum Bureau. By the turn of the century, there were twelve lyceum bureaus in operation, and each was booking programs for more than three thousand events a year.

Following the lead of the Redpath Lyceum Bureau, by the late 1870s most lyceum agencies had in place a system of "star" lecture courses. Star courses were designed to promote distinguished, and high-fee lecturers. Late-nineteenth-century star courses were built around such individuals as Susan B. Anthony (1820–1906), Henry Ward Beecher (1813–1887),

William Jennings Bryan (1860–1925), Edward Everett Hale (1822–1909), Wendell Phillips (1811–1884), Henry M. Stanley (1841–1906), Charles Sumner (1811–1874), and Mark Twain (1835–1910). Although lyceum programs were sponsored in urban areas, they remained predominantly a small-town phenomenon, with the vast majority of programs being sponsored by communities of fewer than fifteen hundred people. These were towns in which the *McDuffy Readers* dominated elementary education.

As lyceums became more commercial, they moved closer to show business. Programs were expanded to include animal acts, singers and dancers, readers, humorists, impersonators and magicians, and play productions. Post–Civil War lyceum bureaus supplied programs to three types of gatherings: social clubs, lyceum theaters or opera houses, and, eventually, community chautauquas. The traditional lecturers were booked most often by social reading circles to lead literary discussions, as had been the practice before the war. The typical program built around a single lecture usually lasted an entire day and sometimes two.

The vast expansion of the railroad in the 1870s, following the 1869 completion of the first transcontinental line, not only sent lyceum lecturers westward; now large eastern theater companies could be transported to the frontier. To encourage cultural activities, many midwestern communities financed and built spacious lyceum theaters and opera houses during the last quarter of the nineteenth century. They then booked theater productions and other attractions through the eastern lyceum bureaus. By 1890 more than thirteen hundred midwestern towns each year were booking touring companies for their lyceum theater or opera house. In areas not reachable by rail, the bureaus arranged to have the production company transported by wagon, along with a tent to serve as the theater.

Development of Chautauquas

While the lyceums were moving westward, in 1874 the Methodist minister John Heyl Vincent (1832–1920) and businessman Lewis Miller (1829–1899) began the chautauqua movement, a summertime cultural encampment on the northern shore of Chautauqua Lake in western New York. Largely through Vincent's efforts, the word "chautauqua" became associated with education, culture, and inspiration.

The first several sessions at Chautauqua Lake provided training for Sunday School teachers in how to conduct and organize classroom lessons. Beginning in the late 1870s general educational programs, various

platform arts, and entertainment were integrated into the summer curriculum. Chautauqua participants, Vincent believed, needed something "constructive" to do between lessons in religion and Sunday School instruction. He turned, in part, to the commercial lyceum agencies to fill this void. Star lyceum personalities who appeared at the New York Chautauqua in the last quarter of the century included Jane Addams (1860–1935), Thomas A. Edison (1847–1931), Ulysses S. Grant (1822–1885), Rutherford B. Hayes (1822–1893), Upton Sinclair (1878–1968), Billy Sunday (1862–1935), Ida M. Tarbell (1857–1944), Leo Tolstoy (1828–1910), Booker T. Washington (1856–1915), and George Westinghouse (1846–1914).

The summer programs attracted more people to the New York Chautauqua each season. By the early 1900s literally thousands of people from all over the United States attended. To reach those who could not come to the New York Chautauqua, in 1878 Vincent began a home-study course called the Chautauqua Literary and Scientific Circle. More than eighty-four hundred people, primarily in rural areas of the Midwest, joined a local circle during its first year. Circle enrollment climbed to one hundred thousand in 1888, and by 1900 almost two hundred thousand belonged.

The desire for adult education, however, was not met only by the New York Chautauqua or the lyceums. After 1880 many local circles began their own community chautauquas. By combining local talent with the star lecturers and other performers booked through lyceum bureaus, community chautauqua programs were created. A typical local program lasted from five to seven days and covered such areas of study as Bible reading, literature and interpretive reading, health and science, history and social studies, and public speaking.

Some attempts were made by the managers of smaller community chautauquas to negotiate lyceum bookings cooperatively. But none of these plans succeeded for the same reason that collaborative efforts among the lyceum groups had failed: local chautauquas did not want outsiders interfering with or having control over their programs. Nonetheless, the community-based chautauquas paved the way for the commercialized, lyceum-operated circuit chautauquas of the early twentieth century.

Starting in 1903, the Redpath Lyceum Bureau capitalized on the disputes between local chautauquas. The bureau offered a weeklong, standardized program of high-quality lyceum talent to a circuit of towns at a cost far less than having each town book it individually. What the community lost under the Redpath circuit chautauqua scheme was the ability to control the program makeup and dates. By 1910 other lyceum bureaus were operating chautauqua circuits. Yielding to the pressures of the radio, sound movies, and efficient transportation as alternative avenues to education and entertainment, circuit chautauquas ended in the late 1920s.

See also **Literacy and Reading Habits; Orators and Oratory; Popular Culture.**

Bibliography

Bode, Carl. *The American Lyceum: Town Meeting of the Mind.* New York: Oxford University Press, 1956.

Gould, Joseph Edward. *The Chautauqua Movement: An Episode in the Continuing American Revolution.* New York: State University of New York, 1961.

Redpath Chautauqua Collection. Special Collections, University of Iowa, Iowa City, Iowa.

Slout, William Lawrence. *Theatre in a Tent: The Development of a Provincial Entertainment.* Bowling Green, Ohio: Bowling Green University Popular Press, 1972.

Tapia, John E. *Circuit Chautauqua: From Rural Education to Popular Entertainment in Early-Twentieth-Century America.* Jefferson, N.C.: McFarland, 1997.

JOHN EDWARD TAPIA

LYNCHING

LYNCHING   The term "lynching" is applied to various forms of summary punishment inflicted by self-appointed groups without regard to established legal procedures. While not uniquely American, lynching has been conspicuous throughout American history, especially during the nineteenth century.

The term probably entered the American vocabulary during the Revolutionary War when Charles Lynch (1736–1796), a justice of the peace in Bedford County, Virginia, conducted a vigilante campaign against suspected loyalists. In subsequent decades popular tribunals throughout the nation inflicted "Lynch's law" on transgressors of community standards. As lynching spread across the nation during the early nineteenth century, two trends emerged. Mobs ignored existing legal institutions and meted out extralegal punishment, and lynchers discarded older nonlethal forms of discipline. By the 1830s lynching had become synonymous with death at the hands of a mob.

Regional patterns in lynching also emerged in the 1830s. In the North extralegal violence declined as economic development and urban growth promoted the consistent exercise of state authority. Courts and new police forces defended public order by suppressing violent crowds. Although race and ethnic riots periodically erupted, lynchings occurred infrequently. In the West vigilante justice invaded mining camps and boomtowns, reaching a climax in the San Francisco vigilance committees of the 1850s. Lynchings also occurred frequently in the antebellum South. Although no reliable count of lynchings in the region exists, the practice almost certainly was common, because the institution of slavery required the coercion of slaves and free blacks and the intimidation of nonslaveholders by white slave owners.

During the Civil War, Southern slaveholders, gripped by fears of slave insurrections, executed slaves in gruesome spectacles aimed at intimidating blacks into submission. In the mountain South and border regions, where residents were divided in their allegiances to the Union and the Confederacy, partisans periodically executed their opponents in a manner indistinguishable from lynching.

The practice of lynching increased after the Civil War. Following Emancipation, southern whites lynched blacks as punishment for insufficient deference and for disputing work conditions. The Ku Klux Klan and various informal white paramilitary groups inflicted lynchings in their campaigns of political terrorism against both black and white Republicans.

Lynching during Reconstruction. African Americans were the main targets of lynchings, but Northern "carpetbaggers" and "scalawags" were also lynched. Wood engraving. *Harper's Weekly,* 23 March 1867. LIBRARY OF CONGRESS

Lynchings did not end with the restoration of white control over the region. Instead the proportion of lynchings that occurred in the South rose from 82 percent of all lynchings in the nation during the 1880s to more than 95 percent after the turn of the century. The connection between lynching and racism in the South also became more glaring. Outside the South and border states 83 percent of the mob victims during the late nineteenth century were white. In the South and the border states, in contrast, 85 percent of the lynching victims during the late 1800s were black. While lynching had deep roots throughout the nation and its victims included whites, Native Americans, Chicanos, and Asians, by the late nineteenth century it had become primarily a southern racial phenomenon.

An objective assessment of the transgressions that provoked lynchings is difficult because contemporary sources are rife with prevailing racial, ethnic, and class prejudices. Roughly one-half of the lynchings in the South were prompted by alleged murders and violent assaults. One-third of the black lynching victims in the South purportedly committed sexual assaults. The elastic definition of sexual assaults when black men and white women were involved meant that everything from consensual interracial sexual liaisons to rude behavior by a black man could spark a lynching. The remaining 20 percent of the lynchings in the South were punishments for such offenses as arson, theft, conjuring, trying to vote, and using obscene language.

In the West alleged murders precipitated the largest number of lynchings, and purported theft, especially of livestock, triggered most of the remaining lynchings. Although extralegal executions of labor activists and radicals account for only a small percentage of Western lynchings, they demonstrate that labor disputes and overt dissent, as in the South, could provoke lynchings.

The power of lynching to intimidate was a consequence of the savagery of lynch mobs. The majority of lynchers in the South and West simply shot or hanged their victims with little ceremony. But many lynchings in the South, probably more than a third, were conducted by huge mobs, numbering in the hundreds, even thousands, who murdered with considerable ritual and exceptional brutality, including torture, the severing of body parts, and other forms of sadism. Victims of these mobs who survived torture were sometimes burned alive or were hanged and riddled with bullets. Such lynchings did not have to occur often or be witnessed directly to cast a shadow over all other forms of mob violence. The extreme brutality of lynch mobs became one of the most graphic symbols of bigotry and racial oppression in nineteenth-century America.

See also **Crime; Ku Klux Klan; Vigilantes; Violence.**

Bibliography

Brown, Richard Maxwell. *Strain of Violence: Historical Studies of American Violence and Vigilantism.* New York: Oxford University Press, 1975.

Brundage, W. Fitzhugh, ed. *Under Sentence of Death: Lynching in the South.* Chapel Hill: University of North Carolina Press, 1997.

Moses, Norton H., comp. *Lynching and Vigilantism in the United States: An Annotated Bibliography.* Westport, Conn.: Greenwood, 1997.

Senkewicz, Robert M. *Vigilantes in Gold Rush San Francisco.* Stanford, Calif.: Stanford University Press, 1985.

Tolnay, Stewart E., and E. M. Beck. *A Festival of Violence: An Analysis of Southern Lynchings, 1882–1930.* Urbana: University of Illinois Press, 1995.

Wright, George C. *Racial Violence in Kentucky, 1865–1940: Lynchings, Mob Rule, and "Legal Lynchings."* Baton Rouge: Louisiana State University Press, 1990.

W. FITZHUGH BRUNDAGE

M

MAGAZINES During the nineteenth century, American magazines evolved from a handful of religious or literary journals aimed at an eastern elite to thousands of publications catering to a nation of avid readers. In 1800 a dozen or so magazines existed. Although expansion was steady, publication costs and distribution difficulties early in the century limited growth. Subscribers were mostly the educated and cultured.

Religious periodicals like the *Christian Magazine* (1803–1805) or the *Herald of Gospel Liberty* (1806–1816) allowed clergymen to spread their views beyond the pulpit, but often did not survive beyond the life or financial well-being of their publishers. Most cities and many towns developed weekly literary miscellanies during the first third of the century. There were few truly national magazines at this time. Early literary journals often expressed a partisan political perspective. The best known and most widely read was Joseph Dennie's *Port Folio*, published in Philadelphia from 1801 to 1827. Dennie, a Harvard classmate of John Quincy Adams (who contributed to the publication) and an unreconstructed Tory, created an early forum for American writers, but welcomed only those with a Federalist stance.

It is sometimes difficult to distinguish magazines from newspapers in these early days, since most newspapers were weeklies, and magazine printing styles and formats were similar to those of newspapers. In the first issue of *Port Folio,* Dennie set forth an early definition of a magazine as containing "something of politics to interest Quidnuncs, and something of literature to engage Students." Similarly, *Niles' Weekly Register* (Baltimore, 1811–1849) reported political speeches and government actions, but also included commentary and literary essays. College publications were more clearly literary. Daniel Webster wrote for the *Dartmouth Gazette* (1799–1820), Yale published the *Literary Cabinet* from 1806, and Harvard started its *Lyceum* in 1810.

The target audiences for the many literary and religious journals were the elite of society. Dennie addressed the *Port Folio* to "Men of Affluence . . . Liberality, and . . . Letters." The most influential and longest-lived magazine to appear in this era, the *North American Review* (1815–1878), also aimed at people with power and political influence. If they were elitist, these early magazines were also distinctly American. The *North American Review,* the *Saturday Evening Gazette* (Boston, 1821), and the *New York Mirror* (1823) published British writers, to be sure, but increasingly sought to present American essayists, poets, and storytellers.

1825–1850

Jacksonian Democracy contributed to a surge in periodical publication. But it was less presidential politics than changes in technology and readership that led to the huge proliferation of magazines. A cylinder press process and the development of wood-based paper manufacturing permitted faster and more economical printing. A more literate population, passionate about religion and reform, sought expression of significant ideas. And an economy that allowed more people to take at least some time off provided opportunities for leisure reading. As many as five thousand magazines were started from 1820 to 1850, and about six hundred were in active publication in 1850.

Leading American literary figures like Washington Irving, James Fenimore Cooper, and William Cullen, Bryant published essays, poetry, and fiction in the *Saturday Evening Post* (founded 1821), *Knickerbocker Magazine* (1833–1865), and *Graham's Magazine* (1841–1858). Americans thus had unprecedented access to the best of their national literature. Primary circulation of *Graham's*, which pioneered the use of mezzotint drawings and engravings, reached forty thousand by the mid-1840s, and the *Post* rose to ninety thousand in circulation by the Civil War. Magazines also achieved a strong secondary circulation as they were passed among family and friends.

Smaller literary magazines like New England's *The Dial* (1840–1844), sponsored by Ralph Waldo Emerson, the *Southern Literary Messenger* (1834–1864), and *DeBow's Review* (New Orleans, 1846–1880) gave voice to regional literature and to new currents in thought ranging from transcendentalism to radical proslavery theory. Established churches and upstart sects put out hundreds of magazines; a single denomination might have several journals representing different strains of belief.

Then as now, magazines presented both entertainment and analysis of events and ideas. Some offered instruction as well. *Youth's Companion* (1827–1929) for over a century taught practical lessons and offered "suitable fiction" for its target audience. Journals like *Agricultural Museum* (1810–1812), *American Farmer* (1819–1897), *American Agriculturalist* (1842), and *Country Gentleman* (1853) exposed the husbandman to scientific farming.

Many magazines presented perspectives on party politics and on reform issues. Democrats read the *United States Magazine and Democratic Review* (1837–1859). Whigs read the *American Whig Review* (1845 to 1862). Antislavery magazines began with the Quaker *Manumission Intelligencer* (1819–1820) and the *Emancipator* (1820). Benjamin Lundy's *Genius of Universal Emancipation* (1821–1839) and William Lloyd Garrison's *Liberator* (1831–1865) used newspaper formats but magazine-style content in spreading the antislavery message. The first periodicals edited by African Americans were New York's *Mirror of Liberty* and Philadelphia's *National Reformer,* both begun in 1938. Nine other African-American-edited magazines would appear before the outbreak of the Civil War.

Perhaps the most extraordinary publishing phenomenon of this age was the first successful nonreligious magazine devoted to the interests of women,

Godey's Lady's Book (1830–1898). Founded in Philadelphia, *Godey's* reached its zenith under the direction of Sarah Josepha Hale, who edited the magazine from 1837 to 1877. It said little about politics (although Hale did campaign in its pages for proclaiming a national Thanksgiving), it seldom addressed non-Protestants or women of color, and its stories and poems were more sentimental than daring. But it powerfully influenced American life by giving middle-class women an organ of their own in which to explore their changing roles and identity. It published women writers when other journals did not, led discussion of moral issues, and reinforced family values. It was also a pioneer in illustration: *Godey's* "fashion plates," hand-colored engravings of the latest fashion designs, helped to set the style of an age.

Magazines played an important role in educating the public in the first half of the century, when there were few schools, fewer public libraries, and colleges available only to a few. In a magazine one could find fashion, travel, short stories and poetry, historical and personality sketches, and serious discussion of political and social issues.

1850–1870

The Civil War era witnessed the rise of the general interest magazine and the popularity of the illustrated journal. The five Harper brothers brought out *Harper's Monthly* in 1850, and *Harper's Weekly* in 1857. Both published serials, short stories, biographical sketches, and book reviews. The *Monthly* was strictly literary, featuring reprints from other magazines and serializations of Charles Dickens, Thomas Hardy, Herman Melville, and Englishman Wilkie Collins. The *Weekly* carried more news and articles on current events, and was extensively illustrated with woodcut drawings. Subtitled "A Journal of Civilization," *Harper's Weekly* aimed at the educated and upper classes, featuring leading writers and illustrations by such luminaries as Winslow Homer.

The *Atlantic Monthly* (1857–present), founded in Boston, also sought an elite readership. First edited by James Russell Lowell, the *Atlantic* published Emerson and Henry Wadsworth Longfellow. The third of the leading magazines of this age was the *Nation* (1865–present), founded by E. L. Godkin. Godkin, an immigrant from Ireland only eight years before, quickly established his journal as a leading national editorial voice on issues of public policy. More accessible to the larger public were the inexpensive newsprint weeklies, like Robert Bonner's *New York Ledger* (1855–1903). A cheap story paper, the *Ledger* achieved a weekly circulation of 400,000, far more than the "quality" literary journals, and made its

Harper's Monthly Magazine. A portrait of the upper-class readership of this prestigious literary journal, which published essays, book reviews, and serialized novels of major American and British writers. LIBRARY OF CONGRESS

publisher a millionaire. The general interest magazines were so successful that writers could now earn a living contributing mainly to magazines. Edgar Allen Poe wrote for magazines almost everything for which he is now remembered, while Nathaniel Hawthorne pioneered the magazine-length short story.

Frank Leslie's Illustrated Newspaper (1855–1922), despite its title, was more magazine than newspaper. "Frank Leslie" was Englishman Henry Carter, who had already tried his hand at a ladies' magazine and a romance journal when he launched *Leslie's*. It was a phenomenon: news accounts were graphically illustrated with engraved illustrations so people could see events as well as read about them. *Leslie's* was magazine-like in the scope of its coverage, featuring reports on news, fashion, sports, theater, and the art world. Carter also included engravings unrelated to current news, including pictures of nature and animals and idealized views of home, hearth, and historical events. While *Leslie's* is most famous for its Civil War drawings, by 1860 it had already covered—and illustrated—such important events as Commo-

dore Matthew Perry's "opening" of Japan, the Crimean War, the Panic of 1857, the Dred Scott decision, and the laying of the transatlantic cable. *Leslie's* even pioneered muckraking, with a late 1850s series on unsanitary milk production in the cities.

The Civil War created a passion for news and information. Magazines joined newspapers as the common currency of social and political life. Those that could not adapt to the readers' news hunger or that were politically suspect (such as the Southern literary journals) died during the war or at least suspended publication for the duration. Those that had the resources to provide ample news coverage, like *Leslie's Weekly* and *Harper's Weekly,* thrived. A few, notably the *Atlantic,* kept above the fray.

1870–1900

The number of magazines published, and their circulations, increased dramatically in the 1870s and 1880s. Advances in education and literacy, the sharpened need for information that the war had stimulated, and a growing economy created a vast public ready for reading. Rotary presses allowed faster printing and improved engraving technology produced clearer illustrations. A national railroad network allowed better and quicker delivery. By 1870 there were 1,200 American magazines, and the number rose to 3,300 in 1885, more than a fourfold increase since the end of the war. Many, of course, lived only briefly. Journalism historian Frank L. Mott estimated that between 8,000 and 9,000 magazines existed at some point between 1865 and 1885.

The great general interest magazines shared the "New Journalism" philosophy of the 1870s. The main tenet of this movement was a focus on accuracy and professionalism, and it flourished under the direction of editorial giants like E. L. Godkin of *The Nation,* Joseph Holland at *Scribner's,* and William Dean Howells at the *Atlantic.* They continued to publish the best writers, such as Mark Twain, Bret Harte, Frank Stockton, and Joel Chandler Harris.

This era also saw the emergence of many more special interest periodicals, as diverse segments of the public for the first time existed in sufficient numbers and had sufficient capital to support them. Moreover, the Postal Act of 1879 gave economical second-class mailing privileges to any publication devoted to "the dissemination of information of a public character, or devoted to literature, the sciences, arts, or some special industry."

Some special interest publications, like the *United States Army and Navy Journal* (1863–1921), were direct products of the Civil War. Reconstruction, the process of rebuilding the Union and assimilating former slaves into society, was the impetus for the birth of many journals edited by African Americans. *Freedman's Torchlight,* for example, was published by African American editors from 1866 on to help disseminate skills and knowledge among the freedmen.

Susan B. Anthony addressed suffrage and political rights for women in *The Revolution* (1869–1872), and Alice Blackwell began editing *The Woman's Journal* (1870–1917). Black activist Ida B. Wells presented her views in the *Free Speech and Headlight* (1888–1892) until her outspoken attacks on lynching spurred Memphis mobs to destroy her presses and drive her from the South. Mary Seymour edited the cutting-edge *Business Women's Journal* (1889–1896). In addition to these political magazines, popular magazines for women found a strong and loyal readership. The heavily illustrated *Harper's Bazaar* (1867–present) presented the latest and best of European and American fashion. *Woman's Home Companion* (1873–1957), *Ladies' Home Journal* (1883–present), *Good Housekeeping* (1885–present), *Vogue* (1892–present), and *House Beautiful* (1896–present) all hit the market before the turn of the century.

St. Nicholas (1873–1943) was beloved by genera-

Lippincott's Magazine. The December 1896 cover of *Lippincott's Magazine.* Published in Philadelphia, this monthly periodical featured literary poetry and prose. LIBRARY OF CONGRESS

tions of children. Music magazines proliferated—there were over one hundred by 1885. The *American Art Review* (1879–1881) brought Currier and Ives before the public. New sports and recreations, from cycling to stamp collecting, produced special interest publications. Humor magazines emerged: *Puck* (1877–1918), *Judge* (1881–1939), and *Life* in 1883. The small literary magazine persisted, including *The Literary Digest* (1890–1938) and *The Smart Set,* (1900–1930), which carried O'Henry's first short story.

Trade and business magazines reflected the maturation of the American economy. The new science stimulated publication of many scientific and educational publications, such as *National Geographic* (1888–present), and the *Annals of the American Academy of Political and Social Science* (1890–present). Nurses, dentists, physicians, and lawyers looked to professional journals for information and ethical guidelines. *McClure's* (1893) was just beginning to develop the muckraking style that would later make its exposes famous.

African American intellectuals used periodicals to help establish their own voice. Over forty journals edited by African Americans were founded in the 1880s and 1890s. White interests backed some, like *Voice of the Negro,* and Booker T. Washington's *Colored American Magazine. The Negro American* (1887) and *Howard's Negro-American Magazine* (1889) joined W. E. B. Du Bois's *Horizon* in rejecting white support and seeking to present an independent African-American position. Publications of the Black churches, like the *A.M.E. Church Review* (1884–present), and of alumni associations of colleges like Hampton, Tuskegee, and Lincoln, provided thoughtful discussion of racial issues.

By the 1890s consumer magazines were modern in look and substance. General interest monthlies like *Harper's, Scribner's, Munsey's,* the *Century,* and *Ladies' Home Journal* dominated circulation. These periodicals delivered quality illustrations and good writing, and sophisticated cover art teased prospective purchasers. Revenue from national advertising paved the way for greater accessibility; even the glossiest of the magazines cost no more than thirty-five cents, and many sold for just a dime.

American magazines were a mature phenomenon by 1900, having played a critical role in educating and entertaining Americans and in keeping before them the critical social and political issues of the nineteenth century.

See also **Literacy and Reading Habits; Literature,** *sub-entries on* **African American Literature** *and* **Women's Literature; Newspapers and the Press.**

Bibliography

Primary Works

Mott, Frank Luther. *A History of American Magazines.* 5 vols. Cambridge, Mass.: Harvard University Press, 1938–1968.

Pickett, Calder M., ed. and comp. *Voices of the Past: Key Documents in the History of American Journalism.* Columbus, Ohio: Grid Publications, 1977.

Secondary Works

Bartow, Edith Merwin. *News and These United States.* New York: Funk and Wagnalls, 1952.

Bullock, Penelope L. *The Afro-American Periodical Press, 1838–1909.* Baton Rouge: Louisiana State University Press, 1981.

Endres, Kathleen L., and Therese L. Lueck, eds. *Women's Periodicals in the United States: Consumer Magazines.* Westport, Conn.: Greenwood, 1995.

Endres, Kathleen L., and Therese L. Lueck, eds. *Women's Periodicals in the United States: Social and Political Issues.* Westport, Conn.: Greenwood, 1996.

Hutton, Frankie. *The Early Black Press in America, 1827 to 1860.* Westport, Conn., Greenwood Press, 1993.

Leonard, Thomas C. *News for All: America's Coming-of-Age with the Press.* New York: Oxford University Press, 1995.

Mott, Frank Luther. *American Journalism: A History of Newspapers in the United States through 260 Years, 1690 to 1950.* New York: Macmillan, 1950.

Tebbel, John, and Mary Ellen Zuckerman. *The Magazine in America, 1741–1990.* New York: Oxford University Press, 1991.

Wood, James Playsted. *Magazines in the United States.* 3d ed. New York: Ronald, 1971. The original edition was published in 1956.

DAVID L. JAMISON

MAGAZINES, WOMEN'S Women's magazines in the nineteenth-century United States contributed substantially to the transformations of the national culture and influenced the gender system of the Victorian era. This genre of publication reflected and molded public opinion on the role of women in the society and economy of the emerging industrial, urban nation. Appealing to mainstream women, these varied periodicals became a significant segment of the publishing industry, itself an important sector of the dynamic national economy both before and after the Civil War. Women's magazines supplied entertainment, advice, and instruction for their readers and employment for women, who as editors and writers contributed the poetry and prose, fiction and nonfiction, that constituted the content. "Embellishments" that adorned the pages, woodcuts and engravings pictorially illustrating the text and displaying fashion trends, influenced developments in the fashion industry, commercial art, and women's literature. In the Jacksonian era of the 1830s editors of women's periodicals nurtured the emergence of the national and the distinctly regional literature by recruiting U.S. authors as contributors. Publishers utilized technological advances, stimulating the developing consumer culture of the nineteenth century. The impact of women's magazines on U.S. Victorian culture marked the convergence of significant social, economic, literary, and women's history trends in the nineteenth-century United States.

These popular monthly publications played a major role in the growth of the mass media and consumer culture from 1820 to 1900. Having established the viability of their specialized market, women, as a significant sector of the literate public and of those affluent enough to be subscribers, publishers and editors of women's magazines developed a format that sustained only minor changes after the Civil War. The earliest of U.S. women's magazines, appearing during the Federalist era (1789–1800), were commercial expressions of the postrevolutionary construct of republican motherhood, a role for women of the new nation that defined women's patriotism by the performance of their maternal duties. The content of these periodicals reflected the intent of male publishers and editors, often members of the ministry, to divert women readers from the dissolutory influence of contemporary works of fiction from abroad. Male authorities offered young women readers, instead, poetry and prose that simultaneously entertained and instructed them in their proper role and duty. These eighteenth-century pioneering publications did not survive into the nineteenth century.

The earliest nineteenth-century women's magazines were published as commercial ventures aimed at the privileged class. Women recruited as editors and writers were conservative advocates of advancing women's education and enlarging the paid employment available to middle-class women. They judiciously extended the proper place of women beyond the confines of the home but eschewed overtly political or feminist commentary. The most successful mainstream periodicals, such as *The Ladies' Companion and Literary Expositor* (1834–1844), *Peterson's Ladies National Magazine* (1842–1898), and *Harper's Bazaar* (1867–1913), began monthly issues that included sheet music, hand-painted color fashion plates, and illustrative engravings that were suitable for framing. Short stories and sentimental poetry, by writers who garnered fame as contributors to women's magazines, followed the visual features. Mildly instructive nonfiction features and articles, arts and crafts instructions, and household advice preceded editors' or publishers' columns that characteristically concluded the issues. The few women's journals that addressed social reform movements

Sarah Josepha Hale and *Godey's Lady's Book*

Sarah Josepha Buell Hale (24 September 1788–30 April 1879) developed a career as an editor and writer that became the prototype for antebellum women editors and writers in the United States. Born in New Hampshire, Hale promoted her regionally based patriotism as well as her conservative "womanist" advocacy of improvements in nineteenth-century women's education and employment opportunities as the editor of the premier U.S. women's magazine of the Victorian era, *Godey's Lady's Book and American Ladies' Magazine,* from 1837 to 1877. Educated at home before institutions of higher education for women had been established, Hale taught common school before she married a lawyer, David Hale, on 28 September 1813. Nine years later, at the age of thirty-four, she became the sole supporter of her five children, the last born four days after her husband's sudden death.

As a widow Hale tried the few available occupations for women of her generation. Her effort at establishing a dame school failed, as did her millinery shop. Her husband had encouraged her writing, which subsequently offered her the means of supporting and educating her children. Her book of poems, *The Genius of Oblivion and Other Poems* (1823), dedicated to her late husband, brought her to the attention of the publisher of *Ladies' Magazine,* which she edited in Boston until 1837. While in Boston she participated in the founding of the Seaman's Aid Society, a landmark organization among early-nineteenth-century women's benevolence associations, and the women-led effort to complete the Bunker Hill Monument.

In 1837 Hale merged her magazine with that of Louis A. Godey (1804–1878), beginning a successful professional association that lasted for forty years. As she had in Boston, she lived in a boardinghouse in Philadelphia, where *Godey's* was published. Although she had ceased to have a home to manage after 1822, as the editor of *Godey's Lady's Book and American Ladies' Magazine* she became the high priestess of the "cult of true womanhood" (Welter, 1966) and the authority on woman's sphere, woman's role, woman's influence, and woman's work. From her influential position she promoted advances in women's education, especially women's entry into the professions of medicine and teaching, and increased employment opportunities in the paid labor force. The circulation and reputation of *Godey's,* both as a literary magazine and as a women's magazine, peaked in the 1850s. Because a significant portion of *Godey's* readers were southerners, the Civil War, which was never mentioned in its pages, marked the beginning of the magazine's decline. Nevertheless Hale publicized the efforts of the Ladies Association of the Union to purchase and establish Mount Vernon as a national historical site in 1860, and she consulted with the founder of Vassar College, the first liberal arts college for women, established in 1861 and opened in 1865. In 1877, shortly before his death, Godey sold the magazine, and Hale retired as its editor. She died two years later.

The new owners maintained the title of the publication, but its contents lacked the vision and purpose that Hale had contributed. Its lavish hand-painted fashion plates, no longer a feature unique to *Godey's,* were replaced by printed embellishments available in other newly established women's magazines. *Godey's* ceased publication in 1898.

---

reached only small audiences usually affiliated with women's organizations. For example, Amelia Bloomer's *Lily* (1849) and Paulina Wright Davis's *Una* (1853) appeared before the Civil War. *Revolution* and the *Woman's Journal,* published by the National Woman Suffrage Association and the American Woman Suffrage Association respectively, appeared after 1870.

Northern women's magazines outnumbered southern periodicals before and after the Civil War. All such publications judiciously and discreetly advocated only respectable women's benevolence activities. As examples of prescriptive literature, issues of

these mainstream periodicals contributed to the emergence of the "cult of true womanhood," which urged the improvement of women through the cultivation of purity, piety, domesticity, and submission. Women's magazines also provided instructions for the increasingly professionalized role of the urban wife and mother while offering diversion to enrich a lady's leisure moments.

Early-nineteenth-century women's magazines depended upon individual subscribers to fund the publication costs, but publishers used paid advertisements to keep the newsstand rates and subscriptions as low as possible by the turn of the twentieth cen-

Godey's Ladies Book. Women wear stylish clothing in this fashion plate from *Godey's Ladies Book*, a prominent Victorian women's publication, 1855. LIBRARY OF CONGRESS: PRINTS AND PHOTOGRAPHS DIVISION.

Home Companion, Good Housekeeping, Delineator, Pictorial Review, and *McCalls.* Several publications, like *McCalls,* began as pattern magazines. The magazines directed to late-nineteenth-century U.S. women offered housekeeping advice, fashion news, and nonfiction by some of the prestigious writers of the Progressive era. Just as some of their antebellum predecessors had launched nationally renowned writers, these magazines introduced fiction by authors whose works became important contributions to twentieth-century American literature.

See also **Advertising; Gender,** *subentry on* **Interpretations of Gender; Literature,** *subentry on* **Women's Literature; Woman's Rights; Women.**

Bibliography

Endres, Kathleen L., and Therese L. Lueck, eds. *Women's Periodicals in the United States: Consumer Magazines.* Westport, Conn.: Greenwood, 1995.

Humphreys, Nancy K. *American Women's Magazines: An Annotated Historical Guide.* New York: Garland, 1989.

Welter, Barbara. "The Cult of True Womanhood, 1820–1860." *American Quarterly* 18 (summer 1966): 151–174.

Zuckerman, Mary Ellen. *A History of Popular Women's Magazines in the United States, 1792–1960.* Westport, Conn.: Greenwood, 1998.

———. *Sources on the History of Women's Magazines, 1792–1960.* New York: Greenwood, 1991.

ANGELA M. HOWARD

tury. The best-known Victorian women's magazines, *Godey's Lady's Book and American Ladies' Magazine,* a market leader during the 1840s and 1850s, and *Peterson's Ladies' National Magazine,* which dominated the genre from the 1860s into the 1880s, had circulations approximating 150,000.

After 1865 women's magazines adapted advances in technology and distribution to maintain a reasonable monthly issue price while increasing their circulation within a truly national market. Editors adjusted the established format of the contents—fiction, poetry, nonfiction, fashions, and features—to consolidate the importance of their magazines among popular mass-circulation publications. By the 1890s periodicals for women dominated the industry as a whole through their hegemony over the specialized readership of the "new woman," the mainstream concept that encompassed the expanded post–Civil War public role of single and married women among the working class and the rising middle class. The "big six" of the new periodicals of the Gilded Age (1880s–1890s) included *Ladies Home Journal, Woman's*

MAINE   Rugged and rocky Maine, the easternmost state in the continental United States, had prospered in the seventeenth century through fishing, trapping, and the lumber industry (especially white pine for the masts of sailing ships). By 1800, the "District of Maine" saw a revived movement to win independence from Massachusetts, which had seized Maine during the 1650s. With Maine's few remaining Native Americans (mostly Penobscots and Passamaquoddys) confined to small reservations, a massive influx of new settlers poured into Maine's interior, increasing the population from 96,540 in 1790 to 298,335 in 1820.

Squatter resentments against the absentee landowners, mostly Massachusetts Federalists, fueled the separation movement led by a "junto" of Jeffersonian Republican lawyers and businessmen, including John Holmes, William Pitt Preble, and, most importantly, William King, known as the "Sultan of Bath" because of his dominance of that coastal town's political and economic life. Separated by New Hampshire from the more densely populated Massachusetts, Maine had often been ignored by authorities in Boston, and the perceived indifference of Massachusetts to British incursions into Maine in the War of 1812 boosted support for separation. King secured the aid of his Federalist half-brother, Senator Rufus King of New York, in repealing the "coasting law," a system of fees for each state passed in a coastal voyage, eliminating the strongest antiseparation argument advanced by the Federalists in coastal towns. With Massachusetts Federalists eager to rid themselves of a Republican district, Maine voted to separate in 1819, but its bid for statehood became entangled in the controversy over Missouri's admission as a slave-holding state. The resulting Missouri Compromise of 1820, engineered in part by John Holmes (then a Massachusetts congressman), admitted Maine into the Union as a free state with a liberal constitution, and admitted Missouri without slavery restrictions.

In the early years of statehood, a long-running border dispute with Canada led to the "Aroostook War" of 1839, settled by the Webster-Ashburton Treaty of 1842. Of more lasting importance, Maine sparked the nationwide liquor prohibition, or "Maine Law," movement with a new prohibition law in 1851, after agitation led by Portland Mayor Neal Dow. The prohibition issue split the dominant Democratic Party by 1853, and, after a period of chaos, many in its prohibition (and antislavery) faction, led by Anson Morrill, joined with the Whigs to form the new Republican Party, which dominated the state for the remainder of the century. Among the leading former Democrats among the Republicans was Hannibal Hamlin, Abraham Lincoln's first vice president, with Senator William Pitt Fessenden and Congressman Israel Washburn prominent among the former Whigs.

Although the Civil War found Maine with a population twice what it had been at statehood, postwar emigration to the West radically slowed population growth, which increased from only 628,279 in 1860 to 694,466 in 1900. Despite the development of the pulp industry to supplement lumbering, the post-1873 depression led to the election of a Greenback-Democrat governor, Alonzo Garcelon, in 1879. Maine senator, and former Speaker of the House, James G. Blaine, resolved the crisis caused when Garcelon attempted to falsify legislative election returns. Boosted in part by his handling of this homestate conflict, Blaine served as secretary of state under President James A. Garfield (and again under Benjamin Harrison) and was the Republican presidential nominee in 1884. Though dogged by scandal, Blaine led the national Republican Party for two decades. With Thomas B. Reed (dubbed "Czar" for his allegedly autocratic methods) serving as Speaker of the House, Maine

ended the nineteenth century having enjoyed national influence far beyond its size.

See also **Missouri Compromise; New England; Temperance Movement.**

Bibliography

Banks, Ronald F. *Maine Becomes a State: The Movement to Separate Maine from Massachusetts, 1785–1820.* Middletown, Conn.: Wesleyan University Press, 1970.
Muzzey, David Saville. *James G. Blaine: A Political Idol of Other Days.* New York: Dodd, Mead, 1934.
Robinson, William A. *Thomas B. Reed: Parliamentarian.* New York: Dodd, Mead, 1930.
Vexler, Robert I. *Chronology and Documentary Handbook of the State of Maine.* Dobbs Ferry, N.Y.: Oceana Publications, 1978.
Works Progress Administration, Federal Writers Project. *Maine: A Guide "Down East." American Guides Series.* Boston: Houghton Mifflin, 1937.

R. SCOTT BURNET

MANIFEST DESTINY In 1780 Timothy Dwight published "America," the first of his many patriotic poems that both captured and inspired a national sense of destiny and empire:

> Hail land of light and glory! Thy power shall grow
> Far as the seas, which round thy regions flow;
> Through earth's wide realms thy glory shall extend,
> And savage nations at thy scepter bend.
> And the frozen shores thy sons shall sail,
> Or stretch their canvas to the ASIAN gale.
>
> (Cohen, *The Cambridge History of American Foreign Relations,* vol. 1, p. 7)

Dwight's paean anticipates and summarizes the apparent destiny of the United States to pursue a westward course of American empire in the antebellum era. Long before the term "Manifest Destiny" became the coin of this expansive realm, James Madison and Thomas Jefferson, among others, committed themselves to an unfolding empire of liberty premised on western expansion, commercial liberalism, and an open international commercial order.

By the 1820s the idea of a national destiny—a Manifest Destiny—began to emerge. Speaking for millions of Americans, John Quincy Adams maintained that the United States was destined to be "coextensive with the North American Continent, destined by God and by nature to be the most populous and powerful people ever combined into one social contract" (Cohen, *The Cambridge History of American Foreign Relations,* vol. 1, p. 4). The sentiments Manifest Destiny embraced—natural right, virtue, mission, geographic predestination, and national destiny—were melded into a powerful if often disingenuous argument for territorial expansion and commercial growth. By the 1840s the term encompassed a broad spectrum of expansionist rationalizations.

A Destiny Manifest: 1840s

Between 1845 and 1848 a surge of territorial expansion took the nation to the Pacific Coast and made it a true continental empire. With the annexation of the Texas Republic in 1845 and the Mexican Cession of 1848, the United States acquired more than one million square miles of land. The rhetoric of Manifest Destiny that had begun to take shape in the 1820s became even more florid, exaggerated, and protean. National security, natural boundaries, and a divine destiny were alternatively argued to justify and explain expansion. John L. O'Sullivan, editor of the *United States Magazine and Democratic Review,* looking to the design of the almighty and the working of history, wrote in the July and August 1845 edition of the magazine that the nation's Manifest Destiny was "to overspread the continent allotted by Providence for the free development of our yearly multiplying millions." The altruistic sentiments expressed by O'Sullivan and other advocates of Manifest Destiny had a hard edge to them, however. The natural, predestined right to expand came at the expense of other peoples, Native Americans and Mexicans in the Southwest. Extension of the nation's domain over those peoples' lands and resources reflected a contempt for what white Americans considered "mongrel races."

As O'Sullivan perhaps understood, Manifest Destiny was less a reification of noble principles than a reflection and extension of the political principles that defined the second party system. The desire to maintain and expand freedom, the essence of American nationalism, proved the catalytic element in expansion. Instructed by a political culture whose purpose was to realize and extend the basic republican tenets of equality and liberty, those who boomed Manifest Destiny understood the political power of territorial aggrandizement. It expanded freedom over space by extending American institutions to the Southwest and Pacific Coast. It also preserved personal liberty by meeting the territorial needs of a nation of autonomous, self-reliant, footloose agrarians. Finally, it enhanced freedom through time by providing the means of upward mobility through increased commercial opportunities and newly opened, thinly populated lands.

The Eclipse of Manifest Destiny: 1850s

Once anxious to escape enslavement themselves and to release individual energies and potential, Americans felt their enthusiasm for further annexations cool after the Mexican Cession. Expansion became associated with the spread of slavery or antislavery rather than the spread of freedom. Beginning with the introduction of the Wilmot Proviso in 1846, which would have banned slavery in any territory acquired from Mexico, the nation was forced to address the problem of slavery's relevance to their empire of republican liberty.

As the issue was played out in the context of the expansionist designs of the 1840s and 1850s, it spoke to the present and future. Were the institutions of the West and future acquisitions to resemble those of the North or the South? Slavery, northerners believed, retarded the progress of the nation, degraded white workingmen, and contravened the fundamental republican principles of liberty and equality. Southerners, slaveholders and nonslaveholders alike, replied that slavery promoted both equality, by meliorating class conflict, and liberty, by making exploitation and manipulation of white workers unnecessary. They, therefore, linked slavery restriction to their constituents' and the nation's future progress or decline.

The origin and force of expansion had deep roots that stretched from Jefferson to the Jacksonian political system. The breakup of that political system explains the lack of consensus on national destiny and the absence of widespread territorial growth in the 1850s. That is, the free-soil conflict, pitting one section against the other for the right to expand and control the government, disrupted Jacksonian party differences and then displaced them altogether. When Manifest Destiny and its concomitant expansion became identified with sectional, not national, objectives, the future of the nation became uncertain, and territorial aggrandizement ceased.

The case of Cuba is instructive. Narciso López, a Venezuelan by birth, resuscitated the issue of territorial expansion with two unsuccessful filibustering raids against Cuba in 1850 and 1851. The second raid cost him his life. Although López's supporters came from the free and slave states and he had a particularly strong following in New York City, widespread objection to the raids in both sections of the country reflected a diminished sense of national confidence and a sensitivity to residual sectional tensions. Even though Manifest Destiny was not yet in eclipse, to a growing number of Americans in 1851 expansion no longer appeared to promote automatically the ideals of liberty.

When in 1859 the Buchanan administration proposed a $30 million appropriation to purchase Cuba, Republicans and Democrats alike reacted warily. Some Republicans suggested opening up Central America to free African Americans. Asserting that an "isothermal" line prevented whites from settling in the tropics, they argued that colonization had many advantages. It would rid the North of its race problem and keep Anglo-Saxon institutions and blood pure. Assuming that all African American colonists were incipient capitalists, they further maintained that colonization would produce the commercial advantages of annexation without the trouble and expense of acquisition. Finally and most importantly, colonization of free African Americans would produce something of a fire wall that would prevent the spread of slavery.

Separately and together, failed attempts to acquire Cuba reflected a diminished sense of boundlessness that had characterized expansionism in the 1840s. Editors in the North and the South, while reiterating a belief in the nation's Manifest Destiny, also cautioned that territorial expansion, if it came at all, had to be by means honest and fair. Moreover, editors and congressmen alike insisted that new territory must be either unoccupied or peopled by a race sympathetic to and supportive of the republican institutions of the United States. William Henry Seward, for example, envisioned territorial expansion as an extended process of peaceful emigration to and Americanization of Central America.

The conflict over slavery in the newly acquired lands of the Southwest and potential acquisitions in Mexico, Central America, and the Caribbean engendered an immutable battle between the North and South for control of the government. Filibustering expeditions to Cuba, Mexico, and Central America only exacerbated and inflamed that struggle. By the end of the decade opposition to territorial acquisitions reflected a growing conviction among many that the failure of American institutions to expand was due to moral retrogression. The destiny of slavery, so it seemed, had to be resolved before any further expansion of the empire of liberty, and so the war came.

Manifest Destiny Transformed: 1860–1880s

Though dwindling in numbers in the 1850s, proponents of Manifest Destiny continued to advocate for the acquisition of overseas colonies. They talked of seizing or acquiring by more traditional means Formosa, Hawaii, Okinawa, the Bonin Islands, and Santo Domingo. The more deluded even called for the purchase of the island of Rhodes or the principality of Monaco. Understandably, public response was underwhelming. Reflecting, perhaps, popular opinion, Secretary of State William Marcy maintained: "Remote colonies are not a source of strength to any Government, but of positive weakness, in the

cost of their defense, and in the complications of policy which they impose to the prejudice of home-interests. Their supposed advantage to the mother-country, is the commercial monopoly, secured by such connection" (Brauer, "1821–1860: Economics and the Diplomacy of American Expansionism," p. 64). The U.S. government and members of both political parties, however, had opposed such monopolies, advocating at the very least commercial reciprocity. At most they urged a liberal economic order based on free trade and open access to global markets.

On the eve of the Civil War commercial expansion, which had been a function of and a necessary adjunct to an expansive agrarian empire of independent yeomen, eclipsed territorial aggrandizement. After the war commercial expansion transcended territorial aggrandizement altogether. In the postwar era and throughout Reconstruction governmental and public interest in territorial acquisitions, including Alaska, the Isthmus of Panama, the West Indies (particularly Santo Domingo), and islands in the Pacific, were means to an end. Global commercial supremacy, not territorial hegemony, redefined the concept of the nation's Manifest Destiny and gave shape to an American empire if not an empire of the Americas.

The acquisition of Alaska in 1867 makes the case

Great Stretches. Frank Bellew, an illustrator for *Harper's Weekly,* depicted the United States' Pacific expansion to the Sandwich Isles (now Hawaii) while Russia crept eastward through China. By the 1870s, when this illustration was published, belief in Manifest Destiny had become less prominent. LIBRARY OF CONGRESS

exactly. The Connecticut newspaper editor Gideon Welles once complained that Secretary of State William Henry Seward was "almost crazy on the subject of territorial acquisition" (Paolino, *The Foundations of the American Empire,* p. 14). The purchase of Alaska from tsarist Russia for $7.2 million seemed to prove Welles correct. Alaska, totaling some 571,000 square miles, was twice the size of Texas and equal to nearly one-fifth the size of the continental United States. At two cents an acre, Alaska was indeed a bargain.

Yet the purchase represented no simple, indiscriminant land grab. Rather, Seward's interest in Alaska reflected his desire to secure an entrepôt in the Pacific Northwest for Pacific and Asian trade. Seward's son Frederick Seward remembered that his father believed the purchase would give Americans "a foothold for commercial and naval operations accessible from the Pacific states" (Cohen, *The Cambridge History of American Foreign Relations,* vol. 2, p. 14). On 31 March 1867 the *New York Times* discussed the treaty under the head "Bright Prospects for Our Japan and China Trade" while assuring its readers that the purchase of Alaska would "influence in our favor the vast trade of the Pacific." Writing in the *Albany Argus,* Seward envisioned a very different destiny for the United States. "The day is coming," Seward predicted, "when the commerce of the Pacific will rival the Atlantic and be almost entirely under our control" (Paolino, *Foundations of American Empire,* p. 113).

Manifest Destiny Reascendant: 1890s

In February 1899 *McClure's* magazine published Rudyard Kipling's poem "The White Man's Burden." Americans, like their British counterparts, were now called to a higher duty:

> Take up the White Man's burden—
> Send forth the best ye breed—
> Go bind your sons to exile
> To serve your captives' need.
>
> (in Bailey, *A Diplomatic History
> of the American People,* p. 476)

That same month the U.S. Senate ratified by a 2 to 1 margin the Treaty of Paris that added to American territory Puerto Rico, Guam, and the Philippines. President William McKinley, who confessed that he could not locate the Philippines within two thousand miles, asserted without irony that national honor, commerce, racial superiority, and altruism underlay this imperialist grab.

Such historians as Richard Hofstadter and Robert Beisner have maintained that this renewed sense of a national Manifest Destiny issued from three interrelated factors. In the 1880s and 1890s a social malaise gripped the country, as Americans began to doubt the viability of their institutions and the quality of a population that immigrants from southern and eastern Europe were rapidly transforming. In 1893 a severe economic depression crippled the U.S. economy. At the same time American export markets in Europe and the Far East seemed to be in decline and in danger. The perhaps illogical response was a dramatic upsurge of aggressive energy, which evinced itself in reform movements at home and an aggressive foreign policy abroad.

Reinforced by social Darwinism, which applied Darwinian principles of change and struggle of the fittest to social and national progress, and Anglo-Saxonism, which posited the superiority of that "race," Manifest Destiny became inextricably interwoven with imperialism. In stark contrast to the uneasiness that characterized the expansionism of the antebellum era, imperialists of the late nineteenth century asserted that the nation's duty no less than its destiny required that it should not simply and passively provide a model for other nations to follow. Secretary of State Richard Olney put it baldly in 1898, "The mission of this country is not merely to pose but to act . . . to forego no fitting opportunity to further the progress of civilization" (Beisner, *From the Old Diplomacy to the New,* p. 76).

Thus as the nineteenth century gave way to the twentieth, Manifest Destiny again embraced noble aims that unhappily issued in ignoble ends, but with a difference. In the 1840s and 1850s expansionist projects contained peoples that Americans refused to rule and to absorb. Antebellum Americans had never viewed their ever-expanding frontier as a home for native peoples, and it is suggestive that the enormous tract of land the United States wrested from Mexico contained only a few thousand inhabitants. Indeed the Gadsden Purchase of 1853, which secured a small swath of Mexican territory comprising the southern portions of what became Arizona and New Mexico, was so desolate that Kit Carson reported that "a wolf could not make a living on it" (Bailey, *A Diplomatic History of the American People,* p. 266).

By the late nineteenth century Manifest Destiny mandated the subordination of peoples and lands allegedly incapable of governing themselves. Senator Albert Beveridge of Indiana proclaimed that the nation's destiny at the dawn of the twentieth century was both "elemental" and "racial." "God has not been preparing the English-speaking and Teutonic peoples for a thousand years for nothing but vain and idle self-contemplation and self-admiration," Beveridge informed the Senate in 1900. "He has made us the master organizers of the world to establish system where chaos reigns. He has given us the spirit of progress to overwhelm the forces of reaction throughout the earth. He has made us adepts in government that we may administer government among savage and senile peoples" (Weinberg, *Manifest Destiny*, p. 308). Unlike the relatively cost-free arrogance of the 1840s, the national and human price of this *mission civilizatrice* were apparent in Beveridge's final observation that God "has marked the American people as His chosen nation to finally lead in the regeneration of the world" (Weinberg, *Manifest Destiny*, p. 308). Payment for such conceit came due in full in the twentieth century.

See also **Alaska Purchase; American Indians,** *subentry on* **U.S. Government Policies; Expansion; Filibusters; Foreign Relations; Frontier; Gadsden Purchase; Mexican Americans; Mexican Cession; Nationalism; Northwest Territory; Race and Racial Thinking; Sectionalism; Spanish-American War.**

Bibliography

Articles and Essays

Bailey, Thomas A. *A Diplomatic History of the American People*. 9th ed. Englewood Cliffs, N.J.: Prentice-Hall, 1974.

Brauer, Kinley J. "1821–1860: Economics and the Diplomacy of American Expansionism." In *Economics and World Power: An Assessment of American Diplomacy since 1789*. Edited by William H. Becker and Samuel F. Wells Jr. New York: Columbia University Press, 1984.

Crapol, Edward M. "Foreign Policy in the Early Republic Reconsidered: Essays from a SHEAR Symposium." *Journal of the Early Republic* 14 (winter 1994): 453–495.

Books

Beisner, Robert L. *From the Old Diplomacy to the New, 1865–1900*. Arlington Heights, Ill.: AHM, 1975.

Cohen, Warren I., ed. *The Cambridge History of American Foreign Relations*. Volume 1: *The Creation of a Republican Empire, 1776–1865*, by Bradford Perkins. Volume 2: *Empire for Opportunity, 1865–1913*, by Walter LaFeber. New York: Cambridge University Press, 1993.

Graebner, Norman A. *Empire on the Pacific: A Study in American Continental Expansion*. New York: Ronald, 1955.

Haynes, Sam W., and Christopher Morris, eds. *Manifest Destiny and Empire: American Antebellum Expansionism*. College Station: Texas A & M University Press, 1997.

Hietala, Thomas R. *Manifest Design: Anxious Aggrandizement in Late Jacksonian America*. Ithaca, N.Y.: Cornell University Press, 1985.

Hofstadter, Richard. *Social Darwinism in American Thought, 1860–1915*. Philadelphia: University of Pennsylvania Press, 1944.

Horsman, Reginald. *Race and Manifest Destiny: The Origins of American Racial Anglo-Saxonism*. Cambridge, Mass.: Harvard University Press, 1981.

Hunt, Michael H. *Ideology and U.S. Foreign Policy*. New Haven, Conn.: Yale University Press, 1987.

Jones, Howard, and Donald A. Rakestraw. *Prologue to Manifest Destiny: Anglo-American Relations in the 1840s*. Wilmington, Del.: Scholarly Resources, 1997.

Merk, Frederick. *Manifest Destiny and Mission in American History*. New York: Knopf, 1963.

Miller, Stuart Creighton. *"Benevolent Assimilation": The American Conquest of the Philippines, 1899–1903*. New Haven, Conn.: Yale University Press, 1982.

Paolino, Ernest N. *The Foundations of the American Empire: William Henry Seward and U.S. Foreign Policy*. Ithaca, N.Y.: Cornell University Press, 1973.

Rosenberg, Emily S. *Spreading the American Dream: American Economic and Cultural Expansion, 1890–1945*. New York: Hill and Wang, 1982.

Stuart, Reginald C. *United States Expansionism and British North America, 1775–1871*. Chapel Hill: University of North Carolina Press, 1988.

Van Alstyne, Richard Warner. *The Rising American Empire*. New York: Oxford University Press, 1960. Reprint, Chicago: Quadrangle, 1965.

Weinberg, Albert K. *Manifest Destiny: A Study of Nationalist Expansionism in American History*. Baltimore: Johns Hopkins University Press, 1935.

Williams, William Appleman. *The Tragedy of American Diplomacy*. Cleveland, Ohio: World, 1959.

MICHAEL A. MORRISON

MANLINESS   Among British immigrants to the American colonies, the words "manly" and "manliness" evoked virtues desired in males ranging from qualities associated with aristocratic and military ideals, like honor and boldness, to those esteemed by merchants, artisans, yeomen, and religious dissenters, like frankness and fortitude. These traits all presumed male superiority, especially in reason and self-mastery and therefore in capacity to govern. George Washington's famous composure and aloofness in public made him an ideal head for a gentry-led patriarchal social order. In contrast the qualities attributed to women and to American Indian and African men, such as being emotional, impulsive, or naive, justified their submission. White males deemed weak, irresolute, or self-indulgent deserved contempt for being "unmanly" or "effeminate."

Such ideas of manhood and womanhood would be redefined in the new United States. The social construction of gender was already evident after the Revolution, which saw democratic rejection of the very foundation of the colonial gentry's ideal of itself as a natural aristocracy of virtue and cultivation devoted to public usefulness. Leisure came under assault from tradesmen, artisans, and farmers, who instead exalted labor as fundamental to manliness. In the nineteenth century the "breadwinner" would become the model of responsible manhood, and political democracy would displace the aristocratic dignity of a president like Washington with the rougher masculine style of one like Andrew Jackson.

Character and the Self-Made Man

The following account of change in American ideals of masculinity during the nineteenth century is most applicable to those white middle- and upper-class northeasterners better positioned to influence others through their writings and leadership in public and private institutions. This limitation reflects the heavy dependence by historians studying the male gender on such sources as advice books for young men; novels, essays, and fiction in popular magazines; diaries; and correspondence. These sources suggest that the highly competitive marketplaces and temptations to sin of nineteenth-century cities made the achievement of manly self-control an anxious subject for young men and their parents. The purer moral values learned at home, increasingly defined as women's sphere, now seemed constantly threatened by the evils of men's sphere, the world outside the home where males earned the family's livelihood.

Democratic individualism added to that anxiety by creating a new hero, the "self-made man," who made his way to success, especially riches, against every obstacle and mostly without assistance from others. In the 1840s and 1850s popular biographies like Charles Seymour's *Self-Made Men* (1858) had appeared, showcasing the climb of poor boys to prosperity through diligence. Even earlier advice books by clergymen and other evangelical Protestant writers warned of degradation by the practices of alcohol consumption, masturbation, gambling, and other sinful indulgences that weakened the will and enervated the body. They exhorted their readers to attain self-discipline, good manners, and moral purity. Developing "character"—the summary term for this ideal of manliness—also would make them more productive and economically successful.

Although as late as 1900, 68 percent of the American population lived in places with less than 10,000 inhabitants, both the opportunities for self-made men and the moral dangers seemed greatest in rapidly growing cities. For the novelist Horatio Alger, the ideal situation for a young man "struggling upward" remained a clerkship with a kindly Christian merchant who would serve as surrogate father and role model of "respectability." Alger depicted this ideal situation in *Ragged Dick*, the first of his many best-sellers, in 1867. That kind of opportunity was about to be displaced by a new world of big business, in which many middle-class males would do sedentary, white-collar office work with little prospect of becoming independent through self-employment.

This new breed of worker stood in contrast to the hardy farmer working his own acres, so often praised as the backbone of the American Republic. How could the new man prove himself manly?

Aggressive Masculinity

Even before the Civil War some Americans seeking to restore male vigor and valor found inspiration in European innovations, notably the German gymnasium. The "muscular Christianity" promoted in the 1850s by the athletic English clergyman Charles Kingsley urged young men to take up combative "manly sports" like football. The Civil War renewed respect for martial virtues and was followed by increasing preoccupation among white middle-class males with bodily strength and prowess. The 1880s and 1890s saw both a sports craze and the celebrity of strong men like the prizefighter John L. Sullivan and the bodybuilder Eugen Sandow.

By the turn of the century a national periodical press and metropolitan newspapers facilitated the promotion of national ideals of manliness, not least through the celebration of models like Sullivan and Theodore Roosevelt, military hero and U.S. president (1901–1909). Influential university faculty and graduates led the way in urging recovery of a more virile manhood. Intellectuals like the psychologists William James and G. Stanley Hall and the writers Owen Wister, Frank Norris, and Jack London praised the warlike, even primitive, instincts of men as antidotal to an overcivilized refinement. Those who shared this desire for a more aggressive masculinity worried that the predominance of women among America's teachers and church members would turn boys into "sissies." In response, "manliness" advocates favored the creation of special programs for boys under adult male leadership that would inculcate hardier virtues, not least by holding up noble savages and pioneer backwoodsmen like Daniel Boone and Davy Crockett as exemplars.

This redefining of "manliness" by middle- and upper-class writers reduced the distance between their ideal and that of some working-class and immigrant groups since the beginning of the century. A bachelor subculture developed in antebellum cities. The young men who came to dominate volunteer fire companies were notorious for violent competition, and illegal blood sports like prizefighting drew crowds. Maintaining honor by avenging insults was central to the conception of manhood, especially among southerners, even those of evangelical persuasion in religion.

While dueling became disreputable in the North after the killing of Alexander Hamilton by Aaron

Burr in 1804, planters and lower-class whites, especially in the Old Southwest, continued to prepare themselves for such tests of honor as well as for demonstration of their skills in riding, shooting, and hunting. For African-American men, by contrast, manhood meant above all becoming independent, being one's own master; and combat, whether individually or as soldiers during the Civil War, with those who had controlled them felt especially "manly."

Not enough is known yet about the relative influence on rural males in the settled Midwest and Northeast of antebellum ideals and styles of masculinity, ranging from Jackson's prowess and bellicosity to evangelical self-discipline. Most probably, throughout the century agricultural workers expected their sons to grow into adult male tasks and attitudes as quickly as possible. The physical demands of farm life made it unlikely they would share the worries of middle-class city dwellers about boys and men becoming soft and feminized.

See also **Agriculture; Corporations and Big Business; Business; Character; Cities and Urbanization; Clubs,** *subentry on* **Fraternal Societies and Clubs; Cowboys and Cowgirls; Dueling; Gender,** *subentry on* **Interpretations of Gender; Manifest Destiny; Sports,** *subentry on* **Sports and the Sporting Life; Work,** *subentry on* **Middle-Class Occupations.**

Bibliography

Carnes, Mark C., and Clyde Griffen, eds. *Meanings for Manhood: Constructions of Masculinity in Victorian America.* Chicago: University of Chicago Press, 1990.

Gorn, Elliott J. *The Manly Art: Bare-Knuckle Prize Fighting in America.* Ithaca, N.Y.: Cornell University Press, 1986.

Kimmel, Michael S. *Manhood in America: A Cultural History.* New York: Free Press, 1996.

Rotundo, E. Anthony. *American Manhood: Transformations in Masculinity from the Revolution to the Modern Era.* New York: Basic, 1993.

Townsend, Kim. *Manhood at Harvard: William James and Others.* New York: Norton, 1996.

CLYDE GRIFFEN

MANNERS   A perusal of some foreign travelers' accounts of the pre–Civil War decades, such as Frances Trollope's famously derisive *Domestic Manners of the Americans* (1832), raises the question: *what* manners in nineteenth-century America? But those accounts can be misleading, especially as their descriptions of overly inquisitive, underdressed, tobacco-spitting Americans tended to focus on new settlements in the West. American manners were better in eastern towns and cities. Indeed, Americans, especially the white middle class, which grabbed the reins of cultural leadership in the first half of the century, were keenly interested in etiquette. This makes sense, considering that they were trying to figure out how citizens of this new republic should behave.

Historians have learned from anthropologists and sociologists that manners are not trivial. Manners are the basis of ritual and symbolic behavior, and they allow people to act out power relations in a nonverbal fashion in every encounter. They can therefore be quite revealing, sometimes disclosing social facts that Americans do not wish to acknowledge openly. In some ways manners of the past are a little hard to trace because people did not generally record every bow or curtsy. Historians are helped by the fact that these behaviors had to be learned, and many Americans, especially in the nineteenth century, turned to conduct manuals for those lessons. The nineteenth century was the great age of the etiquette book, rivaled only by the Renaissance, when a plethora of treatises on courtly behavior helped transform knights into gentlemen.

One would think that Americans would have desired a new code of behavior immediately upon winning independence from Britain and thereby trading in a monarchy for a republic, but they continued to rely on British tutelage for several decades. It was only in the 1820s and 1830s that American publishers began to bring out books that purported to offer manners suitable for a republic. In fact, these volumes were not very different from new advice works appearing at the same time in Victorian Britain. In both cases the books described a self-contained world wherein bourgeois adults presented themselves as respectable in the parlors and dining rooms of their peers. Scholars differ as to when middle-class manners began to develop, but all agree that the middle class was in charge by the 1820s. For the most part—again in etiquette books produced on both sides of the Atlantic—lower-class people only appear as servants. In contrast to advice works of the previous centuries, the nineteenth-century books no longer regarded servants as young charges to be educated but rather as silent props and stagehands for middle-class performances. The similarity between British and American manuals in this respect suggests that the major forces behind manners were the economic developments that lifted the middle class to prominence. Despite patriotic affirmations of the democratic nature of American society in the prefaces of the new American manuals of the antebellum era, the differences between them and British versions were few. One dissimilarity was a slight reluctance on the part of American authors to go as far as British authors in acknowledging distinctions between the middle and upper classes.

Is Polite Society Polite
And Other Essays *By*
MRS·JULIA WARD HOWE
Lamson,Wolffe, & Co.
Boston·Six Beacon St·   New York·Life Building

Essays on Etiquette. As wealthy Americans turned back to European standards of politesse after the Civil War, books devoted to social codes were published. Julia Ward Howe, author of the "Battle Hymn of the Republic," wrote this collection of essays in 1895. LIBRARY OF CONGRESS

Americans denied the class-communicating functions of their social rituals. The nineteenth century saw the advent of the precept of "ladies first," and this new notion of according social preeminence to women was especially useful as a way of disguising both class and gender inequality in supposedly democratic America. While both British and American advice books gave women precedence, etiquette writers and travelers alike remarked on the degree to which American manners were marked by civility toward women. Reading between the lines of the etiquette manuals indicates that a gentleman did not need to bestir himself to aid a servant girl. Nevertheless, the attention those manuals paid to deference to women distracted their audience from the persisting if not increasing class and gender inequality in the United States.

Thus by mid-century Americans were using manners to enact the rise of the middle class and to make clear socially the power relations that were muddied by growing electoral democracy among white men. The bourgeois code Americans embraced was hegemonic. "Out groups," whether native-born working-class "swells," Irish servant girls, or African Americans of any class or status, could either imitate or satirize the code, but they could not compete with it. Even very wealthy Americans could only go along

with the bourgeois America presented in antebellum advice literature.

While these ritual accommodations of the contradictions of a liberal capitalist society were long lasting, especially ladies first, the situation did change somewhat after the Civil War. The maturation of industrial capitalism in the final decades of the century thrust up many fortunes, and new ideological justifications of inequality, such as the "gospel of wealth," lessened the need for covert communication of class through manners. Rich Americans now openly imitated and asserted parity with aristocratic Europeans. The very wealthy were once again the acknowledged leaders of society, and etiquette books registered their leadership. Perhaps the best example is descriptions of table settings, which became frightening in their complexity. New forms of reporting on social rituals also developed, as etiquette manuals were supplemented with magazine articles and newspaper "society" columns. Still, this was the age of Horatio Alger, and the fiction that in America anyone could become a lady or a gentleman did not die. Indeed, some authors offered conduct instruction to Americanize the wave of new and, from the native-born perspective, more "alien" immigrants from southern and eastern Europe. Of course, those specific instructions tended toward advising on suitable industrial work habits as much as toward instructing about gentility.

Added to the foundation laid in the antebellum decades, these developments set the stage for proper behavior in "the American century": both assertive of and blind to class and especially concerned with gender. Nineteenth-century manners reveal how Americans conceived ritual solutions to some central problems of American culture.

See also **Character; Class, Social; Gender,** *subentry on* **Interpretations of Gender; Social Life.**

Bibliography

Bushman, Richard L. *The Refinement of America: Persons, Houses, Cities.* New York: Vintage, 1993.

Halttunen, Karen. *Confidence Men and Painted Women: A Study of Middle-Class Culture in America, 1830–1870.* New Haven, Conn.: Yale University Press, 1982.

Hemphill, C. Dallett. *Bowing to Necessities: A History of Manners in America, 1620–1860.* New York: Oxford University Press, 1999.

Kasson, John F. *Rudeness and Civility: Manners in Nineteenth-Century Urban America.* New York: Hill and Wang, 1990.

Schlesinger, Arthur M. *Learning How to Behave: A Historical Study of American Etiquette Books.* New York: Cooper Square, 1968.

C. DALLETT HEMPHILL

MAPS.   See **Geography and Cartography.**

MARINES, U.S.   The history of the U.S. Marine Corps in the nineteenth century is characterized by Marine historian Allan Millett as a history of "institutional adaptation and survival" (Millett, p. xv). Officially organized on 11 July 1798, the marines of the Early Republic served primarily as ship guards and on-board sharpshooters. While proponents hoped that the service would develop as an infantry for the U.S. Navy, the so-called tin soldiers were little appreciated by that service, the U.S. Army, or the American public. During the first half of the nineteenth century, marines participated in numerous land operations in far-flung places, such as Peru, China, the Falkland Islands (1832), and even on the American frontier fighting Indians in the Seminole War (1836–1842). These campaigns, as they were small in scale, did little to change or enhance public perception of the corps, and for the most part marines performed no better or worse than the sailors and soldiers fighting by their side. With the corps suffering from inadequate funding to undertake more extensive training and internal problems relating to re-

cruitment, pay, command authority, and discipline, Archibald Henderson, who served as Marine Corps commandant from 1820 to 1859, had great difficulty justifying the corps' continuing existence until the Mexican War (1846–1848), when he created an elite status for his men by exaggerating their contributions in capturing "the halls of Montezuma."

Despite this development, the Civil War and the years following proved to be difficult times for the Marine Corps. While the navy found joint operations with the army contentious and could have benefitted from the marines assuming their future amphibious assault mission, few within or without the corps visualized such a role for the marines at this time, nor would the army have willingly acceded such a role to their rival service. Following the war, Congress drastically cut appropriations for all the armed forces and even considered absorbing the corps into the other services. Calling for either a "funeral or a resuscitation," young marine officers took steps to modernize and professionalize their ranks as well as to secure an independent mission. The Spanish-American War (1898) and the resulting acquisition of an American empire in 1898 provided the turning point in U.S. Marine Corps history. With a new, aggressive foreign policy, the "Gallant Marines" who had been "First in the Fight" proved their worth as the best force for "immediate and sudden call" when establishing forward bases. In 1899 Congress passed the Naval Personnel Act, which authorized substantial increases in funding and manpower for the once meager corps.

See also **Army; Military Service; Navy.**

Bibliography

Millett, Allan R. *Semper Fidelis: The History of the United States Marine Corps.* New York: Free Press, 1991.

Simmons, Edwin Howard. *The United States Marines: A History.* Annapolis, Md.: Naval Institute Press, 1998.

Shulimson, Jack. *The Marine Corps' Search for a Mission, 1880–1898.* Lawrence: University Press of Kansas, 1993.

LORI LYN BOGLE

MARITIME TECHNOLOGY   Advances in U.S. maritime technology in the nineteenth century were an outgrowth of international developments that included the introduction of steam power; the development of ironclad, iron-hulled, and finally steel ships; and many other mechanical, electrical, and structural improvements. In some instances American inventors led the way, and in others they followed leads that developed elsewhere in the North Atlantic world. The concept of steam-engine propulsion for both merchant and naval ships led to some practical experiments in the late 1700s, and the early decades of the nineteenth century were alive with experimentation and invention as steam power attempted to drive out wind power.

The Role of Professionalization

These technical developments were proceeded by a period in the late eighteenth century during which the art of ship construction was professionalized in Britain, France, and the United States. In France the *Genie Maritime,* that is, the profession of naval engineers, was formed in 1765 within the Marine Ministry. In the United States an act passed on 27 March 1794 provided for the construction of six frigates, and Joshua Humphreys was appointed principal constructor. Professionalization of shipwrights in Britain took longer, with the formal emergence of the term "constructor" or "naval constructor" appearing in the 1840s.

In the United States Humphreys designed the six 44-gun frigates authorized under the 1794 act, and many of the details were planned by his assistant Joshua Fox, who was an expatriate British shipwright. Both Fox and Humphreys submitted plans for the frigates to Secretary of War Henry Knox, who compromised by merging aspects of both of the plans. The use of heavy timbers and close framing of the ship structures, as planned by Humphreys, contributed to the great strength of the ships and improved their resistance to cannon fire. Both Humphreys and Fox were dismissed in 1801, and a wide variety of private yards built a series of sixty-foot sloops as planned by Thomas Jefferson.

Although the profession of naval constructor was reinstituted in the United States in 1813, the U.S. Navy's first steamship was designed in New York in 1814 by an outside entrepreneur. An innovative design by Robert Fulton for the *Demologus,* a 24-gun catamaran frigate, was decades ahead of its time. The ship was completed too late for the War of 1812, and after some initial trials, it was laid up. No other steamship was constructed for the U.S. Navy until 1842.

The Earliest Steam-powered Vessels

Steam propulsion for merchant ships took off in the United States under the leadership of several inventive men who came from backgrounds entirely outside the world of naval constructors and shipwrights. Between 1784 and 1787 James Rumsey, an innkeeper, experimented with a craft driven by steam and pole on the upper Potomac River in what is now West Virginia. Another early experimenter, John Fitch, worked in Philadelphia between 1785 and 1798 to

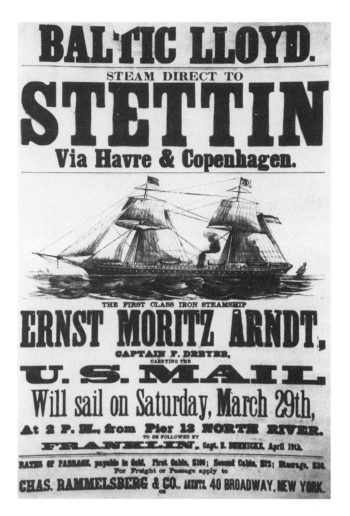

Trans-Atlantic Steam Power. An announcement of departure for the first-class iron steamship *Ernst Moritz Arndt* and its mail delivery to Stettin, a Prussian seaport in present-day Poland. Printed by H. D. Gerdts & Co., 1873. LIBRARY OF CONGRESS

perfect his design, which used a steam engine to power a set of paddles. The credit for the first commercial steamboat goes to Fitch, who operated a regular line in 1790 between Trenton, New Jersey, and Philadelphia, Pennsylvania, on the Delaware River. Between 1790 and 1804 several experiments were tried on the Connecticut, Hudson, and Delaware Rivers by other inventors.

The New York patrician and politician Robert R. Livingston became interested in the possibility of steam power, and he obtained a monopoly on the use of steam in New York waters. In 1804, with the help of several others who had experimented through the 1790s, he built a steam-powered, propeller-driven open boat. Fulton, an American artist studying in Britain, became interested in experiments there. He met Livingston in France, where Livingston was serving as U.S. minister. Fulton bought a British steam engine built by the firm of Boulton and Watt, and with the support of Livingston, launched a successful riverboat, which made a round trip from New York to Albany on the Hudson in September 1807. It was called the *Steam-Boat*, after 1809 was known as the *North River Steam-Boat*, and even later was named the *Clermont*. Fulton's craft saw river service for several years, providing reliable though expensive service on the Hudson.

For this reason Fulton is often credited as the "inventor" of the American river steamboat. Fulton-designed steamboats, operating under the Livingston monopoly in New York State, were soon widely imitated. Over the next four years steamboat services by other firms opened up on the Delaware River, on the St. Lawrence River, on Lake Champlain, and on the Ohio and Mississippi Rivers out of Pittsburgh. When the War of 1812 intervened, plans were well underway for integrated stagecoach lines and river steamers to link through lakes, rivers, and highways from the Canadian border at the northern end of Lake Champlain to Charleston, South Carolina, and New Orleans, Louisiana.

Following the War of 1812 steam-powered riverboats flourished, and side-wheelers and stern-wheelers grew in size and reliability through the 1820s. With the dredging of rivers to clear sandbars and snags of logs and stumps, regular transportation for both freight and passengers became possible and played an important part in the rapid population and economic growth of the United States in the decades before the Civil War. The steamboats of the period were ideally suited to solve one major transportation problem in the country. While it was possible to float barges downstream or to move downstream in large oar-powered rowboats, long-distance travel upstream was nearly impossible before the introduction of steam. Powered by firewood, the steamers could stop frequently to load logs for the hungry fireboxes. The paddle-wheel systems were also ideal for river waters, since a vessel with shallow draft could mount all engines and the transmission gear to the paddle wheels, well above the waterline.

However, early steam engines were unreliable and underpowered for ocean-going vessels, and nearly all ocean-going steamboats before the 1880s combined both sail and steam power. Steam could prove useful for entering and leaving harbors or for propulsion on windless days at sea, but for long-distance travel across the ocean, wind power tended to be more reliable. Steam engines were greasy, demanding, hazardous, and unfamiliar to sailors trained to handle and repair sails and rigging.

The *Savannah*, originally intended for the U.S. coastal trade, made the first transatlantic crossing under partial steam power in May and June 1819. Captain Moses Rogers, who had worked in a packet line on the Delaware River, hoped to sell the ship in Britain for the Russians to use in the Baltic Sea. When the sale fell through, Rogers brought the ship back to the United States by wind power and later removed the engines.

Over the next twenty years a variety of companies attempted to establish regular ocean-going, steam-powered travel between Europe and the United States. Finally in 1840 the British entrepreneur Samuel Cunard established a subsidized steam-powered shipping line that operated between Liverpool, England, and Halifax, Canada, with an additional stop in Boston. New York City was added as a destination in 1847.

The Perfection of Sail

In the 1840s and the 1850s the old maritime technology of sail and wind power reached new heights of perfection and remained quite competitive, while the new maritime technology of steam power struggled to overtake and surpass the sailing ship.

Sailing ships from the early and mid–nineteenth century took many forms. Operating out of New Bedford and Nantucket, Massachusetts, American whalers cruised Arctic seas, the South Atlantic, the South Pacific, and the Indian Ocean in search of the sperm whale. Built low to the water, the typical whaling bark had single topsails and high lookouts, enabling men to scan the ocean for signs of whales. On the deck a characteristic pair of bricked boilers made up the tryworks, and many whaling ships were steered with a huge tiller rather than a wheel. Large wooden davits suspended up to five whaleboats from both sides of the ship. A crew of some thirty men would handle the five boats and the ship itself. In the late twentieth century one surviving whaler, the *Charles W. Morgan*, resided at Mystic River Seaport, Connecticut. Built in 1841, this classic 105-foot, black and white painted ship operated for eighty years, making some thirty-seven voyages, each lasting two to three years.

Whales were harvested for their oil, which was an excellent source of indoor lighting in much of the United States through the 1840s and 1850s. The growth of city lighting systems based on coal gas piped to homes and businesses and, later, kerosene refined from petroleum supplanted whale oil, putting an end to the demand for and the reckless killing of thousands of whales.

As the foreign trade of the United States expanded throughout the century, trading vessels plied the sea-lanes to Europe, Asia, and the South Pacific. Yankee merchants had opened the trade to the Far East as early as 1783, carrying American products like dried fish, flour, cheese, potatoes, onions, and candles. Their vessels returned, loaded with tea. Under the tea chests, captains often packed heavy pottery as ballast, bringing chinaware to the United States. Operating out of Salem and Boston, Massachusetts, many of these traders opened up fur trade with Native Americans on the Pacific Coast.

Traveling aboard such a "China trader" bound for the island of Mauritius as a merchant seaman, Nathaniel Bowditch of Salem, Massachusetts, identified and corrected 8,000 errors in British navigation tables that used astronomical observations to help determine latitude and longitude on the trackless ocean. Bowditch's *The New American Practical Navigator,* published in 1802, went through many editions in his lifetime. Together with improved chronometers, the navigation tables made a major contribution to solving the technological problems of ocean navigation.

Perhaps the best remembered and most beautiful of American sailing craft during the years of compet-

ing technologies was the clipper ship. With sleek, flush decks, excellent hull design, and a mass of sail with strong masts and rigging, the ship could speed through the water under full sail even in strong winds. The best-known clipper shipbuilder was Donald McKay, who produced many ships in his East Boston yard.

The culmination of the clipper ship may have come with McKay's *Great Republic,* built in 1853, with four masts and an auxiliary steam engine used not for propulsion but to raise the anchor. Between the years 1847 and 1854 a number of McKay-built clipper ships set records for speed on the long voyage from New York and Baltimore, around Cape Horn, to San Francisco. Over and over the record was broken, coming down from more than ninety days to seventy-six days. Clipper ships also set speed records for transatlantic crossings and for trips to Canton, China, during these same years. Part of the success of clipper ships was due to advances in charting by the U.S. Naval Observatory, which published detailed guides to winds and currents that supplemented Bowditch's tables.

While the 1848 California gold rush and the set-

The Great Mississippi Steamboat Race. In July 1870 the *R. E. Lee* beat the *Natchez* in a race up the Mississippi from New Orleans to St. Louis. Lithograph by Currier & Ives, 1870. LIBRARY OF CONGRESS

tlement of Oregon drove clipper ship captains to new speed records, other entrepreneurs planned steamship lines that ran from New York to Panama, took a short overland road or rail journey to the Pacific side, then a second steam run to San Francisco or to Astoria in Oregon Territory. Before the Civil War competition from the steam lines began to spell the end of the clipper ship era.

Yankee traders, Baltimore and Boston clipper ships, and New England whalers were the most famous of the sailing vessels produced in the United States in the early decades of the nineteenth century. Other types included small sailing packet or passenger ships, which operated from port to port in the United States, and a wide variety of special-cargo ships. Among the latter were round-bottomed or "kettle-bottom" ships, especially designed to carry bales of cotton, that were built in several ports, including Kennebec and Bath, Maine. Hundreds of these cargo carriers regularly operated in the 1830s and 1840s from rivers and bays in the South to the textile mills of New England. Steam-powered packet lines and steam-powered merchant cargo ships began to supplant the coastal sailing packets and kettle bottoms by the 1850s. Steam offered some advantages, but the sailing vessels cost less to operate and continued to compete.

For instance, immigrants flooded to the United States aboard sail-driven, transatlantic packet lines, and a much smaller, steam-powered packet service attracted only a wealthier class of traveler until long after the U.S. Civil War. In some of the bulk trades, such as nitrates imported from the West Coast of South America and coastal lumber and coal transport, sailing vessels, with their cheaper operating costs, continued to work their humble trades from port to port long after steam had proven reliable. Coal was shipped by schooners from the Pennsylvania fields to small New England ports to fire steam engines in trains and factories ashore well into the twentieth century.

Naval Technology

Steam began to have a major impact on U.S. naval vessels following the establishment in 1842 of the system of navy bureaus to procure ships, equipment, and supplies. The Bureau of Construction, Equipment, and Repair was in charge of building ships. The world's first propeller-driven warship was the *Princeton*, designed in 1844 by John Ericsson, a Swedish engineer who had immigrated to the United States from Britain in 1842. Ericsson had patented a system of propeller-driven ships in 1836, and he solved one of the main problems confronting those who wanted to use propellers rather than paddle wheel propulsion. Propellers required that a moving shaft pierce the hull below the waterline without creating a leak, and Ericsson's system of lubricated packing around the shaft made rapid advances in propeller-driven ships possible.

John Lenthall, an experienced naval constructor who had designed in 1842 the navy's first iron warship, the *Michigan*, became chief constructor of the navy in 1853. He served in that post through 1871. Working with Benjamin Isherwood, who became chief of the Bureau of Steam Engineering in 1862, Lenthall designed many mass-produced gunboats, sloops, and other warships that saw service in the Civil War.

The most famous of the Civil War ironclad warships, the *Monitor*, was designed by Ericsson. He completed the ship in a remarkable three months from a cardboard model he had devised. The *Monitor* included several innovations, including a rotating gun turret; very low freeboard, that is, the distance between the waterline and the deck; and power by steam and propeller. Ericsson ignored navy orders to install a mast and sails on the ship. The famous gun duel in March 1862 between Ericsson's "cheesebox on a raft" and the Confederate ironclad *Virginia*, the former steam frigate *Merrimac*, was the first battle between steam-powered, ironclad ships. The *Monitor*, the smaller and faster ship, only had two eleven-inch guns in the turret, while the *Virginia* mounted ten nine-inch guns. Although neither vessel sank, the fact that the *Monitor* prevented the *Virginia* from destroying more of the Union navy or moving on Washington was seen as a victory. The Union, the Confederacy, and, later, foreign navies all began building "monitors" along the lines originated by Ericsson.

Following the Civil War the U.S. Navy formally established a Construction Corps, which included engineers who had graduated from the Naval Academy. Unlike the prior naval constructors, who had all been civilians, this new group of naval officers emulated the system already established in Britain and France of a coherent professional group working for the national naval service. Some of the first officers in this corps, including Francis Bowles, Robert Gatewood, and David W. Taylor, trained in Britain at the Royal Naval College. Others went to France or Scotland for training over the next few years.

In 1881 the U.S. Navy began to modernize in an organized fashion, first with the construction of four all-steel, steam-powered ships, the "squadron of evolution." These "ABCD" ships, *Atlanta, Boston, Chicago,* and *Dolphin,* were soon joined by others. All were built with steel hulls, mounted modern guns, and were driven by improved steam engines fired by coal. With the appointment in 1887 of George Melville as chief of the Bureau of Steam Engineering, propulsion innovations rapidly progressed. Melville, a full-bearded hero of Arctic exploration, was a strong proponent of a professional approach to engineering. He advocated the establishment at or near the Naval Academy of an experiment station to perfect mechanical devices, engines, and propulsion gear for the navy. His dream was not realized until several years after his retirement in 1903.

Even though Melville could not arrange support for an experiment station for engines, he and Isherwood convinced the navy to accept double and triple expansion steam engines and to experiment with turbine engines. Steam engines used steam from boilers to drive piston engines much like a modern automobile engine. In double and triple expansion systems, the steam, rather than venting after it was exhausted from a piston, was reused in a second or third cylinder, greatly increasing efficiency. In turbine systems, developed in the 1890s by British and Swedish inventors, steam from boilers continuously turned a multibladed turbine instead of feeding into pistons. With fewer moving parts, turbines made even more efficient use of steam power and held promise for greater speed or for ample generation of electric power for large electric motors.

Meanwhile Captain David W. Taylor of the Construction Corps advocated the establishment of a towing tank to be used to scientifically model and design new ship hull forms. He won congressional approval for funding of the tank in the mid-1890s, and the first Experimental Model Basin in the United States was completed at the navy yard in Washington, D.C., in 1898.

The "new navy," which had been built between 1881 and 1898, saw action during the Spanish-American War in battles in Manila Bay in the Philippines and off Santiago, Cuba. The gunboats and cruisers of the U.S. Navy fired exploding shells, some propelled by a new smokeless powder. Smokeless powder allowed gunners to fire rapidly since they did not need to wait for the smoke to clear before sighting their targets. Gun designers through the 1890s had worked on improving gun breeches to take advantage of smokeless powder, enabling loaders to rapidly eject a used shell casing, inset a new shell, and fire the next round within a few seconds. The devastating fire from rapid-fire, five-inch guns and larger weapons proved decisive in both naval battles of the Spanish-American War.

By the end of the century steam had proven itself, both in merchant shipping and in the modern navies. As the new century dawned, new technologies were imminent that would change the world of sea travel and naval warfare even more: wireless telegraphy, submarines, turbine electric drives, and aircraft. The advent of these innovations brought the era of the great sailing vessels to its end.

See also **Civil War,** *subentry on* **Battles and Combatants; Coal; Inventors and Inventions; Military Technology; Naval Academy, U.S.; Naval Technology; Navy; Spanish-American War; Steam Power; Transportation,** *subentry on* **Canals and Waterways; Travel, Technology of; War of 1812.**

Bibliography

Bauer, K. Jack. *A Maritime History of the United States: The Role of America's Seas and Waterways.* Columbia: University of South Carolina Press, 1988.

Carlisle, Rodney P. *Where the Fleet Begins: A History of the David Taylor Research Center.* Washington, D.C.: Naval Historical Center, 1998.

King, R. W., ed. *Naval Engineering and American Sea Power.* Alexandria, Va.: American Society of Naval Engineers, 1993.

Villiers, Alan, ed. *Men, Ships, and the Sea.* Washington, D.C.: National Geographic Society, 1973.

Whipple, A. B. C. *The Clipper Ships.* Alexandria, Va.: Time-Life Books, 1980.

RODNEY CARLISLE

MARKET REVOLUTION   During the nineteenth century the U.S. economy underwent a major transformation. In 1800 almost all commercial activity involved foreign rather than domestic trade. Markets for the sale of foreign goods and domestic manufactures hardly existed outside the major cities, and these localized markets had more interaction with markets in Europe and China than with one another. After the War of 1812 developments in transportation, law, and banking enabled the local markets to expand into the hinterlands, so a number of large regional markets came into existence. Following the Civil War the continued development of transportation and industrialization permitted these regional markets to form one large national market by the end of the century. In the process traditional values and lifestyles gave way to a modern, consumer-based culture.

Prior to 1815 the U.S. domestic market was utterly undeveloped. Outside of the major commercial cities—Boston, New York, Philadelphia, Baltimore, Charleston, and New Orleans—and the large tobacco and cotton plantations of the South, the vast majority of Americans engaged in subsistence farming. Isolated from the outside world in tiny communities scattered across the nation's interior, these farmers cultivated holdings as small as twenty acres, on which they raised or produced enough, in terms of variety and quantity, to satisfy nearly all of their own material needs. These communities were imbued with a spirit of communalism. Land was rarely sold to strangers but instead was handed down to offspring. When one needed assistance with virtually any problem, the neighbors came to the rescue with little thought for monetary reward. Although most subsistence farmers also produced a small cash crop, wheat or corn in the North and tobacco or cotton in the South, the income raised in this way was used only to pay taxes and to purchase from country storekeepers the few things that could not be produced on the farm.

The Antebellum Market Revolution

Merchant capitalists operating out of the major commercial cities devoted their energies to exploiting the foreign trade. The most lucrative aspects of this trade involved importing tea, silk, and porcelain from China and exporting U.S. agricultural products to Europe. Because most of Europe was at war between 1800 and 1815, American foodstuffs were in such great demand that U.S. merchants were able to compete very successfully in the European market.

After 1815, when the cessation of the Napoleonic Wars brought peace to Europe, this situation changed. Not only did the European demand for American foodstuffs decline, but the energies that the British and French had devoted to war were now rededicated to trade. For example, the British government began to subsidize British steamship lines, which made American sailing ships uncompetitive. U.S. merchant capitalists continued to play an active and important role in foreign trade, but they also began to devote themselves with more vigor to exploiting the domestic market.

Several major obstacles stood in their way. Most important, transportation networks linking the commercial cities with the nation's interior were practically nonexistent. Rivers still served as the nation's principal highways, and very few good roads existed more than twenty miles from a city. Other obstacles included the primitive nature of state and federal business law, the existence of many state and private banknotes that served as currencies along with federal money, and intense competition from foreign merchants and manufacturers.

The transportation problem was solved by the construction of roads, canals, and railroads. Although several attempts, such as the Gallatin Plan and the American System, were made to involve the federal government in the development of internal improvements, most transportation projects resulted from local initiatives and were funded with state, municipal, and private monies. For example, commercial interests in New York City played a fundamental role in securing state funding for the Erie Canal, which by 1825 connected that city to communities in the western part of the state over three hundred miles away. By 1840 an elaborate network of canals crisscrossed New York, New Jersey, Pennsylvania, Maryland, Virginia, and Ohio. In addition to linking the older commercial cities to the interior, these canals extended the hinterlands of growing commercial centers such as Richmond, Virginia, and Cleveland, Ohio.

After 1840 railroads supplanted canals as the best means of connecting the country to the city. Spurred on by men of business, Baltimore spent more than $20 million in municipal funds on the construction of the Baltimore and Ohio and other railroads, thus extending its hinterland into the interiors of Maryland, Pennsylvania, and what is now West Virginia. Similarly, commercial interests in New York City played a fundamental role in connecting their city to the growing port cities along the Great Lakes, and businessmen in Philadelphia were major underwriters of the Pennsylvania Railroad, which connected their city to Pittsburgh and points west. By 1860 thirty thousand miles of rail lines crisscrossed the United States, bringing a great number of rural folk within reach of urban merchants.

Greater access to the interior increased the number and dollar amounts of contracts entered into by merchant capitalists. Because they no longer had the time for informal arbitration of a broken contract, merchants turned increasingly to formal litigation in state courts. The courts were dominated by judges with formal legal training, most of whom came from mercantile families and therefore favored commercial interests over communal interests. Their decisions adapted the English common law of contracts so that instead of protecting the community from the depredations of commercial activity, they opened the door to the development of a no-holds-barred free market. Common-law notions of fairness regarding profits, warranties, and contractual obligations gave way to unregulated prices and interest rates, "let the buyer beware," and absolute freedom to make and enforce contracts that favored one party over the other. These legal developments greatly enhanced merchants' ability to do business in the domestic market.

As merchants began to conduct business across state lines, the need arose for a uniform currency. State-chartered banks could issue banknotes, but these notes were rarely redeemable for gold or silver. Consequently their value depended on the time and place in which they were traded for goods and services, thereby diminishing their value as a national medium of financial exchange. A major step toward rectifying this confusing monetary system came in 1816, when the second Bank of the United States was chartered. Although this bank could not prohibit state banks from issuing notes, it did issue notes of its own that were backed by a federal charter and a guarantee that the national government would accept them at face value, thereby making them more attractive than state banknotes. State banks were forced either to stabilize their own notes by backing them with hard money or to remove them from circulation.

Many merchant capitalists withdrew from foreign trade to invest in domestic manufacturing. To raise revenue and to protect these nascent industries from intense European competition, the U.S. Congress, responding to the commercial interests, passed a new tariff bill in 1816. This bill imposed a high import duty on foreign manufactures in order to give American industries a competitive advantage in the domestic market. With the tariff's assistance the new manufacturers supplied the burgeoning American market.

The results of the first wave of the market revolution were staggering. Although subsistence farming persisted in many places until 1860, by that date virtually all U.S. citizens were participating in the marketplace to a significant degree. Now able to purchase things they had once been forced to make themselves, such as shoes, clothing, and certain tools, farmers devoted most of their energies to growing cash crops. These crops were sold for enough money to buy the material necessities of life as well as luxuries, such as chewing tobacco for men and stylish dresses for women. This revolution also affected American society in other ways. The lucrative nature of market production led many young people to abandon family homesteads in favor of more productive land in the West, thus weakening family ties. Instead of pitching in together to build and harvest, members of agricultural communities contracted for such services in a much more impersonal way. Many Americans decried the shift away from traditional values. However, they also rejoiced over the inexpensive material bounty delivered to their front doors.

The Post–Civil War Market Revolution

Although the market revolution slowed down during the Civil War, it picked up speed again in the 1870s. The second wave transformed the several regional markets that had come into being during the first wave into one national market. In this respect the market revolution dovetailed with the rise of "big business" between 1870 and 1900. During this period regional industrial firms developed into national organizations that integrated manufacturing, shipping, and marketing operations. Railroads evolved from a number of regional lines into a truly national transportation network by standardizing the gauge of the rails and coordinating the movement of passengers and freight among several connecting railroads linking the two coasts. The combination of mass production and mass distribution made available huge quantities of inexpensive consumer goods to the general public nationwide.

At the same time the way in which these goods were merchandised to customers changed dramatically. Large mail-order houses, such as Sears, Roebuck and Company and Montgomery Ward, offered customers in virtually any part of the country prompt service and reasonably priced, quality merchandise. These customers shopped in the comfort of their own homes by browsing through attractive, well-organized catalogs. In the larger cities, department stores—such as Macy's in New York and Marshall Field in Chicago—designed displays of upscale consumer goods to catch the discriminating consumer's attention, while in the smaller cities and larger towns, chain stores—such as S. S. Kresge Company, forerunner of the twentieth-century K-Mart Corporation—offered consumers a variety of inexpensive food, clothing, and household items. The development of big-city newspapers and national magazines made it possible to advertise new and improved wares to consumers in the comfort of their own homes in much the same way catalogs did.

The two most important social changes wrought by the second wave of the market revolution involved diet and dress. After 1880 average Americans no longer had to make, preserve, and store enough food to last for several months to a year. Instead they could purchase a variety of canned foods as well as fresh fruits, vegetables, meats, and dairy products at nearby chain grocery stores, such as the Great Atlantic and Pacific Tea Company, better known as the A&P. By the end of the century Americans no longer had to make their own clothing. They could purchase ready-to-wear fashions off the rack at nearby department or chain stores, as well as from several mail-order houses. This wave of the market revolution created a national consumer society, in which people bought rather than made what they needed.

The market revolution began because merchant capitalists sought to offset plummeting profits in foreign trade by cultivating the previously unexploited domestic market. Despite its effect on traditional values and ways of life, or perhaps because of it, the market revolution continued because the American public saw the opportunity for a better standard of living. During the nineteenth century American society was transformed from a self-sufficient, materially limited culture into one that was more dependent and more comfortable.

See also **Advertising; Banking and Finance,** *subentry on* **The Banking Industry; Industrialization and the Market; Internal Improvements; Law,** *subentry on* **Common Law; Merchandising,** *subentries on* **Chain Stores, Department Stores,** *and* **Mail Order.**

Bibliography

Boorstin, Daniel J. *The Americans: The Democratic Experience.* New York: Random House, 1973.

Horowitz, Daniel. *The Morality of Spending: Attitudes toward the Consumer Society in America, 1875–1940.* Baltimore: Johns Hopkins University Press, 1985.

Leach, William. *Land of Desire: Merchants, Power, and the Rise of a New American Culture.* New York: Pantheon, 1993.

Sellers, Charles. *The Market Revolution: Jacksonian America, 1815–1846.* New York: Oxford University Press, 1991.

Strasser, Susan. *Satisfaction Guaranteed: The Making of the American Mass Market.* New York: Pantheon, 1989.

CHARLES W. CAREY JR.

MARRIAGE   Marriage in the nineteenth century was both a consensual, private relationship symbolizing a couple's commitment to each other and a coercive, public relationship through which the state allocated rights and responsibilities to men and women. While marriage was a contract between a man and a woman, the state defined the terms of the relationship in ways that the couple could not alter. Over the course of the century, the practice and regulation of marriage shifted in response to social, political, economic, and legal developments.

State Control over Marriage

The state jealously guarded its interest in the practice of marriage. Lawmakers and judges carefully regulated the institution and its legal effects. Throughout the nineteenth century, racial prejudices infused state laws governing the availability and effects of marriage. Slaves were not legally permitted to marry, though many enslaved people entered into extralegal marriages that were recognized in their own communities. In addition, most states prohibited interracial marriage. These prohibitions, which were known as "antimiscegenation" laws (a term that originated in the 1860s), gained strength after the Civil War as Reconstruction-era politicians feared increased numbers of interracial unions. For most of

the century, these laws applied only to marriages between African Americans and whites. Toward the end of the century, however, some states banned unions between Native Americans and whites, and other western states banned marriages between whites and Asians. Racial prejudices also affected the government's use of marriage as a way to confer citizenship. In 1855 Congress passed a law granting citizenship to foreign women who married American men. The carefully worded law, however, excluded women who could not be "naturalized under existing laws," such as women of African descent (until 1870) and Asian women.

States also regulated marriage by legislating monogamy as its sole legal form. Every state thus made bigamy a crime, as did the 1862 Morrill Act with respect to the American territories. Different groups contested the supremacy of monogamous marriage. Various utopian groups, including free lovers, Oneidans, and Shakers, experimented with nonmarital forms of sexual ordering. Members of the Church of Jesus Christ of Latter-day Saints, however, with their official embrace of plural marriage, became the prin-

Domestic Sewing Machine. A husband introduces his wife to domesticity in this part of a larger illustration entitled "The Life and Age of Woman," which outlined the phases of a woman's life. Lithograph by W. J. Morgan & Co., 1882. LIBRARY OF CONGRESS

cipal target of the national campaign against polygamy. In *Reynolds v. United States* (1878), the Supreme Court held that the First Amendment's guarantee of religious liberty did not include the right to multiple marriages.

Courtship and Marriage Rituals

Over the course of the nineteenth century, northern middle-class whites embraced the ideal of romantic love as the key element of marriage. Courtship rituals thus became increasingly private and focused on shared emotional intimacy. Although premarital sexual relations were still frowned upon, especially among the middle class and those with middle-class aspirations, the language of romantic love and eroticism characterized the courtship period. The custom of giving an engagement ring as the culmination of courtship originated in the mid–nineteenth century, as did the bridal custom of wearing a white dress and veil.

Such norms, however, varied across communities. Slaves developed their own rituals to mark commitment outside the bounds of legal marriage. Among whites, class and region affected the meaning and rituals of marriage. For many upper-class whites, for instance, marriage remained an important economic institution for the transmission of property. Among many urban, working-class youth, and southern whites, courtship rites remained more public. In addition, many couples never participated in the formalities of marriage. Even as rituals proliferated, most states accepted the doctrine of common law marriage, which granted marital status to couples who, absent a formal ceremony, "held themselves out" to their communities as married. After the Civil War and emancipation, many southern states passed laws that automatically legitimized slaves' marriages when freedpeople were living and acting like husband and wife.

Separate Spheres and Coverture

Once married, husbands and wives assumed distinct social and legal roles. Socially, the ideology of separate spheres and the "cult of true womanhood" exerted powerful influences over white, middle-class married life. The family, the quintessential private sphere, stood in sharp contradistinction to the world of politics and employment, the so-called public sphere. Gender clearly marked each sphere: women inhabited the private sphere; men defined the public sphere.

Despite its dominance, however, no ideology could accurately reflect the lives of all married women across a century. Race and class, for instance, excluded many women from the separate spheres framework. Indeed, poor white women and black women faced accusations of laziness if they shunned work outside the home and attempted to model their lives on the separate spheres structure of white, middle-class society. Even within white, middle-class society, by the end of the century more women were working outside the home and challenging the rigid boundaries of separate spheres ideology.

Legally, coverture ordered the lives of married couples. Under this common law regime, a husband and wife had a single legal identity: the husband's. A wife, therefore, lost significant legal rights. She could not enter contracts, sue or be sued, or control any property (unless her family was wealthy enough to create an equitable trust). A husband, by contrast, had the right to sue on his wife's behalf, to use all his wife's property, and to assume the value of all her paid and unpaid labor. Some states protected a husband's right to chastise his wife. Along with these rights, came responsibilities: A husband was legally obligated to provide for his wife and legally responsible for her conduct. A wife also had a dower right to one-third of all her husband's property if she outlived him.

Legal changes over the course of the century affected the status of married women, altering their rights and opportunities. Activists in the woman's rights movement decried the inequalities of marriage, some comparing it to a form of slavery. The Declaration of Sentiments from the Seneca Falls Woman's Rights Convention of 1848, for example, denounced married women's "civilly dead" status. Agitation by woman's rights activists, along with concerns such as protecting family assets from a husband's creditors, contributed to the passage of reform laws beginning in the 1840s. By 1865, twenty-nine states had passed married women's property laws, allowing wives to hold property in their own names. In addition, by 1887, two-thirds of the states had passed married women's earning statutes, giving wives legal title to their labor and wages for nonhousehold labor. While these acts represented a formidable attack on the coverture regime, judicial reluctance to enforce them to their full potential severely dampened their practical significance for married women.

See also **Divorce and Desertion; Domestic Life; Gender,** *subentry on* **Gender and the Law; Law,** *subentry on* **Women and the Law; Miscegenation; Women,** *subentry on* **Women's Rights.**

Bibliography

Basch, Norma. *In the Eyes of the Law: Women, Marriage, and Property in Nineteenth-Century New York*. Ithaca, N.Y.: Cornell University Press, 1982.

Cott, Nancy F. *Public Vows: A Political History of Marriage in the United States*. Cambridge, Mass.: Harvard University Press, 2000.

Edwards, Laura F. *Gendered Strife and Confusion: The Political Culture of Reconstruction*. Urbana: University of Illinois Press, 1997.

Franke, Katherine M. "Becoming a Citizen: Reconstruction Era Regulation of African American Marriages." *Yale Journal of Law and the Humanities* 11 (1999): 251–309.

Grossberg, Michael. *Governing the Hearth: Law and Family in Nineteenth-Century America*. Chapel Hill: University of North Carolina Press, 1985.

Hartog, Hendrik. *Man and Wife in America: A History*. Cambridge, Mass: Harvard University Press, 2000.

Rothman, Ellen K. *Hands and Hearts: A History of Courtship in America*. New York: Basic Books, 1984.

Siegel, Reva B. "Home as Work: The First Woman's Rights Claims Concerning Wives' Household Labor, 1850–1880." *Yale Law Journal* 103 (1994): 1073–1217.

Stanley, Amy Dru. *From Bondage to Contract: Wage Labor, Marriage, and the Market in the Age of Slave Emancipation*. Cambridge, U.K.: Cambridge University Press, 1998.

Stevenson, Brenda E. *Life in Black and White: Family and Community in the Slave South*. New York: Oxford University Press, 1996.

ARIELA R. DUBLER

MARYLAND Maryland has been described as "America in miniature," because it contains the main topographical features of the contiguous United States. It is split into unequal parts by the Chesapeake Bay, producing an isolated eastern shore and an irregular pistol shape bounded on the east, north, and west by the Mason-Dixon line and on the south by the Potomac River. Before the arrival of Europeans the bay and Potomac shores were home to more than twenty tribes of Algonquin Indians.

Maryland's revolutionary constitution established a republican plutocracy, with high property qualifications for public office, and shifted power from the executive to the legislative branch. During the nineteenth century the state experienced increased democratization, including the elimination of the property qualifications for public office and the retrocession of powers to the governorship.

The population of Maryland was heterogeneous from its beginnings. The settler stock included English, Scots, Irish, Scots-Irish, Germans, and Africans. There was no significant addition in numbers until after the War of 1812, when a notable influx of Irish and Germans began. Opposition to immigrants, especially Irish Catholics, grew in the 1840s into a potent political movement that was formally known as the American Republican Party but was familiarly called the Know-Nothings because the members professed ignorance of what their party stood for. They were so strong a force in both the state legislature and Baltimore city government that any show of opposition or failure to vote for American Party candidates was an invitation to mayhem or even murder. In 1856 Maryland gave its electoral votes for the presidency to the Know-Nothing candidate.

In 1860 Maryland had 687,049 residents—515,918 whites, 87,189 slaves, and almost as many free blacks, 83,942. In the presidential election of 1860 a majority of Maryland voters (54 percent) supported the pro-Union candidates John Bell, Stephen Douglas, and Abraham Lincoln, but the secessionist John C. Breckinridge obtained a plurality of fewer than eight hundred votes. During the ensuing secession crisis Governor Thomas Holliday Hicks stymied the Confederate sympathizers until Federal troops occupied the state. Although it straddled invasion routes, Maryland was not the site of any major Civil War battle except the bloodiest, Antietam. As the 1860 election returns suggested, the division among Marylanders was close, but pro-Union sentiment was somewhat greater. In 1864, late in the war, a new state constitution abolished slavery. Nearly 63,000 Marylanders served on the Union side and 22,000 served with Confederate troops.

Maryland's post–Civil War politics was controlled by a Democratic Party machine. Its operations never suffered the notoriety of similar organizations elsewhere because it promoted candidates who were capable and honorable if, by and large, undistinguished. Briefly the Republicans gained control of both the state and city governments between 1895 and 1899, but this interlude ended with a major census fraud scandal.

Roger Brooke Taney

Among the Maryland figures of national importance must be numbered Roger Brooke Taney (1777–1864), who served as chief justice of the U.S. Supreme Court from 1836 to 1864. He is remembered primarily for his execrable opinion in *Dred Scott v. Sandford* (1856), in which he ruled that a former slave could not sue in a federal court. But he also bravely challenged the constitutionality of President Lincoln's suspension of habeas corpus. His enduring constitutional legacy, however, is leaving intact Chief Justice John Marshall's precedents upholding national power and undergirding them with equally sound supports for state authority.

Frederick Douglass

Marylander Frederick Douglass (1817/1818?–1895) was born a slave on the Eastern Shore, but because of an attempt to escape and his successful resistance to an effort to break his will, in 1836 he was sent to Baltimore, where he worked in the shipyards; he had to yield his pay to his master. Douglass was taught to read and write partly by the wife of his master, who was furious when he found out what she had done. In 1838 Douglass escaped to Massachusetts by borrowing a black sailor's passport. In 1841 he joined the abolitionist movement and later published a narrative of his life and feelings while he was a slave (1845). He moved to Rochester, New York, in 1847 and for seventeen years published a newspaper, the *North Star* in the cause of abolitionism. Unlike the more radical abolitionist William Lloyd Garrison, Douglass favored political action to more violent forms of opposition. Douglass attended the Seneca Falls convention for women's rights in 1848. During the Civil War he recruited two regiments of black troops that included his own two sons. After the war he held several minor offices in the government of the District of Columbia. In 1891 he was sent as minister-resident to Haiti. He died in 1895 upon returning home from a meeting to promote women's rights.

The economy of the state underwent transformations in the nineteenth century. In colonial times its wealth came primarily from tobacco cultivation augmented by commerce, shipbuilding, and fishing. Even before independence farmers had begun substituting grain for tobacco as their money crop. This trend resulted in the migration of people from the older settlements on the eastern shore and in southern Maryland to the northern and western counties. There was also a notable shift from family farms to large villas, whose prospering owners could afford to buy newer and larger machines, especially after the Civil War. By 1888 farmers in the middle counties were converting from grain production to dairy farming to supply the developing urban populations nearby.

In the first half of the nineteenth century Maryland had an economic orientation toward the Midwest. When the opening of the Erie Canal in 1825 seriously threatened Baltimore's geographical advantage over the port of New York, a local group under the leadership of Phillip Thomas and George Brown proposed the building of the Baltimore and Ohio Railroad, while another group revived the long-dormant effort to build a westerly canal. These projects were financed by a combination of private, state, and city capital. Both enterprises were inaugurated with groundbreaking ceremonies on 4 July 1828, but the canal never extended beyond Cumberland, and the railroad did not reach Cincinnati until 1873.

Meanwhile, Baltimore's earlier focus on commercial enterprises was gradually supplemented with industrial investments. Sugar refineries, the first factories, were soon joined by mills processing coffee, vegetables, seafood, leather, and guano (a natural fertilizer imported from Latin America). Foundries producing iron, steel, copper, and tin products followed. By 1860 one-half of all industrial workers in the state lived in Baltimore. The climax in the city's industrial production came in the 1890s, when 82 percent of the state's total output was manufactured in Baltimore.

Just as its topographical features mimic those of the other lower forty-eight states, Maryland's development in the nineteenth century imitated that of the rest of the nation, only on a smaller scale. Economically, its agriculture yielded dominance to industrialization. Socially, Maryland absorbed wave after wave of immigrants, at first from northern Europe and toward the end of the century from the eastern and southern regions of Europe. In 1800 its population was largely derived from Great Britain and from Africa and numbered somewhat less than 380,000. In 1899 Maryland was home to almost 1.2 million and contained a much broader spectrum of nationalities and ethnicities. Politically, Maryland like the rest of the nation became increasingly democratic, and although after the Civil War its government was dominated by the Democratic Party, the Republican Party was a force that could not be ignored. The potency Maryland displayed during the nineteenth century continued well into the succeeding century.

See also **Baltimore; Immigration and Immigrants;** *subentries on* **Ireland, Great Britain, Germany; Transportation,** *subentries on* **Canals and Waterways, Railroads.**

Bibliography

Baker, Jean H. *Ambivalent Americans: The Know-Nothing Party in Maryland.* Baltimore: Johns Hopkins University Press, 1977.

Brugger, Robert J. *Maryland: A Middle Temperament, 1634–1980.* Baltimore: Johns Hopkins University Press, 1988.

Lewis, H. H. Walker. *Without Fear or Favor: A Biography of Chief Justice Roger Brooke Taney.* Boston: Houghton Mifflin, 1965.

Manakee, Harold R. *Maryland in the Civil War*. Baltimore: Maryland Historical Society, 1961.

Wagandt, Charles Lewis. *The Mighty Revolution: Negro Emancipation in Maryland, 1862–1864*. Baltimore: Johns Hopkins University Press, 1964.

Walsh, Richard, and William Lloyd Fox, eds. *Maryland: A History, 1632–1974*. Baltimore: Maryland Historical Society, 1974.

White, Frank F., Jr. *The Governors of Maryland, 1777–1970*. Annapolis, Md.: Hall of Records Commission, 1970.

NICHOLAS VARGA

MASONS   The Masonic fraternity, the "Ancient and Honorable Fraternity of Free and Accepted Masons," was established in America almost simultaneously in Philadelphia and Boston in the early 1730s. By the time of the American Revolution, in which Masons (also called Freemasons) played conspicuous roles, subordinate lodges functioned in all thirteen colonies and four future states along with a number of military lodges and four grand lodges. Growth was even more pronounced in the Federalist period. By 1800 several hundred lodges had been founded within all sixteen states, two future states, and the District of Columbia, while the number of grand lodges had risen to fourteen.

Origins and Development

The founders of Freemasonry or "speculative" Masonry, as opposed to "operative" masonry or actual stonemasons, were British scientists and clergymen who in the early eighteenth century translated the rhetoric of the building trades into intellectual and spiritual contexts. They successfully blended emerging scientific and enlightened ideas about the natural world with nonrational and mystical elements. This vague synthesis was set within the context of brotherhood and conviviality found in popular gentlemen's clubs. Through impressive quasi-religious ceremonies, Freemasonry offered a means of obtaining personal moral regeneration and of working toward the common goal of social reformation.

Initially three basic and theatrically presented "degrees" emerged, which led an initiate through successive stages of self-education toward greater esoteric knowledge. Over time deeper layers of symbolism developed, and "higher," more mysterious degrees were added, including twenty-nine degrees according to the "Scottish Rite" and ten according to the "York Rite."

As Freemasonry quickly spread throughout the British Isles and the overseas empire, complicated disputes arose over authenticity and purity of ritual ("ancients" versus "moderns"), over the social composition of membership and leadership (nobility versus commoners), and over jurisdiction (which grand lodge legally established and controlled which subordinate lodges). American Freemasonry was also very much influenced by internecine disagreements and by the addition of more elaborate degrees and rituals.

Beliefs and Membership

Ideologically, the fraternity taught natural rights philosophy, deism, Lockean psychology, scientific progress, the advancement of human happiness, and representative government. Socially, it began with an elitist and hierarchical orientation appropriate to a rising provincial patriciate. But claiming noninvolvement with politics, religion, and class antagonism and undergoing several transformations, American Freemasonry by the early nineteenth century had attracted men of less prominence who had absorbed contemporary ideals of republicanism, egalitarianism, and evangelicalism. Offering an extensive network of affective connections and shared values and providing a source of stability in the midst of radical social and economic change, the Masonic fraternity expanded rapidly.

The moralistic ideals espoused by American Freemasons came to be identified with democratic individualism as well as such middle-class virtues as sobriety, thrift, industry, honesty, temperance, piety, self-discipline, devotion to country, charity, respectability, and honor. At the outset of the nineteenth century, Freemasons profusely praised the exemplary life and accomplishments of their recently deceased and most illustrious brother George Washington; the century ended with eight more Masons having been elected president (34.8 percent of the century's presidents) and thirteen vice presidents (52 percent). The thousands of rank-and-file American Masons, representing a wide variety of professional, commercial, and artisanal occupations, usually joined during their youth, and often became leaders in their fields. Freemasonry remained essentially urban and small town in character, with comparatively few farmers joining. Some Masons used the lodge to make business connections and to enhance personal prestige.

Membership requirements were liberal, only specifying possession of high moral character and a belief in the Supreme Being among freeborn, physically sound, adult white men. Each subordinate lodge set its own levels of various dues and fees, which determined the socioeconomic character of any particular organization. The extensive demands on leisure time required to actively participate in fraternity func-

Nineteenth-Century American Freemasonry[a]

Year	No. of States/Territories with Masonic Lodges	No. of Grand/ Subordinate Lodges	No. of Members	No. of Adult White Males[b]	Masons as % of Adult White Males[b]
1800	23	14/ 375	17,000+	890,645[c]	1.91
1810	27	18/ 655	32,750+	1,210,631[c]	2.71
1820	29	22/ 1,405	90,000	1,649,363[c]	5.46
1830	30	27/ 802	40,000	2,362,466	1.69
1840	31	29/ 843	50,000+	3,325,105	1.50
1850	36	32/ 1,678	68,071	4,885,220	1.39
1860	42	37/ 4,872	202,309	6,940,208	2.92
1870	49	42/ 6,850+	466,481	8,692,047	5.37
1880	49	47/ 8,750+	544,513	11,792,610	4.62
1890	49	49/10,450	636,332	15,715,273	4.05
1900	49	49/11,765	838,325	19,550,538	4.29

Sources: Steven C. Bullock, *Revolutionary Brotherhood: Freemasonry and the Transformation of the American Social Order, 1730–1840* (Chapel Hill: University of North Carolina Press, 1996), 371, 181; Henry Wilson Coil, *Coil's Masonic Encyclopedia* (New York: Macoy, 1961), 39; Bobby J. Demott, *Freemasonry in American Culture and Society* (Lanham, Md.: University Press of America, 1986), 46: Lynn Dumenil, *Freemasonry and American Culture, 1880–1930* (Princeton, N.J.: Princeton University Press, 1984), xi, 4, 7, 225; Leon Hyneman, *World's Masonic Registrar* (Philadelphia: Lippincott, 1860), 442, *passim*; Fred L. Pick, G. Norman Knight, and Frederick Smyth, *The Pocket History of Freemasonry*, 5th ed. (London: Frederick Muller, 1969), 308–309; *Proceedings of the Grand Lodge of Free and Accepted Masons of the State of New York* (New York: J. J. Little, 1891), 182; *The Statistical History of the United States from Colonial Times to the Present* (New York: Basic, 1976), 16; Henry Leonard Stillson and William James Hughan, eds., *History of the Ancient and Honorable Fraternity of Free and Accepted Masons and Concordant Orders* (Boston: Fraternity Publishing, 1912), 877–893; William Preston Vaughn, *The Anti-Masonic Party in the United States, 1826–1843* (Lexington: University Press of Kentucky, 1983), 11, 187; *Proceedings* of each grand lodge for each appropriate decade, where available.

[a]A comprehensive time series of Masonic membership and subordinate lodges does not exist. The above statistics are drawn from various incomplete and often contradictory sources.

[b]This category is actually native-born free adult white males.

[c]Calculated by taking one-half the number for the category 16–25 years old and adding the result to those of older ages.

tions, especially among holders of higher degrees, also helped to determine who became Masons.

Anti-Masonry

The watershed event of American Freemasonry was sparked by the dramatic disappearance and presumed murder in 1826 of a renegade Mason, William Morgan, from Batavia, New York, who had threatened to publish the secret rituals of the fraternity. A series of legal investigations led to only light sentences for allegedly responsible, well-placed Masons, who appeared to have successfully subverted justice. This event, combined with Masonic secrecy, high-sounding titles of Masonic offices, and bloodcurdling Masonic oaths, produced a widespread conviction in the public mind that Freemasonry was exclusivist, anti-Christian, undemocratic, misogynist, and anti-American. Zealous politicians, clergy, and social reformers effectively capitalized on these fears.

The virulence of the anti-Masonic movement (1826–1843) in both religious and political manifestations drove the fraternity underground and almost destroyed it, especially in the eastern states. Overall membership fell by as much as two-thirds, and sev-

eral grand lodges temporarily ceased their operations. The anti-Masonic movement soon burned itself out, but not without leaving a permanent imprint on Freemasonry.

Although the fraternity's membership recovered and exceeded all expectations, its former intellectual vigor was missing. That attribute was replaced by vague repetitions of time-tested, universalistic principles, emphasis on fraternalism, dedication to charitable enterprises and public service, erection of meeting halls, and greater organizational refinement. Freemasonry had become demystified and more privatized.

The Late Nineteenth Century

The Masonic fraternity carefully avoided official statements on controversial political, social, or religious issues and relied on harmony and brotherly love within and outside of the lodge to soothe tempers. The Civil War was a significant example, as Masons took up arms against one another yet remained committed to their brothers. Comradeship on the front lines translated into a flurry of Masonic activity. More than 250 military lodges were founded during the war, 98 in Northern states and 153 in Southern states, and membership in civilian lodges grew dramatically in the following decades (see table).

Masonic ritual became strongly religious in character, thus reflecting the prevailing cultural context, but without any specific denominational content. Vague religious notions permitted a great latitude of personal belief, and Masons were left alone in their individual consciences as long as they upheld the moral principles of Freemasonry in their personal behavior.

Freemasonry became more respectable and popular. The fraternity engaged in frequent and newsworthy civic processions and public ceremonies. Twenty additional associated but separate Masonic bodies were founded, including five specifically for female relatives of Masons. Attracting fewer professional and mercantile elites and more white-collar workers, small shopkeepers, and skilled craftsmen, the fraternity offered elevated status and opportunity for distinction through an established hierarchy. Although allowing for considerable heterogeneity, Freemasonry remained essentially a native, Protestant, middle-class organization.

By 1900 Freemasonry was the oldest, most prominent, and largest voluntary association in the United States and a model frequently imitated. In reaffirming traditional beliefs and values, it provided a refuge from a materialistic, competitive, and immoral world. Freemasonry seemed to have become a permanent feature of American life.

Bibliography

Bullock, Steven C. *Revolutionary Brotherhood: Freemasonry and the Transformation of the American Social Order, 1730–1840.* Chapel Hill: University of North Carolina Press, 1996.

Demott, Bobby J. *Freemasonry in American Culture and Society.* Lanham, Md.: University Press of America, 1986.

Dumenil, Lynn. *Freemasonry and American Culture, 1880–1930.* Princeton, N.J.: Princeton University Press, 1984.

Vaughn, William Preston. *The Anti-Masonic Party in the United States, 1826–1843.* Lexington: University Press of Kentucky, 1983.

WAYNE A. HUSS

MASSACHUSETTS   First settled by the Pilgrims in 1620, Massachusetts was one of the thirteen original colonies. The state has poor farmland, almost no mineral resources, and mountains in the west. Its chief natural advantages are the superb harbor, which led to the growth of its major city, Boston; excellent fishing grounds off its coast; and dense forests, which initially produced wood and naval stores.

Massachusetts's rivers and streams were not useful as water highways in the colonial period, but proved to be extremely valuable as sources of waterpower in the nineteenth century. From its beginnings the colony's greatest asset was its human capital. The early Puritan settlers were particularly hard working, and were dedicated to creating an educated clergy to serve well-educated congregations. In 1636 Massachusetts became the site of America's first college, Harvard, which had evolved by 1800 into the nation's foremost university. In addition, the colony's seventeenth-century "common schools" evolved, in the mid-1800s, into the nation's strongest public school system.

The first gunshots of the American Revolution were fired in Massachusetts, and its residents were leaders in the movement toward American independence. Massachusetts was one of the first states to abolish slavery, with the adoption of its constitution in 1780. (Massachusetts has the oldest state constitution still in use in the United States.) Massachusetts's leading citizen, John Adams (1735–1826), helped to draft the Declaration of Independence, served as a diplomat during and after the Revolutionary War, and was the nation's first vice president. At the dawn of the nineteenth century, Adams was serving his last year as president of the United States. His son, John Quincy (1767–1848), also served as president, but no other Bay Stater reached that high office in the nineteenth century. Nevertheless, the state was always central to the U.S. political process, with citizens serving in the cabinet and on the Supreme Court. Daniel Webster (1782–1852), Charles Sumner (1811–1874), and Henry Cabot Lodge (1850–1924) ensured that Massachusetts was represented by a famous and powerful member of the House or Senate for almost the entire length of the century.

Massachusetts, 1800–1860

In 1800, Massachusetts had 422,845 residents, making it the fifth-largest state in the nation. By 1850, immigration and a vibrant economy had boosted the population to 994,514, while it ranked as the sixth-largest state. At the end of the century, there were 2,805,346 people, and Massachusetts had the seventh-largest population in the nation. Massachusetts has, however, always been one of the smallest states in physical size. Thus, its population has always been dense—packed into Boston, the largest city, and numerous medium-sized, industrial cities. Throughout the nineteenth century the population was overwhelmingly of European origin, with a small African

American population and even fewer Native Americans.

State industry was dominated by shipbuilding, fishing, whaling, and international commerce during the first quarter of the nineteenth century; these activities remained important until the Civil War. Beginning in the 1820s, Massachusetts rapidly developed an industrial economy based on textiles, shoe making, ironworks, and furniture. Rivers and streams provided the power for factories, while steam provided power for railroads, which came to the state early. Business innovators like Francis Cabot Lowell (1775–1817), Patrick Tracy Jackson (1780–1847), Abbott Lawrence (1792–1855), and Amos Lawrence (1786–1852) transformed the textile industry, starting with the creation of the Boston Manufacturing Company in 1812. Meanwhile Chief Justice Lemuel Shaw (1781–1861), the most significant state judge of the century, transformed the state's legal regime to accommodate the new technologies and industries. Massachusetts's factories first drew on rural New En-

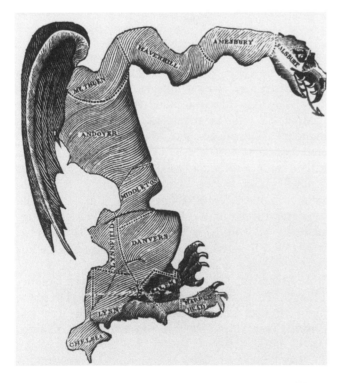

"The Gerrymander." In 1812, Republican governor of Massachusetts Elbridge Gerry divided the state into new voting districts, fashioning Essex County as overwhelmingly Republican. The curved county, thought to resemble a salamander, was depicted in this famous cartoon that brought about the American political term "gerrymander." Outraged by what they considered cheating, Federalists forced a repeal of this gerrymander the following year. Published in the Boston *Weekly Messenger*, 1812. LIBRARY OF CONGRESS

glanders, especially the daughters of farmers, for labor. They then increasingly turned to Irish immigrants, who flooded into the state beginning in the 1840s. By the end of the nineteenth century, new immigrants from eastern and southern Europe were coming to the factory towns of Lowell, Lawrence, Waltham, Lynn, Holyoke, and Worcester, as well as to Boston. By 1900 the state was producing half of the nation's shoes and a quarter of its woolen goods.

Massachusetts had an even greater impact on the national culture. Harvard College produced an overwhelming number of intellectuals, such as Ralph Waldo Emerson (1803–1882) and Henry David Thoreau (1817–1862). Other famous native writers included Herman Melville (1819–1891), Henry Wadsworth Longfellow (1807–1882), and Nathaniel Hawthorne (1804–1864). The state court, led by Shaw at mid-century and Oliver Wendell Holmes Jr. (1841–1935) at the end of the century, set the pace for common law developments, while Joseph Story (1779–1845) was the leading intellectual on the U.S. Supreme Court from 1811 until 1845. Story also taught at Harvard Law School, which emerged before mid-century as the national center for legal education. At the end of the century, the Harvard Law professor Christopher Columbus Langdell (1826–1906) transformed legal education with his "case method" and set the pattern for more than a century of legal training. By mid-century Boston had a science museum, an athenaeum, a public library, and numerous other cultural centers. This trend continued after the Civil War as more libraries, museums, and other cultural institutions—such as the Boston Symphony Orchestra, founded in 1881—appeared throughout the state.

In the 1830s Massachusetts emerged as the center of American social reform. In 1837, Horace Mann (1796–1859), as president of the Massachusetts senate, presided over the passage of the state's historic education bill. The bill's provisions led to the creation of the country's first modern public school system, which Mann shaped as secretary of the state board of education from 1837 to 1848. The New England Tract Society, the American Bible Society, and the Sunday School Union brought the ideas of Protestant theology, good works, and public morality to towns and villages across the Northeast and Midwest, as well as to China and other foreign missions. Dorothea L. Dix (1802–1887) almost single-handedly created a movement to improve the conditions of mental institutions and asylums in the 1840s. Her crusade carried over to national prison reform. After studying at Harvard Medical School in the 1820s, Samuel Gridley Howe (1801–1876) created the nation's first serious school for the blind, which emerged, with the help of the philanthropist Thomas H. Perkins (1764–1854), as the Perkins Institute.

More radical forms of social change dominated Massachusetts from the 1830s until the end of the century. Women like Lucy Stone (1818–1893) and Lydia Maria Child (1802–1880) were prominent leaders in the movement for gender equality and woman suffrage, which had great strength in Massachusetts. Other state reformers campaigned against the death penalty and violence, and formed organizations for world peace. However, antebellum Massachusetts also became a center of nativism. In the mid-1850s the anti-immigrant, anti-Catholic Know-Nothing Party gained control of the Massachusetts legislature, the governorship, and most of the U.S. congressional delegation.

Antislavery in Massachusetts

The most important humanitarian movement of the century, the crusade against slavery, was centered in Massachusetts. In 1829, David Walker (1785–1830), a free black living in Boston, published *Walker's Appeal*, a small pamphlet that warned masters to free their slaves or face violent resistance. Walker died the following year under mysterious circumstances, and many believed he was murdered by agents from the South. In 1831, William Lloyd Garrison (1805–1879) began publishing the nation's most important abolitionist newspaper, the *Liberator*. Garrison organized the New England Anti-Slavery Society, and later helped to found the American Anti-Slavery Society. He recruited numerous antislavery speakers to the cause, including the ablest orator of the era—perhaps of the century—Wendell Phillips (1811–1884). Garrison's organization was racially integrated and surprisingly egalitarian for its time. His chief printer was a leader of the African American community, William C. Nell (1816–1874), and many of his followers, especially Phillips, were uncompromising advocates of equality. Garrison himself often spent the night at the homes of blacks while traveling, something almost unheard of for white Americans of the period. Among Garrison's protégés was a young fugitive slave from Maryland, Frederick Douglass (1817–1895), whose half-century career as a reformer, social activist, and politician began when Garrison invited him to address the 1841 convention of the Massachusetts Anti-Slavery Society.

The antislavery movement spread beyond the relatively small number of people who joined Garrison's organization, as Massachusetts challenged racism and slavery in America. The first school desegregation case, *Roberts v. City of Boston* (1849), took place in Massachusetts. The state court ruled against the black parent, Sarah C. Roberts, who was represented by Charles Sumner and Robert Morris (1823–1882), one of the nation's first black lawyers. However, in 1855 the Massachusetts legislature effectively reversed this ruling by prohibiting segregation in the public schools. By the time of the Civil War the state legislature had in fact repealed all forms of legal segregation.

The state and its people stood squarely against the enforcement of the fugitive slave laws. In the 1840s Massachusetts led the North in prohibiting its public officials from participating in the return of fugitive slaves. In 1854, in the most celebrated fugitive case of the decade, Boston was turned into an occupied city as the federal government sent soldiers, marines, and the coast guard to remove the fugitive slave Anthony Burns (1834–1862) from Boston, after a mob had failed to rescue him from the custody of the U.S. marshal. In 1860 the state elected an avowed abolitionist, John Andrew (1818–1867), as its governor. By this time two other uncompromising opponents of slavery, Sumner and Henry Wilson (1812–1875), represented Massachusetts in the U.S. Senate.

Massachusetts, 1861–1900

During the Civil War, Massachusetts continued to lead the charge against slavery. Even before President Abraham Lincoln called for troops, Governor Andrew offered the president three Massachusetts regiments. During the war, Massachusetts organized one of the first northern black regiments, the famous Fifty-fourth Massachusetts Infantry Regiment (known today as the "Glory Brigade"). Its white colonel, Robert Gould Shaw (1837–1863), was the son of elite Bostonians. Two sons of Frederick Douglass traveled from New York to sign up with the unit. When the Fifty-fourth went off to battle, Massachusetts organized a second black brigade, the Fifty-fifth, which was led by a Unitarian minister, Colonel Thomas Wentworth Higginson (1823–1911). More than 146,000 Massachusetts men fought for the United States, and just under 14,000 gave their lives for the cause.

After the Civil War, Massachusetts remained a leader in the fight for racial equality and public reform. Senator Sumner sponsored his last successful civil rights legislation, which was passed after his death as the Civil Rights Act of 1875, and in 1890 Congressman Henry Cabot Lodge sponsored an unsuccessful attempt to provide federal protection for black voters. Lodge moved to the Senate in 1893, where he advocated civil service reform, but he also supported the newest nativist movement, the American Protective Association. Its members, like the

Know-Nothings of a half-century earlier, advocated an end to Catholic immigration.

At the end of the nineteenth century, Massachusetts became the center of higher education in the nation. Numerous new colleges joined older institutions like Harvard, Williams, and Amherst. These new institutions included Boston College, Boston University, Tufts, Northeastern, and four major women's colleges—Mount Holyoke, Smith, Radcliffe, and Wellesley. The state remained an industrial power as well, particularly in producing textiles, clothing, shoes, and machine tools, although banking and insurance led to new fortunes. Led by the lawyer Louis D. Brandeis (1856–1941), reformers helped to ease the social costs of industrialization, urbanization, and immigration. By 1900, Massachusetts offered more social protections to workers, children, and women than almost any other state.

See also **Abolition and Antislavery; Boston; Education; New England.**

Bibliography

Brown, Richard D. *Massachusetts: A Bicentennial History.* New York: Norton, 1978.

Handlin, Oscar. *Boston's Immigrants, 1790–1865: A Study in Acculturation.* 1941. Rev. and enl. ed., Cambridge, Mass.: Belknap Press of Harvard University Press, 1991.

Handlin, Oscar, and Mary Flug Handlin. *Commonwealth: A Study of the Role of Government in the American Economy: Massachusetts, 1774–1861.* 1947. Rev. ed., Cambridge, Mass.: Belknap Press of Harvard University Press, 1969.

Horton, James Oliver, and Lois E. Horton. *Black Bostonians: Family Life and Community Struggle in the Antebellum North.* 1979. Rev. ed., New York: Holmes and Meier, 1999.

Kaestle, Carl F., and Maris A. Vinovskis. *Education and Social Change in Nineteenth-Century Massachusetts.* New York: Cambridge University Press, 1980.

Levy, Leonard W. *The Law of the Commonwealth and Chief Justice Shaw.* Cambridge, Mass.: Harvard University Press, 1957.

Tager, Jack, and John W. Ifkovic, eds. *Massachusetts in the Gilded Age: Selected Essays.* Amherst: University of Massachusetts Press, 1985.

PAUL FINKELMAN

MATHEMATICS AND NUMERACY The history of mathematics in the nineteenth century can be loosely divided into two major periods: 1800–1875 and 1875–1900. Practical usage of mathematics by the layman in the earlier period remained essentially unchanged from that of centuries past. Merchants and farmers required little more than simple arithmetic: the ability to add and subtract numbers and, occasionally, to multiply and divide them. Technical applications of the day were mainly in maritime navigation, land surveying, and astronomy, including the determination of Easter and other movable Christian feasts. The need to understand such calendar-related problems resulted in certain religious orders, notably the Jesuits, emphasizing proficiency in mathematics. However, mathematics as a science advanced little during this period, and pursuit of mathematics for its own sake was rare. For the most part, dedicated programs of study had yet to appear at American colleges. Instead, only a few low-level introductory courses were offered and their instructors typically had no specialized mathematical training.

This same period did, however, experience a rapid growth in the application of statistical information. Economic and trade statistics began appearing in almanacs early in the century and statistical figures soon found a role in debates of important social issues, such as temperance and causes of prostitution. The public rapidly embraced the ability to quantitatively measure such things and it was amid this excitement that the American Statistical Association was founded in 1839. However, by scientific standards, statistical techniques, especially the methods of classification and sampling, remained somewhat crude. Specifically, objective data-gathering practices and mutually exclusive, easily identifiable categories were not yet understood nor appreciated by the average surveyor. Federal censuses experienced particular difficulties since incentives to file inaccurate reports could not be effectively eliminated. For example, there was a widespread fear that census results would be used to increase taxes and military duties. Moreover, low pay rates invited some census takers simply to make up reported figures instead of completing their required house calls. These problems were eventually addressed through several venues, including legislation, later in the century.

After 1875, the nature of mathematics as an academic and research discipline in America began a radical transformation, though its utility for the layman would remain primarily in arithmetic. Events in three separate areas were responsible for this awakening. First was the formalization of mathematics as an independent academic program in the higher education system, with major emphasis being placed on attracting qualified faculty. Johns Hopkins University was the first institution to create a modern mathematics department (1875–1877), and Harvard, Yale, Columbia, Princeton, and Brown quickly followed. In turn, these institutions prompted similar departments in colleges around the country. Formal graduate research work also commenced around this time. Johns Hopkins, Harvard, and Yale reported thirty-two, nine, and eighteen doctoral dissertations in mathematics, respectively, before 1900. Graduates accelerated expansion of the subject by returning to academe to carry on their own research and to train the next generation of investigators.

The second event that significantly stimulated mathematics was the founding in 1888 of the New York Mathematical Society (later renamed the American Mathematical Society [AMS] in 1894) by Thomas Fiske and colleagues at Columbia. The society published research developments in several journals, including its *Transactions*, which first appeared in 1900, and fostered dissemination and further collaboration through technical meetings. For example, it was instrumental in organizing the Chicago Congress of 1893, held in conjunction with the Columbian Exposition, the most important mathematical conference in America up to that time. Among those attending or sending papers were several of the most eminent international figures, including Felix Klein and David Hilbert from Germany. In addition to AMS periodicals, several other journals founded during this time facilitated dissemination of research, the most notable of which were the *American Journal of Mathematics* (1878), the *Annals of Mathematics* (1884), and the *American Mathematical Monthly* (1894).

The third major factor was the European influence: European mathematicians transplanted to America and Americans who had been schooled or had obtained postgraduate training in Europe. Mathematics was a substantially more mature science in Europe during the period, and this gradient of knowledge naturally flowed into the United States. Germany, whose universities at Göttingen, Berlin, and Leipzig were perhaps the most prestigious of the time, was particularly responsible for this influence. Mirroring activities in Germany and the rest of Europe, research work spanned the spectrum of major topics in pure and applied mathematics. In particular, Americans contributed to advances in abstract algebras, functional and vector analysis, calculus and differential equations, number and group theory, probability, and geometry.

A number of prominent American mathematicians are associated with this era. One of the leading individuals in pure mathematics was undoubtedly Benjamin Peirce, who graduated from Harvard (1829) and was appointed professor of mathematics and natural philosophy there in 1833. He devised methods to determine the number of real roots of an arbitrary algebraic equation and extended Lagrange's theorem on the development of functions. His main work, *Linear Associative Algebra,* was published in 1870. George William Hill graduated from Rutgers (1859) and was primarily an astronomer concerned with the practical application of mathematics. His interest in

lunar theory led him to study differential equations and series. Results concerning the lunar perigee laid the foundation in 1877–1878 for the theory of linear differential equations having periodic coefficients. So important was this work that it directly influenced a number of eminent mathematicians abroad, including Henri Poincaré. Other notable mathematicians were Josiah Willard Gibbs, who originated vector analysis and its associated notation in 1881, and Simon Newcomb, who improved the tables of celestial motion around 1885. These developments, along with numerous others occurring in America near the close of the nineteenth century, paved the way for mathematics as it is known today.

Bibliography

Cohen, Patricia Cline. *A Calculating People: The Spread of Numeracy in Early America.* New York: Routledge, 1999.

Klein, Felix. *Development of Mathematics in the Nineteenth Century.* Translated by M. Ackerman. Brookline, Mass.: Math. Sci. Press, 1979.

Smith, David E., and Jekuthiel Ginsburg. *A History of Mathematics in America Before 1900.* Chicago: Mathematical Association of America, 1934. Reprint, New York: Arno Press, 1980.

Struik, Dirk J. *A Concise History of Mathematics.* 3d ed. New York: Dover, 1967.

MICHAEL C. WENDL

MEATPACKING In the first half of the nineteenth century most meat was prepared for family or local consumption immediately after slaughter. Thereafter meat increasingly was preserved and packed in containers for transportation and sale in urban and foreign markets. Late-nineteenth-century demand in the growing urban populations and among foreign consumers created a large U.S. industry of refrigerated dressed beef, pork, and mutton. By 1900 meatpacking was the largest industry in the United States.

Slaughtering and Meatpacking before the Civil War

Early in the century most cattle, hogs, and sheep were slaughtered and butchered during the winter months for immediate consumption. A farm family that slaughtered its own stock dry-cured or pickled the meat under the supervision of the housewife. Better cuts of ham, bacon, and dried beef were traded for sugar and coffee at country stores that in turn sent the meat to city markets. As cities grew, some farmers drove live hogs and cattle to urban slaughterhouses, which sold the carcasses to butchers and households.

Commercial packing began in the early nineteenth century, when European retailers sought meat supplies for long sea voyages and plantation owners needed meats to feed their slave workforces. Packed meats also were traded for sugar and molasses from the West Indies. Pork was the only product suitable for curing and packing, as beef, lamb, and mutton did not retain their flavor, color, or tenderness in the salting process.

Producers found that hogs were best killed and processed close to where they were raised. Costly to move, the animals lost weight and quality when transported great distances. Hog raising and subsequently packing became a major activity in the newly settled areas of the Ohio River valley in the 1810s and 1820s.

The first commercial packer in Cincinnati opened in 1818, and by the 1830s the city was the first major meatpacking center. Its location on the Ohio River facilitated trade with the East Coast and down the Mississippi River. The city had winter temperatures cold enough to limit meat spoilage but not so cold as to freeze the meat. Moreover, Cincinnati was near large deposits of salt, which was used to cure and pickle pork, as well as near forests of hardwoods, which were used to smoke meats. Cincinnati also had superior banking facilities and a large population to purchase surplus products. The city was much more convenient for midwestern farmers than driving hogs to eastern cities. By 1855 Cincinnati had forty-two packinghouses and had achieved a worldwide reputation as "Porkopolis."

Cincinnati reached its peak as a meatpacking center about 1850. Soon thereafter it was replaced by the fast-growing city of Chicago, which by 1840 had become a railroad and transportation hub and the gateway for trade to the West. Midwestern farmers began shipping their livestock to Chicago's central markets, where after 1848 the animals were sold at the Chicago Board of Trade. By 1864 the city was home to fifty-eight meatpackers. The following year the Union Stock Yards and Transit Company opened as a large, centralized cash market for livestock sales and transportation.

Commission merchants purchased slaughter animals from farmers and arranged their transport to packinghouses. Slaughtering and packing were wholly separate enterprises before the 1840s. Because of the odors and waste, slaughterhouses usually were on the outskirts of towns. Packing plants, however, were in the warehouse district near wharves and centers of trade. Most packing plants were associated with icehouses, which provided the means to keep meats cold for a few weeks beyond the winter.

Meat was packed in winter, when the weather was cold enough to prevent quick meat spoilage. In the few beef-packing plants cattle were slaughtered from mid-October to early November, just after the first frost killed pasture grasses. Hogs were fed recently harvested corn for a final three to six weeks before going to the slaughterhouse from early November to mid-January. Packing operations were not steady, as weather conditions had to be right for the transportation of animals to the slaughterhouse and for proper meat preservation. By the 1840s in Cincinnati and the 1850s in Chicago, most meatpackers slaughtered their own animals.

Though packing plants were not identical, the slaughtering process was fairly standard. Animals were led to small pens on the roof, where they were knocked unconscious, killed, then dragged inside to drain. Hogs were scalded, scraped of their hair, and hung by their rear feet so gutters could remove the entrails. The carcasses were sent into a cooling room, often in the basement, because any remaining internal heat would cause fermentation when the pork was pickled. Usually on the next day the carcasses were divided into smaller parts and butchered into finer cuts or "dressed." After the meat was smoked, pickled, or salted for several days to a few weeks, it was packed. Some trimmings were retained to make sausage. Most packing plants included a small lard house and a smokehouse. Cattle were slaughtered in a similar fashion, though little beef was packed for sale.

The slaughtering process produced much inedible waste, fat, trimmings, and bones. In Cincinnati most of this waste was dumped into the Ohio River, but a few small companies in the city began using this material to create new by-products (see sidebar "By-Products of Meatpacking" on the next page).

By 1850 meatpacking was an established industry. Its labor force worked an average of twelve hours a day for fifteen weeks a year, earning $26.85 a week. In the late 1850s several packinghouses successfully experimented with "ice packing" in the summer, using ice supplies gathered during the previous winter. Slaughter animals cost less during the summer, and customers preferred fresh cured hams and lard over even the best winter-packed products.

The Late-Nineteenth-Century Industry

Before refrigeration, fresh meat was obtainable only from a local farmer, butcher, or slaughterhouse. Cattle were shipped live to these small businessmen, but tended to lose weight and quality and become sick during transit. After the introduction of the refrigerated railroad car in 1867, meatpackers shipped dressed beef instead of the entire steer. Although the

By-products of Meatpacking

Along with the early packing operations in Cincinnati, a small by-products industry developed to use the waste products generated in slaughtering and butchering animals. Much of the waste was discarded, but small companies, like Procter & Gamble, established in the late 1830s, removed the waste and made various products from fertilizer to soap to lard oil. Even hog bristles were used to make brushes and mattresses.

As meatpacking operations increased in size, particularly after 1850, meatpackers recognized the potential for creating their own by-product industries. They employed chemists to analyze the animals and find uses for every part. Several dozen commodities resulted, and packers were soon credited with "using every part of the hog except the squeal," although the statement was similarly applicable to cows.

The largest by-product industry produced hides. Fats and other edible products became lard, cooking oil, oleomargarine, chewing gum, and candy. Bones became buttons, knife handles, and combs. Animal hair was used in mattresses, upholstery, and brushes. Several types of fertilizer products were derived from slaughter or by-product waste, and fertilizer production became a major side industry. Glue, soap, glycerin, cosmetics, pharmaceuticals, lubricating oils, and dyes also were derived by-products.

With the exception of tanneries, the meatpackers either set up or purchased the businesses that made these by-products and made them part of the overall meatpacking operation. In most cases the income from sales of by-products made the difference between profit and loss for the meatpackers.

networks. In large urban areas they established "branch houses," cold-storage wholesale facilities that often included sausage-making equipment and a smokehouse. In 1888 the largest packers owned two dozen branch houses; these were so successful that by the next year they had 544 in most of the major cities in the eastern United States.

For smaller cities and rural areas, packers set up "peddler car" service along major rail lines. Salesmen took orders from small retailers or sold directly to consumers from railcar shipments made once or twice a week. Armour & Company established the first two "car routes" in 1887. By World War I this service served more than sixteen thousand small towns in the central and western United States.

Meatpackers also introduced dressed beef to international markets. Refrigerated storage rooms on transatlantic steamships took the first dressed beef to England in 1875, and that year U.S. companies exported thirty thousand pounds of dressed beef to England. Two years later they shipped more than fifty-five million pounds. Profits were immense, as each carcass brought a net profit of $64 after shipping costs.

The meatpackers' rapid expansion into the dressed beef trade in the 1870s and 1880s met several obsta-

The Mince Meat Department. Meat packing houses depended on the cheap, unskilled labor of immigrants and women, shown here at Armour's packing house in Chicago. Photograph published by Strohmeyer and Wyman, c. 1893. LIBRARY OF CONGRESS: PRINTS AND PHOTOGRAPHS DIVISION.

meat was not packed, this beef became the major product of the meatpacking industry.

In 1869 G. H. Hammond of Detroit made the first long-distance shipment of refrigerated meats—dressed beef, pork, and lamb. Gustavus Swift opened his first plant in 1875 and started sending dressed beef eastward two years later. In the early 1880s two large pork packers, Armour & Company and Nelson Morris, built new plants to join the dressed beef trade.

Each company developed extensive distribution

cles, including opposition from railroad companies that had substantial investments in cars, feed yards, and pens to serve a livestock trade. In 1878 Swift improved the refrigerated car design and began constructing them for his meatpacking plants. He arranged to bypass lines that would not transport the new rail freight.

Local butchers and slaughterhouses also opposed the dressed beef trade, seeing it as a direct threat to their livelihoods. They circulated propaganda about the alleged deficiencies of refrigerated beef, led boycotts, and called for federal investigations into packing plant conditions and company operations. Packers had difficulty overcoming the resulting prejudice against western beef. By the late 1880s, however, most consumers concluded that dressed beef was as good as or better than local sources, was wholesome, and was safe.

In addition to dressed beef and packed pork products, meatpackers introduced canned meats in tin containers. While some canning took place as early as 1825, it did not become a substantial commodity until the late 1870s. The military was the largest consumer of canned meats. The U.S. Navy began carrying canned meats on its ships during the Civil War. Alleged problems with canned meats and dressed beef during the Spanish-American War prompted further investigations. Major General Nelson Miles claimed in 1898 that "embalmed beef" had caused outbreaks of illness among his troops. Subsequent investigations blamed improper distribution and handling of dressed beef and canned products by commissary officers and cleared the meatpacking industry of wrongdoing. Nevertheless, the canned meat and foreign dressed beef trade suffered from the scandal for several years.

European consumers and governments also raised questions about the quality and safety of American dressed beef. Several countries banned imports of dressed beef and pork as well as live animals. Several U.S. investigations found that American products had less disease than European products but at the same time recognized the need for a federal inspection system to satisfy international concerns. In 1891 Congress passed a meat inspection act to provide a rigorous system of safeguards at every stage of production, from slaughter yard to finished product. But as a concession to the politically powerful meatpackers, only meats destined for export to foreign countries were inspected.

By the 1870s the bulk of slaughter animals left packinghouses as dressed meat. Though some packing was still done, its importance declined. With increasing volume, packers standardized their plant designs and incorporated new refrigeration equipment,

electric lighting, and specialized machinery, such as hog hair scrapers. A trolley system to transport pork and beef carcasses evolved into a formal "disassembly line" by the 1890s. Processing, though, still required many laborers, and few steps could be fully mechanized.

Tasks were divided and simplified to employ cheaper, unskilled labor and to increase the speed and efficiency of meatpacking operations. Immigrants filled most unskilled positions, which paid about fifteen cents an hour for an eight- to ten-hour workday. Skilled workers, such as finishing butchers, earned as much as fifty cents an hour. From 1870 to 1900 children were about 3 percent of the total workforce, and women were 2 to 4 percent. Women and children trimmed fat from smaller cuts of meat or worked in sausage rooms. The average annual salary for a packing plant worker increased slowly from $305 in 1870 to $553 in 1890. A national depression in the 1890s and strong competition among meatpacking companies drove wages down to $488 a year, and workdays were lengthened from eight to ten or twelve hours by 1900.

Labor unions tried to organize workers in the meatpacking industry in the early 1880s, when year-round operations became common, but efforts were sporadic, disorganized, and often crushed by the corporations. Most walkouts were spontaneous, short-lived, and generally unsuccessful. Companies simply hired replacement workers or shifted production from a struck plant to another and waited out the strikers. In 1897 the Amalgamated Meat Cutters and Butcher Workmen, the first industrywide union, was founded. Its membership grew to four thousand in 1900 and to seventy-five thousand in 1904. The union called its first strike in 1904, seeking reforms and wage increases for unskilled, ethnic workers. The strike collapsed after about two months. Union membership fell and did not recover until the 1910s.

Work conditions in the industry were appalling, including poor lighting, unventilated chilled rooms, and the carnage of slaughtered animals. The public was particularly incensed by stories of water and waste dripping into meat processing areas, primitive toilets adjacent to butchering lines, widespread pneumonia and tuberculosis among workers, and numerous disabling job accidents, particularly among unskilled workers. In 1906 Upton Sinclair published *The Jungle*, a novel about immigrants working at a meatpacking plant that focused public attention on these issues. In the resulting fervor Congress later that year passed the comprehensive Meat Inspection Act and the Pure Food and Drug Act, and public opinion forced more industry efforts to improve working conditions and wages.

Conclusion

By 1886 four companies controlled the American meatpacking industry: Swift & Company, Armour & Company, Nelson Morris, and George H. Hammond Company. That year the four companies created a pooling arrangement in the Northeast, dividing territory and business to avoid competition, fix market shares, and assure uniform profit margins. Although temporarily shaken by the entry of two new corporations, Cudahay Packing Company in 1892 and S&S (later Wilson & Company) about 1896, the pooling arrangements expanded and continued into the twentieth century. The meatpackers claimed they were not fixing prices or conspiring but seeking to keep markets evenly supplied to avoid gluts and scarcities. These pools, however, were the kind of collusion that the Sherman Anti-Trust Act of 1890 sought to stop. In 1903 an injunction against the packers put a temporary end to what some labeled a "beef trust." The packers continued other questionable marketing practices until the 1920s. In every investigation and trial, however, the packers were found innocent of collusion or antitrust violations.

At the end of the nineteenth century, meatpacking was the largest and most important industry in the United States, and it continued to hold that position until after World War I. Though the industry did not employ the most workers, meatpacking products, valued at more than $4 billion in 1919, were a larger contributor to the gross national product than iron and steel, automobiles, or cotton goods. While a handful of large corporations controlled national distribution and trade, local butchers provided services relatively unchanged from those they had offered in the early 1800s.

See also **Chicago; Cincinnati; Food; Railroads; Ranching and Livestock Raising; Regulation of Business; Transportation,** subentry on **Railroads; Trusts.**

Bibliography

Clemen, Rudolf Alexander. *The American Livestock and Meat Industry.* New York: Ronald, 1923.

Institute of American Meat Packers. *The Packing Industry: A Series of Lectures Given under the Joint Auspices of the School of Commerce and Administration of the University of Chicago and the Institute of American Meat Packers.* Chicago: University of Chicago Press, 1924.

Mayer, Oscar Gottfried. *America's Meat Packing Industry: A Brief Survey of Its Development and Economics.* Princeton, N.J.: Newcomen Society, American Branch, 1939.

Skaggs, Jimmy M. *Prime Cut: Livestock Raising and Meatpacking in the United States, 1607–1983.* College Station: Texas A&M University Press, 1986.

Wade, Louise Carroll. *Chicago's Pride: The Stockyards, Packingtown, and Environs in the Nineteenth Century.* Urbana: University of Illinois Press, 1987.

Walsh, Margaret. *The Rise of the Midwestern Meat Packing Industry.* Lexington: University Press of Kentucky, 1982.

CAMERON L. SAFFELL

MEDICINE   While all the sciences in America developed from amateur traditions into professional disciplines in the nineteenth century, the most dramatic changes occurred in medicine. As a result of the Revolutionary War, American medicine had become cut off from its traditional European sources and had reverted to its early-eighteenth-century condition, typified by apprentice-based medicine, reliance on bloodletting, and use of massive doses of dangerous drugs. Only in Philadelphia (College of Philadelphia), New York (King's College), Boston (Harvard), New Hampshire (Dartmouth College), and Kentucky (Transylvania University) was medical education available in any form that approximated the sophistication of European medicine. As a result, most physicians were poorly educated, poorly trained, and poorly regulated. In turn, patients were poorly served.

Benjamin Rush

The most influential physician of the early nineteenth century was Benjamin Rush (1745–1813) of Philadelphia, who, despite his exposure to European medicine, rejected the new approaches to disease classification in favor of his own idiosyncratic belief that all illness had one fundamental cause, "vascular tension." According to Rush, those suffering from illness had a predisposition to disease that was exacerbated by either external or internal stimuli acting on the body, resulting in convulsive excitement in the walls of the blood vessels. These events were common features of all disease and, furthermore, could not be addressed by the natural and noninvasive healing associated with traditional Hippocratic medicine. Instead, Rush recommended bleeding and massive purging, claiming that "desperate diseases require desperate remedies." Rush even invented his own purgative, "Rush's Thunderbolt," a powerful concoction that featured calomel (mercuric chloride) as the active ingredient, an extremely dangerous drug that remained a standard part of nineteenth-century materia medica until at least 1870. Believing that the body had large stores of blood, Rush recommended the removal of substantial amounts of the vital fluid. (Courses in bloodletting were part of the curriculum of medical schools until the Civil War.) Thus, early-nineteenth-century medical practice was harsh, prompting historians to describe this period as the "heroic age" of American medicine, referring not to the practitioners but to the bravery needed by patients to undergo treatment.

Although popular literature often pilloried medicine and its reliance on dangerous methods and drugs, Rush-inspired medicine predominated during the first half of the century. Nevertheless, the abuses of heroic medicine, the poor training of many practitioners, and the proliferation of poorly remunerated and low-status physicians, prompted the formation of alternative practices. By mid-century there were numerous "irregular" practitioners; chief among them were the Thomsonians (naturopathic), inspired by the methods of Samuel Thomson (1769–1843); eclectic physicians; and homeopathic providers. The expansive spirit of 1840s Jacksonian democracy encouraged the spread of these alternatives. Politicians eventually prevented "regular" physicians from passing licensure laws to regulate medical practice, and by 1865, all of the states had repealed licensure requirements. As the report of the Sanitary Commission of Massachusetts claimed in 1850, "Anyone . . . can assume the name of physician. . . . It's a free country."

Rise of Alternative Medicine

Samuel Thomson, the farmer who founded the nature-based medical practice bearing his name, was led to oppose the allopathic medicine of regular practice, which relied on bloodletting or harsh treatments. He believed herbal remedies not only were sufficient to cure all disease but also offered much more gentle healing regimens, especially when accompanied by cooling or warming baths. Obtaining a patent for his first herbal cure in 1813, he went on to write the *New Guide to Health; or, Botanic Family Physician* in 1822, a best-seller in the largely rural nation. Eclectic physicians followed the teachings of Dr. Wooster Beach (1794–1859), who borrowed freely not only from naturopathic sources but from any other source that proved successful, including several mineral-based therapies. Several medical schools offering instruction in Beach's eclectic medicine emerged between 1830 and 1840.

Finally (although there were many other minor medical sects), homeopathy reached the United States with the translation of the German physician Samuel Hahnemann's work, *Organon of Medicine*, in 1810. Hahnemann's emphasis was similar to other "irregular" practices in that he offered an alternative to the harsh remedies of traditional medicine. Claiming that drug therapy should be based on the notion of *similia similibus curantur* ("like cures like"), ho-

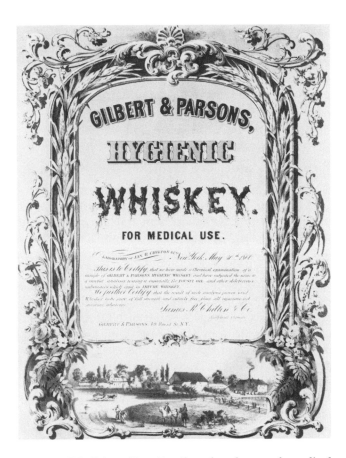

Dubious Medicine. Despite the abundance of medical schools and physicians, the quality of American medicine was tenuous until after the Civil War. Lithograph by Robertson, Seibert and Shearman, c. 1860. LIBRARY OF CONGRESS: PRINTS AND PHOTOGRAPHS DIVISION.

meopathy stressed the curing power of drugs that produced symptoms similar to those of the disease. The physician's job was to isolate the essential symptom of the disease and then to prepare a drug, diluted to an almost infinitesimal degree, that would produce the same effect; in the diluted form, however, the drug became the cure. By mid-century, these sects enjoyed great popularity in the United States, in large measure because, while their efficacy could be questioned, they offered gentle therapies, doing less harm to patients than heroic medical methods.

One notable exception to the excesses of heroic medicine was the introduction of Edward Jenner's method of protecting from the ravages of smallpox, referred to as vaccination. Benjamin Waterhouse (1754–1848), a physician who trained at two of Europe's leading medical schools, Edinburgh and Leiden, became a faculty member at Harvard in 1783. Happening to read Jenner's account of vaccination in 1799, he successfully inoculated his son in 1800 and then used the procedure on no fewer than six other patients before demonstrating it to the Boston medical community and public in 1802. Vaccination became immediately popular, so much so that the explorers Meriwether Lewis and William Clark expressed their desires to vaccinate Native Americans when they reached the western reaches of the United States in 1805.

Birth of the American Medical Association

The setting for the formation of the American Medical Association, therefore, featured a chaotic array of medical systems, a vast armamentarium of unproved drugs (including "Rush's Thunderbolt"), and little if any regularized medical training. There was particular concern about the state of medical education, since by 1840 medical schools had proliferated and many were proprietary enterprises offering little if any standard training. A series of National Medical Conventions held in the 1840s aimed to improve medical education. Following the meeting in Philadelphia in 1847, the American Medical Association was formally organized to carry out these reforms. But reaching agreement on a program of reforms was another matter, since many recommendations would increase the cost of operating proprietary schools and thus directly affect the owner-physicians. Not until 1860 did the association agree on educational requirements that included a three-year study program, education prior to medical school, a four-month clinical experience, and an examination for the medical degree. Even after consensus was achieved, the Civil War prevented implementation of these educational reforms.

The other major objective of the American Medical Association was to curb "irregular" medical practitioners, especially the homeopaths. The writer and physician Oliver Wendell Holmes Sr. (1809–1894), presented one of the earliest attacks on homeopathy, "Homeopathy and Its Kindred Delusions," to the Massachusetts Medical Society in 1842, shortly before the American Medical Association was founded. When the association developed its code of ethics, it incorporated many of Holmes's sentiments, including prohibiting physicians from consulting with homeopaths and from attending any patient who was under homeopathic care. Chicago municipal hospitals almost immediately denied homeopaths the right to practice medicine in the hospitals, and the U.S. Army ruled against the entrance of homeopaths to the Army Medical Corps during the Civil War. The net effect was to reverse the open, free-market atmosphere of the Jacksonian era and replace it with a clear separation between regular medical practice and the "irregulars" by 1870.

Benjamin Rush (1745–1813). Rush, past surgeon general of the Continental army (1777–1778), set an austere tone for American medicine at the beginning of the nineteenth century by endorsing the practices of bloodletting, purging, and his own "Rush's Thunderbolt." LIBRARY OF CONGRESS

The separation of medical practitioners became more pronounced during the Civil War, especially in the Union Army. The need to regularize and militarize the medical community created demands to determine qualifications for physicians and surgeons. Working closely with the American Medical Association, most military doctors were selected from the ranks of regular medical practitioners; these physicians then occupied the hierarchic structure of the medical corps. At the same time, medical practice during the country's bloodiest war did not increase in sophistication. Casualties from malaria, typhoid fever, and dysentery and other infectious diseases associated with poor sanitary conditions far exceeded the casualties from the battlefield. Those soldiers severely injured by gunfire also did not fare too well, since subsequent infection often led to septicemic infections, especially if the wound required amputation. The only medical advances included new developments in evacuating the wounded, the building of new hospitals in rural areas adjacent to battlefields, and the appreciation for the role of women in health care.

The Civil War marked the beginning of a new period in the history of nineteenth-century medicine. American Medical Association–sponsored reforms, which had been nobly intended and highly praised but usually ignored in the 1850s, now became guideposts to American medicine. More and more practitioners and educators realized that the critical problem facing medicine was the poor quality of medical education. President Charles Eliot of Harvard, one of the prominent reforming administrators, wrote that "until the reformation of the School in 1870–1871, the medical students were noticeably inferior in bearing, manners, and discipline to the students in other departments." His statement is not too surprising, given that most medical schools had eliminated the requirement of a bachelor's degree prior to admission. Yale offered a medical curriculum lasting four months for each of two years; the second year simply repeated the first! But many medical schools rejected reforms based on market considerations: if they adhered to the reforms, they would lose their paying clients.

Post–Civil War Reforms

By 1870, American medicine found itself in dire straits. There were too many medical schools, too many physicians, and too many glaring deficiencies in the practice of medicine. Furthermore, European medical innovations demanded medical practitioners who were well versed in the sciences. Addressing the problem, President Eliot forced the reluctant medical faculty at Harvard to accept a three-year graded curriculum and a lengthened school year and to require written examinations. Despite a dramatic reduction in the number of applications to Harvard between 1870 and 1872, other leading institutions (Pennsylvania, Syracuse, and Michigan) implemented similar measures. Then, in 1876, the new graduate university in Baltimore, Johns Hopkins University, opened, with the ultimate aim of creating a medical school centered around a teaching hospital. When the Johns Hopkins medical school opened in 1893, it offered the best medical education then available in the United States. Modeled after leading European institutions, it stressed research in medical laboratories, clinical work prior to medical practice, the teaching of basic sciences in medical school, and continued examinations to measure proficiency. Changes at Harvard and Johns Hopkins set the stage for the wholesale reformation of American medicine in the early twentieth century, led by the American Medical Association's Council on Medical Education and enacted through implementation of Abraham Flexner's recommendations in his *Flexner Report* (1910). The essential character of modern medical education had been set by 1910: clearly stated premedical requirements, two years of basic sciences followed by two years of clinical experience, and national board examinations.

Scientific Advances

Important as these reforms were, they would not have altered the practice of medicine were it not for advances in science that completely changed the understanding of disease and the way medicine could be practiced. Part of medicine's historical problem, not just in the United States but throughout the Western world, was that it was an empirical discipline that lacked a well-accepted theoretical foundation supported by science. This changed in the nineteenth century, in large part because of new developments in the study of physiology (nutrition, metabolism, and nerve action yielded to science for the first time during the mid-1800s) that informed physicians about how the body worked and how the diseased state could interfere in this action. Animal research in France during the first half of the century, conducted by François Magendie and Claude Bernard, contributed much information in this regard. But even armed with these new insights, the physician still lacked effective therapies to offer the diseased patient.

The discovery of microbial disease agents and the development of anesthetic procedures during the latter half of the nineteenth century changed medicine profoundly. As early as 1842, Holmes had noted the alarming infection rate in maternity wards attended by physicians who had just come from performing autopsies. Ignaz Semmelweiss in Austria warned of the same problem, calling for physicians to wash carefully after performing autopsies, but neither physician's warnings were heeded, since the prevailing attitude was that contagion was spread through the air ("fetid emanation") or water, not by bodily contact. Finally, the French researcher Louis Pasteur (1822–1895) demonstrated unequivocally in the 1860s that microorganisms caused fermentation and, slightly later, that infection also had microbial causes. In the early 1870s, physicians and surgeons began to experiment with aseptic methods, usually some form of phenolic acid applied to the patient or phenolic spray applied during surgical procedures. Gowns, gloves, and masks were added to the surgical theater to prevent chafing and staining from the aseptic chemicals; by the end of the century, these accoutrements, along with instruments, were cleaned and sterilized routinely.

It was one thing to reduce infection and quite another matter to deal with the pain of heroic medicine. Here again, science contributed crucially to medicine. During the early part of the century, recreational gases were experimentally applied, first in dentistry and then in obstetrical operations. Nitrous oxide was the first anesthetic used, but it was soon replaced by ether, due to its ease of application. Samuel T. G. Morton, Crawford Long, and Horace Wells played instrumental roles in the development of ether and chloroform as anesthetic agents between 1846–1848. In the mid-1840s the Scottish surgeon James Young Simpson began to experiment successfully with chloroform, a substance less dangerous than ether, and by the end of the 1860s, it was widely used in obstetrical practice.

Aseptic (and then antiseptic) procedures and anesthesia were the necessary preconditions for invasive surgery. Because of its traditional limitations, surgery was not added to medical education at Harvard until the late 1870s, but its full installation into the medical curriculum was one of the goals at Johns Hopkins. William Halsted (1852–1922), the foremost pioneer in American surgery, built the Hunterian Laboratory for experimental medicine adjacent to the medical school, where, with his colleague Harvey Cushing (1869–1939), he began to develop experimental protocols for surgery using dogs as subjects. Surgical interventions in disease were still relatively rare at the end of the nineteenth century, with the abdominal cavity, thorax, and brain considered completely off-limits except for drastic procedures in terminal illnesses. Nevertheless, the new breakthroughs enabled surgical practice to begin to take its place as a central part of American medicine.

Pasteur's work in microbiology had a profound and immediate impact on public health and the understanding of how disease was spread. By 1870, the compelling nature of his research demonstrated that contagion was not a "fetid emanation" but was caused by microbial agents. Soon, Pasteur's German collaborator Robert Koch identified the microbes responsible for anthrax (1876), tuberculosis (1882), and cholera (1884). Typhoid (1880) and diphtheria (1884) also were traced to their microbial origins. These findings were so impressive and their application so immediate that some scientists, physicians, and laypeople began to anticipate the creation of a disease-free world through the elimination of disease-causing microbes. Life expectancy in the United States increased 40 percent between 1880 and 1925, and the great killers of the nineteenth century (typhoid, cholera, and diphtheria) were all but eradicated by the 1930s.

Thus, the most dramatic changes in American medicine during the nineteenth century occurred in the arena of public health. These changes were not directed at individual patients but at large public works (water supply and sewage treatment) and outbreaks of diseases like typhoid and cholera. Patient care remained little altered for much of the century, save for the gradual disappearance of Rush's heroic treatments. Medical intervention in disease was limited, and patent drugs of dubious efficacy still filled American pharmacies and were still being prescribed by physicians. Only patients who required emergency surgery or palliative treatment for pain were better served at the end of the century than they would have been in 1800.

Additionally, the setting of medical practice remained virtually unchanged. Most medical procedures were conducted within the physician's office, often adjacent to the physician's home. The country's Civil War experience certainly underscored the value of medical evacuation services and hospital care, but these ancillary medical options were usually available only in large cities. Hospitals were still associated with serving the poor and, consequently, with being havens for the spread of disease. Hence, for the middle-class and wealthy, hospital care was an option that was avoided until the twentieth century.

Economic and Social Dimensions

A final transformation of modern American medicine that had to await the twentieth century was its emergence as an honored and lucrative profession. With the proliferation of charlatans and self-trained practitioners during the first half of the nineteenth century, this may not be surprising. But economic success did not immediately follow the reforms of the second half of the century. Most physicians were able to support themselves only at a level that frequently left them economically behind other professional occupations. As the century progressed, medical groups organized themselves in an attempt to control entry into the profession in an effort to address these concerns. One net effect was to limit the entry into medicine of less empowered parts of the American population.

Women made gains in medicine as a result of the women's rights agitation that began in the 1840s. Some women were allowed, often grudgingly, to practice, but usually in obstetrics and gynecology or other areas of medicine that were connected to women's health and that were not financially well compensated. Many hospitals did not accept female physicians, however, and many medical schools limited enrollment to males. In response, a few women's medical schools and hospitals emerged at mid-century. Several examples are the Women's Medical College (New York), the Female Medical College of Pennsylvania, the Boston Female Medical College, and the New York Infirmary for Women and Children. Prominent women doctors were Elizabeth Blackwell, Marie Zakrzewska, and Ann Preston. More important, when Mary Garrett presented Johns Hopkins University with the crucial funding to complete its hospital, she attached the proviso to her gift that the university would admit women to its medical schools, a reform that did not have a lasting impact in twentieth-century medicine. Thus, while about 4 percent of the medical students were female at the end of the century, these numbers declined during the first two decades of the twentieth century. Similarly, blacks were not allowed to enroll in most medical schools during the nineteenth century, so black physicians formed their own schools, including Howard in Washington, D.C. (1867), and Meharry Medical College in Nashville, Tennessee (1876). These became the only two schools to survive the post-Flexner reforms, and black medical education remained separate in the United States until after World War II.

The major legacies of the nineteenth century to the development of American medicine were, therefore, the improvement of medical education, the beginnings of scientific medicine, the full incorporation of antiseptic procedures and anesthetic agents, and the application of microbiology to the investigation of disease entities. Fortified by these important developments, American medicine confidently entered the twentieth century.

See also **Academic and Professional Societies; Health and Disease; Hospitals; Patent Medicines.**

Bibliography

Duffy, John. *The Healers: A History of American Medicine.* Urbana: University of Illinois Press, 1979.

Ludmerer, Kenneth M. *Learning to Heal: The Development of American Medical Education.* New York: Basic Books, 1985.

Rosenberg, Charles E. *The Care of Strangers: The Rise of America's Hospital System.* New York: Basic Books, 1987.

———. *The Cholera Years: The United States in 1832, 1849, and 1866.* Chicago: University of Chicago Press, 1962.

Starr, Paul. *The Social Transformation of American Medicine.* New York: Basic Books, 1982.

KEITH R. BENSON

MEMORIALS.   See **Monuments and Memorials.**

MENTAL ILLNESS   The nineteenth century was a time of profound changes in the diagnosis and definition of mental illness, in the treatment and placement of those people categorized as mentally ill, and in the organization and professionalization of individuals caring for and treating the mentally ill. The issues surrounding mental illness were closely related to the significant adjustments being made as the United States moved from a rural, agricultural nation to an industrial, urban one. Far from being a static medical category, mental illness was a rapidly changing set of social problems, tied to attempts to cope with dizzying societal change. In 1800 Americans generally considered disorders of the mind an inescapable though unfortunate part of community life, and churches, public almshouses, and poorhouses treated persons exhibiting behaviors associated with mental illness as charity cases. Manifestations of bizarre mental behavior were handled almost exclusively at the local level, often by family members. By 1900, however, almost every facet of this situation had changed. By that time mental illness was seen as a discrete category of medical problem usually caused by organic brain diseases. Medical doctors specializing in mental disorders formed their own professional organizations and provided the expertise to diagnose and treat mental illness. People classified with these diseases were often placed in large congregate institutions or asylums, where they could possibly be cured and released, meanwhile protecting society from the problems they caused.

Beginnings of Institutionalization

The shift to an institutionally based approach to solving the issues of insanity or mental illness involved a variety of major social changes. First, the intellectual climate of the French Enlightenment forced scientists and medical doctors to reexamine the causes of and treatments for the variety of mental problems known as madness, lunacy, or insanity. Before this paradigm shift most people believed that madness was a part, albeit an unpleasant one, of the unchanging and unchangeable plan of God or nature. In the last decade of the eighteenth century Philippe Pinel, a French physician who literally and figuratively unchained the mad in the Bicêtre asylum in Paris; William Tuke, an English reformer who revolutionized care at his York Retreat; Benjamin Rush, a Philadelphia doctor instrumental in implementing "moral treatment" at the Pennsylvania Hospital; and a few others theorized that environmental changes could influence and alter behavior. Thus the reformers felt that cure rather than simply care was a real possibility. This curing, however, would have to take place in a controlled environment under the auspices of a doctor professionally trained in the treatment of madness. Separate facilities designed specifically to handle problems of madness and lunacy developed, but often they were small, private asylums that catered to those who could afford to pay.

Simultaneously, social and demographic changes in society influenced how Americans viewed mental illness. The years 1815 to 1860 saw the beginnings of the Industrial and Market Revolutions, a rapidly growing proletarianized urban population, and a swell of immigrants into the United States. These changes caused problematic dislocations in the American social landscape and a rise in the rates of madness. Reformers were divided as to whether madness was a consequence of these societal changes or a cause of them. Some, particularly professional institutional superintendents, saw the proliferation of lunacy as a logical outcome of the increasing numbers of immigrants and poor people, and they viewed these individuals as threats to the social order. Others, especially eclectic reformers like Dorothea Dix, influenced by the moral power of the religious revival known as the Second Great Awakening, saw the mentally ill as victims of changing societal patterns. The debate between social control and humanitarian methods for handling the mentally ill has infused historical analysis, generating too much heat and not enough light. Undoubtedly most reformers had mixed motivations for their ideas about insanity, but whatever their motivations, their programs proved quite similar. They removed the mentally ill from society and placed them in large public institutions, well away from urban population centers.

By the 1820s those concerned with the plight of the mentally ill perceived that small private institutions could not handle the burgeoning numbers of persons considered mentally ill. The move to large public asylums was part of a broader trend toward formalized public agencies and institutions designed to handle the increasing number of poor and dependent individuals, and away from the private, ad hoc, and church-related organizations previously assigned those functions. Although dependent on public funding, these asylums remained infused with the benevolent Christianity that marked prior attempts to ameliorate the plight of the insane. While Virginia, Kentucky, and South Carolina had public facilities by 1830, the first major public mental hospital opened its doors to patients in Worcester, Massachusetts, in 1833. Its national reputation was secured when its first superintendent, Dr. Samuel Woodward, was elected the first president of the Association of Medical Superintendents of American Institutions for the Insane (AMSAII) in 1844. By 1860 thirty states ran public institutions to house the mentally ill. Because they did not stem the swelling tide of insane persons, these facilities rapidly filled up, necessitating the establishment of new asylums. Although the asylum became the programmatic foundation for dealing with the insane, its function remained unclear and difficult to determine.

The establishment of institutions led to the formation of a professional group that medicalized the study of lunacy. Psychiatrists, or alienists, were medical doctors who usually held a position on the staff at a state hospital. The setting in which they practiced shaped their ideas concerning their patients and the mental disorders they exhibited. Almost exclusively male, these doctors posited that mental disorder could develop as a consequence of immoral action, and therefore was the result of conscious choice. Intemperate action, excessive emotion, sexual desires, and overwork were considered causes of mental disorder, and all were tied to the changing American social and economic world. Despite the increase in the number of insanity cases, asylum doctors remained positive about the possibility of a cure that could come through a change in environment. Removal to an institution, where exposure to moral and religious training, combined with an eclectic regimen of medical practices from narcotics and localized bleeding to massage and hydrotherapy, would bring about a change in the patient's behavior and attitude. This optimistic outlook, however, did not reflect the realities of asylum life for patients. Most did not get better, and stays were measured in years or decades rather than months.

Chronic Cases and the New Psychiatry

During the years after the Civil War the numbers of chronic asylum patients increased markedly. Institutions often solved overcrowding problems by discharging patients who did not benefit from the medical and moral regimen practiced within their walls. Frequently these individuals were unable to care for themselves, and they joined the rolls of county and state almshouses and other charitable agencies designed to help, house, or simply control the poor. American psychiatry in the second half of the nineteenth century struggled with the disparity between the desire of superintendents to admit and keep only curable patients and the burgeoning numbers of chronic insane persons both in and out of the asylum system. By 1900 institutions had lost their optimistic outlook and instead warehoused a large population of long-term, aging patients with little hope of cure.

As the twentieth century dawned, institutional

psychiatry had lost much of its prestige and intellectual clout. Neurologists and alienists not affiliated with hospitals scathingly attacked asylums and the moralistic underpinnings of institutional psychiatry itself. In 1882 the trial of Charles Guiteau, President James Garfield's assassin, demonstrated the wide gap between the two camps. Although Guiteau was found guilty and hanged, the ideas expressed in his insanity defense clearly represented a new examination of the issues surrounding mental illness. By 1892 the AMSAII had changed its name to the American Medico-Psychological Association, reflecting the declining status of institutional leaders. The emphasis had shifted from inpatient care to understanding the etiology and course of mental disorder. The new "dynamic psychiatry" viewed mental illness as a continuum of normal to abnormal, not as an either-or situation. Infused with the visions of the Progressive era, Americans expected to solve the problems associated with mental illness. However, by ignoring the needs of chronic patients, this new attitude perpetuated the asylum as a warehouse, marginalizing not only institutional psychiatry but institutional patients as well.

See also **Health and Disease; Hospitals; Psychology; Welfare and Charity.**

Bibliography

Dain, Norman. *Concepts of Insanity in the United States, 1789–1865.* New Brunswick, N.J.: Rutgers University Press, 1964.

———. *Disordered Minds: The First Century of Eastern State Hospital in Williamsburg, Va., 1766–1866.* Williamsburg, Va.: Colonial Williamsburg Foundation, 1971.

Dwyer, Ellen. *Homes for the Mad: Life inside Two Nineteenth-century Asylums.* New Brunswick, N.J.: Rutgers University Press, 1987.

Foucault, Michel. *Madness and Civilization: A History of Insanity in the Age of Reason.* New York: Pantheon, 1965.

Fox, Richard W. *So Far Disordered in Mind: Insanity in California, 1870–1930.* Berkeley: University of California Press, 1978.

Gollaher, David. *Voice for the Mad: The Life of Dorothea Dix.* New York: Free Press, 1995.

Grob, Gerald N. *The Mad among Us: A History of the Care of America's Mentally Ill.* New York: Free Press, 1994.

———. *Mental Illness and American Society, 1875–1940.* Princeton, N.J.: Princeton University Press, 1983.

———. *Mental Institutions in America: Social Policy to 1875.* New York: Free Press, 1972.

———. *The State and the Mentally Ill: A History of Worcester State Hospital in Massachusetts, 1830–1920.* Chapel Hill: University of North Carolina Press, 1966.

Hughes, John S., ed. *The Letters of a Victorian Madwoman.* Columbia: University of South Carolina Press, 1993.

McCandless, Peter. *Moonlight, Magnolias and Madness.* Chapel Hill: University of North Carolina Press, 1996.

McGovern, Constance M. *Masters of Madness: Social Origins of the American Psychiatric Profession.* Hanover, N.H.: University Press of New England, 1985.

Rosenberg, Charles E. *The Trial of the Assassin Guiteau: Psychiatry and Law in the Gilded Age.* Chicago: University of Chicago Press, 1968.

Rothman, David J. *Conscience and Convenience: The Asylum and Its Alternative in Progressive America.* Boston: Little, Brown, 1980.

———. *The Discovery of the Asylum: Social Order and Disorder in the New Republic.* Boston: Little, Brown, 1971.

Scull, Andrew. *Social Order/Mental Disorder: Anglo-American Psychiatry in Historical Perspective.* Berkeley: University of California Press, 1989.

Thielman, Samuel. "Southern Madness: The Shape of Mental Health Care in the Old South." In *Science and Medicine in the Old South.* Edited by Ronald L. Numbers and Todd L. Savitt. Baton Rouge: Louisiana State University Press, 1989.

Tomes, Nancy. *A Generous Confidence: Thomas Story Kirkbride and the Art of Asylum-keeping, 1840–1883.* New York: Cambridge University Press, 1984.

STEVEN NOLL

MERCHANDISING

[This entry includes four subentries: **The General Store, Chain Stores, Mail Order,** and **Department Stores.**]

THE GENERAL STORE

Providing goods and services in a central location, the general store found in every rural community dated from colonial times. During the nineteenth century, general stores developed into vital centers of economic and social activity, where expanding services over time deepened long-established rituals of reciprocity. Trading goods and services among kin and neighbors in early rural America proved necessary for subsistence and strengthened social relations that were hampered by great distances and poor roads between family farms. By the late 1800s, general stores had added more variety and choice to their shelves but retained their basic organization: they remained individually owned and operated, community-oriented small businesses. Photographs from late in the century portray stores with potbellied stoves, bright and colorful advertisement placards, a postal service, ornate coffee grinders, flour and cracker barrels, countertops lined with glass candy jars, tea canisters, and balance scales. A place of commerce and socializing, the general store was an integral part of America's growing market system.

Seaport towns were the first to experience population density, draw artisans, and have access to im-

Original Convenience Store. Port city grocery stores, such as this one in Boston, were stocked with imported goods as well as a variety of everyday items packaged to sustain shelf life. Photograph, 1895. LIBRARY OF CONGRESS

ported goods that supported centralized merchandising. Merchants in such cities as Boston; Philadelphia; and Charleston, South Carolina, provided the template for the general store of the nineteenth century. Usually one-story single-room structures, early stores were attached to the proprietor's house. (Frontier stores at first were crude log structures, but by the nineteenth century, many areas were rebuilding and owners erecting stores from frame and brick.)

Early American settlement outside port cities did not develop centralized marketplaces uniformly over time and place. In the Northeast commercial and artisan services remained loosely grouped around meetinghouses until after the Revolutionary War. In most rural regions, and particularly in the South, settlement consisted of dispersed family farms. The advent of court days in the 1740s and colonial defenses, such as those built during the 1750s for the French and

Indian War, focused local activity on a central marketplace. Where a garrison or a courthouse and jail existed, one could conduct business and count on the regular visits of local families. The rise of capitalistic practices provided the necessary economic activity for town centers to grow. Regional economies expanded and backcountry towns developed as a function of consumer demand for imported goods driven by increased farm profits. The earliest development following this model was in eighteenth century Pennsylvania, the western Carolinas, and the Shenandoah Valley.

Merchants

The early nineteenth century was a period when the merchant became a critical figure in economic growth. Shopkeepers served their communities by fostering the distribution of imported goods and the sale of agricultural surpluses for export. These practices integrated rural and urban economies. Stores were also centers for the redistribution of local goods, matching crop surpluses to deficits. With few banks available, customers employed stores to keep their money and would then draw on the accumulated credit. As there were many currencies circulating during the century, stores served as a means for currency exchange, too. In frontier areas merchants combined taverns and general stores. By the 1870s many owners found it profitable to merge their general store business with other local needs, including gristmills, ginning shops, and smith work.

Store owners and employees tended to be white males. Clerkships in seaports were often hard-won indentures, and the sons of professionals usually filled them. Many clerks went on to distinguished political careers, such as President Grover Cleveland, New York governor Horatio Seymour, and Kansas senator Samuel Pomeroy.

Owning a profitable general store came with significant risk and considerable local influence. Owners were sophisticated when calculating the price of their goods and took into consideration the costs of transportation, spoilage, measures, bad credit, and interest. The most difficult problem was carrying bad credit. Proprietors might expect to recover a third or less of the overdue bills on their books. With currency scarce, merchants accepted goods in lieu of cash: hides, hemp, tobacco, wheat, livestock, and land titles were exchanged. After the Civil War merchants faced consumers with little to barter for merchandise.

During the 1870s and 1880s southern store owners, who also tended to be large planters, supported legislation allowing farmers to offer part of their future crop as credit. The result of the crop-lien system was that merchants charged high interest on credit, making it impossible for farmers to avoid substantial debt. Merchants would extend lien credit only on certain cash crops—notably cotton. Farmers trying to diversify could not gain the credit necessary to plant other crops, despite the regular decline of cotton prices. Crop liens further hurt farmers by requiring them to sell their crop through the merchant, thus limiting the farmer's ability to obtain a better price.

Consumers

All kinds of people held accounts in general stores: enslaved, free, rich, poor, male, and female. Early daybooks indicate that only single and widowed women involved themselves directly in consumer activity in some areas. But all women increased their patronage as the century progressed. The individual accounts of slaves in store records indicate their participation in commerce, but it is unlikely that such activity was widespread.

Patrons were always interested in a variety of goods from basic to luxury items. Early records from Kentucky show purchases for diverse textiles: forest cloth, durant, shalloon, corduroy, silk, velvet, and chintz. Traveling salesmen often proclaimed their knowledge of the latest styles in Baltimore and Philadelphia, indicating a demand for fashion in rural areas. When it came time to pay for goods, nineteenth-century consumers bought primarily on credit. By the later part of the century, the differences between cash and credit prices could be more than double, a testament to the cost of credit to merchants.

Goods

General stores carried all types of items, one of the earliest being crackers, prized by sailors, soldiers, and settlers because they kept for long periods without spoilage. Over the course of the century, new items made their way to store shelves. During the nineteenth century businesses developed tea in teabags, granulated sugar, fruit and nut extracts, commercially made soap, scouring powder, starch, steel implements, canned goods, condensed milk, boxed friction matches, kerosene glass lamps, and ready-made clothing. Indeed by the 1890s industrialization and advertising had converged to offer customers a plethora of items to make everyday life more convenient.

By the turn of the century, the modern office was superseding the marketplace; for example, during the early twentieth century, consumer-oriented businesses developed regional and national infrastructures, increasingly reaching customers through mail order catalogs. The general store persisted, however, by offering more goods provided through improved communication and transportation. Not until the advent of chain stores, such as F. W. Woolworth's, in the 1920s did general stores fade in significance. More efficient quantity buying, warehousing, and distribution left individually owned general stores unable to compete in the marketplace that they had done so much to establish.

See also **Advertising; Cities and Urbanization; Consumerism and Consumption.**

Bibliography

Atherton, Lewis E. *The Southern Country Store, 1800–1860.* Baton Rouge: Louisiana State University Press, 1949.

Carson, Gerald. *The Old Country Store.* New York: Oxford University Press, 1954.

Clark, Thomas D. *Pills, Petticoats, and Plows: The Southern Country Store.* Indianapolis: Bobbs-Merrill, 1944.

Johnson, Laurence A. *Over the Counter and On the Shelf: Country Storekeeping in America, 1620–1920*. Edited by Marcia Ray. Rutland, Vt.: Charles E. Tuttle, 1961.

Rothenberg, Winifred. *From Market-Places to a Market Economy: The Transformation of Rural Massachusetts, 1750–1850*. Chicago: University of Chicago Press, 1992.

DAVID F. HERR

CHAIN STORES

Chain stores in America trace their modern origins back to the founding in New York City of the Great Atlantic and Pacific Tea Company (A&P) in 1859. Although there were, according to a Federal Trade Commission study, only fifty-eight chains in existence in 1900, nineteenth-century chain stores served as one of the new forms of mass distribution institutions in the U.S. economy and were harbingers of the consolidation of many sectors of retailing in the early twentieth century.

Antecedents of the chain store (defined as a retail establishment owned by a firm that controls at least one other establishment selling similar merchandise) existed as far back as China in 200 B.C. The Hudson's Bay Company operated a chain of trading posts in North America beginning in 1670, and scattered examples of multiple-store ownership can be found in early-nineteenth-century America. At first primarily a mail-order vendor, the Great Atlantic and Pacific Tea Company was operating eleven tea stores by 1870. The chain expanded to about 200 shops with total sales of about $5.6 million by the end of the century, and to 15,671 stores in 1927. Tea and coffee remained the core of the firm's business until about 1890, when it gradually began to diversify its grocery offerings. Although A&P's share of the grocery market was still minimal at the end of the nineteenth century, the company had innovated strategically. Selling high-priced, high-profit-margin tea and coffee, A&P developed sales volume by setting its prices below those of the competition. This was a foretaste of the high-volume, low-service "economy stores" that A&P introduced in 1913. Other major grocery chains that trace their origins to the late nineteenth century are Grand Union, Kroger, and Jewel Tea.

After working for a retailer in Watertown, New York, Frank W. Woolworth opened his first successful five-and-ten-cents store in 1879 in Lancaster, Pennsylvania. Seven years later he operated seven stores, all in the Middle Atlantic states, and at the turn of the century the chain had fifty-nine stores with sales of about $5 million. Other variety chains founded before 1900 included McCrory, S. H. Kress, and S. S. Kresge. A few chains in drug, shoe, restaurant, and cigar retailing also existed by the end of the nineteenth century, but none of these had given hints of their rapid growth in the following decades.

In operating chain stores the keys to success were expanding the product lines each store carried, high-volume sales, and rapid stock turnover. The economies of speed that mass retailers achieved were more important than the economies of scale they may have gained. Both grocery and variety chains had to develop a managerial hierarchy to coordinate activity in diverse locations, to move goods rapidly, and to recruit, train, and supervise reliable, capable sales staffs. As they grew, they were able to take advantage of backward vertical integration, assuming the functions of independent wholesalers. Most early chains sought locations in towns and smaller cities, and few spread beyond their original geographic regions. In the case of Woolworth's at least, expansion came from bringing in ambitious business partners willing to finance growth. The hardworking young men Woolworth recruited as partners and managers supervised a sales force of low-paid young women whose tasks were usually limited to taking payment, making change, and wrapping packages. The chain stores' advantages mirrored the weaknesses of traditional retailers, who were often undercapitalized, unable to maintain profitable accounts, and dominated by their large wholesale suppliers.

At the end of the nineteenth century, chain stores were poised for the expansion that was to make them the focus of intense political debate in the early twentieth century. Like urban department stores and the large mail-order houses, chains represented a threat to the interests of local retailers and independent wholesalers. In calling for regulation, taxation, and even dissolution of the chains, their opponents employed antimonopoly rhetoric and evoked memories of harmonious nineteenth-century communities. Yet the economic advantages and political weight of chain stores and their allies ultimately prevailed. They remain a pervasive part of the nation's business environment.

See also **Industrialization and the Market; Market Revolution.**

Bibliography

Beckman, Theodore N., and Herman C. Nolan. *The Chain Store Problem: A Critical Analysis*. New York: McGraw-Hill, 1938.

Lebhar, Godfrey M. *Chain Stores in America: 1859–1962*. New York: Chain Store Publishing, 1963.

Tedlow, Richard S. *New and Improved: The Story of Mass Marketing in America*. New York: Basic, 1990.

DANIEL POPE

MAIL ORDER

Mail-order merchandising in the nineteenth century both reflected and stimulated some of the broad trends of American development during that time—the transportation revolution and westward expansion, the growth of big business, and the standardization and consolidation of American material culture.

Mail order refers to marketing in which the buyer orders the product by mail. In the late twentieth century, the process has been subsumed in the wider category of direct marketing, which includes such phenomena as telemarketing and Internet sales. But in the 1800s mail order constituted the dominant, if not exclusive, form of nonstore merchandising. Mail order, along with department stores and chain stores, was one of the new forms of mass distribution to arise in post–Civil War America.

Although some retailers and manufacturers had sold goods by mail since the colonial era, the large-scale growth of mail-order marketing in the nineteenth century is associated with two major firms, Montgomery Ward and Company and Sears, Roebuck and Company. Although Sears eventually grew to greater stature (both shifted most of their retailing from mail order to stores), Ward's mail-order operations preceded those of Sears by a generation and set the pattern for mail-order sales through general merchandise catalogs.

Mass distribution by mail order depended on a national transportation and communication infrastructure. The U.S. Post Office had begun issuing postage stamps in 1847, but free city delivery was instituted only in 1863. The railroad network, which had reached 53,000 miles by 1870, covered more and more of the nation and provided the physical means for carrying both orders and goods. Railway express companies, which handled shipping arrangements, were the most common means of delivering products in the era before the post office instituted parcel post service in 1913. To deliver the ever expanding mail-order catalogs, rural free delivery, begun in the 1890s, was a great boon.

Aaron Montgomery Ward's insight—that he could acquire goods in Chicago and advertise for buyers in rural America—led to his first merchandise circular, issued in August 1872. Ward sought his customers among members of the Grange, calling his firm the "original grange supply house." The company encouraged Grangers and others to join together in buying clubs to reap the cost savings of large shipments. Montgomery Ward was highly successful during the Gilded Age. In less than four years its initial price list grew into a catalog of 152 pages and nearly four thousand items. In 1887 Montgomery Ward moved into a six-story warehouse on Chicago's Michigan Avenue. Farmers could buy everything from groceries to barbed wire, and the firm could handle five thousand orders a day.

Retailing at a distance, selling goods that could not be inspected before sale, required sellers to establish a basis of trust. As early as 1875, Ward's catalog provided a strong money-back guarantee on all of its goods and promised to pay all expenses as well. The firm offered practical advice on saving money on shipping costs, identified with the grievances of farmers against monopolistic manufacturers, and established a reputation for honesty: "We endeavor to avoid make-believes and subterfuges of every description," stated one advertisement.

Richard W. Sears, a railroad station agent in Minnesota, entered the mail-order business in 1886 as the result of a commercial mishap. When a local jeweler refused shipment of a package of watches sent from Chicago, the company offered Sears the watches for $12 apiece. Sears offered to sell the watches to other station agents along the line for $14. In turn, the agents could find customers and make a profit at prices below the $25 that local jewelers would charge. Sears's profit from this serendipitous incident was enough to induce him to try again, this time ordering the watches from a Chicago wholesale house. Six months later, Sears had made $5,000 in the watch trade. He quit the railroad to devote full time to it, setting up a small office in Minneapolis and moving to Chicago the next year. By 1893, in partnership with Alvah C. Roebuck, Sears was publishing a 196-page catalog offering a spectrum of merchandise from shoes to musical instruments to wagons. In 1895 Roebuck decided to withdraw from the company (although he allowed continued use of his name), and Julius Rosenwald, a men's clothier, joined as an investor and as vice president. Sears, Roebuck's expansion continued, and the company reached $50 million in sales by 1906.

In his catalog copy and in his advertisements in newspapers and magazines destined for the nation's farm families, Richard Sears showed a flair for vivid prose and a taste for bombastic exaggeration. Both to promote particular items and to induce readers to order the catalog, Sears in the 1890s became one of the leading advertisers in low-cost magazines aimed at a rural market. These mail-order magazines, often with six-figure circulations, featured saccharine popular fiction and advice for farm families combined with endless pages of agate-type ads for mail-order products. At the same time, however, the firm's slogan, "Cheapest supply house on Earth," indicated that low prices were its greatest appeal. As one executive put it, "We are a supply house. We deal in

Catalog Shopping. The catalog of Chicago-based Sears, Roebuck and Company standardized American fashion; the 1899 catalog displays a wide variety of women's hats ranging from $1.69 to $1.98, weighing up to two pounds, nine ounces, and available in assorted colors. LIBRARY OF CONGRESS

necessities. Our constant effort is to furnish these necessities at the lowest possible price, so that the farmer at a distance can get his goods from us."

Yet even as mail-order merchandising thrived on the isolation of rural Americans, it played an important role in breaking down that separation. It disseminated standardized products across the country. Advertisements and catalogs spread a national language of consumption. At least a few customers shared their most personal concerns with the mail-order firms, writing to ask for help in finding a wife, describing their recent medical problems, or relating their business travails. In these ways mail order linked rural Americans to an urbanizing, industrializing American society.

See also **Advertising; Consumerism and Consumption; Post Office.**

Bibliography

Boorstin, Daniel J. *The Americans: The Democratic Experience.* New York: Random House, 1973.

Chandler, Alfred D., Jr. *The Visible Hand: The Managerial Revolution in American Business.* Cambridge, Mass.: Harvard University Press, Belknap Press, 1977.

Emmet, Boris, and John E. Jeuck. *Catalogues and Counters: A History of Sears, Roebuck and Company.* Chicago: University of Chicago Press, 1950.

Latham, Frank B. *1872–1972, A Century of Serving Consumers: The Story of Montgomery Ward.* Chicago: Montgomery Ward, 1972.

DANIEL POPE

DEPARTMENT STORES

Department stores were new institutions of mass retailing that both emerged from and helped to shape the cities of late-nineteenth-century America. Some department stores originated as dry goods emporiums, and expanded their lines of products; others began as retailing arms of wholesale establishments whose main business was to stock small town and rural general stores. The great downtown department stores became more than distribution mechanisms: they came to exemplify many of the key features of an emerging consumer society.

Distinguishing Features

No single definition of the term has won general favor, but, in general, department stores sold a variety of product lines: apparel, linens, and other textiles; furniture and home furnishings; and other household goods. As the name implies, products were grouped into departments, both physically and organizationally, each with its own managers. Other features also came to characterize the department stores of the late nineteenth century. Department stores erected large buildings to hold and display their merchandise. They adopted a "one price" basis, eliminating bargaining. Usually they sold for cash, though some pioneered the offering of consumer credit. High sales volume and a rapid turnover of merchandise were their marketing objectives. For example, R. H. Macy's in New York City had a stock turn (ratio of annual sales to inventory) of about twelve in 1887, a far higher figure than most stores achieved in the next century. Most advertised heavily in local newspapers and other urban media, such as streetcars and billboards. The advertisements of John Wanamaker's Philadelphia, Pennsylvania, store gained distinction for their plain-speaking style. Others relied more on visual display, superlatives, and exhortation.

Revolutions in transportation and communications and the growth of cities were the preconditions for downtown department stores. The railroad and telegraph moved the goods; ads in mass-circulation newspapers informed and enticed customers. Dense urban populations and streetcar networks brought buyers to the stores. Similar developments in Western Europe had comparable effects, and the Bon Marché in Paris, France, is often accorded the title of the world's first department store. Because the definition itself is ambiguous, it is unclear which establishment deserves to be called the first in the United States. A. T. Stewart established his dry goods "marble palace" store in New York City in 1846, arranging his merchandise in departments. His retail sales may have reached five million dollars annually by 1862. Stewart took pride in his policies of buying and selling for cash, eliminating haggling, and maintaining low markups. But his stores never diversified beyond dry goods, and most of his business remained at the wholesale level. Other dry goods merchants, such as Rowland Macy, John Wanamaker, and Chicago's Marshall Field, made the transition to the full-blown department store. Macy added items like china, toys, and dolls to his dry goods assortment in 1860 and in the following decade introduced home furnishings, book, and candy departments. By the 1880s, most substantial American cities had at least one large department store, some of which survived into the twenty-first century, like Rich's in Atlanta, Georgia; Filene's in Boston, Massachusetts; and Hudson's in Detroit, Michigan.

Innovations

Department store business practices, especially during the last two decades of the century, changed in several ways. The stores integrated backward to deal directly with manufacturers and bought merchandise for cash. They introduced varied services: package wrapping and delivery, rest rooms, child care areas and restaurants on the premises, and periodic sales with merchandise discounted. They became the most prominent regular large-scale newspaper display advertisers. Although colorful and powerful entrepreneurs gave their names and images to the stores, the departmental structure of their businesses required a substantial degree of decentralization. Edward A. Filene's definition of a department store as "a holding company for its departments" has some validity. Departmental merchandise buyers became the central figures in the stores, in charge not only of acquiring goods but also of arranging their display and managing the sales force.

The stores themselves were striking new urban landmarks. Broad entrances at street level, revolving doors, wide aisles, elevators, and, eventually, escalators were introduced around 1900 and became design standards. They made dramatic use of new building technologies to create an environment of color, glass, and light. Window displays from the late 1880s onward became forms of spectacle, enticing shoppers but physically separating those who could not afford to buy the goods exhibited. By the end of the century, the craft of window designing was becoming professionalized, with a trade journal and a national association of "window trimmers." Innovations in color printing and dye making allowed stores to use a vivid spectrum of colors to advertise and present the products. Department stores were pacesetters in using incandescent lights for spectacle, not just for illumination.

The new department stores were distinctly gendered institutions—places where mostly female shoppers encountered a predominantly female sales staff. Although there were a few women pioneers among store executives and buyers (Margaret Getchell, a former schoolteacher, worked her way up at Macy's from cashier to store superintendent in the 1860s, eventually managing a staff of more than two hundred employees), for the most part men supervised young, single women sales clerks. The salespeople took part in an intricate three-sided game of cooperation and conflict with their bosses and their customers. For the mostly middle-class customers, the department store shopping experience represented a large step for women out of the home and into public space, but the space was dominated by the corporate designs of the store owners. By the early twentieth century, the stores gave lessons in the duties and opportunities of the middle-class consumer. Their staffs offered interior decorating services, taught customers how to use home appliances, and demonstrated the advantages of featured products. The stores also became centers of cultural uplift, with art displays and musical and theatrical performances.

By the end of the nineteenth century, department stores had become central institutions of urban life. Their business methods had transformed the process of marketing products to millions of Americans. Their new methods of display, spectacle, and service gave the process of shopping new meanings and heightened significance. In John Wanamaker's words, the task of department stores was to "educate desire." In so doing, they helped to create modern consumer culture.

See also **Advertising; Consumerism and Consumption; Cities and Urbanization; Merchandising;** *subentries on* **The General Store, Chain Stores.**

Bibliography

Barth, Gunther. *City People: The Rise of Modern City Culture in Nineteenth-Century America.* New York: Oxford University Press, 1980.

Benson, Susan Porter. *Counter Cultures: Saleswomen, Managers, and Customers in American Department Stores, 1890–1940.* Urbana: University of Illinois Press, 1986.

Chandler, Alfred D. *The Visible Hand: The Managerial Revolution in American Business.* Cambridge, Mass.: Belknap Press, 1977.

Hendrickson, Robert. *The Grand Emporiums: The Illustrated History of America's Great Department Stores.* New York: Stein and Day, 1979.

Hower, Ralph M. *History of Macy's of New York, 1858–1919.* Cambridge, Mass.: Harvard University Press, 1943.

Leach, William. *Land of Desire: Merchants, Power, and the Rise of a New American Culture.* New York: Pantheon Books, 1993.

DANIEL POPE

MEXICAN AMERICANS

MEXICAN AMERICANS   People of Mexican descent arrived in the Far Northern territories claimed by Spain as early as the sixteenth century. The earliest *pobladores* (settlers) established them-

selves in northern New Mexico. Others who followed made their way into central and eastern Texas during the 1710s, into southern California in the 1760s, and into the modern-day Tucson area of Arizona in the 1770s.

Part of this population resided in urban areas preselected by the Spanish crown. But since the Far North during that era was a frontier hinterland, most settlers lived in ranchos, self-sustaining rural entities that generally belonged to the well-to-do of Spanish society who had received land grants from the Spanish and, after 1821, from the Mexican government. Though worked by the lower class, the rancho required everyone associated with it to contribute to its daily tasks. This entailed tending to the livestock, miscellaneous ranch chores, and family and household duties as well as fighting off Native Americans. Most essentials for life derived from what the rancho produced.

Aftermath of the Mexican War

In 1848 residents of Mexico's Far North became citizens of the United States in accordance with the Treaty of Guadalupe Hidalgo, which ended the war between the United States and Mexico (1846–1848). The number of residents of Mexican descent who lived in the U.S. Southwest during the last half of the nineteenth century is unknown, but some of the figures cited by demographers place the population in 1850 between 86,000 and 115,000 and perhaps as high as a quarter of a million by 1900. Such increases resulted from natural reproduction and, more important, from continued migration from Mexico. Movement north from the old country accelerated with the gold rush of 1849; one scholar estimates that some twenty-five thousand people from Sonora and its neighboring states headed for California mines in the four-year period following the Treaty of Guadalupe Hidalgo. During the 1880s and 1890s immigrants sought work on the California farms, Arizona ranches, and South Texas cattle and sheep ranges, and in deep-shaft mines.

White Americans dominated the post-1848 political and economic orders in Texas, New Mexico, Arizona, and California. Consequently Mexican Americans encountered numerous problems finding a niche in the new society. In an effort to disfranchise Mexican American citizens, whites employed such mechanisms as bossism, the practice by which influential political figures offered rewards from local government to manipulate Hispanic constituencies. Coercion, intimidation, and threats of hostility ranked among other means to dispossess Hispanics of the vote. To be sure, Mexican Americans launched efforts either to win representation in the political system or to end their subordination; however, patronage and appointments remained the chief means for holding office. A semblance of self-rule, on the other hand, existed in those places where Mexican Americans maintained a demographic advantage—South Texas, southern Arizona, and northern New Mexico.

Political disfranchisement was not the only problem Mexican Americans dealt with in the aftermath of the war with Mexico. While the Treaty of Guadalupe Hidalgo had guaranteed the right of individuals to lands given them by the Spanish or Mexican governments, grantees faced obstacles to protecting their property, including defending it from land swindlers, squatters, and hostile state courts. The federal judiciary proved sympathetic to Mexican American claims until 1889, when the Supreme Court ruled in the case of *Botiller et al. v. Domínguez* that the defendants, the Domínguez family, had erred in not validating the rancho's legal papers with the U.S. Land Commission in 1851. In ruling against the Domínguez family, the high court asserted that land recipients could no longer depend on the guarantees of the Treaty of Guadalupe Hidalgo.

On several occasions Mexican Americans resorted to individual and group resistance to protest white injustices. In 1859 Juan N. Cortina led an anti-white movement in the lower Rio Grande Valley of Texas. The campaign, which denounced white newcomers to South Texas for abusing Mexican Americans, garnered a sizable following before Texas Rangers and the U.S. Army suppressed the movement. In California Joaquín Murietta in the 1850s and Tiburcio Vásquez in the 1870s similarly gained sympathy and support for attacks on the white interlopers. Although both were outlaws, common folks aided them by concealing their whereabouts, extending shelter to them, and providing them with food and supplies. The activities of these bandit heroes, however, resulted in white retaliation against Mexican Americans.

Hispanic Culture

Much of Mexican American life centered around ethnic enclaves in the growing southwestern cities and around ranch settlements. Culture, though strongly tied to the pre-1848 heritage and to the heritage imported from Mexico by new immigrants, took on syncretic dimensions in the second half of the century. Some Hispanics learned to speak English, converted to Protestant denominations, and joined white Americans in the commemoration of U.S. patriotic days.

The family unit also experienced modification. Until the mid–nineteenth century the Mexican American family retained many tenets common to family structures in the Iberian Peninsula and Latin America. Anchored in patriarchal customs, the Hispanic family recognized the preeminence of the male head, the subservience of the wife, and certain traditions governing relations between parents and their offspring, especially between father and children. Since custom dictated that women stay at home, wives could not engage in business or political affairs, attend schools, or enjoy the social freedoms available to men. But circumstances after 1848 undermined the old structure as the demands of frontier living—including finding work to supplement the household income—influenced women to reassess traditional roles. Hispanic women entered the workforce in increasingly large numbers in the 1880s and 1890s and, once in the public sphere, were introduced to U.S. institutions that suggested different ways of conducting their lives. Pulling shift work with other women who entertained grand dreams and ambitions, experiencing modern technology at work on the job, or coming in closer contact with the capitalistic world outside segregated neighborhoods and villages all offered new exposure otherwise impossible to women who were constrained by older traditions. Many now found it easier to leave the house without supervision, feel a new independence as a wage earner, appreciate their spending power (however limited their earnings), and take pride in their ability to contribute to the family budget.

At the end of the nineteenth century, however, the Mexican American family still remained loyal to most of its traditional values and customs. For instance, the institution of *compadrazgo*, which called for the *padrinos*, those baptizing a child, to assume the responsibility of instructing young adults in religion and in proper family protocol and even to adopt the child should something happen to its biological parents, remained intact.

See also **Barrios; Mexican War; Mexico.**

Bibliography

Camarillo, Albert. *Chicanos in a Changing Society: From Mexican Pueblos to American Barrios in Santa Barbara and Southern California, 1848–1930.* Cambridge, Mass.: Harvard University Press, 1979.

Griswold del Castillo, Richard, and Arnoldo De León. *North to Aztlán: A History of Mexican Americans in the United States.* New York: Twayne, 1996.

Mirandé, Alfredo, and Evangelina Enríquez. *La Chicana: The Mexican American Woman.* Chicago: University of Chicago Press, 1979.

Montejano, David. *Anglos and Mexicans in the Making of Texas, 1836–1986.* Austin: University of Texas Press, 1987.

Nostrand, Richard L. *The Hispano Homeland.* Norman: University of Oklahoma Press, 1992.

Sheridan, Thomas E. *Los Tucsonenses: The Mexican Community in Tucson, 1854–1941*. Tucson: University of Arizona Press, 1986.

ARNOLDO DE LEÓN

MEXICAN CESSION   The Mexican Cession refers to the large expanse of territory ceded to the United States by Mexico after the latter's defeat in the Mexican War in 1848. Comprising all or parts of the present-day states of Arizona, California, Colorado, Nevada, New Mexico, Utah, and Wyoming, the total area of the cession amounted to more than 500,000 square miles. With this cession of land, Mexico, which also relinquished any claims on Texas, lost one-half of its national territory.

That the United States demanded the Mexican provinces of California and New Mexico during the negotiation of a peace treaty in 1848 was hardly surprising. Such a demand was repeated by American politicians during the 1830s and 1840s, a campaign historians have called Manifest Destiny. During these decades trade through the New Mexico Territory was increasing yearly, turning the sleepy village of Santa Fe into a major mercantile outpost. Even more enticing to American expansionists was California. Rich in resources in itself, it would also be America's window on the Pacific and the Far East. A call to annex all of Mexico was short-lived. Racist concerns about America's ability to assimilate millions of nonwhites and abolitionists' arguments that the "all-Mexico" campaign was simply a plot by proslavery forces to expand the "slavocracy" eventually put an end to the idea.

Thus, when representatives from Mexico and the United States sat down to hammer out a treaty ending the Mexican War in 1848, the Americans made it clear that the issue of the Mexican Cession was not negotiable. Mexico, in no shape to contest the American demands, gave in and signed the Treaty of Guadalupe Hidalgo. The United States acquired an immense amount of land, virtually completing the contiguous continental expansion of the nation, for a mere $15 million payment to Mexico. Some critics made sarcastic remarks at the time to the effect that the payment represented "guilt money."

While the cession represented the crowning glory of Manifest Destiny, it also resulted in a number of unforeseen problems. The first was a pragmatic issue: exactly what were the borders of this new territory? The northern border had already been established by the settlement of the Oregon Territory question with Great Britain in 1846. The southern boundaries of the cession, however, were in doubt. Both the United States and Mexico jockeyed to gain any advantage they could in the negotiations and subsequent surveys. The United States discovered just how costly mistakes in this process could be. When setting the border between Mexico and much of the New Mexico Territory, unreliable maps and U.S. haste to conclude the surveys and negotiations resulted in the forfeiture to Mexico of a sizable chunk of territory comprising present-day Arizona and New Mexico. The land was considered vital to a transcontinental railroad through the Southwest, and thus the United States demanded that the negotiations be reopened and that Mexico relinquish the land. Tempers in Washington and Mexico City flared, and for a time it looked as though another war would be fought. Neither side relished the thought of more bloodshed, however. Eventually the United States purchased the land, known as the Gadsden Purchase, from Mexico in 1853.

Another problem was the clash of cultures that occurred in the territories seized from Mexico. Though relatively lightly populated, the territories did contain a number of Spanish-speaking, Catholic Mexicans. As the Mexican population in Texas had earlier discovered, Americans were not always the best neighbors. The racial attitudes, arrogance, and anti-Catholicism of the Americans were of constant concern to the Mexican populations of the New Mexico and California Territories, and on more than one occasion violence between the two groups flared up.

Of larger consequence to the United States as a whole, the Mexican Cession became a battleground between proslavery and abolitionist forces. Though neither California nor New Mexico ever became another Bleeding Kansas, the debate over whether or not to allow slavery in the new lands was hotly contested in Congress and the editorial pages of newspapers. It was evident to both sides that the destiny of the nation lay in these new territories. The states carved out of these lands could change the balance of political power, and their votes in Congress and the electoral college could be absolutely critical. The Wilmot Proviso, proposed during the Mexican War, had tried to ban slavery outright in any territory taken from Mexico, but it was defeated. The Compromise of 1850 attempted to resolve the debate by declaring California a free state, making Texas a slave state, and instituting in the other new territories the notion of popular sovereignty, whereby the citizens of those territories would decide the issue of slavery for themselves. Whether popular sovereignty would have resulted in a violent struggle between proslavery and antislavery forces in the territories has remained uncertain. The population in those lands grew too slowly for the issue of statehood to arise prior to the Civil War.

See also **Abolition and Antislavery; Gadsden Purchase; Manifest Destiny; Mexican Americans; Mexican War.**

Bibliography

Billington, Ray Allen. *Westward Expansion: A History of the American Frontier.* 4th ed. New York: Macmillan, 1974.

Connor, Seymour V., and Odie B. Faulk. *North America Divided: The Mexican War, 1846–1848.* New York: Oxford University Press, 1971.

Pletcher, David M. *The Diplomacy of Annexation: Texas, Oregon, and the Mexican War.* Columbia: University of Missouri Press, 1973.

MICHAEL L. KRENN

MEXICAN IMMIGRANTS. See **Immigration and Immigrants,** subentry on **Mexico and Latin America.**

MEXICAN WAR

Background to the War

The Mexican War (also called the Mexican-American War and the United States–Mexican War) had its roots in the United States's desire to expand its boundaries to the Pacific Ocean. This movement, usually described as Manifest Destiny, actually began much earlier, as evidenced by U.S. involvement in the independence movements in Spanish and former Spanish territories throughout the early decades of the nineteenth century. Relations between Mexico and the United States were strained by the Texas Revolution (1835–1836) in which men and supplies from Louisiana, Alabama, Georgia, Kentucky, and other states enabled white colonists in Texas to win their independence from Mexico and establish the Republic of Texas. Although Texas failed to gain admission to the Union in 1837, many Texans and Americans believed that annexation was inevitable. Mexico, fearing that Texas was just the first attempt by the United States to expand at Mexico's expense, refused to admit that Texas was lost, denying the right of one country to annex territory belonging to another.

The 1844 presidential election forced the issue of Texas. The previous year a pro-annexation movement developed in the United States partly prompted by fears that Texas would fall under the influence of Great Britain. President John Tyler backed the proposal and in April 1844 signed a treaty annexing Texas to the United States, which after much debate the Senate rejected in June. Opponents viewed the annexation of Texas as an attempt on the part of slaveholders to subvert the Missouri Compromise and add new slave territory to the nation—a charge that resurfaced once the war began. The Democratic Party included two expansionist planks in its platform for the upcoming election: the occupation of Oregon and the "reannexation" of Texas. Supporters of reannexation claimed that Texas had been included in the Louisiana Purchase and that the former secretary of state John Quincy Adams had lost Texas to the Spanish in 1819 in the Adams-Onís Treaty. According to this line of reasoning, Texas had belonged to the United States since 1803, in spite of any claim by Mexico to the contrary. Tyler did not wait for the newly elected Democratic president, James Knox Polk, to take office before acting to make annexation a fact, signing on 1 March 1845 a joint resolution of Congress inviting Texas to join the Union. Mexico severed diplomatic relations with the United States on 28 March. Voters in Texas met on 4 July and approved the agreement. On 29 December 1845 Polk signed the treaty, admitting Texas as the twenty-eighth state.

The location of the southern boundary of Texas complicated the issue of annexation. Republic officials, and therefore the United States, claimed that the state extended to the Rio Grande (Río Bravo). Mexico, on the other hand, asserted that as a Mexican province, Texas had ended at the Nueces River, more than one hundred miles north of the Rio Grande. Anticipating that Mexico might try to block annexation militarily, Polk ordered Brigadier General Zachary Taylor, with a thirty-four-hundred-man force designated the Army of Occupation, to Corpus Christi, at the mouth of the Nueces River. While Taylor's presence was intended to deter attacks on Texans by Indians and Mexicans, it was a clear statement to Mexico that the United States was there to stay.

Polk attempted to settle the dispute over Texas diplomatically. In October 1845 the Mexican president, José Joaquín Herrera, agreed to accept a representative to discuss the worsening situation. Polk sent the diplomat John Slidell to Mexico with instructions to restore peace by settling outstanding issues between the two republics. Specifically, Slidell was to offer to relieve Mexico of several million dollars of damages claimed by U.S. citizens in return for recognition of the Rio Grande as the southern boundary of Texas. Moreover, Slidell was to offer to purchase New Mexico and California, which would not only prevent the latter region from falling into European hands but would also give U.S. shippers ex-

Attack on Chapultepec. On 13 September 1847, Major General Winfield Scott and his army seized Chapultepec Castle, the western gate of Mexico City, and by nightfall would penetrate the city. Lithograph by E. B. and E. C. Kellogg, c. 1847. LIBRARY OF CONGRESS: PRINTS AND PHOTOGRAPHS DIVISION

cellent Pacific ports. Polk's representative, who arrived at Veracruz in November 1845, never had the opportunity to carry out his instructions, as pressure in Mexico mounted to resist the United States. The situation worsened after General Mariano Paredes y Arrillaga and his supporters overthrew Herrera for what was perceived as Herrera's soft stand against the United States, forcing Slidell to leave Mexico in March 1846.

Failure on the diplomatic front prompted Polk to apply military pressure on Mexico in an attempt to break the deadlock. In January 1846 Polk ordered Taylor to move his base of operation from Corpus Christi to the north bank of the Rio Grande. Taylor received the order on 2 February but did not commence the move until 8 March. By the end of the month Taylor had arrived opposite Matamoros, where he ordered an earthen fortification, dubbed Fort Texas, built, also establishing a supply base at the mouth of the river at Point Isabel. Besides occupying the disputed territory, the United States had effectively blockaded Matamoros, the primary port

of entrance for northern Mexico. General Pedro de Ampudia, the Mexican commander in the region, reported to his government that a state of war existed. On 24 April 1846 General Mariano Arista, who arrived to replace Ampudia, ordered his cavalry to cross the Rio Grande and encircle Taylor. The next day this force, which consisted of several thousand lancers and rancheros, surprised and captured two companies of U.S. Dragoons following a brief skirmish. On 1 May, Taylor learned that more Mexican troops had crossed the river, prompting him to leave a small garrison at Fort Texas while he raced to Point Isabel to secure his supply base. On 3 May, the sound of cannon fire at Fort Texas some twenty miles away alerted Taylor that the fort was under attack. He set off to relieve the fort on 7 May, encountering and defeating along the way the main Mexican force at Palo Alto on 8 May and Resaca de la Palma on 9 May. Fort Texas, rechristened Fort Brown to honor Major Jacob Brown, who was killed during the siege, was the nucleus of the postwar city of Brownsville, Texas. On 17 May, Arista evacuated Matamoros, which Taylor occupied the following day. No one doubted that U.S. troops were on Mexican soil now and that the United States and Mexico were at war.

Polk's patience with Mexico had run out even before he learned of the new turn of events. The president and his cabinet had already discussed declaring war when news of the 25 April skirmish on the north bank of the Rio Grande reached Washington on 9 May. Revising an earlier draft of a war message to include this new information, Polk sent the document to Congress on 11 May. Citing the death of at least eleven men of Captain Seth Thornton's squadron (one officer and ten enlisted men) as evidence, Polk told Congress that "Mexico has . . . shed American blood upon the American soil" and asked it to recognize that a state of war already existed. With war a fact, he requested money and troops with which to carry the conflict forward to a swift end.

Military Campaigns

The war was fought in two phases in two theaters, northern Mexico and central Mexico.

Phase One: Northern Mexico

Polk's war message spurred Congress into action. On 12 May, Congress authorized the president to call fifty thousand volunteers into service. Polk signed the bill the next day, clearing the way for Secretary of War William L. Marcy to levy a quota of volunteers against various states. Geography played a role in the allotments, with troops from states closest to the front being called up first. There was no shortage of men willing to enlist in these early days of the war and, in fact, many volunteers feared the war would be over before they had the opportunity to fight. The scene of men rushing to enlist was repeated in towns and cities across the United States. One major difference existed between soldiers of the volunteer army and the regular army: unlike the regular army, where Congress appointed the officer corps, volunteers were allowed to elect their own officers. Because of this democratic aspect, the spirit of equality permeated volunteer ranks, making them more difficult to control. The ramifications of this situation were not yet evident, as the volunteers entered the service throughout the early summer months of 1846.

On 30 May 1846 Polk met with his cabinet to discuss strategy. The challenge was to successfully conclude the war with all possible speed while gaining the territory that Polk and his supporters had sought before the outbreak of hostilities. This meeting was the genesis for occupation of Mexico's northern states. Taylor was ordered to leave the Rio Grande and advance into Nuevo León. Brigadier General

Battle of Buena Vista. American forces under General Zachary Taylor defeated Mexican general Santa Anna's army near Buena Vista, Mexico, on 23 Feb 1847. Taylor's reputation as a military hero would grow, resulting in his election as president two years later. From a sketch taken on the spot by Major Eaton, aide-de-camp to General Taylor, c. 1847. LIBRARY OF CONGRESS

Stephen W. Kearny was placed in command of the Army of the West and charged with the task of seizing New Mexico. Another expedition was to be outfitted at New York and sent by sea to occupy California. An additional column, under Brigadier General John E. Wool, was sent to capture Chihuahua. Unable to achieve his goals through diplomacy, Polk intended to claim these territories as indemnity for the war.

While Taylor waited for reinforcements on the Rio Grande, Kearny and Wool gathered their forces and set off on their missions. Kearny launched his sixteen-hundred-man expedition from Fort Leavenworth, Kansas, in June 1846. After spending several days in late July at Bent's Fort on the Arkansas River (near present-day La Junta, Colorado) to allow his men to rest, Kearny advanced into New Mexico, occupying Santa Fe on 18 August. With his mission accomplished, Kearny set about forming a government for the newly conquered territory even as he prepared to carry out secondary tasks. On 25 September 1846 Kearny and an escort of U.S. Dragoons headed west from Santa Fe to aid in the capture of California. Wool had also been on the move, having left San Antonio, Texas, in late September with approximately thirty-four hundred men. Reaching the Rio Grande at Presidio on 8 October, he crossed several days later. By November, Wool was at Monclova, where he halted after learning news of an armistice between the United States and Mexico.

The armistice was the result of the Battle of Monterrey. In late August 1846, augmented by newly arrived volunteers, Taylor left his base at Camargo and began the advance on Monterrey, the capital of Nuevo León, reaching the city on 19 September. The following day he divided his 6,640-man army into two wings and sent one under Brigadier General William Jenkins Worth to cut off the road to Saltillo, a move designed to prevent the Mexicans from either receiving reinforcements or retreating. Over the next two days, Worth's troops not only cut off the road but captured the Mexican defenses guarding the western sector of Monterrey. On the morning of 21 September, Taylor ordered a diversionary attack against the eastern approach to the city, which developed into a pitched battle in which the U.S. forces made substantial gains but at a high cost. On 24 September General Pedro de Ampudia, the Mexican commander, asked for terms after Taylor and Worth's troops had fought their way into the center of Monterrey. Representatives from both sides worked out an agreement whereby the Mexicans surrendered the city to Taylor and in return were allowed to withdraw to San Luis Postosí with most of their arms and equipment. Moreover, an eight-week-long armistice

was declared to allow Taylor and Arista to communicate with their governments.

Events had proceeded in California independent of the actions of Taylor, Wool, and Kearny. Earlier in June, even while the War Department was busy gathering troops, American settlers in California had already declared independence from Mexico in an episode called the Bear Flag Revolt. The actors in the affair had help from Captain John Charles Frémont, a U.S. Army officer commanding a mapping expedition in the region. The following month, the U.S. Navy seized the ports of Monterey, San Pedro, San Diego, and San Francisco; Santa Barbara and Los Angeles fell in August. Frémont and Commodore Robert F. Stockton cooperated in the occupation as they awaited directions from Washington.

Polk was not pleased with the course of the war even though a vast amount of territory was falling under U.S. control, because the Mexican government seemed no closer to capitulating than when hostilities began. Taylor's armistice enraged the president, who quickly ordered the general to resume operations. On 5 November 1846 Taylor notified the Mexican authorities that the armistice was over, advanced through Rincondada Pass, and entered Saltillo without opposition. Polk, however, had decided against marching on Mexico City via the northern route and ordered Taylor to send the bulk of his troops, especially his regulars, to Tampico. The president had chosen a new commander to head up the campaign against the Mexican capital, Major General Winfield Scott, the commanding general of the army. Wool was ordered to abandon his march on Chihuahua and join Taylor in order to assist his depleted command.

As 1846 came to a close and the new year arrived, events threatened to undo the earlier successes. In California the Californios rose up and attempted to recapture key ports and drive Stockton and Frémont's forces from the region. General Kearny, who entered California unaware of the new development, was met by rancheros who scored a victory over his worn-out dragoons on 6 December at San Pasqual. U.S. land and sea forces regrouped and defeated the Californios at the Battle of San Gabriel near Los Angeles on 8 January 1847. Stockton reoccupied Los Angeles two days later, and on 13 January the Treaty of Cahuenga was signed, ending the fighting in California. That same month, however, a revolt broke out in New Mexico, where insurgents killed U.S.-installed government officials. Brigadier General Sterling Price marshaled U.S. forces and defeated the rebels at Taos on 4 February 1847. Even Taylor faced a difficult time at Saltillo. Persistent rumors of a counteroffensive proved true and on 22 February 1847, an approximately fifteen-thousand-man Mexi-

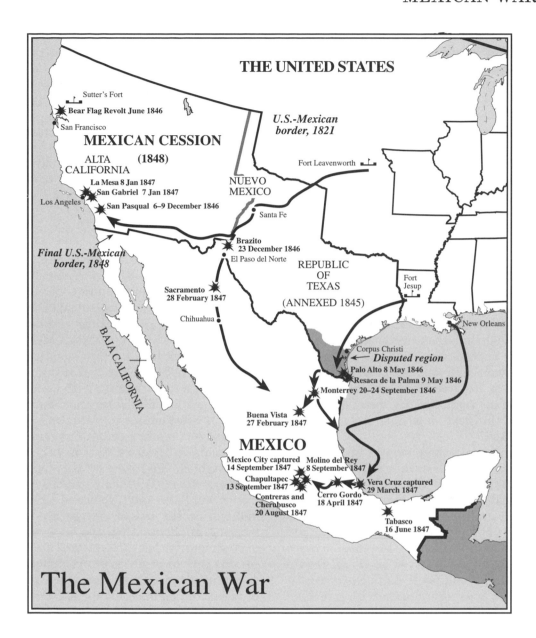

THE UNITED STATES

Sutter's Fort

★ **Bear Flag Revolt June 1846**

San Francisco

U.S.-Mexican border, 1821

MEXICAN CESSION

(1848)

ALTA CALIFORNIA

Fort Leavenworth

La Mesa 8 Jan 1847
San Gabriel 7 Jan 1847

NUEVO MEXICO

Los Angeles

★ **San Pasqual 6–9 December 1846**

Santa Fe

Brazito 23 December 1846
El Paso del Norte

Final U.S.-Mexican border, 1848

REPUBLIC OF TEXAS

(ANNEXED 1845)

Sacramento 28 February 1847

Fort Jesup

Chihuahua

BAJA CALIFORNIA

New Orleans

Corpus Christi

← *Disputed region*

Palo Alto 8 May 1846
Resaca de la Palma 9 May 1846
Monterrey 20–24 September 1846

Buena Vista 27 February 1847

MEXICO

Mexico City captured 14 September 1847   **Molino del Rey 8 September 1847**

Chapultepec 13 September 1847

Vera Cruz captured 29 March 1847

Contreras and Cherubusco 20 August 1847

Cerro Gordo 18 April 1847

Tabasco 16 June 1847

The Mexican War

can army led by General Antonio López de Santa Anna appeared at the hacienda of Buena Vista several miles south of the city to challenge Taylor's force of some forty-eight hundred men, mostly volunteers. Fierce fighting on 23 February nearly forced the Americans from the field, but Santa Anna failed to renew the attack the following day and withdrew from the area. This sudden turn of events allowed Taylor to claim victory.

One campaign that went well at this time was the invasion of Chihuahua. In New Mexico, Colonel Alexander Doniphan and his First Missouri Mounted Volunteers left Santa Fe on or about 14 December 1846, on a trek across the desert to capture Chihuahua City. On Christmas Day, while encamped near El Paso del Norte (present-day El Paso, Texas), the

Missourians were attacked by a force of some twelve hundred Mexicans but emerged the victors of the Battle of Brazito. Doniphan marched into Chihuahua and captured its capital after scoring another victory at Sacramento on 28 February.

Phase Two: Central Mexico

Winfield Scott's campaign to capture Mexico City developed out of Polk's frustration at not being able to force the Mexican government to the peace table, even after having defeated its armies and occupying its northernmost states. Scott arrived in Mexico in December 1846 and, in accordance with his orders, began shifting units from Taylor's army to his own. Cooperating with the U.S. Navy, Scott marshaled his forces at Lobos Island in February, preparing for an amphibious assault on Veracruz. On 9 March 1847 U.S. forces landed unopposed on a stretch of beach south of Veracruz and began an investment of the city. The siege guns opened fire on 22 March; on 29 March, the Mexican Army turned over the city and marched away after being paroled.

Scott began moving inland along the National Highway in early April. His vanguard discovered that a Mexican army under General Santa Anna had fortified a mountainous pass called Cerro Gordo, which the Americans would have to pass on their way to Mexico City. Scott brought his main body of troops forward and on 18 April attacked and drove the Mexicans from their positions. Key to Scott's victory had been the discovery by Captain Robert E. Lee of a passage around the Mexican's right flank that allowed U.S. soldiers to circle behind the enemy's lines unnoticed. During the night preceding the battle, Scott's men also succeeded in planting several cannon on a high hill that overlooked important earthworks. So sudden and complete was the U.S. victory that advancing troops captured Santa Anna's coach containing his treasury chest, camp equipment, and even his spare cork leg. Scott quickly occupied Jalapa the next day. U.S. troops entered Puebla on 15 May.

Scott spent the next three months at Puebla rebuilding his army. On 4 May, while still at Jalapa, he had released almost all of the volunteers from his command so that they could return home. The War Department, in its first call for volunteers, had assumed that the fighting would be over in a year and, therefore, had allowed volunteers to enlist for twelve months. With their term of service nearly up, the volunteers with Taylor and Scott declined to reenlist. Congress tried to avoid this situation when it issued a second call for volunteers in November and December of 1846 by requiring new enlistments to be "for the war." Congress also passed the Ten Regiment Bill on 11 February 1847, which increased the size of the regular army. These measures, however, had not yet yielded results, and Scott could advance no farther until reinforcements arrived. Scott used his time at Puebla to rest his veterans and train his new units. By early August, Scott was ready for the final leg of the campaign—the capture of Mexico City.

Scott began his advance from Puebla on 7 August and within a few days arrived in the Valley of Mexico. The U.S. commander had sent engineers and spies ahead to examine the Mexican defenses and determine the best way to enter the city. The most direct route was guarded by a hilltop fortress called El Peñon, which Scott decided to avoid. He had approximately ten thousand men under his command, compared with more than twenty thousand Mexi-

cans whom Santa Anna had raised to defend the city. Wishing to avoid a costly battle at this stage, Scott instead sent his army south around Lake Chalco. On 19 August he encountered resistance at the village of San Antonio. Using the rain-soaked night to position his troops for the next day's action, Scott defeated separate Mexican forces at both Contreras and Churubusco. Routed defenders fell back to the protection of the walls of the city with Scott's men on their heels. There was to be no entrance yet, however, as Scott and Santa Anna agreed to an armistice while negotiators met to discuss peace.

Scott, convinced that the Mexicans were using the cease-fire to strengthen their defenses, broke off negotiations and prepared to take the city by force. On 8 September 1847 he ordered an assault on an old mill known as Molino del Rey just south of Chapultepec Castle, where it was rumored that Santa Anna was casting cannon. The Mexican defenders put up a fierce resistance before retiring. Morale in Scott's army sank after it was determined that the rumored foundry did not exist and that many American lives had been lost for no reason. With his army weakened through battle and disease and needing to end the war soon, Scott pressed forward. On 13 September he launched a two-pronged assault against the western approaches to Mexico City. Chapultepec Castle fell that morning, and by sunset U.S. forces had fought their way to the very walls of the city, seizing the San Cosmé and Belén gates. Prepared for house-to-house fighting, Scott's troops entered the city the next morning, but Santa Anna and his army had left during the night. Although Mexican officials surrendered Mexico City to Scott, rooftop sniping continued for several days until Scott threatened to turn his soldiers loose on a plundering spree. Calm gradually settled on the captured capital, but peace seemed no closer.

The fighting that lay ahead proved vital to the U.S. war effort. In the summer of 1847 the Mexican government had issued a call for a guerrilla war against the U.S. rear echelons. Supply trains sent from Veracruz were routinely attacked by bands of Mexican irregulars: even trains with escorts of one thousand men were not safe. Without sufficient troops to guard every point along the National Highway, Scott severed communications with the coast, depending on his own forces to carry out his campaign. He left a small garrison at Puebla to protect the warehouses and hospitals that had been established there. On 14 September, Mexican forces laid siege to Puebla, intending to capture the city and thereby force Scott either to abandon Mexico City or to remain there isolated with little chance for relief. On 22 September, Santa Anna arrived at Puebla with the remnants of his army and joined in the siege. On 12 October, U.S. reinforcements marching inland from Veracruz reached Puebla and raised the siege. Guerrilla activity along the National Highway continued for several months, although many writers attribute the attacks to bandits. Colonel John C. Hays's regiment of Texas Mounted Volunteers, commonly called Texas Rangers, proved particularly effective in antiguerrilla operations.

The Treaty of Guadalupe Hidalgo

In May 1847 President Polk's handpicked negotiator, Nicholas Trist, joined Scott's column with a draft treaty. The document required Mexico to give up any claim to Texas as well as recognize the Rio Grande as the international boundary. In addition, Mexico was to cede New Mexico and Upper California to the United States as a war indemnity. Less strongly emphasized were demands for the right of transit across the Isthmus of Tehuantepec and the cession of Lower California. Polk authorized Trist to pay up to $20 million for these concessions.

Trist's arrival marked the beginning of an acrimonious feud between the diplomat and Winfield Scott, the U.S. commander in central Mexico. Scott resented the fact that he would essentially be taking orders from a civilian employee of the State Department. Trist and Scott refused to meet at first, both sending letters of protest about the other to their superiors in Washington. The two men eventually patched up their differences and worked together for a negotiated peace whenever the opportunity arose. Following the Battle of Cerro Gordo in April 1847, Scott and Trist dispensed a million dollars to unknown Mexican officials after it was hinted that money in the right pockets would enhance the likelihood of peace talks. The plan, called a bribe by some, failed to achieve the desired results. Scott halted hostilities following his victories at Contreras and Churubusco to allow Trist the opportunity to open negotiations with Santa Anna, although this attempt failed. Once Mexico City was firmly in U.S. hands, Trist started to work again. He faced two obstacles: first, the Mexican Congress was in disarray, and thus there was no authorized body with which to negotiate; second, Trist's own government had lost confidence in him and had called him home. On the advice of Scott and others, Trist defied Polk and persisted in bringing representatives of a newly organized government to the table. On 2 February 1848 Mexican officials signed the treaty at a suburb of Mexico City called Guadalupe Hidalgo, and Trist forwarded it to the president. Polk reviewed the document with his cabinet and realized that Trist had

achieved nearly all demands set forth in the original draft he had carried to Mexico. Although Mexico denied the right of transit across the Isthmus of Tehuantepec and the cession of Lower California, it relinquished title to more than five hundred thousand square miles of territory, which would one day become the U.S. states of California, Arizona, and New Mexico as well as parts of Utah, Colorado, Nevada, and Wyoming. Mexico was in turn to receive $15 million plus $3,250,000 to settle outstanding claims by U.S. citizens. Polk sent the Treaty of Guadalupe Hidalgo to the U.S. Senate, which ratified it on 10 March 1848. The document was sent back to Mexico, where it was approved by the Mexican Congress on 25 May 1848. Shortly thereafter, U.S. troops returned home.

Opposition to the War

Not all Americans had favored the war. Much of the opposition centered in New England and the states north of the Ohio River, where abolitionist sentiment existed. Antislavery elements both within and outside the Whig Party claimed that the Texas Revolution and the subsequent annexation of the Lone Star Republic were part of a sinister plot on the part of the slave states to acquire more slave territory. Although the War Bill of 11 May 1846 passed by a wide margin, fourteen Whig members of the House of Representatives voted against it. This block, which included John Quincy Adams and Joshua Giddings, routinely opposed the administration's request for congressional support. Most congressmen, however, suppressed whatever qualms they had about the war and voted to send men and supplies to the front, explaining that their failure to do so would endanger American soldiers already in the field. This did not prevent some congressmen from speaking out. Representative Abraham Lincoln of Illinois questioned Polk's assertion that American blood had been shed on American soil. More vitriolic was Senator Thomas Corwin of Ohio's remark in a speech in which he opposed the Ten Regiment Bill of 11 February 1847: "If I were a Mexican I would tell you, 'Haven't you not room in your own country to bury your dead men. If you come into mine, we will greet you with bloody hands, and welcome you to hospitable graves.' " Such talk caused the war's supporters to call Corwin and others Mexican Whigs and Tories, claiming their opposition aided the enemy and prolonged the fighting. Hanging over the Whigs was the specter of the Federalist Party and its opposition to the War of 1812 culminating in the Hartford Convention. The desire not to be labeled traitors kept more moderate Whigs in line with the administration's desires.

The slavery issue drove a wedge between members of Polk's own party. The Wilmot Proviso, introduced by Democratic Representative David Wilmot of Pennsylvania, both reflected this division and exacerbated it. First introduced in August 1846, the bill would have prohibited the extension of slavery into any territory gained as a result of the war. Northern Democrats voted for the proviso because it enabled them to support the war, territorial expansion, and Manifest Destiny, while simultaneously opposing the extension of slavery. Although defeated, the bill resurfaced again in February 1847 during the debate over additional money and troops for the war. Voting on the bill tended to be along sectional lines, with northerners supporting it and southerners opposing it. The issue helped split the Democratic Party and led to the formation of the Free-Soil Party in 1848.

Many of the country's intellectual elite opposed the war. Although he did not speak out publicly, Ralph Waldo Emerson, the unofficial leader of the transcendentalist movement, recorded his opposition in his private journal. James Russell Lowell wrote and published *The Biglow Papers* (1848), a series of satirical poems that lampooned Polk and the war. The most famous antiwar work was Henry David Thoreau's essay "Civil Disobedience" (1849), which in large part laid the groundwork for the modern peace movement. These writings, however, had little impact on public thought during the war.

Members of the American Peace Movement offered a strong argument against the conflict: the inevitable losses from death and destruction and the endless suffering for the wounded and those who fell ill. U.S. casualties amounted to 1,429 killed in action, with an additional 10,885 deaths from disease. Mexican numbers are more difficult to ascertain. Abiel Abbot Livermore, a proponent of the peace movement, estimated their losses at more than 4,000 killed and 30,000 sick or wounded.

The Mexican War affected the 1848 presidential election. Polk had pledged not to run for a second term. The Whigs had two candidates in mind: Generals Zachary Taylor and Winfield Scott. Taylor's victories along the Rio Grande and in northern Mexico had significantly enhanced his reputation and popularity with the American public, who found comfort in his sobriquet, Old Rough-and-Ready. Polk worked to undermine both Taylor and Scott by commissioning Democratic politicians as generals in order to create a hero for his own party. Relations between the Democratic administration and the two generals were extremely partisan. Taylor believed that Polk had deliberately stripped him of his best troops and set him up for a defeat by Santa Anna. Following Scott's capture of Mexico City, Polk recalled the victorious general home to face a court of inquiry over a dispute that had developed between Scott and several high-ranking Democratic officers. Taylor easily won the Whig nomination for president. The Democrats turned to Lewis Cass of Michigan, a war hero from a previous conflict. Cass's campaign included the call for "squatter sovereignty," a notion that would allow inhabitants of newly acquired territories to decide whether or not slavery would be permitted, thereby relieving Congress of the difficult decision. Taylor won, although not necessarily on the strength of the Whig Party, which was unraveling. A major factor in the outcome was the defection of many New York Democrats to former president Martin Van Buren, the nominee of the newly formed Free-Soil Party. The emergence of this third party cost the Democrats enough votes to allow a Whig victory. The election demonstrated that both of the great Jacksonian parties were in turmoil as Americans began to realign themselves along sectional lines, heading steadily toward a civil war.

The War's Significance

Although short in duration, the Mexican War was a pivotal event of the nineteenth century, the culmination of the movement to extend the nation's boundaries to California. The drive for additional territory would next be seen in the filibuster expeditions of the 1850s, a time when private armies attempted to conquer portions of Lower California, Sonora, Cuba, and Nicaragua. This interest in new territory also manifested itself on the eve of the Civil War with the rise of the Knights of the Golden Circle, whose goal was to bring the Caribbean under the control of the southern slave-based economy and even possibly form a separate republic from the United States. Halted by the Civil War, the movement emerged again in the drive for Hawaii, the Philippines, and Cuba as the United States entered the age of imperialism. It is no exaggeration to state that the Mexican War was directly responsible for the Civil War, because the territory gained from Mexico reopened the national debate on the expansion of slavery, calling into question the very existence of the institution and creating an irreparable rift with no possibility of compromise. The Mexican War also destroyed the two great parties that had developed around Andrew Jackson, splitting the Democrats along sectional lines and driving the Whig Party out of existence. It would be the newly formed Republican Party and a realigned Democratic Party that would dominate the political scene during the last half of the century. In an effect that extended well beyond the century, the war created a distrust of the United States in Mexico that continues to color relations between the two nations. While many Americans know little about the war, Mexicans remember it well, because it resulted in the loss of more than one-third of Mexico's national territory to the United States.

See also **Expansion; Filibusters; Foreign Relations,** *subentry on* **1789–1860; Manifest Destiny; Mexico; Missouri Compromise; Texas.**

Bibliography

Alcaraz, Ramon. *The Other Side; or, Notes for the History of the War between Mexico and the United States.* Translated and edited by Albert C. Ramsey. New York: Wiley, 1850.

Bauer, K. Jack. *The Mexican War, 1846–1848.* New York: Macmillan, 1974.

Brack, Gene M. *Mexico Views Manifest Destiny 1821–1846: An Essay on the Origins of the Mexican War.* Albuquerque: University of New Mexico Press, 1975.

Frazier, Donald S., ed. *The United States and Mexico at War: Nineteenth-Century Expansionism and Conflict.* New York: Macmillan, 1998.

Henry, Robert Selph. *The Story of the Mexican War.* Indianapolis, Ind.: Bobbs-Merrill, 1950.

Johannsen, Robert W. *To the Halls of the Montezumas: The Mexican War in the American Imagination.* New York: Oxford University Press, 1985.

McCaffrey, James M. *Army of Manifest Destiny: The American Soldier in the Mexican War, 1846–1848.* New York: New York University Press, 1992.

Ohrt, Wallace. *Defiant Peacemaker: Nicholas Trist in the Mexican War.* College Station: Texas A&M University Press, 1997.

Pletcher, David M. *The Diplomacy of Annexation: Texas, Oregon, and the Mexican War.* Columbia: University of Missouri Press, 1973.

Schroeder, John H. *Mr. Polk's War: American Opposition and Dissent, 1846–1848.* Madison: University of Wisconsin Press, 1973.

Singletary, Otis A. *The Mexican War.* Chicago: University of Chicago Press, 1960.

Smith, Justin H. *The War with Mexico.* 2 vols. New York: Macmillan, 1919.

Winders, Richard Bruce. *Mr. Polk's Army: The American Military Experience in the Mexican War.* College Station: Texas A&M University Press, 1997.

RICHARD BRUCE WINDERS

MEXICO   The United States' relations with Mexico during the nineteenth century can be divided into two fairly distinct periods. From Mexico's independence in 1821 into the 1840s, the relationship between the two nations was determined by mutual suspicion, distrust, and animosity, eventually culminating in the outbreak of the Mexican-American War in 1846. The last half of the century, however, was a time of peace between Mexico and the United States, cemented by increasingly close economic contacts.

The Age of Anxiety

In 1810 Mexico began its long rebellion against Spanish rule. The uprising was generally applauded by citizens of the United States, who saw in it reflections of their own recent revolution against European domination. Some even joined in filibustering expeditions to aid in the fighting against Spanish forces.

Mexican independence

Officially, however, the United States remained neutral in the conflict between the Mexican rebels and Spain, even going so far as to ban arms shipments to Mexico in 1814. Mexico sent several agents to the U.S. government seeking support, aid, and recognition, but none was forthcoming. Of the factors at work in the U.S. decision to maintain a policy of neutrality in regard to the revolt in Mexico, the unwillingness to needlessly antagonize Spain was first and foremost. By 1812 the United States was at war with Great Britain; it did not need a further conflict with another European power. In addition, U.S. policymakers did not want to disturb ongoing negotiations with Spain concerning the territory of Florida. And the expansionist desires of the United States did not end with Florida; its policymakers had their eyes on the Texas territory and even California. Spain, facing economic difficulties at home and coping with revolutions throughout its New World empire, might be amenable to the sale or cession of these territories; an independent Mexico might not prove as flexible.

While official U.S. contacts with the events in Mexico were kept in check, the activities of private citizens would prove decisive. In 1820 a Missouri miner named Moses Austin visited the Texas territory of Mexico to inquire into the possibility of land grants for American colonists. He assured Spanish officials that the settlers would live according to Spanish rules and respect their customs. Spain considered the American settlers to be a calculated risk. The Texas territory was sparsely populated. The influx of thousands of new homesteaders would provide a buffer against incursions by Native Americans and would, in any case, create a new source of revenue for the depleted Spanish treasury. Spanish officials were not unaware of the U.S. interest in Texas; perhaps offering land and opportunities to settlers (in exchange for loyalty to Spanish rule) would forestall the loss of the territory. The decision was made that same year to allow the colonists entry into Texas.

At the same time Spanish rule in Mexico was coming to an end. In 1821 the Mexican revolt was successful, and the next year Augustín de Iturbide was made emperor of the new nation. The United States moved quickly to establish economic contacts with Mexico, but diplomatic recognition was slower in developing. Joel R. Poinsett, who had experience in serving as a U.S. agent in Latin America, was appointed to serve in that capacity to Mexico in 1822. After a short while in the country, Poinsett concluded that Iturbide's rule was ineffective and unpopular, and recommended that recognition be withheld. Despite Poinsett's arguments, President James Monroe asked Congress for diplomatic recognition of Mexico and four other Latin American republics, and relations with Mexico were formally established in December of that year. Iturbide was overthrown and executed the next year. Although formal relations had been established, securing a U.S. minister to Mexico proved to be a problem. The first man selected, Andrew Jackson, hero of the War of 1812, declined the office; the second, Ninian Edwards of Illinois, never left to assume the post. Finally, in 1825, Poinsett was given the job. In the meantime, the United States had lost valuable time, which the British used to their advantage to establish economic and political contacts with the Mexican government, including extending to them a series of loans.

The American delay in recognition and in sending a minister to Mexico City was, at least partially, due to the fact that the early U.S. enthusiasm for the Mexican revolt against Spanish rule had begun to wane almost immediately. The brief Iturbide empire convinced some Americans that the Spanish colonial heritage exerted too great a hold on Mexico for that nation ever to develop into a functioning republic. The political strife and instability in Mexico after 1821 were also seen as evidence that the Mexican people were not ready for the demands of a democratic system of government. By the mid-1820s many Americans judged the revolution in Mexico a failure.

Also largely a failure was Poinsett's diplomacy in Mexico. His directions from his own government had been relatively simple: promote democracy in Mexico; caution Mexico against becoming involved in any attempts to free Cuba from Spanish control; protect and encourage American trade; and try to straighten out the border problems between the United States and Mexico. Trade with Mexico did grow during Poinsett's stay: by 1830 its annual trade with the United States had risen from $2 million in 1825 to more than $10 million. And Mexico did refrain from direct action in regard to Cuba. In attempting to "promote democracy," however, Poinsett antagonized many Mexicans (who viewed his actions and rhetoric as interference with Mexican sovereignty).

His efforts to settle border disputes (often by offering to purchase Mexican territory) only increased Mexican suspicions about the expansionist plans of its northern neighbor. Mexico requested that Poinsett be recalled in October 1829.

American settlers in Texas

Forgotten in all of this confusion was the Spanish agreement to allow American settlers into Texas. Moses Austin's son, Stephen, had begun leading colonists into what was now Mexican territory. The Mexican government came to the same conclusion as the Spanish government before it: it was better to encourage the American settlers than to try to stem their flow into Texas, an action that might bring on military conflict with the United States. By the early 1830s, nearly thirty thousand Americans had crossed into Texas to claim lands.

Despite the fact that Mexico made rather generous land grants to the new colonists, friction soon developed. Mexico, which in 1829 had banned slavery, allowed the Americans to bring their slaves to Texas. However, they could not buy or sell slaves in the territory, and children born to the slaves would

General Antonio Lopez de Santa Anna (1794–1876). Santa Anna endured a tumultuous military and political career: as president of Mexico (1833–1836) he and his army suffered defeat during the Texan Revolution; he became dictator of Mexico in 1844 but was deposed and exiled a year later, only to return as president (1853–1855) and face exile a second time (1855–1874). LIBRARY OF CONGRESS

be legally free. Mexico also required that the colonists be subject to Mexican law, and offered citizenship within three years of their arrival. Finally, Mexican officials insisted that the American settlers profess Catholicism. None of this sat well with the newcomers, many of whom were slaveowners, were fiercely American in thought and behavior, and carried with them the anti-Catholic biases of most of their Protestant fellow Americans. A clash of cultures ensued.

The American settlers brought with them the perceptions of Latin American peoples and cultures built up over the years in the United States. They believed that Latin people were lazy, shiftless, prone to criminal behavior, and hot-tempered, yet also cowardly and craven; that years of colonial rule by the autocratic Spanish had extinguished Latin America's ability to form stable or democratic governments; and that the Catholic Church, viewed as a decadent and corrupting Old World institution, further degraded the people of Latin America. Generations of race-mixing had led to what many observers in the United States referred to as a "mongrel race" of people in Latin America. Nothing that the American colonists in Texas saw caused them to reevaluate these perceptions. The Mexicans seemed particularly lazy, leaving thousands of acres of land and vast resources virtually untouched and undeveloped. Americans felt that Mexicans, instead of working to improve their lot, spent their days drinking, gambling, and dancing. Mexican women were judged particularly licentious. The Mexicans' seeming subservience to the Catholic priesthood also galled the Americans.

From the Mexican viewpoint the Americans in Texas represented the best and the worst Yankee traits. They were indeed industrious and were intent on improving and modernizing the territory. Yet they were also viewed as uncultured, grasping materialists whose arrogance was matched by a lack of gratitude. It was felt that the Mexican government had been more than fair in its dealings with the settlers, who showed no inclination to be governed by Mexican law and customs. The settlers seemed to consider Texas an extension of the United States rather than part of another sovereign nation. The racism and air of superiority of the colonists were palpable, antagonizing both Mexican officials and citizens.

More disturbing to the Mexican government than these cultural differences was the increasing awareness that the United States seemed intent on eventually annexing the area. Mexican diplomats and visitors to the United States were shocked to hear discussions about the annexation of Texas, New Mexico, and even California—by force, if necessary—on the streets, in the halls of Congress, and in the press. American presidents from the early nineteenth century to Andrew Jackson had had their eyes on Texas and the lands farther west, and many attempts had been made to purchase the territories from Mexico. What American officials did not seem to understand was that these offers angered Mexicans and created deep suspicions. Mexico was not another European colonial power being asked to sell far-off, detached pieces of land; Texas, New Mexico, and California were part of Mexico's sovereign territory, and any suggestion that these lands be auctioned off to the highest bidder created intense waves of nationalism among the Mexican people.

Hostility in Texas

In 1830 Mexico issued a proclamation prohibiting further American settlement in Texas. The expectation that the settlers would provide an economic windfall for the Mexican government and might serve as a buffer to U.S. annexation of the territory had been disappointed. Mexican officials reported that the American colonists carried out most of their economic dealings with U.S. traders and businessmen; Mexico saw little, if any, economic benefit from these arrangements. And instead of staving off possible annexation, the settlers seemed to be the advance agents of such an eventuality. The Mexican proclamation did nothing to stem the tide of colonists into Texas. It did, however, produce more hostile reactions among the settlers already in Texas, some of whom began to revolt against Mexican rule.

In addition, the proclamation further increased friction between Mexico and the United States. Mexican officials began to demand that the United States stop the flow of settlers into Mexican territory. The American government responded that it did not have the power to stop U.S. citizens from traveling where they desired to go. The new American minister in Mexico did little to alleviate these tensions. Following Poinsett's recall in 1829, President Andrew Jackson had appointed one of his political cronies, Anthony Butler, as the new U.S. minister to Mexico. It was an unfortunate choice. Butler was brusque, undiplomatic, and given to drink. His intemperate outbursts in dealing with Mexican officials drove the two nations farther apart. During his tenure, the British gained more and more influence in Mexico; Mexican suspicions of America's territorial goals increased; and Mexican criticisms of slavery in the United States gained momentum. Only in the area of trade did relations between Mexico and the United States improve. By the time Butler left his post in 1835, annual trade between the countries had increased to more than $18 million.

Problems in Texas continued to mount. In 1833 Stephen Austin traveled to Mexico City to negotiate a settlement of differences between the Mexican government and the settlers in Texas. The talks foundered, and on his way back to Texas, Austin was arrested; he languished in prison for nearly a year. By the time he was released and allowed to return to Texas, many of the American settlers were openly discussing revolution. Sam Houston, a former governor of Tennessee, was one of the leading voices for this position. In 1835 fighting broke out between the Texans and Mexican troops. From Mexico City, President Antonio López de Santa Anna declared that he would personally lead the Mexican army into Texas and crush the revolution. His forces' victories at the Alamo and at Goliad brought a declaration of independence from the Texas rebels on 2 March 1836. On 21 April, Santa Anna's army was routed by the Texas militia, led by Houston, at the Battle of San Jacinto, after which the Mexican leader promised to withdraw Mexican armed forces south of the Rio Grande and recognize the independence of Texas.

The official U.S. response to the events in Texas was measured but could not conceal American moral support for the rebels; most of the public saw them as chips off the American block and were disturbed about the killing of prisoners by Santa Anna at both the Alamo and Goliad. However, the nation remained officially neutral. This did not stop hundreds of Americans from crossing into Texas to join the fight, or the shipment sent by private citizens and businessmen of large amounts of weapons and other supplies to the Texans. The Mexican government and people, stunned by their defeat in Texas, turned their wrath on the United States. Mexican newspapers and politicians clamored for some response, and relations between the two nations continued to deteriorate. Santa Anna, disgraced by his defeat at San Jacinto, regained stature in Mexico following his loss of a leg while fighting French invaders in 1838 and now demanded the recapture of the lost territory. Trade also diminished. By 1840 annual trade between Mexico and the United States had plummeted to less than $7 million; by 1845 it was less than $3 million.

After 1836 Texas was an independent republic. Many Americans demanded its annexation; Mexico, which did not recognize the agreement signed by Santa Anna, declared that such an action would mean war. The future of Texas was complicated by the issue of slavery. Antislavery forces in the United States fought against the annexation of Texas with its large population of slaves. Proslavery expansionists were equally vigorous in calling for action. For eight years neither Mexico nor the United States took direct action on the issue of Texas. American officials were disturbed over French and British political maneuvering in Texas; both had recognized the republic and signed treaties of commerce and friendship. In addition, the United States still had its eyes on Texas and the Mexican territories of New Mexico and California. Mexican officials merely restated their position: annexation would mean war. Relations between Mexico and Texas were rocky, at best. Sporadic border battles erupted throughout this period, and in 1842 a group of Texans tried unsuccessfully to capture the city of Santa Fe in the New Mexico territory.

War with the United States

By 1844 the United States had decided it could wait no longer for annexation. The concept of "Manifest Destiny"—the notion that the United States had a right, even an obligation, to expand—was at its high point in the American consciousness, and visions of a United States literally stretching from sea to sea dominated the nation's culture. Texas was merely a stepping-stone. Concern over British and French influence in Texas was also a factor. And southern congressmen kept up a steady chant for the annexation of the territory. Democratic presidential candidate James Polk based his successful 1844 presidential campaign on the issue of expansion, calling for the annexation of Texas, California, and the Oregon Territory. Early in 1845 outgoing president John Tyler, keen on making his mark on history, secured a joint resolution from Congress annexing Texas to the United States. Mexico immediately broke off diplomatic relations.

President Polk made one clumsy attempt to arrive at a peaceful solution to U.S.-Mexican differences. In 1845 he sent John Slidell to Mexico as the new U.S. minister. His goal was to arrange the purchase of California and New Mexico and the settlement of the Texas problem. Mexican officials were incensed. They refused to accept Slidell's credentials, for such an act might indicate acceptance of the Texas annexation. When news leaked out about Slidell's proposal to buy the other Mexican territories, a nationalistic wave of criticism erupted in Mexico. Slidell left Mexico City after only a few months.

Angry over what he perceived as Mexican intransigence, President Polk ordered U.S. troops to the Rio Grande in January 1846. It was a provocative move, since the border between Mexico and Texas had never been definitively determined. Mexico responded by also sending forces to the Rio Grande. It seemed only a matter of time before matters erupted, and they did so in May 1846 when fighting broke out between U.S. and Mexican forces. Polk, arguing the dubious position that "Mexico . . . has invaded our territory and shed American blood upon American soil," asked for and received a declaration of war from Congress. Despite some opposition in the United States, especially from opponents of the expansion of slavery, Polk had cleverly portrayed the war as one to defend American honor and the nation's fighting men. Over the next two years the United States would suffer more than thirteen thousand deaths, of which nearly twelve thousand were due to disease and other causes; more than seventeen hundred men were killed in action.

The Mexican War lasted until February 1848, when the Treaty of Guadalupe Hidalgo was negotiated. Under this treaty, Mexico ceded half of its territory to the United States in exchange for a $15 million indemnity and the assumption by the American government of more than $3 million in claims against Mexico by U.S. citizens. The United States had acquired the vast California and New Mexico territories and settled the issue of Texas, nearly doubling the nation's size. There had even been a call to annex all of Mexico, but this had withered quickly. Mexico was shattered. Not only had it lost half of its territory, but also thousands of lives and millions of pesos spent on the conflict. Animosity toward the United States had never been higher.

Yet in one particular instance there was an interest on the part of some Mexicans to become part of the United States. In 1847 Mexican officials in the Yucatán region asked for American assistance in putting down a revolt of the Mayan natives. By 1848, with the situation in the Yucatán deteriorating, the Mexican governor went to so far as to offer the region as a protectorate of the United States. Polk and his aides took the offer seriously, and Congress was informed of the situation. The ensuing debate in Congress, however, indicated that there was little interest in annexing the Yucatán, aside from that of some expansion-minded southerners. When officials in the region hinted that they might make the same offer to various European nations, Polk responded with a reaffirmation of the Monroe Doctrine, declaring that areas in the Western Hemisphere could not offer themselves to the rule of other sovereign nations.

Civil war and empire

Events following the war did nothing to lessen the hatred of most Mexicans for the United States. A filibustering expedition by William Walker into Lower California in 1853 suggested that the United States harbored additional territorial designs on Mexican land. The decision by Santa Anna (who had once again returned to power, this time as "perpetual dictator") to negotiate the sale of additional Mexican territory to the United States in 1854 (the Gadsden Purchase) rearoused Mexican nationalism, which eventually drove him from power in 1855. In 1858 the American minister in Mexico, John Forsyth, urged his government to use its military to force the Mexicans to negotiate more favorably on issues such

as the U.S. purchase of more territory, additional claims emanating from the recent war, and other matters. From that point on, relations between Mexico, embroiled in civil war, and the United States, drifting toward a civil war of its own, remained tense.

In 1860 the revolutionary forces of Benito Juárez claimed success, and in early 1861 Juárez entered Mexico City as the new leader of Mexico. His Liberal regime was popular with many Americans, and the new president seemed determined to improve relations between the two nations. When America's Civil War broke out in April 1861, Juárez committed his country to a policy of neutrality, but it quickly became apparent that it was a decidedly pro-Union neutrality. None of this, however, meant an end to the fighting in Mexico. The continuing civil war in Mexico (and the outbreak of the Civil War in the United States) provided an opportunity for Great Britain, Spain, and France to organize a military effort against Mexico in 1861 that was designed to collect debts and other claims. While settlements with Great Britain and Spain were quickly worked out, France's actions indicated that it had a larger plan in mind. After an initial setback French troops defeated Juárez's forces and drove the Mexican president from the capital. Napoleon III seemed intent on reestablishing a French empire in the New World, and when Mexican Conservatives asked him to help in providing a new monarch for Mexico, he obliged by putting Maximilian, archduke of Austria, in power in 1864. Juárez and his supporters turned to guerrilla warfare against the regime.

The United States protested the French action and did not recognize the government of Maximilian. Nevertheless, despite pleas from the deposed Juárez, no direct U.S. action was taken. The attention of President Abraham Lincoln and his government was focused, not surprisingly, on the Civil War; problems in Mexico would have to wait. When the war ended in 1865, more than fifty thousand U.S. troops were dispatched to the border with Mexico and U.S. diplomats expressed their desire that the French leave. Unofficially, shipments of arms and supplies, along with some American volunteers, continued to come across the U.S. border to aid Juárez. Napoleon III needed only a little prodding; the Mexican experiment had been a financial sinkhole. In 1867 the last of the French troops departed. Maximilian's government quickly fell to the attacks of Juárez's forces, and the "emperor" was captured and executed.

Warmer Relations

While Mexican suspicions of the United States were never to dissipate entirely, the U.S. stand against the French occupation did serve to produce somewhat warmer relations between Mexico and the United States. President Juárez, now restored to power as president, was grateful for the American help during his struggle against Maximilian and the French. He acted quickly to settle two of the most troublesome matters existing between the United States and Mexico: claims and border problems.

Claims and border problems

The claims issue dealt with claims by American citizens for damage to property during Mexican civil uprisings; claims by Mexico for damages caused by American filibusters; and a dizzying host of others. In 1868 the U.S. and Mexican governments signed an agreement whereby a joint commission would judge the validity of the claims. By late 1877, the commission had finished its work. More than two thousand claims were studied; fewer than four hundred were approved. As in most such cases, few of the claimants on either side were entirely satisfied with the decisions, but an annoying diplomatic matter had been resolved in a peaceful manner.

The border issue was much more problematic. No longer was this matter concerned with territorial acquisitions by the United States. The focus now was on protecting American and Mexican citizens on both sides of the border from raids by bandits and Native Americans. There were constant complaints about robberies, personal depredations, and cattle rustling. The United States charged that Mexican officials were incompetent and uninterested in the problem, and that American citizens were suffering constant losses. U.S. military men on the border requested permission for "hot pursuits" into Mexican territory. Mexico responded that it, too, was suffering, and that according to the 1848 treaty ending the Mexican-American War, the United States was responsible for controlling the Native American attacks along the border. Juárez, and his successor Sebastian Lerdo de Tejada, grappled unsuccessfully with this problem.

The Díaz era

In 1876 Lerdo was overthrown by Porfirio Díaz, a general in the Mexican army. Díaz eventually established a dictatorship that lasted until 1911. In the United States his assumption of power was looked upon with skepticism and concern. Juárez's Liberal regime, and the peaceful transfer of power to Lerdo, had convinced some Americans that Mexico was achieving political maturity. Relations between the United States and Mexico had improved dramatically since the 1850s. Díaz's revolt seemed a throwback to the chaotic 1840s and 1850s in Mexico, raising concerns that this military figure might not be as committed to good U.S.-Mexico relations as his predecessors were. On the basis of these concerns, the United States postponed de jure recognition of the regime.

Díaz sensed that a successful settlement of the border problems might be enough to push the United States into recognizing his government. To that end he increased the number of Mexican troops along the border area to better police it, and he also entered into negotiations with the United States to permit mutual border crossings in pursuit of criminals or rampaging Native Americans. These actions, together with the demands by American businessmen and investors for an end to the diplomatic limbo, persuaded the U.S. government to grant official recognition in April 1878.

From that point on, economic issues dominated the relations between Mexico and the United States. The days of territorial expansion by the United States at the expense of Mexico were over, and the animosities of the Mexican-American War were slowly fading. Settlement of the claims and border problems and the recognition of the Díaz regime ushered in a new era in U.S.-Mexican relations. Díaz was an ardent supporter of foreign investment and foreign trade, and his rule during the late nineteenth century coincided with a tremendous growth of U.S.-Mexican trade as well as direct U.S. investment in Mexico.

Despite the gradual warming of relations during the Juárez-Lerdo years, U.S.-Mexican trade had not increased significantly. By 1870 total trade amounted to only about $9 million. Under Díaz's regime, tax systems were overhauled, laws that had inhibited trade and commerce were scrapped or modified, and Mexico welcomed American investors. As a result by 1890 total trade had increased to $36 million. By the 1890s the United States purchased more than three-quarters of Mexico's total exports and accounted for nearly 60 percent of Mexico's imports.

Growth in investments

The growth of American investment in Mexico was even more striking. By the end of the Díaz dictatorship in 1911, U.S. citizens and companies had invested more than $600 million in Mexico. Mexico had become the only nation in Latin America in which direct U.S. investments outstripped British investments. The lion's share of that amount was invested in two areas: railroads and mining. Railroads were essential to the bustling Mexican economy and to its links with the United States. U.S. investors poured more than $250 million into railroad concessions in Mexico. American money was also heavily invested in mining in Mexico. By the 1890s the Díaz government had rescinded laws that kept subsoil minerals as the property of the nation and had established new laws that allowed for the development of the oil industry. Nearly $270 million in U.S. investment was in mining by 1911, not only for gold and silver but also for iron, copper, and oil. American investors were also attracted to real estate in Mexico. New, more liberal laws concerning the foreign ownership of land attracted more than $40 million of U.S. money. By 1910 nearly one-fourth of Mexico's total land was owned by foreigners, with Americans accounting for half of that total.

American investors (and investors from Great Britain, France, and elsewhere) were attracted by the liberal economic policies of the Díaz regime and by the stability of his dictatorship. For Mexico and the United States, the last decades of the nineteenth century were quiet and, for some, profitable. Yet the seeds of future conflicts were being planted. By the late nineteenth century some Mexican politicians and citizens were raising the alarm against the foreign economic penetration—and possible domination—of Mexico. The foreign ownership of vast tracts of land, mines, and oil fields seemed to some Mexican nationalists a selling-out of the national heritage and future. The United States, as the nearest of these foreign threats, drew some especially harsh criticism, indicating that the wounds of 1848 had not entirely healed. In 1911 Mexico exploded in revolution against Díaz. His fall, and the repercussions of the Mexican Revolution, in which the United States would intervene extensively, would dramatically change the U.S.-Mexican relationship into one resembling the suspicion and rancor characteristic of the 1840s and 1850s.

See also **Expansion; Filibusters; Gadsden Purchase; Manifest Destiny; Mexican War; Texas.**

Bibliography

Cline, Howard Francis. *The United States and Mexico.* Cambridge, Mass.: Harvard University Press, 1963.

De Léon, Arnoldo. *They Called Them Greasers: Anglo Attitudes toward Mexicans in Texas, 1821–1900.* Austin: University of Texas Press, 1983.

Garber, Paul N. *The Gadsden Treaty.* Gloucester, Mass.: P. Smith, 1959.

Gregg, Robert D. *The Influence of Border Troubles on Relations between the United States and Mexico, 1876–1910.* Baltimore: Johns Hopkins University Press, 1937.

Hanna, Alfred, and Kathryn Abbey Hanna. *Napoleon III and Mexico: American Triumph over Monarchy.* Chapel Hill: University of North Carolina Press, 1971.

Hatfield, Shelley Ann Bowen. *Chasing Shadows: Indians along the United States–Mexico Border, 1876–1911.* Albuquerque: University of New Mexico Press, 1998.

Joseph, Gil. *Revolution from Without: Yucatan, Mexico, and the United States, 1880–1924.* New York and Cambridge, U.K.: Cambridge University Press, 1982.

Liss, Sheldon B. *A Century of Disagreement: The Chamizal Conflict, 1864–1964.* Washington, D.C.: University Press of Washington, 1965.

Manning, William R. *Early Diplomatic Relations between the United States and Mexico.* Baltimore: Johns Hopkins University Press, 1916. Reprint, New York: AMS, 1971.

Moseley, Edward H. "The United States and Mexico, 1810–1850." In *United States–Latin American Relations, 1800–1850: The Formative Generations,* Edited by T. Ray Shurbutt. Tuscaloosa: University of Alabama Press, 1991.

Nelson, Anna. *Secret Agents: President Polk and the Search for Peace with Mexico.* New York: Garland, 1988.

Raat, W. Dirk. *Mexico and the United States: Ambivalent Vistas.* Athens, Ga.: University of Georgia Press, 1992.

Schmitt, Karl M. *Mexico and the United States, 1821–1973: Conflict and Coexistence.* New York: Wiley, 1974.

Schoonover, Thomas D. *Dollars over Dominion: The Triumph of Liberalism in Mexican–United States Relations, 1861–1867.* Baton Rouge: Louisiana State University Press, 1978.

Vázquez, Josefina Zoraida, and Lorenzo Meyer. *The United States and Mexico.* Chicago: University of Chicago Press, 1985.

MICHAEL L. KRENN

MIAMI In 1566 Pedro Menéndez de Avilés, charged by the Spanish government with exploring Florida, arrived in south Florida, where the Tequesta Indians lived along the Miami River. De Avilés established the first white settlement in the region. Between 1570 and 1704 the Tequestas were decimated by European diseases and warfare and eventually disappeared. Creeks from Georgia and Alabama moved into the area and combined their tribes as the Seminoles. White settlers began to trickle into the area during the early 1800s, and by 1830 a few plantations along the Miami River produced sugarcane, bananas, corn, and tropical fruits. White migration threatened Seminole communities and precipitated a series of wars between whites and American Indians that began in 1816. Finally defeated in 1858, the Seminoles were forced to resettle in Indian Territory and those who remained scattered throughout the Everglades. During Reconstruction the federal government offered 160 acres of free land to homesteaders in south Florida. Moving into the region for the free land, many settlers earned money salvaging cargo ships wrecked on the Florida reefs.

Henry Morrison Flagler extended his Florida East Coast Railway into the Miami area in April 1896 and then built the Royal Palm Hotel. More than three hundred local voters decided to incorporate the area on 28 July 1896, creating the city of Miami. Flagler ensured that the city would grow by dredging a ship channel, building homes for workers, and donating land for schools, churches, and public buildings. The black workers who arrived around 1896 provided most of the labor used to build the city, but their housing was restricted to an area called Overtown. By 1900 Miami was beginning to develop a cosmopolitan flavor.

See also **Florida; Seminole War(s).**

Bibliography

Buchanan, James E., ed. *Miami: A Chronological and Documentary History, 1513–1977*. Dobbs Ferry, N.Y.: Oceana Publications, 1978.

Didion, Joan. *Miami*. New York: Simon and Schuster, 1987.

Smiley, Nixon. *Yesterday's Florida*. Miami: E. A. Seemann, 1974.

ABEL A. BARTLEY

MICHIGAN   An American Indian word sometimes translated as "great water" or "land between the lakes," Michigan was the name the French gave to one of the Great Lakes. In 1787, when Thomas Jefferson helped design political plans for the huge Northwest Territory, he named part of it "Michigania." From the time Michigan was admitted to the Union in 1837, it has been the only state consisting of two peninsulas and bordered by four Great Lakes. It owns the longest shoreline of any state except Alaska.

Their strategic Great Lakes location made Michigan's two peninsulas desirable, and the French were the first to visit and claim Michigan. In 1754, French and British rivalry erupted into the French and Indian War in North America, and in 1760 the British flag went up over Michigan's forts. The Ottawa Indian leader Pontiac ultimately failed in his effort during the summer of 1863 to lead a rebellion against the English, and, later that year, a peace treaty signed in Paris formally gave New France (Canada) to Great Britain.

During the American Revolution (1775–1783), Michigan became the center of British power in the West. According to the treaty that ended the war, Britain agreed to hand over Michigan and its forts, but for thirteen years it delayed on the grounds that the United States had not lived up to its treaty obligations. When the U.S. flag finally went up over Michigan forts in 1796, Detroit was the only settled community, a village of about five hundred people.

Under the Northwest Ordinance of 1787, each territory could apply for statehood once its population reached sixty thousand. The ordinance outlawed slavery, but a ruling early in the nineteenth century allowed owners to retain slaves they had held before 1796. Slaves remained in the census count when the Michigan territorial legislature made slavery illegal in 1833.

In 1805, Michigan became a separate territory with Detroit as its capital and William Hull, an easterner, its first governor. Just before Hull's arrival, ashes from a baker's pipe caused a fire that burned down most of Detroit, and residents were still struggling to rebuild the city when Congress declared war on Britain in 1812. Within the first weeks of war the British captured the fort on Mackinac Island, and Governor Hull surrendered the fort at Detroit. U.S. forces recaptured Detroit after Admiral Oliver Hazard Perry's small fleet defeated the British on Lake Erie in 1813. The British did not relinquish Fort Mackinac until 1815, when the Treaty of Ghent reestablished the prewar borders.

To increase settlement in Michigan, Lewis Cass, territorial governor from 1813 to 1831, attempted to counter the effects of the Detroit fire, the war, and unflattering images of the territory that had been spread by government surveyors, who promoted Ohio, and by John Jacob Astor's American Fur Company agents, who wanted to protect the Mackinac Island fur supply. In 1820 Michigan had only 8,765 non-Indian residents, but several events coincided to promote development in the next two decades. Cass sent out his own surveying expedition, which reported favorably on Michigan's opportunities, and in 1820 Congress reduced the price of land to $1.25 per acre and the minimum purchase to eighty acres. Cass personally negotiated treaties with Indians that opened most of Michigan's land for purchase by the mid-1830s, and improved transportation helped bring farm families from the East. Steamboats began to traverse the Great Lakes in 1817, and the Erie Canal opened in 1825. The Ohio Turnpike joined Michigan's new Chicago Road and Territorial Road edging westward, and stagecoaches linked Detroit with Saint Joseph on Lake Michigan by 1834. The first railroads were running by 1840.

"Michigan fever" made it the fastest growing state or territory in the nation. In 1835, with well over sixty thousand residents, Michigan adopted a constitution. Drawing on the constitutions of eastern states but incorporating frontier convictions, the Michigan constitution granted the vote to every white male over twenty-one, including aliens, and established Michigan as a leader in providing funding and direction for public education.

A border dispute with Ohio, grandiosely termed the Toledo War, delayed congressional approval of statehood until Michigan agreed to compromise. Michigan reluctantly accepted the western part of the Upper Peninsula, and Ohio gained the mouth of the Maumee River, which Ohioans wanted for a canal. Michigan became a state in January 1837. The capital remained in Detroit until 1847, when legislators voted to relocate it to a new town they named Lansing. Only farmland at the time, the site was more centrally situated than Detroit and more acceptable to rural voters, who mistrusted the city, its immigrants, and its vulnerability to Canada.

By the eve of the Civil War, Michigan's population had reached 749,113 people, only one-third of whom had been born in the state. American-born residents arrived from New York, New England, Ohio, and Pennsylvania. Nearly one-fifth of Michigan residents were foreign-born, of whom 38,787 came from the German states and 30,049 came from Ireland. In distinctive settlements, immigrants from the Netherlands established Holland in 1847 and Zeeland in 1848 and were a significant presence in most towns along the west side of the Lower Peninsula. Michiganders created political, religious, and social organizations to meet their various concerns, including temperance organizations; ethnic churches; denominational colleges; Catholic, Lutheran, and Dutch parochial schools; German singing clubs; and the Republican Party.

Cass, now a prominent U.S. senator, ran for president as a Democrat in 1848. Praised by the *Detroit Free Press,* he won support among those Michigan Democrats who, like Cass, preferred to let voters in the territories decide on slavery for themselves. But the state had also become home to ardent abolitionists. In July 1854, meeting in Jackson, antislavery Democrats, Whigs, Free-Soilers, and assorted dissidents wrote a platform and nominated a slate of candidates they called Republicans. The ticket was a success in the fall election, and Kingsley Bingham became the nation's first Republican governor. Thereafter Michigan claimed that Jackson was the birthplace of the national Republican Party. Republicans advocated tariffs that pleased Michigan lumber and mining interests, and they supported railroads, roads, the Homestead Act, and an agricultural college, which pleased farmers. Immigrants and the working class kept Detroit a Democratic stronghold, but elsewhere most Michigan voters chose Republican candidates. The Republican Party won nearly every state and national election from 1854 until 1932.

Michigan Republican leaders, more radical than Abraham Lincoln in 1860, nevertheless offered their support when the party chose him over a staunch abolitionist. When the Civil War started Michigan residents came forward to save the Union regardless of party affiliation or place of birth. Between 1861 and 1865 Michigan contributed ninety thousand troops, nearly 23 percent of its male population.

Lumber, mining, industry, and a farm market

Logging in Michigan, 1893. Due to its abundance of "green gold," Michigan became a center of the timber industry, as well as the furniture industry. LIBRARY OF CONGRESS: PRINTS AND PHOTOGRAPHS DIVISION

economy were just beginning to flourish in Michigan when the Civil War spurred rapid and continuing growth. Specialized farmers produced sheep, potatoes, wheat, cherries, apples, and dairy products. Industries began to produce woolen underwear, leather shoes, ginger ale, beer, cold cereals, and other products.

By 1870 Michigan was the leading lumber producer in the country, often accounting for about one-fourth of the nation's lumber. Michigan's "green gold," more profitable than the gold found in California, gave rise to production of doors and barrels and to the furniture industry in Grand Rapids.

The products of Michigan's mines transformed the national economy. Michigan became a leading producer of gypsum and salt, materials essential to the plaster, chemical, pharmaceutical, and paint industries. More importantly, rich deposits of iron ore and copper were discovered in the Upper Peninsula in the 1840s. The Gogebic, Marquette, and Menominee Ranges made Michigan the largest producer of iron ore in the nation until 1900. In the last decades of the nineteenth century Michigan's Keweenaw Peninsula jutting into Lake Superior produced more copper than any other state, sometimes 90 percent of the nation's output. Mining companies created towns around their mines and recruited miners from Europe. The Upper Peninsula soon boasted the largest Finnish population in the United States.

Transporting raw materials and manufactured goods to and from the mines was initially difficult and expensive because Lake Superior was several feet higher than Lake Huron. Cargo had to be unloaded, carted around rapids, and then reloaded. In 1855, with state and federal land as an incentive, an engineering company opened the Saint Marys Canal and a system of locks at Sault Sainte Marie, providing a navigable waterway between the two lakes.

When the century drew to a close, the auto industry was positioned to take root and flourish in Michigan. Lumber and mines had created an industrial base. Farms supplied city dwellers with food, while farm families bought manufactured goods. Detroit had skilled and semiskilled workforces, and unskilled immigrants were arriving from Europe in search of work. And among Michigan's lumber, railroad, and copper barons were entrepreneurs with capital to risk on interesting ideas. By the spring of 1896, when Charles King and Henry Ford first drove their autos on Detroit streets, Michigan residents were poised to contribute to changes that would reach well beyond the state's borders.

See also **Detroit; Hunting and Trapping; Iron; Lumber and Timber Industry; Mining and Extraction; Natural Resources; Northwest Territory; War of 1812.**

Bibliography

Dunbar, Willis F., and George S. May. *Michigan: A History of the Wolverine State.* 3d ed., revised by George S. May. Grand Rapids, Mich.: Eerdmans, 1995. The single most valuable book for a detailed and comprehensive history of Michigan; original edition published in 1965.

Hathaway, Richard J., ed. *Michigan: Visions of Our Past.* East Lansing, Michigan State University Press, 1989.

Kestenbaum, Justin L., ed. *The Making of Michigan, 1820–1860: A Pioneer Anthology.* Detroit, Mich.: Wayne State University Press, 1990.

JoEllen McNergney Vinyard

MID-ATLANTIC STATES The Mid-Atlantic region—traditionally defined as the grouping of the states New York, Pennsylvania, and New Jersey—has never been as distinctive as other geographic regions such as New England or the South. Delaware is sometimes considered part of this region, though it is more accurately associated with the South because it was a slave state. Geographically, Delaware is heavily influenced by Pennsylvania and therefore is in some ways a Mid-Atlantic state. Though the region's boundaries are sometimes blurred, its undefined status is, in fact, the region's most important characteristic. The key to understanding the Mid-Atlantic throughout the nineteenth century is to view its complexity, diversity, and fluidity as a model for understanding the problems, issues, and relationships of the rest of the nation.

The region is united through its relationship to the Atlantic Ocean and its corresponding connections to the Hudson, Ohio (formed by the confluence of the Monongahela and Allegheny), Delaware, and Susquehanna Rivers, as well as a host of other smaller rivers and tributaries. The Mid-Atlantic region was also the preeminent region of the construction of canals throughout the 1800s. Using their natural waterways as connection points, these canals provided a route over which boats carried manufactured products from the East to the West and farm products and raw materials from the West to the East. The most important and notable of these canals, the Erie Canal, opened a water passage from the Hudson River in eastern New York to the Great Lakes in the Midwest, and was completed in 1825. It was enlarged several times over the next three decades, testifying to both its importance and need. Port cities were an important part of the region's cultural and economic character. With such centers as New York and Philadelphia, as well as Camden, New Jersey, Buffalo, New York, and Erie, Pennsylvania, the region flourished in the maritime trade, shipping both the nation's and the world's goods.

The region was dominated throughout the nineteenth century by two of the country's major states, New York and Pennsylvania, along with the urban centers of New York City and Philadelphia. These areas were major economic, agricultural, shipping, and population centers in the early national period, and they continued to dominate in these aspects in the antebellum and industrial periods through to the end of the century. For the entire century, New York and Philadelphia were the two largest cities in America in terms of population and wealth, were two of its busiest ports, and were among the major industrial centers.

Though the Mid-Atlantic led the nation in these areas, it was also marked by its changing character. Within the first two decades of the century, New York replaced Virginia as the most heavily populated state and became the center of immigration and migration through its links to the Erie Canal and New York City's position as the main clearing port for immigrants. Pennsylvania grew in population by some 480 percent from 1800 to 1860, adding over 2.3 million inhabitants and a growing diversity of ethnic cultures. New Jersey's population increased over 300 percent during the same period.

English, Welsh, Dutch, Scots-Irish, Irish, and German immigrants made up the bulk of the region's population growth during the first half of the century. As the Mid-Atlantic led the transformation of the nation into industrialism during the last two decades of the century, eastern Europeans, the predominant group, and others joined these groups. This caused a shift in the ethnic mixture and attendant culture of the region. This transition also caused the region's population to double again in the last forty years of the century. Immigration was of vital importance to the region and influenced many of its social, political, and economic concerns. At times the region's population was almost 25 percent foreign born. The area's position as one of the major entry points (New York City being the principal entry point in the nation) for those seeking a haven in the United States also helped define its character.

The ethnic diversity contributed to a wide array of religious diversity and a demand for religious toleration throughout the region. The religions of the various groups included Anglican, Quaker, Huguenot, Amish, Catholic, and Russian Orthodox. Two of the most important black congregations in the nation, the African Methodist Episcopal and African Methodist Episcopal Zion churches, founded in Philadelphia in 1787 and in New York in 1796, respectively, flourished during the nineteenth century, as blacks at that time made up a large percentage of the Methodists in the United States. Religious toleration, which emerged out of necessity, and through mostly voluntary channels, had a significant impact on the religious debates and directions of the nation as these matters were worked into law and custom.

At the beginning of the century the Mid-Atlantic region was very much a product of its past. As the location of the nation's first two capitals; home to a very diverse political, religious, and cultural landscape; and possessor of a high concentration of the nation's intellectual and cultural elite, the region entered the century already important in shaping the institutions, the laws, and the future of the young country. One of the most important positions occupied by the Mid-Atlantic was as the agricultural backbone of the nation. With the exception of New Jersey, the states in the region were predominantly rural and involved in agriculture. Crops such as wheat, corn, and rye made the region an essential supplier of the nation's food—a position that it relinquished as the nation grew and the Midwest became the nation's dominant agricultural area. Neverthe-

less, the Mid-Atlantic continued to remain important agriculturally.

New Jersey was one of the first great industrial centers. As early as 1792, Paterson had become a textile center. Later the city became known for the manufacture of locomotives and for silk production. Trenton specialized in clay products, iron, and steel. Many of New Jersey's harbor areas and coastal areas focused on maritime industries of fishing, whaling, and shipping. New Jersey's position between the two states of Pennsylvania and New York made it ideal for this, and little agriculture took place there.

By the end of the century, exemplifying the transition taking place throughout the nation, the Mid-Atlantic shifted away from agriculture as its primary economic base and moved more toward solidifying its position as the nation's manufacturing base. The area became the single largest steel manufacturing region in the world and a growing center of commerce, finance, and advertising. In addition to steel, the coal and oil industries also began in this region and quickly expanded their reach and influence to the rest of the nation. These industries had a marked impact on the region and on the character of its people. Around these industries grew a series of small cities, or "regional capitals," such as Pottsville, Pennsylvania, which grew into the economic and political center of the coal region. These second-tier cities, small-scale versions of the larger urban centers, grew up around particular industries and would later collapse with their demise. In fact, in every state within the region, the most dominant cities were not the capitals, but rather these industry-based centers.

The major industries within the Mid-Atlantic brought with them major conflicts and labor troubles. The Molly Maguires, a secret miners' society, fought against oppressive conditions in the coal mines. Their methods were sometimes violent, and ten members were executed in 1877 for their supposed crimes. A strike against the steel industry in Homestead, Pennsylvania, in 1892 turned violent, resulting in ten deaths. Throughout all the major urban centers and in the smaller industrial towns the inequality in wealth was readily apparent as one group grew rich from the labor of another.

The issues of slavery and race did not escape the region, precisely because of its location between the North and South. All of the states in the region had slaves in the late 18th century, though gradual emancipation laws were passed in Pennsylvania in 1780, in New York in 1799, and in New Jersey in 1804. The neighboring border states of Maryland and Delaware remained slave states during the Civil War. In 1860, Pennsylvania, New Jersey, and New York had a little over 131,000 free blacks. But the issue of race was no simpler in the Mid-Atlantic than in the nation. New Jersey was one of three states to vote against Lincoln's reelection; and New York witnessed the outbreak of draft riots during the war to protest both the war's direction and the cause of abolition. Not fully in the South and not quite in New England, this region suffered from its central geography almost as much as it prospered.

The defining issues for the region in Congress and in national politics were as varied and complicated as the region itself. Tariffs, immigration, trusts, abolition, secession, political machines, labor disputes, corruption, monetary reform, regulation, veterans' pensions, imperialism, and progressive reforms all found their way into the politics of the Mid-Atlantic. Tariffs were often supported by some to protect the growth of the region's industries, but opposed by others due to the region's dependence on maritime transportation. Immigration brought the workers necessary to fuel the economic and agricultural expansion of the Mid-Atlantic, but also brought with it the problems of a varied ethnic and racial culture. These were not easy problems to work out, often resulting in the development of distinct neighborhoods, open ethnic and religious clashes, and a cacophony of calls for change. Both Republicans and Democrats claimed dominance in the region at various times throughout the period, and people followed shifts in the issues of race, foreign affairs, and domestic troubles according to their party loyalties.

In the area's major cities the nation's largest and most important urban political machines rose to power. Tammany Hall in New York and the organization run by Matthew Quay and Boies Penrose in Philadelphia controlled politics in those cities for several decades. While their efforts were sometimes beneficial to the cities' residents, these groups came to define corruption in the United States.

Several presidents also came out of the region, including the ineffectual James Buchanan of Pennsylvania, who served from 1857–1861, to the more popular and progressive Teddy Roosevelt, who became President in 1901 but made his mark as the chief of police in New York City and as the governor of New York State.

Despite the cultural diversity within the region, the inner workings were sometimes less open, and residents often viewed the region from within their own isolated perspectives. There was little actual identification of the collection of states as a unified region, a condition that persisted throughout the following century. Though each state possessed common traits with the others, no two seemed enough alike to ever have more than a partial connection, and this was oftentimes only with a particular part of another

state. The coastal areas of New Jersey became resorts and playgrounds for the elite from both New York and Pennsylvania throughout the latter part of the century. The famed resorts of Cape May and Atlantic City were two of the most popular for Pennsylvanians, while Asbury Park, Long Branch, and Sea Bright became havens for New Yorkers.

Those who lived in the Mid-Atlantic often saw the people and organizations of other regions as allies, reaching out to them on more occasions than the other regions reached back. They interacted, as a matter of course, with other regions, and with other countries through immigration (and emigration) and trade.

Addressing the Mid-Atlantic region as a collective whole necessarily eliminates consideration of the myriad details and particulars of each state, though certainly one can find similarities in many areas among the states. Frederick Jackson Turner called this the "typically American region" and spoke of a legacy that was present in all other regions. But Turner's idea compounds the difficulty in understanding both the region and America. As Tocqueville wrote sometime earlier, no one was totally sure what the "new American" was.

See also **Buffalo, N.Y.; Coal; Delaware; Immigration and Immigrants; Labor Movement,** *subentry on* **Unions and Strikes; New Jersey; New York City; New York State; Pennsylvania; Philadelphia; Politics,** *subentry on* **Machines and Bosses; Steel and the Steel Industry.**

Bibliography

Bliven, Bruce, Jr. *New York: A Bicentennial History.* New York: Norton, 1981.

Flemming, Thomas. *New Jersey: A Bicentennial History.* New York: Norton, 1978.

Klein, Philip S., and Ari Hoogenboom. *A History of Pennsylvania.* 2d ed. University Park: Pennsylvania State University Press, 1980.

Smallwood, Arwin D., and Jeffrey Elliot. *The Atlas of African-American History and Politics: From the Slave Trade to Modern Times.* Boston: McGraw-Hill, 1998.

Thompson, Daniel G. B. *Gateway to a Nation: The Middle Atlantic States and Their Influence on the Development of the Nation.* Rindge, N.H.: R.R. Smith, 1956.

JEROME D. BOWERS II

MIDWEST, THE   Discussions of the Midwest rarely get beyond questions of definition. No one can agree on where it is, let alone on what it is. Even residents of the region are perplexed by the label. Nebraskans generally do not believe that they have anything peculiarly regional in common with Ohioans, and vice versa. This conceptual confusion follows directly from the diversity of terrains and peoples in the most generously defined Middle West—that is, the area west of Pennsylvania, north of the Ohio River, south of Canada, and east of the 100th meridian, encompassing all of Ohio, Indiana, Illinois, Michigan, Wisconsin, Minnesota, and Iowa, and parts of Missouri, Kansas, Nebraska, and the Dakotas.

Nineteenth-century Americans referred to this region as the "West" or the "Old Northwest." The term "Middle West" became commonplace only in the early twentieth century. It then conjured up images of Jeffersonian pastoralism, of a place in a middle stage of economic and social development, frozen somewhere in between undeveloped forests and prairies and elaborate industrialized cities. In a nation half-rural and half-urban, half-agricultural and half-industrial, half-traditional and half-modern, the Middle West became in popular culture the American touchstone, a place without extremes, an area that mixed the best of the old and the new so well that it seemed more homogeneous than distinctive.

This construction of the Midwest as a bland, flat world of boosters and businessmen, farms and frustrations, was an intellectual response to the rapid emergence of the region in the nineteenth century. While individual studies have treated urban development in Chicago and Cincinnati, immigrant enclaves in Milwaukee and Cleveland, religion and ethnicity in the upper Mississippi Valley, politics in individual states, and labor, race, and gender in cities, little is known about the Midwest as a whole, about whether there existed a regional culture that was more than the sum of its parts.

A search for midwestern regionalism leads beyond the inherently fragmentary subjects of geography and demography and into the exercise of national political power and its influence on the representations of cultural identity. The area that came to be called the Midwest was the creation of national political decisions and a debate over social values and economic structures that took place within conceptual borders established by those decisions. In the end, the only substantial differences between the southern and northern banks of the Ohio River or the Great Lakes are political. Ohio, Indiana, and Illinois are midwestern states because the Ohio River was a political border as well as a commercial artery. Wisconsin and Minnesota's northern borders resulted from decades of war and diplomacy between Canada and the United States. Only in the West, where the 100th meridian marks the emergence of an arid landscape, were the borders of the Midwest anything other than arbitrary lines on a map drawn primarily for political reasons.

Origins

The origins of the Midwest lie in the actions of the American government in the 1780s. Thousands of American Indians and hundreds of French settlers lived between the Great Lakes and the Ohio River. Great Britain claimed control of the region, but its power was more asserted than demonstrated. Meanwhile, a multitude of American citizens were beginning to migrate west from Pennsylvania and northward from Kentucky. The U.S. Congress, eager to establish its claim to the area and to collect revenue from land sales, passed a series of laws intended to organize the region as a U.S. territory. The Land Ordinance of 1785 provided for the survey and auction of square townships. Not only did this system make it easier to speculate in lands at a distance, it literally marked the claim of the United States.

More important, the Ordinance of 1787 created the procedures whereby the region could be assimilated into the United States and laid down basic principles about the character of society in what Congress called the Northwest Territory. A nationally appointed governor, secretary, and three judges would govern the territory until there were five thousand "free male inhabitants of full age." Residents were then permitted to elect a lower house, which, with a nationally appointed upper house, would constitute a territorial legislature. When there were sixty thousand people and Congress had certified the existence of a plan for a republican government (willing to bear its share of national debts and to submit to national authority), the people could form a state.

Widely praised for creating a mechanism whereby conquered regions could become equal parts of the American Union, the ordinance was also a remarkably strong assertion of national authority. The president and Congress were in loco parentis to the residents of the territory until they decided they were ready for the responsibilities as well as the rights of citizenship. Over the course of the nineteenth century, the residents of Ohio (1803), Indiana (1816), Illinois (1818), Missouri (1821), Michigan (1837), Iowa (1846), Wisconsin (1848), Minnesota (1858), Kansas (1861), Nebraska (1867), North Dakota (1889), and South Dakota (1889) met those qualifications.

Statehood campaigns dominated early politics in the region. Details varied, depending on personalities, economic conditions, and national politics. In general, however, advocates of statehood attacked the arbitrariness and corruption of their territorial government and demanded more democracy and local control, while opponents warned of the financial and political costs of giving up territorial status.

Iowa City, Iowa. Suggestions of commercial development along a road in Iowa City, only eight years after Iowa achieved statehood in 1846. Photograph by Carrie Weatherby, 1854. LIBRARY OF CONGRESS

Some also suggested that unrefined frontierspeople were ill-prepared for the responsibilities of citizenship.

Territorial residents could argue about statehood and lobby for or against it. But they could not achieve it without the permission of the federal government. Statehood was granted, not won. In the end, the admission of a state to the Union served the dual function of affirming local control and national authority. Congress granted the residents the right to form their own government. In so doing, the electorate often chose a more "democratic" form, with a weak governor and judiciary and a strong legislature, but one that remained within the parameters of a national political system.

Regional Identity

The Northwest Ordinance did more than outline a process for transforming territories into states. It was also a charter document, laying down expectations about life in the Northwest Territory and the states created from it. The citizens were to support public education and tolerate religious diversity in order to promote morality and good government. They were to honor contracts and treat the Indians with "good faith." They were forbidden to introduce slavery or involuntary servitude.

Historians have detailed the myriad ways in which settlers violated these injunctions. Treaties with Indians were ignored almost from the moment they were signed. Some blacks were held in bondage in Illinois as late as the 1840s. Support for public education lagged well behind the economic development of the region. Still, the territorial experience established basic principles that residents began to rally around as characteristics of regional identity in the 1830s and 1840s. If the national government did not dictate the course of midwestern history, it decisively shaped its contours. The national government defeated Indians and acquired their lands; it defeated the British in Canada in the War of 1812 and established the permanent northern border of the United States. In the first decades of the nineteenth century, Congress created a system for public land sales that oversaw the transfer of millions of acres of land into the hands of American citizens.

These actions attracted particular kinds of people to the region north of the Ohio River. New Englanders spread across the Burned-Over District of New York into northern Ohio and Michigan in the 1820s and 1830s. Upland southerners, many of them Quakers or Methodists with religious scruples about slavery, if not racism, ventured into the Ohio Valley. Large numbers of German immigrants arrived in the

Cincinnati, Ohio. With its location on the Ohio River and development after the opening of the Erie and Miami canals, Cincinnati—the "Queen City"—secured its place as a major city in the growing American landscape. Photograph by Charles Waldock, 1870. LIBRARY OF CONGRESS

1840s and 1850s and gave a distinctive tone to areas in which they concentrated, as did Scandinavians and eastern Europeans in the second half of the century.

Most of these immigrants were committed to a free-labor ideology and small-scale capitalism in which slavery had no place. Indeed, the absence of slavery was as central to the definition of the Midwest as its presence was to the South. It was the fact that slavery was illegal on its northern shores and legal on its southern ones that made the Ohio River a border. Although demographically and geographically much of Kentucky was very similar to southern Ohio, Indiana, and Illinois, it was not part of the Midwest because it was a slave state. Its politics were not affected by the antislavery forces that dominated parts of northern Ohio and Illinois. Slavery and the presence of large numbers of blacks made Kentucky different from Indiana.

Hundreds of white men in southern Ohio, Indiana, and Illinois flaunted the prohibition on slavery, using indentures and other legal means to secure their "servants" into a permanently inferior condition. But voters in territorial Indiana and Illinois refused to legalize the institution. Their decision had little to do with sympathy for African Americans. Rather, they feared the impact of slavery on their developing worlds. They did not want the presence of enslaved African Americans driving down wages, driving up land prices, creating a class of aristocratic "nabobs," and encouraging white immorality. The Old Northwest was no haven for African Americans. For the first half of the nineteenth century, state legal codes restricted the movement of blacks and required them to post bonds to take up permanent residence. Abolitionist sentiment and the Underground Railroad notwithstanding, it was not by accident that the Midwest remained an overwhelmingly white region until the early twentieth century. As late as 1900 fewer than 3 percent of the people in the region were African Americans.

Slavery made Missouri and Kansas ambiguous regionally. In both places, people bitterly contested the strong presence of slavery. The Missouri Compromise of 1820 admitted Missouri as a slave state despite opposition to the institution within its borders. As Dred Scott (the black plaintiff in an unsuccessful suit for freedom in 1857) discovered and the author Mark

Twain's characters Huck Finn and Jim knew, it was this political decision that made Missouri different from Illinois and Iowa, not geography or demography. The reverse was true in Kansas when, after years of bloody civil war, it entered the Union as a free state in 1861. On the critical issues of slavery and race, political decisions and national authority were central to an emerging regional identity.

By the 1850s the Midwest had achieved stability. Ohio, Indiana, and Illinois were exporting more people farther west than they were importing. Cincinnati, Chicago, Detroit, and Milwaukee had become major American cities. Railroads linked the region internally and with the rest of the continent. Public education was taking root in state-supported systems. Dozens of small colleges and public universities dotted the landscape. Above all, there were hundreds of small communities dominated by networks of persister families interested not only in economic development and social improvement but in constructing a mythological past for their towns and states. Their stories, encapsulated in a plethora of county histories, depicted the settlement of the region as the transformation of an Indian "wilderness" by respectable pioneers into a model vision of commerce and culture. In general, leading midwesterners emphasized the importance of free labor and individual autonomy. They were committed to a Euroamerican society in which economic development and social improvement went hand in hand.

On the eve of the Civil War, Ohio, Indiana, Illinois, Michigan, Iowa, Wisconsin, and Minnesota constituted a region whose distinctiveness rested on real and perceived differences from the slaveholding states, particularly in its commitment to free labor, capitalist development, and Protestant-tinged moral improvement. The sectional crisis solidified this self-image. The Civil War was the defining moment in the history of the Midwest. Its most influential residents increasingly saw themselves as living in between the industrializing, urban Northeast and the backward, plantation South. The fact that they were in the middle figuratively as well as geographically became a point of pride. They were people of common sense and compromise. Others were southerners or easterners; midwesterners were Americans. Why should they accept a regional label when they were defining the nation?

Contesting Regional Identity

After the Civil War, the Midwest was arguably the most influential section of the United States. Compared to the South or the West, it was a prosperous place; its residents had little sense that other parts of the United States were getting more than their fair share of federal largesse and attention. In the last third of the nineteenth century, national power seemed to be shifting to the region. Between 1860 and 1900, the Midwest supplied six of nine U.S. presidents (Abraham Lincoln, Ulysses Grant, Rutherford B. Hayes, James Garfield, Benjamin Harrison, William McKinley). Meanwhile, Chicago became the central interior city of the nation, processing and marketing the natural resources and agricultural products of the Great Lakes and the Great Plains to markets throughout the world.

The Midwest was never a land of consensus, however. Regional values had been contested from the beginning in everything from politics to manners. Southern migrants and their descendants often continued to identify with their place of origin, voting for Democrats and sympathizing with resistance to a Republican-controlled federal government. European immigrants, especially Catholics, also fought efforts to create homogeneous systems of public education and popular culture. The very diversity of the region encouraged the formation of identities around religion or ethnicity rather than place.

Religion was the most important factor dividing midwesterners. Even rural states such as Iowa contained a kaleidoscope of Christian denominations. There was, moreover, a tribal character in the overlap of religious and ethnic identities. Because immigrants tended to migrate as families and to settle in the same areas, the region was a checkerboard of ethnic enclaves.

After the Civil War, Republicans were under enormous pressure from their core base of support—middle-class Protestants—to do something about restricting the consumption of alcohol and encouraging tighter state control of public education. Efforts to enact prohibition met with huge opposition from Democratic voters, many of whom were southern whites or Catholic immigrants. They saw prohibition as an attack on their cultural traditions and the rights of local communities. There was a similar division over control of public education and a demand that English be the only language in public schools. The key voters in these cultural wars were Germans, many of them Republican voters who nonetheless had no interest in promoting cultural uniformity at the expense of their way of life.

The political debates of the late nineteenth century resolved very little. But they demonstrated the dynamism that the diversity of peoples brought to the Midwest. Regional culture was never fixed. It was fluid negotiation, constantly shifting to meet the demands of particular peoples in particular times and places. A middle-class preoccupation with character and capitalism dominated but never controlled the region. The vitality of the Midwest lay in the regularity and intensity with which its residents contested its cultural parameters. This struggle involved class as well as ethnicity and religion. Not all midwesterners strove to attain a middle-class life of respectability; many never had the opportunity to do so.

The region was unique in the late nineteenth century in its balance of agriculture and industry, countryside and cities. The lack of a depressed hinterland meant that midwestern industries depended on a strong influx of immigrant workers willing to endure harsh conditions in coal and iron mines, lumbering operations, or meatpacking and steel factories. Workers, however, frequently found conditions intolerable, especially given low and declining wages and unsympathetic employers. In the 1880s, the average annual earnings of unskilled industrial workers was around $250, half the minimum middle-class income.

Skilled and unskilled workers organized to deal with their plight. In the 1880s the Knights of Labor's efforts to create an umbrella labor union that would unite all workers in their campaigns for higher wages, better conditions, and working-class cooperation and improvement were very popular. But they disintegrated by the 1890s, destroyed by ethnic and religious differences, economic hard times, reams of bad publicity associated with the Haymarket incident in Chicago in 1886, in which eight police officers were killed, other violent "anarchist" incidents, and, above all, the coercive power of the states. Time after time, local and state governments used their police power to coerce workers to stop strikes and accede to the wishes of their employers.

Working men and women probably achieved greater success in resisting efforts to regulate their lives away from the workplace. Many lived in ethnic communities with members of extended families; they went to the same church and belonged to the same clubs. They took pleasure in drinking at local taverns and participating in various sports. Young women flaunted middle-class conventions about morality and sexuality in the ways that they dressed and the places they went.

Farm families and working-class families alike sought to protect and defend their ways of life, organized around the customs of the household and local kinship communities, from the transforming impact of machinery and national corporations. Their activities ranged from membership in the Patrons of Husbandry (the Grange) or neighborhood associations to the maintenance of traditional notions about gendered divisions of labor and the importance of social as well as economic relationships. For a few years

in the early 1890s the People's (or Populist) Party's innovative schemes for combating perennial currency and credit problems won considerable support among rural midwesterners, particularly in Minnesota, Kansas, and Nebraska. Midwestern farm families organized to develop strategies to deal with change. But they were never comfortable for extended periods of time with third-party politics or broad-based social movements; their focus was on the local and the particular.

These controversies were critical moments in the development of regional identity in the Midwest. They revealed that residents believed that the most dangerous threats to the Midwest lay in divisions within the region, rather than in the actions of the federal government or institutions in other parts of the United States or the world. If they occasionally complained bitterly about the power of railroad companies and eastern banks, they rarely united for long against outside forces, whether they were governments or corporations. Without a common enemy after the Civil War, midwesterners talked about the importance of their local, ethnic, religious, and political communities with greater regularity and far more passion than they did about any kind of overarching regional identity.

See also **American Indians,** *subentry on* **Indian Removal; Chicago; Illinois; Indiana; Iowa; Kansas; Michigan; Minnesota; Missouri; Nebraska; North Dakota; Ohio; South Dakota; Wisconsin.**

Bibliography

Cayton, Andrew R. L., and Peter S. Onuf. *The Midwest and the Nation: Rethinking the History of an American Region.* Bloomington: Indiana University Press, 1990.

Conzen, Kathleen Neils. *Immigrant Milwaukee, 1836–1860: Accommodation and Community in a Frontier City.* Cambridge, Mass.: Harvard University Press, 1976.

Cronon, William. *Nature's Metroplis: Chicago and the Great West.* New York: Norton, 1991.

Doyle, Don Harrison. *The Social Order of a Frontier Community: Jacksonville, Illinois, 1825–1870.* Urbana: University of Illinois Press, 1983.

Faragher, John Mack. *Sugar Creek: Life on the Illinois Prairie.* New Haven, Conn.: Yale University Press, 1986.

Gjerde, Jon. *The Minds of the West: Ethnocultural Evolution in the Rural Middle West, 1830–1917.* Chapel Hill: University of North Carolina Press, 1997.

Gray, Susan E. *The Yankee West: Community Life on the Michigan Frontier.* Chapel Hill: University of North Carolina Press, 1996.

Jensen, Richard. *Winning the Midwest: Social and Political Conflict, 1888–1896.* Chicago: University of Chicago Press, 1971.

Nelson, Daniel. *Farm and Factory: Workers in the Midwest, 1880–1990.* Bloomington: Indiana University Press, 1995.

Ross, Steven J. *Workers on the Edge: Work, Leisure, and Politics in Industrializing Cincinnati, 1788–1890*. New York: Columbia University Press, 1985.

Shortridge, James R. *The Middle West: Its Meaning in American Culture*. Lawrence: University Press of Kansas, 1989.

Teaford, Jon C. *Cities of the Heartland: The Rise and Fall of the Industrial Midwest*. Bloomington: Indiana University Press, 1993.

ANDREW R. L. CAYTON

MIDWIVES   Throughout history, midwifery has been the almost exclusive province of women. The definition of midwife, "a woman who assists other women in childbirth," reinforces the idea that midwifery is "women's business." During the colonial era of American history, midwives were the recognized experts in the conduct of childbirth. As such, they dominated the practice of midwifery.

At the beginning of the nineteenth century, the vast majority of American women continued to rely on midwives as birth attendants. Early-nineteenth-century midwives, like their colonial counterparts, were highly esteemed members of their communities. The typical midwife of this era was an apprenticeship-trained, older, married woman who had borne several children and who combined running a household with her midwifery practice. Most early-nineteenth-century midwives were experienced and self-assured, and their maternal and infant mortality rates compared favorably with those of medical practitioners, who most often attended the births of urban, upper-class women.

As the evolution of scientific obstetrics accelerated, increasing numbers of physicians began to serve as birth attendants. The growing reliance on "men-midwives" in the early decades of the nineteenth century brought forth a vociferous debate about the propriety of men serving as birth attendants. Many midwives and physicians supported midwifery in the name of preserving decency and morality in the birthing room. However, proponents of man-midwifery, most of whom were physicians, persuaded American women that the skill and expertise of medical men necessitated that notions about the "delicacy of the sexes" be cast aside. By mid-century, physicians had succeeded in convincing many middle- and upper-class Americans that the well-being and safety of the pregnant woman took precedence over protecting female modesty.

The growth of medical professionalism and the advancement of scientific obstetrics seemed to ensure that by century's end the midwife would be replaced by the physician. By the second half of the nineteenth century, most physicians, as well as most middle- and upper-class Americans, complacently ignored the midwife. Yet just as it appeared that the midwife would disappear from the American setting, a new and vociferous debate over her present and future role began to take shape.

The arrival of millions of immigrants from eastern and southern Europe after 1880 brought new visibility to the midwife. Midwifery was a long established and highly respected profession throughout most of Europe. After immigrant women arrived in the United States, they continued to employ midwives. By the turn of the twentieth century, many cities and towns of the urban Northeast and Midwest, where immigrants most often settled, had begun to experience an unexpected revival of midwifery.

African Americans, too, depended on the assistance of midwives. In the southern states as many as 90 percent of all African American births were attended by midwives at the close of the nineteenth century. Throughout rural, impoverished areas of America, friends and relatives were sometimes called upon to act as midwives. All told, approximately 50 percent of births in the United States were attended by midwives in 1900.

Immigrants from southern and eastern Europe, African Americans, and other poor Americans preferred midwives for a variety of reasons. Immigrants sought out midwives because they spoke the same language and shared similar traditions and customs. African American women turned to African American midwives rather than rely on an often hostile, white-dominated medical establishment. Economic considerations also caused many women to favor midwives over physicians. Generally speaking, the midwife's fee was less than half that of the physician. Moreover, midwives allowed informal payment "in kind" or on a neighborly give-and-take basis, and they often performed housekeeping and nursing services not offered by physicians.

Statistics, although limited, suggest that the maternal and infant mortality rates of late-nineteenth-century midwives, most of whom were empirically trained, were equal to or better than those of physicians. A few privately funded schools for immigrant midwives were founded during the later years of the century. However, the establishment of formal, state-regulated training programs for midwives did not occur until several decades later, when public health officials began to call for training and regulation of midwives as a way to protect them from the attacks emanating from a powerful medical establishment determined to bring about the midwife's demise. At the dawn of the twentieth century, therefore, the American midwife tenaciously held on to her time-honored position as the nation's principal birth attendant.

See also **Birth and Childbearing.**

Bibliography

Donegan, Jane B. *Women and Men Midwives: Medicine, Morality, and Misogyny in Early America.* Westport, Conn.: Greenwood, 1978.
Leavitt, Judith Walzer. *Brought to Bed: Childbearing in America, 1750–1950.* New York: Oxford University Press, 1986.
Litoff, Judy Barrett. *American Midwives, 1860 to the Present.* Westport, Conn.: Greenwood, 1978.
Ulrich, Laurel Thatcher. *A Midwife's Tale: The Life of Martha Ballard, Based on Her Diary, 1785–1812.* New York: Knopf, 1990.

JUDY BARRETT LITOFF

MILITARY ACADEMY, U.S.   An act of Congress of 16 March 1802, signed by President Thomas Jefferson, formally established the Military Academy at West Point, New York, on the site of a strategic Revolutionary War fortress. The academy was begun in part as a result of desires expressed by George Washington, among others, to train Americans in the technical arts of war (artillery and engineering). It was also established to enhance scientific education in the nation and to diversify the nation's military leadership. In 1843 Congress formally ensured a national representation for U.S. military leadership when it specified that the academy's cadets would be selected from each congressional district as well as from the territories and the nation at large.

In 1817, after years of governmental neglect and institutional disarray, Sylvanus Thayer was named commanding officer, or superintendent, at West Point. For the next sixteen years he improved administrative and organizational efficiency and established the foundation for future institutional success. He formalized a prescribed four-year curriculum grounded in mathematics, science, and engineering, and utilized some of the more advanced pedagogical thinking of his day. He continued the practice of daily recitations in small classes, provided instruction in all courses at various levels based on the abilities of cadets, and directed that each cadet pass every course in order to graduate. He improved military instruction, tightened discipline, and emphasized earlier efforts to instill ethical conduct and integrity in cadets. That emphasis continued throughout the academy's subsequent history. Thayer is recognized as the father of the Military Academy because the academy is based on the foundations and traditions he established.

To accomplish his academic goals Thayer gathered an impressive faculty, often graduates of the Military Academy, who offered a superb education in mathematics, physical sciences, and engineering. Their efforts established the academy as the first, and for several decades the premier, engineering school in the nation. Faculty members Charles Davies in mathematics, William H. C. Bartlett in engineering, mechanics, and physics, and Dennis Hart Mahan in engineering and military science provided cadets with scientific and technical skills rarely taught elsewhere in the new nation. The faculty's scholarship was widely used in courses at other colleges, and the academy's graduates helped establish technical departments at many leading universities. In addition, Mahan's writings had a major impact on the tactics used by military leaders on both sides in the Civil War.

Due to limited promotion opportunities in the nation's small peacetime army, graduates in the first half of the nineteenth century provided their greatest service through civilian contributions to the nation. Thayer's prescribed scientific and technical education, largely unprecedented among America's early colleges, enabled academy graduates to make important contributions in the design and construction of the nation's expanding railroad lines, harbors, bridges, and roads.

Although graduates served in the War of 1812 and the Seminole Wars, and with great distinction in the Mexican War, it was not until the Civil War that the Military Academy had a profound impact on America's military history. The "band of brothers" who were trained and educated in West Point's demanding environment fought side by side, or in opposition, on the battlefields of the Civil War. During that conflict academy graduates quickly rose to senior leadership positions and contributed more than four hundred generals to lead the armies of the North and South. Academy graduates Ulysses S. Grant, William T. Sherman, and Philip Sheridan became some of the most honored heroes in the North, as did Robert E. Lee and Thomas "Stonewall" Jackson in the South. Although the Military Academy has a congressionally mandated geographical diversity, and a degree of social diversity, it was not until after the end of the Civil War, in the 1870s, that the first African Americans entered the academy. During the final decades of the century, prior to the reinstitution of social segregation, a handful of African Americans attended the academy and three graduated.

Encouraged by the success of its graduates in the Civil War, the academy saw little reason to expand its curriculum beyond a focus on engineering and military science. The most notable advance after the war was in the area of physical education. Under the guidance of Herman J. Koehler, later called the Father of Army Physical Education, the academy began an extensive exercise program to supplement fencing and horsemanship. By the turn of the century, the institution that had begun as the nation's premier engineering school and had provided officers of superior talent in wartime was also training cadets to meet the physical demands of war.

Near the end of its first century, the academy selected the motto "Duty, Honor, Country," a phrase that formalized Thayer's ideals. An emphasis on character development instilled in a rigorous military environment and enhanced by a demanding academic, military, and physical program enabled academy graduates to provide both military and civilian service to the nation throughout the nineteenth century.

See also **Civil Engineering.**

Bibliography

Ambrose, Stephen E. *Duty, Honor, Country: A History of West Point.* Baltimore: Johns Hopkins University Press, 1966.

Crackle, Theodore J. *The Illustrated History of West Point.* New York: Abrams, 1991.

Pappas, George S. *To the Point: The United States Military Academy, 1802–1902.* Westport, Conn.: Praeger, 1993.

STEPHEN B. GROVE

MILITARY SERVICE

From the beginning of the Republic, American leaders have found themselves faced with a dilemma. How does a free nation, with a history of persecution by a foreign standing army, maintain its freedom while guaranteeing its security? This question, in effect, defined how the United States in the nineteenth century attempted to meet military threats within the limits of the Constitution. As society changed, so did the nature of and commitment to military service, from the volunteer armies of the Civil War to the regular troops on the frontier. Consequently, the U.S. military system in 1900 would have been unfamiliar to a citizen-soldier of 1800, who in the milieu of the early Republic would have seen a "horse soldier" of the frontier army as a threat to liberty. Conversely, the American "Regular" of 1900, in the best spirit of the Progressive Era, would have seen the 1800 militiaman as ineffectual and incompetent. Much as the political, social, and economic systems of the United States changed after 1800, the military system underwent a dramatic and irreversible transformation.

The Militia

From the beginning of the century, service in the U.S. military could be divided into several different categories. Initially, the militia was intended to be the backbone of the American military system. Following colonial traditions, it was subdivided into the standing militia (all able-bodied men of military age, usually eighteen to forty-five), the volunteer militia (voluntarily organized militiamen who paid for their own equipment and training; usually specialized units like artillery or cavalry), war volunteers (militiamen who volunteered for singular expeditions and campaigns, such as the Black Hawk War of 1832), and involuntary servers (such as draftees during the Civil War).

The militia's readiness for war varied and was based on state support for the organization. Semiannual "muster days" were common in the first decades of the century. According to John K. Mahon, the muster training day was a major event in the local community, equivalent to a county fair. He summarizes a muster training day as:

George Armstrong Custer. Custer held numerous positions in the military, serving as a brigadier general of volunteers in the Civil War at age twenty-three (1863). At Little Bighorn on 25 June 1876, he led a contingent of the Seventh Cavalry and was killed in battle. LIBRARY OF CONGRESS

start[ing] with drill, first company, and then, if numbers warranted it, battalion exercises. Officers inspected all firearms, but were lenient since many a yokel had only a shotgun. Toward noon the general or even the governor might arrive, and then all units would combine for regimental maneuvers. At the appropriate break, local folk often served a heavy repast accompanied by much imbibing. After a rest period, there would be more drill, and finally, the day's climax, a sham battle. The cavalry charged; the infantry rattled away with blank cartridges; even the artillery, wadding their guns with rags, blasted until their pieces were hot. With the noise and smoke, ladies screamed and children yelled. When all was over at sunset, the crowd, desperately tired, straggled home. (*History of the Militia and National Guard*, pp. 57–58)

Whatever the quality of muster drill days, they were too few to provide the level of competency demanded against a determined foe. President Thomas Jefferson, despite his firm belief that the militia should serve as the center of defense, fully understood the shortcomings of the militia system. These weaknesses led him to fund the establishment of a military academy at Fortress West Point in 1802, and to expand the standing army after the 1807 *Chesapeake-Leopard* affair, in which HMS *Leopard*, while searching for two damaged French ships, fired upon the USS *Chesapeake* in Norfolk Harbor. When war came in 1812, the militia system, weakened by years of general neglect and governmental indifference and lacking training and equipment, failed abysmally. More than one hundred thousand militiamen bravely responded to President James Madison's call. Their use was limited, however, by individual state governors and by short tours of duty. As a result, the militia never gained the level of unit cohesion and competence exemplified by the Regular Army at Lundy's Lane (1814) and Chippewa (1814); even the great "militia" victory at New Orleans in 1815 was due to a hefty backing of the "Cottonbalers" of the Regular Seventh Infantry Regiment.

The Volunteer Militia

The militia's failure in the War of 1812 led to a further decline of the system. By the Jacksonian era, only a few states maintained an organized militia, others depended upon the volunteer militia units for their military needs. The volunteers, much like Freemasons, took advantage of the wave of clubs, fraternities, and other organizations that swept America during the period. For many, the well-drilled and colorfully dressed volunteer units became the nineteenth-century equivalent of a country club, complete with formal dinners, members-only dances and balls, and strict rules of membership. Participation in an elite regiment, such as the New York Seventh Infantry, the "Park Avenue Seventh," could cost hundreds of dollars per year—a considerable sum at the time—for fees, dues, uniforms, and equipment.

The volunteers gained a level of training and experience unequaled by the standing militia. Since their charters were granted by the state legislatures, the volunteers were, in effect, the forerunners of the modern National Guard, and they performed many of the same duties—quelling riots, enforcing state laws, and offering their services in times of national emergency. During wartime, volunteers often served as organized units under their own leaders. This paid great dividends in military efficiency and competence; for example, some of the best volunteer regiments of the Civil War era performed better than Regular Army regiments.

However, the volunteer system began to fall apart after the Civil War. The bloody battlefields were filled with men who had sought military duty as peacetime volunteers; when those men were gone, few came forward to replace them. In the post–Reconstruction era, states were hesitant to fund or organize volunteer militia units, and most were left to wither. By the Spanish-American War of 1898, few well-drilled volunteer regiments remained, and many of these (along with the states that still had a militia) were considered under the new title of "National Guard." Their training and experience varied from state to state; many had become no more than social organizations for overage and untrained scions of prominent families. In effect, by 1898 the volunteer system had failed to supply citizen-soldiers much as the militia system had failed in 1812. After 1898 the system was scrapped, and in 1903 the National Guard was born in an attempt to ensure standardized training and equipping of state troops, and to provide a ready backup force for the standing army.

The Regular Army

The development of a standing army in the United States is a story of political ideology, wartime experience, and national change. In 1800 the tiny standing force was scattered in a handful of frontier outposts and undermanned arsenals. By 1900 the U.S. Army had regular troops from the Philippines to Puerto Rico. American "Regulars" were considered as competent as their European counterparts, and, in the racist outlook of the day, superior to technologically inferior "backward peoples."

Of the three military organizations of nineteenth-century America, the standing army, the Regulars, for several reasons had the highest level of training and competence. First, they had the time to conduct training, especially at the small-unit (company) level, unlike the militia or the volunteers. Second, the bulk of the officer corps of the Regular Army was West Point–trained, providing a sense of professionalism and cohesion lacking in the non-Regular forces. Last, many of the Regulars, especially the officers, had years of frontier combat experience against Native Americans.

The Regular Army was formed of individual volunteers. Many enlisted soldiers saw the army as an opportunity to gain clothing, food, and pay. Consequently, enlistments skyrocketed during times of economic hardship. In addition, many immigrants, especially those lacking useful skills, joined the army to find employment and fit into their new country. According to Edward Coffman, one English traveler stated in the late 1830s that the U.S. Army was formed of "the scum of the population of the older states, or . . . the worthless German, English or Irish emigrants [sic]" (*The Old Army,* p. 137). In the 1850s nearly two-thirds of the U.S. Army's recruits had been born outside the United States. Recent statistical studies of Regular Army regiments of the antebellum and post–Reconstruction periods have found a wide variety of skills in the ranks—craftsmen from blacksmiths to bookbinders, for example, were found in a survey of troops at Fort Snelling, Minnesota, in 1833. This indicates that many of the new immigrants, far from being incompetent or unemployable, were using regular service for other reasons, such as gaining citizenship quickly, learning English, or seeing the frontier.

The recruitment of troops for regular service was left to regimental "recruiting parties" until 1825, when the War Department established the General Recruiting Service in an attempt to centralize the system. Not surprisingly, most of the new recruits came from the large cities of the eastern seaboard; the Deep South provided relatively few enlisted men but many officers. In general, the Regulars throughout the century were underpaid. Cadets graduating from West Point were warned not to marry before they made the rank of captain, since their pay would be insufficient to provide for a family. Several of the most famous leaders of the Civil War, such as Ulysses S. Grant, left the Regular Army for financial reasons. For the enlisted men, pay would seem to have been sufficient. However, this belies the realities of army service in the nineteenth century. Poor food and shoddy equipment led many soldiers to spend their pay on better food (such as fresh vegetables, eggs, and "luxury" items such as alcohol and tobacco) and better uniforms. As a result many of the troops found themselves in debt to the post traders and were forced to reenlist to pay debts—the equivalent of the "company store" system employed by industrialists of the Gilded Age.

Despite these limitations the Regular Army somehow provided the soldiers necessary for national expansion. Following the Civil War the Regulars offered employment to freed slaves, the "Buffalo Soldiers." African American troops had served extremely well during the Civil War, and afterwards they were members of volunteer regiments and Reconstruction-era state militias. On the basis of their service, Congress authorized the raising of all-black (but white-led) cavalry and infantry regiments, the most famous of which were the Ninth, Tenth, Twenty-fourth, and Twenty-fifth Cavalries. Attempts to train African American officers failed because of the inherent racism of American society at the time. The experience of Lieutenant Henry O. Flipper, the first black graduate of West Point, exemplifies the problems with race and military service in the era. Ostracized at West Point, Flipper persevered and graduated in 1877, to the applause of his classmates and General William T. Sherman. Upon leaving West Point, Flipper was assigned to the all-black Tenth Cavalry. Although seemingly integrated into the "Army family," Flipper saw his career come to an abrupt end in 1882, when he was accused and convicted of making a false report. Despite the fact that white officers had not been punished for the same offense, and despite the impassioned defense of Flipper by his white regimental commander, the first African American graduate of West Point was dismissed. Not until 1998 was Flipper's court-martial overturned by presidential order and his rank restored.

Military service in nineteenth-century America reflected the concerns and goals of the society. Early fears of standing armies led to dependence upon a weak militia system, but the realities of global responsibilities at the end of the century demanded a competent professional army. The poor pay and conditions of the Regular Army never seemed to deter new recruits, although desertions were extremely numerous, especially in areas where economic booms were occurring (such as California in the 1850s). The lack of governmental support, at both state and federal levels, hampered the development of either a strong and competent militia system or a professional standing force. It was not until the United States found itself with a global empire in 1898 that permanent and lasting reforms changed the nature of military service in America.

See also **African Americans,** *subentry on* **Blacks in the**

Military; Army; Civil War, *subentry on* Battles and Combatants; Militia, State; Navy; War of 1812.

Bibliography

Coffman, Edward M. *The Old Army: A Portrait of the American Army in Peacetime, 1784–1898.* New York: Oxford University Press, 1986.

Doughty, Robert A., Ira Gruber et al., eds. *Warfare in the Western World.* 2 vols. Lexington, Mass.: D. C. Heath, 1996.

Huntington, Samuel P. *The Soldier and the State: The Theory and Politics of Civil–Military Relations.* Cambridge, Mass.: Belknap Press of Harvard University Press, 1957.

Mahon, John K. *History of the Militia and National Guard.* New York: Macmillan, 1983.

Skelton, William B. *An American Profession of Arms: The Army Officer Corps, 1784–1861.* Lawrence: University Press of Kansas, 1992.

ROBERT MACKEY

MILITARY TECHNOLOGY   The technological explosion of the nineteenth century was not a pacifistic endeavor. To a great extent the rise of American competitiveness in industry, science, and applied technology with the nations of Europe owes much to the growth of the arms industry in the United States. Like many other industrial endeavors of the century, the American arms industry was dramatically changed by sudden increases in government funding, driven by new inventions, and often crippled by a lack of public support.

The Industrial Revolution and the "American System" of Weapons Manufacture

The small arms industry provided one of the first examples of modern industrialization in America. Eli Whitney's development of interchangeable parts in 1800, meant to quickly build ten thousand muskets under a 1798 government contract, spelled the doom of the craftsman system of manufacture. Whitney, in simplest terms, developed an assembly-line style of production and standardized the parts of the weapons. This provided two distinct advantages. First, it meant that weapons could be repaired easily on the battlefield by cannibalizing parts from other weapons with the confidence that the weapon would function. Second, and more important to the rising industrialization of the nation, standardized parts and assembly-line methods meant that inexperienced workers could be trained quickly and efficiently to do small, repetitive tasks. Later in the century, immigrants, women, and others considered "nonemployable" by the crafts-based system of manufacture found work in factories applying Whitney's method of weapons manufacture to other products.

As the century progressed, small arms, artillery, and machine guns from American factories played a major role in making the nation a world-class industrial power. The federal government, at its chain of arsenals stretching from across the nation, funded the research and development of innovative weapons. Examples include the heavy coastal artillery pieces designed by Robert Parrott and Thomas Rodman at arsenals at Cold Spring, New York, and Alleghany Arsenal (near Pittsburgh), Pennsylvania, respectively. Testing and experimentation with stronger and lighter bronze, iron, and steel alloys for cannon and small arms paid enormous dividends for civilians as well, providing the technology for steel-hulled steamships and iron and steel beams for building construction.

Small Arms

The development of small arms in the nineteenth century mirrored the technological explosion in other facets of American life. At the beginning of the century, military-issue muskets differed little from their civilian counterparts. Military side arms' only real difference was in the uniformity of issue. Prior to the War of 1812, American soldiers were armed with a variety of different models of flintlock muskets, mostly copies of the British army's famous "Brown Bess," and later of the French army's "Charleville." Most muskets were of .69 to .74 caliber (the caliber determines the size of the shot, or bullet, that fits the muzzle of the weapon) at the beginning of the century, and by mid-century were between .50 and .60 caliber.

The weapons were simple in design, and directly determined the tactics of the day. Because of their smoothbore design, muskets were notoriously inaccurate over one hundred meters. Consequently, musket-armed troops were organized in large bodies standing shoulder to shoulder. The intent of this formation was to overcome the inaccuracy of the musket by firing many of them at once at other large troop formations. After exchanging volleys with an opposing force, the troops advanced with bayonets to force the enemy from the field. The battles, due to these tactics, were bloody and often inconclusive. The flintlock smoothbore musket remained the basic infantry weapon of the United States until the 1850s, when the rifled musket gradually replaced it. During the Civil War both sides initially armed their hastily raised forces with flintlocks, and those weapons were used throughout the conflict.

Rifles had long been a part of colonial life, but were almost exclusively civilian-owned. The rifled musket took nearly three times as long to load as a smoothbore, and was not designed to accommodate a bayonet. Consequently, the few "riflemen" in the U.S. Army were either attached militiamen, as at the Battle of New Orleans in 1815, or were used as skirmishers (soldiers sent forward a short distance to find the enemy, make contact with them, and begin fighting) for musket-armed units. However, rifled weapons were much more accurate than smoothbore ones, capable of hitting targets up to five hundred meters away. The dilemma of the rifle continued to puzzle small arms manufacturers and soldiers until 1849, when French army officer Claude-Etienne Minié invented a conical bullet that came to be known as the "minié ball." This deceptively simple invention allowed for the practical use of rifles on the battlefield, thereby greatly expanding the range and deadliness of the individual soldier. The bullet, slightly smaller than the bore of the rifle, was hollow and allowed for the expansion of its base by gases released by the exploding gunpowder. The bullet essentially filled the rifle grooves of the musket, spinning as it left the barrel. When combined with the mercury fulminate percussion cap (which replaced the flint as the gunpowder ignition mechanism), the rifled musket became the single most deadly weapon of the Civil War, responsible for over 70 percent of casualties.

During the Civil War, the first repeating, cartridge-using rifles and carbines were introduced, along with the first practical machine guns. Weapons such as the Spencer, Sharps, and Henry repeating rifles, though not widely distributed in either the Union or the Confederate army, could be devastating on the battlefield. The new metal-jacketed bullet allowed soldiers to fire in all sorts of weather, to fire multiple rounds before reloading, and to load and fire in positions other than standing shoulder to shoulder. Additionally, the weapons were, in general, lighter and less cumbersome than the five-foot musket.

The most familiar repeating rifle, the Winchester Model 73, which became known as the "gun that won the West," was never adapted to military use. The U.S. Army's conservative Ordnance Bureau, despite the lessons of the Civil War and the Franco-Prussian War of 1870–1871, continued to resist the introduction of repeating or magazine-fed rifles until the 1890s, arguing that soldiers would "waste ammunition" if issued multiple-shot weapons and thus create a logistical nightmare for quartermasters. The U.S. Army, due to conservative leadership and lack of funds, preferred either to modify rifled muskets as single-shot cartridge rifles, such as the 1871 "Breechblock" Springfield, or to use Civil War–issue carbines (Spencer, Sharps) well into their obsolescence.

Consequently, the U.S. Army found itself technologically inferior to many of its opponents, including Native American tribes, who had obtained more advanced weaponry. For example, some historians and archaeologists studying the 1876 Battle of Little Bighorn ("Custer's Last Stand") have discovered mounds of Winchester cartridges surrounding the area where Custer and his men died. This suggests that the Native Americans simply overwhelmed the cavalrymen (who were armed with Civil War–issue repeaters) with firepower from more advanced rifles. In the Spanish-American War of 1898, a similar situation arose when U.S. troops armed with Springfield "Breechblocks" faced Spanish troops armed with the newest model of the German Mauser rifle. In the late 1890s, the U.S. Army finally adopted a bolt-action, magazine-fed rifle, the Krag-Jörgensen; however, limited numbers were available in 1898. It was well into the twentieth century when the United States re-emerged as the preeminent manufacturer of military small arms.

Artillery

In contrast with the often stagnant and sometimes innovative small arms industry in America, the United States was one of the world's leaders in artillery technology from the 1840s onward. Before that time American artillery differed little from its European counterparts; guns were usually bronze smoothbores capable of ranges from several hundred to several thousand yards, depending upon the size of the artillery piece. The increasing sophistication of metallurgical techniques during the century encouraged the development of alloys and metals that made cannon more dependable and effective. For example, a bronze 12-pound howitzer in 1800 ("pound" or "pounder" refers to the weight of the shot, which determined the size of the gun) could weigh up to 3,800 pounds; a twelve-pound "Napoleon" of the Civil War era weighed approximately 1,600 pounds due to changes in metallurgy and industrial techniques.

By the mid–nineteenth century most American artillery pieces were still bronze smoothbore muzzle-loading cannons that had a variety of uses, from large, coastal artillery designed for harbor defense to light field artillery issued at the regimental level. In general, three classifications for artillery were used in the nineteenth century—guns, howitzers, and mortars. Guns were long-range (up to five thousand feet, varying with the size of the gun), flat-trajectory weapons, usually carried by warships or used in coastal fortifications. The gun was designed to fire a projectile directly at a target, much like a rifle. In general, guns were designed and employed as antiship weapons, where accuracy was paramount. In the decade before the Civil War, the first rifled guns were adapted for use both in the fortification system defending major seaports and as field artillery. Rifled field pieces, although smaller than howitzers or mortars, were excellent for "counterbattery," or anti-artillery, uses because of their increased accuracy.

The mortar was a stubby, high-trajectory, short-range cannon meant for siege warfare. In general, mortars were heavy (weighing up to several tons) and capable of causing massive damage to enemy fortifications. During the Civil War mortar boats were employed along the riverways of the South, giving mobility to these behemoths. Following the conflict mortars were employed as part of coastal fortifications as "close defense" weapons. The term "howitzer" encompassed the wide range of artillery pieces that were neither guns nor mortars. These are the classic "cannons," intended to be direct-fire antipersonnel weapons. The howitzers also varied in caliber and size, from small three-pounders to massive thirty-two-pounders. The most famous howitzer of the era, the twelve-pound "Napoleon," was capable of a multitude of uses, from antipersonnel weapon to counterbattery fire.

The artillery of the period employed a variety of shell types, including explosive shell, canister (antipersonnel rounds that resembled coffee cans filled with lead shot), and solid cannonballs. Although both rifled guns and howitzers could fire all of these munitions, howitzers were (in general) used as close-range antipersonnel weapons. Even with the development of breech-loading artillery after 1865, the basic types of munitions remained the same.

Coastal Artillery and Fortifications

By the end of the century, American artillery, especially large coastal artillery, was larger and more accurate. Smoothbore artillery of impressive size, including Colombiads and Parrott guns capable of firing projectiles of 350 (or more) pounds up to six thousand yards, were common in coastal fortifications in the latter part of the Civil War. These weapons continued to be used in the handful of permanently manned coastal emplacements in the United States until the 1890s. New techniques, many duplicating the work of German arms manufacturer Alfred Krupp, introduced more accurate and longer-range rifled coastal artillery by the Spanish-American War. Lighter field artillery also underwent changes by the 1890s, based on the explosion of artillery-related technologies (munitions, metallurgy, and optics) in Europe. The introduction of rapid-fire, breech-loading artillery by France in the closing years of the century signaled a change in artillery technology. Much as with small arms, American artillery technology had fallen behind its European counterparts; it did not regain superiority until after World War II.

From 1800 on, the United States invested heavily in fixed fortifications. Following the War of 1812, the nation began to implement a large-scale plan of coastal forts designed to delay or stop transatlantic invasions. However, these forts, guarding such cities as New Orleans and Charleston, never saw a "foreign" invasion; ironically, they become the focus of brutal battles during the Civil War. Following 1865 the United States, with its powerful fleet of seagoing ironclads and lack of a credible threat, allowed the coastal forts to become dilapidated. The Spanish-American War of 1898 changed that. Although the nation had invested in a modern, steel-hulled, and steam-powered fleet, the bulk of the U.S. seaports remained undefended from assault. Fearing raids by Spanish warships along the East Coast, the government invested heavily in a crash project of fixed fortifications with long-range artillery emplacements, varying from small, temporary earthworks to large concrete-and-steel gun emplacements. By the early twentieth century many U.S. coastal cities had returned to the armed status of a hundred years earlier, with permanent batteries guarding the entrances to vital seaports.

Military Technology and the Development of the United States

Weapons use in the Civil War serves as a perfect example of the changes in American military technology that took place in the nineteenth century. In addition to the minié ball and percussion cap, which made rifles practical in mass numbers, other technological innovations shaped warfare forever after. Repeating rifles, metal cartridges, the widespread use of standardized weapons, and newer and more effective artillery all formed the century to come. Much like the rest of American society, the military was shaped and changed by the emergence of the railroad and telegraph, which allowed for the logistical support of large armies and for effective, centralized command. However, it was one inventor, Dr. Richard Gatling, who changed the nature of warfare in the modern era, in the United States and elsewhere. Gatling's machine gun, which had only limited use in the final year of the Civil War, became the forerunner of modern machine guns and a major export for the American arms industry during the rest of the century. The Gatling gun was a hand-cranked .58 caliber machine gun with a rate of fire of nearly four hundred rounds per minute. It became the first machine gun of the U.S. Army, serving until replaced by more advanced models after the Spanish-American War. Gatling's machine gun became the model that other inventors, including Hiram Maxim, imitated for their weapons.

The United States became a major industrial power in the nineteenth century in part because of the arms industry. American weapons saw action on battlefields from Virginia to Peking. Most European armies possessed some American weapon in their arsenals, be it Colt's revolver or Gatling's machine gun. For example, the Gatling gun was standard issue on many British warships, especially those in "colonial waters." Later, licenses were sold to foreign nations to produce many of the weapons mentioned, and it became common for American-style firearms to be produced in European nations. From actions against the Native American tribes to international business, American military technology played a powerful, but often forgotten, role in the development of the United States during the nineteenth century and beyond.

See also **Firearms; Naval Technology.**

Bibliography

Chinn, George M. *The Machine Gun: History, Evolution, and Development.* 5 vols. Washington, D.C.: U.S. Government Printing Office, 1951–1987.

Clary, David A. *Fortress America: The Corps of Engineers, Hampton Roads, and United States Coastal Defense.* Charlottesville: University Press of Virginia, 1990.

Coggins, Jack. *Arms and Equipment of the Civil War.* Garden City, N.Y.: Doubleday, 1962.

Doughty, Robert A., Ira D. Gruber et al. *Warfare in the Western World.* 2 vols. Lexington, Mass.: D. C. Heath, 1996.

Hazlett, James C., Edwin Olmstead, and M. Hume Parks. *Field Artillery Weapons of the Civil War.* Newark: University of Delaware Press, 1983.

Hogg, Ian. *The Weapons That Changed the World.* New York: Arbor House, 1986.

Trask, David A. *The War with Spain in 1898.* New York: Macmillan, 1981.

Wahl, Paul, and Donald Toppel. *The Gatling Gun.* New York: Arco, 1965.

Weigley, Russell F. *The American Way of War.* New York: Macmillan, 1973.

———. *Towards an American Army: Military Thought from Washington to Marshall.* New York: Columbia University Press, 1962; Westport, Conn.: Greenwood Press, 1974.

ROBERT MACKEY

MILITIA, STATE   Throughout the nineteenth century the state militias were the backbone of national defense and the arm of the state governors. Initially meant to serve as *the* army of the United States, the militia was, in many respects, a military system suited to the relative isolation of the New World from the Old, and reflective of a deep-seated mistrust of a standing army. The legal basis of nineteenth-century militias was the Uniform Militia Act of 1792. Seen by many historians as a toothless tiger, the act provided the legal process to call out, maintain, and organize the state militias. Additionally, it enshrined universal military service, naming all able-bodied men between eighteen and forty-five as members; this became the basis of conscription during the Civil War, when men were technically "drafted" from the militia and not from civilian life.

The militia, especially on the frontier, served as a ready force to repulse invasion by foreign powers (British from Canada, French from the Louisiana Territory, the Spanish from Florida); a posse comitatus (the Whiskey Rebellion, slave rebellions, and labor unrest in the latter half of the century); and a force to use against local Native American tribes. The first true test of the militia system came during the War of 1812, and it failed miserably. Internal divisions over the conduct of the war between New England and the rest of the Union hampered efforts to arm and mobilize the state militias. New England governors, concerned over their lucrative trade relations and long-standing pro-British sympathies, refused to mobilize their forces for the invasion of Canada, claiming that President James Madison had no constitutional right to send the militia outside the United States. When British forces marched on Washington in 1814, the militia responded by digging in fortifications at Bladensburg, Maryland, along the route of approach. The British swept the militia aside after a few volleys, beginning what would later be derisively called the "Bladensburg Races," as the hastily raised and untrained militia ran in all directions. Unlike the defense of Washington, the Battle of New Orleans (January 1815) would later be summoned as "proof" of militia competence and skill under General Andrew Jackson, an untrained "militia" officer. However, many supporters of the militia system neglected to note that the British made fatal mistakes at New Orleans, and that the militia force was strongly backed by Regular Army infantry and artillery.

1815–1865

Following the War of 1812, the state militia system became as neglected as the Regular Army and the navy. Luckily for the fledgling nation, only the continual conflicts between the United States and the Native American tribes presented a challenge, one easily met with a small Regular Army backed by the militia. Militiamen traditionally supported these anti-Indian campaigns, which they saw as directly helping their state or territory expand against a foe

Camp Cameron, Washington, D.C. Union soldiers of the Seventh New York State Militia responded to President Lincoln's call to arms by volunteering their forces until the Civil War ended. Photograph, 1861. LIBRARY OF CONGRESS

they had vilified for generations. Militia forces took part in a series of U.S.–Native American conflicts, including the Seminole Wars, the Black Hawk War (in which a young Abraham Lincoln was an Illinois militiaman), and scattered conflicts along the frontier. With these few exceptions, the Jacksonian era militia had become a dinosaur of an earlier age, replaced in the bulk of its military duties by the Regular Army and by the growing "volunteer" movement as a representative of popular military ardor. Although attempts were made to repair the militia system, all were halted due to lack of funds, bitter political quarrels, or lack of interest. Historian John K. Mahon notes that "cornstalks and brooms appeared with greater frequency in place of firearms on training days. The First Regiment, Iowa Territorial Militia, listed 950 men but only 63 muskets" (*History of the Militia and National Guard*, pp. 81–82). Similar conditions obtained in many militia organizations. Additionally, the militia units came under attack from peace groups and even temperance societies, who claimed that the organizations were nothing more than a continuation of a violent system and pro-

moted drunkenness and idleness, the twin demons of the temperance reformers. By the 1850s many states north of the Mason-Dixon Line had scrapped the system altogether, including Delaware, most of New England, and even frontier Missouri.

The volunteer system, which provided many of the best-trained and equipped units for the Civil War and the Spanish-American War, filled the role abandoned by the militia system. Volunteer units were just that—military organizations outside the normal governmental system whose members paid for their own weapons and uniforms. Among the wealthy, membership in an elite volunteer regiment, such as the New York Seventh Infantry Regiment or the Washington Light Artillery of Charleston, South Carolina, was seen as an important social indicator, much like membership in an elite country club in the twentieth century. Men with such last names as Tiffany, Roosevelt, and Vanderbilt paid hundreds of dollars per year to serve as privates or noncommissioned officers in the exclusive organizations. Not all of the volunteer regiments were exclusive, however. The fire brigades of New York City, for instance, also served in a volunteer militia organization and became famous in the opening days of the Civil War as "Fire Zouaves," wearing the baggy pantaloons and fezzes of the elite French Algerian troops. Another New York regiment, the Sixty-ninth Infantry, consisted entirely of Irish immigrants, who planned to use their training and experience to fight against the British occupation of their native land. From 1830 to 1860 volunteers put down riots in New York, enforced the Fugitive Slave Act in both the North and the South, suppressed slave rebellions, and acted as reserve police forces—to the pleasure of both volunteers and public officials—with a minimum of state funding and support.

By 1861 volunteers had served with distinction during the Mexican-American War of 1846–1848, and the "Mormon War" of 1856, and against the Seminoles in Florida. When the Civil War began, volunteer organizations, with their training, elan, and organization, formed the core of both Confederate and Union armies. In 1861, for example, a force of 143,155 officers and men was formed in Virginia after secession; at the core of this army were nearly 12,000 organized volunteers, including twelve well-trained artillery companies. In the South most of the states had kept their pre-war militia system intact, and used militia troops to seize arsenals, forts, and other federal property after secession. However, these troops suffered greatly from a lack of training, organization, and especially weapons. For example, one historian notes that Virginia, North Carolina, and South Carolina possessed some artillery; however, "[o]nly Arkansas among the western Rebel states was reported to have had any militia artillery at all—one howitzer" (McMurray, *Two Great Rebel Armies*, p. 98).

Union volunteer regiments responded to President Abraham Lincoln's 1861 call for 75,000 militia to put down the rebellion in huge numbers—in 1861 nearly 40 percent of the 93,000 militiamen were members of organized volunteer regiments. Entire regiments, such as the New York Seventh and Sixty-ninth Infantry, offered their services to the federal government for the duration of the war. The rapid mobilization of Union manpower owed much to the existence of these volunteer regiments, who volunteered for duty en masse several times during the war. More significantly, these volunteer regiments provided amazing numbers of junior officers to the rapidly expanding Union Army; the New York Seventh alone provided six hundred of its alumni to the Union cause as officers.

1865–1900

Following the Civil War many of the Northern volunteer organizations, disrupted by the war, never re-formed, whereas new state militia regiments, consisting of freed blacks led by white pro-Union officers, were raised in the former Confederate states. Some states, such as Missouri, had disbanded their militia systems entirely by the 1880s. Missouri allowed instead for the formation of new volunteer units, but expected the units to pay for themselves. Consequently, the Missourians had to go as far as soliciting local businessmen to support the state's military system—a situation ripe for corruption and favoritism. From 1865 to 1898, the state militias and volunteer units performed summer encampments, training, and other preparations for war without federal support, despite the hard lessons learned during the Civil War. As a result of a lack of federal oversight and state indifference, the state military organizations, both volunteer and organized militia (now known as the National Guard), often became nothing more than well-organized and well-armed police forces. During the numerous labor difficulties of the Gilded Age, members of the National Guard were summoned by the state governors almost five hundred times, for missions as diverse as preventing lynching in the South and breaking strikes in Idaho.

The Spanish-American War forever changed the state militia system. When President William McKinley called for volunteers against Spain, the U.S. Army found itself swamped with ill-trained, undisciplined, and poorly equipped militiamen more reflective of the War of 1812 than of the beginning Progressive Era. A handful of competent volunteer National Guard regiments, including the First U.S. Cavalry Volunteers ("The Rough Riders") and the Seventy-first New York, emerged, but the majority of units were woefully unprepared for war. Nearly 233,000 men volunteered for the war, almost all of whom came from the ranks of the National Guard, but in contrast to 1861, few complete units were taken into federal service. The war revealed glaring problems with the organization, equipment, and competence of the National Guard, beginning a series of reforms that would culminate in the 1903–1904 "Root reforms," which finally eliminated the last vestiges of the state militia system and replaced it with a centrally organized and federally controlled military organization.

See also **Military Service.**

Bibliography

Coakley, Robert. *The Role of Federal Military Forces in Domestic Disorders, 1789–1878*. Washington, D.C.: U.S. Government Printing Office, 1989.

Crackel, Theodore. *Mr. Jefferson's Army: Political and Social Reform of the Military Establishment, 1801–1809*. New York: New York University Press, 1987.

Karsten, Peter. "Armed Progressives: The Military Reorganizes for the American Century." In *The Military in America: From the Colonial Era to the Present.* Edited by Peter Karsten. New York: Free Press, 1980.

Mahon, John K. *History of the Militia and National Guard.* New York: Macmillan, 1983.

McMurray, Richard M. *Two Great Rebel Armies: An Essay in Confederate Military History.* Chapel Hill: University of North Carolina Press, 1989.

Millett, Alan, and Peter Maslowski. *For the Common Defense: A Military History of the United States of America.* New York: Free Press, 1984; 1994.

Weigley, Russell. *The American Way of War.* New York: Macmillan, 1973.

Williams, Thomas Harry. *Americans at War.* Baton Rouge: Louisiana State University Press, 1960.

ROBERT MACKEY

MILLENNIALISM AND ADVENTISM

The concept of the millennium derives from the early Christian belief that Jesus Christ would come to earth a second and final time to establish a messianic kingdom that would last for a thousand years (a millennium). At the end of the millennium there would be an apocalyptic battle between God and Satan, to be followed by a final judgment (from which true believers would be protected by a "rapture," whereby they would be transported to heaven) and the creation of "a new heaven and a new earth." This expectation of the second coming of Christ has led Christians at various times to heightened anticipation that the millennium is upon them. Such anticipation inevitably places believers in critical tension with their surrounding culture. Response to this tension can lead religious movements either to condemn and withdraw from society or, on occasion, to work for its transformation, as the Social Gospel movement did. Separation from the culture has characterized what is called "premillennialism"; transformation of the culture has been associated with "postmillennialism."

Premillennialism is the belief that the second coming of Christ will occur before the inauguration of the one thousand years of glory. Postmillennialism holds that the one thousand years will precede the Second Coming of Christ and will arrive as a result of progress in morality and belief. Premillennialists tend to emphasize missionary activity that seeks the conversion of individual souls from the influences of a corrupt world. They remain uneasy about supporting church organizations and social structures, which they believe will soon pass away. Postmillennialists, by contrast, seek to reform the moral life of society as a whole, bringing about the kingdom of God on earth as a precursor of the return of Christ. Established churches are usually seen as instrumental to this reforming activity.

The "pursuit of the millennium" has occurred in various periods of Christian history. The Puritans brought with them a form of postmillennialism, believing that the Reformation of the sixteenth century had inaugurated the kingdom of God in their time. Religious revivals or evangelical "awakenings" could be used to stoke the fires of millennialism. During the first Great Awakening in the 1740s, clergy such as Jonathan Edwards (1703–1758) expounded strong postmillennial views in which America itself was to play a leading role in bringing to completion the kingdom of God (albeit under God's providential actions). The millennialism of the nineteenth century was stimulated in particular by a second Great Awakening, which began in the 1790s in New England with scattered renewals of piety in various towns and gathered momentum in the early decades of the new century. (The most dramatic of the new revivals began in 1800 at camp meetings in Kentucky.) Much of the millennialism that stemmed from it was postmillennial in character. Given the general optimism that followed the success of the American Revolution, Americans were often given to the conviction that America was the place where the kingdom would be established, provided that through evangelical activity the anarchic potential of the new nation could be made subject to moral control. Postmillennialism contributed directly to evangelical attacks on slavery, agitation for women's rights, and many other reform movements in the antebellum period. Adding to this religious zeal was the postmillennial belief, preached by revivalists such as Charles Grandison Finney (1792–1875), that people could become spiritually and morally perfected through a conversion experience. It was thought that the perfection of society as a whole would flow from individual perfection. Revivalists argued that evangelicals were committed to the reformation of the world as a whole and to the "general renewal of society."

One major exception to this postmillennial optimism and social reformist impulse was the premillennialism that first achieved popularity in the early 1800s through William Miller (1782–1849). Miller embraced a formula for predicting the date of Christ's second coming that used biblical prophecies. When these predictions failed to materialize in the mid-1840s, many of his followers joined the Seventh-Day Adventist Church. Its organization, stimulated by James (1821–1881) and Ellen (1827–1915) White, was the subject of much debate over how an "organized" church was consistent with the expectation of an imminent return of Christ.

Other religious groups that thrived in the nineteenth century because of millennial beliefs included the Shakers, the Mormons, and the Oneida Community. Each group tried to establish isolated societies in which values consistent with a communal view

William Miller

William Miller was born in 1782 in Massachusetts and raised near Lake Champlain, New York. For a time he became a deist (giving up the Christian belief in a God who intervenes in history). During service in the War of 1812, he came to believe that God had had a hand in the American victories. After the war he returned to Low Hampton, New York. He apparently had a religious conversion (coincident with the revivalism of the second Great Awakening) and joined the Baptist Church in 1816. Determined to make the Bible self-consistent in order to meet deist criticism, Miller studied it diligently. He came to the conclusion that there was a clear prediction in its verses of the second advent of Christ. Using a passage from the book of Daniel, and assuming a translation principle that "days" equals "years," Miller foretold that the premillennial Second Coming would occur in about the year 1843 and that nonbelievers would be denied entry to the kingdom. He began to speak publicly in 1831. A number of people, including members of the clergy, were moved by his talks, even though he was speaking against the predominant postmillennial social reformist tendencies of the time.

Miller preached across New England, New York, and Canada. He estimated that he had spoken to about 500,000 people by 1844. Miller was joined by an expert publicist, Joshua V. Himes, in 1839. Himes helped put out a paper for Miller's movement, *Signs of the Times,* in 1840, followed in 1842 by *Midnight Cry.* Under Himes's leadership the Millerites became organized by 1842. Their message was carried across the country through revival preaching at camp meetings, often with elaborate charts detailing the biblical predictions of the upcoming advent. Millerism reached as far as Ohio and Great Britain. As the year 1843 approached, millennial fervor accelerated. Stories (usually denied by the Millerites themselves) circulated that followers of Miller were preparing ascension robes to greet the Second Coming. Under pressure Miller finally set the exact date of the event as 18 April 1844. When that day came and went, Miller confessed his error but did not renounce his belief that the coming was near. Shifting interpretations by others led to a new date being set, 22 October 1844. Many people (the exact number is uncertain) began to close their businesses and settle their affairs. When this date also failed to witness the advent (a day known as the Great Disappointment), Miller urged patience and a continuation of faithfulness to the expectation. He later admitted that human calculation of the end might have been erroneous. His evangelical missionizing slowed considerably, and he died on 20 December 1849. From the ashes of the failed prophecy came the Seventh-Day Adventist Church under James and Ellen White, which continues to this day.

of the millennium (and not with the individualism of American society generally) could be lived out. They drew heavily upon the practices of the earliest Christian churches.

The Shakers (the United Society of Believers in Christ's Second Appearing), founded by a charismatic named Ann Lee (1736–1784), believed that the millennium had already come in the presence of Lee herself and simply had to be accepted by those who would live by its principles, which included celibacy, simplicity, and a common sharing of all goods and property.

The Mormons (the Church of Jesus Christ of Latter-day Saints), who owe their ideas and structure to the visions of Joseph Smith (1805–1844), also believed that they were called to live out their idea of what millennial life should look like (which included, for a period of time, polygamy) in a place free from non-Mormon persecution. They eventually settled in the area around the Great Salt Lake in Utah.

The most extreme example of millennialism was the Oneida Community, established by John Humphrey Noyes (1811–1886) in upstate New York. It was founded on Noyes's belief that the millennium actually began shortly after Christ's death and needed to be implemented fully in the present. The group practiced "Bible communism" and introduced a new idea: complex marriage, based on Noyes's belief that in heaven there would be no marriage between individuals. Members of the Oneida Community considered themselves married to one another; children were raised collectively.

Millennial belief has also, in a different form, influenced the practice of non-Christian groups. One of the most dramatic examples is the emergence in the latter half of the nineteenth century of the Ghost

Dance among many Native American tribes. The dance was an attempt to respond to the disasters of defeat, disorganization, and despair among the Indians, whose way of life was rapidly disappearing under the onslaught of white encroachment beginning in the 1880s.

See also **Mormonism; Revivalism; Social Gospel.**

Bibliography

Barkun, Michael. *Crucible of the Millennium: The Burned-over District of New York in the 1840s.* Syracuse, N.Y.: Syracuse University Press, 1986.

Butler, Jonathan M. "Adventism and the American Experience." In *The Rise of Adventism: Religion and Society in Mid-Nineteenth-Century America.* Edited by Edwin S. Gaustad. New York: Harper and Row, 1974. This collection of original scholarly essays is a gold mine of material on the era as a whole.

Dick, Everett N. "The Millerite Movement 1830–1845." In *Adventism in America: A History.* Edited by Gary Land. Grand Rapids, Mich.: Eerdmans, 1986.

McLoughlin, William G. "Revivalism." In *The Rise of Adventism: Religion and Society in Mid-Nineteenth-Century America.* Edited by Edwin S. Gaustad. New York: Harper and Row, 1974.

Sandeen, Ernest R. "Millennialism." In *The Rise of Adventism: Religion and Society in Mid-Nineteenth Century America.* Edited by Edwin S. Gaustad. New York: Harper and Row, 1974.

Smith, Timothy L. *Revivalism and Social Reform: American Protestantism on the Eve of the Civil War.* Baltimore: Johns Hopkins University Press, 1980.

FRANK G. KIRKPATRICK

MINING AND EXTRACTION

In 1800 the United States had a pre-industrial economy and an overwhelmingly rural population. By 1900 it was an urban and industrial powerhouse whose economy had overtaken that of Great Britain, France, and Germany combined.

Arguably, America's emergence as an economic superpower was marked by the organization of United States Steel in 1901. This event projected America to the world as the premier manufacturing nation. But there was another aspect to America's economic development that made the manufacturing base possible: its extractive industry, including coal and metal ore mining, petroleum, and timber.

Historian David Potter has characterized the United States as a nation conditioned by abundance. The wealth of natural resources this country had at its disposal contributed to the rise of the United States as a modern nation.

Coal

Invented in 1690, the steam engine was perfected in the late eighteenth century. This coincided with American independence and the frontier's westward movement. When steam power became a driving force behind technological progress in the early nineteenth century, part of the frontier's expansion involved the search for fuel, specifically coal.

In 1866 a mining expert estimated that the United States had a reserve of four trillion tons of mineable coal. While this figure included less desirable varieties, such as lignite and sub-bituminous, it primarily represented available deposits of both anthracite

Polish Miners Strike. Armed guards of the Pennsylvania coal and iron police, endorsed by the federal government, attempt to suppress Polish strikers at this Shenandoah mine. Cover of *Frank Leslie's Illustrated Newspaper,* 1888. LIBRARY OF CONGRESS: PRINTS AND PHOTOGRAPHS DIVISION

(hard) coal and bituminous (soft) coal. The difference between the two is their geological age. Anthracite is older and subjected to a greater degree of pressure in formation, making it a purer form of coal than bituminous.

America's bituminous coalfields are extensive, running westward from Pennsylvania to Indiana, and southward from Maryland to Alabama. In contrast, the nation's anthracite deposits are found in only one region: eastern Pennsylvania, in and around the Susquehanna, Schuylkill, and Lehigh River basins. Although the field is small in its geographic extent, it is unusually rich in the coal it has produced, and continues to produce.

Of the two major coal varieties, bituminous was discovered first during the early colonial era. By the Revolutionary War a primitive bituminous coal industry had been established. But the anthracite field's discovery proved to be a far more important event.

Credit for its initial uncovering goes to Obadiah Gore, a Connecticut blacksmith who settled in eastern Pennsylvania during the 1760s. Gore initially used various outcroppings (where the coal protruded through the ground) to fuel his forge. By 1769 he was trying to mine the coal on a larger scale. His efforts to mine and use anthracite were stymied by a number of different problems, ranging from technological limits to lack of reliable transportation. But the biggest problem was the difficulty in igniting anthracite. Between 1795 and 1812 countless attempts were made to introduce it to Philadelphia as a domestic fuel. But it did not burn readily, and it failed to respond to stoking methods used with bituminous coal. Then in 1812 it was discovered by accident that anthracite burnt satisfactorily if simply packed in a furnace and left alone. The air passing through the heated mass in a closed firebox created a natural hot blast producing intense heat.

After this discovery anthracite became highly prized. Demand grew in the major urban markets. Schuylkill County in Pennsylvania, still a wilderness in 1828, was the anthracite field's center. By 1844 the area was sending half a million tons of coal to Philadelphia annually by a myriad of small railroads, an illustration of the close connection between the nation's coal industry and the creation of the nation's transportation system. As early as 1798, the Pennsylvania legislature chartered a company to improve navigation on the Lehigh River. Most notable were the improvements to the Schuylkill River in 1822 and the completion of the Delaware and Hudson Canal in 1829. These arteries still shipped large amounts of coal as late as 1864.

Impressive as they were, the canals were overshadowed by the railroads. In 1827 the nation's oldest rail line, the Baltimore and Ohio, was chartered by the state of Maryland. In 1842 another major line, the Philadelphia and Reading Railroad, opened its corridor between Philadelphia and Pottsville, Pennsylvania. Despite a precarious start marked by poor management, the line was shipping two million tons of coal a year by 1855.

Meanwhile, America's coal industry took shape. It lagged behind Great Britain's mature mining companies in technology and extractive technique, but those advantages were mitigated by the sheer volume of America's coal deposits and the ease with which they were accessed. A notable case in point was the large open mine located at Mauch Chunk (later Jim Thorpe), Pennsylvania. Here, an anthracite coal seam of unprecedented size was discovered very close to the surface and was quarried.

Otherwise, there were three types of mining: drift, slope, and deep shaft. With drift and slope mining, the method was to follow a coal seam from a surface outcropping, either horizontally into a hillside or at an angle into the ground. In deep shaft, a vertical shaft was dug first, and the coal seams then worked off of it.

Two methods prevailed for extracting the coal: room and pillar and long-wall. Room and pillar was the older method, where a honeycomb of individual "rooms" was cut into the area where coal was worked. This area, known as the coal face, was interconnected by tunnels, their roofs supported by coal pillars. Once the coal was removed from an area, the pillars were taken out, allowing the roof, or "overburden," to subside.

In the long-wall method, a central tunnel was dug from the shaft to the coal seam's end. Once a working coal face was established, miners cut the coal in a single room running the width of the seam, working back toward the shaft. As the mining crew dug, the overburden was permitted to subside behind them.

Pioneered in England, long-wall mining did not gain a significant footing in the American coal industry until the twentieth century. Although it was less wasteful than room and pillar, long-wall was not attractive to American coal operators because it took much longer to establish a working coal face with long-wall than with room and pillar. Miners also preferred room and pillar because it offered greater work autonomy than long-wall did.

This was an important matter. Coal mining was a skilled occupation, requiring a practical knowledge of engineering and geology. The usual method of digging the coal was for the miner to undercut the coal face by digging a wedge-shaped trough into it at its base, running the width of the room in which he and his

"**Mining on the Comstock.**" Cross section of a mine, showing a sloped shaft and room and pillar method in the center, and a vertical shaft and long-wall method on the right. Drawing by T. L. Dawes engraved by Le Count Bro's., c. 1877. LIBRARY OF CONGRESS: PRINTS AND PHOTOGRAPHS DIVISION.

assistant worked. He then took an auger or hand drill and made several holes in the coal face. The holes were filled with black powder and fused. After lighting the fuses, the miner went to a safe place, yelling "fire in the hole!" The resulting explosion was known as a "shot." The pieces would then be loaded by the miner's assistant (or "buddy") into a cart and taken to the surface to be screened, cleaned, and weighed. This part of the process was a constant source of contention since most miners were paid by the ton. Small coal pieces and impurities were not counted.

Coal and mineral or "hard rock" mining was extremely dangerous. In addition to cave-ins and slate falls, gases and coal and mineral dust were constant hazards. The three most dangerous gases in mines were methane (fire damp), carbon monoxide (white damp), and carbon dioxide (black damp). Methane was the most hazardous. It is highly volatile, tasteless, colorless, odorless, lighter than air, and usually seeped from the coal face to gather in a pocket at the mine's ceiling. Testing for it involved applying flame to a suspected pocket, which was very risky.

Carbon monoxide is also colorless, odorless, and tasteless, in addition to being highly poisonous. Since there was no way to test for this gas during the nine-

teenth century, it was common for miners to take canaries into the mine with them as an early warning system. If the birds were overcome, it meant a carbon monoxide pocket had built up and it was time to get out.

The danger presented by coal dust was twofold. It too is highly volatile: if sufficiently concentrated, a simple spark can set it off. Also, miners subjected to long-term exposure to high concentrations of coal dust developed a degenerative respiratory condition popularly known as miner's asthma, in which the lung becomes clogged with coal dust, causing loss of elasticity and impaired breathing. First identified in England in the 1830s, the condition came under scrutiny in the United States between 1869 and 1881 by physicians John Carpenter and H. A. Learhman. Originally dubbed anthracosis, it later became known as coal workers' pneumoconiosis, or black-lung disease.

Another dust disease, primarily afflicting hard-rock miners, was silicosis. Like black lung, the condition resulted from sustained exposure to high concentrations of fine dust particles, in this case sand. The disease differed from black lung in that instead of coating the lung, the dust cut into the lung tissue, which impaired

Titusville Oil Wells. These wells in Venango County, Pennsylvania, were among the first to be pumped in the United States. Photograph c. 1860. LIBRARY OF CONGRESS

breathing and made the miner susceptible to infectious diseases, especially tuberculosis.

While methods were developed to reduce dust levels, the first line of defense against both dust and gases was effective ventilation. Of all the engineering challenges presented by deep mining, providing sufficient breathable air was one of the most daunting. One early method involved sinking a ventilation shaft at a different height from the mine's opening. The idea was to create a partial vacuum by allowing warmer air to rise and escape out of the mine, causing a column of fresh air to rush in from the surface. Based on the same theory, another system used a furnace connected to a ventilation shaft to promote air flow. Still another produced the same effect with a cascade of cold water flowing down the central shaft. While each method worked to some degree, they were not adequate to meet the needs of deeper mines. Moreover, use of a ventilation furnace in a deep mine

could be hazardous. An example was the Avondale disaster in Luzerne County, Pennsylvania, in 1869. More than one hundred men were asphyxiated in a mine three hundred feet deep when the ventilation furnace burned the main shaft.

The introduction of the fan was a major breakthrough for the mining industry. Experiments with fans had been made as early as 1621, but these efforts failed because they attempted to force air into the mine. Air has mass and resistance, making a forced-air approach useless. Eventually, engineers discovered that fans were more effective when they drew stale air out of the mine, thereby promoting an upward flow of fresh air in. The mainstay device until well into the next century was the Guibal fan, first demonstrated in 1854.

Other innovations were comparatively minor. For most of the nineteenth century a miner's tools consisted of the pick, shovel, auger, black powder, and fuses; large-scale mechanization was a phenomenon of the twentieth century. Nevertheless, efforts were made to introduce machinery to increase productivity. One device, originally demonstrated in 1850, was a compressed-air jackhammer to replace the pick for undercutting the coal face. This device began to come into greater use around 1875. A far more important development for miners was the safety lamp. Introduced in 1815, it featured a wire mesh that prevented methane from getting to the flame in sufficient quantity to cause an explosion.

As the nineteenth century continued, America's coal output grew phenomenally. Starting from just a few hundred tons in 1800, the United States was producing a total of 22 million tons a year by 1864. During this time and immediately following the Civil War, anthracite was the leader, accounting for 52.33 percent of total coal production between 1850 and 1869. By 1870 the United States had become a major coal producer, topping all other coal-mining nations by 1890. In 1870 America's bituminous coal production began to outdistance anthracite due to the rise of the steel industry.

Iron

Like coal mining, iron making had a long history in the United States, dating back to 1619 in Virginia. Iron making was a complicated matter in which raw ore was smelted and then refined by three distinct processes: puddling, blooming, and rolling. The purpose of these was to take the very brittle smelted product (pig iron) and reduce its carbon and silica content, converting it into stronger and much more malleable wrought iron. Each of these processes required a great deal of skill. Puddling alone had nine distinct steps.

The traditional fuel source for iron making had been charcoal. But in the nineteenth century the iron industry turned its attention to anthracite and bituminous coal. Nicholas Biddle (1786–1844), who had headed the Second National Bank of the United States, offered a five-thousand-dollar reward to anyone who could produce pig iron for one hundred consecutive days using anthracite. A similar prize was offered by Philadelphia's Franklin Institute for anyone who managed to do the same with bituminous. Neither fuel, as things turned out, could replace charcoal. But an alternative was found with the development of coke.

Coke was bituminous coal heat-treated in an oven to burn off impurities. Refined in this manner, it produced heat with charcoal's intensity. Although experiments were made with it during the 1830s, it was not until 1850 that the use of coke came into vogue. By 1876 coke had displaced all other fuels in the iron industry.

It was during these same years that iron making underwent a revolution. Working independently of each other, William Kelly (1811–1888) in the United States and Henry Bessemer (1813–1898) in England developed a new way of making wrought iron between 1851 and 1855 that did away with skilled labor. Dubbed the Bessemer process, it refined pig iron by blowing excess carbon and silica off the molten mass with blasts of compressed air. The process, as perfected by Robert F. Mushet (1811–1891), paved the way to the cheap mass production of the purest and strongest of all iron products: steel.

In the years following the Civil War, demand for steel grew at a geometric rate. In 1868 total steel production in the United States stood at 26,786 tons. By 1890 that figure had grown to 4.28 million tons. As more steel was being made for buildings, bridges, and rails demand for bituminous coal also grew. From 1870 to 1890 the coal beds of south-central Appalachia were opened. By 1900 bituminous coal was the nation's, and the world's, most important fossil fuel, a position it held well into the twentieth century until displaced by petroleum.

Oil

Known in the ancient world, oil was used for heating and other purposes. It did not come into general use, however, until the second half of the nineteenth century. The major problem was how to extract it. Oil usually appeared in swamps and other bodies of water, and attempts were made to skim or channel it off the water's surface. But neither of these efforts proved very effective. A better method had to be found, especially since a new market for petroleum was emerging.

Although oil had been sold for many purposes, even as a cancer cure, demand was growing for a new lighting source. Until the 1850s, lamps were fueled by whale oil, which led to the near extinction of several whale species. With whale oil prices rising to exorbitant levels, petroleum promised to be a good and inexpensive replacement.

The stumbling block was that no technology existed to get the oil out of the ground. However, Edwin Drake (1819–1880), who assumed the honorific title of colonel, developed the basic method still in use today. Working near Titusville, in the heart of northwest Pennsylvania's oil field, Drake came upon the idea of forcing pipes into the ground and then drilling. In this way, when the pool was finally reached, the oil would flow up by force of hydrostatic pressure.

After drilling sixty-seven feet, Drake's well hit oil and began flowing on 27 August 1859.

This marked the beginning not only of an oil boom in northwest Pennsylvania, but the start of the oil industry itself. Although petroleum products replaced whale oil and found other uses, demand for petroleum would receive its greatest boost with the invention of the diesel engine in the 1890s and the introduction of the internal combustion engine.

Minerals and Precious Metals

Contemporary with the coal and oil industry's development was the rise of metal or hard-rock mining. Since stone ores are incredibly dense, hard-rock mining became a generic expression for the extraction of metals from gold and silver to copper, iron, and lead.

Like coal mining, hard-rock mining presented problems related to working underground, including ventilation, safety from dust exposure, and gas explosions. Metal mining too was a skilled occupation, but the two industries diverged in the degree of difficulty, complexity, and danger involved. Whereas a colliery that reached three hundred feet was considered a deep mine, metal mines regularly went to a depth of one thousand feet to reach the principal deposit, or lode. In Nevada alone, by 1880, no fewer than thirty-seven metal mines had exceeded a depth of one thousand feet, and five had reached three thousand.

Another area of divergence was the hard-rock industry's ethnic composition. Certainly, both coal and metal mining employed a wide diversity of workers, including Native Americans, Irish, Slavs, and African Americans. In the hard-rock industry, however, one group predominated and was actively recruited: Cornish miners. Their native Cornwall was England's principal metal-ore producing region. Referred to as Cousin Jacks, these men had the experience and practical know-how needed for cutting through bedrock and reaching the mineral deposits.

As in the coal industry, metal mining relied on blasting and open extraction of surface outcroppings. Blasting in this industry was extensive, since mining through bedrock and granite was such a challenge. In addition, hard-rock miners regularly applied fire to the bedrock to crack it in order to break through.

Hard-rock mining was a midwestern and western enterprise that included the iron and copper ore deposits of Michigan and Wisconsin, the lead deposits of Montana, and especially the gold and silver deposits that ran from Colorado to California. When these territories were first explored by Lewis and Clark in 1805 and 1806, coal was already being mined in the East. Metal mining was primarily a late-nineteenth-century industry; it was not until 1850 that iron manufacturers began using Michigan iron ore.

Although the government sought to promote the development of these resources, the major impetus behind the opening of the ore fields was the coming together of supply and demand, as in the case of the Michigan copper rush of the 1840s. This not only attracted prospectors and miners, but also needed investment capital from the East and abroad, primarily Great Britain. The most famous such instance was the discovery of gold in California in 1848, which attracted people and investment in large quantities. British investors poured $250 million into western mining interests between 1860 and 1901 and held $400 million in U.S. railroad stock. By 1852 California was producing 45 percent of the world's gold supply, with the major gold and silver strikes of Colorado and Nevada yet to happen.

Timber

Another resource that seemed almost endless in its abundance was timber. From Maine to California, to the Pacific Northwest and Appalachia, the lumberman was a constant presence. Like coal mining, the lumber industry fed demand created by the growth of America's eastern cities. The Erie Canal, completed in 1825, provided access to the pine forests in and around the Great Lakes. Later, railroads expanded that access.

Timber was the most visibly profligate of the extractive industries, primarily for two reasons. With wood so plentiful, it was much more cost-effective to clear-cut entire forests and then move on. Also, it had long been believed that forested areas represented untamed wilderness and that clear-cutting announced civilization's arrival. Fed by an ever-growing demand the lumber industry expanded at a prodigious rate, producing 44.5 billion board-feet per year by 1919.

Economic Concentration and Labor

The question of how these industries were structured is neither easily nor quickly addressed. Whereas iron and steel witnessed a myriad of smaller companies at first, as did hard-rock mining, it was eventually marked by the rise of corporate giants such as Carnegie Steel and the Anaconda Copper Company. The same corporate control is true of the oil industry, with John D. Rockefeller (1839–1937) and Standard Oil driving smaller companies into bankruptcy.

Coal was a different matter, however. While some large companies were formed during the nineteenth century, such as Pittsburgh Consolidated, most coal production remained in the hands of small producers.

It was not until the twentieth century that the industry was concentrated and rationalized, with smaller companies being driven out of business.

Although the rate of economic growth achieved by the extractive industries during the nineteenth century was impressive, it came at a cost paid chiefly by American workers. One estimate set the coal industry's average daily wage at $1.50 in 1868. While this masked the disparity between skilled and unskilled labor, skilled workers rarely made more than $3 a day. Many occupations in the extractive industries were unskilled and so commanded much less.

Almost without exception local, state, and federal authorities sided with employers, even to the point where basic legal and constitutional protections were suspended. Hand in hand with such suspensions went the regular use of armed guards, such as Pennsylvania's coal and iron police, and private detective agencies, including the Pinkertons and the Baldwin-Felts organization. In addition, during times of labor strife, vigilantes were regularly deputized by county sheriffs and given a license to use whatever force was deemed necessary.

Workers' attempts to improve their situation fostered a culture of opposition. This took many forms, ranging from local benevolent associations to violence, as in the case of the Molly Maguires in the anthracite coalfield in the 1870s. Ultimately, this culture led to the creation of organized labor. While the creation of labor unions was hampered by such things as ethnic and racial diversity and economic downturns, unions were established nevertheless and won some impressive results for their members.

Most notable were the United Mine Workers of America (UMWA), founded in 1890, which represented coal miners, and the Western Federation of Miners (WFM), established in 1893, which sought to organize the hard-rock industry. In 1902 the UMWA was able to fight and win a long strike for the eight-hour day against eastern Pennsylvania's largest coal operator, the Philadelphia and Reading Railroad. This strike was one of the first instances where the federal government, under President Theodore Roosevelt, intervened in a labor dispute as an impartial arbitrator. That enabled the union to make its case to the wider public as never before and marked the start of a new and less hostile relationship between organized labor and the federal government.

Reevaluation of Resource Use and Labor Issues

Taking the long view, American economic development between 1800 and 1899 was nothing less than remarkable. The country, however, paid handsomely for it in terms of the waste of resources and human suffering. As the twentieth century began, these concerns were beginning to be addressed. In the area of conservation, the influence of Gifford Pinchot (1865–1946) and John Muir (1838–1914) would be felt. Although Muir and Pinchot disagreed on what shape conservation should take, wise use or preservation, both worked to end the profligate expending of resources.

Similarly, both the government and the courts were beginning to reevaluate their positions on such social policy issues as child labor and employer liability. Whereas the courts had originally held that the workers could not sue employers for negligence, since employees were free to seek work elsewhere, this trend was eventually reversed. By the early 1900s, the courts were awarding workers compensatory and punitive damages for injuries sustained as a result of a hazardous workplace. This ultimately led to passage of workers' compensation laws in most states between 1912 and 1920.

As for child labor, although this was not finally outlawed until the passage of the Social Security Act in 1935, the practice was coming to public attention. A great deal of the credit for this goes to the nation's first investigative journalists, the so-called muckrakers, and labor advocates such as Mary Harris "Mother" Jones (1830–1930). Thus, as the nineteenth century came to an end, its philosophy of an unlimited individualism was coming under increasing fire. Although it was not replaced by a communitarian ethic, a basic sense of social responsibility was beginning to take shape.

See also **Industrialization and the Market; Labor Movement,** *subentry on* **Unions and Strikes; Natural Resources.**

Bibliography

Asbury, Herbert. *The Golden Flood: An Informal History of America's First Oil Field.* New York: Knopf, 1942.

Broehl, Wayne G., Jr. *The Molly Maguires.* Cambridge, Mass.: Harvard University Press, 1964.

Derickson, Alan. *Black Lung: Anatomy of A Public Health Disaster.* Ithaca, N.Y.: Cornell University Press, 1998.

Dix, Keith. *What's a Coal Miner to Do? The Mechanization of Coal Mining.* Pittsburgh, Pa.: University of Pittsburgh Press, 1988.

Eller, Ronald D. *Miners, Millhands, and Mountaineers: Industrialization of the Appalachian South, 1880–1930.* Knoxville: University of Tennessee Press, 1982.

Fahey, John. *Hecla: A Century of Western Mining.* Seattle: University of Washington Press, 1990.

Giddens, Paul Henry. *Early Days of Oil: A Pictorial History of the Beginnings of the Oil Industry in Pennsylvania.* Princeton, N.J.: Princeton University Press, 1948.

Giebelhaus, August W. *Business and Government in the Oil Industry: A Case Study of Sun Oil, 1876–1945.* Greenwich, Conn.: JAI Press, 1980.

Holbrook, Stewart Hall. *Iron Brew: A Century of American Ore and Steel.* New York: Macmillan, 1939.

Knowles, Ruth S. *The Greatest Gamblers: The Epic of American Oil Exploration.* 1959. 2d ed. Norman: University of Oklahoma Press, 1978.

Letwin, Daniel. *The Challenge of Interracial Unionism: Alabama Coal Miners, 1878–1921.* Chapel Hill: University of North Carolina Press, 1998.

Lewis, Ronald L. *Transforming the Appalachian Countryside: Railroads, Deforestation, and Social Change in West Virginia, 1880–1920.* Chapel Hill: University of North Carolina Press, 1998.

Mussey, Henry Raymond. *Combination in the Mining Industry: A Study of Concentration in Lake Superior Iron Ore Production.* 1905. Reprint, New York: AMS Press, 1968.

O'Connor, Richard. *The Oil Barons: Men of Greed and Grandeur.* Boston: Little, Brown, 1971.

Rowe, John. *The Hard-Rock Men: Cornish Immigrants and the North American Mining Frontier.* New York: Barnes and Noble, 1974.

Wallace, Anthony F. C. *St. Clair: A Nineteenth-Century Coal Town's Experience with a Disaster-Prone Industry.* Ithaca, N.Y.: Cornell University Press, 1987.

Wyman, Mark. *Hard Rock Epic: Western Miners and the Industrial Revolution, 1860–1910.* Berkeley. University of California Press, 1979.

RICHARD P. MULCAHY

MINNESOTA

Minnesota, meaning "land of sky-colored waters" in Dakota, is known for its forests, prairies, lakes, rivers, and farmland and for its weather swings to extremes in winter and summer. The Ojibwas (or Chippewas) inhabited the pine forests in the northeastern portion of the state, and the Dakotas (or Sioux) lived on the prairies of southern Minnesota. Both groups were seminomadic, moving as seasons changed and various foods were ready to harvest. French explorers arrived in Minnesota during the mid-1600s, seeking to form trade relations with Indian tribes and to explore the upper Mississippi River, hoping to find a route to China. War with England ended France's hold on the region by 1763. Instead of establishing permanent settlements, the English formed the North West Company, whose trading posts remained in British hands until the Jay Treaty in the 1790s.

On 29 April 1808 Congress granted a monopoly on trade throughout Minnesota to the newly created American Fur Company. Fort Snelling, built at the confluence of the Minnesota and Mississippi Rivers, secured the holding. The treaties of 1837 with the Dakotas and Ojibwas opened the large delta between the St. Croix and the Mississippi Rivers to white settlement. Throughout the 1840s lumber milling made Stillwater, located on the St. Croix, the center of commerce; this distinction shifted to St. Paul, the future capital of Minnesota, with the growth of fur trading with the Pembina métis (mixed-blood people of the Red River Valley) and banking and commerce with downriver businesses. Upriver, entrepreneurs harnessed waterpower for milling and lumbering at the Falls of St. Anthony, which became Minneapolis. Wheat overtook fur as the centerpiece of Minnesota's economy.

On 3 March 1849 Minnesota became a territory and Alexander Ramsey was appointed its governor. Treaties with the Sioux in 1851, and the Chippewas in 1854 and 1855, opened up millions of acres to settlement, thereby stimulating a dramatic population increase. Democrats, led by Henry Hastings Sibley, a director of the American Fur Company, dominated territorial politics throughout the 1850s, until the Republican Party, founded as an antislavery party in 1854, competed for control of state government. As Minnesota moved toward statehood, the Democrats and Republicans each held a constitutional convention in 1857. After a compromise on the issue of black suffrage (the matter would be submitted to the electorate at some unspecified future date) was struck, Minnesota achieved statehood on 11 May 1858. The panic of 1857 had thwarted plans to construct railroads throughout the state, and had damaged the state's credit, town development, and business.

Minnesota's triracial society evoked conflict in the Civil War era, as the state moved toward black equality but Indian removal. The *Dred Scott* decision (1857) brought slavery to Minnesota through a burgeoning trade with southern visitors that was dampened by an 1860 hearing in Minneapolis that resulted in the freeing of a slave named Eliza Winston. Later that year Republicans supported Abraham Lincoln and swept congressional and state elections. When war began in 1861, Alexander Ramsey was the first governor to offer volunteers to the Union Army. In 1862 the Dakotas, frustrated by delays of annuity payments, attacked settlers in southwestern Minnesota in what was called the Sioux Uprising. The leaders were executed and the remaining band was removed from Minnesota. Concurrently, black contrabands attempting to land in St. Paul were repulsed at the docks by striking Irish laborers. In 1868 Minnesota passed a black suffrage bill, predating the Fifteenth Amendment, and banned school segregation. The Ojibwas were forced onto reservations.

Jobs in iron mining, flour milling, and lumbering, together with railroad construction, liberal landownership laws, and the end of the Civil War and Indian hostilities, stimulated more settlement. Wheat production increased as a result of new farm machinery and railroads that connected farms with markets more easily, making Minneapolis the flour-milling center of the world. From the 1870s to the 1890s, farmers protested the discriminatory practices of railroads and grain elevators, excessive rates, unfair grading of grain, high interest rates, and a biased tax system. Reflecting national trends, they organized the Grange, Farmers' Alliance, Antimonopoly Party, Greenback Party, and Populist Party, all of which had an impact on national politics. In 1875 and 1899 the legislature passed civil rights bills. John Lind, fusion candidate of the Populists and the Democrats, was elected governor in 1898. The state promoted campaigns to attract immigrants, most of whom came from Scandinavia, Germany, or Great Britain.

The 1900 census counted 1,751,394 residents of Minnesota, ten times the 1860 figure; 29 percent of them were foreign-born.

See also **American Indian Societies,** *subentries on* **The Great Lakes, The Plains; Fur Trade; Lumber and Timber Industry.**

Bibliography

Anderson, William. *The History of the Constitution of Minnesota.* Minneapolis: University of Minnesota Press, 1921.

Blegen, Theodore C. *Minnesota: A History of the State.* Minneapolis: University of Minnesota Press, 1975.

Folwell, William Watts. *A History of Minnesota.* 4 vols. 1921–1930. Reprint, 2 vols. St. Paul: Minnesota Historical Society, 1961.

Holmquist, June Drenning, ed. *They Chose Minnesota: A Survey of the State's Ethnic Groups.* St. Paul: Minnesota Historical Society, 1981.

WILLIAM D. GREEN

MINSTREL SHOWS   American minstrel shows consisted of white entertainers who painted their faces black with burnt cork, then in front of large, raucous audiences, parodied the dance, song, and dialect of southern slaves. They played instruments that were associated with plantation music, including fiddles, banjos, tambourines, and the jawbones of animals. This native form of American entertainment originated at the end of the eighteenth century when white musicians began impersonating slaves in front of small crowds. In between acts of plays and as part of traveling circuses, they managed only a small following, but in the next century things would change. On a stage in Louisville, Kentucky, in 1828, an aspiring white actor and comedian from New York, Thomas Dartmouth "Daddy" Rice, put on blackface makeup and played a character that he named "Jim Crow." The performance made him famous, and the chorus of his "Jim Crow" song became legend:

First on de heel tap, den on de toe,
Ebery time I wheel about I jump Jim Crow.
Wheel about and turn about and do jis so,
And every time I wheel about I jump Jim Crow.
  (quoted in Wittke, p. 26)

Soon other solo artists tried to duplicate Rice's success. The first organized minstrel show was put on more than a decade later, when Dan Emmett and his Virginia Minstrels, consisting of Emmett, along with a banjo player, a bone player, and a tambourine player, performed together in New York City.

Popularity and Influence of Minstrelsy

For the rest of the century, these "Ethiopian concerts" were America's most popular form of entertainment. In a typical show, an all-male band sat in a semicircle on stage. In the 1840s, most bands consisted of only four or five members, but years later their sizes increased significantly. With faces painted

Black Stereotype. An advertisement for George Thatcher's Greatest Minstrels Show, 1899. With a pitchfork, the interlocutor funnels stereotypical elements of the black South, such as watermelon and plantation musical instruments, into a machine that churns out energetic, childlike, large-lipped blacks. LIBRARY OF CONGRESS: PRINTS AND PHOTOGRAPHS DIVISION

black and wearing straw hats, worn shoes, and torn clothes, minstrels lampooned southern slaves. After the Civil War, they caricatured northern free blacks as well. The performance included singing, dancing, and comedic and theatrical acts. Usually an interlocutor sat in the center of the semicircle and served as the vocal director. Nearly every minstrel show included a frenzied dancing finale called the "breakdown," when troupe members joined together and danced to loud, dissonant music and screams from the crowd.

Minstrel shows attracted huge audiences, and their appeal was widespread. President Abraham Lincoln and writer Mark Twain were enthusiasts. No group patronized minstrelsy more avidly, however, than the northern working class. In Boston, Philadelphia, New York, and other urban centers, men who worked in shops and factories gathered in large numbers to watch, listen, and laugh. The majority of them were native-born Americans, but many were immigrants. Few had ever encountered an African American slave, or seen a southern plantation.

The popularity of minstrel shows reflected the deep racism that pervaded nineteenth-century American culture. Minstrels played on commonplace stereotypes of African Americans. They satirized both the southern "plantation darky" and the northern "dandy Negro" as lazy, licentious, and hapless. In supposed imitation of blacks' speech, they pronounced "the" as "de," and "that" as "dat." Minstrels' gaudy striped trousers, enormous shirt collars, and kinky black wigs indicated that their impersonations were strictly fiction, but it appears that audiences chose to see in them substantial measures of truth. It was possible to sympathize with the slave characters that minstrels portrayed as gentle, childlike people. Nevertheless, the racial stereotypes these shows fostered were relentlessly negative, and the shows plainly promoted the institution of slavery. Song lyrics emphasized slaves' contentment and affinity for their masters. By the 1850s, abolitionist characters were being inserted into minstrel shows and portrayed as ignoramuses. In a version of a popular skit entitled "Happy Uncle Tom," minstrels ignored the plight of a runaway slave who had come to New York City in search of Harriet Beecher Stowe, the author of *Uncle Tom's Cabin*, only to find that she had taken the profits from the sale of her novel and gone to England. After minstrel shows, intoxicated audience members sometimes blackened their own faces and assaulted free blacks in the streets, as well as in their homes and churches.

Some of the appeal of minstrelsy may have derived from its capacity to unify a diverse white population in mutual antipathy to blacks. At these shows audience members were not Protestant, Catholic, or Jewish; they were not American, Irish, or German; instead, they were white. Minstrelsy invited whites to revel in their whiteness and the privileges that whiteness conferred; it helped create a kind of community on the basis of color. Still, racism does not wholly explain minstrelsy's popularity. Minstrel shows also provided relief for white, working-class anxiety brought about by rapid social, economic, and demographic changes spurred by merchant capitalists and mechanization. During the antebellum period, white workers lost much of the security and independence that they had previously enjoyed as self-employed artisans. At the same time, they felt that their jobs were being threatened and their neighborhoods transformed by the influx of new immigrants. The impersonation of plantation slaves provided a crude form of escapist entertainment and indirectly evoked an idealized past, when American farmers and workers controlled their own destinies.

Furthermore, in an era of both industrialization and evangelical religious reform, white working-class men struggled to adapt to harsh and impersonal work routines that required them to repress desires, or rewarded them for doing so. Again minstrel shows provided an outlet. Male performers in blackface danced in a sexually suggestive manner. They chased women characters that were played by cross-dressing male actors. Simultaneously, audience members drank, swore, and carried on riotously. They jeered, taunted, and threw items at the minstrels. Fistfights among audience members were customary. Clearly, minstrel shows provided more than entertainment for its working-class audience.

African American Performers

While most performers were white, a select number of African Americans were able to make a name for themselves as minstrels. William Henry Land, who went by the name of Master Juba, was the most famous. A native New Yorker, Land perfected his routine in the city's notorious Five Points district. He received his big break in 1841, when the celebrated showman P. T. Barnum asked him to perform in one of his shows. Considered the greatest "heel and toe" dancer of his time, Juba toured with all-white minstrel companies and on occasion received top billing. He earned hundreds of dollars per performance across the United States and in London, England. In addition to performing, African Americans also wrote many of the thousands of minstrel songs that were published. Some managed and owned their own successful troupes, among them the Original Georgia Minstrels and the McCabe and Young Minstrels. In spite of its racist nature, minstrelsy placed African American song and dance at the forefront of American popular entertainment for the first time. In the twentieth century, jazz, blues, rock and roll, and rap music continued the legacy of original African American music, first made popular by minstrel shows.

See also **Bands and Band Concerts; Circuses; Humor; Music,** *subentry on* **Spirituals and African American Music; Race and Racial Thinking; Recreation; Vaudeville and Burlesque.**

Bibliography

Bean, Annemarie, James V. Hatch, and Brooks McNamara, eds. *Inside the Minstrel Mask: Readings in Nineteenth-Century Blackface Minstrelsy.* Hanover, N.H.: University Press of New England, 1996.

Lhamon, W. T., Jr. *Raising Cain: Blackface Performance from Jim Crow to Hip Hop.* Cambridge, Mass.: Harvard University Press, 1998.

Roediger, David R. *The Wages of Whiteness: Race and the Making of the American Working Class.* New York: Verso, 1991.

Toll, Robert C. *Blacking Up: The Minstrel Show in Nineteenth Century America.* New York: Oxford University Press, 1974.

Wittke, Carl. *Tambo and Bones: A History of the American Minstrel Stage.* Durham, N.C.: Duke University Press, 1930.

MATT CLAVIN

MISCEGENATION   Miscegenation, the practice of interracial sex and marriage, became a social and political issue in British North America as early as the seventeenth century, when Maryland and Virginia banned marriages between whites and people of other races. Relations between white men and black women generally caused legislators far less concern than did relations between white women and men of color. The laws were designed to curtail formal relations that exemplified racial equality; interracial competition for white women; the birth of mixed-race children to white women; and access by people of color to property by means of marriage or inheritance.

By law and custom, interracial relations were discouraged in the United States, although the specifics varied from place to place and from time to time, and miscegenation laws were not always enforced. Some statutes established penalties of ten years or even life in prison; others imposed neither fines nor imprisonment. Among the thirteen original states, all had laws against interracial marriage except New Hampshire, Connecticut, New York, and New Jersey; Pennsylvania repealed its law in 1780, as did Massachusetts in 1843. Among the thirty-five new states

that joined the Union by 1912, only Kansas, New Mexico, and Washington (aside from a brief period each prior to statehood), and Vermont, Minnesota, and Wisconsin failed to enact such laws. Some far western states demonstrated as much concern regarding whites' marriages with people of Asian ancestry as with those of African ancestry.

The term "miscegenation" originated during the Civil War, replacing "amalgamation," when two Democratic newspapermen from the New York *World,* David Goodman Croly (1829–1889) and George Wakeman (d. 1870), published a hoax pamphlet during the 1864 presidential campaign, designed to portray Republicans as avowed advocates of interracial sexual relations, particularly between black men and white women. The mere fabrication by Croly and Wakeman indicates how salient the question was, as Republicans in the 1860s struggled to foster enhanced rights of African Americans.

In 1865 to 1866, in the immediate aftermath of the Civil War and emancipation, southern white legislators displayed their continued commitment to white power and privilege by retaining miscegenation laws or even imposing greater penalties than before. During the Republican years of Reconstruction, however, those laws often came under political attack or were challenged on constitutional grounds. Mississippi, South Carolina, and Louisiana dropped their prohibitions of interracial marriage for a time during Reconstruction, and courts in Alabama, Louisiana and Texas briefly overturned miscegenation laws then. By the 1890s, however, those states had restored such laws and all the former Confederate states banned interracial marriage. Virginia had established a two-to-five-year term in the penitentiary for each partner in an interracial marriage; Alabama legislated a two-to-seven-year term.

Especially after the 1870s, courts almost uniformly ruled that miscegenation laws did not violate the Fourteenth Amendment's clause requiring "equal protection of the laws." The U.S. Supreme Court upheld a miscegenation statute in *Pace v. Alabama* (1883), a case in which Tony Pace, a black man, challenged an Alabama law that—in a legal environment in which he could not marry a white woman—established a higher penalty for his living with her outside marriage than he would have suffered had both parties been black or both white. Meanwhile, a number of northern states repealed their miscegenation statutes—Illinois in 1874; Rhode Island in 1881; Maine and Michigan in 1883; and Ohio in 1887—so such laws became an increasingly southern phenomenon. Miscegenation laws remained on the books in every former Confederate state until the U.S. Supreme Court outlawed them in *Loving v. Virginia* in 1967, when a white man and a black woman successfully challenged a Virginia law that made their marriage a felony.

See also **Marriage; Race and Racial Thinking; Race Laws; Reconstruction; Segregation,** *subentry on* Segregation and Civil Rights; **Sexual Morality.**

Bibliography

Hodes, Martha. *White Women, Black Men: Illicit Sex in the Nineteenth-Century South*. New Haven, Conn.: Yale University Press, 1997.

Kaplan, Sidney. "The Miscegenation Issue in the Election of 1864." *Journal of Negro History* 34 (July 1949): 274–343.

Wallenstein, Peter. "Race, Marriage, and the Law of Freedom: Virginia and Alabama, 1860s–1960s." *Chicago-Kent Law Review* 70, No. 2 (1994): 371–437.

Williamson, Joel. *New People: Miscegenation and Mulattoes in the United States*. New York: Free Press, 1980.

PETER WALLENSTEIN

MISSIONS

[This entry includes three subentries: **North American Indians, Indian Responses to White Missionaries,** and **Foreign Missions.**]

NORTH AMERICAN INDIANS

Efforts to Christianize Native Americans commenced soon after the first encounter between American Indians and whites in the late fifteenth century. Throughout the remainder of America's colonial period and during most of its national era, missionaries worked in collaboration with their respective governments to achieve political, economic, and spiritual dominion over the continent's aboriginal peoples.

The enduring cooperation between church and state was based on a philosophy of history that posited a unilinear course of development of the lifeways of human societies, from the reputed savagery and heathenism of American Indian communities to European and Euro-American civilization and Christianity. Most missionaries considered that, in addition to their duty to convert Indian heathens, an essential part of their "burden" was to hasten the Indians' progress by assimilating them into institutions and mores of Western culture. For their part, Indians were expected to acquiesce gratefully to European theories and policies concerning who they were and what they should become. However, their reactions to missionization were not always what their mentors anticipated or desired.

Following the American Revolution the work of missionizing American Indians passed largely into the hands of the denominations and interdenominational societies of the new nation. Nevertheless, their methods and goals remained practically identical with those of their colonial predecessors. In collaboration with government Indian policy, they worked toward the "civilization and Christianization" of North American Indians.

During the nineteenth century the Roman Catholic Church drew upon its sizable pool of diocesan and ordered priests, sisters, and brothers to continue and expand its 300-year-old ministry among American Indian tribes. The Protestant churches for the most part entrusted their missionary activities to denominational and interdenominational societies. Among the earliest and most notable of these organizations were the Presbyterian Board of Missions, organized in 1804, and the American Board of Commissioners for Foreign Missions (ABCFM), a cooperative body of the Congregational, Presbyterian, and Reformed Churches founded in 1810.

While much of the funding for Native American missions came from the pockets of denomination members, both Catholic and Protestant churches came to depend on the federal government and its Indian Bureau to underwrite their initiatives. A major source of these subsidies was the so-called "civilization" fund, which Congress initiated in 1819, primarily to help subsidize church schools in native communities. The initial annual appropriation for this fund was $10,000.

The cooperation between government and missionaries reached its apogee during the administration of President Ulysses S. Grant. In an effort to eliminate the corruption pervading the Indian Bureau, Grant, in concert with the society of Friends (Quakers) and a group of prominent Protestant reformers, formulated a policy that meted out political and spiritual oversight of the seventy-one Indian reservations among twelve mainline churches and the ABCFM. Because of the great influence that the Friends and other Christian humanitarians exerted on it, this reform of the Indian service soon came to be known as the Grant "Peace Policy." Upon receiving its share of reservations, each church was requested to nominate agents who would assume full responsibility for the Christianization and civilization of their respective tribes. One of the powers conferred on these agents was the right to expel members of other denominations discovered proselytizing on their reservations.

A major springboard by which the proponents of the Peace Policy sought to catapult Indians from savagery to civilization was the on-reservation boarding school. Missionaries and government officials believed that in such a self-contained environment children could be systematically trained in the habits of civilized society while they were simultaneously protected from the primitive conditions that characterized their home lives. The Indian Bureau therefore drew up plans to build, furnish, and operate a number of boarding school facilities and at the same time encouraged Christian denominations to establish and maintain such schools. As an incentive the government agreed to furnish churches with food, clothing, and tuition for the students under their care.

In little more than a decade after the inauguration of the Peace Policy, bickering among the participating denominations, especially the Catholic and Protestant churches, prompted the Indian Bureau to abandon this experiment in Christian Indian administration. The Indian Bureau's growing concern that government support of denominational schools violated the principle of separation of church and state further undermined the policy. By the conclusion of the nineteenth century formal subsidies for Christian Missions were reduced, even though the Indian Bureau continued to consider Christianization an essential part of its solution to the "Indian problem."

An examination of the ideas and reactions of Native Americans reveals that, despite the limited role prescribed for Indian people in the mission process, they responded to Christianity and missions in highly creative and diverse ways. Despite the wide variation of Indian reactions, it is possible to devise a spectrum of Indian response types. At one pole of this spectrum are Indians who abandoned their traditional religions for Christianity. While some of these Indians accepted the tenet that Christianity was the only true faith, many others were intimidated by federal laws that prohibited aboriginal practices or assumed that Indian ceremonies would soon be stamped out by "civilization" policy. At the other extreme were Indians who rebuffed everything to do with Christianity. Many among these joined religious movements that adapted elements of Christianity to customary beliefs and practices, such as the Native American Church, the Indian Shaker Church, and the Ghost Dance.

Most Indian reactions to Christian missions fell between complete acceptance and complete rejection. Belonging to one or another Christian denomination, most Indian communities found ways to keep their traditional religious beliefs and practices alive. One strategy they employed was to introduce elements of their traditional beliefs and ceremonies into Catholic and Protestant rituals. For example, the Catholic Sioux Indian Congress boasted many subtly transformed practices of the Lakota sun dance. An even more widespread strategy was dual participation in both Christianity and native religions. Because of the hostility of the government and church officials to

Indian religions, most dual participants found it necessary to practice their traditional ceremonies in secret.

Many of the tenets and goals of nineteenth-century American Indian missionization continued to dominate church work in native communities until the mid-1960s, when the Indian self-determination and multiculturalism movements compelled churches to reconsider and transform some of the basic assumptions of their missiologies. In spite of those changes, the beliefs and practices of nineteenth-century missions left an indelible mark on church relations with American Indians.

See also **American Indians,** *subentries on* **American Indian Religions, U.S. Government Policies, Indian Removal; Education,** *subentry on* **Indian Schools.**

Bibliography
Bowden, Henry Warner. *American Indians and Christian Missions: Studies in Cultural Conflict.* Chicago: University of Chicago Press, 1981.
Tinker, George E. *Missionary Conquest: The Gospel and Native American Cultural Genocide.* Minneapolis, Minn.: Fortress Press, 1993.

HARVEY MARKOWITZ

INDIAN RESPONSES TO WHITE MISSIONARIES

In the nineteenth century American missionary societies followed the lead of Catholic, Puritan, and Moravian missionaries who had been active among Native Americans in the colonial era. American Indians along the Mississippi River had been exposed in the seventeenth and eighteenth centuries to Catholicism through the efforts of French Jesuits and Récollets (Franciscans). Franciscans had made their mark among the Pueblo peoples of the Southwest, and John Eliot's Praying Towns of Protestant Christian converts had established a model for religiosity in New England in the seventeenth century.

The Congregationalist and Presbyterian ministers of the American Board of Commissioners for Foreign Missions, established in 1810, brought a strongly Calvinist doctrine to the Cherokees, Choctaws, and Chickasaws in the Southeast. The sons of several mixed-blood families, including Elias Boudinot and Leon Hicks of the Cherokees and Israel Folsom and McKee Folsom of the Choctaws, were sent to the board's Foreign Mission School in Cornwall, Connecticut. The Methodist doctrine of free will and the evangelical nature of that religion attracted other Indians to missionary work. William Apess (1798–

1839), a Pequot, was converted to Methodism in 1818 and ordained a minister in 1829 or 1830. He preached to diverse audiences, became a leader of the Mashpee community, one of Eliot's Praying Towns, in 1833, and published an autobiography, *A Son of the Forest* (1829). Two Mississauga Ojibwa Methodist ministers, Peter Jones (1802–1856) and George Copway (1818–1869), preached in their respective communities in northern Canada. Jones translated scriptures and hymns into the Ojibwa language, and Copway wrote three books dealing with his life and with Ojibwa history and culture.

While they disrupted traditional religions, missions provided native people with unprecedented educational opportunities. With strong encouragement from David Folsom, a mixed-blood Choctaw leader, the three Choctaw chiefs Apukshanubbee, Pushmataha, and Mushulatubbee in 1819 committed $2,000 annually in treaty annuity money to American Board missionaries for the support of schools and blacksmith shops. The leaders were not so interested in converting to Christianity as in learning the ways of white society to be better able to deal with their white neighbors.

More overt resistance to Christianity came in the form of new native religious movements. After 1805 the Shawnee Prophet Tenskwatawa and his brother Tecumseh gained a large following among tribes along the East Coast. Tenskwatawa's visions and prediction of an eclipse of the sun in 1806 consolidated a religious movement, and Tecumseh attempted to build a pan-Indian armed rebellion against white Americans. He attracted warriors from a number of tribes, but his death and the American defeat of British forces at the Battle of the Thames (1813) put an end to the hope of a unified Indian resistance to white dominance.

The Seneca spiritual leader Handsome Lake had a series of visions from 1799 to 1801 from which he evolved a doctrine that melded aspects of Christian teaching, including the notions of sin and punishment and an emphasis on the nuclear family, with traditional elements of Seneca ceremonialism to create the "longhouse" religion that persisted on Seneca reservations in New York State into the twentieth century.

In the West, Catholic influence spread to the Salish, Kootenai, and Blackfeet through the agency of Pierre Jean De Smet (1801–1873), a Belgian Jesuit who established a mission on the Flathead reservation in Montana in 1841. Apparent conversion did not, however, mean full acceptance of Catholic doctrine. As one Jesuit recalled, converts prayed for a long life, that they would kill many animals, and that they could steal many horses. In November 1847 a party of Cayuse Indians killed Marcus Whitman, a missionary of the American Board of Commissioners for Foreign Missions, his family, and several mission workers, whom they blamed for an outbreak of smallpox in the tribe.

In 1870 a Ghost Dance ceremony began among the Paviotso in Nevada and spread to tribes in California and Oregon. Dancers believed that dead ancestors would be brought back to life and that white people would disappear. In 1890 a second Ghost Dance was inspired by the vision of Wovoka, a Paiute who worked for a white family. Both dances promised a return of the buffalo and restoration of dead ancestors. The movements were a response to the many changes in Indian lifestyles that were imposed by U.S. policies and contact with white missionaries, settlers, and the U.S. Army.

The massacre of some three hundred Lakota people at Wounded Knee Creek in South Dakota in 1890 was the result of the army's attempt to suppress the Ghost Dance on the Pine Ridge reservation. One of the witnesses at the massacre site was Black Elk, an Oglala Lakota spiritual leader and healer who converted to Catholicism around 1904 and became an active catechist for the Catholic Church. He did not, however, reject his Lakota beliefs entirely but maintained a balance between the two ways of thinking.

The variations in Christian religious practice led the Seneca leader Red Jacket to question a missionary in 1805, "If there is but one religion, why do you white people differ so much about it?" The varieties of Indian responses to Christianity ranged from armed resistance to full conversion to a melding of native and Christian beliefs.

Christian missionary activities, supported by the U.S. government through various acts, such as the Civilization Act of 1819, became part of federal policy to assimilate Indians into American society, and many Indian children in mission schools and adults in their homes and in camp meetings underwent strong emotional conversion experiences and gave up traditional beliefs in cultural practices such as ceremonies. Missionaries also became the defenders of Indian tribes against forcible removal and assimilation because of what they saw as the lack of godliness in white society, particularly frontier society. Jeremiah Evarts of the American Board of Commissioners for Foreign Missions lobbied vigorously against President Andrew Jackson's Indian removal policy of the 1820s and 1830s. Isaac McCoy, a Baptist missionary, proposed the establishment of an Indian state where tribes could be consolidated. Missionaries sought basic justice for tribes faced with forced removal, but they also wanted to protect the gain in converts, whom they feared would be lost if Indians were totally assimilated into American society.

See also **American Indians,** *subentry on* **Overview.**

Bibliography

Bowden, Henry Warner. *American Indians and Christian Missions: Studies in Cultural Conflict.* Chicago: University of Chicago Press, 1981.

Keller, Robert H., Jr. *American Protestantism and United States Indian Policy, 1869–1882.* Lincoln: University of Nebraska Press, 1983.

Milner, Clyde A., II, and Floyd A. O'Neil, eds. *Churchmen and the Western Indians, 1820–1920.* Norman: University of Oklahoma Press, 1985.

CLARA SUE KIDWELL

FOREIGN MISSIONS

Spreading Christianity in diverse parts of the world was the major cross-cultural activity for nineteenth-century Protestant churches. The sending of foreign missionaries began in 1810 with the organization of the American Board of Commissioners for Foreign Missions, a voluntary association of New England Congregationalists, later joined by Presbyterians and other Reformed Christians. Inspired by British missions in India and earlier Puritan efforts to convert Native Americans, the American Board dispatched the first five men and three women to India in 1812. After three of the missionaries became Baptists, American Baptists held the Triennial Convention in 1814 to organize support for missions abroad, ultimately choosing Burma as their main mission field. In 1819 Methodists in New York City organized a missionary society to support Methodist work, initially among Wyandot Indians and in Liberia. Also in 1819, the American Board sent missionaries to Hawaii, where response to the missionary message was so positive that Hawaii was considered fully evangelized by the 1870s. African Americans began organizing their own missionary associations by 1836. As different denominations, notably Congregationalists, Presbyterians, Methodists, and Baptists, organized mission societies, they selected their own mission fields. The chief locations for American missions in the early nineteenth century were India, the Middle East, the Pacific islands, North American Indian territories, and Liberia.

Motivated by religious convictions about the necessity of belief in Jesus Christ for eternal salvation, by desires to glorify God and be useful to others, and by the optimism and activism that characterized much of American culture, early nineteenth-century missionaries translated the Bible into indigenous languages, preached, opened schools, engaged in charitable and social service, and started churches. The ordained male was considered the chief missionary, with wives and lay workers considered assistants. By mid-century, mission boards generally shared the view that the chief aim of missions was planting self-supporting, self-governing, and self-propagating native churches. This "Three Self" theory became standard mission policy. Volunteer supporters raised funds and sent the missionaries supplies. By 1870, approximately two thousand Americans had served abroad in mission work. Conversions remained few in number among adherents of world religions, but greater numbers were reported from tribal mission fields, such as the Karens in Burma, Cherokee Indians, and Micronesians.

Anti-slavery motivation was very important for British missions but less so for Americans. The mission of Methodists to Liberia was in a response to requests by African Americans who had settled there beginning in 1820, and Liberia missions were related more to the issue of colonization than to abolitionism. After the *Amistad* affair (1839) and the founding of the American Missionary Association as an abolitionist break-off from the American Board in 1846, opposition to slavery served as a factor within missions themselves. But the American Missionary Association was never very successful as a foreign mission. Its real impact was among freedmen in the South after the Civil War.

Women in Missions

Beginning with the nondenominational Woman's Union Missionary Society, in 1860 women began organizing their own missionary societies to send unmarried women to distant territories to teach and care for the sick. By the end of the century, there were more than forty denominational women's mission boards working alongside their parent bodies. Under the slogan "Woman's Work for Woman," women missionaries provided education, medical care, and spiritual sustenance to women and children, especially those in gender-segregated societies like India, China, Japan, Korea, and the Middle East. Not allowed to preach in most denominations, women missionaries concentrated on developing social service agencies, such as schools, hospitals, leprosaria, and orphanages. Accompanied by indigenous "Bible Women" as partners, missionary women also conducted village evangelism. Some women missionaries agitated for social changes to benefit women by, for example, opposing foot-binding and female infanticide in China, condemning prostitution in British colonies, and petitioning the Indian parliament to raise to twelve the age at which girls could marry. Local mission circles held prayer meetings, raised funds, and studied missionary literature in support of their "sisters" abroad, thus making foreign missions the most popular social movement among American Protestant women in the late nineteenth century. Going abroad as missionaries provided women professional opportunities unavailable to them in the United States. By 1909, there were 2,368 American women, 10 percent of whom were medical doctors, serving under women's missionary societies.

Motivated by increased wealth and education, search for new markets, and growing political self-awareness, American eyes increasingly turned abroad as the century waned. In a period marked by rising enthusiasm for gunboat diplomacy, Americans maintained missions in China, opened them in Japan, and, after the Spanish-American War (1898), entered the Philippines, Cuba, and Puerto Rico. In 1884 Presbyterian and Methodist missionaries in Korea provided support for its king's efforts to maintain independence from other imperial powers. Popular American support for missions grew in proportion to their identity as bringers of Western education, democracy, and "civilization" to less advanced peoples. Missionary interest among university students increased with the formation of the Student Volunteer Movement for Foreign Missions in 1888. Spurred by piety, the social gospel, and international interests, increasing numbers of college students volunteered for mission work under the watchword "the evangelization of the world in this generation." By the 1880s, theological conservatives were founding independent evangelical "faith" missions in new mission fields.

The collaboration between evangelism and social works that had characterized earlier nineteenth-century American missions began to splinter late in the century, as denominational missions gravitated increasingly toward social and institutional solutions to world problems, while faith missions saw widespread evangelism as their proper goal. Despite growing conservative unease about theological liberalism and political progressivism, missionary advocates cooperated broadly in the Ecumenical Missionary Conference in New York City in 1900. The height of missionary triumphalism, the conference featured missionary presentations at Carnegie Hall and in churches throughout New York City, and an ethnographic exhibit that became the founding collection of the Museum of Natural History. Two hundred thousand people and U.S. presidents of the present, future, and past, William McKinley, Theodore Roosevelt, and Benjamin Harrison, all attended.

By the end of the century, approximately 5,850 North Americans were serving as cross-cultural missionaries under the major Protestant mission agencies. At least 57 percent of mainline missionaries were women, with the percentage of women even higher in independent faith missions. India was the largest American mission field, with China a close second. Since the United States was still considered a mission field by the Vatican, only small numbers of American Roman Catholics went abroad as missionaries. In their letters home, articles, and personal appearances at churches during their furloughs, missionaries interpreted global realities for ordinary Americans. Not only did missions represent Western values and energy abroad, but they shaped American perceptions of non-Western peoples. As the United States grew interested in global issues, missionary rhetoric about saving and uplifting the downtrodden masses of the world provided, in the historian William Hutchison's words, a "moral equivalent for imperialism." Although missionaries themselves were driven primarily by specific religious and humanitarian motives, their presence abroad was broadly emblematic of American cultural identity vis-à-vis the rest of the world.

See also **Asia, Foreign Relations with; Diplomatic Corps; Evangelicalism; Foreign Relations,** *subentries on* **1789–1860, 1865–1917; Hawaii; Protestantism,** *subentries on* **Congregationalists; Presbyterians, Methodists, Baptists.**

Bibliography

Beach, Harlan P. *A Geography and Atlas of Protestant Missions.* New York: Student Volunteer Movement for Foreign Missions, 1901–1903.

Dwight, H. O., H. A. Tupper, and E. M. Bliss. *The Encyclopedia of Missions.* 2d ed. New York and London: Funk and Wagnalls, 1910.

Hutchison, William R. *Errand to the World: American Protestant Thought and Foreign Missions.* Chicago: University of Chicago Press, 1987.

Montgomery, Helen Barrett. *Western Women in Eastern Lands.* New York: Macmillan, 1910.

Robert, Dana L. *American Women in Mission: A Social History of Their Thought and Practice.* Macon, Ga.: Mercer University Press, 1996.

DANA L. ROBERT

MISSISSIPPI   Lying between thirty and thirty-five degrees north latitude, Mississippi is the heart of the Deep South. Diverse geographically, its physiographic regions range from coastal meadows to piney woods, from hills to prairies and alluvial delta plains, the state's most pronounced topographical feature. With its warm summers, mild winters, and abundant rainfall, the state experiences few climatic extremes. Although in some geographic areas its soil is poor, historically the state's greatest resource has been its land—in several broad belts, some of the most fertile in the South.

Congress established the Mississippi Territory in 1798. On 10 December 1817 President James Monroe signed the Mississippi admission bill, making Mississippi the twentieth state in the Union. Its new status culminated more than one hundred years of existence as a colony of France, then England, and then Spain, and an additional nineteen years as a federal territory.

Understandably, in the nineteenth century it was Mississippi's fertile virgin soil that attracted land-hungry yeomen farmers and cotton planters. The federal government's Indian removal policy eliminated the titles to millions of acres of Choctaw and Chickasaw lands and forcibly banished the two tribes, Mississippi's largest, to Oklahoma. Their departure sparked a migration into the cession areas, especially in the 1830s and 1840s, that had increased the state's total population 175 percent by 1840. According to census figures (which did not count preremoval Indians), Mississippi's total population grew from 75,448 in 1820 to 791,305 in 1860. By the 1830s, blacks outnumbered whites, and a black majority persisted into the 1930s.

The expansion of Mississippi's plantation culture aggravated long-standing regional problems. Originally as much class conflicts as they were political differences, controversies between the yeomen-dominated eastern counties and the aristocratic Mississippi River counties eased marginally in the 1830s. However, new sectional disruptions manifested themselves as the older southern region experienced a loss of power and influence to the recently organized central and northern areas. The fissures became so great that occasionally lawmakers from the two sections refused to sit in legislative sessions with each other. What seemed more ominous to some in the late antebellum period was a short-lived but vain movement in the southwestern counties to secede and become part of Louisiana.

These kinds of sectional disputes shaped much of Mississippi's political development during the antebellum period. Questions concerning land policy, internal improvement programs, banking, and democratic constitutional reform presented similar challenges if not similar responses. But there were also areas of consensus. Few whites in Mississippi, particularly after the watershed 1830s, found much to criticize about slavery. In 1860 Mississippi had the South's second largest percentage of slaves (55 percent); bondmen were concentrated largely in the fertile cotton belt—the Brown Loam, Tombigbee Prairie, and Mississippi Delta regions. But even in less agriculturally productive regions where slave numbers were small and the economic impact of slavery was negligible, criticism was muted and leaders sided with the slave-dominated plantation counties to bolster the system.

Mississippi ardently defended states' rights and secession. If the narrow 1851 gubernatorial victory of the Unionist Henry S. Foote over the states' rights leader Jefferson Davis was a barometer of public sentiment, clearly Mississippi did not regard congressional passage of the Compromise of 1850, the campaign's major issue, as important enough to spark disunion. But the state affirmed the right to secede in 1861 following Abraham Lincoln's election as president. To be sure, cleavages manifested themselves over both secession and the outbreak of civil war, but in the end they were small and of little consequence. Hence in 1861 there was considerable unity about the course Mississippi undertook, although later war developments, with their mounting physical and human consequences, dampened optimism and enthusiasm about Southern nationhood.

The war's destructive effects on Mississippi were widespread. Few counties escaped some form of physical damage. A cotton- and slave-dependent economy lay in ruin long before the surrender at Appomattox, but the Confederacy's collapse proved especially devastating to slave owners. Collectively, the class lost through uncompensated emancipation 436,000 slaves valued at $218 million. It was the human toll, however, that Mississippi felt the most. Nearly 27,000 of 78,000 white men, one-fourth of the males over the age of fifteen, died as a result of the war. Seventeen thousand black Mississippians fought as Union soldiers, but their casualty statistics are difficult to verify. Still, literally thousands of Confederate and Union veterans returned home debilitated in some way. The problem was so acute that in 1865 the legislature spent 20 percent of Mississippi's budget to buy artificial limbs for former Confederates. Mississippi had staked its fortunes with the Confederacy and lost; in many ways it paid dearly for the gamble.

Reconstruction in Mississippi brought a brief period when the majority population enjoyed historic and unparalleled citizenship rights. The freedmen voted, and black leaders such as Blanche K. Bruce and John R. Lynch went to Congress; many blacks served in state and local government. But their political activism angered whites, provoking a violent counterrevolution that initially curbed the power and influence of blacks and eventually relegated them to second-class citizenship.

The determination to find and maintain the "proper place" for Mississippi blacks consumed much of the state's attention in the late nineteenth century. Problems in public education, industrial development, and infrastructure were often neglected. Largely influenced by the cries of dirt farmers from the white counties who were burdened by debt, crop liens, and a languishing agricultural economy, Mississippi constitutionally resolved a superficial race problem. Conservative leaders convinced poor whites that race rather than economics lay at the root of their problems. By the end of the nineteenth century, blacks were effectively disfranchised and thoroughly segregated. Yet Mississippi as a whole remained dreadfully poor, overwhelmingly rural and provincial, and hamstrung by one-crop agriculture.

See also **Race Laws; Reconstruction,** *subentry on* **The South; Sectionalism; States' Rights.**

Bibliography

McLemore, Richard A., ed. *A History of Mississippi.* 2 vols. Hattiesburg: University and College Press of Mississippi, 1973.

Moore, John Hebron. *The Emergence of the Cotton Kingdom in the Old Southwest: Mississippi, 1770–1860.* Baton Rouge: Louisiana State University Press, 1988.

Skates, John Ray. *Mississippi: A Bicentennial History.* New York: Norton, 1979.

ROBERT L. JENKINS

MISSOURI   Located in the center of the United States, Missouri has been a microcosm of the nation. Blessed with a diverse topography that varies from the lowlands of the boot heel to the broad plains north of the Missouri River to the lovely Ozark Mountains, Missouri offered settlers two of the nation's most important rivers for ease of travel. The great Mississippi River formed the area's eastern border, and the turbulent Missouri River bounded the northwest corner of the territory before angling through the middle of the state to deposit its waters in the Mississippi.

Missouri's population joined its geography in mirroring the nation. Native Americans included the Missouris, who gave the territory its name, Sacs, Foxes, Otoes, and Osages, the most important tribe. Slaves came to the territory long before statehood, and Missouri's black population usually approximated that of the nation as a whole. The French established their first permanent settlement at Sainte Genevieve in 1750 and founded Saint Louis in 1764, but the Louisiana Purchase of 1803 transferred the territory to the United States. President Thomas Jefferson sent Meriwether Lewis and William Clark on their famous adventure in 1804, and after their return in 1806 even more Americans knew about the land west of the Mississippi River. The territory quickly filled up with people from Tennessee, Kentucky, and Virginia. Dominant during the late eighteenth and early nineteenth centuries, the Osages gave up their territory in Missouri by treaty in 1808. By 1818 Missouri's population exceeded 60,000, and the territory petitioned for statehood. The 1820 census counted 56,017 whites, 347 free blacks, and 10,222 slaves.

Missouri exemplified the contest between North and South over the expansion of slavery into new territories and over who would control the state's land and politics. Members of Congress voted on statehood for Missouri according to whether or not their own states allowed slavery. The Missouri Compromise finally resolved the issue in 1820, when Congress voted to admit Maine as a free state and Missouri as a slave state, with the provision that no more slave states would be admitted in territory above Missouri's southern boundary. Missouri became the twenty-fourth state in 1821.

Besides the beginnings of commercial agriculture in the form of tobacco and hemp, the Missouri economy depended on the fur trade for income. Traders such as Auguste Chouteau, Pierre Chouteau, and William Ashley established Saint Louis as the center of the trade, and in 1824 Ashley invented the rendezvous system of acquiring furs. Members of his Rocky Mountain Fur Company met trappers at a location in the West, where the company exchanged trade goods for furs. As a result of this new system, Missouri fur traders served as the vanguard in opening the West, and Independence, Missouri, became the launching point for the Santa Fe Trail, the Oregon Trail, and the California gold rush of 1849.

Politically, the new state was dominated by Jacksonian democracy during the 1820s. President Andrew Jackson's chief spokesman in the U.S. Senate was Thomas Hart Benton, who represented Missouri in that body from 1821 until 1851. A hard-money man who believed in cheap land and limited influence by the federal government, Benton eventually lost his position because he could not abide slavery's expansion. During the 1850s the question of slavery so divided Missouri politics that between 1854 and 1856 the state had only one U.S. senator. The legislature was so torn it could not decide on another.

These divisions played themselves out in "Bleeding Kansas" between 1856 and 1858, when proslavery Missourians fought antislavery immigrants for control of that territory. Kansas served as a prelude to the terrible destructiveness of the Civil War, during which Missouri sent 40,000 men to fight for the Confederacy and 110,000 to fight for the Union. In 1861 Governor Claiborne Fox Jackson tried but failed to lead the state out of the Union. He established a government in exile, while Hamilton R. Gamble served as Missouri's pro-Union provisional governor. Guerrilla warfare plagued the state. William Quantrill, "Bloody" Bill Anderson, Frank James, Jesse James, and Cole Younger and his brothers supposedly represented Confederate interests, while the equally detestable James Lane, James Montgomery, and Charles R. "Doc" Jennison killed and plundered in the name of the Union.

Although Missouri experienced Radical Republican rule after the Civil War, urban and economic growth marked the remainder of the nineteenth century. Even with industrial and urban growth, Missouri remained primarily agricultural during the last half of the nineteenth century. During the 1890s the number of farms in Missouri increased from 238,043 to 284,886. The number of improved acres increased from nearly twenty million to almost twenty-three million. Even with that increase, about half of the state's farmland remained unimproved, because total acreage exceeded forty-five million acres. The federal government still operated land offices in Boonville, Ironton, and Springfield in 1903. In 1900 more than two-thirds of Missouri's residents lived on farms and earned their living directly from the land.

For a time Missouri was known as the "Outlaw State." Reaching notoriety in the 1870s, Jesse and Frank James did not end their careers as thieves until 1882, when Bob Ford, a member of their gang, murdered Jesse, and Frank surrendered to Governor Thomas Crittenden. The Younger brothers ended their outlaw careers in 1876 by taking part in a failed bank holdup in Northfield, Minnesota, with Frank and Jesse James. Authorities captured the Younger brothers and placed them in the state penitentiary. After the 1900s began, Cole Younger, the eldest of the Younger clan, joined a Wild West show, a nostalgic reminder of the Missouri of the 1800s.

Immigrants from Germany, Ireland, Italy, and other southeast European countries swelled the populations of Kansas City and Saint Louis, the state's largest city with 575,238 people in 1900. The 1900 census counted 3,106,665 residents of Missouri—2,944,843 whites and 161,822 blacks. As the new century began, Saint Louis hosted a world's fair of unprecedented size, the Louisiana Purchase Exposition, and Kansas City began construction of the park and boulevard system that would make it the first urban area to experience the City Beautiful movement. Despite the division and trauma of the Civil War, Missouri had become a center of industry and urban development during the nineteenth century.

See also **Abolition and Antislavery; American Indian Societies,** *subentry on* **The Plains; Bleeding Kansas; Border States; Civil War,** *subentry on* **The West; Com-**promise of 1850; Jacksonian Era; Kansas City; Lewis and Clark Expedition; Louisiana Purchase; Missouri Compromise; Outlaws; Reconstruction,** *subentry on* **The West; St. Louis; Supreme Court,** *subentry on* **Slavery; Trails to the West; World's Fairs.**

Bibliography

Christensen, Lawrence O. "Missouri." In *Heartland: Comparative Histories of the Midwestern States.* Edited by James H. Madison. Bloomington: Indiana University Press, 1988.

Christensen, Lawrence O., and Gary R. Kremer. *A History of Missouri, 1875–1919.* Volume 4 of *A History of Missouri,* edited by William E. Parrish. Columbia: University of Missouri Press, 1997.

McCandless, Perry. *A History of Missouri, 1820–1860.* Volume 2 of *A History of Missouri,* edited by William E. Parrish. Columbia: University of Missouri Press, 1972.

Parrish, William E., Charles T. Jones Jr., and Lawrence O. Christensen. *Missouri: The Heart of the Nation.* Arlington Heights, Ill.: Harlan Davidson, 1992.

LAWRENCE O. CHRISTENSEN

MISSOURI COMPROMISE

In 1787 the U.S. Congress under the Articles of Confederation passed the third Northwest Ordinance, which, among its many provisions, prohibited slavery in the Northwest Territory, which comprised the area north of the Ohio River and east of the Mississippi River. At the time the Mississippi River was the western border of the nation, and thus the geography of the antislavery provision was clear. The Louisiana Purchase (1803), however, extended American territory all the way to the Rocky Mountains, and the new land was not covered by the provisions of the Northwest Ordinance.

Achieving a Missouri Compromise

From 1817 to 1819 the Missouri Territory sought entrance into the Union as a slave state. Slaves had been in the territory at the time of the Louisiana Purchase, and between 1803 and 1819 no one had ever suggested that the Northwest Ordinance of 1787 applied to the territory west of the Mississippi. Nevertheless, in the debate over Missouri statehood, Congressman James Tallmadge (1778–1853) of New York proposed an amendment that would ban new slaves in the state and create a gradual abolition scheme similar to that in his home state. No existing Missouri slaves would be emancipated, but any slave children born after statehood would be freed at age twenty-five. At the time, Missouri had only about 10,000 slaves, representing 16 percent of the territory's population. Gradual emancipation would have harmed few masters, and all could have sold their slaves in existing slave states.

The southern members of Congress, however, re-acted fiercely to Tallmadge's proposal. His amend-ment threatened the South in two ways. It repre-sented the first direct assault on the morality of slavery since the debates over the slave trade in the 1790s. Southerners were quick to defend the justice and good policy of slavery, and they denounced northerners for their interference in southern insti-tutions. In addition, the amendment threatened the political power of the South. If Missouri came in as a free state, it would deprive the South of new votes in the House, Senate, and electoral college, while en-hancing the North's already substantial power in the House and giving it a slight advantage in the Senate.

On 16 February 1819 the House of Representa-tives, by a vote of 87 to 76, prohibited the entry of future slaves into the Missouri Territory. With the exception of one member from Delaware, every southerner voted against this provision. The next day the House passed Tallmadge's gradual emancipation provision by a vote of 82 to 78 (two "yes" votes were cast by southerners). Among northerners, 10 voted against the first provision and 14 opposed the sec-ond. In the Senate, however, the slavery ban lost 22 to 16, while the gradual emancipation provision lost 31 to 7.

The Missouri issue was revived in December 1819. By this time Maine had voted to separate from Mas-sachusetts, and was requesting entry to the Union as a free state. On 30 December 1819, Henry Clay (1777–1852), the slave-owning Speaker of the House from Kentucky, warned that Maine could not become a state unless Missouri was admitted as a slave state. In February 1820, Senator Jesse B. Thomas (1777–1853) of Illinois offered a compromise: Maine would enter as a free state, Missouri would come in as a slave state, and slavery would be banned forever in the remainder of the Louisiana Purchase north of 36°30′ north latitude. The Senate quickly adopted this scheme and the House, just as quickly, rejected it, with both southerners and northerners voting "no." Washingtonians soon flocked to the House and Senate to hear what seemed like endless, and point-less, debates on the Missouri question. Some south-erners, led by Congressman John Randolph (1773–1833) of Virginia, talked about secession. They warned that the debate could be settled only by bloodshed, while some northerners asserted that the extension of slavery would be worse than disunion. Senator Rufus King (1755–1827) of New York, who in 1787 had represented Massachusetts at the Con-stitutional Convention, was one of the most promi-nent supporters of a ban on slavery. On the other side was Congressman Charles Pinckney (1757–1824) of South Carolina, who had represented his state at the Constitutional Convention.

On 1 March 1820 the House, continuing to disre-gard Senator Thomas's proposal, agreed to admit Missouri as a free state. The Senate responded by striking any slavery restrictions on Missouri and sup-porting the Thomas plan. Thanks to the leadership of Congressman Clay, a compromise finally was reached. On 3 March, Congress accepted Maine's pe-tition to enter the Union as a free state. Three days later, Congress gave Missouri permission to write a constitution that would not limit slavery in the new state. Congress also agreed that the rest of the Loui-siana Purchase north of 36°30′ latitude would remain free.

A year later the Missouri issue still festered, due to a provision in Missouri's proposed constitution that would ban the migration of free blacks into the future state. In early 1821 a number of senators and representatives privately expressed the fear that the nation might divide over this issue. In late February, however, Congressman Clay managed to bring about a Second Missouri Compromise. Congress legislated that Missouri could not enter the Union if its state constitution violated the rights of U.S. citizens. Al-though Senator Thomas of Illinois initially had au-thored the Missouri Compromise, Clay was respon-sible for its ultimate passage. By assembling a working coalition of southerners and northern mod-erates, Clay was able to push both compromises through the divided House.

Growing Sectionalism

The Missouri Compromise settled the issue of slavery in the territories for the next quarter century. After 1821, Congress informally agreed to pair new states from the North with those from the South, ensuring an equal number of free and slave states. This process worked relatively well in the 1830s and 1840s, but the long-term prospects for the compromise were poor. Arkansas became a state in 1836, followed by Michigan in 1837. The annexation of Texas in 1845 and the entry of Florida that same year gave the South a temporary majority of two states. The entry of Iowa (1846) and Wisconsin (1848) brought both sections to fifteen states. At this point, based on the 36°30′ latitude rule, the South could expect only one more slave state—Oklahoma—while the North could look to the admission of multiple states from the remaining Louisiana Purchase Territory and the former Oregon Country.

It soon became clear that the Missouri Compro-mise had outlived its time. In addition to changing U.S. geography, the Mexican Cession acquired at the end of the Mexican-American War (1846–1848) changed the politics of slavery and territorial expansion. Southerners saw the new land from Mexico as a source of political power, because most of it was below the Missouri Compromise line. However, there was heated congressional debate over the status of slavery in these territories. The Compromise of 1850 forestalled civil war by, among other provisions, admitting California to the Union as a free state and giving the residents of the New Mexico and Utah Territories self-determination on the slavery question.

To accommodate southern demands for new slave territories, Congress extended this principle of "popular sovereignty," which allowed territorial settlers to decide for themselves whether to enter the Union as a free or slave state. The Kansas-Nebraska Act (1854) granted those two territories popular sovereignty on all slavery issues, even though, under the Missouri Compromise, Kansas and Nebraska were to have been admitted as free states. The act's passage led to a small civil war, known as Bleeding Kansas. Finally the U.S. Supreme Court ruled in *Dred Scott v. Sandford* (1857) that the Missouri Compromise violated the Constitution. According to Chief Justice Roger B. Taney's majority opinion, slaves were property and did not qualify as U.S. citizens. Because, based on the Fifth Amendment, the government could not deprive slave owners of their property without due process of law, Congress did not have the power to forbid slavery in the territories.

Just as the Missouri Compromise helped to glue the nation together, its demise set the stage for the country's breakup. The Kansas-Nebraska Act led to the formation of the Republican Party, and the *Dred Scott* decision catapulted its most articulate critic—Abraham Lincoln—to the White House. Lincoln was the first president dedicated to abolishing slavery, and fear of his policies led to secession by eleven of the slave states, civil war, and an end to slavery in the United States.

See also **Civil War**, *subentry on* **Causes of the Civil War; Compromise of 1850; Kansas-Nebraska Act; Statehood and Admission.**

Bibliography

Freehling, William W. *The Road to Disunion.* Vol. 1. *Secessionists at Bay, 1776–1854.* New York: Oxford University Press, 1990.

Moore, Glover. *The Missouri Controversy, 1819–1821.* Gloucester, Mass.: Smith, 1967.

Robinson, Donald L. *Slavery in the Structure of American Politics, 1765–1820.* New York: Norton, 1979.

PAUL FINKELMAN

MONETARY POLICY   Banking was highly decentralized in the early days of the United States. State banks, like state governments, formed the backbone of the system during the antebellum period. A central bank of sorts did exist during the first third of the nineteenth century—the First Bank of the United States from 1791 to 1811 and the second Bank of the United States from 1816 to 1836—but states could and did charter banks at will. The 28 banks that existed in 1800 swelled to 88 by 1811 and to nearly 250 in 1816. The coin of the realm depended principally upon location. Although U.S. banknotes circulated widely, currency printed by local banks fueled many business transactions. State banks issued their own currency, and local paper commanded up to twice as much value as notes issued elsewhere, in part because people could more easily ascertain the reputation of local banks and in part because of transportation costs to redeem "foreign" currency.

Bank of the United States

The first Bank of the United States was largely of Alexander Hamilton's making. George Washington signed its twenty-year charter on Valentine's Day 1791. The bank held most of the Treasury Department's deposits, collected customs bonds, facilitated payment of interest on the public debt, and carried on foreign-exchange transactions for the Treasury. The bank was not required by law to assist other banks, but in practice it became a lender of last resort. Despite these apparent successes, a Jeffersonian Republican Congress in 1811 refused to renew the bank's charter because it had been created and run by the Federalists and because many Americans continued to fear centralized power and foreign ownership. Although they had little direct influence over the bank, foreigners owned nearly 70 percent of its stock.

The difficulty of financing the War of 1812 and the inflation of 1814 made it clear that a central bank was necessary, and in 1816 Congress chartered the second Bank of the United States. Nicolas Biddle took the helm in 1823 as the bank's third president and soon placed his imprimatur upon the banking system. Under Biddle the bank actively managed its loan portfolio and streamlined currency exchange throughout the nation.

Federal banking ceased with the presidency of Andrew Jackson. Jackson hated banks due to unfortunate financial deals he had made early in his life, and he had vowed to torpedo the second bank as soon as he took office. The bank continued operation until its charter expired in 1836. Shortly thereafter the United States experienced the devastating panic of 1837. A

"Capitol Fashions for 1837." A political cartoon depicting President Martin Van Buren as successor to Andrew Jackson, whose opponents nicknamed him "King Andrew the First." Van Buren was held responsible for the panic of 1837 by continuing Jackson's unpopular hard-money policies. As a result, this cartoon portrayed the new president as being crowned by a devilish creature, cloaked in the worthless currency his policy created, and treading on the Constitution and the rights of Indians. Delt Forbes, 1837. LIBRARY OF CONGRESS: PRINTS AND PHOTOGRAPHS DIVISION

central bank might have combated the panic somewhat better than the loose state banking system, but the principal cause of the panic stemmed from the nature of the American economy. As with any small, open economy, domestic monetary policy was largely at the mercy of outside forces. In 1836 Britain raised interest rates to stanch the outward flow of specie, which had an immediate effect on the vulnerable former colonies. U.S. banks found the cost of obtaining precious metals much higher than anticipated. Consequently they could not redeem their own notes for gold, which led to a major loss of confidence among note holders.

Free Banking

As the country recovered from these financial shocks, a new era in banking arrived, free banking (1837–1863). Aspiring bankers no longer had to convince state legislatures of their competence or the need for a new bank; they simply had to have a small amount of capital to set up shop. By 1860 more than fifteen hundred state banks were issuing on average six different denominations of notes. Although some commentators call this time chaotic and cited it as a reason for bank regulation, others argue that free banking worked reasonably well. Although about half of the banks closed during the period, most redeemed their notes at or slightly below par. At the same time consumers and businesses enjoyed the benefits of competition among banks. The free-banking era also led to the widespread use of paper currency, which released gold and silver stocks for productive uses. Yet the proliferation of note types and the ease of counterfeiting also meant that the costs of doing business were greater than if a credible, easily verifiable currency had been established.

National Banks

National fiat money arrived with the Civil War. The federal government created national banks to increase its borrowing power, and these banks issued "greenbacks," non–interest bearing notes used for legal tender. The value of greenbacks fluctuated with the fortunes of the Union army, plummeting to an all-time low after the June 1864 loss at Cold Harbor, Virginia.

National banks faced two entry barriers: a minimum capitalization requirement and loan restrictions. As a result national banks encountered stiff competition from state banks until the federal government imposed a 10 percent tax on state bank notes in March 1865. Later it inhibited branch banking among state banks as well. Consequently national banking restrained the growth of banks over much of the United States for several decades. Despite these constraints, a vigorous system of state banks survived. The number of state banks dwindled to 261 in 1870, supplanted by 1,612 national banks and 2,318 private banks. But state banks rebounded in following years; their numbers grew to 8,696 by the century's end as compared with only 3,731 national banks. Increasingly close correspondent banking arrangements, which tied local to regional and national banks, helped integrate capital markets and eliminate regional differences in interest rates by the century's end.

Gold and Silver Standards

After the Civil War the United States sought to resume its position in the international trading community. To do so required adherence to a universally approved metal standard. Before the war the United

Monetary Policy and the Democrats. This 1896 political cartoon from the *Washington Post* depicts a donkey labeled Democracy bearing the weight of opposing politicians in the monetary debate. William Jennings Bryan and other free-coinage advocates sit in the sack on the right labeled "silver"; in the "gold" sack on the left, President Grover Cleveland stands among gold standard proponents. Cleveland's efforts to repeal the 1890 Sherman Silver Purchase Act in 1893 returned the standard of exchange to gold and triggered deflation. LIBRARY OF CONGRESS

States had been on a bimetallic standard. The official exchange rate of gold for silver was set at 15 to 1 in 1792, but since the market valued gold more highly, the United States was effectively on a silver standard for the first third of the century. Americans had to rely for many years on foreign coins for legal tender. The original U.S. silver dollar was slightly lighter than the Spanish dollar, so newly minted U.S. dollars were exported and exchanged at par for Spanish dollars, which were then reminted into more American dollars. Thomas Jefferson therefore suspended the coinage of silver dollars in 1806, and Americans had to use foreign money instead. The Currency Act of 1834 revised the exchange rate between gold and silver to 16 to 1. Because the market rate for gold then fell below the official rate, the United States effectively enjoyed a gold standard until the end of 1861. The war suspended metal standards in favor of greenbacks, but the peace at Appomattox revived the desire for a metal standard.

The major problem facing monetary authorities at the end of the Civil War was that gold dollars sold at a premium of about 50 percent above the value of a paper dollar. Secretary of the Treasury Hugh McCulloch proposed to eliminate the premium by retiring greenbacks with budget surpluses, thus raising their value. Because paper currency remained the monetary standard, the contraction meant lower prices for goods as well as for gold in terms of paper dollars. McCulloch's scheme was unpopular among business owners and farmers, who typically carried heavy debt loads. Deflation meant that debtors had to pay back loans in dollars worth more than those originally lent to them. Because demand for food is inelastic, its price varies more than its quantity, relative to other goods. Consequently food prices fall faster than other prices in deflationary periods, so farm income fell precipitously as the money supply contracted after the war. Responding to the resultant public outcry, Congress reversed its contractionary policy in 1868.

Then came the Coinage Act of 1873, dubbed by some the "crime of 1873." The act eliminated the silver dollar as a medium of exchange and placed the United States on a virtual gold standard. The Coinage Act came about in part because Britain decided to adopt a gold standard, and, as in many other instances, the United States followed. Britain abandoned silver partly because the noted economist David Ricardo thought that silver was easier to mine and therefore monetary authorities could not control the stock of silver as readily as they could the stock of gold. Congress tried to reverse the Coinage Act with the Sherman Silver Purchase Act of 1890. President Grover Cleveland convinced Congress to repeal the latter law in 1893, and gold remained the reigning medium of exchange from 1873 until well after the turn of the century. Foes of a gold-backed currency naturally included silver producers, but a confluence of events also turned debtors, especially farmers, against it. For them the primary evil of committing to gold was the continuing deflation that plagued the country in the last part of the century.

Why did deflation occur after the 1873 act? The interaction of domestic and international metal, currency, and output markets provides the answer. Demand for gold expanded radically as a number of countries went on the gold standard. Discoveries of gold deposits lagged behind, so gold's market value went up substantially. By the time William Jennings Bryan delivered his "Cross of Gold" speech in 1896, the market value of gold relative to silver was 30 to 1. If the United States had kept a bimetallic standard, people simply would have sold their gold coins at the market rate and used silver as a medium of exchange. Because Americans could not switch to silver, markets had to reach equilibrium another way, by deflation. Scholars conclude that the American money stock grew between 1 and 2.6 percent annually from 1869 to 1879, while real output grew at 5 percent per year. Relatively fewer dollars were chasing relatively more goods, and prices fell at the rate of nearly 5 percent annually from the end of the Civil War to 1879.

In a classic essay on this tumultuous period, Hugh Rockoff claimed that the *Wonderful Wizard of Oz* (1900) by L. Frank Baum was really intended as a monetary allegory. Among other symbols, Dorothy represents the American people, Oz is the abbreviation for ounce, the cyclone is the free silver movement out of the West, Cleveland is the Wicked Witch of the East, and William McKinley is the Wicked Witch of the West. The good witches are the northern and southern farmers' alliances that gave birth to the Populist Party. McKinley's campaign manager Mark Hanna is the Wizard, Bryan is the Cowardly Lion, the Scarecrow represents western farmers, and the Tin Man stands for industrial workers. Water, like inflation, melts the powers of the Wicked Witch of the West. The road to Oz is golden, and Dorothy's shoes are silver, not ruby, in the original story.

See also **Banking and Finance; Investment and Capital Formation; Money and Coins; Panics and Depressions.**

Bibliography

Atack, Jeremy, and Peter Passell. *A New Economic View of American History.* New York: Norton, 1994.

Friedman, Milton. *Money Mischief: Episodes in Monetary History.* New York: Harcourt Brace Jovanovich, 1992.

Friedman, Milton, and Anna Jacobson Schwartz. *A Monetary History of the United States, 1867–1960.* Princeton, N.J.: Princeton University Press, 1963.

Rockoff, Hugh. "The 'Wizard of Oz' as a Monetary Allegory." *Journal of Political Economy* 98 (August 1990): 739–760.

Rolnick, Arthur J., and Warren E. Weber. "New Evidence on the Free Banking Era." *American Economic Review* 73 (1983): 1080–1091.

Sylla, Richard Eugene. *The American Capital Market, 1846–1914.* New York: Arno, 1975.

Walton, Gary M., and Hugh Rockoff. *History of the American Economy.* Fort Worth, Tex.: Dryden, 1994.

JENNY BOURNE WAHL

MONEY AND COINS   The nineteenth century was a pivotal period in the story of American numismatics. The century began during a lively and ongoing debate over who was actually responsible for the provision of exchange media in the United States. People generally agreed that the federal government should enjoy a monopoly over the supply of coinage to the American people, and indeed a mint had been set up for the purpose in 1792. But this new facility was an inept coiner, and Americans had yet to discover large sources of precious metals. People relied on foreign coins, barter, and a variety of paper instruments ranging from bills of exchange to private banknotes. The use of foreign coins and private banknotes underscores an important fact about money in nineteenth-century America. Simply put, no agreement had established who bore responsibility for supplying the inhabitants of the young nation with currency.

By the time the nineteenth century ended, the federal government operated three mints (at Philadelphia, San Francisco, and New Orleans) and had operated three more at one time (at Carson City, Nevada; Charlotte, North Carolina; and Dahlonega, Georgia). The mints' industrial expertise, married to vast new supplies of western gold and silver, produced all of the coinage needed by Americans and, in a neat turnabout, much of the coinage required by other nations as well. The federal government had driven its currency competitors from the field by that time and was in the process of establishing a monopoly over paper money fully comparable to the one it enjoyed over coinage. The modern American monetary system acquired most of its basic characteristics during the nineteenth century.

The creation of a national mint was inherent in the Federalist vision of the United States. The mint would provide a constant reinforcement of the majesty of the new government and would drive out unsupported paper currency, that bane of the business community and unwelcome legacy from the past. Congress passed the Mint Act in 1792, and a federal coiner was erected in Philadelphia that year. After that, nothing went according to plan.

The first U.S. Mint proved an indifferent practitioner of the coiner's craft. Its employees learned their work as they went along, and their machinery consisted of tools unwanted elsewhere or originally meant for other work. The mint lacked native supplies of gold and silver, so the tyro coiners were therefore obliged to wheedle gold coins and silver teapots from members of the public, purify and assay the metal, roll it out, cut it into coining blanks, and strike those blanks—all for free. Of course, this meant that the U.S. Mint lost money every year. Adding to the facility's other woes, a succession of senators and congressmen demanded that Americans find another source for the coinage they required.

The monies of foreign nations were a readily available alternative source. If a coin could be weighed and tested, someone somewhere in the United States would use it in trade. Latin American gold and silver coinage predominated. In fact, the Mexican peso, or piece of eight, had served as the template for the

American dollar. Coins from the Spanish Empire and its successor states continued to circulate in the United States with official approval for many years. So did British sovereigns, French coins worth five francs, and Brazilian ones worth 960 reals. The latter were recycled Latin American pesos that had been restruck in Bahia and Rio de Janeiro. The laws making foreign coinage legal tender were not wiped from American statute books until February 1857.

By 1857 the main mint in Philadelphia had been joined by the two small mints in Charlotte and Dahlonega, built in response to modest gold strikes in those districts. The New Orleans mint was more important because its supply of metal was far larger— the seemingly inexhaustible supply of gold escudos and silver pesos entering the Crescent City from Central and South America. These southern mints opened for business in 1838, and all closed during the Civil War. The New Orleans mint was eventually reopened and continued to coin through the remainder of the nineteenth century and beyond.

A fourth branch mint opened in direct response to larger events. In 1848 gold was discovered in California. Within a year private coiners were on the scene, turning California dust and ore into rough-and-ready but useful coins whose weights and fineness approximated those of legal American issues. In the spring of 1854 an official U.S. branch mint opened in San Francisco to drive its free-market competitors from the field. The Carson City mint opened in 1870 and operated until 1893.

All of the new facilities and the parent one in Philadelphia were equipped with modern, steam-powered machinery built in the United States. The industrialization of the country required increased production of coins and also provided the means by which to achieve that expansion. By the middle of the nineteenth century the U.S. government was poised to acquire a monopoly over the circulation of coinage.

Paper currency was another matter. The Constitution of 1787 reflected the views of the seaboard business community that had inspired its drafting. The unsupported state and federal paper issues of the Revolutionary War were worthless by that war's end, convincing the mercantile community and the drafters of the Constitution that public paper money should play no role in the new Republic. The framers banned state currency outright and were deliberately silent on whether the new national government could or could not print money. But if public authorities could not or would not circulate paper currency, private ones would do so. Banks, railroads, insurance companies, city governments, land companies, and even a hotel and an orphans' institute circulated their own currency with a minimum of outside control. Predictably, the results were widespread speculation and fraud; counterfeit, spurious, and altered notes; and annoyance for many and misery and ruin for a few. But the notes also paid for clearing land, construction of railroads and factories, and building of cities.

The problem of printing a note that could be mass produced yet was difficult to forge was triumphantly solved by Jacob Perkins of Newburyport, Massachusetts. Perkins created a master image on soft steel, hardened the steel, transferred the design onto a soft steel roller, hardened the roller, and transferred the image to several soft steel plates that, once hardened, could print identical notes. Perkins perfected his method by 1805 and secured a monopoly to print paper money for Massachusetts and Maine, which then was part of the Bay State, in 1809. A succession of engravers developed the artistry of nineteenth-century U.S. banknotes into the world's most beautiful currency, portraying Americans in the field, in the factory, at leisure, and at work.

Between 1860 and 1865 the U.S. currency situation changed. The private note became a slightly discredited memento of the past, and the national government took a major step toward establishing a monopoly over the issue of paper currency. During the Civil War authorities in both the North and the South found that they needed larger sums of money than ever before and that the usual expedients were inadequate. The South, where circulating specie had always been scarce, and the North, where people now hid coins, turned to paper currency, but the traditional issuers quickly became insufficient. The governments of the United States and the Confederate States of America injected themselves into the emergency, because unlike banks they could issue vast amounts of paper backed only by promises and force its acceptance.

The Confederacy had the easier time. In the spring of 1861 the Confederacy issued its first currency, which was joyfully accepted at full value across the South. But as the war became more general and the prospects of Southern independence more remote, depreciation set in. By 1865 the real value of its paper had sunk to a fiftieth of its stated value. Northern victory that spring rendered it worthless along with the wartime issues of state and local governments, individuals, and private banks.

The Union reacted to the need for a national currency in stages. In the summer of 1861 the United States created demand notes payable in specie "on demand." That convertibility may have satisfied the fiscally conservative, but it did little to provide the sinews of an expanding war. In the following year the government was obliged to create a species of fiat money, that is, currency backed by promises but little more, called legal tender. Since this new federal money was not backed by silver or gold, its value fluctuated against precious metal, rising when victory appeared near and falling when victory appeared to recede. At the low point of the war, one paper legal tender dollar was worth about 37 cents in gold.

The Lincoln administration was aware of another potential source of money, private Northern banks, but bank owners were not sufficiently interested in a Union victory to help pay for it. Late in the winter of 1863 Congress passed the National Banking Act, which created a national banking system. Each bank that joined would use its resources to purchase war bonds. The bank would then be chartered as a national bank, giving it the right to issue national bank notes against the value of the bonds it acquired. The Union government received money with which to prosecute the war, and the bank got prestige but not much more. That being the case, very few institutions joined the new arrangement, so the administration exerted force, using the power of taxation modestly at first but more onerously later. The private banks took the hint. They either joined the national system, thereby giving up their own currency notes for federal money, or they ceased to issue fiscal paper.

The Civil War began the federal government's movement toward a monopoly over currency, but the process did not end until 1935, when an expanded Federal Reserve system replaced the note-issuing national banks. America's money continued to reflect larger events during the remainder of the nineteenth century. Those events ranged from domestic political and economic concerns, such as the debate over silver versus gold coinage in the presidential campaigns of 1896 and 1900, to foreign affairs, including trade coinage for the Orient, normal coinage for Hawaii, and coinage and currency for several old and new countries in Latin America. But the central question of nineteenth-century numismatics in the United States was resolved in the factory towns of the East, the gold fields of the West, and the battlefields of the South.

See also **Banking and Finance; Currency Policy; Gold Rushes and Silver Strikes; Monetary Policy.**

Bibliography

American Numismatic Society. *America's Copper Coinage, 1783–1857.* New York: American Numismatic Society, 1985.
———. *America's Currency, 1789–1866.* New York: American Numismatic Society, 1985.
———. *America's Gold Coinage.* New York: American Numismatic Society, 1990.
———. *America's Silver Coinage, 1794–1891.* New York: American Numismatic Society, 1987.
Doty, Richard. *America's Money—America's Story.* Iola, Wis.: Krause, 1998.
Haxby, J. A. *Standard Catalog of United States Obsolete Bank Notes, 1782–1866.* 4 vols. Iola, Wis.: Krause, 1988.
Schilke, Oscar G., and Raphael E. Solomon. *America's Foreign Coins.* New York: Coin and Currency Institute, 1964.
Taxay, Don. *The U.S. Mint and Coinage.* New York: Arco, 1966.

RICHARD G. DOTY

MONROE DOCTRINE   The Monroe Doctrine originated in President James Monroe's message to Congress on 2 December 1823. It concerned the governments of newly independent Latin America and the role of Europe in the New World. While it had limited meaning and application at the time, it became the cornerstone of U.S. policy in the Western Hemisphere.

By 1823 a confluence of events prompted President Monroe and Secretary of State John Quincy Adams to prepare a definitive statement of U.S. policy toward colonization and European interference in the hemisphere. Russia had been moving southward from its colony in Alaska, threatening, at least in the minds of U.S. officials, the Pacific coast. Meanwhile, revolutions had removed the Spanish and Portuguese from most of Latin America. In 1822 the United States was the first power to begin recognizing the new governments. In 1823 ominous rumors circulated that Spain, France, and other members of the Holy Alliance, a loose confederation of European reactionary regimes, would try to reconquer the former colonies. Both Monroe and Adams were gravely concerned, for such actions threatened the economic and territorial goals of the United States. The United States had emerged from the War of 1812 with new economic energy and more certain territorial designs. The moment was propitious for a declaration of American goals.

At this time British Foreign Minister George Canning proposed that the United States and Great Britain issue a joint declaration supporting Latin American independence and vowing that they would take no more territory in the New World. Some in the Monroe administration were flattered that Britain, the most powerful nation in the world, would want to join with the United States in such a policy. Secretary of State Adams, however, went on the attack. The proposal, he argued, was purely self-serving for the British. They certainly did not need the United States to help protect the Western Hemisphere—the British navy did that. In addition, the vow not to engage in territorial expansion would preclude the United States from moving to acquire Cuba or Texas, which Adams especially had his eye on. Adams insisted that a unilateral declaration of U.S. policy was needed, and he ultimately persuaded President Monroe. From this decision was born the Monroe Doctrine.

The section of Monroe's message dealing with these matters was quite brief and made three major points. First, no further European colonization in the New World would be tolerated. Second, the United States pledged to remain aloof from European wars and politics, implying that the Old and New Worlds were quite distinct entities. Finally, Monroe warned against European interference with the independent republics in the New World.

This rather sweeping declaration drew a mixed reception. In the United States it was generally applauded in spite of some fears (groundless, as it turned out) that Monroe was pledging the United States to militarily defend the Latin American nations from European attack. Latin America responded with cautious optimism. While the American warning to the Europeans was certainly welcome, the facts that the statement was issued without consultation with the Latin American governments and that it said nothing about U.S. intentions caused some concern. In Europe the statement was either virtually ignored or pilloried as American arrogance. How could the United States hope to back up its implied threat against European intervention in the New World? Adams knew the answer: the United States did not have to. The British, as he was well aware, no more wanted the recolonization of Latin America than did the United States. The British fleet would be all the protection that was needed.

The immediate impact of the Monroe Doctrine was slight. Europeans constantly interfered in Latin America, often sending military forces to collect debts, protect European property and investments, or simply to punish insults. The United States was powerless to stop them. Little by little, however, the Monroe Doctrine was expanded upon and used more aggressively. In the 1840s President James Polk modified the doctrine somewhat by arguing that areas of Latin America could not offer themselves as protectorates or colonies of European powers. During and immediately after the Civil War the United States brandished the Monroe Doctrine, which was then backed by a large and modern military, and warned the French and Spanish to remove their forces occupying Mexico and Santo Domingo, respectively. In 1895 Secretary of State Richard Olney further elaborated on the meaning of the Monroe Doctrine. In the midst of Great Britain's dispute with Venezuela

over the boundaries of British Guiana, Olney warned the British that the United States was "practically sovereign on this continent" and that its "fiat is law." Taken aback, the British eventually gave in to U.S. demands for an arbitrated settlement.

What had begun as a relatively general and straightforward statement of American policy in the New World had evolved into something more aggressive and clear-cut. The United States assumed the position of dominance in the Western Hemisphere once held by the European powers. Latin Americans feared that the Monroe Doctrine, far from being a guarantee of Latin American freedom and security, was merely the foundation for U.S. economic and territorial expansion at their expense. In the years to come the scope of the doctrine would be widened even further, demonstrating to Latin Americans that their fears were justified.

See also **Central America and the Caribbean; Europe, Foreign Relations with; Great Britain, Foreign Relations with; South America, Foreign Relations with.**

Bibliography
May, Ernest. *The Making of the Monroe Doctrine.* Cambridge, Mass.: Harvard University Press, 1975.
Perkins, Dexter. *A History of the Monroe Doctrine.* Boston: Little, Brown, 1963.
Weeks, William Earl. *John Quincy Adams and American Global Empire.* Lexington: University Press of Kentucky, 1992.

MICHAEL L. KRENN

MONTANA Migrating Indians crossed Montana's high plains and mountains long before the nineteenth century. They found generally mild weather that could turn sweltering in the summer and bitter in the winter. Arriving in the sixteenth century, the Flathead Indians lived west of the Continental Divide. Migrating Crows reached the Powder River Basin in what is now western Montana between 1400 and 1600. The Crows found the Apaches and, perhaps, some Kiowas already established. Tribes of Cheyenne arrived later.

Soon after the United States acquired the vast Louisiana Purchase in 1803, Meriwether Lewis and William Clark explored Montana, encountering its Indian population in 1805 and again on their return trip a year later. Fur trappers followed, many in the employ of the American Fur Company, owned principally by John Jacob Astor. In 1841 the first wagon train of emigrants bound for Oregon passed through, alarming the Cheyennes and Sioux by their consumption of scarce wood and grass. By the 1850s the U.S. government had launched an effort to control the Indians by limiting their hunting grounds. In 1876 federal authorities dispatched three U.S. Army columns against the Sioux and Cheyennes, ultimately forcing both tribes onto reservations, but not before Crazy Horse and his warriors had wiped out George Armstrong Custer's Seventh Cavalry detachment at the Battle of the Little Bighorn. The next year the U.S. Army chased the Nez Percé tribe through Montana, at one point killing women and children before Nez Percé warriors could organize a counterattack.

Portions of what is now Montana fell within the Oregon Territory in 1848 and the Idaho Territory in 1863. But these territorial governments scarcely touched the remote settlers huddled in Montana, a population greatly enlarged by a gold rush starting in 1862. Many settlers followed the Montana Trail from Salt Lake City to Fort Benton while others chanced the Bozeman Trail, named for the pioneer John Bozeman. The Union Pacific Railroad made the Bozeman Trail obsolete by 1868, and the Utah and Northern Railroad replaced the Montana Trail in 1882.

Mining proved central to the Montana economy. Young men dominated the early mining camps, which became known for their violence, drinking, and prostitution. With alarming frequency the *Montana Post* and the *Boise News* reported murders and assaults. Miners governed themselves by means of town meetings called "miners' courts." Unauthorized by any legislature, these courts set up rules and elected officers. In Bannack, miners elected Henry Plummer sheriff, but vigilantes accused him of leading local bandits and hanged him and his deputies in 1864. Some Montanans used this vigilantism to justify their calls for territorial status, pointing out that Idaho's capital was remote from Montana's mining camps.

In 1864 Congress created Montana Territory, and President Abraham Lincoln named the former Ohio congressman Sidney Edgerton its first governor. A quarter-century later, in 1889, Congress made Montana a state, and Democrat Joseph K. Toole became Montana's first elected governor. In the 1892 presidential race Republicans narrowly carried Montana, and thereafter Democrats and Republicans waged hard-fought battles for control of the state. Regardless of party, the "war of the copper kings"—notably Marcus Daly and William Andrews Clark—dominated Montana's politics. The economy's mainstays continued to be cattle and copper. The new state had 243,329 residents in 1900, up from 20,595 thirty years earlier.

See also **American Indian Societies,** *subentry on* **The Plains; Frontier; Gold Rushes and Silver Strikes.**

Bibliography

Hampton, Bruce. *Children of Pride: The Nez Percé War of 1877.* Henry Holt, 1994.

Malone, Michael, Richard Roeder, and William Lang. *Montana: A History of Two Centuries.* Seattle: University of Washington Press, 1991.

Spence, Clark C. *Montana: A Bicentennial History.* New York: Norton, 1978.

CHRISTOPHER WALDREP

MONUMENTS AND MEMORIALS Historical monuments, particularly those erected publicly rather than on family plots in cemeteries, tell more than their manifest stories. They also reveal much about the ideas dominant when they were erected. They went up slowly at first. Fewer than twenty public monuments dating from the first three decades of the nineteenth century appear in the "Smithsonian Inventory of American Sculpture," admittedly an incomplete list. Most of those honor George Washington or the War of 1812. In the 1820s alone statues of Washington appeared at the state capitols of North Carolina, Virginia, and Massachusetts and atop the Washington Monument in Baltimore.

An important shift in how and where Americans buried their dead affected monument building in the United States in the 1830s and 1840s. The cemetery as a "rural" landscaped park dates to 1831 and the Boston physician Jacob Bigelow, a founder of Mount Auburn Cemetery in Cambridge. This park also initiated the American use of the euphemism "cemetery," which means "sleeping place" in Greek, in place of "burial ground." Immediately Mount Auburn and its imitators became tourist attractions, and tombstones grew more monumental. As the century wore on American sculptors received more of the monument commissions that previously were monopolized by Italians and other Europeans.

In the 1840s and 1850s new public monuments honored founders, like Benjamin Franklin, Thomas Jefferson, Patrick Henry, and George Mason, but also local heroes, such as the Palmetto Regiment in South Carolina and King Gambrinus, the patron of brewing, in Milwaukee. Massachusetts citizens dedicated the Bunker Hill Monument, a 221-foot granite obelisk, in 1843. When Scottish Americans put up the monument to Sir Walter Scott in Manhattan's Central Park in 1845, ethnic groups literally made their appearance on the landscape. German Americans put up a monument to Martin Luther, and Polish Americans erected one to the Revolutionary War hero Casimir Pulaski. This trend reached its crescendo in the final decade of the century, when Italian Americans put up statues of Christopher Columbus across the country.

In 1848 construction began on America's largest single monument, the Washington Monument in the capital. Work stalled in 1854, however, and did not resume until the end of Reconstruction. A visible line marks where construction stopped, emblematic of America's waning ability to unite behind major undertakings as the Civil War approached. Another Washington landmark, *Freedom*, the bronze woman atop the Capitol, also bears witness to the growing division. The sculptor's prototype wore a "liberty cap" similar to those worn by freed slaves in ancient Rome, but Secretary of War Jefferson Davis, a powerful man in the Buchanan administration, objected as a slave owner. He suggested stars overlaid by an eagle's head and feathers, making most tourists think *Freedom* is a Plains Indian.

One of America's most famous monuments received its iconic name in the late 1830s. Delighted with the Bible verse cast into the bell that hung in the Pennsylvania Statehouse when the Continental Congress adopted the Declaration of Independence, "Proclaim LIBERTY throughout all the Land unto all the Inhabitants thereof," abolitionists christened it the Liberty Bell. During the 1840s and 1850s they adopted the bell as a symbol, to the discomfort of those who wished the slavery issue would go away. The movement for black freedom also inspired America's other foremost iconic monument, the Statue of Liberty (1886), which stemmed from connections forged during the Civil War between American abolitionists and the French Anti-Slavery Society.

Yankees put up busts of Daniel Webster in Central Park (1853) and Boston (1858). Meanwhile supporters of slavery erected a statue of the disunionist John C. Calhoun in Charleston (1851) and renamed counties for him in Alabama and Florida. An incident during the Civil War continued the American tradition of ideological altering of the landscape. After his forces took New Orleans in 1862, Union commander Ben Butler had the words "The Union Must And Shall Be Preserved" carved onto the base of the monument to Andrew Jackson in the French Quarter. Confederates fumed but had to admit that the words paraphrased Jackson's toast in defiance of Calhoun, "Our Federal Union: it must be preserved."

After the war a great rush to erect monuments to memorialize the heroes and victims of the struggle ensued. The Union put up its monuments first. In *War Memorials as Political Landscape* (1988) James M. Mayo claims that the lag in southern monument building is attributable to the South's war-induced poverty (p. 171). Yet the parts of the South least affected by the war and most prosperous afterward, such as Florida and much of Texas, erected Confederate monuments no earlier than the harder hit sections. In contrast, German Americans in Comfort, Texas, who were devastated when Confederates killed thirty-nine of their band trying to flee the Confederate draft, put up a *Treue der Union* (True to the Union) stone in 1866. In fact, war monuments are usually erected by the victors. Not until Congress in 1890 defeated the last nineteenth-century bill supporting black voting rights, the Lodge Force Bill, were neo-Confederates confident that they had secured white supremacy and thus sufficiently confident to erect monuments honoring the Confederacy. Of the Civil War monuments honoring the United States, 52 percent went up in the nineteenth century, and another 21 percent went up in the first decade of the twentieth century. Only 27 percent of the Confederate monuments went up in the nineteenth century and another 18 percent between 1900 and 1909. The dedications of these monuments were major events. Businesses closed, bands played, organizations paraded through the streets to the site, and dignitaries gave marathon speeches.

Many Civil War monuments have become landmarks in their communities, such as Grand Army Plaza in Brooklyn, New York. Dedicated in 1892, it was designed by John Duncan, famous also for Grant's Tomb in Manhattan, the largest tomb in America and the most expensive monument built in the nineteenth century (1897). Perhaps no city is more defined by its Civil War monuments than Washington, D.C., whose nineteenth-century public monuments include Lieutenant General Winfield Scott in Scott Circle (1874), General Grant's aide John Rawlins in Rawlins Park (1874), Brigadier General James McPherson in McPherson Square (1876), the Navy or Peace Memorial northwest of the Capitol (1877), General George Thomas in Thomas Circle (1879), and Admiral David Farragut in Farragut Square (1881), as well as two statues of Abraham Lincoln (1868 and 1876). Frustrated in their attempts to put up an outdoor statue of Robert E. Lee inside the District of Columbia, Democrats responded in 1896 with General Winfield Scott Hancock on Pennsylvania Avenue, and in 1901 with Albert Pike, Confederate general and Arkansas Ku Klux Klan leader, in Judiciary Square.

Some later Confederate monuments were counterfactual, such as one labeled "A Loving Tribute to Our Confederate Soldiers in Helena, Montana" (1916). Not only did no one from Montana fight for the Confederacy, but most of Montana was still Indian country until well after the Civil War, as George Armstrong Custer found out to his sorrow at the Little Big Horn in 1876. But the Confederacy dominates the landscape in many places it did not dominate during the nineteenth century. Kentucky, for example,

Washington Monument Under Construction. After a twenty-year delay in construction because of the Civil War and insufficient funds, the Washington Monument was finally crowned in 1884 with an eight-inch aluminum pyramid. An interruption in its construction is evident in the different shades of marble, with darker stone making up the bottom third. The obelisk was outfitted with a steam elevator which, while acceptable for men's use, was considered too dangerous for women—thus forcing them to climb up 898 steps while their male companions ascended with general ease. LIBRARY OF CONGRESS

did not secede, and ninety thousand Kentuckians fought for the United States in contrast with only thirty-five thousand for the Confederate States. Nevertheless, according to the historian Thomas Clark, the state erected seventy-two Confederate monuments and only two Union ones.

Reconstruction influenced the landscape even in states that were not directly affected by it. A statue of Andrew Hendricks stands on the west side of the Indiana Statehouse and bears a plaque that says, "Lifelong opponent of Republican Oliver P. Morton, Indiana's Civil War Governor and postwar United States Senator, whose statue stands on the east side of the Capitol." Hendricks particularly opposed Re-

publican policies of citizenship for African Americans, and his monument indicates that white supremacists controlled the state government in 1890, when the monument was erected. Similarly, a statue of Chief Justice Roger B. Taney dominates the south lawn of the Maryland Statehouse. Placed in 1872, it honors Taney for his opinion in *Dred Scott v. Sandford* (1857), which proclaimed that blacks had "no rights which the white man was bound to respect." In 1996 Maryland put up a conflict partner for Taney, a monument to Supreme Court justice Thurgood Marshall, at the north entrance of the capitol.

New Orleans claims its 1884 statue of Margaret Gaffney Haughery was America's first monument to a woman. A widow, she started a successful bakery and devoted its profits to orphans. Women were rarely represented in stone in the nineteenth century, but they often played large roles in erecting the monuments. In the 1880s the Woman's Christian Temperance Union supported a plethora of temperance monuments, often fountains proclaiming the superiority of water over liquor.

Monuments seem silent, consensual, and faithful—history written in stone. But some American monuments, like their counterparts in eastern Europe, have been scenes of turbulence. Robert E. Cray wrote of the 1879 monument built in Tappan, New York, to Major John André, a British spy in the Revolutionary War, that was thrice toppled by angry patriots. The 1889 monument to the policemen killed in Chicago's Haymarket riot took much abuse over the years and was eventually surrounded by the Chicago Police Academy. Several nineteenth-century monuments were altered by official action in the twentieth century. San Francisco's 1894 Pioneer Monument, in part a paean to the subjugation of the American Indians, in 1996 received a corrective plaque pointing out the continuing presence of Native Americans in California. An 1889 statue of John Mason adorned Mystic, Connecticut, where Mason led British colonists in exterminating the major village of the Pequots. In the 1990s descendants and supporters of the Pequots mounted a campaign that finally removed it to a less offensive location in Windsor, near Mason's original homesite. Other nineteenth-century monuments have become controversial as Americans face the unvarnished facts of their ancestors' actions.

Tied to the nineteenth century is the hierarchy that many monuments embody. The sheer size of the Washington Monument is an example, as is the portrayal on horseback of leaders who were deskbound in life. All across the United States sculptors depicted whites in dominant positions over people of color. This was even true of the 1876 Emancipation Monument in Washington, D.C., which was paid for by donations from African Americans.

Two monuments placed late in the nineteenth century hint in opposite ways at the direction many monuments took in the twentieth century. In 1890 Richmond erected its first Confederate statue, a huge, triumphant-looking Robert E. Lee, on what became Monument Row. In 1898 Augustus Saint-Gaudens completed one of the most praised monuments in the United States, Boston's memorial to Colonel Robert Gould Shaw and the Fifty-fourth Massachusetts Colored Regiment, heroes of the failed 1863 assault on Fort Wagner, South Carolina. The Lee monument presaged the parade of Confed-erate leaders and soldiers soon to rise in bronze across the South. The Shaw memorial, on the other hand, was a dinosaur. Later United States war memorials, whether to the Union dead, veterans of the Spanish-American and Philippine Wars, or the World War I doughboy, were generally devoid of ideological intensity and artistic innovation.

See also **Cemeteries and Burial; Civil War,** *subentry on* **Remembering the Civil War; History; Nationalism; National Parks; Patriotic and Genealogical Societies; Sculpture.**

Bibliography

Cocke, Edward J. *Monumental New Orleans.* Jefferson, La.: Hope, 1974.

Cray, Robert E., Jr. "The John André Memorial: The Politics of Memory in Gilded Age New York." *New York History* 77, no. 1 (January 1996): 5–32.

Goode, James M. *The Outdoor Sculpture of Washington, D.C.* Washington, D.C.: Smithsonian Institution Press, 1974.

Loewen, James W. *Lies across America: What Our Historic Sites Get Wrong.* New York: New Press, 1999.

Mayo, James M. *War Memorials as Political Landscape.* New York: Praeger, 1988.

JAMES W. LOEWEN

MORMONISM   The Church of Jesus Christ of Latter-day Saints, otherwise known as the Mormon Church, had its origins in the religious experiences of Joseph Smith Jr. Smith was born on 23 December 1805 in Vermont and moved with his family in 1816 to Palmyra in western New York State. Farming and laboring, the Smith family lived in the Second Great Awakening's Protestant culture.

Origins

Many early-nineteenth-century Americans were seekers, primitivists (those expecting to find Christ's primitive church), millennialists (those expecting Christ's imminent return to inaugurate a thousand-year reign), and believers in magic. In this climate of intense religious yearning, revivalists scoured the region for converts. In the year between mid-1819 and mid-1820 Protestant ministers conducted numerous revivals in the communities around Palmyra. Somewhat partial to Methodism but confused by conflicting religious claims and worried about his personal worthiness, Smith, in the spring of 1820 when he was fourteen years old, sought guidance and forgiveness through prayer. He experienced a vision in which Christ forgave his sins, cautioned him not to join any of the churches, and told him he would receive further instructions.

Between 1823 and 1827 Smith experienced visitations from an angel named Moroni, who revealed the location of golden plates covered with ancient writings about Christianity in ancient America. Using a seer stone, Smith translated the text, which he published as the Book of Mormon, giving rise to the term "Mormon." He collected a group of followers and built theology and practice on the Bible, the Book of Mormon, and additional revelations. Smith organized the Church of Jesus Christ of Latter-day Saints on 6 April 1830, and its missionaries called on Americans, Canadians, and Europeans to repent and to prepare for Christ's return.

Almost immediately the Saints encountered opposition, some of it violent. Partly in response to the persecution, in December 1831 Smith moved to Kirtland, Ohio, where a sizable body of converts had gathered. Shortly thereafter, impelled by Smith's revelations, converts began to gather in Independence, Missouri, to build the center of a Zionistic kingdom, a place of refuge from the tribulations promised before Christ's second coming. Interpreting the First Amendment's free exercise of religion clause literally, Mormons conducted all facets of their lives according to religious precepts. They purchased land for distribution to converts, established a communitarian system called the Law of Consecration and Stewardship, and voted as a bloc. Such practices aroused violent opposition from neighboring Missourians. Driven from Independence by mobs in 1833, the Mormons relocated in northern Missouri, from which they fled after a civil war in 1838 that pitted Missourians against Mormons.

Settling in Nauvoo, Illinois, in 1839, the Mormons gathered converts from the United States, Canada, and Europe. Distinctive doctrines and practices, such as continuous revelation, the gathering of Mormon believers into one place, community economics, bloc voting, the corporeality of God, salvation for the dead, temple endowment ceremonies, marriage for eternity, and plural marriage, drew the Mormon community together and rankled its neighbors. Smith ordered the destruction of a Nauvoo city newspaper published by the church's critics, and he and his brother Hyrum Smith were subsequently imprisoned. A mob stormed the jail and assassinated the brothers on 27 June 1844.

Continued hostility toward the church led most of the Mormons to follow Joseph Smith's disciple Brigham Young to Utah. Smaller groups followed James J. Strang to Lake Michigan; Sidney Rigdon, who had served as Smith's counselor, to Pittsburgh; and Granville Hedrick, whose group owned the original site designated for the temple, to Independence. In 1860 Joseph Smith III, the eldest son of Joseph

Joseph Smith (1805–1844). Smith believed that he had been chosen by God to restore the church of Christ and translate the history of America's true church. Following these beliefs he founded the Church of Jesus Christ of the Latter-day Saints, commonly known as the Mormon Church. LIBRARY OF CONGRESS

Smith, was called to the presidency of the Reorganized Church of Jesus Christ of Latter-day Saints (RLDS), made up at first of many believers who had remained in the Midwest. Joseph Smith Jr.'s first wife, Emma, and Smith's brother, William Smith, joined the RLDS as well. After settling in Illinois and Iowa, the RLDS established its headquarters in Independence, and Joseph Smith III served as the church's president until 1914. While accepting the Book of Mormon and Smith's revelations, the RLDS rejected plural marriage and some of the other doctrines preached in Nauvoo.

Settlement in Utah

In July 1847 Young's followers settled in Utah. Gathering in converts, the Saints built communities throughout the West. By 1910 the church numbered about 393,000 members. By 1930 they had established at least 742 settlements, principally in Utah but also in Idaho, Arizona, Nevada, Wyoming, Colorado, New Mexico, Montana, California, Oregon, and Washington in the continental United States; Alberta in Canada; Chihuahua and Sonora in Mexico; and Hawaii and Samoa in the Pacific. The settlers laid out towns and farms, built irrigation works, and organized wards or congregations presided over by bishops and stakes, or units of a number of wards, presided over by stake presidents. Their settlements encroached on Ute, Shoshoni, Paiute, Gosiute, and Navajo lands, and settlers engaged in a number of battles with American Indians.

After Congress organized Utah Territory in 1850, President Millard Fillmore appointed Brigham Young as governor and superintendent of Indian Affairs. Most of the territory's federal appointees, however, were Protestants and Catholics who had decided prejudices against the Saints. Early conflicts led President James Buchanan in 1857 to dispatch an army to escort Young's replacement as governor. Hysteria over the coming army led a unit of the Mormon Utah territorial militia and a band of Paiute allies to massacre more than one hundred non-Mormon immigrants at Mountain Meadows in southwestern Utah. In spite of his subsequent removal from the governorship, Young remained a powerful Mormon leader in the West.

Intent on building the kingdom of God on earth, Mormons cooperated to a high degree. Between 1864 and 1874 they established a series of communitarian enterprises called United Orders in towns and cities throughout the mountain West. In 1868 they set up a merchandizing and manufacturing cooperative called Zions Cooperative Mercantile Institution, and they boycotted non-Mormon businesses. Young died in 1877, and his successor, John Taylor, lifted the boycott in 1882.

Distressed by the Latter-day Saints' political, social, and economic control and by the polygamy practiced by perhaps 20 percent of Mormon men, Protestant and Catholic organizations lobbied Congress to force the Mormons into more commonplace patterns of American conduct. Congress responded with a series of laws in 1862, 1874, 1882, and 1887 that imprisoned more than one thousand Mormons for terms of six months to five years for practicing polygamy. Laws also limited the power of local government, disfranchised Mormon women, and confiscated the church's property.

Bowing to external pressure, Taylor's successor, Wilford Woodruff, in a successful effort to save the church from destruction, announced the end of plural marriage in 1890. In addition the Mormons dissolved their political party in 1891, cooperated in organizing national political parties, and joined non-Mormons in various business enterprises. These changes constituted a shift from building a literal kingdom of God on earth to promoting personal piety. Recognizing the revolution in Mormon society that had taken place, Congress admitted Utah as a state in 1896. Conversion to the modified form of Mormonism continued, and by the end of the twentieth century membership in the Church of Jesus Christ of Latter-day Saints and its affiliated churches had grown to more than 10 million.

See also **Anti-Mormonism; Communitarian Movements and Groups; Polygamy, Mormon; Religion,** *subentry on* **Religion in Nineteenth-Century America; Revivalism; Utah.**

Bibliography

Allen, James B., and Glen M. Leonard. *The Story of the Latter-day Saints.* 2d ed., revised. Salt Lake City: Deseret, 1992.
Arrington, Leonard J. *Brigham Young: American Moses.* New York: Knopf, 1985.
———. *Great Basin Kingdom: An Economic History of the Latter-day Saints, 1830–1900.* Cambridge, Mass.: Harvard University Press, 1958.
Brodie, Fawn M. *No Man Knows My History: The Life of Joseph Smith, the Mormon Prophet.* 2d ed., revised. New York: Knopf, 1971.
Bushman, Richard L. *Joseph Smith and the Beginnings of Mormonism.* Urbana: University of Illinois Press, 1984.
Campbell, Eugene E. *Establishing Zion: The Mormon Church in the American West, 1847–1869.* Salt Lake City, Utah: Signature, 1988.
Launius, Roger D. *Joseph Smith III: Pragmatic Prophet.* Urbana: University of Illinois Press, 1988.
Lyman, Edward Leo. *Political Deliverance: The Mormon Quest for Utah Statehood.* Urbana: University of Illinois Press, 1986.

THOMAS G. ALEXANDER

MOVIES   While the production, distribution, and presentation of motion pictures began in the final years of the nineteenth century, these were years of failure. The era of the movies as mass entertainment would not begin until 1905, when the nickelodeon explosion began in urban America. The nineteenth century is thus properly labeled as the prehistory of the cinema.

The new technology of making movies required a camera to record the images, a printer to develop them, and a projector to present them. Thomas Alva Edison (1847–1931) is most frequently credited for these inventions; his laboratory did develop the kinetoscope, a peep show–like viewing device. But dozens of other inventors, in particular the Kodak company, which developed the flexible film base, also contributed, along with many inventors from other nations. The development of printers and projectors was pursued by the Lumière brothers of France.

In 1894 came peep shows for individual users; a year later screen projection premieres were held in both France and the United States. The first films were simple in form and style and short in length, usually the one-shot recording of a vaudeville performer or the static representation of a newsworthy event such as activities surrounding the Spanish-American War of 1898. Movie presentations piggybacked on other forms of mass entertainment, sometimes forming one act of a vaudeville show or a special attraction at an amusement park. Thus, typical audiences were made up of the middle class, who could afford the relatively high prices of vaudeville and the time free from work necessary to spend a day in the country at an outlying amusement park.

See also **Interpretations of the Nineteenth Century,** *subentry on* **Twentieth-Century Film and Media; Photography.**

Bibliography
Gomery, Douglas. *Shared Pleasures: A History of Movie Presentation in the United States.* Madison: University of Wisconsin Press, 1992.

Musser, Charles. *The Emergence of Cinema: The American Screen to 1907.* New York: Scribners, 1990.

DOUGLAS GOMERY

MUCKRAKERS

From the moment it entered the literary lexicon, the term "muckraker" has had conflicting connotations: a badge of honor, a mark of opprobrium. Debates over the meaning of muckraking reflect the uncertain status of investigative journalism in America. The muckraking impulse produced such groundbreaking exposés as Upton Sinclair's *The Jungle* (1906) and the Watergate reporting of Woodward and Bernstein in the 1970s. Some would say that it is also responsible for the worst excesses of modern tabloid culture.

Muckraking as a label dates from the early twentieth century. Theodore Roosevelt, deploring the stridency of the popular press, coined the term in a much-acclaimed speech in 1906. "There is filth on the floor," Roosevelt thundered,

and it must be scraped up with the muck-rake, and there are times and places where this service is the most needed of all the services that can be performed. But the man who never does anything else, who never thinks or speaks or writes save of his feats with the muck-rake, speedily becomes, not a help to society, not an incitement to good, but one of the most potent forces of evil.

Christened in the twentieth century, muckraking was born in the nineteenth. Its growth may be tied to the rise of reporting as a reputable profession and the unstable balance of power that resulted between politics and the press.

The modern era of American newspaper publishing began in the 1830s, when rapidly growing cities such as New York, Boston, and Philadelphia found themselves host to a profusion of competing papers. Early newspapers had been sold on a subscription basis; the new "penny papers," priced at a pittance, were hawked on street corners. Local news—not, as in earlier days, editorial opinion—was the hallmark of the nineteenth-century urban paper. The age of the all-powerful editor was giving way to the age of the reporter. Newsrooms bustled with correspondents covering fires, murders, sports, and social scandals.

The brash spirit of the penny press flowed into the newspapers of the late nineteenth century. The "yellow press" (a term inspired by R. F. Outcault's controversial comic strip, "The Yellow Kid") was bankrolled by its titans, Joseph Pulitzer (1847–1911) and William Randolph Hearst (1863–1951), but it was brought to life by the men and women who wrote the copy, took the photos, and sketched the cartoons that riveted the masses. If the penny papers professionalized the trade of reporting, the yellow journals stretched the boundaries of that profession.

Correspondent Nellie Bly traveled around the world in seventy-two days. Stephen Crane, author of *The Red Badge of Courage* (1895), honed his craft as a reporter for both Pulitzer's *World* and Hearst's *Journal*. Richard Harding Davis, perhaps the most dashing of the lot, filed reports from Cuba, North Africa, and the Middle East. And Jacob Riis exposed slum conditions in New York's Lower East Side with his searing photo-essay, *How the Other Half Lives* (1890). Many of these journalists became celebrities; many cultivated highly placed political "sources"; and all recognized that narrative flair, more than mere fact-gathering, was the key to a good story.

The heyday of the yellow press coincided with an era of innovation in magazine publishing. Muckraking, incubated in the daily press, reached maturity in the magazines. And despite a multitude of hosts, a single journal, *McClure's Magazine*, deserves credit as the cradle of muckraking.

S. S. McClure (1857–1949), the magazine's editor, is remembered today as a publishing maverick whose personal eccentricities ultimately cost him control of his publishing empire. In truth, by hiring an in-house staff that included such figures as Ida Tarbell, Ray Stannard Baker, Lincoln Steffens, William Allen White, Finley Peter Dunne, Willa Cather, and Frank Norris, he established that writers, not editors, were a magazine's lifeblood.

Newspapers had long relied on staff reporters, but no magazine before *McClure's* did so. The leading magazines of the mid–nineteenth century—*The Atlantic Monthly, Scribner's, Harper's, The Century,* and *The North American Review*—were dominated by their editors. Contributors supplied content, but the editors ensured, through selective solicitation of material and force of personality, that each journal maintained a distinctive tone.

When *McClure's* began publication in 1893, it joined *Cosmopolitan* (founded in 1886) and *Munsey's* (founded in 1889) in the ranks of upstart mass-market monthlies. *Collier's, Everybody's,* and others soon followed. With its innovative use of staff reporters, *McClure's* set itself apart from the pack and set in motion the creative process that eventually became known as muckraking.

The January 1903 issue of *McClure's* featured a trio of groundbreaking reports: Ida Tarbell on the Standard Oil trust, Lincoln Steffens on municipal corruption, and Ray Stannard Baker on labor union politics. McClure insisted in a back-page editorial, "We did not plan it so; it is a coincidence that the January *McClure's* is such an arraignment of American character as should make every one of us stop and think."

Between 1903 and 1906, dozens of popular magazines followed the example of *McClure's* and showcased investigative reports. This "reform" journalism seemed, for a time, a perfect accompaniment to the progressive politics of the Roosevelt administration. But as the exposés became more sensational, the president grew more fretful. When *Cosmopolitan,* newly acquired by William Randolph Hearst, launched a particularly rabid attack entitled "The Treason of the Senate," Roosevelt countered with his "muck-rake" speech.

Labeled, but hardly crippled, the muckrakers carried on. The first wave of muckraking magazines thrived, the investigative spirit persisted, and the epithet "muckraker" endures as both a tribute to and a warning against the persuasive powers of the American journalist.

See also **Magazines; Newspapers and the Press; Politics,** *subentry on* **Corruption and Scandals.**

Bibliography

Filler, Louis. *Crusaders for American Liberalism.* 1939. Reprint, Yellow Springs, Ohio: Antioch Press, 1964.

Fitzpatrick, Ellen F., ed. *Muckraking: Three Landmark Articles.* Boston: Bedford Books of St. Martin's Press, 1994.

Sinclair, Upton. *The Brass Check: A Study of American Journalism.* 1920. Reprint, New York: Arno Press, 1970.

Steffens, Lincoln. *The Autobiography of Lincoln Steffens.* 1931. Reprint, New York: Harcourt, Brace, and World, 1968.

Wilson, Christopher P. *The Labor of Words: Literary Professionalism in the Progressive Era.* Athens: University of Georgia Press, 1985.

JESSICA DORMAN

MUSEUMS

[This entry includes two subentries, **Art Museums** and **Science and Technology Museums.**]

ART MUSEUMS

With the Italian Renaissance and its system of art patronage as a model, the new United States in the nineteenth century fostered the growth of artistic creativity, art collecting, and the American art museum. In the eyes of many, the art museum became a symbol of American progress, power, and pride. Through the art museum, the growing national commitment to educational opportunity; democratic values; and the preservation of history, knowledge, morality, and culture was reinforced.

The principal credit for establishing the American museum movement belongs to the esteemed portrait painter Charles Willson Peale (1741–1827) and members of his family, most of whom were also artists. In 1786 Peale opened his initial museum venture, celebratory of American life and multidisciplinary in scope, in Philadelphia. It featured works from his earlier portrait gallery of Revolutionary War figures. Peale was also a major force and inspiration behind the Pennsylvania Academy of the Fine Arts, founded in Philadelphia in 1805, and still flourishing today as this country's oldest art school. Of those museums created by Peale's sons, the Peale Museum in Baltimore stands out. Its original building (1814) is the oldest museum structure still standing in the United States.

The American art museum also traces its origins to private collectors, and to the exhibition of works of art at the nation's early historical societies, college teaching galleries, and libraries. Established in 1791 by Jeremy Belknap (1744–1798) as the first American organization of its kind, the Massachusetts Historical Society in Boston acquired and displayed portraits and prints. Initiated by John Pintard (1759–1844), the New-York Historical Society (1804) was the most active of the earliest historical societies in building and exhibiting art collections, in large part due to its acquisition of the collections of Luman Reed (1787–1836) in 1858 and Thomas J. Bryan (d. 1870) in 1867. A major American artist, Colonel John Trumbull (1756–1843), was instrumental in the creation of the pioneering Yale University Art Gallery (1832), whose building Trumbull designed to accommodate his collection of miniatures and grand historical paintings. The addition of the James J. Jarves (1818–1888) collection to Yale's holdings in 1871 made it a more eclectic university art museum. Bowdoin College's collection of paintings, primarily portraits and many the bequest of the collector James Bowdoin III (1752–1811), came to the school in 1813 and was displayed after 1850. One of the oldest private or proprietary libraries, the Boston Athenaeum, incorporated in 1807, exhibited its own American paintings and sculpture as well as loan items. Its collection later formed the basis of the Boston Museum of Fine Arts. All of these institutions and their counterparts elsewhere in the country were primarily devoted to collecting, research, and exhibition for a limited, often specifically defined audience—primarily male intellectuals and elites. They did not engage in educational activities. Nonetheless, they played an important role, through their connections with artists and patrons, in fostering artists' careers and encouraging the development of a distinctly American school of art in the nineteenth century.

Prior to the Civil War, the first seeds were sown for a more democratic art museum, dedicated to increasing audience diversity and to the broad educational purposes for which American institutions eventually became known worldwide. The Smithsonian Institution, established in Washington, D.C., in 1846, was committed to art collections early in its history, laying the basis for the future National Gallery of Art, National Portrait Gallery, and National Museum of American Art. America's first truly public, civic, and continuing art museum was housed at the Wadsworth Atheneum (1842) in Hartford, Connecticut, founded by paintings collector Daniel Wadsworth (1771–1848), and devoted to art, as well as to history and literature. Other notable institutions of this era were New York's Albany Institute of History and Art (1791) and the Peabody Museum of Salem, Massachusetts, whose forerunner, the East India Marine Society, was set up in 1799. Before the Civil War, however, no American museums were devoted exclusively to art.

The history of the large, urban art museum dates from 1870, with the establishment of the Metropolitan Museum of Art in New York City and the Museum of Fine Arts (MFA) in Boston. Today both are housed in immense neoclassical granite complexes that suggest the reverence accorded art in our modern culture. Committed to comprehensive international collecting, public accessibility, and core educational missions, the Metropolitan Museum and the MFA have helped to define the twentieth-century art museum in the United States as well as abroad, and have actively participated in training artists and displaying contemporary artworks. Philadelphia, the third principal center of American art in the nineteenth century, launched its Museum of Art in 1877 as an outgrowth of the Centennial Exposition of 1876. Another major collection of fine arts, notably American painting and sculpture, was formed by the Corcoran Gallery of Art in Washington, D.C., which opened in 1874. Other art museum programs dating from mid-century were established in Charleston, South Carolina (1858), in Buffalo, New York (1862), and at New York's Vassar College (1864). At first, this formative group of urban-based institutions served a largely upper-middle- and upper-class audience, male as well as female, but this audience became much more diverse in the twentieth century.

After 1870, the art museum movement, sustained by the money of leading industrial barons, spread to other parts of the country, particularly the Midwest. The largest and most outstanding of these midwestern institutions is the Art Institute of Chicago, dating from 1879. The Detroit Institute of Arts, incorporated in 1885, is another city-based, universal survey museum, ranking with Chicago as one of the country's richest, most comprehensive collections. Private museums built to house personal art collections followed in Minneapolis (the Walker Gallery, 1879) and Milwaukee (the Layton Art Gallery, 1888). Other general nineteenth-century art museums of note in the region were the St. Louis Art Museum (1880), the Indianapolis Museum of Art (originating with the Art Association of Indiana in 1883), the Cincinnati Art Museum (1886), and Ohio's Columbus Gallery of Fine Arts (1878). Elsewhere, the M. H. de Young Museum was established in San Francisco in 1895, the Crocker Art Museum in Sacramento in 1885, the Worcester Art Museum in Massachusetts in 1896, and the Brooklyn Museum of Art in New York in 1897. Each of these museums has developed significant general holdings of paintings, sculpture, and decorative arts in the twentieth century. The years 1870 to 1900 saw the establishment of the art museum in urban and university settings as a major component of American intellectual and cultural life, a reflection of American social values, and a strong influence in shaping and refining the aesthetic tastes of the American people.

Metropolitan Museum of Art. After being founded in 1870 by a group of businessmen, financiers, and artists, the Met moved to its present location in Central Park in 1880. Its original gothic-revival structure has been completely surrounded by neoclassical, granite additions, as evident in this c. 1900–1910 photograph. LIBRARY OF CONGRESS: PRINTS AND PHOTOGRAPHS DIVISION

See also **Painting; Sculpture.**

Bibliography

Alexander, Edward P. "The Art Museum." Chapter 2 in *Museums in Motion: An Introduction to the History and Functions of Museums.* Nashville, Tenn.: American Association for State and Local History, 1979.

Burt, Nathaniel. *Palaces for the People: A Social History of the American Art Museum.* Boston: Little, Brown, 1977.

Einreinhofer, Nancy. *The American Art Museum: Elitism and Democracy.* London and Washington, D.C.: Leicester University Press, 1997.

Tomkins, Calvin. *The Merchants and Masterpieces: The Story of the Metropolitan Museum of Art.* New York: Henry Holt, 1989.

Whitehill, Walter Muir. *Museum of Fine Arts, Boston: A Centennial History.* 2 vols. Cambridge, Mass.: Belknap Press of Harvard University Press, 1970.

BRYANT F. TOLLES JR.

SCIENCE AND TECHNOLOGY MUSEUMS

Science and technology museums in nineteenth-century America advanced scientific knowledge, preserved historical ideas and artifacts, and promoted science education. They also entertained. The nineteenth century was a volatile period for science museum development shaped by two intertwined debates: Was the main mission of science and technology museums education or entertainment? Was the main activity for such institutions research or display? In the early 1800s science museums fell distinctly into one camp or the other. By the end of the century, many institutions had combined education and entertainment through research and display.

In the nineteenth century, science museums took many forms but existed primarily to explain science and technology to people who did not work in the factories, laboratories, or universities where science and technology were put to use in the nineteenth century. Museums of natural history and natural science formed the typical "science museum," but other types also appeared, including zoos, aquariums, botanical gardens, and planetariums. The first major zoos appeared in Philadelphia, Chicago, and Cincinnati in the 1870s.

Early institutions focused on research and teaching, with the serious student or scholar the main audience. In the 1810s some museums pushed for public education, although control stayed with the societal elite. Museums taught the public about science but

Smithsonian Castle. Completed in 1855, the castle was the original Smithsonian building and served as the home of first secretary of the Smithsonian, Joseph Henry, and his family. It was designed by the architect James Renwick, Jr., who also designed St. Patrick's Cathedral in New York City and the Smithsonian's Renwick Gallery. Photograph, c. 1880. LIBRARY OF CONGRESS

kept the public at arm's length. In the 1820s and 1830s the push toward egalitarianism throughout American society encouraged museums to cater to the public. Toward the middle of the century, the movement from amateur practice to professionalism in science prompted many museums to emphasize collections for research and scholarship. Industrial fairs influenced the following generation of museums to concentrate again on the public.

Early Collections

Early American museums followed the model of European institutions based upon the private collections of prominent individuals. In 1782 the Swiss immigrant Pierre Eugène du Simitière (1736–1784) founded the American Museum in Philadelphia with his personal collection. John Scudder took over several private collections and opened Scudder's American Museum in New York in 1810. However, American museums were often founded with more public participation in gathering collections than traditional European institutions, depending on groups of donors rather than individuals. In the case of science

and technology museums, scientists, industrialists, and engineers often played important roles.

The Charleston Museum, the first American institution that might be defined as a science museum, opened in South Carolina in 1773. The museum advertised in local papers for contributions of "natural productions, either animal, vegetable, or mineral," exemplifying trends that became characteristic of many American museums: public involvement, practical application of knowledge, and a focus on natural history.

Several science museums followed the Charleston Museum model. The Maryland Science Center traces its origins to 1797, and the Peabody Museum (later the Peabody Essex Museum) in Salem, Massachusetts, opened in 1799. Other museums founded before the Civil War include Philadelphia's Academy of Natural Sciences (1812), the Western Museum (1820), the New England Science Center (1825), and the Boston Society of Natural History (1830), predecessor of the Boston Museum of Science. These early museums specialized in the natural world, displaying fossils, geological specimens, plants, and stuffed animals. Many universities, such as Harvard and Yale, displayed their collections, primarily as teaching tools, but university museums tended to be passive when it came to public involvement.

In 1816 William Clark (1770–1838), best known for the Lewis and Clark Expedition, founded William Clark's Indian Museum at his home in St. Louis, the first museum west of the Mississippi. The museum featured Indian artifacts gathered by Clark during and after the expedition, including buffalo robes, blankets, and saddles.

Washington, D.C., became a focus for museums in 1816, when the Columbian Institute for the Promotion of Arts and Sciences opened and began to collect natural curiosities. In 1840 the Institute became the National Institution for the Promotion of Science, which collected minerals, Indian artifacts, and botanical and zoological specimens. Congress founded the Smithsonian Institution in 1846 as a scientific research center under the leadership of Joseph Henry (1797–1878). The Smithsonian influenced the later development of both scientific research and museums. The Smithsonian scientists led the way in the study, classification, and publication of new forms of animals, plants, and fossils. They both displayed specimens and sponsored numerous scientific expeditions to study natural history and cultures. With the arrival at the Smithsonian of George Brown Goode, the institution set a standard of practice that American museums began to emulate focusing on active education rather than haphazard curiosity collections or scientific specimen collections.

Science and Technology Museums in Nineteenth-Century America

Museum	Location	Founding Date
Charleston Museum	Charleston, S.C.	1773
American Museum	Philadelphia, Pa.	1782
Peabody (later Peabody Essex) Museum	Salem, Mass.	1799
Elgin Botanic Garden	New York, N.Y.	1801
New-York Historical Society	New York, N.Y.	1804
New England Museum	Boston, Mass.	1810
Scudder's American Museum	New York, N.Y.	1810
Academy of Natural Sciences	Philadelphia, Pa.	1812
William Clark's Indian Museum	St. Louis, Mo.	1816
Columbian Institute for the Promotion of Arts and Sciences	Washington, D.C.	1816
Western Museum	Cincinnati, Ohio	1820
Maryland Academy of Sciences	Baltimore, Md.	1822
Franklin Institute	Philadelphia, Pa.	1824
New England Science Center	Worcester, Mass.	1825
Boston Society of Natural History	Boston, Mass.	1830
National Institution for the Promotion of Science	Washington, D.C.	1840
Barnum's American Museum	New York, N.Y.	1841
State Cabinet of Natural History (later New York State Museum of Natural History)	Albany, N.Y.	1843
Smithsonian Institution	Washington, D.C.	1846
Boston Museum of Science	Boston, Mass.	1851
Missouri Botanical Garden	St. Louis, Mo.	1859
Museum of Comparative Zoology	Cambridge, Mass.	1859
Ward's Natural Science Establishment	Rochester, N.Y.	1862
American Museum of Natural History	New York, N.Y.	1869
California Academy of Sciences Museum	San Francisco, Calif.	1853
Philadelphia Zoological Gardens	Philadelphia, Pa.	1874
New York Botanical Garden	New York, N.Y.	1891
Field Museum of Natural History	Chicago, Ill.	1893

The Museum of Comparative Zoology, founded by natural scientist Louis Agassiz (1807–1873) at Harvard University in 1859, also proved particularly influential. The directors of several American natural history museums in the second half of the nineteenth century were students and protégés of Agassiz. Significantly, Agassiz opposed Darwinism, and his beliefs affected the development of museums run by his students. Agassiz's authority gave scientific weight to anti-Darwinism, but it also separated him and the natural history museums from scientific research. Increasingly, the amateurs who had taken part in natural history explorations by gathering specimens were excluded as Darwinism moved research into the laboratory with more sophisticated tools than classification and taxonomy. Many natural history museums declined in importance and became quiet dusty exhibit halls rather than spaces for science.

Popular Entertainment

Some museums focused on entertainment as much as education. Charles Willson Peale (1741–1827), an artist by profession and a naturalist by inclination, acquired the collection of Philadelphia's American Museum in 1784. The institution became the Philadelphia Museum, a leading public attraction. The museum collected oddities but eventually became an important resource for natural history, reflecting trends in nineteenth-century American culture and science. The museum was both a scholarly institution and a source of entertainment for elite society families. Attractions included lectures, magic-lantern shows, and science demonstrations, as well as the exhibition of some live animals. After Peale's death in 1827 the museum died, but it was an influential example, its small efforts at science and education losing out to entertainment but contributing to the development of museums through habitat arrangement and new methods of taxidermy.

In 1841 Phineas T. Barnum (1810–1891) took over Scudder's American Museum. Unlike Peale, Barnum did not allow scientific principles to stand in the way of amusement. Waxworks, automatons, chemical and electrical experiments, mummies, and magicians dominated the museum. However, Barnum did not completely abandon science, particularly natural history, for "humbuggery." He used the spectacular side-shows to draw audiences into the museum, where they also learned natural history. While Barnum often collected for amazement rather than science or education, he nevertheless produced a valuable natural history collection.

The Western Museum in Cincinnati, founded in 1820, began as an institution dedicated to science but developed a circus atmosphere and survived only until 1867, when the collections went to the Cincinnati Society of Natural History. Throughout most of its existence, its directors strove to enthrall, entertain, and frighten visitors more than enlighten or educate them, reflecting a trend that became even more prevalent after the nineteenth-century expositions.

Expositions

The shift to another stage of development occurred after the rise of international exhibitions, starting in 1851 with the Great Exhibition of London, housed in the Crystal Palace, and the subsequent founding of the South Kensington Museum of Industrial Arts in 1857. The museums influenced by such exhibitions proved less historically oriented than previous institutions. They reflected the contemporary emphasis on the promotion of industry through science and technology, and public education became a major focus. The popularity of the international exhibitions pushed museums toward public display and entertainment. Exhibitions, including the Philadelphia Centennial Exposition in 1876, added substantially to the natural history collections of many museums, such as the Smithsonian. The World's Columbian Exposition, held in Chicago in 1893, also proved influential for science museums. Chicago's fair boasted the Midway, a self-contained entertainment district, and its popularity pushed science museums further toward public entertainment. Numerous regional expositions followed the great success at Chicago. Nashville hosted the Tennessee Centennial and International Exposition in 1897, and Omaha, Nebraska, was the site of the Trans-Mississippi and International Exposition in 1898.

Many universities founded museums to serve as resources for scholars. In the late eighteenth century, Harvard University began a mineralogical and geological museum as a teaching, research, and display collection. It became an active public museum in 1891. Similarly, Yale University began a collection of natural and artificial curiosities in the late eighteenth century for the purposes of teaching and research in chemistry and natural history, particularly geology and mineralogy. It became a source of public entertainment and a key attraction in New Haven, Connecticut, and opened as a separate museum building in 1876. The University Museum of the University of Pennsylvania began gathering archaeological collections in 1887 with university-sponsored expeditions to Nippur, Iraq. The museum opened its own building in 1899 to house the growing anthropological and archaeological collections from all over the world.

Modern Museums

Public education and dissemination of knowledge gradually became accepted goals for modern American museums. Natural history museums served as places of popular education and outpaced art museums in attendance and applicability to everyday life. The American Museum of Natural History, founded in New York in 1869, served as a model of true public service, serving as a mediary between its natural history research laboratory and the common New Yorker. The museum adopted the motto "for the people, for education, for science" and blazed a trail for public involvement when the public became a founding partner. In 1882 the city of Milwaukee accepted about 20,000 natural history specimens from the Natural History Society of Wisconsin and founded the Milwaukee Public Museum. The Milwaukee Museum set a standard for museum practice when they presented the first known total habitat diorama.

The Field Museum of Natural History in Chicago, founded in 1893 as the Columbian Museum, became an exemplary institution. Marshall Field (1834–1906) provided funds to establish the museum to house the biological and anthropological collections from the 1893 fair and to "accumulate and disseminate knowledge, preserve and exhibit objects illustrating art, archaeology, science, and history."

Just as Marshall Field brought natural history to Chicago, Andrew Carnegie brought it to Pittsburgh in 1896 with the Carnegie Museum of Natural History, foremost in display and natural history research. It was one part of the Carnegie Institute, or Carnegie Museums of Pittsburgh, which included an art museum opened in 1895.

George Brown Goode (1851–1896), an influential museologist at the Smithsonian's National Museum of Natural History, pushed for an ideal American museum to meet the needs of the people through concern with public education. He urged a move from "bric-a-brac" to informative, thought-provoking collections. By the end of the nineteenth century, the

Smithsonian had become a center for education, display, and entertainment as well as scientific research.

The increasing number and size of science and technology museums in the late nineteenth century coincided with changes in the roles and institutional settings for science and technology in American society. During the late nineteenth century, major technical schools appeared and universities set up engineering and science schools with curricula distinct from the traditional liberal arts. The study of science and technology became further institutionalized in the new research laboratories of scientists such as Thomas Alva Edison (1847–1931). The need for science and technology museums to explain what occurred beyond those laboratory and university walls increased, eventually giving rise to the hands-on "science centers" of the twentieth century.

See also **Recreation; World's Fairs; Zoos.**

Bibliography

Alderson, William T., ed. *Mermaids, Mummies, and Mastodons: The Emergence of the American Museum.* Washington, D.C.: American Association of Museums, 1992.

Hudson, Kenneth. *Museums of Influence: The Pioneers of the Last 200 Years.* Cambridge, U.K.: Cambridge University Press, 1987.

Leon, Warren, and Roy Rosenzweig, eds. *History Museums in the United States: A Critical Assessment.* Urbana: University of Illinois Press, 1989.

Orosz, Joel J. *Curators and Culture: The Museum Movement in America, 1740–1870.* Tuscaloosa: University of Alabama Press, 1990.

Shapiro, Michael Steven, ed. *The Museum: A Reference Guide.* New York: Greenwood Press, 1990.

Winsor, Mary P. *Reading the Shape of Nature: Comparative Zoology at the Agassiz Museum.* Chicago: University of Chicago Press, 1991.

Wittlin, Alma S. *Museums: In Search of a Usable Future.* Cambridge, Mass.: MIT Press, 1970.

LINDA EIKMEIER ENDERSBY

MUSIC

[This entry includes four subentries:
Orchestral Music
Opera
Folk Songs, Parlor Music, and Popular Music
Spirituals and African American Music.]

ORCHESTRAL MUSIC

The development of orchestral music in the United States during the nineteenth century was marked by a strong dependence on European—particularly German romantic—models for validation. Music and musical activities that did not measure up to the high standards ascribed to German romanticism were belittled or attacked. Tension between the cultivated and vernacular traditions persisted in orchestral music throughout the century.

The musician Lowell Mason (1792–1872) was a seminal influence in the development of American musical culture. Mason promoted the European classical tradition not only for its musical qualities, but also for its perceived powers of moral and aesthetic uplift. This attitude was promulgated later in the nineteenth century by such figures as the critic John Sullivan Dwight (1813–1893) and Theodore Thomas (1835–1905), a conductor of his own touring orchestra and a passionate advocate of the German romantic tradition. In the view of these influential musical thinkers, whatever failed to aspire to the standards set by Ludwig van Beethoven (1770–1827) and other German masters had to be considered ephemeral at best, or deleterious at worst.

Dwight, whose *Journal of Music* (1852–1881) was influential far beyond its circulation numbers, developed Mason's theme of musical uplift into a high-minded credo of music as the ultimate language of feeling and the spirit. Like Mason, Dwight looked to German models for his moral uplift. To him, Beethoven, and particularly the Beethoven of Symphony no. 9 (1824), represented the ultimate achievement of spiritual elevation by music. In his journal Dwight published a wide variety of articles, from concert reviews and commentary to translations of German and French treatises on music. Among the contributors to *Dwight's Journal of Music* were Alexander Wheelock Thayer (1817–1897), a significant biographer of Beethoven, and Frédéric Louis Ritter (1834–1891), whose *Music in America* (1883) was the first attempt at a comprehensive survey of the subject. Pointedly, Ritter dismissed folk or vernacular traditions in his survey.

Theodore Thomas's influence on American musical taste was broader and more direct than Dwight's. As conductor of his own orchestra, Thomas took the classical tradition directly to audiences in lengthy tours of the East and Midwest between 1869 and 1878. Thomas's group was not the first to undertake such tours; the Germania Musical Society toured the United States between 1848 and 1854, playing the music of German composers. Thomas, however, blended evangelistic zeal with shrewd programming instincts. In his concerts he frequently wrapped audience-pleasing operatic and light-classical selections around a core of weightier symphonic music by such composers as Beethoven, Felix Mendelssohn (1809–1847), and Richard Wagner (1813–1883). He later conducted the New York Philharmonic Orchestra and became the first conductor of the Chicago Symphony Orchestra in 1891.

The New York Philharmonic was founded in 1842 and remains the earliest American orchestra still in existence. That New York City housed the first permanent orchestra in the country was not surprising; given its booming economy and population, New York alone among the American cities was able to provide the mass audience and capital required to support such an institution. America's second permanent orchestra, the Boston Symphony, was founded in 1881. The Chicago Symphony Orchestra followed a decade later.

The leading solo instrument of the nineteenth century was the piano, in both the parlor and the concert hall. The manufacture and sale of pianos increased dramatically during the first half of the century, and a number of firms grew to prominence in the United States. Such piano builders as Jonas Chickering (1798–1853), William Knabe (1803–1864), and Henry Steinway (born Heinrich Steinweg, 1797–1871) founded companies that supplied a growing market, with twenty-one thousand pianos built in 1860, up from approximately nine thousand in 1851.

The leading American pianists were the English-born Richard Hoffman (1831–1909); William Mason (1829–1908), the son of Lowell Mason; and, above all, Louis Moreau Gottschalk (1829–1869), the New Orleans–born virtuoso pianist and composer. As a youth Gottschalk went to Paris, where Frédéric-François Chopin (1810–1849) and Hector Berlioz (1803–1869) praised his playing. Others spoke warmly of his compositions, which mixed Afro-Caribbean rhythm, Creole-influenced melody, and Chopinesque virtuosity. Such works as *Bamboula* (1844) and *Le Banjo* (1854) represented the first serious effort to bring together the vernacular and cultivated traditions in American music, earning Gottschalk the scorn of Dwight. The best-known pianist of the late nineteenth century was Edward MacDowell (1860–1908), who gained fame as a composer of picturesque miniatures and suites, including his *Woodland Sketches* (1896) and its famous first sketch, "To a Wild Rose."

Contemporary with MacDowell was a loosely affiliated group of composers centered in Boston and trained in the German tradition, including John Knowles Paine (1839–1906), Arthur Foote (1853–1937), George Whitefield Chadwick (1854–1931), Horatio Parker (1863–1919), and Amy (Mrs. H. H. A.) Beach (1867–1944). These composers adhered in varying degrees to the classical-romantic genres of the symphony, the sonata, and chamber music. Paine was an outstanding symphonist; Foote excelled at chamber music; Parker was a brilliant or-

ganist; and Beach, an outstanding pianist, composed prolifically for that instrument. Chadwick wrote skillfully in many genres and took a greater interest in vernacular musical elements. His Symphony no. 2 (1885) anticipated by a decade the "Negro" themes of the 1893 Symphony no. 9 (*From the New World*) by Antonín Dvořák (1841–1904); folklike melodies also appeared in Chadwick's string quartets and other orchestral works.

Dvořák's tenure at New York's National Conservatory of Music (1892–1895) exposed him to the African American spiritual, which he proclaimed the foundation of a distinctively American musical style. He later amended this declaration to include Native American music and eventually to include a broader array of folk, vernacular, and popular musical traditions. His declaration was rejected by a few, but others, most notably Arthur Farwell (1872–1952), began to explore the use of Native American musical materials as a basis for composition. The popular reception of Dvořák's remarks and the tentative exploration of vernacular musical materials by Chadwick and others suggest that the dominance of the Mason-Dwight-Thomas doctrine of musical separation was breaking down by the end of the nineteenth century.

See also **Bands and Band Concerts; Romanticism.**

Bibliography

Chase, Gilbert. *America's Music, from the Pilgrims to the Present.* 3d ed., rev. Urbana: University of Illinois Press, 1987.

Dwight, John Sullivan, ed. *Dwight's Journal of Music.* 1852–1881. Reprint, New York: Johnson Reprint, 1968.

Gottschalk, Louis Moreau, ed. *Notes of a Pianist.* With a prelude, a postlude, and explanatory notes by Jeanne Behrend. New York: Knopf, 1964.

Saloman, Ora Frishberg. *Beethoven's Symphonies and J. S. Dwight: The Birth of American Music Criticism.* Boston: Northeastern University Press, 1995.

Starr, S. Frederick. *Bamboula! The Life and Times of Louis Moreau Gottschalk.* New York: Oxford University Press, 1995.

Tawa, Nicholas E. *The Coming of Age of American Art Music: New England's Classical Romanticists.* New York: Greenwood, 1991.

Thomas, Theodore. *A Musical Autobiography.* Edited by George P. Upton. 1905. Reprint, with a new introduction by Leon Stein, New York: Da Capo, 1964.

CHARLES S. FREEMAN

OPERA

In nineteenth-century America, English ballad opera, a type represented by the rollicking celebration of lower-class life in *The Beggar's Opera* (1728) and dominant throughout the previous century, was overthrown by the appearance of French and Italian opera.

Earliest Opera Companies

French opera flourished in New Orleans, where by the 1820s two opera companies directed by two of the notable operatic impresarios of the century competed for audience favor. John Davis headed the French company, which added new operas by Daniel Auber and Giacomo Meyerbeer to the older repertory of André Grétry, Étienne Méhul, and Luigi Cherubini. Davis's company achieved national importance by conducting a series of northern tours between 1827 and 1833 to New York, Boston, Philadelphia, and Baltimore. James Caldwell, who headed the rival company, sustained the English-language repertory but also brought (from Havana, Cuba) Italian companies that introduced the operas of Vincenzo Bellini and Gaetano Donizetti to the city. In addition, in 1835 he built in New Orleans the largest theater of the day, the St. Charles Theater.

Meanwhile, Manuel García's tiny company brought Italian opera to New York City in November 1825, staying nine months and presenting nine different operas, most notably Gioacchino Rossini's *Barber of Seville, Cinderella,* and *Otello* and Wolfgang Amadeus Mozart's *Don Giovanni.* Americans also heard the first of the great divas, young Maria García, later famous under her married name Maria Malibran.

European opera had arrived in the United States. Soon Bellini, Meyerbeer, Donizetti, and Giuseppe Verdi operas were introduced, but whether opera was permanently established remained uncertain for many years. Institutional and material limitations and deeply rooted cultural antipathies to opera shaped its subsequent development. In the absence of ecclesiastical support and governmental patronage, opera had also to struggle against resistance to the foreign and a puritanical fear of the exotic, associations that supposedly marked it as hostile to democratic culture. As the United States had no schools of music, American singers went to Europe to study, sing, and establish reputations. Americans welcomed and depended on touring European companies and especially star singers. Many of the most famous artists came to the United States in the wake of Jenny Lind's concert tour sponsored by P. T. Barnum in 1850–1851. Among those artists were Giovanni Mario and Giulia Grisi, Marietta Alboni, Henriette Sontag, Christine Nilsson, Italo Campanini, and Therese Tietjens. They came, captivated audiences, and made a good deal of money, adding to the image of opera as costumed vocal pyrotechnics, not

as dramatic ensemble. Their novelty appearances obscured the need to plant opera in native grounds.

Building Opera Audiences

The social and financial leadership of the emerging American opera audience was assumed by wealthy members of the middle class, who saw themselves emulating their aristocratic European counterparts. They found it easier to build opera houses than to establish and maintain opera companies. So although the 1800s saw construction in New York City of the Italian Opera house (1833), the Astor Place Opera House (1848), and the Academy of Music (1854); in Philadelphia, the handsome Academy of Music (1857); and in Chicago, the magnificent Auditorium Building (1889) by Dankmar Adler and Louis Sullivan, one of the architectural glories of the nation, in each instance buildings were established, but no resident companies.

Support of opera depended on a wider audience than that represented by the generally well-meaning plutocracy who built the buildings. This audience cut across social lines to a far greater extent than the elite, adhering to the archaic notion of opera as limited to the few, cared to acknowledge. The numbers of artisans, workers, clerks, and shopkeepers attending operas swelled as the century progressed, with the influx of knowledgeable and music-loving German and Italian immigrants. Above all, women filled the audiences. Observers noted that women often constituted a majority of those present, and in small towns and cities women were indispensable in attracting visiting companies. Many people labored to expand the audience and to present opera in modest surroundings at affordable prices. Max Maretzek, an impresario and conductor, worked tirelessly to produce popular operas at the New York Academy of Music, and others attempted to "democratize" opera at Palmo's Opera House and Niblo's Garden in New York City and at San Francisco's Tivoli Theater. In 1867 the New England and the Boston Conservatories of Music were founded, but thereafter conservatory building faltered. American singers still had to go abroad to gain experience. Without the production of opera in English in the major operatic places, the effect of American composers' efforts remained marginal, although William Henry Fry's *Leonora* (1845) and George Frederick Bristow's *Rip Van Winkle* (1855) later proved influential.

Continental Expansion

The primary story of opera in the United States in the last half of the century is one of continental expansion. Opera had reached Cincinnati, St. Louis,

"Grand Opera Celebrities." As opera pervaded the continental United States by the 1890s, American opera singers achieved a stardom and recognition comparable to that of European opera singers. Lithograph by the Strobridge Lithograph Company, 1896. LIBRARY OF CONGRESS

Chicago, and San Francisco by the 1850s, and the South outside New Orleans, the Great Plains, and the Northwest by the 1890s. European touring companies garnered most of the publicity, exemplified by Adelina Patti's tours in the 1880s. However, of greater lasting influence were touring companies, such as those of Clara Louise Kellog and Emma Abbott, that produced opera in English. Numerous other companies, many headed by women such as Alice Oates, Emily Melville, and Emma Howson, also sustained the English-language repertory of Michael W. Balfe and W. S. Gilbert and Arthur Sullivan as well as introducing Jacques Offenbach's comic operas. Two French operas, Georges Bizet's *Carmen* and Charles Gounod's *Faust,* became very popular. In the last quarter of the century small towns throughout the nation experienced a mania for building modest opera houses—such as the Bardavon Opera House in Poughkeepsie, New York, and the Eureka Opera House in Eureka, Nevada—many of which survive as a tribute to opera's ineradicable appeal.

The last major development of the century was the introduction, first in New York City and then slowly in other major cities, of Richard Wagner's music dramas by orchestral conductors, such as Carl Bergmann, Theodore Thomas, and Leopold Damrosch, in the form of concert hall excerpts. In the "German" season at the Metropolitan Opera in the late 1880s, full productions of Wagner's *Tristan and Isolde* and *Die Meistersinger* and the four operas of *The Ring of the Niebelung* gained the stage. The talents of the conductor, Anton Seidel, and of the brilliant singers, Jean and Edouard de Reszke, Albert Niemann, Lilli Lehmann, and the American Lillian Nordica, were equal to Wagner's demands. While the Metropolitan Opera was most famous in the 1890s for its remarkable casts of internationally famous singers, the "nights of stars," its enduring historical achievement was the introduction of Wagner to the United States.

See also **Music,** *subentry on* **Orchestral Music; Theater.**

Bibliography

Dizikes, John. *Opera in America: A Cultural History.* New Haven, Conn.: Yale University Press, 1993.

Kolodin, Irving. *The Metropolitan Opera, 1883–1966: A Candid History.* 4th ed. New York: Knopf, 1966.

Zietz, Karyl Lynn. *National Trust Guide to Great Opera Houses in America.* New York: Wiley, 1996.

JOHN DIZIKES

FOLK SONGS, PARLOR MUSIC, AND POPULAR MUSIC

Since colonial times popular and folk music have been significant components in the creation of a unique musical culture in America. Popular music in the nineteenth century dealt with love, work, games, festivals, ceremonies, politics, famous people, historical events, places of interest, and numerous other topics. Though rooted primarily in the heritage of white Americans, which included the influences of British tunes as well as the songs and dances of cowboys, mountain men, and lumberjacks, popular music was also shaped by the musical traditions of African Americans, Native Americans, and other racial and ethnic groups.

The Purpose, Instruments, and Lure of Folk Music

The term "folk music" originated in the nineteenth century to refer to the music of the peasantry and other groups of common people for whom folk musicians created their songs. The origins of an English-language folk music tradition in America began with the first noticeable immigrations of British settlers to the North American continent in the 1600s. A folk song was usually passed down orally instead of in written form, leading to the development of many variants of each song. Scholars have argued that the "simple" and "catchy" melodies of folk music were what made it quickly appealing to large numbers of people. Folk music was typically composed by uneducated people who remained anonymous. The vast majority of songs were written by nonprofessional musicians who worked by improvisation. Though created by individuals, songs did not belong to one person; they belonged to communities of people. They were not only played and sung in leisure but also accompanied work and other ritual events. Folk music was as important for cultural communication as it was for its aesthetic value, especially among people whose culture was largely oral. It was profoundly

Parlor Piano. In parlor music, the piano gave melody to urban northerners' sentimental recollections of the South. The piano pictured was designed and manufactured by Henry P. Miller & Sons Piano Company in Boston. Photograph c. 1890. LIBRARY OF CONGRESS: PRINTS AND PHOTOGRAPHS DIVISION

social, played in groups and serving to bond people.

Folk music used a variety of instruments, and some folk music was monophonic—a melody played or sung without accompaniment. Native Americans made music with drums, rattles, whistles, and notched sticks. The white folk-musical tradition, on the other hand, made use of the banjo, guitar, mandolin, violin, and the mouth organ. Native American folk music expressed resistance against the physical encroachment of whites, but it also incorporated many linguistic influences from the whites' culture as well. Much Native American music centered on the power of nature and the supernatural. It included dances, children's songs, lullabies, and love songs.

African American slave music relied in part on the banjo, drum, tambourine, dances like the juba, and the practice of clapping hands as a rhythmic accompaniment. Slave music was largely transmitted orally. Songs such as *Roll, Jordan, Roll* became very popular. These songs expressed a longing for freedom from slavery, and they often celebrated familial values and cooperation as defenses against the hardships of slavery. Some slave songs were variations on African songs; others were original, made in America.

Most popular and folk music told a story. The most significant kinds of songs were ballads and epics. The short pieces, called ballads, were divided into sets of stanzas. They were more common in the United States than the longer epic songs, which typically described historical events centered on a hero. Often relaying the story of a significant incident in history or in local myth, folk ballads became very influential in the white musical tradition. Authors created and sang the lyrics of ballads in a way that reinforced the speaking patterns of the region or group where the tune originated. Folk music was especially popular right before and during the Civil War.

Since folk music was not written down, scholars have had a difficult time discovering how it was created and how it evolved. One aspect, however, is evident. If people did not warmly receive a folk song, it quickly died. Even if it was accepted, a folk song went through many changes over the years. This music remained close to the people for whom it was composed, or who later inherited it and played it.

The Influence of Popular Music

Folk music was often thought to be inseparable from "popular music." They were both "music of the people," learned through hearing the tunes performed, though popular music tended to be written down. But popular music was not as diverse or as varied as folk music, and it was more likely to tell less-personal stories of political, military, or religious events. Popular music, like folk music, was produced for the general public. But unlike folk songs, which were highly local in origin and flavor, popular music was not specific to one region of the country or one particular ethnic group. Circulating widely across the country, it was written to inspire people, to stir emotions, and to reinforce all the values and traditions associated with the American culture.

Nineteenth-century popular music reflected the influences of British cultivated music and utilized the diatonic scale (a scale composed of five whole tones and two semitones) of musical tonal patterns. Americans often borrowed tunes from England and gave them new lyrics. Indeed, much popular music was set to the melody of non-American songs. Some examples of popular music included *Amazing Grace* (composed probably between 1760 and 1770), *The Star-Spangled Banner* (1814), *Battle Hymn of the Republic* (Civil War), *Dixie* (Civil War), *Oh, Shenandoah!* (Civil War), and *America the Beautiful* (1913). Popular music, unlike folk music, tended to be created and performed by professionals. Nevertheless, people learned songs without having to read the music sheets for them. Tunes like *Oh! Susanna* (1846), *Camptown Races* (1850), and *My Darling Clementine* (late 1800s), were simple but very effective in their emotional, usually sentimental appeal.

Shape Notes

Music and religion often complement each other. As a consequence, nineteenth-century popular music found its way into churches, especially in New England. During the first half of the century, New England popular music traveled south where it influenced the revivals of the Second Great Awakening and took root in southern religious traditions. Popular music was relatively easy to play because some of it was written down, with various shapes called shape notes, representing the notes, or syllables, on a scale (but not all such music was written down in this fashion). The four-shape notational system, which used shaped noteheads, was born in the early 1800s. Books such as *Southern Harmony* (1835), *Kentucky Harmony* (1815), *Missouri Harmony* (1820), *Repository of Sacred Music* (1820), and the *Sacred Harp* (1844) were published in this four-shape notation form. These notes represented the popular syllables "fa," "sol," "la," and "mi," which were employed in a method for ear training and assisted a singer's memory and practice of musical pitch. Each of the syllables was represented by a specific shape. The position of these shapes on the musical staff told the reader their pitch. Out of this four-shape note system emerged a myriad of musical notations that domi-

Emancipation Train. Cover sheet for music written by abolitionist Jesse Hutchinson, Jr., entitled "Get Off the Track!" Hutchinson came from an abolitionist New England family that performed antislavery concerts. This 1844 illustration is an allegory for the victory of abolitionism, depicting an engine called "Liberator" pulling along the railroad car "Immediate Emancipation," which is decorated with flags of freedom. LIBRARY OF CONGRESS: PRINTS AND PHOTOGRAPHS DIVISION

nated popular music in the 1800s, especially gospel and other religious hymns. The songs of the southern religious camp meetings incorporated this four-shape note musical method, and it soon spread throughout the South and as far west as Texas.

Minstrel Shows

With the rise of popular and folk music there also arose an interesting genre of song and dance—the minstrel show. Whites painted their faces black and then sang and danced in a fashion that mimicked or satirized black music and behavior. Minstrelsy was freighted with ambivalent attitudes toward African American culture—it provided an outlet for the admiration and enjoyment of black music (or white music masquerading as black), while expressing amusement with or contempt for blacks' appearance, customs, and values. Folk dances like the juba were an important component of minstrel shows. These song and dance shows grew in popularity and commercialism on the eve of the Civil War, moving well beyond their folk beginnings. After the war, professional minstrel troupes continued to tour the country, performing for both white and black audiences.

Parlor Songs

The European influence on the creation of American folk, popular, and parlor music cannot be denied. Political tunes, dance music, and instrumental music were all imported from England. All this music was played in one form or another on the piano, which

was itself a European import. The piano became the principal instrument for the composition and performance of parlor music, a genteel genre of popular music that spread widely through the middle class beginning in the middle decades of the century. Many parlor songs had their beginnings in the North but bore the romantic spirit of the South. Their lilting sentimentality helped make them so attractive to the northern urban middle-class. People wanted an escape from the harsh and driven qualities of an industrializing society, and they found comfort in the pastoral and saccharine qualities of parlor music, which was filled with celebrations of nostalgia, love, motherhood, and home. Pianos were in fashion and appeared in more American homes than in any other time in U.S. history. Songs of minstrel and folk origins made their way into parlor music along with the "rag" craze at the beginning of the 1900s.

See also **Bands and Band Concerts; Folk Arts; Minstrel Shows; Music**, *subentry on* **Spirituals and African American Music; Popular Culture.**

Bibliography

Abrahams, Roger D., and George Foss. *Anglo-American Folksong Style*. Englewood Cliffs, N.J.: Prentice-Hall, 1968.

Brand, Oscar. *The Ballad Mongers: Rise of the Modern Folk Song*. New York: Funk & Wagnalls, 1962.

Browne, C. A. *The Story of Our National Ballads*. New York: Crowell, 1931. Revised 1960.

Elson, Louis C. *The National Music of America and Its Sources*. Boston: L. C. Page, 1924.

Malone, Bill C. *Southern Music, American Music*. Lexington: The University Press of Kentucky, 1979.

Nettl, Bruno. *Folk and Traditional Music of the Western Continents*. Englewood Cliffs, N.J.: Prentice-Hall, 1965.

———. *Folk Music in the United States: An Introduction*. Detroit: Wayne State University Press, 1976.

Studwell, William E. *The Americana Song Reader*. New York: Haworth Press, 1997.

DAVID TREVIÑO

SPIRITUALS AND AFRICAN AMERICAN MUSIC

Music played a major role in slave life. Drawing at once on West African traditions and those learned in the colonies, music in slave communities served three primary functions: entertainment, accompaniment to labor, and companion to prayer and praise.

Recreational Music

Slaves used music in their own recreational activities and to provide musical entertainment for those who owned them. During feasts and holidays, such as the Pinkster celebrations and slave festivals, slaves often performed African dances and songs. These gatherings were elaborate affairs that sometimes featured parades and large bands of slaves playing fiddles, drums, banjos, and wind instruments. Slaves also used their bodies in this music making, stomping their feet and slapping their legs and chests in time to the singing. In this way their bodies became instruments and provided an African-derived rhythmic counterpoint to the music performed. Some of the songs sung in slave quarters poked fun at the master class. In these songs that "sang the master," slaves ridiculed their masters' courting habits, manner of dress, and treatment of slaves, for example:

> Dere's Mr. Travers lub Miss Jinny;
> He thinks she us good us any.
> He comes from church wid her er Sunday,
> Un don't go back ter town till Monday.

This music was largely improvisatory: slaves composed the music and created the witty, often condemnatory, words on the spot, encoding them in such a way that the slave owners did not understand that they were being mocked.

Slaves were frequently called upon to entertain their masters. Chroniclers of slave life in the nineteenth century, as well as paintings and sketches from the period, illuminate the important role of the slave musician. Slave fiddlers were especially popular, and were the staple of the masters' dances and cotillions. Solomon Northup, a violinist born a free man but kidnapped into slavery as an adult, recounted his trials as a slave musician in *Twelve Years a Slave* (1853). He described being forced to sing, dance, and make music. For Northup the ability to play his violin well brought both solace and misery. The instrument that was his daily companion offered, in his words, its "melodious consolations" but also became a symbol of slavery's cruelties when his owners made him play.

Work Songs

As an accompaniment to labor, music helped slaves endure long hours of tedious work. Slaves sang as they picked cotton, shucked corn, and harvested crops. Rhythm was the most important aspect of the work songs, for it determined the pace of the labor. Boat songs were sung slowly, to match and regulate the rhythm of rowing, whereas corn songs had fast tempos that reflected the quick movements of hands shucking corn. Slave work songs often served as a means of communication. Field hollers and cries by one slave would be responded to by others. These antiphonal, or "call and response," hollers and cries served at least two practical communicative purposes: to let others know where the slave was working

"Songs of the Jubilee Singers." Program for an 1871 concert tour to raise money for the fledgling Fisk University, with an image of Jubilee Hall (for which they raised the money to build) and list of traditional spirituals. The Fisk Jubilee Singers played a key role in spreading spirituals across the United States, Europe, and around the world. Published in 1881. LIBRARY OF CONGRESS

and to signal boredom, fatigue, or loneliness. Festivals were often associated with slave and other rural labor in the antebellum South. Corn shucking festivals, which featured competitions, dancing, games, and colorful slave masters of ceremonies, were especially popular among both slaves and planters.

Religious Music

Prayer and praise music belonged to two main categories: religious folk songs, known as spirituals, and a dancelike genre known as the "shout." Slaves sang spirituals as part of worship services, often at clandestine gatherings. The spiritual was a conglomeration of African musical forms and traditions and white hymnody. Although its origins are not precisely known, the spiritual is believed to have derived from slave adaptations of hymns used in religious worship by white Americans. Some spirituals combined material from several hymns, while others were improvisations of preexistent music with new words and

MUSIC   381

new tunes added. Spirituals were passed from one slave community to another orally, altered with each transmission. They were usually performed antiphonally, with a soloist and a body of singers. Psalms and paraphrases of texts from the New Testament were used frequently in spirituals. In the post–Civil War years the Fisk Jubilee Singers, a celebrated group of student vocalists from Fisk University in Nashville, made this body of music known through the United States and Europe.

The shout was a sacred dance that accompanied slaves' worship. African in origin, the shout was an energetic ring dance characterized by hand clapping and foot shuffling. White writers in the nineteenth century regarded the shout, sometimes referred to as a "ring spiritual," as savage and barbaric. They commented on the wild, dervishlike trembling and whirling body movements of the dancers ("shouters"), the monotonous thud of stamping feet, the peculiar chanting of the singers, and the hysterical pitch reached by both singers and dancers as the pace of the circle dance gradually quickened. Although the shout was usually described by white observers as a dance, the slaves took care to distinguish between shouting and dancing. During a shout the feet were neither crossed nor lifted from the ground, as occurred in dancing, and only religious songs were sung.

Postbellum Music

In the years following emancipation, slave traditions in music led to a variety of popular musics, including blues and black minstrelsy. Early blues reflected the changes brought about by the Civil War. Large slave communities were broken apart, and the musical practices common to communal living, such as field hollers and cries, gradually evolved into music that conveyed individual expression. Postbellum blues musicians were often itinerant. Traveling from place to place, they sang their personal stories and accompanied themselves on a guitar or banjo. Black minstrel troupes abounded in the last quarter of the nineteenth century. Many former-slaves who had entertained slave owners as musicians, acrobats, and comedians became professional entertainers in minstrel companies. Small troupes consisted of only two or three musicians, while larger companies, like the Georgia Minstrels, included singers, an array of instrumentalists, comedians, and dancers. Most minstrel troupes in the nineteenth century were all-male. The best-known minstrels were James Bland, who was billed as the "World's Greatest Minstrel Man" and whose songs were performed by black and white minstrels; Samuel Lucas, known as the "Grand Old Man of the Stage"; and Gussie Lord Davis, who

wrote many songs for black minstrels and later became popular as a Tin Pan Alley songwriter. W. C. Handy, popularly known as the "Father of the Blues," was a minstrel in the 1890s.

By the end of the century, small numbers of black musicians, some of them former minstrels, had established themselves as performers in the white domain of classical music. Foremost among these was the soprano Sissieretta Jones, called the "Black Patti" after the white diva Adelina Patti. Jones concertized throughout Europe, Africa, and Asia, and in 1896 began a career in a vaudeville troupe, Black Patti's Troubadours, that toured in the United States and in Europe. Thomas Green "Blind Tom" Bethune was a slave who became a popular concert pianist in the second half of the century. He could play by ear any piece of music he heard and had a performing repertoire of several thousand works, including compositions by Bach, Beethoven, Chopin, and Liszt. Blind Tom was also well regarded as an improviser and composer.

See also **Minstrel Shows; Theater.**

Bibliography

Abrahams, Roger D. *Singing the Master: The Emergence of African American Culture in the Plantation South.* New York: Pantheon, 1992.

Allen, William Francis, Charles Pickward Ware, and Lucy McKim Garrison, eds. *Slave Songs of the United States.* 1867. Reprint, New York: Books for Libraries, 1971.

Andrews, William L., ed. *The Oxford Frederick Douglass Reader.* New York: Oxford University Press, 1996.

Douglass, Frederick. *My Bondage and My Freedom.* 1855. Reprint, New York: Dover, 1969.

Epstein, Dena J. *Sinful Tunes and Spirituals: Black Folk Music to the Civil War.* Urbana: University of Illinois Press, 1977.

Floyd, Samuel A., Jr. *The Power of Black Music: Interpreting Its History from Africa to the United States.* New York: Oxford University Press, 1995.

Johnson, James Weldon, and J. Rosamond Johnson. *The Books of American Negro Spirituals.* 1926. Reprint, New York: DaCapo, 1977.

Jones, LeRoi. *Blues People.* New York: Morrow, 1963.

Levine, Lawrence W. *Black Culture and Black Consciousness: Afro-American Folk Thought from Slavery to Freedom.* New York: Oxford University Press, 1977.

Northup, Solomon. *Twelve Years a Slave.* 1853. Reprint, edited by Sue Eakin and Joseph Logsdon. Baton Rouge: Louisiana State University Press, 1968.

Southern, Eileen. *The Music of Black Americans.* 3d ed. New York: Norton, 1997.

———. *Readings in Black American Music.* 2d ed. New York: W. W. Norton, 1983.

Spencer, Jon Michael. *Black Hymnody: A Hymnological History of the African-American Church.* Knoxville: University of Tennessee Press, 1992.

GAIL HILSON WOLDU

N

NATIONALISM

[This entry includes two subentries, the first on nationalism to the end of the Civil War, the second from 1861 to 1900.]

1800–1865

Founded at different times and under different auspices, the American colonies slowly developed the historical memory, shared emotional attachments, and sentiments of nationalism associated with protracted residence of a homogeneous people in a well-defined territory. But by the late eighteenth century the colonies shared a sense of apartness from Britain and Europe. Recognizing the uniqueness of their social and physical environment in the New World, Americans had begun to believe this uniqueness promised a higher destiny than that of Old Europe. Behind the controversies in the 1760s over taxes and representation was a confidence in American moral superiority and importance. By 1776 the colonists were prepared to see their Revolution as a turning point in the history of human liberty and an experiment that would demonstrate to the world the full potential of mankind for self-government.

From the Federalists to Manifest Destiny

The revolutionary generation was fond of applying to itself a verse from the prophet Isaiah (66:8) that refers to a nation being "born at once," yet it was long uncertain whether the universalist ideals of the Declaration of Independence (1776) wedded to the framework of the Constitution (1787) had erected a stable structure. The short-lived Articles of Confederation (1781) confusingly declared that the states were each sovereign and their union perpetual, while the Constitution reflected the unsettled status of the matter by reinforcing neither provision. It was the aim of the Federalist Party, as the first leaders of the new Republic, to establish the prestige and authority of the national government, and after they left office their program was carried forward by the federal judiciary under the direction of Chief Justice John Marshall between 1801 and 1835. In the early decades of the nineteenth century Marshall's Supreme Court established itself as the ultimate interpreter of the Constitution, with power to strike down congressional and state legislation in conflict with it, and widened the scope of congressional action through a doctrine of implied powers and an expansive interpretation of the commerce clause (Article I, section 8) of the U.S. Constitution. This judicial groundwork laid the foundation for a grand vision of economic nationalism identified with Henry Clay and the Whig Party, successors to the Federalists.

Clay's American System was designed to bind the sections together through a network of protective tariffs for manufactured goods coupled with a subsidized program of internal improvements (roads, bridges, canals) to transport the agricultural products of the West to the areas of industrial population. Although Clay's hopes were frustrated by political divisions over the tariff and slavery, the speedy expansion of the national territory stimulated a strong spirit of nationalism. After the Louisiana Purchase (1803), which doubled the size of the nation, and the acquisition of Florida (1819), a powerful popular sentiment of martial bellicosity combined with a mystical faith in the providential direction of an American "Manifest Destiny" to urge on the absorption of Oregon (1846) and the large conquests of the Mexican War (1848), which carried the western boundary of the nation to the Pacific.

Popular Nationalism

At the same time numerous cultural expressions of national sentiment had been gaining wide acceptance. The life and character of George Washington, glorified and mythologized in orations, sermons, and schoolbooks, and his features, familiarized through the portrait engravings by Gilbert Stuart and Charles Willson Peale, came to be identified with the meaning of the Republic itself. His birthday was annually celebrated, and his name was attached more frequently to new towns and counties than that of any other revolutionary patriot. Hailed as truly Roman, his virtues were seen to support the common notion that the United States was a re-creation of a classical republic and harmonized with the eagle, shield, and sheaf of arrows on the Great Seal of the United States, adopted in 1776, with its Latin motto "E pluribus unum." Other familiar slogans included "I have not yet begun to fight," "I only regret that I have but one life to lose for my country," "Millions for defense, but not a cent for tribute," and "Our country, right or wrong!" The "Star-Spangled Banner," adopted as the national anthem in 1931, was a product of the War of 1812, a war that also elevated Andrew Jackson, the hero of the Battle of New Orleans, to rank with the founding fathers. Unquestionably the most significant demonstration of national feeling was annually evoked by the tumultuous celebration of the nation's birthday, the Fourth of July. By the 1820s and 1830s this day had become the occasion for massive patriotic parades, lavish banquets, flowery orations, innumerable toasts, cannonading, and fireworks, accompanied everywhere by the ceremonial recitation of the Declaration of Independence, as the citizenry rededicated itself to the principles of liberty.

Literary and Artistic Nationalism

The spirit of nationalism began to make an appearance in literature and art as writers and painters turned their attention to the special qualities of the American scene. Among novelists, James Fenimore Cooper depicted the romance of the American forest, Nathaniel Hawthorne the influence of Puritanism, and Herman Melville the drama of the whale fishery. The poets William Cullen Bryant, Oliver Wendell Holmes, Henry Wadsworth Longfellow, James Russell Lowell, and John Greenleaf Whittier illustrated characteristic aspects of American experience, while the essayists Ralph Waldo Emerson and Henry David Thoreau pondered the ethical implications of American culture. Walt Whitman expounded the significance of American democracy in poetry of striking originality. Painters of the Hudson River School, such as Thomas Cole, Frederick Church, and Asher Durand, discovered sublimity and moral grandeur in the waters, hills, and woodlands of the American landscape, and the historian George Bancroft launched a multivolume *History of the United States* (1834–1882), which justified and confirmed for Americans the transcendent providential destiny in which they already believed.

The Role of the Civil War

It remained for the Civil War to sweep away to the strains of the "Battle Hymn of the Republic" numerous barriers still remaining to the full exercise of federal authority. The war saw the enactment of the first conscription act, the beginnings of a national banking system, the first national banknotes, and a wartime income tax. It also made possible the Thirteenth Amendment, barring slavery, and the Fourteenth Amendment, establishing a national citizenship exempt from state jurisdiction. By 1863, when President Abraham Lincoln spoke at Gettysburg, it was clear to him that the war had made explicit what had always been implicit. His "Four score and seven years ago our forefathers brought forth on this continent a new nation" meant that Isaiah's prophecy had already been realized in 1776, when a new nation had indeed been "born at once."

See also **Federal-State Relations,** *subentries on* **1800–1833, 1831–1865; Holidays; Nationalism,** *subentry on* **1861–1900; Slogans, Songs, and Nicknames, Political; Washington, George.**

Bibliography

Boorstin, Daniel J. *The Americans: The National Experience.* New York: Random House, 1965. Intellectual and cultural history from the Revolution to the Civil War.

Nagel, Paul C. *This Sacred Trust: American Nationality, 1798–1898.* New York: Oxford University Press, 1971. Development of the national idea in various forms.

Nye, Russell Blaine. *Society and Culture in America, 1830–1860.* New York: Harper and Row, 1974. Comprehensive and detailed.

Zelinsky, Wilbur. *Nation into State: The Shifting Symbolic Foundations of American Nationalism.* Chapel Hill: University of North Carolina Press, 1988. Valuable quantification of nationalist symbols.

FRED SOMKIN

1861-1900

The growth of a unified national culture was slow and uneven before the Civil War. American nationalism took shape during the struggle for independence, but unlike many other nation-states, the central government did not play an activist role in its construction. Indeed the government did not significantly intervene until World War I. Instead, the glorification of national heroes and the celebration of holidays depended on local initiatives. The construction of nationalism as a political doctrine, in which an individual's identity and interests connect to the destiny of the nation-state, followed no overall plan. Local and regional cultures predominated. On the eve of the Civil War the flag was not yet sacred, no pledge of allegiance existed, and July Fourth held vastly divergent meanings for abolitionists, proslavery advocates, workers, and capitalists.

The Civil War involved more than the issue of two nations or one. Also at stake was whether or not the ideal of liberty extended to all Americans. When President Abraham Lincoln signed the Emancipation Proclamation in 1863, he expanded the meaning of patriotism from a willingness to die for the United States to include the the obligation of the government to grant freedom to slaves in the Confederacy. This act endowed the war with a moral dimension.

During the Civil War an American and a Confederate nationalism vied for people's allegiance. The Stars and Stripes and the Stars and Bars emerged as the two sides' most sacred symbols. The U.S. Army awarded medals of honor to men who captured enemy flags or kept the Stars and Stripes from touching the ground. At the war's end the endeavor of constructing an American nationalism moved into a cultural milieu.

Between the Civil War and the dawn of the twentieth century self-conscious patriots launched far-reaching campaigns to create rituals, symbols, and national narratives to assure loyalty to the nation. In the United States, where being an American was seen as a choice rather than a birthright, diverse groups contested the meaning of American nationalism. The Grand Army of the Republic (GAR), a mass organization of Union veterans founded in 1866, was a significant force in this development. To assure that the wartime sacrifices of its members were compensated and that their place in history was remembered, the GAR orchestrated campaigns to teach love

of the flag in the public schools and inaugurated the ritual of veterans' parades.

The GAR promoted the male warrior as the preeminent patriot. When women, who had demonstrated their loyalty as nurses on the front lines and as fund-raisers on the home front, petitioned for inclusion within its ranks, the fraternity barred their entry. Women, galvanized by their Civil War experiences, formed their own mass organization in 1883. The Woman's Relief Corps moved beyond charitable work for GAR veterans to create Memorial Day, the most important new national holiday of the nineteenth century. But while nationalism gave women a route into public culture, the Relief Corps did not fundamentally challenge gender relations, and more often than not it perpetuated the metaphor of "love paying tribute to valor" in its memorial rituals.

Elite groups, most notably the Daughters of the American Revolution (DAR), founded in 1890, admitted only women who could trace their American ancestry back to the American Revolution and before. The DAR, infused with a middle-class sensibility and grounded in the superiority of white culture, promoted the Americanization of immigrants and placed markers, built monuments, and held colonial teas in memory of their ancestors. Businesspeople also incorporated national iconography into their advertising in recognition that patriotism pays. In 1876 business leaders sponsored the Centennial Celebration in Philadelphia. Progress had always been a theme in patriotic oratory, but business made industry and commerce, not liberty and emancipation, the cultural centerpiece of America's first hundred years.

Still other groups focused on the next generation of students. Progressive educators initiated the study of civics and American history in public schools, welcoming the efforts of the *Youth's Companion,* a national publication that applied modern advertising techniques to popularize the schoolhouse flag movement. In anticipation of the 1892 Columbian Exposition, the *Youth's Companion* asked Francis Bellamy to organize a national public school celebration. Different versions of a pledge of allegiance already existed, but Bellamy wanted to write a pledge that resonated with U.S. history. He initially considered using the French Revolution's slogan "Liberty, Equality, and Fraternity" but settled on "with liberty and justice for all." He left it to future generations to decide if the United States was an "individualist or a socialistic state" (Bellamy, Francis Bellamy Papers, 12 July 1923).

During the nineteenth century capitalist expansion and industrialization coupled with military victories in the Mexican War, the Civil War, the Indian wars, and the Spanish-American War assured the ex-

Pledge of Allegiance. Beginning in 1892, children in New York City schools recited the Pledge of Allegiance daily in assemblies and classrooms. Reciting the Pledge of Allegiance became part of the Americanization process for millions of immigrant children, like the students pictured at the Mott Street Industrial School in New York's Little Italy. Photograph by Jacob A. Riis, 1892. LIBRARY OF CONGRESS

istence of a territorial United States and launched the nation as a world power. Popular imperialism merged with conceptions of American nationalism and Manifest Destiny, as expansionists argued that the flag should be planted halfway around the world in the Philippines.

A racialized Americanism gained ground after the government ended Reconstruction in 1876 and returned the control of race relations to the white South. Black Americans and their white allies envisioned an Americanism based on equality. Black leaders such as Frederick Douglass even stated that emancipation was one of the great moments in American annals, since it reconciled the nation's ideals with its practices. But the failure of Reconstruction and the participation of white southerners in the Spanish-American War in 1898 strengthened a shared racism favorable to the rewriting of Civil War history. Confederates, once denounced as traitors, were transformed into brothers and warriors who had also shed their blood. Blue and gray reunions celebrated reconciliation at the cost of excluding black Americans from the national fraternity. Black Americans were the backbone of patriotic celebrations in the South

during Reconstruction. With its end white southerners paraded a revived Confederate culture, in which they honored Robert E. Lee, commemorated their own Confederate Memorial Day, and continued to fly the Stars and Bars.

By the end of the nineteenth century numerous groups participated in creating and promoting the cultural meanings of American nationalism. Debate, conflict, negotiation, and contest characterized the shaping of a national ideology. Within both the GAR and the Relief Corps, white and black members struggled over whether loyalty or the color line defined membership. Workers seeking their share in profits claimed that a living wage was a fundamental part of citizenship, while capitalists called the growing immigrant working class "un-American." Militarists supported intervention and preparedness as the way to national greatness, while pacifists and anti-imperialists argued that the Republic contradicted itself by acquiring colonies. Nativists urged immigration exclusion and a view of national identity defined by Anglo-conformity. Americanizers confidently promoted the melting pot theory of national identity and tried to convert the children of immigrants through schoolhouse flag rituals. Some reformers developed a concept later described as cultural pluralism, in which groups maintained dual allegiances and identities.

At the dawn of the twentieth century various constructions of American nationalism contended for cultural authority. The question remained: Would nationalism represent the promise of democracy for all, or would the imposition of a racialized, militarist, and politically intolerant interpretation come to predominance in the twentieth century?

See also **Civil Rights; Education,** *subentry on* **Public Policy toward Education; Emancipation; Expansion; Gender; Holidays; Immigration and Immigrants,** *subentry on* **The Immigrant Experience; Liberty; Monuments and Memorials; Patriotic and Genealogical Societies; Republican Motherhood; Veterans Organizations.**

Bibliography

Bellamy, Francis. Letter to Mrs. Lue Stuart Wadsworth, 12 July 1923. Francis Bellamy Papers. University of Rochester, Rush Rhees Library, Rochester, New York.

Bodnar, John, ed. *Bonds of Affection: Americans Define Their Patriotism.* Princeton, N.J.: Princeton University Press, 1996.

Curti, Merle. *Roots of American Loyalty.* New York: Columbia University Press, 1946.

Gillis, John R., ed. *Commemorations: The Politics of National Identity.* Princeton, N.J.: Princeton University Press, 1994.

Kammen, Michael. *The Mystic Chords of Memory: The Transformation of Tradition in American Culture.* New York: Vintage Books, 1993.

Lind, Michael. *The Next American Nation: The New Nationalism and the Fourth American Revolution.* New York: Free Press, 1995.

Silber, Nina. *The Romance of Reunion: Northerners and the South, 1865–1900.* Chapel Hill: University of North Carolina Press, 1993.

O'Leary, Cecilia Elizabeth. *To Die For: The Paradox of American Patriotism.* Princeton, N.J.: Princeton University Press, 1999.

CECILIA ELIZABETH O'LEARY

NATIONAL PARKS   The United States in the late nineteenth century was a nation composed of both civilization and wilderness—one symbolized its progress and the other bore witness to its past. As the nation developed, however, it turned with growing concern to the preservation of its wilderness. What was once seen as an obstacle to be overcome was now invested with spiritual meaning. Americans learned what Edward Abbey would later note in *Desert Solitare,* that "a civilization needs wilderness." By 1900 there were five national parks and thirty-eight forest reservations, as well as a growing number of national monuments, military battlefields, memorials, and historic sites.

The leading factors in the late-nineteenth-century efforts to set aside areas of land for preservation and public enjoyment—a unique historical experience with nature; democratic idealism; the sheer vastness of the landscape; and the growing affluence of American society—each contributed to the creation of the parks.

Reverence for undeveloped land took time to emerge as a part of the national consciousness. President Thomas Jefferson recognized the potential for the wilderness in his 1803 instructions to the Corps of Discovery, carried out in the expedition of Meriwether Lewis and William Clark (1804–1806). But, in 1831 French observer Alexis de Tocqueville noted that Americans were still scarcely aware of their own natural resources and undeveloped lands. Then in 1854, with the publication of *Walden,* writer Henry David Thoreau made America aware of its ability to discover itself in the woods. His reflections, added to the actual physical process of expansion and the attempts to find transportation routes across the continent, brought the wilderness to the forefront of American society. But it had not been accomplished through nor did it result in any systematic approach.

While there were European precedents in the development of formal parks, the development of natural parks was a uniquely American idea. Americans encountered the wilderness through exploration and migration westward as part of the continuous expansion of the nation. The development of the Hudson River school of art matched this movement west and focused on the wilderness landscapes of New York and various other areas of the United States from 1825 until the late 1800s.

The origins of the national parks remain shrouded in uncertain, competing claims. Two such claims enjoy widespread support. One holds that John Muir, the famed naturalist and founder in 1892 of the Sierra Club conceived the idea that the federal government might preserve and protect the Yosemite region of California for the public in perpetuity, during his four-year camping trip in the region (1869–1873). Another holds that members of the Washburn-Doane Expedition of 1870, sent to explore the scenic wonders of the Yellowstone area (in Wyoming, Idaho, and Montana), sat around a campfire and dreamed up the idea of setting aside the scenes they had witnessed for all to see, an idea they carried back to Washington, D.C. Neither hypothesis can be proven with any certainty, since the designation "national park" was used prior to both claims, and similar ideas were already circulating in many circles. Stewart L. Udall, a former secretary of the interior, in his work *The Quiet Crisis and the Next Generation* called the creation of the parks a "fluke," an idea with implications that were not fully understood at the time.

In April 1832, Hot Springs Reservation in Arkansas was the first federal area of land set aside for the purposes of preservation and recreation. The site was a popular attraction for its medicinal and healing powers, as well as for the unique beauty of its geothermal springs. Although the Arkansas site was a federally protected area, it was not until 1872, when Yellowstone was placed under the control of the secretary of the Interior, that the words "national park" were used consistently to refer to a particular site and its status within the nation's political and environmental identity. The preservation of Yellowstone was followed in 1875 by that of Mackinac National Park in Michigan, a much smaller and less stunning area, but also remote and picturesque. The creation of three parks fifteen years later, in 1890—General Grant, Sequoia, and Yosemite (all in California)—inaugurated a massive effort to increase the amount and quality of land set aside. That these areas were all in the West was no accident; as Americans pushed west they saw sites that they were afraid would not be seen again if left to the forces of economic development and expansion. Such was the case with the designation of Mount Rainier National Park in Washington State, the largest accessible single-peak glacier system, in 1899.

The ideas of conservation and progressive reform combined to form the backbone of the incipient park movement. This can especially be seen in the creation of Mount Rainier, typical of most of the natural sites designated as parks in the early years. The glacier-fed streams, mountain meadows, and imposing mountain, which could be seen from as far away as the city of Seattle, were preserved through the efforts of both national and local groups. European dignitaries, educators, the Sierra Club, the National Geographic Society, the Seattle Chamber of Commerce, the National Geologic Society, the American Association for the Advancement of Science, and even the Appalachian Club all took part in the efforts to establish the park. The area was valued for its scientific and natural resources (as evidenced by the opposition to its creation as a national park by the timber, grazing, and mining interests of the Northwest) and also valued for its recreational and scenic value. By 1900 approximately one hundred people, including Muir, had already climbed to the mountain's summit—a feat used to support the claim that the site would be well used. Like the parks that had preceded it, Rainier was preserved for both its natural beauty and for its potential as a place of recreation and enjoyment.

Railroads should not be overlooked as forces in the creation of the national parks and in the later tourism promotions of the national park system. The remoteness of the scenic wonders led many railroad companies to build and develop special lines to these sites, construct facilities that served as base sites to explore parks, and then to promote their own tourism services. Western agricultural interests were also a concerted force for the creation of many of the parks. Their interests were in the protection of water, clean soil, and lands that could not be fenced off or bought out by rivals.

The federal government was concerned for more than natural parks. During the nineteenth century, the government established two national monuments, a national historic site, a national memorial, and six national military parks (all of them Civil War battlefields). These sites (with the exception of the Casa Grande Ruins in Arizona) were all symbols of the growth of the Republic and monuments to its struggles. The Washington Monument, constructed in 1848, was a glorious structure, rising into the sky of the capital and celebrating the nation's permanence as well as honoring the memory of the great military and political leader. The Civil War sites, such as Antietam in Maryland, Gettysburg in Pennsylvania, and Shiloh in Tennessee, were incorporated into the growing list of national parks at the very moment when the nation was undergoing a process of emotional reunification and redemption and were part of the flurry of park creation throughout the century's final decade.

In an early example of the administrative conflicts that later plagued attempts to unify the parks under one single administrative unit, the military parks were originally under the control of the War Department, while the other sites were under the control of the Department of the Interior. This division not only created a series of conflicting policies and procedures that governed the parks but also a dualistic sense of purpose for the American public—scenic wonder and national honor. Many of the natural parks were patrolled and staffed during the nineteenth century by U.S. Army personnel, a situation that later gave rise to the Park Service's corps of rangers, who wore military-style uniforms and hats.

Although the National Park Service was not created until 1916, its holdings were already being preserved, protected, and presented to the American people in the latter half of the nineteenth century as the legacy of both the American civilization and environment. By creating national monuments, national historic sites, natural parks, and forest reserves, nineteenth-century America originated the recognition of natural areas as among the nation's most treasured possessions.

See also **Exploration and Explorers; Federal Land Policy; Geography and Ecology; Lewis and Clark Expedition; Recreation.**

Bibliography

Abbey, Edward. *Desert Solitaire: A Season in the Wilderness.* New York: Simon and Schuster, 1990.

Muir, John. *Our National Parks.* San Francisco: Sierra Club Books, 1991. This book was originally published around 1901.

Pyne, Stephen J. *How the Canyon Became Grand: A Short History.* New York: Viking Penguin, 1998.

Rothman, Hal. *America's National Monuments: The Politics of Preservation.* Lawrence: University Press of Kansas, 1994.

Sellars, Richard West. *Preserving Nature in the National Parks: A History.* New Haven, Conn.: Yale University Press, 1997.

J. D. BOWERS

NATIVE AMERICANS. See **American Indians.**

NATIVISM. See **Immigration and Immigrants,** subentry on **Anti-Immigrant Sentiment.**

NATURAL RESOURCES

Natural resources are products of nature. Indeed, pairing the words "natural" (landscapes, forests, rivers, minerals) with "resource" (how nature is employed and manipulated within a human context) is largely descriptive of the American relationship to the land in the 1800s. How, why, and to what extent the nation uses this bounty at any particular moment depends upon a complex combination of resource supply, political direction, technological development, and economics. In the nineteenth century these activities clustered in three broad time periods. First was the era of political consolidation (1800–1830); second was the period of eastern industrialization (1830–1860); and finally a period of increased industrial development and westward expansion (1860–1900).

Natural Resources in an Era of Political Consolidation

In 1781 Thomas Jefferson, in *Notes on the State of Virginia,* proposed that the United States should "let our workshops remain in Europe." He argued that America should be primarily an agricultural nation whose greatest natural resources were the fertile land and the industrious people who worked it. Jefferson envisioned a country populated by the yeomenry, a body of farmer-citizens who would work the land and either grow household foods locally or trade for them with neighbors. In Jefferson's mind this dream was assured by the Louisiana Purchase of 1803.

Contrary to this vision, other prominent political figures, such as Alexander Hamilton and Daniel Webster, expressed a desire to develop industrial manufacturers rapidly and to exploit the new nation's abundant natural resources. They argued that it was necessary to industrialize in order to create wealth and place the new country on a secure international footing. The War of 1812, which revealed the nation's dependence on others for weapons and industrial production, and a general public enthusiasm for capitalist enterprise, settled the dispute. America was to be a nation of manufacturers as well as of farmers, and the nation's natural resources were a key element in the achievement of this goal.

In the early nineteenth century the technology and capital that flowed into the new nation, and the manufacturing infrastructure it subsequently created, rapidly gained momentum. In many instances this growth fed upon itself, setting a cycle in motion. Profitable manufacturing enterprises required larger and more sophisticated industrial technology. New technologies increased the need for natural resources. Increased extraction of resources (water, coal, iron, timber) spurred further industrial activity, which in turn required more land and material to support it. Viewed in this light, there was always a symbiotic relationship between the "industrial East" and the agrarian "frontier West."

Westward Expansion, Industrialization, and Natural Resource Exploitation

Cheap land and settlement policies like the 1862 Homestead Act formed a magnet that drew the population to occupy and farm western regions. However, the interests of established eastern manufacturers and nascent western industrial concerns were just as responsible for attracting people to the West well before passage of the Homestead Act. Indeed, to a large degree both causes were intertwined. For every frontier agricultural settlement and village, there were mining towns and lumber camps extracting natural resources for the growing American economy. The agricultural character and frontier spirit of the American West was culturally strong during and after the nineteenth century. However, mechanization, both on the rural farm and in the urban factory—along with the communication and transportation networks that linked them—more accurately characterizes the American West.

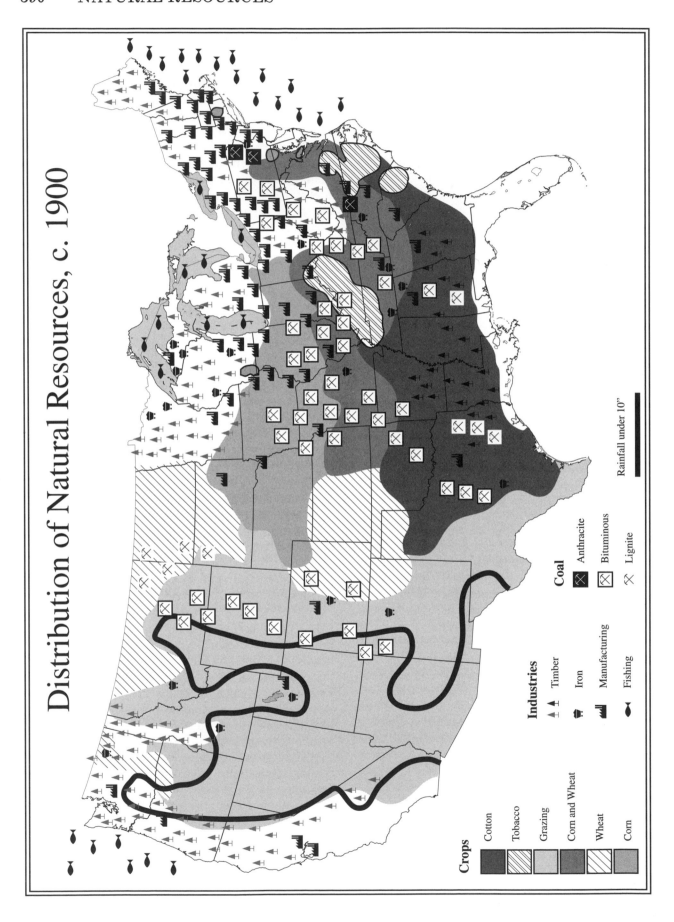

Distribution of Natural Resources, c. 1900

Crops

	Cotton
	Tobacco
	Grazing
	Corn and Wheat
	Wheat
	Corn

Industries

Timber	
Iron	
Manufacturing	
Fishing	

Coal

Anthracite	Bituminous
Lignite	

Rainfall under 10"

Rivers, canals, roads, railroads, and by mid-century the newly developed telegraph system created transportation and communication networks. At important intersections of these networks, towns and villages rapidly developed into urban manufacturing and transportation centers such as Chicago, St. Louis, and Cincinnati. In nineteenth-century America the transformation, exploitation, and extraction of natural resources rapidly advanced as railway networks expanded, as people flocked to urban areas, and as the tall-grass prairie was transformed into rangelands and grain fields. All these events were inexorably tied; each fed the others concurrently.

American railroads made their debut in the late 1820s. By 1830 the United States had twenty-three miles of track in operation. Forty years later there were more than 50,000 miles. In the decade 1880–1890 alone more than 70,000 miles of railway were constructed. By 1900, on 140,000 miles of track, trains transported timber, coal, oil, grain, vegetables, cotton, ores, meat, and thousands of people.

Increasingly, people settled in urban centers like Chicago. About half a million people lived in towns numbering twenty-five hundred residents or more in 1810. By 1900 the number was close to thirty million people. Home for most of these people was in houses and apartments built from wood products. In 1880 the Chicago lumberyards alone shipped over a billion board feet of wood products taken from the surrounding forests and from as far away as Oregon and Washington.

With permanent urban homes came durable goods, and on the surrounding farms larger and more sophisticated tools and machines, like the McCormick reaper and combine, became ubiquitous. Much of this hardware was increasingly made of metal manufactured in mills, from ore extracted in numerous mining regions. From roughly the turn of the century to the Civil War, per capita iron consumption climbed from 20 to 120 pounds per year.

In the nineteenth century large mechanized farms were uniquely American, and they produced vast amounts of grain during the period 1860–1900. Flour production, for example, rose from 40 million barrels per year to 106 million. Chicago (an insignificant trading post in the 1820s) exported 21 million bushels of grain in 1856 alone. The next year, that city's gigantic grain elevators stored four million bushels.

The capital for all this commercial and industrial enterprise came from a number of sources, much of it from the buying and selling of the natural resources that supplied the rapidly growing demand. Other currency was produced in a more old-fashioned way, but with a new industrial twist. In one operation in the mining regions of California, one ounce of extracted gold required 1.5 million gallons of water diverted through six thousand miles of pipeline and ditches.

These figures are both impressive and alarming. What was once dense forest, vast expanses of tall-grass prairie, and free-flowing rivers and streams had been transformed into a network of roads, railways, navigable watercourses, large agricultural concerns, and urban manufacturing centers by 1900. All this activity changed the American landscape forever. By century's end the largely unrestrained resource exploitation began to arouse concern within economic and industrial circles.

Conservation, Efficiency, and Waste

By the late 1880s it was evident that the incredible level of natural resource extraction could not continue indefinitely, yet it was politically and economically impractical, indeed almost impossible, to halt industrial growth. So the focus became one of efficiently developing the remaining natural resources and employing increasingly sophisticated technology and techniques that would keep waste to a minimum. Thus the idea of efficiently extracting the remaining resources and the concept of natural resource conservation emerged in the 1890s. This initiative continued to be an important political topic in the next century.

In its first century the new nation struggled to define itself culturally and politically. The tremendous amount of natural resources provided a portion of this identity. America had always been, in some way or another, associated with abundance and novelty. How this abundance would be utilized and exploited was somewhat unclear in 1800, but a political and economic direction soon emerged. A cycle of industrial development, resource extraction, and further industrial development followed.

After about 1830 the United States rapidly expanded westward. While the natural resources and landscape of the West were in many ways different from those of the East, the economic, technological, and political direction of the country bound the two sections together. America's industrial and economic power grew at an unprecedented rate from 1830 to 1900. The extraction and exploitation of natural resources mirrored the pace of growth and was key to the nation's national and international identity. However, by the late 1880s some industrialists, a few politicians, and experts in the new fields of hydrology, forestry, and agronomy questioned this rapid exploitation and the methods employed over a century of progress, and asked if the waste and pace could continue. Therefore, natural resource conservation became a topic of political discussion.

See also **Coal; Conservation; Lumber and Timber Industry; Mining and Extraction; Transportation,** *subentries on* **Canals and Waterways, Railroads.**

Bibliography

Cronon, William. *Nature's Metropolis: Chicago and the Great West.* New York: W. W. Norton, 1991.

Hays, Samuel P. *Conservation and the Gospel of Efficiency: The Progressive Conservation Movement, 1890–1920.* Cambridge, Mass.: Harvard University Press, 1959.

Jefferson, Thomas. *Notes on the State of Virginia.* New York: Harper & Row, 1964. The original edition was published in 1861.

Marx, Leo. *The Machine in the Garden: Technology and the Pastoral Ideal in America.* New York: Oxford University Press, 1964.

———. "Does Improved Technology Mean Progress?" In *Technology and the Future.* Edited by Albert H. Teich. 7th ed. New York: St. Martin's Press, 1997.

Pursell, Carroll. *The Machine in America: A Social History of Technology.* Baltimore: Johns Hopkins University Press, 1995.

Williams, Michael. *Americans and Their Forests: A Historical Geography.* New York: Cambridge University Press, 1996.

CHARLES L. SMITH

NATURE   Attitudes toward nature in the nineteenth century often reflected America's fascination with economic development and nation-building. In the rapidly industrializing East, the Enlightenment concept of nature as a mechanical system gained credence from experience in the mill and factory. Ecological processes were likened to the workings of a well-oiled machine. Thomas Ewbank's *The World a Workshop* (1855) compared the planet to a factory, designed by a divine engineer for human operators to run according to their needs. Imbued with a sense of their rightful dominion over the earth, Americans read nature as a resource to be utilized. For eastern industrialists and western pioneers alike, the natural world represented a vast repository of raw materials to be converted into economic wealth. Commentators perceived the American West as a limitless storehouse of minerals and furs. Ecosystems were parceled up into rectangular plots and subjected to frenzied speculation. Aggressively exercising their rights as property owners, settlers cut down trees, plowed up native grasses, and eradicated indigenous creatures.

The transformation of wild nature into "improved" land resounded with notions of social progress. Thomas Jefferson's vision of the United States as an agrarian republic, a nation of virtuous yeoman farmers, identified nature—the land itself—as a vital nurturer of American values. Expansionists portrayed the West as a fertile ground for liberty and democracy, with "free land" and abundant resources promising freedom and prosperity for poverty-stricken urbanites. Promulgators of the notion of "Manifest Destiny," a mid-century expansionist concept that was revived in the 1890s, meanwhile couched western migration in patriotic tones, inspiring white Americans to assert a 'natural right' to control both the landscape and other races. The conquest of nature thus came to be represented as a robust enterprise of individual, social, and national betterment.

Pioneers often considered the natural world as a hostile force. W. H. Venable, a settler in Ohio, described trees as "the backwoodman's enemy, for they occupy his ground. They will not run away, like the buffalo and the Indian, so they must be hewn down and cremated" (Simpson, p. 23). Reminiscent of colonial sentiments toward wilderness, western settlers displayed a vehement antipathy toward untamed land. Diarists cast the rippling prairie as a godless place and feared that, without the accouterments of civilization, communities would descend into barbarism. Pioneers imbued the settlement enterprise with moral and religious purposes. Floods, fallen trees, grasshoppers, and wolves became spiritual enemies as well as economic impediments.

Appreciation and Preservation

Those who had wandered the American woods and prairies for thousands of years considered nature very differently. Native Americans saw themselves as part of a vibrant and hospitable community of nature. Powerful animal spirits roamed the landscape, imparting valuable lessons and knowledge to their human brethren. Native Americans used and manipulated their environment but retained a kinship with the natural world.

During the nineteenth century, a number of white Americans entertained romantic views of nature that ran counter to the dominant materialism of the age. A few of these intellectuals recognized their affinity for the worldviews of Native Americans. Most, however, drew on imported strains of European romanticism, which fostered an appreciation of wild landscapes as sublime and mystical places for solitary contemplation, refuges from the apparent artificiality and soullessness of city life. Romanticism flourished among the artistic and literary elites of antebellum New England, who despaired over the industrialization and urbanization sweeping the region. The Transcendental Club, founded in Boston in

Yellow Shank. John James Audubon, the nineteenth-century ornithologist, demonstrated his examination and appreciation of nature with detailed, colorful prints. Engraving, c. 1827–1830. © THE ACADEMY OF NATURAL SCIENCES OF PHILADELPHIA/CORBIS

1836, emerged as a center of American romantic thought. Transcendentalists revered unspoiled landscapes as pure and spiritual places where humans could elevate themselves above cold reason and connect with a divine Oversoul. Leading exponent Ralph Waldo Emerson advocated in his book *Nature* (1836) looking at nature through "new eyes." On 4 July 1845, Emerson's protégé Henry David Thoreau embarked on a two-year sojourn at Walden Pond, near Concord, Massachusetts, to live a simple life and contemplate the tangible beauty and intangible meanings of the natural world. Thoreau recalled his experiences in *Walden* (1854), espousing an eloquent view of the intrinsic value of organic nature that continues to inspire American environmentalists.

Other nineteenth-century naturalists, writers, poets, and artists also extolled the virtues of wild nature as quintessentially American. Building on romantic notions, cultural nationalists asserted the superiority of wild American scenery, unmarred by Old World corruption and decadence. Patriots interpreted the size and grandeur of such places as Yosemite Valley and the Grand Canyon as proof of American exceptionalism, and earnestly promoted the natural monuments of the West as sources of national identity and pride. Huge paintings by Albert Bierstadt and Thomas Moran conveyed a sense of permanence, grandeur, and godliness in nature. Woodcuts and

picture books of famous American scenes adorned middle-class walls and tables.

Natural history became increasingly popular during the century. Ornithologists John James Audubon and Alexander Wilson depicted American birds in painstaking detail, while explorers of the West Meriwether Lewis and William Clark compiled a vast body of information on western flora and fauna. Nature writing, botany, and plant collecting emerged as popular pastimes, especially among upper- and middle-class women. The theories of the English biologist Charles Darwin spurred further interest in natural history, although his account of evolution as an amoral and violent process posed a potent challenge to the religious and romantic views of nature previously favored by Americans.

In the early part of the century, only the wealthy could afford to tour natural attractions, such as Trenton Falls, Catskill Mountain House, or Niagara Falls. By the 1870s, however, vacations at the coast or in the mountains had become a part of the urban middle-class calendar. City parks provided a natural playground for those who could not afford to travel. The landscaped knolls, tree-lined avenues and rugged grottoes of New York's Central Park (designed by Frederick Law Olmsted and Calvert Vaux in 1858) offered urbanites a place for physical and spiritual renewal away from the grime of the street and the factory. The notion of a healthy and strenuous outdoor life as guarantor of American virtue contributed to the rise of sportsmen's clubs during the 1870s.

In the latter years of the nineteenth century, a growing number of Americans lamented the loss of wild nature. As industrialization took hold of the land and the culture alike, especially in the West, a tincture of romantic idealization of nature countervailed in sectors of public opinion. Taking stock of the wastefulness of frontier life, utilitarian conservationists led by forester Gifford Pinchot argued for a measured and rational use of remaining natural resources. In the 1850s, Pinchot campaigned for lands set aside under the Forest Reserve Act of 1891 to be scientifically managed. Preservationists, meanwhile, perceived undeveloped landscapes as priceless remnants of a vanishing America. John Muir, cofounder of the Sierra Club (1892), emerged as a prominent advocate of protecting nature for its own sake. The setting aside of more than thirty-three hundred square miles of scenic wonderland in Wyoming as Yellowstone National Park (1872) marked a milestone in nature preservation. A provision of the New York state constitution, adopted in the 1890s, declared the Adirondack Mountains to be "forever wild." As the nineteenth century drew to a close, Americans embraced spectacular vistas as national treasures, but still judged many landscapes by their dollar value alone. Contested meanings of nature would continue to frame American relations with the physical environment throughout the next century.

See also **Conservation; Expansion; Federal Land Policy; Frontier; Geography and Ecology; Manifest Destiny; National Parks; Natural Resources; Painting; Recreation; Romanticism; Transcendentalism.**

Bibliography

Dorman, Robert L. *A Word for Nature: Four Pioneering Environmental Advocates, 1845–1913.* Chapel Hill: University of North Carolina Press, 1998.

Huth, Hans. *Nature and the American: Three Centuries of Changing Attitudes.* New ed. Lincoln: University of Nebraska Press, 1990. The original version was published in 1957.

Nash, Roderick. *Wilderness and the American Mind.* 3d ed. New Haven, Conn.: Yale University Press, 1982. The original version was published in 1967.

Norwood, Vera. *Made From This Earth: American Women and Nature.* Chapel Hill: University of North Carolina Press, 1993.

Runte, Alfred. *National Parks: The American Experience.* Lincoln: University of Nebraska Press, 1979.

Simpson, John Warfield. *Visions of Paradise: Glimpses of Our Landscape's Legacy.* Berkeley: University of California Press, 1999.

Worster, Donald. *Nature's Economy: A History of Ecological Ideas.* 2d ed. Cambridge, U.K.: Cambridge University Press, 1994. The original edition was published in 1977.

KAREN JONES

NAVAL ACADEMY, U.S. The U.S. Naval Academy was established in 1845, but the idea for a school to train future naval officers went all the way back to the turn of the nineteenth century, when Congress created the U.S. Navy. Indeed, Alexander Hamilton, with President John Adams's support, proposed that the military school envisioned for West Point, New York, include separate and detailed training in naval affairs. Congress, however, rejected the plan when it founded the U.S. Military Academy.

Succeeding presidents and secretaries of the navy continued to lobby for the creation of a naval school, but in every instance the established naval leadership and the Congress balked. Typical of the reaction to such a proposal was one senior officer's opinion: "You could no more educate sailors in a shore college than you could teach ducks to swim in a garret." A mutiny on the brig *Somers* in 1842 shocked previously hostile officers, and Congressmen were swayed to support proposals to train midshipmen more formally.

Secretary of the Navy George Bancroft succeeded in convincing the navy's old guard that the army's Fort Severn, located on the banks of a river by the same name in Annapolis, Maryland, was a more suitable site to train midshipmen than the Philadelphia Naval Asylum, which had been established in 1838. On 10 October 1845 the Naval School opened with Commander Franklin Buchanan as superintendent, seven faculty members, and two hundred midshipmen, most of whom already had over six years of service in the navy. The curriculum at the new Naval School emphasized natural philosophy, mathematics and chemistry, English and foreign languages, and ordnance and navigation. Although the organization of the curriculum and the academic board were patterned after West Point, the Naval School lacked one major component: military training.

During the Mexican War, Commander Buchanan's return to a ship command necessitated the selection of a successor. No sooner had a new superintendent and commandant, Commander George P. Upshur, reported than discipline broke down, and it was not until the academic board reformed the entire educational system in 1850 that things improved. In that year, the Naval School was renamed the U.S. Naval Academy, and the course of instruction was expanded to four years, with a three-year tour at sea between the second and third years. A system of demerits and punishments for errant midshipmen was placed in effect, and midshipmen were finally required to wear uniforms. The academic board decided in 1851 that midshipmen would stay at the Naval Academy for all four years and would receive their nautical training during summer cruises, rather than between the second and third years of instruction.

With these reforms the Naval Academy was well on its way to becoming what Superintendent Buchanan hoped would be a school "second to none." Throughout the 1850s academic and dormitory buildings were added to the school and the faculty was enlarged. From its inception the Naval Academy had both civilian and military instructors, a tradition that continues to this day.

The election of Abraham Lincoln as president in 1860 ushered in crisis years for the country in general and for the Naval Academy in particular. Many midshipmen and naval officers resigned and returned to their home states to offer their services to the newly formed Confederacy. Turmoil in Maryland and fears of Confederate invasion prompted the Naval Academy to relocate to Newport, Rhode Island, for the duration of the war. Union victory in 1865 brought the academy back to Annapolis, where Rear Admiral David Dixon Porter became its superintendent. During Porter's tenure the academy tightened standards, modernized the curriculum, allowed midshipmen to work off demerits, and added athletics to the program of study.

In the late nineteenth century the academy continued to refine its curriculum and expand its physical plant. In the 1870s the school briefly admitted its first black midshipmen, but none of the three graduated and the school remained all white at the end of the century. In 1898 the academy had a crest emblazoned with the words "Ex Scientia Tridens" (from knowledge, seapower). As the century neared its end, the Naval Academy stood poised to train the leaders of the Great White Fleet of the 1900s and the future heroes of the Pacific War in World War II.

See also **Navy.**

Bibliography

Hagan, Kenneth J. *This People's Navy: The Making of American Sea Power.* New York: Free Press, 1991.

Howarth, Stephen. *To Shining Sea: A History of the United States Navy, 1775–1991.* New York: Random House, 1991.

Sweetman, Jack. *The U.S. Naval Academy: An Illustrated History.* Annapolis, Md.: Naval Institute Press, 1979.

MARY A. DECREDICO

NAVAL TECHNOLOGY Naval technology changed dramatically during the nineteenth century. A naval officer serving in Britain's *Royal Sovereign* in 1637 could have adjusted easily to service in the American *Philadelphia* almost two hundred years later. However, an early-nineteenth-century naval officer would have been confounded by the state-of-the-art warships of the 1890s. The warships the U.S. Navy took to war against the Barbary corsairs and Britain during the first two decades of the century were sail-powered, wooden ships armed with smooth-bore, muzzle-loading cannon. Against Spain in 1898 the navy employed warships made of steel, propelled by steam engines, protected by steel-alloy armor, and armed with powerful cannon capable of firing exploding shells to a range of several miles.

National maritime policy defines a country's naval strategy, which in turn dictates the types of ships a country constructs. Nineteenth-century maritime nations adopted one of two strategies: the strong-navy strategy of *guerre d'escadre*, which involved fleet-versus-fleet battles, or *guerre de course*, usually the strategy of weaker maritime powers, which involved indirect attacks on an enemy's commercial shipping.

Starting with the Revolutionary War, American naval strategy regarding a stronger naval power, such as Britain, focused on commerce raiding. When confronting a weaker naval power, such as the Barbary corsairs in 1801 and 1816, Mexico in 1846, the Confederacy in 1861, and Spain in 1898, the U.S. Navy pursued the strategy of *guerre d'escadre* and sought first to destroy the enemy fleet if it existed, including Spanish ships in the Philippines and Cuba in 1898, and then to blockade the enemy coastline and project power ashore.

Navies have always been technologically complex, and naval officers identify with the hardware they operate as much as workers in any profession do. Within such a technologically defined society, new advances have the potential to destabilize the existing order. Naval officers were generally conservative and viewed new technologies skeptically. Innovations that clearly enhanced the status quo, such as a more powerful gun, were accepted readily. Technologies and their supporters that challenged the status quo often were dismissed. Some technological innovations—such as the affixing of an iron plate to the outside of a wooden-hulled ship (France's *La Gloire*, 1857)—resulted in obvious improvements, even though the latter sparked a race for more powerful naval guns to penetrate the iron plate. Larger guns mandated larger ships, made possible by iron and steel hulls. More powerful guns could be resisted only by stronger and heavier armor. Larger, heavier ships required more powerful engines, and the result was larger, more capable, and more expensive warships as the century came to a close. In general naval officers considered larger ships, with their bigger guns and

Sailboats on a Stormy Sea. "American Squadron at Sea," painted by Robert Walker, 1839. LIBRARY OF CONGRESS

heavier armor, more capable than smaller ones. The advantages of new, nonweapon technologies were less clear. Steam engines, for example, threatened both the traditional sailor's role and the warrior ethos within the naval profession.

Replacing Sail with Steam

During the War of 1812 the U.S. Navy was much weaker than the British navy and pursued a strategy of *guerre de course* on the high seas. A series of victories by large, heavily gunned U.S. frigates over smaller British frigates brought the U.S. Navy international recognition. However, the war against British commerce, including the American naval officer David Porter's eradication of the British whaling trade in the Pacific during the cruise of the frigate *Essex*, hurt Britain dearly.

During the war the United States expended $320,000—more than the cost of the famous frigate *Constitution*—to build *Demologos*, Robert Fulton's steam-propelled "floating battery," to defend harbors from the British navy. *Demologos*, which was not completed before the end of the war, was delayed by

the mistrust of its captain, David Porter, of steam engines and his insistence on additional sails.

Steam propulsion appeared to have limited utility for the navy. Porter later used a small, steam-powered ship, *Sea Gull*, during his operations to suppress Caribbean piracy stemming from the wars of Latin American independence. While steam propulsion proved useful in chasing pirates up rivers, its inefficiency offered no assistance to the navy's increasing worldwide mission of protecting American commerce. Without overseas bases, American warships could only reach the distant East India Squadron by sail power.

By the 1830s America's rivers hosted seven hundred commercial steamships. In 1835 Secretary of the Navy Mahlon Dickerson began acquisition of the steam-powered *Fulton the Second*. Some officers opposed steamships because the side-mounted paddle-wheels had significant military disadvantages. They were vulnerable to gunfire and displaced many broadside guns.

More surprising than opposition to technological change were the nonengineer naval officers of the line, such as Matthew C. Perry, who championed steam propulsion. By 1842, in spite of the aesthetically motivated disdain of Secretary of the Navy James Paulding, the navy had two paddlewheel frigates, *Missouri* and *Mississippi*. The attraction of steam propulsion for naval officers—independence from natural forces—was similar to that felt by early users of waterwheels and windmills. The weaknesses of the engines—the inefficient transmission of engine power and the engines' voracious appetite for coal—limited the potential of these early steam-propulsion systems to provide added speed during pursuit, evasion, or battle.

Fuel problems persisted in the years before the Civil War. Steamship operations during the Mexican War (1846–1848) proved difficult. Keeping ships coaled in Mexico, more than eight hundred miles from the nearest U.S. naval base, was a significant logistical problem. In 1851 the 2,450-ton side-wheel steamer *Susquehanna* departed Norfolk on its maiden voyage for duty as flagship of the East India Squadron. The eight-month trip covered 18,500 miles, and the ship consumed its weight in coal and eleven hundred sticks of wood. The sailors spent 25 percent of the voyage coaling the ship.

Thanks to John Ericsson's development of the submerged screw propeller in 1837 (first used by the U.S. Navy in 1839), the navy was able to construct more efficient screw frigates during the 1850s. By the mid-1850s paddlewheel steamers had given way to new classes of propeller-driven ships with improved steaming and sailing qualities. However, the problem of coal was far from resolved. The demand for it translated into a need for overseas possessions that would later feed into a circular argument in favor of imperialism to provide naval coaling bases for the protection of U.S. trade.

During the Civil War both the United States and Confederate navies made use of steamships. Steam warships were well suited for Confederate commerce raiding, maintaining the Federal naval blockade, attacking Confederate coastal forts and ports along the Atlantic and Gulf Coasts, and in the decisive Federal campaign in the western river system.

Officers and Engineers

The growth of the U.S. Navy from 42 warships in 1861 to a wartime high of 671 ships expanded the officer corps. The need for steam-engineering officers outstripped the supply. Line officers resented the large number of socially inferior and often inept mechanics brought into the wartime navy as junior officers.

Secretary of the Navy Gideon Welles and his assistant secretary Gustavus Fox considered steam-propelled warships as the technological basis of the future U.S. Navy. They proposed making every officer an engineer—a future most line officers rejected. Line officers routinely discriminated against naval engineers, who were given nonnaval ranks and lesser pay and were excluded from ship command. Engineers' power was vested in the navy's bureau system, established by legislation in 1842 and subsequently supported strongly by Congress.

At the outbreak of the Civil War the Confederacy had little naval or industrial infrastructure. Confederate naval strategy centered on coastal defense and commerce raiding. The Confederates bolstered their naval campaign with innovative technologies, such as torpedoes (underwater mines) and the human-powered submarine *Hunley*.

The war validated the work of Rear Admiral John Dahlgren, a naval ordnance expert. He measured the pressure along the length of a cannon barrel as it was fired and developed the Dahlgren gun, which was thicker near the breach, where the pressure was greatest. Dahlgren guns were smooth-bore muzzle loaders and were lighter and more efficient than traditional cannon. Warships equipped with steam propulsion, ironcladding, and Dahlgren guns firing exploding shells could destroy land fortifications.

During the war Benjamin Franklin Isherwood was chief of the U.S. Navy's Bureau of Steam Engineering and the driving force behind the design of the steam frigate *Wampanoag*. *Wampanoag* and similar ships were fast *guerre de course* ships, which the U.S. Navy began to build to threaten British commerce should Britain decide to aid the Confederacy. Unfinished at the war's end, *Wampanoag* was tested for acceptance in 1869. It proved to be the fastest warship in the world and held that record for almost twenty years. Isherwood had many enemies within the navy, and his ship seemed inappropriate to a navy returning to its prewar strategic mission of worldwide commerce protection. Admiral David Dixon Porter considered *Wampanoag* ill suited for service on far stations. Line officers dominated the Board on Steam Machinery Afloat and the Board of Inspection and Survey, which condemned *Wampanoag* as vulnerable to attack because of its size, as an inefficient sailing ship, and as liable to roll. Porter ordered half of *Wampanoag*'s machinery and two of her four propeller blades removed in order to improve her sailing quality. In this way Porter humiliated Isherwood while adapting the ship to the worldwide commerce-protection strategy unchanged from before the Civil War.

In 1873, when the Spanish in Cuba seized the gun-runner *Virginius* and executed some of her American crew, the navy concentrated in Key West and prepared for war. Diplomacy prevailed, but the resulting

Sailors on Deck. Sailors aboard the USS *Monitor* voyage to fight the Atlantic coast Confederates during the Civil War. The iron-clad exterior of the ship indicates that naval technology was in its middle stages. Photograph, 9 July 1862. LIBRARY OF CONGRESS: PRINTS AND PHOTOGRAPHS DIVISION

naval exercise demonstrated the navy's weaknesses. Nevertheless, the nation was unwilling to fund new ships, and the navy made few effective arguments on their behalf. The technological base of the navy stagnated, and the bloated officer corps, promoted solely on the basis of seniority, became the catalyst for change.

Foreign developments in naval technology were dynamic, but the U.S. Navy became a floating museum during the 1870s. Trapped within a profession commanding obsolete technology, naval officers established the U.S. Naval Institute (1873) and the Line Officers Association. The Naval Institute served as a professional forum on issues such as strategy, and the Line Officers Association lobbied for a large, modern navy, which the officers insisted was essential for expanding American trade.

The Naval Appropriations Act of 1882 provided the line officer hierarchy another chance to suppress naval engineers. The act limited the officer corps to its 1882 size and ordered a ceiling of one hundred officers in the Engineering Corps. The separate engineering curriculum at the Naval Academy, awarded the Diplôme de Medaille d'Or at the 1878 Paris Universal Exposition, was terminated. The line finally had engineers under control, and Secretary Welles's ideal of "every officer an engineer" was dead.

Creating a World-Class Navy

The post–Civil War naval stagnation ended with congressional authorization for the construction of four steel-hulled warships in 1883. Equipped with steam engines, the ships also carried a full comple-

Steam Technology. Oilers and machinists maintain one of the 4,400 horsepower, triple-expansion engines aboard the U.S. cruiser *Newark*. This cylinder assembly, like those in other navy cruisers built during the 1880s, had to be installed on its side to fit under the protective deck. This use of steam engines represented a later stage in naval technology. LIBRARY OF CONGRESS

ment of sails. By the time they came into service near the end of the 1880s, the British had adopted the two-power standard, holding that Britain would have a navy equal to the second and third best navies in the world combined, which joined with a broad spectrum of navalist opinion to create an environment favorable to construction of a first-rate American navy.

In 1890 Captain Alfred Thayer Mahan published *The Influence of Sea Power on History, 1660–1783,* which reached a wide audience. Mahan linked Britain's wealth to the empire it achieved and maintained through a large navy that adhered to a *guerre d'escadre* strategy. According to Mahan and other navalists, such as Theodore Roosevelt and Henry Cabot Lodge, the growing United States needed a first-class navy composed of modern steel battleships serving a strategy of *guerre d'escadre*.

In 1890 Congress authorized the construction of three steel battleships to serve the new American strategy. The modern battleship owed its creation to developments in metallurgy, steam engineering, and ordnance. The Bessemer process provided less-expensive steel that made construction of large ships affordable. Large ships could carry powerful breech-loading, rifled guns, and the resultant technological race focused on more powerful guns versus improved armor.

Warship armor, specifically armor in battleships, benefited from metallurgical advances. Steel manufacturers were reluctant to produce armor, so the navy underwrote the capital expenditures required. These steel firms began to sell armor more cheaply abroad, creating a scandal. By the end of the century steel armor had been strengthened by the addition of nickel and chrome alloys, resulting in a need for increased gun power.

Steam engine efficiency had improved steadily after the Civil War with the development of double-expansion and eventually triple-expansion engines. These more efficient engines allowed U.S. ships to sail a greater distance using the same amount of fuel. By the end of the 1890s the British inventor Charles Parsons perfected the marine steam turbine. Tested in England, the turbine would become the standard for warship propulsion for the first half of the twentieth century.

When the Spanish-American War began in 1898, the U.S. Navy possessed four battleships. Ironically, Commodore George Dewey had none when he achieved fame by defeating the Spanish naval force in Manila Bay in 1898. Admiral William Sampson demonstrated the effectiveness of the modern battleship in defeating the weak Spanish naval force of Admiral Pascual Cervera off Cuba. The war brought the United States an empire that included the Philippines, Guam, and Puerto Rico and validated a *guerre d'escadre* strategy based on the modern battleship. Congress, between 1898 and 1905, authorized the construction of fourteen more battleships, enabling the United States to rise to the status of a world naval power. The United States became enmeshed in an international naval race and considered Britain, Germany, and Japan its principal rivals. This naval rivalry proved quite expensive, consuming an average of 17 percent of the annual federal budget during the administrations of Presidents Theodore Roosevelt and William Howard Taft.

A first-rate navy required excellent technology, and technology required naval engineers. During the 1890s Assistant Secretary of the Navy Theodore Roosevelt presided over a study that resurrected Secretary Welles's Civil War idea of every officer an engineer. The resulting Amalgamation Act of 1899 merged naval engineers into the line and set the stage for a more technocratic naval profession in the twentieth century.

During the nineteenth century the U.S. Navy evolved from an inexpensive, weak-navy strategy of *guerre de course* to an expensive, strong-navy strategy of *guerre d'escadre*. The United States became a major power based on its navy. The officer corps established professional standards, largely as a result of changes in naval technology. The naval profession in 1899 was more attuned to technology, providing the foundation for the technology-based American naval profession of the twentieth century.

See also **Maritime Technology; Military Technology; Steam Power.**

Bibliography

Bennett, Frank M. *The Steam Navy of the United States: A History of the Growth of the Steam Vessel of War in the U.S. Navy, and of the Naval Engineering Corps.* Pittsburgh, Pa.: Warren, 1896.

Buhl, Lance C. "Mariners and Machines: Resistance to Technological Change in the American Navy, 1865–1869." *Journal of American History* 59 (1974): 703–727.

Calvert, Monte A. *The Mechanical Engineer in America, 1830–1910: Professional Cultures in Conflict.* Baltimore: Johns Hopkins University Press, 1967.

Hagan, Kenneth J. *This People's Navy: The Making of American Sea Power.* New York: Free Press, 1991.

Herrick, Walter R. *The American Naval Revolution.* Baton Rouge: Louisiana State University Press, 1966.

Karsten, Peter. *The Naval Aristocracy: The Golden Age of Annapolis and the Emergence of Modern American Navalism.* New York: Free Press, 1972.

Morison, Elting E. *Men, Machines, and Modern Times.* Cambridge, Mass.: MIT Press, 1966.

Shulman, Mark Russell. *Navalism and the Emergence of American Sea Power, 1882–1893.* Annapolis, Md.: Naval Institute Press, 1995.

Sloan, Edward William, III. *Benjamin Franklin Isherwood, Naval Engineer: The Years as Engineer in Chief, 1861–1869.* Annapolis, Md.: Naval Institute Press, 1965.

WILLIAM M. MCBRIDE

NAVY

At the beginning of the nineteenth century the United States followed the traditional maritime policy of a nation unable to rival the offensive power of the British fleet. The new U.S. Navy, reorganized under the Naval Act of 1798, sought naval allies whenever possible and devoted its meager appropriations to smaller ships (frigates, sloops, and brigs) augmented by the domestic merchant service, commercial fisheries, and privateers (state-licensed pirates) during wars. While the American frigate, designed by Joshua Humphreys, was larger, sturdier, faster, and more heavily armed than any other ship in its class (it carried a minimum of forty-four guns), it was no match for the British ship of the line, which had at least seventy-four guns and controlled the important sea lanes of the world. During nineteenth-century conflicts, American officers raided enemy commerce (*guerre de course*), protected the Republic's maritime trade, and engaged an isolated enemy warship when the opportunity arose. But with little exception the ships under their command were incapable of fleet combat (*guerre d'escadre*).

The Emerging Navy

After the American Revolution a conflict developed over what kind of navy, offensive or defensive, would best serve the needs of the young nation. After the American victory in the Quasi-War against France (1798–1800), the first secretary of the navy, Benjamin Stoddert (1751–1813), and other "navalists," called for a large maritime force patterned after the British model to deter the nation's enemies. Conversely, "antinavalists" pointed to the tremendous success of privateers during the Revolution as proof that a strong fleet was unnecessary. Not only would it cost more than the country could afford, it would also weaken national security by serving as a catalyst to war. Instead of new construction they demanded drastic demobilization, leaving a small navy for defense purposes only. Any hopes of a navy capable of offensive action were dashed in 1800 when the newly elected president and leading antinavalist, Thomas

Jefferson, proposed abolishing the Department of the Navy altogether and adopting a naval militia system. In desperation, Stoddert presented Congress with a postwar naval plan so modest—centered on a fleet of only six active, undermanned frigates with seven warships held in reserve—that the president would be forced to concede or appear unconcerned with national security. Jefferson, however, was unsatisfied by Stoddert's attempts at republican economy and moved to cut the fleet further until the ongoing troubles with the Barbary pirates necessitated the rapid construction of several new frigates.

The Barbary pirates were corsairs from the North African states of Morocco, Algiers, Tunis, and Tripoli who operated a loosely allied naval confederacy under the mantel of the sultan of Turkey. The pirates patrolled the seas, seizing ships and imprisoning the crews of any nation that had not paid a tribute. After the Revolution, the United States was eager to participate in the rich Mediterranean trade, but could no longer operate in the region under British protection. War broke out when Tripoli increased its monetary demands and cut down the flagpole in front of the U.S. embassy. Jefferson believed that a short war would be less expensive than paying the new tribute and he authorized a series of naval expeditions to ensure American prerogatives in the Mediterranean.

During the War with Tripoli (1801–1805) the navy functioned as a blockading "squadron of observation." The fundamental weakness inherent in the antinavalist stance was clearly demonstrated in 1801, when Jefferson was able to dispatch only three frigates and one sloop of war to the Mediterranean. With little firepower at their disposal, commanders were ordered to avoid combat. Action was permitted during the second year, but Commodore Richard Morris lacked the initiative to engage the enemy. Progress finally came in the third year, when Commodore Edward Preble, who was ill with cancer, took charge aboard the forty-four-gun *Constitution*. Lieutenant Stephen Decatur daringly burned the *Philadelphia*, which had been captured earlier by the pirates. Besides these heroics, a five-hundred-mile land campaign, organized by the diplomat William Eaton and including Europeans, Arabs, and a few American marines, gave the fledgling navy the heroes it needed to begin building its heritage. Although the U.S. Navy was not able to conduct fleet warfare in the early nineteenth century, it proudly pointed to the personal courage and honor of many veterans of the War with Tripoli in its pleas for public support.

With pressure mounting from the Eaton campaign and the guns of the American brigs *Argus* and *Hornet* and the schooner *Nautilus* aimed at his shores, the bashaw of Tripoli agreed in 1805 to negotiations that favored the American cause. Jefferson ransomed the imprisoned crew of the *Philadelphia*, paid a one-time "reduced" tribute in exchange for peace, and ordered the nation's seventeen frigates largely sold or mothballed. The president claimed that, instead of maintaining expensive warships, a passive naval defense would better serve American security needs. According to Jefferson, strong coastal fortifications and two hundred small gunboats (open vessels carrying one or two large-caliber guns and twenty to thirty citizen soldiers commanded by a few regular officers) stationed along the coastline would prevent enemy landings without provoking a preemptive strike by the Royal Navy, which was fearful of the creation of a rival offensive fleet. While gunboats were effective on the Great Lakes and in fortified harbors, they were impractical on the high seas. To the president's dismay, gun for gun they were three times as expensive as Humphreys's frigates. Great Britain, with over eight hundred commissioned vessels at its disposal, worried little about the maritime capability of the United States as war threatened in 1812.

In the years preceding the War of 1812 it was unclear which power, Great Britain or France, the United States would confront next. After the British defeated the French fleet at the Battle of Trafalgar (21 October 1805), a stalemate ensued in the longterm conflict between those two powers. With the Royal Navy controlling the seas and Napoleon's army commanding the Continent, the British and French fought each other indirectly by violating the neutral trade rights of the United States. Nonmaritime factors played a role in America's war declaration against England, but the rallying cry of free trade and free men, demanding the end of British impressment of American seamen, brought naval interests to the forefront of the groups demanding war.

In 1812 the United States was materially unprepared for war against the greatest sea power of the day. But with new frigate construction underway and with officer morale bordering on arrogance, the service embraced the opportunity to prove its usefulness to the nation. Secretary of the Navy Paul Hamilton, an alcoholic, South Carolinian rice planter with little maritime knowledge, sought the advice of his leading captains on how best to prosecute the naval war. The most senior officer, John Rodgers, convinced the secretary to mass his seventeen ships in one or two squadrons for a preemptive strike against the small British fleet then stationed in American waters. However, young, ambitious, and resourceful officers who had seen action in the Quasi-War and against the Barbary pirates refused to be reigned in by their superiors and pursued commerce raiding and single-ship engagements that netted several important victories.

Spectacular frigate duels, such as the *Constitution* versus the *Guerrière*, the *Constitution* versus the *Java*, and the *United States* versus the *Macedonian*, raised American morale considerably, but they were not decisive. More important to the war effort were the American operations on the Great Lakes defending New York from an imminent British invasion from Canada. On the lakes, Isaac Chauncey, Oliver Hazard Perry, and Thomas Macdonough built "instant" navies out of local materials, forcing the British to do likewise. Chauncey's delaying actions on Lake Ontario created a shield for Perry, who successfully engaged the British at Put-in-Bay on Lake Erie. Macdonough was also victorious on Lake Champlain. The young master commandant defeated eleven thousand British regulars, even though his crew was inexperienced in nautical skills, by keeping his ships at anchor and on springs. After raking the bows of the British with one broadside, rigged cables turned the ships around and presented fresh cannons to the enemy. Unable to counter such resourcefulness, Great Britain canceled its invasion plans and entered negotiations to end the war on the basis of status quo antebellum.

Before news reached America that the Treaty of Ghent had restored the prewar status of the warring nations, Andrew Jackson's volunteer forces at New Orleans defeated Sir Edward Pakenham's British regulars, giving the impression that the army rather than the navy had brought Great Britain to terms. The navy profited materially from the War of 1812, however. The nation maintained its prewar maritime policy of not antagonizing the major powers with an offensive fleet, but the navy's strong public approval spurred Congress to allocate $10 million to build a permanent naval force much stronger than the previous one. Ironically, not a single vessel of the nine ships of the line and twelve heavy frigates authorized by the Gradual Increase of the Navy Act of 1816 ever fired a shot in anger, and they were rarely deployed. Between 1815 and 1860 the navy built smaller, handier vessels that incorporated the new steam technology and deployed them in diverse missions, including exploration, diplomacy, scientific expeditions, suppression of the African slave trade, fighting Caribbean pirates, and protection of American commerce.

Early steamships, such as the steam battery *Demologos* (1815) and the paddle wheelers *Fulton II* (1837), *Mississippi* (1841), and *Missouri* (1841), were impractical, and the officer corps disdained them. The ships had low-pressure, coal-hungry engines and were forced to carry a full rigging of sail because of their limited range and the lack of inter-national refueling stations open to the United States. In addition the large paddle wheels reduced by a third the number of guns a ship could mount. Advancements such as the screw propeller (1842), which eliminated the need for paddle wheels; iron hulls; smooth-bore cannons; and solid shot gave the navy much to be proud of. Yet the ever-present soot, the inability to freely pursue commerce raiders because of inefficient engines, and the emergence of engineers as a new class of officers who competed for privileges, prompted many old line officers to suppress steam technology at the very time they sought to modernize and professionalize their service.

As the navy grew in size, technology, and complexity of mission, its conservative, even reactionary management proved ineffective. The Board of Navy Commissioners, established in 1815 and consisting of three senior officers who advised the civilian secretary of the navy, resisted technological advancements. In 1842 Congress replaced the board with five "bureaus" or departments to oversee the material requirements of the service. The individual bureaus, Navy Yard and Docks; Ordnance and Hydrography; Construction, Equipment, and Repair; Medicine and Surgery; and Provisions and Clothing, were periodically revised, but the system remained intact through the rest of the nineteenth century. While the secretary of the navy maintained operational control, real power rested with the bureau chiefs, who generally remained in their positions of power and patronage throughout their careers.

In addition to reorganizing its bureaucracy, the navy enacted a number of reforms to improve officer education and acquire the specialization and corporate knowledge needed to fashion the service into a true profession. Prior to 1845, "midshipmen," appointed through political or naval connections and often as young as thirteen, received on-the-job training and tutoring aboard ships and at "cram schools" located at a number of shore stations. Seasoned midshipmen who secured their commanding officer's recommendation and passed an exam of questionable rigor were promoted to lieutenant. Because of a glut of officers appointed during the War of 1812 and a promotion system that relied on seniority, however, many midshipmen remained at their original rank well into their thirties, and few ever advanced beyond the rank of lieutenant.

A number of officers unhappy with the low standards in the commissioning process called for a naval school patterned after the U.S. Military Academy at West Point. Opponents had earlier claimed that such an institution was unconstitutional and would promote a "naval aristocracy." By 1845, however, naval officers critically needed advanced instruction in steam technology. The public called for a safer training environment after the nineteen-year-old midshipman Philip Spencer, the son of Secretary of War John Canfield Spencer, was executed at sea in December 1842 for planning a mutiny aboard the training brig *Somers*. With the coming of the Mexican War, Secretary of the Navy George Bancroft established the U.S. Naval Academy at Annapolis, Maryland, in October 1845, and then secured congressional approval for his actions. Instructed in engineering and the liberal arts, academy students received the status and privileges accorded to members of the middle and upper classes that primarily made up its student body.

While the Naval Academy instructed "young gentlemen," the navy's enlisted personnel during the nineteenth century primarily were members of the lower class. The navy recruited a multiracial, about 5 percent black in 1842, and transient lot from the seafaring populations of the eastern seaboard and from various ports around the world. American sailors endured inadequate pay, strict discipline, and unpleasant shipboard living conditions, lightened only in part by a daily ration of whiskey and water, known as grog. A number of captains won the love and obedience of their men through their personal examples of honor and selfless duty, but few officers avoided using the lash to enforce discipline. To improve its public image, the navy abolished flogging in 1850 and ended the grog ration in 1862.

By the time of the Mexican War (1846–1848) the navy had made great advancements in technology, management, education, and recruitment. It also changed its traditional wartime strategy. For the first time the United States possessed the superior naval force because Mexico had sold its ships. Consequently, the United States employed fleet tactics of blockading, amphibious landings, troop transportation, and convoying to its advantage. Lessons learned here would play an important role in the Civil War. In addition the navy played a major role in the conquest of California that netted for the nation several important new ports and an urgent need for a Central American isthmus canal to quickly concentrate its overextended fleet in the event of a war with a formidable naval adversary. During the opening days of the Civil War such an adversary seemed possible as the Confederacy lobbied for a naval alliance with Great Britain, France, or both.

The Civil War

The U.S. navy was woefully unprepared for armed conflict when the South seceded from the Union. President James Buchanan's secretary of the navy Isaac Toucey, a Southern sympathizer and antina-valist, weakened the nation's maritime defenses considerably before the war. Of the forty-two commissioned war vessels, only eight were modern steam vessels mounting Dahlgren guns and most had fallen into disrepair or had been dispatched to distant stations. It took up to two years for some of these ships to return to the United States. With so few ships, and the loss of the Federal naval yards in the South, Secretary of the Navy Gideon Welles scrambled to build the large and diverse maritime force required to implement General Winfield Scott's plan to divide and strangle the Confederacy. Welles's first task was to fashion a blockading force for the 3,500 miles of Southern coastline, using any vessel, no matter how small, he could secure. Historians have disagreed about the effectiveness of the naval blockade. While it was never complete, it became more effective over time and largely confined Southern shipping to shallow-draft blockade-runners quiet enough and fast enough to slip past blockaders.

The Confederate navy had few officers, fewer experienced sailors, and no European alliance to augment its fleet of ten old ships mounting a total of fifteen guns. The Confederacy therefore sought alternative means to counter the Union's rapidly increasing naval forces. Jefferson Davis issued letters of marque authorizing privateers, but international law had banned such activity, and no international prize courts assisted ships in unloading their booty. Commissioned commerce raiders, purchased from Great Britain by the Confederate agent James D. Bulloch, were more successful. Roaming the Atlantic, the *Alabama*, the *Shenandoah*, the *Florida*, and other fast ships built impressive records as they destroyed U.S. shipping, raising international shipping rates and Union frustrations in the process. Confederate secretary of the navy Stephen Mallory also invested time and money in experimental weaponry, such as the ironclad *Virginia*, mines, and the submarine *Hunley*. His attempts produced mixed results. While the initial success of the *Virginia* at Hampton Roads demonstrated that a few ironclads could break the blockade, the South could not keep pace with the U.S. industrial might, which produced ironclads and tinclads, the latter for riverine operations, at a rapid rate.

Once the United States had constructed enough new ships to control American waters the Union moved whole armies and conducted successful joint operations with the army on the Tennessee and Mississippi Rivers. The Union maintained blue water and brown water superiority, but its naval operations never were decisive. The Civil War was foremost a land war and the navies, both North and South, operated as mere auxiliaries of their respective armies.

Squadron of *Evolution*. The USS *Chicago*, *Yorktown*, *Boston*, and *Atlanta* take to the seas in 1889. These ships demonstrated several aspects of nineteenth-century naval technology, with steel-clad exteriors, sails, and steam power. LIBRARY OF CONGRESS: PRINTS AND PHOTOGRAPHS DIVISION

After the Civil War

The navy faced difficult transitions between 1868 and 1880 as it fell from the third-ranked maritime force in the world to the twelfth. At the end of the Civil War the United States possessed nearly seven hundred vessels, a handful of which were state-of-the-art steam vessels, including the experimental *Wampanoag*, then the fastest ship in the world at 17.75 knots. Because of the emphasis on steam during the war, naval engineers had attracted considerable public attention and influence, and they demanded respect from line officers, who jealously guarded their ranks from encroachment. Benjamin Isherwood, the navy's engineer in chief, antagonized many line officers when he claimed, "The Navy is now, and must ever continue to be, exclusively a steam navy."

The navy fell on hard times, however, as the war-weary and debt-ridden nation turned away from maritime concerns and concentrated instead on Reconstruction, industrialization, and western expansion. George Robeson, secretary of the navy during the corrupt Ulysses S. Grant administration, scrapped and sold much of the fleet at a fraction of its cost. In 1870 only fifty-two vessels remained. In addition the navy attempted to save money and keep engineers in their place by requiring that all vessels except tugs and dispatch ships be fitted with a full rigging of sail. Officers who failed to justify their use of coal faced disciplinary actions. While the Naval Academy was a premier engineering institution after the war, it also experienced its most violent period of hazing and violence after Congress added two years to the curriculum and only commissioned 25 percent of its graduates, who seldom advanced beyond the rank of lieutenant. Disgruntled midshipmen, according to Superintendent Francis Ramsay in 1882, were on the verge of mutiny.

The public paid little attention to the state of the navy until 1873, when a disagreement with Spain over the capture and execution of several American citizens illegally running arms to Cuban rebels nearly led to war. During the so-called *Virginius* crisis the navy tried to intimidate Spain by assembling a squadron off Key West but could only muster a rag-tag collection of outdated vessels that were unprepared for war. The declining state of the navy as epitomized by the *Virginius* crisis had a devastating effect on morale in the officer corps. Demoralized officers, especially young, ambitious junior officers with little hope of promotion, cruising far from home under sail power alone felt wounds to their pride as foreign officers laughed at the "old tubs" under their command.

While the American navy degenerated after the Civil War, the great naval powers of Europe, especially Great Britain, forged ahead with new technological advancements in steam engines and ship construction. The U.S. Navy, ready to capitalize on the expensive experimentation of other nations, patiently watched and learned. Three events, and considerable lobbying, convinced Congress to appropriate $1.3 million for new steel construction. First, in July 1882, the United States realized its harbor fortifications were vulnerable to attack after the British fleet bombarded Alexandria, Egypt, destroying forts far stronger than those guarding American ports. Second, Chile purchased the British-built cruiser *Esmeralda*, which completely outclassed anything in the American fleet. Finally, as nations with steam navies scrambled to grab coaling stations around the world, the United States faced the prospect of having American territory within striking distance of imperialistic European powers.

America's first new ships in twenty years were the cruisers *Atlanta*, *Boston*, *Chicago*, and *Dolphin*. Steel-hulled and fitted with modern steam engines, breech-loading guns, and full riggings of sail, the "ABCD" ships, as they were known to the American public, showed the flag abroad, but were only commissioned for defensive action. The United States finally began building battleships capable of *guerre d'escadre* in 1890, when Secretary of the Navy Benjamin Franklin Tracy reassured Congress that such vessels would not roam far from American waters because of the limited size of their coal bunkers. The "coastline battleships," the *Indiana*, *Massachusetts*, and *Oregon*, soon had their bunkers enlarged after Alfred Thayer Mahan (1840–1914), and the success of the Spanish-American War (1898) convinced the nation to build an offensive navy capable of fleet warfare.

The real father of Mahanian doctrine was Rear Admiral Stephen B. Luce, a farsighted leader instrumental in uplifting the navy's intellectual level. After securing approval for a Naval War College in 1884, Luce recruited Mahan to popularize the concept of "sea power" among the American public. In *The In-*

fluence of Sea Power upon History, 1660–1783 (1890), a social Darwinian polemic with a strong dose of Manifest Destiny, Mahan claimed that the United States, if it hoped to survive, needed to build an offensive fleet of ships powerful enough to seize and control the critical sea lanes (main shipping routes) of the world. America's traditional *guerre de course* strategy was ineffective, according to Mahan and his supporters, and should be rejected. Instead of commerce raiding, the United States should concentrate its ships into a single massive fleet and occupy the interior lines of battle to attack its enemies with economy of movement. Mahan claimed that if the nation followed these principles it would become a world power capable of sending its armies and commerce across the ocean with relative ease. Mahan's ideas were widely read in the United States, England, Germany, and Japan after the United States became an imperialistic power as a result of the Spanish-American War.

In 1898 an "unexplained" explosion onboard the USS *Maine* convinced Americans to fight to free the Cuban people from the Spanish Empire. An influential group of navalists, however, saw the call for war as an ideal opportunity to lead the American public

Boiler Room. Crewmen stoke the boilers of the battleship *Massachusetts*, which burned eight to twelve tons of coal per hour when running at full power. Photograph, 1899. LIBRARY OF CONGRESS

Navy Cooks. The cooks aboard the USS *Maine,* a ship that was sunk in Havana Harbor in 1898 immediately before the Spanish-American War. Crews in the navy were integrated (note the African American crew member on the left), unlike the army, where black troops were segregated, although usually under the authority of white officers. LIBRARY OF CONGRESS: PRINTS AND PHOTOGRAPHS DIVISION

into imperialism. Before 1898 the nation had resisted overseas expansion, considered immoral and a violation of American principles. The nation refused to annex "inferior" peoples, even when offered territory from insurgents willing to accept American rule in Hawaii in 1893. But the navy was convinced that national security was endangered unless the country greatly expanded its trade and built a large offensive navy supplied by American-owned coaling stations around the world. Assistant Secretary of the Navy Theodore Roosevelt, backed by Secretary of the Navy John D. Long and President William McKinley, put long-term plans in action when he ordered Commodore George Dewey to immediately attack the Philippines, a Spanish possession and an essential stepping-stone to the China market, if the United States declared war.

Even though the Spanish navy was rated higher than the U.S. Navy, Spanish forces in the Philippines and Cuba were no threat. Early Sunday morning, 1 May 1898, Dewey entered Manila Bay and completely demolished the enemy fleet with no loss of American lives. While the commodore waited for oc-

cupation troops to secure the island from the Spanish and other European powers stationed in the area, fighting broke out in Cuba. Because the American public was terrified that the Spanish fleet commanded by Admiral Pascual Cervera would bombard the eastern seaboard, the navy divided its Caribbean fleet. Commodore Winfield S. Schley waited at Hampton Roads, while Rear Admiral William T. Sampson stationed his ships off Key West, Florida. Suspecting that Cervera had headed for Puerto Rico, Sampson sailed for San Juan. Instead, the Spanish admiral had slipped into Santiago Bay and mined its passage. Schley and Sampson arrived and set up a blockade. On 3 July Cervera attempted to run past the Americans, losing his entire fleet in a dramatic three-hour chase. The army's notable achievements on land added to the navy's sterling record, and hostilities ceased on 12 August 1898, less than four months after the declaration of war.

The "splendid little war," as John Hay called it, held great significance for the navy as it prepared to defend America's new territories of Guam; Puerto Rico; a base at Guantánamo Bay, Cuba; the Philippines; and Hawaii, which Congress annexed during the war. The Philippines proved the most troublesome. Seven thousand miles from the United States and within Japanese striking distance, they were undefendable. The Panama Canal, acquired at the beginning of the twentieth century, helped move ships from ocean to ocean, but with several far-flung territories to police, the United States sought international agreements rather than an expensive second fleet. Such defense agreements were counterproductive in the end, for they inadvertently increased Japanese naval power, which by 1941 was a serious threat to American security.

See also **Army; Barbary War; Civil War,** *subentry on* **Battles and Combatants; Expansion; Foreign Relations; Marines, U.S.; Maritime Technology; Mexican War; Military Technology; Naval Academy, U.S.; Naval Technology; Spanish-American War; Steam Power; War of 1812.**

Bibliography

Barrow, Clayton R., Jr., ed. *America Spreads Her Sails: U.S. Seapower in the Nineteenth Century.* Annapolis, Md.: U.S. Naval Institute Press, 1973.

Bauer, K. Jack. *Surfboats and Horse Marines: U.S. Naval Operations in the Mexican War, 1846–48.* Annapolis, Md.: U.S. Naval Institute Press, 1969.

Dudley, William S., ed. *The Naval War of 1812: A Documentary History.* Washington, D.C.: U.S. Naval Historical Center, Department of the Navy, 1985.

Fowler, William M., Jr. *Under Two Flags: The American Navy in the Civil War.* New York: Norton, 1990.

Hagan, Kenneth J., ed. *In Peace and War: Interpretations of American Naval History, 1775–1984.* 2d ed. Contributions in Military History Series no. 41. Westport, Conn.: Greenwood, 1984.

Howarth, Stephen. *To Shining Sea: A History of the United States Navy, 1775–1991.* New York: Random House, 1991.

Karsten, Peter. *The Naval Aristocracy: The Golden Age of Annapolis and the Emergence of Modern American Navalism.* New York: Free Press, 1972.

Langley, Harold D. *Social Reform in the United States Navy, 1798–1862.* Urbana: University of Illinois Press, 1967.

McKee, Christopher. *A Gentlemanly and Honorable Profession: The Creation of the U.S. Naval Officer Corps, 1794–1815.* Annapolis, Md.: U.S. Naval Institute Press, 1991.

Merli, Frank J. *Great Britain and the Confederate Navy, 1861–1865.* Bloomington: Indiana University Press, 1970.

Millett, Allan R., and Peter Maslowski. *For the Common Defense: A Military History of the United States of America.* New York: Free Press, 1984.

Symonds, Craig L. *Navalists and Antinavalists: The Naval Policy Debate in the United States, 1785–1827.* Newark: University of Delaware Press, 1980.

Trask, David F. *The War with Spain in 1898.* New York: Macmillan, 1981.

Valley, James E. *Rocks and Shoals: Order and Discipline in the Old Navy, 1800–1861.* Annapolis, Md.: U.S. Naval Institute Press, 1980.

Whipple, A. B. C. *To the Shores of Tripoli: The Birth of the U.S. Navy and Marines.* New York: William Morrow, 1991.

LORI BOGLE

NEBRASKA   Geography loomed large in determining the nineteenth-century development of Nebraska, situated on the forbidding upper Great Plains and sloping gradually upward from the Missouri River to the foothills of the Rocky Mountains. The climate brings hot summers and cold winters, a short growing season, and rainfall that averages thirty-two inches in the east and a mere fifteen inches in the west. Although the flat valley of the wide and shallow Platte River, which snakes through central Nebraska, provided a transportation route across the plains, a lack of timber, navigable streams, and water made the rolling land uninviting. In 1834 the federal government, considering Nebraska essentially a great desert, designated it as part of a permanent Indian country.

The United States established the Nebraska Territory in 1854 under the controversial Kansas-Nebraska Act, which in a fundamental policy reversal provided for popular sovereignty regarding slavery in Kansas. The act also reflected the government's desire to build a railroad to the Pacific Ocean over a central route through Nebraska. The Pacific Railroad Act of 1862, enacted early in the Civil War, enabled the construction of the transcontinental Union Pacific Railroad through the Platte River valley. The original Nebraska Territory extended from the Kansas border in the south to Canada in the north, and the white population, only 2,732, included fur traders, wagon freighters, and soldiers. When Nebraska gained statehood on 1 March 1867, it had an estimated non-Indian population of 50,000 people.

In the 1870s a range cattle industry arose in northwestern Nebraska. Stockmen drove Texas cattle on long trail drives to Nebraska, where the Union Pacific and the Chicago, Burlington, and Quincy Railroads connected them to markets. On the Missouri River, in Omaha, the eastern terminus of the Union Pacific Railroad, businesses built impressive stockyards and meatpacking plants. By the turn of the century Nebraska had weathered the demise of the open range and the advent of fenced cattle ranches and developed a major livestock industry.

Ignoring disadvantageous agricultural prospects, farmers swarmed into eastern and central Nebraska. People arrived on Nebraska's "sod house frontier" from all over the United States and from Europe, especially Scandinavia, Bohemia, and Germany. Many took advantage of the Homestead Act of 1862, which allowed a person to claim 160 acres of public domain land for a small price. Between 1863 and 1900 a total of 141,446 homesteaders filed for 19,820,201 acres. In addition, railroads, which owned 16.6 percent of Nebraska's total acreage, sold more than 7 million acres to private parties. Yet farming smallholdings on the prairie proved so difficult that only 68,867 homesteaders stayed long enough to gain clear titles to a total of 9,609,920 acres.

Enough people remained in Nebraska to create out of the wilderness a settled cultural and religious life constructed around farms and small country towns. Though at a high cost, determined tillers of the soil survived calamities ranging from insect infestations to years of continuous dry weather to make Nebraska a prime grain-producing state. Between 1870, the first census year following Nebraska's statehood, and 1900 the state's population increased from 122,993 to 1,066,910. Omaha, the largest city, had 102,559 residents in 1900. (By the end of the nineteenth century most of the new eastern European immigrants had settled in south Omaha, where work was easy to find in the meatpacking industry.)

The Republican Party, strongly backed by railroad interests, dominated Gilded Age politics in Nebraska. The state's Democrats were disorganized and dispirited. A split between urban and rural factions and a rivalry between competing geographical interests north and south of the Platte River complicated matters. A poor grain market and severe drought conditions contributed to the rise of the antimonopoly and antirailroad Nebraska Farmers' Alliance, which was especially active after the panic of 1893 launched a national depression.

The Alliance took a lead in the formation of the Populist Party, which met in a national convention in Omaha in 1892. A cardinal goal of the Populists was the creation of an inflationary economy through the virtual free coinage of silver. In 1896, William Jennings Bryan, a free-silver advocate from Nebraska, ran for president on both the Democratic and Populist tickets. He lost decisively to the Republican candidate William McKinley, a conservative advocate of the gold standard. An agricultural recovery followed the election, and many Nebraska Populists returned to the Republican Party.

At the century's end Nebraska was hardly removed from the frontier. Indians did not relinquish all of their land claims until 1892. Even so, optimism abounded, expressed in the impressive Omaha Trans-Mississippi and International Exposition of 1898, and Nebraska's newcomers hoped for dramatic progress in a golden age of agriculture.

See also **Agriculture; American Indian Societies,** *subentry on* **The Plains; Federal Land Policy; Frontier; Great Plains; Homesteading; Kansas-Nebraska Act; Louisiana Purchase; Meatpacking; Monetary Policy; Panics and Depressions; Populism; Railroads; Ranching and Livestock Raising; Trails to the West; World's Fairs.**

Bibliography

Larsen, Lawrence H., and Barbara J. Cottrell. *The Gate City: A History of Omaha.* Enlarged ed., new conclusion by Harl A. Dalstrom. Lincoln: University of Nebraska Press, 1997.

Luebke, Frederick C. *Nebraska: An Illustrated History.* Lincoln: University of Nebraska Press, 1995.

Olson, James C., and Ronald C. Naugle. *History of Nebraska.* 3d ed. Lincoln: University of Nebraska Press, 1997.

LAWRENCE H. LARSEN

NEVADA   The American and Canadian fur trappers Jedediah Smith and Peter Skene Ogden explored the western portions of the intermontane West in the 1820s, making contact with Shoshone and Paiute Indians. By 1845, the army explorer John C. Frémont identified the land as an area of interior drainage, the Great Basin. Overland travelers soon followed routes through the desolate land to the riches of California and then retraced their steps in the "rush to Washoe," when prospectors discovered the gold- and silver-rich Comstock Lode in 1859–1860. Virginia City emerged as the leading town on the lode in a range of mountains just east of the Sierra and the California border. Carved out of the western counties of Utah, Nevada Territory emerged in 1861 to govern these activities, and Nevada gained its statehood in 1864.

The expansive forces that shaped nineteenth-century American society drove early Nevada. Water and steam provided the mechanical power for transportation, deep-shaft underground industrialized mining, and ore processing. Capital from nearby San Francisco underwrote the huge investment in technology that made possible the mining and successful ore processing, sustaining an urban complex in a mountainous desert. The rapid development of Comstock mining became synonymous with Nevada in the 1860s and 1870s. With a population in 1880 of 62,266, mostly male, the state was barely more than an economic and political colony of San Francisco.

Labor organizations, large corporations, stock speculations, and a varied immigrant population marked the suddenly assembled urban society in Virginia City, Nevada, where the budding novelist Mark Twain began his career as a journalist (1862–1864) with the *Territorial Enterprise.*

By 1872, the Virginia & Truckee Railroad connected Reno, the state capital at Carson City, and the Comstock towns. From Reno, the Central Pacific Railroad, built across Nevada in 1868–1869, brought the world to Nevada from San Francisco and New York. Nevada entered into a twenty-year mining depression after the failure of the Comstock in 1878. Population fell to 45,761 in 1890 and 42,335 in 1900. Eastern newspapers labeled Nevada a "rotten borough" after the depopulated boroughs represented in the British House of Commons.

Without mineral wealth Nevada relied on the scant resources of its land and water. The vast Nevada sage land supported open-range stock raising, but the White Winter of 1889–1890 destroyed many of the free-range cattle operations in the northern counties. Smaller ranchers moved in with the knowledge they must practice winter cattle feeding. Prostrate Nevada sought panaceas for its future. U.S. senator William M. Stewart championed the silver money standard, and Congressman Francis G. Newlands, later a senator, singled out irrigation as Nevada's salvation.

From its nadir in 1900, Nevada faced a slow recovery. The 1902 National Reclamation Act, sponsored by Congressman Newlands, brought a federal irrigation project to northern Nevada. In 1905, a small railroad town called Las Vegas appeared on the route of the new rail connection between Salt Lake City and Los Angeles, and by 1910, Reno prospered with a divorce business, while gold, silver, and copper ore discoveries spurred a mining boom in Nevada.

See also **Divorce and Desertion; Mining and Extraction; Ranching and Livestock Raising; Transportation,** *subentry on* **Railroads.**

Bibliography

Elliott, Russell R. *History of Nevada.* 1973. 2d ed., with assistance of William D. Rowley, Lincoln: University of Nebraska Press, 1987.

Rowley, William D. *Reclaiming the Arid West: The Career of Francis G. Newlands.* Bloomington: Indiana University Press, 1996.

WILLIAM D. ROWLEY

NEW ENGLAND Captain John Smith, sailing north from the Virginia Colony in 1614, gave the name "New England" to a region that English people had not yet settled. The Puritans who arrived in 1630 were part of an endeavor sponsored by the New England Company. In the 1680s England's King James II tried to combine New York with the New England colonies in what he called the Dominion of New England. The name remained in use—without the accretion of New York.

New England's boundaries underwent some changes, but the region continued to be defined as the colonies, and then the states, east of New York. Among the thirteen original states, four were in New England: Massachusetts, New Hampshire, Connecticut, and Rhode Island. Vermont became a state in 1791. The Maine District of Massachusetts entered the Union as a state as part of the Missouri Compromise in 1820, and Maine's northern border was finally

---

The Hartford Convention

Delegates from Massachusetts, Connecticut, and Rhode Island met in Hartford in the winter of 1814–1815. New western states had already been admitted to the Union, states whose votes tended to support the Virginia Republicans in national politics, and any number of additional states seemed on the way. Desperate over the loss of political power in the nation, military costs incurred during the War of 1812, and economic losses suffered as a consequence of a trade embargo, they resolved to address all these unhappy developments.

Delegates insisted that henceforth it would take a two-thirds majority rather than a simple majority in each house to pass a measure admitting a new state, declaring war, or placing an embargo on foreign trade. The Three-Fifths Clause would be amended so that slaves would no longer count in determining power in the U.S. House of Representatives or the electoral college. In two additional thrusts at Virginia's dominance, henceforth no president could serve more than a single term, and successive presidents could not come from the same state.

If the war persisted and these amendments were not adopted, the delegates vowed to meet again. In short, Hartford Convention delegates acted in a way similar to the First Continental Congress of 1774, which urged adoption of various measures by Great Britain and, when refused, led to the Second Continental Congress, which declared independence. The War of 1812 did end, however, and the proposals went nowhere. By the winter of 1860–1861 New England had long since forsaken secession and would not brook it among southerners.

set in the Webster-Ashburton Treaty with England in 1842. The New England states are small. Maine, though nearly as large in area as the other five states combined, ranks thirty-ninth among the fifty states in size, and Rhode Island is dead last.

The region was hardly all of a piece. European fishermen were attracted to the coastline before the Pilgrims arrived at Plymouth Rock, and long before those fishermen stopped by, Native Americans relied on shellfish for a large part of their annual food. Before the colonial period was over British settlers had spread along the coastline and up the rivers, yet colonists left much of the interior unexplored and unsettled until the revolutionary era and later. With regard to population growth rates during the nineteenth century, the region's three northernmost states displayed their greatest growth in the opening decades, but the three southernmost states, reflecting the maturing of an urban and industrial society there, experienced their fastest growth from the 1840s on.

In other ways, too—climate, physical appearance, social behavior—the southern parts differed from the northern, and the region's interior areas often contrasted with the coastal areas. The least accessible areas were not only remote but mountainous. Rhode Island's highest elevation is only 812 feet above sea level; New Hampshire's Mount Washington soars more than a mile. Southern New England's winter days are often cold, but nothing like the lowest temperatures recorded in New Hampshire's White Mountains or in northern Maine. While loggers worked the upcountry, whalers sailed from the region's southern port cities. The spoken language of the Boston area was distinctive, as were the accents farther north, particularly "down east" in Maine.

Social, Cultural, and Economic Transformation

During the seventeenth century a startling rise in the number of European settlers in New England offset a rapid decline in Native Americans' presence. In the eighteenth century natural increase accounted for most of the continued rapid growth of the white population, and settlements pushed up such rivers as the Connecticut and the Merrimack. The dispersal away from the coast continued into the nineteenth century.

In 1800 roughly nineteen of every twenty residents of the region were Caucasians who had been born in New England. Few Native Americans lived there any longer, and the percentage of Africans, even in Rhode Island, held in single digits. Slavery in New England came to a virtual end in the 1780s except in Rhode

The Hartford Convention. A political cartoon depicting three New England states—Massachusetts, Rhode Island and Connecticut—preparing to leap into the arms of King George III. In December 1814, during the War of 1812, delegates from these states met in Connecticut to consider seceding from the United States and establishing an independent peace with England. Cartoon by William Charles. LIBRARY OF CONGRESS

Island and Connecticut, where gradual emancipation laws brought the institution to an end somewhat later. From settlement through the Revolution, in religious terms as well as racial, the region was unusually homogeneous, as virtually all residents were Protestant Christians and most were Congregationalists. Most were English in national background, and virtually all spoke English.

As late as 1900 the percentage of whites in the New England states ranged from a low of 97.8 in Rhode Island to a high of 99.8 in New Hampshire. Yet in other ways the ethnic and religious homogeneity of the colonial era did not survive the nineteenth century. In the century's middle decades, tens of thousands of Irish immigrants settled in Boston and other cities and mill towns, particularly in southern New England, and their Catholicism changed the cultural and political landscape. In the century's final decades French Canadians from Quebec fanned across northern New England, and their French language and Catholic religion brought similar changes to that area. By 1900 New England's population was more heavily immigrant than any other region of the country.

A similar transformation occurred in the region's economy. In 1789 Samuel Slater stepped off a ship from England with his head full of plans to apply in the New World the new technology of industrial production that was maturing in the Old World. In the next few years he launched the early Republic's venture into the industrial revolution and factories began processing wool, cotton, and leather into cloth, shoes, and boots. Slater's world, as it rapidly emerged in New England, brought together raw materials, machinery, waterpower, and workers, all of which, combined with the development of transportation facilities and the growth of markets, foreshadowed the economic demise, for example, of independent shoemakers who produced small quantities through traditional means for local markets.

Educational and Social Welfare Institutions

New Englanders led efforts in the nineteenth-century United States to build up various kinds of public institutions. Horace Mann of Massachusetts led the movement to establish state systems of public elementary and secondary schools. Dorothea Dix, also of Massachusetts, led a movement to establish mental hospitals. Thomas Hopkins Gallaudet led in the establishment of a school in Connecticut for deaf children, and Samuel Gridley Howe did much the same for a school in Massachusetts for blind youngsters.

At the beginning of the nineteenth century New England was home to some of America's oldest and most prominent institutions of higher education. The four original states each had a liberal arts college—Harvard, Yale, Brown, and Dartmouth—that trained elite men for such professions as the ministry and the law. By late in the century these schools had such female counterparts as Smith, Wellesley, Mount Holyoke, and Radcliffe, all in Massachusetts.

Congressman Justin S. Morrill of Vermont inaugurated a new chapter in the educational history of the region and the nation when he spearheaded passage of the Land-Grant College Act of 1862. That act fostered new "agricultural and mechanical" programs and thereby spurred the emergence of institutions of higher education whose constituencies and curricula contrasted with those of the traditional colleges. Morrill's home state attached the new program to the University of Vermont. The state universities of Maine and Massachusetts—both soon coeducational—quickly emerged, and though the other states at first attached their land-grant programs to Yale, Dartmouth, or Brown, they eventually transferred the funds and created the new state Universities of Connecticut, New Hampshire, and Rhode Island.

New England and National Politics

At the Philadelphia Convention of 1787, Virginians often referred to New England as the "eastern states," and the two regions, the South and New England, viewed each other as strangers and rivals for control of the new nation as much as colleagues in establishing independence and creating that new nation. Tensions over power and policy persisted through the nineteenth century.

Virginians controlled the presidency for eight of the first ten terms, as four men from that state each had two terms in the nation's highest office. Two New Englanders John Adams and his son John Quincy Adams were president for one term apiece. Virginians had feared for the future if New England proved preponderant, but New Englanders found themselves subject to southern political priorities as Virginia Republicans ran roughshod over New England Federalists, especially during James Madison's presidency. So desperate were many New Englanders over the course of national and international politics during the War of 1812 that delegates met in a convention in Hartford, Connecticut, to discuss remedies. One option explored was secession.

In national politics, New England long continued to oppose the South. In the 1800 presidential election New England's electoral college votes all went to the Federalist candidate John Adams, whose bid for reelection Thomas Jefferson turned back. In 1856 and 1860 the New England states all supported the new

Maine, Massachusetts, and the Missouri Compromise

Congressmen from New England supported the effort to prevent Missouri from joining the Union as a slave state. They also agreed to a compromise that capitulated on Missouri but limited future expansion of slavery in what remained of the Louisiana Purchase. Exemplifying the region's opposition to expansion of the slave South's power in national life more than opposition to slavery itself, New England agreed to a swap that gave statehood to Maine to offset Missouri's two votes in the Senate.

The Missouri Compromise became possible after a decision in regional politics that matched the one in national politics. A separate statehood movement had grown powerful in the Maine District, and many people in Massachusetts were inclined to let that area go. As late as 1820 a huge amount of public land remained in the district, however, and voters in the rest of the state were not about to give away what they expected to be a bonanza that could fund public spending. The logjam broke when it was agreed that any proceeds from the sale of public land in an independent Maine would be split evenly between the new state and Massachusetts.

When the money was realized, as public domain became private land and public money, Massachusetts divided its share evenly between education and transportation. Half of the proceeds went to the new state system of public schools that Horace Mann presided over from 1837 to 1848, and half funded an exercise in public enterprise, the Boston and Western Railroad, which connected the port city of Boston with Albany, the Hudson River, and the Erie Canal. The variation in political behavior within New England was exemplified by the failure of other New England states to act in the manner Massachusetts did in response to such nontax public revenue in the generation after 1820.

Republican Party. "Beecher's Bibles"—weapons to support a northern preponderance, certainly to prevent a southern preponderance, in Kansas Territory in the 1850s—also demonstrated the region's commitment to preserving the West for the northern variant of western expansion. At the end of the century the New England states all remained heavily Republican.

The Emergence of Modern America: The Persistence of Traditional America

Modern America—indeed many attributes of the modern world—emerged in New England in the first half of the nineteenth century. Slavery ended. Women's social roles changed, and their educational opportunities expanded. By mid-century the Congregationalist Church lost its privileged position wherever it had been previously established, that is, in Massachusetts, Connecticut, and New Hampshire—all of New England's original states except Rhode Island. Meantime, people moved from farms to mill towns; they shifted from cultivating corn and cutting timber to manufacturing shoes and cotton or woolen textiles. By the end of the second century of European settlement an urban, industrial world was growing up, especially in southern New England.

In the years before the Civil War, New Englanders came to see the U.S. South as increasingly out of step with history. Perhaps it was, but New England, not the South, had changed so much that the regions more sharply diverged than ever before. Yet New England changed in ways that transformed the rest of the country. New England's roles in the sectionalization of slavery, the rise of the Republican Party, and the prosecution of the Civil War and Reconstruction led to a partial revolution even in the South and a narrowing of the regional differences. Moreover, just as the early Republic's schools for blind and deaf youngsters, transplanted from France to New England, eventually made their way to states in every U.S. region, the mechanization of production, transplanted from England to New England, led to industrialization in every region.

The beneficiaries of the changes in New England's social and economic patterns invented a past that they could celebrate and that might demonstrate their superior social status and their shared authenticity as New Englanders. In the 1820s New Englanders organized the Pilgrim Society, as settlers' descendants, insular and parochial in the face of enormous change all around them, adopted a creation myth to rival Virginia's Pocahontas story. Historians have discovered that the image of the New England town itself—houses painted white, clustered in villages, surrounded by elm trees—was an invention of the early Republic, emerging two centuries after English settlement.

See also **Boston; Connecticut; Education,** *subentries on* **Colleges and Universities, Education of the Blind and Deaf; Emancipation; Immigration and Immigrants,** *subentries on* **Ireland, Canada; Maine; Massachusetts; Missouri Compromise; New Hampshire; Protestant-**

ism, *subentry on* **Congregationalists; Rhode Island; Sectionalism; Textiles; Vermont.**

Bibliography

Abrams, Ann Uhry. *The Pilgrims and Pocahontas: Rival Myths of American Origin.* Boulder, Colo.: Westview Press, 1999.

Barron, Hal S. *Those Who Stayed Behind: Rural Society in Nineteenth-Century New England.* Cambridge, U.K.: Cambridge University Press, 1984.

Blewett, Mary H. *Men, Women, and Work: Class, Gender, and Protest in the New England Shoe Industry, 1780–1910.* Urbana: University of Illinois Press, 1988.

Clark, Christopher. *The Roots of Rural Capitalism: Western Massachusetts, 1780–1860.* Ithaca, N.Y.: Cornell University Press, 1990.

Cott, Nancy F. *The Bonds of Womanhood: "Woman's Sphere" in New England, 1780–1835.* 2d ed. New Haven, Conn.: Yale University Press, 1997. The original edition was published in 1977.

Melish, Joanne Pope. *Disowning Slavery: Gradual Emancipation and "Race" in New England, 1780–1860.* Ithaca, N.Y.: Cornell University Press, 1998.

Nissenbaum, Stephen. "New England as Region and Nation." In *All over the Map: Rethinking American Regions.* By Edward L. Ayers, Patricia Nelson Limerick, Stephen Nissenbaum, and Peter S. Onuf. Baltimore: Johns Hopkins University Press, 1996.

Peirce, Neal R. *The New England States: People, Politics, and Power in the Six New England States.* New York: Norton, 1976.

Tucker, Barbara M. *Samuel Slater and the Origins of the American Textile Industry, 1790–1860.* Ithaca, N.Y.: Cornell University Press, 1984.

PETER WALLENSTEIN

NEW HAMPSHIRE The Granite State's American Indian past, together with its geological and glacial past, live on in such places and place names as Mounts Kancamagus, Chocorua, and Passaconaway; Lakes Sunapee, Winnesquam, and Winnipesaukee; and Rivers Merrimack, Connecticut, and Pemigewasset. Other place names followed their British counterparts, notably Portsmouth the seafaring center and Manchester the industrial center. Founded by John Mason, the colony was named after Hampshire, his native area of England.

Working with the Materials at Hand

New Hampshire's first English settlement, near Portsmouth, was established in 1623, and subsequent settlements took shape as people from Massachusetts moved north up the Merrimack and Connecticut Rivers. In a hybrid cultural world, settlers were as apt to live on corn and venison as on any diet they had known before they crossed the Atlantic. Fish, fur, and timber were mainstays of the colonial economy.

Water, wood, and stone sang the song of New Hampshire's growth as a colony and as one of the thirteen original states. New Hampshire's first European newcomers arrived through the narrow window on the Atlantic Ocean; rivers provided paths of settlement and trade; and water powered the early factories that brought New Hampshire into the industrial age. Abundant trees made possible large homes, warm winters inside them, and the work of varied artisans; hillsides showcased white pine, white birch, red maple. Granite and mica led to important mining activities, but not before farmers had made stone walls a standard feature of the landscape. English farmers, unlike their Indian predecessors, needed to clear rocks from their fields before plowing, had the four-legged creatures that made it possible, and wanted indelible boundaries to declare the limits of the next family's property.

New Hampshire's population grew rapidly for the hundred years before the 1810s, but as cities and farms beckoned to the West, it failed to double between 1810 and 1900. At mid-century more sheep than people lived in the state. In 1800 Portsmouth (pronounced "pottsmuth") was the state capital and the nation's tenth largest city, but soon even other towns in New Hampshire pulled past it. By 1860 Manchester sported the largest population at 20,107. Concord (pronounced "conquered"), the capital city after 1808, ranked second, and then came Nashua (yet a third town on the Merrimack) and Portsmouth. In an overwhelmingly white social world, black residents numbered 970 in 1810, all free by then, and did not exceed that figure until the twentieth century.

Politics and Culture

The state was routinely Democratic from the 1830s into the 1850s, but after that it was reliably Republican. Many people left the state, and most New Hampshire natives who made a splash in nineteenth-century public life did so elsewhere. Daniel Webster served as a Federalist in the U.S. House of Representatives in the 1810s, but before his second term was over he moved from Portsmouth to Boston. In his subsequent distinguished career in the U.S. Senate he represented Massachusetts. Levi Woodbury remained a New Hampshire resident throughout his tenure in President Andrew Jackson's cabinet and on the Supreme Court, but Salmon P. Chase moved to Ohio before serving in President Abraham Lincoln's cabinet and as chief justice of the Supreme Court. Horace Greeley, who popularized the phrase "Go west, young man, go west," acted on that advice, moved to the nation's largest city, and eventually edited the *New York Tribune.*

Lewis Cass, a New Hampshire native, ran for the presidency in 1848 from Michigan. In 1852 two New Hampshire residents ran for the presidency, John P. Hale as the Free Soil candidate and Franklin Pierce, the winner, as a Democrat. The nation's fourteenth president is memorialized by the Friends of Franklin Pierce in their motto, "to rescue him from the obscurity he so richly deserves" (Peirce, *The New England States,* p. 293).

New Hampshire exemplified various themes of regional and national life. The name "Uncle Sam" is said to have originated with Samuel Wilson, who left his childhood home in New Hampshire to move to Troy, New York, where he supplied barrels of pork and beef to men in uniform during the War of 1812. Most churches in New Hampshire, thus presumably most churchgoers, were Baptist, Congregationalist, or Methodist. Reflecting the slow trend toward freedom of religion in the states, New Hampshire began the process of disestablishing the Congregationalist Church with the Toleration Act of 1819, and in 1877 the state removed from its constitution the requirement that the governor and legislators be "of the Protestant religion." Mary Baker Eddy founded Christian Science in the 1860s. Granite State natives included the first woman lawyer in New Hampshire, Marilla Ricker (1890), and the first in Montana, Ella Knowles Haskell (1889).

Transportation and Industry

Extraordinary change characterized transportation in the nineteenth century. New Hampshire residents who never went anywhere fostered the mobility of people who went everywhere. The Concord coaches that J. Stephens Abbot and Lewis Downing built in Concord, the Model T of the early nineteenth century, helped people move to the American West, and the clipper ships built in Portsmouth supported trade with the Far East. During the Civil War the USS *Kearsarge,* built in Portsmouth in 1861, destroyed the commerce-raiding CSS *Alabama* off the coast of France in 1864. New Hampshire's first few miles of railway track came in 1838, and the greatest force in the state's political life at the end of the century was the Boston and Maine Railroad.

The greatest changes in nineteenth-century New Hampshire accompanied the rise of industry. The state's first shoe factory opened in Weare in 1823. By that time Charles Robbins, who had worked at Samuel Slater's mill in Rhode Island, and Benjamin Prichard, who learned from Robbins, had established wool and cotton factories in New Hampshire. The Amoskeag mills in Manchester later became the largest in the world. In the century's final decades, French Canadians came with large families, parish priests, and a willingness to work in the textile mills of the Merrimack Valley, especially Manchester, and the lumber towns of the North Country, especially Berlin ("ber' lin"), towns that have retained a considerable French Catholic flavor.

At the dawn of the twentieth century, New Hampshire's population reached 411,588. Policy decisions remained focused on town meetings rather than the state capital, and much of public finance in the state remained local too. With 56,987 residents, Manchester still led the cities, and Nashua had 23,898, trailed by Concord, Portsmouth, Dover ("dova"), Keene, Laconia, and Berlin. The leading institutions of higher education were the venerable Dartmouth College in the northwest and the new University of New Hampshire in the southeast. Vacationers visited New Hampshire's mountains and lakes in the summer. During other seasons, they viewed the brilliant colors of fall foliage, happened upon snow-topped covered bridges, or sampled newly made maple syrup.

See also **Maritime Technology; New England; Politics,** *subentry on* **The Second Party System; Textiles.**

Bibliography

Hareven, Tamara K., and Randolph Langenbach. *Amoskeag: Life and Work in an American Factory-City.* New York: Pantheon Books, 1978.

Morison, Elizabeth Forbes, and Elting E. Morison. *New Hampshire: A Bicentennial History.* New York: Norton, 1976.

Peirce, Neal R. *The New England States: People, Politics, and Power in the Six New England States.* New York: Norton, 1976.

Turner, Lynn Warren. *The Ninth State: New Hampshire's Formative Years.* Chapel Hill: University of North Carolina Press, 1983.

PETER WALLENSTEIN

NEW JERSEY   New Jersey changed from an agricultural to an urban-industrial state during the nineteenth century. Improved transportation and growing business advanced population growth and transformed the Garden State into a varied landscape of cities, small towns, and seashore resorts.

New Jersey is located on the Atlantic coast between the Hudson and Delaware Rivers, forming a great peninsula between New York and Pennsylvania. It has four natural regions: the Appalachian ridge and valley, featuring the Kittatinny Mountains; the highlands; the Piedmont lowlands, with the

Watchung Mountains and Palisades; and the Atlantic coastal plain, with an ocean shoreline extending from Sandy Hook to Cape May. Despite its 127-mile (204-kilometer) coastline, New Jersey has a humid continental climate and variable temperatures from the northern to the southern regions.

New Jersey's Native Americans, the Lenni Lenape, a branch of the Algonquian Delaware tribe of eastern woodland peoples, lived near the Delaware River prior to European settlement. Their numbers were depleted by migration and disease, and in 1758 they moved to the Brotherton reservation (Burlington County), the first in America. By 1802 the remaining Lenni Lenape had moved to New York and then westward.

During the colonial period the Netherlands and Sweden made attempts at settlement along the Hudson and Delaware Rivers but failed to encourage their nationals to populate their scattered trading outposts. In 1664, eager to colonize the eastern seaboard, England successfully challenged the Dutch claims to New Netherlands. Lord John Berkeley and Sir George Carteret were granted a charter for a proprietary colony named New Jersey. The colony's liberal political and religious environment attracted a diverse population of English Quakers, Episcopalians, Scotch Presbyterians, Baptists, and Puritans to the colony. On 2 July 1776 New Jersey adopted its first state constitution and actively participated in the Revolutionary War, becoming known as the "Cockpit of the Revolution." On 18 December 1787, it was the third state to ratify the federal Constitution.

Under the 1776 state constitution New Jersey women who met the property qualification could, and did, vote. The privilege was revoked in 1807 by the Suffrage Reform Act, which also denied the franchise to free blacks. In 1844 New Jersey adopted a new state constitution that upheld white male suffrage and removed the property qualification for voting. New Jersey had adopted a gradual emancipation plan for slaves in 1804 but waited until 1846 to abolish slavery, converting the few remaining aged slaves into "apprentices" in service to their masters. Antislavery sentiments were expressed in the activities of Quakers and the Underground Railroad, which had established escape routes in the state.

New Jersey's economic development depended on the movement of goods and resources in the New York City–Philadelphia corridor. Toll roads, turnpikes, canals, and especially railroad lines gradually established New Jersey's unique economic potential. Specialized farming in fruits, vegetables, dairy, and poultry introduced commercial agriculture; and the industrialized cities of Newark, Jersey City, Paterson, Trenton, Camden, Elizabeth, and New Brunswick enlarged the state's manufacturing output of goods, such as iron, leather, paper, glass, and textiles.

By mid-century state politics was dominated by the Democratic Party and its allies in the railroad industry. However, in 1856 and 1859 independent-minded New Jersey voters supported the gubernatorial candidates of the newly formed Republican Party. But the controversy over states' rights, slavery, and potential loss of southern trade divided the state politically as the Civil War approached. In 1860 New Jersey was the only northern state to deny the Republican candidate, Abraham Lincoln, all its electoral support. In 1864 New Jersey backed its favorite son, George B. McClellan, a Democrat, for president. During the war residents contributed in the war effort and met the state's quota for soldiers in spite of some "copperhead" or antiwar sentiments.

The Civil War stimulated New Jersey's economy with orders for military supplies and equipment. During the postwar era the state legislature acted favorably toward business. Corporations such as Standard Oil and American Sugar Refining found their way into the state. In the 1880s immigrants from central and southern Europe provided the workers for urban industries and made up one-fifth of the population. Thomas A. Edison's laboratories in Menlo Park and West Orange forecast the state's future in technology. During the Gilded Age, some of the nation's wealthiest industrial leaders built estates in suburban communities such as Morristown and shore towns such as Long Branch and Lakewood.

New Jersey's population grew from 211,149 in 1800 to 1,883,669 in 1900, with 70.5 percent of its people living in urban areas. By the turn of the century, the state ranked sixteenth in population among the forty-five states and third nationally in population density.

See also **Mid-Atlantic States.**

Bibliography

Brush, John E. *The Population of New Jersey.* 2d ed. New Brunswick, N.J.: Rutgers University Press, 1958.

Cunningham, John T. *New Jersey: America's Main Road.* Garden City, N.Y.: Doubleday, 1976.

Kull, Irving S., ed. *New Jersey: A History.* 4 vols. New York: American Historical Society, 1930.

Myers, William Starr, ed. *The Story of New Jersey.* 5 vols. New York: Lewis Historical Publishing, 1945.

CARMELA ASCOLESE KARNOUTSOS

NEW MEXICO   In the late eighteenth century, as thirteen former British colonies were establishing a new nation on the Atlantic coast, the Spanish colony of New Mexico languished on the northern fringe of Spain's New World empire. Its capital, Santa Fe, had been established in 1607, but its people had been isolated by Spain's mercantile policy that allowed trade only with the mother country or other Spanish colonies. As Spain's empire weakened, that isolation was soon to give way to modern economic influences.

In 1821 William Becknell was heading west from Missouri with a mule train of trade goods when he encountered a group of soldiers from Santa Fe, who told him of Mexico's newly won independence. The soldiers invited him to take his goods to Santa Fe, thereby originating sixty years of trade on the Santa Fe Trail. Americans soon extended their commerce south to northern Mexico and west to California, thus developing a prosperous trade network with Santa Fe as its hub.

The growth of American economic interests over the next twenty-five years paved the way for the peaceful conquest of New Mexico by the U.S. Army during the Mexican War (1846–1848), and in 1850 Congress created New Mexico as a U.S. territory. With the Gadsden Purchase (1853), the United States acquired land across the southern part of the territory that created the present boundary between the United States and Mexico. New Mexico Territory, which extended to the Colorado River, generally remained loyal to the Union during the Civil War, although the southern portion briefly became a Confederate territory. In 1863 Congress separated Arizona Territory from New Mexico.

Native Americans lived in the New Mexico area for thousands of years before the Spanish arrived in the region or the United States annexed it. Pueblo groups lived in settled villages. The Navahos and Apaches, relatively recent arrivals themselves, were more nomadic. During the Civil War, Kit Carson and the U.S. Army attempted to move the Navahos and some Apache groups from their homeland onto a reservation at Bosque Redondo, New Mexico, on the Pecos River. This experiment, a four-year disaster known today as the Long Walk, ended with a treaty in 1868 that allowed the Navahos to return to their homeland in western New Mexico and eastern Arizona. Provided with cattle and sheep, the tribe developed an economy based in large part on the production of wool that was woven into sophisticated rugs and blankets. These were sold to passengers on the transcontinental railroad that came through New Mexico after 1880. The Pueblo people, meanwhile, were able to maintain their agricultural economy in the face of legal challenges to their hereditary land grants and their status as Indians under federal law,

challenges that would not be settled until the next century.

Railroad advertising resulted in an increased awareness of New Mexico's ruggedly beautiful landscape, its healthful climate, and its economic potential. Speculators from the East soon took advantage of cultural and linguistic differences to gain control of the territory's politics and its natural resources. As a result, much of the Spanish-speaking population was dispossessed of its centuries-old landholdings, creating an enduring legacy of bitterness. Problems were often settled by gunfire, leading to the public perception of New Mexico as part of the violent frontier and giving rise to such mythical figures as Billy the Kid and Elfego Baca.

In the late nineteenth century New Mexico was increasingly integrated into the American political and economic systems. Volunteers eagerly joined Theodore Roosevelt's Rough Riders during the Spanish-American War in 1898. By 1900 the territory had 195,310 residents. Anticipating statehood, the territorial legislature drafted a constitution, and New Mexico became the forty-seventh state on 6 January 1912.

See also **American Indian Societies**, *subentry on* **The Southwest; Mexican War; West, The.**

Bibliography

Beck, Warren A., and Ynez D. Haase. *Historical Atlas of New Mexico*. Norman: University of Oklahoma Press, 1969. See especially maps 19–48, 53, 58.

Larson, Robert W. *New Mexico's Quest for Statehood, 1846–1912*. Albuquerque: University of New Mexico Press, 1968.

Moorhead, Max L. *New Mexico's Royal Road: Trade and Travel on the Chihuahua Trail*. Norman: University of Oklahoma Press, 1958. See especially chapters 3–8.

Simmons, Marc. *New Mexico: A Bicentennial History*. New York: Norton, 1977. Reprinted as *New Mexico: An Interpretive History*. Albuquerque: University of New Mexico Press, 1988.

Utley, Robert M. *High Noon in Lincoln: Violence on the Western Frontier*. Albuquerque: University of New Mexico Press, 1987. Story of Billy the Kid.

DOROTHY R. PARKER

NEW ORLEANS   In the middle of the nineteenth century J. D. B. DeBow predicted that New Orleans would be to the Father of Rivers as was "London to the Thames and Paris to the Seine." Because New Orleans was positioned at the foot of a river system that drained nearly half of the continent, DeBow recognized, it competed successfully with those older, more established ports. New Orleans also competed with and even resembled in fundamental ways ports like New York and Boston, yet it differed from those urban ports in one significant way. New Orleans was a slave city.

Nineteenth-century New Orleans, like the other ports that rimmed the South, was rooted in the world of plantation slavery. Slavery defined the political structure of the city and shaped its economic system and even the relations between its inhabitants. The influence of slavery is most evident when nineteenth-century New Orleans is compared with the city of the eighteenth century. New Orleans in the eighteenth century was a colonial port society with slaves. Neither the port nor its surrounds achieved a profitable or stable plantation economy. That began to change, however, as the eighteenth century turned into the nineteenth. During the years that Spain ruled Louisiana (1768–1803), the New Orleans economy became self-sufficient. Lower Mississippi Valley planters produced an adequate food supply along with sugar, hemp, and cotton for profit. In those years Spain opened trade into and out of the port, allowing Americans upriver to float their crops down on barges. The last years of the eighteenth century were a preview of what was to come. Besides the increased profitability of plantation slavery and the commercial growth of the port, the invention of the cotton gin and a successful method to granulate sugar increased productivity even more. Finally, the addition of trade by steamboat, beginning in 1812, completed the process that propelled New Orleans into competition with the world's busiest ports. By 1860 New Orleans was the largest city in the South and the largest cotton market in the world.

The profitability of plantation slavery in the region with its concomitant effect on the commercial success of the city accompanied political and social change. Soon after the French ceded New Orleans to the United States with the Louisiana Purchase Treaty of 1803, Americans flocked into the city, yet it retained much of its original character. For one thing, its population remained remarkably diverse. One commentator described the city's population in 1803 as "fiery Creoles, plain, upstanding Americans, yellow sirens from Santo Domingo, staid and energetic men from the German Coast speaking perfect French, haughty Castilian soldiers, dirty Indians, Negroes of every shade and hue, and the human trash—ex-galley slaves and adventurers." One facet of the population in the early nineteenth century never failed to draw comment. The majority of the inhabitants of New Orleans at that time divided themselves into Americans or Creoles, and little understanding existed between them. Americans were the newcomers, and the Creoles considered them unrefined frontierspeople. Americans thought of the

Creoles, or the *ancienne population,* as lazy and illiterate. In reality culture divided the two dominant segments of the population. The Americans spoke English and were Protestant. The Creoles spoke French and were Catholic.

Other groups laid claim to the city also. Captain Thomas Ashe (1770–1835), who visited the city in 1808, noted the diversity of the city's inhabitants in a summary of his travels published later that year. "Virginians and Kentuckians reign over the brokerage and commission business, the Scotch and Irish absorb all the respectable commerce on exportation and importation; the French keep magazines [warehouses] and stores; and the Spaniards do all the small retail trade." Redemptioners, or indentured Germans, joined the mostly French, Spanish, African, and American inhabitants during the first two decades of the nineteenth century. After 1830 poverty-stricken Irish poured in, competing with the city's slaves and free people of color for work. By 1860 New Orleans was in every aspect an international city. The 1860 census counted 155,000 people who were not black, and of them 41 percent were foreign born. The diversity of the city's population, its divisiveness, its Creole culture, and its position near the mouth of the Mississippi River created a discreet political, economic, and social situation in New Orleans that set it apart from the South's other antebellum ports.

The success of the antebellum period was not to last in New Orleans. From the start of the Civil War the city was garrisoned. In military moves that strangled the city, Union troops placed a blockade downriver, and Confederates placed one upriver. With no supplies coming up or down the river, New Orleans residents faced starvation by April 1862, when the city fell to Union troops led by General Benjamin F. Butler. The desperate circumstances worsened as freed slaves poured into the city.

The years that followed the war were the darkest in Louisiana's history. The Emancipation Proclamation could not rid New Orleans of the pall of slavery. With the region's planters struggling to regain labor to replant crops and former slaves fighting for political rights and control over their own labor and land, the city's economy staggered. Ushered in by the struggle for political control between the Republicans, who wanted to see the freedpeople attain full political rights, and the Democrats, who were mostly former Confederates, a period of violence gripped the city. One historian pointed out that the shooting did not begin in New Orleans until after the war. Throughout Reconstruction, while Federal troops maintained a presence in the city, the streets were racked by riots, armed and unarmed confrontations, and political chaos. In two separate incidents, one in 1864 and an-

Mardi Gras Procession. The Mardi Gras fanfare in New Orleans, with the city's distinctive iron balconies and horse-drawn streetcars in the background and foreground. Photograph taken before 1900. LIBRARY OF CONGRESS

other in 1874, bloody warfare broke out between factions. Even after Reconstruction ended and Democrats had regained power, the agitation continued. Violent behavior had become an acceptable manner of interaction between people who had been bitter political enemies for so many years. After Federal troops were withdrawn, white Democrats increased their efforts to strip blacks of their hard-won rights. By the 1890s whites had segregated public accommodations and schools and had disfranchised most blacks. In a maneuver meant to regain at least some of their rights, a group known as the *Comité des Citoyens* (Committee of Citizens) challenged Louisiana's separate facilities law. On 7 June 1892 Homer Plessy, a light-skinned black man, boarded an East Louisiana Railroad train reserved for whites. Plessy was arrested by prearrangement and was found guilty in state court of violating the law. In 1896 the Supreme Court, in *Plessy v. Ferguson,* upheld the state law, declaring that separate but equal facilities were constitutional.

Inhabitants of New Orleans saw the best and the worst of times during the nineteenth century. They witnessed the rise and fall of plantation slavery and with it the rise and fall of the economy of the city. The city grew from a struggling backwater port to an international commercial center, and then its fortunes dwindled with the Civil War. But through all

of the structural change that transpired over the century, New Orleans retained much of its colorful and diverse character.

See also **Civil War,** *subentry on* **Consequences of the Civil War; Creoles; Louisiana; Louisiana Purchase; Race Laws; Reconstruction,** *subentry on* **The South; Slavery,** *subentry on* **Overview.**

Bibliography

Cowan, Walter G., et al. *New Orleans Yesterday and Today: A Guide to the City.* Baton Rouge: Louisiana State University Press, 1983.

Fischer, Roger A. *The Segregation Struggle in Louisiana, 1862–77.* Urbana: University of Illinois Press, 1974.

Fossier, Albert A. *New Orleans, the Glamour Period, 1800–1840.* New Orleans, La.: Pelican, 1957.

Hall, Gwendolyn Midlo. *Africans in Colonial Louisiana: The Development of Afro-Creole Culture in the Eighteenth Century.* Baton Rouge: Louisiana State University Press, 1992.

Hirsch, Arnold R., and Joseph Logsdon, eds. *Creole New Orleans: Race and Americanization.* Baton Rouge: Louisiana State University Press, 1992.

Reinders, Robert, and John Duffy. *End of an Era: New Orleans, 1850–1860.* New Orleans, La.: Pelican, 1964.

VIRGINIA MEACHAM GOULD

NEWSPAPERS AND THE PRESS The story of American newspapers of the nineteenth cen-

NEWSPAPERS AND THE PRESS   419

tury is rooted in the commerce of ideas that was part of the fabric of the new nation. The earliest Congresses showed their awareness of the importance of enhancing this trade. A reporter was invited to cover the House of Representatives from its earliest sitting, in April 1789. The Senate permitted coverage starting in 1794. For nineteenth-century newspapers, the most important congressional measure was the Post Office Act of 1792, which provided that "Every printer of newspapers may send one paper to every other printer of newspapers within the United States, free of postage. . . . " Editors "borrowed" items from exchange papers, and reprinted them in their own columns, guaranteeing a lively trade in news and anecdotes among the early press. Printers led the lobby for better roads and postal services because they depended so heavily on these exchanges until well into mid-century.

1800–1812: The Press in the Early National Period

While daily newspapers had existed since 1784, the vast majority of the two hundred or so papers in publication in 1800 were weeklies. A mercantile press served the major seaport cities. Editors went to the docks to gather news directly from arriving ships and published this information in journals made available in shipping offices, coffeehouses, and taverns. These papers contained useful news about ship arrivals and departures, commodity prices, and general business intelligence.

Partisan political newspapers in 1800 ranged from official party organs to papers representing the views of individual publishers. Coverage of events was uneven, and reportage was usually heavily colored by partisan sentiment. Gossip, rumors, and scurrilous personal attacks were the order of the day. William Cobbett was the prototype. Calling himself "Peter Porcupine," Cobbett in his pugnacious *Porcupine's Gazette* expressed the prevailing sentiment: "Of professions of impartiality I shall make none." Whether as vitriolic as "Porcupine" or "Lightning Rod Junior" (Benjamin Franklin Bache) of the Philadelphia *Aurora*, or as erudite as Noah Webster of the *American Minerva*, politically engaged printers helped stimulate national political debate.

Thomas Jefferson's election to the presidency in 1800 led to the debut of the most important political newspaper of the early nineteenth century, the *National Intelligencer*. Jefferson believed that effective citizen participation in government required an informed public, and so in 1801 he invited Samuel Harrison Smith to come to Washington to launch a national newspaper. Smith's *Intelligencer* was originally a four-page triweekly, paid for in part by government

subsidy and in part by the advertising it carried on its first and last pages. It reported the "Proceedings of Congress" on page 2 and miscellaneous Washington news on page 3. For the first third of the century the *National Intelligencer* was virtually the sole source of information about the national government. Across America, newspapers "clipped" items from their exchange copy of the *Intelligencer* to include in their own columns.

The *Intelligencer* offered reasonably straightforward congressional news, but partisanship guided editorial policy in virtually every other paper. Alexander Hamilton–John Jay Federalists published the *New York Evening Post* (still published as the *New York Post* at the turn of the twenty-first century), the Aaron Burr faction controlled the *New York Morning Chronicle*, while Jeffersonians countered with the *American Citizen*.

As the frontier moved westward, settlers took their presses with them. By 1805, Pittsburgh, then on the far frontier, had three papers on a regular publication schedule. Newspapering followed the push to each newly founded community. Most of the frontier papers were small and many died quickly, but many more endured and succeeded. A southern press developed in this era, including the first newspapers in Mississippi, Alabama, and Tennessee. By 1810, Louisiana readers had French, English, and bilingual options.

The rough and ready frontier journals were typically personal enterprises, written, typeset, and printed by one man, often on paper he had made. Because there was little cash and few markets in the West and South, papers there carried less advertising than their eastern city counterparts. They also differed in coverage. While they might still carry European news culled from their exchange papers and national political news (from the *Intelligencer*), the frontier papers pioneered local coverage, reporting about crops, new lands opened for settlement, Indian relations, internal improvements like plank roads, bridges or fords, and canals.

Still, the news mainly flowed east to west, and not very quickly in either direction. News of Meriwether Lewis and William Clark's return to St. Louis from their epic journey reached even the best-connected newspapers over a month after the event, and then only when the *National Intelligencer* reprinted a letter from Thomas Jefferson replying to Clark's notification of the completion of the mission.

1810–1830: The War of 1812 and the Era of Good Feelings

As the economy grew, the mercantile press assumed an even more important place in the seaports. Large commercial exchanges had reading rooms with "news books" containing both maritime reports and regular newspapers. Proprietors paid for such devices as semaphore signal systems to get the latest news from the harbor.

The War of 1812 strongly affected newspapers. The question of entry into the war stimulated partisan comment. The Federalist *Connecticut Courant* opposed the war as "wicked, foolish, unnecessary and in no interest to America." Republican sheets like the *Albany Argus,* the *Richmond Enquirer,* and the *National Advocate* (New York) fervently supported the war effort. But more profoundly, the War of 1812 stirred the public's interest in getting the latest available news. The *National Intelligencer* became a daily in 1813, partly to feed this hunger. Newspapers invested in a newly invented power press that could print eight-hundred copies per hour to allow for more frequent and rapid press runs. In his debut editorial for the *Boston Daily Advertiser,* Nathan Hale (nephew of the patriot) wrote in 1817: "One of the peculiar traits [of Americans] is the insatiable appetite which exists in all classes of people in this Country for news. It is . . . so universal that it has given rise to a salutation . . . 'What's the news?'"

By 1820 over 550 newspapers were being published in America. Special interest newspapers first emerged around this time. America was largely agricultural, and farm-oriented newspapers emerged in this period. *The American Farmer* was first published in Baltimore in 1819, and the *Albany Plough Boy* in 1820. The *American Turf Register,* often cited as the first sporting paper, was devoted to the improvement of American breeding stock.

The *Columbian Centinel,* in welcoming President James Monroe to Boston, called the 1820s the Era of Good Feelings. A decline in the most virulent partisanship (albeit temporary) allowed Americans—and their newspapers—to turn their full attention to business. In 1820, each of America's seven largest cities featured newspapers with "Advertiser" or "Mercantile" in their titles. The paper that would become the *Providence Journal* proudly announced in 1820 that its sole editorial task would be the securing of tariff protection for American business.

The best-known special interest presses were the abolitionist newspapers. There were a few antislavery papers in the Upper South, such as Tennessee's *Emancipator* (1819); Benjamin Lundy's *Genius of Universal Emancipation* (1821), first published in Baltimore in 1824; and Kentucky's *Abolition Intelligencer* (1822). By 1834 the *Genius of Universal Emancipation* was being published in Philadelphia. The *Boston Philanthropist* appeared in 1826.

1830–1845: The Penny Press

Political partisans were connected to their factions through party newspapers. Men of commerce could afford the costly mercantile journals. But the growing population of urban working people was largely unserved by the press. Several aggressive publishers saw this opportunity and seized it. They were helped by advances in technology that allowed ever-faster and more economical printing. (The new "Hoe" press, installed in big city papers as early as 1832, could run four thousand papers an hour.) The key stimulus, however, was the realization that the old mercantile and partisan political papers had lost pace with the times, that ship crossings and reprints of lengthy congressional speeches were not what urban readers wanted.

Benjamin H. Day was barely twenty-three years old when he founded the *New York Sun* in September 1833. His vision, grasp of new technology, and interest in a new readership made him a true revolutionary. He sold his paper for a penny a copy. (Six cents was then the going price in New York.) Four months from its founding the *Sun* was selling four thousand and by 1836, thirty thousand copies a day; the *Sun's* circulation led all American papers until the 1850s. Day's formula overturned journalistic conventions of the era. He abstained from partisanship, ignored political speeches, and eschewed detailed analyses of congressional actions. Instead he emphasized news with immediate impact: crime incidents and court cases, local politics, human interest stories, anecdotes, odd happenings, even animal stories. He was not above using hoaxes as circulation builders; a famous story reported the discovery of bat-like creatures living on the moon.

Day also introduced new distribution and advertising concepts. Using a plan then employed only in London, he hired boys and unemployed men to "shout" his papers in the streets. Most importantly, he saw that he could deliver customers, in unprecedented numbers, to his advertisers. The *Sun's* large circulation allowed Day to shift to advertising as a significant revenue source, allowing him to sell his newspaper for a penny.

James Gordon Bennett began the *New York Herald* as a penny paper in 1835. Like Day, he was nonpartisan: "We shall support no faction . . . and care nothing for any election. . . . " He delivered news ("facts, on every proper and public subject") and human interest ("human nature [in] its freaks and vagaries") in a refreshingly direct way. Bennett delighted in reporting the scandals, misdeeds, and hypocrisies of the upper classes, incurring their anger but building an enthusiastic following among his penny press faithful. He went further than anyone in covering finan-

Horace Greeley (1811–1872). Greeley heavily influenced the attitudes of people in the North through his journalistic and political leadership. In addition to founding the New York *Tribune* (1841), Greeley advocated such causes as the Free-Soil movement, antislavery, the Republican Party, and universal suffrage. LIBRARY OF CONGRESS

cial news. His regular "Money Market" reports reflected shrewd attention to America's growing industrialization and developing capital markets. Often Bennett's news approach was sensationalistic. At his behest the *Herald*'s correspondents provided graphic descriptions of fires, floods, and crimes and personally visited gruesome crime scenes to report gory details.

Bennett was also famous for his hard-hitting editorials, for which he was loathed not only by the upper crust but by his competitors, who called him a "loathsome libeller," a "venomous reptile," and an "infamous blasphemer." His success was enormous; by 1840 the *Herald* rivaled the *Sun* in circulation.

Day and Bennett changed the face of urban journalism. By their approaches to pricing, advertising, news concept, speed of reportage, and style of presentation, they reached a new public. American newspaper circulation had been relatively flat from 1820 to 1835; from 1835 to 1840 it grew 8 percent a year.

Horace Greeley, arguably the era's most famous journalist, founded the *New York Tribune* in 1841 and edited it for thirty years. His was a penny paper dedicated to social reform. Politically active and personally committed, Greeley espoused abolition, women's rights, temperance, and workingmen's issues. Greeley deplored the excesses of the *Herald*, but along with Day and Bennett he helped build a new newspaper readership.

New York's three great penny papers were not alone: the *Boston Times*, the *Philadelphia Public Ledger*, and even the long-lived *Baltimore Sun* were all founded as penny papers that gave a new "feel" to the news.

While the nonpolitical urban penny press was a remarkable development, partisan papers continued to dominate the smaller cities and towns. The Whigs and Democrats had their loyal organs, and every new political movement, such as the Anti-Masons, Know-Nothings, and Free-Soilers, set forth their views in often hastily edited sheets. Every faction within the major parties had an editorial voice. "Campaign papers," edited only during a given political contest, were common in this day. As the *Richmond Times* wrote: "Neutrality in this country and in this age is an anomaly."

Americans and their newspapers continued to move west. Although improvements in post roads allowed express mail delivery from the East, every town wanted its own paper. When Alexis de Tocqueville visited America in 1831, he was struck by this proliferation of small-town newspapers. America had between 1,000 and 1,200 papers by 1830, three times as many as in France or in England. In 1835 there were 145 newspapers in Ohio alone. Tocqueville commented that "the number . . . is almost incredibly large . . . there is scarcely a hamlet which has not its newspaper." Tocqueville was less impressed with the quality of American journalists. He argued that editors often had "a scanty education and a very vulgar turn of mind." But if he was elitist about the editors' education, he had little doubt about their activism and their impact: "They attack and defend . . . in a thousand different ways . . . [when they take a stand] their influence becomes irresistible."

The role of the frontier and small-town press went beyond news and politics. In towns with no schools, newspapers might be the only voice of literacy. The press helped to educate the public, and the network of papers, linked by the postal exchange system, provided a mechanism for common dialogue in a nation of small and often scattered communities.

1844–1860: Technology, Politics, and the Newspaper Business

The Mexican War (1846–1848) was the first American war reported by eyewitness reporters. Pioneer

Editorial Staff of the New York *Tribune*. A daguerreotype of the journalists who molded the nationally renowned newspaper. Seated, from left to right: George M. Snow, financial editor; Bayard Taylor, reporter and poet; Horace Greeley, the distinguished editor; George Ripley, literary editor. Standing, left to right: William Henry Fry, music editor; Charles A. Dana, managing editor and later owner and editor of the famous New York *Sun*; Henry J. Raymond. LIBRARY OF CONGRESS: PRINTS AND PHOTOGRAPHS DIVISION

war correspondents George Kendall and James Freaner rode with General Zachary Taylor's troops. Since telegraph lines did not reach the war theater, dispatches went by horseback or boat from the battlefields to New Orleans, the nearest printing center. Once back in Washington, war news was rapidly distributed by telegraphy. Even in war the American press did not abandon its crusty partisanship. Whig and Liberty Party papers blasted "Mr. Polk's War" and the *New York Tribune* wrote: "People of the United States, your rulers are precipitating you into a fathomless abyss of crime and calamity."

In 1844, when the Whigs at their Baltimore convention nominated Henry Clay for President, Samuel F. B. Morse telegraphed the news and Washington had a same-day story. Telegraphy quickly became a staple of newsroom operations. The wires allowed late updates of developing stories and rapid contact with distant places, fostering a new conception of national news.

Advances in printing technology helped editors deliver news faster. By 1850 most big-city papers had installed steam presses that could print twenty thousand newspapers an hour. News coming in as late as the previous evening could be typeset, run, and in a reader's hands by first thing the next morning.

Technology, news hunger fueled by the Mexican War, and the ever-growing ability to deliver large circulations to advertisers changed the economic side of newspapering. Newspapers became businesses, and soon they were big business. Publishers incorporated their enterprises and sought new ways to attract capital. James Gordon Bennett had founded the *Herald* in 1835 on $500; $70,000 in initial capitalization was needed to start the *New York Times* in 1851; and the *Sun*'s 1849 selling price was $250,000.

Nationally, the number of newspapers grew rapidly, to sixteen hundred in 1840 and twenty-three hundred in 1850. Expansion of this newly lucrative business was especially great in the cities. In 1850, New York supported fifteen dailies, Boston twelve, and Philadelphia and New Orleans ten each. The number of daily newspapers increased by 84 percent during the 1840s alone.

Newspapering, politics, and social issues were still intertwined. Joseph Medill bought the eight-year-old *Chicago Daily Tribune* in 1855, and quickly demonstrated the power of even a new member of the press by leading the "Lincoln for President" boom. Medill's paper helped build the legend of the Railsplitter, highlighting Lincoln's homespun wisdom and reporting his speeches in their most favorable light. Henry J. Raymond founded the *New York Times* as a penny paper in 1851. By 1857 the paper was strong enough to publish a powerful series of stories and editorials exposing four members of Congress for having given away to cronies thousands of acres of public land. (The *Times* called it "the iniquitous Minnesota land grab.")

Women registered a few gains in the male-dominated newspaper world in the 1840s and 1850s. Cornelia Walter edited the *Boston Transcript* from 1842 to 1847 and is credited with being the first female editor of a regular newspaper. Jane Gray Swisshelm edited the *Pittsburgh Sunday Visiter* from 1848 to 1852. She also worked as a Capital Hill correspondent for various Pittsburgh papers, the first woman to do so. Such opportunities in the mainstream newspaper press were few; most women who participated in journalism did so through magazines or in reform, especially abolitionist, newspapers.

The abolitionist press reached its peak in these decades. Newspapers with names like *Emancipator, Anti-Slavery Record,* and *Human Rights* put forward the abolition program amid a storm of controversy. Many abolitionist papers suffered property damage to their presses or personal violence to their editors, in some cases both. John Greenleaf Whittier was editor of the *Pennsylvania Freeman* when its office was burned by a mob. Cassius Marcellus Clay edited his *Kentucky True American* with pistols at his sides at all times. Elijah Lovejoy's murder during the destruction of his newspaper at Alton, Illinois, in 1837 became a rallying cry for ardent abolitionists. The burning of the *Kansas Herald* helped prompt John Brown's Osawatomie massacre of proslavery settlers in the Kansas Territory in 1856.

By 1860, newspapers were poised to play a key role in the Civil War. Telegraph technology and the transatlantic cable, completed in 1858, significantly increased the speed of news delivery. Moreover, the reach of the press had become truly nationwide. About 3,700 papers (387 dailies) were being published in 1860, including over 100 in California alone. Circulations had grown dramatically. In 1830 no American newspaper circulated even 5,000 copies. By 1860 America boasted the largest circulating daily newspaper in the world, the *New York Herald,* with an average daily press run of 77,000.

1860–1865: The Civil War

In 1860 the press in the Northern states was a significant institution, influential in business and powerful in national politics. Large circulations grew even larger as interest in war news swelled. The *Herald*'s 77,000 circulation, for example, went to 107,520 copies the day after the firing on Fort Sumter, and did not drop below 100,000 for the rest of the war.

The Southern press resembled that of an earlier America. Most newspapers in the Confederacy were small circulation weeklies. Even a leading daily like the *New Orleans Picayune* ran only five thousand copies. Once the war was joined, Southern papers were in the same straits as the other institutions of the Confederacy, cut off from capital, technology, raw materials, and even personnel. The Press Association of the Confederate States of America never had more than ten correspondents in the field.

The Northern press was a force unto itself. Over three hundred American reporters were in the field (along with dozens more from overseas). The *New York Herald* alone spent $500,000 on salaries, telegraph fees, and logistical support for the fifty to sixty staffers it employed in war coverage. The *Tribune* and the *Times* each had twenty reporters and illustrators in action. *Frank Leslie's Illustrated Newspaper* (founded 1855) and *Harper's Weekly* (1857) had artists at every major encampment and battle site. *Leslie's* eighty artists provided over three thousand sketches and drawings. Reproduced by woodcut technology, these sketches allowed the public to see the news as well as read it. Newspapers regularly published maps and battle diagrams.

In the Civil War, reporters for the first time became news gatherers in a regular and systematic way, going to the scene to provide eyewitness coverage. From the *Herald*'s well-provisioned staff to the three dogged reporters from the *Memphis Daily Appeal* who accompanied Confederate armies, the emphasis was on immediacy and detail.

The Union government's attitude toward the press was ambivalent. The Lincoln administration used the Associated Press as its regular conduit of official news. The unprecedented immediacy of reporting, however, posed a problem: the enemy could read the news. Robert E. Lee regularly read the Yankee papers for information about command structure, troop movement, and morale. Thus, there was pressure for censorship. The Union military commanders imposed self-censorship in October 1861, and in 1862 the secretary of state forbade newspapers from publishing the "number, positions, or strength of the military force of the United States." Generals regularly banned correspondents from theaters of operations. The Confederate Congress made it a felony to publish news of troop movements or naval activity.

Not all Civil War corespondents and artists were ethical or honest; reporters filed "eyewitness" accounts of battles they had not seen, and illustrators well to the rear drew scenes at the front of which they had only been told. Even those on the scene exaggerated or sensationalized and used reportage to inflame partisan sentiment. A disloyal Copperhead press published throughout the War, criticizing Lincoln and his generals, attacking administration policy (especially the draft), glorifying the Confederacy, and urging the end of the war.

Yet an astonishing amount of real war news, direct from battle zones and obtained in the face of danger, reached the public. The newspaper reading habit was now firmly fixed: English visitor Edward Dicey wrote in 1863, "The American might be defined as a newspaper reading animal."

The 1870s and 1880s: The New Journalism

Newspapers came out of the Civil War with a newfound awareness of their potential. National publications like *Harper's Weekly* covered, with text and woodcut illustration, the big stories: westward expansion, Indian wars, industrialization. As in earlier decades, local frontier papers were prized community assets: the *Montana Post* sold out its first press run of nine hundred copies in minutes, at fifty cents a copy. Cheyenne, Wyoming, first laid out as a railroad town in July 1869, had a newspaper, the *Leader,* within three months of its founding. In an age of land speculation, newspaper advertisements and news columns trumpeted the romance of the West and its attractiveness as a destination for settlers. But western journalism was not all rosy promotion. Reporters for frontier papers like the *Black Hills Pioneer* rode with the U.S. Cavalry, came to know Indians and Indian agents, and thrilled the nation with tales of frontier valor.

The Civil War left established newspapers with a more discerning and news-hungry readership, whose loyalty could no longer be taken for granted. Reporters could not wait for news; they had to uncover it, using techniques developed during the war, and it had to be delivered quickly and attractively. The front pages of papers, for most of the century the province of advertising, were much more devoted to news after the war.

Able editors capitalized on the trend. Charles A. Dana bought the *New York Sun* in 1868 and announced a policy of publishing news that was "the freshest, most interesting and sprightliest." Knowing that more sophisticated readers wanted good writing, he was among the first to hire college graduates as reporters. He revived human interest writing and campaigned against scandal. By 1876 Dana had built the *Sun* into a 130,000-copies-a-day giant.

The 1870s were the great age of the *New York Herald* and of James Gordon Bennett Jr., son of the founder. Bennett spent money to make money. He used the costly transatlantic cable freely, continued his Civil War practice of hiring a large reportorial staff, and diversified his newspaper's content (creating the first real estate section, for example). Ben-

nett's famous aphorism, "I make news," was never better demonstrated than in his hiring of reporter Henry M. Stanley to find missionary David Livingstone in Africa. Stanley's three-year mission provided plenty of copy and reader interest for the *Herald.* Like his penny press predecessors, Bennett was not above using a hoax to build circulation. In 1874 he front-paged a story that all the animals had escaped from the New York Zoo and were on a citywide killing rampage.

Direct subsidies from political parties to newspapers had nearly disappeared by the 1870s, but many papers had clear political sympathies. Reconstruction brought these out, as Republican papers attacked President Andrew Johnson and called for his impeachment, while Democratic papers supported Johnson's lenient policies toward the former Confederate states. More papers, though, were adopting an independent editorial stance. Whitelaw Reid of the *Tribune* crowed, "Independent journalism! That is the watchword of the future in the profession."

Editorial independence allowed for social muckraking and crusades against political corruption. The most famous was led by *Harper's Weekly* and the nominally Democratic *New York Times* against the felonious New York City government of Tammany Hall and "Boss" William M. Tweed. *Harper's* provided the scathing cartoons of Thomas Nast and the *Times* did the gritty legwork that would be a model for future investigative reporting, digging through city documents to find cost overruns, padded payrolls, and kickbacks. Tammany allegedly offered the *Times* $5 million not to publish the records and offered Nast an art scholarship to study in Europe.

Tammany was not the only target. The *Sun* coined the slogan "Turn the Rascals Out!" in campaigning against the second Grant administration. The Scripps papers exposed overcharging in the funeral business, mistreatment in workhouses, and the abominable living conditions in slums in Cleveland and Detroit. The unforgettable "Nellie Bly" (Elizabeth Cochrane) pioneered undercover investigative reporting by posing as an unwed mother to expose baby selling and simulating insanity to report on asylum conditions.

The great figure of the "New Journalism" was Joseph Pulitzer. Originally from the German-language press, Pulitzer first ran the *St. Louis Post-Dispatch* and then the *New York World,* both publishing successes. Pulitzer's New Journalism was built on a strong news base. He had a large reporting staff, trained in the importance of accuracy and comprehensiveness. He urged reporting on the city's underclasses, especially the rapidly arriving immigrants. Pulitzer urged his reporters to find "what is original, dramatic, romantic . . . odd, apt to be talked about," yet he also stressed "accuracy, accuracy, accuracy."

Editorially, Pulitzer took on the New York Central Railroad, Standard Oil, and a group of bribe-taking city councilmen he called the "Broadway Boodlers." His crusades were legendary, as were his stunts. He sent the tireless Nellie Bly around the world in an attempt to beat the fictional circumnavigation record in Jules Verne's *Around the World in Eighty Days* (1873). She completed the trip in seventy-two days, and Pulitzer milked a circulation bonanza as the public followed her trip.

The New Journalism was visual. Pulitzer led in the use of illustrations: pen portraits of political figures, a drawing of the new Brooklyn Bridge, maps, cartoons, diagrams, and soon "half-tone" photographic reproductions.

The 1890s: Yellow Journalism

William Randolph Hearst, at the *San Francisco Examiner* and then at the New York *Journal* in 1895, thought of himself at first as a practitioner of Pulitzer-style New Journalism. Hearst's *Journal* stressed hard news, crusaded against special interest and scandals, and generally took an activist stance: "While Others Talk, the *Journal* Acts."

But soon, in a feverish circulation war with Pulitzer's *World*, Hearst's *Journal* turned to lurid sensationalism, gimmicks, and hoaxes. Hearst cut the *Journal*'s price to a penny and hired away Pulitzer's key reporters and his cartoonist, Richard Outcault, creator of the cartoon character the "Yellow Kid." Hearst featured Outcault's character in so many editions that "yellow" came to stand for the brand of journalism that Hearst espoused. Hearst soon completed his conversion to the full yellow style: scare headlines, extensive use of pictures (including faked ones), comics, features, ultra-sensational reporting, and patent pandering to society's underdogs. Hearst's circulation gains were so dramatic that Pulitzer rose to the bait and began to imitate the yellow approach.

The Hearst-Pulitzer battle reached its zenith, and yellow journalism its greatest fame, in the agitation over Spanish colonial rule in Cuba. Both papers used yellow techniques to build war fever in America, including phony "eyewitness" accounts, faked pictures of atrocities, and inflated claims of Spanish treachery, culminating in their irresponsible reporting of the mysterious explosion of the battleship

Yellow Journalism. Roused by Joseph Pulitzer's success with the New York *World*, William Randolph Hearst attempted to increase circulation of his *Journal* by sensationalizing and fabricating its content. This so-called Yellow Journalism, named after a cartoon character called Yellow Kid that symbolized Hearst's phony tactics, grew to its ugliest during the Spanish-American War. Both Pulitzer and Hearst provoked the nation with grossly exaggerated representations of the conflict in Cuba; this cartoon shows Pulitzer *(left)* and Hearst *(right)* spelling out a distorted war to the American public. LIBRARY OF CONGRESS

Maine. (The *Journal* called it "the Work of an Enemy"; the *World* claimed, falsely, to have evidence that a Spanish bomb was the cause.) The results were dramatic. At the height of the 1898 war fever, the *Journal* was circulating a staggering 1.5 million copies a day, with the *World* close behind. The *World* earned $500,000 in profits in 1898.

Newspapering had truly become big business. The age of personal journalism in the cities was over. Small-town papers felt the change too, though much more slowly. Journalist Lincoln Steffens said in 1897: "The magnitude of financial operations of the newspaper is turning journalism upside down."

The profession itself was changing as well. Joseph Pulitzer advocated specialized academic training for journalists, and women were increasingly entering a still largely male bastion. An 1893 survey found 250 working newspaperwomen in the United States, plus scores more doing rewrite and clerical tasks. Nellie Bly filed powerful reports on the Pullman strike in 1894, and conducted a memorable interview with feminist Elizabeth Cady Stanton in 1896. But male reporters and editors saw these as aberrations, and dismissed Bly and her colleagues as "stunt girls."

As the century ended, yellow journalism was fading. Although about one-third of big-city papers in 1899 were still "yellow," many never had been or were turning their backs on these techniques. The press world was dividing into the "serious" newspapers of record, like the *New York Times*, purchased by the Ochs family in 1896, and picture-oriented, popular appeal papers like those in the Scripps group.

In 1800 the American newspaper industry consisted of only 200 barely solvent one-man operations. A century later the American press was made up of 21,000 papers, many with large and complex reportorial, editorial, and business staffs, and generating $96 million in annual advertising revenue. By 1900 the American press was at once a major industry and a mature medium of communication.

See also **Communications; Literacy and Reading Habits; Magazines; Muckrakers; Newspapers, African American; Telegraph.**

Bibliography

Andrews, J. Cutler. *The North Reports the Civil War.* Pittsburgh, Pa.: University of Pittsburgh Press, 1955.

Bartow, Edith Merwin. *News and These United States.* New York: Funk and Wagnalls, 1952.

Emery, Edwin. *The Press and America: An Interpretive History of Journalism.* 2d ed. New York: Prentice Hall, 1962. The original edition was published in 1954.

Jones, Robert W. *Journalism in the United States.* New York: E. P. Dutton, 1947.

Knightley, Phillip. *The First Casualty: From the Crimea to Vietnam, the War Correspondent as Hero, Propagandist, and Myth Maker.* Harcourt Brace, 1975.

Kroeger, Brooke. *Nellie Bly: Daredevil, Reporter, Feminist.* New York: Times Books, 1994.

Leonard, Thomas C. *News for All: America's Coming-of-Age with the Press.* New York: Oxford University Press, 1995.

Marzio, Peter C. *The Men and Machines of American Journalism: A Pictorial Essay from the Henry R. Luce Hall of News Reporting.* Washington, D.C.: Smithsonian Institution, 1973.

Moorcroft, Marilyn. *Investigative Reporting.* New York: Franklin Watts, 1981.

Mott, Frank Luther. *American Journalism: A History of Newspapers in the United States through 260 Years, 1690 to 1950.* New York: Macmillan, 1950.

Payne, George Henry. *A History of Journalism in the United States.* Westport, Conn.: Greenwood Press Reprints, 1970. The original edition was published in 1920.

Schwarzklose, Richard A. *The Nation's Newsbrokers.* Volume I: *The Formative Years from Pretelegraph to 1865.* Evanston, Ill.: Northwestern University Press, 1989.

Sim, J. Cameron. *The Grass Roots Press: America's Community Newspapers.* Ames: Iowa State University Press, 1969.

Sisson, Dan. *The American Revolution of 1800.* New York: Alfred A. Knopf, 1974.

Stephens, Mitchell. *A History of News.* New York: Viking Penguin, 1988.

Stern, M. L. *Under Fire: The Story of American War Correspondents.* New York: Julian Messner, 1968.

Thompson, Robert Luther. *Wiring a Continent: The History of the Telegraphy Industry in the United States, 1832–1866.* Princeton, N.J.: Princeton University Press, 1947.

Thorn, William J., and Mary Pat Pfeil. *Newspaper Circulation: Marketing the News.* New York: Longman, 1987.

Tocqueville, Alexis de. *Democracy in America.* Translated by Henry Reeve. 2 vols. London: Longman, Green, Longman, and Roberts, 1862. The original edition was published in two volumes in 1835 and 1840.

Trimble, Vance H. *The Astonishing Mr. Scripps: The Turbulent Life of America's Penny Press Lord.* Ames: Iowa State University Press, 1992.

DAVID L. JAMISON

NEWSPAPERS, AFRICAN AMERICAN

In nineteenth-century towns and cities African Americans created for themselves institutions white society would not or could not provide. Among others, they established churches, schools, mutual-aid societies, and businesses. One of these institutions was the newspaper.

New York City was the home of the first black newspaper, *Freedom's Journal*, whose initial issue came out on 16 March 1827. Founded by John Russwurm, one of the first black college graduates, and the Reverend Samuel Cornish, *Freedom's Journal* was a forum for black antislavery sentiment and a voice for black demands for equal rights in the North.

Other antebellum black newspapers followed the pattern of *Freedom's Journal.*

Among the more prominent of the other papers were the *Colored American,* published in 1837 by Phillip Bell and Cornish, and the newspapers associated with the abolitionist leader Frederick Douglass, *Ram's Horn* and *North Star,* published in 1847 in New York and Rochester respectively. The *North Star,* later called *Frederick Douglass' Paper,* lasted an unusually long time for black newspapers of that era, ceasing publication in 1860. Edited and published by Douglass, this newspaper gave him one of his major forums. He published *Douglass' Monthly* from 1859 to 1863 and the *New National Era* from 1870 to 1874. All told, forty black newspapers were published between 1827 and the Civil War.

Antebellum black newspapers did more than protest slavery and racism. They reported and commented on events inside and outside of their African American communities; recorded births, deaths, and marriages; advertised black businesses; and advocated the moral uplift of the African American community. They also provided jobs for black journalists and printers and a venue for black intellectuals, poets, and essayists who had no other outlet for their writings.

The postwar era saw tremendous growth in the number of black newspapers. Between 1865 and 1900, one thousand were established. This upsurge had several causes, the first of which was emancipation. Education was a high priority for former slaves, and as they became literate they demanded newspapers. When blacks acquired the vote, political parties created newspapers to reach them. Finally residential segregation in northern and southern cities concentrated African Americans into compact markets that increased black newspapers' potential profitability.

However, most black newspapers had short lives, due in part to their proliferation and competition in black urban communities, which made it difficult for them to amass the circulation or advertising revenue necessary for survival. Most black newspapers survived meagerly if at all. Black journalists often found that zeal and enthusiasm could not make up for the lack of a sound financial base or good business sense. Many were only part-time journalists who made their livings primarily as teachers, politicians, lawyers, or ministers.

As in the antebellum era, black newspapers after the Civil War protested against the exclusion of blacks from the American mainstream and provided news for the black community. Frequently they were little more than organs for the Republican Party or campaign sheets for black politicians, but a few black newspapers in the postbellum period stood out. Among the notables were the *Colored American* (a different newspaper from the 1837 *Colored American*), the South's first black newspaper founded in 1865; Frederick Douglass's *New National Era,* founded in Washington, D.C., in 1870; and the *Washington Bee,* founded by W. Calvin Chase in 1879. Other superior black newspapers included the *New York Globe* (later the *New York Age*), founded in 1881 by T. Thomas Fortune; the *Richmond Planet,* founded in 1884 by John Mitchell; the *Philadelphia Tribune,* founded in 1884 by Chris Perry; and the *Baltimore Afro-American,* founded in 1892 by William Alexander and taken over in 1897 by John H. Murphy. Owing to the talent and tenacity of their founders, these newspapers lasted far longer than their competitors. For example, the longest-lived, the *Afro-American,* lasted through the twentieth century.

The outstanding black editors of this era included T. Thomas Fortune of the *New York Age,* who by 1890 was the preeminent figure in black journalism. Another was Ida B. Wells, whose newspaper *Memphis Free Speech* so vociferously crusaded against lynching that it was destroyed in 1892 by a Memphis mob. Undaunted, Wells escaped to Chicago, where she continued her antilynching crusade with the *Conservator,* which she operated with her husband Ferdinand Barnett. Her activities exemplified the protest mission of the black press of the nineteenth and the twentieth centuries.

See also **Abolition and Antislavery; African Americans; Civil Rights; Education,** *subentry on* **Education of African Americans; Emancipation; Newspapers and the Press; Segregation,** *subentry on* **Segregation and Civil Rights; Voters and Voting,** *subentries on* **Black Voters before the Civil War, Black Voters after the Civil War.**

Bibliography

Dann, Martin E., ed. *The Black Press, 1827–1890.* New York: Putnam, 1971.

Farrar, Hayward. *The* Baltimore Afro-American, *1892–1950.* Wesport, Conn.: Greenwood, 1998.

Hutton, Frankie. *The Early Black Press in America, 1827–1860.* Westport, Conn.: Greenwood, 1993.

Penn, Irvine Garland. *The* Afro-American Press *and Its Editors.* Springfield, Mass.: Wiley, 1891.

Pride, Armistead S. *The Black Press: A Bibliography.* Jefferson City, Wis.: Association for Education in Journalism, Ad Hoc Committee on Minority Education, 1968.

Wolseley, Roland E. *The Black Press U.S.A.* Ames: Iowa State University Press, 1971.

HAYWARD FARRAR

NEW YORK CITY   During most of the nineteenth century New York City meant present-day

Manhattan. Demographically the city paralleled London as a "shock city." In 1800 New York City was home to 60,515 souls, nearly double the population of ten years earlier. As the rush into the city continued, its human populace doubled again by 1820, and in 1860 more than eight-hundred thousand people were crammed into the lower third of Manhattan Island. This demographic explosion was but one feature of the massive changes that doomed colonial mores forever, replacing them with the characteristics of the new metropolis. Even mid-century cosmopolitans could hardly foresee that by 1900 more than three million people would live in a consolidated city of five boroughs.

1800–1865

Late-eighteenth-century Federalist dominance of local politics collapsed with the election in 1800 of President Thomas Jefferson and Vice President Aaron Burr, an expert at ward organization in New York politics. The Republican triumph meant expanded suffrage for the common man as that party chipped away at colonial-era voting requirements. In the next two decades Federalists and Republicans battled for the votes of artisans and laborers, and Federalists benefited from a strong allegiance with black voters. A new state constitution in 1821 eliminated property requirements for white male suffrage, but African Americans had to post a $250 bond and were largely disfranchised. The only prevalent local controversy during the 1820s was anger over immigrant encroachment into licensed trades.

New York City's early-nineteenth-century economy strongly resembled that of the colonial era. Over the course of the century, shipping expanded sharply. Jay's Treaty of 1795 invigorated the urban economy by reopening West Indian and English ports and paving the way for the settlement of western Manhattan Island. In 1811 the New York City commissioners accepted a plan that laid out streets and avenues on the island in a gridiron pattern that incorporated parks.

Following the completion of the Erie Canal in 1825, New York quickly surpassed Philadelphia as the nation's leading port. Termed the "city of masts," New York's waterfront employed thousands of sailors, wharfingers, and cartmen in the transport of goods.

The nineteenth century brought fundamental changes in skilled trades. The traditional career ladder from apprentice to journeyman to master was replaced by factory employment, where workers included boys and young women. Masters became capitalists, and distinct class barriers destroyed trade unity. The panic of 1837 highlighted the weaknesses of the trade unions, and textile manufacture and cabinetmaking underwent dramatic transformations. Unlike the massive factories of New England, local shops in New York were small with few employees. Packet service to the West Coast, railroad construction, telegraph innovations, and inland land speculation fueled new wealth, and college-educated clerks dislodged traditional scriveners. The growth of the middle class created a demand for service workers, and new immigrants displaced African Americans as domestics, sailors, and industrial workers. By 1855 more than thirty thousand Irish women labored as domestics, and Germans dominated as shoemakers, brewers, bakers, tobacconists, and tailors.

A major political battle erupted in 1829, when the Workingmen's Party, influenced by the radicals Thomas Skidmore, Frances Wright, and Robert Dale Owen, demanded equal opportunities for all people to pursue such licensed trades as carter, butcher, baker, grocer, and tavern keeper. Rejected at first, the Workingmen resurrected their reforms at the Democratic Party convention in 1834. When mainstream leaders attempted to end the meeting and stifle debate by turning off the gaslights, "Workies" lit matches or locofocos and took over the meeting. The Whig Party sustained its strength among the city's elite, licensed workers, and emerging middle class. The mayor of New York was elected by popular vote for the first time in 1834, and although the Whigs occasionally secured office, the Democrats dominated city politics for the next two decades. Democratic Party newspapers inflamed racial animosity in the city, fomenting the race riots of 1834, 1835, 1849, and 1857. Self-described as the party of the people, Democrats used patronage skillfully, awarding licenses to immigrants and building a city bureaucracy. In the 1840s, as government work shifted from part-time to full-time and employees changed from amateurs to permanent professional staff, the Democrats built major support among the new police, fire, and sanitation departments. In addition the massive wave of new Irish immigrants supported the Democratic Party. Because the Democratic Party had little interest in African American civil rights or in opposing slavery, the black middle class organized a shadow political party that headed a national movement addressing those issues.

The working-class culture of New York City was an amalgam of English, Irish, German, and African influences. Five Points became an infamous center, where musicians, dancers, prostitutes, and boozers of all nationalities congregated, made love, and, in Walt

New York City Hall. City Hall, constructed between 1803 and 1812, was designed by John McComb Jr. and Joseph-François Mangin. During construction, the architects commissioned a sculpture of Justice for the top of the cupola; during an 1858 firework display, the wooden work crashed through the ceiling, burned, and would be replaced two years later. Photograph by William B. Holmes, c. 1860. LIBRARY OF CONGRESS

Whitman's words, "presaged a grand national opera." The nearby Bowery was a theater of melodrama, minstrelsy, and sports. P. T. Barnum opened his American Museum in New York in 1842, and after 1845 baseball was popular among artisans and laborers. Favored resorts included Battery Park Vauxhall and Jones Wood. Central Park, built in the 1850s, was a refuge for the middle class, and everyone paraded on Broadway.

Just before the Civil War the new Republican Party absorbed what was left of the Whig Party. The Democrats, under Mayor Fernando Wood and the party boss William Marcy Tweed, continued to control the patronage rolls. Wood joined other Democrats in organizing the "Copperheads," who were accused of Southern sympathies during the Civil War. The draft riot of 1863, a manifestation of the deep racial and class animosities in New York City, was sparked by Irish discontent over discriminatory exemptions from military service and President Abraham Lincoln's Emancipation Proclamation. The riot lasted five days, more than one hundred people were killed, and dozens of churches, orphanages, businesses, and homes were destroyed. In the riot's aftermath the New York Common Council instituted exemptions for virtually any white man. Consequently, the Union army and navy turned their sights upon

black recruits, and the following year the Republicans and the Union League sponsored a parade of black soldiers down Broadway.

1865–1900

The scandals surrounding Tweed figured prominently in the city's postwar politics. Tweed, who built his Tammany Hall powerbase into a lucrative network of kickbacks, extortion, and real estate fraud, was by 1870 one of the most powerful men in the city. That year he pushed through a new city charter that allowed his associates to siphon off huge sums of money from bond issues, tripling the city debt. In 1871 Thomas Nast, a *Harper's Weekly* cartoonist, caricatured the Tammany Hall leader and his associates as obese vultures to accompany the newspapers' articles detailing Tweed's corruption in construction projects. During the following two years Tweed was indicted, expelled from the city government, and jailed. As the Republicans regained power, the city returned to elite leadership.

New York suffered another shock in 1872, when Protestants and Catholics in Ireland battled in the Orange riots. Alarmed, New York's middle and upper classes built armories, where young clerks trained in militia and prepared for war against the laboring

Bird's Eye View of New York City. New York City became a mosaic of ethnic neighborhoods—including Irish, Chinese, Russian Jewish, and Italian—owing to the waves of immigration that began in 1820 and continued through the 1970s. Sketched and drawn on stone by Parsons & Atwater. New York, Currier & Ives, c. 1876. LIBRARY OF CONGRESS

class. Similar anxieties characterized the Decency Crusade led by the reformer Anthony Comstock, who capitalized on a story of the alleged adultery of the famed minister Henry Ward Beecher published by Victoria Woodhull, a radical feminist. That scandal along with Woodhull's denunciation of masked balls as promiscuous helped publicize Comstock's crusade. He gained an investigator's rank in the post office, which he used to censor magazines and books and to campaign successfully against the abortionist Madame Restell.

While Comstock captured middle-class cultural attitudes, New York's laboring classes organized unions to combat corporations during economic downturns in the 1870s. Technological innovations, including transportation, electric lights, the telephone, and gas, supercharged corporate profits. Manhattan attracted the financiers John D. Rockefeller, J. Pierpont Morgan, and Jay Gould, as well as ancillary law, advertising, and newspaper firms. Soaring real estate prices, new skyscrapers, and the Brooklyn Bridge symbolized the city's embrace of commerce.

In 1886 the Statue of Liberty, donated by the French government, was installed in New York Harbor, where it beckoned a new wave of approximately

seventeen million immigrants from southern and eastern Europe who arrived in New York between 1880 and 1920. Largely Russian Jews and Italians, these immigrants settled into ethnic neighborhoods on the Lower East Side, near their German and Irish predecessors. Chinatown in lower Manhattan developed after 1880. African Americans from southern states reinvigorated the city's black population, which moved uptown to the Tenderloin District, to Hell's Kitchen, and to Harlem in the early twentieth century.

Poverty inexorably accompanied immigration. Shocked by Jacob Riis's photo essay *How the Other Half Lives* (1890), middle-class New Yorkers rediscovered poverty and sought reform through moral and charitable intervention. Agencies such as the Salvation Army, the Charitable Organization Society, and the Children's Aid Society provided relief while carefully guarding against their notions of sin. Temperance advocates warred against ethnic men enjoying a Sunday beer. Theodore Roosevelt, reviving his political career in the 1890s as president of the New York City Board of Police Commissioners, worsened relations between police and citizens by insisting on Sunday closure of saloons. Colonel George Waring reformed the sanitation department as part of an effort to clean up the city, fight disease and germs, and promote better housing.

In the 1890s New York financiers and politicians lobbied to annex the outer counties into a political entity known as Greater New York. Though opposition arose in Brooklyn and debates lasted for several years, consolidation was achieved in 1898. Consolidation centralized city government, making New York the largest and most populous city in the United States. It brought emerging suburbs under municipal jurisdiction and consolidated property tax rates and assessments. By 1901 problems over planning mandated a new charter, which created a powerful Board of Estimate that included the five borough presidents. At the close of the century New York City's 3,437,202 residents prepared to expand its commercial and cultural reach globally.

See also **Brooklyn; Chinatowns; Cities and Urbanization; City and Regional Planning; Immigration and Immigrants; New York State; Politics,** *subentries on* **Machines and Bosses, Corruption and Scandals.**

Bibliography

Burrows, Edwin G., and Mike Wallace. *Gotham: A History of New York City to 1898*. New York: Oxford University Press, 1999.

Hodges, Graham Russell. *New York City Cartmen, 1667–1850*. New York: New York University Press, 1986.

———. *Root and Branch: African Americans in New York and East Jersey, 1613–1863*. Chapel Hill: University of North Carolina Press, 1999.

Nadel, Stanley. *Little Germany: Ethnicity, Religion, and Class in New York City, 1845–1880*. Urbana: University of Illinois Press, 1990.

Wilentz, Sean. *Chants Democratic: New York City and the Rise of the American Working Class, 1788–1850*. New York: Oxford University Press, 1984.

GRAHAM RUSSELL HODGES

NEW YORK STATE   New York State began the nineteenth century with the passage of a gradual emancipation bill ending slavery; a hotly contested presidential election that spawned a new political party, the Republicans, featuring Vice President Aaron Burr; and rapid interior settlement. Removal of British troops from Oswego and Niagara and expulsion of Iroquois Indians from tribal lands paved the way for white settlement upstate. New Yorkers planned future real estate development by creating new counties in the first twenty years of the century along the southwestern frontier (Allegany, Broome, Cattaraugus, Cayuga, Cortland), up the northeast-ern border with Vermont (Essex, Warren, Franklin, Lewis), and along Lake Ontario (Niagara, Erie, Livingston, Jefferson, Genesee, Monroe, and Orleans). Settlement organization occurred either by individual homestead or, most commonly, by speculation. State population reached 589,000 in 1800; 738,000 in 1830; 3,097,000 by 1850; 5,083,000 in 1880; and 7,269,000 in 1900.

New York State, 1800–1860

New York State was primarily rural in 1800, with the bulk of its urban population in New York City. Fifty years later, after development of cities along the Erie Canal, the urban population reached 873,000, but more than two million residents lived in rural areas. The key engine for upstate urban development was the Erie Canal. Soon after the canal opened in 1825, Albany and the newer cities of Utica, Syracuse, and Buffalo served as market nodes for agricultural hinterlands and industrial development. Canal craze and search for waterpower created such construction projects as the Chenango Canal between Binghamton and Utica, connecting major cities and incorporating remote rural towns into the Atlantic economy. Every new city found an economic specialization. Watertown, for example, located eighty miles north of Syracuse, employed readily accessible wood and abundant waterpower to sustain booming paper production. As the market economy transformed national politics, New York State combined customary state intervention and capitalist methods. Canals and their successors, the railroads, were funded by state bonds, favorable tax policies, and land speculation. Towns more remote from waterpower attracted institutions to gain permanence. Colleges, courthouses, prisons, insane asylums, and orphanages acted as anchors in smaller county seats. Such forces sustained a demographic boom upstate. Albany's population tripled between 1825 and 1855, while Buffalo's soared from 5,000 to 74,000 in the same period, and similar gains were achieved in Syracuse, Troy, and Utica. Even so, the state's urban population did not reach parity with its rural numbers until 1870. By the end of the century most New Yorkers lived in cities.

Politics in the antebellum period mixed national and local concerns. Elections in the 1820s and 1830s, for example, hinged on combinations of anti-Masonry, or fear of secret conspiracies, with national bank wars, dooming the presidency of Martin Van Buren, a New Yorker. Geography and economics also fused to split state political perceptions. New York City, dependent on southern cotton to fuel prosperity and guided by its past history of slavery, was hostile to black civil rights and abolitionism. Central and western counties, in contrast, populated by New Englanders, sent thousands of antislavery petitions to Congress, welcomed fugitive slaves, and fought their owners' agents sent to recapture them. Dramatic events, such as the Jerry Rescue in Syracuse (1851), galvanized upstate public sentiment against slavery. By the 1850s New York City and State were badly fractured over slavery, establishing divisions apparent during the Civil War.

Urban development depended on rural produce. After poor price levels in the early 1820s, farm produce prices rose until the panic of 1837 and recovered again in the late 1840s, only to fall in the panic of 1857. New York State farmers herded sheep and produced wheat, potatoes, and hops. Cattle produced great profits in meat, manure, and dairy products. New York State was the leading state in lumber production by 1850. Labor remained a persistent problem as western lands successfully beckoned young men. The state gradually lost geographic advantage in meat supply with the extension of railroads into the Midwest.

Upstate counties were seedbeds for religious revival. Older denominations were reinvigorated by revivals in the 1830s, and, in burned-over districts in western counties such new sects as the Church of Jesus Christ of Latter-day Saints found fertile ground for their mixture of popular mysticism and revolutionary fervor. Farther east such communitarian groups as the Oneida Community and the Owenites formed towns to pursue social perfection. After dreams fizzled perfectionists remained to serve as the core for new communities. Temperance and food reforms, such as Grahamism, a health diet based on graham flour, had more limited appeal. Of long-term significance was the feminist movement, which sought civil rights for women. Women's rights advocates held their first national meeting in Seneca Falls, New York, in 1848. By 1860, they had secured custodial rights for mothers, improved inheritance rights, authored a new married women's property act, and set the stage for the postwar drive for suffrage.

New York State in the Civil War

The Civil War powerfully affected New York. Despite the popularity of abolitionism in upstate western counties, New York's government was cool to Abraham Lincoln and favored conciliation with the Southern states. In New York City, Democrats were so opposed to Lincoln's policies that their positions throughout the war bordered on treason. While Governor Edwin D. Morgan strongly supported Union calls for men and supplies, Mayor Fernando Wood of New York City at first openly supported the South, but after the outbreak of hostilities, even he upheld federal authority and supported its military effort. Dislike of the president continued throughout the war, with Radical Republicans even trying to deny renomination to Lincoln. Although New York City's economy soared for the wealthy, the cost of war for ordinary people was high. Draft exemptions costing $300 kept the better-off out of the army, but the populous New York State, more than any other state, provided more young men to the draft, supplied the most munitions, paid the highest taxes, bought the greatest number of war bonds, and gave the largest support to relief efforts. New York supplied more than forty generals, more than 460,000 residents enlisted in the Union army, and fatalities numbered more than fifty thousand. Manufacturing, banks, insurance, and munitions suppliers prospered, but the merchant marine was devastated, and farmers lost key labor supplies. Hyperspeculation and fraud produced panics periodically. Inflation and human costs born by working classes were manifested in discontent and contributed to draft riots, which came close to full insurrection in New York City in 1863. Graft and corruption flourished, while casualties broke families.

New York State, 1865–1900

Democrats and Republicans battled for control in postwar politics. Republicans, pointing to Democratic support for the southern cause and to corruption under the Tammany Hall boss William M. Tweed in New York City, won control of both congressional houses after the war. Alliance with Republican presidents during the Reconstruction years provided the state with massive amounts of patronage. After the fall of the Tweed Ring and the reformation of the party, Democrats regained New York's governorship in 1875. Samuel J. Tilden and Grover Cleveland became national figures for state Democrats, who recaptured the majority of the state's congressional seats. Democrats controlled the state's executive office until 1895. For Republicans, the Roscoe Conkling–bossed party enjoyed a close relationship with President Ulysses S. Grant after the war but split with the national party in the 1870s.

Workers responded to the fusion of politics and capital by traditional and revolutionary means. The Orange Riots in New York City in 1871 showed class and ethnic cleavages. Genuine radical movements grew in the city alongside traditional trade unionism. In the countryside, rural women formed associations through churches, ladies' aid societies, and farm organizations. In Albany, worker militancy in the 1860s gave way to trade unionism by the 1880s. Similarly, in Troy workers fought more for short-range, wage and job-conscious goals. By the 1890s they established an enduring union movement, which created a legacy that would reappear in the American socialist movement of the early twentieth century. For middle-class New Yorkers, goals included ties with commercial interests, the "good life," and mobility for their children into professional and entrepreneurial status.

Political anxiety over national and statewide worker dissatisfaction encouraged the movement for labor legislation. After 1895 new labor laws sought to prevent abuses by sweatshops and the labor of women and children. Complicating the issue was the political future of Greater New York, then debating consolidation of the southern five counties into a single metropolis. Nonetheless, the Constitutional Convention of 1894 approved reapportionment of the legislature, reorganization of the judiciary, creation of forest lands (creating the model for later federal protection of forest lands), reform of prison labor, and education. Among its accomplishments was awarding constitutional status (and thus tax support) to the University of the State of New York. Anticipating the Progressive movement, the state assembly called for a return to public regulation of utilities, especially the railroads. Less successful, although spirited, debates occurred over the civil status of women. Feminist organizations battled unsuccessfully for woman suffrage from the passage of the Fifteenth Amendment in 1870 to the Constitutional Convention of 1894 and beyond, while male political figures refused to acknowledge their efforts. The ethnic composition of the state changed dramatically at the end of the century. Waves of immigrants from Eastern Europe and Mediterranean nations transformed New York City and set the stage for twentieth-century migration throughout upstate New York. By the onset of the twentieth century, although New York State was changed radically in economics and geography, certain aspects of life, such as the status of women and rural life, had changed little.

See also New York City; Politics, subentries on Machines and Bosses, Corruption and Scandals; Voters and Voting, subentry on The Women's Vote.

Bibliography

Bliven, Bruce. *New York: A Bicentennial History.* New York: Norton, 1981.

Ellis, David M., et al. *A Short History of New York State.* Ithaca, N.Y.: Cornell University Press, 1957.

Gerber, David A. *The Making of an American Pluralism: Buffalo, New York, 1825–1860.* Urbana: University of Illinois Press, 1989.

Hewitt, Nancy A. *Women's Activism and Social Change: Rochester, New York, 1822–1872.* Ithaca, N.Y.: Cornell University Press, 1984.

Walkowitz, Daniel J. *Worker City, Company Town: Iron and Cotton-Worker Protest in Troy and Cohoes, New York, 1855–1884.* Urbana: University of Illinois Press, 1978.

GRAHAM RUSSELL HODGES

NINETEENTH CENTURY   The nineteenth century was the most dramatic in American history. Few Americans of 1800 would have recognized their nation in 1900. The nation's political geography was totally altered, the population was vastly different, the economic base had changed, and the most divisive social institution of the nation—slavery—existed no more. Although the form of government was the same, the structure of the Constitution had been so radically transformed that in many ways it was a new document. The nature of politics, parties, and campaigns was also fundamentally different. The scope of change and growth in the century is in part understood by considering the centuries that preceded it and followed it.

The English colonies hugging the eastern seaboard of America in 1700 looked very much like American states hugging the eastern seaboard in 1799. At both ends of the eighteenth century animal and wind power moved people from place to place, and roads were few and poor. Technology was mostly unimportant to Americans in 1700 and in 1799. The American Revolution certainly brought about a major political change, but the state governments of 1799 were much like the prerevolutionary colonial governments. Elites ruled and voted throughout the century. Some more territory had also been settled, and many Native Americans had been forced out of the lands settled by whites. But the political geography of America in 1799 remained much as it had been a century earlier. The colonies of 1700, like the states of 1799, were strung along the Atlantic Coast with minimal expansion into the interior. The presence of powerful Indian nations and European armies served to limit growth and threaten the colonies in 1700 and the states in 1799. America in 1700 and in 1799 was predominately a land of white Protestants living on small farms and in small towns. In the South white Protestants and black slaves lived both on small farms and large plantations. Agriculture was the main industry; tobacco and rice were the most important cash crops. Slavery existed everywhere in 1700 and everywhere but a few New England states in 1799. Government was mostly local at both ends of the century. The end of the Seven Years' War and the Revolution and the writing of the national Constitution and state constitutions planted the seeds of enormous change, but that change was for the most part not realized until later.

In many ways America in 1900 was remarkably similar to America in 1999. Surely the technology was different, but only in kind. Oil, steel, electricity, and telecommunications were major industries in 1900 and 1999. Oil, coal, and electricity moved people from place to place in 1900 as they did in 1999. The automobile and the airplane were in their infancies in 1900, but they were on the scene. Interurban and intraurban trains moved people in 1900 and in 1999, often along the same routes, sometimes operated by the same companies, and even on the same tracks. Commuters entered New York, Boston, Chicago, or Cleveland on the same tracks in 1999 that commuters had used in 1900. The same systems that brought water to people in 1900 brought them water in 1999.

Literacy rates were only slightly higher in 1999, but the proliferation of information sources was great at both ends of the century. Except for colorized comic strips and photographs, the newspaper reader of 1900 would instantly recognize the newspaper of 1999, including some of the baseball teams' names on the sports page. By 1999 the franchise had been ex-panded to include women, and the civil rights enforced in 1999 had been ignored in 1900. In 1900 much of the nation focused its attention on the absorption of new immigrants from southern and eastern Europe and from the Middle East and Asia. In 1999 the focus was also on new immigrants, who now came from Latin America, the Caribbean, the Middle East, Asia, and Africa. Latino immigrants had replaced Italian and Jewish immigrants as a source of anxiety for many established Americans. In 1900 and in 1999 the United States was a world power, with a global economic and military presence.

In 1900 people were urban and suburban, increasingly employed in nonfarm jobs, and religiously and ethnically diverse. These trends continued to the end of the century. Native Americans in 1900 and 1999 were at the very margins of society, hardly noticed by the government. In 1900 the United States was legally segregated, and blacks were among the poorest people in the nation. In 1999 de facto segregation had replaced de jure segregation, but black poverty remained a major problem. In 1903 the great black scholar W. E. B. Du Bois declared, "The problem of the [t]wentieth [c]entury is the problem of the color line." The statement remained valid at the beginning of the twenty-first century.

The changes that transformed the agriculture-

Washington in 1800. The west grounds of the capitol and Pennsylvania Avenue, along which Thomas Jefferson planted Lombardy poplars in 1803. From Conrad Malte-Brun, *A System of Universal Geography* (Boston: Samuel Walker, 1834). LIBRARY OF CONGRESS: ARCHITECT OF THE CAPITOL COLLECTION

American Progress. A heroic woman draped in white drifts into the western frontier, guiding explorers and their new technologies, and connecting this land to its eastern origin. Painting by John Gast. Copyrighted by George A. Crofutt, 1873. LIBRARY OF CONGRESS

based colonial America of the 1700s into the industrial power of the 1900s mostly took place in the nineteenth century. The United States in the nineteenth century was marked by enormous physical expansion, huge population growth, radical changes in the makeup of the people, and a startling economic transformation. At the center of this changing nation was the bloody civil war, which took more American lives than were lost in all other wars combined.

At the dawn of the nineteenth century the United States was a tiny nation, hemmed in by European powers and powerful Indian nations. Territorial acquisitions through purchase, annexation, warfare, negotiation, and intimidation expanded the nation to the shores of the Pacific Ocean by 1848 and, with the purchase of Alaska from Russia in 1867, to the western tip of the continent. Conquest and annexation created an empire in both the Pacific and the Caribbean before the close of the century. The tiny and

militarily weak product of a revolution against English colonialism in 1800 had by 1899 itself become a colonial power with a powerful navy and an enormous economic infrastructure. The anticolonial nation of 1800 was itself a colonial power by 1900, with the American flag planted on islands in the Caribbean and the Pacific Ocean.

The century began with a confirmation that the nation's political experiment could work as President John Adams peacefully left his office on 3 March 1801 so his apparent political enemy, Thomas Jefferson, could replace him. This transition was truly a revolutionary event not only in the United States but in world politics. By 1899 the peaceful transfer of power from one president to the next was commonplace. Four presidents, William Henry Harrison, Zachary Taylor, Abraham Lincoln, and James A. Garfield, had died in office and been peacefully replaced by their vice presidents. Political assassination was unknown in the United States of 1800, but by 1900 it had left two presidents, Lincoln and Garfield, dead. William McKinley, elected in 1896, died from an assassin's bullet in 1901. An innocent nation in 1800 was sadly more worldly by 1900.

Other government institutions had also evolved. The Supreme Court was powerless and unimportant in the eighteenth century. That began to change with Chief Justice John Marshall, who took office in 1801, and at the end of the century the Court was a powerful force in society. In the last decade of the century the Court gave its blessing to state-sponsored segregation but struck down state and federal legislation designed to reign in the excesses of the new industrial order and the robber barons, whose wealth seemed to defy imagination. Equally important, bureaucracies emerged at the state and federal levels, as had urban political machines. In addition reform movements, settlement houses, and other attempts to counter urban politics and urban poverty appeared.

In 1800 religious restrictions prevented some Americans from holding office, while racial prejudice excluded others. In 1899 no legal religious restrictions existed, and blacks had been holding public office in the North since the late 1850s and in the South since the late 1860s. In 1800 secret ballot voting was unknown, and the electorate was mostly white and owned property. By 1900 the franchise was open to all adult male citizens without property restrictions. Nonwhites voted everywhere except in the South, which was in the process of vastly restricting black voters in violation of the spirit and goals of the Fourteenth (1868) and Fifteenth (1870) Amendments to the U.S. Constitution. With the brief exception of New Jersey, where women could vote in the first decade of the nineteenth century, voting and political participation in 1800 were strictly limited by gender. But by 1899 women could vote in a few states, and more importantly, the movement for woman suffrage was vibrant, powerful, and on the eve of victory.

The crusade for the women's vote grew out of an earlier reform movement aimed at ending slavery. Abolitionism, temperance, and other reforms of the mid-century profoundly shaped the nation at that time and later. Black and white opposition to the return of fugitive slaves under the Fugitive Slave Acts of 1793 and 1850 set an example later emulated by labor leaders, organizers of the poor, civil rights activists, and opponents of wars. Indeed America's first celebrated antiwar protester was Henry David Thoreau, who in 1846 refused to pay a tax because he opposed the war with Mexico.

The United States of 1800 was mostly populated by white Protestants of northern European background and black slaves. The Louisiana Purchase in 1803 brought Catholics of French and Spanish origin into the nation. In mid-century the acquisition of Texas, California, and territory that became New Mexico and Arizona brought Latinos of Spanish and Indian origin. The nation was overwhelmingly Protestant in 1800, but by 1899 Catholics had become the largest denomination in the country. Large Jewish communities were scattered around the nation, while Muslims, Confucians, Shintos, Buddhists, and Hindus could be found in a few places. Eastern rite Catholics from Greece, Russia, Serbia, and Armenia added to the religious mix, just as their distinctive churches altered many urban skylines. Eastern and southern Europeans, Armenians, Turks, and Syrians had decisively reshaped the ethnic mix of America, and joining them were Chinese, Koreans, Japanese, Pacific Islanders, French Canadians, and Latinos from Mexico, Central America, and South America. Residents of large cities like New York or Chicago could hear almost every language of Europe and a good many from the Middle East and East Asia.

New ideas and new faiths also altered the religious diversity of the United States. During the century two major new religions developed, the Church of Jesus Christ of Latter-day Saints, whose members are commonly known as Mormons, and the Church of Christ, Scientist, whose members are commonly known as Christian Scientists. Various Protestant faiths, including the Seventh-Day Adventist Church, emerged in the United States during the Second Great Awakening in the second quarter of the century. Before the Civil War, major denominations, most importantly the Baptists, Presbyterians, and Methodists, divided over slavery. At the end of the twentieth century the Baptists remained divided over other issues. Late in the nineteenth century the Social Gospel and the rise of the urban mission further altered the nature of American Protestantism.

The population had not only diversified in its ethnic and religious makeup. The demographics of the nation also changed. White birthrates were about 55 per 1,000 people in 1800 and 30.1 per 1,000 in 1900. Statistics are unavailable for African American birthrates. White women had fewer children, and most Americans probably lived longer. The average number of children in white families declined from 7.04 to 3.56 during the century. With declining birthrates and increased life expectancy, the median age of Americans rose from 16.6 to 23.3 years during the century.

In 1800, 95 out of every 100 Americans lived on a farm, but by 1900 only 60 of every 100 lived in a rural area. For all Americans the growth of such huge cities as New York, Chicago, and Philadelphia profoundly changed the nature of the country's population and outlook. By 1899 urban centers dominated a nation that had once had only small towns and villages. Urban growth accompanied expansion in population and national territory. In 1800, 5,308,483 Americans lived in a nation that contained 864,811 square miles. In 1900, 75,994,757 Americans lived in a nation of 3,022,387 square miles.

The most dramatic change of all was the presence of millions of black citizens whose parents and grandparents had been slaves. The central political and social issue of the nation's first eighty-five years, slavery, was destroyed in the country's eighty-ninth year. Slavery was legal in all but three states in 1800 but was illegal everywhere after 1865. By 1868 African Americans were citizens of the nation that had once declared them unfit for anything but bondage. African Americans were mostly rural at both ends of the century, but some had moved out of the South to the North, to places like Kansas, Oklahoma, and California, and increasingly into cities. Indeed urban centers in both the South and the North offered some escape from the extreme poverty and racist violence of the rural South. Despite mob attacks against blacks in cities and towns, the post–Civil War reign of terror and lynching blacks was more pronounced in the rural areas.

Along with the end of slavery came the economic devastation of the South. For sixty years after 1800 this section of the country had boasted of its wealthy planters and political prowess, and the South dominated all national political institutions from 1800 to 1850. By 1899, however, the South was the poorest section of the nation and politically the weakest. The Midwest now dominated, and every elected president but one between 1860 and 1900 was from that region. Meanwhile the Far West had been settled and was clearly rising in significance.

Americans of 1800 moved by animal power, wind, and water on vehicles of wood and iron, much as they had in 1700. But by 1899 they moved in steel machines powered by steam, gasoline, or electricity. Canals, roads, and railroads reshaped the geography of settlement and the possibilities for movement. The limitless frontier of 1800 had disappeared by 1900. The West in 1800 had been unknown to white Americans—unexplored and unsettled. By 1899 white Americans had explored, mapped, crisscrossed, and traveled most of the West. Indeed in the last decade of the century Americans talked about the end of the frontier. Symbolic of the "conquest" of the West was the need, recognized late in the century, to create national parks and preserves, to save the bison, and to conserve the majestic natural wonders of places like Yellowstone. Equally symbolic of the "conquest" of the West was the altered status of Native Americans.

By 1899 once powerful native tribes had been reduced to wards of the state, impoverished on reservations, and increasingly denied the right to perpetuate their culture.

Most Americans lived on small farms in 1800, using animals to plant and harvest their crops. In 1899 massive machines powered by coal or gas harvested huge tracts of wheat and other crops. But farming was no longer the main source of wealth or jobs. In 1800 the total U.S. exports were worth $71 million. In 1900 this figure was over $1.3 billion. In 1825 the United States imported about $13 million worth of tea, coffee, and sugar. In 1900 such imports were worth about $163 million. In addition the nation imported $312 million worth of rubber, silk, wood, copper, tin, petroleum products, and other industrial raw materials that were not brought into the nation in 1800. In 1849 the United States had 123,025 factories, including hand and neighborhood industries. In 1899 such enterprises numbered 509,490. In 1800 the nation had no steel industry. In 1867 the United States produced 19,643 long tons of steel and in 1899, 10,639,857 long tons.

The electric light lengthened the day, indoor plumbing made life more comfortable, the refrigerated railroad car made food more wholesome and interesting, and the commuter rail and streetcar shortened the commute to work. Workers were probably better paid at the end of the century. But their hours were longer, and their jobs were often more dangerous owing to the machines and conditions of factory work. On the other hand, labor unions, which were illegal in 1800, were growing and redefining industrial society. Many union workers were employed by huge companies owned by stockholders with little interest in or direct contact with the conditions of employment. The corporation had been a rare and limited enterprise in 1800, but by the end of the century it dominated the economic landscape. Along the way such great entrepreneurs as Andrew Carnegie, John D. Rockefeller, and J. P. Morgan had become household names as they developed, rationalized, and dominated new industries.

Day-to-day life also changed. The homemade or handmade clothing of 1800 was replaced by mass-produced, factory-made clothing by 1899. The powdered wigs of 1800 were long forgotten, and new fashion trends for men and women altered appearance and style throughout the century. Shoes and shirts came from a department store or a mail-order catalog rather than from cobblers and tailors. Beards, limited to uncouth frontiersmen and a few religious minorities in 1800, were a common fashion statement at the end of the century even though new technology and distribution made shaving easier and safer. Food production and distribution was increasingly centralized. Beef and pork came from the packing centers of Chicago and Cincinnati rather than from local farmers and butchers, and flour, dried cereal, and other packaged foods were more readily available. Furniture was frequently manufactured rather than handcrafted. The telegraph, inexpensive and efficient postage, and, late in the century, the telephone facilitated communications. The penny press, the dime novel, photography, and the earliest motion pictures entertained Americans and disseminated the news.

By any measure, during the nineteenth century the United States reshaped itself from a tiny, powerless, fledgling republic into a huge, powerful, and rich democracy. Punctuated by wars of conquest and a civil war of enormous consequence and bloodshed, the nation became more democratic, more heterogeneous, and more powerful than anyone in 1800 could possibly have imagined. The twentieth century has been called "the American century," but the nineteenth century was "America's century"—a century of growth, expansion, massive change, and political development. It was the century that created the modern United States.

See also **American Indians; Cities and Urbanization; Civil War; Expansion; Immigration and Immigrants; Politics; Population; Race and Racial Thinking; Religion; Slavery; Transportation; Women; Work.**

Bibliography

Bureau of the Census. *Historical Statistics of the United States, Colonial Times to 1957*. Washington, D.C.: U.S. Government Printing Office, 1960.

PAUL FINKELMAN

NON-WESTERN RELIGIONS   The role of non-Western religions in the nineteenth-century United States must be perceived in a way that sharply distinguishes between the intellectual impact of the East on transcendentalists like Ralph Waldo Emerson and Henry Thoreau, or on a poet like Walt Whitman singing of a *Passage to India* (1871), and the quite different experience of immigrants from lands outside the Judeo-Christian orbit. The intellectual influence was institutionally symbolized by the formation in 1875 of the Theosophical Society in New York, which was dedicated to the study of wisdom both Eastern and Western, and above all by the 1873 Parliament of the World's Religion in Chicago, at which such figures as the Hindu swami Vivekananda and the Japanese Zen master Soyen Shaku dazzled Anglo-American audiences. Their presence led directly to the establishment of the first Ramakrishna Mission and Vedanta Society in New York in 1895 and to the founding of Western Zen centers shortly after the turn of the century. For the most part, however, nineteenth-century interest in Eastern religions by occidental Americans was intellectual and poetic rather than concerned with serious worship or practice. At the same time traditional practitioners of Asian religions were arriving on U.S. soil.

Until nearly the end of the century, most ethnic Asians in the United States were Chinese laborers brought to California after the gold rush of 1849 or their families and descendants. By the time the Chinese Exclusion Act of 1882 stopped immigration from East Asia, more than 100,000 Chinese were living in the United States, mostly on the West Coast. Apart from those few who encountered Christian missionaries, almost all were at least nominally adherents of the mix of Confucianism, Taoism, and Buddhism that is the traditional popular religion of China. The first Chinese temple in the popular style, with its characteristic mix of Buddhist and Taoist deities, opened in San Francisco in 1853. By the end of the nineteenth century some four hundred such temples had been founded on the West Coast. These temples were not so much places of congregational worship, except on major festivals like Chinese New Year, as of family-oriented funerals, memorial services, and special devotions. Nonetheless, like all churches and temples based in immigrant communities, they served as symbolic links to the home country, safe havens in a strange and often threatening land, and places where immigrants could congregate to socialize and informally discuss common concerns.

Japanese and Korean Buddhists worked in the sugar fields of Hawaii beginning in the 1880s. The first strictly Buddhist temple in what is now a part of the United States opened in Hilo, Hawaii, in 1889 and was brought under the U.S. flag with the annexation of Hawaii in 1898. This and other early Hawaiian temples were affiliated with the Pure Land (Jodo Shinshu) denomination, the school most active in missionary work among Japanese overseas populations. As Japanese immigrants reached the West Coast at the end of the century, Pure Land missionaries founded the first mainland Japanese Buddhist temple in San Francisco in 1898, founded a Young Men's Buddhist Association (patterned on the Young Men's Christian Association) the same year, and established the Jodo Shinshu Buddhist Mission to North America (later the Buddhist Churches of America) in 1899. The churches of this denomination were firmly rooted in the Japanese American community while boldly adapting Western, particularly Protestant Christian, styles of worship, youth work, and church organization. These religious centers offered community life and symbolic ties to the motherland and at the same time presented powerful modes for assimilation.

Hinduism made a significant impact on American intellectual life in the nineteenth century. Transcendentalists such as Emerson and Thoreau made frequent favorable references to early translations of the Upanishads and the Bhagavad Gita. However, few ethic Hindus, Sikhs, or adherents of other Indian religions made their way to the United States until the 1890s. Little evidence of organized Hindu or Sikh worship exists apart from the rather Protestantized version of it presented by the Vedanta societies.

A scattering of Muslims has long lived in the United States. These included slaves from Islamized regions of Africa, and late in the nineteenth century a growing number of immigrant Levantine merchants. However, the Islamic religion in the United States was generally unorganized until after 1900. The only nineteenth-century mosque was built in New York in 1893 by Alexander Russell Webb, an Anglo-American convert. Webb also began a periodical, *Muslim World,* and was the sole representative of Islam at the Chicago Parliament of Religions, also in 1893.

Nineteenth-century Americans were profoundly aware of non-Western religions as spiritual alternatives and as a growing presence in their traditionally Christian homeland. But it was not until the very end of that century that the spiritual pluralism that marked the next century began to take visible and institutional shape.

See also **Immigration and Immigrants,** *subentries on* **The Ottoman Empire and the Middle East, Asia; Religion,** *subentry on* **Religion in Nineteenth-Century America; Transcendentalism.**

Bibliography
Ellwood, Robert S., ed. *Eastern Spirituality in America.* New York: Paulist Press, 1987.
Haddad, Yvonne Yazbeck. *The Muslims of America.* New York: Oxford University Press, 1991.
Layman, Emma McCloy. *Buddhism in America.* Chicago: Nelson-Hall, 1976.

ROBERT S. ELLWOOD

NORTH AFRICA, FOREIGN RELATIONS WITH. See **Barbary War.**

NORTH CAROLINA At the beginning of the nineteenth century North Carolina was overwhelm-

ingly rural, but by the time the Civil War erupted, the state had experienced significant changes. In 1838 the federal government removed most of the Cherokees, the last major tribe of native Carolinians to control a section of the state, marching them to Indian Territory. Using funds from the sale of more than one thousand square miles of territory that formerly belonged to the Cherokees, the state launched an aggressive campaign of internal improvements. By 1860 almost nine hundred miles of railroads and five hundred miles of plank roads or "farmers' railroads" were in operation. The North Carolina legislature also created a Literary Fund in 1837, and by 1860 the state had built more than twenty-five hundred common schools. Additionally, owing to the private construction of thirty-nine cotton mills and nine woolen mills, the state assumed responsibility during the Civil War for clothing its own troops, an agreement effected by no other Confederate state.

Despite these changes, North Carolina remained primarily rural in 1860, and the vast majority of whites engaged in self-sufficient farming. Most of the large plantations and the slaves who made them possible were concentrated in the southeast near Wilmington, the state's major port. Rice was the main plantation crop. The eastern coastal plain was the next most commercialized region, where farmers, planters, and slaves grew tobacco, cotton, and corn. Commercial agriculture penetrated the piedmont, and slave owning became more concentrated there in the 1850s. The least commercialized area with the smallest slave population was the mountainous west. Despite regional differences, most whites probably supported slavery, although 70 percent did not own any slaves. Abolitionist sentiment was prevalent in only four northern piedmont counties, Randolph, Guilford, Davidson, and Forsyth, the home of Quakers, Moravians, and Wesleyan Methodists.

Although yeomen prevailed numerically in antebellum North Carolina, political, economic, and social power lay largely in the hands of the wealthy. Even though the state constitution was revised in 1835, few of the democratic reforms that were sweeping the South were included, apart from the popular election of the governor. Thus while rivalry between Democrats and Whigs was intense during the thirty years before the Civil War, the state legislature in 1860 had the highest percentage of slaveholders and one of the highest percentages of planters of any southern state. North Carolina avoided overt class conflict primarily because "the rich largely dominated what the poor largely ignored" (Escott and Crow, "The Social Order and Violent Disorder," p. 400).

The Civil War drastically altered this situation. Although forty thousand North Carolinians sacrificed their lives for the Confederacy, wartime hardships produced noncooperation and resistance among the neutral and the disaffected, who questioned the war's legitimacy from the outset. The state had the highest death rate among its soldiers and the highest desertion rate of any Confederate state. A peace movement emerged in 1863 and produced a candidate for governor in 1864.

This disaffection lived on after the war in the Republican Party, which formed in the state in 1867. A successful, biracial Republican Party in the piedmont drew opposition from a virulent Ku Klux Klan, which contributed to the Republican defeat in 1870. Yet strong support from mountain whites and from African Americans in eastern North Carolina produced a Grand Old Party (GOP) that remained vibrant until the end of the nineteenth century. The Democrats who had led North Carolina into the Civil War lost their bid for reelection in 1862. Former Whigs regained control, and renaming themselves Democrats after the war, they continued in power, losing control only in 1868 and in 1896.

As former Whigs, the postwar Democrats helped spearhead a drive for greater industrialization, and by 1920 North Carolina was the leading industrial state in the South. Especially in the piedmont, textile, tobacco, and furniture industries arose. Capital for industrialization accrued to creditors, especially rural merchants, as agricultural prices declined in the 1870s and 1880s and then plummeted in the depression of the 1890s. Yeomen, who had commercialized their farms in the wake of the war and were now losing them, and landless whites, who swelled the ranks of tenant farmers, provided labor for the mills. Most African Americans remained mired in sharecropping in eastern North Carolina, though some in the piedmont worked in tobacco factories.

As Whigs-turned-Democrats continued to promote industrialization, many farmers joined the Populist Party. In 1896 a coalition of Populists and Republicans (Fusionists) won control of all three branches of state government. Democrats returned to power with venomous white supremacy campaigns in 1898 and 1900. African Americans were disfranchised, the Republican Party was shattered, voter turnout declined, and segregation laws were enacted.

See also **Appalachia; Civil War,** *subentry on* **Consequences of the Civil War; Democratic Party; Ku Klux Klan; Reconstruction,** *subentry on* **The South; Republican Party; South, The.**

Bibliography

Clayton, Thomas H. *Close to the Land: The Way We Lived in North Carolina, 1820–1870.* Chapel Hill: University of North Carolina Press, 1983.

Escott, Paul D., and Jeffrey J. Crow. "The Social Order and Violent Disorder: An Analysis of North Carolina in the Revolution and the Civil War." *Journal of Southern History* 52 (August 1986): 373–402.

Hall, Jacquelyn Dowd, et al. *Like a Family: The Making of a Southern Cotton Mill World.* Chapel Hill: University of North Carolina Press, 1987.

Kenzer, Robert C. *Kinship and Neighborhood in a Southern Community: Orange County, North Carolina, 1849–1881.* Knoxville: University of Tennessee Press, 1987.

Kruman, Marc W. *Parties and Politics in North Carolina, 1836–1865.* Baton Rouge: Louisiana State University Press, 1983.

Lefler, Hugh Talmage, and Albert Ray Newsome. *North Carolina: The History of a Southern State.* Chapel Hill: University of North Carolina Press, 1973.

Nathans, Sydney. *The Quest for Progress: The Way We Lived in North Carolina, 1870–1920.* Chapel Hill: University of North Carolina Press, 1983.

Watson, Harry L. *An Independent People: The Way We Lived in North Carolina, 1770–1820.* Chapel Hill: University of North Carolina Press, 1983.

GAIL W. O'BRIEN

NORTH DAKOTA   North Dakota's topography was shaped largely by glacial action during the Ice Age. Most of the state is either gently rolling drift prairie or glacial lake bed. Through recorded history North Dakota has been subhumid grassland, generally averaging between fifteen and twenty inches of precipitation per year, with a continental climate and wide temperature ranges.

At the beginning of the nineteenth century the future state was inhabited mainly by the Mandans, Hidatsas, and Arikaras, who farmed along the Missouri River; the Ojibwas, who lived mainly in the northeast; and several bands of Dakotas (Sioux), who ranged throughout the region.

Fur traders had entered North Dakota as early as 1738, and by 1800 a vigorous trade existed among the Mandans, Ojibwas, North West Company, and Hudson's Bay Company. Much of this trade was carried out by métis, the offspring of European fathers and Ojibwa mothers. The North West Company post at Pembina, founded in 1801, was the first European settlement in the future state.

The American purchase of the Louisiana Territory was followed by the visit to North Dakota of Meriwether Lewis and William Clark, who wintered at the Mandan villages in 1804–1805. In the Convention of 1818 with England, drawing the boundary between the United States and Canada at the forty-ninth parallel, the United States surrendered part of the Missouri River drainage in return for the southern half of the Red River Valley.

North Dakota became part of Dakota Territory in 1861, but settlement was impeded by the hostility of the Dakotas, the difficulty of transportation, and the forbidding climate. Following the Sioux Uprising of 1862 in Minnesota, the military launched a series of expeditions and built a number of small posts in North Dakota. By 1877 most of the Dakotas were confined to reservations. The transportation problem was addressed when the Northern Pacific Railroad crossed the Red River at Fargo in 1871 and built westward toward Bismarck. In 1878 what became the Great Northern Railroad also entered the state, providing transportation to the northern part of the area.

The Cass-Cheney bonanza farm—an establishment of over 13,000 acres founded west of Fargo in 1875 and farmed by hundreds of workers using scores of pieces of machinery—demonstrated the practicality of spring wheat production in North Dakota. This resulted in an influx of settlers to eastern and central North Dakota that swelled the population from 16,000 to 152,000 between 1878 and 1885. Farther west, in the Little Missouri country, Theodore Roosevelt and other open-range cattle ranchers established enterprises.

Dependent on wheat production, economically oriented to Minneapolis and St. Paul, Minnesota, politically dominated by the railroads, and peopled mainly by Canadian, Norwegian, and German immigrants, the northern part of Dakota Territory diverged increasingly from the southern part. In 1889 Congress split the territory in two and admitted both Dakotas to the Union. By 1900 North Dakota had a population of 319,146.

The new state was overwhelmingly Republican, but that fact obscured significant factional divisions, especially between conservatives led by railroad lobbyist Alexander McKenzie and agrarian reformers in the Farmers' Alliance. These divisions continued well beyond the end of the century as the state struggled with the implications of a colonial, commodity-based economy in a remote and difficult environment.

See also **American Indian Societies,** *subentry on* **The Plains; Fur Trade.**

Bibliography

Lamar, Howard R. *Dakota Territory, 1861–1889: A Study of Frontier Politics.* New Haven, Conn.: Yale University Press, 1956.

Robinson, Elwyn B. *History of North Dakota.* Lincoln: University of Nebraska Press, 1966.

Wilkins, Robert P., and Wynona Huchette Wilkins. *North Dakota: A Bicentennial History.* New York: Norton, 1977.

DAVID B. DANBOM

NORTHERN EUROPEAN IMMIGRANTS. See **Immigration and Immigrants,** subentry on **Scandinavia and Finland.**

NORTHWEST TERRITORY   The Northwest Territory, the first national territory, comprised the present-day states of Ohio, Indiana, Illinois, Michigan, Wisconsin, and parts of Minnesota. The territory's creation was a consequence of the creation of the United States. Great Britain ceded its claims to the region in 1783, and the commonwealth of Virginia followed suit a year later. Congress then passed several acts to facilitate land sales and to organize a government, establishing the authority of the United States in fact as well as theory. Most important was the Northwest Ordinance of 1787, which guaranteed certain rights to residents of the region, notably public education, freedom of worship, and the abolition of slavery, in return for their submission to congressional authority in the organization of territorial governments and the sale of public lands.

American Indians hotly disputed the bold claims of the U.S. government and its encroaching citizens. The Miamis, Delawares, Shawnees, and other tribes insisted that the Ohio River was an inviolable boundary. Supported by the British, the Indians asserted their position with great skill in the early 1790s, defeating two American armies in the process. The embarrassed administration of President George Washington brought the full force of the Legion of the United States to bear against the Indians, and the British, unwilling to risk a war with the Americans, deserted them. Defeated at Fallen Timbers in August 1794, most of the Indians signed the Treaty of Greenville in August 1795, exchanging two-thirds of what would become the state of Ohio for peace and a guarantee of annual payments.

Americans moved into the southern reaches of the Northwest Territory so quickly that Congress divided it in 1800, creating the Indiana Territory to the west of a line drawn from the mouth of the Kentucky River north (and slightly east) to the Canadian border. Three years later Congress authorized the admission of Ohio into the United States. Indiana became a state in 1816, Illinois in 1818, Michigan in 1837, Wisconsin in 1848, and Minnesota in 1858. The statehood movements tended to follow a pattern established in Ohio, where calls for local independence and popular democracy were met for a time with objections about taxation and the qualifications of people for the rights and responsibilities of American citizenship.

Slavery was an issue of great importance in Indi-

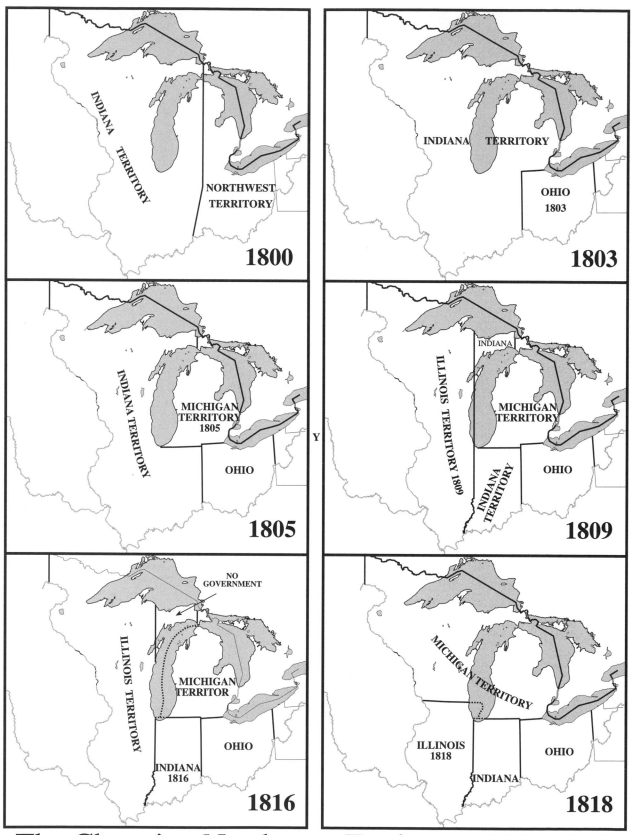

The Changing Northwest Territory, 1800–1818

ana and Illinois in the early 1800s. Many southern-born migrants wished to introduce the institution, and some flaunted the Northwest Ordinance's prohibition of it. In the end territorial voters rejected slavery, although their motivation was hardly altruistic. They did not want African Americans in their states, competing for jobs, creating a class of arrogant slaveholders, and threatening racial mixture.

The Northwest Territory was short-lived. It was also at least initially a creative fiction, since the United States did not conquer the region until years after claiming it. Its significance lies in the precedents established for the governance of future territories and their eventual admission to the Union as equal members.

See also **American Indian Societies,** *subentry on* **The Great Lakes; Midwest, The.**

Bibliography

Cayton, Andrew R. L. *Frontier Indiana*. Bloomington: Indiana University Press, 1996.
Dowd, Gregory Evans. *A Spirited Resistance: The North American Indian Struggle for Unity, 1745–1815*. Baltimore: Johns Hopkins University Press, 1992.
Finkelman, Paul. *Slavery and the Founders: Race and Liberty in the Age of Jefferson*. Armonk, N.Y.: M. E. Sharpe, 1996.
Onuf, Peter S. *Statehood and Union: A History of the Northwest Ordinance*. Bloomington: Indiana University Press, 1987.

ANDREW R. L. CAYTON

NORWEGIAN IMMIGRANTS. See **Immigration and Immigrants,** subentry on **Scandinavia and Finland.**

NULLIFICATION The constitutional theory called nullification held that individual states could set aside an unconstitutional act of the federal government by declaring such an act to be a nullity and interposing state authority between the federal authority and the state's citizens. Before the Civil War six attempts at nullification occurred in the United States. Two instances specifically were called nullifications at the time, and one attempt led to a constitutional crisis.

Instances of Nullification

The first instance of nullification involved the U.S. Supreme Court case of *Chisholm v. Georgia* (1793). Chisholm was the executor of the estate of a Tory whose lands had been confiscated by Georgia during the Revolutionary War. Chisholm sued in the federal courts to recover the lands under the restoration provisions of the peace treaty with Great Britain.

Georgia, objecting to the federal judiciary's taking jurisdiction on the grounds that this impinged on the state's sovereignty, refused to argue the case. With only Justice James Iredell dissenting, the Supreme Court found for Chisholm. The justices held that in regard to the judicial power of the United States, the states had surrendered their sovereignty in ratifying the Constitution.

Georgia refused to comply with the decision and contemplated violent resistance. Several states demanded that Congress submit for ratification the Eleventh Amendment, which restored sovereign immunity to the states. The amendment was ratified in 1795. The reaction to *Chisholm* did not articulate a theory of nullification, but it was at least an example of a protonullification, ultimately constitutionalized by the ratification of an amendment.

The theory of nullification was first proposed amid the political ferment that resulted from the passage of the Sedition Act (1798). Backed by the Federalists, this act added the common-law offense of seditious libel to federal criminal law. Vice President Thomas Jefferson in 1798 secretly wrote a resolution for the Kentucky legislature that claimed the act was unconstitutional because it exceeded the delegated powers, violated state prerogatives, and was directly repugnant to the First Amendment. James Madison prepared a somewhat similar resolution for the Virginia legislature. Although neither resolution used the term "nullification," the Virginia Resolution spoke of the right of each state to "interpose."

Both states passed new resolutions later in 1798 and in 1799, and the second Kentucky Resolution specifically cited nullification as a theoretical justification. The victory of the Jeffersonians in the election of 1800 and the lapse of the Sedition Act ended the crisis atmosphere, but the doctrine of nullification had been imperfectly but prominently announced. According to Jefferson, no ultimate interpreter of the Constitution was so designated, therefore states enjoyed an equal right to interpret when actions by the federal authorities were ultra vires, that is, beyond constitutional powers. When such illicit actions occur, Jefferson stated, a state has the right to nullify those acts and to interpose its force and authority between the citizenry and the national government.

In 1814, delegates from the New England states and observers from New York State met in the Hartford (Connecticut) Convention. In addition to proposing several constitutional reforms, the convention declared that these states would become neutral nonbelligerents and would no longer participate in the War of 1812. This constituted an attempt by these states to nullify a congressional declaration of war, but the rapid end of the war prevented a constitutional crisis.

The most famous instance was the so-called nullification crisis of 1832–1833, involving the federal government, the state of South Carolina, and the Tariff Act of 1828. This confrontation threatened secession and civil war nearly three decades before the election of Abraham Lincoln as president actually triggered those calamities.

The Tariff Act of 1828, called by its opponents the "Tariff of Abominations," spurred South Carolina to contemplate nullification. Initially passed through a parliamentary accident, this statute levied extremely high tariffs on foreign manufactures, alienating southern sympathies for the American System.

In 1828 John C. Calhoun anonymously penned the "South Carolina Exposition and Protest," which set down both the general theory of nullification and specific objections to the 1828 tariff. For four years South Carolina and the other southern states sought repeal or reduction of that tariff law without success. Finally in 1832, when a new tariff law failed to enact significant reforms, South Carolina reacted. A state convention voted to declare the tariffs of 1828 and 1832 null and void and to prevent their enforcement within the borders of the state. Military defenses were organized so the state could enforce its ordinance without federal interference.

President Andrew Jackson proposed a Force Bill that would authorize him to use the military to compel South Carolina's compliance with the tariffs. In the end violence was avoided by Senator Henry Clay's compromise, through which Congress passed both the Force Act and a ten-year reduction of the tariffs back to the levels of 1816.

South Carolina was forced to compromise largely because it failed to enlist the aid of any other states. Nevertheless, it may have been emboldened by its successful nullification of an international treaty in the seamen controversy, wherein it passed and enforced a Seamen Law that provided for the jailing of black sailors while their vessels were in South Carolina's ports. The object of this law was to prevent agitations for liberty and revolutionary conspiracies among the blacks of the state. Nevertheless the act clearly violated an Anglo-American treaty on the treatment of merchant seamen that, under the supremacy clause, Article VI, section 1, of the U.S. Constitution, was the supreme law of the land.

A fifth instance of nullification erupted in the reaction of the Wisconsin Supreme Court to the decisions of the U.S. Supreme Court in *Ableman v. Booth* (1859) and its related cases. One of the most severe clashes ever between federal and state judiciaries, this incident arose from an attempt to implement the Fugitive Slave Act of 1850.

In 1854 the fugitive slave Joshua Glover was captured in Racine by his owner, a Mr. B. S. Garland, and U.S. deputy marshall Stephen V. R. Ableman. Glover was subsequently freed from jail by a mob incited by Sherman Booth and John Rycraft, who were arrested but freed by a writ of habeas corpus issued by Judge A. D. Smith of the Wisconsin Supreme Court. In *In re Booth* (1854), Judge Smith held that the Fugitive Slave Act of 1850 was unconstitutional on the grounds that Article IV of the U.S. Constitution did not grant enforcement power to the federal government and on additional grounds that the 1850 act denied due process and jury trial to Glover.

After his release Booth was rearrested by federal authorities, and the whole Wisconsin Supreme Court in *Ex parte Booth* (1854) declined to interfere with the federal courts during the pendency of a federal criminal matter. After the federal conviction of Booth and Rycraft, however, the Wisconsin Supreme Court again ordered the pair freed on the basis of its original opinion of the unconstitutionality of the Fugitive Slave Act in *In re Booth and Rycraft* (1854).

The U.S. Supreme Court sought review on a writ of error, but the clerk of the Wisconsin court, on judicial instruction, refused to comply with the writ. In *United States v. Booth* (1855), the U.S. Supreme Court directly instructed the clerk to comply. U.S. chief justice Roger B. Taney wrote the Court's decision in *Ableman v. Booth*, holding that state courts could not free federal prisoners through writs of habeas corpus. Although rhetoric in the Wisconsin state case of *Ableman v. Booth* (1860) expressed some further resistance, the state supreme court split evenly on whether to accede to the federal appellate power. In the civil suit of *Arnold v. Booth* (1861) the state court refused to attempt to interfere in the jurisdiction of the federal district court.

Ableman v. Booth rang the death knell for judicial resistance to federal judicial power in the arena of fugitive slave law, although the accession to that authority in *Arnold v. Booth* was accompanied by a rhetoric of defiance. As in the case of *Chisholm, Ableman* was an attempt at nullification of a Supreme Court decision. In *Chisholm* the nullification was attempted by the state legislature, but in *Ableman*, the state supreme court was the instrument of nullification. It might be argued that the Georgia legislature was successful in its nullification owing to the ratification of the Eleventh Amendment, and that the Wisconsin Supreme Court was unsuccessful in its attempted nullification. Yet the ratifications of the Thirteenth, Fourteenth, and Fifteenth Amendments represented the triumph of the cause for which the Wisconsin court undertook its nullification attempt.

The Theory of Nullification

To the extent that nullification theory had any basis in reality, it was as an extralegal device envisioned by the framers of the Constitution as a potential act of rebellion justified only by a usurpation or an actual attempt to impose despotism. Calhoun attempted to transform nullification into an institutionalized legal doctrine by proposing that, if a state undertook to nullify a federal enactment, the various states could propose and ratify a constitutional amendment making the federal act unambiguously constitutional if they supported the enactment. If this occurred, the nullifying state would have to submit to the law or exercise its right to secede.

Calhoun's elaborate theory of nullification was alien to the thought of the constitutional framers and was most likely unworkable. But he did recognize the inadequacy of simple nullification, that the Union could not endure if each state were able to nullify any federal law as it saw fit. Under Calhoun's theory the Union could, in the long run, preserve the uniformity of its laws, and a nullifying state would ultimately face the loss of participation in the Union if it persisted in a stand repudiated by the substantial majorities required for a constitutional amendment.

See also **Constitutional Amendments; Constitutional Law; Courts, State and Federal; Federal-State Relations; Foreign Trade and Tariffs,** *subentry on* **The Politics of Tariffs; Fugitive Slave Laws; Slavery,** *subentry on* **Law of Slavery; Supreme Court.**

Bibliography

Cover, Robert M. *Justice Accused: Antislavery and the Judicial Process*. New Haven, Conn.: Yale University Press, 1975.

Ellis, Richard E. *The Union at Risk: Jacksonian Democracy, States' Rights, and the Nullification Crisis*. New York: Oxford University Press, 1987.

Finkelman, Paul. *An Imperfect Union: Slavery, Federalism, and Comity*. Chapel Hill: University of North Carolina Press, 1981.

Freehling, William W. *Prelude to Civil War: The Nullification Controversy in South Carolina, 1816–1836*. New York: Harper and Row, 1966.

Malone, Dumas. *Jefferson and the Ordeal of Liberty*. Boston: Little, Brown, 1962.

Morris, Thomas D. *Free Men All: The Personal Liberty Laws of the North, 1780–1861*. Baltimore: Johns Hopkins University Press, 1974.

Peterson, Merrill D. *Olive Branch and Sword: The Compromise of 1833*. Baton Rouge: Louisiana State University Press, 1982.

———. "Virginia and Kentucky Resolutions (1798–1799)." In *Encyclopedia of the American Constitution*. 4 vols. Edited by Leonard W. Levy, Kenneth L. Karst, and Dennis J. Mahoney. New York: Macmillan, 1986.

Wiecek, William M. "Nullification." In *Encyclopedia of the American Constitution*. 4 vols. Edited by Leonard W. Levy, Kenneth L. Karst, and Dennis J. Mahoney. New York: Macmillan, 1986.

PATRICK M. O'NEIL

O

OFFICES AND OFFICE WORK The nature of office work and the profile of office workers changed significantly over the course of the nineteenth century. From would-be male entrepreneurs and professionals to permanently salaried male and female employees, nineteenth-century office workers were the forerunners of modern American middle-class workers.

The economy of early nineteenth-century America was primarily agricultural. Market exchanges occurred mostly within local areas, frequently among people who knew each other as neighbors and friends. During the 1820s an expansion in domestic trade and the growth of inland cities fueled an increase in both manual production and industrial manufacturing. American workers produced shoes, hats, and textiles among other goods. By the late antebellum period a network of commission merchants, agents, wholesalers, and jobbers were selling these manufactured goods that more and more American workers were producing. These middlemen were increasingly using banks, insurance companies, and credit-reporting agencies for the services made necessary by the increase in trade.

Characteristically, these antebellum businesses operated on a small scale and required very few office workers. The owner could often make do with as few as one or two assistants in the office. In an environment with so few employees, the work was by necessity performed in a flexible and often informal manner. Clerks needed to be masters of many trades. Besides doing the bookkeeping and accounting, office workers sent out and paid bills, evaded creditors

when necessary, and performed any tasks necessary to keep the business running smoothly. In many offices the clerk might also be called upon to sweep the floor or run errands.

Not all offices were identical. Those that produced a considerable amount of paperwork, law offices for example, might hire a few clerks specifically as copyists. In the days before carbon paper and Xerox machines, men skilled in penmanship made multiple copies of important letters and documents. More common, however, were offices where one or two clerks performed a wide range of jobs, some clerical and others substantive.

Historians who have studied class formation in early nineteenth-century America have identified clerks as important members of the emerging middle class. At a time when skilled, independent artisans were beginning to fall into the ranks of permanently employed manual laborers, office workers were distinguishing themselves as members of this new middle class. Not only did clerks use their brains rather than their hands to earn a living, but—equally important—the promise of autonomy and independence remained within their reach.

In small antebellum offices, good clerks had to do more than push paper. Their duties required that they learn the businesses for which they worked, operating, in effect, as apprentices. Those who succeeded could hope for partnerships, or perhaps to gain enough knowledge and skill to begin businesses of their own. Office workers, therefore, maintained one of the cardinal characteristics of middle-class men—the ability, or at least the potential, to work for themselves. A male clerk was someone on his way to becoming an independent businessman, a professional, or an entrepreneur.

During and after the Civil War both office work and office workers began to change. The first modifications came within the federal government, which in the early 1860s began to hire women to perform some jobs in its offices in Washington, D.C. The war brought with it an expansion in the government's responsibilities, and some federal officials recognized that women provided a good source of cheap labor. At the same time many middle-class women found themselves needing a means of support. With few wage-earning possibilities available, women flocked to Washington in large numbers to take jobs as federal clerks.

Women's entry into government offices was not always smooth or easy. Many government officials and politicians were skeptical, wondering whether women's constitutions could withstand the strain of office life and whether women were able to comprehend the tasks required. More troubling, however, was the question of propriety. Women who became federal clerks crossed a barrier that had divided the worlds of men and women during much of the nineteenth century. While not all middle-class women remained cloistered by their firesides, certain segments of the public world, offices for example, remained decidedly male spaces. Female clerks encountered spittoons, cigars, and rough-talking men in the halls of government—the very things from which women were supposed to be protected. In addition many perceived new sexual dangers. Some people felt that only women of questionable character would put themselves in such an environment, while others worried that the experience of office work would corrupt innocent women. Women employed in the Treasury Department often were dubbed "treasury courtesans."

Given these attitudes, it is no surprise that the private sector was slow to follow the government's example. Not until the 1880s did a significant number of women begin to take jobs as clerical workers in private offices. Prompted by changes in the economy and the growth of new technologies, employers considered reorganizing the work in their offices and hiring female office workers.

The growth of large corporations during the last two decades of the century changed the face of American offices. No longer small, intimate, and informal, offices began to be organized more bureaucratically. The press of paperwork encouraged employers to subdivide clerical labor in much the same way that manual labor had been divided in the mid–nineteenth century. Large corporations employed clerks as ste-

nographers and copyists, and later as typists, bookkeepers, and file clerks. Rather than performing a wide range of tasks, as had early-nineteenth-century office workers, clerks increasingly worked at one job. As a result their work no longer required that they learn the business, and clerkships offered less opportunity for advancement. It became unlikely that a clerk would one day rise to own Armour and Company, the Chicago and Burlington Railroad, or the Metropolitan Life Insurance Company.

Instead, office workers became skilled at primarily—and often exclusively—clerical tasks. They might improve their positions by moving from one company to another, but their work did not afford them the expertise or knowledge to move into the executive suites and board rooms. Clerks became full-time salaried employees. Although fairly well-paid, male office workers lost the autonomy and independence so critical to the definition of middle-class masculinity.

For women the compartmentalization of office work meant more opportunities for employment but few chances for upward career mobility. Jobs were being created that required basic skills and little experience, presenting opportunities for those women with sufficient education to master the tasks. Mechanization of offices followed closely on the heels of the reorganization of clerical labor. Typewriters found their way into offices during the 1880s as employers and businesspeople looked for efficient ways to process increasing amounts of paperwork. Women who had previously done routine copying began to do routine typing.

Employers saw women as nimble-fingered but dull-minded employees who were well suited to repetitive tasks and who would willingly accept less money than their male counterparts. Moreover, many believed that women held no career aspirations and only took office jobs to fill a hiatus before marriage. They regarded women as the ideal labor force to take over the mechanized, routinized aspects of office work.

The work and workplaces of women and men remained segregated in most nineteenth-century offices. Operating certain machines, such as typewriters, quickly became categorized as "women's work." Women, with their polite manners and pleasing voices, also became telephone operators. Other new technologies, like calculating and counting machines, remained within men's purview. Women copied, classified, and filed; men calculated and reconciled.

Certainly not all offices had been compartmentalized, mechanized, or feminized by the end of the century. Only about one-quarter of the nation's clerical workers were women. Many office workers continued to work in small offices, to labor at a range of tasks, and, if they were men, to hope to move from clerkship to entrepreneurship. But the future of office work was clearly established. Large, bureaucratically organized companies employed armies of office workers to staff their businesses. Hired for their skills rather than their knowledge, clerks worked in increasingly mechanized offices. Male and female office workers had distinct career paths. The former found more opportunity and higher pay, and the latter were relegated to the less demanding, lower paid, more routinized jobs.

See also **Corporations and Big Business; Labor Force; Small Businesses; Women,** *subentry on* **Women's Labor; Work,** *subentry on* **Middle-Class Occupations.**

Bibliography

Aron, Cindy S. *Ladies and Gentlemen of the Civil Service: Middle-Class Workers in Victorian America.* New York: Oxford University Press, 1987.

Blumin, Stuart M. *The Emergence of the Middle Class: Social Experience in the American City, 1760–1900.* Cambridge, U.K.: Cambridge University Press, 1989.

Cohen, Miriam. *Workshop to Office: Two Generations of Italian Women in New York City, 1900–1950.* Ithaca, N.Y.: Cornell University Press, 1993.

Davies, Margery W. *Woman's Place Is at the Typewriter: Office Work and Office Workers, 1870–1930.* Philadelphia: Temple University Press, 1982.

Kocka, Jürgen. *White-Collar Workers in America, 1890–1940: A Social-Political History in International Perspective.* Translated by Maura Kealey. London: Sage, 1980.

Ryan, Mary P. *Cradle of the Middle Class: The Family in Oneida County, New York, 1790–1865.* Cambridge, U.K.: Cambridge University Press, 1981.

Strom, Sharon Hartman. *Beyond the Typewriter: Gender, Class, and the Origins of Modern American Office Work, 1900–1930.* Urbana: University of Illinois Press, 1992.

Zunz, Olivier. *Making America Corporate, 1870–1920.* Chicago: University of Chicago Press, 1990.

CINDY S. ARON

OHIO   Ohio, the first state born in the nineteenth century and the first admitted under the Northwest Ordinance, had by the end of that century achieved political, economic, and social significance enjoyed by few other states in the federal union. Ohio derives its name from the Iroquoian word *oyo,* meaning "great," a reference to the Ohio River, which forms the state's southern boundary. Between the river and Lake Erie to the north, Ohio is topographically quite flat, with the highest point only 1,550 feet and the lowest 440 feet above sea level. The mean temperature is 52.7 degrees Fahrenheit, and rainfall averages thirty-eight inches.

The Native Americans

In the late eighteenth century the Indians of Ohio included the Wyandots and Ottawas in the valleys of the Maumee and Sandusky Rivers, Mingos and others of Iroquoian blood in the upper Ohio Valley, Delawares in the Muskingum watershed, Shawnees in the valley of the Scioto, and Miamis along the rivers of western Ohio. Siding with the French during the French and Indian War (1756–1763) and with the British during the American Revolution (1775–1783), most of Ohio's tribes looked upon the frontiersmen who crossed the Allegheny Mountains and the Ohio River into their homeland as the primary threat to their way of life. Led by Little Turtle, chief of the Miamis, the tribes fought unsuccessfully to halt white migration in the Indian Wars of 1790–1795. The Treaty of Greenville, which ended those wars, opened southern and eastern Ohio to permanent settlement. Subsequent treaties eroded Indian claims in northwestern Ohio until finally, in 1843, with the removal of the Wyandots from their reserved lands along the Sandusky River, no Indian lands remained in Ohio.

The Birth of a State

Though organized settlements in the Northwest Territory had been made in 1788 at Marietta and Cincinnati (Losantiville) under the provisions of the Ordinance of 1787, it was the Treaty of Greenville that sparked a tidal wave of migration to the Ohio country. Settlers from New England, following the lakeshore, poured into Connecticut's Western Reserve in northeastern Ohio. Those from the Middle Atlantic states and the South, following the Ohio River and its tributaries, journeyed to southern Ohio, particularly the Virginia Military District. Cleveland, Chillicothe, and Dayton were settled in 1796; Columbus and Athens, in 1797; and Youngstown, in 1798. So considerable was the migration that in April 1802 Congress authorized the election of delegates to a state constitutional convention. Drafted that November in Chillicothe (the third capital of the Northwest Territory, following Marietta and Cincinnati), the Ohio Constitution of 1802 concentrated power in the hands of the state legislature, a reaction to the arbitrary rule of the Federalist territorial governor, Arthur St. Clair. (In 1851 a second constitution, still in effect today though many times amended, provided a more balanced distribution of power among executive, legislative, and judicial branches of government.) In March 1803, in the same stone building in Chillicothe that had been the capitol of the Northwest Territory, the government of the state of Ohio, the seventeenth state in the federal union, began to function. A Jeffersonian Republican, Edward Tiffin, was the first governor, supported by substantial Republican majorities in both houses of the General Assembly. The state capital remained at Chillicothe until 1810, when it was moved to Zanesville. It returned to Chillicothe in 1812 and moved to Columbus in 1816, where it has remained.

The War of 1812

Expansionist interest in neighboring Canada as well as continued British intrigue with America's Indians assured the support of most Ohioans for war with England in June 1812. Much of the war was fought on Ohio land and in Ohio water. In the most significant naval action of the entire conflict—the Battle of Lake Erie at Put-in-Bay in September 1813—Commodore Oliver Hazard Perry's victory ended British control of the Great Lakes. The war ended in stalemate, but it also ended British intrigue with the Indians and assured the neutralization of the Great Lakes along the U.S.-Canadian border.

Canals and Railroads

Beneath the forest that covered most of Ohio was soil so fertile, particularly in the north and west, that most settlers turned to farming for their livelihood. Once the trees had been cleared, wheat, corn, oats, rye, barley, tobacco, pork, beef, and dairy products were produced in abundance, but getting surpluses of these commodities to market on trails across the mountains to the east and south was extremely difficult. Though the National Road, built across Ohio between 1825 and 1840, presaged a network of roadways in all parts of the state, canals linking the Great Lakes and the Ohio-Mississippi river system constituted a more immediate solution for Ohio's transportation needs.

With the completion of the Erie Canal across New York in 1825, construction began on two Ohio canals, the Ohio and Erie, to connect Cleveland on Lake Erie with Portsmouth on the Ohio River, and the Miami and Erie, to connect Toledo and Cincinnati. Though a short-lived boundary "war" with Michigan in 1835 over rival claims on Toledo prolonged work on the Miami and Erie, the canals were completed by 1845. Produce from the interior regions of the state now had access to the markets of the world through the port cities of New York and New Orleans. Reflecting increasing prosperity, the population of Ohio surged from 581,434 in 1820 to 2,339,511 in 1860, third behind New York and Pennsylvania.

By 1860 the canals were experiencing competition from a new form of transportation that would soon displace them, the railroads. Beginning in 1836 with the Erie and Kalamazoo (connecting Toledo with Adrian, Michigan) and in 1838 with the Sandusky and Mad River (connecting Sandusky with Springfield), Ohio was soon crisscrossed with ribbons of steel. By the end of the century, every Ohio county seat but one had a rail connection, and in total railway mileage Ohio was ranked second among the states. In 1913 Ohio's canals were finally closed.

The Abolitionist Crusade and the Civil War

By the 1830s a railroad of another sort had made its appearance in Ohio. Sharing 436 miles of common border along the Ohio River with Kentucky and Virginia, both slave states, Ohio represented the shortest distance between slavery in the Upper South and freedom through fugitive slave laws in Canada. The "Underground Railroad" emerged to help runaway slaves, through a covert network of stations, reach Canada and freedom. No northern state had more stations or helped more runaways than Ohio. And no state had more abolitionist leaders of consequence than Ohio, including John Brown, Harriet Beecher Stowe, Levi Coffin, Benjamin Lundy, James G. Birney, John Rankin, and John Parker.

After a new Republican Party emerged in the wake of the Kansas-Nebraska Act of 1854, Ohio elected a Republican governor, Salmon P. Chase, in 1855. When Abraham Lincoln became president and the Civil War began at Fort Sumter, South Carolina, Ohio sent the first militia regiments into the South, invading the thirty-four westernmost counties of Virginia that emerged in 1863 as the new state of West Virginia. And Ohio contributed some of the foremost generals to the Union cause, including Ulysses S. Grant, Philip H. Sheridan, and William Tecumseh Sherman.

Industrialization and the Rise of the Cities

Not only was the Union preserved and slavery ended, but the Civil War also accelerated profound economic change. Before the war Ohio had led the nation in agricultural production. But during the conflict demand for the materials of war stimulated the development of a number of industrial centers across the state. In the years that followed, the processes of industrialization and urbanization continued, until by 1900 Ohio had become one of the three principal industrial states in the nation. Though farming continued to be the occupation of the majority, an increasing number of Ohioans turned to industry for their livelihood. Cleveland, a sleepy canal town of eighteen thousand in 1850, became a major industrial center of more than three hundred thousand by 1900. Leading its transformation were such captains of industry as Samuel Mather, in steel and shipping; Marcus A. Hanna, in coal; Amasa Stone, in railroading; and John D. Rockefeller, in oil. Akron emerged as the nation's rubber capital by century's end, thanks to Benjamin F. Goodrich, Frank Seiberling, and Harvey Firestone. Toledo became the glass capital through the leadership of Edward Libbey, Michael Owens, and Edward Ford. In Cincinnati, William Procter and James Gamble developed the world's largest soap-manufacturing company. John Henry Patterson made Dayton and cash registers virtually synonymous. The combination of productive agriculture and expanding industry made Ohio attractive as a place to live and work; its population reached 4,157,545 by 1900.

Mother of Presidents

As one of the most populous states in the Union (assuring a large bloc of delegates both at national nominating conventions and in the electoral college); as a state that was a leader in both agriculture and industry; and as one of the most Republican of all the states in an era of Republican hegemony, Ohio produced more presidents than all other states combined in the late nineteenth century. Of the seven men who served as president between 1869 and 1901, five were Ohioans. All five were veterans of the Civil War: Ulysses S. Grant (1869–1877); Rutherford B. Hayes (1877–1881); James A. Garfield (1881); Benjamin Harrison (1889–1893); and William McKinley (1897–1901). In the early twentieth century two other men from Ohio went to the White House: William Howard Taft (1909–1913) and Warren G. Harding (1921–1923).

See also **American Indian Societies,** *subentry on* **The Great Lakes; Cincinnati; Northwest Territory; Underground Railroad; War of 1812.**

Bibliography

Cayton, Andrew. *The Frontier Republic: Ideology and Politics in the Ohio Country, 1780–1825*. Kent, Ohio: Kent State University Press, 1986.

Havighurst, Walter. *Ohio: A Bicentennial History*. New York: Norton, 1976.

Knepper, George W. *Ohio and Its People*. 2d ed. Kent, Ohio: Kent State University Press, 1997.

Murdock, Eugene C. *The Buckeye Empire: An Illustrated History of Ohio Enterprise*. Northridge, Calif.: Windsor, 1988.

Roseboom, Eugene H., and Francis P. Weisenburger. *A History of Ohio*. Edited by James H. Rodabaugh. Columbus: Ohio Historical Society, 1967.

Scheiber, Harry N. *Ohio Canal Era: A Case Study of Government and the Economy*. Athens, Ohio: Ohio University Press, 1969.

Wittke, Carl, ed. *History of the State of Ohio* 6 vols. Columbus: Ohio Historical Society, 1941–1944.

PHILLIP R. SHRIVER

OIL.   See **Petroleum.**

OKLAHOMA.   See **Indian Territory.**

ORATORS AND ORATORY   From Thomas Jefferson's presidential inaugural address of 1801, which helped steer the young republic through the modern world's first democratic transfer of power, to Theodore Roosevelt's "Strenuous Life" speech of 1899, which articulated the vibrancy of a secure and increasingly industrialized nation, oratory played a central role in virtually every facet of nineteenth-century American life. The power of the spoken word was felt in all regions of the country and among all social classes. Political leaders used it to conduct the business of the nation, reformers to confront a host of social evils, preachers to build churches and save souls, public lecturers to edify a people hungry for knowledge. "The highest bribes are at the feet of the successful orator," exclaimed Ralph Waldo Emerson. "All other fames must hush before his. He is the true potentate."

In no setting was this more true than the U.S. Congress, which produced, in the years between 1820 and 1860, the most concentrated outpouring of political eloquence in the nation's history. It was the golden age of American oratory. The speeches of Henry Clay, John C. Calhoun, Daniel Webster, Robert Hayne, Charles Sumner, Thomas Hart Benton, Stephen Douglas, and others drew swarms of listeners to the Senate gallery and were regularly reprinted in newspapers and magazines for all to read and discuss. Arguably the greatest oratorical contest in the history of Congress occurred in late January 1830 when Webster and Hayne clashed over the nature of the Union and the meaning of the Constitution. Twenty years later, the nation's attention was fixed on Webster, Clay, and Calhoun as the great triumvirate debated compromise measures that would forestall civil war for another decade.

Congress continued to produce its share of notable speeches after the Civil War, but changes in political culture, as well as in congressional procedures, afforded fewer opportunities for the kind of grand debates that occurred in the antebellum era. During the war years, however, Abraham Lincoln produced three of the most celebrated presidential speeches in all of American history. Presented in the midst of the secession crisis, his first inaugural address masterfully delineated the constitutional issues in such a way as to place responsibility for civil war squarely and unequivocally on the South. The Gettysburg Address, regarded today as the finest speech in the English language, played a key role in redefining the war from a contest to save the union to a quest to free the slaves and perfect the principles of American democracy. Lincoln's second inaugural address, delivered at the end of the war, invoked God's judgment on America for the long existence of slavery and sought to lay the foundation for a just and lasting peace in the principles of charity and forgiveness. While it would be another half century before Theodore Roosevelt transformed the presidency into a "bully pulpit," Lincoln wielded the rhetorical power of his office with an eloquence unmatched by any chief executive before or since.

Virtually all the century's major reform movements were fueled by the spoken word, and none more so than abolitionism. Shortly after its creation in December 1833, the American Anti-Slavery Society created its agency system. Soon the first group of agents was in the field, moving from town to town, village to village, lecturing about the evils of slavery and the moral necessity of abolition. By all accounts, the most effectual speaker in this group was Theodore Weld. His powers of persuasion were legendary, but after two years in the field, he had lost most of his voice. Thereupon he turned to training the next wave of agents, known as "The Seventy," whose efforts allowed the AASS to boast of more than 1,300 subsidiary societies, with more than 250,000 members, by the end of 1838. Over the next two decades, a galaxy of talented speakers that included Wendell Phillips, Theodore Parker, Frederick Douglass, Charles Lenox Remond, and Henry B. Stanton expanded and strengthened the hold of abolitionist organizations and ideas throughout the North.

After the Civil War, African American speakers such as Douglass, Alexander Crummell, Henry McNeal Turner, and T. Thomas Fortune took the lead in championing the cause of equal rights for the freed slaves. Possessing a powerful intellect, a thunderous voice, and a charismatic platform presence, Douglass was the acknowledged spokesman for his race until his death in 1895. He was succeeded in that role by Booker T. Washington, the president of Tuskegee Institute, who rose to national prominence on the strength of his Atlanta Exposition Address of September 1895. Stressing the need for economic development while eschewing political agitation and social equality between the races, Washington hoped to ally the future of southern blacks with the region's dreams of industrial progress. In contrast to Washington's public silence on many of the injustices facing his race, during the 1890s the African American journalist Ida B. Wells led what is often referred to as a one-woman crusade against lynching. Her powerful and scrupulously documented speeches gained her national fame and remain one of the most compelling bodies of discourse indicting this heinous crime.

Nor was Wells the only female orator to raise her voice in behalf of social and political justice. Before the 1830s few dared violate the social and religious prescriptions against women speaking in public. But commitment to the antislavery cause motivated Maria Stewart, Angelina Grimké, Abigail Kelley, and others of similar outlook to defy tradition and speak publicly on behalf of the slave. Faced with ridicule for violating social norms, these women were forced to defend their right to speak in public. In the course of doing so, they began to articulate a rationale for women's rights. Justifying the right of women to speak in public proved to be an important precursor to the organized movement for women's suffrage, which drew on the oratorical abilities of such advocates as Elizabeth Cady Stanton, Susan B. Anthony, Sojourner Truth, Lucy Stone, and Ernestine Rose. Most enduring of the countless orations in behalf of suffrage was Stanton's "The Solitude of Self" (1892), in which she justified giving women the vote by arguing that every human soul must be fit for independent action.

Religion, like politics, was inextricably bound up with the oratorical culture of the nineteenth century. As wave after wave of religious revivals swept across the land at regular intervals, thousands of people gathered in rural camp meetings and urban churches alike to hear evangelical preachers ranging from itinerant exhorters to such luminaries as Charles Finney and Dwight Moody. It was also through sermons and addresses that William Ellery Channing and Theodore Parker articulated the doctrines of religious liberalism. Later in the nineteenth century the sermons of Henry Van Dyke and Washington Gladden helped spread the creed of Christian service to the poor and dispossessed that came to be called the social gospel. Foremost among the century's pulpit orators was Henry Ward Beecher, whom Sinclair Lewis dubbed "a combination of St. Augustine, Barnum, and John Barrymore." A major figure on the national stage for four decades, Beecher captivated the congregation of Brooklyn's Plymouth Church as well as lecture audiences at home and abroad with his magnetic delivery and message of humanistic religion, evolutionary theology, and social reform.

In addition to its political and religious functions, oratory served as a means of education and entertainment. Beginning in the mid-1820s with the development of the Lyceum movement of community-

The Orator as Presidential Candidate. A promotional poster outlining the platform of William Jennings Bryan for the election of 1900. The phrases "no crown of thorns" and "no cross of gold" refer to Bryan's famous speech at the 1896 Democratic convention. LIBRARY OF CONGRESS

based adult education, the lecture platform provided a highly visible, and lucrative, venue for speakers throughout the rest of the century. Many lectures were educational in tone and content; others focused on consequential social, political, or religious issues; some were pure dross and sensationalism. But whether connected with the Lyceum or the Chautauqua circuit that sprang up in the last quarter of the century, scores of professional speakers gained great popularity by taking their talents to towns in every corner of the land. Major lecturers before the Civil War included Wendell Phillips, Ralph Waldo Emerson, Edward Everett, Horace Greeley, James Russell Lowell, and Oliver Wendell Holmes. Phillips, who was known as the King of the Lyceum, continued to tour regularly until the late 1870s, presenting popular lectures such as "The Lost Arts" and promoting a variety of reform causes from women's rights and labor reform to temperance and freedom for Ireland.

In 1884 Russell Conwell, whose platform appeal rivaled that of Phillips, founded Temple University with the profits from his perennially popular "Acres of Diamonds," which he presented, with little variation, as many as 200 times a year for more than five decades. Other stars of the Gilded Age lecture circuit included Mark Twain, Robert G. Ingersoll, Chauncey Depew, Anna Dickinson, Robert B. Gough, and Mary A. Livermore.

Although contemporaries often bemoaned the fallen state of American public address in the decades after the Civil War, it is clear from the vantage point of history that while the tone, tenor, and topics of public discourse changed with time, oratory remained a vital part of the American experience throughout the nineteenth century. As William Jennings Bryan, himself one of the century's most storied speakers, stated in 1906, "As long as there are human rights to be defended . . . as long as there are great interests to be guarded; as long as the welfare of nations is a matter for discussion, so long will public speaking have its place."

See also **Congress; Lyceums.**

Bibliography

Baskerville, Barnet. *The People's Voice: The Orator in American Society.* Lexington: University Press of Kentucky, 1979.

Benson, Thomas W., ed. *Rhetoric and Political Culture in Nineteenth-Century America.* East Lansing: Michigan State University Press, 1997.

Campbell, Karlyn Kohrs. *Man Cannot Speak for Her.* 2 vols. New York: Praeger, 1989.

Cmiel, Kenneth. *Democratic Eloquence: The Fight over Popular Speech in Nineteenth-Century America.* Berkeley: University of California Press, 1990.

Duffy, Bernard K, and Halford R. Ryan, eds. *American Orators before 1900: Critical Studies and Sources.* New York: Greenwood, 1987.

STEPHEN E. LUCAS
SUSAN ZAESKE

OREGON The state of Oregon was originally a part of the Oregon Country, which extended from the forty-second parallel to 54° 40′ and from the Rocky Mountains to the Pacific Ocean. The major geographical features of the state are the coast and Cascade Mountains running from north to south and the Columbia River on the north. East of the Cascades the climate is colder and drier than in the area to the west. The major linguistic stocks of the native peoples who occupied this area were Oregon Coast Penutian, including Chinookan and Kalapuya, and Athapascan west of the Cascades, and Sahaptin and northern Paiute east of the Cascades. Americans had engaged in the maritime fur trade beginning with Robert Gray in 1788, but the first U.S. citizens who resided for long in the area were the members of the Lewis and Clark expedition who lived at Fort Clatsop, near the mouth of the Columbia River, from November 1805 to March 1806.

The first American beaver fur–trading company was John Jacob Astor's Pacific Fur Company, which had its base at Astoria from 1811 to 1813. It was bought out by the British North West Company, which in turn was absorbed by the Hudson's Bay Company (HBC) in 1821. The HBC dominated the economy of the region until 1846 but later coexisted with American missionaries and farmers. The first missionaries were Methodists led by Jason Lee, who arrived in the Willamette Valley in 1834. The Catholic missionaries François Blanchet and Modeste Demers came to this fertile region in 1838. By the early 1840s the first pioneers came over the Oregon Trail from the Middle West in search of economic opportunities, to escape ill health, and to seek adventure. Some justified their 2,000-mile journey, which took four to six months, according to the tenets of Manifest Destiny, a belief that they were doing the will of God in extending the American empire. The agricultural pioneers settled first in the Willamette Valley and later east of the Cascades. The gold rush in California stimulated exports of wheat, beef, and lumber to that state after 1848 and gave Oregon a viable economy. A gold rush to southern Oregon began in 1851 and to eastern Oregon in 1862. These developments made Portland the principal city in the state as it became the hub of transportation routes to California and within Oregon.

The advent of the pioneers and the businessmen destroyed many of the American Indian peoples. Disease introduced by the fur traders took heavy tolls. Wars were fought in southern Oregon in the 1850s, and Oregon was also the location of wars with the Modoc Indians (1872), the Nez Percé (1877), and the Bannock (1878). As the Euro-Americans encroached upon their lands, the Indians were placed on reservations. The Warm Springs (1855), Umatilla (1855), Grande Ronde (1855), and Klamath (1864) reservations were to be "schools," where federal agents and clergy would convert the Indians to white culture. The results were disastrous. The native peoples lost much of their culture without gaining acceptance into the white world.

In 1846 the Oregon Country was divided at the forty-ninth parallel between Great Britain and the United States, largely because of the growing numbers of American settlers. In 1848 Oregon became a federal territory, from which Washington was separated in 1853, and in 1859 Oregon entered the Union as the thirty-third state. The 1860 census counted 52,465 residents. Oregon was little touched by the Civil War, and few of its citizens fought in the conflict. Most notable of those who did fight was Edward Baker, who had resigned from the U.S. Senate and was killed at Ball's Bluff, Virginia, while fighting for the Union.

The most important event after the Civil War was the completion of the Northern Pacific Railroad to Portland in 1883. This stimulated exports and imports, changed land use patterns, and brought larger numbers of immigrants to the state. With the railroad and increasing urbanization, political movements took on new forms after the Civil War. Grangers and Populists unsuccessfully attempted to obtain effective legislation regulating railroad and grain elevator rates, and prohibition and woman suffrage became significant movements, although they were not successful until the twentieth century. The most important newspaper—the *Portland Oregonian*, edited from 1870 to 1910 by Harvey Scott—had a national reputation. Oregon was a Democratic territory before the Civil War and a Republican state afterward, although the Democrats remained strong challengers. The most famous political Oregonians after Chief Joseph were Joseph Lane, who ran for the vice presidency on the John C. Breckinridge ticket in 1860, and Abigail Scott Duniway, a well-known woman suffrage leader. The population reached 413,536 in 1900.

See also **American Indian Societies,** *subentry on* **The Northwest Plateau; Fur Trade; Lewis and Clark Expedition.**

Bibliography

Dodds, Gordon B. *Oregon: A Bicentennial History.* New York: Norton, 1977.

O'Donnell, Terence. *That Balance So Rare: The Story of Oregon.* Portland: Oregon Historical Society Press, 1988.

Robbins, William G. *Landscapes of Promise: The Oregon Story, 1800–1840.* Seattle: University of Washington Press, 1997.

GORDON B. DODDS

ORPHANS AND ORPHANAGES   Orphans, not always parentless, were often simply the children of the poor. Similarly, orphanages were the institutional response to their poverty. Although dramatic events like cholera epidemics occasionally robbed children of both parents, most "orphans" had at least one parent who was unable to care for his or her child because of unemployment, physical or mental disability, or the death or desertion of a spouse. These parents asked that orphanages or orphan asylums care for their children. Timothy A. Hacsi, in *Second Home: Orphan Asylums and Poor Families in America* (1997), describes orphanages as "often the final desperate step in a series of attempts [by a parent] to deal with poverty brought on by some family calamity" (p. 143). Children might also be placed in orphanages by public officials who judged the parents negligent and incapable of caring for their offspring. Orphanages provided what the children's families could not: food, clothing, shelter, medical care, and some secular and religious education. In keeping with contemporary child-rearing practices, institutions attempted to discipline the children and to teach job skills so orphans could avoid their parents' poverty. Some children spent years in orphanages; most spent months or weeks. They usually rejoined their parents or relatives after families had been reconstituted or family fortunes had been recouped, but they were discharged from the orphanages at fifteen or sixteen regardless of their family situations.

Orphanages developed in a period when institutions seemed the solution to many problems, including poverty, and public poorhouses or almshouses were the first shelters for indigent children. Most entered with family members. In 1866 Ohio became the first state to encourage the removal of dependent children from these facilities, where the children were often housed with the ill, the insane, and with criminals. Subsequently many states sponsored public institutions, such as county homes or large state-managed schools, for dependent children. Some cities and other states, like New York and California, provided public subsidies to private orphanages. States, cities, and private organizations also established juvenile asylums or houses of refuge for delinquent children, although the distinctions between dependence and delinquency were never clear-cut.

The vast majority of orphanages were privately funded and staunchly sectarian, established by Protestants, Catholics, or Jews for their coreligionists. By 1860 Americans had founded almost 200 orphanages. Catholic dioceses, responding to their large immigrant and often impoverished constituencies, led the way until 1880. Orphanages sustained the religious traditions of Catholics and Jews against Protestant hegemony and at the same time eased the transition of immigrant children into American life.

Founded by local philanthropists, congregations, or dioceses, most orphanages were located in cities, where energetic religious rivalries existed and where the hazards of urban life created visible poverty and middle-class fears of social disorder and unrest. Most orphanages were near the neighborhoods of the families they served, and parents could visit their children and were supposed to contribute to their sup-

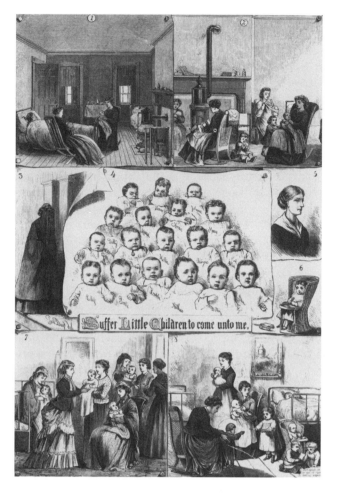

An Infant Asylum. Illustration from *Frank Leslie's Illustrated Newspaper,* 19 July 1873, of the New York Infant Asylum, No. 24 Clinton Place. The picture documents various stages of an orphan's life, including the arrival of the mother to bear the child, the activities of the orphans, and reception day. LIBRARY OF CONGRESS

port. Volunteer boards of local women managed the orphanages, raising funds, hiring staff, screening the families of applicants, and arranging for the placement and release of the children. Nuns performed these roles in Catholic orphanages.

A minority of orphanages placed children in boarding homes, where children were supposed to learn a skill or trade and help around the house or farm, a variation of the older custom of indenturing the poor. Most parents, however, preferred the orphanages to foster families who might win their children's love and loyalty. Less frequently, orphanages placed children for permanent adoption if all parental rights had been relinquished.

By 1890, due to the ravages of the Civil War, a series of economic downturns, and continued rapid urbanization, 564 orphanages housed 50,000 children. Only a few institutions were racially integrated. According to LeRoy Ashby, 27 orphanages served nonwhite children exclusively (*Endangered Children*, p. 64). Sectarianism persisted, and orphanages reflected the new waves of urban newcomers as the children of immigrants from southeastern Europe joined the children of Irish, German, and native-born Americans.

The mean population of orphanages in 1890 was 85 children, but Catholic and Jewish institutions on average sheltered 140 and 187 children, respectively, according to Hacsi (*Second Home*, p. 53). Some institutions were much larger. By the turn of the century the Jewish Orphan Asylum in Cleveland, Ohio, housed 500 children; the Hebrew Orphan Asylum in New York City housed about 1,000; and the New York Catholic Protectory housed more than 2,500.

These huge congregate facilities drew criticism from public and private social welfare administrators. Gathering annually at the National Conference on Charities and Corrections to exchange information and opinions about the rapidly proliferating private and public charitable agencies, these critics formed the vanguard of the emerging social work profession. They maintained that orphanages stifled the individuality of children and the initiative of parents, who allowed the children to be raised at public expense. Children, they believed, should be raised in private homes by their own families, and if this proved impossible, by foster families. Although the orphanages had their defenders, especially among Catholics, the preference for "home life" over institutional life became official social work doctrine at the 1909 White House Conference on Dependent Children. But child-care workers recognized how difficult it was for an indigent parent to raise a child and how difficult it was to find appropriate foster homes. In the 1910s the states intended to solve these problems and allow families to raise their own children at home by initiating mothers' or widows' pensions, the forerunners of Aid to Dependent Children.

In theory, the children of the poor were now the responsibility of the states, and orphanages should have disappeared. But the stipends were too small to support a family, and too few mothers were judged eligible to receive them. So the number and mean population of orphanages continued to grow through the 1910s as the newest immigrants, Orthodox Jews, for example, founded their own institutions. In 1933 the Great Depression forced a record number of the children of the poor, more than 140,000, into child-care institutions (U.S. Department of Commerce, *Children under Institutional Care and in Foster Homes, 1933*, p. 4). After the Social Security Act of 1935 created old age insurance, unemployment in-

Orphan Trains

Orphan trains were created as an alternative to orphanages and asylums for juvenile delinquents by the Reverend Charles Loring Brace, the founder of the New York Children's Aid Society. Alarmed by the thousands of homeless children earning their living on the streets of New York as newsboys, beggars, prostitutes, and petty criminals, Brace determined to remove these "dangerous classes" from the corrupting influences of urban life and their impoverished families. He believed that children could not be reformed in institutions, where regimentation and anonymity robbed inmates of initiative, preparing them badly for "practical life." His own solution to the children's poverty and delinquency was to send them by train to live on farms, where families would teach them Christian values and useful agricultural skills in the healthy outdoors in return for the children's labor. Parents often requested that Brace take their children, but the Children's Aid Society also recruited children from the alleys and tenements of New York.

From 1855 to 1929 the society placed out at least 150,000 children. Almost all were American or western European, very few of them were Catholic or Jewish, and almost none were black (Holt, *The Orphan Trains*, pp. 69–71). Adults accompanied these children on the train and arranged for their placement with obliging families at each stop. Children who could not be placed in one town would continue on to the next.

No legal contract bound the children and the families with whom they were placed; either party could withdraw from the arrangement. Families sent disobedient or disagreeable children away, and children often returned home or simply ran off. The society did little prior investigation of the receiving families and lost contact with the children after placement. Their own parents often could not find them again.

Some Catholic orphanages in Boston and New York also experimented with orphan trains. By 1900 these were replaced by "streetcar orphan trains," which took children to local churches, where parishioners were urged to take an orphan home.

As early as the 1870s Brace's critics pointed out that the "orphans" were sometimes abused and overworked. Brace's system came under increasing attack from the emerging social work profession for careless placement and supervision. The last of the orphan trains ran in 1929.

surance, and Aid to Dependent Children to mitigate the poverty and economic insecurity of families, orphanages finally ceased to shelter the children of the poor.

Modern historians, like nineteenth-century observers, disagree about how well orphanages cared for children. One argument concerns whether they were overcrowded, harsh, purely custodial institutions or sympathetic shelters that were at least better than the alternatives of homelessness and destitution. Another dispute centers on whether orphanages deliberately tore children from their families or hoped to preserve the families. Historians also debate the effectiveness of orphanages as child-care providers. Hacsi maintains that "more children whose families, including extended families, were for a time unable to care for them were helped in orphan asylums than by any other means" (*Second Home*, p. 1). Matthew A. Crenson argues that orphanages aided only a tiny fraction of the children in need (*Building the Invisible Orphanage*, p. 254).

The hundreds of orphanages, large and small, represented the vast ethnic, religious, and geographic diversity of nineteenth-century America. Although the care of dependent children would take different forms in the twentieth century, nineteenth-century orphanages established that such care was a significant community responsibility.

See also **Asylums; Domestic Life; Hobos, Tramps, and the Homeless; Life Cycle,** *subentry on* **Childhood and Adolescence; Welfare and Charity; Work,** *subentry on* **Child Labor.**

Bibliography

Ashby, LeRoy. *Endangered Children: Dependency, Neglect, and Abuse in American History.* New York: Twayne, 1997.

———. *Saving the Waifs: Reformers and Dependent Children, 1890–1917.* Philadelphia: Temple University Press, 1984.

Bogen, Hyman. *The Luckiest Orphans: A History of the Hebrew Orphan Asylum of New York.* Urbana: University of Illinois Press, 1992.

Cmiel, Kenneth. *A Home of Another Kind: One Chicago Orphanage and the Tangle of Child Welfare.* Chicago: University of Chicago Press, 1995.

Crenson, Matthew A. *Building the Invisible Orphanage: A Prehistory of the American Welfare System.* Cambridge, Mass.: Harvard University Press, 1998.

Folks, Homer. *The Care of Destitute, Neglected, and Delinquent Children.* New York and London: Macmillan, 1902.

Friedman, Reena Sigman. *These Are Our Children: Jewish Orphanages in the United States, 1880–1925.* Hanover, N.H.: University Press of New England for Brandeis University Press, 1994.

Goldstein, Howard. *The Home on Gorham Street and the Voices of Its Children.* Tuscaloosa: University of Alabama Press, 1996.

Hacsi, Timothy A. *Second Home: Orphan Asylums and Poor Families in America.* Cambridge, Mass.: Harvard University Press, 1997.

Holloran, Peter C. *Boston's Wayward Children: Social Services for Homeless Children, 1830–1930.* London and Cranbury, N.J.: Associated University Presses, 1989.

Holt, Marilyn Irvin. *The Orphan Trains: Placing Out in America.* Lincoln: University of Nebraska Press, 1992.

Polster, Gary Edward. *Inside Looking Out: The Cleveland Jewish Orphan Asylum, 1868–1924.* Kent, Ohio: Kent State University Press, 1990.

U.S. Department of Commerce, Bureau of the Census. *Children under Institutional Care and in Foster Homes, 1933.* Washington, D.C. 1935.

Zmora, Nurith. *Orphanages Reconsidered: Child Care Institutions in Progressive Era Baltimore.* Philadelphia: Temple University Press, 1994.

MARIAN J. MORTON

OUTLAWS

OUTLAWS   The outlaw was a major component of the romantic image of life on the desolate, untamed American frontier. The exploits of American outlaws, while not unique in relation to the activities of ruffians and lawbreakers in any region or period, were transformed into semiheroic deeds of admirable but flawed men. This cultural phenomenon, which began with the dime novels of the late 1800s, continued to flourish during the twentieth century. The modern-day infatuation with outlaws began with the European legend of Robin Hood, which itself was an exaggeration of the real-life exploits of a Scottish bandit named Robert Hod.

After the Civil War, with westward expansion reaching the Pacific coast, the age of the outlaw in the American West began. Although crime increased throughout the country during the last quarter of the nineteenth century, lawlessness was especially central to life on the frontier. Many outlaws had fought in the Civil War or were cultural products of it: guerrilla leaders such as William Quantrill and "Bloody Bill" Anderson carved out careers that were mimicked by bandits in the late nineteenth century.

Two of Quantrill's protégés became the most feared outlaws on the frontier. Frank and Jesse James, along with Cole Younger, organized the James-Younger gang, a band of frontier ruffians who robbed several banks and murdered nearly a dozen people across the Midwest. The 1870s, during which criminal activity escalated, was the period of the greatest number of successful bank and train robberies committed by the James and Younger brothers. In 1876, after six members of the gang were killed or captured during a bank robbery in Northfield, Minnesota, Jesse and Frank James were limited to small-time train robberies. But their exploits fueled the romanticized stories about the American West.

Although several hundred individuals helped to create the legend of the outlaw, a few affected its propagation more than most. James "Wild Bill" Hickok, John Wesley Hardin, Clay Allison, and Sam Bass, whose capture by Texas Rangers is reenacted annually in Round Rock, Texas, figured prominently in the development of the gunfighter mystique. Robert Leroy Parker and Harry Longabaugh, better known as Butch Cassidy and the Sundance Kid, had careers as bank robbers that captured the public's imagination. Most legendary, however, was Henry McCarty, who achieved hero status as William Bonney or Billy the Kid. Billy died when he was twenty-two and was involved in only half a dozen gunfights; thus his reputation as the deadliest man in the West may have been the most exaggerated outlaw legend of the century.

The western figure who was most successful at forging a positive image from questionable activities such as gambling and cattle rustling was Wyatt Earp. He and his brothers became the most famous clan of western personalities. In 1881 the Earp brothers, who sometimes served as peace officers, sparked the legendary shootout at the O.K. Corral in Tombstone, Arizona. Like many of his contemporaries, Wyatt Earp was an opportunist who contributed to his legendary status by publishing an account of his own exploits.

Bandits in other parts of the country also contributed to the public's following of outlaw activities. In Mississippi and Tennessee, highwaymen along the Natchez Trace were infamous for raiding merchants' wagons and stealing the earnings of flatboatmen who had sold their wares after transporting them down the Mississippi River. In contrast to the typical western gunfighter, these larcenists were not surrounded with a quasi-positive aura: both law enforcement personnel and the citizenry demanded their capture. Natchez Trace bandits, led by Samuel Mason and Wiley Harpe, were active thieves before the introduction of the steamboat *New Orleans* in 1811; after that year, and especially by 1830, decreased traffic along the Trace resulted in fewer criminal incidents in the region.

Rivermen who worked on the Ohio and Mississippi Rivers came closer to the mystique of the western gunfighter than did the land-based highwaymen in Mississippi and Tennessee. Rivermen were perceived as rough, independent "Jacksonian men": they worked hard, drank heavily, and gambled fervently. The river cities of New Orleans, Natchez, and St. Louis became centers of activity for these men, who rarely committed crimes but whose exploits could easily be romanticized.

The most famous water-based personality in outlaw lore was Jean Laffite. Based in the swampy Barataria region of southeastern Louisiana, he became a hero after his men helped Andrew Jackson win the Battle of New Orleans in 1815. Neither Laffite's mysterious allegiances nor his confrontations with political leaders diminished his stature as a hero of the common classes. Laffite's legend as an American Robin Hood, like that of the western gunfighters, has persisted throughout succeeding generations.

That the popularity of shady characters, whether gunfighters, highwaymen, or pirates, continues to capture the public's interest is a testament to the cultural fiber within which the outlaw legend was born. Outlawry—both in deed and in legend—was one of the distinct features of nineteenth-century American culture.

See also **Crime; Gunfighters.**

Bibliography

Allen, Michael. *Western Rivermen, 1763–1861: Ohio and Mississippi Boatmen and the Myth of the Alligator Horse.* Baton Rouge: Louisiana State University Press, 1990.
Boessenecker, John. *Gold Dust and Gunsmoke: Tales of Gold Rush Outlaws, Gunfighters, Lawmen, and Vigilantes.* New York: Wiley, 1999.
Prassel, Frank Richard. *The Great American Outlaw: A Legacy of Fact and Fiction.* Norman: University of Oklahoma Press, 1993.
Seal, Graham. *The Outlaw Legend: A Cultural Tradition in Britain, America, and Australia.* New York: Cambridge University Press, 1996.

KEVIN ROBERTS

OVERSEAS POSSESSIONS

OVERSEAS POSSESSIONS   The acquisition of overseas possessions by the United States occurred at the end of the nineteenth century as a result of the expansionist impulses of the 1890s and the victorious outcome of the Spanish-American War. The administration of President Ulysses S. Grant attempted to annex the Dominican Republic, but Congress blocked it. By the end of the century, as policymakers focused on a possible canal across Central America and expanded trade and influence in Asia, the issue of bases and potential possessions emerged as a central concern for presidents and Congress.

Hawaii

The Hawaiian Islands were the first overseas territory to fall under U.S. control. In 1893 a rebellion toppled the Hawaiian monarchy, and President Benjamin Harrison signed an annexation treaty with the new government. Grover Cleveland repudiated the pact when he took office later that year, and Congress

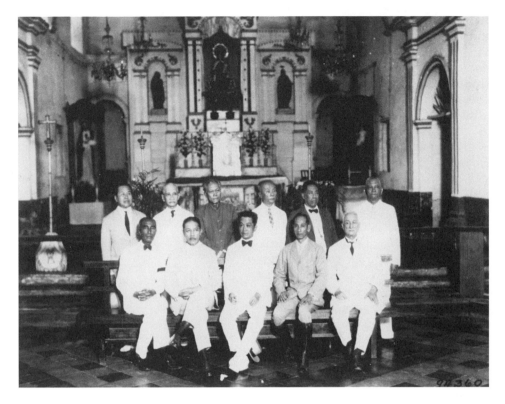

Philippine Independence Leaders. General Emilio Aguinaldo *(seated, center)* and ten of the delegates to the first Assembly of Representatives that passed the Constitución Política de la República Filipina on 21 January 1899. Photographed in 1929. NATIONAL ARCHIVES

left the situation as it was. Four years later William McKinley sought to gain congressional support for an annexation treaty, but lawmakers again hesitated. Only with the outbreak of the Spanish-American War in April 1898 was McKinley able to induce Congress, as a wartime measure, to annex Hawaii by a resolution of both houses.

Guam, Puerto Rico, and Cuba

The defeat of Spain in August 1898 brought more new territories under American sovereignty. The Treaty of Paris (December 1898) ceded Puerto Rico, Guam, and the Philippines to the United States. In the case of Guam, no particular controversy developed over its new situation. The Foraker Act (1900) established Puerto Rico as unorganized territory whose residents were not deemed to be full citizens of the United States. As for Cuba, over which the war had originally been fought, the Teller Amendment (1898) barred annexation, and Washington settled for a political dependency relationship with a nominally independent Cuba through the Platt Amendment (1901).

The Philippines

The major focus of controversy regarding overseas possessions at the end of the century was the Philippine Islands. Attacked by Commodore George Dewey on 1 May 1898, the archipelago was viewed first as a potential bargaining chip in wartime negotiations with Spain. As the American military presence broadened during the summer of 1898, however, the McKinley administration became persuaded that the islands could not be returned to Spain. With the prospect of the Philippines coming under the control of either Japan or Germany, the idea of allowing the inhabitants of the islands to determine their own destiny seemed unwise to American leaders. A consensus developed in the McKinley administration that it would be best to acquire the Philippines as a whole and administer them as a possession of the United States. That was the outcome envisioned after the signing of the peace treaty.

Filipinos under the leadership of Emilio Aguinaldo saw the matter in more nationalistic terms, and they rose up against American forces in February 1899. The ensuing conflict lasted for more than two and a half years. The Filipinos, unable to defeat the Americans in conventional battles, waged a guerrilla campaign that saw savagery and atrocities on both sides. By 1901 the Filipino revolt had largely been ended, but the experience tempered American enthusiasm for further imperialistic adventures.

While waging war against the insurrection, the McKinley administration put in place a civil government for the Philippines. In 1899 the president named a civilian commission that visited the islands and began the process of establishing a framework for a colonial government. Early in 1900 McKinley dispatched a second commission, headed by William Howard Taft, that endeavored to govern the islands during the rest of the year. To clarify the authority of the commission and its rulings, Congress adopted the Spooner Amendment in early 1901 to create the post of governor-general for the Philippines. Once the measure was adopted McKinley named Taft as the first governor-general; his term began on 4 July 1901.

The problems of subduing the Philippine uprising reduced American enthusiasm for acquiring additional overseas possessions as the nineteenth century ended. Puerto Rico and the Philippines were deemed to be possessions of the United States, but their in-habitants were not full citizens of the nation. The Supreme Court upheld this doctrine in the Insular Cases (1901–1922). American expansionism produced a kind of constitutional empire that blended direct rule of the peoples involved with some of the procedural safeguards granted to American citizens. This mixed result reflected the ambiguity and tentativeness of the way in which the United States became a world power at the end of the nineteenth century.

See also **Expansion; Foreign Relations,** *subentry on* **1865–1914; Hawaii; Puerto Rico; Spanish-American War; Virgin Islands.**

Bibliography

Campbell, Charles S. *The Transformation of American Foreign Relations, 1865–1900*. New York: Harper and Row, 1976.

Fry, Joseph A. "Phases of Empire: Late-Nineteenth-Century U.S. Foreign Relations." In *The Gilded Age: Essays on the Origins of Modern America*, edited by Charles W. Calhoun. Wilmington, Del.: Scholarly Resources, 1996.

Gould, Lewis L. *The Presidency of William McKinley*. Lawrence: University Press of Kansas, 1980.

LEWIS L. GOULD

P

PAINTING Nineteenth-century American art may be divided into three periods: the Federal Period, which began with the close of the Revolutionary War and ended with the election of Andrew Jackson to the presidency in 1828; the Jacksonian Period, which extended to 1865; and the Gilded Age, which completed the century but, some scholars would say, lasted to 1913, the year the Armory Show in New York City introduced modernism to the United States.

The Federal Period: 1780s–1828

The American Revolution brought a cultural revolution in addition to political liberation from England. The young Republic expressed its spirit strongly in neoclassicism in the arts (a revival of the classical styles of ancient Greece and Rome), especially in architecture and sculpture but also in painting. An artistic nationalism arose, and Americans searched for a national character in the arts. As in colonial times, portraiture was the popular and practical genre, and painters preferred the founding leaders of the country as subjects. Art museums and academies, such as the Peale Museum in Philadelphia, the American Academy of Arts and Sciences in Cambridge, Massachusetts, and the National Academy of Design in New York were founded during the Federal Period. Instead of becoming wholly neoclassical, American painters, feeling independent, explored new areas, including the still life, history

painting to document revolutionary events, nature themes, mythology and allegories, landscape, panorama, genre, and trompe l'oeil (deception) painting.

By 1800 American painting demonstrated two main styles, neoclassicism and romanticism. The older, established painters, such as Charles Willson Peale, Gilbert Stuart, John Trumbull, and Robert Fulton, studied these styles with Benjamin West (1732–1820), an American-born artist who had been exploring neoclassicism and romanticism at the Royal Academy of Art in London since the 1760s. Younger artists, born during the American Revolution or later, chose art centers other than London during their European travels. John Vanderlyn traveled throughout Europe but spent more time in Paris and Rome than elsewhere. Washington Allston spent some time in London with West, but his trips to Italy had a strong impact on his romantic nature.

Peale (1741–1827) is representative of Federal Period painters in his exploration of various subjects in addition to his portraits of American leaders. Peale trained under West from 1767 to 1769 and then returned home. He painted George Washington as a general and as a president. Peale's brother James Peale, also a painter, specialized in miniatures, small portraits on ivory. Both Peale brothers taught their children to paint, and at least eighteen Peales became famous, among them Sarah Miriam Peale and Margaretta Angelica Peale.

Charles Peale had vast interests as a naturalist and an excavator of prehistoric animals. In addition to running the family art studio, he directed his own museum in Philadelphia, where he collected likenesses of the aging founders of the United States. He arranged sittings with Washington, during which many of his children also painted the famous leader. In an early portrait, *George Washington after the Battle of Princeton*, oil on canvas (c. 1779), Peale conformed to the typical American style with his linear, sharpedged forms. While he represented Washington in the proper, formal manner of the English, Peale's experiments with new subjects influenced his children and other young American painters. His portrait of two of his sons, *The Staircase Group*, oil on canvas (1795), was conceived as a trompe l'oeil, a painting intended to make the viewer believe the two-dimensional image is real. The portrait is life scale, and his sons stand at the turn of an early colonial-style staircase that spirals upward behind a wall. Peale framed the painting with a real door frame and placed a real wooden step at the bottom of the painting to complete the illusion that his sons are actually standing on the stairs. Another experiment, *Mastodon Excavation*, oil on canvas (1808), combines history painting, actual portraits of individuals involved in a historic event, and genre painting. *Artist's Studio*, oil on canvas (1822), is both a self-portrait and a perspective of the Peale Museum interior, in which Peale dramatically opens a curtain to reveal the curiosities of the museum.

The Peale children painted a variety of subjects. Rembrandt Peale (1778–1860) specialized in portraiture, sometimes employing trompe l'oeil effects. For instance, *George Washington*, the "Porthole Portrait," oil on canvas (c. 1802), appears to be mounted behind an extravagant, oval aperture made of stone. Raphaelle Peale (1774–1825) preferred still life, which was new to the United States.

Trumbull (1756–1843) painted historical, religious, and landscape subjects in addition to portraits. He studied history painting with West in London between 1780 and 1789, returning in 1794 and 1808. Four of Trumbull's history paintings, commissioned in 1817, hang in the rotunda of the U.S. Capitol. While all of these works illustrate American history texts, perhaps the most recognizable is *Declaration of Independence, July 4, 1776*, oil on canvas, twelve feet by eighteen feet (c. 1820), which is reproduced on the back of the U.S. $2 bill. He used the neoclassical approach to composition with his symmetrical frieze of notables, who are sharply delineated, like sculptures.

For a period of time Vanderlyn (1775–1852) was probably the strictest American neoclassicist. Rather than in London, he chose to study art in Paris, where Jacques-Louis David, founder of French neoclassi-

Charles Willson Peale, *The Staircase Group: Raphaelle and Titian Ramsay Peale*. Oil on canvas, 1795. Philadelphia Museum of Art. © FRANCIS G. MAYER/CORBIS

cism, headed the French Academy of Art. *Marius amid the Ruins of Carthage*, oil on canvas (1806), is a portrait of a republican Roman general of the period 155–186 B.C. This subject impressed Napoleon, who awarded it a gold medal at the Paris Salon of 1808.

Allston (1779–1843) also painted a few neoclassical subjects, but he is better remembered as the most romantic painter in the United States during the Federal Period. He spent time in the German Nazarene colony outside Rome, where he was influenced by their spiritual rendering of nature in landscape subjects. He traveled throughout Europe and spent some time with West in London, where he absorbed the aesthetic category of the sublime that Edmond Burke introduced in eighteenth-century England. The sublime depicts the inadequacy of humans in the face of an awesome nature. Artists usually depicted the stormy side of nature with people at its mercy, as in Allston's *Elijah in the Desert*, oil on canvas (1818), and *Ship in a Squall*, oil on canvas (1837). Another remarkable landscape by Allston depicts a different romantic mood, *Moonlit Landscape*, oil on canvas (1819). Perhaps the earliest American moonlight painting, it is a quiet, peaceful setting with figures representing no specific narrative or allegory.

Landscapes were the most successful experiment during the Federal Period and were immensely popular by the mid–nineteenth century. Early landscapes in the United States were wide, information-oriented views designed to convey knowledge of the area's geographic features. The topographic view was still popular at the beginning of the Federal Period, but it began to lose its wide, horizontal format. An example is *A Winter Scene in Brooklyn*, oil on canvas (1820), by Francis Guy, the first American painter to have a one-person exhibition of landscapes. While Trumbull and Vanderlyn both painted Niagara Falls in the topographic-view tradition, Vanderlyn added a dead tree as a picturesque element, which anticipated the tastes of the mid–nineteenth century. Vanderlyn also experimented with a subcategory of landscape, the panorama. A panorama is a large-scale painting designed to fit a rotunda. The viewer standing in the center is surrounded by the painting and, turning around, has a 360-degree view. Vanderlyn's panorama of Versailles and gardens in France (1819) measures 12 feet in height by 165 feet in circumference.

Rubens Peale, who painted the stuffed birds in the Peale Museum, and John James Audubon (1785–1851), a Creole born in Santo Domingo, also became naturalists. Audubon spent much of his life in the wild, recording the birds and mammals of America in pen and watercolor. *Black-billed Cuckoo* (1822) (figure 4) appeared in his first printed volume in 1827. He traveled to Europe to supervise the printing of huge volumes on birds and mammals.

The Jacksonian Period: 1828–1865

With the election of Jackson as president in 1828, a new cultural era began in the United States. Most of the revolutionary leaders had died, and westward expansion had pushed beyond the Mississippi River. The West joined the North and the South as a regional force in the mid–nineteenth century and gave the United States a new sense of identity and nationalism. With the democratization of culture, the government increasingly supported art. Mass circulation through prints, plaster copies, traveling exhibitions, and traveling panoramas made art accessible to the new cities of the West. Neoclassicism and romanticism continued to prevail, and neoclassicism still dominated in architecture and sculpture, as it had during the Federal Period. Genre and western subjects replaced the portrait in popularity as industrialization and urbanization spread west.

Landscape painting matured during the mid–nineteenth century. Initially a few independent painters exhibited landscapes of the disappearing wilderness of the Northeast. Never organized as a formal group, these painters became known as the Hudson River school, made up of three distinct groups. The first group, 1820s–1850s, included Thomas Doughty, Thomas Cole, and Asher Brown Durand. The second group, 1850s–1870s, was called the luminists and included John Kensett and Martin Johnson Heade. The third group, 1850s–1870s, included John Kensett, Frederick E. Church, and Albert Bierstadt.

American landscape painting followed two romantic traditions, the sublime and the picturesque. The picturesque tradition depicts domesticated landscapes in an asymmetrical, lyric manner. Artists created various moods, and the first generation of the Hudson River school often produced allegorical pieces. Cole (1801–1848) combined elements of the sublime with his picturesque views of the American wilderness. His *Landscape with Dead Tree*, oil on canvas (1828), is both factual, with specific tree trunks in the foreground that Cole sketched on trips, and generalized, representing the cycle of life in nature. He also produced imaginative landscape allegories, such as *The Voyage of Life*, oil on canvas (1840), a series of four canvases dedicated to the cycle of life.

The luminists were influenced by the invention of the camera and strived for factual, hard realism pervaded by a poetry of light, which inspired the term "luminism" in 1854. Luminism is an attitude toward light and things in nature. It is a realistic tradition that goes beyond realism to encompass superreal overtones. Luminist paintings tend to be smaller than the first-generation Hudson River school paintings, yet they are filled with more realistic details. Most of the subjects depict coastal areas from Maine to Connecticut, such as *Schooners before Approaching Storm off Owl's Head, Maine,* oil on canvas (1860), by Fritz Hugh Lane. Some painters of this group expanded their subjects from the Northeast to scenes in South America, such as Heade's series of hummingbirds and exotic flowers of Brazilian jungles.

The third generation of the Hudson River school painted the monumental "epic landscapes." Like the luminists, this group was interested in realism and lighting, eliminating the brown overtones of the first generation. These artists painted subjects in the Far West and in wildernesses around the world. Church (1826–1900), for example, traveled to Virginia, the upper Mississippi, Colombia, Ecuador, Panama, Mexico, Jamaica, Newfoundland, and countries in the Mediterranean and the Near East. In 1858 Bierstadt (1830–1902) traveled with Frederick Lander's army expedition to the Wyoming Rockies, Lake Tahoe, and the giant redwoods of the West Coast. Congress paid ten thousand dollars each for a number of Bierstadt's paintings, including *The Rocky Mountains,* oil on canvas (1863).

Genre subjects, which depict common people in everyday activities, also peaked during the Jacksonian Period. Nathaniel Currier and James Merritt Ives established a lithography firm that popularized genre subjects through works paying tribute to American baseball, steamboat races, farm scenes of all seasons, and pioneers in the West. William S. Mount was one of the most successful genre painters who dwelled on rural Americana scenes. The most famous of his works, *The Power of Music,* oil on canvas (1847), is one of the series of barn paintings he began in 1831 depicting musicians and dancers on the barn floor. This particular painting, as in all genre subjects, expresses the prevailing American social attitudes of the time. A black man listening to the music remains outside the barn door, knowing he is not accepted socially on the dance floor. A branch of genre called western painting evolved during the Federal Period and reached its height during the Jacksonian Period. These painters specialized in western subjects, such as the everyday life of cowboys, wilderness characters, and Indians. A mid-century painter, George Caleb Bingham (1811–1879) grew up in frontier Missouri and painted western subjects. *Fur Traders Descending the Missouri River,* oil on canvas (1845), is typical of his pictures of frontier men. He also painted raftsmen and politicians in rural Missouri. Other painters traveled into the West to paint the last American Indians in the wild. George Catlin (1796–1872) lived with Indians for eight years and put together a portfolio of portraits and daily activities of Native Americans. In Rock Island, Illinois, in 1832, for example, he recorded Black Hawk's last powwow east of the Mississippi River before relocating his tribe on the west side. C. M. Russell and Frederic Remington extended the taste for western painting into the late nineteenth century.

The Gilded Age: 1865–1913

In 1860 the United States was still largely an agricultural society, yet by 1900 the nation was the leading industrial power in the world. The 1860 population of thirty million people grew to seventy-six million by 1900, fifteen million of whom were recent immigrants. After the Civil War old and new industries expanded. Cities grew, drawing workers in from rural America along with immigrants. America's rapid expansion posed new problems in the equitable distribution of wealth, recurring depressions, and fraud at the public expense in the private sector and in government. Mark Twain named this period the "Gilded Age." Art activity expanded in the postwar era with other aspects of American culture. American artists began to study abroad in new art centers like Munich and Düsseldorf in addition to Paris. This period experienced the establishment of several art museums, art institutions, art schools, and art collecting among the new rich, and the number of art dealers and artists increased. While aesthetic tastes were still roughly divided between late neoclassicism, realism, and romanticism, the public accepted a broader range of expression among independent artists.

While the luminists and the third generation of the Hudson River school dominated landscape painting without interruption until about 1870, a group of independent landscape painters introduced wider concepts. George Inness (1825–1894) started out in 1845 in the tradition of Church, but by the end of the 1860s he added brushwork, more atmosphere, and unique poetic touches to create picturesque, romantic displays of inner emotion, such as *The Coming Storm,* oil on canvas (1878). A landscape group known as the "Ten," consisting of John Henry Twachtman, Childe Hassam, Julian Weir, Theodore Robinson, and others, introduced impressionism to the United States. They experimented with impressionism in Paris and continued American impressionism into the twentieth century. Hassam (1859–1935) studied art in Paris in 1886, then returned to New York City, where he painted New England and urban scenes. *Washington Arch in Spring,* oil on canvas (1890), demonstrates his French technique of broken brushwork.

The individual figure painters who emerged may be divided between the native school and the expa-

William Sidney Mount, *The Power of Music.* Oil on canvas, 1847. Cleveland Museum of Art. © FRANCIS G. MAYER/ CORBIS

triates. The most famous of the expatriates were Mary Cassatt, John Singer Sargent, Henry Ossawa Tanner, and James Abbott McNeill Whistler. Cassatt (1844–1926) was one of the few American women painters who attained international fame and was the only American invited to join the impressionist movement in Paris. After training at the Pennsylvania Academy of Fine Arts, she settled permanently in Paris and exhibited with the impressionists in 1877. She made periodic trips to the United States and in 1892 painted a mural in the Women's Building of the 1893 World's Columbian Exposition in Chicago. She painted mainly portraits and figure studies of women and children, such as *Mother and Child,* oil on canvas (1890).

Sargent (1856–1925) studied and exhibited in Paris before settling in London. Influenced by the French painter Claude Monet for a time, he later was in great demand as a portrait painter in London and in the United States. He quickly absorbed and understood the devices of the formal, proper English portrait derived from Sir Joshua Reynolds of the eighteenth century. While Sargent's style was eclectic, he evoked character in his sitters and the ambiance of late-nineteenth-century society. Tanner (1859–1937), son of a bishop of the African Methodist Episcopal Church in Pittsburgh, first studied under Thomas Eakins in Pennsylvania but moved to Paris in 1891. Being black, Tanner found life as a painter in the United States a struggle, so he spent the remainder of his life in Paris. He developed a loose style related to impressionism but painted American genre subjects of black folk, such as *The Banjo Lesson,* oil on canvas (1893). His other genre subjects

Albert Bierstadt, *Rocky Mountains.* Oil on canvas, c. 1860s. International Business Machines Corporation Collection, Armonk, N.Y. © GEOFFREY CLEMENTS/CORBIS

possess a spiritual quality, and by 1900 his paintings were principally religious in content, perhaps because of a small demand for genre pictures of African Americans in Paris. Whistler (1834–1903) also passed through Paris before settling in London. He painted figures and landscapes in a simplified, flattened composition based on "musical harmonies" or art for art's sake. *Arrangement in Gray and Black No. 1: Portrait of the Artist's Mother,* oil on canvas (1872), his most recognized work, is a study of rectangles with some curvilinear patterns painted for contrast over the rectangular base.

Several Americans went to Europe and returned home with European influences. William Morris Hunt (1824–1879) attended the École des Beaux Arts and was in part responsible for the Beaux Arts taste in the United States. Frank Duveneck (1848–1919) attended the Royal Academy in Munich, where he developed a loose style consisting of puddles of paint on canvas. William Chase (1849–1916), an eclectic, combined his Munich bravado with impressionism.

While native school figurative painters often took trips to Europe, they were more influenced by their native training. Winslow Homer (1836–1910) trained as an illustrator in a lithography firm in Boston. He sold drawings to *Harper's Weekly* in New York and painted genre subjects ranging from Civil War prisoners to lawn scenes to cotton pickers. After a trip to England, he returned home to paint epic themes, such as *The Fog Warning,* oil on canvas (1885), which shows rising sea fog threatening to separate a fisherman from his parent fishing ship. Dynamic diagonals heighten the drama of the gloomy situation. Living in Maine in the summer and in the Bahamas during the winter, Homer alternately painted hunting scenes of the Northeast and the sublimity of humans at the mercy of the seas. Besides painting in oils, Homer was a master of watercolor, learning to control the medium effectively.

Thomas Eakins (1844–1916), another notable figure painter of the native school, studied at the Pennsylvania Academy of Fine Arts and at the École des Beaux Arts and later taught at the Pennsylvania

Academy. Men rowing in single and double sculls are typical of the works he executed in hard-edged realism and carefully placed compositions. *The Clinic of Dr. Gross*, oil on canvas (1875), depicts an actual medical operation with assistants and students looking on. John La Farge (1835–1900) grew up in the Caribbean and studied art in Europe from 1856 to 1858. Searching for his own style, he loosened his brushwork and recorded the unusual lighting he found in the Caribbean (in the 1880s before the arrival of Gauguin) and travels to Tahiti, as in *Afterglow*, oil on canvas (1891). La Farge was also a noted stained glass artist, working with translucent and iridescent glass. He invented a double glass technique he called "plated" glass, in which the colors of the subject change with the position of the sun.

Some American artists during the late nineteenth century continued to paint in a full romantic mood with personal, inner visions. Elihu Vedder (1836–1923) spent much of his career as an expatriate in Europe. *The Questioner of the Sphinx*, oil on canvas (1863), portrays the Great Sphinx at Giza when it was mostly covered by sand. An Arab questions it for its knowledge of the future in mystical quietness. Ralph Blakelock (1849–1919) had no formal art training and did not travel to Europe. After visiting the West, he painted dark, mysterious, nocturnal landscapes with Indian encampments, such as *Moonlight, Indian Encampment*, oil on canvas (1889), influenced by his personal experiences. He used a thick impasto paint that gives his works a flattened, abstract quality as well as introspective, expressive traits. Albert Pinkham Ryder (1847–1917) had only a few painting lessons, and although he did make trips to Europe, they were not to study art. Typical of his style are dark, flat objects in front of a glowing sky, such as *Moonlight Marine*, oil on canvas (c. 1880s). Ryder also illustrated mysterious literary and operatic episodes, such as *Siegfried and the Rhine Maidens*, oil on canvas (1891), which represents silhouetted maidens in a nocturnal landscape with a stormy sky.

Genre and still life subjects continued to be popular into the late nineteenth century. The trompe l'oeil experiments of Raphaelle Peale were regenerated in works by William Michael Harnett and John Frederick Peto. Harnett's *After the Hunt*, oil on canvas (1885), is a painting of objects associated with hunting—hunting horn, rifle, pistol, hat, canteen, dead game—hanging on a barn door with rusty hinges. The work simulates textures with photographic realism and cast shadows to the point of fooling the observer into believing that those items are hanging on the wall like a sculpture assemblage.

Minority Artists

Tanner and Audubon are the best-known black painters of the nineteenth century, but African Americans had participated in the profession since colonial times, taught by white painters in the traditional manner. Like whites, blacks relied on portraiture as the main means of earning a living in a studio. Joshua Johnston (1789–1825), a Federal Period painter, was the first African American artist to gain public recognition as a portrait painter. Johnson applied a flattened, simplified style of realism to represent his sitter. Posed in front of a bare background, the sitter in *Portrait of a Cleric* (c. 1805) recalls the tradition used by colonial limner portrait painters. Up to the Civil War black artists had difficulty acquiring professional training and received limited portrait patronage. Audubon turned to watercolors of precise, realistic representations of birds and mammals in North America. The earliest black landscape painter was Robert Stuart Duncanson (1821–1872), who painted in the tradition of the Hudson River school. *The Blue Hole, Flood Waters, Little Miami River,* oil on canvas (1851), exhibits an interest in realistic lighting and reflections in the water similar to Church's landscapes. Like Church and Bierstadt, Duncanson found his subjects west of the Appalachian Mountain range to Ohio. He was a photographer in Cincinnati during the 1850s, which may explain his penchant for realistic details. Edward Mitchell Bannister (1828–1901), a landscape painter, was born in Canada and settled in Boston, a liberal U.S. city, in the 1850s. He received national recognition at the 1876 Centennial Exposition in Philadelphia. Bannister developed personal, expressive power with impasto brushstrokes in his picturesque landscapes, such as *Approaching Storm*, oil on canvas (1886). Some of his landscapes achieve a lyrical quality not too different from Inness's works of the postwar period. Grafton Tyler Brown (1841–1918) traveled to the West to establish a career. Working in San Francisco as a lithographer, he produced an aerial view, *San Francisco* (c. 1877). Other minority painters joined Tanner in Europe, where they found greater acceptance, recognition, and patronage.

Throughout the nineteenth century many American painters felt a need to experience recent European developments, yet at the same time they developed an American tradition of painting. While searching for this tradition, they experimented with new subjects or took old subjects to new levels. While most Americans faithfully depicted their subjects with straightforward, hard-edged realism, by the end of the century, influenced by impressionism in Paris or the Munich schools, some became more abstract, preferring looser brushwork.

See also **Folk Arts; Gilded Age; Jacksonian Era; Jeffersonian Era; Lithography and Prints; Museums,** *subentry on* **Art Museums; Photography; Realism and Naturalism; Romanticism; Sculpture.**

Bibliography

Brown, Milton W., et al. *American Art.* New York: Abrams, 1979.

Craven, Wayne. *American Art: History and Culture.* Madison, Wis.: Brown and Benchmark, 1994.

Davidson, Abraham A. *The Story of American Painting.* New York: Abrams, 1974.

Green, Samuel M. *American Art: A Historical Survey.* New York: Ronald Press, 1966.

Lewis, Samella. *African American Art and Artists.* Berkeley: University of California Press, 1990.

Mendelowitz, Daniel M. *A History of American Art.* New York: Holt, Rinehart and Winston, 1970.

Novak, Barbara. *American Painting of the Nineteenth Century: Realism, Idealism, and the American Experience.* 2d ed. New York: Harper and Row, 1979.

Pierson, William H., Jr., and Martha Davidson, eds. *Arts of the United States: A Pictorial Survey.* New York: McGraw-Hill, 1960.

Richardson, Edgar Preston. *A Short History of Painting in America.* New York: Crowell, 1963.

PHILIPPE OSZUSCIK

PALEONTOLOGY.   See **Archaeology.**

PANICS AND DEPRESSIONS The U.S. economy in the nineteenth century followed a pattern of expansion and contraction, with major growth spurts occurring in the 1830s and 1850s and major depressions beginning in 1819, 1837, 1857, 1873, 1884–1887, and 1893. Intertwined in the downward swings of the economy were moments of banking crisis in which financiers were often unable to maintain specie payment of their notes, as they were required to do by law. These suspensions of specie payment, along with the emotional turmoil of the weeks leading up to the deed, were called "panics." Thus banking operations were inevitably involved in all depressions, with the result that banking and currency questions dominated politics throughout the century.

That prosperity and stagnation have so obviously alternated for so long has led economists to seek the sources of this seemingly consistent fluctuation of business conditions. After many decades of empirical work, theorizing, and model building, no one doubts that a pattern exists, but it lacks consistency: the durations, periodicity, and amplitudes of the fluctuations are idiosyncratic. It would seem that the basic process that generates the business cycle is investment. Entrepreneurs take risks in anticipating the goods the public will consume; the risk takes the form of using their money, others' money, and bank loans to build plants and buy equipment to provide the product or service. At some point entrepreneurs become overly optimistic—through lack of information, irrational expectations, or easy access to credit—and create too much capital stock.

In the nineteenth century this process was usually called speculation. However, consumption ultimately could not sustain speculative investment revealed in low profits or actual losses; entrepreneurs then could not repay their loans, and the excess capacity had to be liquidated. Panics occurred when it became clear that banks would not be receiving repayment of loans. Retiring bad debts by one means or another was the depression phase of the cycle; when new investment began, a boom and a new business cycle commenced.

Another explanatory scheme of the business cycle is that it results from monetary policy, essentially changes in the money supply. Bankers confronted one liquidity crisis after another, because though they might have had responsible loans and currency emissions, they kept on hand only enough specie to take care of normal daily transactions. The amount of specie, referred to as the specie reserve, was only a fraction of their liabilities. The liquidity problem arose in times of panic when the demand for redemption vastly exceeded specie holdings. A central bank or a bank of last resort could stop these liquidity crises quickly and allow only insolvent banks to fail.

The banking system of the United States in the nineteenth century had one other feature that induced instability and made matters worse. There was a very good reason why times of financial pressure were called "panics." People who placed money on deposit in a bank or who relied on banks to redeem their notes had no assurance that the bank would do so. When a bank failed, all the depositors and noteholders lost whatever money was owed them. For persons who placed their life savings in a bank, failure was catastrophic. Thus, when rumors swirled that some banks were failing and unable to pay noteholders and depositors, hordes of people surged into the banking district, demanding specie. If they got there early and got their money, they would not be crippled by bank failure. This fear depleted banks of their specie and produced suspensions of specie payment.

Another source of the panics of the nineteenth century was what economists call exogenous shocks, problems arising outside the economy. Exogenous shocks certainly did exist in the nineteenth century: persistent agricultural famines, gold and silver dis-

Business Cycles in the Nineteenth Century

Business Cycle			Ayres (Cleveland Trust Company) Index of Business Activity: Change		Unemployment Rate (%)
Peak	Trough	Peak	High to Low	Low to High	
Panic of 1819: no data, 1818–1822					
N/A	1834	1835	− 13.5	+ 28.4	4
1836	1838	1839	− 32.8	+ 27.0	6–8
1839	1843	1845	− 34.3	+ 23.6	
1845	1846	1847	− 5.9	+ 15.7	
1847	1848	1853	− 19.7	+ 20.0	
1853	Dec. 1854	Jun. 1857	− 18.4	+ 13.9	
Jun. 1857	Dec. 1858	Oct. 1860	− 23.1	+ 17.7	6–8
Oct. 1860	Jun. 1861	Apr. 1865	− 14.5	+ 19.6	
Apr. 1865	Dec. 1867	Jun. 1867	− 23.8	+ 18.9	
Jun. 1867	Dec. 1870	Oct. 1873	− 9.7	+ 19.4	
Oct. 1873	Mar. 1879	Mar. 1882	− 27.3	+ 24.4	10
Mar. 1882	May 1885	Mar. 1887	− 32.8*	+ 26.0*	6–8
Mar. 1887	Apr. 1888	Jul. 1890	− 14.6*	+ 21.3	
Jul. 1890	May 1891	Jan. 1893	− 22.1*	+ 21.1*	
Jan. 1893	Jun. 1894	Dec. 1895	− 37.3*	+ 27.8*	18
Dec. 1895	Jun. 1897	Jun. 1899	− 25.2*	+ 27.9*	

Sources: Victor Zarnowitz, *Business Cycles: Theory, History, Indicators, and Forecasting* (Chicago: University of Chicago Press, 1992), tables 7.3 and 7.4; and Stanley Lebergott, *Manpower in Economic Growth: The American Record since 1800* (New York: McGraw-Hill, 1964), 172–187, 522.

*The index in the column changes to a three-trend adjusted indexes average change.

coveries, immigration waves, and wars. Indeed, it may be that the exogenous shock interpretation holds the most analytical power for the U.S. economy in the nineteenth century. This economy was distinctly immature in its institutional and economic structure. Its overseas markets were still being developed; its financial structure was unsettled; its communications ability was weak; and its stock of knowledge was highly imperfect. In such a condition outside shocks could have profound consequences.

The Panic of 1819

The panic of 1819 was a result of the War of 1812. That conflict altered important aspects of the economy. Manufacturing was enormously stimulated, and the difficulties in acquiring money to finance the struggle led to a proliferation of banks (sanctioned by state governments) outside of New England; the number in the country rose from 88 in 1811 to 392 in 1818. Congressional leaders responded to the financial experience of the war by chartering a new national bank, the second Bank of the United States (BUS), in 1816. At the same time foreign trade was readjusting to peacetime conditions but doing so very unevenly—Americans purchased from abroad much more than they sold. The balance of trade (value of exports minus imports) was − $60 million in 1815, − $65 million in 1816, and − $12 million in 1817. Some of this deficit was covered by service and finance charges, but some portion of it had to be paid in specie.

These were the conditions that brought about the panic of 1819. It became clear to the president of the BUS, William Jones, that an expansionary policy was unsupportable, and he began a contractionist policy by demanding that state banks redeem their notes in specie. A new bank president, Langdon Cheves, increased the contractionist policy so that banknotes in circulation fell from an estimated $68 million in 1816 to $45 million in 1820. This contraction produced bankruptcies throughout the nation as state banks curtailed loans and tried to hoard specie. Prices fell perhaps 10 to 20 percent, and imports and exports reached lows in 1821. Sometime in early 1822 the panic of 1819 and its associated depression seem to have run their course. But a boom did not immediately appear; the BUS, under Nicholas Biddle after 1823, continued a deflationary policy by demanding immediate redemption of state banknotes.

Information about the panic of 1819 and its attendant depression is scarce. The indexes of economic behavior that give the information most wanted about the business cycle, such as changes in gross national product, unemployment, real wages, and net capital investment, do not exist. It is generally considered, however, that the contraction had limited repercussions. Undoubtedly the "infant" manufacturers of the United States were crushed and unemployment rose in the cities. But in 1820 the United States was nearly 92 percent rural. Unemployment during the ensuing depression probably did not exceed 5 percent. The damage the panic of 1819 wrought was commercial and agricultural: it brought a sharp halt to land speculation in the West and South, and curtailed the growth of the Cotton Kingdom.

The Panic of 1837

Inflation suddenly appeared in 1834 and peaked in 1837, the price index rising from 90 to 115. At approximately the same time, a vast speculation in land emerged. In 1829, 1.2 million acres of public land were sold; in 1833, 3.9 million acres; in 1834, 4.7 million acres; and in 1836, 20 million acres. This ballooning of land sales was directly connected to the expansion of the Cotton Kingdom. Historians used to believe that President Andrew Jackson's decision to destroy the BUS was responsible for this inflation and land speculation. By removing government deposits from the BUS and giving them to state banks,

Jackson unwittingly let the state banks expand their banknotes. The money supply increased dramatically, and this availability of money led to speculation. In trying to end the land speculation by demanding that purchasers pay for land in specie, Jackson helped to bring on the inevitable crash. The speculation could not be sustained in any event; loans were not repaid and banks were forced to contract credit (i.e., contract loans and discounts of other banknotes), thus generating a panic mentality. This then became the panic of 1837, and it produced a suspension of specie payment in May.

Since the work of the economic historian Peter Temin in 1969, the political explanation for the panic of 1837 has fallen into disfavor. Instead, it appears that specie movements in the international arena were the real triggers for both the panic and the depression that followed. Three key elements were responsible. First, merchants in China no longer demanded gold and silver in payment of debts but were willing to accept bills of exchange or other internationally recognized commercial paper; that meant less of a drain of specie out of the United States. Second, Mexico discovered silver deposits and began flooding the world market with the metal. The ultimate result was a rise in specie holdings in American banks, from a total of $31 million in 1832 to $88 million in 1837. The increase in specie did not induce bankers to act irresponsibly; they expanded banknotes—but the specie reserve ratio held constant from the 1820s through the 1830s (with a few excep-

The Panic of 1837. A reaction to Van Buren's support of Andrew Jackson's Specie Circular of 1836, a monetary policy whereby banks could receive payment in only gold or silver ("specie") for public lands. LIBRARY OF CONGRESS: PRINTS AND PHOTOGRAPHS DIVISION

tions). It was a third agent that brought about the panic of 1837: the Bank of England. The directors of the Bank of England saw specie flowing out of the country and determined to end it; they did so by raising the interest rate (the rediscount rate), making it more profitable to keep specie in England than to ship it overseas. In the United States this produced a contraction of the specie flow, inaugurating the financial crisis.

The economic tumult that followed actually was brief. The suspension lasted for about one year, and then the banks resumed specie payment. It seemed that the country was to be spared an underperforming economy. Then a second panic hit in 1839, producing a partial suspension of specie payments (New England and New York banks did not suspend payments). This financial stringency arose because England suffered a poor wheat harvest and thus had to import grain; at the same time prices for American cotton rose because of a lackluster harvest. Once again it looked as if England would endure a specie drain, and once again the Bank of England raised the rediscount rate. This produced a lowered specie inflow into American banks, setting off the panic of 1839. It should be noted that usually the panic of 1839 is subsumed in the panic of 1837, and the panic of 1837 usually refers to the period 1837–1843.

Economic conditions appeared depressed until 1843, but a number of qualifications need to be made. The United States suffered a price deflation but not necessarily lowered production. Prices fell from their 1837 index high of 115 to a low of 75 in 1843. But this price deflation did not diminish production, which evidently adjusted to the new price regime. The gross national output grew by an estimated 16 percent over these years; unemployment in 1838, the worst year of the panic of 1837, is thought to have been between 6 and 8 percent.

The economy revived after 1843, and several factors propelled the nation into a new boom period in the 1850s. The Cotton Kingdom grew into its glory years, and the demand for cotton by European and U.S. textile companies rose at a brisk rate, sustaining high cotton prices. Just as interesting was the development of the grain-growing area of the Great Lakes region. In 1846 Great Britain repealed the corn laws, which had placed high import duties on foreign grains. This opened the door for American wheat producers to enter the European, and especially the English, markets. Coincident with development of the Great Lakes region was the emergence of the railroad industry, which would take fifty years to mature. Finally another exogenous shock appeared. Gold was discovered in California in 1849, and in the years thereafter silver and gold were found in the mountainous West. Once more specie flowed into the banks, enabling bankers to expand their note issues. The result was inflation; the price index rose from 82 in 1848 to 108 in 1854.

The Panic of 1857

The stage was now set for the panic of 1857. Actually, the economy had experienced tremors earlier. In both 1846 and 1848 it had had momentary slowdowns that probably were overborne by the deficit spending of the Mexican War and the impact of the repeal of the corn laws. In late 1854 New York City had a brief banking panic, and perhaps the country had a short recession in 1855. This 1854–1855 trough probably should have developed into what occurred three years later, since an overexpansion of currency, inflation, and high investment had occurred. But international affairs intervened. France, Russia, and Great Britain went to war in the Crimea between 1853 and 1856. At the same time crop failures in other parts of Europe, particularly the Baltic states, led to an increased demand for American grains. Thus war abroad spared the United States from facing a crash. Peace in 1856 and the return of the European states to normal business activity, however, ended the high demand for American products, and when foreign trade collapsed, the banks realized they were not going to earn the specie they had expected. The failure of the Ohio Life Insurance and Trust Company in August 1857 created a general fear that the banks were in trouble, and a panic mood set in among noteholders and depositors, resulting in a general suspension of specie payments in October 1857.

If the panic of 1857 was the product of specie infusion from the California goldfields and from investment in railroads, it was also an example of how changes in international trade affected the American economy. Exports of wheat fell from 14.8 million bushels in 1857 to 3.0 million bushels in 1859; exported corn dropped from 10.3 million bushels in 1856 to 1.7 million bushels in 1859. The contraction particularly damaged the Great Lakes region and activities in the eastern part of the country that relied upon exchange with the Old Northwest. The panic of 1857 had almost no impact on the South. This was reflected in export tables: in 1857–1858 some 2.5 million bales of cotton were exported; by 1859–1860 the number had risen to 3.8 million bales. The effects on manufacturing probably produced an unemployment rate of 6 or 7 percent in 1858, and then manufacturing activity resumed.

The Civil War and Its Aftermath

By the spring of 1860, European demand for American crops was rising, and it seemed the nation was ready for a new round of prosperity. That potential was ended by secession and the outbreak of the Civil War. The North endured a recession in 1861–1863 owing to the loss of the cotton trade and the unpaid debts of Southerners. After 1863 the North commenced a startling boom that fortified people's belief in the rectitude of their free-labor economy. Overall, however, the Civil War period was an economically stagnant time. The years 1861 to 1865 saw no great leaps in technology, organization of production, productivity in general (except in agriculture), or output. After the war two small recessions, probably resulting from the readjustment of the country from war production to peacetime pursuits, occurred: one in 1866 and another in 1869–1870.

The Civil War did not dominate the contours of the economy between 1865 and 1900, although it certainly affected the institutions and investment patterns of the South. Rather, the postbellum economy in general battled the effects of a massive deflation. The Civil War produced an inflation that reached its height in 1864. Taking that year as a general price index number of 100, prices fell to 34 by 1894. By any standard, using whatever year one wishes, the deflation of the Gilded Age is impressive. The general reason is that growth in the money supply was insufficient to match growth in output, thereby forcing prices down. Unlike the years 1816–1857, no new supplies of gold were found, although new silver discoveries were constantly made. For reasons of ideology and international reputation, the United States went on the gold standard in 1873 and 1879. Silver discoveries no longer influenced specie totals held as reserves by banks, and with the international supply of gold essentially stagnant, it seemed that the downward pressure on prices was due to the gold standard. This condition produced political movements that sought to create a bimetallic standard, using both gold and silver as standards of value and thereby inflating the money supply. However, banks could inflate the money supply by issuing more banknotes—in short, the bimetallic standard was not necessary to halt the deflation.

The Panic of 1873

The distinct cause of the depression between 1873 and 1878 was evidently overinvestment in railroads. Railroad construction would dominate investment in the American economy for the rest of the nineteenth century, and a recurrent dilemma was finding ways for railroad companies to make profits. Railroads were a new enterprise that had unusually high fixed costs, and they became profitable only after consolidation, a process that would take nearly three decades. In 1865 the nation had 35,085 miles of oper-

ating track and by 1873, 70,268 miles. Connected with excess railroad construction was the inadequate growth in the money supply. Contractions in money supply were not constant between 1866 and 1898 but tended to be concentrated around the years of depression; this certainly was true for the years 1873–1878. The continuing problem was debt. People who contracted debt found it difficult to earn sufficient income to pay it off when prices for their goods or services were falling. Farmers were one of the groups that were especially vociferous about the debt problem.

The panic of 1873 was one of the strongest in American history. It commenced with the failure of Jay Cooke's banking house, a center for the sale of railroad securities. The ensuing depression lasted nearly six years, and recovery commenced only in 1879. The average unemployment rate for the decade was about 10 percent, and in its worst year, evidently 1876, a high of 13 percent unemployment was reached. Yet this depression has received the least scholarly attention of all the nineteenth-century fluctuations and is the least understood even though its political and social impact was the greatest of all the nineteenth-century economic slumps.

A small recession occurred between 1884 and 1887, the bottom being reached in 1885. However, a banking crisis did not accompany this downturn, and on the whole it seemed moderate, unemployment reaching about 7 or 8 percent.

The Panic of 1893

The greatest economic contraction of the nineteenth century occurred with the panic of 1893 and its attendant depression, lasting until 1897. In early 1893 commodity prices began to fall, as did stock prices, setting off fears of a general deflation. In February the Philadelphia and Reading Railroad declared bankruptcy, and within two months it appeared that the federal government's gold reserve was going to fall beneath the $100 million minimum. Failures elsewhere established a panic mentality, and by May the panic of 1893 had begun, producing a general suspension of specie payment by August. Again, this panic and the depression that followed were apparently the results of excessive railroad investment—and perhaps as well the incapacity of railroad companies to operate efficiently—along with another contraction of the money supply. According to Milton Friedman and Anna Schwartz, this contraction resulted from the attempt of politicians to placate the silver forces with the Bland-Allison Act (1878), which partially took the country off the gold standard and thereby caused hoarding of the precious metal.

The severity of the 1893–1897 depression is revealed in its high unemployment rate of more than 18 percent in 1894 (second in severity only to the Great Depression of 1929–1939). As late as 1897 the unemployment rate still was 14.5 percent. The steepest decline came in 1894, followed by a significant recovery in 1895, and then another plunge in 1896. The estimated gross national product in 1892 of $30 billion (1929 constant dollars) fell to $27.8 billion in 1894, then recovered to $33.3 billion in 1897. The economic historian of this crash, Charles Hoffman, finds that while consumption held steady, the great collapses were in construction and railroad building. The cycle ended as old debts were liquidated. Reinforcing the return to expansion was a surge in the money supply brought about by gold discoveries in Australia and Alaska in 1898. Indeed, the two decades following the depression of 1893–1897 were marked by a return to inflationary times, with prices rising more than 80 percent between 1897 and 1916.

Certain things must be said about the nineteenth-century business cycle. This article has kept to the economics of the cycle and has not gone into the profound political and social upheavals that the economic fluctuations caused—and they may be more important than any other feature of these contractions. Economic life in the nineteenth century was brutal, and its brutality reached a high point between 1865 and 1896. There should be no sentimentalism about the period, no paeans to the gold standard, to financial responsibility, or to the glories of falling prices. The last three decades of the nineteenth century were written in blood and class warfare. Falling prices may have their advantages, but not if they result in the destruction of the community. No one need bid a tearful farewell to the business cycle that characterized the American economy in the nineteenth century.

See also **Banking and Finance; Federal-State Relations; Gold Rushes and Silver Strikes; Monetary Policy.**

Bibliography

Excellent studies of the American banking system include Charles P. Kindleberger, *Manias, Panics, and Crashes: A History of Financial Crises,* 3d ed. (New York: Wiley, 1996), and Bray Hammond, *Banks and Politics in America from the Revolution to the Civil War* (Princeton, N.J.: Princeton University Press, 1957). A difficult but vital book for the end of the period is Jeffrey G. Williamson, *Late Nineteenth-Century American Development: A General Equilibrium History* (London: Cambridge University Press, 1974). The classic work on the last three decades of the century is Milton Friedman and Anna J. Schwartz, *A Monetary History of the United States, 1867–1900* (Princeton, N.J.: Princeton University Press, 1963).

Studies of panics and depressions include Murray N. Rothbard, *The Panic of 1819: Reactions and Policies* (New York: Columbia University Press, 1962); Reginald Charles McGrane, *The Panic of 1837: Some Financial Problems of the Jacksonian Era* (Chicago: University of Chicago Press, 1924; reprint, New York: Russell and Russell, 1965); Peter Temin, *The Jacksonian Economy* (New York: Norton, 1969); James L. Huston, *The Panic of 1857 and the Coming of the Civil War* (Baton Rouge: Louisiana State University Press, 1987); Rendigs Fels, *American Business Cycles, 1865–1897* (Chapel Hill: University of North Carolina Press, 1959); and Charles Hoffmann, *The Depression of the Nineties: An Economic History* (Westport, Conn.: Greenwood, 1970).

JAMES L. HUSTON

Coxey's Army, 1894. Jacob Sechler Coxey (1854–1951) led hundreds of unemployed from Ohio to Washington, D.C., to petition Congress for public works programs. Coxey's well-publicized march on Washington ultimately had no effect on public policy. LIBRARY OF CONGRESS: PRINTS AND PHOTOGRAPHS DIVISION

PAPERMAKING.   See **Printing Technology.**

PARKS AND LANDSCAPE ARCHITECTURE   The art of improving the natural beauty of the land had a considerable head start in America, where the luxuriant unkempt wilderness, the spacious landscape, and a predominantly rural culture provided experiences ranging from the sublime to the idyllic. The American nineteenth century opened with President Thomas Jefferson, who sponsored Meriwether Lewis and William Clark's western expedition, and closed with President Theodore Roosevelt, whose concern for the conservation of wilderness brought thousands of acres of unspoiled nature into public ownership. By mid-century, with Jefferson's vision of the United States as an agrarian utopia in jeopardy, the public park emerged as a counterforce against both the exploitation of the wilderness landscape and the rapid growth of industrial cities. Beginning in the nineteenth century and extending into the twentieth century, the United States created a system of parks, parkways, and garden suburbs that eclipsed European precedents and became a model worldwide.

The seminal figure in the development of parks in the nineteenth century was Frederick Law Olmsted (1822–1903). On the urban front Olmsted designed New York's Central Park in 1858. In the unsettled wilderness he guided the administration of Yosemite Valley and the Mariposa Big Tree Groves, conserved as a California state park (1864). He became the lead advocate for the establishment in 1872 of Yellowstone National Park, a reservation with more than two million acres. Between 1869 and 1895 Olmsted advocated for conservation of Niagara Falls, New York, and developed park systems for Boston, Buffalo, and Chicago, among other cities.

Andrew Jackson Downing (1815–1852) was a significant transitional figure in the development of landscape architecture in nineteenth-century America. His writings helped democratize gardening as he promoted a picturesque view of domestic architecture in harmony with landscape. He opened the way for Olmsted's concept of community planning in preserved and designed natural settings. Downing was also a scientific gardener, a recognized horticulturist, and a pomologist. Editor of the popular magazine *Horticulturalist*, Downing also wrote books on architecture and landscape, most notably *A Treatise on the Theory and Practice of Landscape Gardening, Adapted to North America* (1841) and *Cottage Residences or, A Series of Designs for Rural Cottages and Cottage Villas, and Their Gardens and Grounds* (1842).

Downing encouraged transplanting English ideas regarding informal gardening to the United States while casting these ideas in a peculiarly American "democratic" light. He crossed disciplines in his exhortations that architects design houses as scenic compositions in harmony with the landscape and rich

Floor Plan, U.S. Capitol Grounds, by Frederick Law Olmsted, July 1874. Although best known as an architect of parks, Olmsted (1822–1903) designed other features such as the Bronx, N.Y., street system, academic campuses, and residential communities. LIBRARY OF CONGRESS: ARCHITECT OF THE CAPITOL COLLECTION

in associative meaning. He derived the latter point of view from England as well, most notably from John Claudius Loudon's theories of association that envisioned relationships between domestic form and client character, between building type and purpose, and between content and form. Downing also bridged art and morality, asserting, as the English art critic and sociologist John Ruskin did, that appreciation of art and nature reflected an ethical position, a moral stance evidencing a religious and virtuous character. American democracy's unique art was an art of freedom, a spatial art of the natural and the out-of-door.

Downing was the first American landscape architect and theorist who attracted attention overseas. He brought Calvert Vaux (1824–1895) from England to be his partner in 1850, and they promoted the adaptation of scenic design to domestic architecture and the grounds of rural American villas. When Downing died two years later, Vaux continued Downing's practice for five years. Then, in association with Olmsted, Vaux entered and won the most significant

Gondola and Terrace in Central Park, New York City. Looking south toward Bethesda Fountain, an example of the blend of turf, wood, and water that characterized Olmsted's landscapes. Photograph c. 1894. LIBRARY OF CONGRESS

competition of the period, the design of New York's 830-acre Central Park.

After designing Central Park, Olmsted dominated landscape design in the United States until his death. He defined the quintessential American landscape tradition and established the profession of landscape architecture. The principles he instituted in his Greensward Plan (1857–1858) for Central Park were embodied in Olmstedian landscapes ranging from small urban parks to large suburban communities. His plan was the model for park design and landscape well into the twentieth century.

Olmsted viewed a park as a work of art—nature embellished, as gardeners had historically interpreted the art of garden layout. Rooted in the informal English romantic garden, Olmsted conceived his park as a place for rest and recreation with soft, open, country settings set apart as an "opposite class of conditions" from the clamorous cacophony of the city. Fundamentally informal, the Olmsted landscape was characterized by variety in light and shadow, in space and form, in hard and soft landscaping, with artistically composed plants, natural clusters of trees and woods, and an integrated architecture that included park furniture and, in suburban communities, private residences. Architecture, however, always deferred to landscape. Trees and other plants created a sense of natural habitat appropriate to the site, whether escarpment, open meadow, or wooded re-

treat. He employed formal accents as organizing elements, such as, in Central Park, the Mall with its cascading elm trees, terrace, Bethesda Fountain, and vista to the Belvedere; and in Prospect Park, Brooklyn, the Concert Grove with radial walks and Music Island.

Olmsted coordinated topographic changes, creating at Central Park a public works project of unprecedented scale. He designed circulation systems, water, and plantings and coordinated Vaux's designs for architecture, bridges, lamps, and park furniture, all composed as a harmonious whole or, as Olmsted expressed it, "framed in a single noble motive." Olmsted's landscapes are typically marked by bold landforms that balance spatial elements of turf, wood, and water and accommodate, indeed orchestrate, experiences in sequence. To separate vehicular traffic from pedestrians he positioned pathways and roads at different levels or in parallel lanes. Bridle paths, parkways, service roads, pedestrian walkways, and pleasure drives cross each other on forty-six bridges of individual designs in Central Park. Provisions for recreation and sport *en plein air* (in open air) reflect Olmsted's view that communion with nature is the ultimate leisure activity.

Moreover, Olmsted's landscapes embody a clear social intention. City parks, freely open to all, offered a new kind of civic space appropriate for individuals living in a democratic society. The informality of these parks is in contrast to their Old World precedents, where the avenue led to the palace or some other symbol of traditional authority. Olmsted's parks, though carefully composed, are nonhierarchical and open to suggestion. In his view the park should convey to immigrants, factory workers, rich, and poor the status of citizen.

Olmsted replayed the principles embodied in Central Park in subsequent designs nationwide, among them Prospect Park, Brooklyn (1865–1888); the suburban village of Riverside, Illinois (1868–1869); Mount Royal Park, Montreal, Quebec (1873–1881); the Capitol grounds, Washington, D.C. (1874); the park system of Boston (1875–1895); Stanford University (1886–1889); Biltmore Estate, Asheville, North Carolina (1888–1894); the Chicago World's Columbian Exposition (1890–1893); and Druid Hills, Atlanta (1893).

The site of the "White City" was Jackson Park, a swampy reservation of about five hundred acres set aside for a park, yet to be constructed at the time of the fair in 1893. Olmsted and Vaux had prepared a plan for the park, then known as "South Park," in 1871. Further, it was Olmsted and Harry Codman who recommended it as the site of the fair in their report of 1890. Jackson Park was joined to what was then called "North Park" by a strip of land called the "Midway." Several sources list Olmsted as the landscape architect of Jackson Park. The precise relationship between Daniel H. Burnham as the chief architect of the fair and Olmsted as landscape architect is beyond the scope of this entry. The authors are of the opinion that Burnham's specific contributions to the parks of Chicago date from his plan of 1909. In this document, Burnham makes reference to the creation of the "Special Parks Commission" in 1899, and the further creation by Cook County of the Outer Belt Commission in 1903. The majority of Burnham's contributions are in the twentieth, not the nineteenth, century.

Moreover followers and sometime partners of Olmsted promoted the new profession of landscape architecture and applied Olmsted's ideas to other sites during the nineteenth century. Those architects include H. W. S. Cleveland (1814–1900), whose Twin Cities metropolitan park system (1872–1895) is notable; Jacob Weidenmann (1829–1893), who designed parks in Connecticut, Chicago, and New York; and Charles Eliot (1859–1897), who worked with Olmsted on the Boston park system and on Belle Isle Park in Detroit (1884) before opening his own office in Boston in 1886. Eliot's greatest triumph was successful promotion of legislation to create in 1892 the Boston Metropolitan Park System, one of the first in the world. In 1895 Olmsted's son, Frederick Law

Olmsted (1870–1957), founded Olmsted Brothers, the firm that continued Olmsted's work. Olmsted Brothers earned more than 3,500 commissions. In the twentieth century Frederick Olmsted Jr. served on the Senate Park Commission; guided the McMillan Plan of Washington, D.C.; and, most notably, extended his design interests into a system of regional parks in the surrounding Washington suburbs. Among his other noteworthy designs are Forest Hills Gardens in Queens, New York, for the Russell Sage Foundation (1910–1912); Roland Park, Baltimore (1920s); Palos Verdes Estates in southern California (1923); and, with William Lyman Phillips (1885–1966), Mountain Lake Sanctuary (Bok Towers) in Florida (1922–1931). The niece of writer Edith Wharton, Beatrix Jones Farrand trained with private teachers and traveled extensively before setting up a practice in New York City in 1895. Her principal teacher was Charles Sprague Sargent, the first director of the Arnold Arboretum in Boston. Farrand was a consultant and designer of over two hundred projects, including Dumbarton Oaks in Washington, D.C.

The nineteenth century closed with two key events in the history of landscape architecture. The first was the establishment in 1899 of the American Society of Landscape Architecture, of which John Charles Olmsted (1852–1920), stepson of the senior Olmsted and a partner in Olmsted Brothers from 1898 to 1920, was the first president. Other founding members included Frederick Law Olmsted Jr., Warren H. Manning (1860–1938), and Beatrix Jones Farrand (1872–1959). The second was the beginning of professional education in landscape architecture. Harvard University established the first degree program in the United States in 1900. Its distinguished graduates included Henry Vincent Hubbard (1875–1947), Elbert Peets (1886–1968), and Thomas Church (1902–1978). Hubbard became Harvard's pioneer educator in the field, establishing the School of City Planning in 1929.

Olmsted, the initiator of the regional perspective that influenced twentieth-century landscape architects, environmental designers, and planners, formulated the fundamental concepts of parkway, urban park, and suburb to define nineteenth-century landscape architecture in the United States. His example shaped American landscape well into the twentieth century.

See also **Architecture; City and Regional Planning; National Parks; Nature.**

Bibliography

Beveridge, Charles E., and Paul Rocheleau. *Frederick Law Olmsted: Designing the American Landscape.* New York:

Rizzoli, 1995. A lavishly photographed and informed discussion of Olmsted's works by the editor of the Olmsted papers and the major scholar on Olmsted.

Creese, Walter L. "Yosemite National Park," "The Boston Fens," and "Riverside: The Greatest American Suburb." In *The Crowning of the American Landscape: Eight Great Spaces and Their Buildings*. Princeton, N.J.: Princeton University Press, 1985. An analysis of notable landscape spaces associated with Olmsted.

Fabos, Julius Gy, Gordon T. Milde, and V. Michael Weinmayr. *Frederick Law Olmsted, Sr.: Founder of Landscape Architecture in America*. Amherst: University of Massachusetts Press, 1968. A tribute to Olmsted that contains drawings and plans of his work in celebration of the centennial for Olmsted's coining of the term "landscape architect."

Kelly, Bruce, Gail Travis Guillet, and Mary Ellen W. Hern. *Art of the Olmsted Landscape*. New York: New York City Landmarks Preservation Commission Arts Publisher, 1981. An exhibition catalog defining the design elements of the Olmsted landscape.

Major, Judith K. *To Live in the New World: A. J. Downing and American Landscape Gardening*. Cambridge, Mass.: MIT Press, 1997. A discussion of Downing's theories.

Mumford, Lewis. "The Renewal of the Landscape." In *The Brown Decades: A Study of the Arts in America, 1865–1895*. New York: Harcourt, Brace, and Company, 1931. An early recognition of Olmsted as one of the dominant figures of the period.

Olmsted, Frederick Law, Jr., and Theodore Kimball, eds. *Frederick Law Olmsted, Landscape Architect, 1822–1903: Forty Years of Landscape Architecture*. 2 vols. New York and London: Putnam, 1922–1928.

Olmsted, Frederick Law, Sr. "The Landscape Architecture of the World's Columbian Exposition." *Inland Architect and News Record* (September 1893): 20.

———. *Preliminary Report upon the Proposed Suburban Village of Riverside, near Chicago*. In *Civilizing American Cities*. Edited by S. B. Sutton. Cambridge, Mass.: MIT Press, 1979.

———. "Public Parks and the Enlargement of Towns." In *Civilizing American Cities*. Edited by S. B. Sutton. Cambridge, Mass.: MIT Press, 1979.

Olmsted, Frederick Law, Sr., and Calvert Vaux. "The Conception of the Winning Plan Explained by Its Authors." In *Forty Years of Landscape Architecture*. Edited by Frederick Law Olmsted, Jr. Vol. 1. New York and London: Putnam, 1928. Reprint, Cambridge, Mass.: MIT Press, 1973.

Roper, Laura Wood. *FLO: A Biography of Frederick Law Olmsted*. Baltimore: Johns Hopkins University Press, 1973. The first full-length biography of Olmsted.

Rybczynski, Withold. *A Clearing in the Distance: Frederick Law Olmsted and America in the Nineteenth Century*. New York: Scribners, 1999. A full-length biography of Olmsted.

Tatum, George B., and Elisabeth Blair MacDougall, eds. *Prophet with Honor: The Career of Andrew Jackson Downing, 1815–1852*. Eleventh Dumbarton Oaks Colloquium on the History of Landscape Architecture, 1987. Washington, D.C.: Dumbarton Oaks Research Library and Collection, 1989. A collection of scholarly papers presented on the life, work, and legacy of Downing.

Tishler, William H., ed. *American Landscape Architecture: Designers and Places*. Washington, D.C.: Preservation Press, 1989. Brief summaries of major contributions and contributors to parks and landscapes in the United States.

Van Rensselaer, Schuyler, Mrs. "Frederick Law Olmsted." In *Accents as Well as Broad Effects: Writings on Architecture, Landscape, and the Environment, 1876–1925, Mariana Griswold Van Rensselaer*. Selected and edited by David Gebhard. Berkeley: University of California Press, 1996. A biographical account by one of the leading architectural critics of Olmsted's day.

ROBERT M. CRAIG
DOUGLAS C. ALLEN

PATENT MEDICINES   The term "patent medicine," commonly used to describe remedies sold in the nineteenth century, is actually a misnomer. In almost all cases the medicines were not patented, which would have required revealing the ingredients. Instead only the trademark and the name were registered with the patent office. The correct term, "proprietary medicine," was little known and seldom used outside the trade.

The nineteenth century witnessed the heyday of patent medicines. While the common image of the traveling snake-oil salesman had some basis in fact, not all patent medicines were produced by charlatans and frauds. Some grew out of domestic practice, often carried on by women who brewed medicines for their families and shared them with neighbors. One example is Lydia Pinkham's Vegetable Compound, advertised as a "sure cure for female complaints." Lydia Estes Pinkham (1819–1883), whose face appeared on the trademark, began selling her home medicine in 1875 after her family suffered financial reverses following the panic of 1873.

Dissatisfaction with medical practice in the nineteenth century contributed to the popularity of patent medicines. The heroic measures employed by doctors in the first half of the century often relied on bleeding and purging, therapies that did little to restore health. Later in the century doctors resorted to the use of quinine, alcoholic tonics, and opiates believed, erroneously, to sustain the vital forces.

Patent medicine firms pioneered national newspaper advertising, making names and faces like the Smith Brothers and their cough drops recognizable across the country. The advertising budget for a typical nineteenth-century proprietary medicine company could run as high as 80 percent of the company's annual budget, proving that printer's ink was the lifeblood of patent medicine.

Advertising increasingly marked the difference between patent medicines and those doctors prescribed. As the field of medicine struggled to professionalize in the nineteenth century, the American Medical Association, founded in 1847, attempted to prohibit doctors from advertising either their services or the medicines they prescribed. Similarly, pharmaceutical companies advertised to doctors, but their so-called

Advertisement for Patent Medicines. Marketing patent medicines to the public did not mean disclosing the ingredients; advertisements were a promise for a cure. Clay, Cosack & Co., lithograph, 1874. LIBRARY OF CONGRESS

ethical (prescription) drugs were distinguished by the fact that they were not advertised directly to the public.

Throughout the nineteenth century, makers of patent medicines were free to make grandiose claims for their products. Ads generally began with a paragraph of symptoms, ranging from headache to kidney failure, followed by testimonials supporting the cure-all claims. A medicine's ingredients remained secret. Thus a local chapter of the Women's Christian Temperance Union endorsed Lydia Pinkham's Vegetable Compound, unaware that it was 19 percent alcohol. Chemical analysis of Mrs. Winslow's Syrup, which promised to soothe fussy babies, revealed that it contained a hefty dose of opiates.

A fierce muckraking campaign combined with the work of the U.S. chief chemist Harvey Washington Wiley led to the passage of a Pure Food and Drugs Act in 1906. The law required that ingredients be listed on the label and stipulated that bottles containing dangerous ingredients display a skull and crossbones. Federal regulation put the worst offenders out of business and forced others to modify their formulas but did little to undermine the popularity of proprietary medicines. In the twentieth century

these medications shed the pejorative label "patent medicines" and became known simply as over-the-counter remedies.

See also **Advertising; Health and Disease; Medicine.**

Bibliography

Garvey, Ellen Gruber. *The Adman in the Parlor: Magazines and the Gendering of Consumer Culture, 1880s to 1910s.* New York: Oxford University Press, 1996.

Stage, Sarah. *Female Complaints: Lydia Pinkham and the Business of Women's Medicine.* New York: Norton, 1979.

Young, James Harvey. *The Toadstool Millionaires: A Social History of Patent Medicines in America before Federal Regulation.* Princeton, N.J.: Princeton University Press, 1961.

SARAH STAGE

PATRIOTIC AND GENEALOGICAL SOCIETIES   The oldest patriotic society in America is the Society of Cincinnati (1783), formed after the Revolutionary War by Continental Army officers. Named for the Roman hero Lucius Quinctius Cincinnatus, who laid down his plow to lead Roman armies to victory in the fifth century B.C., the society continued through the nineteenth century and is still in existence as the twenty-first century begins. Its membership is composed of male descendants of those who fought in the Revolution. There is a companion organization for women for female descendants, the Daughters of the Cincinnati, which dates from 1894.

Members of the General Society of Mayflower Descendants, founded in 1897, claim as their direct ancestors the Pilgrims, who arrived in North America on the *Mayflower* in 1620. The Sons of the Revolution (1883) and the Daughters of the American Revolution (DAR, 1890) are descendants of veterans of that conflict. Other national hereditary societies formed in the nineteenth century are the Colonial Dames of America (1890), the Society of Colonial Wars (1892), and the Military Order of Foreign Wars (1894).

During the Mexican War, American officers founded the Aztec Club in 1847. Veterans of the War of 1812 did not meet to start an organization—the Society of the War of 1812—until 1854, when they held a large gathering for veterans of all ranks. The Civil War was followed by the founding of several veterans' societies, including the Military Order of the Loyal Legion (1865), mainly for officers, and other societies made up of former officers of particular armies (e.g., the Society of the Army of the Cumberland, 1868). The Grand Army of the Republic (1866) was by far the largest and most influential. A powerful lobbying force to gain veterans' benefits between 1880 and 1890, its membership peaked at more than 400,000 in 1890. *The National Tribune* was founded in 1877 to keep GAR members posted on pension matters. The GAR was instrumental in securing the adoption of Memorial Day in 1868 and continued its influence into the first half of the twentieth century. It had two women's auxiliary groups, the Women's Relief Corps (1883) and the Ladies of the GAR (1886). In the South, the United Confederate Veterans was founded in 1889, followed by the United Daughters of the Confederacy in 1894 and the United Sons of Confederate Veterans in 1896.

Some hereditary societies were of state or regional orientation. Examples of these are the St. Nicholas Society, in New York City (1835); the Native Sons of the Golden West (1875); the Native Daughters of the Golden West (1886); and the Holland Society, in New York (1885). The Huguenot Society, composed of descendants of Protestant French immigrants, was founded in 1883. One of the earliest American genealogical societies was the New England Historical and Genealogical Society (1847). Similar groups were formed in other regions and states, such as New York and Pennsylvania.

See also **Nationalism; Veterans Organizations.**

Bibliography

Damon, Allan L. "Veterans' Benefits." *American Heritage* (June 1976): 49–53.

Davies, Wallace Evan. *Patriotism on Parade: The Story of Veterans' and Hereditary Organizations in America, 1783–1900.* Cambridge, Mass.: Harvard University Press, 1955.

Konrad, J. *Genealogical Societies and Historical Societies in the United States.* Munroe Falls, Ohio: Summit Publications, 1987.

BARBARA HUGHETT

PATRIOTISM.   See **Nationalism.**

PATRONAGE OF THE ARTS.   See **Philanthropy.**

PEANUTS   The peanut, also known as a groundnut, pinder, or goober (particularly in Africa), is, in fact, not a nut but a legume, like the different types of peas and beans. Thus it might be referred to as the ground pea, because after the plant flowers it bends downward to produce pods below the soil's surface.

Peanuts are native to South America and were introduced first in Africa, then in the North American colonies, by slave traders. They stocked their ships with peanuts because of the legume's small size, high nutritional content, and acceptance as food by the African slaves.

U.S. peanut production was limited to scattered parts of the South prior to the Civil War. Southeast Virginia and North Carolina had the largest areas of peanut production during this period. Many people viewed peanuts as a "free Negro crop" because it was grown by poor African American freedmen and slaves in garden plots for family use. Other families grew small crops for their own consumption, as hog feed, or to furnish hay. Farmers rarely grew more peanuts than they could use, leaving few for sale to the public or for use in commercial candies and confections. But by the 1850s street vendors in New York, Boston, and Philadelphia were selling freshly roasted peanuts in the shell by the pint, creating a small commercial demand for the crop.

Peanut growing expanded rapidly after the Civil War. During the war Union soldiers in Virginia had discovered that peanuts were a light, well-balanced, and tasty food that could be packed easily. The soldiers helped increase demand for the legumes both during and after the war.

Farmers found that peanuts could be grown in the same areas of the country as cotton. They were quicker and easier to grow than cotton, but they provided much less profit. Peanut growing was concentrated in Virginia, the Carolinas, Georgia, and Tennessee. The national output of approximately 150,000 bushels in 1860 expanded to 1.7 million bushels by 1879 and reached 14 million bushels by 1905. These figures represented only a fraction of world production but approximately equaled U.S. peanut consumption in the late nineteenth century. A lack of mechanization and relatively light consumer demand slowed further expansion. The first cleaning machines were patented in the 1870s; the first reliable harvesters did not come out until about 1900.

Nineteenth-century consumers used peanuts in several ways. Peanut oil was a low-cost cooking substitute for olive oil and a cheap industrial lubricant. Peanuts were used as ingredients in bread and soap and as a substitute for coffee. Peanut butter, a paste of crushed peanuts, became popular after 1890 when a St. Louis physician discovered it was a nutritious, easily digested, high-protein food source for his elderly patients. Livestock producers fed peanuts and peanut plants (peanut hay) to their hogs because it fattened them faster than corn. Peanuts did not reach mass popularity until the early twentieth century, however, when the scientist George Washington Carver, working at the Tuskegee Institute, found hundreds of applications for peanuts and encouraged southerners to grow them instead of cotton.

See also **Agriculture; Food.**

Bibliography

Johnson, F. Roy. *The Peanut Story.* Murfreesboro, N.C.: Johnson Publishing, 1977. Originally published in 1964.

Woodroof, Jasper Guy, ed. *Peanuts: Production, Processing, Products.* 3rd ed. Westport, Conn.: AVI Publishing, 1983.

CAMERON L. SAFFELL

PENNSYLVANIA Pennsylvania in the nineteenth century was one of the most diverse states of the Atlantic coast in both topography and population. The population multiplied tenfold, from 602,365 in 1800 to 6,302,115 in 1900. At the beginning of the century, English Quakers dominated culture and politics in the coastal plain around Philadelphia; before 1800 they dominated the state as well. German Pietists (Amish and Mennonites) and Lutherans settled in the fertile farm country of the interior, while Scots-Irish Presbyterians moved on to the rugged Alleghanies and the frontier regions of the northwest. Cosmopolitan Philadelphia was no longer the national capital by 1800, but it remained nationally preeminent in art and science.

Forging an Industrial State

Nineteenth-century Philadelphia was a center of commerce and banking and of production of cloth and other commodities. Elsewhere several towns exploited the plentiful iron ore of the state, but none to such an extent as Pittsburgh in the southwestern corner of the state. Smoke from its many factories powered by bituminous (soft) coal already filled its skies early in the century, but between 1830 and 1860 anthracite (hard) coal and coke (made from soft coal) replaced charcoal in blast furnaces, rapidly increasing iron production. By 1860 Pennsylvania produced more than half of the nation's iron. Despite its reputation as an industrial state, however, Pennsylvania at mid-century was just surrendering its position as breadbasket of the nation.

Situated where the Allegheny and Monongahela Rivers form the Ohio, Pittsburgh's iron and glass industries benefited from river connections to the West. But the rivers in central and eastern Pennsylvania were of little use in commerce, giving impetus to the transportation boom of the 1820s and 1830s. Canals and railroads transported goods to market, but the railroads also demanded iron from Pittsburgh and engines from Philadelphia's Baldwin Locomotive Works. Although the debt-laden State Works had become a political issue by the 1850s, railroad growth continued through the Civil War, dominated by Tom Scott's Pennsylvania Railroad, which bought the rail components of the State Works.

The Civil War boosted Pennsylvania's manufacturing and transportation industries. The navy yard and the Sharps Armory in Philadelphia proved especially important. Even greater changes in manufacturing came after the war. At the end of the Civil War, Pittsburgh produced five times more iron than steel, but by the 1880s and 1890s Pittsburgh had become the steel capital of the United States, taking advantage of local coke and the city's easy access to the new ore fields around the Great Lakes. There the Scottish-born Andrew Carnegie created his steel empire, aided by his associate Henry Clay Frick, who controlled the region's coke production. Frick also broke a massive steelworkers' strike at Carnegie's Homestead plant in 1892.

By 1900 Pittsburgh had grown to 321,616 people, more than five times its 1860 population. In large part this increase was because of the influx of Italian and eastern European immigrants, who answered the demand for unskilled labor in the steel mills and coal mines. Although industries developed elsewhere in the state, Pittsburgh was also the headquarters of the innovative food-bottling company founded by H. J. Heinz, as well as the companies of George Westinghouse, who revolutionized the railroad industry with a new air brake and pioneered the distribution of electric power. In another important economic development, the discovery of oil near Titusville in 1859 made Pennsylvania the nation's leading petroleum producer until the Texas and Oklahoma oil fields opened around 1900. By the end of the century Pennsylvania was the keystone of American industrialization, but the state was also struggling with the concomitant problems of pollution and oppressive working conditions.

Politics: From Quaker Commonwealth to Party Machines

The Whiskey Rebellion of 1794, sparked by hostility to the excise taxes on whiskey, damaged the image of the Federalists, who were accused of overreacting. By 1799 the Federalist Party lost control of the Pennsylvania state government to the Jeffersonian Democratic-Republican Party supported by many of the Germans and the Scots-Irish. The new dominant party broke into factions by the 1820s. In the 1830s even the overwhelming popularity of Andrew Jackson in Pennsylvania could not guarantee unity and success for the Democrats, as an Anti-Mason-Whig coalition, led by such shrewd politicians as Thaddeus Stevens, elected Joseph Ritner as governor in 1835. Disputes over their defeat in 1838 led to the brief "Buckshot War," which contributed to the decline of the Anti-Masons. The Whigs gained support in the aftermath of the panic of 1837 with their support of protective tariffs, favored by most manufacturers.

Led by James Buchanan, Pennsylvania Democrats mollified the state's business interests by abandoning their national party's opposition to the tariff and to banks, but some voters still blamed the Democrats for tariff reductions in 1846. The party also split over the Wilmot Proviso in 1846, a measure introduced by the Pennsylvania Democrat David Wilmot that was intended to block slavery from new lands acquired from Mexico. Equally portentous was the rise of the anti-Catholic Native American movement of the 1840s and anti-Catholic riots in Philadelphia in 1844.

Despite the popularity of the Whig Party's opposition to the Kansas-Nebraska Act and its call for the sale of the State Works, the party fell apart in the mid-1850s. So did the faction-ridden Democratic Party, while the nativist, anti-Catholic Know-Nothing movement swept Pennsylvania. An anti-Nebraska and largely Know-Nothing coalition elected James Pollock governor in 1854, but a confusing array of local party alignments contested the congressional elections that year. The opportunistic Democratic leader Simon Cameron eventually joined the coalition, along with Wilmot and his protégé Galusha Grow. Years later the Republican Party was forged from the Whigs, Know-Nothings, and defecting Democrats. Buchanan, serving as minister to Britain, was safely away from the political chaos. He was elected president in 1856, but he proved ill suited for the job and for the times.

Cameron was ineffective as Abraham Lincoln's secretary of war, but the Radical Republican Stevens was a dominant figure in Congress during the Civil War and Reconstruction. The key wartime Republican within the state was the energetic governor Andrew Curtin, who was in office at the time of the 1863 battle at Gettysburg, Pennsylvania, the only major battle fought in a free state. After the war, however, Cameron, aided by Robert W. Mackey and Matthew S. Quay, pushed Curtin aside and established himself as the boss of the Pennsylvania Republican machine. The canny Cameron passed on his U.S. Senate seat and his control of the machine to his son Don Cameron in 1877, but by the end of the century Quay was the almost undisputed boss of Pennsylvania Republicans. Corrupt machine politics, coupled with the growing political influence of corporations, caused a reform backlash as early as 1873, when a new reform constitution was ratified. Despite Republican protariff rhetoric, the Democratic and Republican Parties in this period in Pennsylvania substantially agreed on economic policies, so corruption and reform became the key political issues of the 1880s and 1890s. Despite the persistence of vocal reform minorities in both parties and occasional elections of reformist governors, Pennsylvania ended the century controlled by a political machine beholden to the titans of industry, who had established the state's preeminence in the national economy.

See also **Kansas-Nebraska Act; Petroleum; Philadelphia; Railroads; Steel and the Steel Industry.**

Bibliography

Coleman, John F. *The Disruption of the Pennsylvania Democracy,1848–1860.* Harrisburg, Pa.: Pennsylvania Historical and Museum Commission, 1975.

Holt, Michael F. *Forging a Majority: The Formation of the Republican Party in Pittsburgh, 1848–1860.* New Haven, Conn.: Yale University Press, 1969.

Snyder, Charles McCool. *The Jacksonian Heritage: Pennsylvania Politics, 1833–1848.* Harrisburg, Pa.: Pennsylvania Historical and Museum Commission, 1958.

Stevens, Sylvester K. *Pennsylvania: Birthplace of a Nation.* New York: Random House, 1964.

Vexler, Robert I., ed. *Chronology and Documentary Handbook of the State of Pennsylvania*. Dobbs Ferry, N.Y.: Oceana Publications, 1978.

Wall, Joseph Frazier. *Andrew Carnegie*. New York: Oxford University Press, 1970.

SCOTT BURNET

PERIODICALS.   See **Magazines.**

PERSONAL APPEARANCE   The personal appearance of nineteenth-century Americans differed by gender, ethnicity, religion, social class, age, and geographical region. Photographs, diaries, newspaper advertisements, and other historical documents reveal diverse individual choices in cosmetics, hairstyles, jewelry, and social demeanor. At the same time, certain conventions reflected that society's need for limitations on individual expression. Thus ensued very specific and sometimes rigid expectations and norms for various groups' demeanor.

Most historians agree that several key events in the nineteenth-century United States affected the population's diverse physical appearance. Industrialization spurred movement of workers from the farm to urban factories. The subsequent growth of the white middle class and a working class with disposable income fueled the growing mass consumer marketplace. The postbellum movement of freed African Americans to urban centers created a market for beauty products to enhance their particular skin and hair. The changing role of women in the nineteenth century was a critical factor in changes of styles and appearance. On the one hand, middle-class women were the central figures in the "private sphere" of domesticity, which served as an increasingly important shelter for escaping urban values and conventions. On the other hand, women began to lobby for a larger role in the "public sphere," so that by the turn of the century many wanted to cultivate an attractive personal appearance for their exciting new public lives.

These dramatic changes in social structure excited anxiety in nineteenth-century America. Standards and expectations of personal appearance became a means for that chaotic society to create boundaries, using visual cues, and to impose some sort of structure for societal functioning. People of all social classes learned these guidelines in etiquette books, character manuals, household guides, and fashion magazines, such as the 1850s' *Godey's Lady's Book*. Periodical topics ranged from the evils of the city, to the home preparation of beauty creams, to the proper demeanor at funerals.

A set of popular ideas reinforced these boundaries of difference in personal appearance. One was "physiognomy," the notion that outer appearance reflects inner character. Thus a "pure" woman's inner radiance appears as a natural blush on her cheeks. Such books as Judith and Hannah Murray's *The American Toilet* (1827) used riddles and puzzles to inspire middle-class women. A prostitute, in contrast, needed paint to "mask" her inner evil nature, which allowed her to seduce innocent rural youth flocking to the cities for work. American Indian paint was considered to be a mark of the "savage," and Indians were thus typically photographed in seminudity during the nineteenth century. By 1900 some of these ideas gave way with the mingling of social groups in urban areas, and people's use of personal adornment to celebrate newly won freedom from the farm, the home, or the plantation. By the early twentieth century, it was perfectly acceptable to use cosmetics and even etiquette as a way to enhance social discourse and to express individuality—within limits.

Cosmetics and the Beauty Business

In the early decades of the century, the term "cosmetic" referred to complexion preparations, part of the folk traditions of all cultures, with formulas handed down within families. Most white American women did not wear foundation to cover the face but, rather, used handmade preparations to improve the complexion. White skin and pink cheeks were the ideal, so skin whiteners were the most popular nineteenth-century cosmetic. Paints were used only by such "public" women as prostitutes, or sometimes by bold high-society women. White American men had rejected their eighteenth-century penchant for wigs, powder, and paint after the American Revolution. By the nineteenth century, such ornament was considered emasculating, and only shaving lotion, talcum powder, and hair dye were acceptable cosmetics.

By mid-century, the prohibition against adding color to the face began to relax for some groups. There was a publishing boom in beauty guides and household encyclopedias for white women, who were now encouraged to use personal appearance and movement to improve their social status. Typical books were Sarah Josepha Buell Hale's *Mrs. Hale's Receipts for the Million* (1857), and Thomas Webster's *The American Family Encyclopedia of Useful Knowledge* (1859).

As the U.S. interior developed transportation networks, so demand for cosmetics grew in all regions. Recipes for creams, often made of indigenous herbs and oils, had been prepared in the kitchen. Eventually, successful formulas became "patented" and peddled. Others were packaged and sold in pharmacies. By the turn of the century, many beauty products were sold by poor white and working-class women, who bypassed the traditional retail and distribution networks to sell products door-to-door or at social gatherings. The famous California Perfume Company, later renamed Avon, began in 1886. Many builders of the beauty business were women. Helena Rubinstein, a Polish-Jewish immigrant, sold a family face cream formula to friends and eventually opened her own beauty salon in 1900.

For African Americans, too, commercial cosmetics were available by the early twentieth century. Madame C. J. Walker, born Sarah Breedlove to former slaves, became a St. Louis agent for Poro African American beauty products, formulated by another notable black businesswoman, Annie Turnbo Malone. Walker experimented with hair preparations and developed a system that would soften and straighten African American hair without damage.

Beauty Is Business. Beauty products proliferated in the marketplace as such enhancements became socially acceptable. Woodcut by Ringwalt & Brown, 1870. LIBRARY OF CONGRESS

She eventually added face powder for dark skin tones to her line. At the same time, she was a visible and vocal advocate for the distinctive physical beauty of African Americans, and for their rights, expecially for women as entrepreneurs.

Hair Styles and Wigs

In the early 1800s white men abandoned the elaborate hair styles of the previous century for natural, unpowdered, shorter hair. Older men and such professions as law, the ministry, and the military changed their hairstyle conventions more slowly, but before mid-century there were virtually no wigs left. At the same time there was a growing popularity of beards, moustaches, and sideburns, in an astonishing diversity of styles. Some men did use hair oil, and hair dye to touch up grayness.

Women began the century with classically inspired wisps, braids, and ringlets, worn close to the head. Then hairstyles got "bigger." By the 1830s, women added large topknots and intricate braids and ringlets, enhanced with hairpieces and adorned with feathers and flowers. They applied dyes and conditioning oils and combed out their hair once or twice daily. By the 1860s, white women still wore numerous hairpieces and large chignons drawn to the back of the head—often the object of satirical cartoons in the press. The 1890s saw notable changes in women's hairstyles. False hair was discarded in favor of long, natural hair tied in a topknot. This style was easier to maintain. Fashion publications began to advise women to choose the hairstyle that suited them best.

Until white children reached the age of six or so, there was minimal gender distinction between boys' and girls' hairstyles, which were often arranged in ringlets. Traditionally, boys received their first haircut when they began to wear "breeches"—short pants instead of a dress—around the age of five. By about twelve years their appearance imitated their father's. Girls wore braids or loosely curled hair with a ribbon until adolescence, when they adopted more elaborate styles.

Scholarly research about African American hairstyles remains controversial and important. It is probably true that some African Americans chose hairstyles to emulate their white masters, while others retained styles with African influence. In yet other cases, hairstyle was not a personal choice. Slaves' heads might be shaven voluntarily, or as a punishment. Throughout the nineteenth century, some African Americans straightened their hair with a painful egg-lye formula. Others carried on well-developed West African hairstyling traditions, which were considered a medium of expression especially suited to thick, tightly curled hair. Straightened or curly, communal hair care was an important tradition, as families and friends assisted each other in combing, shaving, braiding, and styling their hair and adorning it with beads and shells. On the plantation, the colorful bandana was an important item of self-adornment, as well as a way to conceal hair when there was no time to comb it. Historical documents indicate that as the century progressed, African American hairstyles became shorter and less complex. Madame Walker's hair-care system was taught and adopted widely, causing a movement of African American hair care from the kitchen to black-owned beauty salons in the early twentieth century. This two-part hair-care system began with shampoo formulated to enhance softness and minimize breakage of African American hair. The next "hair grower" step consisted of a light oil that, when used with the hot, wide-toothed steel comb, put less strain on the scalp and hair while straightening it somewhat.

Jewelry

At the beginning of the century, white women's jewelry, like clothing and hairstyles, reflected classical influences. Recent excavations at Pompeii figured in the designs of cameos and earrings, and bracelets were worn high on the arms in imitation of women on classical vases. Later, small scent bottles, lockets, and crosses on chains were popular. By mid-century, jewelry became more extravagant, in keeping with the hairstyles. Larger lockets and crosses were worn on velvet ribbons, and pendant earrings became popular now that hair was pulled back. Most women owned at least one unique brooch and several rings with precious stones. For the turn-of-the-century high necklines, there were "dog collars" of diamonds and pearls. Nineteenth-century white men's jewelry consisted of watch chains, jeweled buttons, rings, cravat pins, and sometimes brooches to secure shirt openings. Men wore less and less jewelry as the twentieth century approached—just a tie tack, an adorned watch, and cuff links—with the exception of ceremonial buttons and badges, especially those related to military service, which were worn on some occasions. After 1865, formal photographs of black and white U.S. Army veterans often include a G.A.R. (Grand Army of the Republic) badge on a pocket or lapel.

Etiquette

Given the import of appropriate personal appearance and behavior in nineteenth-century society, people of all cultural backgrounds learned etiquette from formal and informal sources. Early in the century, an unmasked physical appearance and sincere demeanor was praised. This was in keeping with the idea of "republican etiquette," in which all people should have the opportunity to be genteel, regardless of social class. Later it became acceptable to embody these republican ideals in more rigid social forms, in order to preserve decorum, practice self-restraint, and still achieve middle-class gentility. This led to very detailed instructions for physical gestures and verbal communication. Popular etiquette books such as *The American Chesterfield* (1827) recommended that all bodily movement and social conversation should reflect the importance of self-restraint. By 1900, many of the intricacies of social convention were relaxed, and clothing adapted accordingly.

For African Americans and other working classes, the republican ideal did not always apply. There were strictly prescribed expectations for proper deference to their social "superiors." African Americans were not to stand or walk too erectly. Instead of looking white people directly in the eye, they used the "down look." Historical documents of urban blacks at the turn of the century reveal their joy at being able to stroll down the street confidently, looking at people directly. However, failure to observe the social etiquette of segregation and racism in the postbellum South could have serious, even fatal, consequences for African Americans. Some southern blacks died at the hands of lynch mobs for insulting whites by failing to observe this unwritten code.

The limited documentary record does suggest that there were ethnic and regional differences in personal appearance of nineteenth-century Americans. However, until more research is completed in this very important area, it is difficult to generalize.

For example, there is documentary evidence that the Chinese in California did dress in traditional garb and kept their hair in queues. There are photographs of San Francisco's Chinatown and of the railroad and mine workers to confirm this. However, there is equally compelling evidence that some Chinese spent their hard-earned dollars on western clothing, in a desire to assimilate. They also tucked their queues under a hat or were shaved by a barber.

For American Indians, there was a vast variety of self-decoration to enhance personal appearance. Various tribes and regions adopted very different appearances for war, ritual occasions, and for everyday life. There was face painting in such cultures as the Great Plains Indians. They used mineral pigments mixed with water and grease. Often face painting and featherwork expressed mood, or even served as protection. In the nineteenth century, some Indian tribes were already expert at the beadwork and turquoise and silver jewelry making for which they are renowned.

By 1900 there was increased physical self-display in the public sphere, whether through lipstick or a longer walking stride. "Personal disguise" became acceptable, whether manifested in polite table manners or rouge. People believed that appearance was not just a reflection of inner character but also of personal taste. For white women this relaxed attitude made it easier to move into the public sphere with a time-saving short hairstyle and freedom to gesture with one's hands. For such groups as African Americans, opulent "stylin'" for public strolling or church became an important symbol of their freedom to express their aesthetic through personal appearance.

See also **Class, Social; Clothing; Manners; Race and Racial Thinking.**

Bibliography

Corson, Richard. *Fashions in Hair: The First Five Thousand Years.* New York: Hillary House, 1969.

Halttunen, Karen. *Confidence Men and Painted Women: A Study of Middle-Class Culture in America, 1830–1870.* New Haven, Conn.: Yale University Press, 1982.

Kidwell, Claudia Brush, and Valerie Steele, eds. *Men and Women: Dressing the Part.* Washington, D.C.: Smithsonian Institution Press, 1989.

Peiss, Kathy. *Hope in a Jar: The Making of America's Beauty Culture.* New York: Henry Holt, 1998.

Severa, Joan L. *Dressed for the Photographer: Ordinary Americans & Fashion, 1840–1900.* Kent, Ohio: Kent State University Press, 1995.

Tortora, Phyllis, and Keith Eubank. *A Survey of Historic Costume: A History of Western Dress.* New York: Fairchild, 1998.

White, Shane, and Graham White. *Stylin': African American Expressive Culture from Its Beginnings to the Zoot Suit.* Ithaca, N.Y.: Cornell University Press, 1998.

BARBARA M. JONES

PETROLEUM   The inhabitants of North America have always known about petroleum. Until the nineteenth century, however, it was as much a nuisance as it was a curiosity. Native Americans valued petroleum as a medicine, and European settlers followed their lead. But its utility depended on the physical state in which it was found. Liquid petroleum from an oil spring was easily applied as an ointment, while the hard, sticky asphaltum found above ground in some oil regions made a perfect construction material. Virtually every group who came in contact with natural asphalt used it for caulking, paving, and roofing. And although many people thought of profiting from oil, the economic exploitation of petroleum did not occur until the 1850s, when several factors combined to create a market for the product.

After the invention of a fuel-burning lamp in the 1780s people in both Europe and North America depended on sperm whale oil to light their homes and businesses. But seventy years of relentless hunting reduced the number of whales, and New England whalers were sailing around Cape Horn and far out into the Pacific to meet the demand. Prices for illuminating oil shot up alarmingly, and the fear of an impending fuel crisis generated a search for a substitute. After experimenting with other products, like lard oil, which gave off too little light, and camphene, a mixture of turpentine and alcohol that tended to explode, entrepreneurs settled on petroleum as the most likely alternative. Abraham Gesner, a Canadian physician and geologist, first distilled a clean-burning lamp oil, kerosene, from hardened petroleum in the late 1840s. Gesner's experiments led to the formation of the New York Kerosene Works, which used imported Scottish coal for raw material. James Young, a close competitor in the "coal oil" trade from Scotland, joined the New York organization. Like Gesner, Young had patented several methods for refining coal and shale oil and had already experimented with the direct distillation of petroleum into gas and lighter oils.

The First Commercial Well

In 1855 Benjamin Silliman, a renowned scientist from Yale University, submitted a report for the Pennsylvania Rock Oil Company supporting its founders' claim that the local oil would yield a number of useful products. What they lacked was a large enough supply to put it on the market. Several shareholders in the Pennsylvania company split off to form the Seneca Oil Company of Connecticut and hired Edwin L. Drake, a former railroad conductor from New Haven, to investigate their property and the prospect of finding more oil. Unemployed at the time due to poor health, Drake gambled his life savings on Seneca Oil stock and was determined to justify the decision.

While Drake had no practical experience with wells of any kind, he had the common sense to recognize the best way to go about the job. Rather than digging a mining shaft into the seeps, Drake surveyed the area and decided to drill for oil employing the cable tool techniques used by salt well drillers. Oil production had always been an incidental and unwanted consequence of drilling for brine. Drake was merely the first person to attempt it deliberately. The cable tool method involved repeatedly dropping a heavy drill bit, suspended from a derrick on a rope or

The Pennsylvania Oil Industry, c. 1864. The first functioning oil well was drilled at Titusville, Pennsylvania, in 1859. LIBRARY OF CONGRESS: PRINTS AND PHOTOGRAPHS DIVISION

cable, to cut out the well. In the method's roughest form the driller jiggled the tools up and down using his own weight to counterbalance the bit. But Drake had just enough capital behind him to purchase a small boiler and steam engine for power in the fashion of the most advanced salt well rigs. He hired an experienced driller to make the tools and drill the well. When cave-ins and water infiltration almost stopped their progress, Drake encased the hole with iron piping, an innovation that would be universally adopted. Drake completed the first successful well on 27 August 1859 at Titusville, Pennsylvania, and thus became the founder of the U.S. oil industry.

Drake's success did not immediately change the public's attitude about petroleum, but his work set the stage for a Pennsylvania oil rush in the early 1860s similar to the one that had sent thousands of people recklessly searching for gold in California a decade earlier. This boomtown phenomenon, and the army of get-rich-quick schemers that promoted it, gave the oil industry a dubious reputation. Nevertheless, from the 1860s through the 1890s the petroleum industry gained strength in the eastern and midwestern oil fields of Pennsylvania, West Virginia, Kentucky, Ohio, Illinois, and Indiana. U.S. oil production grew from a few barrels a day drawn out of the Drake well to an annual output of some sixty million barrels by the end of the century.

This massive increase in the volume of oil spawned numerous technical innovations. Oil went from being haphazardly collected in empty bottles, tubs, and buckets to being stored in wooden barrels and eventually iron tanks that held tens of thousands of barrels. In the course of this evolution, the forty-two-gallon barrel became a standard measure for the industry. Transportation methods also improved. Horse-drawn wagons hauled oil from the fields until the development after 1865 of large and sophisticated pipeline systems that linked wells directly to storage yards and railroad termini. Railway tank cars soon carried crude and refined products throughout the nation.

The Standard Oil Company

While the mechanical and technological changes that occurred during this period made the industry more efficient, producing and refining petroleum remained a chaotic and unnerving business. Drilling for oil was one of the few ways for an individual prospector, or wildcatter, to make money in a hurry, and the oil could be refined using rudimentary techniques. One of the hallmarks of the industry, therefore, was the continuous presence of small, independent operations. Another was the "rule of capture," a common-law concept of ownership that made oil the property

The California Oil Industry, c. 1898. The Century Oil Company, in the Kern River District, was indicative of a trend toward southwestern industries, which would broaden the market at the end of the nineteenth century. NATIONAL ARCHIVES

of the person who brought it to the surface regardless of its origin. Since oil migrates across wide areas through underground rock and sand, anyone drilling a well was inclined to extract as much as possible before someone else did. Consequently, the early industry in particular was troubled by successive waves of overproduction, massive waste, and volatile price fluctuations that tore the foundation out from under the market at every turn. Oil that sold profitably for several dollars a barrel one day could be worth ten or twenty cents the next day if a new field or a large gusher came into production. Most often these discoveries were the work of individuals who did not have the means to store their oil or the desire to control their production. They simply flooded the market with little thought as to what the next day might bring. For those who could see the longer-term potential of oil, this was an intolerable situation.

One way out of this predicament was for producers and refiners to form voluntary associations and exchanges to limit production and output. Unfortunately, few of these agreements lasted beyond the next big discovery. John D. Rockefeller, an up-and-coming refiner from Cleveland, devised a more certain solution. Rockefeller set up the Standard Oil Company of Ohio in 1870 to stabilize the industry and his own profits. He began by integrating other refineries into his operation, and he then protected his organization through successive arrangements with railroad companies and pipeline operators. These deals gave him a virtual monopoly of the illuminating oil trade by the 1880s. Rockefeller's tactics were shrewd and deliberate and left little room for the individual producer to compete against him. His actions were not necessarily illegal at the time, but by the end of the century numerous state and federal laws had been aimed directly at the rebates, kickbacks, and secret agreements that characterized Rockefeller's methods. Although the company delivered improved service, safe products, and relatively low prices, Standard Oil was condemned by reformers and journalists as an enemy of the public and a threat to the nation.

Despite Rockefeller's best efforts, which essentially defined the initial phase of the industry, Standard Oil was actually losing some of its power by the end of the 1890s. Increasing foreign competition and a shift in domestic production from the eastern oil fields to those in the Southwest and California changed the dynamics of the market and the requirements for success. The retail trade for petroleum moved away from illuminating oil toward a wider mix of products. Fuel oil, in particular, came into demand as a replacement for coal to run locomotives, ships, and industrial machinery. The market for petroleum shifted from the home to the factory, creating a need for more lubricants and other industrial materials. The desire for vast quantities of gasoline for motor vehicles would soon follow. All of these changes enabled new independent companies like Gulf Oil, the Texas Company, and Union Oil to assert their dominance in these areas and become major competitors as the industry entered the 1900s.

See also **Coal; Corporations and Big Business; Mining and Extraction; Natural Resources; Regulation of Business; Trusts.**

Bibliography

Ansell, Martin R. *Oil Baron of the Southwest: Edward L. Doheny and the Development of the Petroleum Industry in California and Mexico.* Columbus: Ohio State University Press, 1998.

Beaton, Kendall. "Dr. Gesner's Kerosene: The Start of American Oil Refining." *Business History Review* 29, no. 1 (March 1955): 28–53.

Centennial Seminar on the History of the Petroleum Industry, Harvard University. *Oil's First Century: Papers.* Cambridge, Mass.: Harvard Graduate School of Business Administration, 1960.

Chernow, Ron. *Titan: The Life of John D. Rockefeller Sr.* New York: Random House, 1998.

Giddens, Paul H. *The Birth of the Oil Industry.* New York: Macmillan, 1938.

———. *Early Days of Oil: A Pictorial History of the Beginnings of the Industry in Pennsylvania.* Princeton, N.J.: Princeton University Press, 1948.

Tait, Samuel W. *The Wildcatters: An Informal History of Oil-Hunting in America.* Princeton, N.J.: Princeton University Press, 1946.

Williamson, Harold F., and Arnold R. Daum. *The American Petroleum Industry.* Volume 1: *The Age of Illumination, 1859–1899.* Evanston, Ill.: Northwestern University Press, 1959.

MARTIN R. ANSELL

PHILADELPHIA

When the nineteenth century began, Philadelphia was America's leading commercial port and the nation's largest city with nearly 68,000 residents, including neighboring Southwark and Northern Liberties. Moreover, as the site of the signing of the Declaration of Independence, the host of the U.S. Constitutional Convention, the home of the First Bank of the United States, and the recent capital of both Pennsylvania (until 1799) and the United States (until 1800), Philadelphia enjoyed an undisputed dominance in national public affairs. By the 1810 census New York had passed Philadelphia in size and as the dominant commercial center, but the Pennsylvania city remained the nation's second-largest city until 1890, when Chicago surpassed it.

From Federal City to Consolidation

In the first half of the century Philadelphia expanded physically while its growing population became increasingly diverse. By mid-century the relatively compact city, as laid out in William Penn's careful grid, was bordered by five built-up suburbs to the north and south, and the surrounding Philadelphia County included an additional twenty-three townships, boroughs, and districts. In 1850 center city Philadelphia had a population of 121,376, while the rest of the county had 287,376 residents. Four years later concerns about public disorder, administrative chaos, and inefficient delivery of services prompted the 1854 Consolidation Act, which expanded the city's boundaries to include the surrounding jurisdictions.

As Philadelphia grew, its economic focus shifted from commerce to manufacturing. In the second quarter of the century the city emerged as the world's leading textile center, with major manufacturing enclaves in Frankford, Kensington, and Manayunk. In the meantime the city's heavy industry prospered, led by the Baldwin locomotive works and an assortment of iron and steel manufacturing. Antebellum Philadelphia also had a large free black population, approaching twenty thousand at mid-century, that supported a wide array of churches, businesses, and separate institutions. In 1850 nearly 30 percent of Philadelphians were foreign-born, mostly from Ireland, Germany, and England.

In the second quarter of the century Philadelphia experienced repeated episodes of public disorder that often reflected ethnic and racial differences. In the 1830s and 1840s the city confronted antiblack violence as well as several attacks on abolitionists. The worst rioting occurred in 1844, when Irish Protestants and Catholics battled in two destructive clashes. Throughout the entire period the city was plagued by street battles between rival gangs or volunteer fire companies. These ethnic hostilities spilled into politics, and local nativists rose to prominence in the mid-1850s before giving way to the new Republican Party.

To the Centennial City and Beyond

Despite strong economic and social ties with the South, Philadelphians remained staunchly loyal to the Union during the Civil War, earning a reputation among traveling regiments for the two volunteer refreshment saloons in Southwark. The always colorful and often corrupt Republican Party machine controlled local politics for decades after the war. Despite an important abolitionist minority, white Philadelphians resisted calls for racial equality both before and after the war. Black troops drilled at Camp William Penn, but Philadelphia remained geographically and institutionally segregated. It took state legislative action to desegregate the streetcar lines in the late 1860s, and African Americans faced economic discrimination that effectively barred them from high-paying industrial employment. By 1900 the black population had reached 62,000 but W. E. B. Du Bois's pathbreaking study, *The Philadelphia Negro* (1899), documented persistent geographic and economic segregation.

In 1876 Philadelphia hosted the national Centennial Exposition, entertaining more than ten million visitors from across the globe. By this point the city had expanded across the Schuylkill River into West Philadelphia. In 1890 the population passed one million topped only by New York and Chicago. But unlike other leading U.S. cities, Philadelphia remained a "city of homes," with blocks of modest row houses expanding outward rather than tenements and apartment buildings reaching toward the sky. While other

Bustling Northeast Metropolis Scene. Crowded Philadelphia street, 1897. LIBRARY OF CONGRESS

cities filled with the newly arriving immigrants, Philadelphia's immigrant population remained below national urban norms, largely because most of the city's industrial jobs called for skilled or semiskilled labor. The traditional mix of Irish, German, and English immigrants expanded in the 1890s to include Italians, Russian Jews, and other eastern European newcomers.

During the final quarter of the century Philadelphia truly emerged as a dominant industrial center. Local textile manufacturing and iron and steel production remained strong, and the Pennsylvania Railroad became the nation's leading corporation. Philadelphia, long renowned for its medical training facilities, blossomed as an intellectual center with the growth of the University of Pennsylvania in West Philadelphia and the founding of Temple University, Drexel University, the Free Library of Philadelphia, and the Philadelphia Museum of Art. In the final decades of the century Mary Cassatt, John Singer Sargent, and Walt Whitman joined Thomas Eakins in establishing the city's cultural reputation.

See also **Pennsylvania; Steel and the Steel Industry; World's Fairs.**

Bibliography

Cutler, William W., III, and Howard Gillette Jr., eds. *The Divided Metropolis: Social and Spatial Dimensions of Philadelphia, 1800–1975.* Westport, Conn.: Greenwood, 1980.

Davis, Allen F., and Mark H. Haller, eds. *The Peoples of Philadelphia: A History of Ethnic Groups and Lower-Class Life, 1790–1940.* Philadelphia: Temple University Press, 1973.

Scranton, Philip. *Proprietary Capitalism: The Textile Manufacture at Philadelphia, 1800–1885.* Cambridge, U.K., and New York: Cambridge University Press, 1983.

Weigley, Russell F., ed. *Philadelphia: A 300-Year History.* New York: Norton, 1982.

J. MATTHEW GALLMAN

PHILANTHROPY   No phenomenon is more characteristic of nineteenth-century America than philanthropy, voluntary donations of money and time for public purposes. Philanthropy took many forms, including gifts and bequests to public institutions, such as James Smithson's bequest to the federal government that created the Smithsonian Institution; freestanding charitable trusts, such as Boston's Lowell Institute; pledges of money by large numbers of citizens to support new enterprises, such as the Massachusetts General Hospital; purchases of shares to sustain churches and libraries; and spontaneous subscriptions of goods and money to relieve victims of disasters. The willingness to give was accompanied and facilitated by an unprecedented proliferation of voluntary associations and eleemosynary corporations supported by the money and energy of individual citizens. Philanthropic efforts varied enormously in scope and scale, ranging from multimillion-dollar endowments, like the Philadelphia merchant Stephen Girard's bequest for the establishment of a school for orphans, to pennies contributed by children to Sunday Schools and tract societies. Some philanthropies aspired to grand goals, such as ending slavery or intemperance; others aimed at more limited ends, such as providing citizens with funds for decent burials or building loans.

This list hardly exhausts the possibilities. Though philanthropy is often associated with gifts of money, in the nineteenth-century United States the practice was just as likely to be associated with personal gestures directed to relatives and neighbors. Perhaps the most famous, albeit fictional, charitable act of the century was the impulsive decision of the sisters Jo, Meg, Beth, and Amy March in Louisa May Alcott's *Little Women* (1868) to take their Christmas breakfast to an impoverished immigrant family in their neighborhood. Religious Americans were more likely to define philanthropy as a spiritual transaction than a financial one.

Whatever form it took, the practice of private citizens contributing money and time for charitable, educational, religious, and other public purposes is arguably the nineteenth century's most important contribution to American institutional life. This was a major achievement given the hostility of the founding fathers to voluntary associations, the suspicion with which the public regarded private giving, and the lack of legal mechanisms for ensuring that charitable funds would be used for the purposes designated by donors.

"Experimental Knowledge of Republican Institutions"

Occasional private philanthropic gestures were not unknown in the eighteenth century, but they were uncommon. Schools and colleges depended primarily on user fees and government grants for revenue. Religious bodies in most of the colonies were supported by taxation and pew rents rather than by donations. Private charitable and health care institutions were virtually unknown until after the Revolution. With the exception of a few fraternal organizations, such as the Freemasons, voluntary associations were nonexistent.

Even after independence most Americans remained intensely suspicious of corporations of every kind, and this suspicion lingered well into the nineteenth century. In the 1790s many states, including New York, Pennsylvania, and Virginia, repealed the Elizabethan Statute of Charitable Uses and stoutly resisted efforts to establish private institutions. In other states, like Connecticut, where private charities flourished after 1790, people fretted about the tendency to "parcel the commonwealth into little aristocracies" and sought to constrain privatist tendencies through a variety of regulatory mechanisms.

More than anyone else, Benjamin Franklin inspired nineteenth-century Americans with his energetic civic philanthropies, which included organizing the nation's earliest subscription library, volunteer fire company, and mechanics society (the Junto). He established under his will two large charitable trusts in Philadelphia and Boston. The trusts, which were given a duration of two hundred years, were ordered invested in loans "to assist young married Artificers in setting up their Business" and, when terminated, were to be used to found institutions that would have "a good effect on the conduct of Youth" and be "of Service to many worthy Characters and useful Citizens" (Benjamin Franklin, "My Last Will and Testament Dated July 17, 1788, with a Codicil or Addition Dated June 3, 1789," Archives of the Pennsylvania Historical Society). The Franklin Trusts endured and were finally distributed in 1990.

Franklin's example inspired his fellow Philadelphian, the merchant Stephen Girard (1750–1831), to leave the bulk of his fortune, then the largest in the United States, to the city of Philadelphia to establish a "college" for "poor white male orphans, between the ages of six and ten years." In 1844 litigation by covetous relatives produced a landmark U.S. Supreme Court decision upholding the legality of charitable trusts.

Despite its status as America's largest and wealthiest city, Philadelphia did not set the pace for American philanthropy because of the hostility of Pennsylvania law to private charities. Boston, in contrast, was exceptionally friendly to such efforts. Favored by a conservative state constitution and legal establishment, wealthy Bostonians after 1800 used philanthropically supported institutions, such as Harvard College and the Boston Athenaeum, to counter the rising influence of popular democracy. On his death in 1836 the textile heir John Lowell Jr. (1799–1836) left a quarter-million dollars, second in size only to Girard's bequest in this period, to establish a free-standing charitable trust to support free public lectures and other educational activities. The huge resources of the Lowell Institute attracted quality lecturers and intellectual celebrities from throughout the world and helped make Boston the primary intellectual center in the nineteenth-century United States.

Grand philanthropic gestures like Franklin's, Girard's, and Lowell's represented only one of the philanthropic traditions that emerged in the decades before the Civil War. Perhaps more typical were efforts that drew on the collective resources of larger groups of citizens. In 1810, when a number of leading citizens of Boston determined to establish a hospital, they wrote a circular letter that begged its recipients to contribute $100,000 for "a hospital for the reception of lunatics and other sick persons." Promising that individual contributions would be matched dollar for dollar by the state, the effort yielded sufficient funds to establish the Massachusetts General Hospital. This form of fund-raising soon became the characteristic support for hospitals, colleges, and other eleemosynary institutions in the Northeast.

While Boston's citizens appealed to the mercantile elite for support of benevolent objects, Protestant evangelicals in Connecticut tapped the generosity of national constituencies and small donors for support of their initiatives. In 1828, after losing its endowment in a financial panic, Yale College, then the largest institution of higher education in the country, launched its first national appeal for funds. Outlining its educational goals in the famous *Yale Report of 1828*, the college organized an association of alumni and launched a national campaign that raised an endowment of $100,000 and became the model for other college fund-raising efforts.

A third philanthropic tradition exposed abuses and organized humanitarian advocacy for government interventions. Such efforts included antislavery and abolitionist crusades, the temperance movement, and reforms in the care of the mentally and physically disabled.

Dorothea Dix (1802–1887) exemplified this philanthropic style as she went from state to state exposing abuses of the mentally ill, lecturing, and lobbying for the establishment of mental hospitals. In 1852 she persuaded Congress to pass a bill that would have set aside the proceeds from sales of five million acres of public lands for support of the indigent insane. After months of delay, President Franklin Pierce vetoed the bill, arguing in his veto message that he could "not find any authority in the Constitution for making the Federal Government the great almoner of public charity throughout the United States" (James D. Richardson, *A Compilation of the Messages and Papers of the Presidents, 1789–1897*, 1898). In restricting federal social welfare initiatives for the next half-century, the Pierce veto stimulated private philanthropy.

The fourth and most widespread philanthropic tradition centered around the charitable activities of such fraternal orders as the Freemasons and Odd Fellows, "friendly" and young men's societies, savings and loan associations, and other mutual benefit membership organizations. These entities provided members with fellowship, access to capital and political influence, training in civic skills, and basic social insurance in the form of death, sickness, and burial benefits. Introduced to the United States by Franklin, fraternal orders were originally elite organizations. Easily emulated, they were quickly embraced by artisans and the swelling ranks of small businesspeople in commercial centers. The early political parties were modeled on fraternal societies. Later in the nineteenth century fraternal orders supplied the pattern for temperance organizations, early labor unions like the Knights of Labor, student societies such as the Greek-letter fraternities, and after the Civil War, veterans groups, such as the Grand Army of the Republic.

Fraternal and other mutual benefit associations were organized distinctively as federated or franchiselike entities, with local units nested in state bodies that were in turn affiliated with national, and in the case of the Freemasons international, frameworks. This form gave them an extraordinary capacity to disseminate information, which is why they played such important roles during the American Revolution, and to cement commercial and political relationships. In the second half of the nineteenth century these national associations grew rapidly, becoming the dominant form of American voluntary associations.

Such visitors to the United States as Alexis de Tocqueville proclaimed that philanthropic and voluntary associations were examples of the genius of American democracy. Yet not all Americans shared the Frenchman's enthusiasm. In 1829 the Unitarian leader William Ellery Channing, citing the power of these associations to sway masses of people, branded them "perilous instruments" that, as "a kind of irregular government created within our Constitutional government," should be "watched closely." In 1832 Henry St. George Tucker, a Virginia jurist, worried about their tendency to accumulate vast wealth and warned against "the wretched policy of permitting the whole property of society to be swallowed up in the insatiable gulph of public charities."

Tensions between Religious and Scientific Philanthropy, 1860–1890

The Civil War put the range of American philanthropic traditions into play, often in opposition to one another. The Union was not prepared for the immense challenge of providing relief to the hundreds of thousands of wounded and sick who fell victim to this first modern war, nor did the federal government have plans to deal with the millions of emancipated slaves and the catastrophic devastation of the southern economy and polity.

Ultimately these tasks fell to voluntary bodies, the largest of which, the U.S. Sanitary Commission and the U.S. Christian Commission, responded very differently to the suffering produced by the war. The Sanitary Commission, a tightly centralized, nationally federated organization supported by voluntary contributions of money, goods, and labor, used professional sanitarians and physicians to provide public health and relief services to the military. Its measured bureaucratic responses to problems set precedents for the methods of "scientific philanthropy" that dominated later in the century. Where the Sanitary Commission rationed relief according to the "worthiness" of recipients and abstract criteria of efficiency, the U.S. Christian Commission, drawing on the religious tradition of "friendly visiting," used volunteers to respond to the needs of suffering individuals. Viewing charity as a spiritual transaction rather than an allocation of resources and personnel, the Christian Commission was frequently at odds with its more bureaucratic rival.

This tension between philanthropic styles persisted for the rest of the century. During Reconstruction voluntary agencies fought fiercely over how best to rebuild the South's shattered economic and political institutions and how to help emancipated slaves acquire the skills needed for self-sufficiency and citizenship. Although these disagreements ensured the failure of the most ambitious humanitarian initiative of the period, they did leave an enduring legacy in the first grant-making foundations, the Peabody and Slater Funds, which supported black colleges throughout the South.

The panic of 1873 and the decade of depression and economic disruption that followed produced widespread unemployment, and thousands of men and their families took to the road in search of work. Many ended up in cities, where public and private welfare agencies were better equipped to address their needs. Early on, tensions developed between the "scientific philanthropists," who regarded poverty and dependency as products of idleness and vice and "sentimental" and "spontaneous" responses to poverty as socially dangerous, and the religious philanthropists, including Protestant evangelical groups, Roman Catholics, and Jews.

Although religious impulses underlay the efforts of all groups involved in poor relief, their differences reflected both the increasing heterogeneity of religious life and the emerging splits between "liberal" and "conservative" Protestants. The perfectionist and progressive theologies and the privileged status of their members led the liberals to embrace social readings of Darwinian biology that treated poverty as an inevitable outcome of the struggle for existence necessary to the progress of the race. They contended that the propertied classes emerged from that struggle as the most "fit" to govern society. Conservative Protestants rejected Darwinian biology as unscriptural and dismissed its social and political implications as violations of their deeply held convictions about spiritual equality.

In the late 1870s the scientific philanthropists, drawing on the work of British reformers, proposed a program for systematizing municipal poor relief efforts through "charity organization societies." These societies proposed to identify, register, and classify all applicants for welfare assistance and, on that basis, determine their eligibility for relief. By 1890 virtually every city of any size in the United States had a charity organization society.

These initiatives received material encouragement from such wealthy industrialists as Andrew Carnegie (1835–1919), whose 1889 essay "Wealth" in the *North American Review* proclaimed, "It were better for mankind that the millions of the rich were thrown into the sea than so spent as to encourage the slothful, the drunken, the unworthy." Nonetheless Carnegie went on to urge the wealthy to dispense their fortunes during their lifetimes rather than cursing and corrupting their heirs with great unearned fortunes. Carnegie donated much of his wealth in support of public libraries and educational institutions, which presumably served the worthy poor by providing opportunities for them to improve themselves through reading and education.

The increasingly secular and elitist character of scientific philanthropy stimulated more humanitarian initiatives. The British reform journalist W. T. Stead (1849–1912) dismissively retitled Carnegie's essay "The Gospel of Wealth" then wrote an influential critique of American conditions, *If Christ Came to Chicago* (1893). The evangelical clergyman Charles

Andrew Carnegie (1835–1919). Although Carnegie's philanthropic activities did not commence until 1900, in 1899 he wrote an article in the *North American Review* in which he espoused his views on distributing large portions of personal wealth for the benefit of society. LIBRARY OF CONGRESS

Sheldon (1857–1946) moved readers to apply scriptural principles to their economic, social, and political dealings by asking "What would Jesus do?" in his best-selling novel *In His Steps* (1896). Jane Addams (1860–1935) and other young Christian reformers, following the model of London's Toynbee Hall, established settlement houses that brought the privileged and the poor together for mutual understanding and civic activism. Though his own motives were more political than religious, the pioneer photojournalist Jacob Riis (1849–1914) studied New York slum conditions. His book *How the Other Half Lives* (1890) was one of the most powerfully influential tracts on the Protestant social gospel, an important constituent of the Progressive movement of the early twentieth century.

The Rising Tide of Reform and the Reintegration of American Philanthropy

At the end of the century Americans finally acknowledged that progress would not inevitably and irresistibly eradicate poverty. Whether moved by faith or motivated by enlightened self-interest, the wealthy, the learned, and the respectable who controlled the wealth of the nation began to grasp what Carnegie had said about the obligation of the privileged to place within the reach of their fellow citizens "ladders upon which the aspiring can rise" and in doing so return "their surplus to the mass of their fellows in the forms best calculated to do them lasting good."

The deepening political and economic crisis of the 1890s led reformers to launch a "mission to the millionaires," warning that failure to follow Carnegie's advice would force a wrathful nation to strip them of their riches. The Populist takeover of the Democratic Party in 1896 and its demands for an income tax and nationalization of banks, railroads, and other core industries underscored the necessity for major institutional changes.

The great social reforms of the Progressive Era came about under the leadership of the Republican standard-bearer, the New York patrician Theodore Roosevelt, and through the organizational genius of the Ohio coal and iron tycoon Marcus Alonzo Hanna rather than through the efforts of statesmen of more humble origins, indicating the extent to which the privileged classes embraced their public responsibilities. Chief among these, as the grant-making foundations created by Olivia Slocum Sage, John D. Rockefeller, and Carnegie early in the twentieth century demonstrated, was an appreciation for the power of wealth coupled with moral imagination.

See also **Abolition and Antislavery; Asylums; Clubs; Hospitals; Poverty; Progressivism; Reform, Idea of; Reform, Social; Settlement Houses; Social Gospel; Sociology; Temperance Movement; Wealth.**

Bibliography

Addams, Jane. *Twenty Years at Hull-house.* New York: Macmillan, 1910.

Carnegie, Andrew. *The Gospel of Wealth and Other Timely Essays.* New York: Century, 1900.

Carnes, Mark C. *Secret Ritual and Manhood in Victorian America.* New Haven, Conn.: Yale University Press, 1989.

Clawson, Mary Ann. *Constructing Brotherhood: Class, Gender, and Fraternalism.* Princeton, N.J.: Princeton University Press, 1989.

Curti, Merle, and Roderick Nash. *Philanthropy in the Shaping of Higher Education.* New Brunswick, N.J.: Rutgers University Press, 1965.

Cutlip, Scott M. *Fund Raising in the United States: Its Role in America's Philanthropy.* New Brunswick, N.J.: Rutgers University Press, 1965.

Dumenil, Lynn. *Freemasonry and American Culture, 1880–1939*. Princeton, N.J.: Princeton University Press, 1984.

Fischer, David Hackett. *Paul Revere's Ride*. New York: Oxford University Press, 1994.

Fleming, Walter Lynwood, ed. *Documentary History of Reconstruction: Political, Military, Social, Religious, Educational, and Industrial, 1865 to the Present Time*. Gloucester, Mass., P. Smith, 1960.

Franklin, John Hope. *Reconstruction after the Civil War*. Chicago: University of Chicago Press, 1961.

Gamm, Gerald, and Robert D. Putnam. "The Growth of Voluntary Associations in the United States, 1840–1940." *Journal of Interdisciplinary History* 29, no. 3 (Spring 1999): 511–557.

Griffin, Clifford Stephen. *Their Brothers' Keepers: Moral Stewardship in the United States, 1800–1865*. New Brunswick, N.J.: Rutgers University Press, 1960.

Hall, Peter Dobkin. *The Organization of American Culture, 1700–1900: Private Institutions, Elites, and the Origins of American Nationality*. New York: New York University Press, 1982.

Huggins, Nathan Irvin. *Protestants against Poverty: Boston's Charities, 1870–1900*. Westport, Conn.: Greenwood Press, 1971.

Katz, Michael B. *In the Shadow of the Poorhouse: A Social History of Welfare in America*. New York: Basic Books, 1986.

Miller, Howard Smith. *The Legal Foundations of American Philanthropy, 1776–1844*. Madison: State Historical Society of Wisconsin, 1961.

Scott, Anne Firor. *Natural Allies: Women's Associations in American History*. Urbana: University of Illinois Press, 1991.

Skocpol, Theda. "The Tocqueville Problem: Civic Engagement in American Democracy." *Social Science History* 21, no. 4 (Fall 1996): 455–479.

Story, Ronald. *The Forging of an Aristocracy: Harvard and Boston's Upper Class, 1800–1870*. Middletown, Conn.: Wesleyan University Press, 1980.

Watson, Frank Dekker. *The Charity Organization Movement in the United States: A Study in American Philanthropy*. New York: Macmillan, 1922.

Weeks, Edward. *The Lowells and Their Institute*. Boston: Little, Brown, 1966.

Wilson, Dorothy Clarke. *Stranger and Traveler: The Story of Dorothea Dix, American Reformer*. Boston: Little, Brown, 1975.

PETER HALL

PHILIPPINES.   See Overseas Possessions.

PHILOSOPHY   What is philosophy and who is a philosopher are questions that are always answered relative to contemporary conceptions and concerns. Preachers and theologians, such as Jonathan Edwards, are sometimes considered philosophers, as are statesmen and politicians, from James Madison and Thomas Jefferson to John C. Calhoun and Abraham Lincoln; college philosophy teachers; independent sages and intellectuals like Ralph Waldo Emerson, Henry David Thoreau, and Oliver Wendell Holmes; and scientists such as Louis Agassiz. The story of philosophy in the nineteenth century ends with its professionalization, which occurred along with the professionalization of learning in general and the development of the research university. Colleges and universities were transformed from places of indoctrination where teachers transmitted accepted truths to students into places of inquiry where the job of the professor was to find new knowledge. Pragmatism, often regarded as the uniquely American philosophy, emerged out of all these stories, either as continuation or reaction, and it occupied an important place in the professionalization of American philosophy. Since pragmatism is covered in its own article, this entry briefly surveys the other antecedents of contemporary American philosophy.

In the early nineteenth century the dominant philosophy in America was derived from Scottish common sense. Common sense viewed moral perception, judgment, and ideas as innate and universal, similar to perception of the external world through the senses. It thus could be deployed against skepticism and in favor of an autonomy of science from religion.

The most influential and widely known development in American philosophy early in the nineteenth century emerged neither from the university nor from the pulpit but in the writings of the transcendentalists, especially Ralph Waldo Emerson (1803–1882) and Henry David Thoreau (1817–1862). Using Samuel Taylor Coleridge's version of Immanuel Kant as a way of revolting against the dominant American philosophies that had come from England and Scotland, Emerson espoused a philosophy of individualism and democracy that departed from the established schools, which were designed to reinforce conventional values. To followers of John Locke, both in England and in the United States, individual feeling was the source of schism and war, and the faculty of understanding was the source of peace, truth, and republican government. In contrast Emerson saw feeling as the route to authenticity and its own sort of truth. Initially ordained as a Unitarian minister, Emerson wrote inspiring secular sermons, which he published in essay form. The transcendentalists were "idealists," not in Plato's sense but in opposition to commercial materialism and in support of the uses of experience to find the ideal within the real. The Civil War made a revolt against conventional values in the name of democracy attractive, and the prophetic character of Emerson's and Thoreau's writing fit perfectly with the needs of the times, being neither skeptical nor a ratification of traditional values. Thoreau was educated at Harvard but earned his living through pencil making and surveying. In "Civil Disobedience" (1849) he applied transcendental themes to political issues. Both Emerson and Thoreau were far more influential across the world than other American philosophers of the time. Emerson and Thoreau influenced such diverse thinkers as Friedrich Nietzche, the American pragmatists, and Mohandas K. Gandhi.

Throughout the nineteenth century American philosophy continued to turn from Scottish common sense to the philosophy of the Germans. New attention to the importance of time, history, and progress, which led to the Darwinian revolution in science, prompted Americans to look for a philosophy that would protect their religious beliefs and their morality, now suddenly vulnerable to attack as the continuity between common sense and the latest science became questionable. The religion and the politics that Americans defended was individualistic and democratic, and Hegelian idealism seemed the appropriate philosophy for defense of these ideals.

As part of a democratic movement of self-education, philosophical clubs and lecture series sprang up throughout the country. The so-called St. Louis Hegelians were led by William Torrey Harris (1835–1909), who was later the U.S. commissioner of education. Harris founded the St. Louis Philosophical Club in 1866, and in 1867 he founded the *Journal of Speculative Philosophy,* the first professional philosophy journal published in English.

The most important eastern counterpart of the St. Louis Hegelians was the Cambridge Metaphysical Club, founded in 1868 by William James (1842–1910) and Oliver Wendell Holmes Jr. (1841–1935). With the addition of Charles Sanders Peirce (1839–1914) among its members, this club is considered the fountainhead of pragmatism. Members of the Metaphysical Club shared a faith in evolution, although not necessarily Darwinian evolution. They developed an idealism that rejected a priori knowledge but continued to search for a unity of theory and practice.

Philosophers from the Midwest and the East met at the Concord School in the summers of 1879 through 1883. The school was founded in Concord, Massachusetts, by Emerson and Bronson Alcott (1799–1888), and the faculty included Harris, James, and Charles Sanders Peirce's father, Benjamin Peirce (1809–1880), a noted mathematician. Midwestern philosophers, whose idealism was derived from Germany, and eastern philosophers, whose idealism was the more romantic transcendentalism, tried to formulate a unified research program. American philosophy became less autodidactic and more professional as precise communication was adopted as vital to the discipline. The popularity of idealism was so complete that when the *Philosophical Review* was founded

in 1892 at Cornell, its editor claimed that all American philosophers agreed that mind is the only absolute reality.

Apart from the pragmatists, Josiah Royce (1855–1916) emerged at the end of the nineteenth century as the leading creative thinker in American philosophy. Royce was a professor of philosophy and as such a professional philosopher. After studying in Germany and at Johns Hopkins, he taught English at Berkeley before moving to the Department of Philosophy at Harvard in 1882. Royce's idealism confirmed the priority of mind as ultimate reality but rejected interpretations that designated mind as individual mind rather than as the intelligible structure of the universe. His most important works from this time include *The Religious Aspect of Philosophy* (1885) and *The World and the Individual* (1900–1901).

When the nineteenth century ended, pragmatism was a flourishing school and philosophy was an established professional activity. Twentieth-century philosophers found a continuity of enterprise with the philosophers of the late nineteenth century but not those of a hundred years earlier.

See also **Evolution; Pragmatism; Transcendentalism.**

Bibliography
Kuklick, Bruce. *Churchmen and Philosophers.* New Haven, Conn.: Yale University Press, 1985.
———. *The Rise of American Philosophy, Cambridge, Massachusetts, 1860–1930.* New Haven, Conn.: Yale University Press, 1977.
Schneider, Herbert. *A History of American Philosophy.* 2d ed. New York: Columbia University Press, 1963.
White, Morton Gabriel. *Science and Sentiment in America.* New York: Oxford University Press, 1972.

EUGENE GARVER

PHOTOGRAPHY   Photography, introduced into the United States in late 1839, irrevocably changed the means by which Americans conceptualized their world. Once dependent on the spoken or written word, or on artists' conceptions rendered in paint or ink, Americans now could turn to "writing with light" for authentic, truthful images of events, personages, and faraway scenes, seeing for themselves in a photograph as if they were viewing the scene in person.

The proliferation of photographs, photographic equipment and materials, and technical expertise throughout the nineteenth century was a response to the ever increasing demand for photography. The history of the business and technology of photography in and of itself is a success story of capitalistic enterprise. Although photography was a commercial practice, it also abetted and reified the great sweep of social and cultural change Americans experienced throughout the century. The many forms of photography altered Americans' relationships with each other as it altered visual perception of the world. Personal relationships could be confirmed and one's character inspected through a visit to the daguerreotypist or photographer. By mid-century, relatives, strangers from afar, and celebrities could be known through the cheap, fashionable paper photograph known as a *carte de visite* sent through the mail. Distant places, current events, wars, and newsworthy personages could be instantly apprehended through stereopticon slides and, later, paper stereographs studied through the lenses of a stereoscope—while sitting in the comfort of one's parlor. By the end of the century Americans took camera in hand, creating that class known as amateur photographers.

The history of photography is, at its core, a history of technological innovation not in cameras alone, but also in the photosensitive medium upon which the image was fixed. According to the historian of technology Reese V. Jenkins, the history of the American photographic industry in the nineteenth century may be charted in four stages: the daguerreotype (1839–1855), wet collodion (1855–1880), dry gelatin on glass plates (1880–1895), and gelatin on celluloid roll film, commonly known as the amateur roll film system (1895–1909). Within each of these stages the contours of American society and culture may be discerned.

Daguerreotypy

Daguerreotypy, the first commercially viable photographic process, was developed by two Frenchmen, Joseph Nicéphore Niepce, and the better known Louis Jacques Mandé Daguerre, who announced the process in August 1839. By the end of the year the procedure was known in the United States, and commercial photography, despite an economic depression that lasted until 1843, began to take shape. The daguerreotype, known for its clarity, was a silver-coated copper plate exposed to iodine vapors just prior to exposure to light through a camera. Once exposed, the plate was treated with mercury vapors to develop the latent image and then fixed in a bath of sodium thiosulfate (known as "hypo"). This produced a direct-positive image that could not be reproduced. In subsequent years, small-scale "operators" learned technical and chemical processes from manuals or from each other, and depended on European supply

houses or small American manufacturers for the necessary chemicals, cameras, and optical equipment.

The business of daguerreotypy quickly changed, however. By the eve of the Civil War, Americans had enthusiastically embraced daguerreotypy, especially for portraiture. They flocked to urban "daguerreian rooms" or "daguerreian parlors" in the commercial centers of cities and towns, near fashionable shops and hotels, and along fashionable avenues, such as New York City's lower Broadway. There they sat for their portraits drawn truthfully by the sun (the "pencil of nature") or admired the variety of portraits and landscapes displayed in these commercial photographic galleries. Just as the daguerreotype of Judge Pyncheon reveals his true character in Nathaniel Hawthorne's 1851 romance, *The House of the Seven Gables*, so the daguerreotype portraits of Americans were thought to be revelatory agents in which one's character traits could be discerned (and corrected, if necessary). Even viewing a daguerreotype seemed an exercise in this "natural magic," dependent on the cultural belief in scientific positivism. The mirrorlike surface of the silvery daguerreotype could hide as well as reveal, however, necessitating booklike cases to protect the fragile image from scratches and to shade light so that the image could be revealed. Ralph Waldo Emerson confided to his journal, "People who go Daguerreotyping have a pretty solemn time. They come home confessing and lamenting their sins. A Daguerreotyping Institute is as good as a national Fast" (Rudisill, *Mirror Image*, p. 191). Charles and Henry Meade and Mathew B. Brady in New York City, M. A. Root in Philadelphia, Albert Sands Southworth and Josiah Johnson Hawes in Boston, and similar operators in cities large and small enjoyed business success and celebrity. Other entrepreneurs prospered through supplying the demand for photographic materials. By the early 1850s, the Scovill Manufacturing Company and the E. & H. T. Anthony Company were leaders in photographic supplies for the lucrative New York City market and for the nation.

"Brady of Broadway" became the best-known photographic parlor in mid-nineteenth-century America. Mathew B. Brady (1823/1824–1896) opened his Daguerrean Miniature Gallery at 205–207 Broadway in 1844, and attracted a clientele by soliciting those whom he termed "the great and the good" to sit for their portraits. In 1849, Brady opened a gallery in Washington, D.C., to acquire portraits of statesmen and politicians, and the next year he announced the publication of his *Gallery of Illustrious Americans*, twelve lithographs made after his daguerreotypes of personages such as President Zachary Taylor and the ornithologist John James Au-

Mathew Brady (1823/1824–1896). Lithograph of the first photo of Mathew Brady, age twenty-six. LIBRARY OF CONGRESS: PRINTS AND PHOTOGRAPHS DIVISION

dubon. Brady is best remembered, however, for his Civil War reportage through photography, obtained by sending an army of photographers, including Alexander Gardner and Timothy O'Sullivan, to the battlefields to capture the dead with light. Brady's 1862 exhibition, "The Dead of Antietam," shocked visitors with its graphic depiction of corpses. After the Civil War, Brady's fortune and fame fell, and although Congress purchased his collection of negatives in 1875 for $25,000, the nearly blind photographer-entrepreneur-historian died penniless in 1896.

Photography on Paper

Daguerreotypy was practiced into the twentieth century, but by the 1860s the process was overtaken by the wet collodion process that had been developed, again in Europe, in the 1840s. In the United States, the durable tintype, a direct-positive on sheet iron, and the fragile ambrotype, a direct-positive on glass, employed this process. Tintypes and ambrotypes were cheap and popular, but eventually photographers and consumers turned to photography on paper. This process offered photographers the means to make multiple prints from a collodion-covered glass plate negative treated with silver nitrate. This created a photosensitive silver halide surface that, when exposed in a camera, converted part of the silver halide grains into metallic silver. The latent image was then revealed with other chemicals that furthered this process, and was finally fixed with hypo. When this glass-plate negative was placed atop paper coated with silver chloride and exposed to the sun, then fixed again with hypo, many positives could be produced. The continuing boom in photography led to high demand for albumen (egg whites) paper, necessary to retain detail when the image was transferred from the glass plate negative to the surface of the paper positive.

Photography on paper, in the form of the *carte de visite* (approximately two and a half by four inches) and the later, larger cabinet card (five by seven inches) satisfied American consumers' desires for multiple prints—not only of themselves but also of celebrities and of the politicians, generals, and statesmen whose newsworthiness warranted a trip to the photographer. The temporary and permanent dislocations caused by the Civil War also abetted the *carte de visite* boom, and many a parlor album from this era tells the sad story of families, neighbors, and friends parted by distance and by death. Oliver Wendell Holmes (1809–1894), a photography enthusiast, observed that the *carte de visite* was a form of "social currency, the sentimental 'green-backs' of civilization." As a form of emotional, if extralegal, tender, portrait photographs served to reify emotional bonds.

However, photographic periodicals, such as *Humphrey's Journal* and *Anthony's Photographic Bulletin*, carried articles about the social limits of commercial photographic practice, as did popular journals such as *Harper's New Monthly Magazine*. In both nonfiction and fiction, working-class behavior was decried, the Irish were disparaged, and African Americans were rarely mentioned at all. Indeed, not until the post–Reconstruction era were African Americans depicted fictionally in photographic parlors—and then only to ridicule attempts at adopting what was by then a white, middle-class commodity. Embedded in photographic portraiture was the power of self-representation, and those groups at the margins, although most certainly depicted, were thought to be unworthy of genteel self-culture. Photography has often been called a democratic art, but in the nineteenth century photography mirrored the classist and racist limits of American democracy.

Stereography

Another form of paper photography, the stereograph, gained a popularity in the 1850s and 1860s that did

Stereograph of the Senate Chamber. The widespread popularity of the stereograph is attested by its depiction of government landmarks. When placed in a special viewer called a stereoscope, the two halves appear to be three-dimensional. Photography by Bell and Brothers, 1867. © HULTON-DEUTSCH COLLECTION/CORBIS

not wane until the 1920s. Stereographs were taken with a camera having two lenses about two and a half inches apart—replicating the distance between human eyes. When pasted side by side upon cardboard and viewed through a stereoscope, the image appeared in three dimensions. With the perfection in the early 1860s of a cheap stereoscope by Oliver Wendell Holmes (who refused to patent it, thus allowing widespread duplication), what was once an optical curiosity became a popular pastime for the family. "I think there is no parlor in America where there is not a Stereoscope," remarked Dr. Hermann W. Vogel in 1883. Stereography quickly became a profitable business—a primary line of some firms, a sideline for many photographers across the United States. The American Stereoscopic Company was formed in Philadelphia by the Langenheim brothers, who had earlier attempted stereo-daguerreotypes. The E. & H. T. Anthony Company imported stereographs and also manufactured them, purchasing negatives from itinerant professional and amateur photographers. By the end of the century, the Meadville, Pennsylvania, Keystone View Company had purchased the negatives of many other firms, and by 1898 it had organized production geared to schools and libraries.

Amateur Photography

The technically complex wet collodion process restricted photography to professionals for the most part, and to a few amateurs who possessed the wealth, leisure, and patience to master the difficult procedures. In addition, photographic materials were highly perishable, a condition that proved to be a barrier to the expansion of the industry. In the late 1870s, however, gelatin-coated glass plates, sensitized in the factory, solved both concerns. Gelatin dry plates, perfected in Great Britain, promised greater sensitivity to light and a longer shelf life.

With this new technique, photographers could offer a more varied array of portraits, landscape views, and advertising cards. And consumers themselves availed themselves of this new process. Armed with sets of bulky and fragile dry plates and "detective cameras" disguised as fishing tackle boxes, briefcases, or paper bags, amateur photographers tramped through the rural countryside and in urban parks, testing their skills—and trying the patience of unsuspecting subjects.

George Eastman was one of these amateurs, and his avid interest led him to manufacture dry gelatin plates. Competition forced him to innovate, and beginning in 1884 he sought and received patents for a variety of products and processes known as roll film. Eastman, however, wanted to tap the large amateur market with an easy-to-use, lightweight portable camera. In 1887 he coined the term "Kodak" and introduced his system. Enclosed in a leather-covered box, the camera held a one-hundred-exposure roll of

The Eastman Dry Plate and Photographic Products Factory. Women working in the print mounting department, c. 1890. GEORGE EASTMAN HOUSE/ARCHIVE PHOTOS

film that, when fully exposed, was returned, inside the camera, to the Eastman Company. After development, the snapshots along with the camera loaded anew with another roll of film, would be returned to the amateur. At the cost of twenty-five dollars, the camera did for the amateur what the professional photographer could not: it captured the incidental and the private, the purely individualistic tastes of an individualistic society.

Bibliography

Earle, Edward W., Jr., ed. *Points of View: the Stereograph in America: A Cultural History.* Rochester, N.Y.: Visual Studies Workshop Press, 1979.

Hales, Peter Bacon. *Silver Cities: The Photography of American Urbanization, 1839–1915.* Philadelphia: Temple University Press, 1984.

Jenkins, Reese V. *Images and Enterprise: Technology and the American Photographic Industry 1839 to 1925.* Baltimore: Johns Hopkins University Press, 1975.

Jussim, Estelle, and Elizabeth Lindquist-Cock. *Landscape as Photograph.* New Haven, Conn.: Yale University Press, 1985.

Krauss, Rosalind. "Photography's Discursive Spaces: Landscape/View." *Art Journal* 42 (Winter 1982): 311–319.

Mensel, Robert E. " 'Kodakers Lying in Wait': Amateur Photography and the Right of Privacy in New York, 1885–1915." *American Quarterly* 43 (March 1991): 24–35.

Newhall, Beaumont. *The History of Photography from 1839 to the Present Day.* 5th ed. New York: Museum of Modern Art, 1982.

Panzer, Mary. *Mathew Brady and the Image of History.* Washington, D.C.: Smithsonian Institution Press for the National Portrait Gallery, 1997.

Rudisill, Richard. *Mirror Image: The Influence of the Daguerreotype on American Society.* Albuquerque: University of New Mexico Press, 1971.

Sobieczek, Robert, and Odette M. Appel. *The Spirit of Fact: The Daguerreotypes of Southworth and Hawes, 1843–1862.* Boston: Godine, 1976.

Taft, Robert. *Photography and the American Scene: A Social History, 1839–1889.* 1938. Reprint, New York: Dover, 1964.

Trachtenberg, Alan. *Reading American Photographs: Images as History, Mathew Brady to Walker Evans.* New York: Hill and Wang, 1989.

SHIRLEY TERESA WAJDA

PLANNING.   See **City and Regional Planning.**

PLANTATION, THE   Colonial Americans referred to all large rural estates as "plantations," but by the turn of the nineteenth century the term was reserved for slave-based agricultural operations in the southern United States. Modern scholars have refined their definition of the phrase even further, applying it to properties worked by at least twenty slaves. Only a tiny minority (some 3 percent in 1860) of white southern families acquired such large concentrations of human property. Still, the region's unique identity came to be associated with plantations tended by a multitude of African American slaves. In fact, the plantation system that sprang into existence in the American South illustrated the many ways in which the region was firmly integrated into a global capitalist economy.

The first English colonists to create a plantation complex in North America initially relied upon white indentured servants as field hands. But after the 1670s a steady influx of African slaves oriented plantation life toward African bondage. The American Revolution (1775–1783) temporarily disrupted the production of staple crops in the South as landowners fled from their properties and slaves sought refuge or were forcibly taken behind British lines. With the establishment of an American republic in the 1780s, however, plantation owners quickly reestablished their businesses, acquiring new slaves when necessary and reorienting their crop production to meet the era's changing demands.

The Antebellum Plantation System

In the nineteenth century the southern plantation economy hinged upon the production of four primary staple crops: tobacco, rice, cotton, and sugar. The first

Plantation of Octave J. Darby. Built by François St. Marc Darby, 3 March 1813. New Iberia, Louisiana. LIBRARY OF CONGRESS

two had served as mainstays of the colonial plantation system. In the 1790s technological breakthroughs enabled planters to introduce several new crops that dramatically restructured the entire southern economy. Thanks to the rapid growth of the English textile industry in the late eighteenth century, the demand for cotton increased exponentially. The southern climate was ideal for the cultivation of cotton, but the difficulty of cleaning tenacious cotton seeds from cotton lint vexed southern growers until 1793, when Eli Whitney, a Massachusetts-born tutor residing on a Georgia plantation, perfected a new cotton gin. "King Cotton" soon reigned supreme over the plantation South. In 1800 southern growers produced 73,000 bales; in 1820 that number jumped to 334,000 bales; and on the eve of the Civil War the South produced 4.5 million bales. By 1850 approximately 57 percent of all southern slaves resided on plantations and farms that produced cotton. At about the same time Whitney was working on his cotton gin, Jean Étienne Boré, an expatriate planter from Santo Domingo, improved the sugar refinement process, thereby enabling southerners to create a profitable sugar plantation economy in Louisiana.

Seeking to flee the exhausted soil that was lowering productivity in states such as Virginia and South Carolina—the most important plantation colonies in the eighteenth century—planters moved into Georgia, Alabama, Tennessee, Mississippi, Louisiana, Florida, Missouri, Texas, and Arkansas between

1790 and 1860 (at which time there were some forty-seven thousand slave owners). Although this migration disrupted family relationships for both slave owners and slaves, the new plantations remained ensconced within an intricate financial network, linking seemingly isolated rural properties with resources and markets around the country and, indeed, around the world. In 1860 Great Britain remained the most important consumer of southern cotton, providing a market for 2,344,000 bales. Continental Europe served as the second-most-important market, purchasing 1,069,000 bales. The rapidly expanding textile industry of the northern United States absorbed almost another million bales.

As planters looked to these distant markets, they also forged ties with smaller neighboring farms. White farmers who owned few or no slaves relied upon planters to gin their cotton harvest and, in many cases, to bring it to market. This relationship helped to cement the loyalties of the majority of white southerners to a plantation system that actually concentrated the lion's share of agricultural profits in the hands of a small group of extremely wealthy planters. In 1830 approximately 252,000 white southern families possessed slaves (or 36 percent); by 1860 that figure was approximately 394,000 (or 25 percent of all white southern families). The planters themselves relied heavily upon middlemen known as factors, who extended credit during the planting season and received a brokerage fee in return for marketing

Antebellum Louisiana. The plantation house "Arlington," near Lake Providence, Louisiana. LIBRARY OF CONGRESS

the harvested crops. Planters also looked to their factors to provide consumer goods such as clothing, fine furniture, and books. In short, even the most remote plantations existed only because of the opportunity and incentive created by global financial exchanges.

The Postbellum Plantation System

In the decades following the Civil War, the economy of the South continued to revolve around the production of cotton. The defeat of the Confederacy in 1865, however, had permanently dismantled the slave labor system. Upon acquiring their freedom, African Americans sought land of their own so that they could live as independent agricultural producers. When Reconstruction policies denied them this dream, blacks negotiated new terms of labor with the white landowners who had previously been their masters. After initial experiments with wages proved unsatisfactory to both whites and blacks, a new system of sharecropping became the most common arrangement for cotton production in the postbellum South. Instead of working in gangs under the direct supervision of white overseers, as had been the case in the Old South, individual African American families were assigned small plots of land and were provided with seed, tools, and other supplies. Sharecropping enabled African American families to decrease their workloads some 30 percent below antebellum levels and also afforded these families some degree of autonomy in their daily decisions. Unfair credit and accounting practices, however, denied black sharecroppers their portion of the profits, leaving many

farmers with less than nothing to show for their arduous labor.

By the end of the nineteenth century, increasing numbers of white farmers had themselves become sharecroppers. The average size of the farms on which southern cotton was produced declined dramatically. Although the South remained extremely dependent upon the production of cotton as a cash crop and although regional cotton yields grew steadily, the era of the great plantations had passed. Financial power now rested in the hands of merchants and absentee landowners who did not concern themselves directly with the cultivation of cash crops.

See also **Agriculture; Cotton; Foreign Trade and Tariffs; Slavery,** *subentry on* **Slave Life.**

Bibliography

Fite, Gilbert C. *Cotton Fields No More: Southern Agriculture, 1865–1980.* Lexington: University Press of Kentucky, 1984.

Gray, Lewis C. *History of Agriculture in the Southern United States to 1860.* 2 vols. Reprint, Gloucester, Mass.: Peter Smith, 1958. The original edition was published in 1933.

Roark, James L. *Masters without Slaves: Southern Planters in the Civil War and Reconstruction.* New York: Norton, 1977.

Wright, Gavin. *The Political Economy of the Cotton South: Households, Markets, and Wealth in the Nineteenth Century.* New York: Norton, 1978.

JEFFREY ROBERT YOUNG

POLICE   During the nineteenth century crime rose both in cities and on the frontier as the nation's borders and population expanded. The population of the United States surged from five million to seventy-six million while the borders grew from encompassing 891,000 to 3.6 million square miles. Most of the population growth was concentrated in the large cities of the Northeast and Midwest, whereas the land expansion was in the West. Enforcing the law in crowded cities and on remote frontiers became a complicated matter. Proper law enforcement required an organized police force in cities and towns as well as a system of sheriffs, deputies, and marshals on the rural frontiers.

Urban Police

At the beginning of the nineteenth century, law enforcement activities were primarily carried out by constables during the day and by night watchmen in the evening. The night watchman was usually a volunteer, whereas the constable charged a fee for his service. This system was rife with inefficiency. Since the night watchman was a volunteer, he often fled at any sign of danger. Also, since the constable charged a fee, lower-income people were denied adequate police protection. Further, police forces in the early nineteenth century were fragmented. Watchmen were often posted in sentry boxes throughout the city. They had no communications with one another and did not patrol the streets. In the early nineteenth century it was not uncommon for a single city to have several separate police forces. In 1800 New York City had five different types of police: the mayor, the high constable, constables, marshals, and watchmen. New York and other cities had daytime constables and night watchmen under separate commands.

Large cities were the first locations to have modern police forces. London, England's Metropolitan Police Force, instituted in 1829 by Home Secretary Robert Peel, was the first modern police force. Fifteen years later the United States followed the British lead when New York reorganized its police force on Peel's model. After this, organized public police forces began to appear in large cities in the Northeast. At this time the system of night watchmen was abolished. The Peel model was adopted by Boston in 1849 and by Philadelphia in 1856.

Uniforms

Police officers wore uniforms most commonly fashioned on the style of the Union Army in the Civil War. The very fact that law enforcement officials were easily recognizable served to deter crime. Additionally, the uniforms allowed residents to identify officers easily when seeking assistance with directions and other minor needs.

Political Influences

Prior to the Civil War police were closely tied to the political players in city government. Since salaries were paid and personnel were selected by the city, politicians used police hiring as patronage for their supporters. This was reflected in the ethnic makeup of the police force. Irish politicians gave Irish political supporters jobs on the police force, and politicians of other ethnic groups did likewise. This meant that police were partisans of the local politicians. During elections in cities such as Boston, Cincinnati, and New York, police openly promoted the politicians who had gotten them their jobs. Further, since hiring was done purely on a political basis, many police departments were plagued with incompetent employees. Under the protection of political officials, police extorted money from prisoners, were excessively absent, and, in some cases, assaulted superior officers. In 1894 the Lexow Committee in New York exposed widespread corruption in the police force. This led to a state law mandating the creation of an apolitical police commissioner. Other cities opted to take police control away from politicians as well. Police departments were then directed by appointed or elected city officials. By the end of the century the trend toward bipartisanship led many cities to appoint a chief or commissioner to lead the police force.

Rural Areas and the Western Frontier

Law enforcement in the West had a different pattern of development. In the early part of the century, boomtowns in the West did not have established law enforcement agents. Members of a vigilance committee, or "vigilantes," performed law enforcement. Since vigilantes did not operate under an official mandate, justice was often subjective. At the onset of the Mexican War in 1846, the federal government created the Texas Rangers to assist with raids and reconnaissance. The Rangers remained a constabulary force during the remaining years of the nineteenth century, and in 1901 the organization became the official law enforcement agency of the state. Deputies of the U.S. Marshals served as the official law enforcement on the frontier. The federal marshal system was created by the Judiciary Act of 1789, to serve as enforcement agents of the attorney general. The marshals were empowered to enforce federal laws, as well as to manage prisons, execute court orders, and conduct the census. Cities in the West gradually formed organized police forces. Los Angeles was serviced by a vigilance committee called the Los Angeles Rangers until 1854, when they became an official organization through a $4,000 state grant. In 1869 Los Angeles organized a full-time, twelve-man police force. In areas without large cities or towns, law enforcement was carried out at the county level. The sheriff was in charge of county policing. To fulfill this task, he was granted the authority to enlist deputies to form a posse if circumstances warranted.

See also **Crime,** *subentry on* **Overview; Vigilantes.**

Bibliography

Cresswell, Stephen. *Mormons, Moonshiners, Cowboys, and Klansman: Federal Law Enforcement in the South and West, 1870–1893.* Tuscaloosa: University of Alabama Press, 1991.

Foner, Eric, and John A. Garraty, eds. *The Reader's Companion to American History.* Boston: Houghton Mifflin, 1991.

Hall, James Patrick. *Peacekeeping in America: A Developmental Study of American Law Enforcement: Philosophy and Systems.* Dubuque, Iowa: Kendall/Hunt, 1978.

Kurian, George Thomas. *Datapedia of the United States, 1790–2000: America Year by Year.* Lanham, Md.: Bernan Press, 1994.

More, Harry W., Jr., ed. *The American Police: Text and Readings.* St. Paul, Minn.: West, 1976.

Walker, Samuel. *A Critical History of Police Reform: The Emergence of Professionalism.* Lexington, Mass: D. C. Heath, 1977.

Wood, Daryl. "Police History and Organization." 1996. Web page available at http://www.uaa.alaska.edu/just/just110/police1.html.

BARRY BAIN

POLISH IMMIGRANTS. See **Immigration and Immigrants,** subentry on **Central and Eastern Europe.**

POLITICS

[This entry includes nine subentries:
Political Thought
Political Culture
Party Organization and Operations
The First Party System
The Second Party System
The Third Party System
Parties and the Press
Machines and Bosses
Corruption and Scandals.]

POLITICAL THOUGHT

In the "Author's Preface" to *Democracy in America* (1835), his masterly account of the United States in the early national period, Alexis de Tocqueville described the tasks of the country's new form of government:

> The first duty which is at this time imposed upon those who direct our affairs is to educate the democracy; to warm its faith, if that be possible; to purify its morals; to direct its energies; to substitute a knowledge of business for its inexperience, and an acquaintance with its true interests for its blind propensities; to adapt its government to time and place, and to modify it in accordance with the occurrences and the actors of the age.

Most important, Tocqueville concluded, "A new science of politics is indispensable to a new world."

The most significant issue for historians of American political thought is the relationship between liberalism and republicanism during the revolutionary and early national periods. Louis Hartz, in *The Liberal Tradition in America,* argued that the revolutionary experiment in democratic government was essentially a liberal enterprise, a product of the thought and work of the English liberal tradition found in the work of John Locke, Adam Smith, and Thomas Hobbes. But it was Locke above all who stood as the source of American liberalism: "Locke dominates American political thought, as no thinker anywhere dominates the political thought of a nation. He is a massive national cliché" (Hartz, p. 140). Eighteenth- and early-nineteenth-century liberalism focused on the inviolate rights of the individual to life, liberty, and property and held that the autonomy and independence of each citizen should remain forever free from the imposing power of tyrannical government. This liberal tradition was deeply intertwined with participation in the nascent market economy, and in the nineteenth-century United States the freedom of the marketplace became one of the defining characteristics of political thought.

For some time now, historians of the American Revolution have challenged Hartz's notion that Lockean liberalism pervaded the political thought of the revolutionary and early national periods. Such historians as Bernard Bailyn, Gordon S. Wood, J. G. A. Pocock, and others have found instead a "republican synthesis" that emphasized civic responsibility and the necessity for a virtuous and educated citizenry. In this formulation, Locke played almost no part in the development of American political thought. The "country Whig" intellectuals of England, such as John Trenchard and Thomas Gordon, were cited more frequently in late-eighteenth-century political rhetoric than was Locke, and it is in these traditions that we can find the roots of revolutionary and early national politics.

In fact, the languages of both "country Whig" virtuous republicanism and Lockean rights-based liberalism can be found in early American political discourse, and each intertwined with the Christian language of millennial perfectionism. Over the course of the nineteenth century, and especially under the impact of the Second Great Awakening, the rise of mass party politics, and the market revolution in Jacksonian America, American political discourse underwent a radical shift. The founders' hierarchical republicanism fell apart as the expansion of suffrage and the spread of political democracy extended the opportunities for participation in the republic's politics (at least for the nation's white male citizens). And some historians have identified a divergent tradition of working-class republicanism and "producerism" closely connected to the ideas of Thomas Paine. This tradition, developed most cogently in the workingmen's parties of Jacksonian America's cities, did not focus on the hierarchical ideals of virtue in classical republicanism, but instead emphasized the damaging effects of capitalist growth on the artisans' right to the products of their labor.

The growth of slavery in the South also affected ideas about politics. John C. Calhoun's *Disquisition on Government* and *Discourse on the Constitution and Government of the United States,* both written in the 1840s, proposed a new theory of American governance. Calhoun expanded on his earlier defense of the states' nullification rights over the federal government, developed during the debate on the Missouri Compromise, by arguing that there was concurrently a majority in the various sections of the country that required representation in a republican form of government. In order to protect the South's "peculiar institution" of black chattel slavery, Calhoun argued that the nation needed a dual presidency representing sectional concerns. By the 1850s a number of southern intellectuals, most prominently George Fitzhugh, expanded on Calhoun's ideas, defending slavery as a key ingredient in a just society and as a far more fair labor system than free-market capitalism.

The defense of slavery never attracted a serious political following beyond the South. Most political rhetoric of the antebellum South still relied upon the republican and liberal categories of freedom, liberty, independence, and the common good for whites. But southerners like Calhoun, James Henry Hammond, and Fitzhugh argued that such republican liberty was possible only in a slave society. The articulation of a free labor ideology by such Republican leaders as Abraham Lincoln and Chief Justice Salmon P. Chase in the antebellum North had a far more important impact on American political thinking. That ideology developed in opposition to the idea that a slave system better provided for a just society than market capitalism could. Free labor integrated elements of both the republican and the liberal traditions, emphasizing not only the individual rights of each citizen but also a faith in the power of the small producer. It thus appealed to a wide range of Americans. The coalition of interests in the Republican Party of the 1850s and after testifies to the success of the free-labor ideology in mobilizing political support.

The republican and liberal language of antebellum American politics survived into the late nineteenth century, but they were put to very different uses. In the absence of a true conservative political tradition in the United States, akin to the traditionalism and unease with progress evident in the work of the English social thinker Edmund Burke, liberalism developed at least two strains during the last third of the nineteenth century. One, laissez-faire liberalism, provided a foundation for modern conservatism in the twentieth century; the second, social liberalism, provided the foundation for the modern welfare state. Both laissez-faire liberalism and social liberalism (or what twentieth-century Progressives called the "new liberalism") accepted the core values of individual liberty and the sanctity of property, but they drew on different aspects of the powerful antebellum free labor faith. In the hands of the social thinker William Graham Sumner, a professor of social science at Yale University, and E. L. Godkin, editor of *The Nation,* the American liberal tradition meant support for free trade and the defense of individual rights of self-possession against the tyrannical hand of the federal government. Such social liberals as Lester Frank Ward repudiated the individualist basis of the laissez-faire liberalism of Godkin and Sumner and articulated a vision of government planning as the key to the progress of the nation. The only solution to the difficult social problems of the late nineteenth century—economic expansion, conflict between capital and labor, and the farmers' revolt—was scientific planning and government legislation.

Finally, the republicanism of some antebellum workingmen lived on in the collectivism of socialist intellectuals. Collectivism stretched back to utopian communities in the antebellum era, such as the Owenite and Fourierist cooperatives that dotted the American landscape in the 1830s, 1840s, and 1850s. Although socialism achieved only a limited following at the national level (and that in the early years of the twentieth century), a significant collectivist rhetoric pervaded late-nineteenth-century political thought. Wide-ranging social thinkers as Edward Bellamy, Henry Demarest Lloyd, and Henry George articulated a vision of political thought integrating the republican emphasis on civic virtue, antebellum perfectionist reform, and the expansion of government power for the public good.

The late nineteenth century also witnessed the expansion of women's involvement in the nation's public life. Most nineteenth-century political rhetoric about citizenship and participation dealt exclusively with men. Although women lacked the right to vote, the political participation of women over the course of the nineteenth century had an important effect on politics and American political thought. The antebellum suffrage movement evolved from women's active participation in the abolitionist movement, and by the Civil War their reformist activities brought them substantially into politics. During the late nineteenth century their activities challenged the categories of American political rhetoric. The demand for equality, and the argument that women deserved to participate in the fruits of the democratic experiment, found a wide audience. Many of the reformist activities of American women in the nineteenth century—public welfare, social legislation, and labor reform—found their way into politics and government and contributed to the "new liberalism" of twentieth-century Progressives.

The competing categories of late-nineteenth-century American political thought had a profound impact on the developments of Progressive politics in the early twentieth century. Historians have long argued over the proper definition of American Progressivism. But as James Kloppenberg and Daniel Rodgers have shown, there was a substantial discussion of the meaning of politics and political language among social thinkers in early-twentieth-century Europe and the United States. The constantly evolving language of American political life continues to deal with such terms as freedom, virtue, free labor, and the public good—categories that were developed and defined over the course of the nineteenth century.

See also **Liberalism; Nullification; Republicanism; Slavery,** *subentry on* **Defense of Slavery; States' Rights.**

Bibliography

Appleby, Joyce. *Liberalism and Republicanism in the Historical Imagination.* Cambridge, Mass.: Harvard University Press, 1992.

Bailyn, Bernard. *The Ideological Origins of the American Revolution.* Cambridge, Mass.: Belknap Press of Harvard University Press, 1967.

Baker, Paula. "The Domestication of Politics: Women and American Political Society, 1780–1920." *American Historical Review* 89 (June 1984):620–647.

Foner, Eric. *Free Soil, Free Labor, Free Men: The Ideology of the Republican Party before the Civil War.* New York: Oxford University Press, 1970.

———. *The Story of American Freedom.* New York: Norton, 1998.

Hartz, Louis. *The Liberal Tradition in America.* New York: Harcourt Brace, 1955.

Kloppenberg, James. *Uncertain Victory: Social Democracy and Progressivism in European and American Thought, 1870–1920.* New York: Oxford University Press, 1986.

Pocock, J. G. A. *The Machiavellian Moment: Florentine Political Thought and the Atlantic Republican Tradition.* Princeton, N.J.: Princeton University Press, 1975.

Rodgers, Daniel. *Atlantic Crossings: Social Politics in a Progressive Age.* Cambridge, Mass.: Belknap Press of Harvard University Press, 1998.

Wiebe, Robert. *The Opening of American Society: From the Adoption of the Constitution to the Eve of Disunion.* New York: Knopf, 1984.

———. *The Search for Order, 1877–1920.* New York: Hill and Wang, 1967.

Wood, Gordon S. *The Creation of the American Republic, 1776–1787.* Chapel Hill: University of North Carolina Press, 1969.

———. *The Radicalism of the American Revolution.* New York: Knopf, 1992.

EDWARD RAFFERTY

POLITICAL CULTURE

American political culture in the nineteenth century was fundamentally chaotic, diffuse, and unconsecutive. It mixed but did not blend the dissimilar national obsessions of the pre– and post–Civil War periods with an unchanging set of economic and ethnocultural factors that spanned the century.

On one level the century's political culture can be divided into two epochs separated by the American Civil War. The first began after the adoption of the federal Constitution in 1789. During this period the political culture of the American Union was absorbed with the question of its own identity. The epoch that followed the Civil War concluded only in 1912 with the end of the Progressive Era and the election of President Woodrow Wilson. This was the period of American national political consolidation based on the vision of the victors of the Civil War.

On another level the century's political culture can be understood as a function of a constant set of ethnocultural and economic factors—immigration, language, religion, race, industrialization, and urbanization. Response to these factors shaped the political landscape in consistent ways throughout the century. At the beginning of the century the immigration of non-Protestants, the growth of the slave population, and an accelerating westward expansion began to change the locus of political power within both the states and the Union. By the century's end renewed immigration on an unprecedented scale, industrialization, urbanization, the creation of national markets, and westward expansion substantially altered a Union in which power was increasingly concentrated in the federal government.

American political culture and political parties, the expression of that culture, were in large part produced by the major political event of the century, the Civil War. The conflict over the essence of the Republic, its resolution by the conquest of the Confederate States of America, and the construction of a new nation in the aftermath of that war occupied much of the century. These events provided the background for most of the political struggles of the century, from war with Britain in the early part of the century to slavery, tariff policy, expansion westward, industrialization, imperialism, and infrastructure.

The institutional expression of American political culture began as a diffused and fluid set of political factions among a small elite, whose members considered themselves the guardians of the true meaning of the federal Union. In the 1830s these factions began to resemble the organized political parties that dominated politics into the twenty-first century. Before the Civil War the major political parties were coalitions eager to impose their visions of the nature of Union to further their own political agendas. Among the most important were the Federalist Party of Alexander Hamilton, John Adams, the mercantile elite of the Northeast, and the planter aristocracy of South Carolina that existed from the 1790s through the 1820s; the Democratic-Republican Party (eventually the Democratic Party) of Thomas Jefferson, James Madison, Andrew Jackson, John C. Calhoun, and the farmers and planters in the West and the South, which began as a center of opposition to the more strongly centralist agenda of the Federalists; the short-lived Whig Party of Daniel Webster, Henry Clay, and traditionalist merchant, planter, and industrial elites; and the Republican Party of Abraham Lincoln, the abolitionists, nativists, interventionists, elitists, and nationalists, which became the heir of the antislavery elements of society and of the merchant, industrialist, and planter classes formerly sympathetic to the Whig Party. On the eve of the Civil War all but two of these political parties, the Democratic and Republican Parties, had disappeared. The history of organized politics of national scope after the Civil War is largely the history of these two parties. They along with numerous smaller and more short-lived factions gave political culture tangible expression and became the primary vehicles for the effective expression of political ideas in the United States.

Successive waves of immigration disrupted and fractured politics in the nation and in virtually every state. Immigration created opportunities for new elites to arise and use the instrument of government for their own and their communities' benefit. Corruption and localism were important markers for political culture, and especially after 1865, both were increasingly associated with the large urban political machines that began to affect the business of the political parties. The Tammany Society of New York was a prominent example. Although the campaign to create a merit-based civil service reflected a reaction against the corruption of the machine system, it was also perfumed with the aroma of nativism, the idea that foreigners were introducing "antidemocratic" norms in places they controlled.

Immigration sharpened divisions based on religion and language. For the first half of the nineteenth century the American population was substantially northern European in origin and Protestant in religion. Politics aimed to contain or assimilate the increasingly Catholic, mostly Irish and German, and—after the Civil War—the Jewish, southern and eastern European, immigrants who began to vie for control of the political machinery and culture first at the state level and then at the national level. Whigs before the Civil War and Republicans after 1860, for example, fearing the effects of extending suffrage to immigrants, sought to minimize these effects through campaigns of assimilation and containment. During the 1850s the radical, strongly anti-Catholic, and nativist Know-Nothing or American Party captured the governorships of Massachusetts and Delaware before it split over the slavery question and lost ground to the Republican Party in the early 1860s.

Immigration affected the cultural politics of language. The state was used to preserve the predominance of the English language as a means of preserving the dominance of the first settlers and as a powerful force of national consolidation. Language produced a complex pattern of politics based on absorption, segregation, diffusion, and marginalization of non-English-speaking immigrant populations. Throughout the century native and immigrant groups fought for control of education. The former saw in education a means to assimilate newcomers; the latter saw in education a means to preserve their folkways and group cohesion. In the Midwest English-speaking residents attempted to eradicate first German and then Scandinavian and Slavic languages. Language was an especially prominent issue in the Southwest, where Spanish, the official language of the areas absorbed in 1848, was targeted for extinction.

Immigration also sharpened racial divisions. The century's penchant for fusing race and ethnicity produced a cultural politics based on a belief in the existence of a rainbow of "white races" that distinguished between the English and other European "races." This racial hierarchy produced a constant political division throughout the century, in which the English "race" took precedence over other European "races," and all European "races" took precedence over non-Europeans. Moreover for all European groups, first arrivals or latecomers, the "color line" produced a political culture centered on racial purity. The race hierarchy assigned positions below the whites according to any other "race" in a person's ancestry, and on that basis people were excluded from the political life of the Union to some extent. Whites attempted to push American Indians into small areas of settlement or to make them disappear either by assimilation or extermination. But even successful assimilation did not give Indians social or political parity with even the lowest orders of white society.

Slavery was the prominent political issue between the Missouri Compromise of 1820 and the Civil War. While the major political parties included elements on both sides of the issue, splinter factions arose from time to time. Among the most important was the Free-Soil Party, which formed in 1848 to keep slavery out of the new territories. While abolitionism played a part in the formation of these parties, the availability of land for whites, free of the debilitating competition from slave labor, also played a role. After the Civil War slavery continued to affect political culture. Republicans worked closely with newly freed African Americans in the South, while Democrats opposed black enfranchisement and expanded civil rights. When southern whites regained control of the states of the old Confederacy, the Republicans gradually abandoned their African American allies to a regional political culture of de jure segregation.

Race, religion, and ethnicity fueled the policing of morality in local and national politics. Ethnoculturalists have suggested that antebellum and post–Civil War morality movements are best understood as the cultural expression of a religious reflex. Indeed religion and politics were closely allied. Prohibition, abolition, Sabbatarianism, perhaps even the cultural assimilation movements can be characterized as political manifestations of a Protestant revival movement similar in scope to the Great Awakening of the eighteenth century. However, the imprint of the cultural patterns of religious behavior on the culture of politics was complex. For example, while religious pietists were comfortable using the power of the state to compel moral order, religious liturgicals sought reform through conversion. They joined occasionally, for example, when the suppression of Mormon polygamy became a political issue. Prohibition appealed to nativists and old elites because it promised to control the waves of potentially unruly immigrants, Indians,

and African Americans. In the second half of the nineteenth century prohibitionists were increasingly active in party politics, especially within the Republican Party. The supposedly loose morals of immigrants, people seen as originating from inferior racial, ethnic, or religious stock, fed popular agitation for state removal of children from nonconforming environments and protection against "white slavery," the trafficking in women for the purpose of forced prostitution.

Economic factors, primarily industrialization and urbanization, shaped important aspects of the political culture. The growth of national business enterprises fostered sensitivity to social stratification, urbanization, and class struggle. Industrialization produced elites capable of molding political parties to protect their interests. As the heirs of the Whigs, the post–Civil War Republicans represented merchants, industrialists, and wealthy agricultural landlords. But as the nineteenth century closed the growing power of business linked with political corruption, stimulating reform efforts. Stratification and the class struggle gave birth to radical workers' parties (such as the Locofocos), in northern cities even before the Civil War. The short-lived anti-Jacksonian National Republican Party, an 1830s offshoot of the Democratic Party, and the Whig Party in the 1830s through the 1850s were magnets for the wealthy in both the North and the South who were willing to compromise their sectional differences in defense of their collective wealth and positions in society. Later in the century the class divisions in the cities encouraged other groups with ties to European class radicalism, most notably the Socialist Labor Party, founded in 1877, and the Social Democratic Party, founded by Eugene Debs in 1898, which in 1901 joined with Christian Socialists to form the Socialist Party. The less radical elements of these movements found a home in the Democratic Party machines of northern cities.

Before the Civil War urbanization and concentrations of wealth in the industrial sector in the northern states divided the strong political culture that favored tariffs, in the North, from the southern planters and thus helped fuel the controversy over the power of the central government. After the Civil War those forces compelled numerous factions of farmers to protest against a monetary policy favoring industry. Subsequently populism produced a racist, anti-immigrant antiurbanism as well. Among these factions were the Granger movement, the Farmers Alliances of the 1870s, and the Greenback and Greenback Labor Parties of the 1870s and 1880s. These farm-rural movements joined with the Knights of Labor to create the People's Party or Populist Party, active from the

1890s through the early 1900s. The Populists favored inflationary fiscal policies, nationalization of the railroads, direct election of senators, and an eight-hour workday. Some of the social programs advocated by the Populists were later taken up by progressive Republicans, including the insurgent Bull Moose Party, and later by the Democratic Party.

The two great political parties of the nineteenth century represented opposite poles of institutional responses to the definition of the Union and the steady effects of immigration, language, race, industrialization, and urbanization. Ethnoculturalists have proposed that the parties, the people, were the institutional political manifestations of the division within the culture of religion between pietists, the social interventionists, and their opposites, the liturgicals. Democrats were generally wary of federal power and tended to include many factions that coexisted in uneasy alliances. States' rights and localism provided outlets for the many potentially antagonistic allies within the party. Republicans were a political unit with a more singular vision. They tended to be ardent nationalists, heirs to the ideas of Hamilton and the Federalists. Republicans meant to use the power of the federal government to mold a nation and preserve the power of the traditional elites.

Ironically the complex, chaotic, diffuse, and unconsecutive blending that was the nineteenth century political culture is well illustrated by the two great political parties. As the question of the nature of the Union receded in prominence near the end of a century of change stimulated by ethnocultural and economic factors, these parties each stood poised to completely reverse their respective political philosophies. The Democratic Party, for almost a century the stalwart supporter of states' rights and a more "Unionist" approach to Federalism, became within the next generation the party of national intervention and shrinking state authority. It retained only a minority faction of traditional Democrats based mostly in the states of the former Confederate republic. The Republican Party, within that same generation, transformed from the radical "nationalist party" of its first generation to a more "Unionist" party, advancing the power of business and markets over that of national and even state authority. Yet the Republican Party retained its moral-cultural elitist, Whiggish tendencies. It reserved federal power for the protection and management of the good morals and culture of a hodgepodge of immigrant peoples in need of assimilation for the preservation of business, prosperity, and good conduct.

See also **Cities and Urbanization; Democratic Party; Federalist Party; Government; Immigration and Immigrants,** *subentry on* **Anti-immigrant Sentiment; Industrialization and the Market; Nationalism; Populism; Race and Racial Thinking; Religion,** *subentry on* **Religion as a Political Issue; Republican Party; Third Parties.**

Bibliography

Abbott, Richard H. *The Republican Party and the South, 1855–1877: The First Southern Strategy.* Chapel Hill: University of North Carolina Press, 1986.

Benson, Thomas W., ed. *Rhetoric and Political Culture in Nineteenth-Century America.* East Lansing: Michigan State University Press, 1997.

Blocker, Jack S., Jr. *American Temperance Movements: Cycles of Reform.* Boston: Twayne, 1989.

Borden, Morton. *Jews, Turks, and Infidels.* Chapel Hill: University of North Carolina Press, 1984.

Finkelman, Paul. *An Imperfect Union: Slavery, Federalism, and Comity.* Chapel Hill: University of North Carolina Press, 1981.

Gienapp, William E. *The Origins of the Republican Party, 1852–1856.* New York: Oxford University Press, 1987.

Haas, Garland A. *The Politics of Disintegration: Political Party Decay in the United States, 1840–1900.* Jefferson, N.C.: McFarland, 1994.

Holt, Michael F. *Political Parties and American Political Development: From the Age of Jackson to the Age of Lincoln.* Baton Rouge: Louisiana State University Press, 1992.

———. *The Rise and Fall of the American Whig Party.* New York: Oxford University Press, 1999.

Kleppner, Paul. *The Cross of Culture: A Social Analysis of Midwestern Politics, 1850–1900.* 2d ed. New York: Free Press, 1970.

———. *The Third Electoral System, 1853–1892: Parties, Voters, and Political Cultures.* Chapel Hill: University of North Carolina Press, 1979.

Levine, Lawrence W. *Highbrow/Lowbrow: The Emergence of Cultural Hierarchy in America.* Cambridge, Mass.: Harvard University Press, 1988.

Mink, Gwendolyn. *Old Labor and New Immigrants in American Political Development: Union, Party, and State, 1875–1920.* Ithaca, N.Y.: Cornell University Press, 1986.

Montgomery, David. *Beyond Equality: Labor and the Radical Republicans, 1862–1872.* New York: Knopf, 1967.

———. *Citizen Worker: The Experience of Workers in the United States with Democracy and the Free Market during the Nineteenth Century.* Cambridge, U.K., and New York: Cambridge University Press, 1993.

Rutland, Robert. *The Democrats, from Jefferson to Carter.* Baton Rouge: Louisiana State University Press, 1979.

Scheckel, Susan. *The Insistence of the Indian: Race and Nationalism in Nineteenth-Century American Culture.* Princeton, N.J.: Princeton University Press, 1998.

Silbey, Joel H. *The American Political Nation, 1838–1893.* Stanford, Calif.: Stanford University Press, 1991.

———. *The Partisan Imperative: The Dynamics of American Politics before the Civil War.* New York: Oxford University Press, 1985.

Skowronek, Stephen. *Building a New American State: The Expansion of National Administrative Capacities, 1877–1920.* New York: Cambridge University Press, 1982.

Summers, Mark W. *Railroads, Reconstruction, and the Gospel of Prosperity: Aid under the Radical Republicans, 1865–1877.* Princeton, N.J.: Princeton University Press, 1984.

LARRY CATÁ BACKER

PARTY ORGANIZATION AND OPERATIONS

Political parties were ubiquitous in the nineteenth-century United States, managing political activities, articulating partisan policies, and mobilizing voters to turn out on Election Day. Much of their success stemmed from the organizational structures that each built to conduct party business, structures designed to deal with a growing electorate inhabiting a broad geographic expanse. These organizations were never as extensive nor as fully formed as party leaders desired, but for their time they made up an unprecedentedly elaborate institutional network. The federal Constitution and state constitutions mandated regular elections, often annually, certainly at least every other year. At the same time, deep divisions over policies—among different social and economic groups and between different regional blocs—fueled constant conflict to be decided at the polls.

State and Local Parties

State parties organized as early as the first party system after 1793. Stimulated by the need to compete in closely contested elections on a regular basis, Aaron Burr in New York took the lead in building the characteristic structure of caucuses and committees of partisan leaders. Burr's most prominent successor, Martin Van Buren, also of New York, made his name as the strongest proponent of the permanent need for a tight, effective organization and the benefits the parties would derive from such. By the mid-1830s Van Buren's template was widely accepted.

The parties largely built their organizations from the same template. They appeared at every geographic level in a pyramidical structure originating in local settings, where village and town party committees came together to agree on delegates to a county or district leadership caucus and later to a mass-based convention. The caucus or convention in turn selected delegates to a statewide meeting to nominate candidates for that year, to draw up a party platform based on proposals that originated both among the leaders and in rallies of committed followers, and to form state campaign committees to manage election activities in each contest.

At the top of this structure were clusters of leaders who came together to direct party business. Such groups were quickly labeled the "Albany Regency," the "Richmond Junto," the "Concord Cabal," and other often derogatory names, suggesting that they were manipulative and undemocratic. These party activists, some of whom were full-time professionals, negotiated and worked together to raise money and direct the parties' foot soldiers—the local postmen, land agents, newspaper editors, and others—who managed party affairs at the village and district levels. All of them kept an especially wary eye on potential schisms. Their organizational watchwords always stressed unity behind a collective quest, "everything for the cause, nothing for men," as partisan publications constantly declaimed.

National Coalitions

As the parties grew into national coalitions, their organizational structures also became nationwide. Congressional caucuses echoed local ones, and national conventions and national campaign committees repeated the style and structure of those originally established at the local and state levels. The first national convention in the nineteenth-century era, called by the third-party Anti-Masons, met in 1831. By 1840 such meetings were a regular feature of American politics. Party loyalists from different regions, "delegates fresh from the people," in Andrew Jackson's phrase, often with different priorities and candidates, sat down together as the supreme party authority to select nominees, write platforms, and establish the organizational nexus for each campaign. Occasionally serious splits occurred, but most of the time the party organizations were able to tame internal dissent and to compromise on behalf of their collective purpose.

The campaign committees established by the convention and later the more permanent state and national party committees elected by the conventions reflected the meetings' will and did the work necessary to maximize the party vote. Each drew up elaborate schedules for their best speakers and most prominent leaders, schedules they carried through to Election Day. Groups of committed volunteer supporters—the "Tippecanoe clubs" in 1840, the "Wide-Awakes" in 1860—were created to lead mass rallies and raise the roof on behalf of their party, and their energy in the streets was an important dimension of organizational success.

Activities and Finances

Undergirding all of these activities was each party's wide-ranging network of partisan newspapers, whose editorials, reprinted as pamphlets and circulated through local party meeting rooms, promoted the party outlook everywhere. Speeches of the candi-

"I AM CONFIDENT THE WORKINGMEN ARE WITH US."

Political Cartoon of Mark Hanna Wielding Power over Labor. Hanna's control over labor and the resources he had amassed for William McKinley's campaign fund indicate that he was considered a formidable political organizer. *New York Journal*, 8 October 1896. LIBRARY OF CONGRESS

dates were similarly reprinted and distributed. They became the sources for speeches by local leaders at campaign rallies. At these rallies the leaders, the candidates, and other notables appeared, met, even caroused with the voters.

On polling day the party organizations were especially active. They provided printed ballots to be cast by their supporters, kept close tabs to see that everyone appeared at the voting sites, sent wagons to bring the faithful to the polls, and stationed poll watchers to look out for trickery by their opponents, a not infrequent occurrence. Party workers rounded out the day by participating in the counting of the ballots and the announcement of the results.

Party organization also extended to government. When Congress and the state legislatures met, partisan legislative caucuses coordinated strategy and directed the behavior and votes of each party's representatives. Appointments to government offices, from clerks and building watchmen to land surveyors and customs inspectors, were governed by the spoils system, which guaranteed that only members of the party in power were named in the expectation that they would spend some of their time supporting partisan objectives.

All of these organizational activities needed money. Parties raised what they could from their wealthiest supporters, receipts from the sale of party publications, and contributions from their officeholders, who understood that part of their salary was to be returned to the organization as payment for the position that the party had given them. Party newspapers were paid to print the official records of government activities, of which some income went to the party. These sources never seemed to be enough, however, and party leaders constantly scrambled for more, opening up the possibilities of corrupt exchanges between those who had money and the partisans who needed it and who had something to give in return at the governmental level.

Machines and Reform

New political organizations developed in mid-century, especially in the growing urban centers, but these party "machines" were similar in structure, activities, and purpose to those that had previously developed in the countryside. Party leaders claimed that their organizations reflected the nation's democratic values: all decisions were based on consultation and consent, beginning with the expressions of the will of the party members in committee meetings and conventions at every level. Such claims contained much truth. However, a second level of decision making existed in which the party leaders, after hearing from their supporters, considered in addition what their experience suggested was the best policy or who were the best candidates for the party at that particular moment. Sometimes these two levels conflicted, and democratic impulses gave way to pragmatic considerations.

The decisions made by the party leaders, allegedly in "smoke-filled rooms," became the basis of a growing anger directed against the party organizations for being oligarchic, not democratic. (It is not clear that this charge was true, although party organization in the late nineteenth century had evolved into more complex, larger, and more routinized bodies in which professional politicians were able to exercise more authority and control than had been the case in more informal, more loosely structured times.) Such attacks became more and more widespread in the 1870s and 1880s, an era in which political corruption was on the increase as the parties continued their scramble for more money to contest some of the closest elections in American history. Good government proponents, often led by reform-minded newspapers, mounted campaigns against the alleged sins of Tammany Hall, the Whiskey Ring, and other partisan "spoilsmen" whose behavior threatened the American political experiment. The parties' political organizations had served their purpose well, but it was clear that their activities contained the seeds of their ultimate destruction.

See also **Democratic Party; Federalist Party; Reform, Political; Republican Party; Third Parties.**

Bibliography

Marcus, Robert. *Grand Old Party: Political Structure in the Gilded Age, 1880–1896.* New York: Oxford University Press, 1971.

Nichols, Roy F. *The Invention of the American Political Parties: A Study of Political Improvisation.* New York: Macmillan, 1967.

Remini, Robert. *Martin Van Buren and the Making of the Democratic Party.* New York: Columbia University Press, 1959.

Silbey, Joel H. *The American Political Nation, 1838–1893.* Stanford, Calif.: Stanford University Press, 1991.

JOEL H. SILBEY

THE FIRST PARTY SYSTEM

The first American party system, lasting from 1793 to 1815, was marked by ferocious political confrontation. The founders of the United States strongly opposed political parties, believing, in good eighteenth-century style, that such "factions" promoted debilitating internal divisions that threatened America's fragile national unity. This notion gave way before the realities of the new nation, specifically the need to press for or resist a range of aggressively pushed policy initiatives. The Constitution had superimposed a national political framework on the existing state systems. At every level persistent divisions engendered by religious, economic, cultural, and ideological conflicts, many originating in colonial days, remained constant facts easily provoked to stir up political confrontation.

The policies pushed by President George Washington's administration further raised the political temperature. The extreme nationalism of Secretary of the Treasury Alexander Hamilton provoked a sharp reaction on behalf of local power against the rising authority of the central government. At first, working within the administration, Secretary of State Thomas Jefferson and Congressman James Madison became convinced of the necessity to organize a national coalition to elect enough congressmen to defeat the Washington administration's centralizing plans. Calling themselves Republicans, they allied with political leaders in various states—for example, Aaron Burr in New York—and formulated an appeal that stressed the primacy of states' rights, agricultural enterprise, and a French alliance in foreign affairs. They opposed Hamilton's plans for a national bank, a protective tariff, a British alliance, and other policies that enormously enhanced national power.

America's first two presidential elections were relatively orderly because, generally, everyone supported George Washington. Then the political landscape shifted turbulently. The persistent challenge of the Republicans (later called Democratic Republicans) provoked a response from the Hamiltonians, now calling themselves Federalists, who, after Washington refused to run again, reluctantly organized themselves to enter the electoral arena. Their foot-dragging stemmed from their fear of party divisions and a desire not to have their policies subject to the vagaries of popular electoral behavior, a situation they thought detrimental to the national interest.

By the mid-1790s, despite the Federalists' hesitancy, two programmatic coalitions confronted each other at the ballot box, in Congress, and in the state legislatures. The coalitions were held together by the power of their commitments, their fears, and the developing organizational networks that communicated their ideas and the reasons why they should be supported to their followers. Partisan newspapers on both the national and the state levels and widespread pamphleteering against the other side became campaign norms. These expressed what was at stake by means of a destructive demonology that precluded any tolerance for alternative views or even of the other side's right to exist.

From the presidential election of 1796 through that of 1800, these coalitions struggled bitterly, with the Republicans finally winning out in the extraordinarily divisive "revolution of 1800." The results demonstrated that some states overwhelmingly supported one party over the other; elsewhere, as in New York and Pennsylvania, two-party conflict appeared early and remained a constant. The Republicans drew electoral strength from much of the South, agrarian areas of New York, and Scotch-Irish enclaves in Pennsylvania and elsewhere. The Federalist electoral strength lay largely in mercantile New England and in Anglican-dominated areas elsewhere.

Despite the high temperature continually manifested in campaigns, this party conflict did not survive very long into the nineteenth century. Partisan consciousness and divisions never penetrated deeply everywhere. Federalists not committed to the notions of permanent partisan conflict withdrew from politics after 1800, cursing the country that had forsaken them. Moreover, the parties' organizational development was incomplete and haphazard. Neither built up the elaborate institutions—committees, caucuses, conventions—characteristic of later stages of American political development. As a result voters were never as fully mobilized as the intensity of party expression suggested. Turnout at the polls on Election Day was low in comparison with later times, only about 20 percent of those eligible to vote. Few voters were loyal to the same party from election to election, suggesting that as yet no intense commitment to a permanent system of partisan confrontation existed.

Around 1810 the Federalists came surging back as the successive Republican administrations of Presidents Thomas Jefferson and James Madison ran into trouble over their foreign policy initiatives and the severe economic difficulties that such initiatives caused for the trading areas of the nation. When the War of 1812 broke out between Britain and the United States, the Federalist position became even stronger. The Federalist Party's leaders chose to oppose the Republicans not only at the polls but by also threatening, at the Hartford Convention in 1815, to take Federalist New England out of the Union if the Republicans' anti-British foreign policy was not reversed and the war ended. This Federalist particularism and what the Republicans argued was their anti-Americanism severely affected the Federalist political situation when the United States won a great military victory at New Orleans and made peace with Britain. Sorely wounded by their own behavior, the Federalists could not recover and disappeared as a national party after 1815, leaving the field to the increasingly factionalized Republicans.

See also **Democratic Party; Federalist Party.**

Bibliography

Elkins, Stanley, and Eric McKitrick. *The Age of Federalism.* New York: Oxford University Press, 1993.

Fischer, David Hackett. *The Revolution of American Conservatism: The Federalist Party in the Era of Jeffersonian Democracy.* New York: Knopf, 1965.

Formisano, Ronald P. "Federalists and Republicans: Parties—Yes, System, No." In *The Evolution of American Electoral Systems.* Edited by Paul Kleppner et al. Westport, Conn.: Greenwood, 1981.

JOEL H. SILBEY

THE SECOND PARTY SYSTEM

The second party system, which began about 1828 and collapsed in 1854, revolved around the programs of Andrew Jackson and his new Democratic Party. The system featured very close contests between the Democrats and the Whigs, with the Democrats usually controlling the White House. The Whigs, however, won the 1840 and 1848 presidential elections, and they often controlled Congress and governorships: in the 1840s they won, on average, 47 percent of the House seats and 49 percent of the governorships.

Characteristics of the System

The second party system was characterized by widespread white male suffrage, high voter interest and turnout, intense party loyalty, dependence on nominating conventions, hierarchical party organizations at the local, county, state, and national levels, and the systematic use of government jobs as patronage for party workers. The invention of high-speed printing presses and the creation of a telegraph network facilitated the growth of newspapers, most of which were political allies of the Whig Party. Horace Greeley made his *New York Tribune* a nationally influential organ of the Whigs. Thomas Ritchie, editor of the *Richmond Enquirer* (1804–1841), headed the "Richmond Junto," which controlled Democratic politics in Virginia in the 1830s and 1840s.

Both parties contained broad-based voting coalitions. Throughout the country, businessmen, factory owners, bankers, clerks, and professionals favored the Whigs, as did commercially oriented farmers and planters. Planters who favored geographical expansion rather than technological modernization favored the Democrats, as did subsistence farmers and day laborers. Irish Catholic immigrants were loyal to the Democrats, and by the 1840s were themselves the target of nativist and anti-Catholic fears. The 1830s had been an era of religious revivals, with a strong growth of pietistic denominations. Politicians soon discovered that the pietists had an interest in public affairs. Congregationalists, Presbyterians, and other pietistic Protestants injected a moralistic element into the Whig ranks, as well as a commitment to public schools, private colleges, and cultural institutions. Nonreligious individuals, annoyed by applications of pietistic moralism such as the call for prohibition, found relief in the Democratic ranks. Both parties cut across the class structure. The Democrats attracted more support from the underprivileged, while free blacks in the North, seeing the Democrats as racist and hostile to their interests, favored the Whigs.

The Domination of Jackson

Andrew Jackson was a reform candidate in 1828, crusading against the bargain made between Henry Clay and John Quincy Adams that had made Adams president and Clay secretary of state in 1825. One reform Jackson instituted as president was to open up government jobs to his supporters, with party support being the main criterion for employment. The patronage system thereby became a powerful engine driving the ambition of political wanna-bes. By reform, Jackson also meant a return to pure, simple Republicanism.

The Whigs rejected Jackson's small-government notions and adopted Henry Clay's vision of the "American system," with government sponsorship of industrialization through high tariffs, more versatile money supplies based on the semiofficial Bank of the United States, and a vigorous program of "internal improvements," especially expansion of the nation's transportation system.

The Democrats returned to the Jeffersonian ideal of a vast agricultural society, and for that they needed geographical expansion and the removal of the southeast Indian tribes. They achieved these goals over strong Whig opposition. In 1830 Jackson vetoed the Maysville Road Bill, signaling the end to federal sponsorship of internal improvements. In 1832 he vetoed the renewal of the charter for the Bank of the United States, shrugged off a censure motion in the Senate, and campaigned for reelection as the champion of the people. After his reelection Jackson removed the federal deposits from the bank, causing its virtual collapse. In towns and cities across the land, alarmed businessmen and financiers surged into the Whig Party and denounced Jackson for dam-

Andrew Jackson, Upholder of the Constitution. A portrait of Andrew Jackson depicting him as an arbiter of democracy and an adherent to the Constitution. 4 March 1829, the date of his inauguration. LIBRARY OF CONGRESS

aging the economy. Frightened by the surge of dubious paper money that followed the collapse of the regulatory powers of the bank, Jackson in 1836 issued the Specie Circular, which required payment in gold for land purchases, thus bringing to a shattering close the land boom in the West.

The Democratic Party originated as a coalition of Jackson's supporters in the Southwest, Martin Van Buren's New York base, and Ritchie's Richmond Junto. Although Jackson alienated many of his original followers, he replaced them with new supporters prior to his reelection over Clay in 1832. By the mid-1830s Van Buren succeeded in adding to the party critical political factions in every state. Democrats met at their 1835 national convention to ratify the nomination of Van Buren, Jackson's choice to succeed him. The opposition, which included the Anti-Masonic Party, was coalescing into the Whig Party; the Whigs ran three regional candidates against Van Buren, who easily prevailed. Economic

REPUBLICAN BANNER, (*Extra*).
NASHVILLE, Monday Evening, Oct. 21th, 5 o'clock.

SAVE ME SAVE ME

ONWARD IS THE CAUSE OF
CLAY & FRELINGHUYSEN
Glorious Whig Triumph!!!
THE OLD MARYLAND LINE FOREVER!!!

By the official returns from all the counties it appears that the Whigs of this gallant State have elected a Whig Governor, a Whig Senate and a Whig House of Representatives.

NEW JERSEY,
Hurra for the Jersey Blues!!!
The Whigs of this patriotic State have shown themselves to be what their fathers were in '76, good and true; they have swept every thing, electing a Whig Governor by 1855, the largest majority ever given in the State, carrying both branches of the Legislature.

OHIO,
Make way for the young Lion of the West!!
Now as in 1840, this noble State is on the side of correct principles, she too has elected a Whig Governor by a majority of not less that **2500**, and the Legislature by a majority of 16 on joint ballot. Well done noble and gallant and patriotic Ohio.

GEORGIA.
Stand aside and let the South embrace the North in the great cause of **LIBERTY** and the **UNION**. In the election for Members of Congress the Whigs have elected 5 out of the 8 Congressmen. She will stand proudly and firmly by **HARRY OF THE WEST** by a majority of thousands.

PENNSYLVANIA.
The old Key Stone State safe for Clay and Frelinghuysen!!
Shunk, the Locofoco Candidate hardly elected; his majority will not exceed 3000. Porter, the Democratic Governor was elected in 1841 by a majority of **23.003**, a loss of about **20.000**. This is a glorious result indeed, one that should dispel every doubt as to the election of Henry Clay. That the vote of Pennsylvania is safe for the Whigs no well informed man can doubt.

DELAWARE.
Small in numbers but mighty in spirit and good works, has given another decisive demonstration of her devotion to Whig principles, by electing a majority of Whigs good and true.

TENNESSEE,
SHE TOO IS COMING!
Let the Whigs of Tennessee rejoice at the bright and still brightening prospects that surround them. Let them buckle on their armour afresh and resolve that she too shall take her position in the great Whig line, rallying under the time honored banner of **LIBERTY AND UNION, NOW AND FOREVER**. To your posts Whigs! do your duty, your whole duty, and the **VICTORY** will be ours, **CLAY** elected and our **COUNTRY** saved.

A Whig Campaign Advertisement. The Whig party began in about 1833. Its heyday was in the 1840s. Whig presidents assumed office in 1840 and 1848; by the mid-1850s, however, the party had collapsed. LIBRARY OF CONGRESS

hard times, however, ruined Van Buren's term. A solid Whig opposition, coupled with some Democratic defections, blocked passage of his "independent treasury." By 1840 the Whigs had proved that they too could rouse excitement and loyalty on behalf of their hero, General William Henry Harrison. Har-

rison swept to victory in the "Log Cabin and Hard Cider" campaign, which ignored issues and promoted personalities. He died one month after taking office, and the Whigs discovered to their horror that his successor, John Tyler, was largely opposed to their programs for a national bank, tariffs, and internal improvements.

End of the System

James K. Polk, the leader of the Jacksonians in the House of Representatives and the chief enemy of the Bank of the United States, was tapped by Jackson for the 1844 nomination. Polk defeated Clay, primarily by promising to annex Texas, a move Clay opposed. Polk's aggressive war with Mexico was bitterly opposed by the Whigs. The war issue split the Democrats, and a new Free-Soil Party nominated Van Buren in 1848. Victory in the war brought to the fore the issue of whether slavery would be allowed in the new territories. With the Democrats split, the Whig war hero Zachary Taylor was elected president in 1848.

By then, however, the classic Whig issues had faded away—most states promoted banks, industry was satisfied with the moderate Polk tariffs, and private enterprise was building railroads with the help of British investment. The question of slavery in the territories seemed impossible to solve, but Taylor's death in 1850 facilitated the Compromise of 1850, which temporarily postponed the issue. When the Democrats reunited in 1852, the Whigs realized their time was over. Local leaders, such as Abraham Lincoln, had lost enthusiasm. After the defeat of their candidate, General Winfield Scott, in the 1852 presidential election, the Whigs disintegrated as a party. In the North, most Whig supporters joined the new Republican Party. In the South, former Whigs dominated the American Party, and when the Confederacy was established they put away their partisanship. Despite the disintegration of the Whig Party, Whig programs for banking, tariffs, and internal improvements were enacted by the Lincoln administration.

The second party system taught America the techniques of practical democracy. The vast majority of eligible voters became active partisans and through rallies, newspapers, and speeches gained a strikingly sophisticated understanding of complex national political issues, such as tariffs and banks. As voters debated these issues, local candidates joined in and tied their fortunes to the national leaders. For politicians the system provided a clear blueprint for partisanship, gaining nominations, campaigning, and governing. Although the Whigs had done well previously, in the early 1850s they began to slip so fast that aspiring officeholders realized the futility of ever gaining national office and readily abandoned the party. The Democratic Party survived because it could guarantee office in return for energetic partisanship. As the slavery issue ripped the Democrats apart, a new party arose. By controlling all the major northern states, the newly formed Republican Party changed the entire political calculus and opened the third party system.

See also **Jacksonian Era; Politics,** subentries on **The First Party System, The Third Party System.**

Bibliography

Holt, Michael F. *The Rise and Fall of the American Whig Party: Jacksonian Politics and the Onset of the Civil War.* New York: Oxford University Press, 1999.

McCormick, Richard P. *The Second American Party System: Party Formation in the Jacksonian Era.* Chapel Hill: University of North Carolina Press, 1966.

Van Deusen, Glyndon G. *The Jacksonian Era, 1828–1848.* New York: Harper and Row, 1959.

Watson, Harry L. *Liberty and Power: The Politics of Jacksonian America.* New York: Hill and Wang, 1990.

RICHARD JENSEN

THE THIRD PARTY SYSTEM

The third party system, which began in 1854 and changed over to the fourth party system in the mid-1890s, revolved around the issues of nationalism, modernization, and race. It was dominated by the new Republican Party, which claimed success in saving the Union, abolishing slavery, enfranchising the freedmen, and adopting many Whig modernization programs such as national banks, railroads, high tariffs, homesteads, and college aid.

Characteristics of the System

Like its predecessor, the third party system was characterized by intense voter interest, high voter turnout, unflinching party loyalty, dependence on nominating conventions, hierarchical party organization, and systematic political patronage. Cities with populations of fifty thousand or more developed ward and citywide "bosses," who could depend on the votes of constituents, especially recent immigrants. Newspapers continued to be the primary communication system, with the great majority closely linked to one party or the other.

Both parties were composed of broad-based voting coalitions. Throughout the North, businessmen, shop owners, skilled craftsmen, clerks, and professionals favored the Republicans, as did more modern, commercially oriented farmers. In the South the Republicans won strong support from the newly enfranchised African Americans, but the party was usually controlled by local whites (scalawags) and opportunistic Yankees (carpetbaggers). The race issue and identification with the lost cause of the Confederacy pulled the great majority of white Southerners into the Democratic Party. They were joined by traditional Democrats in the North, especially Catholic Irish and German immigrants, unskilled laborers, and hardscrabble old-stock farmers. Methodists, Congregationalists, Presbyterians, Scandinavian Lutherans, and other pietists in the North were tightly linked to the Republican Party. In sharp contrast, liturgical groups, especially the Catholics, Episcopalians, and German Lutherans, looked to the Democratic Party for protection from pietistic moralism, especially its call for prohibition.

Modernization, Slavery, and War

The collapse of the Whig Party in 1852 created political chaos. Various prohibitionist and nativist movements emerged, especially the American Party, based originally on the secret Know-Nothing lodges. The Republican Party was more driven in terms of ideology and talent, and it surpassed the hapless American Party in 1856. By 1858 the Republicans controlled majorities in every northern state, and hence controlled the electoral votes for president in 1860.

The ideological force driving the new party was modernization, including opposition to the antimodern threat of slavery. By 1856 the Republicans were crusading for "Free Soil, Free Labor, Frémont, and Victory."

The Democratic response was to warn in 1856 that the election of the Republican candidate, John Frémont, would produce civil war. The leader of the Democrats was the Illinois senator Stephen A. Douglas, whose vision of democracy included the conviction that voters in each state should decide the issue of slavery for themselves. When President James Buchanan tried to use political leverage to bring about the approval of slavery in Kansas Territory, Douglas broke with him, presaging the split that ruined the party in 1860.

In that year Northern Democrats nominated Douglas for president while the party's Southern wing looked to John Breckinridge as the upholder of the rights of property and of states' rights, which in this context meant slavery. In the South, former Whigs organized an ad hoc Constitutional Union Party, which pledged to keep the nation united on the basis of the Constitution, regardless of democracy, states' rights, property, or liberty.

The Republicans played it safe in 1860, passing over better-known radicals in favor of a moderate border-state politician known to be an articulate advocate of liberty. Abraham Lincoln made no speeches, letting the party apparatus march the armies to the polls. It was a measure of Lincoln's political genius that he drew upon and synthesized the sentiments of antislavery, free soil, democracy, and nationalism.

Within the Union, the Republican Party gained strength from the war effort. The Democrats at first supported a war for Union, and in 1861 many Democratic politicians became colonels and generals. Announced by Lincoln in September 1862, emancipation was designed primarily to destroy the economic base of the slave states; however, it also energized the Confederates to fight to the bitter end and it also alienated most Northern Democrats. They were reluctant to support a war that used what they believed were unconstitutional means and that benefited what they considered an inferior race. Despite considerable gains in 1862, the Democrats were unable to stop the war, and in 1864 the Republicans made "copperhead treason" (a Northerner's sympathizing with the Southern cause) a successful campaign issue. The Union Army increasingly became the fighting arm of the Republican Party. It is likely that a majority of Democrats who enlisted, including such key leaders as John Logan and Benjamin Butler, marched home Republican.

War issues resonated for decades after the Civil War's end in 1865. Republicans waved the "bloody shirt" (of dead Union soldiers), and Democrats warned against black supremacy in the South and plutocracy in the North. The modernizing Republicans who had founded the party in 1854 looked askance at the corruption of Ulysses S. Grant and his war veterans, bolstered by the solid support of the freedmen. The dissenters formed the Liberal Republican Party in 1872, only to have it smashed by Grant's reelection.

By the mid-1870s it was clear that Confederate nationalism was dead. All but the most ardent Republican stalwarts agreed that the Republican coalition of African Americans, scalawags, and carpetbaggers was corrupt and incompetent. In 1874 the Democrats won big, with economic depression a major issue. People wondered how much longer the Republicans could use the army to impose control in the South. The Republican candidate Rutherford B. Hayes became president in 1876 after a highly controversial electoral count, which to many demonstrated that the corruption of southern politics threatened the legitimacy of the presidency itself. After Hayes removed the last federal troops in 1877, the Republican Party in the South sank into oblivion, kept alive only by the crumbs of federal patronage.

End of the System

New issues emerged in the late 1880s, as Grover Cleveland made the low tariff "for revenue only" a rallying cry for Democrats, and the Republican Congress in 1890 legislated high tariffs and high spending. At the state level, moralistic pietists pushed hard for prohibition and, in some states, for the elimination of foreign-language schools serving German immigrants. The millions of immigrants divided politically along ethnic and religious lines, with enough Germans joining the Democratic Party to give the Democrats a national majority in the early 1890s.

In 1896 William Jennings Bryan and the radical silverites seized control of the Democratic Party, denounced their own president, Grover Cleveland, and called for a return to Jeffersonian agrarianism. William McKinley and Mark Hanna took control of the Republican Party with a campaign of education that made lavish use of new advertising techniques. McKinley promised to make everyone prosperous through strong economic growth based on sound money and business confidence and an abundance of high-paying industrial jobs. Every racial, ethnic, and religious group would prosper, and the government would never be used by one group to attack another.

McKinley thus introduced the central theme of twentieth-century American values, pluralism. Hanna systematically told nervous businessmen and financiers that he had a business plan to win the election and then billed them for their share of the cost. Under the second and third party systems, parties financed their campaigns through patronage; now civil service was undercutting that revenue, and entirely new, outside sources of funding became critical. Hanna spent $3.5 million in three months for speakers, pamphlets, posters, and rallies that all warned of doom and anarchy if Bryan should win and offered prosperity and pluralism under McKinley.

The overwhelming Republican victory, repeated in 1900, restored business confidence, inaugurated a long epoch of prosperity, and swept away the issues and personalities of the third party system. Most voting blocs continued unchanged, but others realigned themselves, giving a strong Republican dominance in the industrial Northeast. This cleared the way for the Progressive movement to impose a new way of thinking and to create a new agenda in politics.

See also **Democratic Party; Politics,** *subentry on* **The Second Party System; Republican Party; Whig Party.**

Bibliography

Gienapp, William E. *The Origins of the Republican Party, 1852–1856*. New York: Oxford University Press, 1987.

Jensen, Richard. *The Winning of the Midwest: Social and Political Conflict, 1888–1896*. Chicago: University of Chicago Press, 1971.

Josephson, Matthew. *The Politicos: 1865–1896*. New York: Harcourt Brace, 1938.

Keller, Morton. *Affairs of State: Public Life in Late Nineteenth Century America*. Cambridge, Mass.: Harvard University Press, 1977.

Kleppner, Paul. *The Third Electoral System, 1853–1892: Parties, Voters, and Political Cultures*. Chapel Hill: University of North Carolina Press, 1979.

Schlesinger, Arthur M., Jr., ed. *History of American Presidential Elections*, 1789–1968. 4 vols. New York: Chelsea House, 1971.

Silbey, Joel H. *The American Political Nation, 1838–1893*. Stanford, Calif.: Stanford University Press, 1991.

RICHARD JENSEN

PARTIES AND THE PRESS

Nineteenth-century political parties financed American newspapers through government patronage. Party papers provided a means of informing constituents and attracting voters. By the end of the century commercial advertisers had replaced political parties as the newspapers' chief source of revenue, although most papers remained identifiably partisan.

When the federal government moved to Washington, D.C., in 1800, the *National Intelligencer* spoke for the Democratic-Republicans, while the *Federalist* served the opposition Federalist Party. With their party in power, the editors of the *Intelligencer* received lucrative printing contracts from the executive department and became the official printers of Congress. By contrast, declining revenues soon caused the *Federalist* to disappear along with its party. Mailed with no charge, the *National Intelligencer* provided news from the national government, which newspapers nationwide reprinted.

As the old Republican Party split into factions in the 1820s, each financed its own newspaper. When Andrew Jackson won the presidency in 1828, he shifted government patronage from the *Intelligencer* to his own official printers, Duff Green, Francis P. Blair, and John C. Rives. Each presidential administration until that of Abraham Lincoln had a paper identified as its "official organ," a practice that gave presidents considerable control over the flow of news from Washington. Minority party members regularly complained of the majority's unfair use of government press patronage to retain power.

State party organizations, governors, and legislative majorities similarly subsidized newspapers. Thurlow Weed, editor of the *Albany* (New York) *Evening Journal* from 1830 to 1863, epitomized the journalist as state party "boss." First for the Whigs and later for the new Republican Party, Weed distributed patronage to other papers in return for their editorial endorsements.

State party leaders launched newspapers during the months prior to an election and closed them as soon as the votes were counted. In 1838 Weed arranged for the young Horace Greeley to edit a campaign weekly, the *Jeffersonian*, and during the 1840 presidential election Greeley edited another short-lived paper, *The Log Cabin*.

American political and commercial competitiveness eventually demolished government control of mass communications. During the three decades before the Civil War, the number of American newspapers more than doubled, with most towns having multiple papers representing different parties. An independent "penny press" also emerged, relying on sex, scandal, and sensationalism to sell papers. Dependent on circulation and advertising for revenue, the penny papers gradually aimed for balanced reporting over ideology and partisanship. Telegraph news further encouraged objectivity. Because the Associated Press serviced papers from all parties, it tried to keep opinion out of its dispatches.

Even after they emerged from overt party control, newspapers continued to proclaim their partisanship on their mastheads, and news articles revealed political bias. Papers like the *Chicago Tribune* and the *Springfield* (Massachusetts) *Republican* played active roles in building the Republican Party in their states, while the *Chicago Times* and *New York World* consistently promoted Democratic issues and candidates. Editors and publishers sought state and national office. In 1872 Greeley, then editor of the *New York Tribune*, ran as the presidential candidate on a fusion ticket of Democrats and liberal Republicans. After Greeley's defeat, the *Tribune* became the unofficial voice of the Republican Party, which nominated editor Whitelaw Reid for vice president in 1892.

Political subsidies proved inadequate as technological innovations vastly increased the cost of printing presses and other equipment. Newspapers drew their financial support from advertisements for local stores and national brand products rather than political organizations. However, parties continued to purchase newspaper advertisements at election time, which many smaller papers counted on for financial survival. Smaller weekly papers often made their endorsements of candidates contingent on candidates taking out ads.

By the end of the nineteenth century, publishers like Joseph Pulitzer and William Randolph Hearst had built enormously profitable newspapers on mass circulation and commercial advertising. The emergence of national chains, such as the Hearst papers in larger cities and those owned by E. W. Scripps in smaller industrial centers, further freed newspapers from local party influence.

See also **Advertising; Newspapers and the Press.**

Bibliography

Baldasty, Gerald J. *The Commercialization of News in the Nineteenth Century.* Madison: University of Wisconsin Press, 1992.

Cook, Timothy E. *Governing with the News: The News Media as a Political Institution.* Chicago: University of Chicago Press, 1998.

Dicken-Garcia, Hazel. *Journalistic Standards in Nineteenth-Century America.* Madison: University of Wisconsin Press, 1989.

Ritchie, Donald A. *Press Gallery: Congress and the Washington Correspondents.* Cambridge, Mass.: Harvard University Press, 1991.

Smith, Culver H. *The Press, Politics, and Patronage: The American Government's Use of Newspapers, 1789–1875.* Athens, Ga.: University of Georgia Press, 1977.

DONALD A. RITCHIE

"Can the Law Reach Him?" Political cartoon of Boss Tweed (1823–1878) being accosted by a New York City policeman. Drawing by Thomas Nast, 6 January 1872. © BETT-MANN/CORBIS

MACHINES AND BOSSES

Political machines and the bosses who ran them were central elements of late-nineteenth-century urban life. Machines, mass organizations based on the exchange of material benefits for electoral loyalty, originated in the social and political ferment of the industrializing United States. They were not the inevitable result of urbanization, nor were they simply outgrowths of immigrant cultures that stressed personal fealty over rational decision making. Rather they were institutions shaped by political factors and constrained by limited resources and substantial opposition. As a result they were neither as beneficent as their apologists claimed nor as omnipotent as their opponents charged.

Origins and Evolution

Machines were political innovations created by urban party politicians in response to the changing economic, social, and political order of the United States in the mid–nineteenth century. By the 1830s industrialization and immigration began to make traditional political distinctions between merchant and mechanic obsolete. Mass democratization simultaneously shattered the politics of deference that had prevailed in the early Republic. Faced with these altered circumstances, municipal party leaders devised new ways of organizing and mobilizing the expanding urban electorate.

New York City's Tammany Hall pioneered this new politics. Originally a merchant-dominated Jeffersonian political club formed in 1786, Tammany became the principal arm of the Democratic Party in New York City during the 1840s and 1850s. Under Mayor Fernando Wood, it established itself as the representative of the city's working-class ethnics. Wood and Tammany began distributing food, clothing, and fuel in poor neighborhoods, and the organization aggressively naturalized recent immigrants. Party leaders also set up workingmen's Democratic clubs in these districts, maintaining their allegiance by defending ethnic interests and distributing a growing number of municipal and federal patronage jobs to club members. These efforts formed the skeletal structure of the powerful machine that would flourish later in the century. (The term "boss" first entered the American political lexicon during the 1850s, when it was used to describe Brooklyn Navy Yard political leader Hughie McLaughlin.)

The Tammany style only gradually prevailed as a significant form of nineteenth-century urban politics. Similar activity developed in a few cities before the Civil War, including Newark, Philadelphia, and Pittsburgh, but the great age of boss rule came later in the century. Tammany itself did not fully consolidate its power in New York City until the late 1880s under the leadership of "Honest John" Kelly and Richard Croker. By the 1890s centralized machines dominated public life in ten of the nation's twenty largest cities. Republican organizations governed Philadelphia, Pittsburgh, Cincinnati, and Buffalo, while Democratic machines ruled in San Francisco (briefly), Albany, Jersey City, Brooklyn, and New York. The men who headed these organizations were the most powerful politicians in urban America.

Boss rule featured massive patronage armies and impressive levels of organization and electoral activity. As the public sector grew after the Civil War, machine leaders created elaborate patronage networks. By one estimate 140,000 federal, state, and local offices existed in New York City during the late 1870s, or one position for every eight voters. To deliver majorities in the multitudinous elections held in Gilded Age America required organizations encompassing every neighborhood and every block in the working-class sections of a city, each called to action for the dozens of party caucuses and general elections held throughout the era.

The machine method was impressive not only in its scale but in its corruption. Vote fraud of all types was rampant, although charges usually proved difficult to verify. Bribes and kickbacks were commonplace and often proffered openly as part of the price of doing business. Huge, ornate, and costly city halls, such as those in San Francisco and Philadelphia, arose less as celebrations of civic pride than as byproducts of the machine's thirst for patronage and graft. Some cases were even more excessive. Construction on the New York County Courthouse cost $13 million between 1869 and 1871, yet it was never completed.

Though infamous, machine rule was not automatic. In the late nineteenth century as many large U.S. cities functioned without centralized machines as with them. Major urban centers such as Boston and Chicago did not see machine rule before 1900. Machines were not uniformly successful, even in cities where they dominated public affairs. Tammany battled rival organizations for local supremacy through the early 1880s and suffered defeats at the hands of reformers in 1871 and 1901. Not until 1887

did Philadelphia Republicans consolidate their hold on power in that city, and San Francisco's Christopher "Blind Boss" Buckley maintained his grip on local politics for a scant nine years.

Factional conflict was at least as typical as centralized machine rule. In a few cities a handful of politicians dominated politics in their neighborhoods and jockeyed for citywide power. Martin Lomasney of Boston's West End and Johnny Powers of Ward Nineteen in Chicago were classic ward bosses, but neither these men nor their rivals proved powerful enough to permanently extend their reach beyond their home districts. Perhaps even more typical was the internecine feuding that characterized most urban neighborhoods. In Boston, New Orleans, Chicago, and numerous other cities, widespread factional infighting within wards prevented centralized machine rule, as various interests battled over an inadequate supply of patronage.

The greatest impediment to machine consolidation was the constricted flow of resources. Rarely were sufficient money and patronage available to maintain organizational discipline. Demands for low property taxes (the chief source of local revenue) and limited government tied bosses' hands. Fearful of middle-class tax revolts, even those machines that held a firm grip on power acted cautiously, careful not to increase spending too far or too fast. Benefits from the machine in the form of jobs and services thus flowed to a small circle of constituents, while most working-class immigrants received little direct assistance.

Where centralized machine rule developed, local bosses usually had firm connections with the state government. Tammany after 1885, the Durham-McNichol organization in Philadelphia, San Francisco's Buckley machine during its heyday, and Democratic organizations in Albany and Jersey City all had close ties to party leaders in state government who supplemented the local patronage supply. Limited municipal budgets made it almost impossible to hold together a cohesive citywide organization without outside help. Boston and Chicago Democrats both faced hostile state legislatures unwilling to support machine-building efforts, preventing would-be bosses in those cities from enforcing party discipline.

Institutional arrangements and political strategies also influenced machine viability. Republicans in Philadelphia consolidated power partly because an 1887 revision of the city charter gave the mayor control over municipal patronage. They also rewrote party rules to allow the city committee to distribute party revenues and determine nominations for local offices, powers previously resting with ward leaders. In most cities bosses sought alliances with businesspeople, who provided needed financial support through bribes and contributions in exchange for limited municipal spending, debt reduction, and low tax rates.

Faced with fiscal and political constraints, urban machines grew stingy. In their formative years machines sought support and wielded patronage freely. Tammany Hall under Wood and his successor William Marcy "Boss" Tweed dramatically expanded the public payroll, tripling the city's debt in the process, and worked feverishly to naturalize and register new immigrants. Between 1856 and 1867 Tammany naturalized 9,207 immigrants per year. But as reform opposition grew and the threat of tax revolts intensified, machines grew more conservative. Patronage flowed more slowly from headquarters, and the pace of naturalization diminished markedly after 1880. By the late 1880s New York City's electorate was growing at half the rate it had two decades earlier, despite massive increases in the city's population. Similarly conservative patterns developed in San Francisco, Albany, Jersey City, Philadelphia, and Pittsburgh.

This shift in machine strategy meant that machines provided jobs and other tangible benefits for only a fraction of their constituents. In many cases Irish Americans, the group that had been a mainstay of the machines from the outset, captured plum patronage positions and derived most of the material benefits. Later immigrants, particularly southern and eastern Europeans who began arriving in large numbers after 1880, found the machines far less interested in assisting them. In fact both neighborhood and citywide machines had an incentive to limit the participation of these newcomers in order to preserve their power. If new immigrants voted in large numbers, machines would not have enough resources to maintain their loyalty. In the long run this mass of potential new voters spelled trouble for the machines, but their failure to vote in large numbers allowed machines to ignore most of them until well into the twentieth century.

State-level machines required even greater financial resources. Although Martin Van Buren engineered the transformation of the Bucktail faction of the Democratic-Republican Party into the Albany Regency machine as early as the 1820s, the true heyday of state bosses arose later in the century, as party politicians gained access to deep corporate pockets. The most successful included Matthew Quay of Pennsylvania and Thomas Platt of New York, each of whom solidified Republican machines in their respective states during the late 1880s. They did so by drawing large contributions from corporations and wealthy businessmen in exchange for political favors, which they used to maintain party discipline and fund massive vote-getting operations. The degree of organization in these enterprises was staggering. Quay reputedly kept a card file with the names of 800,000 Pennsylvania voters, each classified by their degree of political reliability.

The culmination of nineteenth-century machine politics came when the Ohio businessman Mark Hanna forged a cohesive national Republican organization during the 1890s. Frustrated by the party's failures and lack of discipline during the 1888 presidential campaign, Hanna aggressively tapped the wealth of big business, which he used to propel William McKinley to the presidency in 1896. Using these resources, he directed a national "educational campaign" that featured a corps of orators and a series of pamphlets dedicating to praising the virtue of sound money and attacking the free silver idea espoused by Democratic candidate William Jennings Bryan. Most importantly, he centralized party operations in the Republican National Committee, which exercised almost full control over state and local activities during both the 1896 and 1900 McKinley campaigns.

Power

Although faced with sharp constraints, machines exercised substantial power in the United States in the late nineteenth century. In cities where machines consolidated their power, they dominated local affairs despite occasional defeats. Bosses, few of whom held elective office themselves, frequently dictated who served as mayor and in the city council. They also delivered substantial majorities in state and national elections, which gave them significant clout in an era of extraordinarily close party balance. Even in cities where machine rule never fully materialized, neighborhood bosses such as Lomasney and Powers were able to shape local affairs to some extent. If they could not determine who served as mayor, they often prevented an enemy from capturing the office or made alliances with others to win power temporarily.

Machines also provided the foot soldiers of the late-nineteenth-century American state. Bosses determined who delivered the mail, inspected customs, lit street lamps, cleaned streets, and performed a range of other governmental services. The growing regulatory impulse of the late nineteenth century enlarged the patronage pool, allowing party members to fill positions as inspectors, clerical workers, and managers of new municipal agencies. While demand for civil service regulation and expertise in government intensified by the end of the century, machines still controlled large segments of the public payroll, and their loyalists did a substantial portion of the government's work.

Urban machines powerfully shaped the nineteenth-century electorate, determining which forms of political action and political ideology were possible and which were not. The mobilization of working-class urbanites into patronage-fueled parties steered them away from more radical forms of politics. Conservative, organizationally driven machine politics helped snuff out an Irish American radical tradition derived from the anti-British Fenian and Land League movements of nineteenth-century Ireland. Tammany helped draw blue-collar support away from the 1886 mayoral bid of the single-taxer Henry George, contributing significantly to the demise of an effective worker's party in late-nineteenth-century New York City. The power of urban machines, particularly as they became less committed to mobilizing recent immigrants, also impeded other forms of grassroots politics that might have been more responsive to community needs.

Reform

The rise of bosses and machines also spurred the development of reformers. These critics argued that machines were corrupt and antidemocratic, charges that had considerable merit. They also claimed that urban political organizations exercised almost untrammeled power derived from the thoughtless loyalty of working-class immigrants, an assertion that shaped historical accounts of machine politics. But this latter criticism proved inaccurate, and historians have effectively challenged the notions that bosses and machines governed with few constraints and that they served the immigrant poor effectively.

Typically perceived as quintessential nineteenth-century institutions, bosses and machines most fully developed in the early twentieth century. Fully centralized machines did not emerge until the late 1880s, just as the size and scale of state and municipal government—and available patronage—began to expand. The climate for machine formation improved further after 1900, as the middle class began retreating to the suburbs, taking their demands for lower property taxes and limited public debt with them. The consolidation, expansion, and increasing activism of city governments also helped machines by providing them with more jobs and services to distribute. A more activist state also enabled bosses to provide collective benefits in the shape of reforms and policies that helped the working class without consuming precious patronage resources. Ironically, bosses and machines prospered in the era of the activist state far more than they did in the relatively parsimonious world of nineteenth-century American public life.

See also **Cities and Urbanization.**

Bibliography

Bridges, Amy. *A City in the Republic: Antebellum New York and the Origins of Machine Politics.* Ithaca, N.Y.: Cornell University Press, 1987.
Brown, M. Craig, and Charles N. Halaby. "Machine Politics in America, 1870–1945." *Journal of Interdisciplinary History* 17 (1987): 587–612.
Erie, Steven P. *Rainbow's End: Irish-Americans and the Dilemmas of Urban Machine Politics, 1840–1985.* Berkeley: University of California Press, 1988.
Keller, Morton. *Affairs of State: Public Life in Late Nineteenth Century America.* Cambridge, Mass.: Harvard University Press, 1977.
McCaffery, Peter. *When Bosses Ruled Philadelphia: The Emergence of the Republican Machine, 1867–1933.* University Park: Pennsylvania State University Press, 1993.
McDonald, Terrence J. *The Parameters of Urban Fiscal Policy: Socioeconomic Change and Political Culture in San Francisco, 1860–1906.* Berkeley: University of California Press, 1986.
Shefter, Martin. *Political Parties and the State: The American Historical Experience.* Princeton, N.J.: Princeton University Press, 1994.
Teaford, Jon C. *The Unheralded Triumph: City Government in America, 1870–1900.* Baltimore: Johns Hopkins University Press, 1984.

JAMES J. CONNOLLY

CORRUPTION AND SCANDALS

Political corruption was an old phenomenon in a new nation by the time the United States entered the nineteenth century. It had been a major American grievance of the years leading to the Revolution, when British officials ranging from customs agents to colonial governors were criticized regularly for profiting illegally from their positions. Delegates to the Constitutional Convention of 1787 sought to limit corruption in the new United States government, though the concentration of unchecked political power appeared to be the primary danger, from which bribery, theft, and lesser degrees of corruption naturally flowed.

The bitterly contested presidential election of 1800 was characterized by charges of public malfeasance against the Federalist administrations of George Washington and John Adams. Jonathan Dayton (1760–1824), Federalist Speaker of the House of Representatives in the Fourth and Fifth Congresses, was accused of using monies appropriated for House members' salaries to speculate in western lands. Similarly, Treasury and War Department officials, including Alexander Hamilton, were alleged to have skimmed funds for personal use or land speculation. Dayton eventually paid eighteen thousand dollars to cover shortfalls in House accounts, but the destruction of Treasury and War Department records in suspicious fires shortly after the election made further investigation in these cases impossible.

From 1802 to 1814, Congress struggled over the Yazoo fraud, which originated on the state level before the turn of the century. In 1795, Georgia's legislature approved the sale of thirty-five million acres of state-owned lands to the Yazoo Companies, a consortium of private investors, for about 1 percent of its retail value. It was later discovered that the companies had made generous gifts of stock, and some outright bribes, to legislators; a new legislature, elected the following year by outraged voters, rescinded the sale. Georgia ceded claim to the land to the federal government in 1802, after which the Yazoo associates bombarded every succeeding Congress with demands for restitution. Finally, prodded by a favorable Supreme Court decision (*Fletcher v. Peck*, 1810), Congress appropriated $4,282,000 to compensate the investors in 1814.

Customs collections always presented opportunities for corruption during this period, and perhaps no official was better placed to profit than the federal collector of customs for the port of New York, through which almost 80 percent of the nation's imports passed. In 1838, Samuel Swarthout, appointed collector because of his contributions to the presidential election of Andrew Jackson, fled to Europe, leaving a shortfall of $1,226,000 in his office accounts, an enormous sum for the time.

Continuity and Change

Such classic instances of political corruption were repeated with variations throughout the century, not always without redress. Congress and state and local government authorities investigated, prosecuted, and reformed, but public malfeasance remained a factor in American society throughout the period. The persistence of corruption was due to a combination of factors.

The United States underwent an extraordinary evolution during the nineteenth century. The nation grew from a predominantly agrarian republic of five million to an increasingly urbanized industrial giant of seventy-two million; the steady flow of immigration became a flood in the 1840s, gradually altering the nation's population from relative homogeneity to broad diversity. The industrial revolution changed America's way of life even more dramatically.

Government at all levels was ill-equipped to meet the challenges of this transformation, not to mention maintaining standards of honesty and efficiency. There was little effective scrutiny of public expenditures. Efficiency and honesty in performing official duties were less important than the incumbent's party loyalty. The presence of financial temptations was enhanced by the fact that government services, such as Indian agencies, postal delivery, and military supply, were provided by private contractors. Bribes in exchange for contracts, delivery of substandard goods (or nondelivery of goods), and skimming remained common until, and even after, the establishment of the professional civil service later in the century.

Government, especially at the state and local levels, was called on to perform services for which they were initially poorly equipped. Public agencies commissioned roads, paved streets, erected schools and hospitals, and constructed sewers and waterworks. Here again, opportunities for malfeasance were always present.

A Political Revolution

The comparative stability of national government in the century's first three decades ended with the dramatic triumph of the military hero Andrew Jackson (1767–1845) in the presidential election of 1828. Jackson and his followers moved to cement their grip on national power. One weapon they used was the widespread adoption of the spoils system, in which public officials were selected according to party affiliation. It was epitomized in Senator William Marcy's remark in 1832 that "to the victors belong the spoils of the enemy." Jobs were often auctioned off to the highest bidder, and officeholders sought to recoup the cost of obtaining employment and further enrich themselves by demanding bribes from would-be contractors and franchisees.

Machine Politics

The spoils system and the development of the political machine went hand in hand. New York's Society of Saint Tammany, better known as Tammany Hall, was perhaps the most famous example, although dozens of similar organizations sprang up in cities across the country. Originally incorporated in 1805 as a mutual benefit society, Tammany came to dominate the Democratic Party in New York City, and often New York State, for much of the century. It regulated patronage employment in government, provided relief for indigent families, controlled city contracts, and regularly delivered enormous electoral majorities that influenced the outcomes of city, state, and even national elections.

Tammany Hall's domination grew through the

century, culminating in the reign of William Marcy "Boss" Tweed (1823–1878), who controlled the organization from 1860 to 1871. During Tweed's reign, construction contracts and franchises frequently were awarded to the highest bidder, city payrolls were padded with nonexistent employees, and jobs were auctioned. One source estimated that the boss and his circle, known as the Tweed Ring, pocketed one of every two dollars spent by the city. Tammany eventually ran afoul of a combination of growing public outrage, New York State Democratic leader Samuel J. Tilden's (1814–1886) presidential aspirations, crusading investigations by several New York newspapers, and attacks by *Harper's Weekly*, whose editorial cartoonist, Thomas Nast (1840–1902), mercilessly pilloried the boss and his associates. The ring was broken up, and Tweed fled to Europe in 1876, where he was apprehended after being identified from one of Nast's cartoons.

On the national level, the Civil War presented unprecedented opportunities for theft. The need for supplies and equipment was so acute that lucrative orders were placed with firms that supplied spoiled food, shoddy uniforms and boots, defective weapons and ammunition, and unseaworthy ships. Would-be suppliers soon learned to retain politically connected agents and "fixers" in Washington to guarantee contracts from the War Department, usually in return for 5 percent of the contract's value. The confusion was complicated by Secretary of War Simon Cameron (1799–1889). Selected by President Abraham Lincoln for political reasons—he was the Republican boss of Pennsylvania—Cameron steered business to friends, business associates, and firms in which he was an investor. Cameron proved as inept as he was corrupt, and Lincoln was forced to replace him in 1862 with the arbitrary but efficient and uncorruptible Edwin M. Stanton (1814–1869).

Corporate Power and Gilded Age Corruption

Following the Civil War, corporate wealth and power emerged as a major source of increased political corruption. The Gilded Age of the century's closing decades was also a golden age for corporate influence. With vast financial resources, wealthy individuals and corporations influenced municipal authorities, state legislatures, and Congress itself. Although small-scale corruption endured, now there were larger targets, including favorable treatment in tariff legislation; corporate bounties and subsidies, particularly from state governments; and generous land grants for railroad construction from Congress. Favor seekers used such tools as election campaign contributions to cooperative candidates and party authorities, generous fees to favored law firms, railroad passes, and insider investment information for lawmakers and other officials.

President Ulysses S. Grant's two administrations (1869–1877) were wracked by scandals. One of the most notorious involved Secretary of War William W. Belknap, who, along with his wife, sold a lucrative Indian trading post contract for a bribe of twelve thousand dollars per year. The House of Representatives voted to impeach the Secretary when the scandal was uncovered, but the Senate did not convict, on the grounds that since Belknap had hastily resigned in March 1876 he was no longer a federal official and therefore not subject to impeachment.

Perhaps the greatest scandal of the era involved Crédit Mobilier of America, a Union Pacific Railroad subsidiary established to finance construction of part of the transcontinental railroad. The railroad's directors poured proceeds from stock and bond sales, including U.S. government bonds, into Crédit Mobilier, where much of the money was subsequently passed directly to stockholders in the form of enormous dividends. Moreover, the cost of the firm's actual construction projects was grossly inflated. In 1867, when it appeared likely that Congress would investigate the arrangement, Crédit Mobilier president Oakes Ames (1804–1873), who was also a member of the House of Representatives, distributed company stock to U.S. senators and representatives at par value, that is, less than half its market price. Ames's largesse had the desired effect: there was no investigation of Crédit Mobilier until 1873, at which time he was censured by the House of Representatives; outgoing Vice President Schuyler Colfax (1823–1885) was disgraced; and the reputations of several other senators and representatives, including the future president James A. Garfield (1831–1881), were damaged.

Reform Beginnings

As corruption reached new heights of scale and sophistication in the last third of the nineteenth century, a reform movement began to emerge. Reformers such as Charles Eliot Norton (1827–1908), George William Curtis (1824–1892), and E. L. Godkin (1831–1902), publisher of the *Nation*, urged structural change in government and moral renewal in the private sector. These well-to-do professionals could not create a sustained grassroots movement for change, but there was progress in the last decades of the century. States and cities improved their procurement and contracting procedures, established professional civil service requirements to replace the spoils system, passed corrupt practices legislation, and imposed more severe penalties for malfeasance.

Election fraud was reduced by voter registration, ballots printed by state authorities, and the introduction of the secret ballot.

On the federal level, President Rutherford Hayes (who held office from 1877 to 1881) prohibited political activity by government employees and authorized an extensive cleanup of the customs houses in 1877. The assassination of President Garfield by a disappointed office seeker in 1881 so shocked the nation that Congress passed the Pendleton Act of 1883. That law prohibited solicitation of campaign contributions from covered federal employees and established a professional civil service appointed on the basis of qualification and exempt from dismissal on political grounds.

Clearly, much remained to be done at the century's close. Petty corruption remained entrenched in many jurisdictions throughout the nation, and corporate power was approaching the peak of its influence over all levels of government. These and other factors contributing to public malfeasance were addressed more systematically after the turn of the century, following the birth of the Progressive movement, with its muckraking journalists, mass political support for reform, and regulatory legislation enacted by newly energized federal and state authorities.

See also **Corporations and Big Business; Gilded Age; Politics,** *subentry on* **Machines and Bosses; Reform, Political.**

Bibliography

Benson, George Charles Sumner. *Political Corruption in America.* Lexington, Mass: Lexington Books, 1978.

Eisenstadt, Abraham S., Ari Hoogenboom, and Hans L. Trefousse, eds. *Before Watergate: Problems of Corruption in American Society.* Brooklyn, N.Y.: Brooklyn College Press, 1978.

Feinberg, Barbara Silberdick. *American Political Scandals, Past and Present.* New York: Franklin Watts, 1992.

Garrison, Webb B. *Behind the Headlines: American History's Schemes, Scandals, and Escapades.* Harrisburg, Pa.: Stackpole Books, 1983.

Lawson, Don. *Famous Presidential Scandals.* Hillside, N.J.: U.S.A. Enslow Publishers, 1990.

Loth, David Goldsmith. *Public Plunder: A History of Graft in America.* New York: Carrick, and Evans, 1938. Reprint, Westport, Conn.: Greenwood, 1970.

Miller, Nathan. *Stealing from America: A History of Corruption from Jamestown to Whitewater.* New York: Marlow, 1996.

Ross, Shelley. *Fall from Grace: Sex, Scandal, and Corruption in American Politics from 1702 to the Present.* New York: Ballantine Books, 1988.

Summers, Mark W. *The Plundering Generation: Corruption and the Crisis of the Union, 1849–1961.* New York: Oxford University Press, 1987.

THOMAS H. NEALE

POLYGAMY, MORMON The patriarchal Mormon form of plural marriage based on Old Testament Hebrew models (and technically known as polygyny) was the largest and most controversial alternative to monogamous marriage in nineteenth-century America. Between 1841 and 1844 in the rapidly growing Mormon settlement of Nauvoo, Illinois, along the Mississippi River, the Mormon prophet-founder Joseph Smith privately began to introduce the idea and practice of plural marriage among his most trusted followers. Smith argued that plural marriage was the highest form of marriage, and he took plural wives himself. He also convinced about thirty of his closest male associates to engage in the practice under his guidance. Not surprisingly, these actions led to tensions within the officially monogamous group, and on 27 June 1844, Joseph Smith and his brother Hyrum were murdered in a jail in Carthage, Illinois, while awaiting trial on charges arising in part from the dissatisfaction of some of their followers with the new polygamous beliefs and practices.

Smith's tragic death might have been expected to cripple the young Church of Jesus Christ of Latter-day Saints and lead to its abandonment of polygamy. Instead, under Brigham Young's leadership, and following a heroic trek to the Great Basin region that began in 1846, polygamy became fully established among the Mormons. Publicly presented in 1852 as an integral part of the Mormon religious and social system, plural marriage spread throughout the more than three hundred settlements that Brigham Young helped found in Utah and adjacent territories before his death in 1877. By the 1880s, there were more than 100,000 Mormons in the intermountain West ideologically committed to polygamy as the highest form of marriage, and approximately one-quarter of all Mormon families were polygamous. Intense federal pressure nevertheless forced the Mormon church in 1890 to discontinue authorizing further plural marriages in the United States, and after 1904 recalcitrant polygamists were excommunicated from the church. Mormons today are among the staunchest defenders of monogamy, although Mormon splinter groups with tens of thousands of adherents continue to advocate and practice plural marriage.

Mormon polygamy in the nineteenth century was the focus of intense controversy. Non-Mormons denounced it as a vile system of debauchery perpetrated upon Mormon women by an unscrupulous male leadership, while Mormons defended it as a way of enlarging kinship ties and conforming to God's will. Recent Mormon and non-Mormon scholarship on polygamy has recognized the difficult emotional challenges that plural marriage posed for women, while also stressing the paradoxical ways in which polygamy sometimes could free women to play a more active role in society. Plural wives in Utah, for instance, sometimes acted as "heads of households," managing family businesses in the absence of their husbands, cooperating in handling child care so that other wives could gain professional training, and publishing a distinguished independent women's newspaper, the *Woman's Exponent*, during the late nineteenth and early twentieth centuries. Many present-day Mormons were both proud of and ambivalent about their polygamous frontier Mormon heritage.

See also **Anti-Mormonism; Mormonism.**

Bibliography

Embry, Jessie L. *Mormon Polygamous Families: Life in the Principle.* Salt Lake City: University of Utah Press, 1987.

Foster, Lawrence. *Religion and Sexuality: The Shakers, the Mormons, and the Oneida Community.* Urbana: University of Illinois Press, 1984.

Newell, Linda King, and Valeen Tippetts Avery. *Mormon Enigma: Emma Hale Smith.* 2d ed. Urbana: University of Illinois Press, 1994.

Young, Kimball. *Isn't One Wife Enough? The Story of Mormon Polygamy.* New York: Henry Holt, 1954.

LAWRENCE FOSTER

PONY EXPRESS   The Pony Express, a private postal service, was established in 1860 by Russell, Majors, and Waddell, a western freighting company. The creation of the express was inspired by the sectional rivalry over the location of a transcontinental railroad.

The U.S. acquisition of California in 1848 kindled the nation's interest in building a transcontinental railroad, but the desire of both the North and the South to have the railroad connect with their section stalled the project. Unable to decide on the rail's location, Congress appropriated $600,000 in 1857 for a contract to carry semiweekly mail overland from the Missouri River to California. Postmaster General Aaron Brown, a southerner, awarded this contract to John Butterfield, whose long, indirect southern route was presumed to be the best all-weather route to California and was also expected to be the site of the future railroad.

Frustrated by this choice, William H. Russell and associates in the North organized the Pony Express over the northern, or central, route to demonstrate its suitability as a mail route. They hoped ultimately to secure a mail contract over that route. The network over which the express route ran was hastily

---

Mark Twain's Reflections of the Pony Express

In a little while all interest was taken up in stretching our necks and watching for the "pony-rider"—the fleet messenger who sped across the continent from St. Joe to Sacramento, carrying letters nineteen hundred miles in eight days! . . . There was no idling-time for a pony-rider on duty. . . . He rode a splendid horse that was born for a racer and fed and lodged like a gentleman; kept him at his utmost speed for ten miles, and then, as he came crashing up to the station where stood two men holding fast a fresh, impatient steed, the transfer of rider and mail-bag was made in the twinkling of an eye, and away flew the eager pair.

Mark Twain, *Roughing It,* from chapter 8

---

built. Altogether some ninety way stations were erected and stocked with the finest horses available. To carry the mail, as many as eighty riders—hardy, light of weight, and brave—were employed at between $50 and $150 a month. The route ran past familiar landmarks—Marysville, Kansas; Fort Kearney, Nebraska; Julesburg, Colorado; and Chimney Rock to Fort Laramie, Wyoming, over South Pass, and down to Salt Lake City, Utah. From there the route ran south of Salt Lake to Carson City, over the Sierra Nevada, south of Lake Tahoe, to Sacramento, California, and from there to San Francisco by boat.

On 3 April 1860, from San Francisco and from St. Joseph on the Missouri River, the riders began their first trip to unite the country with a speedy mail service. Seventy-five horses were needed to make the journey over the extended route, and each rider rode thirty to fifty miles at first, but later each rider would travel between seventy-five and one hundred miles. Two minutes were allowed to exchange horses at the way stations. Their ride completed, the horses would rest until an incoming rider transferred his mailbags to them for their return trip. The mailbags could weigh as much as twenty pounds. At first it cost five dollars to mail a half-ounce letter, but the charge was later reduced to one dollar.

The trip of nearly two thousand miles normally took ten days, but President Abraham Lincoln's inaugural address in 1861 was carried to California in seven days and a few hours. It was a speed that astounded and thrilled Americans, who heaped praise on the riders and their rugged ponies.

The Pony Express lasted nineteen months and was

The Overland Pony Express. The mounted rider waves to workers setting up telegraph lines, foreshadowing the decline of pony express. Photographed by Savage. A wood engraving of the picture was published in *Harper's Weekly* in 1867. LIBRARY OF CONGRESS

seriously delayed only once, because of an Indian uprising. In October 1861, however, the telegraph spanned the nation, making the Pony Express obsolete. The express had made no money, but it had proved the feasibility of the central route. In the end, however, Russell, Majors, and Waddell received no large contract to carry the mail. When the Civil War began, the Butterfield Company was moved from the southern to the central route by the federal government, and the company was then sold to Wells Fargo and Company.

See also **Post Office; Telegraph.**

Bibliography

Driggs, Howard R. *The Pony Express Goes Through: An American Saga Told by Its Heroes.* New York: Frederick A. Stokes, 1935.

Fike, Richard E., and John W. Headley. *The Pony Express Stations of Utah in Historical Perspective.* Cultural Resources Series, monograph 2. Washington, D.C.: Government Printing Office, 1979.

Hafen, LeRoy R. *The Overland Mail, 1849–1869: Promoter of Settlement, Precursor of Railroads.* New York: AMS Press, 1969.

Ingraham, Prentiss, ed. *Seventy Years on the Frontier: Alexander Major's Memoirs.* Lincoln: University of Nebraska Press, 1989.

Reinfeld, Fred. *Pony Express.* Lincoln: University of Nebraska Press, 1966.

WAYNE E. FULLER

POPULAR CULTURE

Origins and Genealogy of the Term

Nineteenth-century critics would have considered the term "popular culture" an oxymoron. To them "popular" connoted something of inferior quality—common, low, or base—as well as an attempt to win favor, while "culture" implied the opposite—refinement, cultivation, and what was thought of in the twentieth century as "high" culture. It was not until the last decade of the nineteenth century that critics began to believe anything "popular" could have aesthetic merit. This newfound respect did not come without a backlash. One late-nineteenth-century magazine lamented the lowering of aesthetic standards, and singled out critics who had begun to treat popular entertainment as serious art and a synonym for excellence. When "popular culture" first appeared in the critical vocabulary, it was used pejoratively by the gatekeepers of high culture, who sought to preserve aesthetic and moral standards. As a result, producers and enthusiastic consumers avoided using the term. It was not until the 1960s, when "camp" and pop art emerged, that artists and consumers began to embrace popular culture as a respectable category for art. At that point the study of popular culture first became a serious subdiscipline for scholars.

Popular culture now refers to the cultural objects and forms of industrial society that have widespread appeal and are widely accessible. It is still distinguished from "elite" or "highbrow" cultural forms, and scholars who study nineteenth-century America include in it everything from photography, blackface minstrelsy, novels, the penny press, illustrated newspapers and magazines, and Shakespearean drama and opera to spiritualism and phrenology, the songs of Stephen Foster, and P. T. Barnum's museum and circus.

Because it is inextricably linked to a commercial marketplace, popular culture is typically seen as a category separate from folk culture. While both forms appeal primarily to the "folk" and "common people," their difference lies in how the product is transmitted. The producers of popular culture rely on a marketplace to sell their goods. They produce for an audience or clientele they do not know directly. In conceiving and designing their wares, they can only hazard guesses at who their audiences are and what they want. Folk culture typically does not rely on a capitalist marketplace for its dissemination, and the producers thus do not stand at a remove from their audiences. Folk artists know who their consumers are; they can see them and hear them as they sing, dance, narrate, and ply their wares.

The separation between producer and consumer in a capitalist society has been a source of confusion and has caused a blurring of boundaries between the categories of mass culture and popular culture. Historians tend to treat mass culture as synonymous with popular culture. Cultural critics, however, usually distinguish between the two, defining popular culture as the ways in which the "people"—who consume and enjoy the products of mass culture—interpret those products to fit their own ideological needs and understandings. In this conceptualization, popular culture is bound up with the products and technology of mass culture, but it represents a process rather than

a product—a process of using and creatively interpreting the products of mass culture. As a result, there is a continual interaction—and often tension—between the commercial interests of mass culture and the popular interests of the people, who use mass culture for their own purposes.

These two different scholarly approaches to popular culture have led to widely different interpretations of the effects of popular culture in nineteenth-century America. At the risk of overgeneralization, one might say that scholars who equate popular culture with mass culture view consumers as more or less passive players in a capitalist society, consumers who helped to fuel the market revolution and create a consumer culture of standardized products in nineteenth-century America. By contrast, critics influenced by postmodern and Marxist-based theories of culture are more inclined to interpret popular culture as a pas de deux between producers and consumers, with the consumers ultimately choreographing the dance. In this scenario, consumers use mass culture in ways that signify resistance and protest against an encroaching capitalist economy and the standardization and alienation that result from it. By reinterpreting the products of commercial society, consumers subvert the intentions of cultural producers, even though they accommodate and reinforce the producers' designs by purchasing their products.

Forms of Nineteenth-Century Popular Culture

The rise of popular culture in nineteenth-century America paralleled the rise of the middle class, which in turn was fueled by the market revolution. The dissemination of popular goods and entertainment depended upon a network of accessible roads, canals, and other forms of transportation, along with a standard currency (as opposed to barter) to buy the products—and enough leisure time to enjoy them. These social preconditions were linked closely to the market revolution, which began in port cities such as Boston and New York in the colonial era, and spread throughout the countryside in the antebellum period. Although some scholars argue that popular culture did not develop until the third or fourth decade of the nineteenth century, there are numerous examples of thriving popular forms of entertainment at the start of the nineteenth century. The two earliest were published execution sermons (which gave way to trial reports) and the novel.

Popular literature

Execution sermons had enormous popularity in Boston as early as the second decade of the eighteenth century. In 1717 the prominent Boston minister Cotton Mather (1663–1728) sold thousands of copies of

Minstrelsy. Advertisement for Primrose & West's all-white performers, 1897. LIBRARY OF CONGRESS: PRINTS AND PHO-TOGRAPHS DIVISION. (MINSTREL POSTER COLLECTION)

his execution sermons through local booksellers. They were so popular that, on average, every other household in Boston contained a copy of them, often cracked in the corners and dirty from many hands. By the beginning of the nineteenth century, execution sermons had begun to be replaced by racy trial reports, which achieved even greater popularity. This change in genre for reporting violent crimes was caused by many factors. It reflected a gradual shift in cultural leadership from the ministry to the legal profession. It was a sign of New England's growing diversity, which meant that trial reports—far more than moralizing and pedantic sermons—enabled and often encouraged readers to interpret crimes and punishments according to their own ideological beliefs. The production, packaging, and dissemination of adversarial trials thus provided an arena in which social tensions and conflicts could be played out. For example, the murder trials of an Irishman and a Federalist lawyer elicited widely differing responses from readers, depending on their social and political orientations.

The novel experienced a meteoric rise in popularity and became the first popular form of entertainment to reach Americans in all regions. Like execution sermons and trial reports, the novel's greatest appeal was in the Northeast, in large part because extensive transportation networks permitted easy access to markets and facilitated the rise of the middle class. The rise of both the novel and trial reports also coincided with a cultural gap left by the loss of power by the church. In fact, trial reports often blurred the boundaries between fact and fiction, thus becoming a subgenre of the novel. Novels and trial reports were in many respects ideal forms for a society in the throes of rapid social change. They subverted notions of literacy and cultural capital sponsored by the upper class. They undermined what were considered suitable forms of writing. And they redefined the very meaning of literature: novels and trial reports did not rhyme or adhere to meter; they were colloquial in style, written in the language of the people.

Cultural elites vigorously attacked the novel even

Barnum's Museum. New Yorkers sleighing in front of Barnum's Museum, Broadway. Lithograph printed in 1855 by Thomas Benecke. LIBRARY OF CONGRESS: PRINTS AND PHOTOGRAPHS DIVISION

before its extraordinary ascent. Perhaps anticipating the expansion of transportation networks, commercial activity, and the middle class, elites sought to stem what they considered an abuse of the written word in order to preserve their place as interpreters of culture. Although in the 1780s and 1790s novels were still largely restricted to upper-class elites in seaport towns, they were decried by elites (many of whom read them) as serpents, friends of the devil, and a serious threat to the peace of the family, community, and nation. Some of the early Republic's most esteemed men took time out from their work to publicly condemn the novel, including Timothy Dwight (1752–1817), the president of Yale College; Jonathan Edwards (1703–1758), the Puritan theologian; Benjamin Rush (1745–1813), the famous physician and statesman; and Thomas Jefferson and John Adams. Despite these efforts, by the year 1855 novels constituted over half of all books published in the United States.

Other forms of popular writing followed the rise of the novel. In the eighteenth and early nineteenth cen-turies, newspapers were narrow in scope and geared to the interests of the economic and political elites. They focused on foreign news, commercial information, and partisan politics. By the 1830s, with the advent of the cylinder press and steam power, newspapers could print tens of thousands of copies and sell them for pennies. The "penny press" appealed to a heterogeneous mass audience by offering local news and lurid accounts of crime and vice. And like trial reports, penny papers blurred the boundaries of fact and fiction.

As the costs of producing magazines and newspapers declined, the short story similarly emerged as a popular middle-class genre. Short stories were a staple of newspapers and popular magazines from the antebellum era through the end of the century. Even more than the novel, the short story was a genre perfectly suited to the rising middle classes. Not only were short stories written in the language of the people; they could be read and absorbed in one sitting and then discarded. The vast majority of the works in short-story collections were first published in newspapers or magazines, and by the 1850s the most popular novels in America—such as *Uncle Tom's Cabin* (1852) by Harriet Beecher Stowe (1811–1896)—were first serialized in newspapers and magazines.

Photography

While print media reached millions of readers and witnessed an extraordinary rise in popularity, photography was unquestionably the most popular cultural phenomenon in nineteenth-century America. Although the Frenchman Louis J. M. Daguerre (1787–1851) is credited with inventing photography in 1839, it was in America that the photograph gained its greatest popularity. Almost from the beginning, Americans had an exuberant love affair with photography. Within a decade of photography's invention, a photographer was available for hire in almost every county of every state, as well as in the territories. The public demand for photography seemed insatiable. In New York City there were more than seventy daguerreotype studios by 1850, where customers could go to have their portraits taken. Photography, like the novel and the newspaper, stood apart from other forms of popular culture in its widespread appeal in all regions of the country. And unlike the novel and the newspaper, photography was not dependent upon a network of roads for distributing products. With a horse, a covered wagon, a camera, and a few supplies, an ambitious entrepreneur could set up shop as a daguerreotypist. Most of the early photographers came to their trade from other professions, having no art or aesthetic background, and abandoned it within a decade. With few barriers to entry, little training required, and an ever-growing demand, it was a business that was easy to enter and relatively painless to leave.

The demand for photographs corresponded with the rise of the middle class (especially in America and France), who wanted portraits of themselves but could not afford expensive paintings. By 1850, after improvements in lenses and shutter speed, every American in possession of pocket change could have his or her portrait taken. The demand for portraits was so high that from 1850 to 1870 over 90 percent of all photographs were portraits. The portrait also satisfied the desire among the emerging middle class for self-transformation. Indeed the very desire to become a part of the middle class represented a transformation in one's identity. And as Americans rose and fell in status, making and remaking themselves anew, they wanted a visible and tangible record of themselves at a given moment as a marker to help them chart their future. In one sense, Americans created pictures of themselves and then sought to become that picture.

Photography also offered a way to replace an obsolete way of life with an alternate vision of America. Its emergence coincided with a radical transformation of the cultural landscape. Railroads and steamboats had transplanted enormous numbers of people to distant places and had changed irrevocably the face of cities and towns. A widespread depression began with the panic of 1837, continued into the mid-1840s, and was followed by another depression in the 1850s. The result was a further erosion of old communities and ways of life. In the face of this retreat and disintegration, photography, much like the print culture, recaptured lost, "real" communities and served as a source for imagining new ones. The daguerreotype, the first popular form of photography, was packaged like a book. The image was contained inside a leather case with a velvet backing, and one opened the case to discover a new world and another reality. It is no coincidence that books were the most common prop in daguerreotype portraiture, and many portraits feature the sitters reading, drawn into another world. Together, photographs and books provided Americans with new visions of themselves and of their country.

By the end of the 1850s, *cartes de visite*, or visiting cards, had replaced daguerreotypes in popularity and represented the precursor to the modern, wallet-sized snapshot. Unlike daguerreotypes, which were one-of-a-kind, "precious" metal objects, *cartes de visite* were infinitely reproducible as prints on paper. They were distributed as calling cards, purchased as souvenirs, and could be produced en masse quite cheaply. Hundreds of thousands of copies of images of famous men and women could be made in short order, based on demand. The night before Abraham Lincoln's famous Cooper Union Address of 27 February 1860, which helped to put him in the White House, Mathew Brady photographed him, and sold over 100,000 *cartes-de-visite* copies. Following the attack on Fort Sumter, one thousand *cartes de visite* a day were sold of the Union commander Major Robert Anderson (1805–1871). Thanks to this new, wet-plate collodion process, Americans were able to collect portraits of themselves, their families, and their friends, as well as of the rich and famous. They housed the portraits in photo albums in their parlors. It was a way for Americans to identify themselves with well-known people whom they had never met, and to become a visible part of a national identity created by portraits.

With George Eastman's (1854–1932) Kodak camera, which allowed Americans to take their own pictures, snapshots finally replaced *cartes de visite* in popularity. First introduced in 1888, the camera sold for twenty-five dollars and came with a roll of paper negative film that allowed one hundred exposures. Kodak's slogan, "You press the button, we do the rest," famously summed up a system of creating pictures of oneself that has remained the most popular form of photography.

Blackface minstrelsy

Despite its widespread popularity, photography has received comparatively little attention from cultural historians and critics, primarily because photography does not fit neatly into the traditional methods and sources of historians or critics, and almost requires an interdisciplinary approach for its interpretation. Conversely, blackface minstrelsy, a nineteenth-century theatrical practice limited primarily to the urban North, has been the focus of numerous books and articles. This is because the subject has provided a window into some of the complex racial dilemmas of the nineteenth century. Blackface minstrelsy was a theatrical style performed principally by whites for white audiences in a way that exploited racist stereotypes of blacks. Musicians and dancers performed in black facial paint with exaggerated ruby lips and grins, tattered clothes, and oversized shoes. Their costumes and performances characterized blacks as buffoons whose only skill was that of the entertaining clown. Dan Emmett (1815–1904), the composer of "Dixie" (1859), and Thomas Dartmouth "Daddy" Rice (1808–1860), the first minstrel dancer to "jump Jim Crow" on stage, were among the first minstrel megastars. They and other early performers took pride in claiming to be students of black music, song, and dance, and therefore authentic performers, despite their overt use of parody, caricature, and stereotyping. While many early scholars viewed the performers and their white audiences as emblematic of the intense antiblack racism that was so pervasive in America, late-twentieth-century critics have recognized a dialectic at work. Performers and especially the artisanal urban audiences identified with and were fascinated by black culture and consciousness—particularly the liberation from white mores that came with being "black." At the same time, the performances reflected whites' disdain and hatred of the culture they mimicked and parodied. Blackface minstrelsy thus offered a way for urban artisans to liberate themselves from middle-class norms while reaffirming their sense of white superiority and distancing themselves from other races.

No matter what form popular culture took in the nineteenth century, a recurring trend was the assimilation of each form into respectable aesthetics and newfound status. The novel, which was despised by elites at the beginning of the century, was considered an elite and cultured aesthetic form by the century's end. The same was true of cheap newspapers and illustrated magazines. Photography, which critics called a science rather than an art in its first twenty years, began to be viewed as a respectable art form by the end of the century, albeit below painting and sculpture in the aesthetic hierarchy. And blackface minstrelsy in many respects became the precursor to the Broadway musical, although with the overt racist expressions stripped away. Popular cultural forms that declined or disappeared by 1900, such as phrenology and spiritualism, did so in large part because they were unable to adapt to changing tastes and audiences. The initial formula for success could not be repackaged or redesigned in a way that appealed to large numbers of people in later generations.

See also **Literacy and Reading Habits; Literature,** *subentry on* **Fiction; Lithography and Prints; Minstrel Shows; Music,** *subentry on* **Folk Songs, Parlor Music, and Popular Music; Photography.**

Bibliography

Bode, Carl. *The Anatomy of American Popular Culture, 1840–1861.* Berkeley: University of California Press, 1959. Reprint, Westport, Conn.: Greenwood, 1983.

Cohen, Daniel A. *Pillars of Salt, Monuments of Grace: New England Crime Literature and the Origins of American Popular Culture, 1674–1860.* New York: Oxford University Press, 1993.

Crouthamel, James L. *Bennett's* New York Herald *and the Rise of the Popular Press.* Syracuse, N.Y.: Syracuse University Press, 1989.

Davidson, Cathy N. *Revolution and the Word: The Rise of the Novel in America.* New York: Oxford University Press, 1986.

Emerson, Ken. *Doo-Dah!: Stephen Foster and the Rise of American Popular Culture.* New York: Da Capo, 1998.

Geist, Christopher D., and Jack Nachbar, eds. *The Popular Culture Reader.* Bowling Green, Ohio: Bowling Green University Popular Press, 1983.

Halttunen, Karen. *Confidence Men and Painted Women: A Study of Middle-Class Culture in America, 1830–1870.* New Haven, Conn.: Yale University Press, 1982.

Harris, Neil. *Humbug: The Art of P. T. Barnum.* Chicago: University of Chicago Press, 1981.

Levine, Lawrence W. *Highbrow/Lowbrow: The Emergence of Cultural Hierarchy in America.* Cambridge, Mass.: Harvard University Press, 1988.

Lott, Eric. *Love and Theft: Blackface Minstrelsy and the American Working Class.* New York: Oxford University Press, 1993.

Taft, Robert. *Photography and the American Scene: A Social History, 1839–1889.* 1938. Unabridged reprint, New York: Dover, 1964.

Trachtenberg, Alan. *Reading American Photographs: Images as History, Mathew Brady to Walker Evans.* New York: Hill and Wang, 1989.

JOHN STAUFFER

POPULATION   When the new U.S. Constitution went into effect in 1789, it contained a provision for a decennial census. The census's purpose was to allow apportionment of the House of Representatives every ten years, but it quickly became an important source of demographic, social, and economic information. Much of what we know about the nation in the nineteenth century comes from census documents. These published volumes grew from a spare set of aggregate statistics in 1790 to multivolume descriptions of the population, economy, and society by the end of the century. The census of 1890 alone had over thirty volumes. Manufacturing censuses were collected in 1810, 1820, and each census year from 1840 to 1900. Similarly, agricultural censuses were taken in 1840 and each census year thereafter until the twentieth century. Original manuscript returns exist for all of the censuses except 1890; samples for public use have been (or will be) made available for all the surviving censuses since 1850, when each individual was enumerated separately. Some states also took censuses, usually in years between the federal censuses. The census has been the major historical source for studying population growth, structure, redistribution, and fertility prior to the twentieth century.

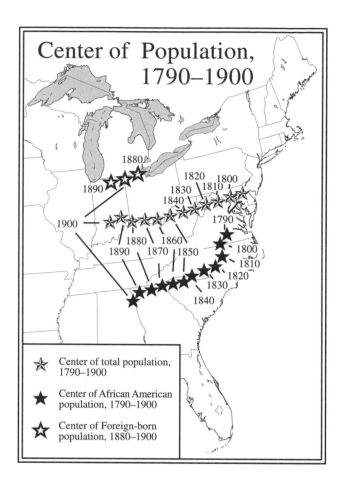

Center of Population, 1790–1900

☆ Center of total population, 1790–1900

★ Center of African American population, 1790–1900

☆ Center of Foreign-born population, 1880–1900

Population Trends from 1790 to 1900

The U.S. population was modest at the outset of the Republic in 1790, when the first decennial census was conducted. This census counted 3.2 million whites (81 percent of the total population) and 760,000 African Americans, most of whom were slaves (see Table 1). No other groups were counted. These individuals were crowded into a narrow strip of coastline that comprised the original thirteen states. The majority were in the largest states: Massachusetts, New York, Pennsylvania, Virginia, and North Carolina. Most of the white population was of ancestry from the British Isles or Germany; however, the proportion of foreign-born individuals is not known. The largest city was New York, with 33,131 persons. Philadelphia was second with 28,522, although if the Northern Liberties had been included it would have been first. The United States only had 24 urban places by the present Census Bureau definition (incorporated places of 2,500 or more persons), comprising 5.1 percent of the population. The population in 1790 was very young, with a median age of about 16 years. This was mostly because of very high birth rates, which widen the base of the age pyramid. There were slightly more men than women (4 percent more) because of the young population (male births

usually outnumber female births by 5 percent) and also because of gender selectivity in migration.

By 1900 the situation had changed dramatically. The total U.S. population now numbered 76 million, having grown at an average rate of 2.7 percent per year since 1790. This implied a doubling of the population every 26 years. About three-quarters of that growth was due to natural increase, and one-quarter was attributable to net immigration, mostly from northern and western Europe. The white population (66.9 million) had grown to 88 percent of the total, both because of high, though falling, birth rates and because of substantial migration from Europe. Blacks were now over 11 percent of the population. Among the other groups enumerated in 1900 were 237,000 Amerindians and 114,000 Asians, mostly Chinese and Japanese.

Over the course of the period 1820 to 1900 (for which we have official statistics), approximately 19.1 million immigrants entered the United States. Some additional migrants came in ways not recorded, such as over the land border with Canada, as first-class passengers, and as arrivals at minor ports; a small though growing proportion of immigrants returned home. The foreign-born were 13.6 percent of the population in 1900, up from 9.7 percent in 1850. The

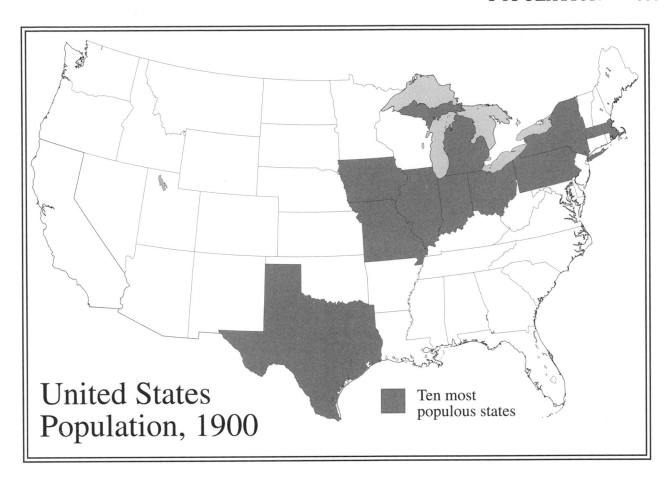

United States Population, 1900

Ten most populous states

Table 1: Population by Race, Residence, Nativity, Age, and Sex in the United States, 1790–1900 (population in thousands)

Census date	Total	Percent per annum growth	White	Black	Other	Urban	Percent	Foreign born	Percent	Median age	Sex ratio (b)
1790	3,929	—	3,172	757	(NA)	202	5.1	(NA)	—	(NA)	103.8
1800	5,308	3.01	4,306	1,002	(NA)	322	6.1	(NA)	—	16.0 (a)	104.0
1810	7,240	3.10	5,862	1,378	(NA)	525	7.3	(NA)	—	16.0 (a)	104.0
1820	9,639	2.86	7,867	1,772	(NA)	693	7.2	(NA)	—	16.7	103.3
1830	12,866	2.89	10,537	2,329	(NA)	1,127	8.8	(NA)	—	17.2	103.1
1840	17,070	2.83	14,196	2,874	(NA)	1,845	10.8	(NA)	—	17.8	103.7
1850	23,192	3.06	19,553	3,639	(NA)	3,544	15.3	2,245	9.7	18.9	104.3
1860	31,443	3.04	26,923	4,442	79	6,217	19.8	4,104	13.1	19.4	104.7
1870	39,819	2.36	33,589	4,880	89	9,902	24.9	5,567	14.0	20.0	102.2
1880	50,156	2.31	43,403	6,581	172	14,130	28.2	6,680	13.3	20.9	103.6
1890	62,948	2.27	55,101	7,489	358	22,106	35.1	9,250	14.7	22.0	105.0
1900	75,994	1.88	66,809	8,834	351	30,160	39.7	10,341	13.6	22.9	104.4

(a) White population.
(b) Males per 100 females.

Source: U.S. Bureau of the Census, *Historical Statistics of the United States* (Washington, D.C.: GPO, 1975). U.S. Bureau of the Census, *Statistical Abstract of the United States, 1992* (Washington, D.C.: GPO, 1992).

proportion of both first- and second-generation immigrants was, of course, higher—34.2 percent in 1900. Of those, 70 percent were from northern and western Europe (including Germany); that proportion had been 78 percent in 1890 and was declining. After 1880 the traditional sources of European migration began to shift from the British Isles and Germany to Scandinavia and southern and eastern Europe (Italy, Russia, the Balkans, and Polish-speaking areas in Germany, Austria-Hungary, and Russia).

By 1900 the United States was moving toward being a more urban society. Nearly 40 percent of its population lived in officially classified urban places, of which there were now 1,737. The largest city by far was New York, with a population of 3.4 million in its recently created five boroughs. Next was Chicago at 1.7 million, followed by Philadelphia (1.3 million), St. Louis (575,000), and Boston (560,000). The process of suburbanization also had begun, especially with the advent of cheap urban transport by railway and streetcar. The population had aged: the median age had risen to 23 years, largely because of the declining birth rate. There was still a slight surplus of males (104 males per 100 females) due to the gender selectivity of the migration process.

The rapid population growth of the nineteenth century was predominantly a consequence of a high rate of natural increase, due in turn to high birth rates and moderate death rates. Table 2 provides three measures of fertility for the period 1800 to 1900 (crude birth rate, child-woman ratio, and total fertility rate) and two of mortality (expectation of life at birth and infant mortality rate) for the white and black populations. In the late colonial period and the early nineteenth century, the high birth rates, large families, and early marriage age of American women had been the subject of comment by contemporary observers, including Benjamin Franklin (1706–1790), Thomas Robert Malthus (1766–1834), and Samuel Blodget (1757–1814). The crude birth rate of 55 estimated for the white population in 1800 was very high. Each woman would have had an average of seven live births in her lifetime (a total fertility rate of seven). The marriage age was probably nineteen to twenty years for white women, and only 5 to 6 percent of white women never married. This is in sharp contrast to the later marriage ages and much greater nonmarriage rates in western Europe in this period. We know less about the mostly rural black population, but birth rates were likely high, and marriage ages even earlier than among the white population. This was certainly true from the 1850s to end of the century, a period for which only estimates exist.

An Unusual Transition in Fertility and Mortality

The United States underwent a demographic transition from high to low levels of fertility and mortality during the nineteenth century. This transition process is essential to the modernization of a society. The usual statistical model has death rates declining before, or at least in conjunction with, birth rates. Often a period of rapid population growth marks such a transition era. The United States experienced a demographic transition quite different from this ideal type. First, the American fertility decline began quite early, and from very high levels of fertility. The transition commenced at least from 1800, if not from the late colonial era, in the white population. In European nations, the fertility transition began between 1870 and 1910, even in England. The one exception, France, probably began its fertility transition even earlier than the United States. Conventional explanations for the fertility transition involve structural and societal changes (such as increased urbanization and industrialization, declining infant and child mortality, rising literacy, new roles for women, compulsory schooling, and child labor laws). Several more recent views emphasize changes in attitudes toward family size. But the American transition occurred before the nation was very urban or industrial; it took place in both urban and rural areas, and it involved both declining marital fertility and rising ages of marriage. Indeed, it is apparent that the U.S. female age at marriage and the proportion of unmarried females both rose during the nineteenth century, reaching a peak in 1900.

The most widely accepted explanations for the antebellum fertility transition in the United States involve the increasing scarcity of good agricultural land and the resulting higher prices for it. As the frontier moved westward during the nineteenth century, more and more people were living in areas that had a history of white settlement; with more inhabitants, land became scarcer and more expensive. Endowing children with a farmstead thus grew more costly. One reaction was to reduce the number of children. A complementary explanation is that parents who sought support and care from their children during old age had to provide an endowment of land or other wealth as an inducement to stay nearby. Otherwise the children would be attracted to opportunities in the wage-labor markets of nearby cities or to the cheap land of the frontier. For urban populations after the Civil War the more conventional explanations of structural and societal change are relevant. How did Americans in the nineteenth century limit their families? We have little direct evidence, but information from medical literature, marriage manuals,

Table 2:   Fertility and Mortality in the United States, 1800–1900

Approx date	Birth rate (a)		Child-woman ratio (b)		Total fertility rate (c)		Expectation of life (d)		Infant mortality rate (e)	
	White	Black	White	Black	White	Black	White	Black	White	Black
1800	55.0		1,342		7.04					
1810	54.3		1,358		6.92					
1820	52.8		1,295	1,191	6.73					
1830	51.4		1,145	1,220	6.55					
1840	48.3		1,085	1,154	6.14					
1850	43.3		892	1,087	5.42		39.5	23.0	216.8	340.0
		58.6 (f)				7.90 (f)				
1860	41.4		905	1,072	5.21		43.6		181.3	
		55.0 (g)				7.58 (g)				
1870	38.3		814	997	4.55		45.2		175.5	
		55.4 (h)				7.69 (h)				
1880	35.2		780	1,090	4.24		40.5		214.8	
		51.9 (i)				7.26 (i)				
1890	31.5	48.1	685	930	3.87	6.56	46.8	50.7		
1900	30.1	44.4	666	845	3.56	5.61	51.8 (j)	41.8 (j)	110.8 (j)	170.3 (j)

(a) Births per 1,000 population per annum.

(b) Children aged 0 to 4 per 1,000 women aged 15 to 44. Taken from U.S. Bureau of the Census, *Historical Statistics of the United States* (Washington, D.C.: GPO, 1975), Series B67–98 for 1800–1970. For the black population 1820–1840, W. S. Thompson and P. K. Whelpton, *Population Trends in the United States* (New York: McGraw-Hill, 1933), Table 74, adjusted upward 47 percent for relative under-enumeration of black children aged 0 to 4 for the censuses of 1820–1840.

(c) Total number of births per women if she experienced the current period age-specific fertility rates throughout her life.

(d) Expectation of life at birth for both sexes combined.

(e) Infant deaths per 1,000 live births per annum.

(f) Average for 1850–1859.

(g) Average for 1860–1869.

(h) Average for 1870–1879.

(i) Average for 1880–1884.

(j) Approximately 1895.

Source: U.S. Bureau of the Census, *Historical Statistics of the United States* (Washington, D.C.: GPO, 1975). U.S. Bureau of the Census, *Statistical Abstract of the United States*, 1986 (Washington, D.C.: GPO, 1985). *Statistical Abstract of the United States*, 1997 (Washington, D.C.: GPO, 1997). Ansley J. Coale and Melvin Zelnik, *New Estimates of Fertility and Population in the United States* (Princeton, N.J.: Princeton University Press, 1963). Ansley J. Coale and Norfleet W. Rives, "A Statistical Reconstruction of the Black Population of the United States, 1880–1970: Estimates of True Numbers by Age and Sex, Birth Rates, and Total Fertility," *Population Index*, 39, no. 1 (1973): 3–36. Michael R. Haines, "Estimated Life Tables for the United States, 1850–1900," *Historical Methods*, 31, no. 4 (fall 1998): 149–169. Samuel H. Preston and Michael R. Haines, *Fatal Years: Child Mortality in Late-Nineteenth-Century America* (Princeton, N.J.: Princeton University Press, 1991), Table 2.5. Richard H. Steckel, "A Dreadful Childhood: The Excess Mortality of American Slaves," *Social Science History* (winter 1986): 427–465.

personal accounts, and the amazing survey by Clelia D. Mosher (1863–1940) suggest they resorted to a variety of traditional birth-control measures, as well as to abortion. It is somewhat easier to control fertility during a period of high birth rates. It became more difficult as the small-family norm became more pervasive at the end of the century. The Mosher survey was especially illuminating. Mosher was a physician who surveyed forty-five married middle-class women from Madison, Wisconsin, and Palo Alto, California between 1892 and 1920. Well in advance of her time, she administered a lengthy questionnaire about these women's sexual lives, including birth his-

tories and use of contraception. These survey forms constitute the earliest systematic attempt to understand this area of American life.

Another unusual feature of the American demographic transition was the delayed decline in mortality. Table 2 lacks information on the expectation of life at birth and the infant mortality rate for the nation prior to 1850 because there is not a good statistical basis for such estimates. A major reason is that, although the federal government took responsibility for census enumeration, no such charge was made for the collection of vital statistics (births, deaths, marriages). Since determining vital statistics was left to the states, it was done unevenly and piecemeal. A number of cities (New York, Boston, Baltimore, Philadelphia, New Orleans) began collecting adequate mortality statistics early in the nineteenth century, but birth statistics were usually less accurate until later in the century. Massachusetts was the first to institute vital registration statewide; this process was begun in 1842 and largely complete by 1855. But a death registration area (consisting of the six New England states, New York, New Jersey, Michigan, Indiana, and the District of Columbia) was not formed until 1900; a birth registration area (consisting of the six New England states, New York, Minnesota, Michigan, Pennsylvania, and the District of Columbia) was not put together until 1915. Neither area covered the entire nation until 1933. Hence much of what is known about vital processes has been learned from demographic estimates using the census and other sources.

Fragmentary sources for the antebellum era indicate that U.S. death rates were moderate. There was a crude death rate of 25 in normal years, with a higher rate in cities than in rural areas and a higher rate in the South than in the Northeast, the Middle Atlantic area, and the Midwest. Mortality among blacks was much higher than among whites (see Table 2). The Amerindian population actually declined in size over the century because of excessive mortality and, in some cases, low birth rates; both were the result of forced relocation onto reservations. The Amerindian population within the present boundaries of the United States fell from 600,000 in 1800 to 240,000 in 1900.

The modern mortality transition in the United States did not begin until the 1870s. This was several decades after the onset of the fertility transition, in sharp contrast to the conventional model of demographic transition. The fertility decline took place earlier because mortality was already moderate early in the century, and thus child survivorship was relatively favorable. There is also substantial evidence that mortality increased from the 1820s to the 1850s. This was a consequence of urbanization, increased population density, and the transportation revolution of the antebellum period (that is, advances in the construction of canals, railroads, and turnpikes, and in steamboat river navigation and lake and coastal shipping). The environment for new diseases was being nationalized and, indeed, internationalized. When Asiatic cholera first arrived in western Europe in 1832, it was thought the disease would not spread to the Americas; and when the disease did, in fact, spread rapidly to American ports, it was believed that it would not spread to rural areas. These expectations were false. The global cholera epidemics of 1832, 1849, and 1866 spread rapidly throughout the United States. The isolation of rural life was much less of a protection than in the past, although mortality continued to be lower in the countryside than in cities until the twentieth century.

The mortality transition affected both blacks and whites. Mortality fell more rapidly in cities than in rural areas, although cities continued to be less healthy places until after World War I. The major source of this transition was the decline in deaths from infectious and parasitic diseases. Much of the transition originally involved waterborne diseases, such as cholera, typhoid fever, and dysentery; but airborne diseases, such as respiratory tuberculosis, bronchitis, pneumonia, measles, and scarlet fever also declined. Better living standards (food, shelter, heating, clothing) played a role in increasing the population's resistance and survivability, but early public health efforts also played a part, especially in cities. The germ theory of disease, put forward by pioneers such as Louis Pasteur (1822–1895) and Robert Koch (1843–1910) in the 1860s and 1870s, was a major impetus to public health improvements. But even before that, many cities were endeavoring to secure clean water supplies, provide adequate sewerage and refuse disposal, and ensure quarantines. These measures were augmented by efforts to gain sanitary milk and food supplies and to provide health education to change behavior patterns. A whole complex of structures and policies was in full swing by the early 1900s and was achieving visible results. For example, between 1880 and 1900, the white expectation of life at birth rose from 40 years to 52 years, while the infant mortality rate fell from 215 to 111 infant deaths per 1,000 live births.

Mobility Patterns

Over the course of the nineteenth century, the American population was very geographically mobile. From the outset of the century, there was a remarkable movement from east to west. Similarly, rural to urban migration took place throughout the century, despite the rapid expansion of new farmsteads in the West. City growth rates often far exceeded any reasonable natural increase, and the net growth was not entirely, or in many cases even largely, from foreign immigrants. From 1790 to 1900, urban population growth averaged 4.6 percent per year while that for rural areas was only 2.3 percent. Toward the end of the century, suburbs began to attract both rural and urban migrants. The black population was an exception to these migration patterns. In 1790, 91 percent of slaves and free blacks lived south of the Mason-Dixon Line, and very few lived in urban areas. By

1900, 90 percent of blacks still lived in the South and only 20 percent lived in urban places. Many slaves had been moved to newer lands in the West, but the great migration by African Americans to northern cities was still in the future. The Amerindian population was concentrated in the West and was almost entirely rural, while the Asian population was 43 percent urban and centered in the Far West.

Migration changed the character of the American population, making it more urban and altering the ethnic mix, although this mostly occurred among the white population before 1900. The rapid development of the American economy in the nineteenth century was made possible in no small part by the additional labor supplied by immigrants from Britain, Ireland, Germany, and Scandinavia, and later from Italy, Russia, Austria-Hungary, the Balkans, and Polish-speaking areas in eastern and central Europe. Native-born migration to the farming frontier and to the cities was also essential.

This mobility was not confined to geographical changes. There was substantial social, occupational, and economic mobility for the white population. Many advanced up the agricultural ladder from landless laborers to landowner farmers, and from urban workers to business proprietors. Nonetheless, income and wealth distribution worsened in the mid-nineteenth century. Not everyone shared in the fruits of growth and development. Many new immigrants did not do well. The Amerindian population continued to suffer from warfare, disease, and forced removals. And close to 90 percent of the black population was enslaved up to the 1860s. Even after emancipation, most blacks remained poor. In the census of 1870, the value of real and personal property of adult white males (aged 20 and over) averaged $2,622; that for blacks was only $117. Even for those who had some wealth, there was a great difference: $4,503 for whites and $586 for blacks. About 60 percent of adult white males reported some wealth, while only 20 percent of blacks made such reports.

One indicator of human well-being, terminal adult stature, deteriorated for those born from 1830 to the 1870s. Americans got shorter in the nineteenth century. This was accompanied by, and likely partly caused by, an increase in mortality from the 1820s to the 1850s. Thus, although real income and wealth per capita rose fairly consistently from the 1830s onward (with the exception of the Civil War period), there were negative side effects.

The nineteenth century was a period of extraordinary demographic and economic growth and transformation in the United States. The country grew from a relatively small, new nation strung along the Atlantic coast of North America to a world economic power with a population larger than any European nation except Russia. It also experienced a very early fertility transition throughout the century, but had a delayed mortality transition, from the 1870s onward. All of this was accompanied by huge in-migration (at least 19 million in the nineteenth century alone) and a persistent movement of the population westward and into burgeoning urban places. For many it was a land of opportunity, but for some groups, particularly blacks, Amerindians, and Asians, social and economic mobility would not come until the twentieth century.

See also **Birth and Childbearing; Cities and Urbanization; Contraception and Abortion; Death and Dying; Expansion; Health and Disease; Immigration and Immigrants,** *subentry on* **An Overview.**

Bibliography

Bodnar, John. *The Transplanted: A History of Immigrants in Urban America.* Bloomington: Indiana University Press, 1985.

Easterlin, Richard A. "The American Population." In *American Economic Growth: An Economist's History of the United States,* edited by Lance E. Davis, et al. New York: Harper and Row, 1972.

Ferrie, Joseph P. *Yankeys Now: Immigrants in the Antebellum United States, 1840–1860.* New York: Oxford University Press, 1999.

Haines, Michael R. "Long-Term Marriage Patterns in the United States from Colonial Times to the Present." *History of the Family* 1 (1996): 15–39.

———. "The Population of the United States, 1790–1920." In *The Cambridge Economic History of the United States,* edited by Stanley L. Engerman and Robert E. Gallman. Vol. 2, *The Long Nineteenth Century.* New York: Cambridge University Press, 1996–.

Haines, Michael R., and Richard H. Steckel. *A Population History of North America.* New York: Cambridge University Press, 2000.

Preston, Samuel H., and Michael R. Haines. *Fatal Years: Child Mortality in Late-Nineteenth-Century America.* Princeton, N.J.: Princeton University Press, 1991.

Schapiro, Morton Owen. *Filling Up America: An Economic-Demographic Model of Population Growth and Distribution in the Nineteenth-Century United States.* Greenwich, Conn.: JAI, 1986.

Steckel, Richard. "Stature and Living Standards in the United States." In *American Economic Growth and Standards of Living before the Civil War.* Edited by Robert E. Gallman and John Joseph Wallis. Chicago: University of Chicago Press, 1992.

Vinovskis, Maris A., ed. *Studies in American Historical Demography.* New York: Academic Press, 1979.

Wells, Robert V. *Revolutions in Americans' Lives: A Demographic Perspective on the History of Americans, Their Families, and Their Society.* Westport, Conn.: Greenwood, 1982.

———. *Uncle Sam's Family: Issues in and Perspectives on American Demographic History.* Albany: State University of New York Press, 1985.

MICHAEL R. HAINES

POPULISM   One of America's most significant third-party movements, the People's Party of America, was organized nationally in Cincinnati, Ohio, in May 1891. A few months later party members began to refer to themselves as Populists or members of the Populist Party. They were proponents of a provocative democratic political-economic agenda that came to be called Populism, a term first used by the movement's detractors. After the 1950s the term "populism" referred in a generic and frequently pejorative manner to a wide variety of mass political movements—particularly those reflecting the right wing of the political spectrum, such as those associated with George Wallace, Barry Goldwater, Ronald Reagan, and Newt Gingrich, among others—which in fact have a stronger relationship and connection to the *anti*-Populism of the 1890s.

Until nearly the midpoint of the twentieth century, 1890s Populism was seen by most interpreters as a benign but somewhat idiosyncratic by-product of a quarter-century of western and southern agrarian unrest precipitated by the passing of the frontier in the late nineteenth century, a theory first expounded by Frederick Jackson Turner. Later studies, less influenced by the frontier explanation, emphasized that the movement accommodated a deeper, more enduring, and ultimately more original brand of thought than previously believed. Whereas the movement's dominant agrarian orientation goes unquestioned, the party did garner support from the laboring and small-business elements of towns. The leaders also were by and large well-educated, middle-class reformers whose backgrounds and ideological roots were rural and egalitarian.

Gilded-Age Origins

American society experienced unparalleled dislocation and discombobulation after the midpoint of the nineteenth century. The post–Civil War economic revolution was especially unsettling. Populism, though meeting with the resistance of conservative, mainstream America, offered a forward-looking, instructive response to this new world in the making.

The Populist critique of industrial society owed much to a deeply embedded tradition of democratic radicalism as well as two decades of thought and agitation sparked by the revolutionary transformation of the United States into the world's foremost industrial power by the early 1890s. In those frenetic years a multitude of forces were at work, pulling American society first one way and then the other. New values challenged those of the older agrarian society; agriculture and industry were mechanized; transportation accelerated at a fantastic pace; vast segments of the western domain were populated precipitately and the urbanization process intensified.

In the interest of a common humanity, growing numbers of Americans questioned the nation's course. What could or should be done to ensure and strengthen the promise of American life? To a great extent, farmers initiated the search for solutions with the aim of restoring agriculture's position of primacy in the nation's economy. By the mid-1870s U.S. farmers had organized legislation, usually associated with the National Grange, aimed at regulating railroads and grain elevator operators. The farmers' movement also produced various independent political organizations, such as the Greenback-Labor Party and the Union-Labor Party, that championed important political and economic reforms, some of which were taken up by the mainstream parties.

From the early 1870s to the late 1880s a number of farmer organizations were formed. In the Old Northwest and the Midwest, early strongholds of the Patrons of Husbandry, the National Farmers' Alliance, the Farmers' Mutual Benefit Association, and the Farmers' League competed for support. In the South the National Farmers' Alliance and Industrial

"The Farmer and the Railroad Monster: Which Will Win?" The railroad industry as emanating from national policy is indicated by railroad cars wound about the Capitol's dome. Wood engraving by Thomas Nast. Published 14 August 1873. LIBRARY OF CONGRESS

The National Grange Movement. Values of an agrarian life were promoted by farmers in the 1870s in the face of technological progress. Printed by Strobridge & Co., 1873. LIBRARY OF CONGRESS

Union, created through a merger of several state and regional organizations, the Colored Farmers' Alliance, and the Agricultural Wheel emerged. Among these associations, the National Farmers' Alliance (Northern Alliance) and the National Farmers' Alliance and Industrial Union (Southern Alliance, which absorbed the Wheel) gained membership rapidly as the 1880s came to a close. By 1890 the Southern Alliance, which incidentally included active contingents from Kansas and South Dakota, had one to three million white members and more than one million more in an African American affiliate. The Northern Alliance put its membership at more than one million.

The People's or Populist Party combined these organizational drives among western and southern farmers with the reform thought and energies that were not confined to any single region or economic endeavor. In the 1880s new settlements stretched from Texas northward through Oklahoma Territory, Kansas, Nebraska, and the Dakotas. The economic collapse in 1887 set in motion a train of events that culminated in the formation of the People's Party in 1891.

Organize or Perish

The farm organizations, contrary to proclaimed intentions, turned increasingly to the political arena to achieve their goals for the agricultural community and to democratize American politics in the process. In December 1889 the two regional Alliances met in St. Louis, Missouri, to discuss a merger. The consolidation effort failed except in Kansas, North Dakota, and South Dakota, states that had already converted to the Southern Alliance, but at the convention both Alliances agreed on a set of reform demands that would provide the core for the later Populist program.

At the outset the Alliances aimed to capture political power at the state level. In the South this meant taking control of the Democratic Party, which dominated every southern state, and by 1890 this approach had met with some success. In the North and West the Alliances pursued a similar strategy with the Republican Party as the object. Several western states, however, led by Kansas, resolved to wage a third-party fight. Early in 1890 Kansans organized a Citizens' Alliance, which coordinated activities with the Farmers' Alliance, Single-Tax Clubs, Bellamy Nationalist Clubs, the Knights of Labor, and other groups. In June 1890 this coalition created the Kansas People's Party. South Dakotans moved even more quickly that same month to organize an Independent Party.

The results of the 1890 elections were encouraging. The movement did not win outright control of any state government, but in four—Kansas, Nebraska, South Dakota, and Minnesota—it gained serious support. In the South, Alliance candidates, running as Democrats, won the governorships in North Carolina, South Carolina, and Georgia, and Alliance members dominated eight southern legislatures. The new political alignment elected eleven congressmen—two senators and nine representatives—in its political debut. Counting third-party men and friends of the Alliance together, as many as forty-four congressmen were allied with the movement. Among Southern Alliance congressmen, however, only one, Thomas E. Watson of Georgia, proclaimed his independence from the Democratic Party.

Actually, the conversion of the southern Democratic Party to the Alliance cause was far from complete. In the southern states resistance to third-party action remained strong and troubled the progress of the Alliance and the reform cause. Intellectual baggage remaining from the Civil War and Reconstruction was intensely complicated by notions of white supremacy, making it difficult for most southern white Democrats to join with the North and West to create a formidable new party. At the same time, members of the Colored Farmers' Alliance were eager to lend their support to an independent movement.

The Omaha Platform

The movement to create a national third party gained considerable momentum in 1891, especially in the Midwest, leading to the creation of the People's Party, which held its first nominating convention in Omaha, Nebraska, in July 1892. This convention produced the Omaha platform, which soon became the bible of 1890s Populism. Best known for the stinging indictment of the prevailing political and economic system in its preamble, written by one of the era's more versatile and colorful reformers, Ignatius Donnelly of Minnesota, the platform contained a recipe to rescue an older, predominantly agrarian America from the onslaught of a largely uncontrolled urban-industrial juggernaut. It consisted of three planks that challenged the nation's solidly entrenched capitalist, so-called free-market system at its core. The first addressed financial and monetary arrangements under the heading "Money." The second pertained to the transportation and communications systems. The third addressed land as the ultimate source of all "wealth" and the "heritage" of all "the people." The Populists reasoned that these three areas existed or were meant to exist to benefit all the people, not just the favored few. In the Populist view, corporate and individual interests had usurped these vital areas, which needed to be reclaimed and conducted by agencies owned and administered by the public.

This agenda, the sum of Populism's first national platform, was followed by ten resolutions, measures the delegates supported but emphasized were "not . . . part of the platform of the People's party." A surprising majority of historians have misunderstood or ignored the platform and have wrongly highlighted one or more of these nonplatform, generally noneconomic, protoprogressive reforms—such as restriction of immigration, initiative, referendum, direct election of U.S. senators, single terms for the president and vice president, and the secret ballot—to illustrate the meaning of Populism.

With this remarkable platform, destined to be of far greater importance than the candidates nominated in support of its program, the People's Party became the first political party of any consequence to argue forthrightly that the federal government had responsibility for the nation's general welfare. The Populists' national agenda found its only national stage in Congress, where over and over again Populist congressmen urged the major parties to give up promoting special interests and utilize the government's immense powers on behalf of the general welfare and democratic reform. The call was indeed historically significant, coming as it did at the high point of an age that condoned only a minimal role for government, with the important exception of government intervention to aid business and propertied interests.

Populist Legacy

In 1896 the Democratic Party coopted a minor portion of the Populist Party's economic program, a call for the restoration of a bimetallic monetary standard, on behalf of its candidate, William Jennings Bryan. The Populists felt themselves compelled to also nominate and support Bryan's fight against the gold standard as the only hope of defeating William McKinley and the foes of financial reform. McKinley and the Republicans won anyway, and in the aftermath the Populist Party was gradually and discordantly dismantled. Populists were left to console themselves with the realization that they had contributed to the conversion of one of the major parties to the cause of reform.

During its brief existence, the Populist Party was strongest in Kansas, Nebraska, Colorado, Texas, and North Carolina, although its influence was felt in a number of southern and western states. Out of its ranks emerged a number of talented and colorful men and women, among them Jeremiah Simpson, William A. Peffer, Mary E. Lease, and Annie L. Diggs from Kansas; William V. Allen and William Neville from Nebraska; Thomas E. Watson from Georgia; Marion Butler from North Carolina; and James Harvey Davis from Texas.

From 1891 to 1903 fifty individual Populists representing sixteen states and one territory served in the U.S. Congress. Although only a tiny fraction of the total representation at any point, they waged a significant educational campaign on the floor of Congress on behalf of the Populist program, elevating the debate on issues ranging from economic depression to imperialism. Populist ideas continued to be a vital source of insight throughout the next century and serve as a powerful critique of American society.

See also **Currency Policy; Democratic Party; Economic Regulation; Industrialization and the Market; Monetary Policy; Radicalism; Reform, Political; Republican Party; Third Parties.**

Bibliography
Argersinger, Peter H. *The Limits of Agrarian Radicalism: Western Populism and American Politics.* Lawrence: University Press of Kansas, 1995.
Clanton, Gene. *Congressional Populism and the Crisis of the 1890s.* Lawrence: University Press of Kansas, 1998.
———. *Populism: The Humane Preference in America, 1890–1900.* Boston, Mass.: Twayne, 1991.
Goodwyn, Lawrence. *Democratic Promise: The Populist Moment in America.* New York: Oxford University Press, 1976.
Hicks, John D. *The Populist Revolt: A History of the Farmers' Alliance and the People's Party.* Minneapolis: University of Minnesota Press, 1931.
McMath, Robert C., Jr. *American Populism: A Social History, 1877–1898.* New York: Hill and Wang, 1993.
Pollack, Norman. *The Just Polity: Populism, Law, and Human Welfare.* Urbana: University of Illinois Press, 1987.

GENE CLANTON

PORNOGRAPHY   Very little is known about the nature or distribution of pornography in the nineteenth-century United States, and it is unlikely that much more will ever come to light. The term "pornography" did not come into general use until the 1920s; before then, when sexually arousing words and pictures were mentioned at all (they rarely were), people labeled them "obscene," "indecent," "filthy," and other vague, subjective terms. Much of what nineteenth-century Americans found indecent would strike present-day readers as hardly arousing at all; words and pictures were likely to be termed obscene on the basis of religious unorthodoxy rather than sexual offensiveness, although the two qualities often overlapped. Court trials, the chief source of evidence about modern attitudes toward the obscene, were rare in the first three-quarters of the nineteenth century. The first federal antiobscenity statute, enacted by Congress in 1842, as part of a customs act intended to police all imports from Europe, left the definition of "obscenity" to the discretion of local inspectors. There appears to have been no significant domestic manufacture of sexually explicit material before the 1840s. In 1821 a certain Peter Holmes was prosecuted in Massachusetts for attempting to publish what would have been the first American edition of John Cleland's 1748 erotic novel *Fanny Hill; or, Memoirs of a Woman of Pleasure*, but except for that and a couple of other early cases, the public record is silent.

Erotic material, whether imported or domestic, probably circulated in an informal, clandestine way, but since it was very rarely mentioned in writing, next to nothing is known about it. In 1859, in the raw frontier village of Eugene City (now Eugene), Oregon, nineteen-year-old Henry Cummins made this rather surprising entry in his diary: "Read 80 pages in the *Life of Fanny Hill*, a book which has a good aim in view that of giving us peep behind the curtain of the life of woman of pleasure. Yet it enters rather much into detail and the scenes represented are not much fitted to cultivate virtuous thoughts in the minds of its readers." Cummins did not record how he had obtained the book, though an itinerant peddler seems the most likely source. Beyond a few such tantalizing glimpses, the subject is shrouded in probably permanent obscurity.

The situation changed dramatically in 1873, when President Ulysses S. Grant signed into law "An Act for the Suppression of Trade in, and Circulation of, obscene Literature and Articles of immoral Use." This act, which remains the basis of American antipornography legislation, had already been dubbed the Comstock Law, after Anthony Comstock (1844–1915), its chief lobbyist. By an informal arrangement, Comstock was made a "special agent" of the Post Office Department, charged with seeking out "obscene" and "immoral" items wherever they might enter the mails. Until his death, he pursued the task with incredible vigor, often overstepping the bounds of his job to invade pool parlors and saloons. In 1913 Comstock told a newspaper reporter that, since 1873, he had disposed of 160 tons of "obscene literature" and brought about the conviction of "persons enough to fill a passenger train of sixty-one coaches, sixty coaches containing sixty passengers each and the sixty-first almost full." It is one of the curiosities of American history that, for forty-two years, the enforcement of public morality was entrusted to one man, whose zeal impressed some as fanatical and others as lunacy.

Comstock's idea of the obscene (he never used the word "pornography") was broad, covering everything from risqué playing cards to classical statuary; it included any mention of sexual organs or functions, especially in regard to birth control. If Comstock's views had represented majority opinion, nineteenth-century America might have been characterized as prudish. But Comstock encountered resistance from the very start of his career, and near the end of it he became a public laughingstock, frequently caricatured in magazines and newspapers. Then as now, American attitudes toward sexual representations were multiple, complex, and often self-contradictory. The irony is that, although Comstock desired to cleanse America, he lent purveyors of filth far more publicity than they could have afforded to buy, thereby abetting the pollution he sought to purge.

See also **Sexual Morality**.

Bibliography

Broun, Heywood, and Margaret Leech. *Anthony Comstock: Roundsman of the Lord*. New York: Albert and Charles Boni, 1927.

Kendrick, Walter. *The Secret Museum: Pornography in Modern Culture*. Berkeley: University of California Press, 1996.

Marcus, Steven. *The Other Victorians: A Study of Sexuality and Pornography in Mid-Nineteenth-Century England*. 1966 2d ed., New York: New American Library, 1974.

WALTER KENDRICK

POST OFFICE　"To establish Post Offices and post Roads" was one of the specific powers given to Congress by the Constitution in 1787. After much debate on how that power should be used, in 1792 Congress passed an act founding the Post Office Department. The act provided the regulations by which the department was to be governed, set postage rates on letters and newspapers, gave members of Congress the frank (the privilege to send their mail free), and created the Office of Postmaster General, with vast powers to contract for mail carriers, establish post offices, and appoint postmasters and other employees. The Post Office Department was organized into various divisions. At its head was the postmaster general, who ruled over an auditor; an assistant attorney general; and four assistant postmasters general, to whom various division chiefs reported and carried on the work of managing the railroad mail, dispensing stamps, supervising money orders, employing mail carriers, mail clerks, and postal inspectors, and appointing postmasters.

Congress, however, retained the right to establish the nation's post roads and by so doing inevitably shaped the growth of the Post Office. The power Congress retained gave the people a voice in the development of their mail service and curtailed the postmaster general's authority to slow its expansion. As they moved into the nation's empty spaces, Americans petitioned Congress for mail service, and their senators and representatives responded by establishing post roads over which their mail was brought to them. In 1792 the nation had only 194 post offices and 6,000 miles of post roads. At the end of the nineteenth century, there were 76,688 post offices and about 500,000 miles of post roads. By then the Post Office was the government's largest business, its greatest bureaucracy, and its principal bond with its citizens. The department's auditor reported in 1900 that the number of its officers and employees exceeded "all other departments of Government combined" (Report of the Postmaster General for 1900, p. 846).

Politics and the Post Office

The close connection between the people and their representatives on postal matters made the Post Office the most political of all government entities. Providing their constituents with mail service was the one way members of Congress could serve them directly and themselves politically in the nineteenth century. Moreover, the Post Office offered politicians an opportunity to share in the appointment of postmasters who often became the nucleus of local political machines.

Politics was firmly fastened on the Post Office in 1829 when President Andrew Jackson elevated the postmaster general to cabinet rank. That official, John McLean, dismissed postmasters who had favored John Quincy Adams in the election of 1828 and replaced them with men loyal to the president and his party. "To the victors belong the spoils," became the slogan for this practice, and from Jackson's presidency onward throughout the century, each change of administration was followed by the removal of postmasters of the defeated party and the appointment of those whose party had won.

Postal Policy

Politics—and Congress's conviction that the postal service must inform the people of political affairs if democracy was to prevail—were responsible for a unique postal policy grounded on three principles: that the Post Office was not to produce a revenue for the Treasury Department; that its revenues were to be used to pay for itself; and that the excess revenues were to be used to expand the mail service so that knowledge might be widely diffused among the people.

This policy endured until mid-century, when private carriers, carrying letters outside the mails over the rapidly expanding railroads for less than the postage rate, undermined the Post Office's monopoly of letter transportation, deprived the Post Office of revenues, and threatened to create a postal deficit. Northerners demanded a reduction in postal rates to solve the problem, but southern members of Congress objected to this. They feared that any reduction of postage rates would further diminish postal revenues and force the abandonment of those post roads and post offices in their area that did not pay for themselves. Some southerners also feared that reduced postage on newspapers would spread antislavery sentiments.

The prolonged debate between northern and southern members of Congress over an issue that was to trouble the postal service for years was temporarily solved by compromise in 1851. That year Congress reduced the postage rate on letters to three cents for a half-ounce letter mailed up to three thousand miles. In return, southern legislators were promised that no post road or post office would be abandoned because of any reduction in revenues that might follow this lowering of postage. Furthermore, the postmaster general was required to continue the expansion of postal service in sparsely populated areas as if this act had not been passed.

This compromise ended the self-sustaining policy, leaving it to the government to make up any postal deficit that might result from reduced postage rates. Thereafter, the postal service rarely paid its way, although postmasters general usually tried to manage the Post Office according to the old policy.

Postal Innovations

After the modification of the postal policy, Congress made many changes in the postal service. To help publishers, it reduced the postage on newspapers in 1852, admitted books to the mails the same year, and in 1855 authorized a registered letter service. In that decade, too, envelopes replaced the folded letters sealed with a wafer, and stamps became commonplace.

The mandatory use of stamps had long been delayed because of concerns that they would not be used. In the beginning, postmasters "rated up" the letters to be mailed, fixing the postage on them with pen and ink according to the distance to be traveled and the number of sheets in the letter. The postage was paid by the addressee. The inefficiency of this practice became apparent when the Post Office was inundated with letters that followed the postage reduction. Consequently, Congress made the prepayment of postage with stamps mandatory in 1855.

More extensive postal innovations were made during the Civil War, when Congress was no longer restrained by either the pay-as-you-go postal policy or by the presence of southern congressmen wary of postal changes. Door-to-door free delivery of mail was created for the burgeoning cities of fifty thousand or more people in 1863, and the next year Congress provided a money order system.

Following the war Congress quickly reestablished the mail service in the South to bind the nation together again and made more additions to the system. In 1872 it admitted merchandise into the mails and thus began a small parcel service. Because of special interests, primarily express car companies, packages were limited to four pounds and postage was set at a penny an ounce. Nevertheless, the small package service allowed rural people to receive city goods through the mails, which affected the economy of small towns and farms of rural America in the 1880s and 1890s.

Throughout the 1870s and 1880s people living in the countryside eyed with envy the cities' free, door-to-door delivery system. Although some letters and packages could be delivered to rural addresses for a price by special delivery (a service initiated in 1885), small-town and rural citizens and their representatives wanted the same free delivery service the cities had. Congress found it difficult to refuse these demands, and gradually brought free delivery to towns of ten thousand people by 1887.

In the meantime, the people in villages and farmers still received their mail at small fourth-class post offices to which mail carriers under government contract carried the mail on horseback or buggy from railroad centers over star mail routes once, twice, or three times a week. It was a sluggish system, and in the 1890s the farmers' agitation forced Congress to provide for an experiment in rural free delivery. This immensely popular experiment began in 1896, and was finally made permanent in 1902. Rural free delivery was the last of the postal services to be established in the nineteenth century.

Railway Mail

While southern members of Congress were still absent from the U.S. Congress, a railroad mail service was developed in 1864 that would revolutionize the nation's communication system. In the early years of the postal service, the mails were carried in portmanteaus from post office to post office along the main post road. At each post office the postmaster would take the mail for his office from the bag, lock it, and send it on its way. As the mails multiplied, this process became unmanageable, and the Post Office Department built distribution centers, where mail was gathered, sorted, and sent to area post offices.

In 1838 Congress declared all railroads to be post roads, and the department resorted to the railroads instead of stagecoaches to carry the mail wherever possible. The mails were handled by mail agents who rode the trains on designated routes, picked up the mail along the way, sorted it, and, if any was addressed to a post office along their route, dropped it there. The "through mail" addressed to destinations beyond their route was sent on to distributing offices, where by the 1860s the mail was so voluminous it clogged the distributing post offices, caused delays, and forced the department to develop railway post offices.

A railway post office was a railroad car equipped like a post office, with sorting boxes, mailbag holders, and a long mechanical arm that reached from the car to snatch mailbags from cranes along the track as the train sped by. Aboard were railway mail clerks, highly trained specialists who retrieved the mail from the cranes and connecting trains and sorted it into mailbags. Those bags addressed to places along the way they deposited at the appropriate places; the rest they transferred to connecting trains that took them to their destinations in one of eleven postal districts scattered around the country in 1889.

The railway mail was a model of efficiency and endured for more than one hundred years. It eliminated the distribution post offices, fulfilled the department's goal of sending the mail as fast as a man could travel, and made possible the distribution of more than a billion pounds of mail at the end of the century.

Diffusion of Knowledge

Beginning in 1792 and continuing through the nineteenth century, members of Congress defended the rapid expansion of the postal service demanded by their constituents as necessary for diffusing knowledge among the people to assure the success of self-government. "However firmly liberty may be established in any country," Connecticut's Representative Elbridge Gerry remarked in the postal debate in 1791, "it cannot long subsist if the channels of information be stopped." To prevent that from happening, Congress admitted newspapers into the mail in 1792 and favored them with a postage rate that was exceedingly generous compared to that on letter postage. It set the latter at twenty-five cents for a one-

The Railway Postal Service. Mail was sorted in special cars designed for this task. It could then be routed directly for delivery to stops along the train's route or to other trains. From engravings in *Harper's Weekly,* 9 October 1875. LIBRARY OF CONGRESS

page letter mailed over 450 miles, but charged newspaper publishers just one cent for a paper sent under a hundred miles and one and a half cents for longer distances. Moreover, newspaper publishers were given the privilege of exchanging their newspapers with each other throughout the nation free of charge.

In the next half-century, the proliferation of newspapers nurtured by this benign policy amazed foreigners who visited the country. The French visitor Alexis de Tocqueville wrote in his *Journey to America* that while traveling in the wilds of Michigan in 1831 he found "no cabin so isolated, no valley so wild, but that letters and newspapers arrive at least once a week" (p. 70). In 1851 Congress favored the press with a law that permitted weekly papers to be mailed free throughout the county of publication, and in 1852 it virtually eliminated distance as a factor in determining the postage on newspapers.

Congress divided the mails into three classes in 1863 and placed letters in the first class, newspapers and periodicals in the second, and the rest in the third. By this act it also attempted to force publishers to prepay the postage on their publications but to no avail. Publishers had become so powerful that Congress hesitated to offend them, with the result that they were mailing many of their papers virtually free to subscribers who often failed to pay the postage.

Faced with a growing postal deficit, the postmaster general, Congress, and the publishers agreed on a law in 1874 that permitted newspaper publishers to mail their papers in bulk, prepaying the postage at two cents a pound; the postage on periodicals was set at three cents a pound, prepaid.

This law, which reduced the postage of publications by about 40 percent, was the price the government paid to win the publishers' consent to the prepayment of postage. It was a generous subsidy, but it was not enough. The publishers returned in 1879, lobbying for a new law, which Congress passed, that reduced the postage on periodicals to the same as that on newspapers. It also broadened the definition of second-class mail to include any publication containing information of a public character or "devoted to literature, the sciences, arts, or some special industry," and not bound by "board" or other substantial binding. A short time later, in 1885, Congress reduced the postage on second-class matter to a penny a pound and to two cents for a one-ounce letter.

The new laws achieved Congress's goal of diffusing knowledge. They opened the floodgates to a vast array of publications, all to be mailed for a penny a pound. Many that previously would have been classified as third-class mail were made second-class merely by the addition of a bit of "public information" scattered among their advertisements. Books, too—those not bound by "board" but prepared with paper covers—were mailed by the thousands in the second-class mail and sold for a dime. Many of these were reprints of classic English, French, and American novels or poems, but for the most part they were "blood and thunder" novels that appealed to a wide audience. Evidence of the success of Congress's policy of diffusing knowledge lay in the statistics. The amount of second-class mail rose from more than 58 million pounds in 1879 to more than 382 million pounds in 1900.

By 1897 the postal deficit had risen to more than $11 million. This was attributed to the abuse of the second-class mail privilege, and from that time to the end of the century Congress attempted to eliminate the abuses of the second-class privilege but failed. Endowed with wealth and the power of the written word, publishers blocked each attempt, and as the century ended the Post Office was still subsidizing their publications.

Mail Censorship

In all this mail there was much that was mailed by unscrupulous men designed to lure their unwary victims to invest in fraudulent schemes that promised much and gave nothing. Fraudulent mining stock, deceptive lottery tickets, and bogus money advertisements filled the mails, overwhelming the ability of hard-working postal inspectors to arrest all the perpetrators.

The rapidly expanding postal service also became a conduit for obscene publications. Postal authorities first became aware of this problem during the Civil War when they found the soldiers' mail laden with obscene material. Congress forbade this matter in the mails in 1865, but the law was unenforced. Although that law was rewritten in 1872, it was not until 1873, when the Comstock Law was passed, that Congress acted forcefully to rid the mails of pornographic material. Not only did that law forbid the mailing of "lewd, lascivious, or obscene" material, it brought Anthony Comstock, the controversial but honest morals crusader, into the Post Office as a special agent to enforce the law. That same year, Comstock's efforts resulted in fifty-five arrests and twenty convictions under the new law.

At the end of the century censorship had refined the content of the mails to accommodate middle-class American values. But the communication revolution provided by the improved mail service and cheap postage were as advantageous to the unscrupulous as to the honest, and the problems of fraudulent and obscene mail were inherited by the next century.

See also **Merchandising,** *subentry on* **Mail Order; Pony Express; Pornography.**

Bibliography

Cushing, Marshall. *The Story of Our Post Office: The Greatest Government Department in All Its Phases.* Boston: A. M. Thayer, 1893.

Fowler, Dorothy Ganfield. *The Cabinet Politician: The Postmasters General, 1829–1909.* New York: Columbia University Press, 1943.

———. *Unmailable: Congress and the Post Office.* Athens, Ga.: University of Georgia Press, 1977.

Fuller, Wayne E. *The American Mail: Enlarger of the Common Life.* Chicago: University of Chicago Press, 1972.

———. *R.F.D.: The Changing Face of Rural America.* Bloomington: Indiana University Press, 1964.

John, Richard R. *Spreading the News: The American Postal System from Franklin to Morse.* Cambridge, Mass: Harvard University Press, 1995.

Kelly, Clyde. *United States Postal Policy.* New York: D. Appleton, 1931.

Scheele, Carl. *A Short History of the Mail Service.* Washington, D.C.: Smithsonian Institution Press, 1970.

WAYNE E. FULLER

POVERTY   At the beginning of the 1800s most poor Americans outside the South resembled the poor of Europe. They were chiefly orphans, widows, people too old or too sick to work, or seasonal workers out of season. Wealthy people or local governments gave them "outdoor relief," consisting of food, firewood, or small amounts of money known as alms, primarily from a sense of paternalism or community responsibility. State poor laws, generally inherited from English tradition, required towns to take care of their poor.

Industrialization and immigration brought poverty of a new kind and on a new scale to American cities in the 1820s, intensifying in the economic crises

A New York City Slum about 1890. Photo by Jacob A. Riis (1849–1914), who began his career as a police reporter. He is best known for his many articles and books documenting New York City's tenement life and for his efforts for reform. LIBRARY OF CONGRESS

of the late 1830s and the 1850s. The number of people needing help increased dramatically, in part from the sporadic nature of all industrial jobs and in part from recurring financial panics. Urban builders for the first time constructed housing exclusively for the poor. Growing numbers of the poor were foreign-born, especially Irish immigrants fleeing the potato famine in the 1850s and eastern European immigrants later in the century. Chinese immigrants to the West Coast faced both racial discrimination and especially low wages.

Poor people coped in various ways, usually turning to organized relief only when less-public strategies failed. Believing, often correctly, that their poverty was temporary, poor people survived through small savings, rigid thrift, help from family members, odd jobs, debt, and aid from churches, fraternal associations, and trade unions. More and more in the late 1800s men traveled from cities to surrounding areas looking for work. In the 1870s the term "tramp" became a commonplace description of apparently rootless men who walked the highways or illegally rode the railroads. Most tramps were unmarried men who

learned to survive an irregular, frustrating pattern of work followed by struggle. Poor women traveled far less than men, more often working as seamstresses in crowded tenements. Poor children, especially during economic crises, added to household incomes by scavenging from city garbage.

The poorest part of the country after the Civil War was the South, where both whites and African Americans struggled with debt, low cotton prices, laws favorable to employers and creditors, paltry alternatives, and the general postwar devastation. Under sharecropping, by the 1870s the dominant labor system for African Americans, workers farmed year-round for landowners in exchange for a share of the value of the crop. Sharecroppers' main strategies were strenuous labor, thriftiness, large families, and, perhaps above all, movement. Like tramps farther north, sharecroppers moved frequently. But unlike tramps, they usually moved as families, relocating from one plantation to another at the end of crop seasons. Many white families in the Upper South, suffering from debt and the loss of the open range on which they had kept livestock, also became sharecroppers.

In the early and mid-1800s American policies about poverty shifted away from outdoor relief to efforts to teach the poor how to escape their poverty. Antipoverty efforts became more organized, antipoverty rhetoric became more judgmental, and policy shifted, in Christine Stansell's phrase, "from meliorism to active reform" (*City of Women*, p. 34). Beginning in 1817 with New York's Society for the Prevention of Pauperism, institutions collected the poor under one roof, oversaw their actions, and forced them to work. The state of New York formalized this policy in 1824 with the County Poorhouse Act, which required every county to build at least one institution to house its poor and, ideally, to teach them the emerging middle-class ethics of thrift, constant industry, and sobriety. In the 1840s the New York Association for Improving the Condition of the Poor encouraged wealthy male volunteers to visit the poor to share lessons about surviving and thriving in the American economy. In the 1850s the Children's Aid Society attempted to reform the environment of poor boys, especially by sending the boys out of cities into the supposedly healthier environment of the rural American West.

The absence of poverty became a lightning rod in mid-century regional debates. Northern Republicans saw the chance to rise from poor to independent to wealthy as crucial to the definition of American freedom and believed that slavery violated that freedom. Southern proslavery theorists replied that their region had no poor people. Slavery, they said, saved the

POVERTY

South from poverty, insecurity, crime, and possible revolution.

Regional arguments over poverty policy continued in the postbellum period. In 1865 and 1866 southern legislatures passed the Black Codes, the vagrancy and apprenticeship laws designed to keep former slaves working as dependent agricultural laborers. Many Americans outside the South were outraged that these laws tried to reinstate central elements of slavery. From the 1860s through the 1880s, however, northeastern and midwestern states passed or enhanced their own vagrancy laws, making begging a crime punishable by forced labor. Supporters of those laws argued that they were upholding the virtues of work for all people, while the South's Black Codes applied only to former slaves and did not mean to teach lessons.

To deal with the growing numbers of wandering poor, urban police departments in the late 1800s started allowing poor people to sleep in their stations. In the 1880s over 600,000 people did so. But charitable organizations always pressed for approaches that taught more lessons. The Charity Organization Society formed in 1877 with the motto Not Alms but a Friend. Its Friendly Visitors included numerous women trying to teach cleanliness and thrift to poor, especially immigrant women. Toward the end of the century antipoverty efforts took on an increasingly scientific tone. In 1878 the Massachusetts Bureau of Statistics of Labor made the country's first effort to measure unemployment, and in the 1880s the term "unemployment" was coined to convey both a condition of joblessness and the problems it caused.

The idea that government programs and cultural assimilation could overcome poverty also characterized U.S. policies toward American Indians. After military conquest and forced reservation status had undercut the basis of most American Indians' economies, many Americans interpreted the poverty of Indians as a sign of their backward cultures. Thus, the 1887 Dawes Act forced Indians either to become independent farmers or to risk forfeiting reservation land.

America's poor people rarely coalesced into a unified political group, whether because they viewed poverty as temporary or because they divided over ethnicity or levels of occupational skill. But two movements in the 1890s demonstrated their political potential. The Populist movement tried to unite farming people of the South, Southwest, and Great Plains around the goals of inflationary currency policies, railroad regulation, and cooperative marketing. In 1894 Coxey's Army, consisting of thousands of unemployed midwestern and western men, marched into Washington, D.C., demanding assistance from the federal government.

See also **Agriculture; Economic Regulation; Hobos, Tramps, and the Homeless; Housing; Immigration and Immigrants,** *subentry on* **The Immigrant Experience; Panics and Depressions; Populism; Reform, Social; Settlement Houses; Sociology.**

Bibliography

Boyer, Paul. *Urban Masses and Moral Order in America, 1820–1920.* Cambridge, Mass.: Harvard University Press, 1978.

Jones, Jacqueline. *The Dispossessed: America's Underclasses from the Civil War to the Present.* New York: Basic Books, 1992.

Katz, Michael B. *Poverty and Policy in American History.* New York: Academic Press, 1983.

Keyssar, Alexander. *Out of Work: The First Century of Unemployment in Massachusetts.* Cambridge, U.K., and New York: Cambridge University Press, 1986.

Mohl, Raymond A. *Poverty in New York, 1783–1825.* New York: Oxford University Press, 1971.

Monkkonen, Eric H., ed. *Walking to Work: Tramps in America, 1790–1935.* Lincoln: University of Nebraska Press, 1984.

Stanley, Amy Dru. *From Bondage to Contract: Wage Labor, Marriage, and the Market in the Age of Slave Emancipation.* Cambridge, U.K., and New York: Cambridge University Press, 1998.

Stansell, Christine. *City of Women: Sex and Class in New York, 1789–1860.* Urbana: University of Illinois Press, 1987.

Takaki, Ronald T. *Strangers from a Different Shore: A History of Asian Americans.* 1st Back Bay ed., updated and revised. Boston: Little, Brown, 1998.

Thernstrom, Stephan. *Poverty and Progress: Social Mobility in a Nineteenth-Century City.* Cambridge, Mass.: Harvard University Press, 1964.

Trattner, Walter I. *From Poor Law to Welfare State: A History of Social Welfare in America.* 6th ed. New York: Free Press, 1999.

White, Richard. *"It's Your Misfortune and None of My Own": A History of the American West.* Norman: University of Oklahoma Press, 1991.

TED OWNBY

PRAGMATISM The three great American pragmatists, Charles Sanders Peirce (1839–1914), William James (1842–1910), and John Dewey (1859–1952), differed in many important ways, yet they all sought to construct a philosophy devoted to the unity of theory and practice. Peirce took the term "pragmatism" from Immanuel Kant, for whom pragmatic ideas regulated conduct rather than correspond to an independent reality. While for Kant the pragmatic, which included the teleological subjects of art, biology, and history, was subordinate to the more authoritative truths of natural science and morality, Peirce held that the meaning of an idea derived from its ability to guide behavior as a universal maxim. Founded on this principle, pragmatism resisted the separation of logic, known a priori, from psychology, known from experience. Logic instead became a theory of inquiry. Peirce took this pragmatic idea of meaning as the basis both for scientific research and for a systematic philosophy of science. James personalized both meaning and action, and Dewey saw meaning and action principally as guides for addressing the practical problems of politics and education. All these thinkers reformulated philosophy in accordance with the newly popular ideas of evolution, although not necessarily Darwinian evolution.

For Peirce the purpose of all thinking was to eliminate doubt in order to "fix" belief and make it stable. Beginning with the essays "The Fixation of Belief" (1877) and "How to Make Our Ideas Clear" (1878), he argued that only experimental science, since it is fallible yet can be corrected by reference to a reality outside our control, can be a successful method for removing doubt and fixing belief. Although personal troubles prevented Peirce from holding an academic position or publishing many of his ideas during the last thirty years of his life, his works have been collected and published, and their brilliance and importance are evident. Believing that the meaning of an idea is found in the actions it guides, he developed that pragmatic maxim into an elaborate and systematic theory of meaning, which he called a theory of signs or semiotics. His idea of "evolutionary love" made room for meaning and order in a world of probability and chance.

James, trained first as a chemist and biologist and then as a physician, began his academic career in 1872 teaching anatomy, physiology, and hygiene at Harvard. In 1875 he offered a psychology course also. His book The Principles of Psychology (1890) was influential both in philosophy and in psychology. While James did not call himself a pragmatist until 1898, Principles embraces the important pragmatic theme that thinking, sensing, and feeling are not a series of atomic events but should be regarded instead as habits, interactions of the active and passive, voluntary and involuntary. Mind is an evolutionary adaptation of interaction between self and world. This pragmatic conception of thought in opposition to more passive versions of thinking reappears in The Will to Believe and Other Essays in Popular Philosophy (1897). In an 1898 lecture James finally introduced the term "pragmatism," whose origination he credited to Peirce.

James turned the pragmatic criterion of meaning in a different, more personal and individualistic direction. Peirce's scientific interpretation of pragmatism meant that the external world regulated the meaning of ideas. James thought that truth lives on credit, not cash, and that holding ideas makes them come true. What is "good to believe" regulates the truth as much as truth regulates what is good to believe.

Dewey, whose career lasted through almost half the twentieth century, was both a professional philosopher and a public intellectual throughout his career. After studying at Johns Hopkins with Peirce among others, he taught first at the University of Michigan. He then taught at the University of Chicago, where his engagement with the public problems of the day became crucial, and he spent the final part of his teaching career at Columbia University. Like the other pragmatists, he opposed the distinction between formal logic and psychology, and he formulated a logic of inquiry. With Peirce and against James, Dewey saw science as the paradigm for knowledge in general. While in Chicago, Dewey published Studies in Logical Theory (1903). However, Dewey was more interested in the uses of experimental methods to address what he called "the problems of men" than in Peirce's recondite scientific orientation. For Dewey the function of philosophy was to mediate between science and society.

For the pragmatists and other American philosophers of the nineteenth century, philosophy was a concept of individuality and democracy that united theory and practice. Their approaches differed on the meaning of individuality and democracy and on the meaning of theory and practice.

See also **Evolution; Philosophy.**

Bibliography

Dewey, John. *The Early Works, 1882–1898.* 5 vols. Carbondale: Southern Illinois University Press, 1967–1972.

———. *The Later Works, 1925–1953.* 17 vols. Edited by Jo Ann Boydston. Carbondale: Southern Illinois University Press, 1981–1990.

———. *The Middle Works, 1899–1924.* 15 vols. Edited by Jo Ann Boydston. Carbondale: Southern Illinois University Press, 1976–1983.

Diggins, John P. *The Promise of Pragmatism: Modernism and the Crisis of Knowledge and Authority.* Chicago: University of Chicago Press, 1994.

James, William. *The Principles of Psychology.* New York: Dover, 1950.

———. *The Will to Believe and Other Essays in Popular Philosophy.* Edited by Frederick H. Burkhardt, Fredson Bowers, and Ignas K. Skrupskelis. Cambridge, Mass.: Harvard University Press, 1979.

Peirce, Charles S. *Collected Papers.* 8 vols. Edited by Charles Hartshorne and Paul Weiss. Cambridge, Mass.: Belknap Press of Harvard University Press, 1931–1960.

———. *Writings of Charles S. Peirce: A Chronological Edition.* Edited by Max Fisch. Bloomington: Indiana University Press, 1982–.

Thayer, H. S. *Meaning and Action: A Critical History of Pragmatism.* 2d ed. Indianapolis: Hackett, 1981.

EUGENE GARVER

PRESIDENCY

[This entry includes an overview on **The Presidency as an Institution** and subentries on the periods 1801–1829, 1829–1849, 1849–1861, 1861–1877, and 1877–1901.]

THE PRESIDENCY AS AN INSTITUTION

The most notable feature of the U.S. presidency during the nineteenth century was how little it changed despite the shifting historical circumstances confronting each chief executive. Tentative outlines of the modern institution began to emerge only at the century's end, during the presidency of William McKinley (1843–1901). Until then the presidency was a small, intimate part of a modestly sized U.S. government.

The First Citizen

The underlying principle of the nineteenth-century presidency was that while the temporary occupant of the office was considered the first citizen of the land, he was not someone who kept aloof from or stood above his fellow citizens. The White House was not heavily guarded despite the assassinations of Abraham Lincoln (1809–1865) and James A. Garfield (1831–1881). Indeed, it was possible for any person with a desire to see the president to enter the White House and pursue whatever business might be on his or her mind. In addition, the president was expected to hold regular public receptions where anyone so inclined could stand in line to shake the president's hand. Several thousand people did so each week.

When a visitor went in to see the president, no large bureaucratic apparatus stood between the guest and the chief executive. Most presidents in the nineteenth century did their work with only one or two secretaries. There were a growing number of clerks by the end of the century, but nothing similar to today's presidential staff existed. The president received several hundred letters each week, and it was still possible to keep track of his correspondence by dividing it into incoming and outgoing mail. More elaborate filing systems did not appear until the twentieth century.

Press coverage of the presidency was also informal. Reporters waited outside the doors of the executive mansion to interview visitors. Until McKinley had his secretary create a table outside his office for reporters in 1897, there was no designated place for the press in the mansion. Sometimes the press's relations with the president were quite distant, as happened during the second administration of Grover Cleveland (1837–1908), when one reporter compared gathering news at the White House to the methods of highwaymen robbing a stagecoach. By tradition, the president was never quoted directly, and reporters had to use guarded language, such as "the president is known to believe," to indicate when the news came from the top.

Thomas Jefferson (1743–1826) abandoned the practice of delivering his annual message and other communications to Congress in person in 1801, and no president diverged from that course during the rest of the century. Sending the president's written annual message to Congress each December became a national ritual, and congressional clerks read out the chief executive's message. Direct presidential appeals to Congress to pass legislation or enact a specific program did occur but were regarded by the lawmakers as an intrusion on their sovereign prerogatives.

In the years before the Civil War, the presidency had lost much of whatever prestige it had gained from the administrations of Jefferson, Jackson, and James K. Polk. The inept and ineffectual terms of Millard Fillmore, Franklin Pierce, and James Buchanan left many citizens looking to Congress for national programs and political leadership. The inability of these executives to handle the slavery issue contributed to the sense of drift from the White House.

Presidential Traditions

Several long-standing traditions governed presidential behavior. The chief executive was expected to stay within the continental United States during his term of office. McKinley planned to break this custom during his second term, and Theodore Roosevelt (1858–1919) finally did so with a 1906 trip to Panama. Travel outside of Washington, D.C., except for summer vacations, often elicited public disapproval, as was the case with Rutherford B. Hayes (1822–1893), who became known as "Rutherford the Rover." Presidents were not supposed to make campaign tours either for themselves in seeking reelection or on behalf of their party's candidates. The disastrous "swing around the circle" tour of Andrew Johnson (1808–1875) in 1866 was a cautionary case in point. In 1898 McKinley began to undermine this tradition when he toured to celebrate the end of the war with Spain in a way that advanced his foreign-policy goals and helped Republican congressional candidates. The most time-honored taboo in this area was against a president campaigning for his own re-election. McKinley honored that custom in 1900 and let Theodore Roosevelt, his running mate, do the speaking tours for their campaign.

An even more hallowed tradition stood against pursuing a third term, and no one dared flout that custom during the nineteenth century. When the nomination of Ulysses S. Grant (1822–1885) for a third, nonconsecutive term was advocated in 1880, the public reacted strongly against the idea. Grover Cleveland did run for the presidency three times, and was the only person in U.S. history to achieve two nonconsecutive terms in the White House.

The Slow Growth of Presidential Power

The powerful presidents of the nineteenth century were Thomas Jefferson, Andrew Jackson (1767–1845), James K. Polk (1795–1849), Abraham Lincoln, Grover Cleveland, and William McKinley. Of these, Jackson and Lincoln had the largest impact on popular perceptions of the institution. Lincoln used the Civil War to build up the power of the state to preserve the Union. After Lincoln's death, the presidency receded in influence for three decades and Congress took the initiative in policymaking. Even Cleveland's strong assertion of presidential prerogatives in the 1890s did not put the institution on anything like a modern footing. That task was left to McKinley, who initiated many of the practices associated with twentieth-century presidential leadership. He managed Congress, brought the press into the White House, wielded the power of war to govern the new empire, and traveled extensively to seek popular support for his policies. Even before Theodore Roosevelt took office in September 1901, there was talk in newspapers and magazines that the presidency was becoming more monarchical and imperial in its techniques. As the twentieth century would show, these premonitions were both premature and prescient. By the end of the nineteenth century, the historical model of the presidency on a human scale that had existed since the founding of the Republic was about to give way to the more imperial and bureaucratic model that has been standard ever since.

See also **Assassinations; Congress; Elections,** *subentry on* **Presidential Elections; Jacksonian Era; Jeffersonian Era.**

Bibliography

Cunliffe, Marcus. *American Presidents and the Presidency.* New York: American Heritage, 1972.

Levy, Leonard W., and Louis Fisher, eds. *Encyclopedia of the American Presidency.* 4 vols. New York: Simon and Schuster, 1994.

McDonald, Forrest. *The American Presidency: An Intellectual History.* Lawrence: University Press of Kansas, 1994.

Skowronek, Stephen. *The Politics Presidents Make: Leadership from John Adams to George Bush.* Cambridge, Mass.: Belknap Press of Harvard University Press, 1993.

LEWIS L. GOULD

1801–1829

In the twelve years preceding Thomas Jefferson's inauguration as the third president, a number of precedents were set by George Washington and John Adams. Both eschewed partisan politics, yet both became enmeshed in bitter controversies with strong partisan overtones. Washington, magisterial and universally popular, took office reluctantly and left with the nation's reverence and awe. Adams barely won his first term and was in part betrayed by his own party when he sought reelection.

By the election of 1800 the two-term tradition was already in place as were precedents regarding relations with Congress. Washington stopped meeting with Congress and its committees, and Adams found himself at odds with his cabinet but insisted on his right to remove his appointees. The Federalist Party took form under the tutelage of Alexander Hamilton, both as a cabinet officer and as the man behind the scenes during the 1790s. The Democratic-Republican Party, later called simply the Republican Party and the precursor of the modern Democratic Party, grew out of the fundamental differences exemplified by Jefferson's agrarian instincts in conflict with Hamilton's mercantilist bent. During the controversy over Jay's Treaty of 1794, the two-party system was born.

As the French Revolution hurtled forward, American politicians became enmeshed in its backlash. When an undeclared naval war with France erupted in 1797–1798, Federalists were convinced that a pro-French party existed in the United States and carried on treasonable activities. Jefferson and his supporters looked on the Federalists as pro-British, willing to imitate the Bank of England and other facets of a governmental system that favored trade and finance over the interests of farmers and small merchants.

In such a political climate Jefferson as vice president presided over the Senate and became the unofficial candidate of the newly formed Democratic-Republican Party. The majority of voters, mainly farmers who opposed higher taxes, flocked to Jefferson's support in 1800 as he promised to cut taxes, protect civil liberties, and whittle down the national

Thomas Jefferson (1743–1826). Despite his strict constructionist view of the Constitution and his professed mistrust of national power, Jefferson greatly expanded the power of the presidency and the national government. Portrait by A. Day, 1801. LIBRARY OF CONGRESS: PRINTS AND PHOTOGRAPHS DIVISION

debt. Despite intrigue promoted by Aaron Burr's friends that produced a tie in the electoral college—seventy-three votes for Burr, seventy-three for Jefferson—Jefferson was chosen president on the thirty-sixth ballot in the House of Representatives.

Thus Jefferson moved into the barely finished White House and began his eight-year tenure in what he would later call the "splendid misery" of the presidency.

Thomas Jefferson (1801–1809)

Simplicity was embodied in Jefferson's inauguration on 4 March 1801. He walked to the ceremonies, delivered his speech in a barely audible voice, and tried to dispel the clouds of partisanship that overhung the political atmosphere. "We are all Republicans—we are all federalists," Jefferson insisted, seeking to quiet fears that his would be a vindictive administration. With a Congress that boasted a heavy Republican majority, Jefferson knew that his legislative program would be enacted if party discipline prevailed. Every president has had a brief "honeymoon" with Congress during the first months of his term, and Jefferson hoped to utilize this goodwill period as one trump card. The other trumps related to the selection of a cabinet of loyal Republicans who were competent and committed to the president's program.

The Revolution of 1800

Neither Washington nor Adams had been close to congressional leaders, and in a sense both tried to stay aloof from partisan intrigue in deference to the constitutional dictum for the separation of powers (legislative, judicial, and executive branches). Cabinet members and influential senators had carried much of the burden for providing the leadership required to finance and operate the federal government. Jefferson abandoned his predecessors' practice of appearing before Congress. He let clerks read his messages, but during his first term he moved deftly behind the scenes. Not until Woodrow Wilson took office would a president go before Congress again.

Taxes, always a sore subject, had caused defections among Federalists, as had the problems created by Great Britain in implementing the Treaty of Paris (1783). The war between England and France that occupied Europe from 1793 until 1815 also proved difficult for a struggling nation that favored neutrality.

Jefferson discerned the mood of the country and led a willing Congress to a vigorous response. The detested Alien and Sedition Laws were allowed to expire, and among the taxes cut was an unpopular levy on carriages. To lower federal expenses the small army was reduced in size, and ships were left unfinished in naval yards. American diplomatic missions in several European countries were either closed or curtailed, and Jefferson instructed Albert Gallatin, his secretary of the Treasury, to make plans to reduce the national debt until it would eventually disappear. Customs (taxes on imported goods) became almost the sole source of federal income as Congress responded to the president's recommendations by enacting the necessary legislation, which Jefferson promptly signed. During his eight years in the White House, Jefferson never vetoed a single piece of legislation, and his cabinet formed in 1801 stayed intact until he left office. No president before or since could boast such an appearance of approval and unity.

Not everything was perfect in Washington, but Jefferson's first administration was remarkable for its accomplishments. The national debt of $83 million that Jefferson inherited in 1801 was scaled down each year, and an actual surplus was accumulated by the federal Treasury during Jefferson's first six years in office. Jefferson relied on his secretary of state, James Madison, for advice and counsel, and Gallatin was also a member of his closest circle. Jefferson believed he was guided by loyal Republicans who shared his commitment to what he called "the revolution of 1800." The president thought his administration had overturned the Federalists' goals of a semiaristocratic national government that favored mercantile and financial interests over those of the great majority of the American people, who were small farmers and tradesmen. The nation grew to sixteen states populated by five million whites and one million slaves, with a majority supporting Jefferson.

Only the Supreme Court was aligned against Jefferson it seemed. The Court consistently decided against the Republicans, beginning with *Marbury v. Madison* in 1803, which established the Court's power to declare acts of Congress unconstitutional. A string of decisions establishing the supremacy of the federal government was frustrating to Jefferson as he championed the rights of states to exercise broad powers.

The Louisiana Purchase

Jefferson's prejudices often misled him. He thought the British were committed to the eventual destruction of the United States as a sovereign nation, and he had an abiding faith in the American farmer as a patriot-citizen. When the British navy began to roam American waters and seize Yankee sailors off American ships within sight of the shore, Jefferson believed this high-handed action was part of the British scheme to humiliate his country. He hoped diplomacy would prevent American involvement in a European war and sent envoys to London seeking an end to impressment. Disillusioned by the antics of Napoleon, Jefferson was not eager to rush from a British frying pan into a French fire. So he waited and pondered the proper course for a country that had no striking power in the world's sea-lanes even though American shipping was expanding at a remarkable rate.

Expansion was also on Jefferson's mind. The Spanish imposition of a ban on American trading on the Mississippi, an act that had been long threatened, forced Jefferson to seek control of New Orleans. A series of Napoleonic disasters, including the decimation of a French army sent to recapture Haiti, put the French leader in a mood to compromise. American emissaries sent to bid on New Orleans wound up with all of the Louisiana Territory on the bargaining

table. In short order the United States purchased for $15 million the vast domain west of the Mississippi River, some 828,000 square miles of land, almost doubling the size of the country.

The world had never before seen so massive a transfer of territory by peaceful means, and the lesson was not lost. Early in his second term Jefferson sought to negotiate the purchase of East and West Florida from Spain and hoped Congress would again provide the cash needed should Madrid be interested in a sale. The ensuing fight in Congress alienated John Randolph, the eccentric representative from Virginia, from Jefferson's trusted circle. Opposition to Jefferson thereafter was always a factor in the political balance, as the New England leadership gravitated to the dwindling but dogged Federalists.

Reelected in 1804 with only nominal opposition from the Federalists, Jefferson reminded voters in his inaugural address that he had kept his promise on cutting taxes. "What farmer, what mechanic, what laborer, ever sees a tax-gatherer of the United States?" the president boasted. In the next breath Jefferson alluded to his Indian policy and admitted that changing Native Americans' traditional way of life would be difficult. Nevertheless the president insisted that America's "aboriginal inhabitants" would benefit from a program that made them farmers instead of hunters. "Humanity enjoins us to teach them agriculture and the domestic arts," Jefferson said.

Jefferson hailed the Lewis and Clark expedition he had sent to explore the Louisiana Territory as a scientific triumph. But all was not well in the West. Aaron Burr, dropped from the ticket in 1804, had been recruiting followers for a half-baked scheme for an empire carved out of Spanish territory. Jefferson got wind of the tiny force Burr was leading and ordered Burr's arrest. During the ensuing trial, which ended in Burr's acquittal, Jefferson refused to honor a subpoena from Chief Justice John Marshall, thereby setting a precedent for presidential conduct.

Diplomacy and the embargo

Before Burr's release, Jefferson had to face a crisis brought on by the Royal Navy. The HMS *Leopard* had fired on the USS *Chesapeake* off the Virginia coast in June 1807, all but destroying the American vessel and seizing part of its crew. The nation reacted with rage, and Jefferson could have asked Congress for a declaration of war and won a majority. But he searched instead for an alternative to war, and in December 1807 Congress passed in a single day the Embargo Act, which closed the world's sea-lanes to American ships.

Thereafter Jefferson's second term was marred by

sectional resistance to the embargo, as New England citizens evaded the law and made the Canadian border a smugglers' cove. Frustrated by the British Orders in Council, which allowed the Royal Navy a free hand in impressing crew members from Yankee ships, Jefferson was bewildered by Americans who skirted the law enacted to save the peace. An act calling for stricter enforcement of the embargo was defied by New Englanders, although the rest of the country seemed prepared to suffer the loss of international commodity markets out of loyalty to Jefferson's program.

Dissension in Congress was obvious during Jefferson's last year in office. American diplomatic overtures in London and Paris led to no concessions from the belligerents, and once it was clear that Madison would succeed him in office, Jefferson appeared to be willing to let both his diplomatic and his domestic programs glide without much direction. The Senate's unanimous rejection on 27 February 1809 of William Short, Jefferson's nominee for minister to Russia, was a stunning insult. Repeal of the embargo was set for 1 March 1809, during Jefferson's final week in office as a gesture of its failure. Jefferson kept his reaction to these last-minute acts of rudeness to himself, and he left Washington on 11 March 1809, never to return. Few presidents have had Jefferson's impact. His relentless efforts to cut the cost of government, even at the expense of national defense, became national policy. Jefferson's concern for civil liberties, for strict separation of church and state, and his confidence in majority rule overshadowed the failure of his efforts to avoid war with England.

James Madison (1809–1817)

As Jefferson's longtime political ally, Madison won his party's nomination at the congressional caucus and faced only token opposition from Federalists. Madison took office committed to carrying out the programs of his predecessor. The problem was that the aura of a strong executive had disappeared in the nation's capital. John Randolph had tried to thwart Madison's presidential bid by maneuvering James Monroe's name before the caucus that backed Jefferson's choice, Madison. The Federalists barely made the presidential election a real contest, for they controlled only the New England states, with scattered support in Maryland and South Carolina. But the Republican majority in Congress was not led by men firmly loyal to Madison. Even worse, several senators believed they could bully Madison. They warned him, days before his inauguration, that they would not confirm Gallatin if Madison nominated him for secretary of state.

Fearing an internecine party battle, Madison backed away from a fight. Perhaps mindful of the embargo fiasco, he listened to his critics instead of his friends. Gallatin was already secretary of the Treasury, so he could be left in that vital post without a Senate fight, and a compromise candidate could be placed in the key State Department office. Cowed by the Senate "invisibles" who sought to embarrass him, Madison played into their hands by choosing as secretary of state Robert Smith, who had been Jefferson's secretary of the navy. Smith, the brother of Senator Samuel Smith of the "invisibles," proved to be both inept and disloyal, and most of Madison's cabinet appointments were not much better. To his critics it seemed that Madison was more interested in geographical balance than in proved competence when selecting his departmental chieftains.

Launched into his presidency with bickering in Congress and little backbone in his cabinet, Madison took control of the State Department himself. Between the British Orders in Council and decrees issued by Napoleon in a steady stream, American ships were being seized, their cargoes sequestered, and their seamen imprisoned in British and French jails. The American shipbuilding industry was strangled, and American farmers saw prices of their commodities fall for lack of outlet markets.

Congress went its way, too. On the domestic front the battle to renew the charter of the Bank of the United States revealed sectional animosity. Gallatin favored recharter, but party leaders from the South and West wanted to eliminate the bank as the tool of eastern financiers. Vice President George Clinton cast the vote needed to kill the bank. Madison was troubled by the consequences, and Gallatin's ability to float government loans was soon crippled.

The War of 1812

After long and tedious debate, a strange law known as Macon's Bill No. 2 was passed and sent to Madison in 1810. The gist of this act was that a carrot would be dangled before the French and British warmakers. Whichever power agreed to treat American shipping as neutral and free to proceed would be recognized, and all commerce with the other power would be prohibited.

Meanwhile an eager young British diplomat, David Erskine, assured Madison that his diplomacy had paid off and claimed that the Orders in Council would not be enforced against American ships. When the British cabinet denied that this was true, Madison ran out of patience. Napoleon added to the president's bafflement with a diplomatic trick of his own. Using all his guile, he announced that all French decrees against American shipping were withdrawn, so by the provisions of American law, a prohibition against the British must follow.

Madison never bothered to ask the French for proof of Napoleon's claim and in effect sent an ultimatum to London. Would the British follow suit, and also recognize the rights of American neutral shippers? When the British hemmed and hawed and asked for proof, Madison gave up. In April 1812 he asked Congress to declare war, and despite some foot-dragging by Federalists in the Senate, on 4 June the United States went to war against Great Britain for the second time. The House voted 79 to 49 for war, but in the Senate the vote was closer: 19 to 13. Congressman John C. Calhoun predicted "that in four weeks from the time a declaration of war is heard on our frontier, the whole of Upper Canada and part of Lower Canada will be in our power."

No such luck, for at the outset everything seemed to go wrong for the American cause. The Royal Navy, with eighty ships of the line compared with three American warships, bottled up American ports with a coastal blockade. The congressmen who expected to capture Canada and use it as a diplomatic bargaining chip overestimated American strength on land. Instead of making a quick sweep into Canada, General William Hull surrendered Detroit to a smaller British-Canadian force and left American border defenses in a shambles. Inept generals and balky New England governors, who would not allow state troops to take part in offensive moves, plagued efforts to invade Canada. To pay for the war Gallatin tried to float loans but found New England financiers unresponsive. He settled for a costly plan involving discounted bonds that made Philadelphia and New York bankers rich, but with customs receipts dried up and the party's no-tax policy in place, he had no choice.

President Madison stood for reelection without being able to boast of any military success. The 1812 presidential campaign was notable only for the fact that DeWitt Clinton, a New York Republican, became the Federalists' best hope of ousting Madison. Dark rumors of disaffection in New England gained some credence from the election results. Clinton carried all of New England except Vermont, but Madison won the electoral college vote, 128 to 89. Elbridge Gerry, who became vice president, claimed that, had Madison lost, "G. Britain would have had a well founded prospect of a triumph over our liberty."

The British mounted an offensive after several American campaigns ended in crippling defeats or ignominious standoffs. The British invasion of Chesapeake Bay was capped by the fall of Washington, D.C., to the Royal Marines in August 1814. Many public buildings in the nation's capital were burned, and Madison was forced to flee from the White House before it was torched. Calls for moving the capital inland were loud until Madison quashed the idea. He rearranged his cabinet and briefly made James Monroe secretary of both state and war.

Only the fierce defensive efforts of American seamen on the Great Lakes and courageous militia at the siege of Baltimore gave Americans cause for pride. A diplomatic mission sent to negotiate a peace wrestled with British indifference for over a year, when suddenly a shift in direction became evident. The defeat of Napoleon and England's weariness of war dramatically changed the British cabinet's stance. On Christmas Eve 1814 a treaty was signed that left all territorial matters where they stood before hostilities began.

News of the peace reached Washington as envoys from a rump convention of antiwar Federalists arrived, intent on humiliating Madison with threats of splitting the Union. The ensuing celebration of the peace quieted the New England Federalists, and the nation trumpeted the Treaty of Ghent as proof of an American victory. A tragic aftermath was the Battle of New Orleans, fought in January 1815. It was a resounding defeat of a crack British force by troops led by General Andrew Jackson. As Gallatin noted, the war's outcome had boosted American morale greatly. "The war has renewed and reinstated the national feelings and character which the Revolution had given, and which were daily lessened," Gallatin surmised. "The people . . . are more Americans; they feel and act more as a nation; and I hope the permanency of the Union is thereby secured."

The return of prosperity

Madison's final years in office saw a return of prosperity at home and a widespread belief that American nationhood had at last been achieved. A plan to recharter the Bank of the United States, which had been killed by Republicans in 1811, was revived. Financing the war had been excessively difficult because no central bank existed, and Gallatin saw the need for a national bank to handle government business. Madison vetoed one version of the bill but approved a revised law in 1816, thus moving federal finances to an even keel. Despite the heavy war expenses, the national debt, which was $83 million in 1801 when the Republicans took over and had dipped to $45 million in 1813, was over $120 million in 1816.

The return of peace had also seen efforts to demilitarize the U.S.-Canadian border, and Madison approved plans to keep warships off the Great Lakes through an international treaty. The long-festering troubles with Algerian pirates, who had sent hundreds of American sailors into dungeons as part of a ransom scheme, finally came to an end when Madison sent an American squadron, commanded by Stephen Decatur, that pounded the marauders into submission. Thereafter the American shipping industry prospered, and the Stars and Stripes was carried into world sea-lanes as a booming cotton industry supplemented cash markets for American wheat, tobacco, and other farm products. Historian Henry Adams conceded that Madison "seemed to enjoy popularity never before granted to any President at the expiration of his term." Adams's great-grandfather John Adams was more blunt. "Notwithstanding a thousand Faults and blunders," the former president noted, Madison's administration "has acquired more glory, and established more union; than all his three predecessors . . . put together."

James Monroe (1817–1825)

With the Federalist Party in disarray, the nomination of James Monroe as Madison's successor was hardly contested. His position as secretary of state seemed a fitting precedent, as both Jefferson and Madison had served their apprenticeships at the State Department. Monroe was popular, the country was at peace, and the electoral vote proved that the Federalist Party had all but withered away.

Monroe followed Washington's example and toured the Atlantic coastal states in the summer after his inauguration in 1817. Everywhere enthusiastic crowds cheered the tall Virginian. In Boston, once the hotbed of Federalist opposition, a converted editor proclaimed that Monroe deserved credit for "an era of good feeling."

Monroe appointed John Quincy Adams secretary of state, and negotiations with Spain to acquire Florida began. Sympathetic toward the revolting Spanish colonies in South America, Monroe eventually declared that the United States would resist European intervention in Latin America. France, Russia, and Spain were put on notice, and the Monroe Doctrine became the bedrock of American foreign policy.

At home Monroe weathered one crisis after another. Missouri and Maine were ready for statehood, but the slavery issue held up the required legislation. Finally a compromise admitting both states but forbidding slavery above 36 degrees, 30 minutes north latitude, Missouri's southern boundary, was passed in 1820. Missouri itself was exempted from this rule. Angry slaveholders advised Monroe to veto the legislation, but he ignored rabid opposition in his home state of Virginia and signed the measures.

Amid the tension in Congress, the collapse of dozens of banks and the drying up of circulating cash created a crisis in 1819. Forty new banks in Kentucky closed their doors, cotton fell from 33 cents a pound to 18 cents, and tobacco dipped from 30 cents to 4 cents a pound in June 1819. Land prices plunged in the South, mortgages were foreclosed, and Monroe used the word "depression" in describing the young nation's first economic crisis. Slowly the country emerged from the recession, but land values in the Old South remained at rock-bottom level.

Despite a slow economic recovery and political echoes from extremists who opposed the Missouri Compromise, Monroe had no real opposition in the 1820 presidential election; the Federalist party was leaderless, had no real program, and had turned into a regional and only nominal "opposition" party. His sweep in the electoral college was 231 to 1. Economic recovery was under way, Spain had agreed to sell Florida, and there were now twenty-three stars on the flag. When Jefferson took office, the country had 957 post offices; when Monroe was inaugurated for the second time, the number had grown to 3,459. Canals and turnpikes were being built, farm prices climbed back to their pre-1819 levels, and Congress kept land prices for the public domain around two dollars an acre.

Monroe's presidency ended as it had begun, on a note of national confidence. Little-noticed at the time, the Monroe Doctrine, enunciated in 1823, warned European powers that the Western Hemisphere was henceforth off limits for future colonization. In time, the Doctrine became the bedrock of American foreign policy.

Monroe's presidency was memorable for its political blandness. Partisan bickering and the specter of slavery were temporarily brushed aside as the nation plunged into a new wave of prosperity while most of the world was at peace. Completion of the Erie Canal in 1825 touched off a frenzy of building waterways and turnpikes. The age of transportation was dawning in a nation still peopled by small farmers and their families. But the days of the Virginia dynasty in the White House were soon to end.

John Quincy Adams (1825–1829)

Adams was probably the best-trained and most disappointed president ever to hold the office. The last caucus-nominated candidate, Adams trailed in the popular voting because of the rousing campaign of the military hero Andrew Jackson. The close ballot threw the election into the House of Representatives, where Henry Clay maneuvered enough votes to make Adams president. Jackson's supporters claimed a backstage "deal" tainted the whole process and vowed revenge.

As a National Republican, Adams found dwindling support when he took office in 1825, despite his selection of Clay as secretary of state (part of the alleged "deal"). The high-minded Adams could not

John Quincy Adams (1767–1848) President from 1825 to 1829, Adams was the only elected president to enter Congress after the end of his term. LIBRARY OF CONGRESS

control Congress, and opposition from defectors (who soon claimed to be Jeffersonian-style Democrats) tied the president's hands regarding domestic reforms. Academies to train officers for the army and navy had been created and funded, but Adams's call for a national university to foster the arts and sciences was derided as impractical.

As a northerner, Adams was sympathetic toward the growing abolitionist movement, but in the South and West voters liked Jackson's call for broader suffrage and an expansionist policy. At the first political convention ever held, Jackson was nominated and easily swamped the incumbent, 178 electoral votes to Adams's 83. A new era in American presidential politics had dawned with a loud bang.

See also **Democratic Party; Internal Improvements; Lewis and Clark Expedition; Louisiana Purchase; Monroe Doctrine; War of 1812.**

Bibliography

Adams, Henry. *History of the United States of America during the Administrations of Thomas Jefferson and James Madison.* 2 vols. New York: Library of America, 1986.

Ammon, Harry. *James Monroe: The Quest for National Identity.* New York: McGraw-Hill, 1971.

Brant, Irving. *James Madison.* 6 vols. Indianapolis, Ind.: Bobbs-Merrill, 1941–1961.

Coles, Harry. *The War of 1812.* Chicago: University of Chicago Press, 1965.

Cunningham, Noble E., Jr. *The Jeffersonian Republicans: The Formation of Party Organization, 1789–1801.* Chapel Hill, N.C.: University of North Carolina Press, 1957.

———. *The Presidency of James Monroe.* Lawrence: University Press of Kansas, 1996.

———. *The Process of Government under Jefferson.* Princeton, N.J.: Princeton University Press, 1978.

Dangerfield, George. *The Era of Good Feelings.* New York: Harcourt Brace, 1963.

Elkins, Stanley, and Eric McKitrick. *The Age of Federalism.* New York: Oxford University Press, 1993.

Ellis, Joseph J. *American Sphinx: The Character of Thomas Jefferson.* New York: Knopf, 1997.

Johnstone, Robert M., Jr. *The Jefferson Presidency: Leadership in the Young Republic.* Ithaca, N.Y.: Cornell University Press, 1978.

Ketcham, Ralph. *James Madison: A Biography.* New York: Macmillan, 1971.

Levy, Leonard W. *Jefferson and Civil Liberties: The Darker Side.* New York: Quadrangle, 1973.

Malone, Dumas. *Jefferson and His Time.* 6 vols. Boston: Little, Brown, 1948–1981.

McCoy, Drew R. *The Last of the Fathers: James Madison and the Republican Legacy.* Cambridge, Mass.: Harvard University Press, 1989.

McDonald, Forrest. *The Presidency of Thomas Jefferson.* Lawrence: University Press of Kansas, 1976.

Rutland, Robert Allen. *James Madison: The Founding Father.* New York: Macmillan, 1987.

———. *The Presidency of James Madison.* Lawrence: University Press of Kansas, 1990.

Smelser, Marshall. *The Democratic Republic, 1801–1815.* New York: Harper and Row, 1968.

Stagg, J. C. A. *Mr. Madison's War: Politics, Diplomacy, and Warfare in the Early Republic, 1783–1830.* Princeton, N.J.: Princeton University Press, 1983.

Tucker, Robert W., and David C. Henrickson. *Empire of Liberty: The Statecraft of Thomas Jefferson.* New York: Oxford University Press, 1990.

White, Leonard D. *The Jeffersonians: A Study in Administrative History, 1801–1829.* New York: Macmillan, 1951.

ROBERT ALLEN RUTLAND

1829–1849

During the first forty years of its existence (1789–1829), the presidency of the United States was held by six men, each a member of either the Virginia dynasty or the Adams family from Massachusetts. Although most of these individuals championed the cause of the common person, all were aristocrats in terms of education, social upbringing, and lifestyle. In addition, each was elected president via a process that denied direct participation to the general citizenry.

The election of Andrew Jackson in 1828 marked the beginning of a new era for the presidency. For the next twenty years each occupant of the White House cherished his credentials as a man of the people, a self-made person of supposedly humble origins who attained the nation's highest office by appealing directly to the mass of voters. Jackson's presidency also set another standard for his successors to follow, that of the forceful executive seeking to limit the power of the federal government to affect the economic well-being of the common person. Most of the other presidents who served between 1829 and 1849 tried to adhere to the Jacksonian model of presidential performance, with varying degrees of success.

The Age of Jackson also ushered in a new system of political parties and a new style of presidential politics. The Federalist Party, which offered no presidential candidate after 1816, was replaced by the Whig Party. Whigs generally supported vigorous federal stimulation of the economy and stood in direct opposition to the presidential policies of Jackson and his fellow Democrats. Meanwhile, the Democratic-Republican Party of Thomas Jefferson evolved into the Democratic Party of Jackson. Unlike their Jeffersonian predecessors, Democrats ceased trying to represent the interests of the entire country. Instead, they focused on protecting the common person from unfair competition with economic elites and from ruinous federal intervention in economic matters. National conventions, which were open to a large number of people, replaced congressional caucuses as the vehicle by which presidential candidates were nominated. Presidential campaigns, which had once been genteel, almost intellectual events driven in large part by political principle, became boisterous, emotional popularity contests.

Andrew Jackson (1829–1837)

With the exception of George Washington, Jackson was the first president who did not serve in a number of other federal government positions before his election to that office. His prior experience consisted of significant military service in war and peace and brief stints in the Tennessee legislature, on the bench of the Tennessee superior court, and in the U.S. Congress as both a representative and a senator. Except for his military confrontations with the British, the Spanish, and Native Americans, he had no experience in foreign policy. Like George Washington, his chief claim to fame was as a general who had achieved victory against the British. Also like Washington, his tall physical stature, rugged good looks, and quiet

but forceful manner gave him much charismatic appeal. As a Tennessean, Jackson was also the first candidate from west of the Appalachian Mountains to be elected president. These facts heightened his popularity among average citizens, who considered Jackson one of them. In fact Jackson was a man of means, a lawyer, plantation owner, and investor, whose scanty legislative record marked him more as a conservative than as a friend of the people. Nevertheless, he was certainly no aristocrat, and once in the White House, he worked assiduously to make sure that the policies of the federal government did not favor any elite group.

In so doing Jackson followed his own lead. Whereas earlier presidents had relied heavily on their department heads for advice, Jackson paid little heed to his cabinet, preferring instead to draw on the counsel of a small group of political allies. His forceful temperament, which when exercised in the military had earned him the nickname "Old Hickory," and his refusal to compromise when he believed that he was in the right led his critics to label him "King Andrew the First." These traits also may have inspired the first presidential assassination attempt in U.S. history, when on 30 January 1830 a gunman discharged two pistols at Jackson at point-blank range. Fortunately, the pistols misfired.

Jackson considered himself the direct representative of the American people, and he revived the practice, which had fallen dormant under his three immediate predecessors, of suggesting to Congress the types of bills he believed it ought to consider. He also insisted on being consulted whenever a new bill was making its rounds through Congress, and he called for the adoption of three constitutional amendments: the creation of two supreme courts, one for each side of the Appalachians; the abolition of the electoral college, the body that had prevented him from becoming president in 1824; and restricting the president's tenure in office to one term of either four or six years.

As part of his determination to lead the nation, Jackson often treated Congress and the Supreme Court with what many observers of the day termed contempt. During his eight years in office he vetoed twelve bills, more than the total number of vetoes exercised by the first six presidents combined. He also refused to consult the Senate on matters of foreign policy, preferring instead to let the Department of State conduct diplomacy unhindered by congressional input. The Senate was outraged by Jackson's efforts to play an active role in its deliberations, and for the last few years of his presidency, senators refused to accept communiqués from the White House. When Georgia annexed nine million acres of Cherokee Indian land in violation of a treaty between the federal government and the Cherokee tribe, Jackson refused to take action despite a ruling by the U.S. Supreme Court in favor of the Indians. Roger B. Taney, his attorney general and future chief justice of the Supreme Court, advised Jackson that the president was not bound by the Court's decisions.

Jackson instigated controversy when he sought to remove a number of career public servants from office. At the time the federal bureaucracy consisted of about ten thousand appointive positions, the vast majority of which fell under the purview of the army, navy, or Post Office. Of these positions, about six hundred were filled by direct appointment of the president. Jackson actually removed less than 20 percent of all federal officeholders or approximately the same percentage that his predecessors had removed. Moreover, most of the ones he did remove had either misused government funds or were guilty of some other form of corruption. However, his public denunciation of permanent officeholding coupled with the remarks of William L. Marcy, a political ally, that "to the victor belong the spoils" fixed in the public mind the desirability of rotating public offices with each incoming president and established this practice as standard procedure for future chief executives.

Unfortunately, rotation of office also established the president as the federal government's chief clerk of personnel. Future presidents, who until 1857 labored without so much as a clerk to assist them, spent up to half their time receiving, reviewing, appointing, and placating tens of thousands of would-be federal employees. Not until the passage of the Pendleton Act in 1883, two years after President James Garfield was assassinated by a disappointed office seeker, was civil service reform instituted, thus greatly curtailing presidential responsibility for federal appointments.

Jackson also moved forcefully to preserve the Union in the face of its most serious threat prior to the Civil War. After Congress passed the so-called Tariff of Abominations in 1828, South Carolina declared the tariff null and void within its borders. Jackson, although he agreed with South Carolinians that the tariff was too high, threatened in 1833 to send federal troops into the state to enforce the law. A compromise tariff was enacted at the same time that Jackson threatened to take military action, and South Carolina was able to back down without losing face, a constitutional crisis was avoided, and the Union was preserved.

Jackson believed that the federal government should play as small a role as possible in the nation's economic affairs. Consequently, when Congress passed a bill in 1832 rechartering the Bank of the United States, he vetoed the bill on the grounds that the bank enriched a small elite at the expense of the

vast majority of the American public. However, the bank's charter did not run out until 1836, so in 1833 Jackson attempted to kill the bank by ordering Louis McLane, the secretary of the Treasury, to withdraw federal funds from the bank. When McLane refused, Jackson fired him and appointed William John Duane in his place. When Duane also refused, Jackson named his friend and political ally Roger B. Taney to the position. Taney redeposited federal monies in a number of state, or "pet," banks per Jackson's orders, thus earning for the president the censure of the Senate in 1834.

Jackson also reduced the federal government's expenditures to a minimal level to retire the national debt. Part of his drive stemmed from the reason the national debt was created in the first place. In the Republic's first decade Alexander Hamilton and the Federalists believed that, by issuing government securities that only the wealthy were likely to purchase, the nascent Republic could secure the loyalty of important men in return for regular interest payments. Jackson rejected that reasoning, believing that such instruments served only to enrich a small elite at the expense of the general populace. By 1836, his last full year in office, the national debt was reduced to zero.

Jackson left office in 1837 at the height of his popular appeal. His charismatic and energetic discharge of presidential duties, his firm conviction that he was the direct representative of the American people, his seemingly sincere efforts to act in the people's best interests, and his role in the rise of a more popular, grassroots democratic politics endeared him to the populace in a way that had not occurred before. Jackson, the only president between 1825 and 1861 to serve two terms in office, placed his personal stamp on the presidency, making it a much more dynamic and popular institution than it had been in the hands of his predecessors. In so doing he made himself the model after which future nineteenth-century presidents and presidential candidates would fashion themselves and by which they would be evaluated.

Martin Van Buren (1837–1841)

A founder of the Democratic Party, Martin Van Buren gained considerable political experience by serving his home state of New York as state senator, attorney general, governor, and U.S. senator. He also served as secretary of state and minister to Great Britain during Jackson's first term and vice president during Jackson's second. Like Jackson, Van Buren opposed a strong federal government and did not favor government intervention in the U.S. economy. Of his cabinet members, Jackson most often turned to Van Buren for advice. Van Buren played an impor-

Martin Van Buren (1782–1862). Democratic Party president from 1837 to 1841, Van Buren witnessed the Panic of 1837. LIBRARY OF CONGRESS

tant role in getting Jackson elected in 1828 and 1832 and associated with Old Hickory socially as well as politically. For these reasons Jackson chose Van Buren to succeed him as president. Having received the blessing of the enormously popular outgoing president, Van Buren was easily elected to the presidency in 1836.

Although Van Buren greatly admired Jackson and strove to follow in his footsteps, he lacked many of the assets that had made Jackson the darling of the American people. A man of unimpressive physical stature and quiet demeanor, Van Buren was a career politician who had never served in the military. Moreover, he was linked politically with a group in New York known as the Albany Regency, and his reputation for political craftiness had earned him the nicknames "the Sage of Kinderhook," "the Little Magician," and "the Red Fox," the latter designation a reference to his reddish gold sideburns as well as to his political skill. To make matters worse, Van Buren was plagued by an economic depression that lasted for the duration of his term in office.

The panic of 1837 was brought on by a number of interrelated events, including Jackson's removal of federal deposits from the Bank of the United States, a financial panic in Europe that led European investors to withdraw their funds from American enterprises, and widespread crop failures throughout the United States. The result was the foreclosure on thousands of American farms and the bankruptcy of hundreds of state and local banks. A distraught populace looked to Washington to take action, but the few measures Van Buren undertook, such as borrowing money to pay government debts and demanding that federal taxes be paid only in gold or silver instead of paper money, probably only heightened the depression's deleterious effects. His one major attempt to end the panic, which was his only significant legislative victory, came in 1840, when he succeeded after a four-year struggle in getting Congress to pass a bill creating an independent treasury system. This system established a national banking network without placing control of the network in the hands of a financial elite, which had been Jackson's primary objection to the Bank of the United States.

Because Van Buren lacked Jackson's charisma, he was unable to placate the American public during the dark days of the panic. His political problems were compounded by opposition within his own party over his refusal to support the annexation of Texas and by the U.S. Army's inability to quickly terminate a war with the Seminole Indians in Florida. Van Buren's public failures and personal shortcomings left him vulnerable to attack during the election of 1840. His political opponents accused him of being an aristocrat, which in the Age of Jackson was the most damning charge of all. When Van Buren left the White House in 1841, the stature of the presidency was significantly lower than it had been when he assumed the office four years earlier.

William Henry Harrison (1841)

Sensing that Van Buren's political and personal weaknesses presented it with an excellent chance to win the presidential election of 1840, the Whig Party searched diligently for a candidate who resembled Jackson as much as possible. The party leaders rejected the candidacy of Henry Clay, a career politician and one of the party's founders, in favor of William Henry Harrison. Like Jackson, Harrison was a former general who had achieved distinction against the British during the War of 1812, a successful Indian fighter who was nationally known for his victory over the Indians of the Old Northwest at the Battle of Tippecanoe, and a longtime resident of the West, in Harrison's case Ohio. Also like Jackson, Harrison was a man of considerable means, but his political handlers portrayed him as a simple man of the people. He was widely touted as having an abiding fondness for log cabins and hard cider, neither of which was particularly true. Nevertheless, the campaign ploy worked, and Harrison easily defeated Van Buren to capture the White House.

Although the candidate Harrison closely resembled Jackson, the president Harrison did not. The Whigs had come into being to oppose what they considered Jackson's heavy-handed, imperious style, and a strong president was precisely what party leaders did not want. Harrison, his years advanced and his health suspect, was all too happy to oblige. His inaugural speech, most of which was written for him by Daniel Webster, another party founder and Harrison's secretary of state, clearly indicated that he considered the president merely the first among equals in the cabinet. Furthermore, during his brief administration all matters requiring a presidential decision were put before the cabinet for a vote, with the majority prevailing.

One month after taking office Harrison died of pneumonia, which he supposedly contracted because he had stood in the snow without a hat during his inaugural ceremonies. Had he lived to complete his term in office, he clearly would have presided over a substantial weakening of the power and prestige of his office. Indeed, the Whigs seemed intent on transforming the president into a prime minister of the European variety, thus effectively placing the locus of power on Capitol Hill rather than in the White House. At any rate, Harrison's occupation of the presidency, because of its extremely limited duration, neither strengthened nor weakened the office to an appreciable degree.

John Tyler (1841–1845)

Harrison's death elevated his vice president, John Tyler, to the presidency, the first time such an event had occurred. A Virginia aristocrat, Tyler had served his home state as a state legislator, U.S. representative and senator, and governor. A strong believer in states' rights, he was a Democrat until he broke with the party because he considered Jackson too egalitarian and high-handed. He was chosen by the Whigs to be Harrison's running mate because they hoped he would generate enthusiasm for the ticket throughout the South, where the Whigs were weak.

Although Tyler's background differed greatly from Jackson's, he believed like Jackson that the nation should be governed by a strong president in charge of a passive federal government. Immediately following Harrison's death the Democrats insisted that Tyler was merely the acting president, calling him "His Accidency," and therefore not competent to exercise

John Tyler (1790–1862). Called "His Accidency" by his opponents, Tyler was the first vice president to become president as a result of the death of a sitting president. Photographic print, c. 1860. LIBRARY OF CONGRESS: PRINTS AND PHOTOGRAPHS DIVISION

the full duties of the office. But Tyler rejected that line of reasoning and succeeded in claiming presidential privileges and performing presidential duties. Although he signed into law a bill abolishing Van Buren's independent treasury system, he vetoed a Whig-sponsored measure to create a new Bank of the United States. After he vetoed several internal-improvement projects dear to the hearts of Whigs, they expelled him from the party, and his entire cabinet save one member resigned in protest. Undaunted, Tyler appointed a new cabinet composed of former Democrats whose political views were more in keeping with his own.

For the rest of his term in office Tyler was a president without a party, the Whigs having disowned him and the Democrats refusing to recognize the legitimacy of his administration. In addition the House of Representatives censured Tyler because of his economic policies. Nevertheless, he presided over a number of accomplishments during his administration, including the reorganization of the navy, the termination of the Seminole War, the suppression and successful reconciliation of a civil disturbance in Rhode Island, the signing of a treaty authorizing the annexation of Texas, and the establishment of diplomatic relations and favorable trading privileges with China. The partisan brouhaha resulting from Tyler's refusal to play politics ensured that he would be a one-term president. Although he was a strong leader, his term did not strengthen the presidency appreciably other than to smooth the way for future vice presidents succeeding to the office after the death of a chief executive.

James K. Polk (1845–1849)

In 1844 three party regulars, Martin Van Buren, Lewis Cass, and James Buchanan, sought the Democratic nomination for president, but none of them could muster enough support to capture it. On the ninth ballot cast at their national convention the Democrats chose as their standard-bearer James K. Polk, the first dark horse candidate in U.S. history. Although Polk had no military background, he like Jackson had pursued a political career in Tennessee, where he served as state legislator, U.S. representative, and governor. His two primary qualifications for the nomination were his workmanlike performance as

James K. Polk (1795–1849) The Mexican War was fought during Polk's one-term presidency. LIBRARY OF CONGRESS

speaker of the House and his close personal friendship with Jackson, who was Polk's mentor throughout his early career and who enthusiastically endorsed Polk's candidacy. So powerful was Jackson's influence upon Polk that the latter was sometimes referred to as "Young Hickory."

Also like Jackson, Polk had a forceful personality. Although Henry Clay, the Whig nominee for president, refused to commit himself to a clear stand for or against the annexation of Texas and Oregon, Polk unhesitatingly demanded that the United States acquire both territories. His clear stance reflected the popular mood of the American public and propelled him to a close but decisive victory over Clay.

As president Polk exercised complete control over the executive branch. He filled his cabinet with trusted, competent men who obeyed his instructions almost without question. His experience as speaker of the House enabled him to push for legislation that had a good chance of passage and to relent when measures he favored did not have sufficient support. Like Jackson, he regarded himself as the direct representative of the American people, and he was not reluctant to veto congressional measures that he thought were contrary to the best interests of the populace.

Polk envisioned a United States that stretched from coast to coast, and he pursued policies that permitted his vision to become reality. He settled the question of Oregon, which the British also claimed, by agreeing to split that territory along the forty-ninth parallel, which constituted the boundary between the United States and Canada east of the Rocky Mountains. The Texas question was settled in part by his predecessor, Tyler, who signed a bill admitting Texas into the Union just days before Polk's inauguration. However, Polk also believed that the United States should exercise jurisdiction over California and New Mexico, both of which were integral parts of Mexico. He allowed a dispute, which his critics claimed he engineered, with Mexico over the boundary between that country and Texas to escalate into the Mexican War, then he personally developed the military strategy that resulted in a decisive American victory. In these matters Polk demonstrated clearly the enormous administrative powers available to the president in time of war, a lesson that later presidents, especially Abraham Lincoln, would put to good use while prosecuting other conflicts. Finally, he successfully managed, although not without difficulty, the treaty negotiations with Mexico in an effort to appease those Americans who wanted to annex all of Mexico as well as those who did not favor the acquisition of any Mexican territory. The addition of such vast quantities of real estate reopened the question of the spread of slavery, which the Missouri Compromise had presumably settled once and for all more than twenty years earlier. Consequently, Polk was forced to contend with diametrically opposed sectional views regarding the advisability of the treaty, which neither he nor his successors were able to reconcile.

Polk's leadership as president resulted in the settlement of other matters related to foreign affairs. A treaty with New Granada (modern-day Colombia) granted U.S. citizens access to the Isthmus of Panama, and a treaty with Great Britain established lower tariffs on British manufacturing goods, thus placating both the British and the South. He also convinced Congress to create the Department of the Interior to manage the territories acquired during his administration.

Had Polk served a second term, he might have found a way to use his formidable political skills to mediate the sectional crisis over slavery and thus avoid the Civil War. But failing health precluded him from running for reelection. Instead of further securing the Jacksonian model as the standard for future presidents to follow, Polk's retirement after one term opened the door of the White House to a string of eminently forgettable occupants.

Conclusion

In terms of the presidency, the period between 1829 and 1849 was clearly the Age of Jackson. Old Hickory transformed the presidency by making it the federal office most responsive to the will of the American people. Jackson's charisma, energy, and military style of leadership made him one of the most popular presidents in U.S. history, and the presidents who came after him attempted to follow in his footsteps. None was able to dominate to the same extent and for the same duration as Jackson. Van Buren, whose political skills might have allowed him to achieve considerable success if not a Jacksonian measure of popularity, could not overcome the bad fortune of a major depression. Harrison's disinclination to lead and untimely death ensured his relegation to the back ranks of presidential effectiveness. Tyler's refusal to cooperate with members of his own party precluded him from winning a term in his own right. Polk, who most closely resembled Jackson in terms of philosophy, energy, and effectiveness, was forced for reasons of health to step aside prematurely. Not until 1861, when Lincoln took office, would the presidency again be occupied by a leader of Jackson's stature.

See also **Banking and Finance,** *subentry on* **The Politics of Banking; Elections,** *subentry on* **Presidential Elections; Expansion; Foreign Relations,** *subentry on* **1789–1860; Jacksonian Era; Mexican War; Oregon; Panics** and Depressions; Politics, *subentries on* The First Party System, The Second Party System; Texas.

Bibliography

Cunliffe, Marcus. *American Presidents and the Presidency.* 2d. ed., revised and enlarged. New York: McGraw-Hill, 1976.

McDonald, Forrest. *The American Presidency: An Intellectual History.* Lawrence: University Press of Kansas, 1994.

Peterson, Norma Lois. *The Presidencies of William Henry Harrison and John Tyler.* Lawrence: University Press of Kansas, 1989.

Quaife, Milo Milton, ed. *The Diary of James K. Polk during His Presidency, 1845 to 1849.* Chicago: A. C. McClurg, 1910.

Remini, Robert V. *The Life of Andrew Jackson.* New York: Harper and Row, 1988.

Wilson, Major L. *The Presidency of Martin Van Buren.* Lawrence: University Press of Kansas, 1984.

CHARLES W. CAREY JR.

1849–1861

Between 1829 and 1849, the presidency was dominated first by the person, and then by the shadow, of Andrew Jackson. Of the three other elected presidents who served during this period, two—Martin Van Buren and James Polk—were protégés of Jackson, and one—William Henry Harrison—was nominated in part because, as a war hero, he resembled Jackson. The leadership failures of these presidents set the stage for the crisis of the 1850s and the Civil War of the 1860s.

From 1849 to 1861 Jackson's legacy continued to affect the presidency. However, the failure of leadership continued, and increased, with each president being less competent and successful than his predecessor.

Two of the elected presidents in this period, Franklin Pierce and James Buchanan, had been early supporters of Jackson. Pierce even acquired a Jacksonian nickname, "Young Hickory." The only non-Democrat elected in this period, Zachary Taylor, resembled Jackson as a war hero and general. The fourth president in this period (and the second non-elected president in U.S. history), Millard Fillmore, ended up much like John Tyler (the first nonelected president), disaffected from his party and with political support only in the slave states. None of the presidents in this period provided the forceful, Jackson-like leadership that might have guided the nation away from the crisis that ultimately led to secession and civil war. Only Taylor, the former general, had the potential to do this, and he died sixteen months into his term.

For the first time in American history northerners,

and nonslave owners, controlled the presidency for a sustained period of time. However, all three northern presidents—Fillmore, Pierce, and Buchanan—were classic "doughfaces": northern men with southern principles. They surrounded themselves with proslavery advisers like Jefferson Davis, John B. Floyd, and Howell Cobb while ignoring the antislavery sentiments within their parties and throughout the North. All three presidents attempted to vigorously enforce the Fugitive Slave Law of 1850, and all three worked to allow, or even encourage, the spread of slavery into the West. During the Civil War all three became vocal opponents of Lincoln, the war effort, and, most of all, emancipation.

The Sectional Crisis

The Mexican War (1846–1848) left the United States in possession of vast new western territories. Even before the war was over, the status of slavery in these territories had emerged as the central political issue of the moment. Serious political debate began in 1846 when David Wilmot, a Pennsylvania Democrat, offered an amendment to an appropriations bill—known as the Wilmot Proviso—which declared "Provided, That, as an express and fundamental condition to the acquisition of any territory from the Republic of Mexico by the United States, by virtue of any treaty which may be negotiated between them, and to the use by the Executive of the moneys herein appropriated, neither slavery nor involuntary servitude, shall exist in any part of the said territory." The Proviso passed the House in 1846 and 1847 but died in the Senate, where the South had a majority. The proviso nevertheless set the tone for the presidential election of 1848.

President Polk proposed extending the Missouri Compromise line into the new territories, which would have made California a slave state; southern nationalists, personified by Senators John C. Calhoun of South Carolina and Jefferson Davis of Mississippi, wanted all the new territories—indeed, all existing territories—opened to slavery. Mainstream northern Democrats, led by Lewis Cass of Michigan, who would be the party's presidential candidate in 1848, wanted to allow the settlers of the territories to decide the issue through something called popular sovereignty. Many northern Whigs, and a good number of northern Democrats, like Wilmot, wanted to ban slavery in all the new territories. When Polk left office, the issue was still undecided.

The territorial question led to the creation of a new, and formidable, party, the Free Soil Party. Led by former president Martin Van Buren, who had now abandoned the proslavery policies he implemented as president, the party appealed to many northern Democrats, who were tired of constantly having to please the southern majority in their party. Van Buren won no states as the Free Soil presidential candidate in 1848, but his 291,263 popular votes came mostly from Democrats, and probably cost Cass the election. Ironically, this antislavery party helped propel a slaveowner, Zachary Taylor, into the White House. Even more ironic, Taylor was less friendly to slavery than any other president up to that time except John Adams and John Quincy Adams.

Zachary Taylor (1849–1850)

In 1848 the Whig Party nominated Zachary Taylor, the son of a minor Kentucky politician, who, like Jackson, was a victorious general. He had earned the nickname "Old Rough and Ready" during the Second Seminole War, and emerged from the Mexican War as a national hero after he repeatedly crushed the numerically superior Mexicans in a number of battles, conquering the northern portion of that country as a result. Even opponents of the war could admire his victories over unfavorable odds. Unlike Jackson, who had gained some rudimentary experience in politics at the state and national level before running for president, Taylor had no political background whatsoever. Indeed, he had never even voted in a presidential election before 1848. By nominating Taylor, the Whigs followed the route they had used in their only previous successful presidential campaign, when they ran William Henry Harrison, also a successful general, although one with far more political experience.

Losing to Taylor was Lewis Cass of Michigan, a longtime party regular with an undistinguished political record. Like Jackson, Cass had been a general in the War of 1812, and he had served as Jackson's secretary of war from 1831 to 1836. The spoiler, as noted above, was Martin Van Buren, running on the Free Soil ticket.

The most serious problem Taylor faced as president was the question of how to organize the territories acquired from Mexico. The problem was also urgent. The discovery of gold in California in 1848 had led to a huge influx of settlers. But, because of the stalemate over the Wilmot Proviso, Congress had been unable to create any government for that region, or any of the other new territories. By 1849 California had more than the sixty thousand settlers required for statehood, and by the end of the year an ad hoc convention in Monterey had drawn up a constitution that prohibited slavery. Southerners were virtually unanimous in opposition to a free California. A free California would tip the balance in the

Senate in favor of the North, and with no new slave states likely to be admitted soon, free state domination of both houses of Congress would probably become permanent.

Taylor pushed for immediate statehood for California and New Mexico, thus avoiding the issue of slavery in territories, at least for those places. However, at the time everyone expected both to vote for freedom. Complicating this was a claim by Texas to a substantial portion of what later became the state of New Mexico. Taylor promised to defend slavery where it existed; as a Louisiana sugar planter, no one could accuse him of being a secret abolitionist. But he was also determined to protect the borders of New Mexico from overly enthusiastic Texans, and to allow the people of both California and New Mexico to create free states, because that was clearly what they wanted. Despite the efforts of several delegations from both sides to modify his stand, some by threatening to secede from the Union if their wishes were not upheld, Taylor refused, and indicated that he would meet disunion with force of arms. Like Jackson, Taylor stood ready to confront southern radicals and, like Jackson, he was able to stare them down.

His position on the Wilmot Proviso further agitated the South. Consistent with Whig deference to Congress, Taylor said he would sign a bill with a proviso in it, even though he thought such a proviso potentially dangerous, probably useless, and surely unnecessary. Further annoying to the South were Taylor's close ties to William H. Seward, a leading New York Whig with strong and well-known antislavery views.

In 1850 Congress began to debate what would eventually become the Compromise of 1850. Taylor opposed some of the compromise, and was clearly ambivalent about a new and harsher fugitive slave law. He correctly believed that the debate over the whole package was slowing California statehood, which was his highest priority, as well as interfering with New Mexico statehood. He did not indicate any strong opposition to the compromise, as long as it did not cede large portions of New Mexico to Texas, but he did not want to hold California hostage to the other issues, including the divisive fugitive slave bill. In June 1850 Texas made preparations to invade New Mexico, and Taylor forcefully responded that he would send the U.S. Army to the disputed region to protect New Mexico. This once again put an end to threats of violence from the slave South. Had Taylor not died a month later (July 9, 1850), it is likely that most of the provisions of the compromise would have been passed and he would have signed them, but the harshness of the fugitive slave law might have been diminished, at least in part because southern

threats of disunion would have been met with Jackson-like promises of military intervention by a successful and skilled former general.

Taylor's foreign policy was more successful than his domestic agenda; he never lived to see California statehood, his main goal. He won minor disputes with France and Portugal, and in the Clayton–Bulwer Treaty with Great Britain, he obtained canal rights for the United States in Central America. He refused to be pushed into filibustering adventures against Cuba, despite the hopes of southerners that the United States would seize the island, with its huge slave population and fertile land, from Spain. Taylor stopped at least one filibustering expedition; and when another failed, leading to the capture of fifty-two Americans, he was able to negotiate their release. On the northern border, he was equally firm in convincing Americans not to interfere in the internal politics of Canada.

Taylor was further troubled by a cabinet that proved to be more of a liability than an asset. With the exception of Secretary of State John Middleton Clayton and Attorney General Reverdy Johnson, they were a thoroughly undistinguished group who had been thrust upon Taylor by party leaders. As a result of a ruling by Attorney General Johnson, Taylor's secretary of war, George W. Crawford of Georgia, received a legal fee of $115,000 (an astounding sum at the time) for work he had done before entering the cabinet. Though perfectly legal, this huge payment smacked of corruption. As a result of this scandal, Taylor supposedly decided to fire his entire cabinet and restock it with men of a higher caliber. He died suddenly before he could take such an action.

Taylor's sixteen months in office did little to enhance the prestige of the presidency. His background, lack of political experience, and forceful opposition to anything that resembled treason or secession were reminiscent of Jackson. But his short time in office, his weak cabinet, and his lack of a large popular following left him with a weak legacy. Nevertheless, he was probably the strongest president of the decade, and had he survived, the direction of politics might have been different.

Millard Fillmore (1850–1853)

Taylor's untimely death elevated Millard Fillmore to the presidency. Fillmore was born into abject poverty, and as a child was virtually illiterate. With the help of his wife, Abigail Powers, he became relatively well educated, taught school, opened a law office, and became a successful attorney in Buffalo, New York. He rose in politics as a Whig Party leader, serving in the state legislature and in Congress, where he

Millard Fillmore (1800–1874). Whig president from 1850 to 1853, Fillmore took office upon the death of Zachary Taylor. Fillmore signed the Compromise of 1850, which included the highly controversial Fugitive Slave Act of 1850. Photo by Mathew Brady. LIBRARY OF CONGRESS: PRINTS AND PHOTOGRAPHS DIVISION

became a protégé of Henry Clay, one of the founders of the Whigs. He was serving as state comptroller when, much to his surprise, the Whigs chose him as Taylor's running mate, partly because Clay pushed his candidacy and partly because he balanced the ticket geographically.

Fillmore replaced Taylor's entire cabinet with men of a higher caliber; among the newcomers were Daniel Webster and John Crittenden, who had served as secretary of state and attorney general, respectively, during the Harrison and Tyler administrations. Initially Fillmore seems to have been able to avoid being controlled by his cabinet without alienating the Whig Party, which Tyler had failed to do. He set about putting an end to the sectional crisis by urging Congress to pass the various measures that made up the Compromise of 1850, and it did so.

Fillmore was opposed to the expansion of slavery into the territories won from Mexico in 1848. In New York his chief political rival had been William H. Seward, who was aggressively antislavery. Fillmore

appealed to those less concerned about the issue. As president, when forced to choose sides, he invariably lined up with conservatives and the South. One exception was the Texas–New Mexico border dispute. Following Taylor's policies, Fillmore sent fifteen hundred soldiers to protect New Mexico's territorial integrity.

Fillmore supported the passage of the Fugitive Slave Law of 1850 and aggressively enforced it. For example, his secretary of state, Daniel Webster, went to Syracuse, New York—the heart of abolition country—where he promised that the fugitive slave law would soon be enforced. The administration then worked with a Missourian to arrest a fugitive named Jerry McHenry in Syracuse in October 1851. This led to one of the most famous rescues of the decade—the "Jerry Rescue"—which embarrassed the Fillmore administration throughout the North. In response to armed resistance by fugitive slaves at Christiana, Pennsylvania, in which a slaveowner was killed trying to seize his runaway slave, Fillmore's aggressive action led to the arrest of more than forty men who had refused to help the U.S. marshal. With Fillmore and his attorney general directly involved in the case, the local U.S. attorney had thirty-eight men indicted for treason. What would have been the largest treason trial in U.S. history collapsed when U.S. Supreme Court Justice Robert Grier ruled that opposition to a law did not constitute making war on the United States. Fillmore's fugitive slave policy gained him great support in the South, but doomed his chance to run on his own as a Whig in 1852.

Fillmore's greatest success in foreign affairs involved Commodore Matthew C. Perry's diplomatic mission to Japan. For this historic voyage, Fillmore assigned to Perry a naval force that included almost one tenth of the men then serving in the U.S. military. As a result of the impressive showing this armada made, Japan began to end its self-imposed isolation from the West by opening its doors ever so slightly to American trade. Like Taylor, Fillmore opposed filibustering efforts to start a revolution in Cuba, and was able to negotiate the release of 160 Americans captured after yet another failed invasion of Cuba. However, he refused to sign a multilateral treaty with Britain and France promising not to annex Cuba.

Fillmore failed to gain the Whig nomination in 1852. His only support at the convention came from the South, which rewarded his vigorous enforcement of the fugitive slave law. Northern Whigs totally rejected him. In 1856 he ran on the anti-Catholic Know-Nothing ticket, getting only Maryland's eight electoral votes and about 21 percent of the popular vote. In 1856, almost all of his support came from the South, where he carried 43 percent of the popular vote. He initially supported the effort to maintain the Union during the Civil War, though he continued to believe that the root cause of the war was not slaveholding secessionists but Republicans and anti-slavery agitators. After Lincoln moved firmly against slavery, Fillmore denounced the administration and the war effort. He campaigned for the Democratic candidate, George B. McClellan, in 1864 and was now willing to see the South leave the Union. He was, as his critics said in 1850, a doughface to the end.

Franklin Pierce (1853–1857)

When the Democratic convention of 1852 deadlocked over the choice among three party regulars, the party's nomination for president was finally given to Franklin Pierce. A native of New Hampshire, Pierce

Franklin Pierce (1804–1869). Pierce gained the Democratic nomination because he was a northerner who supported slavery. His term (1853–1857) was marked by passage of the Kansas-Nebraska Act, which led to a mini–civil war known as Bleeding Kansas. Portrait taken as Democratic candidate for president in 1853. LIBRARY OF CONGRESS

had represented that state in the House and Senate, but he was virtually unknown in the rest of the country. Having served briefly and without distinction as a brigadier general during the Mexican War, he came as close as any Democrat to resembling the nation's last great president, Andrew Jackson. However, the resemblance ended there; Pierce lacked the forceful demeanor of Jackson, possessing instead a more convivial and superficial personality. Despite being little known, Pierce was elected president, largely because the Democratic platform took a strong stand in favor of the Compromise of 1850, whereas the Whigs were in total disarray. His Whig opponent, Winfield Scott, failed to excite anyone in what was truly a boring campaign. Pierce won 254 electoral votes to Scott's 42. But this lopsided victory was deceiving. Pierce had less than fifty thousand more votes than the combined total of Scott and the Free Soil candidate, John Parker Hale.

Pierce's greatest challenge as president was the sectional crisis growing out of the Compromise of 1850. His first attempt to seek peace was the appointment of representatives of various segments of his party in a geographically balanced cabinet. Pierce, however, ignored both the Young America faction of the Democratic Party, best represented by Senator Stephen A. Douglas of Illinois, and the strong antislavery wing, led by senators Salmon P. Chase and Hannibal Hamlin. These antislavery Democrats would bolt the party in 1854–1855 to create the new Republican Party. The slave South, on the other hand, was strongly represented by Secretary of War Jefferson Davis of Mississippi, and Secretary of the Treasury James Guthrie of Kentucky.

In his inaugural address Pierce endorsed the Compromise of 1850, and foolishly acted as if it had settled, forever, the problem of slavery in the United States. Limited in his vision, and unable to comprehend northern hatred for slavery, he probably believed this as well.

Like the last Democratic president, James Polk, Pierce sought to expand the United States. Working closely with Secretary of War Davis, he secured more land from Mexico through the Gadsden Purchase, in order to prepare for a southern route for a transcontinental railroad. He encouraged American annexation of uninhabited islands in the Pacific, under the Guano Islands Act of 1856, and thus embarked on the creation of America's first overseas empire. He failed, however, in his attempts to annex the Sandwich Islands (Hawaii), at least part of the Dominican Republic, and, most important of all, Cuba. In 1854 his representatives in Europe, in a secret memo that was leaked to the press as the Ostend Manifesto, indicated that the United States was prepared to use force to seize Cuba if annexation failed. Northerners viewed this policy as part of Pierce's overall proslavery strategy.

Meanwhile, William Walker, a proslavery American soldier of fortune, seized control of Nicaragua in 1855 and set himself up as dictator. Pierce extended official recognition to Walker's regime in 1856, thereby outraging Latin Americans, the British (who had extensive interests in Central America), and opponents of slavery alike. Continuing negotiations with the British over the provisions of the Clayton-Bulwer Treaty were handled poorly; Pierce tried to use trade agreements in the treaty to set the stage for the annexation of Canada.

Dovetailing with Pierce's disastrous foreign policy was a catastrophic policy on slavery in the territories that led to a rehearsal for the Civil War in Kansas. In 1854 Congress passed the Kansas-Nebraska Act, which Pierce supported in return for senatorial approval of his appointments and foreign treaties. The act stipulated that the transcontinental railroad should take a northerly route. To gain southern support for this route, the act allowed the settlers of the territory, under a theory called "popular sovereignty," to decide the issue of slavery for themselves. This act thus repealed the slavery ban in the Missouri Compromise for most of the remaining territory of the Louisiana Purchase. The result was a mini–Civil War in Kansas between anti- and proslavery forces over the establishment of a state government, thus escalating the antagonism between North and South to a dangerous new level. Thousands of "border ruffians" entered Kansas from Missouri, voting in fraudulent elections and killing some free state settlers. Northerners fought back with armed bands such as one led by John Brown.

Rather than easing the sectional crisis, Pierce's shortsighted and ill-advised solutions served only to exacerbate it. Pierce fired the first territorial governor, Andrew H. Reeder, because he would not support the proslavery faction, even though it was clearly a minority in the territory. His replacement, Wilson Shannon, was blatantly proslavery but ultimately incompetent. Finally, in September 1856 John White Geary, a former mayor of San Francisco, brought order to Kansas through the judicious use of federal troops.

The public fury that the Kansas-Nebraska Act unleashed worked against Pierce in the congressional election of 1854, in which the Democrats performed woefully. As a result, Pierce received little support from Congress during the last two years of his term; of his nine vetoes, five were overridden, one of the highest ratios of unsuccessful presidential vetoes in U.S. history and a clear indication of Pierce's ineffectiveness as president.

In supporting the Kansas-Nebraska Act, Pierce callously rejected the principles of the Missouri Compromise. Although this pleased his southern supporters, especially Secretary of War Jefferson Davis, it infuriated huge numbers of northerners, who left the Democratic Party and the moribund Whig Party to form a new political organization. Initially called "Anti-Nebraska Men," both the leaders and the rank and file soon called their organization the Republican Party. In the 1854 midterm elections, Republicans, as well as nativist Know-Nothings (American Party) emerged as powerful parties in the North, while the Whigs all but disappeared. Indicative of the new party alignments was the speaker of the House in the new Congress, Nathaniel P. Banks of Massachusetts. He had served in the 33d Congress (1853–1855) as a Democrat, but returned in 1855 as a Know-Nothing, and was the first speaker in anyone's memory to oppose slavery. In the following Congress, the 35th, he would serve as a Republican.

Indicative of Pierce's poor political judgment was his confidence that he would be nominated for a second term in 1856. At the Democratic convention in Cincinnati, Pierce ran second to James Buchanan for fourteen ballots; then all his supporters shifted to Stephen A. Douglas on the fifteenth and sixteenth ballots. However, on the seventeenth ballot the convention nominated James Buchanan, a sixty-five-year-old professional politician who had held one public office or another for more than forty years. He had been a congressman, a senator, secretary of state, and an ambassador. A lifelong bachelor, he had shared his Washington lodging with a series of southerners, and was as sympathetic to slavery as most southerners. He had supported allowing slavery in the territories and had been instrumental in trying to annex Cuba, which would have added more slaves, and more potential plantation lands, to the nation. Indeed, on slavery he was the ultimate doughface. Buchanan's most important asset was his absence from the country, as ambassador to Great Britain, throughout Pierce's administration. Thus, he was not held accountable for the utter failure of Pierce and had made no enemies within the party during the previous four years. The party rejected the charismatic and nationally popular Stephen A. Douglas, who would probably have been a far more able and successful president. But Buchanan was safe and reliable, as reflected in his nickname, "Old Buck."

Facing Buchanan were John C. Frémont, running under the banner of the new Republican Party, and a former president, Millard Fillmore, running on the anti-immigrant American, or Know-Nothing, Party.

The election was essentially two separate contests. In the South, Buchanan ran against Fillmore. The Republicans, committed to stopping the spread of slavery in the West, were an insignificant force in the upper South and not on the ballot in the deep South. All three candidates were on the ballot in the North, but the contest was between Buchanan and Frémont. Buchanan carried every slave state but Maryland, and Frémont carried eleven of the sixteen free states. Pierce, meanwhile, finished his term and faded into obscurity, attacking Lincoln during the Civil War and opposing emancipation. As one of his biographers, Larry Gara, concluded, his administration was "a disaster."

James Buchanan (1857–1861)

Buchanan viewed his election as a mandate to fully implement the southern position on the territories

James Buchanan (1791–1868). Buchanan's presidency is generally considered to be the most unsuccessful in U.S. history. By the time Buchanan left office, seven states had seceded from the Union and the nation was headed toward civil war. LIBRARY OF CONGRESS

and to open all of them to slavery. He further believed that he should work to ensure the sectional balance in the Senate by encouraging the creation of new slave states. His cabinet contained four southerners, including Howell Cobb of Georgia and John B. Floyd of Virginia, and two prominent northern doughfaces, but no one from the Douglas wing of his party. This put Buchanan on the road to one of the least successful presidencies in U.S. history.

On his way to the podium to deliver his inaugural address, Buchanan briefly chatted in whispers with Chief Justice Roger Taney. He then urged in his speech that the nation accept the pending Supreme Court decision in *Dred Scott v. Sandford* (1857) on the status of slavery in the territories. Republicans would later charge that in this brief chat Taney told him the Court would strike down all bans on slavery in the territories. Whether Taney told him this will never be known, but we now know that Buchanan already had learned about the pending decision from other justices on the court who were his longtime Democratic allies and friends. *Dred Scott* did not, however, help Buchanan much. It merely energized Republicans to oppose him more vigorously. In the midterm election of 1858 the new party, unalterably committed to stopping the spread of slavery, would take control of the House of Representatives.

Buchanan exacerbated sectional tensions by trying to bring Kansas into the Union as a slave state. His appointed territorial governor, Robert J. Walker, although a slaveowner, was determined to administer the law fairly and to ensure a fair election. Walker did not believe slavery could survive in Kansas, and for that he was vilified in the South. When he tried to prevent a fraudulently elected proslavery legislature from taking office in 1857, Buchanan refused to support him. The proslavery legislature called a constitutional convention to meet at Lecompton, Kansas. Free staters substantially outnumbered supporters of slavery, but the six proslavery counties had thirty-seven delegates at the convention, whereas the thirty free soil counties had only twenty-seven delegates. The convention then wrote a proslavery constitution, and when it was submitted for ratification, there was no mechanism for the people to vote against statehood under this constitution.

When Buchanan tried to force Congress to admit Kansas under the Lecompton Constitution, members of his own party, led by Stephen A. Douglas, balked. Douglas favored popular sovereignty and was no opponent of slavery—his wife in fact owned slaves. But he would not tolerate a fraud that mocked popular sovereignty and democratic institutions. In Congress, Republicans combined with Douglas democrats to defeat Kansas statehood under the Lecompton Constitution. Buchanan then tried to bribe the people of Kansas, offering Kansas millions of acres of public land and immediate statehood if the population endorsed the Lecompton Constitution. In the only fair election in Kansas during this period, the voters defeated the constitution 11,300 to 1,788.

Buchanan now turned his wrath on Douglas and the other anti-Lecompton Democrats. In the Senate, Douglas lost his chairmanship of the powerful Committee on the Territories, and in the 1858 election Buchanan tried to unseat Douglas and his allies. The strategy backfired as administration Democrats were defeated throughout the North, and the new House of Representatives was badly fractured. When southern Fire-Eaters refused to support a northern Democrat as speaker, the Douglas Democrats in the House helped elect a Republican speaker. Buchanan further alienated the North by vetoing a homestead act and supporting a congressional bill to establish a slave code in the federal territories. Similarly, he supported a tariff bill favorable to the South. Ever the doughface, he sought thirty million dollars from Congress to purchase Cuba and turned a blind eye to filibustering activities in Nicaragua by William Walker, who claimed in fact that Buchanan secretly supported his attempts to seize Nicaragua in order to turn it into an American colony. Consistent with his proslavery foreign policy, Buchanan tacitly gave protection to the illegal African slave trade by threatening to use force if the British navy stopped suspected slavers flying the American flag. At the same time, he refused to use American ships to stop the illegal trade.

Republicans in Congress investigated corruption in the War Department, and the Buchanan-appointed postmaster in New York fled the country after stealing $160,000 from the government. The Panic of 1857 further undermined his administration. Northerners blamed the panic on the Tariff of 1857, which had been passed to please the South. Unable to break with his Jacksonian past, Buchanan tightened the money supply at the beginning of the panic, when in fact the economy needed more cash. The nation was barely out of the depression when the election of 1860 arrived.

Eight years of Pierce and Buchanan had finally forced the Democratic Party to implode. The majority of the party supported Douglas, the only Democrat capable of winning in the North. But his apostasy on the Lecompton Constitution was too much for the South to bear, and southern delegates nominated their own candidate, John C. Breckinridge of Kentucky. Disaffected Whigs and Know-Nothings nominated John Bell of Tennessee on a ticket that advocated the status quo. Republicans turned to Abraham Lincoln of Illinois. Although he was a newcomer with limited political experience, Lincoln had impressively challenged Douglas in the 1858 senatorial election in Illinois. More important, he had developed a sophisticated attack on the *Dred Scott* decision, Buchanan, and the Democrats that resonated throughout the North.

Buchanan backed Breckinridge, hoping Lincoln, Douglas, and Bell would split the northern vote and that no candidate would win the election outright. But, as he had throughout his presidency, Buchanan miscalculated. Lincoln carried every northern state, and was swept into office. In the last three months of his administration Buchanan presided over the breakup of the United States. In December 1860, South Carolina adopted an ordinance of secession. Southerners in his cabinet began to resign, although not before Secretary of War John B. Floyd tried to ship newly manufactured cannon to the southern states for use by their militias. Buchanan stood idly by, denouncing secession but doing nothing about it. Though he had been a Jacksonian since he served as Old Hickory's ambassador to Russia, Buchanan had none of the old hero's strength or nerve. Whereas Jackson had threatened to personally lead the army into South Carolina to confront nullification, Buchanan did nothing to stop secession.

On March 4, 1861, Buchanan left the presidency, and the nation, in disarray. He was the only president to see the size of the nation diminish while in office. His administration consisted of one failure after another. In the year 2000 a poll of historians rated him the worst president in U.S. history. It is a title he richly deserved.

Conclusion

With the possible exception of Zachary Taylor, the presidents who served between March 1849 and March 1861 were collectively the most incompetent in U.S. history. They lacked vision, creativity, and a sense of the issues they faced. Their names have rightly become synonymous with political ineptitude. The weakest of them all was Buchanan, who left the presidency, and the nation, in the worst situation it had ever been in. Ironically, he set the stage for a successor who turned out to be America's greatest president, and who in the end would redeem not only the office but also the promise of America itself.

See also **Bleeding Kansas; Compromise of 1850; Democratic Party; Federal-State Relations,** *subentry on* **1831–1865; Filibusters; Fugitive Slave Laws; Gadsden Purchase; Kansas-Nebraska Act; Panics and Depressions; Republican Party; Sectionalism; Whig Party.**

Bibliography

Bauer, K. Jack. *Zachary Taylor: Soldier, Planter, Statesman of the Old Southwest*. Baton Rouge: Louisiana State University Press, 1985.

Birkner, Michael J., ed. *James Buchanan and the Political Crisis of the 1850s*. Selinsgrove, Pa.: Susquehanna University Press, 1996.

Finkelman, Paul. *Dred Scott v. Sandford: A Brief History with Documents*. Boston: Bedford Books, 1997.

Gara, Larry. *The Presidency of Franklin Pierce*. Lawrence: University Press of Kansas, 1991.

Gienapp, William. *The Origins of the Republican Party, 1852–1856*. New York: Oxford University Press, 1987.

Holman, Hamilton. *Prologue to Conflict: The Crisis and Compromise of 1850*. Lexington: University of Kentucky Press, 1964.

Nichols, Roy F. *Franklin Pierce: Young Hickory of the Granite Hills*. Norwalk, Conn.: Easton Press, 1988.

Potter, David. *The Impending Crisis, 1848–1861*. New York: Harper & Row, 1976.

Rayback, Robert. *Millard Fillmore: Biography of a President*. Buffalo, N.Y.: Stewart, 1959.

Sewell, Richard H. *Ballots for Freedom: Antislavery Politics in the United States, 1837–1860*. New York: Norton, 1976.

Smith, Elbert B. *The Presidency of James Buchanan*. Lawrence: University Press of Kansas, 1975.

———. *The Presidencies of Zachary Taylor and Millard Fillmore*. Lawrence: University Press of Kansas, 1988.

PAUL FINKELMAN

1861–1877

Presidents Abraham Lincoln (1861–1865) and Andrew Johnson (1865–1869) dramatically expanded the powers of the presidency during the Civil War and Reconstruction era. However, Lincoln's claims of power were less expansive than usually portrayed, whereas Johnson's went much further. Johnson's actions so threatened the balance of power between the executive and legislative branches of government that the House of Representatives ultimately felt compelled to impeach him. Although the Senate acquitted Johnson by a single vote, the impeachment process fulfilled its purpose of restraining him. Ulysses S. Grant (1869–1877) attempted to be an activist president within an antebellum model but was unable to fulfill new law-enforcement responsibilities growing out of the Civil War. By 1877 the activist presidency was largely discredited.

Abraham Lincoln

Presidential Power

Abraham Lincoln was inaugurated sixteenth president of the United States on 4 March 1861. He had won the office as the candidate of the antislavery Republican Party, primarily on the issue of preventing slavery from expanding into the territories of the United States. The slaveholding Southern states reacted by passing ordinances of secession from the Union and creating the Confederate States of America.

Lincoln provided the strong executive leadership required to see the United States safely through the civil war that followed. His leadership was so forceful that some analysts have held that he established a "constitutional dictatorship." However, this interpretation greatly exaggerates Lincoln's claims and activities. Lincoln claimed inherent powers as chief executive of the United States and commander in chief of its armed forces. However, he never claimed that these powers superseded those of Congress.

For most of the years before he became president, Lincoln had adhered to the concept of the presidency expounded by the Whig Party, which had organized in response to President Andrew Jackson's aggressive use of presidential power from 1829 to 1837. Whigs insisted that it was Congress's business to establish public policy and the president's business to administer it. Despite their original ideology, however, Whigs had come to terms with the role presidents played in American politics. When their candidates won presidential elections, they expected them to provide party leadership and reward party loyalists with offices.

Lincoln's course had paralleled that of his party. As a Republican he continued to hold many Whig ideas. Like the Whigs, he had decidedly mixed attitudes toward presidential power; these were manifested during the four months between his election in November 1860 and his inauguration in March 1861. Seven Deep South states seceded between December and February. While lame-duck congressmen desperately tried to negotiate a compromise that would hold the nation together, Lincoln remained silent. In part this was a wise decision to refrain from advocating measures he had no governmental power to promote. It also was good politics to avoid becoming the focal point of the controversy before acquiring actual power. But Lincoln's course also comported with the Whig notion that public policy was primarily Congress's responsibility, not the president's.

Despite his reticence Lincoln acted forcefully when it appeared that Republican congressional negotiators might agree to give up the party's central plank opposing the expansion of slavery into the territories. He could never accept such a surrender, and in private he clearly warned Republicans against it. Lincoln was fulfilling the expectation that a president would provide political leadership to his party. Its leaders heeded his advice, and no Republican supported the proposal to expand slavery when it came up in Congress.

At the same time Lincoln fashioned a cabinet that met his responsibility as a Republican president to promote his party's influence and organization. He appointed William Henry Seward and Salmon P. Chase, his strongest competitors for the Republican presidential nomination, to head the most prestigious and powerful government departments: State and Treasury. These appointments also balanced regions and factions: Seward of New York represented the former Whig wing of the Republican Party, while Chase of Ohio represented the party's antislavery, radical Democrats.

Lincoln's other appointments similarly recognized party leaders and the need to balance regions and factions. It was up to the members of the cabinet to make appointments in their departments that would strengthen the party machinery. The customary rule was that the president and each department head could exercise his own discretion in making certain appointments. When making others, however, the members of the cabinet would consult with Republican congressmen and state party leaders. Lincoln set an example for his subordinates by replacing nearly all the Democratic officeholders removable at his discretion with loyal Republicans. Although individual cabinet members tended to favor one party group or another, in general they tried to carry out Lincoln's desire to balance intra-party interests. The exception was Chase, who used Treasury Department appointments to cement his own political alliances with various party factions in the states.

Through his influence over patronage, Lincoln made himself the unquestioned organizational leader of the Union Party, made up of Republicans and pro-war Democrats. Losers in factional quarrels blamed him and later tried to organize opposition to his renomination. Many of them turned to Chase as an alternative to Lincoln. But officeholders and party activists almost unanimously backed the president, guaranteeing that he would be renominated despite the scattered dissenters.

As a party leader Lincoln had strong influence in Congress. Although many congressmen were critical of his abilities and policies, on important matters he was able to get his way. One frustrated Republican critic, Henry Winter Davis, complained in 1865 that Congress had "dwindled from a power to dictate law and policy of the Government to a commission to audit accounts and appropriate moneys to enable the Executive to execute his will and not ours." Lincoln's control of patronage was an important element of this influence. After his reelection another disheartened radical opponent lamented that Lincoln "has just now all the great offices to give afresh & cant [*sic*] be successfully resisted. He is dictator."

Executive Power and the Civil War

In the stalemate that continued after his inauguration on 4 March 1861, Lincoln controlled federal policy, decided against calling Congress into a special session. As chief executive he believed it was up to him to determine how best to enforce the laws. Not wanting to appear the aggressor, he determined not to try to recover federal property or enforce federal law in the Deep South states that had formed the new Confederacy. But he also refused to give up the few places remaining in federal hands—especially Fort Sumter, in the harbor of Charleston, South Carolina. When Lincoln made it clear he would resupply the garrison there, South Carolinians precipitated war by opening fire on the fort. The attack galvanized support for war in the North, and Lincoln's restraint enabled Unionists to maintain control in Missouri, Delaware, Maryland, and Kentucky, with the aid of federal soldiers, even as other slaveholding states seceded and joined the Confederacy.

After fighting broke out, Lincoln refused to call Congress into session immediately, instead calling a special session to meet ten weeks later, on 4 July 1861. Acting under a 1795 law authorizing the president to suppress domestic violence, he issued a proclamation ordering insurrectionists to disband and calling out the state militias to suppress resistance to the laws. Evidently relying on an 1807 amendment that authorized the use of federal armed forces as well as militia, Lincoln proclaimed a blockade of Southern ports. He authorized military commanders to suspend the writ of habeas corpus, at first in a corridor between New York and Washington and then throughout the country.

Lincoln relied on legislative authority for these actions where he could reasonably claim it. Where he did not have such authority, he argued that his constitutional obligation as president to execute the laws gave him the implied power to take whatever steps were necessary. When Chief Justice Roger Taney ordered the release of insurrectionaries held without trial, declaring that only Congress could suspend habeas corpus, Lincoln refused to obey. He raised the question of whether the president might break particular laws in order to preserve the Union and to enforce the rest. But he never actually claimed this power. Instead, he asked Congress to ratify his actions or pass laws directing different ones. (In some instances Congress obliged. For example, in 1862 it passed a Habeas Corpus Act modifying Lincoln's policy suspending the writ.) In effect, Lincoln claimed concurrent power with Congress in the crisis, interpreting the executive power broadly to include far more than mere administration.

At the same time Lincoln held that his constitutional position as commander in chief of the armed

Lincoln on the Battlefield. Abraham Lincoln at Antietam, Maryland. October, 1862. LIBRARY OF CONGRESS

forces gave him primary responsibility for waging the war. He assigned and reassigned military officers in his search for efficient commanders; he also took a leading role in establishing Union strategy. The army seized control of the railroads and the telegraph lines. The Treasury Department established rules for trading with the enemy. Lincoln appointed military governors over conquered Confederate territory, and instructed them to encourage Unionists to hold constitutional conventions, abolish slavery, and reestablish loyal governments. He indicated the conditions upon which he would recognize such governments as entitled to restoration to normal relations in the Union—in effect, a reconstruction policy. After resisting pressure to move directly against slavery, Lincoln finally issued the Emancipation Proclamation, freeing all slaves behind Confederate lines as of 1 January 1863. He undertook this confiscation of hundreds of millions of dollars' worth of human property as a war measure, without congressional authorization. Indeed, he insisted that it could be justified only as a war measure and could not apply where order prevailed. Permanent, complete abolition would require a constitutional amendment.

These broad exercises of power led to clashes with Congress, but Lincoln avoided direct challenges. He cooperated with the Joint Committee on the Conduct

of the War, which tried to pressure him on choices of commanders and on strategy. He signed confiscation laws emancipating slaves, although he denied that Congress could confiscate the property of rebels beyond their lifetimes. The most serious conflict came over reconstruction. Lincoln aimed his policy toward the quick establishment of loyal state governments in order to undermine support for the Confederacy. Most of his Republican allies in Congress wanted to delay reconstruction until war's end and to require states to abolish slavery. When Congress enacted its program in the Wade–Davis Bill at the end of its session in July 1864, Lincoln refused to sign it, killing it with a pocket veto (the failure of the president to sign a bill while Congress is adjourned). Not only did he dislike the delay, but he explicitly denied that Congress could ordain emancipation by simple legislation. In the following session of Congress, which met from 5 December 1864 to 3 March 1865, Lincoln made a futile attempt to persuade the House and Senate to admit representatives and senators from Louisiana and Arkansas, which had complied with his reconstruction program.

Some observers have claimed that Lincoln established a "constitutional dictatorship." However, this is a great exaggeration. Lincoln never argued that his inherent presidential powers as chief executive and commander in chief limited the powers that the Constitution delegated to Congress. He acknowledged Congress's power to reverse his actions or pass legislation modifying his policies, as it did when it passed the Habeas Corpus Act in 1863. Lincoln never claimed an executive privilege to withhold information from the Joint Committee on the Conduct of the War, which encroached on military authority that he might have claimed for himself alone. Even in the area of Reconstruction, Lincoln never denied Congress's final authority.

In fact, Lincoln carefully distinguished between what the Constitution permitted him to do under his war powers as commander in chief, and the far more limited powers he and Congress shared in peacetime. Thus, he believed that the confiscation and emancipation of rebels' slaves was a legitimate exercise of the war power. But abolition of slavery itself went beyond the war powers and required a constitutional amendment. A military commander could require the cleansing of a city to protect his troops and civilians from pestilence, but he could not establish a general system of municipal improvements. Lincoln's vigorous execution of presidential power was confined entirely to matters related to the Civil War. The other great reforms of the Civil War era—the promotion of economic development, the establishment of land-grant colleges by the Morrill Act of 1862, the creation of the national banking system, the nationalization of financial policy—Lincoln left to Congress, urged on by individual members of his cabinet. In many ways, therefore, he retained a Whig conception of the presidency.

Andrew Johnson

Vice President Andrew Johnson succeeded Lincoln following his death on 15 April 1865. Johnson was the only Southern senator who remained loyal to the Union, and Lincoln had encouraged his nomination as vice president to represent the Democratic element of the Union Party. As a Democrat, Johnson had inherited the Jacksonian preference for a strong presidency.

Like Lincoln, Johnson claimed broad war and executive powers. In an effort to restore civil government after the Confederate surrender, he supported cabinet members who appointed officials in the South without regard to laws requiring such appointees to have been loyal throughout the conflict. He established a generous pardon and amnesty policy for former Confederates, and interpreted it to restore property that had been confiscated. This decision gutted the operation of the Confiscation Acts that Congress had passed in 1861 and 1862 and forced the Freedmen's Bureau, established in 1865, to return land being farmed by former slaves under its supervision.

Most important, Johnson claimed authority as commander in chief to carry forward Reconstruction. Rather than call Congress into special session, he pro-

mulgated a detailed policy. Rejecting advice that he include black Southerners in the process, Johnson limited participants to white men. Once the former Confederate states pronounced secession null and void, abolished slavery, repudiated the Confederate war debt, and ratified the Thirteenth Amendment, he would recognize them as entitled to normal relations in the Union. Most of the states had complied by the time Congress met in December 1865. Johnson was purposely vague about whether he believed Congress was obligated to seat their representatives and senators.

Johnson's program would have been radical as a wartime policy, but by 1865 many northerners thought it extremely mild. Under his terms southern voters retained former Confederates in power. Southern legislatures and local governments denied African Americans basic civil rights, leading northerners to worry that the South hoped to preserve some of the features of slavery. Congress delayed seating southern representatives and senators while it considered legislation and further constitutional amendments to settle war issues and secure equal civil rights for all Americans. Johnson vetoed the resulting Civil Rights Act in April 1866 (Congress overrode the veto), and he opposed the ratification of the Fourteenth Amendment proposed by Congress shortly thereafter. When Congress passed its own Reconstruction Act in 1867, Johnson vetoed it as an unconstitutional invasion of states' rights, implying

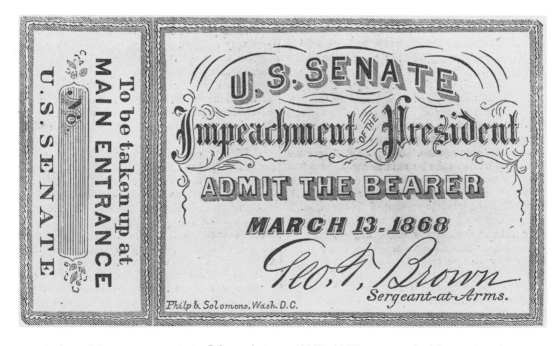

Andrew Johnson (1808–1875). Johnson's term (1865–1869) was marked by acrimonious relations with Congress. His opposition to Military Reconstruction led to his dismissal of Secretary of War Stanton—a move that caused Republicans to impeach him. He avoided conviction and removal from office by one vote in the Senate. LIBRARY OF CONGRESS

that he alone had authority over Reconstruction—a position that went beyond anything Lincoln had claimed.

The conflict between the president and Congress precipitated a dangerous constitutional crisis. After his break with the Republican-dominated Union Party, Democrats hoped Johnson would rejoin their party and use patronage to strengthen it. He never did so, instead inviting conservatives of both parties to support his policy and administration. This course gave the impression that Johnson was using the power of the presidency to create a personal party, an idea that went deeply against the grain of American political tradition. In response Republicans passed the Tenure of Office Act (1867). The law barred the removal of federal officeholders until the Senate confirmed their successors, although it permitted their suspension while the Senate was adjourned, subject to later approval or disapproval. A special proviso limited the way the act applied to members of the cabinet. They were covered during the term of the president who appointed them and for one month thereafter. Senators soon agreed not to confirm replacements for officeholders unless their state's senators agreed to the change. The effect of the law was to make officeholders dependent on senators for their tenure, thereby giving senators tremendous influence over party organizations, which were sustained by activists who received offices as a reward for service.

The Reconstruction Act declared the state governments reestablished under Johnson's program to be provisional and subjected them to control of military commanders. It enfranchised black males and required southerners to frame new state constitutions that established equal civil and political rights, and had to be ratified in special elections. When southern states complied with these terms and ratified the Fourteenth Amendment, they would be eligible for restoration to normal relations in the Union.

As commander in chief of the armed forces, Johnson retained a powerful influence over the enforcement of the Reconstruction Act. To guard against potential interference, Congress refused to adjourn permanently, authorizing its leaders to call it back into session. When Johnson issued instructions narrowly construing the commanders' power, Congress had to reconvene to clarify the law. Worried about what Johnson might do, Congress required all military orders to go through the headquarters of the army administered by General Ulysses S. Grant. Despite these restrictions Johnson removed several of the military commanders whom Grant and Secretary of War Edwin M. Stanton had assigned to administer the Reconstruction Act and replaced them with commanders more sympathetic to his views. As soon as the Senate adjourned, he suspended Stanton, as the Tenure of Office Act allowed, replacing him with Grant.

As the crisis deepened, the House Judiciary Committee investigated whether Johnson had committed impeachable offenses. In November 1867 the committee reported in favor of impeachment, over the objections of its Democratic members and two of its Republican members, including the committee chairman. On 7 December 1867 the House rejected the recommendation. At nearly the same time the Senate refused to agree to Stanton's removal. To Johnson's dismay, Grant turned the secretary of war office back to Stanton.

Emboldened by the failure of impeachment, Johnson renewed his attacks on the Reconstruction Act, removing more commanders and making it unlikely that white southerners would comply with the law before the presidential and congressional elections of 1868. Republicans feared that northern voters would repudiate them in 1868 for failing to complete Reconstruction, and they also worried that there might be violence if Johnson insisted that his southern state governments had the right to participate in the election. As if to confirm their worst suspicions, on 21 February, Johnson removed Stanton in apparent defiance of the Tenure of Office Act. Responding to the provocation, the House impeached Johnson on 24 February.

During the trial Johnson's lawyers insisted that he had only meant to test the constitutionality of the Tenure of Office Act in the courts. They warned that removing Johnson would fatally weaken the presidency and subordinate it to the will of Congress, a concern reinforced by the rhetoric of some of the House managers. Worried by such claims of power, dissenting Republicans nonetheless feared to vote "not guilty" lest Johnson continue his subversion of congressional Reconstruction policy. To protect himself and the presidency, Johnson finally acquiesced in the enforcement of the Reconstruction Act, making it possible for seven Republican senators to join Democrats in acquitting him on 16 and 26 May, on the grounds that the Tenure of Office Act did not cover Stanton.

Johnson's expansive claims of presidential power had nearly led to his removal. The consequence was a severe check to executive pretensions.

The Grant Presidency

Ulysses S. Grant succeeded Andrew Johnson with a very different vision of the presidency. He promised to defer to Congress in the making of public policy and to place the administration of government above partisanship. To carry out his intentions Grant nominated relatively unpartisan Republicans to his cabinet and sought the repeal of the Tenure of Office Act,

Ulysses S. Grant (1822–1885). The military hero Grant did not seek the presidency (1869–1877); it was thrust upon him by a grateful nation. LIBRARY OF CONGRESS

which gave senators so much influence over patronage. This won the praise of civil-service reformers, who wanted to replace the spoils system with professionalized government service.

While Grant's policy comported with the Whig view of presidential power vis-à-vis Congress, he abdicated the president's traditional role as party leader. However, several initial cabinet appointments proved to be unwise choices, and he was forced to turn to more established politicians. Grant's effort to secure the repeal of the Tenure of Office Act also failed. Nonetheless, he remained reluctant to assume political leadership of his party. Republicans were dismayed as their party drifted and began to fray without presidential leadership. Reform-oriented cabinet members refused to use patronage to sustain beleaguered Republican Party organizations in the South against bolters, and they pressed for civil-service reform to deprive traditional party leaders of their base of influence. Republican organizations in the border states and Virginia broke apart, with dissidents joining Democrats to regain control there. Similar fissures began to develop everywhere. Republicans lost ground in local elections, and Grant found himself without the influence to win passage of a fa-

vorite foreign-policy initiative, a treaty annexing Santo Domingo (now the Dominican Republic) to the United States, to serve as a Caribbean naval base and a haven for former slaves.

Grant discerned that the Republican drift and disintegration put his reelection at risk. He began to take firm positions on such issues as violence in the South and financial policy. To strengthen state Republican organizations throughout the country, Grant cooperated with senators on patronage matters. He warned dissidents against bolting regular tickets, and deprived those who did so of access to patronage. With Grant firmly allied with the party bosses, dissidents and reformers became critical and broke away to create the Liberal Republican Party, which cooperated with Democrats in the 1872 elections, promising civil-service and financial reform. But Grant's decision to use the traditional political powers of the presidency succeeded. He was reelected, and the Republican Party retained control of Congress and most northern state governments, as well as those of the Deep South. But reformers persistently and bitterly assailed him. As scandal after scandal erupted, Grant became increasingly identified with political corruption and bossism. In 1876 the Republicans were forced to nominate a candidate for president who promised reform.

Grant's greatest challenge as president was to enforce laws that protected the civil and political rights of Americans against violence by the Ku Klux Klan and other loosely organized bands of white terrorists. Before the Civil War the protection of basic rights had been the responsibility of the states. The Fourteenth Amendment prohibited states from abridging the rights of citizens of the United States; depriving anyone of life, liberty, or property without due process of law; and denying anyone the equal protection of the laws. The Fifteenth Amendment, ratified in 1870, barred racial discrimination in voting qualifications. Under the control of Republicans, southern state governments proved unable to protect their citizens.

Congress passed laws to carry out the provisions of the Fourteenth and Fifteenth amendments, but the president had very limited governmental machinery for enforcing them. There were few U.S. attorneys to seek arrests and few U.S. marshals and deputies to make them. Local white populations were hostile; calling on black citizens to help created the risk of race war. In desperation Grant and his attorney general interpreted laws empowering federal officers to call upon the posse comitatus—the citizens of the community—to help enforce laws as authorizing them to call on locally stationed U.S. military units. But even with this it was difficult to get southern juries to convict.

If violence grew so serious that state authority broke down, federal law authorized the president to respond to state requests for military help. These laws enforced Article IV, section 4 of the U.S. Constitution that guaranteed each state a republican form of government. Grant was extremely reluctant to take this course. However, in 1871 he finally called on Congress to pass more stringent legislation, one provision of which for a limited time authorized him to suspend the writ of habeas corpus and use military force wherever resistance to the law overwhelmed duly constituted authorities. This legislation enabled Grant to suppress the violence temporarily, but Supreme Court decisions began to put its constitutionality in doubt.

While Grant suppressed the worst and most overt violence in 1871 and 1872, fraud and intimidation continued. In several southern states these conditions produced rival claimants for governorships and control of state legislatures. Republican state officials called on the president to protect them under the federal laws enforcing the guarantee clause. But when Grant reluctantly agreed to intervene in these disputes, his position as Republican Party leader made it difficult to convince Americans that he was acting dispassionately. Political support for such interventions rapidly dissipated. By 1874 Grant's hesitation was clear, and southern Democrats successfully tested the use of fraud and violence in elections once again. Grant found it politically impossible to interfere, and by 1876 only three southern states remained under Republican control.

The violence and fraud that had become endemic in southern elections threatened to produce a national calamity in the presidential election of 1876. The situation led not only to rival claimants to the governorships and state legislatures of the last states under Republican control, but also to rival sets of electoral votes. As president, Grant maintained order and urged compromise. Congress averted catastrophe by establishing a commission of ten congressmen and five Supreme Court justices to report which set of electoral votes was entitled to be counted. The commission divided 8–7 along party lines to endorse the Republican electoral votes, and Republican Rutherford B. Hayes succeeded Grant as president on 4 March 1877.

The Civil War had seen a radical expansion of presidential power that culminated in conflict with Congress and impeachment in 1868. After his initial flirtation with a restricted, nonpartisan presidency, Ulysses S. Grant tried to be an active president in the antebellum mold. However, the weakness of the machinery of the federal government made it impossible for him to meet the increased law enforcement responsibilities the Fourteenth and Fifteenth amendments imposed on the president. The failure nearly led to disaster, and his successors turned to other means to try to secure civil and political rights in the South. At the same time pressure grew during the Grant presidency to eliminate the patronage system as the means of maintaining party organization. Successors began to find other tools to do this job.

See also **Civil War,** *subentry on* **Consequences of the Civil War; Elections,** *subentry on* **Presidential Elections; Reconstruction,** *subentries on* **The South, The Politics of Reconstruction.**

Bibliography

Belz, Herman. *Lincoln and the Constitution: The Dictatorship Question Reconsidered.* Fort Wayne, Ind.: Louis A. Warren Lincoln Library and Museum, 1984.

Benedict, Michael Les. "The Constitution of the Lincoln Presidency and the Republican Era." In *The Constitution and the American Presidency.* Edited by Martin Fausold and Alan Shanks. Albany: State University of New York Press, 1991.

———. *The Impeachment and Trial of Andrew Johnson.* New York: W. W. Norton, 1973.

Castel, Albert E. *The Presidency of Andrew Johnson.* Lawrence: Regents Press of Kansas, 1979.

Donald, David. "Abraham Lincoln: Whig in the White House." In *Lincoln Reconsidered: Essays on the Civil War Era.* By David Donald, New York: Vintage, 1961; repr. 1989.

Gillette, William. *Retreat from Reconstruction, 1869–1879.* Baton Rouge: Louisiana State University Press, 1979.

McFeely, William S. *Grant: A Biography.* New York: Norton, 1981.

Paludan, Phillip Shaw. *The Presidency of Abraham Lincoln.* Lawrence: University Press of Kansas, 1994.

Randall, James G. *Constitutional Problems under Lincoln.* New York: D. Appleton, 1926.

Sefton, James E. *Andrew Johnson and the Uses of Constitutional Power.* Edited by Oscar Handlin. Boston: Little, Brown, 1980.

Simpson, Brooks D. *The Reconstruction Presidents.* Lawrence: University Press of Kansas, 1998.

MICHAEL LES BENEDICT

1877–1901

Between 1865 and 1900 the office of the American presidency fell to one of the lowest points in its history in terms of national prestige and authority. However, by the end of the nineteenth century William McKinley had set the institution on its modern course of increasing power and international influence. The experience of Gilded Age presidents remains a lesson in the consequences to the nation of a weakened chief executive.

The decline of the presidency began with the term of Andrew Johnson during the Reconstruction era. Johnson's battles with Congress over the proper policy toward the defeated South and African Americans caused Republican lawmakers between 1865 and 1869 to override Johnson's vetoes, pass such restrictive measures as the Tenure of Office Act (1867), and bring impeachment proceedings against the president in 1868. That year Johnson narrowly escaped conviction and removal from office, but his presidency was thereafter crippled.

The rise of congressional power relative to the president continued under Ulysses S. Grant from 1869 to 1877. Although Grant was a more vigorous executive than historians have generally acknowledged, he took a narrow view of his role and left most policy initiatives to Republican lawmakers. The scandals of his second term further eroded the standing of his office. By 1877 leading senators looked upon the White House as properly subordinate to Capitol Hill.

An Enfeebled Institution

In the 1870s both major political parties viewed presidential power as limited. The Democrats saw the chief executive as a check on Congress, in the mold of their heroic ancestor, Andrew Jackson. They looked to the occupant of the White House to restrain Republican activism in the legislative branch. The Republicans, with their roots in the Whig Party, believed that Congress should take the lead in national governance. While they revered the memory of Abraham Lincoln, the Grand Old Party deemed Lincoln's use of executive power during the Civil War as a departure from constitutional norms.

The political environment of the Gilded Age contributed to the constraints on the presidency. With neither the Republicans nor the Democrats in secure control of both houses of Congress between 1876 and 1892, the Republican presidents—Rutherford B. Hayes, James A. Garfield, and Chester Alan Arthur—faced the obstacles of divided government in pushing their initiatives forward.

In addition, Congress allocated little money for White House operations. The president functioned with only a small staff, usually about ten clerks. A single harried male secretary did most of the office work for the incumbent. The flow of mail to the White House was slow and record keeping erratic. In comparison with today, communication was primitive. Typewriters came into use during Garfield's brief term. During the war with Spain in 1898, Mc-

Kinley became the first president to use the telephone on a regular basis.

By the standards of the turn of the twenty-first century, White House security was exceedingly lax. The American public, who regarded the man who held the nation's highest office as the first citizen of the land rather than as an imperial figure to be held in awe, could visit the executive mansion freely. The president held weekly open receptions, which thousands of ordinary citizens lined up to attend. Washingtonians saw the president and his family on their evening walks or carriage rides. Garfield's assassination in 1881 did not lead to greater protection for the chief executive. As late as the war with Spain, the White House was accessible to anyone who wished to see the president. As a result of this open-door policy, the executive mansion was a relatively ramshackle structure—part office, part museum, part private residence.

Hayes Revives the Presidency

Any prospect of reviving the authority of the presidency seemed remote when Rutherford B. Hayes took office in March 1877. Because the outcome of

Rutherford B. Hayes (1822–1893). Hayes's term (1877–1881) saw the end of Reconstruction in the South. LIBRARY OF CONGRESS

the 1876 election between Hayes and Democrat Samuel J. Tilden had been disputed, Hayes had to overcome questions about his legitimacy. Democrats derided him as "His Fraudulency," and he faced obstacles simply in carrying out the day-to-day duties of his position.

Yet during Hayes's single term, a slow process of revitalization began. The new president proved a more forceful executive than members of his party had anticipated. He rebuffed senatorial efforts to intervene in the selection of his cabinet. He balked when Congress attached to appropriations bills riders blocking the enforcement of federal election laws in the South. Hayes's most controversial battle was over political patronage in the key state of New York. The president eventually won out over his rival, the Republican senator Roscoe Conkling of New York, and established the power of the chief executive to make his own appointments, affirming a key element in presidential autonomy.

Not all of Hayes's initiatives were successful. He failed to bring southern Democrats into the Republican Party, and lawmakers overrode his veto of the Bland-Allison Act (1878), which called for the government coinage of silver. Nonetheless, by the time Hayes retired to Ohio in March 1881, he had established a creditable record on which his successors could build.

The Garfield-Arthur Interruption

Any momentum that Hayes created toward greater presidential authority faltered with the brief term of James Garfield in 1881. An Ohio congressman who won a close race in the presidential election of 1880, Garfield had the potential to be an important president. Like his main political ally, James G. Blaine, Garfield wanted to see the Republicans address the issues of an industrializing society. In his early months in office, Garfield challenged Roscoe Conkling by naming one of the New Yorker's political opponents to the significant patronage position of collector of the port of New York. Conkling rebelled, and an internecine battle ensued. The crucial issue was the right of the president to select his subordinates without deferring in every case to the Republican leaders in the Senate. By late June 1881 it looked as if Garfield had won the battle. Then, on 2 July, as he left for a vacation, a crazed office seeker shot Garfield, who died several months later.

Succeeding to the presidency was Chester Alan Arthur, a New Yorker who had been put on the ticket with Garfield for geographical balance. While many expected the former vice president to be the tool of Conkling and others in the New York Republican or-

ganization, Arthur proved to be both competent and independent. He made some crucial contributions to presidential authority through vetoes of a number of pork barrel spending programs. Enactment of the Pendleton Act in 1883 expanded the federal civil service, taking power away from the politicians and thus working to the advantage of future presidents.

Arthur's presidency ended in anticlimax, however. Democratic victories in the 1882 congressional elections undermined the administration, and the president's failing health eroded his chances to obtain renomination. The Republicans turned instead to their most popular figure, James G. Blaine, as their 1884 nominee. In a close election marred by voter fraud, Blaine lost to the Democratic standard-bearer, Grover Cleveland of New York.

Regression under Cleveland

Cleveland has often been described as a strong president who exhibited courage in office. He gained this reputation because of his ample use of the veto power and his determined advocacy of the gold standard during the 1890s. Yet in terms of the presidential office, Cleveland's record was disastrous. During the twelve years that he led the Democratic Party, it sank to one of the lowest points in its history. By the time Cleveland concluded his second term, in March 1897, the presidency was almost where it had been during the Johnson-Grant era. Cleveland demonstrated that presidential strength did not always translate into enhanced prestige and authority for the occupant of the White House.

Cleveland's political rise was meteoric. He was elected mayor of Buffalo, New York, in 1881 and received his party's nomination for governor of New York the following year. Having carried the state with the largest number of electoral votes, Cleveland became a natural contender for the Democratic presidential nomination in 1884. He was a new face in a party dominated by tired old warhorses. Cleveland embodied the small-government views of the Democrats that the national government should avoid subsidies, keep tariffs low, and stay out of local issues such as racial practices in the South. He also fought with the Tammany Hall machine in a way that added to his credentials as a reformer.

In the race against Blaine, Cleveland overcame disclosures that he had fathered an illegitimate child years before. Cleveland's answer to the scandal was to advise his supporters to tell the truth about the incident. Although ample mud was thrown on both sides, Cleveland won the election because of the Democrats' new electoral strength.

In his first term Cleveland proved to be a competent executive but a lackluster political leader. He did not get along with members of his own party, and his handling of the symbolic issue of the patronage was inept. Mindful of the prerogatives of his office, Cleveland insisted that the president should have the power to remove appointed officials without interference from Capitol Hill, a stance based on precedents established by Hayes and Garfield.

Facing reelection in 1888, Cleveland decided to make the protective tariff the central issue of the race. The president argued that protective tariffs raised consumer prices and fostered the growth of trusts. Republicans countered that protection created jobs and fostered prosperity. To dramatize his point, Cleveland devoted his entire annual message in December 1887 to a plea for lower tariff rates. That dramatic action focused attention on the State of the Union message and provided a precedent for future executives to use this annual ritual to articulate their programs. In the short run, however, Cleveland's move backfired. The president did not carry

Grover Cleveland (1837–1908). Democratic president Grover Cleveland took office as both the twenty-second (1885–1889) president and the twenty-fourth (1893–1897) president. LIBRARY OF CONGRESS

through with his initiative, and he played down the tariff question in the Democratic platform. Observing the custom that incumbent presidents should not campaign for another term, Cleveland left to his party colleagues the task of carrying his message to the voters. The Democratic campaign of 1888 was disorganized and ineffective.

The Harrison Years

The Republicans eagerly took up the tariff issue, which was a question on which their party could unite. They selected Benjamin Harrison, a former senator from Indiana, as their candidate, and he proved to be a superb campaigner. He was able to skillfully address large crowds about the virtues of higher customs duties. Meanwhile, his party raised and spent $3 million, most of which went for printing literature extolling the virtues of protectionism. The new civil service rules barred officeholders from making contributions to election campaigns. As a result, corporations increasingly found themselves being asked for money. The linkage between business and campaign donations grew during the remainder of the century.

The 1888 election was one of only two (1876 was the other) in which the winner received fewer popular votes than the loser. Harrison's majority in the electoral college was secure—233 to 168. Much of Cleveland's popular majority came from the South, where African Americans were largely excluded from the ballot box. Nonetheless, the Republicans won control of both houses of Congress for the first time in years, and they prepared to pursue their activist agenda.

Harrison brought to the presidency the orderly mind of an attorney, which he had been in private life. He created an improved filing system for the White House, and he instituted procedures for monitoring the workings of the government. In an effort to build bridges to Congress, he held frequent conferences with Republican leaders on Capitol Hill. Harrison also liked to travel and make speeches. His tours around the country set a precedent on which William McKinley and Theodore Roosevelt would build a decade later. If he had been a shrewder politician, Harrison might well have made a vigorous contribution to the revitalization of the presidency.

Unfortunately, Harrison lacked both luck in his political circumstances and adroitness in dealing with individuals in Washington. He could charm a throng of twenty thousand people, went a Washington adage, and alienate them one by one as he shook hands. The human side of the presidency escaped him. Political fate also went against Harrison and his party. The Republicans pursued an ambitious program in the Fifty-first Congress. In 1890 they passed the

Sherman Antitrust Act, the Sherman Silver Purchase Act, and the McKinley Tariff. They tried to enact a federal elections bill to safeguard voting rights for all citizens in the South. Democratic opposition from both North and South brought the measure down.

The Republican push for positive government did not sit well with the voters, who went Democratic in large numbers in the 1890 congressional elections. Adding to the woes of Harrison and the administration was the increasing discontent of farmers in the South and West, which led to support for the People's Party. The Democrats benefited most from the spirit of discontent. Harrison won renomination in 1892, but it was a hollow victory. The Democrats selected Cleveland for a third time, and he swept to victory by a margin of 400,000 popular votes. The Democrats also held control of the House and Senate.

A Presidency in Turmoil

Cleveland's attitude toward politicians and the public had not mellowed during his four years out of office. His staff remained small, and his private secretary was not well versed in public relations. Visitors to the White House encountered uniformed guards and a general aloofness from the presidential establishment. Cleveland's relations with the press, never friendly from the outset, worsened during his second term. Reporters covering the president joked that they reminded themselves of highway robbers accosting a stagecoach.

These impressions would have made little difference if Cleveland's second term had been successful. Instead, he clumsily confronted one of the worst economic crises in the nation's history. The panic of 1893 broke out in the spring and evolved into a crippling economic depression that hung on for almost four years. Cleveland grappled with the country's problems with vigor and energy. The specific policies that he followed, however, pleased neither his party nor the voters.

Persuaded that the Sherman Silver Purchase Act of 1890 caused the collapse of business confidence and thus brought on the economic downturn, Cleveland called Congress to meet in a special session in August 1893. In doing so, the president postponed the issue of tariff reform, on which the Democrats were united, in favor of an issue on which they were bitterly divided. To push through repeal of the Sherman Act, Cleveland wielded the power and prestige of his office. He won a victory of sorts, but the price was an alienated party.

Instead of improving, the hard times grew more severe through the winter of 1893–1894. Unemployment and homelessness rose, and unhappiness with the administration mounted. During the summer of 1894 a national railroad strike tied up the country's commerce. Cleveland and his Justice Department used federal power to break the walkout and punish Eugene V. Debs and the railroad union he led. The middle class applauded the president's actions, but industrial workers defected from the Democrats.

In Congress the plight of the president's party became acute. The Democratic promise to lower tariffs resulted in the Wilson-Gorman Tariff of 1894, which actually raised some customs duties. The president tried to blame congressional leaders, adding to his woes with his party. In the 1894 elections, the Democrats suffered one of the worst defeats in the nation's history as a transfer of more than one hundred seats to the Republicans brought the GOP back into power in the House. Democrats complained that Cleveland had been inept in his exercise of presidential authority.

During the last two years of Cleveland's presidency he was almost irrelevant. In 1895 his popularity recovered briefly when his administration took a strong stand against Great Britain in a dispute over the Venezuelan boundary. But that upturn quickly evaporated when the White House aligned itself with Spain over the fate of Cuba. By 1896 Cleveland was virtually a recluse in the White House. His policies had been repudiated, and his aggressive approach to presidential leadership had backfired. On 4 March 1897 Democratic newspapers noted gleefully that it was the last day of the Cleveland administration.

In the 1930s Cleveland's reputation rebounded when biographers depicted him as a courageous chief executive standing against popular clamor for free silver and government interference in the economy. Modern scholarship has been less kind to Cleveland's approach to the presidency. His devastating effect on the Democrats, his insensitivity to the plight of the average American during economic hard times, and the wounds he inflicted to his office have driven his standing downward.

McKinley: The First Modern President

In contrast, presidential scholarship since the 1970s has enhanced the standing of William McKinley. Once scorned for his inability to avoid the war with Spain in 1898, McKinley has been reevaluated as a purposeful and effective president who laid down the standards for the modern form of executive power.

McKinley's efforts to revitalize the office of the presidency began during the early days of his first term. His victory over the Democratic spokesman for free silver, William Jennings Bryan, in the 1896 election ended a generation of political stalemate. In that contest McKinley was not the tool of his industrialist friend, Marcus A. Hanna, but rather a shrewd and effective national leader. His campaign, conducted

William McKinley (1843–1901). Inauguration, 1897. McKinley's term witnessed the Spanish-American War and the Open Door policy for China. He was assassinated on 14 September 1901 in Buffalo, N.Y. LIBRARY OF CONGRESS

largely from his front porch in Canton, Ohio, allowed him to meet a significant slice of the electorate in controlled settings that enabled him to get across his pluralistic, inclusive message. The Republicans had ample money to spend on the campaign, most of it donated by large corporations, but these funds went for pamphlets and campaign literature that spread McKinley's gospel of sound money and tariff protection.

As president, McKinley traveled more than any of his predecessors. Like Harrison he used his travels to put his policies before the voters, but he was more accommodating to the reporters who accompanied him. A formal system of press releases got out McKinley's message. Reporters at the White House were provided with tables and other facilities, and the press was briefed daily. Reporters were sometimes granted personal access to the president to obtain background information.

A central player in this process was McKinley's secretary, George B. Cortelyou. Moving from a secondary role to official recognition as the president's spokesperson by 1900, Cortelyou worked out the procedures for releasing official statements, providing advance texts of speeches, and facilitating coverage of breaking events. By 1901 the White House staff that Cortelyou managed had increased from six people to thirty. They were busy handling the expanded volume of mail addressed to the president, which by 1901 amounted to one thousand letters daily. Cortelyou was a forerunner of the modern-day chief of staff, who oversees the daily routine of the president.

A major cause of the rise of presidential power at the end of the nineteenth century was the Spanish-American War, which began in April 1898. McKinley's diplomacy before the fighting started was more purposeful and courageous than many of his critics realized. Once the fighting got under way, McKinley wielded the war powers of his office in a manner that foreshadowed greater conflicts in the twentieth century.

To oversee the war McKinley had telephone and telegraph lines connected to a White House war room, enabling him to communicate with commanders in the field. Throughout the fighting in Cuba in June and July 1898, McKinley maintained a constant dialogue with his generals about proper strategy and the terms on which a Spanish surrender in Cuba could be negotiated.

A similar arrangement governed events in the Philippines. In April 1898 McKinley ordered Commodore George Dewey to attack Manila Bay. When he learned of Dewey's overwhelming victory on 1 May, he ordered U.S. troops to proceed to the archipelago. The president also used the authority of his office to persuade Congress to annex the Hawaiian Islands as a means of prosecuting the war in the Philippines.

In the peace negotiations with Spain during the summer and fall of 1898, McKinley wielded the powers of the presidency to shape the outcome he desired. He first sought to place members of the Supreme Court on the commission that would hammer out the peace treaty in Paris. When that effort failed, he selected U.S. senators, who were given a voice in ratifying the document they had helped create.

McKinley crisscrossed the Middle West in October 1898, telling his audiences that the nation must accept the burden of its victory, which meant in this case that it must acquire the Philippine Islands. Once the Treaty of Paris had been signed in December, he turned to the same techniques to get it approved by the Senate. Wavering southern Democrats found the president in their region pressing his case before receptive crowds. Other lawmakers heard from their state legislatures and party organizations. When the pact was approved by a narrow margin in February

1899, it was because of McKinley's shrewd exercise of presidential leadership.

When the Philippine Insurrection broke out in February 1899 against the American presence there, McKinley relied on his war powers to justify establishing direct military rule of an overseas possession. A similar rationale allowed the administration to operate a military government in Cuba for several years. The extent to which McKinley had moved toward a modern view of presidential discretion can also be seen in his response to the Boxer Rebellion in China in the summer of 1900. To rescue westerners in Peking, the president deployed twenty-five hundred troops as part of an international relief expedition. Sending his nation's armed forces into a country with which it was not at war exemplifies McKinley's far-reaching view of the implied war powers of his position, especially since he made this move without consulting Congress, which was not in session at the time. Had McKinley lived, there is evidence that during his second term he would have further broken with historical precedent by embarking on official trips outside the continental United States.

Conclusion

The presidency during the late nineteenth century was not the bureaucratized, powerful, media-sensitive institution that dominated American life on the verge of the twenty-first century. When Theodore Roosevelt took office after McKinley's assassination in September 1901, the presidency still resembled the personalized, intimate arrangement of earlier times. Yet the presidents from Andrew Johnson to William McKinley had begun to adapt the institution to the demands of the twentieth century. In the McKinley years critics of the president even charged him with exercising powers beyond the boundaries of the Constitution and acting like an Oriental potentate. Some of this criticism was understandable partisan exaggeration of the deeds of a strong president. Yet the charges recognized that the office and inherent powers of the president had grown during the 1890s in response to the Spanish-American War, the growth of imperialism, and the exigencies of governing an increasingly complex society. There would be ample problems stemming from presidential imperiousness from 1901 onward, but the nation would not experi-

ence a return to the comparative powerlessness and political deference that had characterized holders of the office in the Gilded Age and that later presidents had to overcome.

See also **Democratic Party; Foreign Trade and Tariffs,** *subentry on* **The Politics of Tariffs; Panics and Depressions; Reconstruction,** *subentry on* **The Politics of Reconstruction; Republican Party; Spanish-American War.**

Bibliography

Calhoun, Charles W., ed. *The Gilded Age: Essays on the Origins of Modern America.* Wilmington, Del.: Scholarly Resources, 1995.
Castel, Albert. *The Presidency of Andrew Johnson.* Lawrence: Regents Press of Kansas, 1979.
Doenecke, Justus D. *The Presidencies of James A. Garfield and Chester A. Arthur.* Lawrence: Regents Press of Kansas, 1981.
Gould, Lewis L. *The Presidency of William McKinley.* Lawrence: Regents Press of Kansas, 1980.
Hoogenboom, Ari. *The Presidency of Rutherford B. Hayes.* Lawrence: University Press of Kansas, 1988.
Jones, Stanley L. *The Presidential Election of 1896.* Madison: University of Wisconsin Press, 1964.
Keller, Morton. *Affairs of State: Public Life in Late Nineteenth-Century America.* Cambridge, Mass.: Harvard University Press, 1977.
McDonald, Forrest. *The American Presidency: An Intellectual History.* Lawrence: University Press of Kansas, 1994.
Morgan, H. Wayne. *From Hayes to McKinley: National Party Politics, 1877–1896.* Syracuse, N.Y.: Syracuse University Press, 1969.
———. *William McKinley and His America.* Syracuse, N.Y.: Syracuse University Press, 1963.
Peskin, Allan. *Garfield: A Biography.* Kent, Ohio: Kent State University Press, 1978.
Reeves, Thomas C. *Gentleman Boss: The Life of Chester Alan Arthur.* New York: Knopf, 1975.
Skowronek, Stephen. *Building a New American State: The Expansion of National Administrative Capacities, 1877–1920.* Cambridge, U.K.: Cambridge University Press, 1982.
Socolofsky, Homer E., and Allan B. Spetter. *The Presidency of Benjamin Harrison.* Lawrence: University Press of Kansas, 1987.
Welch, Richard E., Jr. *The Presidencies of Grover Cleveland.* Lawrence: University Press of Kansas, 1988.
Williams, R. Hal. *Years of Decision: American Politics in the 1890s.* Prospect Heights, Ill.: Waveland, 1993.

LEWIS L. GOULD

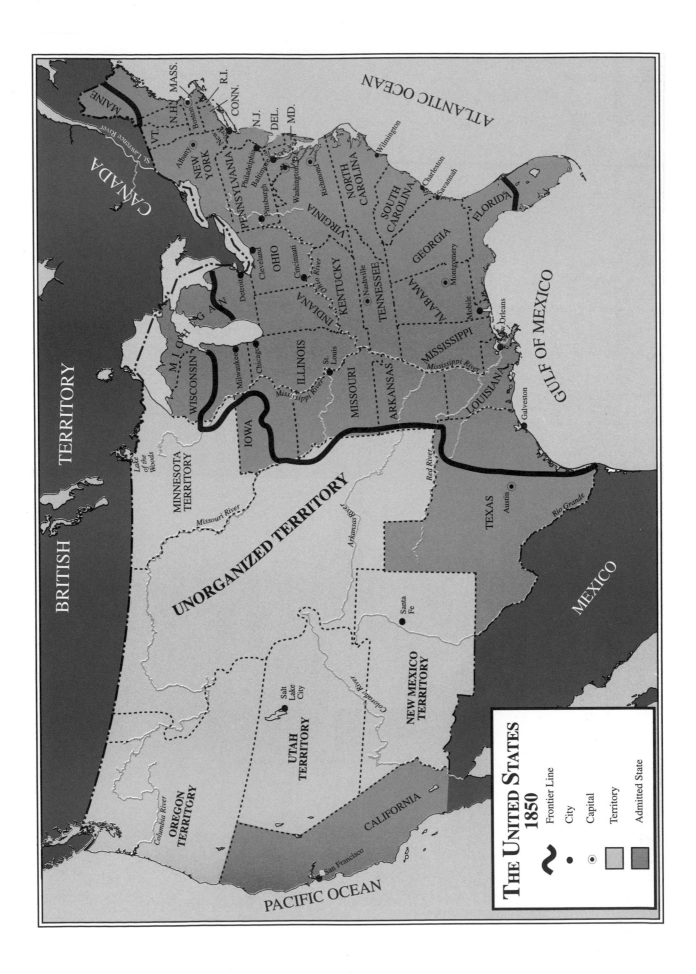

THE UNITED STATES
1850

Frontier Line
City
Capital
Territory
Admitted State